HTML & XHTML: The Complete Reference, Fourth Edition

About the Author

Thomas Powell is a long time Internet and Web industry veteran. After an stint at CERFnet in the early 90s, he founded Powell Internet Consulting (later renamed PINT) in 1994, a Web and network consulting services firm. The firm has grown significantly over the years to become a well-respected player in corporate Web site development and has large clients all over the country in a variety of industries.

Beyond his involvement at PINT, Thomas is well known in the academic community both regionally and internationally. He founded the UCSD Extension Web Publishing program in the late 1990s and continues to teach classes in Web development and design there. He is also an instructor for the UCSD Computer Science Department where he teaches classes in Web design theory, Web Programming and the theory of programming languages.

Mr. Powell is well published and his work has appeared in numerous trade journals. He continues to publish regularly in *Network World* and is a member of the prestigious Network World Test Alliance. He also has published numerous books on Web technology and design, including the best-selling *Web Design: The Complete Reference* and *JavaScript: The Complete Reference*. His books have been translated into over 12 languages and are used around the world both in industry and college settings.

HTML & XHTML: The Complete Reference, Fourth Edition

Thomas Powell

McGraw-Hill/Osborne
New York Chicago San Francisco
Lisbon London Madrid Mexico City
Milan New Delhi San Juan
Seoul Singapore Sydney Toronto

The McGraw-Hill Companies

McGraw-Hill/Osborne
2100 Powell Street, 10th Floor
Emeryville, California 94608
U.S.A.

To arrange bulk purchase discounts for sales promotions, premiums, or fund-raisers, please contact **McGraw-Hill**/Osborne at the above address. For information on translations or book distributors outside the U.S.A., please see the International Contact Information page immediately following the index of this book.

HTML & XHTML: The Complete Reference, Fourth Edition

890 CUS CUS 019876

ISBN 0-07-222942-X

Publisher
Brandon A. Nordin

Vice President & Associate Publisher
Scott Rogers

Acquisitions Editor
Megg Morin

Project Editor
Julie M. Smith

Acquisitions Coordinator
Tana Allen

Technical Editor
Fritz Schneider

Copy Editor
Nancy Rapoport

Proofreader
Susie Elkind

Indexer
Valerie Perry

Composition
Carie Abrew, Tabitha M. Cagan,
Tara A. Davis, Elizabeth Jang

Illustrators
Kathleen Fay Edwards,
Melinda Moore Lytle, Lyssa Wald

Series Design
Peter F. Hancik, Lyssa Wald

This book was composed with Corel VENTURA™ Publisher.

Contents at a Glance

Contents

Part VI Advanced Topics

Part VII Appendixes

Acknowledgments

The fourth edition of this book might as well be the first edition of a brand new series focused on XHTML. Given the amount of rewrite necessary, I want to make sure that all those that helped are given their due. First I want to acknowledge the numerous fixes and improvements that came from the feedback from both my students at UCSD and readers around the world. I write these books for you and I am glad you are putting this information to good use.

I would also like to show my appreciation to the many staff members at PINT who helped on this book project. First, Mine Okano is now three for three on book projects. It may have taken a while for us to get started, but Mine made sure everything proceeded along and I owe her big time, as usual. Once again Dan Whitworth helped out and I especially need to make sure to acknowledge the tenth-anniversary of his first Web site. Rob McFarlane always came through when given a mere afternoon to come up with any desired image changes. Daisy Bhonsle kept up a long standing proofing relationship and I am very glad she always helps out. Plenty of others helped directly or indirectly on examples, proofing, or just running the shop, including Maria Defante, Jimmy Tam, Eric Raether, Meredith Hodge, Cathleen Ryan, Catrin Walsh, James Brock, Jason Gan, David Sanchez, Melinda Serrato, Dave Andrews, Kim Smith, Matt Plotner, Marcus Richard, Cory "TAF" Ducker, Jeremy Weir, Candice Fong-Guleno, Kun Puparussanon, Michele Bedard, Michael Wootton, Heather Jurek, Kevin Griffith, Borrego, and Dutch. Of course Joe Lima, Allan Pister, Christie Sorenson, Chris Neppes, Jared Ashlock, Tad Fleshman, and Perry Herst deserve some credit as well.

The folks at Osborne are always a pleasure to work with. I am not so sure Megg Morin finds my tardiness a pleasure, but somehow our relationship remains intact. Despite skipping our usual long phone calls, Julie Smith was still able to put this monster together. Tana Allen, Nancy Rapoport, Valerie Perry, Roger Stewart, Susie Elkind, Jim Kussow, Elizabeth Jang, and others at Osborne had to deal with all those details and issues that authors take for granted.

My Technical Editor Fritz Schneider, formerly of PINT and now of Google, was of course instrumental in making sure that I was precise. Now that he graduates on to his own books I wish him luck and hope I can edit his tomes someday.

Finally, to my friends and family who tried to give me space to write this thing, you deserve the biggest thanks. However, Tucker and Angus, who can't read, will have to be told of their importance in this production. And finally, Sylvia, I am sure you can appreciate the ironic importance of HTML in our lives.

Thomas A. Powell
tpowell@pint.com
July 2003

Introduction

The fourth edition of this book represents a significant change in order to fully embrace XHTML. Although the previous edition presented XHTML, most of the examples were still in HTML 4 with explanations about differences with XHTML. Today the situation is reversed with the primary focus on the future of markup with XHTML, CSS, and XML rather than the past, filled with tricks and messy table code.

Interestingly, while many books have embraced XHTML, relatively few Web page authors have. Furthermore, at the time of this edition's writing many Web tools do not produce correct markup in traditional HTML, let alone XHTML. Yet the times are changing. During 2002 and 2003 the survivors of the dot com boom have come to take their trade very seriously and more and more sites are truly embracing Web standards.

This book was updated assuming the "embrace the standards" trend will continue. HTML 4 is still well covered and the important table techniques are still presented, but compared to other books on HTML, heavy focus on what Netscape 2 did seven or more years ago is completely purged. Furthermore the focus is very much away from Netscape—especially given that it has been recently discontinued—and more on Internet Explorer, Mozilla, and Opera. Because of this focus on the future, the fourth edition should be both valuable to the standards-conscious designer looking for a reference as well as the newcomer hoping to learn what they need to know for today and tomorrow.

In closing, in my opinion any book that claims to be a "complete reference" has a pretty tough task to complete. But I do honestly believe that readers who study this book carefully will find that they have a complete understanding of HTML, XHTML, CSS, and related client-side technologies. However, if you master this one, remember as I rediscover every day—there is always more to know about Web development. So if you master markup, there are plenty of other books (written both by me and by others) on JavaScript, Web Design, usability, and so on to keep you busy, so get cracking!

Thomas A. Powell
tpowell@pint.com
July 2003

PART I

Introduction

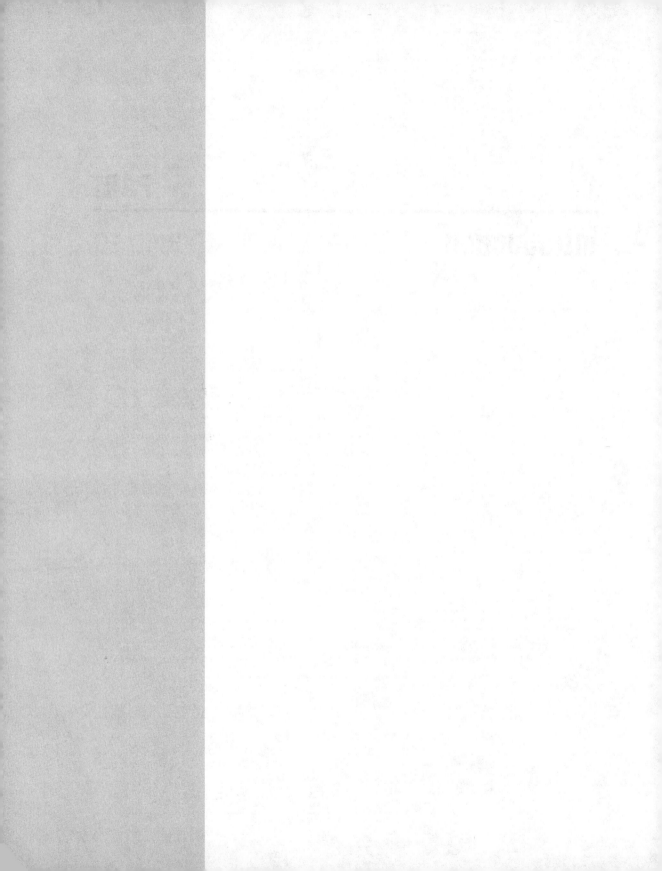

CHAPTER 1

Introduction to HTML and XHTML

Markup is information that is added to a document to convey information about the document's structure or presentation. Markup languages are all around us in everyday computing. While you may not see it, word processing documents are filled with codes indicating the structure and presentation of the document. What you see on your screen just looks like a page of text, but the formatting is done "behind the scenes" by the markup. Hypertext Markup Language (HTML) and its successor, XHTML, are the not-so-behind-the-scenes markup languages that are used to tell Web browsers how to structure and, some may say, display Web pages.

First Look at HTML

In the case of HTML, markup commands applied to your Web-based content relay the structure of the document to the browser software and, though perhaps unfortunate at times, how you want the content to be displayed. For example, if you want to show that a section of text is important, you surround the corresponding text with the markup tags, **<strong>** and **</strong>**, as shown here:

```
<strong>This is important text!</strong>
```

When a Web browser reads a document that has HTML markup in it, it determines how to render the document onscreen by considering the HTML elements embedded within it (see Figure 1-1). Be aware that browsers don't always render things in the way that you think they will. This is due partially to the design of HTML and partially to the differences in the variety of Web browsers currently in use.

So we see that an HTML document is simply a text file that contains the information you want to publish and the appropriate markup instructions indicating how the browser should structure or present the document. These markup *elements* are made up of a start tag such as **<strong>**, and also might include an end tag, which is indicated by a slash within the tag such as **</strong>**. The tag pair should fully enclose any content to be affected by the element, including text and other HTML markup. However, under traditional HTML (not

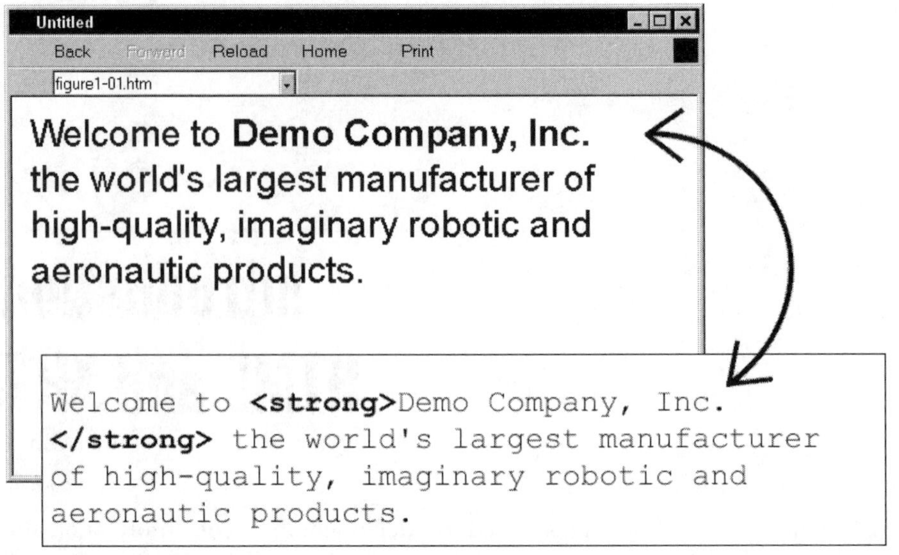

FIGURE 1-1 Interpretation of Web page with HTML markup

XHTML) some HTML elements have optional close tags because their closure can be inferred. Other HTML elements, called *empty elements*, do not enclose any content, and thus need no close tags at all, or in the case of XHTML, use a self-close identification scheme. For example, to insert a line break, use the **
** tag, which represents the empty **br** element as it doesn't enclose any content and has no corresponding close tag.

```
<br>
```

An unclosed tag is not allowed in XHTML, however, so we need to close the tag like so:

```
<br></br>
```

More often, we use a self-identification scheme of closure like so:

The start tag of an HTML element might contain *attributes* that modify the meaning of the tag. The inclusion of the **noshade** attribute in the <**hr**> tag, as shown here,

```
<hr noshade>
```

indicates that there should be no shading applied to the horizontal rule element. Under XHTML, such existence style attributes are not allowed. All attributes must have a value, so instead we use a syntax like the following:

```
<hr noshade="noshade" />
```

As the last example shows, attributes do require value and they are specified with an equal sign; these values should be enclosed within double or single quotes. For example,

```
<img src="logo.gif" alt="Demo Company" height="100" width="100" />
```

specifies four attributes for the **<img>** tag that are used to provide more information about the use of the included image. A complete overview of the structure of HTML elements is shown here:

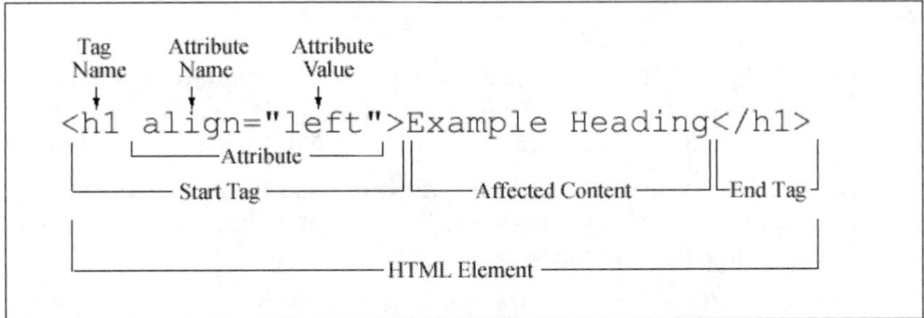

Given these basic rules for HTML tags, it is best now to simply look at an example document to see how they are used. Our first complete example written in transitional HTML 4 is shown here:

```
<!DOCTYPE HTML PUBLIC "-//W3C//DTD HTML 4.01 Transitional//EN"
"http://www.w3.org/TR/html4/loose.dtd">
<html>
<head>
<title>First HTML Example</title>
</head>
<body>
<h1>Welcome to the World of HTML</h1>
<hr>
<p>HTML <b>really</b> isn't so hard!</p>
<p>You can put in lots of text if you want to. In fact, you
could keep on typing and make up more sentences and continue
on and on.</p>
</body>
</html>
```

In the case of XHTML, which is a stricter and cleaner version of HTML, we really don't see many changes yet, as shown in the example that follows:

```
<!DOCTYPE html PUBLIC "-//W3C//DTD XHTML 1.0 Transitional//EN"
"http://www.w3.org/TR/xhtml1/DTD/xhtml1-transitional.dtd">
<html xmlns="http://www.w3.org/1999/xhtml" lang="en">
<head>
<title>First XHTML Example</title>
</head>
<body>
```

```
<h1>Welcome to the World of XHTML</h1>
<hr />
<p>XHTML <b>really</b> isn't so hard!</p>
<p>You can put in lots of text if you want to. In fact, you
could keep on typing and make up more sentences and continue
on and on.</p>
</body>
</html>
```

The preceding example uses some of the most common elements found in HTML documents:

- The **<!DOCTYPE>** statement indicates the particular version of HTML or XHTML being used in the document. In the first example, the transitional 4.01 specification was used, while in the second, the transitional XHTML 1.0 specification was employed.
- The **<html>**, **<head>**, and **<body>** tag pairs are used to specify the general structure of the document. Notice that under XHTML you need to have a little more information about the language you are using.
- The **<title>** and **</title>** tag pair specifies the title of the document that generally appears in the title bar of the Web browser.
- The **<h1>** and **</h1>** header tag pair creates a headline indicating some important information.
- The **<hr />** tag, which has no end tag making its syntax different in XHTML, inserts a horizontal rule, or bar, across the screen.
- The **<p>** and **</p>** paragraph tag pair indicates a paragraph of text.

If you are using a text editor, you could type in the previous listing and save it with a filename such as "firstexample.htm" or "firstexample.html." For a browser to read your file properly off your local disk, it must end either in the .htm or .html extension. If you don't save your file with the appropriate extension, the browser probably won't attempt to interpret the HTML markup. When this happens, the markup elements may appear in the browser window, as shown in Figure 1-2. However, note that some browsers will let you get away with bad file extensions locally, but on a server you could run into problems.

After you save the example file on your system, open it in your browser by using the Open, Open Page, or Open File command, which should be found in the browser's File menu. After your browser reads the file, it should render a page like the one shown in Figure 1-3.

If your page does not display properly, review your file to make sure that you typed in the markup correctly. If you find a mistake and make a change to the file, save the file, go back to your browser, and click the Reload or Refresh button. Sometimes the browser will still reload the page from its memory cache; if a page does not update correctly on reload, hold down the SHIFT key while clicking the Reload button, and the browser should refetch the page. During this simple test, it's a good idea to keep the browser and text editor open simultaneously to avoid having to constantly reopen one or the other. Once you get the hang of HTML design, you'll see that, at this raw level, it is much like the edit, compile, and run cycle so familiar to programmers. However, you certainly don't want to use this manual process to develop Web pages because it can be tedious, error prone, and inefficient for page

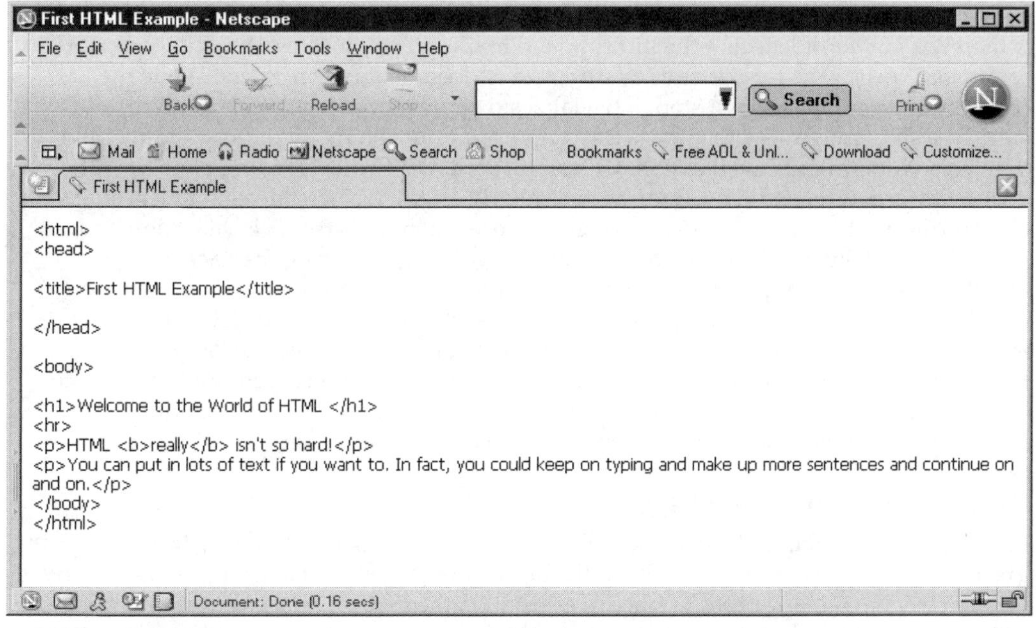

FIGURE 1-2 Raw HTML mistakenly displayed in browser window

structure and visual design. For use here as illustration to learn the language, however, it works fine. Better approaches to HTML document creation are discussed in Chapter 2.

FIGURE 1-3 An HTML page displayed in a browser

Given the simple example just presented, you might surmise that learning HTML is merely a matter of learning the multitude of markup tags, such as **<b>**, **<i>**, **<p>**, and so on, that specify the format and/or structure of documents to browsers. While this certainly is an important first step, it trivializes the role markup plays on the Web, and would be similar to trying to learn writing and print publishing by understanding only the various commands available in Microsoft Word, while disregarding page layout, document structure, and output formats. Similarly on the Web, in addition to learning the various markup tags, you need to consider document structure, visual design and page layout, client and server-side programming, navigation and interface design, and the method by which Web pages are actually delivered. These topics are discussed only to a limited degree in this book as they intersect with HTML and XHTML. However, interested readers are encouraged to reference *Web Design: The Complete Reference, Second Edition* (Powell, 2002), which presents these topics and many others required for full site creation. However, for now let's concern ourselves primarily with understanding basic HTML syntax, as that alone can be a challenge to fully master.

HTML: A Structured Language

HTML has a very well-defined syntax; all HTML documents should follow a formal structure. The *World Wide Web Consortium* (W3C) is the primary organization that attempts to standardize HTML (as well as many other technologies used on the Web). To provide a standard, the W3C must carefully specify all aspects of the technology. In the case of HTML, this means precisely defining the elements in the language. The W3C has defined HTML as an application of the *Standard Generalized Markup Language* (SGML). In short, SGML is a language used to define other languages by specifying the allowed document structure in the form of a *document type definition (DTD)*, which indicates the syntax that can be used for the various elements of a language such as HTML. In 1999, the W3C rewrote HTML as an application of XML (Extensible Markup Language) and renamed it XHTML. XML, in this situation, serves the same purpose as SGML: a language in which to write the rules of a language. In fact, XML is in some sense just a limited form of SGML. The implications of this change are significant and will be touched upon throughout the book. I present both languages and compare them in the chapters that follow so that you can better appreciate the changes. While some standards zealots may disagree with the mere presentation of HTML in the traditional or even loose "tag soup" form, it is still by far the most dominant form of markup on the Web and the author would be remiss in not covering it properly.

From the HTML 4.01 DTD, a basic template can be derived for a basic HTML document, as shown here:

```
<!DOCTYPE HTML PUBLIC "-//W3C//DTD HTML 4.01 Transitional//EN"
"http://www.w3.org/TR/html4/loose.dtd">
<html>
<head>
<title>Document Title Goes Here</title>

...Head information describing the document and providing
supplementary information goes here....
</head>
<body>
```

```
...Document content and markup go here....

</body>
</html>
```


The first line of the template is the **<!DOCTYPE>** indicator, which shows the particular version of HTML being used; in this case, 4.01 transitional. Within the **<html>** tag, the basic structure of a document reveals two primary sections: the "head" and the "body." The head of the document, as indicated by the **head** element, contains information and tags describing the document such as its title. The body of the document, as indicated by the **body** element, contains the document itself with associated markup required for structure or presentation. The structure of an XHTML document is pretty much the same with the exception of a different **<!DOCTYPE>** indicator and a few extra attributes added to the **<html>** tag.

```
<!DOCTYPE html PUBLIC "-//W3C//DTD XHTML 1.0 Transitional//EN"
"http://www.w3.org/TR/xhtml1/DTD/xhtml1-transitional.dtd">
<html xmlns="http://www.w3.org/1999/xhtml" xml:lang="en" lang="en">
<head>
<title>Document Title Goes Here</title>

...Head information describing the document and providing
supplementary information goes here....
</head>
<body>
...Document content and markup go here....

</body>
</html>
```

Alternatively, in either HTML or XHTML we might replace the **<body>** tag with a **<frameset>** tag, which encloses potentially numerous **<frame>** tags corresponding to individual portions of the browser window, termed *frames*. Each frame in turn would reference another HTML/XHTML document containing either a standard document complete with **<html>**, **<head>**, and **<body>**, or perhaps yet another framed document. The **<frameset>** tag also should include a **<noframes>** tag that provides a version of the page for browsers that do not support frames. Within this element often occurs the **<body>** tag for non-framesupporting browsers. An example template for a frameset document is shown here, though we omit the XHTML version, which is nearly identical. Note that the DTD for a framed document is different from that of a normal document.

```
<!DOCTYPE HTML PUBLIC "-//W3C//DTD HTML 4.01 Frameset//EN"
"http://www.w3.org/TR/html4/frameset.dtd">
<html>
<head>
<title>Document Title Goes Here</title>

...Head information describing the frameset and providing
supplementary information goes here...
</head>
<frameset>
...numerous frame elements here...
```

```
<noframes>
  <body>
...Alternative content for non-frame aware browsers...
  </body>
</noframes>
</frameset>
</html>
```

Framed documents are discussed in greater depth in Chapter 8. For now, let's concentrate on a typical document template of **<!DOCTYPE>**, **<html>**, **<head>**, and **<body>** and examine each piece more in depth.

Document Types

HTML follows the SGML notation for defining structured documents. From SGML, HTML inherits the requirement that all documents begin with a **<!DOCTYPE>** declaration. In the most basic sense, this line identifies the HTML "dialect" used in a document by referring to an external document type definition, or *DTD*. A DTD defines the actual elements, attributes, and element relationships that are valid in documents. The **<!DOCTYPE>** declaration allows validation software to identify the HTML DTD being followed in a document, and verify that the document is syntactically correct—in other words, that all tags used are part of a particular specification and are being used correctly. The process of validation is discussed in greater depth in Chapter 2.

NOTE: *Today browsers are aware of the* **<!DOCTYPE>** *and standards-compliant browsers will examine it to determine what rendering mode to enter. This process is often dubbed the "doctype switch" and is used by browsers to quickly determine if a standards-compliant parse of the page should be employed or if the browser should enter into "quirk" mode and assume that a less stringent form of HTML is being used. Because of this, HTML/XHTML document authors should always use the* **<!DOCTYPE>** *statement properly.*

There are numerous HTML and XHTML DTDs that can be used, corresponding to the various standard versions of HTML in existence. In the past, even some proprietary forms of HTML had their own doctype statements. At the time of this edition's writing, the **<!DOCTYPE>** most likely in use is either the HTML 4.0 transitional form, as shown here:

```
<!DOCTYPE HTML PUBLIC "-//W3C//DTD HTML 4.0 Transitional//EN">
```

or the HTML 4.01 transitional specification indicated by

```
<!DOCTYPE HTML PUBLIC "-//W3C//DTD HTML 4.01 Transitional//EN">
```

However, these forms are not quite specific enough and should actually specify the location of the DTD being used, as shown here:

```
<!DOCTYPE HTML PUBLIC "-//W3C//DTD HTML 4.01 Transitional//EN"
"http://www.w3.org/TR/html4/loose.dtd">
```

In the future, the stricter form of HTML—XHTML—probably will be more commonly used. It is indicated by

```
<!DOCTYPE html PUBLIC "-//W3C//DTD XHTML 1.0 Transitional//EN"
"http://www.w3.org/TR/xhtml1/DTD/xhtml1-transitional.dtd">
```

There are numerous document type identifiers that could be used at the start of the document, as shown in Table 1-1.

NOTE *On occasion, you might see other HTML document type indicators, notably one for the 3.0 standard that was never really adopted in the Web community.*

While XHTML is almost certainly the future of HTML, the fact of the matter is there will be multiple forms of HTML in use on the Web for a long time. Document authors should be familiar with the many forms of HTML. A brief explanation of each version of HTML is provided in Table 1-2.

HTML Version	!DOCTYPE Declaration
2.0	<!DOCTYPE HTML PUBLIC "-//IETF//DTD HTML//EN">
3.2	<!DOCTYPE HTML PUBLIC "-//W3C//DTD HTML 3.2 Final//EN">
4.0 Transitional	<!DOCTYPE HTML PUBLIC "-//W3C//DTD HTML 4.0 Transitional//EN" "http://www.w3.org/TR/html4/loose.dtd">
4.0 Frameset	<!DOCTYPE HTML PUBLIC "-//W3C//DTD HTML 4.01 Frameset//EN" "http://www.w3.org/TR/html4/frameset.dtd">
4.0 Strict	<!DOCTYPE HTML PUBLIC "-//W3C//DTD HTML 4.01//EN" "http://www.w3.org/TR/html4/strict.dtd">
4.01 Transitional	<!DOCTYPE HTML PUBLIC "-//W3C//DTD HTML 4.01 Transitional//EN" "http://www.w3.org/TR/html4/loose.dtd">
4.01 Frameset	<!DOCTYPE HTML PUBLIC "-//W3C//DTD HTML 4.01 Frameset//EN" "http://www.w3.org/TR/html4/frameset.dtd">
4.01 Strict	<!DOCTYPE HTML PUBLIC "-//W3C//DTD HTML 4.01//EN" "http://www.w3.org/TR/html4/strict.dtd">
XHTML 1.0 Transitional	<!DOCTYPE html PUBLIC "-//W3C//DTD XHTML 1.0 Transitional//EN" "http://www.w3.org/TR/xhtml1/DTD/xhtml1-transitional.dtd">
XHTML 1.0 Strict	<!DOCTYPE html PUBLIC "-//W3C//DTD XHTML 1.0 Strict//EN" "http://www.w3.org/TR/xhtml1/DTD/xhtml1-strict.dtd">
XHTML 1.0 Frameset	<!DOCTYPE html PUBLIC "-//W3C//DTD XHTML 1.0 Frameset//EN" "http://www.w3.org/TR/xhtml1/DTD/xhtml1-frameset.dtd">
XHTML 1.1	<!DOCTYPE html PUBLIC "-//W3C//DTD XHTML 1.1//EN" "http://www.w3.org/TR/xhtml11/DTD/xhtml11.dtd">
XHTML 2.0 (still in progress)	<!DOCTYPE html PUBLIC "-//W3C//DTD XHTML 2.0//EN" " http://www.w3.org/TR/xhtml2/DTD/xhtml2.dtd ">

TABLE 1-1 Common HTML Doctype Declarations

HTML Version	Description
2.0	Classic HTML dialect supported by browsers such as Mosaic. This form of HTML supports core HTML elements and features such as tables and forms but does not consider any of the browser innovations of advanced features such as style sheets, scripting, or frames.
3.0	The proposed replacement for HTML 2.0 that was never widely adopted, most likely due to the heavy use of browser-specific markup.
3.2	An HTML finalized by the W3C in early 1997 that standardized most of the HTML features introduced in browsers such as Netscape 3. This version of HTML supports many presentation elements, such as fonts, as well as early support for some scripting features.
4.0 Transitional	The 4.0 transitional form finalized by the W3C in December of 1997 preserves most of the presentation elements of HTML 3.2. It provides a basis for transition to CSS as well as a base set of elements and attributes for multiple language support, accessibility, and scripting.
4.0 Strict	The strict version of HTML 4.0 removes most of the presentation elements from the HTML specification, such as fonts, in favor of using Cascading Style Sheets (CSS) for page formatting.
4.0 Frameset	The frameset specification provides a rigorous syntax for framed documents that was lacking in previous versions of HTML.
4.01 Transitional/ Strict/Frameset	A minor update to the 4.0 standard that corrects some of the errors in the original specification.
XHTML 1.0 Transitional	A reformulation of HTML as an XML application. The transitional form preserves many of the basic presentation features of HTML 4.0 transitional but applies the strict syntax rules of XML to HTML.
XHTML 1.0 Strict	A reformulation of HTML 4.0 strict using XML. This language is rule enforcing and leaves all presentation duties to technologies such as Cascading Style Sheets (CSS).
XHTML 1.1	A minor change to XHTML 1.0 that restructures the definition of XHTML 1.0 to modularize it for easy extension. It is not commonly used at the time of this writing and only offers minor gains over XHTML 1.0.
XHTML 2.0	A new implementation of XHTML circa 2003 that may not provide backward compatibility with XHTML 1.0 and traditional HTML. XHTML 2 will likely remove most or all presentational tags left in HTML and will introduce even more logical ideas to the language.

TABLE 1-2 Description of Common HTML Versions

The browser vendors also have provided their own various extensions to HTML. While many of the elements introduced should not be used, some of the innovations made by browser vendors eventually were adopted as part of the standard. Web page authors also should be aware of the primary contributions of each browser as well as the core version of HTML supported, both for browser compatibility as well as understanding the historical changes the Web has undergone. Table 1-3 lists a few of the major browser versions and summarizes some of their element introductions.

Browser	Features Introduced	Standards Support
Netscape 2.*x*	Java, JavaScript, Frames, Plug-ins	2.0 and Netscape extensions, many of which became 3.2 standard.
Netscape 3.*x*	A few proprietary elements such as spacer and multicol	3.2 with Netscape extensions.
Netscape 4.*x*	Basic CSS support and the proprietary HTML element layer	3.2, part of 4.0, part of CSS1, and Netscape extensions.
Netscape 6.*x*	Heavy standards support	4.0, CSS1, much of CSS2, good portion of Document Object Model.
Netscape 7.*x* / Mozilla 1.*x*	Very heavy standards support, minor CSS extensions, link prefetching	4.0, XHTML 1.0, CSS1 and most of CSS2, nearly all DOM 1 and 2.
Internet Explorer 3.0	Frames and Inline Frames, Jscript, ActiveX controls, VBScript, some proprietary HTML elements such as marquee and bgsound	3.2 with some Microsoft extensions and a limited amount of CSS1.
Internet Explorer 4.0	Significant JavaScript access to page elements	Most of 4.0 with Microsoft extensions, most of CSS1.
Internet Explorer 5.0/5.5/6.0	Native XML support, close to full Document Object Model Level 1	4.0 with Microsoft extensions, most of CSS1, most of the Document Object Model 1. XHTML support in IE 6. Still certainly underlying reliance on IE flavored syntax.
Opera 7.0	Very heavy standards focus, focus on accessibility and speed features and related W3C specifications	4.0 and XHTML, most CSS1 and Document Object Model 1. Pre 7.0 versions of Opera had problems with JavaScript and advanced CSS.
WebTV/MSN TV	Proprietary tags useful for television screen layout and integration with television viewing	3.2 with WebTV/MSN TV extensions. Support for many Netscape and Microsoft extensions.

TABLE 1-3 Web Development Feature Overview By Browser Version

It is very important for document authors to know the various versions of **<!DOCTYPE>** declarations, as well as extensions made by the browser vendors. When checking syntax, it is important to understand that strict adherence to W3C specifications is not currently a reasonable goal, given the lack of browser support and widespread use of HTML extensions. One day, if XHTML becomes all that is promised, we will simply follow the specifications as written for correct document construction. Right now, however, that ideal environment seems far off. Even with standards-oriented browsers emerging, bugs and rendering differences continue to plague Web developers. For now, page authors should find the common ground among their browser population, be it HTML 4 or XHTML, and try to stick to what is standard as best as possible.

The <html> Tag

The **<html>** tag delimits the beginning and the end of an HTML document. Given that **<html>** is the common ancestor of an HTML document it is often called the *root element*, as it is the root of an inverted tree structure containing the tags and content of a document. The **<html>** tag, however, directly contains only the **<head>** tag, the **<body>** tag, and potentially the **<frameset>** tag instead of the **<body>** tag. The HTML document template, shown earlier in the chapter, shows the **<html>** tag's typical use in a document, as a container for all other elements.

The <head> Tag

The information in the head of an HTML document is very important because it is used to describe or augment the content of the document. The head of an HTML document is like the front matter or cover page of a document. In many cases, the information contained within the **<head>**tag is information about the information of the page, which generally is referred to as *meta-information*. This is a very important and often overlooked aspect of HTML documents. Search engines use meta-information to index Web pages. Aside from meta-information, the **head** element can include author contact information, scripts, style sheets, comments—and, most importantly, a page title.

The <title> Tag

The most important **head** element is the **title** element, which most browsers display in a title bar at the top of the browser window. The document title is actually the only tag required under traditional HTML specifications and should occur as the first element within the **head** element. XHTML continues the idea of **<title>** being first in the **<head>**, but of course does not allow for the optional use of important structural tags such as **<html>**, **<head>**, or **<body>**. Regardless of specification variations, the **<title>** tag must be used in every HTML document as it gives an HTML document a title by which it is known to browsers and indexing robots. Browsers display the document title while the document is being viewed, and might also use the title in bookmark lists.

NOTE *Most browsers attempt to deduce a title for a document that is missing the **title** element. The browser often uses the URL of the document being viewed, which might indicate nothing about the document's content. However, even this behavior isn't guaranteed. For example, Classic WebTV listed a document without a title as simply "untitled document."*

A document title might contain standard text as well as character entities (for example, **©**), which are discussed later in the chapter. However, HTML markup isn't permitted in the **<title>** tag and doesn't produce the expected result. So, according to the rules of the **title** element,

```
<title><strong>Home Page</strong></title>
```

is not valid, whereas

```
<title>The Demo Company Story &copy; 2003</title>
```

is. However, a well-formed title is not necessarily a meaningful title. Remember that a user sees a title in his or her bookmark list if the page is bookmarked. Search engines that index the Web often place special meaning on the contents of the **title** element when determining what a page is about. Because of this, a title should indicate the contents of a page without ambiguity. Titles such as "My Page" or "Home Page" don't make much sense; "John Smith's Home Page" and "Demo Company, Inc." do. A well-formed title actually can add navigational value to a site by showing an implicit hierarchy among a group of pages. Although "Trainer Robot Datasheet" seems to be a reasonable title, "Demo Company: Products: Trainer Robot Datasheet" is a better title. It not only indicates the company the product is related to, but implies a hierarchy in the site.

NOTE *In the early days of the Web, using characters such as a colon (:), slash (/), or backslash (\) in titles was a problem. An operating system might have a problem with these titles if the document was saved to the local system. For example, the colon isn't allowed within Macintosh filenames, and slashes generally aren't allowed within filenames because they indicate directories. Although this appears to be a problem, most browsers remove the suspect characters and reduce them to spaces during the Save process. To be on the safe side, dashes can be used to delimit sections in the title.*

While titles should be descriptive, they should also be concise. Authors should limit title length to a reasonable number of characters. Netscape and Internet Explorer display around 20–30 characters of a title in their bookmark lists. One way to limit the length of titles is to remove words such as "a," "an," and "the," which provide little extra value.

NOTE *Some browsers are very sensitive to the misuse of the **<title>** tag. Even before the rise of XHTML, according to the HTML 3.2 and 4.0 specifications, the **title** element is mandatory, while the **html, head,** and **body** elements are not. In some versions of Navigator, omitting the **</title>** tag causes a document to not display. So, if you get a bunch of junk on your screen (see Figure 1-4), check the **<title>** tag right away.*

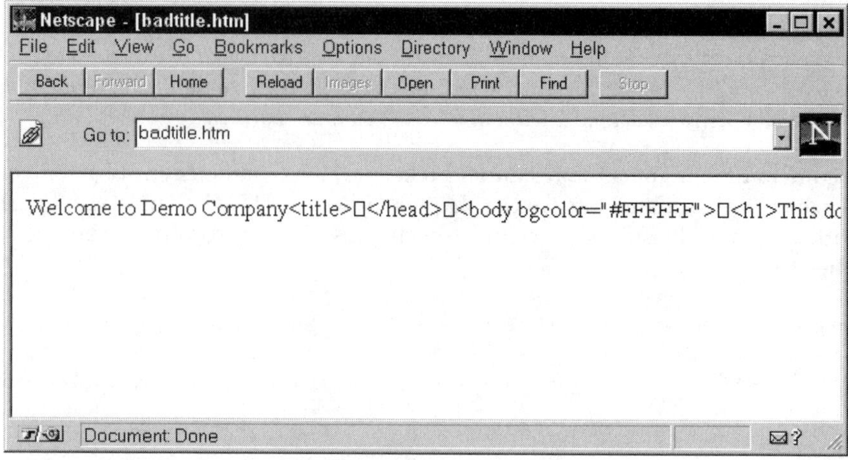

FIGURE 1-4 Problem with **<title>** under Netscape Navigator

According to the HTML and XHTML specifications, only one **title** element should appear in every document. The title should appear in the head of the document. Under extremely old browser versions, multiple **<title>** tags often were used within documents to create an animated title. This was a bug and modern browsers don't support this capability; thus, it shouldn't be used.

Other head Elements

In addition to the **title** element under the HTML 4.01 and XHTML 1.0 transitional DTDs, the elements allowed within the **head** element include **base**, **isindex**, **link**, **meta**, **object**, **script**, and **style.** A brief discussion of the other head elements follows. Complete information is available in the cross-referenced chapters and reference section.

The **<base>** tag specifies an absolute URL address that is used to provide server and directory information for partially specified URL addresses called relative links used within the document. Links and the use of **<base>** are discussed in Chapter 4.

The **<isindex>** tag indicates that the document contains a searchable index. It causes the browser to display a query prompt and a field for entering a query. This element typically was used with simple site searching mechanisms, but is rarely used today, having been mostly replaced by forms. Under the HTML 4.01 and XHTML 1.0 strict definitions, **<isindex>** is deprecated. The element is discussed solely in Appendix A, as its use is discouraged.

The **<link>** tag specifies a special relationship between the current document and another document. It can be used in hypertext navigational relationships including prefetching of documents by browsers, which is discussed in Chapter 4. It can also be used to link the current document to a style sheet, which is discussed in Chapter 10. The **<link>** tag has many interesting possibilities, but unfortunately few of these are implemented even in the most standards-compliant browser.

The **<meta>** tag uses name/value pairs to provide meta-information about a document. The **<meta>** element often provides descriptive information targeted by Web search engines. In a very different use, the **<meta>** tag can define various HTTP request values such as a page refresh or an expiration time. These and other uses are discussed in Chapters 16 and 17, which cover site delivery and site maintenance, respectively.

The **<object>** tag allows programs and other binary objects to be directly embedded in a Web page. The most popular current approaches use Java applets, plug-ins, or ActiveX controls to embed multimedia elements such as Flash animations, sounds, or movies. The **<object>** tag is discussed in Chapter 15.

The **<script>** tag allows programs written in a scripting language to be directly embedded in a Web page. The most popular scripting language in Web documents is JavaScript, which is somewhat standardized in the form of ECMAScript, although few Web practitioners refer to it as that. The **script** element and associated usage of scripts, often dubbed *Dynamic HTML* (DHTML) because it allows HTML elements to be modified dynamically, should simply be considered a form of client-side scripting. It is discussed in Chapter 14.

The **<style>** tag encloses document-wide style specifications relating to fonts, colors, positioning, and other aspects of content presentation. Today, the primary style sheet technology used in Web pages is called Cascading Style Sheets (CSS), which is discussed extensively in Chapters 10 and 11.

The <body> Tag

After the head section, the body of a document is delimited by **<body>** and **</body>**. Under the HTML 4.01 specification and many browsers, the **body** element is optional, but should always be included, particularly as it is required in XHTML. Only one **body** element can appear per document. Because the **body** element delimits the document itself, its attributes are primarily used to effect change across the entire document, such as setting background images, background colors, and link and text color. These attributes are discussed in depth in Chapter 6.

Elements and Characters

Many types of elements are in the body of a Web document. For example, *block-level elements* define structural content blocks such as paragraphs **<p>** or headings **<h1>**. Block-level elements generally introduce line breaks visually. Special forms of blocks such as unordered lists **(<ul>)** can be used to create lists of information. *Inline elements* such as bold (**<b>**), strong (**<strong>**), and numerous others occur within blocks. These types of elements do not introduce any returns. Other miscellaneous types of elements include those that reference other objects such as images (**<img>**) or programs (**<object>**). Other hard-to-characterize elements also could be grouped and defined, but often these are related to browser-specific elements such as **<marquee>** and are not part of the HTML specification, though they may be commonly used. In addition to grouping tags as block, inline, list, miscellaneous, and other, it is common to group HTML tags as logical or physical. *Physical* tags such as **<b>** describe the look of enclosed content, whereas *logical* tags such as **<strong>** describe its meaning. The implication of the logical/physical grouping is significant and is discussed in more detail later in this chapter. However, the specific instances of each of these types of elements will not be discussed now but introduced in subsequent chapters, with the core elements discussed in Chapter 3.

Finally, within the elements in the body, you can type in regular text and insert special characters through the use of character entities. Occasionally, it might be necessary to put special characters within a document, such as accented letters, copyright symbols, or even the angle brackets used to enclose HTML elements. To use such characters in an HTML document, they must be "escaped" by using a special code. All character codes take the form **&*code*;**, in which code is a word or numeric code indicating the actual character that you want to put onscreen. For example, when adding a less than symbol, <, you could use **<** or **<**. Character entities also are discussed in Chapter 3, and a complete list of the character entities is presented in Appendix C.

The Rules of HTML

HTML has rules, even in its standard form. Unfortunately, these "rules" really aren't rules, but more like suggestions because most browsers pretty much let just about anything render. However, under XHTML these rules are enforced, and incorrectly structured documents may have significant downsides, often exposed only once other technologies such as CSS or JavaScript are intermixed with the markup. The reality is that most HTML, whether created by hand or a tool, generally lie somewhere between strict conformance and no conformance to the specification. Let's take a brief tour of some of the more important aspects of HTML syntax.

HTML Is Not Case Sensitive, XHTML Is

These markup examples

```
<B>Go boldly!</B>
<B>Go boldly!</b>
<b>Go boldly!</B>
<b>Go boldly!</b>
```

are all equivalent under traditional HTML. In the past, developers were highly opinionated on how to case elements. Some designers pointed to the ease of typing lowercase tags as well as to XHTML's preference for lowercase elements as reasons to go all lowercase. Other designers pointed out that, statistically, lowercase letters were more common than upper; keeping tags in all uppercase made them easier to pick out in a document, thus making its structure clearer to someone doing hand markup. However, given the XHTML lowercase preference, you should always use lowercase tags.

HTML/XHTML Attribute Values May Be Case Sensitive

One interesting aspect of HTML's case sensitivity is that although HTML element names and attribute names are not case sensitive, we can't assume everything is case insensitive. For example, consider **<img SRC="test.gif">** and **<img src="test.gif">**. Under traditional HTML, these are equivalent because the **<img>** tag and the **src** attribute are not case sensitive. However, for compatibility with XHTML, they should be lowercase. Yet, regardless of the use of XHTML or HTML, the actual attribute values in some tags may be case sensitive, particularly where URLs are concerned. So **<img src="test.gif">** and **<img src="TEST.GIF">** are not necessarily referencing the same image. When referenced from a UNIX-based Web server where filenames are case sensitive, test.gif and TEST.GIF would be two different files, while on a Windows Web server where filenames are not case sensitive, they would reference the same file. This is a common problem and will keep a site from easily being transported from one server to another.

HTML/XHTML Is Sensitive to a Single White Space Character

Browsers collapse white space between characters down to a space. This includes all tabs, line breaks, and carriage returns.

Consider the markup

```
<b>T e s t o f s p a c e s</b><br />
<b>T   e   s   t   o f   s p a c e s </b><br />
<b>T
e s
t o f s p           a c e s</b><br />
```

As shown here, all the spaces, tabs, and returns are collapsed to a single element.

T e s t o f s p a c e s
T e s t o f s p a c e s
T e s t o f s p a c e s

Note that in some situations, HTML does treat white space characters differently. In the case of the **pre** element, which defines a preformatted block of text, white space is not ignored and is preserved because the content is considered preformatted. Also, white space is preserved within the **textarea** element when setting default text for a multiline text entry field.

Because browsers will ignore most white space, HTML authors often format their HTML documents for readability. However, the reality is that browsers really don't care one way or another, and either do end users. Because of this, some sites have adopted an idea called "HTML crunching" to save bandwidth, which is discussed in Chapter 2.

Subtle errors tend to creep into HTML files where white space is concerned; be especially careful with spacing around **<img>** and **<a>** tags. For example, consider the markup here:

```
<a href="http://www.democompany.com">
  <img src="democompany.gif" width="221" height="64"
border="0" alt="Demo Company" />
</a>
```

Notice the line return after the **<img>** tag, just before the **</a>** tag that closes the link. Under some browsers, this will result in a small "tail" to the image, often termed a tick, as shown here:

DEMO COMPANY
Gap in HTML code can cause a "tick" around linked images

Some browsers will fix the tick problem, others won't. What's interesting is that the browsers showing the tick actually are interpreting the specification properly.

The final aspect of spacing to consider is the use of the nonbreaking space entity, or ** **. Some might consider this the duct tape of the Web—useful in a bind when a little bit of formatting is needed or an element has to be kept open. While the ** ** entity has many useful applications, such as keeping empty table cells from collapsing, designers should avoid relying on it for significant formatting. While it is true that markup such as

```
      Look, I'm spaced out!
```

would indent some spaces in the text, the question is, exactly how far? In print, using spaces to format is dangerous and things rarely line up. It is no different on the Web.

XHTML/HTML Follows a Content Model

Both HTML and XHTML support a strict content model that says that certain elements are supposed to occur only within other elements. For example, markup like this,

```
<ul>
   <p>What a simple way to break the content model!</p>
</ul>
```

which often is used for simple indentation, actually doesn't strictly follow the XHTML content model. The **<ul>** tag is only supposed to contain <li> tags. The **<p>** tag is not really appropriate in this context. Much of the time, HTML page authors are able to get away with this, but sometimes they can't. For example, in a strictly conformant browser, the **<input>** tag found outside a **<form>** tag is simply not displayed. HTML documents should follow a structured content model.

Elements Should Have Close Tags Unless Empty

Under traditional HTML, some elements have optional close tags. For example, both of the paragraphs here are allowed, although the second one is better:

```
<p>This isn't closed.
<p>This is.</p>
```

A few tags, such as the horizontal rule **<hr>** or line break **
**, do not have close tags because they do not enclose any content. These are considered empty elements and can be used as is in traditional HTML. However, under XHTML you must always close tags so you would have to write **
</br>** or, more commonly, use a self-closing tag format with a final "/" character, like so: **
**.

Unused Elements May Minimize

Sometimes tags may not appear to have effect in a document. Consider, for example, the **<p>** tag, which specifies a paragraph. As a block tag it induces a return by default, but when used repeatedly, like so,

```
<p></p><p></p><p></p>
```

it does not produce numerous blank lines because the browser minimizes the empty **p** elements. Some HTML editors output nonsense markup such as

```
<p> </p><p> </p><p> </p>
```

to deal with this. This is a misuse of HTML. Multiple **
** tags should have been used instead to achieve line spacing.

Elements Should Nest

A simple rule states that tags should nest, not cross, thus

```
<b><i>is in error as tags cross</b></i>
```

whereas

```
<b><i>is not since tags nest</i></b>.
```

Breaking this rule seems harmless enough, but it does introduce some ambiguity if tags are automatically manipulated using a script; under XHTML, proper nesting is mandatory.

Attributes Should Be Quoted

Although under traditional HTML simple attribute values did not need to be quoted, not doing so can lead to trouble with scripting. For example,

```
<img src=robot.gif height=10 width=10 alt=robot>
```

would work fine in most browsers. Not quoting the **src** attribute is troublesome but should work. But what would happen if the **src** attribute were manipulated by JavaScript and changed to "robot 2.gif" complete with a space? This could cause a problem. Furthermore, XHTML does enforce quoting, so all attributes should be quoted like so

```
<img src="robot.gif" height="10" width="10" alt="robot" />
```

and the empty **img** element would close itself with a trailing slash. Generally, it doesn't matter if single or double quotes are used, unless JavaScript is found in an attribute value. Stylistically, double quotes tend to be favored, but either way you should be consistent.

Browsers Ignore Unknown Attributes and Elements

For better or worse, browsers will ignore unknown elements and attributes, so

```
<bogus>this text will display on screen</bogus>
```

and markup such as

```
<p id="myPara" obviouslybadattribute="TRUE">will also render fine.</p>
```

Browsers make best guesses at structuring malformed content and tend to ignore code that obviously is wrong. The permissive nature of browsers has resulted in a massive amount of malformed HTML documents on the Web. Oddly, from many people's perspective it hasn't hurt as much as you might expect because the browsers do make sense out of the "tag soup" they find. However, such a cavalier use of the language creates documents with shaky foundations at best. Once we add other technologies such as CSS and JavaScript to the mix, brazen flaunting of the rules can have repercussions and may result in broken pages. Furthermore, to automate the exchange of information on the Web we need to enforce stricter structure of our documents. The introduction of XHTML brings some hope for stability and structure of Web documents.

XHTML: The Rules Enforced

The new version of HTML, called XHTML, became a W3C Recommendation in January 2000. XHTML is a reformulation of HTML using XML that attempts to change the direction and use of HTML to the way it ought to be. So what does that mean? In short, rules now matter. In the past, you could feed your browser just about anything and it would render. XHTML ends all that. Now if you make a mistake, it should matter. Theoretically, a conformant browser shouldn't necessarily render the page at all, although this is highly unlikely and browsers tend to resort to a backward compatibility quirk mode to display a document. Yet despite the ability to continue to skirt the rules, you shouldn't. The gains can be significant and the rules are pretty easy to follow, particularly since we already covered them in the previous sections. Briefly, to form a valid XHTML document:

- You must have a doctype indicator and conform to its rules. For example,
```
<!DOCTYPE html PUBLIC "-//W3C//DTD XHTML 1.0 Transitional//EN"
 "http://www.w3.org/TR/ xhtml1/DTD/xhtml1-transitional.dtd">
```
- You must have **<html>**, **<head>**, and **<body>** (or a **<frameset>** containing a **<body>** inside of a **<noframes>** tag).
- **<title>** must come first in the <**head**> element.
- You have to quote *all* your attributes, even simple ones such as **<p align= "left">**.
- You must nest your tags properly, so **<i><b>** is okay **</b></i>**, but **<i><b>** is not **</i></b>**.
- You cannot omit optional close tags, so **<p>** cannot stand alone; you must have **<p>** and **</p>**.
- Empty tags must close, so tags such as **<hr>** become **<hr />**.
- You must lowercase all tags and attribute names.

There's more, but this is most of them. Except for a few changes in syntax, such as the empty tag changes and the forced lowercase, just do your HTML correctly (as you should have done before).

Although XHTML doesn't appear to be a big deal, it is. Enforcing rules is going to cause problems and widespread use will take time, considering the amount of developer education, tool changes, and browser updates required. Most existing Web pages will also have to be restructured to some degree. So the big question is this: Will this really come to pass? Since the third edition of this book little actually has changed in Web development and few major sites use XHTML. However, designers are finally starting to get interested in it, particularly given the modern browsers' support for the technology.

Major Themes

Before finishing the chapter, we need to take a look at some of the major open questions related to HTML/XHTML. You will encounter these issues over and over again throughout the book and while they are pretty easy to describe, they are very hard to answer.

Logical and Physical HTML

No introduction to HTML would be complete without a discussion of the logical versus physical markup battle at the heart of HTML. *Physical HTML* refers to using HTML to make pages look a particular way; *logical HTML* refers to using HTML to specify the structure of a document while using another technology, such as Cascading Style Sheets (CSS) as discussed in Chapters 10 and 11, to designate the look of the page.

Most people are already very familiar with physical document design because they normally use WYSIWYG (*what you see is what you get*) text editors, such as Microsoft Word. When Word users want to make something bold, they simply select the appropriate button, and the text is made bold. In HTML, you can make something bold simply by enclosing it within the **<b>** and **</b>** tags, as shown here:

```
<b>This is important.</b>
```

This can easily lead people to believe that HTML is nothing more than a simple formatting language. WYSIWYG HTML editors (such as Microsoft FrontPage) also reinforce this view. But as page designers try to use HTML in this simplistic fashion, they sooner or later must face the fact that HTML is *not* a physical page-description language. Page authors can't seem to make the pages look exactly the way they want, and even when they can, doing so often requires heavy use of **<table>** tags, giant images or Flash files, and even trick HTML. Other technologies, such as style sheets, might provide a better solution for formatting text than a slew of inconsistently supported tricks and proprietary HTML elements.

According to most markup experts, HTML really was not designed to provide most of the document layout features people have come to expect, and it shouldn't be used for that purpose. Instead, HTML should be used as a logical, or generalized, markup language that defines a document's structure, not its appearance. For example, instead of defining the introduction of a document with a particular margin, font, and size, HTML just labels it as an introduction section and lets another system, such as Cascading Style Sheets, determine the appropriate presentation. In the case of HTML, the browser or a style sheet has the final say on how a document looks.

Even traditional HTML contains mostly logical elements. An example of a logical element is **<strong>**, which indicates something of importance, as shown here:

```
<strong>This is important.</strong>
```

The **strong** element says nothing about how the phrase "This is important" will actually appear, although it probably will be rendered in bold. Although many of HTML's logical elements are relatively underutilized, others, such as headings like **<h1>** and paragraphs **<p>**, are used regularly although they are generally thought of as physical tags by most HTML users. Consider that people generally consider **<h1>** a large heading, **<h2>** a smaller heading, and that **<p>** tags cause returns and you can see that logical or not, the language is physical to most of its users.

The benefits of logical elements might not be obvious to those comfortable with physical markup. To understand the benefits, it's important to realize that on the Web, many browsers render things differently. In addition, predicting what the viewing environment will be is difficult. What browser does the user have? What is his or her monitor's screen resolution? Does the user even have a screen? Considering the extreme of the user having no screen at all: how would a speaking browser render the **<bold>** tag? What about the **<strong>** tag? Text tagged with **<strong>** might be read in a firm voice, but boldfaced text might not have an easily translated meaning outside the visual realm.

Many realistic examples exist of the power of logical elements. Consider the multinational or multilingual aspects of the Web. In some countries, the date is written with the day first, followed by the month and year. In the United States, the date generally is written with the month first, and then the day and year. A **<date>** tag, if it existed, could tag the information and enable the browser to localize it for the appropriate viewing environment. In short, separation of the logical structure from the physical presentation allows multiple physical displays to be applied to the same content. This is a powerful idea that, even today is rarely taken advantage of. We'll take a look at this approach to page design in Chapters 10 and 11 when we cover HTML's intersection with style sheets.

Whether you subscribe to the physical (specific) or logical (general) viewpoint, traditional HTML is not purely a physical *or* logical language yet. In other words, currently used HTML elements come in both flavors—physical and logical—and developers nearly always think of them as physical. Elements that specify fonts, type sizes, type styles, and so on are physical. Tags that specify content or importance, such as **<cite>** and **<h1>**, and let the browser decide how to do things are logical. A quick look at Web pages across the Internet suggests that logical elements and style sheets often go unused because while Web developers want more layout control than raw HTML provides, style sheets are still not well understood by many developers, and browser support continues to be too buggy for some people's taste. Finally, many designers just don't think in the manner required for logical markup and their WYSIWYG page editors generally don't encourage such thinking! Of course, the strict forms of XHTML, particularly XHTML 2, will change all this, returning the language to a primarily logical formatting language.

Standards versus Practice

Just because a standard is defined doesn't necessarily mean that it will be embraced. Many Web developers simply do not know or care about them. As long as their page looks right in their favorite browser, they are happy and they will continue to go on abusing HTML tags such as **<table>** and using various tricks and proprietary elements. In some sense, HTML is the English language of the Web, poorly spoken by many but widely understood. Yet this does not mean you should embrace every proprietary HTML tag or trick used. Instead, acknowledge what the rules are, follow them as closely as possible, and break them only on purpose and only when absolutely necessary. Be careful not to follow the standards or markup validator too religiously in the name of how things ought to be done; your users and clients certainly will not forgive browser errors or page display problems because you followed the rules and the browser vendor did not! With the rise of standards-oriented browsers and the continued refinement of the HTML, XHTML, and CSS specifications, things will improve, but the uptake is still slow, and millions of documents will continue to be authored with no concept of standards-compliant logical structuring. However, this does not mean that XHTML should be avoided. On the contrary, the structure and rigor it provides allows for easier maintenance, faster browsers, the possibility of even higher quality Web tools, and the ability to automatically exchange information between sites. Even with these incredible possible benefits, given the short-term similarity of XHTML and HTML, some developers still think: Why bother? Web page development continues to provide an interesting study of the difference between what theorists say and what people want and do.

Myths About HTML and XHTML

The amount of hearsay, myths, and complete misunderstandings about HTML and XHTML is enormous. Much of this can be attributed to the fact that many people simply view the page source of sites or read quick tutorials to learn HTML. In the text that follows, I cover a few of the more common myths about HTML and try to expose the truth behind them.

Myth: HTML Is a WYSIWYG Design Language

HTML isn't a specific, screen- or printer-precise formatting language like PostScript. Many people struggle with HTML on a daily basis, trying to create perfect layouts by using HTML elements inappropriately or by using images to make up for HTML's lack of screen and font-handling features. Interestingly, even the concept of a visual WYSIWG editor propagates this myth of HTML as a page layout language. Other technologies, such as Cascading Style Sheets (CSS), are far better than HTML for handling presentation issues and their use returns HTML back to its structural roots.

Myth: HTML Is a Programming Language

Many people think that making HTML pages is similar to programming. However, HTML is unlike programming in that it does not specify logic. It specifies the structure of a document. With the introduction of scripting languages such as JavaScript, however, the dynamic HTML (DHTML) is becoming more and more popular and is used to create highly interactive Web pages. Simply put, DHTML is the idea of a scripting language like JavaScript dynamically modifying HTML elements. DHTML blurs the lines between HTML as a layout language and HTML as a programming environment. However, the line should be distinct because HTML is not a programming language. Heavily intermixing JavaScript with HTML markup in the ad-hoc manner that many authors do is far worse than trying to use HTML as a WYSIWYG markup language. Programming logic can be cleanly separated in HTML, as discussed in Chapters 13 to 15. Unfortunately, if this separation isn't heeded, the page maintenance nightmare that results from tightly binding programming logic to content will dwarf the problems caused by misuse of HTML code for presentation purposes.

Myth: Traditional HTML Is Going Away

HTML is the foundation of the Web; with literally billions of pages in existence, not every document is going to be upgraded anytime soon. The "legacy" Web will continue for years, and traditional nonstandardized HTML will always be lurking around underneath even the most advanced Web page years from now. Beating the standards drum upon high might speed things up a bit, but let's face the facts: there's a long way to go before we are rid of messed up HTML markup.

Myth: XHTML Will Take the Public Web by Storm

Wishful thinking, but having taught HTML for years and having seen firsthand how both editors and others build Web pages, I can tell you that it is very unlikely that XHTML will be the norm anytime soon. Since the last millennium, it was predicted that traditional HTML was dead. Yet today, documents are still primarily created both by editor and by hand sloppily, rarely conforming to even traditional HTML standards let alone XHTML.

Although HTML has had rules for years, much of the time people don't really bother to follow them because they see little penalty nor obvious benefit to actually studying the language rigorously. Often, people learn HTML simply through imitation by viewing the source of existing pages, which are not always written correctly, and going from there. Like learning a spoken language, HTML's loosely enforced rules have allowed many document authors to get going quickly. Its biggest flaw is, in some sense, its biggest asset and has allowed millions of people to get involved with Web page authoring. Rigor and structure is coming, but it will take time and require new tools.

Myth: Hand-Coding of HTML Will Continue Indefinitely

Although some will continue to craft pages like mechanical typesetting, as the Web editors improve and produce standard markup perfectly, the need to hand-tweak HTML documents will diminish. I hope designers will realize that knowledge of the "invisible pixel" trick is not a bankable resume item and instead focus on development of their talents as they also pursue a firm understanding of HTML markup, CSS, and JavaScript.

Myth: HTML Is All You Need to Know to Create Good Web Pages

Although HTML is the basis for Web pages, you need to know a lot more than HTML to build useful Web pages (unless the page is very simple). Document design, graphic design, and quite often programming are necessary to create sophisticated Web pages. HTML serves as the foundation for all of these tasks, and a complete understanding of HTML technology can only aid document authors.

Summary

HTML is the markup language for building Web pages and traditionally has combined physical and logical structuring ideas. Elements—in the form of tags such as **<b>** and **</b>**—are embedded within text documents to indicate to browsers how to render pages. The rules for HTML are fairly simple. Unfortunately, these rules have not been enforced by browsers in the past. Because of this looseness, there has been a great deal of misunderstanding about the purpose of HTML, and a good portion of the documents on the Web do not conform to any particular official specification of HTML. The introduction of XHTML attempts to return HTML to its roots as a structural language, leaving presentational duties to other technologies such as Cascading Style Sheets. XHTML also attempts to introduce the required rigor and enforcement of syntax that will make HTML a solid foundation on which to build tomorrow's Web applications. While heavy use of strict XHTML has yet to occur on the Web, document authors following the rules presented, even those using classic HTML, should be well suited to make the transition to perfectly formed documents. Before plunging in to the core elements of HTML, we'll take a look at Web development practices and project planning useful to aspiring HTML document authors.

CHAPTER 2

Web Development Overview

One of the problems with discussing the creation of Web pages is that mastery of HTML often is confused with understanding the process of Web development. HTML is only one part of the process. Graphic design and programming are also important aspects of that Web development process. "Web development" is a more appropriate term than "Web design" to describe the overall process of planning and putting together a Web site, particularly when some degree of forethought, skill, and artistry is employed. Knowledge of HTML alone does not provide all the facilities required to make appealing, usable Web sites. Before you get too caught up in the details of markup tags, you need to understand the Web process and how HTML works in that process. This chapter provides a brief overview of some of the development ideas presented in the companion book, *Web Design: The Complete Reference, Second Edition* (McGraw-Hill/Osborne 2002), with a special focus on the markup aspects of a Web site project.

The Need for Careful Web Development

Today, there is a crisis in Web development similar to the "software crisis" of the late 1960s. A few years ago, most Web sites were little more than digital brochures, or "brochureware." Creating such a site didn't require a great deal of planning—often, it was sufficient simply to develop an interface and then to populate the site with content. Since then, sites have become much larger and more complex. With the introduction of interactivity and e-commerce, sites have clearly moved away from brochureware to become full-fledged software applications. Despite this, many developers have yet to adopt a robust site-building methodology, but continue to rely on ad hoc methods.

NOTE *The "software crisis" refers to a time in the software development field when increasing hardware capabilities allowed for significantly more complex programs to be built. It was challenging to build and maintain such new programs because little methodology had been used in the past, resulting in numerous project failures. Methodology such as structured or top-down design was introduced to combat this crisis.*

Evidence of the crisis in Web development practices is everywhere. Unlike the in-house client/server software projects of the past, the dirty laundry of many failed Web projects is often aired for all to see. The number of pages that seem to be forever "under construction" or "coming soon" suggests that many Web sites are poorly planned. Some sites have been in a state of construction for years, judging by their lack of content or date of last modification. These online ghost towns are cluttered with old information, non-standard HTML, dated technologies, broken links, and malfunctioning scripts. Don't discount some of these problems as mere typos or slight oversights. A broken link is a catastrophic failure, like a software program with menus that just don't go anywhere!

Sites exhibit problems for a variety of reasons. Some sites may deteriorate simply because their builders got bored or moved on. Other sites may fall apart because the site wasn't considered useful or funding was withdrawn. Still other sites probably just couldn't be completed because the sites overwhelmed the developers; the developers may not have understood the tools they were working with, or they were not versed well enough in the medium's restrictions. The vast number of poorly executed sites on the Web suggests that Web development projects are risky and often fail.

Basic Web Process Model

To help reduce the difficulty in constructing sites, we should adopt a *process model* that describes the various phases involved in Web site development. That way, each step can be carefully performed by the developer with help from guidelines and documentation, which tells them how to do things and ensures that each step is carried out properly as they go along. An ideal process model for the Web would help the developer address the complexity of the site, minimize the risk of project failure, deal with the near certainty of change during the project, and deliver the site quickly with adequate feedback for management throughout the process. Of course, the ideal process model also would have to be easy to learn and execute. This is a pretty tall order, and it is unlikely that any single process model is always going to fit the particular requirements of a project.

There are numerous process models used by people to build software and Web sites. However, the most basic process model used should be familiar to most people—at least in spirit, as it is deductive, or more simply, "top-down." Following the top-down method, a Web project begins with the big picture and narrows down to the specific steps necessary to complete the site. Thus, the model starts first with a planning stage, then a design phase, then implementation and testing, and ends with a maintenance phase. The phases might appear to be distinct steps, but the progress from one stage to another might not always be obvious. Furthermore, progress isn't always toward a conclusion, and occasionally previous steps may need to be revisited if the project encounters unforeseen changes. The actual number of steps and their names vary from person to person, but a general idea of the procedure is shown in Figure 2-1.

NOTE *In software engineering, this model often is called the waterfall model, or sometimes the software lifecycle model, because it describes the phases in the lifetime of software. Each stage in the waterfall model proceeds one after another until conclusion.*

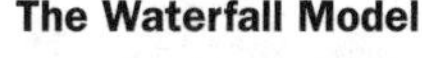

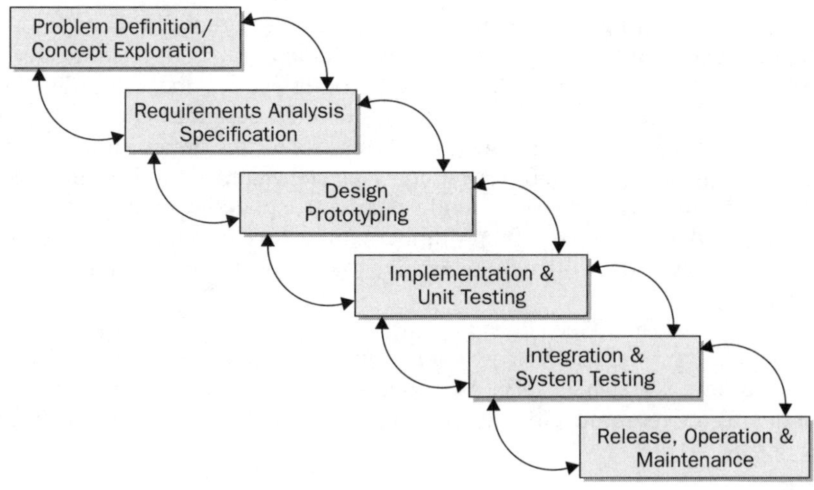

FIGURE 2-1 The Waterfall Model

The good thing about this site development approach is that it makes developers plan everything up front. That also is its biggest weakness. In a Web project, there often is a great deal of uncertainty in what is required to accomplish a project, particularly if the developer has not had a great deal of Web development experience. Another problem with this development model is that each step is supposed to be distinct, but the reality is that in Web development, like software, steps tend to overlap, influence previous and future steps, and often have to be repeated. Unfortunately, the basic Web site development approach can be fairly rigid and might require the developer to stop the project and redo many steps if too many changes occur. In short, the process doesn't deal well with change. However, this simple model for site design continues to be very popular because it is both easy to understand and easy to follow. Furthermore, the distinct steps in the process appeal to management as they can easily be monitored and serve as project milestones.

Approaching a Web Site Project

In theory, Web development process models make sense, but do they work in practice? The answer is a resounding *Yes*. However, site development rarely works in a consistent manner because of the newness of the field, the significant time constraints, and the ever-changing nature of Web projects. Developers should always proceed with caution. With this in mind, regardless of the project, the first step is always the same: set the overall goal for the project.

Goals and Problems

Many Web site projects ultimately fail because they lack clear goals. In the first few years of Web design, many sites were built purely to show that an organization had a site. Somehow, without a site an organization was not considered progressive or a market leader; competitors with sites were considered a threat. Many times, a site provided little benefit because it wasn't really designed to provide anything other than a presence for the organization. As familiarity with the Web has grown, the reasons for having Web sites have become clearer. Today, site goals have become important and are usually clearly articulated up front. However, don't assume that logic rules the Web—a great number of site development projects continue to be driven by pure fancy and are often more reactive to perceived threats than intended to solve real problems.

Determining a goal for a Web site isn't difficult; the problem is refining it. Be wary of vague goals such as "provide better customer service" or "make more money by opening up an online market." These may serve as a good sound bite or mission statement for a project, but details are required. Good goal statements might include something like the following:

- Build a customer support site that will improve customer satisfaction by providing 7/24 access to common questions and result in a 25 percent decrease in telephone support.
- Create an online automobile parts store that will sell at least $10,000/month of product directly to the consumer.
- Develop a Japanese food restaurant site that will inform potential customers of critical information such as hours, menu, atmosphere, and prices as well as encourage them to order by phone or visit the location.

Notice that two of the three goal statements have measurable goals. This is very important, as it provides a way to easily determine success or failure as well as assign a realistic budget to the project. The third goal statement does not provide an obviously measurable goal. This can be dangerous because it is difficult to convince others that the site is successful or to even place a value on the site. In the case of the restaurant site, a goal for the number of viewers of the site or a way to measure customer visits using a coupon would help. Consider a revised goal statement such as the following:

> Develop a Japanese food restaurant site that will inform at least 300 potential customers per month of critical information such as hours, menu, atmosphere, and prices as well as encourage them to order by phone or visit the location.

The simple addition of a particular number of visitors makes the goal statement work. By stating a number of desired visitors, the restaurant owner could compare the cost of placing advertisements in print or on the radio versus the cost of running the site to provide the same effective inquiry rate.

Brainstorming

In general, coming up with a goal statement is fairly straightforward. The challenge is to keep the statement concise and realistic. In many Web projects, team members often want to include everything in the site. Remember, the site can't be everything to everyone; you must have a specific audience and set of tasks in mind. To more fully explore site goals and features, team members often need a brainstorming session. The purpose of a brainstorming session is simply to bring out as many possible ideas about the site as possible. A white board and post-it notes are useful during a brainstorming session to quickly write down or modify any possible ideas for the site.

Oftentimes, brainstorming sessions get off track because participants jump ahead or bring too much philosophy about site design to the table. In such cases, it is best to focus the group by talking about site issues they should all agree on. Attempt to find a common design philosophy by having people discuss what they don't want to see in the site. Getting meeting participants to agree they don't want the site to be slow, difficult to use, and so on is usually easy. Once you obtain a common goal in the group, even if it is just that they all believe that the site shouldn't be slow, future exploration and statements of what the site should be will go smoother.

NOTE *When conducting a project to overhaul a site, be careful not to run brainstorm meetings by ridiculing the existing site, unless no participant in the project has any ownership stake in the site. A surefire way to derail a site overhaul project is to get the original designers on the defensive because of criticism of their work. Remember,* people *build sites, so building a positive team is very important.*

Narrowing the Goal

During the brainstorming session, all ideas should be allowed. The point of the session is to develop what might be called the *wish list*. A wish list is a document that describes all possible ideas for inclusion in a site regardless of price, feasibility, or applicability. It is important not to stifle any ideas during brainstorming, lest this eliminate the creative aspect of site development. However, eventually the wish list will have to be narrowed down to what is reasonable and appropriate for the site. This can be a significant challenge with a site that may have many possible goals. Consider a corporate site that contains product information, investor information, press releases, job postings, and technical support sections. Each person with ownership stakes in a particular section will think his or her section is most important and will want a big link to his or her section on the home page. Getting compromise with so many stakeholders can be challenging!

Audience

Throughout site development and particularly when goals are being discussed, you should always consider the site's audience. What a brainstorming group wants and what an end user wants don't always match. We need to make sure the site's goals are in line with its users' needs. However, to do this we need to accurately describe the site's audience and their reason for visiting the site. Don't look for a generic "Joe Enduser" with a modem who happened upon your site by chance. It is unlikely such a user could be identified for most sites, and most users will probably have a particular goal in mind. Instead, think about what kind of people your end users are. Consider asking some basic questions about the site's users, such as:

- Where are they located?
- How old are they?

- What is their gender?
- What language do they speak?
- How technically and Web proficient are they?
- Are the users disabled (sight, movement, and so on) in any manner?
- What kind of connection would they have to the Internet?
- What kind of computer would they use?
- What kind of browser would they probably use?

Next, consider what the users are doing at the site:

- How did they get to the site?
- What do the users want to accomplish at the site?
- When will they visit the site?
- How long will they stay during a particular visit?
- From what page(s) will they leave the site?
- When will they return to the site, if ever?
- How often do they return?

While you might be able to describe the user from these questions, you should quickly determine that your site would probably not have one single type of user with a single goal. For most sites, there are many types of users, each with different characteristics and goals.

Server Logs

If the site has been running for some time, you have a gold mine of information about your audience—your Web site access logs. Far too often designers don't really look at logs for anything other than basic trends, such as number of page views. However, from looking at log files you should be able to determine useful information, such as the types of browsers commonly accessing the site, the general pattern of when and how visitors use the site such as entry and exit points, the current delivery and server requirements, and so on. Of course, stats logs won't tell you much about user satisfaction and specific details of site usage. For that, you will actually have to get to know users and even talk to them!

User Interviews and Profiling

The best way to understand users is to actually talk to them. If at all possible, you should interview users directly to resolve any questions you may have about their wants and characteristics. A survey may be appropriate, but live interviews provide the possibility to explore ideas beyond predetermined questions. Unfortunately, interviewing or even surveying users can be very time-consuming and will not account for every single type of user characteristic or desire. From user interviews and surveys or even from just thinking about generic users, you should attempt to create stereotypical but detailed profiles of common users.

Consider developing at least three user profiles. For most sites, the three stereotypical users should correspond roughly to an inexperienced user, a user who has Web experience but doesn't visit your site often, and a power user who understands the Web and may visit the site frequently. Most sites will have these classes of users, with the intermediate, infrequent visitor most often being the largest group. Make sure to assign percentages to each of the generic groups so that you give each the appropriate weight. Now name each person. You may want to name each after a particular real user you interviewed, or use generic names like Bob Beginner, Irene Intermediate, and Paul Poweruser. Now work up very specific profiles for each stereotypical user using the questions from the previous section. Try to make sure that the answers correspond roughly to the average answers for each group. So, if there were a few intermediate users interviewed who had fast connections, but most have slow connections, assume the more common case.

Once your profile for each site visitor is complete, you should begin to create visit scenarios. What exactly would Bob Beginner do when he visits your site? What are the tasks he wishes to perform? What is his goal? Scenario planning should help you focus on what each user will actually want to do. From this exercise, you may find that your goal statements are not in line with what the users are probably interested in doing. If so, return to the initial step of the process and modify the goal statement based on your new information.

Site Requirements

Based on the goals of the site and what the audience is like, the site's requirements should begin to present themselves. These requirements should be roughly broken up along visual, technical, content, and delivery requirements. To determine requirements, you might ask questions such as the following:

- What kind of content will be required to meet our goals?
- What kind of look should the site have?
- What types of programs will have to be built?
- How many servers will be required to service the site's visitors adequately?
- What kind of restrictions will users place on the site with respect to bandwidth, screen size, the browser, and so on?

As you determine your requirements, it is likely that site costs will become more apparent and potential implementation problems will surface. The requirements will suggest how many developers are required and show what content is lacking. If the requirements seem excessive in view of the potential gain, it is time to revisit the goal stage or question if the audience was accurately defined. The first three steps of the typical Web project process may be repeated numerous times until a site plan or specification is finally agreed upon.

The Site Plan

Once a goal, audience, and site requirements have been discussed and documented, a formal site plan should be drawn up. The site plan should contain the following sections:

- **Short goal statement** This section contains a brief discussion to explain the overall purpose of the site and its basic success measurements.
- **Detailed goal discussion** This section discusses the site's goals in detail and provides measurable goals to verify the benefit of the site.

- **Audience discussion** This section profiles the users who would visit the site. The section would describe both audience characteristics as well as the tasks the audience would try to accomplish at the site.
- **Usage discussion** This section discusses the various task/visit scenarios for the site's users. Start first with how the user arrives at the site and then follow the visit to its conclusion. This section may also include a discussion of usage measurements, such as number of downloads, page accesses per visit, forms being filled out, and so on as they relate to the detailed goal discussion.
- **Content requirements** The content requirements section provides a laundry list of all text, images, and other media required in the site. A matrix showing the required content, form, existence, and potential owner or creator is useful, as it shows how much content may be outstanding. A simple matrix is shown in Table 2-1.
- **Technical requirements** This section provides an overview of the types of technology the site will employ, such as HTML, XHTML, CSS, JavaScript, CGI, Java, plug-ins, and so on. It should cover any technical constraints such as performance requirements, security requirements, multidevice or multiplatform considerations, and any other technical requirements that are related to the visitor's capabilities.
- **Visual requirements** The visual requirements section outlines basic considerations for interface design. The section should indicate in broad strokes how the site should relate to any existing marketing materials and provide an indication of user constraints for graphics and multimedia, such as screen size, color depth, bandwidth, and so on. The section may outline some specifics, such as organizational logo usage limitations, fonts required, or color use; however, many of the details of the site's visuals will be determined later in the development process.
- **Delivery requirements** This section indicates the delivery requirements, particularly any hosting considerations. A basic discussion of how many users will visit the site, how many pages will be consumed on a typical day, and the size of a typical page should be included in this section. Even if these are just guesses, it is possible to provide a brief analysis of the server hardware, software, and bandwidth required to deliver the site.

Content Item	Description	Content Type	Content Format	Exists?	Owner
Butler Robot Press Release	Press release for new Butler 7 series robot that ran in *Robots Today*	Text	Microsoft Word	Yes	Jennifer Tuggle
Software Agreement Form	Brief description of legal liability of using trial robot personality software	Text	Paper	Yes	John P. Lawyer
Handheld Supercomputer Screen Shot	Picture of the new Demo Company Cray-9000 handheld palm size computer	Image	GIF	No	Pascal Wirth
Welcome from President Message	Brief introduction letter from President to welcome user to site	Text	Microsoft Word	No	President's Executive Assistant

TABLE 2-1 Content Matrix

- **Miscellaneous requirements** Other requirements may need to be detailed in the site plan, such as language requirements, legal issues, industry standards, and other similar considerations. They may not necessarily require their own separate discussion, but instead may be addressed throughout the other sections of the document.
- **Site structure diagram** This section provides a site structure or flow diagram detailing the various sections within a site. Appropriate labels for sections and general ideas for each section should be developed based on the various user scenarios explored in earlier project phases. Organization of the various sections of the site is important and may have to be refined over time. Often, a site diagram will look something like the one shown in Figure 2-2.
- **Staffing** This section details the resources required to execute the site. Measurements can be in simple man-hours and should relate to each of the four staffing areas: content, technology, visual design, and management.
- **Time line** The time line should show how the project would proceed using the staffing estimates from the preceding section combined with the steps in the process model outlined earlier in the chapter.
- **Budget** A budget is primarily determined from the staffing requirements and the delivery requirements. However, marketing costs or other issues such as content licensing could affect the site cost as well.

This is just a suggested site plan—the actual organization and content of a site plan is up to the developer. However, don't skip writing the plan even though it may seem daunting. Without such a document, you can only develop a project in an evolutionary fashion (almost trial-and-error manner), which may result in many false starts and waste time and money. Furthermore, it will be nearly impossible to obtain any realistic bids from outside vendors on a Web site without a detailed specification.

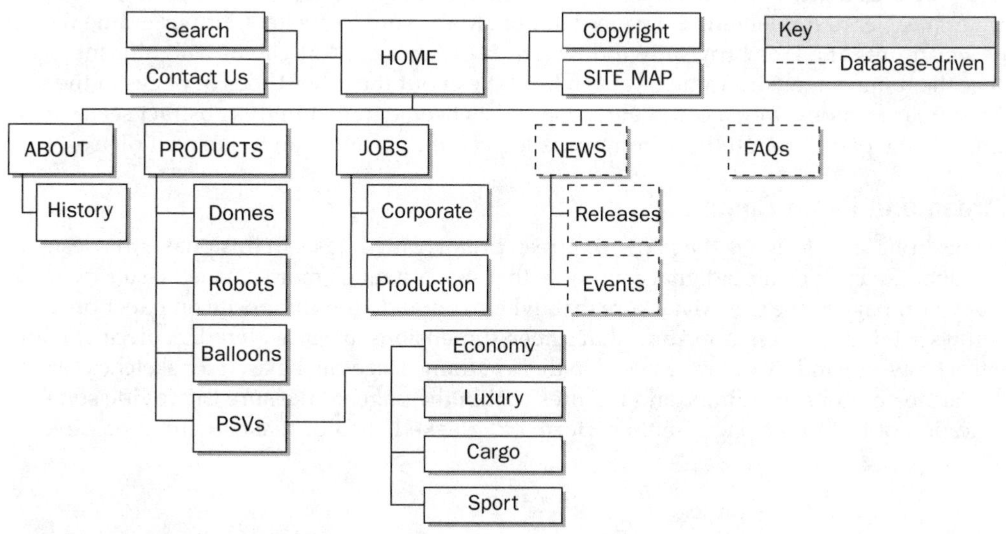

FIGURE 2-2 Typical site organization diagram

A finished plan doesn't allow you to immediately proceed to implementation. Once the specification is developed, it should be questioned one last time, preferably by a colleague or someone with an outside perspective. The completed specification may reveal unrealistic estimates that will throw you back to the stage of questioning initial goals or audience. If it survives, it may be time to actually continue the process with the design and prototyping stage.

Design Phase Dissected

The design or prototyping stage is likely the most fun for Web designers, as it starts to bring form to the project. During this phase, both technical and visual prototypes should be developed. However, before prototypes are built, consider collecting as much content as possible. The content itself will influence the site and help guide its form. If the content is written in a very serious tone but the visuals are fun and carefree, the site will seem very strange to the user. Seeing the content up front will allow the designer to integrate the design and content. Also, consider that content collection can be one of the slowest aspects of site development. Many participants in a Web project are quick to attend brainstorming meetings but are difficult to find once their content contributions are required. Lack of content is by far the biggest problem in Web projects. Deal with this potential problem early.

Wireframes

Like the Web development process itself, visual design for a site should proceed top-down as well. Think first about how the user will enter the site and conclude with how they will leave. In most cases, this means designing the home page first, followed by subsection pages, and finally content pages and subtask pages. First, consider creating page mockups on paper in a block form commonly called a *wireframe*, as shown in Figure 2-3.

Wireframes enable designers to focus on the types of objects in the page and their organization without worrying too much about precise placement and detail of the layout itself. The wireframe approach also helps the designer make templates for pages, which makes it easier to implement the pages later on. Make sure to create your wireframe within the constraints of a Web browser window. The browser's borders can be a significant factor. Once the home page wireframe has been built, flesh out the other types of pages in the site in a similar fashion. Once a complete scenario has been detailed in this abstract sense, make sure that the path through the wireframe is logical. If it is, move on to the next phase.

Screen and Paper Comps

The next phase of design is the paper or screen prototyping phase. In this phase, the designer can either sketch or create a digital composite that shows a much more detailed visual example of a typical page in the site. Make sure that, whether you do the composite on paper or screen, a browser window is assumed and that screen dimensions are considered. A piece of paper with a browser window outline as used in the wireframe stage can be used for sketches. Sketch the various buttons, headings, and features within the page. Make sure to provide some indication of text in the page—either a form of "greeked" text or real content, if possible.

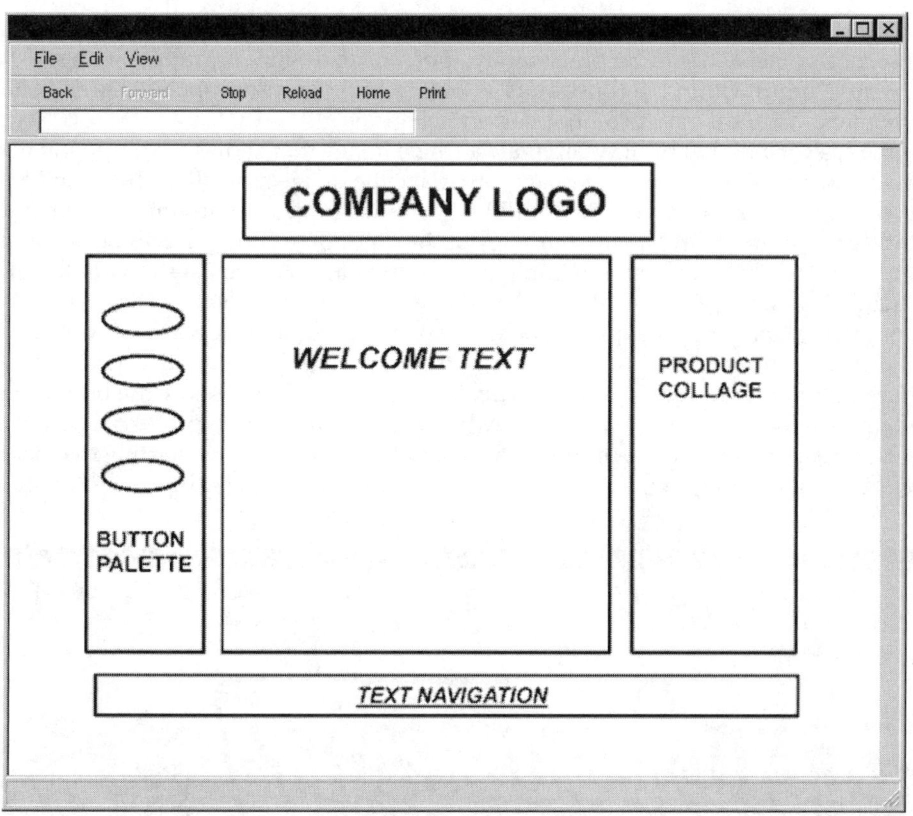

FIGURE 2-3 Sample wireframe

NOTE *Many designers use only temporary "lorem ipsum" or greeking text within screen composites. This approach does bring focus to the designed page elements and should certainly be used in initial comps. However, if real content is available you should eventually use it during the design phase. The more closely your composite simulates what the final result will be like, the more likely it will uncover potential problems before implementation.*

The comping stage provides the most room for creativity, but designers are warned to be creative within the constraints of what is possible on the Web and what visual requirements were presented in the design specification. Thinking about file size, color support, and browser capabilities may seem limiting, but doing so usually prevents the designer from coming up with a page that looks visually stunning but is extremely difficult to implement or downloads very slowly. In particular, resist the urge to become so artistic as to reinvent an organization's look in a Web site. Remember, the site plan will have spelled out visual requirements, including marketing constraints. The difficult balance between form, function, purpose, and content should become readily apparent as designers grapple with satisfying their creative urges within the constraints of Web technology, user capabilities, and site requirements. A typical paper comp is shown in Figure 2-4.

In the case of a digital prototype, create a single image that shows the entire intended screen, including all buttons, images, and text. Save the image as a GIF or JPEG and load it into the Web browser to test how it would look within a typical environment. At this stage, resist the urge to fully implement your page design. You may end up having to scrap the design, and it would be wasteful to implement at this stage. Figure 2-5 shows a digital composite of the Demo Company site created in a graphics program.

Once your paper or digital prototype is complete, it should be tested with users. Ask a few users to indicate which sections on the screen are clickable and what buttons they would select in order to accomplish a particular task. Make sure to show the prototype to more than one user, as individual taste may be a significant factor in prototype acceptance. If the user has too many negative comments about the page, consider starting over from scratch. During prototyping, you can't get too attached to your children, so to speak.

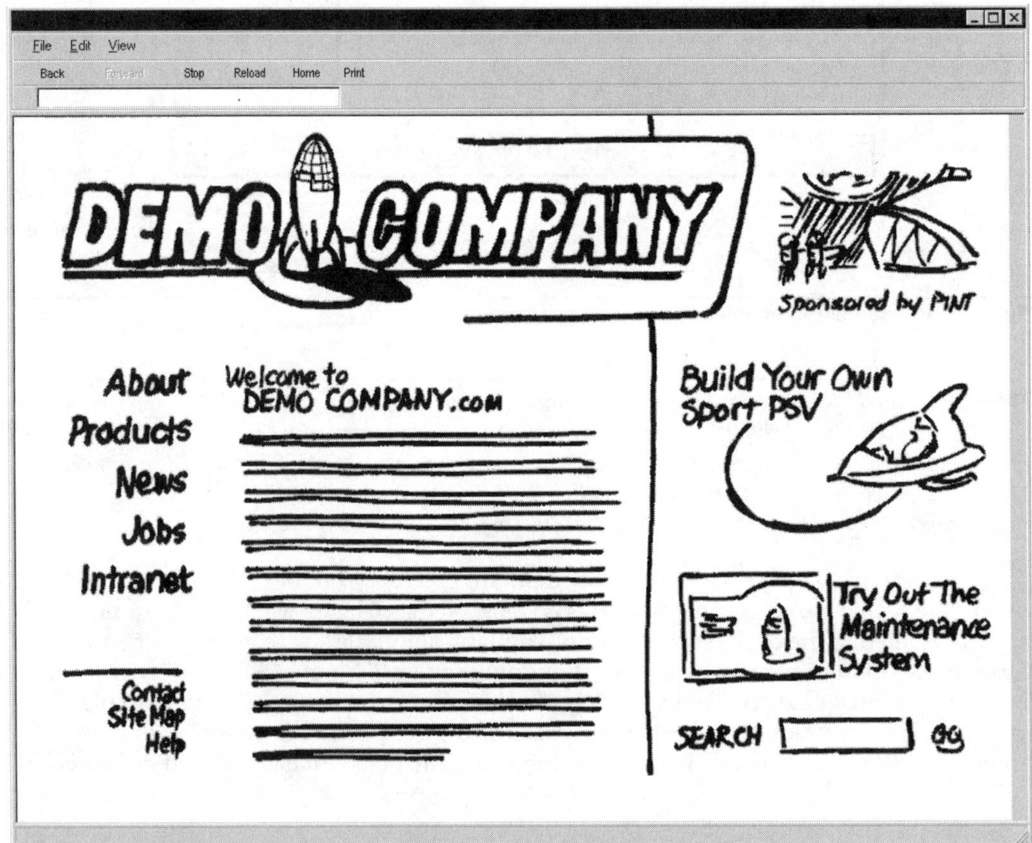

FIGURE 2-4 Paper comp for Demo Company site home page

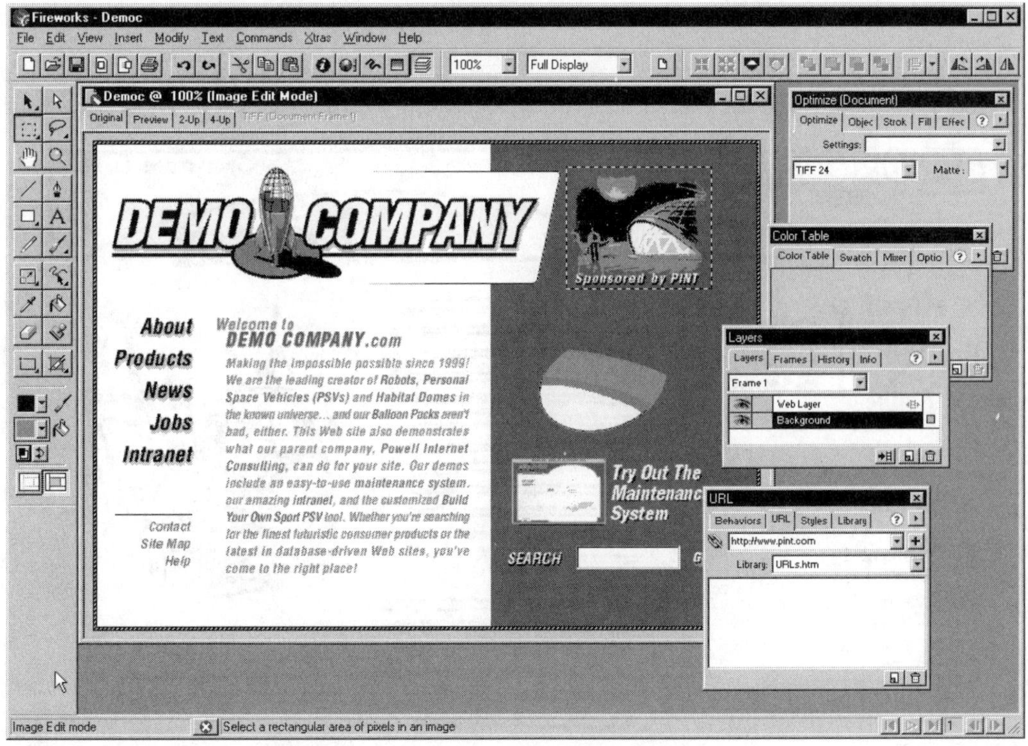

FIGURE 2-5 Digital composite for Demo Company site home page

If you do, the site will no longer be user-focused, but designer-focused. When you finally come up with an acceptable home page design, continue the process with subpages and content pages. A typical subpage composite is shown in Figure 2-6.

In highly interactive sites, you may have to develop prototype pages for each step within a particular task, such as purchasing or download. Prototype pages for the individual steps may have to be more fully fleshed out and include form field labels and other details to be truly useful. A sample paper composite for a more interactive page is shown in Figure 2-7.

While not all sites will require technical prototypes, developers of highly interactive sites should consider not only interface prototypes but also working proof of concept prototypes, showing how technological aspects work, such as database query, personalization, e-commerce, and so on. Unfortunately, what tends to happen is that technical prototypes are not built until a nearly complete interface is put in place, which may result in a heavy amount of rework.

Creating the Mock Site

After all design prototypes have been finalized, it is time to create what might be called the mock or alpha site. Implementation of the mock site starts by cutting a digital comp into its pieces and assembling the pages using HTML or XHTML and, potentially, cascading style sheets. Try building the site using templates so that the entire site can be quickly assembled. However, do not put the content in place during this phase. Many of today's modern

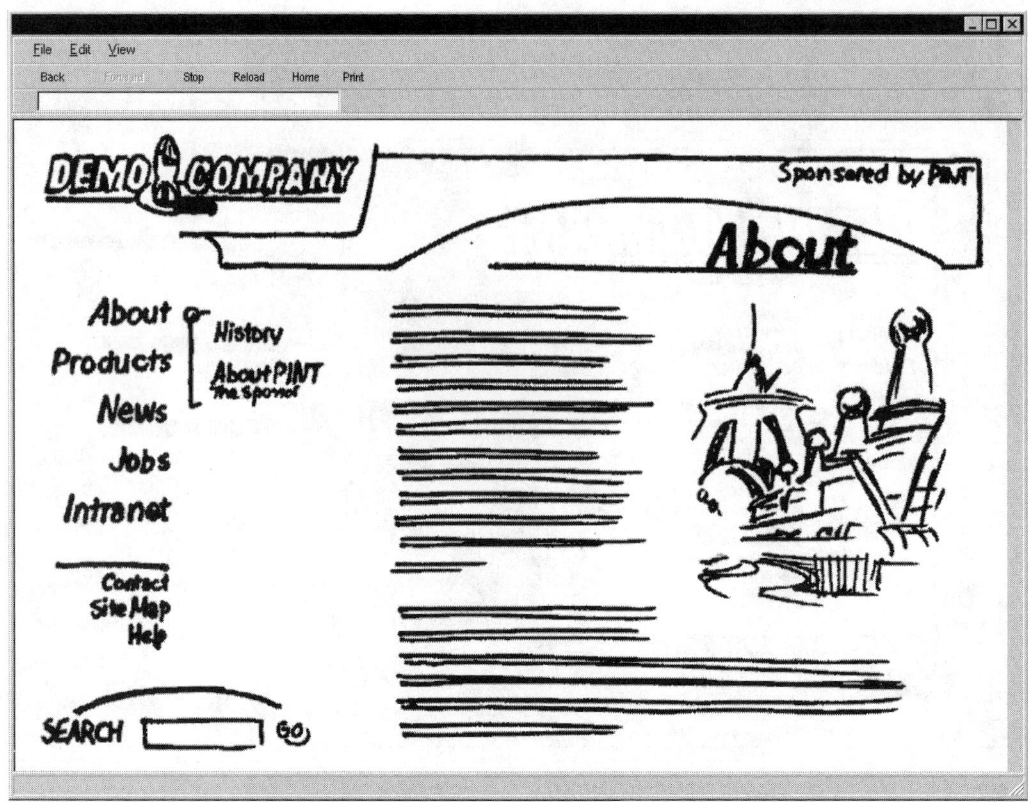

FIGURE 2-6 Subpage paper composite for Demo Company

publishing tools aid in the assembly of sample pages from screen composites. For example, consider the digital home page composite of the Demo Company site shown in Figure 2-5. We then can use a tool such as Macromedia Fireworks (www.macromedia.com/software/fireworks) to "slice" the sample layout into its appropriate pieces, as shown in Figure 2-8.

TIP *Designers should be cautious when using the HTML produced by slice and save features of applications such as Fireworks or Adobe ImageReady. These applications often produce non-standard, very complex, or difficult-to-maintain markup.*

With the various pieces that make up the home page and the various subpages of a site, a Web designer can use a Web editor to assemble the components into fully working pages lacking real content; greeking text of the form "lorem ipsum dolor sit amet" should be used to give pages form. The fully constructed mock site may lack real content, but can give developers and testers a true flavor of how the site will eventually work.

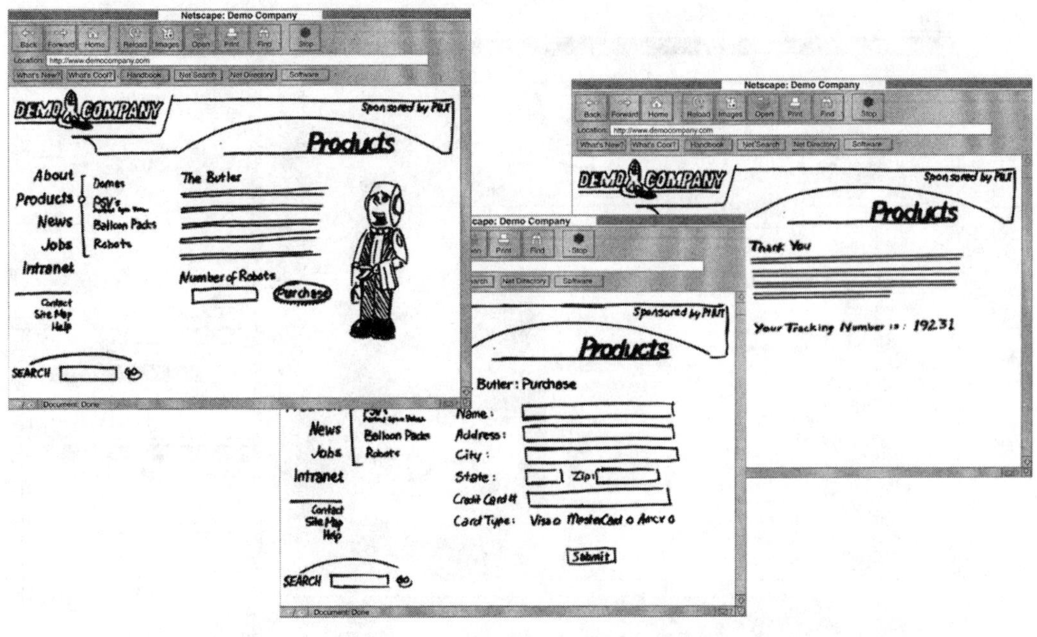

FIGURE 2-7 E-commerce paper composite

Producing the HTML

While visuals and technical elements are very important to Web design, the heart of nearly every modern Web page is still markup. Creation of HTML/XHTML should be taken very seriously as it must be a stable foundation upon which we will build presentation and interactivity.

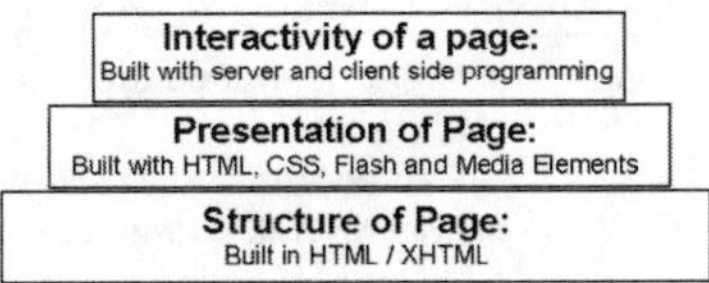

Yet despite its importance as the page's foundation, Web designers often are more concerned with how they create HTML rather than how well they do it, or how appropriate their method of creation is. In truth, there are pros and cons to every method of HTML page creation, from hand editing of markup to the latest WYSIYWG editor. The basic methods and some of their pros and cons are presented in Table 2-2.

The reality of creating HTML documents is that there are occasions to use nearly every approach. For example, making a quick change of a single tag often is fastest in a pure text editor, saving out large existing print documents might make sense using a translator,

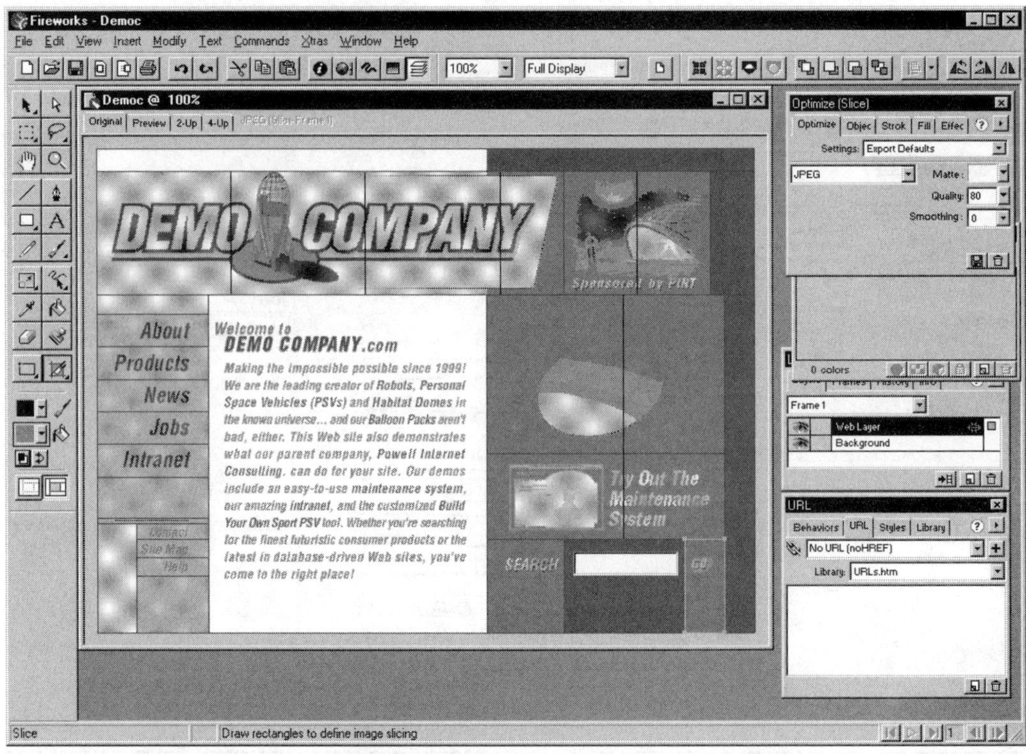

FIGURE 2-8 Slicing comps to build a template

precision coding of an HTML template might best be performed within a tagging editor, and building a modest site in a visual manner is easily done using a WYSIWYG editor. Always consider the applicability of the tool to the job before marrying it.

Method	Example	Pros	Cons
By hand	Coding pages with Notepad	+ Great deal of control over the markup + Can address bugs and new HTML/XHTML elements or CSS properties immediately	– Slow – Error prone – Requires intimate knowledge of HTML/XHTML elements and CSS properties – No direct visual representation
Translation	"Save as HTML" from another tool such as Microsoft Word	+ Quick + Simplifies conversion of existing documents	– Produced markup often is problematic – Often requires editing to add links and clean up problems

TABLE 2-2 Methods of HTML Production

Method	Example	Pros	Cons
Tagging Editor	Using HomeSite	+ Great deal of control + Faster than hand editing + Provides help addressing errors and writing structured markup and correct CSS	– Can be slow – Requires intimate knowledge of HTML and CSS
WYSIWYG Editor	Using Frontpage or Dreamweaver	+ Works on visual representation of page + Requires no significant knowledge of HTML/XHTML or CSS	– Often generates incorrect or less than optimal markup or CSS – Tends to encourage fixed size presentations that do not separate look and structure

TABLE 2-2 Methods of HTML Production *(continued)*

The tools change all the time, but at the time of this writing the HTML tools mentioned in Table 2-3 are popular. Certainly many tools exist—all with their own features and benefits—but given their use at large-scale Web firms, Dreamweaver or HomeSite is suggested for professional developers.

WYSIWYG Promises

Given the HTML creation approaches previously mentioned, many people will wonder why anyone would bother with anything other than the *WYSIWYG* (What You See Is What You Get) variety of tool such as FrontPage or Dreamweaver. Consider the difference between direct markup editing and visual editing shown in Figure 2-9.

Product	Platform(s)	URL	Comments
Dreamweaver	Windows Macintosh	www.macromedia.com/software/dreamweaver	A good visual design tool that balances WYSIWYG design capabilities with code editing. Strong CSS and DHTML support.
HomeSite	Windows	www.macromedia.com/software/homesite	A top-notch text editor for HTML professionals. Incredible code, CSS and markup handling. The original author of HomeSite has a new product called TopStyle (www.bradsoft.com) that appears to pick up where HomeSite left off and may be more appropriate for CSS.
GoLive	Macintosh Windows	www.adobe.com/products/golive	Very popular with Macintosh users, this tool has a visual designer–oriented interface. Some generated markup problems have limited its popularity with some strict standards developers.
FrontPage	Windows	www.microsoft.com/frontpage	Popular with the small developer and internal corporate development crowds. It has improved greatly, but still has a public reputation for generating bad or too Microsoft-specific pages.

TABLE 2-3 A Selection of Popular HTML Development Tools

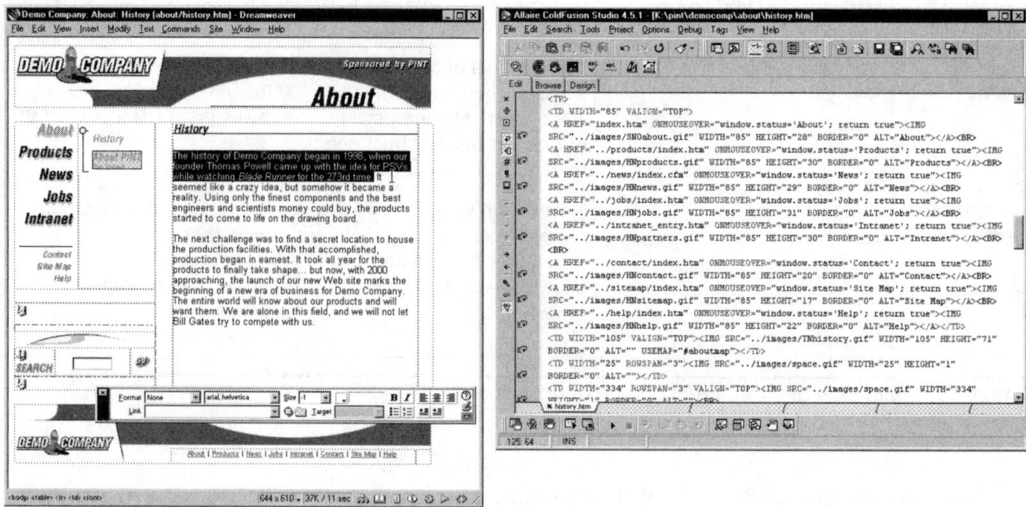

FIGURE 2-9 WYSIWYG editing versus direct HTML/XHTML editing

At first glance, it would be pretty hard to convince any pragmatic individual that direct editing of HTML markup is the way to go. While WYSIWYG page creation tools certainly hide the complexity of markup from the designer, they also don't always deliver on their promises. The reality is that these tools really are somewhat misnamed and instead ought to be called WYSIWYMG (What You See is What You *Might* Get) editors. Remember that the browser is the final display environment for HTML, so what a visual editor shows you might not accurately reflect what the eventual presentation might be, as shown in Figure 2-10.

Even worse than the not-quite WYSIWYG issue, many visual Web page editors have a difficult time dealing with all the various browser quirks. They often seem to introduce their own special ways of using HTML. Often, visual editors simply produce bad or, even when following standards, extremely bulky HTML.

While the ultimate promise of visual Web page editing hasn't quite panned out yet, few pundits would dare suggest that hand production of HTML is the wave of the future. Once HTML becomes more rigorous in the form of XHTML, and CSS becomes better supported, editors will find it far easier to produce quality markup. Hand editing of markup eventually will go the way of mechanical typesetting. For now though, page designers had better know HTML, XHTML, and CSS backward and forward to make sure that pages render correctly.

HTML Production Tips

Regardless of how HTML documents are constructed, special care should be taken when producing markup. Standards should be followed and a style adopted. In this book, it is always suggested to utilize the XHTML rules briefly introduced in Chapter 1 in order to make your markup as future-proof as possible. This section will summarize this approach as well as present some other tips that should lead to better HTML production.

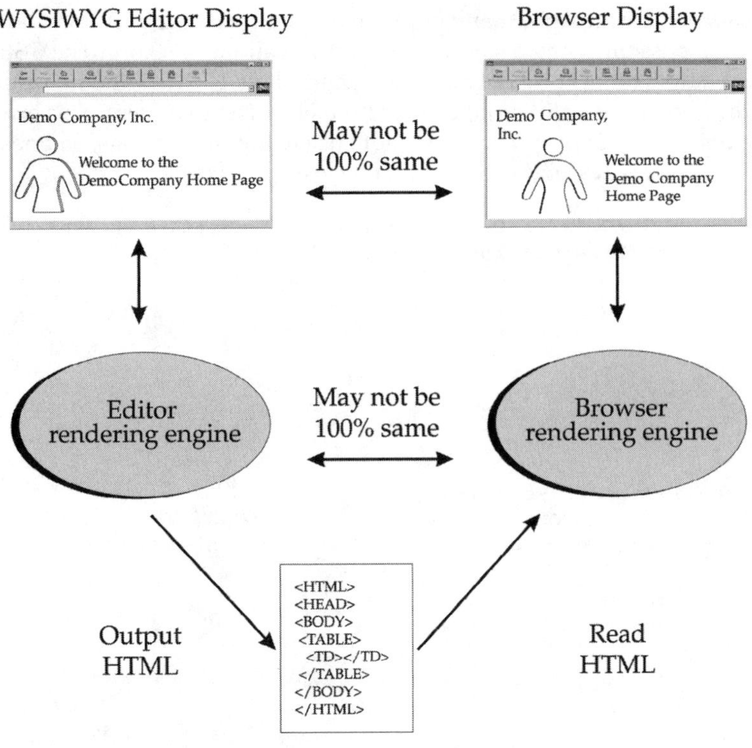

FIGURE 2-10 WYSIWYG editors do not always offer an accurate visual representation

Use Well-Formed Markup

Remember, HTML and XHTML are based on a well-defined specification. Just because a browser lets you get away with bad markup doesn't mean you should. In general, make sure that all markup is well formed—tags closed, nested, and properly used. Quote all your attributes, lowercase your tags, and always specify a DTD line such as

```
<!DOCTYPE html PUBLIC "-//W3C//DTD XHTML 1.0 Transitional//EN"
"http://www.w3.org/TR/xhtml1/DTD/xhtml1-transitional.dtd">
```

at the top of your document to indicate what version of HTML or XHTML you are using, and try to follow the rules indicated by that specification. Of course, mistakes do happen—so make sure to validate, which is discussed next.

Validate

The benefit of validation cannot be overstated. No matter how HTML or XHTML documents are created, they should always be validated. Validation involves checking an HTML or XHTML file to ensure that it meets the appropriate specification and follows the rules previously discussed. Unfortunately, few tools actually create 100 percent correct HTML/XHTML markup and even when building HTML files by hand it is easy to make mistakes.

There will be errors. Fortunately, many popular Web editors offer built-in validation. Online validation also is possible using a site such as http://validator.w3.org. The CSE Validator (www.htmlvalidator.com) is probably the best stand-alone HTML validator available. To understand the benefits of validation, consider the HTML shown here. This example has numerous errors including proprietary attribute usage, missing quotes, bad nesting, tags used in inappropriate ways, and tags that aren't closed.

```
<!DOCTYPE HTML PUBLIC "-//W3C//DTD HTML 4.01 Transitional//EN"
"http://www.w3.org/TR/html4/loose.dtd">
<html>
<head>
<title>Messed <b>Up!</b></title>
</head>
<body bgproperties="fixed">
<h1 align="center">Broken HTML
<hr>
<ul>
<p>Is this <b><i>correct</b></i>?<br>
<a href=HTTP://WWW.DEMOCOMPANY.COM>
Visit DemoCompany</a>
<pre>
      Should we do <b>this?</b>
      How about entities &copy; ?
</pre>
</ul>
</body>
<html>
```

Running the page through a validator catches all the errors, as shown in Figure 2-11.

Don't Mix Script, Style, and Structure

Designers should always try to keep files as simple as possible. With the inclusion of CSS and JavaScript, a web page file can get pretty huge and very complicated. Rather than intermix presentation described in CSS into a page directly, designers should link to an external style using markup such as

```
<link rel="stylesheet" href="styles/globalstyle.css" />
```

as discussed in Chapter 10. For JavaScript, files should be linked using syntax such as

```
<script src="scripts/validate.js" type="text/javascript"></script>
```

as discussed in Chapter 14 to isolate potentially complex code rather than including it in the HTML directly. By cleanly separating look and interactivity to other files, it is far easier to make changes to a page as well as potentially speed up the site because external scripts and styles are cached by the browser.

Name Well

Naming can be a troubling decision for some designers—to use an .htm or .html file extension? There is some benefit to using .htm because it is slightly more transportable,

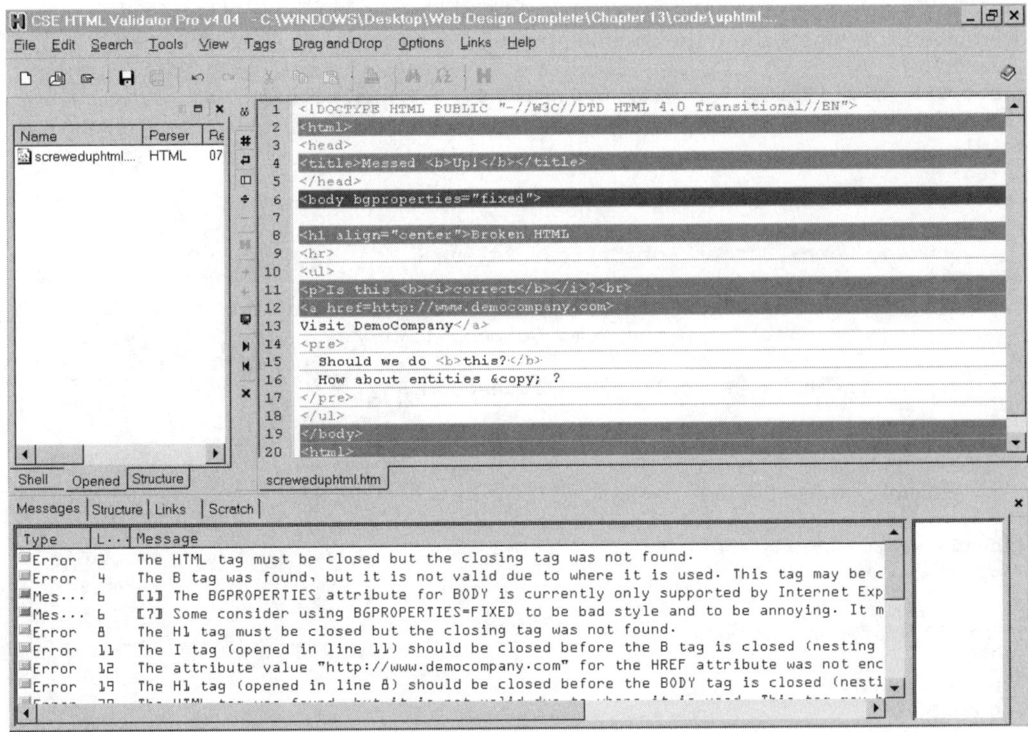

FIGURE 2-11 Validation catches HTML errors

but the reality is that it really doesn't matter. The only important thing is to be consistent. It is sad but somewhat amusing to watch developers struggle with files called index.htm and index.html in the same directory and not understand why changes are not showing up. Save yourself the aggravation and be consistent in whatever you choose. Also, make sure to use common, simple directory names in lowercase, such as /about, /products, and so on. Create simple, well-named directories for common site elements. In particular, you should create a directory for images (/images), style sheets (/styles) , and JavaScripts (/scripts). You also might find it useful to create directories for other media types such as sound, video, and animation files if they are used in the site or even a special directory for all your error pages (/errors). Finally, consider naming graphic elements and other site components in an easy-to-understand manner. Homeheader.gif probably is a better name for an image than r1c1.gif.

Use Comments

Recall that comments can be inserted into an HTML document using <!-- and -->. Use a comment to describe difficult sections and insertions, or simply to leave a note for a future site maintainer. In particular, you might want to put comments at the start of documents indicating important information about the document, the author, and so on. For example, the following document shows how comments could be used in the *head* to inform document maintainers about the document:

```
<!DOCTYPE HTML PUBLIC "-//W3C//DTD HTML 4.01 Transitional//EN"
"http://www.w3.org/TR/html4/loose.dtd">
<html>
<head>
<title>Demo Company Announces Butler 4.0</title>
<!--
    Document Name: Butler Robot Press Release

    Description: The press release announcing the newest Robot
                 Butler in the Demo Company family.

    Author: Thomas A. Powell (tpowell@democompany.com)

    Creation Date: 9/15/00
    Last Updated: 9/25/02
    Comments: Used SuperDuperEdit 7.0 to build the page.
-->
</head>
<body>
...
</body>
</html>
```

Use Templates

One of the best things to consider when authoring HTML pages is not pages, but templates. Why make ten different press releases when you can create and modify a single press release template? Unfortunately, many tools and design books alike tend to take a one-page-at-a-time approach. Avoid this and create generic templates. Using a template will speed up development and make resulting pages more consistent in style and structure. Some designers are hesitant to use templates thinking that it limits design possibilities. Templates don't take the creativity out of design. In fact, using templates takes much of the tedium out of building sites, leaving the designer more time to design. In most cases, if a designer is following the rules of consistency and usability, there really are no restrictions imposed by templates.

Format for Maintenance, Crunch for Delivery

When producing markup by hand, it is a good idea to format the document in a consistent manner. For example, consider matching tags up on tab stops, using white space to separate sections of a document, and ordering attributes within tags alphabetically. Following simple formatting really can make it easier to come back later on and make changes.

On the opposite end of the spectrum, if you end up using a visual editor of some sort and never plan on looking at or editing the underlying markup, you might want to go all the way and "crunch" the page, as shown in Figure 2-12. The idea of crunching is to remove all spaces and other non-required elements such as comments from the final page. This will make the page smaller and thus faster to deliver to the user. Generally, you should use a tool such as W3Compiler (www.w3compiler.com) to do your crunching as the final step before site delivery. With this approach, you keep the original formatted files for maintenance and use the crunched pages only for delivery.

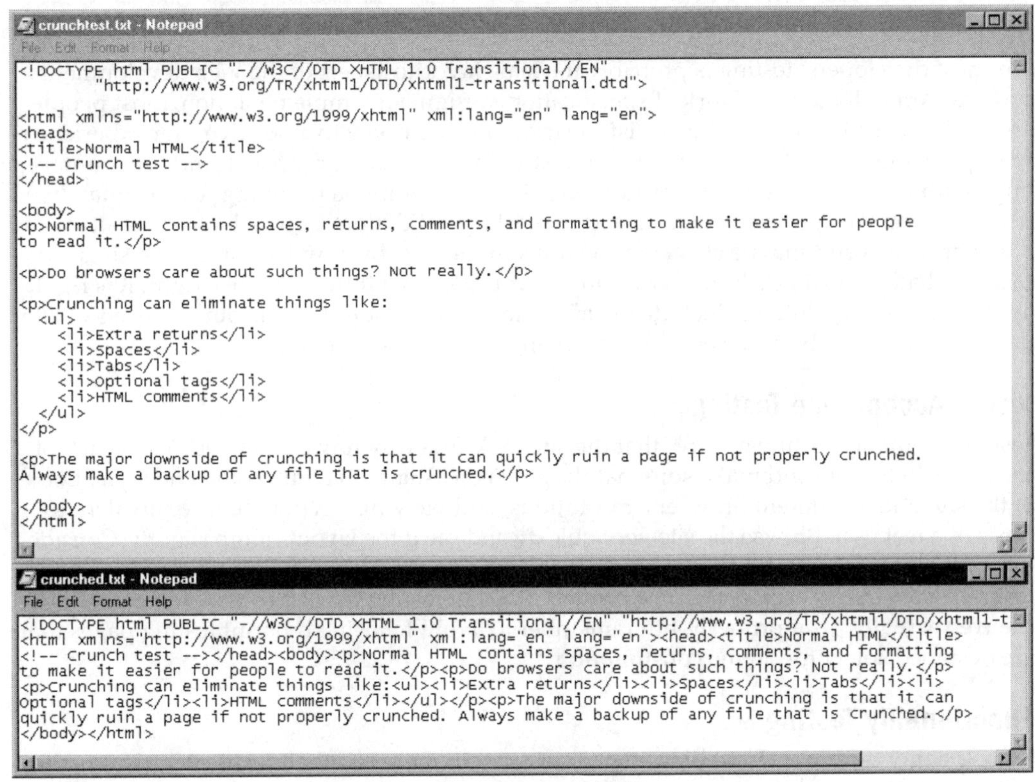

crunchtest.txt - Notepad

```
<!DOCTYPE html PUBLIC "-//W3C//DTD XHTML 1.0 Transitional//EN"
      "http://www.w3.org/TR/xhtml1/DTD/xhtml1-transitional.dtd">

<html xmlns="http://www.w3.org/1999/xhtml" xml:lang="en" lang="en">
<head>
<title>Normal HTML</title>
<!-- Crunch test -->
</head>

<body>
<p>Normal HTML contains spaces, returns, comments, and formatting to make it easier for people
to read it.</p>

<p>Do browsers care about such things? Not really.</p>

<p>Crunching can eliminate things like:
  <ul>
    <li>Extra returns</li>
    <li>Spaces</li>
    <li>Tabs</li>
    <li>Optional tags</li>
    <li>HTML comments</li>
  </ul>
</p>

<p>The major downside of crunching is that it can quickly ruin a page if not properly crunched.
Always make a backup of any file that is crunched.</p>

</body>
</html>
```

crunched.txt - Notepad

```
<!DOCTYPE html PUBLIC "-//W3C//DTD XHTML 1.0 Transitional//EN" "http://www.w3.org/TR/xhtml1/DTD/xhtml1-t
<html xmlns="http://www.w3.org/1999/xhtml" xml:lang="en" lang="en"><head><title>Normal HTML</title>
<!-- Crunch test --></head><body><p>Normal HTML contains spaces, returns, comments, and formatting
to make it easier for people to read it.</p><p>Do browsers care about such things? Not really.</p>
<p>Crunching can eliminate things like:<ul><li>Extra returns</li><li>Spaces</li><li>Tabs</li><li>
Optional tags</li><li>HTML comments</li></ul></p><p>The major downside of crunching is that it can
quickly ruin a page if not properly crunched. Always make a backup of any file that is crunched.</p>
</body></html>
```

FIGURE 2-12 Crunch HTML/XHTML for delivery

NOTE *Some Web designers may feel that nicely formatted HTML is good for people to learn from through the View Source feature in their browser. However, most of a site's customers will not care about format of the markup and will appreciate faster loading pages so crunching really is a good idea. As a developer who wants to learn by "View Source," don't worry, you can always pretty print crunched markup.*

The previous few sections discussed some of the design and production issues required to build a simple mock or alpha site. The mock or alpha site is like the frame of a house. There is much more to fill in. You still might have to add technical "plumbing" and "wiring" and finally populate your site with real content before you can release it.

Beta Site Implementation

Once the mock site is produced and deemed acceptable, it is time to actually implement the beta site. Real content should be placed in pages, and back-end components and interactive elements should be integrated with the final visual design. Although implementation would seem to be the most time-consuming aspect of a project, in reality, if all the components have been collected and prototypes built prior to this stage, the actual site implementation might occur relatively rapidly.

Testing

For most developers, testing is probably the least favorite aspect of the Web development process. After all the hard work of specification, design, and implementation, most people are ready to just launch the site. Resist the urge. Testing is key to a positive user experience with your site. Don't force your users to test your site after its release. If they encounter bugs with what is considered a production site, they won't be forgiving. Unfortunately, testing on the Web generally is relegated to markup validation, a quick look at the site using a few browsers and maybe checking the links in the site. Bugs will exist in Web sites, no matter what. Unfortunately, most developers consider that if the site looks right, it is right. Yet Web design doesn't just include visual design: you must test all the other aspects of site design as well. The basic aspects of Web testing are overviewed here.

Visual Acceptance Testing

Visual acceptance testing ensures that the site looks the way it was intended. View each of the pages in the site and make sure that they are consistent in layout, color, and style. Look at the site under different browsers, resolutions, and viewing environments equivalent to those of a real user. Browse the site very quickly and see if the layouts jump slightly. Consider looking at the pages while squinting to notice abstract irregularities in layout. Visual acceptance testing also requires each page to be printed. It is interesting to see just how few pages on the Web actually print properly, but remember to avoid focusing on print testing pages that are designed solely for online consumption.

Functionality Testing

Functionality testing and visual testing do overlap in the sense that the most basic function of a page is to simply render onscreen. However, most sites contain at least basic functions such as navigation. Make sure to check every link in a site and rectify any broken links. Broken links should be considered catastrophic functional errors. Make sure to test all interactive elements such as forms or shopping carts. Use both realistic test situations as well as extreme cases. Try to break your forms by providing obviously bad data. Remember: users won't think as you do, so prepare for the unexpected.

Content Proofing

The content details of a site are very important. Make sure content is all in place and that grammar and word usage is consistent and correct. Check details such as product names, copyright dates, and trademarks. And always remember to check the spelling! Clients and users often will regard an entire site as being poor just on the basis of one small typo; the importance of this cannot be stressed enough. The best way to perform this test is to print each page and literally read every single line for accuracy.

System and Browser Compatibility Testing

Ideally, system and browser restrictions have been respected during development, but this must be verified during testing. Make sure to access the site with the same types of systems and browsers the site's users will have. Unfortunately, it often seems that designers check compatibility on systems far more powerful and with much more bandwidth than the typical user. The project plan should have detailed browser requirements, so make sure the site works under the specified browsers.

Delivery Testing

Check to make sure the site is delivered adequately. Try browsing the site under real user conditions. If the site was designed for modem users including AOL users, set up an AOL account and a modem to test delivery speed. To simulate site traffic, consider using testing software to create virtual users clicking on the site. This will simulate how the site will react under real conditions. Make sure that you test the site on the actual production server to be used or a system equivalent to it. Be careful to not underestimate delivery influences. The whole project might be derailed if this was not adequately considered during specification. For further information on delivery issues such as hosting, see Chapter 16.

TIP *With a dynamic site, particularly an e-commerce site, it is very wise to add a security testing phase to a project. In this phase, you would try to break into a system through direct form and URL attacks as well as explore any server issues that could compromise security. While well beyond the scope of this book, the author would be remiss not to remind developers of this important consideration.*

User Acceptance Testing

User acceptance testing should be performed after the site appears to work correctly. In software, this form of testing often is called *beta* testing. Let the users actually try the working site and comment on it one last time. Do not perform this type of testing until the more obvious bugs have been addressed. User testing is the most important form of testing because it most closely simulates real use. If problems are uncovered during this phase of testing, you might not be able to correct them right away. If the problems are not dramatic, you can still release the site and correct the problems later. However, if any significant issues are uncovered, it is wise to delay release until they can be corrected.

Release and Beyond

Once the site is ready to be released, don't relax—you are not done. In fact, your work has just begun. It is time now to observe the site in action. Does the site meet user expectations? Were the site development goals satisfied? Are any small corrections required? The bottom line is that the site must live on. New features will be required. Upgrades to deal with technology changes are inevitable. Visual changes to meet marketing demands are very likely. The initial development signifies the start of a continual development process most call *maintenance*. Web development is a process; once you are done it might be time to go back to the beginning of the design process to assess the goals and whether or not they were met and try again—plan, design, develop, release, repeat.

Welcome to the Real World

Although the site development process appears to be a very straightforward cycle, it doesn't always go so smoothly. There are just too many variables to account for in the real world.

For example, consider the effects of building a site for another person such as a boss or client. If someone else is paying for a site to be built, you might still need to indulge their desires regardless of whether the requests conform to what the user wants. Make sure you attempt to persuade others that decisions should always be made with the user in mind. Try to show the benefits of design theories rather than preaching rules. Be prepared to show examples of your ideas that are fully fleshed out. However, accept that they often might be shot down.

NOTE *Experienced designers often will create a variety of site comps to guide discussion, similar to a book of haircuts for customers who can't verbalize what they want.*

Most Web projects have political problems. Don't expect everyone to agree. Departments in a company will wrestle for control, often with battle lines being drawn between the marketing department and the technology groups. To stir up even more trouble, there might be numerous self-proclaimed Web experts nearby who are ready to give advice. Don't be surprised when someone's brother's friend turns out to be a Web "expert" who claims you can build the whole site with Microsoft FrontPage wizards in one hour. The only way to combat political problems is to be patient and attempt to educate. Not everyone will understand the purpose of the site; without a clear specification in place, developers might find themselves in a precarious position open to attack from all sides.

Always remember that the purpose of following a process model such as the one discussed in this chapter is to minimize the problems that occur during a Web project. However, a process model won't account for every real-world problem, particularly people issues. Experience is the only teacher for dealing with many problems. Developers lacking experience in Web projects are always encouraged to roll with the punches and consider all obstacles as learning experiences.

Summary

Building a modern Web site can be challenging, so site builders should adopt a methodology or process model to guide the development process and minimize risk, manage complexity, and generally improve the end result. Software engineering process models such as the waterfall model can easily be applied to most Web projects. Planning during the early stages of a site's development minimizes risk and should improve the end result. A design document that usually includes site goals, audience and task analysis, content requirements, site structure, technical requirements, and management considerations should always be developed. The design document guides the production of the Web site. During the design phase of site production, use wireframes, paper mock-ups, storyboards, and even mock sites to reduce the likelihood of having to redesign the site later on. If a plan is well thought out and the design phase prototypes built, implementation ranging from HTML to JavaScript should proceed rapidly and require little rework. However, once finished, be careful not to rush the site online—adequate testing is required and markup quality should be treated very seriously. If a poorly crafted site is released, maintenance might be required immediately.

II

PART

Core HTML and XHTML

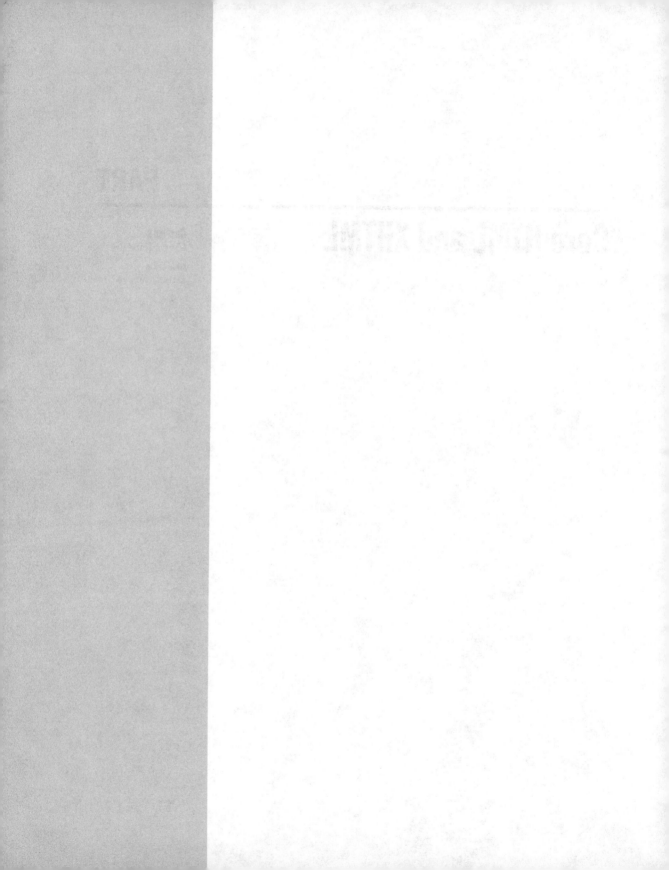

CHAPTER 3

Core Elements

This chapter introduces the basic HTML tags common to nearly every browser, as defined by the HTML 4.01 and XHTML 1.0 transitional specifications. The tags fall primarily into three distinct groups: document structure elements, block elements, and inline elements. In addition to these elements are character entities for inserting special characters into a document. The elements are presented for the most part in a top-down manner: from larger, document and block-oriented structures (such as paragraphs), to smaller units (such as the actual character entities). To speed up the discussion, common attributes to nearly all HTML elements are discussed as a group. Before proceeding, we quickly revisit the structure of HTML documents.

Document Structure Redux

Recall from Chapter 1 that HTML and XHTML are structured languages. All documents should start with a document type definition indicating the type of markup in use and then have a root **html** element that contains a **<head>** and **<body>** tag, or in some situations a **<head>** and **<frameset>** tag. Within the head of the document, information about the document such as its title, character set, style sheets, and scripts is indicated, while the **<body>** tag encloses the actual content of the page. An example structure for an XHTML 1.0 transitional document is shown here:

```
<!DOCTYPE html PUBLIC "-//W3C//DTD XHTML 1.0 Transitional//EN"
"http://www.w3.org/TR/xhtml1/DTD/xhtml1-transitional.dtd">
<html xmlns="http://www.w3.org/1999/xhtml" lang="en">
<head>
<title>Title here</title>
<meta http-equiv="content-type" content="text/html; charset=ISO-8859-1" />

<!-- other head information here -->
</head>
<body>
<!-- other body information here -->
</body>
</html>
```

Given the basic XHTML template, the italicized areas would be modified appropriately per document. All the following examples will continue on with this XHTML 1.0 transitional template except where noted. However, if you prefer to write markup to another specification, all the examples presented in the chapter can be found at the support site (www.htmlref.com) in HTML 4.0 transitional, HTML 4.01 strict with CSS, and XHTML 1 strict with CSS. Now that we have reminded ourselves of the overall document structure, it is time to explore the tags within the body of the document. But before we do that, we should talk about the aspects of these tags that are always similar: the core attributes.

Core HTML Attributes

To accommodate new technologies such as style sheets and scripting languages, some important changes have been made to HTML and XHTML. Since HTML 4.0, a set of four core attributes—**id**, **class**, **style**, and **title**—have been added to nearly all HTML and XHTML elements. At this stage, the purpose of these attributes might not be obvious, but it is important to address their existence before discussing the various HTML elements to avoid redundancy.

id Attribute

The **id** attribute is used to set a unique name for an element in a document. For example, using **id** with the paragraph tag, **<p>**,

```
<p id="FirstParagraph">
This is the first paragraph of text.
</p>
```

names the bound element **"FirstParagraph"**. Naming an element is useful for manipulating the enclosed contents with a style sheet or script. For example, a style sheet rule such as

```
<style type="text/css">
  #FirstParagraph {color: red;}
</style>
```

could be put in the **head** of a document. This style rule says to make an element named "FirstParagraph" red. Naming is key to associating style or interactivity to particular elements. Of course, document authors must make sure objects are named uniquely, as having elements with the same **id** attribute value might cause significant bugs. The uses of the **id** attribute for style sheets and scripting are discussed in Chapter 10 and Chapter 14, respectively.

class Attribute

The **class** attribute is used to indicate the class or classes that a tag might belong to. Like **id**, **class** is used to associate a tag with a name, so

```
<p id="FirstParagraph" class="important">
   This is the first paragraph of text.
</p>
```

not only names the paragraph uniquely as **FirstParagraph**, but also indicates that this paragraph belongs to a class grouping called **important**. The main use of the **class** attribute is to relate a group of elements to various style sheet rules. For example, a style sheet rule such as

```
<style type="text/css">
 .important {background-color: yellow;}
</style>
```

would give all elements with the **class** attribute set to **important** a yellow background. Given that many elements can have the same class values, this may affect a large portion of the document. You can find more examples of the use of **class** and **id** with style sheets in Chapter 10.

style Attribute

The **style** attribute is used to add style sheet information directly to a tag. For example,

```
<p style="font-size: 18pt; color: red;">
   This is the first paragraph of text.
</p>
```

sets the font size of the paragraph to be 18 point, red text. Although the **style** attribute allows CSS rules to be added to an element with ease, it is preferable to use **id** or **class** to relate a document-wide or linked style sheet. The use of CSS is discussed in Chapter 10.

title Attribute

The **title** is used to provide advisory text about an element or its contents. In the case of

```
<p title="Introductory paragraph">
This is the first paragraph of text.
</p>
```

the **title** attribute is set to indicate that this particular paragraph is the introductory paragraph. Browsers can display this advisory text in the form of a *Tooltip*, as shown here:

Tooltips set with **title** values are often found on links, form fields, images, and anywhere where an extra bit of information is required.

The core attributes might not make a great deal of sense at this time because generally they are most useful with scripting and style sheets, but keep in mind that these four attributes are assumed with *every* tag that is introduced for the rest of this chapter.

Core Language Attributes

One major goal of HTML 4 was to provide better support for languages other than English. The use of other languages might require that text direction be changed from left to right across the screen to right to left. Nearly all HTML elements now support the **dir** attribute, which can be used to indicate text direction as either **ltr** (left to right) or **rtl** (right to left). For example,

```
<p dir="rtl">
   This is a right to left paragraph.
</p>
```

Furthermore, mixed-language documents might become more common after support for non-ASCII-based languages is improved within browsers. The use of the **lang** attribute enables document authors to indicate, down to the tag level, the language being used. For example,

```
<p lang="fr">
   C'est Francais.
</p>

<p lang="en">
   This is English.
</p>
```

Although the language attributes should be considered part of nearly every HTML element, in reality, these attributes are not widely supported by all browsers and are rarely used by document authors.

Core Events

The last major aspect of modern markup initially introduced by HTML 4 was the increased possibility of adding scripting to HTML documents. In preparation for a more dynamic Web, a set of core events has been associated with nearly every HTML element. Most of these events are associated with a user doing something. For example, the user clicking an object is associated with an **onclick** event attribute. So,

```
<p onclick="alert('Ouch!');">
Press this paragraph
</p>
```

would associate a small bit of scripting code with the paragraph event, which would be triggered when the user clicks the paragraph. In reality, the event model is not fully supported by all browsers for all tags, so the previous example might not do much of anything. A much more complete discussion of events is presented in Chapter 14, as well as in Appendix A. For now, just remember that any tag can have a multitude of events associated with it, paving the way for a much more dynamic Web experience.

Now that the core attributes have been covered, we can avoid mentioning them for every element presented, and turn to the most common elements used in HTML. The next section begins the discussion with some of the most common elements found in a document— headings.

Headings

The heading elements are used to create "headlines" in documents. Six different levels of headings are supported: **<h1>**, **<h2>**, **<h3>**, **<h4>**, **<h5>**, and **<h6>**. These range in importance from **<h1>**, the most important, to **<h6>**, the least important. Most browsers display headings in larger and/or bolder font than normal text. Many HTML authors erroneously think of heading elements as formatting that makes text bigger or bolder. Actually, heading elements convey logical meaning about a document's structure. However, in most visual browsers, sizing and weight are relative to the importance of the heading. Therefore, **<h1>** level headings are larger and generally bolder than **<h3>** headings, leading developers to interpret these logical tags most often in a physical manner. In addition, as a block element, returns are inserted after the heading unless overridden by a style sheet. The following example markup demonstrates the heading elements:

```
<!DOCTYPE html PUBLIC "-//W3C//DTD XHTML 1.0 Transitional//EN"
"http://www.w3.org/TR/xhtml1/DTD/xhtml1-transitional.dtd">
<html xmlns="http://www.w3.org/1999/xhtml" lang="en">
<head>
<title>Heading Test</title>
<meta http-equiv="Content-Type" content="text/html; charset=ISO-8859-1" />
</head>
<body>

<h1>Heading 1</h1>
<h2>Heading 2</h2>
<h3>Heading 3</h3>
<h4>Heading 4</h4>
<h5>Heading 5</h5>
<h6>Heading 6</h6>

</body>
</html>
```

A sample rendering of this heading example is shown in Figure 3-1.

NOTE *The Lynx text browser renders headings very differently from commercial graphical browsers. Lynx can't display larger fonts, so it might attempt to bold them or align them.* ***h1*** *headings are aligned in the center, and each lower-level heading is indented more than the next-highest level heading.*

Besides the core attributes discussed early in the chapter, the primary attribute used with headings is **align**. By default, headings usually are left-aligned, but the value of the **align** attribute of headings can also be set to **right**, **center**, and **justify** under transitional versions of HTML and XHTML. The following example markup shows the common usage of the **align** attribute for headings:

```
<!DOCTYPE html PUBLIC "-//W3C//DTD XHTML 1.0 Transitional//EN"
"http://www.w3.org/TR/xhtml1/DTD/xhtml1-transitional.dtd">
<html xmlns="http://www.w3.org/1999/xhtml" lang="en">
<head>
<title>Heading Alignment Example</title>
<meta http-equiv="Content-Type" content="text/html; charset=ISO-8859-1" />
</head>
<body>
```

```
<h1 align="left">Aligned Left</h1>
<h1 align="center">Aligned Center</h1>
<h1 align="right">Aligned Right</h1>

</body>
</html>
```

Under the strict version of HTML, as well as under XHTML, the **align** attribute has been deprecated in favor of using style sheets. The example that follows would validate under strict XHTML 1.0 as it uses CSS to align the headings. A full discussion of CSS begins in Chapter 10.

```
<!DOCTYPE html PUBLIC "-//W3C//DTD XHTML 1.0 Strict//EN"
"http://www.w3.org/TR/xhtml1/DTD/xhtml1-strict.dtd">
<html xmlns="http://www.w3.org/1999/xhtml" lang="en">
<head>
<title>XHTML Heading Alignment</title>
<meta http-equiv="Content-Type" content="text/html; charset=ISO-8859-1" />
<style type="text/css">
     h1.left {text-align: left;}
     h1.center {text-align: center;}
     h1.right {text-align: right;}
</style>
</head>
<body>

<h1 class="left">Aligned Left</h1>
<h1 class="center">Aligned Center</h1>
<h1 class="right">Aligned Right</h1>

</body>
</html>
```

FIGURE 3-1 Rendering of heading style example

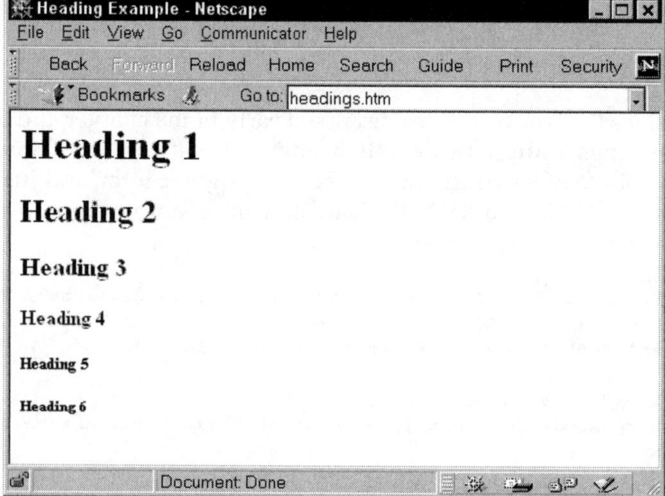

Regardless of appropriateness, given the rise of CSS, many HTML authors often use headings to make text large. As with all HTML elements viewed in a presentational manner, size is a relative concept, not an absolute concept. The actual size of the heading depends on the browser, the browser's settings, and the platform on which it is running. The size of an **<h1>** header under Netscape on a UNIX system may be different from the same **<h1>** header on a Windows machine running Internet Explorer. The headlines are relatively bigger, but the exact size is unknown, making consistent layout difficult.

NOTE *A quick survey of heading use on the Web should reveal that headings beyond* ***<h3>*** *rarely are used. Why? Certainly this is because people use headings in a visual fashion and the look of* ***<h4>***, ***<h5>*** *and* ***<h6>*** *tags can be easily accomplished with other tags.*

Paragraphs and Breaks

Recall that white space handling rules of HTML suggest that multiple spaces, tabs, and carriage returns are often ignored. Word wrapping can occur at any point in your source file, and multiple white space characters are collapsed into a single space. Instead of relying solely on white space, structural elements are used to section a document. One of the most important structuring elements is the paragraph element. Surrounding text with the **<p>** and **</p>** tags indicates that the text is a logical paragraph unit. In general, the browser places a blank line or two before the paragraph, but the exact rendering of the text depends on the browser and any applied style sheet. Text within the **<p>** tags generally is rendered flush left, with a ragged right margin. Like headings, the **align** attribute makes it possible to specify a **left**, **right**, or **center** alignment. Since HTML 4.0, you also can set an **align** value of **justify**, to justify all text in the paragraph. Due to the poor quality of justification in some browsers, this value is used only rarely. The following example in XHTML 1.0 transitional shows four paragraphs with alignment, the rendering of which is shown in Figure 3-2:

```
<!DOCTYPE html PUBLIC "-//W3C//DTD XHTML 1.0 Transitional//EN"
"http://www.w3.org/TR/xhtml1/DTD/xhtml1-transitional.dtd">
<html> xmlns="http://www.w3.org/1999/shtml" lang="en">
<head>
<title>Heading Alignment Example</title>
<meta http-equiv="Content-Type" content="text/html; charset=ISO-8859-1" />
</head>
<body>

<p>This is the first paragraph in the example about the P tag.
There really isn't much to say here.</p>

<p align="center">This is the second paragraph. Again, more of the
same. This time the paragraph is aligned to the center. This might
not be such a good idea as it often makes the text hard to read.</p>

<p align="right">Here the paragraph is aligned to the right. Right
aligned text is also troublesome to read. The rest of the text of this
paragraph is of little importance.</p>
```

```
<p align="justify">Under HTML 4.0 compliant browsers, you are
able to justify text. As you may notice, the way browsers tend to
justify text is sometimes imprecise. Furthermore, some older
browsers do not support this attribute value.</p>

</body>
</html>
```

Because under its default rendering the paragraph element causes a blank line, some HTML authors attempt to insert blank lines into a document by using multiple **<p>** tags. This rarely results in the desired outcome. The browser will collapse empty **<p>** tags because they have no contents and thus desired formatting may not be achieved. To get around this problem, many WYSIWYG HTML editors and even some by-hand HTML authors use a nonbreaking space character within a paragraph, to keep the element from collapsing, as shown here: **<p> </p>**. This approach isn't recommended because it doesn't reduce markup used and further obscures the meaning of the document. A break should be used instead.

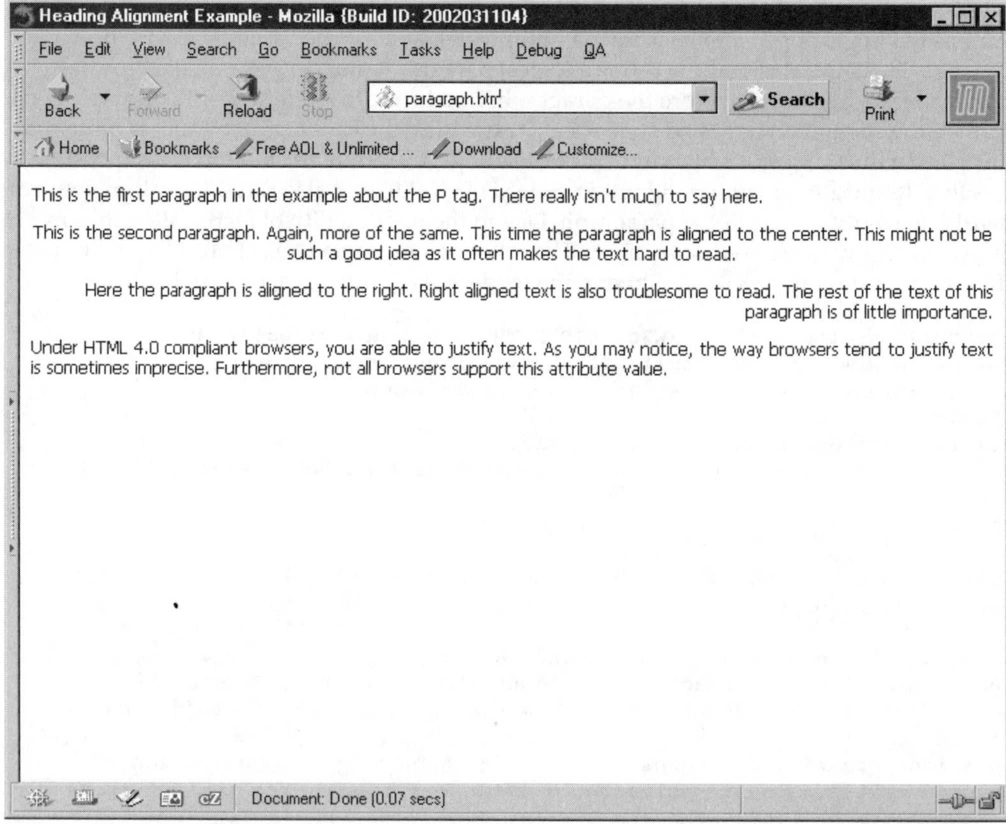

FIGURE 3-2 Rendering of the paragraph example

To insert returns or blank lines in an HTML or XHTML document, the **
** tag is used. This tag inserts a single carriage return or line break into a document. It is an empty element—thus, it has no close tag. Because of this, under XHTML you would use **
** instead of just plain **
**. In addition to the core attributes, the one attribute commonly used with a **
** tag is **clear**. This attribute controls how text flows around images or embedded objects. The use of **
** in this fashion is discussed in Chapter 5.

The following code fragment shows the basic uses of **p** and **br**, and also shows that the two elements are really not equivalent, despite their physical rendering similarities (a screen rendering appears in Figure 3-3):

```
<!DOCTYPE html PUBLIC "-//W3C//DTD XHTML 1.0 Transitional//EN"
"http://www.w3.org/TR/xhtml1/DTD/xhtml1-transitional.dtd">
<html xmlns="http://www.w3.org/1999/xhtml" lang="en">
<head>
<title>Break and Paragraph Example</title>
<meta http-equiv="Content-Type" content="text/html; charset=ISO-8859-1" />
</head>
<body>

<p>This is the first paragraph.<br />
Not much to say here, either. You can use
breaks within a paragraph<br /><br />
like so.</p>

<p></p><p></p><p></p>

<p>This is the second paragraph. Notice that the three paragraph
tags that were just used are treated as empty paragraphs and ignored.</p>

<p>If you use breaks</p>

<br /><br /><br /><br />
<p>you'll get the desired result.</p>
<p>Just because using a non-breaking space to force open a paragraph</p>
<p> </p>
<p> </p>
<p>works doesn't mean you should use it.</p>
</body>
</html>
```

TIP *Users looking for blank lines have to insert multiple* ***
*** *tags into their documents. A single* ***
*** *tag merely goes to the next line rather than inserting a blank line.*

It should be noted that under strict DTDs, the **br** element is not allowed directly in the body as in the previous example and must be present within a heading (**<h1>** - **<h6>**), **<p>**, **<pre>**, **<div>**, or **<address>** tag. Moving the **
** tags within the nearest **<p>** tag like so

```
<p>If you use breaks
<br /><br /><br /><br /></p>
```

PART II

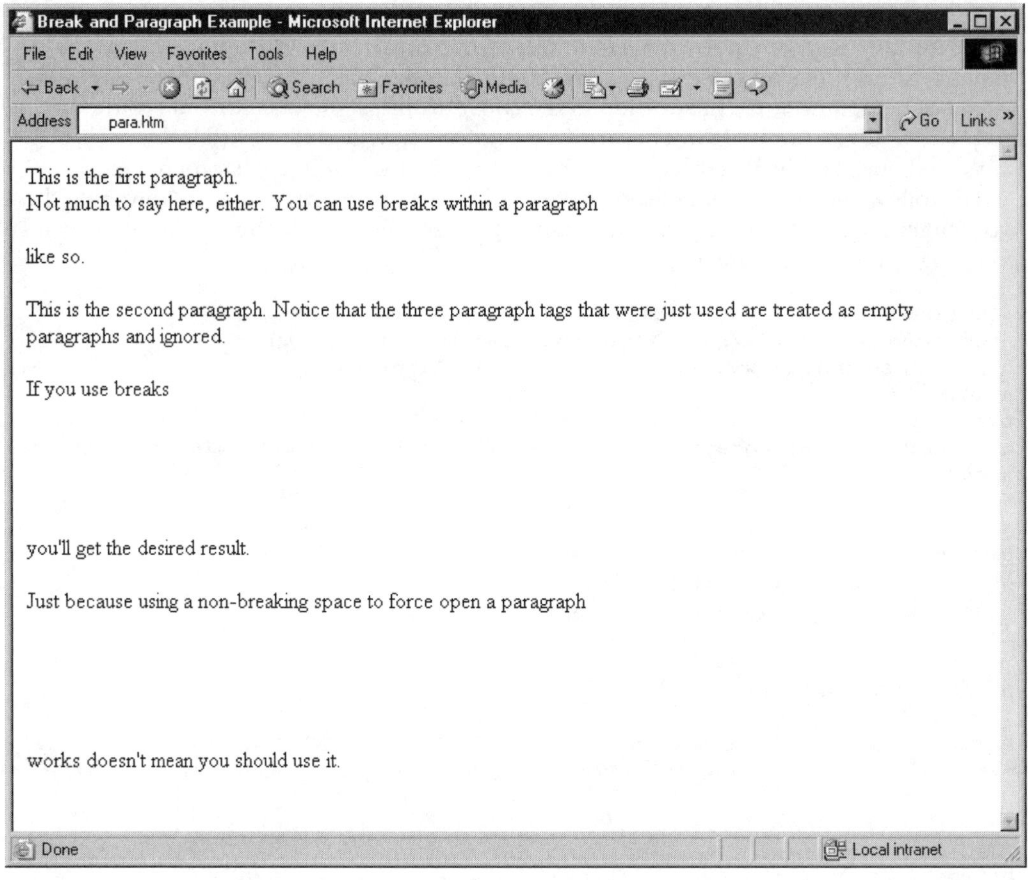
Break and Paragraph Example - Microsoft Internet Explorer
File Edit View Favorites Tools Help
Back Search Favorites Media
Address para.htm
Go Links
This is the first paragraph.
Not much to say here, either. You can use breaks within a paragraph
like so.
This is the second paragraph. Notice that the three paragraph tags that were just used are treated as empty paragraphs and ignored.
If you use breaks
you'll get the desired result.
Just because using a non-breaking space to force open a paragraph
works doesn't mean you should use it.
Done
Local intranet

FIGURE 3-3 Rendering of break and paragraph example

would allow the document to validate under a strict doctype. Given that many HTML authors still do not use strict HTML or XHTML, the tag continues to be commonly found outside block tags.

Divisions and Centering

The **<div>** tag is used to structure HTML documents into sections or divisions. A **<div>** is a logical block tag that has no predefined meaning or rendering. Under traditional HTML, the only major value of the **<div>** tag is to align sections of content by setting the **align** attribute to **left**, **right**, or **center**. By default, content within the **<div>** tag is left-aligned. Divisions are more significantly useful when used in conjunction with style sheets (see Chapter 10).

Aside from using the **<div>** tag to align blocks of text, it is possible to center text using a difficult-to-characterize proprietary tag: **<center>**. Under HTML 2.0-based browsers, centering text was impossible. One of the major additions introduced by Netscape was the **<center>** tag. HTML 3.2 adopted this element because of its widespread use, which continues today. To center text or embedded objects (such as images), simply enclose the content within **<center>** and **</center>**. In this sense, **<center>** appears to be a text-formatting style element, but under the HTML 3.2 and transitional 4.0 specification (and beyond), **<center>** is defined as an alias for a block-level structuring element and eventually will be deprecated under strict versions of HTML. Under the HTML 4.01 DTD, **<center>** is supposed to be simply an alias for **<div align="center">** and is treated exactly the same way. Specification or not, the **<center>** tag is unlikely to go away, considering its simplicity and widespread use. The following example shows the use of **<center>** and **<div>.** (Figure 3-4 shows their screen rendering.)

```
<!DOCTYPE html PUBLIC "-//W3C//DTD XHTML 1.0 Transitional//EN"
"http://www.w3.org/TR/xhtml1/DTD/xhtml1-transitional.dtd">
<html xmlns="http://www.w3.org/1999/xhtml" lang="en">
<head>
<title>Center and Division Example</title>
<meta http-equiv="content-type" content="text/html; charset=ISO-8859-1" />
</head>
<body>
<center>
<h1>This heading is centered.</h1>
<p>This paragraph is also centered.</p>
</center>

<br /><br />

<div align="right">
<h1>Division Heading</h1>
<p>Many paragraphs and other block elements
   can be affected by a DIV at once.</p>
<p>Notice all the paragraphs are right aligned.</p>
</div>
</body>
</html>
```

Spans

Although the **<div>** tag can be used to group large sections of a document for later application of a style sheet or various other formatting, it is not appropriate to put everything within a division. Because **div** is a block element, it will induce a return. If you want to group text without using a block element, use a **<span>** tag, as it provides logical grouping inline with no predefined look. Consider the following markup:

```
<p>In this sentence <span class="important">some of the text is
important!</span></p>
```

In this markup fragment, the **<span>** tag wouldn't necessarily cause any particular presentation under plain HTML. However, as shown, using the **class** attribute, it could be related to a style sheet to make the enclosed text look different, while at the same time providing no particular logical meaning. We could do something directly, like so:

```
<p>In this sentence <span style="color: red; font-size: xx-large;">some of the text
is big and red</span>!</p>
```

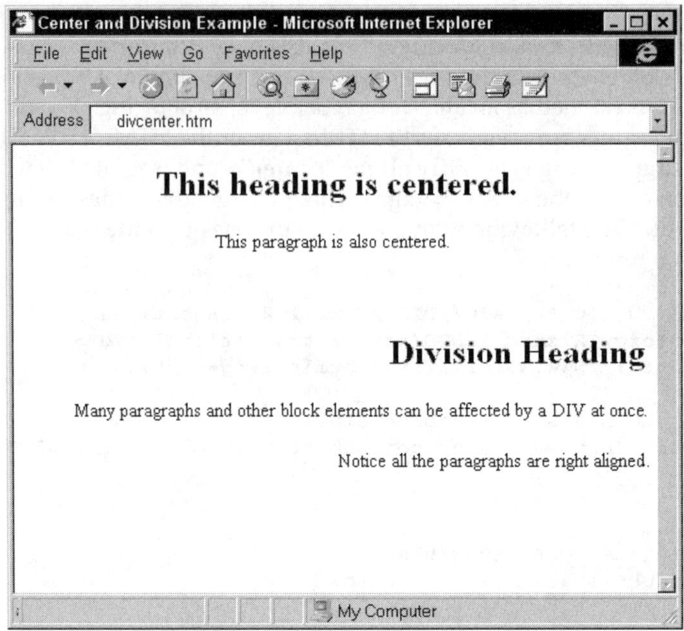

FIGURE 3-4 Example rendering of <div> and <center>

but that would defeat the value of separating presentation from document structure with styles. It would seem at this point the use of **<div>** and **<span>** tags might not make a great deal of sense, but they are some of the most useful of the core elements of XHTML. Their use with style sheets is discussed in Chapter 10.

Quotations

Occasionally, you might want to quote a large body of text to make it stand out from the other text. The **<blockquote>** tag provides a facility to enclose large block quotations from other works within a document. Although the element is logical in nature, enclosing text within **<blockquote>** and **</blockquote>** usually indents the blocked information from both the left and right. In keeping with its meaning, the **<blockquote>** tag supports the cite attribute, which can be set to the Web address of the document or site from which the quotation was pulled, or a brief message describing the quote or its source.

Whereas a **<blockquote>** element will cause a return like other block elements, it is possible to create an inline quotation using the logical **<q>** element. The tag should result in quotation marks around the enclosed text. The tag also should address the rules for switching quotes within quotes. Note that older browsers and even some modern ones such as Internet Explorer 6 do not properly support the **<q>** tag, despite its inclusion in the HTML 4.0/4.01 and XHTML 1.0 specifications. Like the **<blockquote>** tag, **<q>** also supports a **cite** attribute. The following shows an example of **<blockquote>** and **<q>** (rendered in Figure 3-5):

```
<!DOCTYPE html PUBLIC "-//W3C//DTD XHTML 1.0 Transitional//EN"
"http://www.w3.org/TR/xhtml1/DTD/xhtml1-transitional.dtd">
<html xmlns="http://www.w3.org/1999/xhtml" lang="en">
<head>
<title>Quotation Example</title>
<meta http-equiv="content-type" content="text/html; charset=ISO-8859-1" />
</head>
<body>
<h1 align="center">Demo Company Quotes</h1>

<p>See the comments the press has about Demo Company's
futuristic products.</p>

<q>My friend's friend said, <q cite="sounds fishy">My mother's
uncle's cousin thinks that the Demo Company robot is the
greatest invention ever!</q></q>
<br />--George P. Somolovich, Ordinary Citizen

<blockquote cite="http://www.democompany.com">
Demo Company's products are by far the best fictitious products
ever produced! Gadget lovers and haters alike will marvel at the
sheer uselessness of Demo Company gadgets. It's a true shame that
their products are limited only to HTML examples!
</blockquote>
--Matthew J. Foley, Useless Products Magazine

<p>With kudos like this, you need to make sure to buy your
Demo Company products today!</p>
</body>
</html>
```

NOTE *The first Web browsers did not provide any indentation or layout control in regular text. Many HTML authors and HTML editors use* **<blockquote>** *to provide indentation. List elements, particularly the unordered list, are also commonly used for quick indentation in Web pages. While it is poor practice, until style sheets become more common, these workarounds will continue.*

Preformatted Text

Occasionally, spacing, tabs, and returns are so important in text that HTML's default behavior of disregarding them would ruin the text's meaning. In such cases, you might want to preserve the intended formatting by specifying the text to be preformatted. Imagine that programming source code or poetry needs to be inserted into a Web page. In both cases, the spacing, returns, and tabs in the document must be preserved to ensure proper meaning. This situation requires an HTML directive that indicates the preservation of format. The **<pre>** tag can be used to indicate text that shouldn't be formatted by the browser. The text enclosed within a **<pre>** tag retains all spacing and returns, and doesn't reflow when the browser is resized. Scrollbars and horizontal scrolling are required if the lines are longer than the width of the window. The browser generally renders the preformatted text in a monospaced font, typically Courier. Simple forms of text formatting, such as bold, italics,

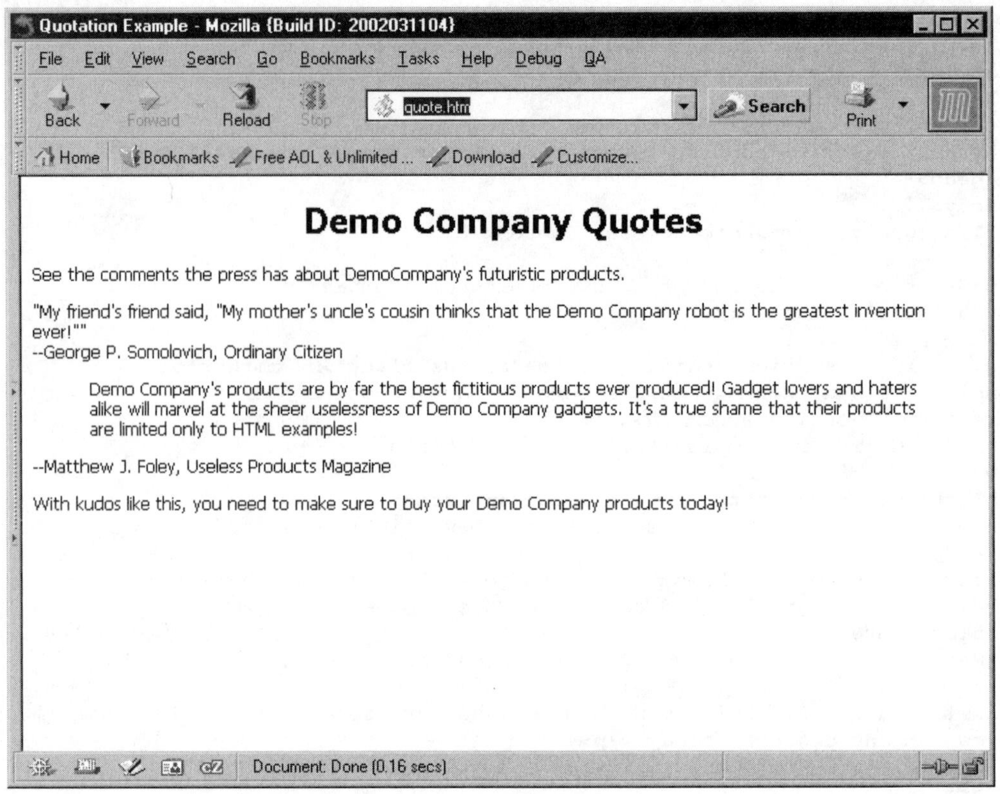

FIGURE 3-5 Rendering of quotations example

or links, can be used within **<pre>** tags. The following example, displayed in Figure 3-6, uses the **<pre>** tag and compares it to regular paragraph text:

```
<!DOCTYPE html PUBLIC "-//W3C//DTD XHTML 1.0 Transitional//EN"
"http://www.w3.org/TR/xhtml1/DTD/xhtml1-transitional.dtd">
<html xmlns="http://www.w3.org/1999/xhtml" lang="en">
<head>
<title>Pre Example</title>
<meta http-equiv="content-type" content="text/html; charset=ISO-8859-1" />
</head>
<body>
<pre>
This is P   R   E   F   O   R   M   A   T   T   E   D
  T
      E
        X
          T

SPACES     are ok!  So are

  RETURNS!
```

```
</pre>
<hr />
<p>
This is NOT P   R   E   F   O   R   M   A   T   T   E   D
    T
      E
        X
          T

SPACES     and
RETURNS are lost.
</p>
</body>
</html>
```

NOTE *According to the HTML and XHTML specifications, only certain HTML elements are allowed within the* **<pre>** *tag, and some elements, such as* **<img>**, *are excluded. Most browsers allow any elements, even those beyond the stated specification, to appear within* **<pre>**, *and render these as expected. Authors should not, however, rely on this. See Appendix A for the* **<pre>** *tag's content model.*

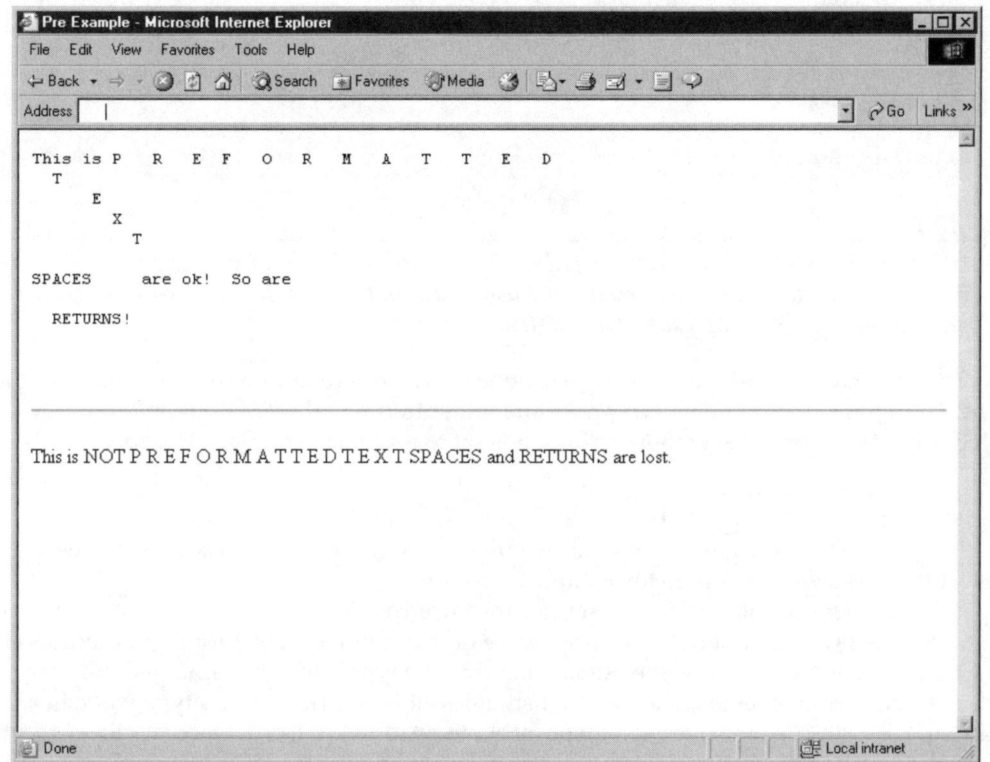

FIGURE 3-6 Rendering of preformatted and regular text

HTML authors should be careful about using **<pre>** to create simple tables or preserve spacing. Unpredictable differences in browser window sizes could introduce horizontal scrolling for wide preformatted content. In these cases, other elements, particularly **<table>**, will provide better formatting control.

Lists

Modern HTML has three basic forms of lists: ordered lists (**<ol>**), unordered lists (**<ul>**), and definition lists (**<dl>**). Lists are block-level, although they can be nested, and their items can contain other block-level structures, such as paragraphs.

Ordered Lists

An ordered list, as enclosed by **<ol>** and **</ol>**, defines a list in which order matters. Ordering typically is rendered by a numbering scheme, using Arabic numbers, letters, or Roman numerals. Ordered lists are suitable for creating simple outlines or step-by-step instructions because the list items are automatically numbered by the browser. List items in ordered and other lists are defined by using the list item tag, **<li>**, which doesn't require an end tag under traditional HTML. For XHTML compliance, however, the use of the closing **</li>** tag is required. List items usually are indented by the browser. Numbering starts from one. A generic ordered list looks like this:

```
<ol>
   <li>Item 1</li>
   <li>Item 2</li>
     . . .
   <li>Item n</li>
</ol>
```

NOTE *In many browsers, the* **<li>** *tag has a rendering outside a list. It often renders as a nonindented bullet. Some books recommend using* **<li>** *in this way. This isn't correct practice given the HTML/XHTML content model. It should be avoided.*

The **<ol>** tag has three basic attributes, none of which is required: **compact**, **start**, and **type**. The **compact** attribute requires no value under traditional HTML but under XHTML, which allows no attributes without values, it is set to a value of compact, like so:

```
<ol compact="compact">
```

It simply suggests that the browser attempt to compact the list, to use less space onscreen. In reality, most browsers ignore the **compact** attribute.

The **type** attribute of **<ol>** can be set to **a** for lowercase letters, **A** for uppercase letters, **i** for lowercase Roman numerals, **I** for uppercase Roman numerals, or **1** for regular numerals. The numeral **1** is the default value. Remember that the **type** attribute within the **<ol>** tag sets the numbering scheme for the whole list, unless it is overridden by a **type** value in an **<li>** tag. Each **<li>** tag can have a local **type** attribute set to **a**, **A**, **i**, **I**, or **1**. Once an **<li>** element is set with a new type, it overrides the numbering style for the rest of the list, unless another **<li>** sets the **type** attribute.

The **<ol>** element also has a **start** attribute that takes a numeric value to begin the list numbering. Whether the **type** attribute is a letter or a numeral, the **start** value must be a number. To start ordering from the letter *j*, you would use **<ol type="a" start="10">** because *j* is the tenth letter. An **<li>** tag within an ordered list can override the current numbering with the **value** attribute, which also is set to a numeric value. Numbering of the list should continue from the value set.

NOTE *Numbering lists to count backward from 10 to 1 or to count by twos or other values is not directly possible in HTML. I believe that a single addition of a step attribute could address this, but it appears that the few remaining holes in HTML have been left unfilled. Instead, CSS is left to address this, which unfortunately is taking far too long.*

PART II

Lists can be nested, but the syntax is widely misunderstood. Commonly, on the Web, markup such as

```
<ol>
   <li>Item 1</li>
    <ol>
      <li>Item a</li>
        . . .
      <li>Item z</li>
    </ol>
    ...
   <li>Item n</li>
</ol>
```

is used. However, the content model of HTML and XHTML lists only allows list items inside of lists, so the correct syntax is actually

```
<ol>
   <li>Item 1
     <ol>
       <li>Item a</li>
. . .
       <li>Item z</li>
       </ol>
   </li>
...
   <li>Item n</li>
</ol>
```

A complete example of ordered lists and their attributes is shown next, the rendering of which is shown in Figure 3-7:

```
<!DOCTYPE html PUBLIC "-//W3C//DTD XHTML 1.0 Transitional//EN"
"http://www.w3.org/TR/xhtml1/DTD/xhtml1-transitional.dtd">
<html xmlns="http://www.w3.org/1999/xhtml" lang="en">
<head>
<title>Ordered List Example</title>
<meta http-equiv="content-type" content="text/html; charset=ISO-8859-1" />
```

```
</head>
<body>
<p>Ordered lists can be very simple.</p>

<ol>
     <li>Item 1</li>
     <li>Item 2</li>
     <li>Item 3</li>
</ol>

<p>Ordered lists can have a variety of types.</p>

<ol>
     <li type="a">Lowercase letters</li>
     <li type="A">Uppercase letters</li>
     <li type="i">Lowercase Roman numerals</li>
     <li type="I">Uppercase Roman numerals</li>
     <li type="1">Arabic numerals</li>
</ol>

<p>Ordered lists can start at different values
and with different types.</p>

<ol start="10" type="a">
<li>This should be j</li>
<li value="3">This should be c
   <ol>
      <li>Lists can nest
          <ol>
             <li>Nesting depth is unlimited</li>
          </ol>
      </li>
   </ol>
</li>
</ol>
</body>
</html>
```

NOTE *When dealing with extremes, use numbering with caution. Negative values or very large values produce unpredictable results. Whereas Navigator ignores negative numbers, Internet Explorer numbers up toward zero. Browsers can allocate a fixed width to the left of a list item to display its number. Under Navigator, a list not embedded in another block structure can accommodate only about four digits; larger numbers can overwrite list elements. A list indented by nesting in another block structure could have more space. Numbering in both Navigator and Internet Explorer loses meaning with large integer values, most likely because of limitations within the operating environment.*

Unordered Lists

An unordered list, signified by **<ul>** and **</ul>**, is used for lists of items in which the ordering is not specific. This can be useful in a list of features and benefits for a product.

FIGURE 3-7 Rendering of ordered list example

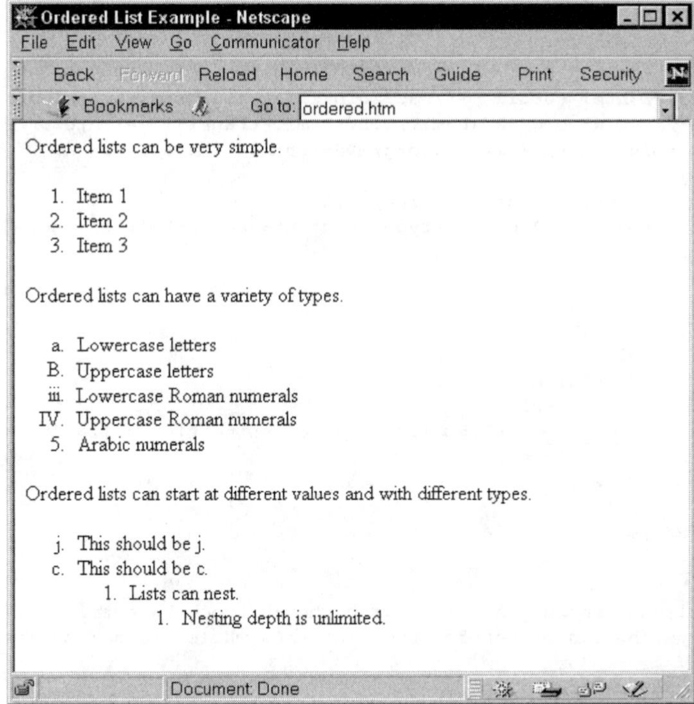

A browser typically adds a bullet of some sort (a filled circle, a square, or an empty circle) for each item and indents the list.

Like ordered lists, unordered lists can be nested. However, in this case each level of nesting indents the list farther, and the bullet changes accordingly. Generally, a filled circle or solid round bullet is used on the first level of lists. An empty circle is used for the second-level list. Third-level nested lists generally use a square. These renderings for bullets are common to browsers, but shouldn't be counted on. Under transitional forms of HTML and XHTML, the **type** attribute can be used to set the bullet type for a list. Under strict variants, CSS should be used instead. The **type** attribute can appear within the **<ul>** tag and set the type for the whole list, or it can appear within each **<li>**. A **type** value in an **<li>** tag overrides the value for the rest of the list, unless it is overridden by another **type** specification. The allowed values for **type** are **disc**, **circle**, or **square**. This is commonly supported in browsers, but small variations exist. For example, in the case of MSN TV (formerly WebTV), a triangle bullet type also is available, because on a television a circle and square generally look the same due to limited resolution. For the greatest level of cross-browser compatibility, authors are encouraged to set the bullet type only for the list as a whole.

NOTE *Internet Explorer 3.0–level browsers under Windows don't render* ***type*** *settings for unordered lists. This has been fixed under Internet Explorer 4.0 and beyond.*

The following is an example of unordered lists, various renderings of which are shown in Figure 3-8:

```
<!DOCTYPE html PUBLIC "-//W3C//DTD XHTML 1.0 Transitional//EN"
"http://www.w3.org/TR/xhtml1/DTD/xhtml1-transitional.dtd">
<html xmlns="http://www.w3.org/1999/xhtml" lang="en">
<head>
<title>Unordered List Example</title>
<meta http-equiv="content-type" content="text/html; charset=ISO-8859-1" />
</head>
<body>
<ul>
    <li>Unordered lists
        <ul>
            <li>can be nested.
                <ul>
                    <li>Bullet changes on nesting.</li>
                </ul>
            </li>
        </ul>
     </li>
</ul>

<p>Bullets can be controlled with the <b>type</b> attribute.
<b>Type</b> can be set for the list as a whole or item by item.</p>

<ul type="square">
    <li>First item bullet shape set by ul</li>
    <li type="disc">Disc item</li>
    <li type="circle">Circle item</li>
    <li type="square">Square item</li>
</ul>

</body>
</html>
```

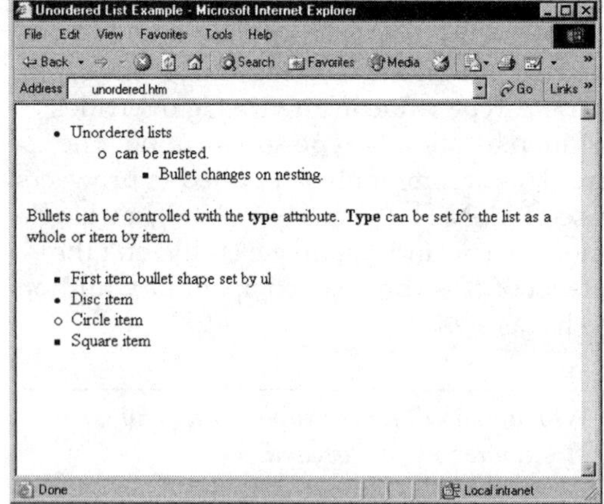

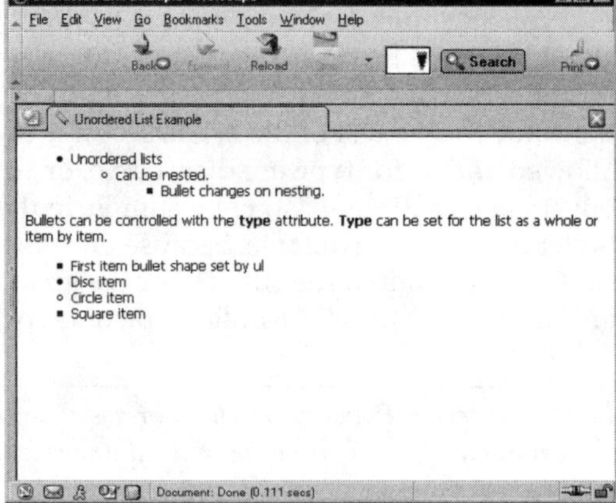

FIGURE 3-8 Rendering of unordered list example

Definition List

A definition list is a list of terms paired with associated definitions—in other words, a glossary. Definition lists are enclosed within **<dl>** and **</dl>**. Each term being defined is indicated by a **<dt>** element, which is derived from "definition term." Each definition itself is defined by **<dd>**. Neither the **dt** nor the **dd** elements require a close tag under traditional HTML, yet given potentially long definitions and conformance to XHTML, the close tags should never be omitted. It is interesting to note that **<dt>** and **<dd>** tags are not required to be used in pairs, although they usually are. The following is a basic example using **<dl>**, the rendering of which is shown in Figure 3-9:

```
<!DOCTYPE html PUBLIC "-//W3C//DTD XHTML 1.0 Transitional//EN"
"http://www.w3.org/TR/xhtml1/DTD/xhtml1-transitional.dtd">
<html xmlns="http://www.w3.org/1999/xhtml" lang="en">
<head>
<title>Definition List Example</title>
<meta http-equiv="content-type" content="text/html; charset=ISO-8859-1" />
</head>
<body>
<h1 align="center">Definitions</h1>
<dl>
   <dt>Gadget</dt>
   <dd>A useless device used in many HTML examples.</dd>

   <dt>Gizmo</dt>
   <dd>Another useless device used in a few HTML examples.</dd>
</dl>
</body>
</html>
```

Vestigial Lists: <dir> and <menu>

Beyond basic ordered, unordered, and definition lists, two other lists are specified under traditional HTML: **<menu>** and **<dir>**. They were supposed to specify short menus of

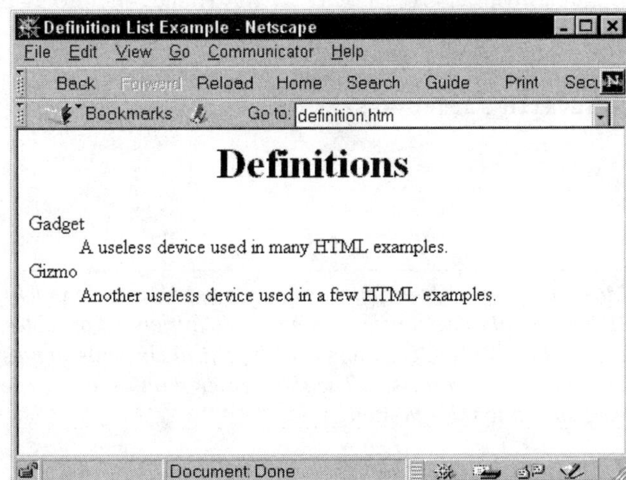

FIGURE 3-9 Rendering of definition list example

information and directory listings respectively, yet these rarely used elements generally appear as unordered lists in most browsers. Presented here solely for completeness, Web developers are warned to avoid using **<menu>** or **<dir>** because they have been dropped from the strict versions of HTML and XHTML.

Using Lists for Presentation

Because definition lists don't add numbering or bullets, many HTML writers have used this element to indent text. Although functionally this is the most appropriate way other than **<blockquote>** to achieve some rudimentary indentation without CSS, the unordered list often is used instead. The use of **<ul>** instead of **<dl>** to indent text quickly is unfortunately very common despite the fact that it is not valid markup. The most likely reason for this preference for **<ul>** is that it requires fewer elements to achieve indentation. A simple example of indenting with lists is shown next, with its rendering shown in Figure 3-10:

```
<!DOCTYPE html PUBLIC "-//W3C//DTD XHTML 1.0 Transitional//EN"
"http://www.w3.org/TR/xhtml1/DTD/xhtml1-transitional.dtd">
<html xmlns="http://www.w3.org/1999/xhtml" lang="en">
<head>
<title>List Indent Example</title>
<meta http-equiv="content-type" content="text/html; charset=ISO-8859-1" />
</head>
<body>
<dl>
  <dd><p>This paragraph is indented. Watch out for
         the left edge. Get too close and you'll hurt yourself!
  </p></dd>
</dl>

<br /><br />

<!-- Warning: markup below is not valid XHTML  -->
<ul><ul>
  <p>This paragraph is even further indented. Many HTML authors
     and authoring tools use this style to indent because
     it takes fewer tags, but it is not standards based and
     really should not be used.</p>
</ul></ul>
<!-- End invalid markup -->

</body>
</html>
```

NOTE *Most HTML purists are offended by the use of* **<ul>** *to indent. If you really must use HTML for presentation, consider using the definition list or tables, if possible, to indent text. However, with WYSIWYG editors spitting out* **ul** *elements in mass numbers, this might be more of a fine point than a real issue. The rise of style sheets and other technologies should, finally in time, put an end to this question.*

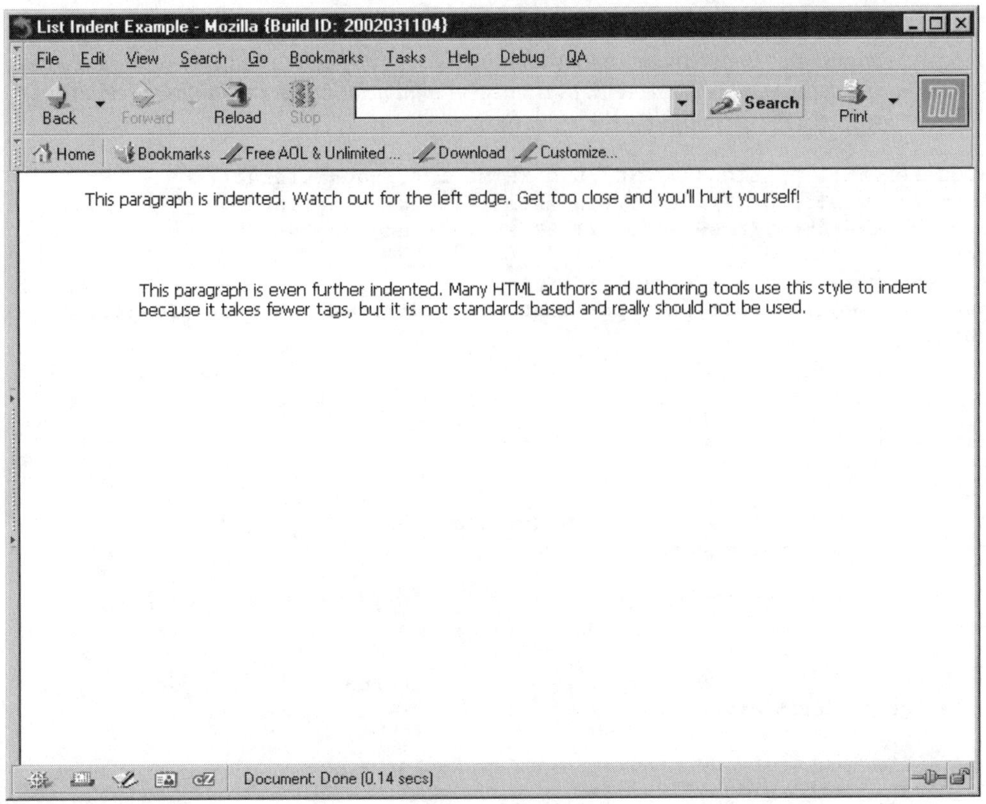

FIGURE 3-10 Example of lists for presentation

Horizontal Rules

As sections are added to an HTML document, it is often useful to break up the document into visually distinct regions. A horizontal rule, indicated by the **<hr>** tag, is an empty block-level element that serves this purpose. As an empty element under XHTML, horizontal rules are written as **<hr />**.

Historically, under HTML 2.0, horizontal rules generally were rendered as an etched bar or line across a browser window. With HTML 3.2 and beyond, more control over the horizontal rule's look and size was added. For example, the **size** attribute sets the bar's thickness (height) in pixels. The **width** attribute sets the bar's width in pixels or percentage. The **align** attribute sets its alignment to left, right, or center. The **noshade** attribute renders the bar without a surrounding shadow. Additional browser-specific attributes (such as **color**) are described in the element reference in Appendix A. Under strict HTML 4.0 and XHTML, the various presentation attributes for the horizontal rule have been removed in favor of CSS, leaving the exact look of the line to the browser rendering the page. An example of horizontal rules and their basic attributes is shown next. A browser rendering is shown in Figure 3-11.

NOTE *Although it looks like a physical element,* **hr** *can have some logical meaning as a section break. For example, under an alternative browser, such as a speech-based browser, a horizontal rule theoretically could be interpreted as a pause. A handheld browser with limited resolution might use it as a device to limit scrolling of the text.*

```
<!DOCTYPE html PUBLIC "-//W3C//DTD XHTML 1.0 Transitional//EN"
"http://www.w3.org/TR/xhtml1/DTD/xhtml1-transitional.dtd">
<html xmlns="http://www.w3.org/1999/xhtml" lang="en">
<head>
<title>Horizontal Rule Example</title>
<meta http-equiv="content-type" content="text/html; charset=ISO-8859-1" />
</head>
<body>


<p>HR size of 10</p>
<hr size="10" />

<p>HR with width of 50% and no shading</p>
<hr width="50%" noshade="noshade" />

<p>HR with width of 200 pixels, size of 3 pixels, and no shading</p>
<hr width="200" size="3" noshade="noshade" />

<p>HR with width of 100 pixels, aligned right</p>
<hr align="right" width="100" />

<p>HR with width of 100 pixels, aligned left</p>
<hr align="left" width="100" />

<p>HR with width of 100 pixels, aligned center</p>
<hr align="center" width="100" />

</body>
</html>
```

Other Block-Level Elements

HTML has many other large tag structures, most notably tables and forms. Many other elements are available under Navigator and Internet Explorer, including frames, layers, and a variety of other formatting and structuring features. Because of their complexity, it makes sense to discuss these tags in later chapters. Tables are discussed in depth in Chapter 7, and forms are discussed in Chapter 12. Before moving on to inline elements, let's cover one element that's somewhat difficult to characterize: **<address>.**

address

The **<address>** tag is used to surround information, such as the signature of the person who created the page, or the address of the organization the page is about. For example,

```
<address>
Demo Company, Inc.<br />
```

```
1122 Fake Street<br />
San Diego, CA 92109<br />
858.555.2086<br />
info@democompany.com<br />
</address>
```

can be inserted toward the bottom of every page throughout a Web site.

The **<address>** tag should be considered logical, although its physical rendering is italicized text. The HTML specification treats **<address>** as an idiosyncratic block-level element. Like other block-level elements, it inserts a blank before and after the block. It can enclose many lines of text, formatting elements to change the font characteristics and even images. However, according to the specification, it isn't supposed to enclose other block-level elements, although browsers generally allow this.

Text-Level Elements

Text-level elements in HTML come in two basic flavors: physical and logical. *Physical elements*, such as **<b>** for bold and **<i>** for italic, are used to specify how text should be

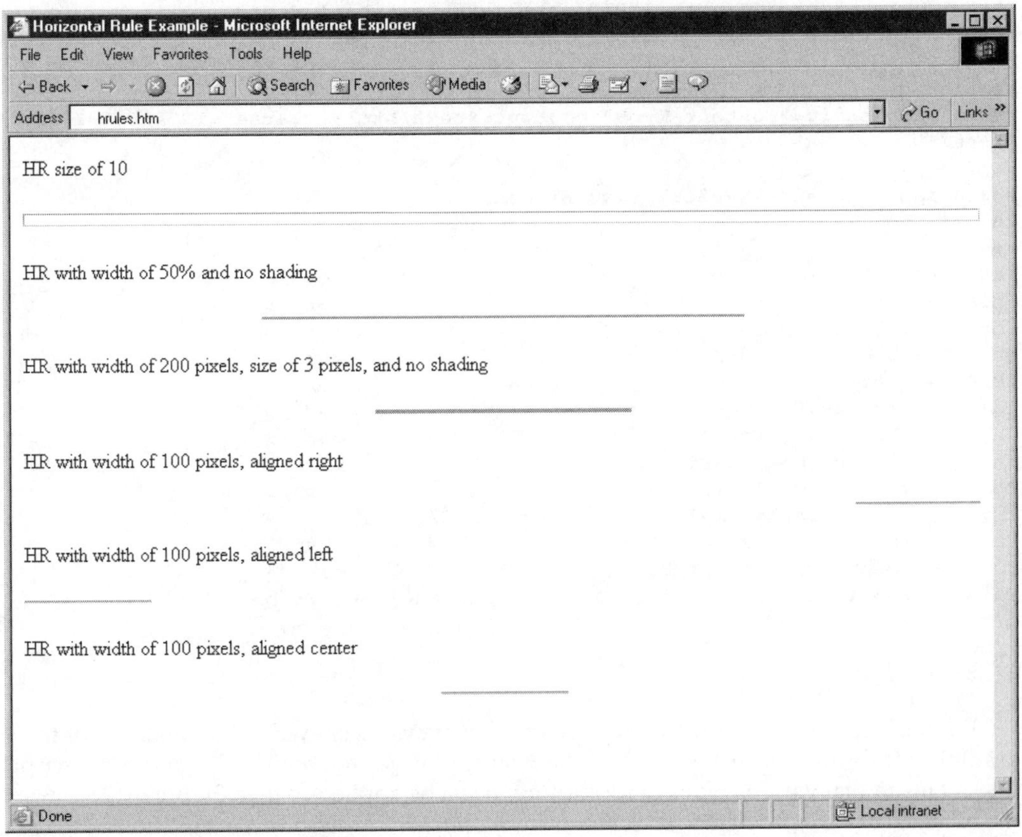

FIGURE 3-11 Rendering of horizontal rule example

rendered. *Logical elements*, such as **<strong>** and **<em>**, indicate what text is, but not necessarily how it should look. Although common renderings exist for logical text elements, the ambiguity of these elements and the limited knowledge of this type of document structuring have reduced their use. However, the acceptance of style sheets and the growing diversity of user agents mean using logical elements makes more sense than ever.

Physical Character-Formatting Elements

Sometimes you might want to use bold, italics, or other font attributes to set off certain text, such as computer code. HTML and XHTML support various elements that can be used to influence physical formatting. The elements have no meaning other than to make text render in a particular way. Any other meaning is assigned by the reader.

The common physical elements are listed in Table 3-1. Note, as shown in the table, under the strict variants of HTML and XHTML, the **<s>**, **<strike>**, and **<u>** tags are deprecated and should not be used.

The following example code shows the basic use of the physical text-formatting elements:

```
<!DOCTYPE html PUBLIC "-//W3C//DTD XHTML 1.0 Transitional//EN"
"http://www.w3.org/TR/xhtml1/DTD/xhtml1-transitional.dtd">
<html xmlns="http://www.w3.org/1999/xhtml" lang="en">
<head>
<title>Physical Text Elements</title>
<meta http-equiv="Content-Type" content="text/html; charset=ISO-8859-1" />
</head>
<body>
<h1 align="center">Physical Text Elements</h1>
<hr />
<p>
This is <b>Bold</b>                                     <br />
This is <i>Italic</i>                                   <br />
This is <tt>Monospaced</tt>                             <br />
This is <u>Underlined</u>                               <br />
This is <strike>Strike-through</strike>                 <br />
This is also <s>Strike-through</s>                      <br />
This is <big>Big</big>                                  <br />
This is even <big><big>Bigger</big></big>               <br />
This is <small>Small</small>                            <br />
This is even <small><small>Smaller</small></small><br />
This is <sup>Superscript</sup>                          <br />
This is <sub>Subscript</sub>                            <br />
This is <b><i><u>Bold, italic, and underlined</u></i></b>
</p>
</body>
</html>
```

Physical elements can be combined in arbitrary ways, as shown in the final part of the example. However, just because text *can* be made monospaced, bold, italic, and superscript doesn't mean that various types of formatting *should* be applied to text. Figure 3-12 shows the rendering of the physical text elements under popular browsers.

Element	Meaning	Notes
<i> … </i>	Italics	
<b> … </b>	Bold	
<tt> … </tt>	Teletype (monospaced)	
<u> … </u>	Underline	Deprecated in HTML and XHTML strict variants.
<s> … </s>	Strikethrough	Deprecated in HTML and XHTML strict variants.
<strike> … </strike>	Strikethrough	Deprecated in HTML and XHTML strict variants.
_…	Subscript	
[…]	Superscript	
<big> … </big>	Bigger font (one size bigger)	
<small> … </small>	Smaller font (one size smaller)	

TABLE 3-1 Inline Physical Tags

FIGURE 3-12 Rendering of physical text formatting elements

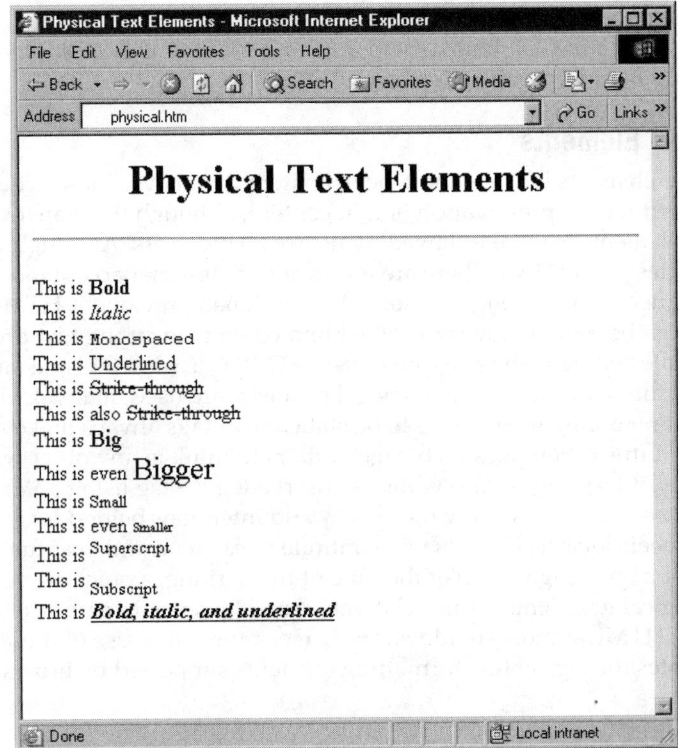

Several physical text formatting elements—particularly **<u>**, **<big>**, and **<small>**—present certain problems that warrant extra discussion.

Confusion Caused by Underlining

Today most browsers support the **<u>** tag, which underlines text. It was not initially defined under HTML 2.0, but was later introduced by Microsoft Internet Explorer and soon after all browsers began to support it. The trouble with this tag is that the meaning of underlined text can be unclear to people who use the Web. In most graphical browsers, clickable hypertext links are represented as blue underlined text. (Link color might vary.) Users instinctively think of underlined text as something that can be clicked. Some feel that the link color sufficiently distinguishes links from text that is underlined purely for stylistic purposes. However, this doesn't take into consideration monochrome monitors or people who are colorblind. Because the underline element could introduce more trouble than it is worth, it should be avoided even if it's allowed in the variant of HTML or XHTML you are using. Fortunately, under strict variants of HTML and XHTML, the tag is removed.

Using <big> and <small>

What do the **big** and **small** elements actually do? On the face of it, enclosing content within a **<big>** tag pair makes it bigger. Putting the **<small>** tag around something makes it smaller. What about when multiple **<big>** and **<small>** tags are nested? HTML has relative fonts ranging from size 1, very small, to size 7, very large. Every application of **<big>** bumps up the font one notch to the next level. The default font for a document usually is relative size 3, so two applications of **<big>** would raise the font size to 5. Multiple occurrences of **<small>** do the opposite—they make things one size smaller. HTML authors familiar with the **<font>** tag discussed in Chapter 6 should note that **<big>** is equivalent to **<font size="+1">** and **<small>** is equivalent to **<font size="-1">**.

Logical Elements

Logical elements indicate the type of content that they enclose. The browser is relatively free to determine the presentation of that content, although there are expected renderings for these elements that are followed by nearly all browsers. Although this practice conforms to the design of HTML, there are issues about designer acceptance. Plain and simple, will a designer think **<strong>** or **<b>**? As mentioned previously, HTML purists push for **<strong>** because a browser for the blind could read strong text properly. For the majority of people coding Web pages, however, HTML is used as a visual language, despite its design intentions. Even when logical elements are used, many developers assume their default rendering in browsers to be static. **<h1>** tags always make something large in their minds. Little encourages Web page authors to think in any other way. Consider that until recently, it was almost impossible to insert a logical tag using a WYSIWYG HTML editor.

Seasoned experts know the beauty and intentions behind logical elements, and with style sheets logical elements will continue to catch on and eventually become the dominant form of page design. Even at the time of this writing, a quick survey of large sites shows that logical text elements are relatively rare. However, to embrace the future and style sheets, HTML authors should strongly reexamine their use of these elements. Table 3-2 illustrates the logical text-formatting elements supported by browsers.

Element	Meaning	Common Rendering
<abbr> … </abbr>	Abbreviation (for example, Mr.)	Plain
<acronym> … </acronym>	Acronym (for example, WWW)	Plain
<cite> … </cite>	Citation	Italics
<code> … </code>	Code listing	Fixed Width
<dfn> … </dfn>	Definition	Italics
<em> … </em>	Emphasis	Italics
<kbd> .. </kbd>	Keystrokes	Fixed Width
<q> … </q>	Inline quotation	Quoted (not in IE 6)
<samp> … </samp>	Sample text (example)	Fixed Width
<strong> … </strong>	Strong emphasis	Bold
<var> … </var>	Programming variable	Italics

TABLE 3-2 Logical Text Formatting Elements

The following example uses all of the logical elements in a test document (shown in Figure 3-13 under common browsers):

```
<!DOCTYPE html PUBLIC "-//W3C//DTD XHTML 1.0 Transitional//EN"
"http://www.w3.org/TR/xhtml1/DTD/xhtml1-transitional.dtd">

<html xmlns="http://www.w3.org/1999/xhtml" lang="en">
<head>
<title>Logical Text Elements</title>
<meta http-equiv="content-type" content="text/html; charset=ISO-8859-1" />
</head>
<body>
<h1 align="center">Logical Text Elements</h1>
<hr />
<p>
  <acronym>WWW</acronym> is an acronym    <br />
  <abbr>Mr.</abbr> is an abbreviation     <br />
  This is <em>Emphasis</em>               <br />
  This is <strong>Strong</strong>         <br />
  This is a <cite>Citation</cite>         <br />
  This is <code>Code</code>               <br />
  This is <dfn>Definition</dfn>           <br />
  This is <kbd>Keyboard</kbd>             <br />
  This is a <q>Quotation</q>              <br />
  This is <samp>Sample</samp>             <br />
  This is <var>Variable</var>             <br />
</p>
</body>
</html>
```

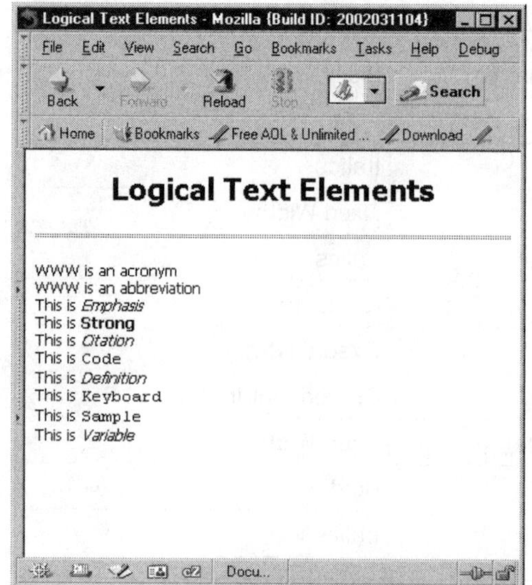

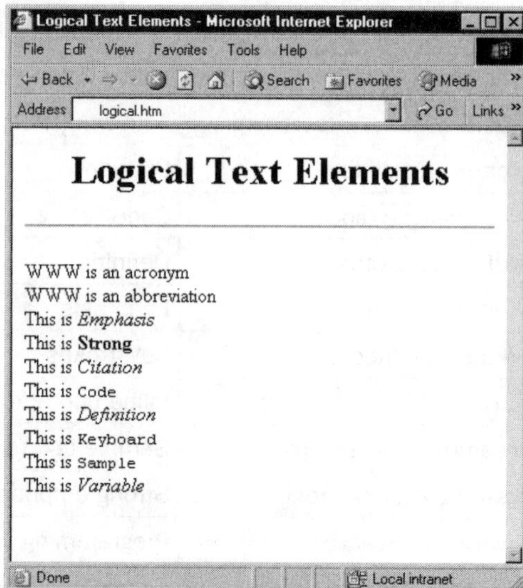

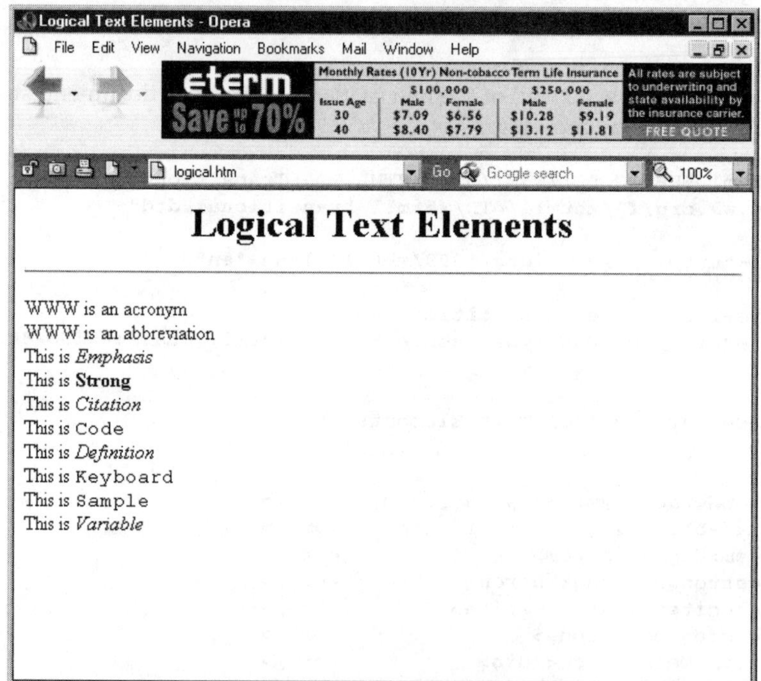

FIGURE 3-13 Rendering of logical text formation under Mozilla, Internet Explorer, and Opera

Subtle differences might occur in the rendering of logical elements. For example, **<dfn>** results in Roman text under Netscape, but yields italicized text under Internet Explorer. **<q>** wraps quotes around content, but does not change rendering in Internet Explorer 6 or earlier. You should also note that the **<abbr>** and **<acronym>** tags lack default physical presentation in browsers. Without CSS, they have no practical meaning, save potentially using the **title** attribute to display the meaning of the enclosed text. In short, there is no guarantee of rendering, and older versions of browsers in particular can vary on inline logical elements, including common ones such as **<em>**. Consult Appendix A for any special browser support details you may encounter.

Inserted and Deleted Text

HTML 4.0 introduced elements to indicate inserted and deleted text. The **<ins>** tag is used to show inserted text and might appear underlined in a browser, whereas the **<del>** tag is used to indicate deleted text and generally appears as struck text. For example, the markup here

```
<p>There are <del>6</del><ins>5</ins> robot models</p>
```

shows how a small modification could be made to content using these two elements. It is possible to provide more information about the insert or delete through the use of the core attribute **title**, which could provide advisory information about the text change as well as the **datetime** attribute, which could be used to indicate when the change happened. Through the use of scripting, it should be possible to hide various revisions made with this element.

A complete example of the use of **<ins>** and **<del>** is shown here; a rendering is given in Figure 3-14. It is important to note that these elements are very difficult to characterize because they can contain any amount of block or inline elements.

```
<!DOCTYPE html PUBLIC "-//W3C//DTD XHTML 1.0 Transitional//EN" "http://www.w3.org/
TR/xhtml1/DTD/xhtml1-transitional.dtd">
<html xmlns="http://www.w3.org/1999/xhtml" lang="en">
<head>
<title>Insert and Delete</title>
<meta http-equiv="content-type" content="text/html; charset=ISO-8859-1" />
</head>
<body>
<del><h1>Old Heading</h1></del>
<ins><h2>New Heading</h2></ins>
<p>This paragraph needs some changes.
<ins datetime="1999-01-05T09:15:30-05:00"
        title="New info inserted by TAP.">
This is a new sentence.</ins>
Here is some more text.</p>

</body>
</html>
```

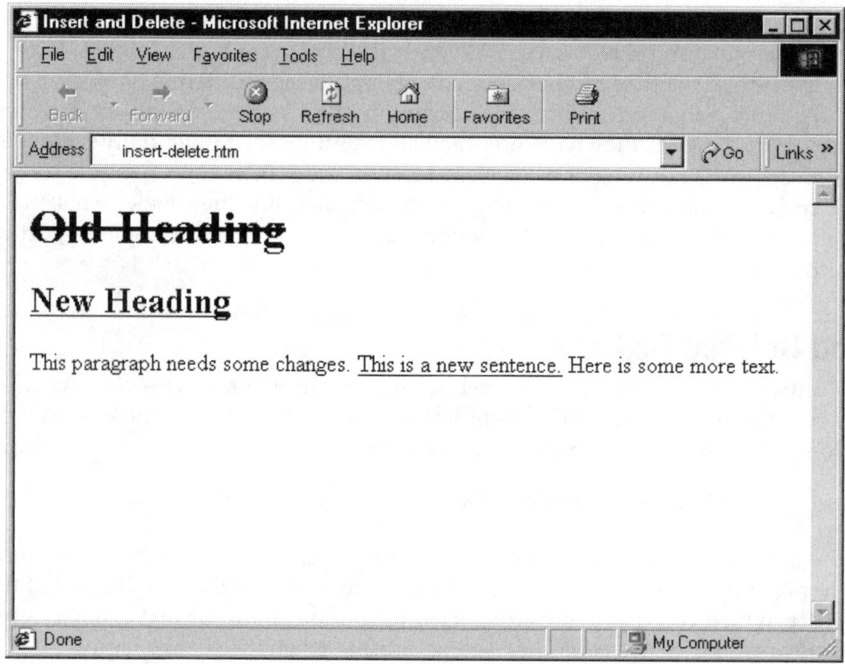

FIGURE 3-14 Rendering of Insert-Delete example

Character Entities

After covering most of the block elements and the basic inline text formatting elements, you might think that nothing remains to talk about—but there is one more level to HTML and XHTML documents: the characters themselves.

Sometimes, you need to put special characters within a document, such as accented letters, copyright symbols, or even the angle brackets used to enclose HTML elements. To use such characters in an HTML document, they must be "escaped" by using a special code. All character codes take the form ***&code;***, in which ***code*** is a word or numeric code indicating the actual character that you want to put onscreen. Some of the more commonly used characters are shown in Table 3-3.

NOTE *The character entity **™** might not always be acceptable as trademark. On many UNIX platforms, and potentially on Macs or Windows systems using various "other" character sets, this entity doesn't render as trademark. **&153;** can be undefined and you may even find trouble with the **™** named entity. However, trademarks are important legally, so they often are needed. The commonly used workaround is **^{<small>**TM**</small>}**. This markup creates a superscript trademark symbol (™) in a slightly smaller font. Because it's standard HTML, it works on nearly every platform.*

Numeric Value	Named Value	Symbol	Description
"	"	"	Quotation mark
&	&	&	Ampersand
<	<	<	Less than
>	>	>	Greater than
™	™	™	Trademark
			Non-breaking space
©	©	©	Copyright symbol
®	®	®	Registered trademark

TABLE 3-3 Commonly Used Character Entities

The following example shows some basic uses of HTML character entities. Figure 3-15 shows how the example might render.

```
<!DOCTYPE html PUBLIC "-//W3C//DTD XHTML 1.0 Transitional//EN"
"http://www.w3.org/TR/xhtml1/DTD/xhtml1-transitional.dtd">
<html xmlns="http://www.w3.org/1999/xhtml" lang="en">
<head>
<title>Character Entity Example</title>
<meta http-equiv="content-type" content="text/html; charset=ISO-8859-1" />
</head>
<body>
<h1 align="center">Character Entities Demo</h1>
<hr />
<p>Character entities like &amp;copy; allow users to insert
special characters like &copy;.</p>

<p>One entity that is both useful and abused is the
non-breaking space.</p>

<p>Inserting spaces is easy with &amp;nbsp;<br />
Look:   S       P      
A       C       E
      S.<br />
</p>

<hr />
<address>
Contents of this page &copy; 2003 Demo Company, Inc.<br />
The <strong>Wonder Tag</strong> &lt;P&gt; &#153; is a registered
 trademark of Demo Company, Inc.
</address>

</body>
</html>
```

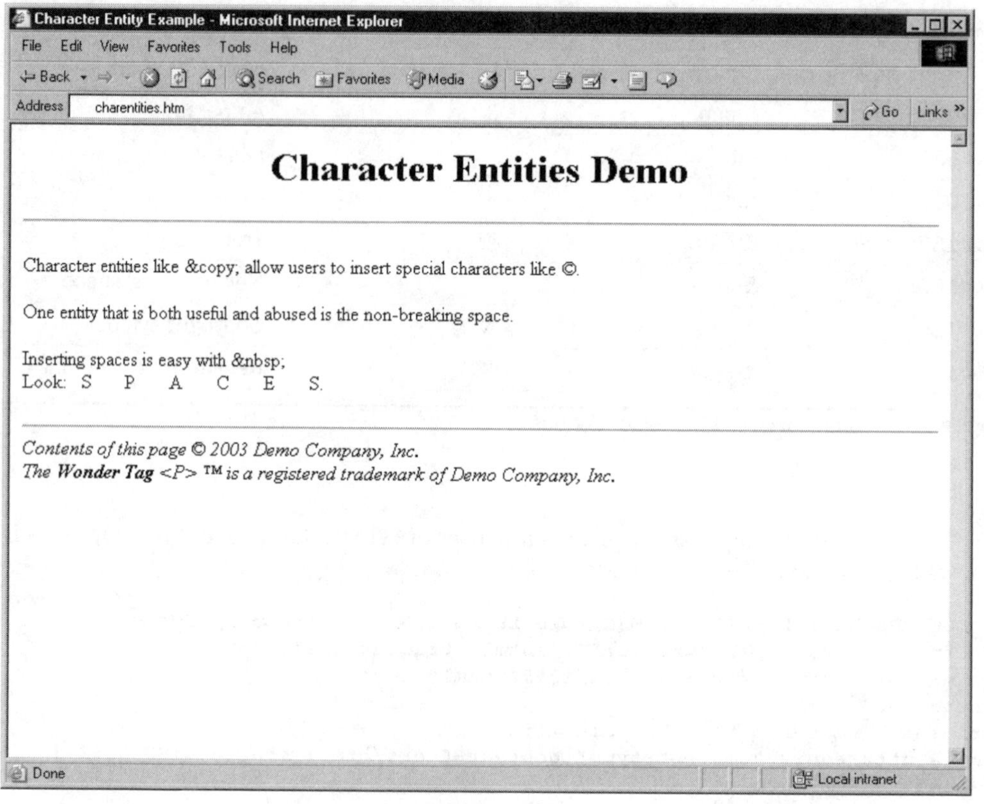

FIGURE 3-15 Rendering of character entities example

NOTE *The use of the nonbreaking space to push text or elements around the screen is an overused crutch. Many HTML editors overuse this technique in an attempt to preserve look and feel.*

While entities are easy to add, excessive use can make markup difficult to read, particularly if the character entities aren't well spaced.

The character set currently supported by HTML is the ISO Latin-1 character set. Many of its characters, such as accents and special symbols, cannot be typed on all keyboards. They must be entered into HTML documents by using the appropriate code. Even if the character in question is supported on the keyboard (for example, the copyright symbol), simply typing the symbol into the document directly may not produce the correct encoding. Of course, many HTML editors make the appropriate insertion for you. A complete list of the character entities is presented in Appendix C.

NOTE *HTML is capable of representing the standard ASCII characters and all the extended characters defined by the ISO Latin-1 character set. However, for non-Western characters, such as Japanese, Russian, or Arabic alphabets, special encoding extensions to a browser or operating system may be required.*

Comments

The last topic that should be considered a core aspect of HTML is the use of comments in an HTML document. The contents of HTML comments are not displayed within a browser window. Comments are denoted by a start value of **<!--** and an end value of **-->**. Comments can be many lines long. For example,

```
<!--
Document Name: Sample HTML Document
Author: Thomas A. Powell
Creation Date: 1/5/00
Last Modified: 5/15/03

Copyright 2000-2003 Demo Company, Inc.
-->
```

is a valid comment. Be careful to avoid putting spaces between the two dashes or any additional exclamation or dashes points in the comment. Comments are useful in the **<head>** of a document to describe information about a document, as the previous example suggested. Comments might also be useful when trying to explain complex HTML markup.

Comments also can include HTML elements, which is very useful for hiding new HTML elements from older browsers, and is commonly used with **<style>** and **<script>** elements, discussed in Chapters 10 and 14, respectively. Recall that a typical browser will output the contents of any tag it doesn't understand onscreen. Thus, we may want to hide the contents of certain tags from nonsupporting browsers. For example, consider trying to hide a style sheet's contents from an older browser. The **<style>** element might occur in the **<head>** of the document and contain various style rules, as shown here:

```
<style type="text/css">
  h1   {font-size: 48pt; color: red;}
</style>
```

A simple use of an HTML comment could mask the content from nonsupporting browsers like so:

```
<style type="text/css">
<!--
h1   {font-size: 48pt; color: red;}
-->
</style>
```

In this case, style sheet-aware browsers are smart enough to know to look within a comment found directly inside the **style** element, whereas older browsers would just skip over the comment, and nothing would happen. The use of comments to mask script code is slightly different as the closing --> symbols are valid code under JavaScript. In this case, hidden script code is wrapped in <!-- //-->. The close comment is preceded with a // because // is a JavaScript comment that hides the --> from the script interpreter.

```
<style type="text/javascript">
<!--
```

```
 alert("Hello I am JavaScript");
//-->
</style>
```

Unfortunately, this comment-out trick does have some problems. Under strict interpretation of XHTML, you should use a CDATA section to mask the content, as shown here:

```
<script type="text/javascript">
<![cdata[
  alert("Hello I am JavaScript");
]]>
</script>
```

It's interesting that this is not supported in the 6 and 7.*x* generation browsers so far; thus, the traditional hiding approach should be used if scripts are embedded in XHTML documents. However, in reality, linked scripts should be used wherever possible to more cleanly separate markup from programming logic.

Summary

The HTML and XHTML elements presented so far are common across nearly all systems. Whether or not they are used, they are simple and widely understood. Yet, despite their simplicity, many of these basic elements are still abused to achieve a particular look within a document, which continues the struggle between the logical and physical nature of HTML. Despite some manipulation, these elements generally are used in a reasonable manner. More complex formatting elements and programming elements are introduced in later chapters. The simplicity of this chapter should provide you with some assurance that HTML rests on a stable core.

A great number of elements have been left out of this discussion. No mention was made of layout-oriented elements, and so far I've completely avoided graphics. These topics and others are covered in upcoming chapters. First, in the next chapter, we'll cover the "H" in HTML, namely hypertext, and explore the concept of linking documents and objects.

4

CHAPTER

Links and Addressing

In previous chapters, you saw how HTML or XHTML can be used to structure a document, but little has been said about the hypertext aspect of the language. HTML/XHTML make it possible to define hyperlinks to other information items located all over the world, thus allowing documents to join the global information space known as the World Wide Web. Linking is possible because every document on the Web has a unique address, known as a *uniform resource locator* (URL). The explosive growth of documents on the Web has created a tangled mess, even when document locations are named consistently. The disorganized nature of many Web sites often leaves users lost in cyberspace. Finding information online can feel like trying to find the proverbial needle in a worldwide haystack. However, it doesn't have to be this way if designers pay attention to site structure.

Linking Basics

In HTML/XHTML, the main way to define hyperlinks is with the anchor tag, **<a>**. A *link* is simply a unidirectional pointer from the source document that contains the link to some destination. In hypertext, the end points of a link typically are called *anchors*, thus the use of the anchor nomenclature in HTML documentation.

For linking purposes, the **<a>** tag requires one attribute: **href**. The **href** attribute is set to the URL of the target resource, which basically is the address of the document to link to, such as http://www.democompany.com. The text enclosed by an **a** element specifies a "hot spot" to activate the hyperlink. Anchor content can include text, images, or a mixture of the two. A general link takes the form **<a href="*URL*">**Visit our site**</a>**. The text "Visit our site" is the link. The URL specified in the **href** attribute is the destination if the link is activated. The following is an example of simple link usage:

```
<!DOCTYPE html PUBLIC "-//W3C//DTD XHTML 1.0 Transitional//EN"
"http://www.w3.org/TR/xhtml1/DTD/xhtml1-transitional.dtd">
<html xmlns="http://www.w3.org/1999/xhtml" lang="en">
<head>
<title>Simple Link Example</title>
<meta http-equiv="Content-Type" content="text/html; charset=ISO-8859-1" />
</head>
<body>
<h1 align="center">Lots of links</h1>
```

```
<hr />
<ul>
<li>Visit <a href="http://www.yahoo.com">Yahoo!</a></li>
<li>Just a <a href="http://www.democompany.com">Demo Company</a></li>
<li>Go to the <a href="http://www.w3.org">W3C</a></li>
</ul>
</body>
</html>
```

When the preceding example is loaded into a Web browser, the links generally are indicated by underlined text, typically in a different color—usually blue or purple, depending on whether the linked object has been viewed before. Links are displayed in a different color after you visit the linked page so that you know in the future which links you have already followed. Status information in the browser generally changes when you position a mouse over a link. The pointer also might change, as well as other indicators showing that the information is a link. See Figure 4-1 for examples of link feedback in various browsers. Note that the cursor over the link looks like a pointing finger, and the URL for the linked page appears in the status area in the lower-left corner of the browser frame.

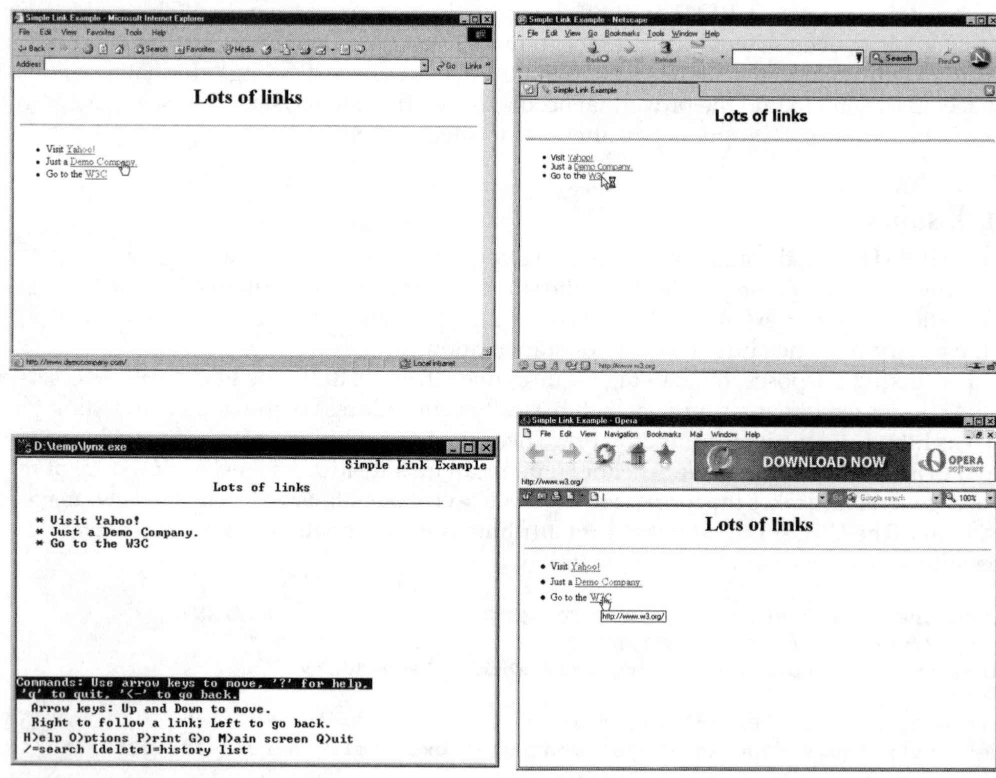

FIGURE 4-1 Example rendering and link feedback in various browsers

It is possible that link rendering does not follow the previously described style. For example, you can turn off link underlining under some browsers or through the use of cascading style sheets. This might cause usability problems for some users, but some designers and users find pages rendered in this way more aesthetically pleasing. Also, in many browsers the status bar is not displayed by default so it is not always obvious where a link leads. We'll talk more about link presentation later as it is an important topic.

NOTE *You can underline any text in an HTML document by tagging it with the underline tag* **<u>***. This practice might lead to confusion between hyperlinks and text that is underlined for stylistic purposes only. This is particularly evident if the link is viewed in a black-and-white environment or by a color-blind individual. Therefore, avoid the* **<u>** *tag if possible in documents to prevent potential confusion.*

PART II

In the previous example, all the **<a>** tags point to external resources with fully qualified URLs. In many cases, however, links are made within a Web site to another document on the same server. In this situation, a shortened URL is used, called a *relative URL*, which omits the protocol, server name, and occasionally even directory path. The following example links to several other documents using relative URLs: a document in the same directory, called specs.html; a document in the "extras" subdirectory, called access.html; and a link back to a page in a directory above:

```
<!DOCTYPE html PUBLIC "-//W3C//DTD XHTML 1.0 Transitional//EN"
"http://www.w3.org/TR/xhtml1/DTD/xhtml1-transitional.dtd">
<html xmlns="http://www.w3.org/1999/xhtml" lang="en">
<head>
<title>Simple Link Example 2</title>
<meta http-equiv="Content-Type" content="text/html; charset=ISO-8859-1" />
</head>
<body>
<h1 align="center">Green Gadgets</h1>
<hr />

<p>Here you will find information about the mysterious green
gadget--the wonder tool of the millennium.</p>
<ul>
   <li><a href="specs.html">specifications</a></li>
   <li><a href="extras/access.html">accessories</a></li>
</ul>
<p align="center">
<a href="../index.html">Back to Home Page</a>
</p>
</body>
</html>
```

As you can see in the previous basic examples, the use of links, at least within text, is simple. However, specifying the destination URL might not be so obvious. Later in this chapter, I cover more advanced HTML/XHTML syntax for forming links, but first, let's take a closer look at URLs because a thorough understanding of URLs is quite important for forming links.

What Are URLs?

A URL is a uniform way to refer to objects and services on the Internet. Even novice users should be familiar with typing a URL, such as http://www.democompany.com, in a browser dialog box, to get to a Web site. Internet users also use URLs to invoke other Internet services, such as transferring files via FTP or sending e-mail. HTML authors use URLs in their documents to define hyperlinks to other Web documents. Despite its potentially confusing collection of slashes and colons, the URL syntax is designed to provide a clear, simple notation that people can easily understand. The following concepts will help you to understand the major components of a URL address.

NOTE *Some people call URLs "universal resource locators." Except for a historical reference to "universal resource locators" in documentation from a few years ago, the current standard wording is "uniform resource locator."*

NOTE *The W3C often calls what users believe a URL to be a URI. The W3C is working from a more advanced view of Web addressing discussed later in the chapter. For this discussion we always use URL, which is more broadly understood.*

Basic Concepts

To locate any arbitrary object on the Internet, you need to find out the following information:

1. First, you need to locate and access the machine on the Internet (or intranet) on which the object resides. Locating the site might be a matter of specifying its domain name or IP address, whereas accessing the machine might be a matter of providing a username and password.
2. After you access the machine, you need to determine the name of the desired file, where the file is located, and what protocol will be used to retrieve the information or access the object.

The URL describes where something is and how it will be retrieved. The *where* is specified by the machine name, the directory name, and the filename. The *how* is specified by the protocol (for example, HTTP). Slashes and other characters are used to separate the parts of the address into machine-readable pieces. The basic structure of the URL is shown here:

```
protocol://site address/directory/filename
```

The next several sections look at the individual pieces of a URL in closer detail.

Site Address

A document exists on some server computer somewhere on the global Internet or within a private intranet. The first step in finding a document is to identify its server. The most convenient way to do this on a TCP/IP-based network is with a symbolic name, called a *domain name*. On the Internet at large, a *fully qualified domain name* (FQDN) typically consists of a machine name, followed by a domain name. For example, www.microsoft.com specifies a machine named *www* in the microsoft.com domain. On an intranet, however, things might be a little different, because you can avoid using a domain name. For example, a machine name of *hr-server* might be all that you need to access the human resources server within your company's intranet.

NOTE *A machine name indicates the local, intra-organizational name for the actual server. A machine name can be just about any name because machine naming has no mandated rules. Conventions exist, however, for identifying servers that provide common Internet resources. Servers for Web documents usually begin with the www prefix or often today have no set machine name. However, many local machines have names similar to the user's own name (for example, jsmith), his or her favorite cartoon character (for example, homer), or even an esoteric machine name (for example, dell-p6-200-a12). Machine naming conventions are important because they allow users to form URLs without explicitly spelling them out. A user who understands domain names and machine naming conventions should be able to guess that Toyota's Web server is http://www.toyota.com.*

The other part of most site addresses—the domain name—is fairly regular. Within the United States, a domain name consists of the actual domain or organization name, followed by a period, and then a domain type. Consider, for example, sun.com. The domain itself is sun, which represents Sun Microsystems. The *sun* domain exists within the commercial zone because of Sun's corporate status, so it ends with the domain type of *com*. In the United States, most domain identifiers currently use a three-character code that indicates the type of organization that owns the server. The most common codes are *com* for commercial, *gov* for government, *org* for nonprofit organizations, *edu* for educational institutions, *net* for networks, and *mil* for military. Recently, the general top level domain (gTLD) name space has been expanded to include domain extensions such as .biz, .info, .name, .aero, .pro, .museum, and .coop. Furthermore, many international names have suggested using their domains as top-level domains such as .cc, .nu, .ws, and .tv. Even more countries, large and small, seem to be allowing global registration of their domain names, which is unfortunate as it somewhat ruins the regional information that geographical domain names provided.

Domain space beyond the United States typically contains more information than organization type with a FQDN, including a country code as well and generally is written as follows:

```
machine name.domain name.domain type.country code
```

Zone identifiers outside the U.S. use a two-character code to indicate the country hosting the server. These include *ca* for Canada, *mx* for Mexico, *jp* for Japan, and so on. The U.S. also uses the *.us* extension although it has only recently caught on outside of local government and k12 educational environments. Within each country, the local naming authorities might create domain types at their own discretion, but these domain types can't correspond to American extensions. For example, www.sony.co.jp specifies a Web server for Sony in the *co* zone of Japan. In this case, co, rather than com, indicates a commercial venture. In the United Kingdom, the educational domain space has a different name, *ac*. Oxford University's Web server is www.ox.ac.uk, whereby ac indicates *academic,* compared to the U.S. edu extension for *education*. In spite of the avoidance of geographical name use for large, multinational companies (such as Sony), regional naming differences are still at this point very much alive. Web page authors linking to nonnative domains are encouraged to first understand the naming conventions of those environments. One special top-level domain, *int*, is reserved for organizations established by international treaties between governments, such as the European Union (eu.int). Top-level domains, such as *com*, *net*, and any new domains, will not necessarily correspond to a particular geographic area.

NOTE *Symbolic names make it convenient for people to refer to Internet servers. A server's real address is its Internet Protocol (IP) numeric address. Every accessible server on the Internet has a unique IP address by which it can be located using the TCP/IP protocol. An IP address is a numeric string that consists of four numbers between 0 and 255 and is separated by periods (for example, 10.0.0.124). This number then might correspond to a domain name, such as www.democompany.com. Note that a server's symbolic name must be translated, or resolved, into an IP address before it can be used to locate a server. An Internet service known as Domain Name Service (DNS) automatically performs this translation. You can use an IP address instead of a symbolic name to specify an Internet server, but doing so gives up mnemonic convenience. In some cases, using an IP address might be necessary because although every server has an IP address, not all servers have symbolic names.*

Investigating all aspects of the domain name structure is beyond the scope of this book. However, it should be noted that domain name formats and the domain name lookup service are very critical to the operation of the Web. If the domain name server is unavailable, it is impossible to access a Web server. To learn more about machine and domain names, see http://www.domainnotes.com.

NOTE *Domain names are not case-sensitive. Addresses can be written as www.Democompany.com or www.DEMOCOMPANY.com. A browser should handle both properly. Case typically is changed for marketing or branding purposes. However, directory and file names following the domain name might be case-sensitive, depending on the operating system the Web server is running on. For example, UNIX systems are case-sensitive, whereas Windows machines are not. Trouble can arise if casing is used randomly. As a rule of thumb, keep everything in lowercase.*

Directory

Servers might contain hundreds, if not thousands, of files. For practical use, files need to be organized into manageable units, analogous to the manila folders traditionally used to organize paper documents. This unit is known as a *directory*. After you have determined the server on which a document resides, the next step toward identifying its location is to specify the directory that contains the file. Just as one manila folder can contain other folders, directories can contain other directories. Directories contain other directories in a nested, hierarchical structure that resembles the branches of a tree.

The directory that contains all others is known as the *root directory*. Taken together, all the directories and files form a file tree, or *file system*. A file is located in a file system by specifying its *directory path*. This is the nested list of all directories that contain the file, from the most general—the root directory—to the most specific. Similar to the UNIX operating system, directories hosted on Web servers are separated by forward slashes (/) rather than backslashes (\), as in MS-DOS and Windows. Figure 4-2 shows a sample file tree for a Web site.

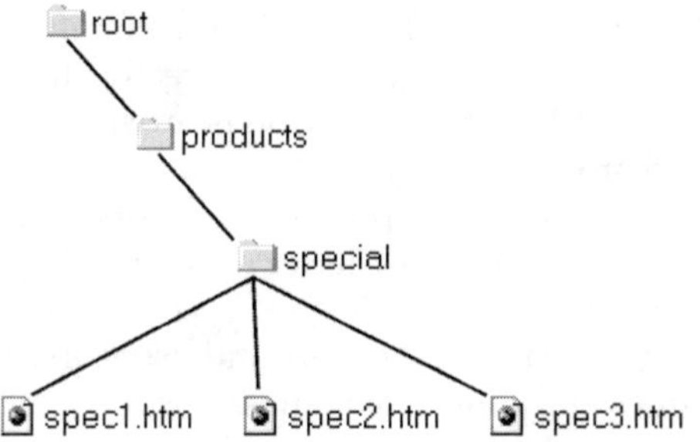

FIGURE 4-2 Sample file tree

Figure 4-2 shows how directories are organized within (or above and below) one another. For example, the directory called **special** is within the **products** directory, which is within the root directory. The full path should be written as /products/special/ to indicate that **special** is an actual directory, not a file in the **products** directory. When linking to other files, you might need to refer to a directory above the current directory, or to the current directory itself. In the scheme presented, ./ means the current directory, whereas ../ means one directory up in the hierarchy. A document in the **special** directory with a link path of ../ will link up to the **products** directory. Interestingly, while this type of information should be common knowledge to even a casual computer user, with the rise of GUI operating systems, many users are not as aware of this notation as they might be. However, for Web site construction it is mandatory to understand this.

NOTE *Directory names might follow conventions specific to an operating system, including conventions for case sensitivity. Authors are cautioned to look carefully at directory casing. Furthermore, directories might follow popular usage conventions (for example, tmp), or they can be arbitrary. Usually, directory names reflect aspects of their content such as media types, subject matter, or access privileges. For example, a directory called "images" might be the name of a directory containing images.*

Filename

After you specify the server and directory path for a document, the next step toward locating it is to specify its filename. This step typically has two parts: a filename, followed by a standard file extension. Filenames can be any names that are applicable under the server's operating system. Special characters such as spaces, colons, and slashes can wreak havoc if used in names of Web-available files. A file named test:1.htm would present problems on a Macintosh system, whereas test/1.htm might be legal on a Macintosh but problematic on a PC or UNIX machine.

A dot separates the filename and the *extension*, which is a code, generally composed of three or four letters, which identifies the type of information contained in the file. For example, HTML source files have a .htm or .html extension. JPEG images have a .jpg extension. A file's extension is critically important for Web applications because it is the primary indication of the information type that a file contains. A Web server reads a file extension and uses it to determine which headers, in the form of a MIME type (discussed in Chapter 16), to attach to a file when delivering it to a browser. If file extensions are omitted or misused, the file could be interpreted incorrectly. When browsers read files directly, they also look at file extensions to determine how to render the file. If the extension is missing or incorrect, a file will not be properly displayed in a Web browser.

Although many operating systems support four or more letters for file extensions, using a three-letter extension (.htm) versus a four-letter extension (.html) may minimize cross-platform incompatibilities. For the greatest flexibility, you should also avoid using spaces, uppercase letters, and special characters. Authors and users, in particular, should be aware of case sensitivity in filenames and directory names.

NOTE *It is possible to have filenames without extensions. Clean URLs that may employ content negotiation such as www.democompany.com/about show no file extension even when addressing files or other objects directly. This advanced idea, though W3C standards based, is still relatively rare and requires modification of a Web server to work. While far beyond the scope of this book, Apache administrators may look into mod_rewrite and mod_negotation to enable this interesting and highly usable URL form, while IIS administrators might use pageXchanger (www.pagexchanger.com) to achieve a similar result.*

Protocol

Finally, we need to specify how to retrieve information from the specified location. This is indicated in the URL by the protocol value. A *protocol* is the structured discussion that computers follow to negotiate resource-specific services. For example, the protocol that makes the Web possible is the Hypertext Transfer Protocol (HTTP). When you click a hyperlink in a Web document, your browser uses the HTTP protocol to contact a Web server and retrieve the appropriate document.

NOTE *Although HTTP stands for Hypertext Transfer Protocol, it doesn't specify how a file is transported from a server to a browser, only how the discussion between the server and browser will take place to get the file. The actual transport of files usually is the responsibility of a lower-layer network protocol, such as the Transmission Control Protocol (TCP). On the Internet, the combination of TCP and IP makes raw communication possible. Although a subtle point, many Internet professionals are unaware of lower-level protocols below application protocols such as HTTP, which are part of URLs.*

Although less frequently used than HTTP, several other protocols are important to Web page authors because they are often invoked by hyperlinks. Table 4-1 lists some examples.

NOTE *Sometimes the protocol javascript: is used in a URL; for example, javascript:alert('hi'). This is not a network protocol per se, but this form of URL is commonly found in Web pages. See Chapter 14 for a more in-depth discussion.*

These are the common protocols, but a variety of new protocols and URL forms are being debated all the time. Someday, such things as LDAP (Lightweight Directory Access Protocol), IRC (Internet Relay Chat), phone, fax, and even TV might be used to reference how data should be accessed. You can read more about the future of URLs and other naming ideas at the end of this chapter.

TABLE 4-1
Some Commonly Used Protocols

Protocol	Description
file	Enables a hyperlink to access a file on the local file system
ftp (File Transfer Protocol)	Enables a hyperlink to download files from remote systems
mailto	Invokes a mail program to enable a hyperlink to send an addressed e-mail message
news	Enables a hyperlink to access a USENET newsgroup using an external news reader
telnet	Enables a hyperlink to open a telnet session on a remote host

Special Features of URLs

In addition to the protocol, server address, directory, and filename, URLs often include a username and password, a port number, and sometimes a fragment identifier. Some URLs, such as mailto, might even contain a different form of information altogether, such as an e-mail address rather than a server or filename.

Username and Password

FTP and telnet are protocols for *authenticated services*. Authenticated services can restrict access to authorized users, and the protocols can require a username and password as parameters. A username and password precede a server name, like this: ftp://*username:password@server-address*. The password could be optional or unspecified in the URL, making the form simply ftp://*username@server-address*.

TIP *HTML authors should avoid including password information in URLs because the information may be readily viewable in a Web page or within the browser's URL box. If the password is omitted, the browser will prompt for the password.*

Port

Although not often used, the communication port number in a URL also can be specified. Browsers speaking a particular protocol communicate with servers through entry points, known as *ports,* which generally are identified by numeric addresses. Associated with each protocol is a default port number. For example, an HTTP request defaults to port number 80. A server administrator can configure a server to handle protocol requests at ports other than the default numbers. Usually, this occurs for experimental or secure applications. In these cases, the intended port must be explicitly addressed in a URL. To specify a port number, place it after the server address, separated by a colon; for example, http://*site-address*:8080. Usually, the reason for port changes is to allow multiple services to run at once or to slightly improve security through obscurity by using a nonstandard port number. However, this security is fairly weak and using different port numbers may confuse users or might even result in difficulty accessing a site.

Fragment

Besides referencing a file, it may be desirable to send a user directly to a particular point within the file. Because you can set up named links under traditional HTML and name any tag using ID under HTML 4 or XHTML, you can provide links directly to different points within a file. To jump to a particular named link, the URL must include a hash symbol (#) followed by the link name, which indicates that the value is a fragment identifier. For example, **<a href="#contents">**. Then, to specify a point called "contents" in a file called test.htm, you would use test.htm#contents. Elsewhere in the file, the fragment name would be set using a named anchor, such as **<a name="contents"></a>** or, more appropriately, by setting an **id** value on an arbitrary tag like **<a id="link1">** or **<p id="firstParagraph">**. This will be discussed later in the chapter in the section "Using name and id to Set Link Destinations."

Encoding

When writing the components of a URL, take care that they are written using only the displayable characters in your character set, which is most likely the ASCII character set. Even when using characters within this basic keyboard character range, you will find certain unsafe characters. You also might find reserved characters that could have special meaning within the context of a URL or the operating system on which the resource is found. If any unsafe, reserved, or nonprintable characters occur in a URL, they must be encoded in a special form. Failure to encode these characters might lead to errors.

The form of encoding consists of a percent sign and two hexadecimal digits corresponding to the value of the character in the ASCII character set. Within many intranet environments, filenames often include user-friendly names, such as "first quarter earnings 1999.doc." Such names contain unsafe characters—in this case, spaces. If this file were to live on a departmental Web server, it would have a URL with a file portion of first%20quarter%20earnings%201999.doc. Notice how the spaces have been mapped to **%20** values—the hex value of the space character in ASCII. Other characters that will be troublesome in URLs include the slash character (/), which encodes as **%2F**, the question mark (?), which maps to **%3F**, and the percent symbol (%) itself, which encodes as **%25**. Only alphanumeric values and some special characters ($ - _ . + ! * '), including parentheses, may be used in a URL; other characters should be encoded. In general, special characters such as accents, spaces, and some punctuation marks have to be encoded. Whenever possible, HTML authors should avoid using such characters in filenames in order to avoid encoding. Table 4-2 shows the reserved and potentially dangerous characters for URLs.

NOTE *Many of the characters in Table 4-2 don't have to be encoded, but encoding a character never causes problems, so when in doubt, encode it.*

Query String

Last but certainly not least, many URLs contain query strings indicated by the question mark (?). When a URL requests a program to be run rather than a file to be returned, a query string might be passed in the URL to indicate the various arguments to be given to the server-side program. Consider, for example,

```
http://www.democompany.com/cgi-bin/comments.exe?
Name=Matt+Folely&Age=32&Sex=male
```

TABLE 4-2 Common Character Encoding Values

Character	Encoding Value
Space	**%20**
/	**%2F**
?	**%3F**
:	**%3A**
;	**%3B**
&	**%26**
@	**%40**
=	**%3D**
#	**%23**
%	**%25**
<	**%3E**
>	**%3C**
{	**%7B**
}	**%7D**
[	**%5B**
]	**%5D**
"	**%22**
`	**%27**
‘	**%60**
^^	**%5E**
~	**%7E**
\	**%5C**
|	**%7C**

In this situation, the program comments.exe is handed a query string that has a name value set to "Matt Folely," an Age value set to "32," and a Sex value set to "male." Query strings are generally encoded as discussed in the previous section. Spaces in this case are mapped to the plus sign (+) while all other characters are in the %hex value form. The various name/value pairs are separated by ampersands (&). While it might look cryptic, query strings are relatively straightforward and their use will be discussed in Chapters 12 and 13 on forms and server-side programming, respectively.

With this brief discussion of the various components coming to a close, the next section presents a formula for creating URLs, as well as some examples.

Formula for URLs

All URLs share the same basic syntax: a protocol name, followed by a colon, followed by a protocol-specific resource description:

```
protocol_name:resource_description
```

Beyond this basic syntax, enough variation exists between protocol specifics to warrant a more in-depth discussion with examples.

HTTP

A minimal HTTP URL simply gives a server name. It provides no directory or file information.

- **Formula** http://*server*/ (with or without trailing /)
- **Example** http://www.democompany.com/

A minimal HTTP URL implicitly requests the home directory of a Web site. Even when a trailing slash isn't used, it is assumed and added either by the user agent or the Web server so that an address such as http://www.democompany.com becomes http://www.democompany.com/. By default, requesting a directory often results in the server returning a default file from the directory, termed the *index file*. Usually, index files are named index.htm or default.htm (or index.html and default.html, respectively), depending on the server software being used. This is only a convention; Web administrators are free to name default index files whatever they like. Interestingly, many people put special importance on the minimal HTTP URL form when, like all other file-retrieval URLs, this form simply specifies a particular directory or default index file to return, although this isn't always explicitly written out.

NOTE *Many sites now configure their domain name service and systems so that the use of www is optional. For example, http://pint.com/ is the same as http://www.pint.com. Although browsers often assist users trying to interpret short hand notation, HTML document authors should be careful to not assume such forms are valid. For example, in some browsers, typing democompany by itself might resolve to http://www.democompany.com. This is a browser usability improvement and can't be used as a URL in an HTML document. Because of misunderstandings with URLs, site managers are encouraged to support as many variable forms as possible so that the site works regardless of browser improvements or slight mistakes in linking.*

Let's make the HTTP URL example slightly more complex. The following is a formula to retrieve a specific HTML file that is assumed to exist in the default directory for the server:

- **Formula** http://*server*/*file*
- **Example** http://www.democompany.com/hello.html

An alternate, incremental extension adds directory information without specifying a file. Although the final slash should be provided, servers imply its existence if it is omitted, and look for a "home" document in the given directory. In practice, the final slash is optional, but recommended:

- **Formula** http://*server*/*directory*/
- **Example** http://www.democompany.com/products/

An HTTP URL can specify both a directory and a file:

- **Formula** http://*server*/*directory*/*file*
- **Example** http://www.democompany.com/products/greeting.html

On some systems, special shorthand conventions might be available for directory use. For example, a UNIX-based Web server might support many directories, each owned by a specific user. Rather than spelling out the full path to a user's root directory, the user directory can be abbreviated by using the tilde character (~), followed by the user's account, followed by a slash. Any directory or file information that follows this point will be relative to the user's root directory:

- **Formula** http://*server*/~*user*/
- **Example** http://www.bigisp.com/~jsmith/

In the previous example, ~jsmith might actually resolve to a path like /users/j/jsmith. This mapping of a tilde character to a user's home directory is a convention from the UNIX operating system and is often used on Web servers, although other Web servers on different operating systems might provide similar shortcut support.

A URL can refer to a named location inside an HTML document, which is called a *marker*, or *named link*. How markers are created is discussed later in this chapter. For now, to refer to a document marker, follow the target document's filename with the pound character, (#), dubbed a fragment identifier, and then with the marker's name:

- **Formula** http://*server*/*directory*/*file#marker*
- **Example** http://www.democompany.com/profile.html#introduction

In addition to referring to HTML documents, an HTTP URL can request any type of file. For example, http://www.democompany.com/images/logo.gif would retrieve from a server a GIF image rather than an HTML file. Authors should be aware that the flexibility of Web servers and URLs often is overlooked due to the common belief that a Web-based document must be in the HTML format for it to be linked to.

To the contrary, a URL can reference any type of file and may even execute a server program. These server-side programs are often termed *Common Gateway Interface (CGI)* programs, referring to the interface standard that describes how to pass data in and out of a program. CGI and similar server-side programming facilities are discussed in Chapter 12. Quite often, server-side programs are used to access databases and then generate HTML documents in response to user-entered queries. Parameters for such programs can be directly included in a URL by appending a question mark, followed by the actual parameter string. Because the user might type special characters in a query, characters that normally are not allowed within a URL are encoded. Remember that the formula for special-character encoding is a percent sign, followed by two hex numbers representing the character's ASCII value. For example, a space can be represented by **%20**.

- **Formula** http://*server/directory/file?parameters*
- **Example** http://www.democompany.com/products/search.cgi?cost=400.00&name=Super%20Part

Forming complex URLs with encoding and query strings looks very difficult. In reality, it rarely is done manually. Typically, the browser generates such a string on the fly based on data provided through a form. A more detailed discussion of HTML interaction with programming facilities appears in Chapters 12–15.

Finally, any HTTP request can be directed to a port other than the default port value of 80 by following the server identification with a colon and the intended port number:

- **Formula** http://*server:port/directory/file*
- **Example** http://www.democompany.com:8080/products/greetings.html

In the preceding example, the URL references a Web server running on port 8080. Although any unreserved port number is valid, the use of nonstandard port numbers on servers is not good practice. To access the address in the example, a user would need to include the port number in the URL. If it is omitted, accessing the server will be limited to the default port 80.

One type of HTTP exists that is, in a sense, a different protocol: secured Web transactions using the Secure Sockets Layer (SSL). In this case, the protocol is referenced as https, and the port value is assumed to be 443. An example formula for Secure HTTP is shown here; other than the cosmetic difference of the *s* and the different port value, it is identical to other HTTP URLs:

- **Formula** https://server:*port/directory/file*
- **Example** https://www.wellsfargo.com

An HTTP URL for a Web page probably is the most common URL, but users might find files or similar types of URLs growing in popularity due to the rise of intranets.

file

The file protocol specifies a file residing somewhere on a computer or locally accessible computer network. It does not specify an access protocol and has limited value except for one important case: it enables a browser to access files residing on a user's local computer, an important capability for Web page development. In this usage, the server name is omitted or replaced by the keyword *localhost*, which is followed by the local directory and file specification:

- **Formula** file://drive or network path/*directory/file*
- **Example** file:///dev/web/testpage.html

In some environments, the actual drive name and path to the file are specified. On a Macintosh, a URL might be the following:

```
file:///Macintosh %20HD/Desktop%20Folder/Bookmarks.html
```

A file URL such as the following might exist to access a file on the C drive of a PC on the local network, pc1:

```
file://\\pc1\C\Netlog.txt
```

Depending on browser complexity, complex file URLs might not be required, as with Internet Explorer, in which the operating system is tightly coupled with the user agent.

Interestingly, in the case of intranets, many drives might be mapped or file systems mounted so that no server is required to deliver files. In this "Web-serverless" environment, accessing network drives with a file URL might be possible. This demonstrates how simple a Web server is. In fact, to some people, a Web server is merely a very inefficient, though open, file server. This realization regarding file transfer leads logically to the idea of the FTP URL, discussed next.

FTP

The File Transfer Protocol, which predates the browser-oriented HTTP protocol, transfers files to and from a server. It generally is geared toward transferring files that are to be locally stored rather than immediately viewed. Today, because of its efficiency, FTP most commonly is used to download large files such as complete applications. These URLs share with HTTP the formula for indicating a server, port, directory, and file:

- **Formula** ftp://server:port/directory/file
- **Example** ftp://ftp.democompany.com:9978/info/somefile.exe

A minimal FTP URL specifies only a server: ftp://ftp.democompany.com. Generally, however, FTP URLs are used to access by name and directory a particular file in an archive, as shown in this formula:

- **Formula** ftp://*server/directory path/file*
- **Example** ftp://ftp.democompany.com/info/somefile.exe

FTP is an *authenticated* protocol, which means that every valid FTP request requires a defined user account on the server downloading the files. In practice, many FTP resources are intended for general access, and defining a unique account for every potential user is impractical. Therefore, an FTP convention known as *anonymous FTP* handles this common situation. The username "anonymous" or "ftp" allows general access to any public FTP resource supported by a server. As in the previous example, the anonymous user account is implicit in any FTP URL that does not explicitly provide account information.

An FTP URL can specify the name and password for a user account. If included, they precede the server declaration, according to the following formula:

- **Formula** ftp://*user:password@server/directory/file*
- **Example** ftp://jsmith:harmony@ftp.democompany.com/products/list

This formula shows the password embedded within the URL. Including an account password in a public document (such as an HTML file) is a dangerous proposition because it is transmitted in plain text and viewable both in the HTML source and browser address bar. Only public passwords should be embedded in any URL for an authenticated service. Furthermore, if you omit the password, the user agent typically prompts you to enter one if a password is required. Thus, it is more appropriate to provide a link to the service and *then* require the user to enter a name and password, or just provide the user ID and have the user agent prompt for a password, as happens in this example:

- **Formula** ftp://*user@server/directory/file*
- **Example** ftp://jsmith@ftp.democompany.com/products/sales

The FTP protocol assumes that a downloaded file contains binary information. You can override this default assumption by appending a type code to an FTP URL. The following are three common values for type codes:

- An **a** code indicates that the file is an ASCII text file.
- The **i** code, which also is the default, indicates that the file is an image/binary file.
- A **d** code causes the URL to return a directory listing of the specified path instead of a file.

An example formula is presented here for completeness:

- **Formula** ftp://*server/directory/file*;type=*code*
- **Example** ftp://ftp.democompany.com/products;type=d

In reality, the type codes rarely are encountered because the binary transfer format generally does not harm text files, and the user agent usually is smart enough to handle FTP URLs without type codes. Like many other URLs, the port accessed can be changed to something other than the default port of 21, but this is not recommended.

mailto

Typically, the mailto protocol does not locate and retrieve an Internet resource. Instead, if possible, it triggers an application for editing and sending a mail message to a particular user address:

- **Formula** mailto:*user@server*
- **Example** mailto:president@whitehouse.gov

This rather simple formula shows standard Internet mail addressing; other, more complex addresses might be just as valid. The use of mailto URLs is very popular in Web sites, to provide a basic feedback mechanism. Note that if the user's browser hasn't been set up properly to send e-mail, this type of URL might produce error messages when used in a link, prompting the user to set up mailing preferences. Because of this problem, page authors are warned to not rely solely on mailto-based URL links to collect user feedback.

NOTE *Some browsers have introduced proprietary extensions to the mailto protocol, such as the ? subject extension. While useful to set subject values and so on in a mail message, they should be used with caution as these extended features are not standardized.*

telnet

The telnet protocol allows a user to open an interactive terminal session on a remote host computer. A minimal telnet URL, shown next, simply gives the remote system's name. After a connection is made, the system prompts for an account name and password.

- **Formula** telnet://*server*
- **Example** telnet://host.democompany.com

As an authenticated protocol, telnet generally requires a defined user account on the remote system. When this is unspecified, the user agent or helper application handling telnet prompts for such information. Like FTP, a telnet URL also can contain an account name and password as parameters. But, as with FTP URLs, be careful about including passwords in public access documents such as HTML files on the Web. Because of the risk of password interception, the password is optional in the formula:

- **Formula** telnet://*user:password@server*
- **Example** telnet://jsmith:harmony@host.democompany.com
- **Example** telnet://jsmith@host.democompany.com

Finally, any telnet URL can direct a request to a specific port by appending the port address to the server name:

- **Formula** telnet://*server:port*
- **Example** telnet://host.democompany.com:94

Some telnet information sources can be configured to run on a particular port other than port 23, the standard telnet port. Consequently, use of the port within a telnet URL is more common than with other URLs.

Other Protocols

A wide variety of other protocols can be used including Gopher, news, NNTP, and so on. Modern browsers may support many of these URL forms. However, some protocols, such as the wais protocol, have little more than historical value. Little evidence suggests that people actually use such older protocols much on the Web, despite their presence in books that are only a few years old. Other unusual URL forms include operating system-biased protocols, such as finger, and esoteric protocols for things like VEMMI video text services. New protocols are being added all the time. In fact, dozens of proposed or even implemented protocols exist that can be referenced with some form of nonstandard URL. If you are interested in other URL forms, visit http://www.w3.org/pub/WWW/Addressing/schemes or http://www.ics.uci.edu/pub/ietf/uri/ for more information.

Relative URLs

Up to this point, the discussion has focused on a specific form of URL, typically termed an absolute URL. Absolute URLs completely spell out the protocol, host, directory, and filename. Providing such detail can be tedious and unnecessary, which is where a shortened form of URL, termed a *relative URL*, comes in to use. With relative URLs, the various parts of the address—the site, directory, and protocol—can be inferred by the URL of the current document, or through the **<base>** tag. The best way to illustrate the idea of relative URLs is by example.

If a Web site has an address of www.democompany.com, a user can access the home page with a URL such as http://www.democompany.com/. A link to this page from an outside system also would contain the address http://www.democompany.com/. Once at the site, however, there is no reason to continue spelling out the full address of the site. A fully qualified link from the home page to a staff page in the root directory called staff.html would be http://www.democompany.com/staff.html. The protocol, address, and directory name can be inferred, so all that is needed is the address staff.html. This relative scheme works because http://www.democompany.com/ is inferred as the base of all future links that omit protocol and domain, thus allowing for the shorthand relative notation. The relative notation can be used with filenames and directories, as shown by the examples in Table 4-3.

When relative URLs are used within a Web site, the site becomes transportable. By not spelling out the server name in every link, you can develop a Web site on one server and move it to another. If you use absolute URLs, however, all links have to be changed if a server changes names or the files are moved to another site.

Of course, using relative URLs also has a potential downside: They can become confusing in a large site, particularly if centralized directories are used for things such as images. Imagine having URLs such as ../../../images/logo.gif in files deep in a site structure. Some users might be tempted to simply copy files to avoid such problems, but then updating and caching issues arise. One solution is to use a **<base>** tag. Another solution is to use symbolic links on the Web server to reference one copy of the file from multiple locations. However, because HTML is the subject here, the focus is the former solution, using the **base** element.

Current Page Address	Destination Address	Relative URL
http://www.democompany.com/ index.html	http://www.democompany.com/ staff.html	staff.html
http://www.democompany.com/ index.html	http://www.democompany.com/ products/gadget1.html	products/ gadget1.html
http://www.democompany.com/ products/jetpackes/modelT.html	http://www.democompany.com/ index.html	/index.html
http://www.democompany.com/ products/gadget1.html	http://www.democompany.com/ index.html	../index.html

TABLE 4-3 Relative URL Formation Examples

The **base** element defines the base for all relative URLs within a document. Setting the **href** attribute of this element to a fully qualified URL enables all other relative references to use the defined base. For example, if **<base>** is set as <**base href="http://www.democompany.com/"**>, then all the anchors in the document that aren't fully qualified will prefix http://www.democompany.com/ to the destination URL. Because **<base>** is an empty element, it would have to be written as <**base href="http://www.democompany.com/" /**> to be XHTML-compliant.

The **<base>** tag can occur only once in an HTML document—within its head—so creating sections of a document with different base URL values is impossible. Such a feature might someday be added to a sectioning element, but until then, HTML authors have to deal with the fact that shorthand notation is useful only in some places. See Appendix A for more information on the **<base>** tag.

Linking in HTML

The discussion thus far has focused solely on the forms of URLs. Little has been said about how to link objects together on the Web. Later in this chapter, the discussion becomes more theoretical and discusses the relationship between URLs, URIs, URCs, and URNs.

The Anchor Element

As briefly introduced at the start of the chapter, the most common way to define hyperlinks in HTML is with the anchor tag, **<a>**. In its most basic form, this element needs two pieces of information: the URL of the target resource, and the document content needed to activate the hyperlink. Assigning a URL value to an **<a>** tag's **href** attribute specifies the target resource like so:

```
<a href="URL">Linked content</a>
```

NOTE *An* ***a*** *element may not enclose another* ***a*** *element. The code* ***<a href="URL1">****Linked****<a href="URL2">****More linked****</a></a>*** *makes no sense.*

Most defined hyperlinks probably use an HTTP URL to link one HTML document to another, but the other URL forms are valid as well. As an example, all the following are syntactically valid links:

```
<a href="http://www.whitehouse.gov/">Visit the White House</a>
<a href="http://www.democompany.com/about/">About Demo Company</a>
<a href="http://www.democompany.com/products/robots.html">Robots</a>
<a href="http://www.democompany.com/products/robots.html#top">Go to top</a>
<a href="products/robots.html">Robots</a>
<a href="../../index.html">Back to home</a>
<a href="ftp://ftp.democompany.com">Access FTP archive</a>
<a href="mailto:info@democompany.com">More information?</a>
```

NOTE *Be careful when using mailto URLs; they often do not work because a browser is not configured to send mail or does not support this URL form properly.*

The following example shows a more complete example of relative and absolute URLs and their use within an XHTML document:

```
<!DOCTYPE html PUBLIC "-//W3C//DTD XHTML 1.0 Transitional//EN"
"http://www.w3.org/TR/xhtml1/DTD/xhtml1-transitional.dtd">
<html xmlns="http://www.w3.org/1999/xhtml" lang="en">
<head>
<title>Link Example 3</title>
<meta http-equiv="content-type" content="text/html; charset=ISO-8859-1" />
</head>
<body>
<h1 align="center">Green Gadgets</h1>
<hr />
<p>Here you will find information about the mysterious green
gadget--the wonder tool of the millennium. </p>
<ul>
    <li><a href="specs.html">Specifications</a></li>
    <li><a href="extras/access.html">Accessories</a></li>
    <li><a href="http://www.democompany.com">Distributors</a></li>
    <li><a href="ftp://ftp.democompany.com/pdfs/order.pdf">
        Download order form</a></li>
</ul>
<div align="center">
<a href="../index.html">Back to Demo Company Home</a>
</div>
<hr />
<address>
Questions?
<a href="mailto:info@democompany.com">info@democompany.com</a>
</address>
</body>
</html>
```

Renderings of the link examples are shown in Figure 4-3.

Link Renderings

In most browsers, text links are indicated by underlined text. Text is blue if the destination has never been visited, purple if it has been visited, and briefly red as the link is activated. If a link includes an image, the border of the image also will be blue or purple, unless the border attribute has been set to zero. HTML authors can override these default link colors with changes to the **link**, **alink**, and **vlink** attributes of the **body** element. The **link** attribute changes the color of all unvisited links; the **vlink** attribute changes all visited links. The **alink** attribute changes the color of the active link, which is the brief flash that appears when a link is pressed. By using a style sheet rule, authors also can change the decoration of links to turn off underlining; change the style in hover mode, where the mouse is over a link; or even display all links in completely different fashion. The approaches using HTML and CSS are summarized in Table 4-4 and demonstrated in the following example:

```
<!DOCTYPE html PUBLIC "-//W3C//DTD XHTML 1.0 Transitional//EN"
"http://www.w3.org/TR/xhtml1/DTD/xhtml1-transitional.dtd">
<html xmlns="http://www.w3.org/1999/xhtml" lang="en">
<head>
<title>Link Style Changes</title>
<meta http-equiv="content-type" content="text/html; charset=ISO-8859-1" />
<style type="text/css">
 a          {text-decoration: none;}
 a:hover    {color: red; text-decoration: underline;}
</style>
</head>
<body link="blue" alink="green" vlink="purple">
<a href="#">Link to this page</a>
<a href="http://www.yahoo.com">Test Link to Yahoo!</a>
</body>
</html>
```


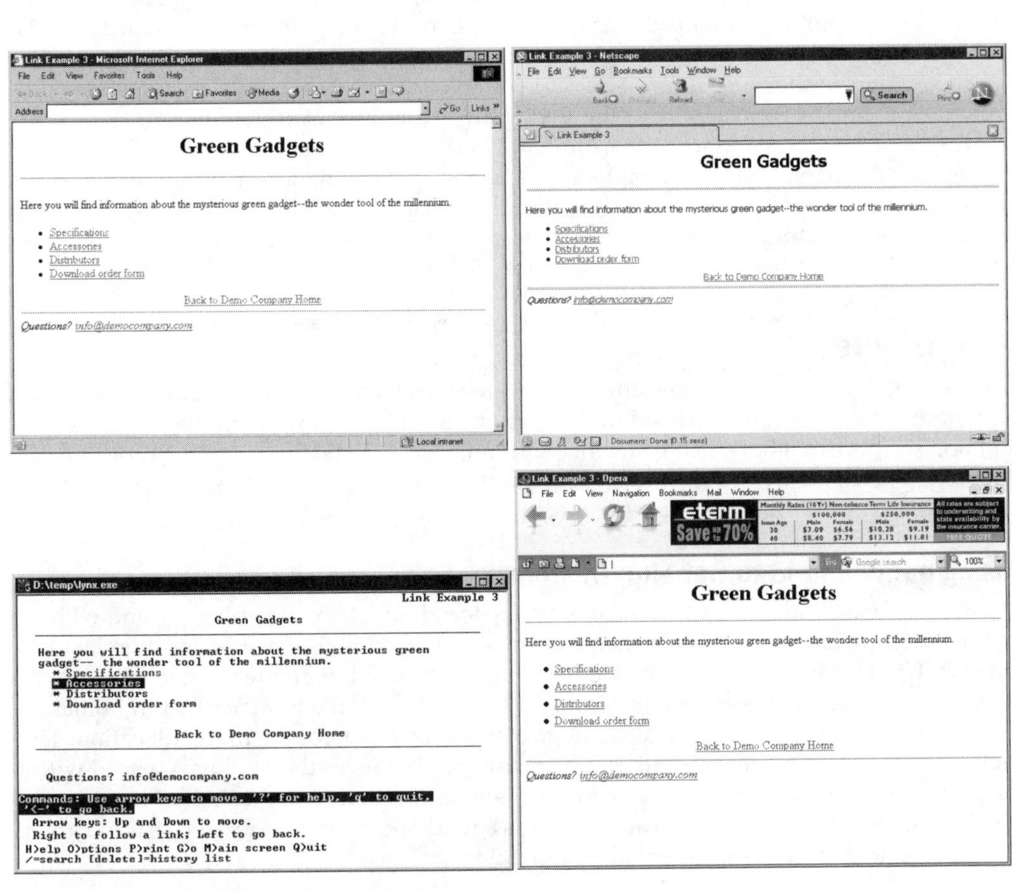

FIGURE 4-3 Browser renderings of combined linked example

Link State	Standard Color	HTML Attribute	CSS Pseudo Class Rule
Unvisited	Blue	<body link="*colorvalue*">	a:link {color: *colorvalue;*}
Visited	Purple	<body vlink="*colorvalue*">	a:visited {color: *colorvalue;*}
Hover	N/A	N/A	a: hover {color: *colorvalue;*}
Active	Red	<body alink="*colorvalue*">	a:active {color: *colorvalue;*}

TABLE 4-4 Link Presentation Summary

NOTE *Except for backwards compatibility, it is preferable to specify all link changes in CSS rather than HTML.*

Changing link colors or removing underlining might seem to make sense aesthetically—but it also can confuse readers who have come to expect a standard color scheme for links. Occasionally, authors try to encourage return visits by changing the setting for visited links to remain blue, or they might reverse colors for layout consistency. Such changes can significantly impair the usability of the site by thwarting user expectations.

Like it or not, the standard Web experience has taught users to click underlined text that is blue or purple. Such user habits suggest that underlining for emphasis should be used sparingly, if at all, in HTML documents. Furthermore, HTML text probably shouldn't be colored blue or purple, unless it obviously isn't a link. Controlling color is very important, but it is only one of many aspects of links that can be controlled.

Anchor Attributes

The **a** element has many possible attributes besides **href**, as shown in Table 4-5. The more important attributes are discussed in the sections to follow, along with the concepts of binding scripts to anchors, using anchors with images, and creating a special type of image link called an *image map*. Refer to the element reference (Appendix A) to see a complete listing of all possible attributes for the **a** element.

Using name and id to Set Link Destinations

An **<a>** tag usually defines a hyperlink's source location: where the link goes, and what you click to go there. One possible destination for a hyperlink is a named location inside an HTML/XHTML document. The **<a>** tag can also be used to define these locations in a special usage known as *setting a fragment identifier*, although the term *marker* might make more sense. To set a marker, set the **name** to a symbolic name for the marker location. The defined name must be unique within the document. Wherever the marker is placed within an HTML document becomes a named candidate destination for hyperlinks. For example, the HTML markup **<a name="marker">** This is a marker**</a>** sets the text "This is a marker" to be associated with the fragment identifier **#marker**.

NOTE *Unlike hyperlink anchors, a marker location is not underlined or in any way visually distinguished.*

Attribute Name	Possible Value	Description
href	URL	Sets the URL of the destination object for the anchor.
name	Text	Names the anchor so that it can be a target of another anchor or script. Traditional HTML superceded by id.
id	Text	Identifies the anchor for target by another anchor, style sheet access, and scripting exposure. HTML 4 or XHTML attribute.
target	A frame name	Defines the frame or window destination of the link.
title	Text	Sets advisory text.
accesskey	A character	Sets the key for keyboard access to the link.
tabindex	A numeric value	Sets the order in the tabbing index for using the TAB key to move through links in a page.
rel	Text	Defines the relationship of the object being linked to.
rev	Text	Defines the relationship of the current object to the object being linked to. In short, rev defines the reverse relationship.

TABLE 4-5 Common Anchor Attributes

In practice, when an <**a**> tag is used solely as a marker, it often doesn't enclose any text, although this doesn't suggest that the close tag should be omitted, as it often is. Setting a marker such as **<a name="top">** is accepted by most browsers, but **<a name="top"></a>** is the valid form that should be used.

An <**a**> tag can serve as both a destination and a link at the same time. For example,

```
<a name="yahoolink" href="http://www.yahoo.com/">Yahoo!</a>
```

creates a link to a site and names the anchor so that it can be referenced by other links. The dual use of the **a** element might cause some confusion, but it is valid.

As discussed in Chapter 3, under the current version of HTML, the **id** attribute also is available for nearly every element. It also can be used to set a marker. The preceding example could have been written **<a id="yahoolink" href="http://www.yahoo.com">**Yahoo!**</a>**, thus exposing the anchor for targeted linking, style sheets, and dynamic manipulation via a scripting language. For backward compatibility, the **name** attribute is often used because many older browsers do not support **id** fully. Thus, we might specify **<a id="yahoolink" name="yahoolink" href= "http://www.yahoo.com">**Yahoo!**</a>** to cover many possibilities. Interestingly, such mixed markup will validate even in strict HTML/XHTML.

The need for named anchors isn't always obvious. Their main purpose is to name a location within a document to jump to; for example, the common "back to top" links found at the bottom of long pages. Such link usage can be accomplished by using **<a name="top" id="top"></a>** to define named locations and then referencing them with links containing fragment identifiers such as **<a href="#top">**Top of the document**</a>.** Be careful to always use the # symbol with marker names. Otherwise, the user agent probably will interpret the link as referencing a file rather than a marker.

In the more general case, a marked location in any HTML document can be referenced by placing # and a marker name after its normal URL. For example,

```
<a href="http://www.democompany.com/products/robots.html#specs">
 Robot Specs</a>
```

will link to a named marker called "specs" in the robots.htm file. A complete example of linking within a file and to markers outside the file is shown here:

```
<!DOCTYPE html PUBLIC "-//W3C//DTD XHTML 1.0 Transitional//EN"
"http://www.w3.org/TR/xhtml1/DTD/xhtml1-transitional.dtd">
<html xmlns="http://www.w3.org/1999/xhtml" lang="en">
<head>
<title>Name Attribute Example</title>
<meta http-equiv="content-type" content="text/html; charset=ISO-8859-1" />
</head>
<body>

<p><a id="top" name="top"></a>
Go to the <a href="#bottom">bottom</a> of this document.<br />
Link right to a
<a href="../examples/chapter4/testfile.html#marker1">marker</a>
in another document.</p>

<p>To make this work we need to simulate the document being very
long by using many breaks.
<br /><br /><br /><br /><br /><br /><br /><br /><br />
<br /><br /><br /><br /><br /><br /><br /><br /><br />
<strong id="middle">the middle</strong>
<br /><br /><br /><br /><br /><br /><br /><br /><br />
<br /><br /><br /><br /><br /><br /><br /><br /><br />
</p>

<hr />
<p><a id="bottom" name="bottom" href="#top">return to top</a>
<a href="#middle">go to middle</a></p>

</body>
</html>
```

NOTE *Named values must be unique, whether they are set using the* ***name*** *attribute or the* ***id*** *attribute.*

title Attributes for Anchors

Often, the **title** attribute will not seem terribly helpful to a user because it provides only basic advisory information about the use of a particular element. In the case of anchors, however, **title** is very useful because it can be used to indicate some information about the link's destination. The following code fragment provides some helpful information for the link:

```
<a href="staff/index.html"
 title="Resumes and information about our staff">Staff</a>
```

A rendering of the previous example might look like this:

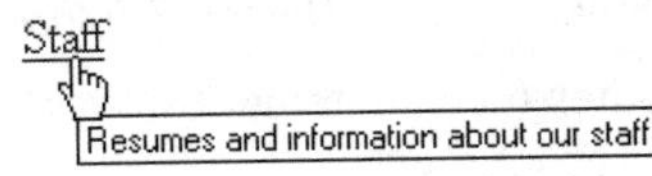

NOTE *Although the* **title** *attribute is usable in nearly every HTML element under Internet Explorer, using it makes sense mainly for links, images, binary objects, and forms.*

The **title** attribute serves another purpose: It provides the title information for a bookmark when a link is bookmarked before the destination page is visited. Although this might not be intuitive, with many browsers, you can right-click a link to access a menu that enables you to bookmark the link before it is visited. Then, when the page is visited, the information enclosed within the **<title>** tag of the destination page is used in the bookmark instead of the information in the **title** attribute of the anchor that loaded the page. (Note that the **title** attribute and the **title** element are two entirely different things.)

Accelerator Keys

The HTML 4 specification added the **accesskey** to the **a** element, as well as to various form elements, as discussed in Chapter 12. With this attribute, you can set a key to invoke an anchor without requiring a pointing device to select the link. The link is activated with the combination of the accelerator key, usually ALT, and the key specified by the attribute. So,

```
<a href="http://www.yahoo.com/" accesskey="Y">Yahoo!</a>
```

makes a link to Yahoo!, which can be activated by pressing ALT+Y. Internet Explore 4 and greater and Netscape 6 and greater support the **accesskey** attribute on links.

Although adding keyboard access to a Web page seemingly would be a dramatic usability improvement, HTML authors are cautioned to be aware of access key bindings in the browsing environment, as detailed in Table 4-6.

Another consideration with accelerator keys is how they should display in the page. In most software, underlining indicates the letter of the accelerator key. Links generally are underlined in browsers, so this approach isn't feasible. Style sheets can be used to change link direction, so underlining the first letter is possible, but then the user might be disoriented, expecting links to be fully underlined. Another approach to indicating the accelerator keys might be to set the access key letter of a text link in bold or a slightly larger size.

TABLE 4-6 Browser Reserved Accelerator Keys

Key	Description
F	File menu
E	Edit menu
V	View menu
N	Navigation menu (Opera 6)
G	Go menu (Netscape/Mozilla), Messaging menu (Opera 6)
B	Bookmarks menu (Netscape/Mozilla only)
A	Favorites menu (Internet Explorer only)
T	Tools or Tasks menu
M	E-mail menu (Opera 6)
S	Search menu (Netscape 6), News menu (Opera 6)
W	Window menu (Netscape 7/Mozilla)
A	Favorites menu (Internet Explorer only)
H	Help menu

tabindex Attribute

The **tabindex** attribute of the **a** element defines the order in which links will be tabbed through in a browser that supports keyboard navigation. The value of **tabindex** usually is a positive number. Browsers tab through links in order of increasing **tabindex** values, but generally skip over those with negative values. So, **<a href="about.html" tabindex="1">** sets this anchor to be the first thing tabbed to by a browser. If the **tabindex** attribute is undefined, the browser tends to tab through links from the top to the bottom of the page.

target Attribute

The **target** attribute is used in conjunction with frames, which are discussed in Chapter 8. To target a link so that the result loads in a particular frame or window, the **target** attribute is added to an **<a>** tag. Generally, a frame has a name, so setting the **target** equal to the frame name results in the link loading in the frame named in the attribute. For example, when selected, a link such as

```
<a href="http://www.yahoo.com/" target="display_frame">Yahoo</a>
```

loads the object referenced by the URL into the frame named **"display_frame"**. If the **target** attribute is left out, the current window or frame the document is in is used. Aside from author-named frames, the following are several reserved names for frames that, when used with the **target** attribute, have special meaning: **_blank**, **_self**, **_parent**, and **_top**. For more information about frames, as well as instructions on how to use the **a** element with frames and the various reserved frame names, refer to the element reference (Appendix A) and Chapter 8.

Anchors and Link Relationships

The **a** element has the following two attributes whose meanings often are misunderstood. These attributes are not widely supported by browsers:

- **rel** This attribute is used to describe the relationship between the document and the destination document referenced by the anchor's **href** attribute. For example, if the destination of the link specifies the glossary associated with a document, the anchor might read:

```
<a href="words.html" rel="glossary">Glossary</a>
```

- **rev** This attribute defines the reverse relationship of what **rel** defines; in this case, what the relationship is from the destination document's perspective. An example of its use is a linear set of documents in which the **rel** attribute is set to **"next"** and the **rev** attribute is set to **"prev"**, as shown in the following code fragment:

```
<a href="page2.html" rel="next" rev="prev">Page 2</a>
```


Although the **rel** and **rev** attributes might seem very useful, few, if any, browsers support them. Currently, the only major use of these attributes is to document the relationship of links with the **<a>** tags themselves. The **link** element (discussed later in this chapter), which has semantic-link purposes similar to the **rel** and **rev** attributes, actually is supported to a limited degree in modern browsers. A list of many of the proposed values for the **rel** and **rev** attributes can be found in this chapter's upcoming section about link relationships.

Scripting and Anchors

Adding logic to anchors is possible through the use of client-side scripting languages such as JavaScript. Under HTML 4 and XHTML 1, core event attributes have been added to the **a** element and include **onclick**, **onmouseover**, **onmouseout**, and other attributes, which can be bound to scripting events. The events named correspond to an anchor being clicked (**onclick**), a pointer being positioned on a link (**onmouseover**), and a pointer leaving a link (**onmouseout**). One obvious use of such events is to animate links so that when a mouse passes over the link, the text changes color, and when the link is clicked, the system issues a click sound. Generically, this is the idea of a *rollover button*. Aside from the basic events that might be useful to create rollover links or trigger programming logic, event models from Microsoft and Netscape can include a variety of other events such as pressing the assigned Help key (**onhelp**) on the keyboard (generally F1), or other keys on the keyboard being pressed or released. HTML authors interested in scripting anchor activities should consult Chapter 14. Combined with images, anchor-oriented scripting additions can be used to create very persuasive Web pages.

TIP *If simple rollover effects are desired, it is often more appropriate to rely on the pseudo selector* ***a:hover*** *than to utilize JavaScript.*

Images and Anchors

As mentioned earlier, **<a>** tags can enclose text and other content, including images. When an anchor encloses an image, the image becomes clickable, thus providing the basic mechanism for a graphic button. Typically, a browser shows an image to be part of an anchor by putting a colored border around the image—generally, the same color as the colored link text, either blue or purple. The browser also can indicate that the image is a link by changing the pointer to a different shape (such as a finger) when the pointer is positioned over an image link. If combined with scripting, the anchor also can modify the size or content of the image, creating a form of animated button. The following markup shows how an anchor can be combined with an **<img>** tag, as discussed in Chapter 5, to create a button:

```
<!DOCTYPE html PUBLIC "-//W3C//DTD XHTML 1.0 Transitional//EN"
"http://www.w3.org/TR/xhtml1/DTD/xhtml1-transitional.dtd">
<html xmlns="http://www.w3.org/1999/xhtml" lang="en">
<head>
<title>Anchors and Images</title>
<meta http-equiv="content-type" content="text/html; charset=ISO-8859-1" />
</head>
<body>
<p>
 <strong>Button with a border</strong><br />
 <a href="about.html">
 <img src="about.gif" alt="About Button" height="55" width="55" />
 </a>
 <br /><br />
 <strong>Same button without a border</strong><br />
 <a href="about.html">
 <img src="about.gif" alt="About Button" border="0" height="55"
 width="55" />
 </a>
</p>
</body>
</html>
```

Notice how the **border** attribute is set to **"0"** to turn off the image's border. Further, note that the code contains a small but significant error. When a space exists between the close of an **<img>** tag and the closing **</a>** tag, a small blue or purple line, or "tick," might occur, as shown in Figure 4-4. To remove a tick, make sure that no space is between the **<img>** tag and the closing **</a>** tag.

NOTE *Although ticks aren't the worst offense on the Web, they indicate a lack of attention to detail in Web page coding. In print literature, spelling errors or small nicks or ticks on an image would be cause for serious alarm. Eventually, the same standards will be applied to Web pages, so HTML authors should begin to look for such small mistakes. Be careful when looking for ticks, though. Internet Explorer actually tries to fix such small spacing problems for you, leading you to believe there isn't a tick if you look at it under only one browser. Testing in many browsers and validation of HTML markup should help catch subtle errors such as ticks.*

All the examples given so far show images with only one destination. Wherever a user clicks on the image link, the destination remains the same. In another class of image links, called *image maps*, different regions of the image can be made hot links for different destinations.

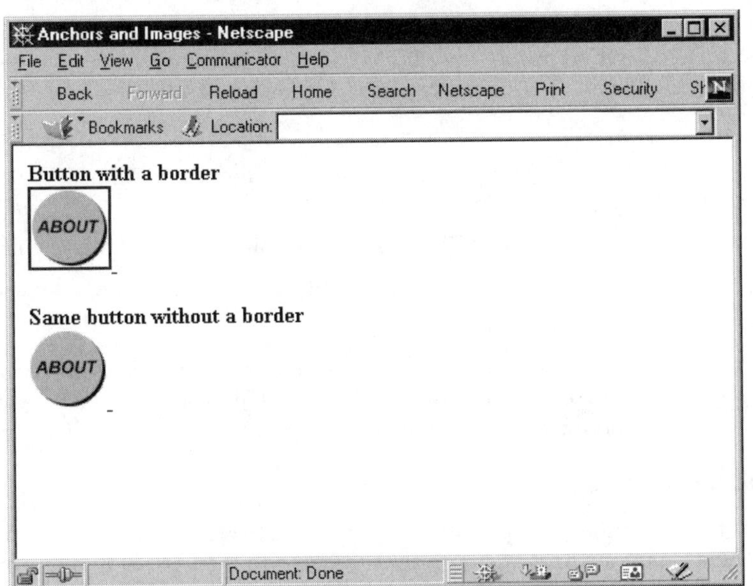

FIGURE 4-4 Ticks—a common problem with image links

Image Maps

An image map is an image that contains numerous hot spots that might result in a different URL being loaded, depending on where the user clicks. The two basic types of image maps are *server-side image maps* and *client-side image maps*. In the server-side image map, the following process is followed:

1. The user clicks somewhere within the image.
2. The browser sends a request to the Web server, asking for the URL of the document associated with the area clicked. The coordinates clicked are sent to the Web server, which decodes the information.
3. After consulting a file that shows which coordinates map to which URL, the server sends back the requested information.
4. After receiving the response, the browser requests the new URL.

Server-side image maps have some major downsides and, fortunately, they are rarely used today. Regardless, they will be covered in this edition to further convince users to not consider this older format. The first downside of server-side image maps is that users really don't have a sense, URL-wise, of where a particular click will take them. All that users see as they run a mouse over the image is a set of coordinates showing the current *x*, *y* value. The second—and more significant—problem is that the server must be consulted to go to the next page. This can be a major bottleneck that slows down the process of moving between pages. The slow speed of decoding, combined with the possibility that a user will click an unmapped hot spot and have nothing happen, makes client-side image maps preferable to server-side maps.

With client-side image maps, all the map information indicating which regions map to which URLs can be specified in the same HTML file that contains the image. Including the map data with the image and letting the browser decode it has several advantages, including the following:

- A server doesn't need to be visited to determine the destination, so links are resolved faster.
- Destination URLs can be shown as the user's pointer moves over the image.
- Image maps can be created and tested locally without requiring a server or system administration support.

Although it's clear that client-side image maps are far superior to their server-side cousins, very old browsers do not support this feature. This doesn't have to be a problem, however, because you can include simultaneous support for both types of image maps.

Server-Side Image Maps

To specify a server-side image map, you use an **<a>** tag to enclose a specially marked **<img>** tag. The **a** element's **href** attribute should be set to the URL of a program or map file to decode the image map. The **<img>** tag then must contain the attribute **ismap** so that the browser can decode the image appropriately.

NOTE *Depending on the Web server being used, support for server-side image maps may or may not be built in. If image maps are supported directly, the particular* **<a>** *tag simply must directly point to the URL of the map file and it will be decoded. This is shown in the next example. On some extremely old servers, however, the anchor might have to point to an image map program in that server's cgi-bin directory.*

As with all linked images, turning off the image borders may be desirable; you can do this by setting the **<img>** tag's **border** attribute equal to 0. A simple example showing the syntax of a server-side image map is shown here; a rendering appears in Figure 4-5:

```
<!DOCTYPE HTML PUBLIC "-//W3C//DTD HTML 4.01 Transitional//EN"
"http://www.w3.org/TR/html4/loose.dtd">
<html>
<head>
<title>Server-side Image Map Example</title>
<meta http-equiv="content-type" content="text/html; charset=ISO-8859-1">
</head>
<body>
<h1 align="center">Server-side Imagemap Test</h1>
<div align="center">
<a href="http://www.htmlref.com/examples/chapter4/shapes.map">
<img src="http//www.htmlref.com/examples/chapter4/shapes.gif" ismap
     alt="shapes map" border="0" width="400" height="200"></a>
</div>
</body>
</html>
```

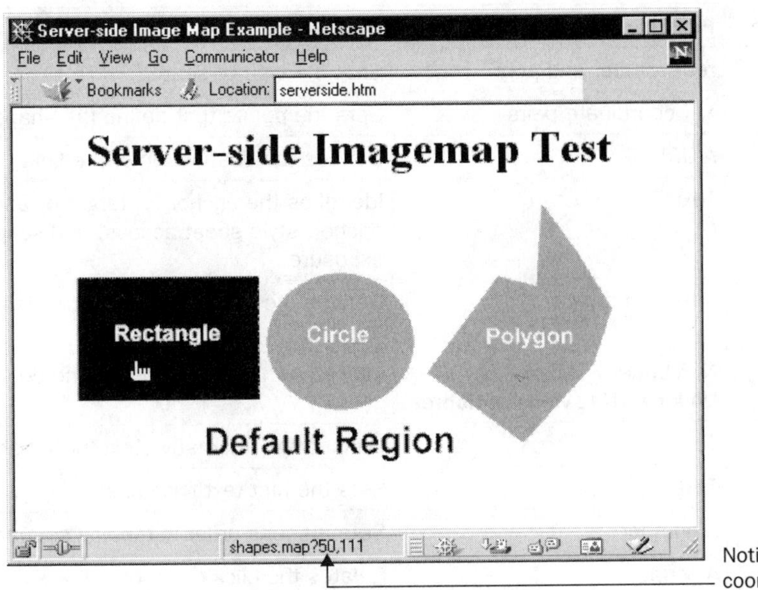

FIGURE 4-5 Server-side image feedback

As previously mentioned, server-side image maps do not provide adequate feedback to the user and could incur performance penalties. Figure 4-5 shows that the browser provides image coordinate information rather than a destination URL with a server-side image map.

HTML authors should favor client-side image maps and use server-side image maps only as needed to support very old browsers.

Client-Side Image Maps

The key to using a client-side image map is to add the **usemap** attribute to an **<img>** tag and have it reference a **<map>** tag that defines the image map's active areas. An example of the **img** element syntax under XHTML is **<img src="controlbar.gif" usemap="#controlmap" />**. Note that unlike server-side image maps, the image will be indicated as a link regardless of the lack of an **<a>** tag surrounding the **<img>**. The **border** attribute should be set to zero or style sheets used to control border appearance if necessary.

The **map** element generally occurs within the same document, although support for it might exist outside of the current document. This is similar, in a sense, to the way server-side maps work. The **map** element can occur anywhere within the body of an HTML document, although it is often found at the end.

The **map** element has two important attributes (**name** and **id**), which are used to specify the identifier associated with the map. The map name is then referenced within an **<img>** tag, using the **usemap** attribute and the associated fragment identifier. The <**map**> tag must have a closing **</map>** tag. Within the **<map>** and **</map>** tags are defined shapes that are mapped onto an image, defining the hot spots for the image map. Shapes are defined by the **area** element, which is found only within the **map** element. The **area** element has a variety of attributes, some of which are summarized in Table 4-7.

Attribute Name	Possible Values	Description
shape	**rect**, **circle**, and **poly**	Sets the type of shape.
coords	*x*, *y* coordinate pairs	Sets the points that define the shape.
href	A URL	Defines the destination of the link.
id	Text	Identifies the anchor for target by another anchor, style sheet access, and scripting exposure.
target	A frame name	Defines the frame or window destination of the link.
nohref	N/A under HTML 4. Under XHTML value of **nohref**	Indicates that the region has no destination.
alt	Text	Defines the alternative text for the shape.
title	Text	Sets the hint text for a shape.
tabindex	A number	Sets numeric order in tabbing sequence.
onclick	A script	Relates the click event of a link with a script.
onmouseover	A script	Relates **mouseover** event with a script.
onmouseout	A script	Relates **mouseout** event with a script.

TABLE 4-7 Common Attributes for <area>

The most important attributes of an **<area>** tag are **href**, **shape**, and **coords**. The **href** attribute defines the destination URL for the browser if that particular region of the image is selected. The **shape** and **coords** attributes define the particular region in question. When the **shape** attribute is set to **rect**, it defines a rectangular region, and the coordinates should be set to provide the top-left and bottom-right coordinates of the image. If the **shape** attribute is set to **circle**, the **coords** attribute must provide the *x*, *y* coordinates of the center of the circle, followed by its radius. If the shape is set to **poly**, it indicates that the area defined is an irregular polygon; each coordinate makes up a point in the polygon, with lines between each successive point, and the last point connected to the first. Areas of the image that are not assigned values might be assigned a value of **shape="default"**.

TIP *If the **shape** attribute is not set or omitted, **rect** is assumed.*

Table 4-8 summarizes the possibilities for the **area** element, and provides examples. The various *x* and *y* coordinates are measured in pixels from the top-left corner (0,0) of the mapped image. Percentage values of the image's height and width also might be used. For example, **<area shape="rect" coords="0,0,50%,50%" />** defines a rectangular region from the upper-left corner to a point halfway up and down and halfway across. Although percentage-style

Shape	Coordinate Format	Example
rect	left-*x*, top-*y*, right-*x*, bottom-*y*	<area shape="rect" coords="0,0,100,50" href="about.html" />
circle	center-*x*, center-*y*, radius	<area shape="circle" coords="25,25,10" href="products.html" />
poly	*x*1, *y*1, *x*2, *y*2, *x*3, *y*3,...	<area shape="poly" coords="255,122,306,53,334,62,255,122" href="contact.html" />

TABLE 4-8 Shape Format and Examples

notation can allow the image to resize, it generally isn't useful for any but the most basic image maps. The biggest difficulty with image maps is determining the coordinates for the individual shapes within the image. Rather than measuring these values by hand, HTML authors are encouraged to use an image-mapping tool. Many HTML editing systems such as Macromedia's Homesite and Dreamweaver (www.macromedia.com) include image-mapping facilities, as shown in Figure 4-6.

TIP *Using any* ***height*** *and* ***width*** *values other than the actual sizes for a mapped image isn't recommended. Once a map has been mapped, resizing will ruin it.*

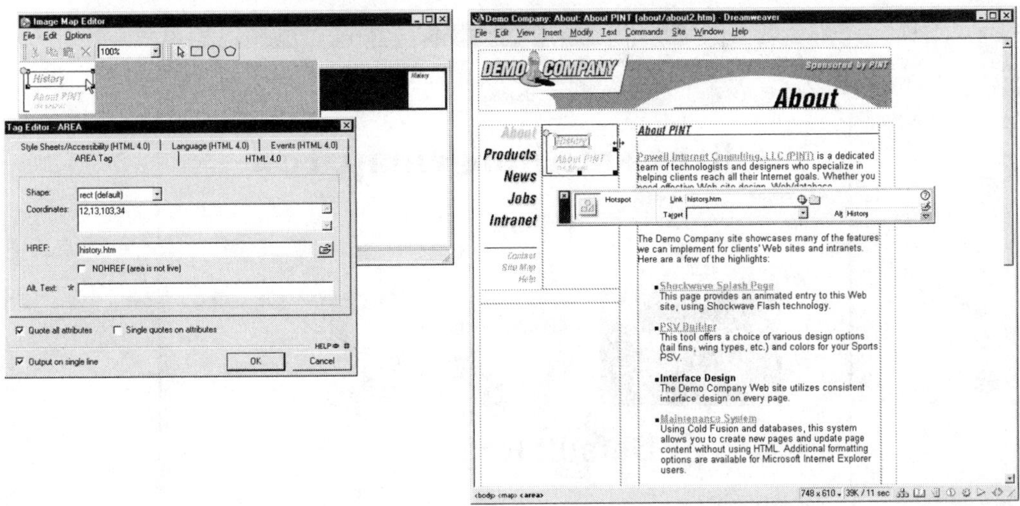

FIGURE 4-6 Image mapping made easy in an editor

The following is an example of a client-side image map, the results of which are rendered in Figure 4-7:

```
<!DOCTYPE html PUBLIC "-//W3C//DTD XHTML 1.0 Transitional//EN"
"http://www.w3.org/TR/xhtml1/DTD/xhtml1-transitional.dtd">
<html xmlns="http://www.w3.org/1999/xhtml" lang="en">
<head>
<title>Client-side Image Map Example</title>
<meta http-equiv="content-type" content="text/html; charset=ISO-8859-1" />
</head>
<body>
<h1 align="center">Client-side Imagemap Test</h1>
<div align="center">
<img src="shapes.gif" usemap="#shapes" alt="shapes map" border="0"
 width="400" height="200" />
</div>
<!-- start of client side image map -->
<map name="shapes" id="shapes">
<area shape="rect" coords="6,50,140,143" href="rectangle.html"
 alt="rectangle" />
<area shape="circle" coords="195,100,50" href="circle.html"
 alt="circle" />
<area shape="poly"
 coords="255,122,306,53,334,62,338,0,388,77,374,116,323,171,255,122"
 href="polygon.html" alt="polygon" />
<area shape="default" href="defaultreg.html" alt="" />
</map>
</body>
</html>
```

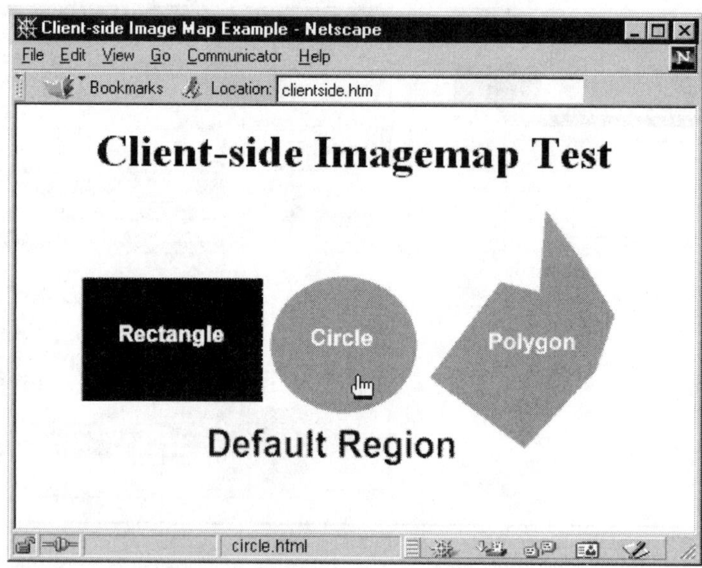

FIGURE 4-7 Rendering of client-side image-map

You can combine support for both server-side and client-side image maps into one file. The browser should override the server-side support with the improved client-side style. This approach guarantees backward compatibility with older browsers. To support both image maps, use the **ismap** and **usemap** attributes in conjunction with an embedded map and a remote map, as shown by the following code fragment:

```
<a href="shapes.map">
<img src="shapes.gif" usemap="#shapes" border="0" ismap="ismap" width="400"
 height="200" alt="" /></a>
```

Image Map Attributes

Client-side image maps have a variety of attributes that can be used with the **area** element. Server-side image maps have no attributes other than those normally associated with the **img** element, such as **border**. The important attributes are discussed here with a full listing in Appendix A.

target

The **<area>** tag for client-side image maps has been extended to support a **target** attribute like the addition to the **<a>** tag. The **target** value should be set to the name of a frame or window. Generally, a frame has a name, so setting **target** to the frame name results in the link loading in the frame named in the attribute. When selected, a link such as

```
<area shape="rect" coords="0,0,50%, 50%"
   href="http://www.yahoo.com" target="display_frame" />
```

loads the page referenced by the URL set by **href** into the frame named **"display_frame"**. If the **target** attribute is omitted, the current window or frame that the document is in is used. In addition to author-named frames, the following are several reserved names for frames that, when used with the **target** attribute, have special meaning: **_blank**, **_self**, **_parent**, and **_top**. For more information about frames, see Chapter 8.

nohref

Although the **nohref** attribute appears to have little use, it can be used to set a region in the map that does nothing when clicked. This might be useful when attempting to cut a hole in something. For example, an image of a donut might make a great image map, particularly if the hole in the middle of the donut isn't an active, clickable area. The **nohref** attribute makes this simple. Just define a large click region for the whole image and then declare the middle of the image nonclickable with the **nohref** attribute. An example of this is shown here:

```
<!DOCTYPE html PUBLIC "-//W3C//DTD XHTML 1.0 Transitional//EN"
"http://www.w3.org/TR/xhtml1/DTD/xhtml1-transitional.dtd">
<html xmlns="http://www.w3.org/1999/xhtml" lang="en">
<head>
<title>Nohref Example</title>
<meta http-equiv="content-type" content="text/html; charset=ISO-8859-1" />
</head>
<body>
<img src="donut.gif" width="300" height="300" border="0"
     alt="A donut" usemap="#donut" />
```

```
<map name="donut" id="donut">
   <area shape="circle" coords="150,150,81" nohref="nohref" alt="" />
   <area shape="circle" coords="150,150,146" href="donut.html" alt="donut" />
   <area shape="default" nohref="nohref" alt="" />
</map>
</body>
</html>
```

If a browser supports **nohref**, the browser will either change the look of the cursor and disallow clicking or simply not allow clicking although the cursor appears to indicate the area is hot. Obviously, the former is the preferred browser action, but cannot be guaranteed.

Given that **nohref** creates an inactive region that sits on top of another, what happens when one region overlaps another? According to the specification, if two or more regions overlap, the region defined first within the **<map>** tag takes precedence over subsequent regions. This rule implies that **area** elements with the **nohref** attribute should be placed before **<area>** tags that are active so that clicking the **<area>** tag with the **nohref** attribute doesn't take the user to a new URL as a result of a previously placed, overlapping active **<area>** tag.

alt and title

Image maps—even client-side image maps—have some major drawbacks when viewed in text-based browsers. The **alt** attribute can be used, as shown in the previous examples, and should provide text labels that are displayed in the status line when the pointer passes over the hot spots. Although the **title** attribute can be added to all elements, and can provide a function somewhat similar to **alt** in graphical browsers, in practice, browsers seem to pick up **alt** before **title**. To be on the safe side, you can use both attributes simultaneously. One unfortunate problem with the **alt** attribute and client-side image maps is that non-graphical browsers don't always pick up the **alt** attributes and build meaningful renderings. Instead of a set of links, the viewer might only see a cryptic message, as shown in Figure 4-8.

Web designers are encouraged to provide secondary navigation that mirrors the choices available in the image map. This secondary navigation should consist of text links located below the image, which makes the site accessible for non-graphical user agents and might improve the site's usability. Users with slow connections can opt to select text links before the image is completely downloaded. An example of text links offered in conjunction with an image map is shown in Figure 4-9. Also, when using server-side image maps, you can make the inactive or default area link to a new page that contains a text menu of the choices provided through the image map. In this way, a user who selects the **ismap** provided by an older browser receives the menu, not the map.

Discussion of the design and navigation issues surrounding image maps is left to books that focus on site design, such as the companion book *Web Design: The Complete Reference Second Edition* (Powell – Osborne 2002). Where possible, however, HTML authors should avoid relying too heavily on single-image–style image maps for navigation purposes.

tabindex

Under HTML 4 and beyond, you can use the **tabindex** attribute of the **area** element to define the order in which hot spots in a client-side image map are tabbed through in a browser that supports keyboard navigation. The value of **tabindex** typically is a positive

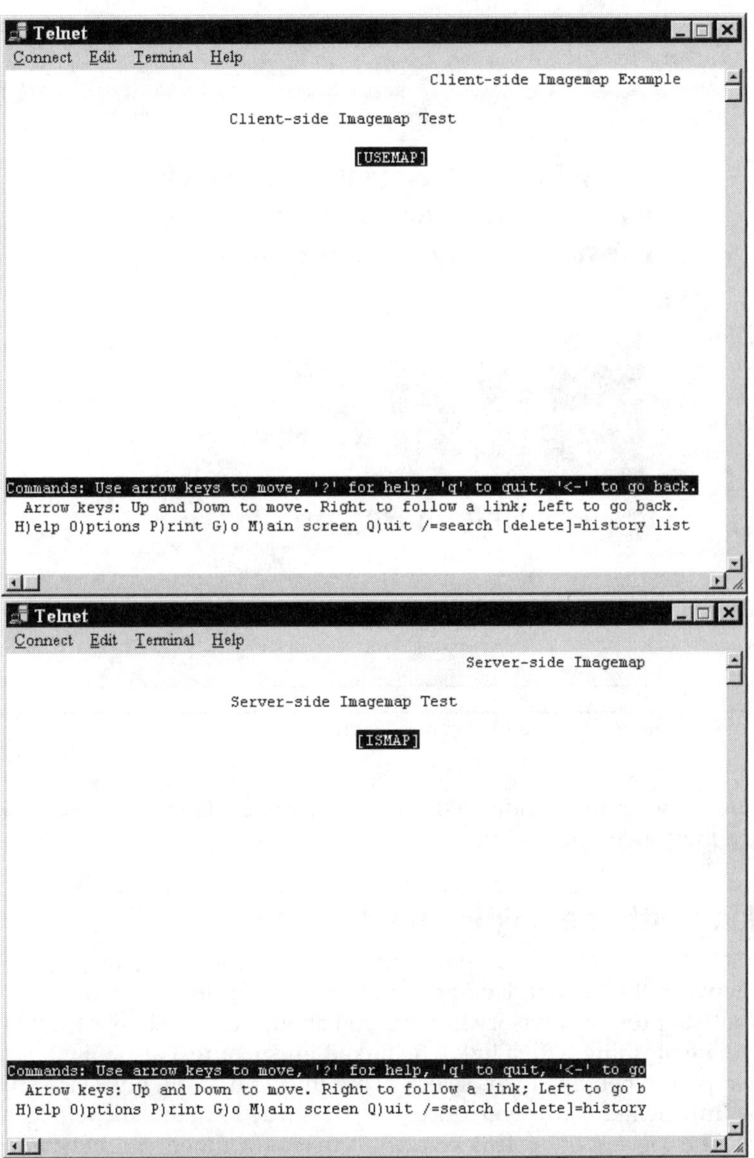

FIGURE 4-8 Non-meaningful image map renderings

number. A browser tabs through links in order of increasing **tabindex** values, but generally skips over those with negative values. So, the following line sets this anchor to be the first thing tabbed to:

```
<area shape="rect" coords="0,0,50%,50%"
   href="http://www.yahoo.com/" tabindex="1" />
```

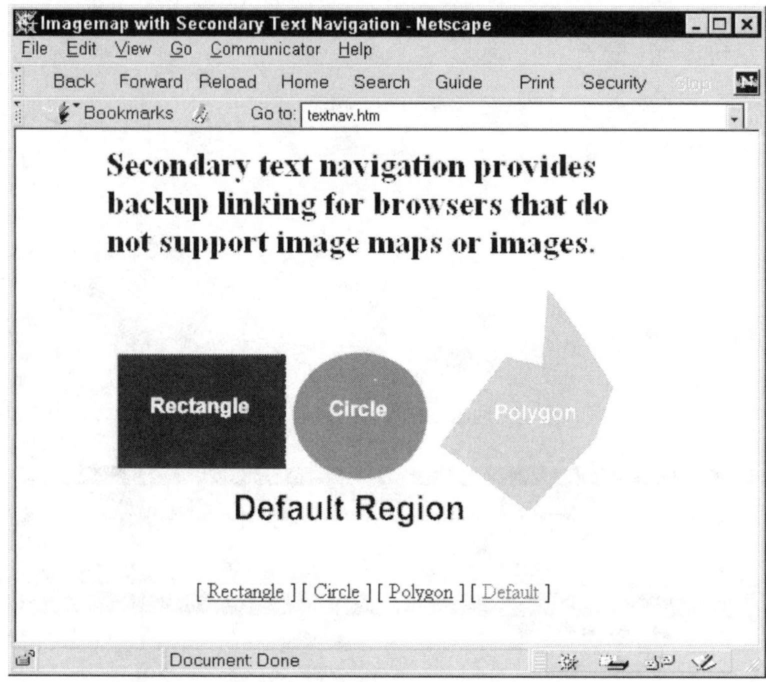

FIGURE 4-9 Image map with secondary text navigation

If the **tabindex** attribute is undefined, the browser tends to tab through links in the order in which they are found within an HTML document.

Semantic Linking with the link Element

Syntactically, a link to another document created by an anchor says nothing about the relationship between the current document and the object being pointed to. You can use the **title** attribute to provide advisory information about the link so that the viewer of a page can associate meaning with a link. The linked image or text also might give some clue about what happens when the link is selected, but in HTML itself, links lack any semantic meaning. The **link** element, however, does provide a way to define the relationship between linked objects. The concept of the **link** element is that a document might have predefined relationships that can be specified, and that some of these relationships might be useful to a browser when offering navigation choices, rendering a page, or preparing a page to be printed. Although **<link>** tags have been around for several years, until recently, few browsers have supported them. However, with the rise of style sheets and even a few proprietary browser features, **<link>** finally is being used.

The **link** element is found in the head of an HTML document, where it might occur more than once. The two most important attributes of the element are **href** and **rel**. Like the **href** attribute for an **<a>** tag, the **href** attribute for a **<link>** tag specifies the URL of another document, whereas **rel** specifies the relationship with that document. The value of **rel** often is called the *link type*. The basic XHTML syntax of the **link** element is **<link href="url" rel="relationship" />**. Under HTML and XHTML, **<link>** also supports a reverse semantic relationship, indicated by the **rev** attribute, as well as the **title** attribute, which can be used to set advisory information for the link. The most mysterious aspect of the **link** element is the value of the **rel** and **rev** attributes.

Link Relationships in Detail

Like the **rel** attribute for the **a** element, the **rel** attribute for **link** defines the relationship between the current document and the linked object. The value of the **rel** attribute is simply a text value, which can be anything the author desires. However, a browser can interpret standardized relationships in a particular way. For example, a browser might provide special icons or navigation features when the meaning of a link is understood. Currently, no standard set of document relationship values exists, but the HTML 4.01 specification lists some proposed relationship values, as shown in Table 4-9. Note that these values are not case-sensitive.

Relationship Value	Explanation	Example
alternate	The link references an alternate version of the document that the link is in. This can be a translated version of the document, as suggested by the **lang** attribute.	**<link href="frenchintro.html" rel="alternate" lang="fr" />**
appendix	The link references a document that serves as an appendix for a document or site.	**<link href="intro.html" rel="appendix" />**
bookmark	The link references a document that serves as a bookmark; the **title** attribute can be used to name the bookmark.	**<link href="index.html" rel="bookmark" title="homepage" />**
chapter	The link references a document that is a chapter in a site or collection of documents.	**<link href="ch01.html" rel="chapter" />**
contents	The link references a document that serves as a table of contents, most likely for the site, although it might be for the document. The meaning is unclear.	**<link href="toc.html" rel="contents" />**
index	The link references a page that provides an index for the current document.	**<link href="docindex.html" rel="index" />**
glossary	The link references a document that provides a glossary of terms for the current document.	**<link href="glossary.html" rel="glossary" />**

TABLE 4-9 Possible rel values

Relationship Value	Explanation	Example
copyright	The link references a page that contains a copyright statement for the current document.	**<link href="copyright.html" rel="copyright" />**
next	The link references the next document to visit in a linear collection of documents. It can be used, for example, to "pre-fetch" the next page, and is supported in some browsers such as MSN TV and Mozilla-based browsers.	**<link href="page2.html" rel="next" />**
prev	The link references the previous document in a linear collection of documents.	**<link href="page1.html" rel="previous" />**
section	The link references a document that is a section in a site or collection of documents.	**<link href="sect07.html" rel="section" />**
start	The link references the first document in a set of documents.	**<link href="begin.html" rel="start" />**
stylesheet	The link references an external style sheet. This is by far the most common use of **<link>** and the most widely supported in browsers.	**<link href="style.css" rel="stylesheet" />**
subsection	The link references a document that is a subsection in a collection of documents.	**<link href="sect07a.html" rel="subsection" />**
help	The link references a help document for the current document or site.	**<link href="help.html" rel="help" />**

TABLE 4-9 Possible rel values *(continued)*

Under Mozilla 1.0 and greater browsers as well as Opera 7 and greater browsers, these link values are finally starting to be recognized. For example, given the following simple example,

```
<!DOCTYPE html PUBLIC "-//W3C//DTD XHTML 1.0 Transitional//EN"
"http://www.w3.org/TR/xhtml1/DTD/xhtml1-transitional.dtd">
<html xmlns="http://www.w3.org/1999/xhtml" lang="en">
<head>
<title>Link Relationship Tests</title>
<meta http-equiv="content-type" content="text/html; charset=ISO-8859-1" />
   <link rel="home" href="http://www.htmlref.com" title="Homepage" />
   <link rel="toc" href="http://www.htmlref.com/overview/toc.html"
         title="Table of contents" />
   <link rel="help" href="http://www.htmlref.com/help.html"
         title="Need help?" />
```

```
   <link rel="up" href="../index.html" title="Chapter 4" />
   <link rel="copyright" href="http://www.htmlref.com/copyright.html"
         title="Copyright statement" />
<link rel="author" href="mailto:tpowell@pint.com" title="Mail the author" />
</head>
<body>
<p>Just a test of link relationships</p>
</body>
</html>
```

you would see the menu items in Opera 7 and Mozilla, as shown in Figure 4-10.

TIP *Under Mozilla, you may have to turn on the preference to show semantic links. Under most 1.x versions of Mozilla, this was found at View | Show/Hide | Site Navigation Tool Bar | Show Only As Needed.*

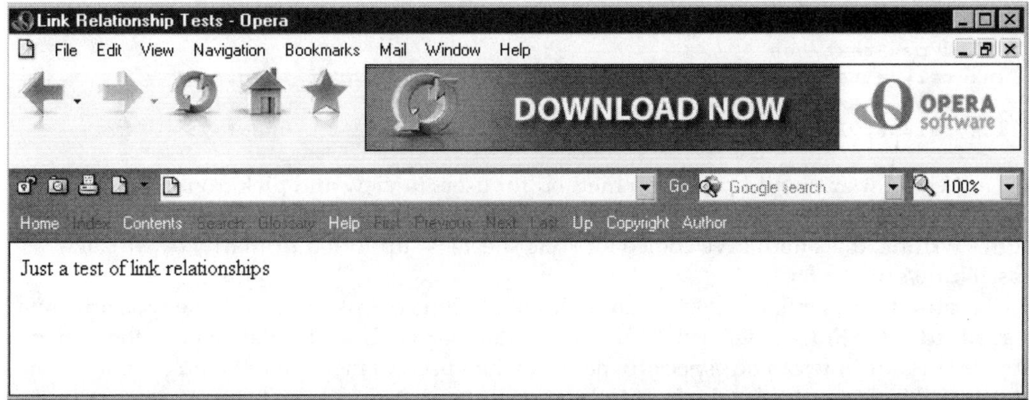

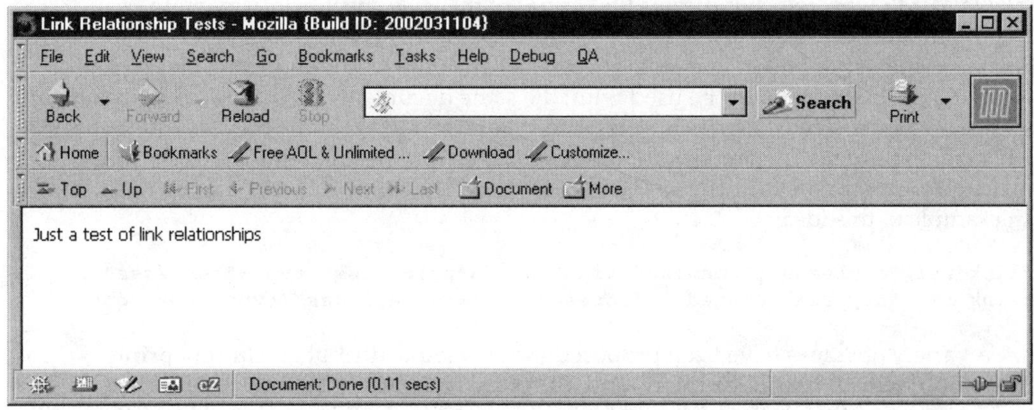

FIGURE 4-10 Browser support for <link> rendering

In addition to the HTML 4.01 proposed relationships, various other relationships are possible. In fact, document authors can make up their own relationships if they desire, but should be careful to avoid the listed values, as they may hold special meaning for browsers.

<link> and Style Sheets

A variety of attributes are defined for the **link** element including **type**, **media**, and **target**. These new attributes are already supported for handling cascading style sheets. The **link** element allows a style sheet for a document to be referenced from a separate file. If the markup code **<link rel="stylesheet" href="corpstyle.css" type="text/css " />** is inserted in the **head** of an HTML document, it associates the style sheet corpstyle.css with the current document. The **rel** value of **stylesheet** indicates the relationship.

The alternate **stylesheet** relationship, which would allow users to pick from a variety of styles, also is defined. To set several alternative styles, the **title** attribute must be set to group elements belonging to the same style. All members of the same style must have exactly the same value for **title**. For example, the following fragment defines a standard style called basestyle.css, and two alternative styles, titled 640x480 and 1024x768, have been added; these refer to style sheets to improve layout at various screen resolutions:

```
<link rel="alternate stylesheet" title="640x480" href="small.css"
      type="text/css " />
<link rel="alternate stylesheet" title="1024x768" href="big.css"
      type="text/css" />
<link rel="stylesheet" href="basestyle.css" type="text/css " />
```

A Web browser should provide a method for users to view and pick from the list of alternative styles, where the **title** attribute can be used to name each choice. At the time of this writing, this alternative choice for style sheets is supported primarily by Mozilla-based browsers.

Because the potential exists for many different kinds of linked objects, the **type** attribute was added to the **link** elements in the previous example to indicate the data type of the related object. This attribute can be especially helpful when used to indicate the type of style sheet being used because other style sheet technologies do exist. For style sheets, **type** usually takes a MIME type, which indicates the format of the style sheet being linked to.

The **media** attribute is also new for the **link** element, but it isn't widely supported beyond printer style sheets. For style sheets, this attribute would indicate what type of media the style sheet should be used with; the same document could thus reference one style sheet when viewed on a computer screen, one on a PDA, and a different style sheet when being printed. The browser then is responsible for filtering out those style sheets that aren't appropriate for the current environment. The following code fragment shows an example of this idea:

```
<link rel="stylesheet" media="print" href="print.css" type="text/css" />
<link rel="stylesheet" media="screen" href="screen.css" type="text/css" />
```

A variety of values have been proposed for the **media** attribute including **print**, **projection**, **screen**, **braille**, **aural**, **tv**, and **all**. When not specified, **all** would be the default type, suggesting that the style should be used in all output environments. More attention will be given to CSS and its relationship with the **<link>** tag in Chapters 10 and 11.

Advanced Browser Support for <link>

Mozilla and MSNTV browsers have used **<link>** to improve performance. If the **rel** attribute is set with the value of **next** (or in Mozilla **prefetch** as well) and an **href** is specified, the browser will "pre-fetch" the page or object in question during the idle time of the browser. If the content of the next page is stored in the browser's cache, the page loads much faster than if the page has to be requested from the server.

In the case of Mozilla, which is far more common than MSN TV, the browser looks either for a **<link>** tag or an HTTP Link: header with a relation type of either **next** or **prefetch**. For example, we might use **<link>** like this:

```
<link rel="prefetch" href="/images/product.jpeg" />
```

This would be the same as providing a prefetching hint using an HTTP `Link:` header:

```
Link: </images/product.jpeg>; rel=prefetch />
```

The Link: HTTP header can also be specified within the HTML document itself by using a **<meta>** tag:

```
<meta http-equiv="Link" content="&lt;/images/big.jpeg&gt;; rel=prefetch" />
```

It is possible to prefetch a variety of objects in a page during a browser's idle time. Consider the following example:

```
<link rel="prefetch alternate stylesheet" title="Designed for Mozilla"
      href="mozspecific.css" />
<link rel="prefetch" href="bigflash.swf" />
<link rel="next" href="2.html" />
```

While prefetching seems to be unique to Mozilla and MSN TV, it is not. Through the use of JavaScript or ActiveX controls, it is possible to prefetch page objects. We'll see in the next chapter that even the simple idea of loading an image with height and width set to 1 so that the loaded image is a barely perceptible dot to the user can be used to simulate the idea of prefetching. The idea here is that because these images are loaded into the browser's cache they will be available for subsequent pages, regardless of if they are shown at their natural size. Be careful though to make sure that the preload of images is controlled with a script or the **<img>** tags are used at the bottom of a Web page so it doesn't disrupt the load of the more visible images on the page.

Now that we have discussed cutting edge browser ideas, let's go even farther and consider some of the theoretical limitations of linking on today's Internet before concluding the chapter.

Beyond Location

An amazing wealth of information is available on the Web. Although many people complain of information overload, the real problem isn't volume. It's relevance. How can a particular piece of information be located quickly and easily? If the Web were ideal, it would be like the computer on the television show *Star Trek*, which always seems to deliver in a matter of seconds any information a user requests. On the Internet, a request to a search tool often yields an overwhelming list of tens of thousands of entries. Some of these entries might be outdated, the documents to which others refer might have moved, or the server that specifies an entry might be unreachable. Although the Web isn't science fiction, many of the computer and information systems presented in science fiction represent valid goals for the Web. The key problem with building a more organized Web is URL-based addressing.

Problems with URLs

The primary problem with URLs is that they define location rather than meaning. In other words, URLs specify where something is located on the Web, not what it is or what it's about. This might not seem to be a big deal, but it is. This issue becomes obvious when the problems with URLs are enumerated:

- **URLs aren't persistent.** Documents move around, servers change names, and documents might eventually be deleted. This is the nature of the Web, and the reason why the **404 Not Found** message is so common. When users hit a broken link, they might be at a loss to determine what happened to the document and how to locate its new home. Wouldn't it be nice if, no matter what happened, a unique identifier indicated where to get a copy of the information?
- **URLs are often long and confusing.** People often have to transcribe addresses. For example, the following is quite a lot to type, read to someone, or avoid not breaking across lines in an e-mail:

  ```
  http://www.democompany.com/about/press/pressdetail.cfm?id=7&view=screen
  ```

  Firms are already scrambling for short domain names and paths to improve the typability of URLs, and most folks tend to omit the protocol when discussing things. Despite these minor cleanups, many URLs are very long and "dirty," filled with all sorts of special characters.

- **URLs create an artificial bottleneck and extreme reliance on DNS services by specifying location rather than meaning.** For example, the text of the HTML 4.01 specification is a useful document and certainly has an address at the W3C Web site. But does it live in other places on the Internet? It probably is mirrored in a variety of locations, but what happens if the W3C server is unreachable, or DNS services fail to resolve the host? In this case, the resource is unreachable. URLs create a point source for information. Rather than trying to find a particular document, wherever it might be on the Internet, Web users try to go to a particular location. Rather than talking about where something is, Web users should try to talk about *what* that something is.

URNs, URCs, and URIs

Talking about what a document is rather than where it is makes sense when you consider how information is organized outside the Internet. Nobody talks about which library carries a particular book, or what shelf it is on. The relevant information is the title of the book, its author, and perhaps some other information. But what happens if two or more books have the same title, or two authors have the same name? This actually is quite common. Generally, a book should have a unique identifier such as an ISBN number that, when combined with other descriptive information, such as the author, publisher, and publication date, uniquely describes the book. This naming scheme enables people to specify a particular book and then hunt it down.

The Web, however, isn't as ordered as a library. On the Web, people name their documents whatever they like, and search robots organize their indexes however they like. Categorizing things is difficult. The only unique item for documents is the URL, which simply says where the document lives. But how many URLs does the HTML 4 specification have? A document might exist in many places. Even worse than a document with multiple locations, what happens when the content at the location changes? Perhaps a particular URL address points to information about dogs one day and cats the next. This is how the Web really is. However, a great deal of research is being done to address some of the shortcomings of the Web and its addressing schemes.

URN

A new set of addressing ideas, including URNs, URCs, and URIs, are emerging to remedy some of the Web's shortcomings. A *uniform resource name* (URN) can locate a resource by giving it a unique symbolic name rather than a unique address. Network services analogous to the current DNS services will transparently translate a URN into the URL (server IP address, directory path, and filename) needed to actually locate a resource. This translation could be used to select the closest server, to improve document delivery speed, or to try various backup servers in case a server is unavailable. The benefit of the abstraction provided by URNs should be obvious from this simple idea alone.

To better understand the logic behind URNs, consider domain names, such as www.democompany.com. These names are already translated into numeric IP addresses, such as 192.102.249.3, all the time. This mapping provides the ability to change a machine's numeric address or location without seriously disrupting access to it because the name stays the same. Furthermore, numeric addresses provide no meaning to a user, whereas domain names provide some indication of the entity in question. Obviously, the level of abstraction provided by a system such as DNS would make sense on the Web. Rather than typing some unwieldy URL, a URN would be issued that would be translated to an underlying URL. Some experts worry that using a resolving system to translate URNs to URLs is inherently flawed and will not scale well. Because the DNS system is fairly fragile, there might be some truth to this concern. Another problem is that, in reality, URNs probably won't be something easy to remember, such as urn: *booktitle*, but will instead be something more difficult, such as urn:isbn: 0-12-518408-5.

URC

A *uniform resource characteristic* (URC), also known as a *uniform resource citation,* describes a set of attribute/value pairs that defines some aspect of an information resource. For example, in the case of a book, a URC might describe a publication date, number of pages, author, and so on. The form of a URC is still under discussion; however, logically what they would provide is already being used often in the form of simple **<meta>** tags.

Combined, a URL, URN, and a collection of URCs describe an information resource. For example, the document "Demo Company Corporate Summary" might have a unique URN such as urn://corpid:55127.

NOTE *The syntax of the preceding URN is fictional. It simply shows that URNs probably won't have easily remembered names and that many naming schemes can be used, such as ISBN numbers or corporate IDs.*

The "Demo Company Corporate Summary" also would have a set of URCs that describes the rating of the file, the author, the publisher, and so on. In addition, the document would have a location(s) on the Web where the document lives, such as one of the following traditional URLs:

```
http://www.democompany.com/about/corp.html
http://www.democompany.co.jp/about/corp.html
```

URI

Taken all together, a particular information resource has been identified. The collection of information, which is used to identify this document specifically, is termed a *uniform resource identifier* (URI).

NOTE *Occasionally, URI is used interchangeably with URL. Although this is acceptable, research into the theories behind the names suggests that the term URI is more generic than URL, and encompasses the ideal of an information resource. Currently, a URL is the only common way to identify an information resource on the Internet. Although technically a URL could be considered a URI, this confuses the issue and obscures the ultimate goal of trying to talk about information more generally than in terms of a network location.*

Although many of the ideas covered here are still being discussed, some systems, such as Persistent URLs, or PURLs (www.purl.org), and Handles (www.handle.net), already implement many of the features of URNs and URCs. Furthermore, many browser vendors and large Web sites are implementing special keyword navigation schemes that mimic many of the ideas of URNs and URCs. Unfortunately, as of the writing of this book, none of these approaches are widely implemented or accepted. Although any of these approaches probably can be considered as true URIs when compared to the URLs used today, URLs are likely to remain the most common way to describe information on the Web for the foreseeable future. Therefore, the system has to be improved slightly and even extended to deal with new types of information and access methods.

Emerging URL Forms

For now, unusable URLs are commonplace but URLs are starting to change for the better. As mentioned earlier in the chapter, URLs might be cleaned particularly when they have long query strings. It is even possible to clean file extensions off of URLs so that a URL such as http://www.democompany.com/about/press/pressdetail.cfm?id=7&view=screen can become http://democompany.com/about/press/pressdetail7. To cleanup a URL, Web designers should first name files and directories well. Further cleaning comes primarily from server-side technologies to rewrite URLs; mod_rewrite for Apache or similar products for IIS such as pageXchanger can do the trick, but obviously require some knowledge of Web server setup as well as site design.

In addition to cleaned URLs, new protocols are emerging as the Web starts to converge with TV, video games, and cell phones. For example, a television channel URL form might look like tv://*channel*, whereby *channel* is either an alphanumeric name (such as nbc or nbc7-39) or a numeric channel number. Similarly, a phone URL might look like phone://*phone-number*, with a numeric value for the phone number and any extra digit information required, such as the country code or calling card information. For example, phone://+1-555-270-2086 might dial a phone number in the United States. New schemes are being proposed all the time. A variety of esoteric schemes are out there already. If you are interested in new URL schemes, take a look at the W3C area on addressing (www.w3.org/Addressing/) for more information.

Summary

Linking documents on the Web requires a consistent naming scheme. URLs provide the basic information necessary to locate an object on the Internet by including the host name, directory, filename, and access protocol. URLs are written in a regular format so that an address can be written for any object. A common shorthand notation, a relative URL, is particularly useful when creating links within a Web site. If a document's URL can be determined, whether it's relative or fully spelled out, it can be specified in an <**a**> tag to create an anchor from one document to another. Links within HTML/XHTML documents can be made with text or with images. A special type of clickable image, called an *image map*, allows areas of an image to be defined as "hot."

Simply linking documents together is the most basic form of hypertext. By using the **link** element, as well as the **rel** and **rev** attributes of the **a** element, you can create relationships between documents. So far, the **link** element primarily is used with style sheets.

Even if Web authors master all aspects of linking, a bigger picture remains to worry about. Chapter 17 covers various topics related to linking, including link management, <**meta**> information, and filtering, but theoretical limitations still exist. The Web is a chaotic environment, and navigating among documents and linking documents presents serious challenges to Web designers. In the future, some of these problems might be solved by URNs, URCs, and improved URLs, which, taken together, make up the uniform resource identifier (URI). However, until URNs or similar technologies are more readily available, HTML authors should be cautious about linking, and do what they can do to improve URLs and link forms.

PART

Presentation and Layout

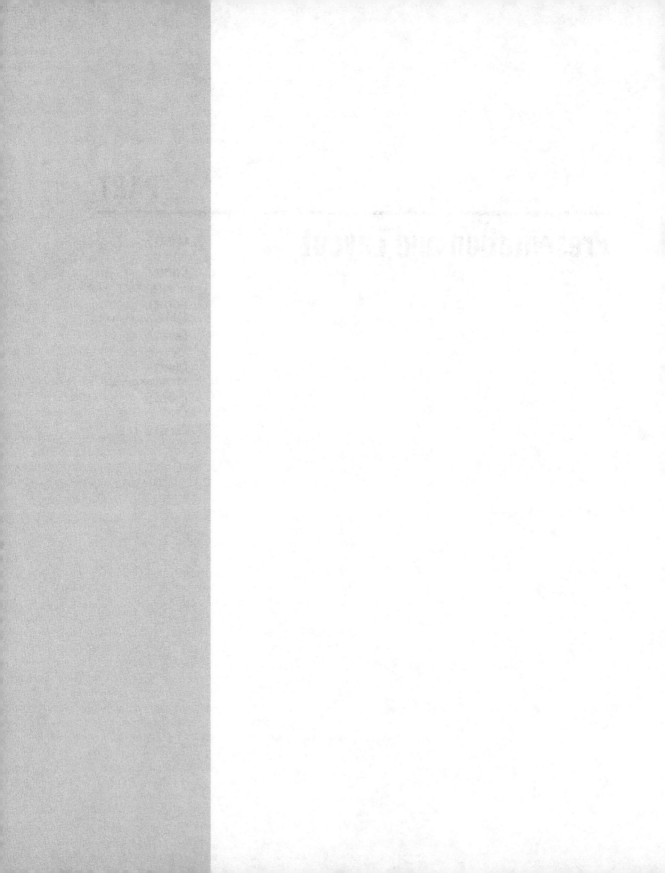

5

CHAPTER

Images

A great Web site isn't just about correct markup. Site organization, navigation, interactivity, content, delivery, and a multitude of other issues affect a user's perception of a site. However, images probably are the most obvious part of a great Web site. Carefully used imagery can add to both the appeal and usability of a Web site. Creation of Web-ready images certainly is beyond the scope of this book, but HTML authors should at minimum be aware of the basics of Web image formats such as GIF and JPEG and know when they are being used appropriately. Although the basic HTML/XHTML syntax of adding images to a page using the **img** element is relatively straightforward, creation of an aesthetically pleasing page is truly more art than it is science. Tools can make Web image creation easier, but readers should be realistic and consider both their own artistic limitations as well as the download constraints of the Web before going overboard with images.

Image Preliminaries

Before discussing image use in HTML/XHTML, it is important to discuss what image formats are supported on the Web today. In general, Web-based images come in two basic flavors: GIF (Graphics Interchange Format), as designated by the .gif extension, and JPEG (Joint Photographic Experts Group), as indicated by the .jpg or .jpeg file extension. A third format, PNG (Portable Network Graphics), as indicated by the .png file extension, is slowly gaining ground as a Web format and is supported fairly well in modern browsers. Table 5-1 details the supported image types found in most browsers. While browsers may support other image types, page authors should use only GIF or JPEG images to ensure that all users can see them.

NOTE *Internet Explorer and many other Windows browsers support the bitmap (BMP) file type popular with Windows users. This format has not been widely adopted on the Web.*

Choosing the correct image for the job is an important part of Web design. In general, GIF images tend to be good for illustrations such as logos or cartoons whereas JPEG images usually are the choice for complex imagery such as photographs. The main concerns for site designers when considering an image format are the size of the file itself and the quality of the reproduction. Table 5-2 provides a concise summary of the qualities of each format.

File Type	File Extension
GIF (Graphics Interchange Format)	.gif
JPEG (Joint Photographic Experts Group)	.jpg or .jpeg
XBM (X Bitmaps)	.xbm
XPM (X Pixelmaps)	.xpm
PNG (Portable Network Graphics)	.png

TABLE 5-1 Selected Web Image File Types

Subsequent sections will explain each of these basic features of the two main image formats in slightly more detail.

GIF Images

GIF is the most widely supported image format on the Web. Originally introduced by CompuServe (and occasionally described as CompuServe GIFs), there are actually two types of GIF: *GIF 87* and *GIF 89a*. Both forms of GIF support 8-bit color (256 colors), use the LZW (Lempel-Ziv-Welch) lossless compression scheme, and generally have the .gif file extension. GIF 89a also supports transparency and animation, both of which will be discussed later in this section. Today, when speaking of GIF images, we always assume the GIF89a format is in use and make no distinction between the formats, regardless of whether or not animation or transparency is actually used in the image.

GIF images use a basic form of compression called *run-length encoding*. This lossless compression works well with large areas of continuous color. Figure 5-1 shows the GIF compression scheme in practice. Notice how the test images with large horizontal continuous areas of color compress a great deal, while those with variation do not. As shown in the demo, simply taking a box filled with lines and rotating it 90 degrees shows how dramatic the compression effect can be. Given GIF's difficulty dealing with variability in images, it is

Format	Compression Scheme	Color Depth Supported	Progressive or Interlaced Rendering	Transparency	Animation
GIF	Lossless (preserves file size for minimal compression of continuous horizontal regions of color)	8-bit (256 colors)	Interlaced	Yes (1 degree)	Yes
JPEG	Lossy (trade image quality for file size)	24-bit (millions of colors)	Progressive	No	No

TABLE 5-2 Web Image Format Overview

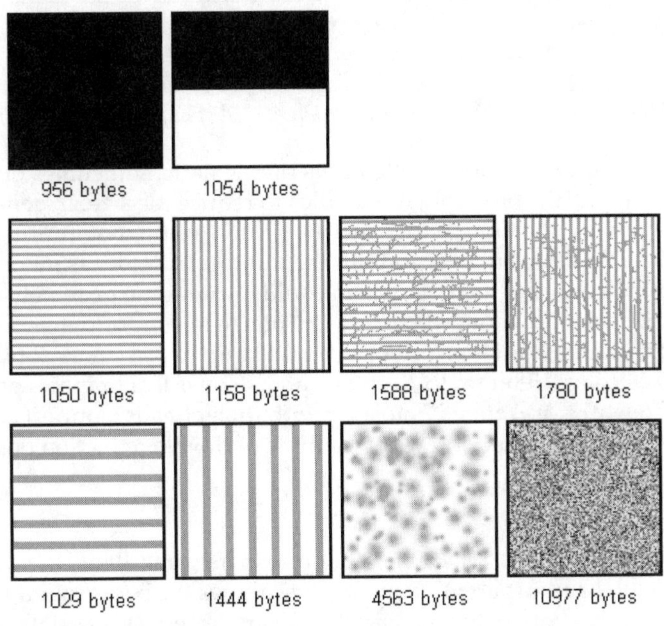

FIGURE 5-1 GIF compression scheme comparison

obvious why the format is good for illustrations and other images that contain large amounts of continuous color.

As mentioned earlier, GIF images only support 8-bit color for a maximum of 256 colors within the image. Consequently, some degree of loss is inevitable when representing true-color images, such as photographs. Typically, when an image is remapped from a large number of colors to a smaller color palette, dithering occurs. The process of dithering attempts to create the desired color that is outside of the palette, by taking two or more colors from the palette and placing them in some sort of checkered or speckled pattern in an attempt to visually create the illusion of the original color.

NOTE *There is a fairly esoteric use of GIF images that allows them to exceed the 256 color barrier by using more than one image block, each with its own color palette within the same GIF file. The so-called "true-color GIF" could provide for thousands of color support, but with a much larger file size. Those looking to exceed the 256 color limitation of GIF should look to JPEG or PNG files.*

While having only an 8-bit color depth seems problematic, sometimes designers will further downward adjust the bit-depth of GIF files to reduce file size. In general, the higher the bit-depth in an image, the more colors and the greater amount of information required. It would make sense then, that if you can limit the number of colors as much as possible without reducing the quality of the image, you could create some extremely small files. The key to doing this is using just enough colors in the image to support what is there or what is reasonable to dither. Standard 8-bit GIFs will contain up to 256 colors, 7-bit up to 128 colors, 6-bit up to 64 colors, 5-bit up to 32 colors, and so on. Most graphics programs, such as Macromedia Fireworks or Adobe Photoshop with ImageReady, support color reduction directly on image save. Figure 5-2 shows an example of the file reduction possibilities using GIF color reduction.

Transparency

GIF images also support *transparency*. One bit of transparency is allowed, which means that one color can be set to be transparent. Transparency allows the background that an image is placed upon to show through, making a variety of complex effects possible.

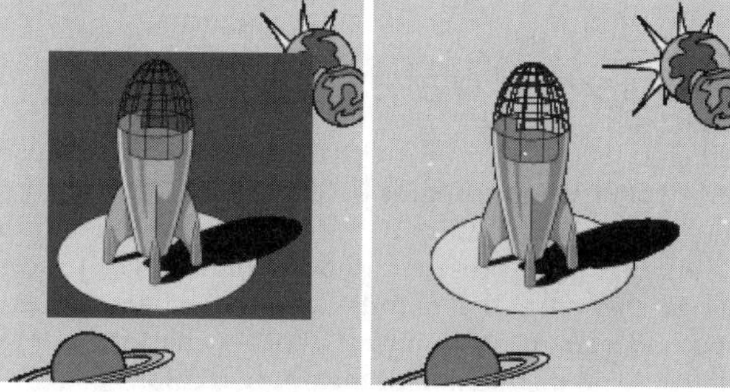

With transparency

GIF transparency is far from ideal. Given that only a single color can be made transparent, it can be difficult to avoid a halo effect when placing transparent GIF images on backgrounds, as shown here:

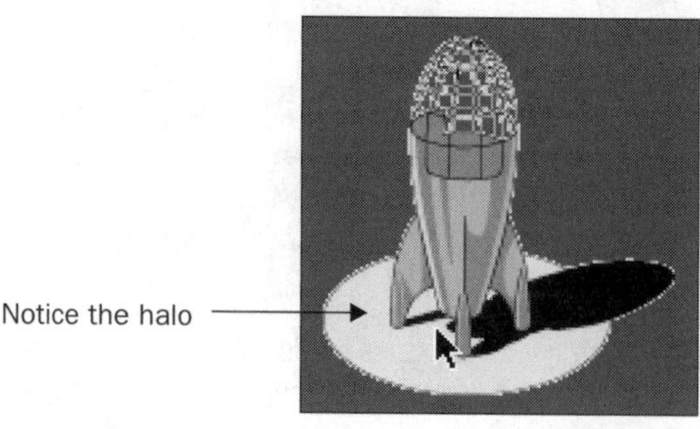

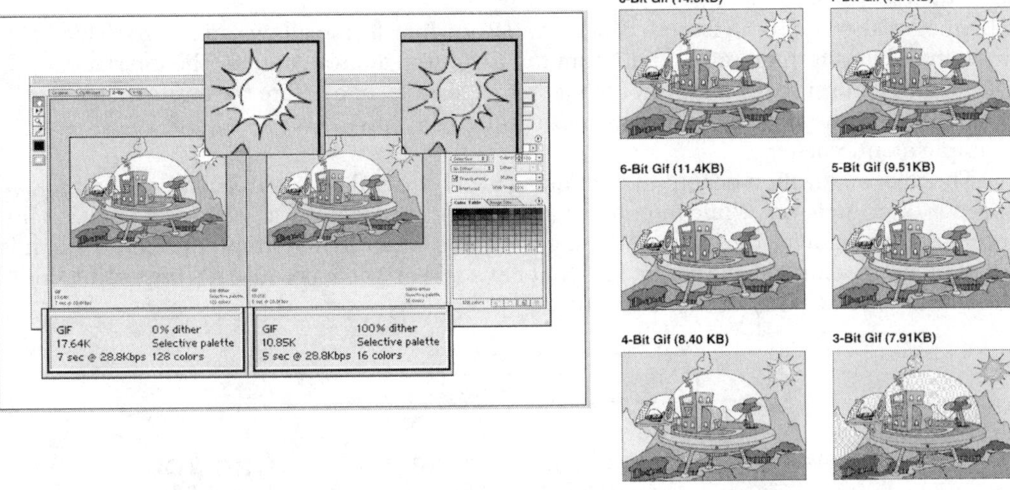

FIGURE 5-2 Color Reduction is useful to reduce GIF file size.

The main problem with 1-bit transparency is that *anti-aliasing* uses variable colors to blur the jagged edges of an image to smooth things out. Recall that everything that is displayed onscreen is made up of pixels and that pixels are square. It should therefore be obvious that creating an image that has rounded edges may pose some problems. Anti-aliasing allows us to create the illusion of rounded or smooth edges by partially filling the edge pixels in an attempt to blend the image into the background, as shown here:

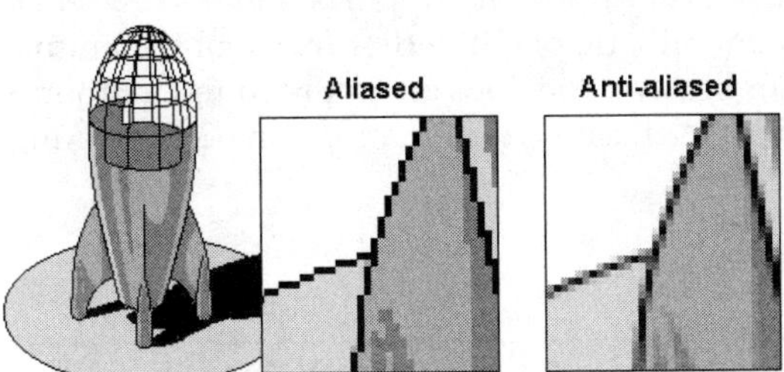

There are a variety of solutions to the anti-aliasing transparency interaction problem. First, you could simply not anti-alias the image, but this can produce unwanted "jagginess" in the image. A second possibility might be to avoid setting the transparency image on a complex background, and instead prefill the image with the appropriate background. This approach is seamless and completely avoids any trace of a halo, but it limits what we can put images on top of. For this reason, designers often avoid transparency in conjunction with complex backgrounds where this effect might be difficult to accomplish.

TIP *When using small text in a graphic, it is often a good idea to leave the text aliased. Anti-aliasing introduces an element of fuzziness, which may make smaller font sizes very difficult to read.*

Interlacing

GIF images also support a feature called *interlacing*. Interlacing allows an image to load in a venetian-blind fashion rather than from top to bottom a line at a time. The interlacing effect allows a user to get an idea of what an image looks like before the entire image has downloaded, thus avoiding user frustration as images download. See Figure 5-3 for an example of interlacing.

The previsualization benefit of interlacing is very useful on the Web, where download speed is often an issue. While interlacing a GIF image is generally a good idea, occasionally it comes with a downside; interlaced images may be larger than non-interlaced images. It is a bad idea to use interlacing for images that have text on them because it's impossible for the text to be read easily until the download is complete.

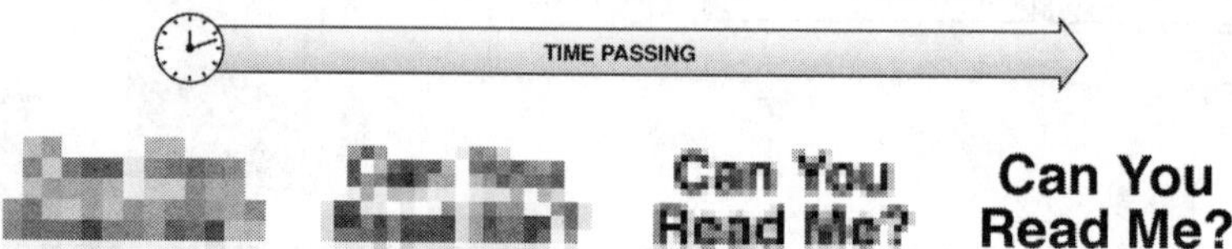

Animation

Finally, the GIF format also supports animation. This works by stacking GIF after GIF to create the animation, in a manner similar to a flip book. The animation extension also allows timing and looping information to be added to the image. Most popular graphics programs, such as Fireworks, support animated GIFs. An example of the interface to control GIF animation in Fireworks is shown in Figure 5-4.

Animated GIFs provide one of the most popular ways to add simple animation to a Web page because nearly every browser supports them. Browsers that do not support the animated GIF format generally display the first frame of the animation in its place. Even though plug-ins or other browser facilities are not required, authors should not rush out to use animation on their pages. Excessive animation can be distracting for the user, and is often inefficient to download.

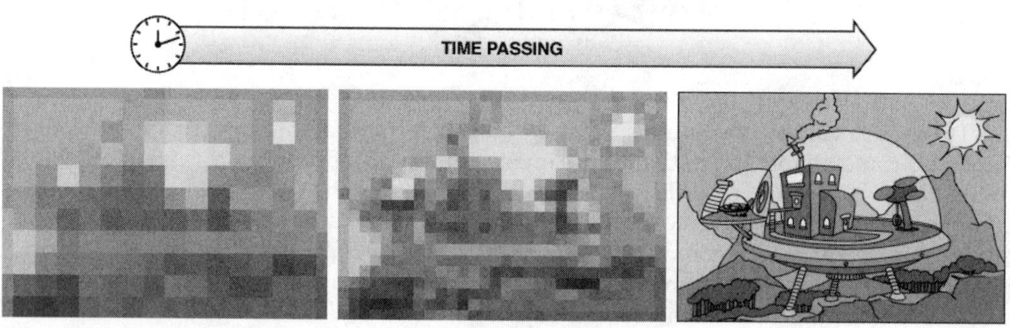

FIGURE 5-3 Interlaced GIF images show the gist of an image quickly

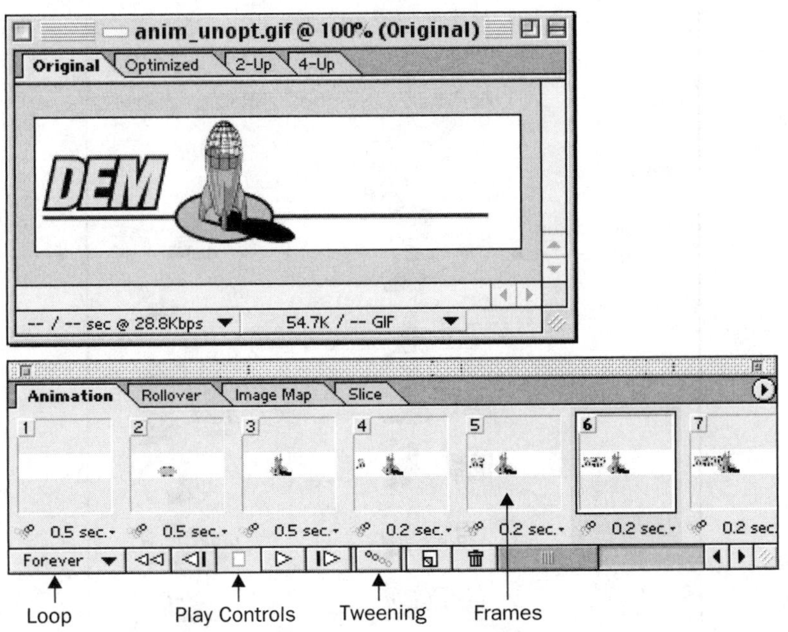

FIGURE 5-4 Animated GIFs provide only basic animation controls.

Because GIF animation is basically image after image, the file size is the total of all the images within the animation combined, which can result in a much larger image than the user is willing to wait for. Thus, it is very important to make sure that every frame of the animation is compressed as much as possible. One approach to combat file bloat is to optimize the image by replacing only the moving parts of an individual animation frame. This is often dubbed *changing rectangles* optimization. By replacing only the portion of the frame that is changing, you can use smaller images in some frames to help cut the file size down. Most of the GIF animating applications have a feature built in that will go through and optimize the images for you. This can result in a dramatic saving of file size, as shown in Figure 5-5.

JPEG

The other common Web image format is JPEG, which is indicated by a filename ending with .jpg or .jpeg. JPEG, which stands for the Joint Photographic Experts Group—the name of the committee that wrote the standard—is a lossy image format designed for compressing photographic images that may contain thousands, or even millions, of colors or shades of gray. Because JPEG is a lossy image format, there is some trade-off between image quality and file size. However, the JPEG format stores high-quality 24-bit color images in a significantly smaller amount of space than GIF, thus saving precious disk space or download time on the

FIGURE 5-5 Example of animated GIF frames and optimization

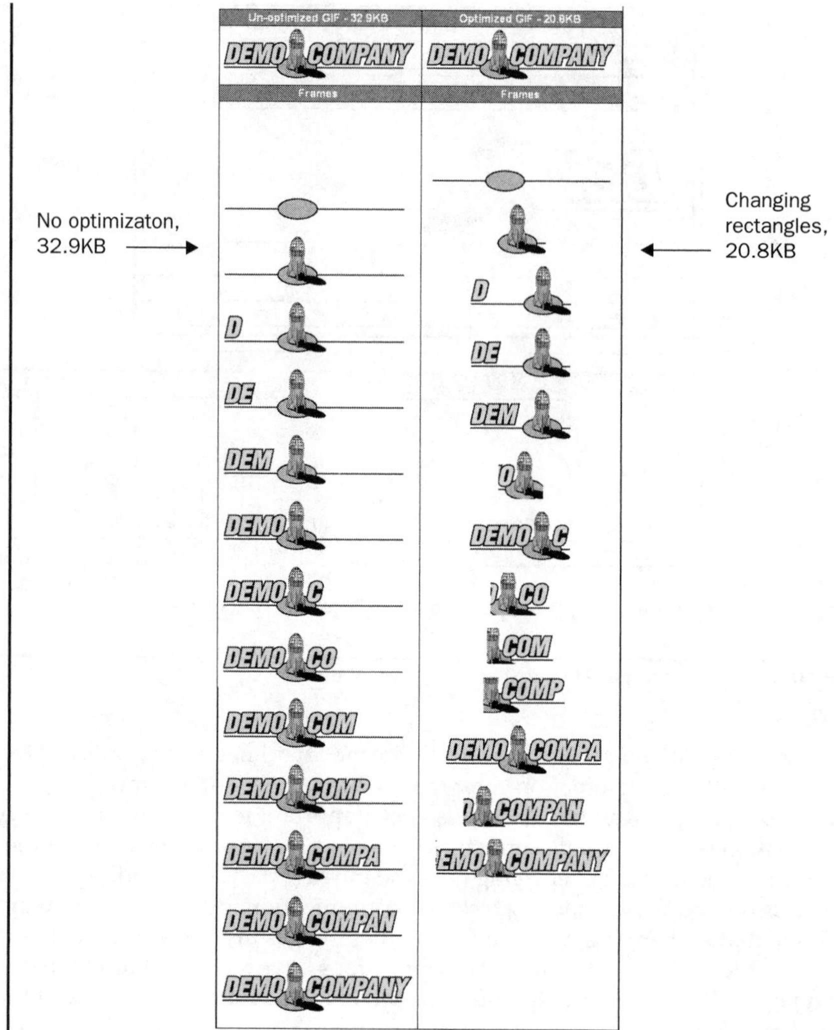

Web. See Figure 5-6 for an example of the quality versus file size tradeoff with JPEGs. Notice the significant file size savings obtained by sacrificing a little quality.

The trick with JPEG's lossy compression is that it focuses on slight smudging in areas of heavy detail that a viewer is unlikely to notice. However, in a situation where continuous color or text is used, JPEG's compression scheme may quickly become evident, as the artifacts introduced into the image will appear heavy in the flat color and text regions. It is possible to avoid this issue by selectively compressing portions of the image using an image manipulation program such as Fireworks or Photoshop.

While the JPEG format may compress photographic images well, it is not well suited to line drawings, flat color illustrations, or text. Notice the comparison between GIF and JPEG file sizes in Figure 5-7.

FIGURE 5-6
JPEG file size and quality comparison

FIGURE 5-7
Comparison of GIF and JPEG files

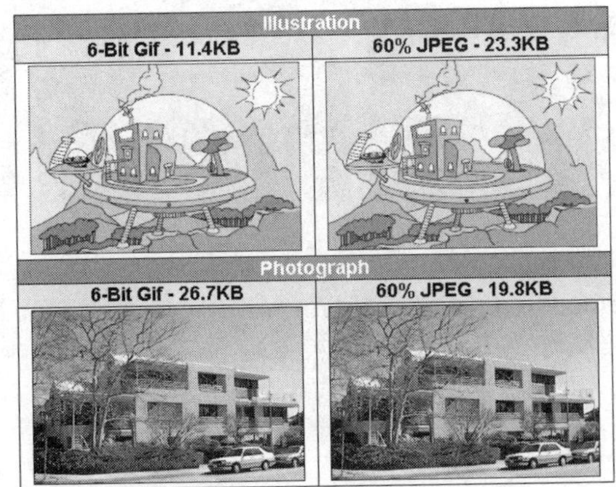

From Figure 5-7, it would seem that choosing between GIF and JPEG is usually very straightforward; photos suggest JPEG and illustrations GIF. However, in certain instances developers may be willing to distort a photo to put it in GIF in order to use the format's features because the JPEG format does not support animation, or any form of transparency. Fortunately, JPEG images do support a similar feature to GIF interlacing in a format called *progressive JPEG*. Progressive JPEGs fade in from a low resolution to a high resolution, going from fuzzy to clear. Like interlaced GIFs though, progressive JPEG images are slightly larger than their nonprogressive counterparts.

Finally, some designers are aware of the fact that because JPEG images are heavily compressed, decompression time can occasionally be a factor. With today's more powerful computers and higher speed lines, the decompression time of a JPEG will not be as noticeable much of the time. However, if you make an extremely large dimension JPEG and compress it highly, you will notice a delay. Of course, if you used a GIF, you'd have a worse looking image that might be just as large.

PNG

The Portable Network Graphics (PNG) format is an emerging format that has all of the features of GIF in addition to several other features. The compression algorithm for PNG is not proprietary compared to GIFs, which use LZW (owned by Unisys). Some designers have worried about the potential problems stemming from Unisys patent claims on LZW compression, but so far this has been a nonissue. PNG's compression algorithm is also slightly better than GIF's, as shown in Figure 5-8, but this alone is probably not much of a reason to give up GIF images given the browser compatibility problems that still plague the PNG format. PNG also supports slightly improved interlacing.

PNG images break the 8-bit color barrier normally found in GIF images, but with the degree of compression available in PNGs today it would not make sense to favor PNG files over JPEGs, as shown here.

A significant plus for PNG images is the improved transparency possibilities. Rather than being limited to a single color for transparency masks, PNG files can use up to 256 colors in a mask, which lends itself to smooth transparent edges and shadow effects.

Another problem addressed by PNG is the apparent color shifting in images that are developed on a system with one Gamma or brightness value and shown on a system with different Gamma. Notice in Figure 5-9 how the images do not quite look the same at different Gamma values. PNG avoids this problem.

Finally, PNG supports animation through its related MNG (Multiple-image Network Graphics) format, similar to what is provided in GIF animations.

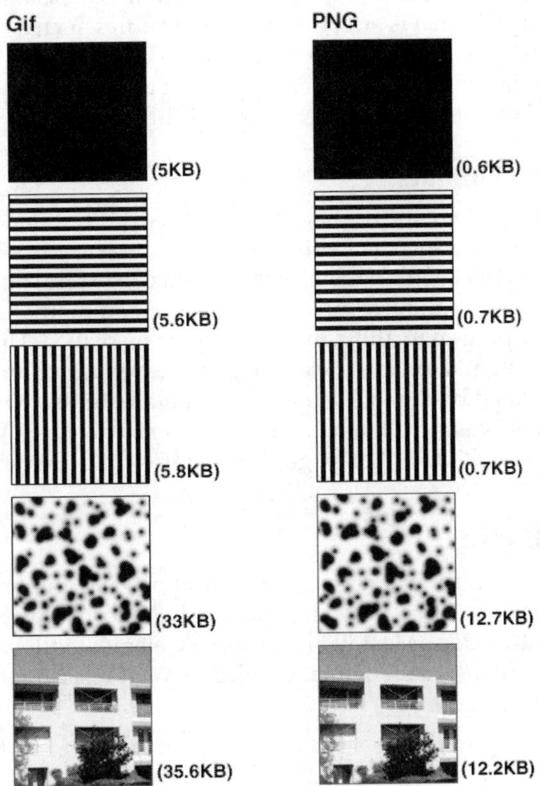

FIGURE 5-8 PNG Compression vs. GIF Compression

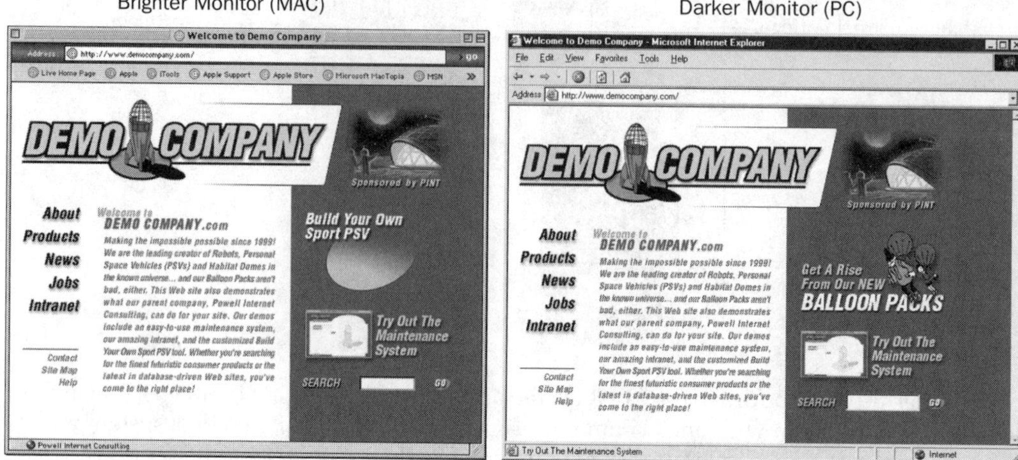

FIGURE 5-9 Different Gamma values can cause images to look different

With all these great features, one wonders why PNG is not more common online. The main reason is that the browser vendors still don't consistently support PNG images. Even when the image format is supported, many features such as transparency are not fully implemented. Still, few browsers except those based upon Mozilla and Macintosh Internet Explorer support PNG well enough to rely on the format, so Web designers are warned to avoid using PNGs unless browser sensing is utilized.

Other Image Formats

There are many image formats in addition to GIF, JPEG, and PNG that can be used on the Web. Vector formats such as Flash (with the file extension .swf) or Scalable Vector Graphics (SVG) are available, and image files may even use exotic compression technology such as fractal or wavelet compression. Most of the less common image formats require a helper application or plug-in to allow the image to be displayed. Unless you have a specific need, you probably should avoid special image types requiring browser add-ons; users may become frustrated by the work involved in obtaining the extra software.

For now, let's assume that a page designer simply has a Web-compatible image that needs to be placed into a Web page and requires the appropriate HTML syntax to do so.

HTML Image Basics

To insert an image into a Web page, use an **<img>** tag and set its **src** attribute equal to the URL of the image. As discussed in Chapter 4, the form of the URL can be either an absolute URL or a relative URL. Most likely, the image element will use a relative URL to an image found locally. To insert a GIF image called logo.gif residing in the same directory as the current document, use

```
<img src="logo.gif">
```

Because **img** is an empty element under XHTML, you would use

```
<img src="logo.gif" />
```

We'll use the XHTML syntax from here on. Of course, in the previous example, an absolute URL also could be used to reference an image on another server.

```
<img src="http://www.democompany.com/images/logo.gif" />
```

Using an external URL is not advised because images can move or cause the page to load at an uneven pace.

NOTE *The* **src** *attribute must be included. Otherwise, browsers that support images might display a placeholder or broken image icon.*

To set up a simple example, first create a directory to hold your images. It usually is a good idea to store all your image media in a directory named "images." This helps you keep your site contents organized as you build the Web site. Now place a GIF format image named robot.gif in that directory. To retrieve an image from the Internet, you can simply right-click with your mouse on an image and save the file to your directory. Macintosh users must hold the mouse button down on an image to access the menu for saving the image. Once you have a GIF image, you should be able to use a short piece of HTML markup to experiment with the use of **img**, as shown in the following:


```
<!DOCTYPE html PUBLIC "-//W3C//DTD XHTML 1.0 Transitional//EN"
"http://www.w3.org/TR/xhtml1/DTD/xhtml1-transitional.dtd">
<html xmlns="http://www.w3.org/1999/xhtml" lang="en">
<head>
<title>Image Example</title>
<meta http-equiv="content-type" content="text/html; charset=ISO-8859-1" />
</head>
<body>
<h2 align="center">Image Example</h2>
  <img src="images/robot.gif" alt="robot" width="156"
  height="251" border="0" />
</body>
</html>
```

NOTE *The name of the image, its path, its width, and height are made up for this example. Your particular attribute values might be different.*

A rendering of the image example is shown in Figure 5-10.

The next few sections cover the basic attributes of **img**.

Alternative Text Using the alt Attribute

The **alt** attribute, which is required under HTML and XHTML specifications, provides alternative text for user agents that do not display images, or for graphical browsers where the user has turned off image rendering.

```
<img src="images/logo.gif" alt="Demo Company Logo" />
```

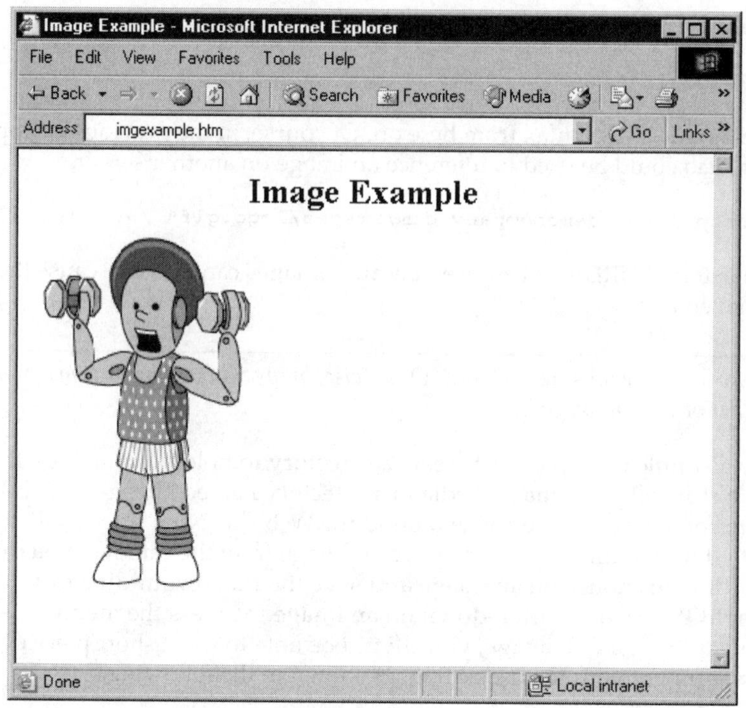

FIGURE 5-10 Rendering of a simple <img> example

The **alt** attribute's value may display in place of the image or be used as a Tooltip or placeholder information in image-based browsers. Any HTML markup found in the **alt** element will be rendered as plain text. If the option to display images is turned off, the browser displays the alternative text, as shown here:

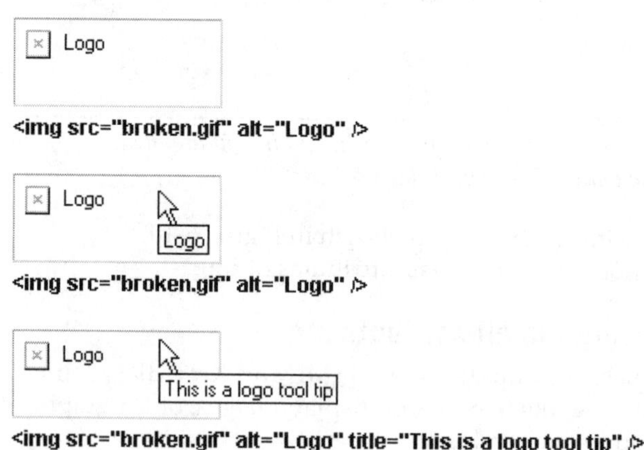

A browser may also show the **alt** text as images load, giving the user something to read as the page renders.

Many modern graphical browsers will also display the **alt** text as the Tooltip for the image once the pointer is positioned over the image for a period of time. However, the core attribute **title** should override this and be displayed instead of the **alt** text in a conformant browser, as shown in the previous illustration.

While theoretically there is no limit to the alternative text that can be used, anything more than a few hundred characters may become unwieldy. Some browsers do not handle long Tooltips and **alt** text properly, and may not wrap the descriptive text. However, be warned that if you insert entities such as **
, which indicates a carriage return, to format the **alt or **title** text, you may wreak havoc in voice browsers that read screen content, though the visual presentation might be improved.

The **alt** attribute's importance becomes clear when you reflect on how many people access the Web from a text-only environment. Unfortunately, much of the alternative text set does not always provide a substantial benefit. Do the previous examples really help by backing up the Demo Company logo graphic with the actual words "Demo Company logo"? Would simply "Demo Company logo" be sufficient, or insufficient? Try to make **alt** text reflect the meaning of an image; if an image is merely decorative, like a graphic bullet for a list item, setting to no value (**alt=""**) is perfectly acceptable.

Although a lot of people might argue that the Web wasn't popular until graphics were integrated or that the Web inherently is a visual medium, the value of textual content on the Web is indisputable. Consequently, it should be made as accessible as possible. There is no arguing that a picture might be worth a thousand words; but if that is the case, why not provide a few words in exchange?

Image Alignment

Probably the first thing a user wants to do after he or she is able to put an image in a Web page is to figure out how to position it on the page. Under the original HTML 2 standard, there was very little that allowed the user to format image layout on a page. Initially, the **align** attribute could be set to a value of **top**, **bottom**, or **middle**. When an image was included within a block element, the next line of text would be aligned either to the top, middle, or bottom of the image depending on the value of the **align** attribute. If the attribute wasn't set, it would default to the bottom. The example that follows illustrates basic image alignment as first defined in HTML 2. The rendering of the image alignment example is shown in Figure 5-11.

```
<!DOCTYPE html PUBLIC "-//W3C//DTD XHTML 1.0 Transitional//EN"
"http://www.w3.org/TR/xhtml1/DTD/xhtml1-transitional.dtd">
<html xmlns="http://www.w3.org/1999/xhtml" lang="en">
<head>
<title>Basic Image Alignment</title>
<meta http-equiv="content-type" content="text/html; charset=ISO-8859-1" />
</head>
<body>
<p><img src="images/aligntest.gif" align="top" alt="" border="1" />
This text should be aligned to the top of the image.</p>

<p><img src="images/aligntest.gif" align="middle" alt="" border="1" />
```

```
This text should be aligned to the middle of the image.</p>

<p><img src="images/aligntest.gif" align="bottom" alt="" border="1" />
This text should be aligned to the bottom of the image.</p>
</body>
</html>
```

One of the problems with image alignment in early HTML was that the text really didn't flow around the image. In fact, only one line of text was aligned next to the image, which meant the inline images had to be very small or the layout looked somewhat strange.

Netscape eventually introduced the **left** and **right** values for **align**, which allowed text to flow around the image. These values were later incorporated into the HTML specification, but eventually, like other image presentation values, were deprecated under strict HTML and XHTML. When setting an image element such as **<img src="logo.gif" align="left" />**, the image is aligned to the left and the text flows around to the right. Correspondingly, when you are using markup such as **<img src="logo.gif" align="right" />**, the image is aligned to the right and the text flows around to the left. It is even possible to flow the text between two objects if things are done carefully. The example presented here shows how the **align** attribute would work under transitional variants not using CSS. The rendering of this example is shown in Figure 5-12.

```
<!DOCTYPE html PUBLIC "-//W3C//DTD XHTML 1.0 Transitional//EN"
"http://www.w3.org/TR/xhtml1/DTD/xhtml1-transitional.dtd">
<html xmlns="http://www.w3.org/1999/xhtml" lang="en">
<head>
<title>Improved Text Flow</title>
<meta http-equiv="content-type" content="text/html; charset=ISO-8859-1" />
</head>
<body>
<p>
<img src="images/redsquare.gif" alt="red square" align="left" />
The top image has its align attribute set to "left," so the text flows
around it to the right. The top image has its align attribute set to
"left," so the text flows around it to the right. The top image has its
align attribute set to "left," so the text flows around it to the right.

<br clear="left" /><br /><br />

<img src="images/redsquare.gif" alt="red square" align="right" />
The bottom image has its align attribute set to "right," so the text flows
around it to the left. The bottom image has its align attribute set to
"right," so the text flows around it to the left. The bottom image has its
align attribute set to "right," so the text flows around it to the left.
</p>
</body>
</html>
```

Notice in the previous example that there is a special attribute to the **br** element. This is necessary to force the text to flow properly and will be discussed shortly.

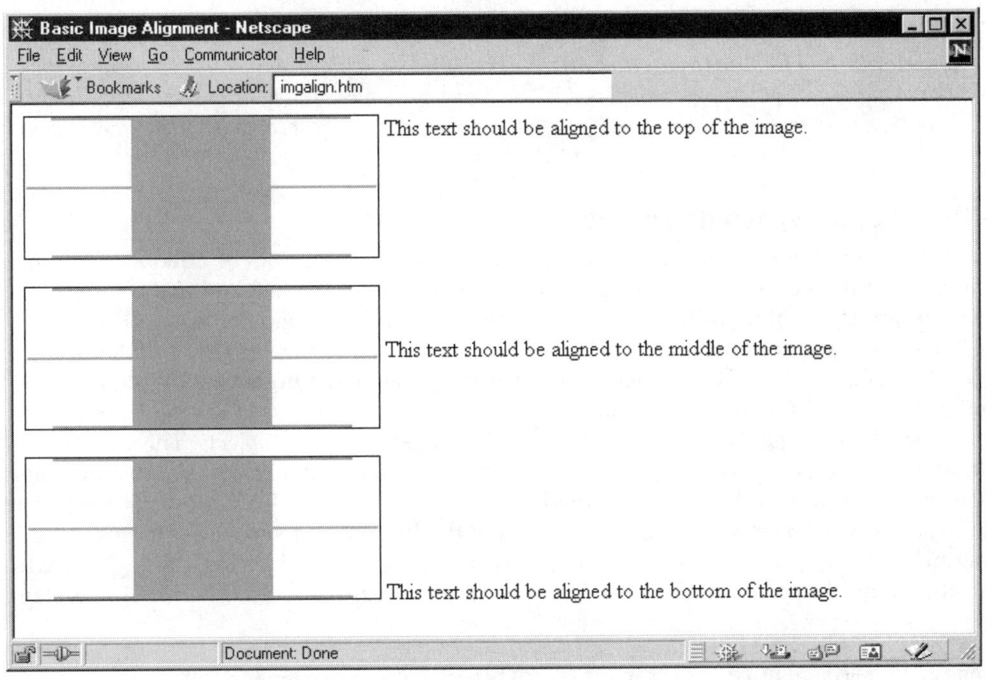

FIGURE 5-11 Image alignment rendering

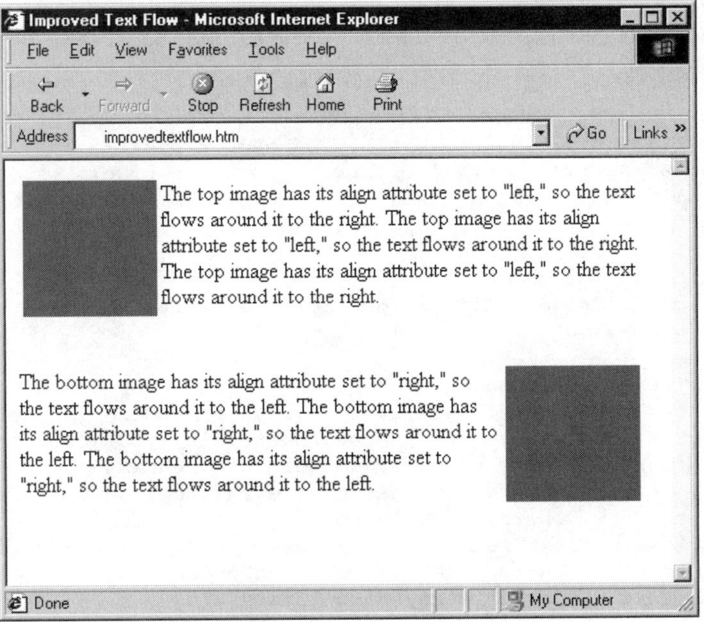

FIGURE 5-12 Image alignment rendering

NOTE *Netscape and Microsoft also support four other values for **align**: **texttop**, **baseline**, **absmiddle**, and **absbottom**. These attributes should be avoided in most cases because they are not standard, not supported consistently across browsers, and have been superseded by style sheets. In fact, formatting and positioning of images in general is handled more precisely by style sheets, which are discussed in Chapters 10 and 11.*

Buffer Space: hspace and vspace

Just floating an image and allowing text to wrap around it might not be adequate. You must also consider how to position the image more precisely with the text and make sure that text breaks where it ought to. Initially introduced by Netscape and made official in HTML 3.2, the **hspace** and **vspace** attributes can be used to introduce "runaround" or buffer space around an inline image. The **hspace** attribute is used to insert a buffer of horizontal space on the left and right of an image, whereas the **vspace** attribute is used to insert a buffer of vertical space between the top and bottom of the image and other objects. The value of both attributes should be a positive number of pixels. It is also possible to set the attribute values to percentage values, although this is inadvisable, as very high values can produce strange results. However, the most problematic aspect of the **hspace** and **vspace** attributes is the amount of buffer space that occurs on both sides of the image. Take a look at the XHTML transitional markup shown here to see how **hspace** and **vspace** work. Figure 5-13 displays a possible browser rendering of the example code.

```
<!DOCTYPE html PUBLIC "-//W3C//DTD XHTML 1.0 Transitional//EN"
"http://www.w3.org/TR/xhtml1/DTD/xhtml1-transitional.dtd">
<html xmlns="http://www.w3.org/1999/xhtml" lang="en">
<head>
<title>HSPACE and VSPACE Example</title>
<meta http-equiv="content-type" content="text/html; charset=ISO-8859-1" />
</head>
<body>

<p>The image below has its <tt><b>&lt;hspace&gt;</b></tt> and
<tt><b>&lt;vspace&gt;</b></tt> attributes set to 50 pixels, so the
text will flow around it at a distance of 50 pixels. The rest of
this text is dummy text. If it said anything interesting you would
certainly be the first to know.

<img src="images/redsquare.gif" align="left" alt="red square"
hspace="50" vspace="50" />

This is dummy text. If it said anything interesting you would certainly
be the first to know. There's really no point in reading the rest of it.
This is dummy text. If it said anything interesting you would certainly
be the first to know. There's really no point in reading the rest of it.
This is dummy text. If it said anything interesting you would certainly
be the first to know. There's really no point in reading the rest of it.
This is dummy text. If it said anything interesting you would certainly
be the first to know. There's really no point in reading the rest of it.
This is dummy text. If it said anything interesting you would certainly
be the first to know. There's really no point in reading the rest of it.
```

```
This is dummy text. If it said anything interesting you would certainly
be the first to know. There's really no point in reading the rest of it.
</p>
</body>
</html>
```

It turns out that in the future, by using style sheets (discussed in Chapter 10), it is possible to avoid these somewhat imprecise layout features altogether. The **hspace** and **vspace** attributes have been very useful, albeit occasionally abused by Web designers.

Extensions to

In flowing text around an image, a designer may encounter a situation in which he or she wants to clear the text flow around the image. For example, it could be problematic to create an image with a caption like the one shown in Figure 5-14 because the text might reflow.

To deal with such problems, a new attribute called **clear** was added to the **br** element; this extension now is part of the HTML standard, though of course it is deprecated under strict HTML and XHTML by CSS, which provides a **float** property that does the same thing. Under older HTML versions and transitional XHTML, the **clear** attribute can be set to **left**, **right**, **all**, or **none** and will clear the gutter around an inline object such as an image. For example, imagine the fragment **<img src="photo. gif" align="left" />** with text wrapping around it. If **<br clear="left" />** is included in the text and the wrapped text is still wrapping around the image, the text will be cleared to pass the image. The **clear="right"** attribute to a **
** tag works for text flowing around right-aligned images. Using a value of **all** ensures

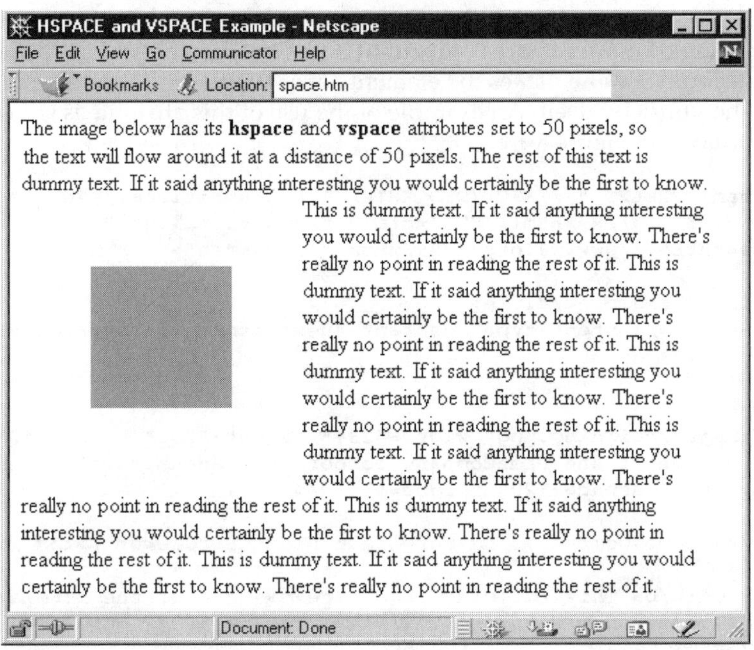

FIGURE 5-13 Rendering of hspace and vspace example

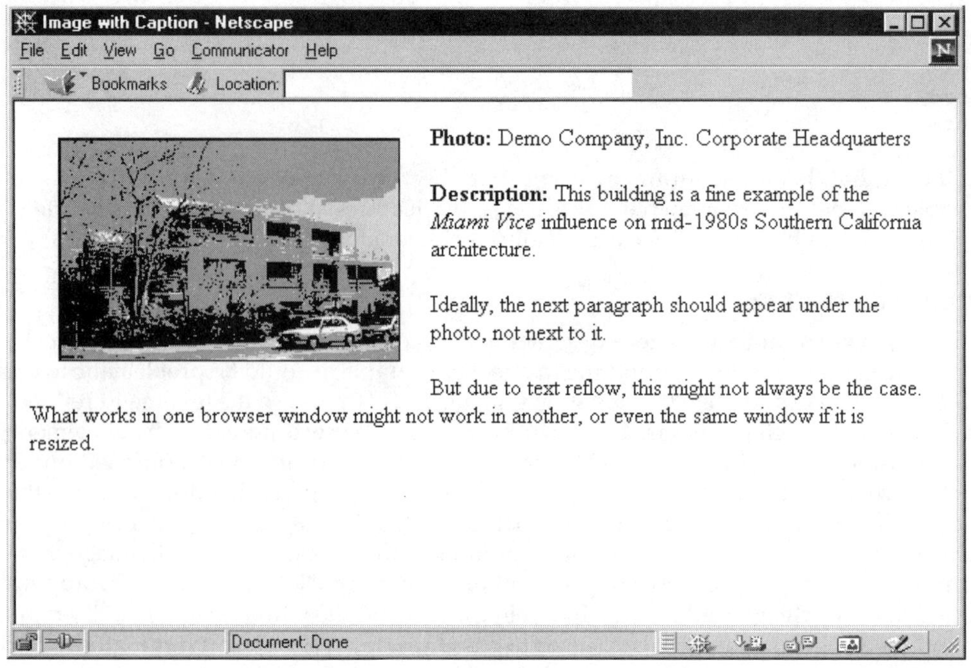

FIGURE 5-14 Image with misaligned caption

that the **
** tag continues to break text until both left and right columns are clear. Setting the attribute to **none** makes the element act as it normally would and is implied when using the **
** by itself. An example of the use of this attribute is shown here; a rendering appears in Figure 5-15.

```
<!DOCTYPE html PUBLIC "-//W3C//DTD XHTML 1.0 Transitional//EN"
 "http://www.w3.org/TR/xhtml1/DTD/xhtml1-transitional.dtd">
<html xmlns="http://www.w3.org/1999/xhtml" lang="en">
<head>
<title>BR Clear Example</title>
<meta http-equiv="content-type" content="text/html; charset=ISO-8859-1" />
</head>
<body>
<p>
<img src="images/building.jpg" width="234" height="150" border="2"
     alt="Outside of the DemoCompany corporate headquarters"
     align="left" hspace="20" vspace="10" />

<b>Photo:</b> Demo Company, Inc Corporate Headquarters<br /><br />

<b>Description:</b> This building is a fine example of the <i>Miami
Vice</i> influence on mid-80s southern California architecture.
<br /><br /></p>
```

```
<p>The next paragraph should appear under the photo, not next to it,
thanks to <b>&lt;br clear=&quot;left&quot: / &gt;</b>.
<br clear="left" />
<i>Photo copyright &copy; 2000 by Demo Company, Inc.</i>
</p>
</body>
</html>
```

height and width

The **height** and **width** attributes to the **img** element, introduced in HTML 3.2, are used to set the dimensions of an image. The value for these attributes is either a positive pixel value or a percentage value from 1–100 percent. Although an image can be stretched or shrunk with these attributes, the main purpose of **height** and **width** actually is to reserve space for images that are being downloaded. As pages are requested by a browser, each individual image is requested separately. However, the browser can't lay out parts of the page, including text, until the space that the image takes up is determined. This might mean waiting for the image to download completely. By telling the browser the height and width of the image, the browser can go ahead and reserve space with a bounding box into which the image will load. Setting the height and width thus allows a browser to download and lay out text quickly while the images are still loading. For an image called test.gif that has a height of 10 and a width of 150, use **<img src="test.gif" height="10" width="150" />**. The usability improvement of using **height** and **width** attributes for images is significant, and they should always be included.

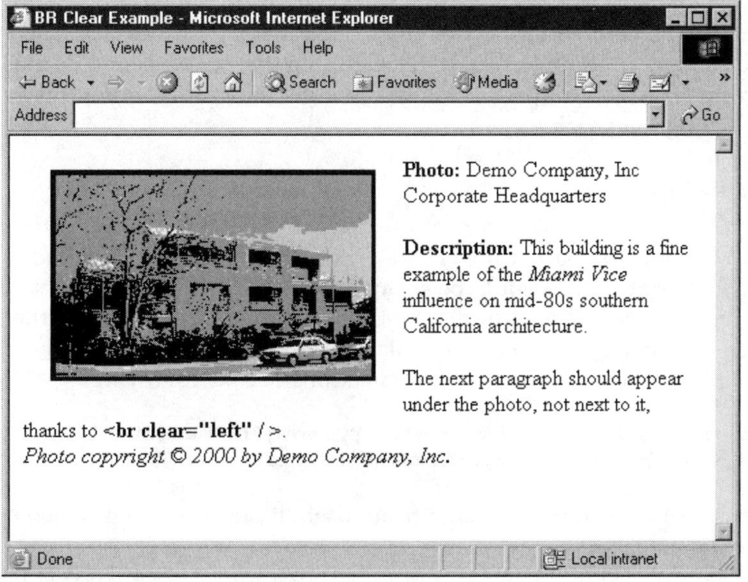

FIGURE 5-15 Rendering of <br clear> example

NOTE *Many people wonder what the measurements of a particular image are. Using Netscape, it is possible to view the dimensions quite easily. First, load the image into the browser by itself without any accompanying HTML. Now look at the title bar of the browser, which should display the dimensions. Also, using the option to view document information for the image within the browser should reveal the dimensions. Most Web editors also can automatically show the dimensions of an image.*

In addition to the prelayout advantages, the **height** and **width** attributes can also be used to size images. This is rarely a good idea, as the image might end up distorted. One way to avoid distortion is to shrink images in a proportional manner. However, if the image is to be made smaller, it is a better idea to size the image appropriately in a graphics program. Shrinking the image with the **height** and **width** attributes does not affect the file size, whereas resizing the image beforehand will shrink the file, hence reducing the download time. Another use of **height** and **width** sizing might be to increase the size of a simple image. For example, imagine an image of a single green pixel, and set the height and width alike: **<img src="greenpixel.gif" height="100" width="100" />**. The resulting image is a large green box with very little download penalty. A few sites even use the **height** and **width** attributes with percentage values such as 100 percent to create interesting effects such as full-screen images or vertical or horizontal color bars.

One other interesting use of the **height** and **width** attributes would be to help preload images. Preloading can be used to create the illusion of a quick download. Imagine that during the idle time on a page, the images on the next page are being downloaded so that they are precached when the user goes to the next page. A significant perceived performance improvement is achieved. One way to perform this prefetching is by putting an image that will appear later on the current page with **height** and **width** both set to **1**. In this case, the image won't really be visible but will be fully loaded into the browser's cache. Once the user visits the next page, the image can be fetched from the local disk and displayed quickly. The **link** element extension for prefetching content discussed in Chapter 4 should really be used over this **<img>** tag trick.

Low Source Images

Another potential speed improvement introduced by Netscape and supported by many browsers despite not being part of the HTML or XHTML standards is offered by the **lowsrc** attribute. The **lowsrc** attribute should be set to the URL of an image to load in first, before the so-called high source image indicated by the **src** attribute. In this sense, the attribute can be set to the address of a low-resolution or black-and-white file, which can be downloaded first and then followed by a high-resolution file. Consider the following:

```
<img src="hi-res-photo.gif" lowsrc="bw-photo.gif" height="100"
width="100" alt="Outside of building photograph" />
```

The **lowsrc** attribute can provide significant usability improvement when large full-screen images must be used.

One interesting aspect of the **lowsrc** attribute is that the browser tends to use the image dimensions of the **lowsrc** file to reserve space within the Web page if the **height** and **width** attributes are not set. Because of this, some strange distortion could happen if the high-resolution image is not the same size as the low-resolution image.

These are only the most common attributes for the **img** element. A more complete listing of **img** element attributes can be found in the element reference in Appendix A.

Images as Buttons

One of the most important aspects of images, as previously discussed in Chapter 4, is how they can be combined with the **a** element to create buttons. To make an image "pressable," simply enclose it within an anchor.

```
<a href="http://www.democompany.com"><img src="logo.gif"
alt="Demo Company" /></a>
```

When the page is rendered in the browser, clicking on the image will take the user to the anchor destination specified. Generally, to indicate that an image is pressable, the browser puts a border around the image, and provides some feedback to the user when the cursor or pointing device is over the hot area, such as turning the pointer to a finger or highlighting the text. For some basic feedback types, see Figure 5-16, which shows a border, finger pointer, and URL destination—all indicating that the image is pressable.

One issue that might be troublesome for page designers is the border that appears around the image when it is made pressable. It is possible to turn this border off by setting the **border** attribute of the image equal to **0**. Consider the following:

```
<a href="http://www.democompany.com"><img src="logo.gif"
alt="Demo Company"  border="0" /></a>
```


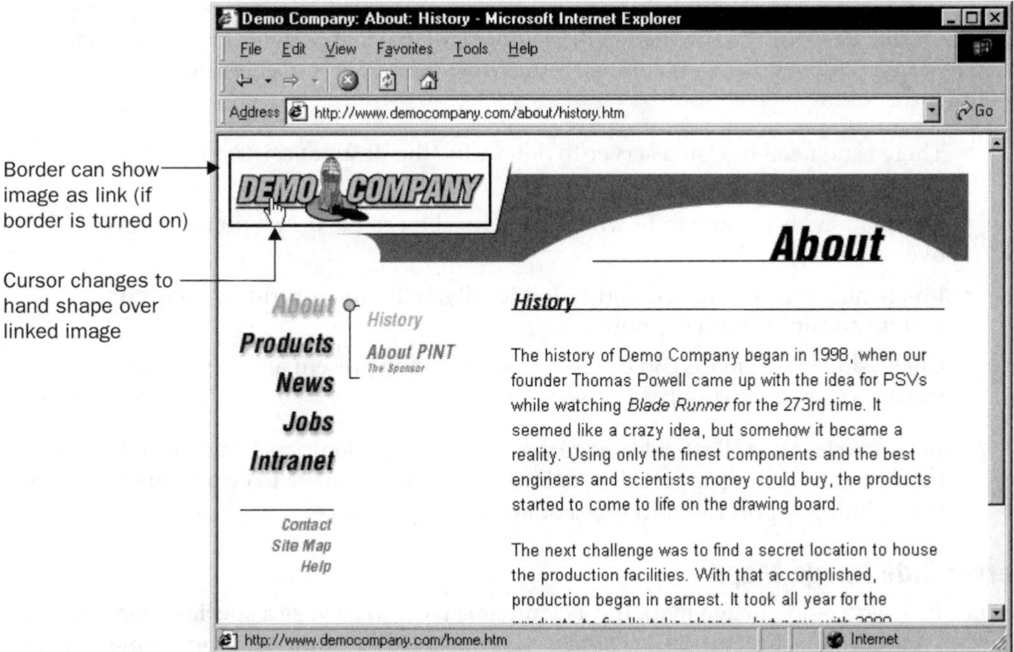

FIGURE 5-16 Image as link feedback

Of course, without the border it may be difficult to determine which images on a page are links and which are not. This can cause users to play a little game of finding the active click region by running their mouse all over the screen. One way to avoid such usability problems is to provide visual cues in images that are made pressable. Although from a design perspective some of these effects, particularly drop shadows, are a little overused, there are tangible benefits to adding feedback information to button graphics. Another approach is to animate the buttons. Using a very simple piece of JavaScript, it is possible to animate a button so that when a mouse passes over an image it comes alive. A brief discussion about how Web pages can be made more dynamic using a scripting language such as JavaScript can be found in Chapter 14.

One nonbutton-oriented use of the **border** attribute is to put a simple stroke around an image. Many times people will use a graphics tool to create a frame on an image, but the **border** attribute is a bandwidth-cheap way to get much of the same effect. Try setting the **border** attribute equal to a positive value on a nonclickable image—for example, **< img src="portrait.gif" alt="" border="5" />**. Borders, particularly when added with CSS, which offers a much richer set of formatting possibilities, provide an easy way to frame an image.

Image Maps

Another form of clickable images, discussed previously in Chapter 4, is the image map. An image map is a large image that contains numerous hot spots that can be selected, sending the user to a different anchor destination. Recall from the previous chapter that there are two basic forms of image maps: *server-side* and *client-side*. In the server-side image map, the user clicks on an image but the server must decode where the user clicked before the destination page (if any) is loaded. With client-side image maps, all of the map information—which regions map to which URLs—can be specified in the same HTML file that contains the image. Including the map data with the image and letting the browser decode it has several advantages, including the following:

- There is no need to visit a server to determine the destination, so links are resolved faster.
- Destination URLs can be shown in the status box as the user's pointer moves over the image.
- Image maps can be created and tested locally, without requiring a server or system administration support.
- Client-side image maps can be created so that they present an alternate text menu to users of text-only browsers.

Although it's clear that client-side image maps are far superior to their server-side cousins, very old browsers may not support this feature. This does not have to be a problem, as it is possible to include support for both types of image maps at once.

Server-Side Image Maps

To specify a server-side image map, the **a** element is used to enclose a specially marked **img** element. An **<a>** tag's **href** attribute should be set to the URL of the program or map file to decode the image map. The enclosed **<img>** tag must contain the attribute **ismap** so the browser can decode the image appropriately. As with all linked images, it might be desirable to turn the image borders off by setting the **<img>** tag's **border** attribute equal to **0**. As mentioned in Chapter 4, server-side image maps do not provide adequate feedback to the user because they show coordinates, and may incur performance penalties. HTML authors are encouraged to use client-side image maps.

Client-Side Image Maps

The key to using a client-side image map is to add the **usemap** attribute to an **<img>** tag and have it reference a **map** element that defines the image map's active areas. An example of this syntax is **<img src="controlbar.gif" usemap="#controlmap" />**. Note that, like server-side image maps, the image will be indicated as a link regardless of the lack of an **<a>** tag enclosing the image. The **border** attribute should be set to **0** if necessary. The **map** element generally occurs within the same document, although it might be possible to link to a **map** element outside the document though this use is uncommon and support in browsers is inconsistent. While the **map** element can occur anywhere within the body of an HTML document, it usually is found at the end of HTML documents.

The **map** element has two important attributes, **name** and **id**, which are used to specify the identifier associated with the map. While **id** is standard XHTML, browser support still often favors **name**, so both are included for safety purposes. The map name then is referenced within an **<img>** tag using the **usemap** attribute and the associated fragment identifier. Within the **<map>** tag are "shapes" defined by **<area>** tags that are mapped onto an image and define the hot spots for the image map. A brief example is shown here with a detailed discussion in Chapter 4 and full syntax of related tags in Appendix A.

```
<img src="shapes.gif" usemap="#shapes" alt="shapes map"
border="0" width="400" height="200" />

<div>
<!-- start of client side image map -->
<map name="shapes" id="shapes">
<area shape="rect" coords="6,50,140,143" href="rectangle.html"
      alt="rectangle" />
<area shape="circle" coords="195,100,50" href="circle.html"
      alt="circle" />
<area shape="poly"
      coords="255,122,306,53,334,62,338,0,388,77,374,116,323,171,255,122"
      href="polygon.html" alt="polygon" />
<area shape="default" href="defaultreg.html" alt="" />
</map>
</div>
```

While the format of the mapping tags is discussed in Chapter 4, memorizing or creating client- or server-side image maps by hand is not advised. Page designers should find that most Web page editors like Macromedia Dreamweaver or HomeSite automate the creation of image hot spots.

Advanced Image Considerations

Although most of the basic uses of images have been discussed, there are some issues that should be mentioned for later discussion. First, because an image can be referenced by a

PART III

style sheet or by a scripting environment, it might be very important to provide a name or identifier for it. The **class**, **id**, and **name** attributes can be used to provide names for images so they can be referenced and manipulated by scripting or style information that usually is found in the head of the document. Names should be unique and in the proper HTML form.

It is possible to include inline scripting or style information directly with an image. For example, setting the **style** attribute allows an inline style to bind to a particular **<img>** tag. Style sheets are discussed in Chapters 10 and 11. Furthermore, it is possible to have images bound to a particular event using an event attribute such as **onmouseover** and tying it to a script. A very simple use of tying an event with an image is to have the image change state depending on the user's action. The most basic use would be to create animated buttons or buttons that make a sound when clicked, but the possibilities are endless. A more detailed discussion and examples of how to bind JavaScript to create animated buttons are presented in Chapter 14.

An important comment concerning the future of **img** is that starting with HTML 4, it is supposed to be possible to include images using an **<object>** tag. For example,

```
<object data="images/logo.gif">Picture of the Demo Company
building</object>
```

Similar to the **<img>** tag, the **data** attribute is set to the URL of the included image while the alternative rendering is placed within the **object** element. Although this new syntax might create some interesting possibilities, the reality is that browsers currently don't support this form of image inclusion. Whereas this generic **<object>** tag for image support makes sense given that an image is no different from any other included binary object, the fact is that until browser vendors embrace this, it should be avoided. A more complete discussion of this element can be found in Appendix A, which provides the full syntax of the **object** element.

Image Toolbar

A special browser-specific feature for images that necessitates some special comment is Internet Explorer 6's image toolbar. If you have ever held your mouse over a large image in a Web page using IE6, you may have noticed a strange pop-up toolbar.

The toolbar supports quick saving of images to a special "My Images" folder. The browser determines what images to show this toolbar for by looking at the dimension of the image. Typically, the image must be fairly large to receive an image tool bar, and using just this simple idea, the browser does a pretty good job of not showing this feature of navigation buttons and banner ads. But for everything else, it depends on if you pass its size threshold. To turn off the image toolbar on an individual image, just add the **galleryimg** attribute and set its value to **no**, like so:

```
<img src="democompanylogo.gif" alt="Demo Company" galleryimg="no"
     height="50" width="100" />
```

If you just want to be rid of the whole feature altogether in a page, either have your server issue an HTTP response header of **Imagetoolbar: no** or, more easily, use a **<meta>** tag in the **<head>** of each page.

```
<meta http-equiv="imagetoolbar" content="no" />
```

Tips on Image Use

Many readers find Web page creation frustrating because it always seems that other sites just look better or load faster. Although this book focuses on HTML and XHTML, it's important to consider a few issues concerning image use. A much deeper discussion of image considerations can be found in *Web Design: The Complete Reference, Second Edition* (www.webdesignref.com).

Image Use

The first thing to consider is that the quality of the image being used certainly will affect the outcome of the page layout. Even when armed with a scanner, digital camera, or appropriate software such as Adobe Photoshop, Adobe Illustrator or Macromedia Fireworks, you might be a long way from being able to produce aesthetically pleasing Web pages. Don't fret—you would never expect that just owning a copy of a word processor would destine you to produce a huge book; it takes skill, patience, and years of practice. Take it from me.

Although this certainly is not a book on Web design, a simple tip is to aim for a minimal design. Straight lines, basic colors, and modest use of imagery should produce a relatively clean and uncluttered design. Furthermore, the simple design probably will load very fast! When you decide to use imagery on your site, whether for pure decoration or information, don't skimp on quality. If you use clip art from some free Web site, your site will reflect this. Fortunately, there are many sites that sell professional quality clip-illustrations and photographs relatively cheaply. While this might save money, don't simply right-click your way to a nice new image free of charge. Web users are sophisticated enough to know when they're having a cheap site foisted on them.

Legal Issues with Images

Unfortunately, the expense of licensing images and the ease with which images can be copied have convinced many people that they can simply appropriate whatever images they need. This is stealing the work of others. Although there are stiff penalties for copyright infringement, it can be difficult to enforce these laws. Also, some page designers tend to bend the rules thanks to the legal concept called *fair use*, which allows the use of someone else's copyrighted work under certain circumstances.

There are four basic questions used to define the fair-use principle:

- **Is the work in question being appropriated for a nonprofit or profit use?** The fair use defense is less likely to stand up if the "borrowed" work has been used to make money for someone other than its copyright holder.
- **Is the work creative or factual?** A creative work could be a speculative essay on the impact of a recent congressional debate; a factual work would be a straightforward description of the debate without commentary. "Fair use" would cover use of the factual work more than use of the creative one.
- **How much of the copyrighted work has been used?** It is possible to use someone else's images if it is changed substantially from the original. The problem is determining what constitutes enough change in the image to make it a new work. Simply using a photo-editing tool to flip an image or change its colors is not enough. There is a fine line between using portions of another person's work and outright stealing. Even if you don't plan on using uncleared images, be careful of using images from free Internet clip art libraries. These so-called "free" images may have been submitted with the belief that they are free, but some of them may have been appropriated from a commercial clip art library somewhere down the line. Be particularly careful with high-quality images of famous individuals and commercial products. Although such groups often might appreciate people using their images, the usage generally is limited to noncommercial purposes.
- **What impact does the image have on the economic value of the work?** Although unauthorized use of a single *Star Trek* related image might not substantially affect the money earned by Paramount Pictures in a given fiscal year, Paramount's lawyers take a dim view of such use. In fact, some entertainment organizations have taken steps to make it very difficult for Web page designers to use such images.

Ultimately we could, perhaps, add a fifth question to the list: Who owns the original work, and how vigorously will the owner defend it? With such a dangerous question it is obvious to see this discussion begs many legal questions that are far beyond the scope of this book. Suffice it to say that in the long run, it's always safer to create original work, license images, or use material in the public domain. Just because many Web designers skirt the law doesn't mean you should.

Images and Download Speed

Even if it is filled with wonderful imagery, few people want to wait literally minutes for your beautifully designed page to load. Page designers should always consider download time when adding images to their pages. Never assume that everyone has the latest high-speed cable connection or that high bandwidth is right around the corner. This section presents a few tips for improving download time of pages:

- **Make sure to use the correct format for the job.** Recall that GIF images are good for illustrations whereas JPEG images are good for photographs. If you break this rule of thumb, you may find that your images are unnecessarily big byte-wise and will take longer to download.
- **Reduce colors if possible.** When using GIF images, reducing the number of colors in the image (the bit-depth) can substantially reduce the file size. If your company logo only has 30 colors in it, why use an 8-bit GIF image when you can use a 5-bit image that supports 32 colors? Tools such as Macromedia Fireworks or Adobe Photoshop make color reduction easy to do.
- **Reduce the number of images in the page.** The number of individual images in a page can substantially affect the load speed regardless of the total number of bytes transferred. Consider that each individual request does have some overhead and that the network might not be quite as effectively utilized compared to a few larger image downloads. Remember, from the user's point of view, time counts—not bytes delivered—so wherever possible try to reduce the number of individual image pieces used.
- **Use the browser's cache.** Once an image has been downloaded once, it should stay in the browser's cache. If the same file is used later on, the browser should be able to reuse the one from the cache. If you can use scripting it might even be possible to download images ahead of time to the browser cache, using precaching or preloading. However, reliance on the cache only works if the complete filenames are the same. This means a single image directory probably is better than copying the files to individual image directories all over your site.
- **Give a preview.** If it is going to take a while to download, give the user something to look at. Interlacing a GIF image or making a JPEG progressive results in images that load incrementally. The user might get the gist of an image long before it completely downloads. Thumbnails of images also are a useful way to let a user take a look at the general idea of an image before committing to a long download. If a long download is required, it is a good idea to warn the user as well.
- **Use markup correctly.** Using **alt**, **height**, and **width** attributes can do a lot to improve page rendering. The alternative text will give the user something to read as an image loads. Setting the **height** and **width** values properly will allow the browser to specify the page layout, quickly allowing the text to flow in right away.

If you have to resort to large file sizes on your Web site, then the ends should justify the means. A big wait for a huge logo or heavily designed page with little content will result in frustrated users who never want to come back again. Could this be why the largest sites such as Amazon and Yahoo! use relatively simple visuals that download quickly? Almost certainly this is the case. In short, always remember when using images to make sure they add something to the overall experience of the user, whether it be to make the site more pleasing visually or provide information.

Summary

Inline images are truly what helped popularize the Web. However, just because images can be used to improve the look and feel of a Web page doesn't mean that they should be used without concern. Although presentation is important, the Web is still fundamentally about the communication of information, some of which does well in image form and some of which does not. Adding images to a Web page is accomplished using an **<img>** tag, which has numerous attributes. Many of the attributes of the **img** element—including **alt**, **height**, **width**, and **lowsrc**—are useful in improving the accessibility and usability of Web pages. As always, the eternal struggle between nice-looking pages and download time continues, and knowledge of markup features is helpful to combat excessive wait time. Many of the other attributes for the **img** element were developed with layout in mind, particularly **align**. However, layout and image formatting are truly better performed using style sheets.

CHAPTER 6

Text, Colors, and Backgrounds

Web page designers strive to create attractive Web pages, but it hasn't always been easy. HTML really wasn't created with design features in mind. In the very early days of the Web, even text color couldn't be set and a simple layout technique such as centering text wasn't initially possible. Browser vendors have added many HTML attributes and elements over the years to provide page developers with more control over the look and feel of their pages. For many layouts, page developers also rely on the default rendering of many standard tags such as **<blockquote>**. Tables, as discussed in the next chapter, handle most of today's layout duties beyond the basics covered here, but ultimately the presentation duties of HTML will be alleviated by Cascading Style Sheets, as discussed in Chapter 10. Despite ongoing improvements in browser support of CSS, markup tricks and workarounds are still occasionally required to create visually appealing pages that work in older browsers. Although, in theory, it would be best to avoid these nonstandard techniques, often they are the grim reality of Web design—at least until CSS is better supported by browsers and better understood by developers.

HTML Approach to Visual Design

While HTML was not designed with layout in mind, it has been abused and extended to support layout as best it can. Today there are many elements, both standard and nonstandard, that can provide layout control. These include the various **align** values for elements, the ubiquitous table tag, and even browser-specific proprietary tags such as **<spacer>** and **<multicol>**. This section covers some of the basic HTML and XHTML elements, both standard and proprietary, that are used to control text and screen layout. Remember that the use of such approaches is best suited to environments that must deal with older browsers—those that do not support technologies such as Cascading Style Sheets. Ultimately, the role of HTML, and of course XHTML, will not be for presentation, but for structure.

Basic Text Layout with HTML Elements

The first thing to consider in the HTML approach to layout is all the elements and attributes used to position text and objects on a page. Web page designers have long tended to use the default presentation of tags such as **<blockquote>** or **<ul>** to attempt to move text around the page, as shown in the example here:

```
<!DOCTYPE html PUBLIC "-//W3C//DTD XHTML 1.0 Transitional//EN"
"http://www.w3.org/TR/xhtml1/DTD/xhtml1-transitional.dtd">
<html xmlns="http://www.w3.org/1999/xhtml" lang="en">
<head>
<title>Simple HTML Layout</title>
<meta http-equiv="content-type" content="text/html; charset=ISO-8859-1" />
</head>
<body>

<blockquote>
This is indented text
</blockquote>

<blockquote><blockquote>
This text is indented more.
</blockquote></blockquote>

<blockquote><blockquote><blockquote><blockquote><blockquote><blockquote>
This is indented heavily, but it may not produce the effect you expect because
it indents from both sides.
</blockquote></blockquote></blockquote></blockquote></blockquote></blockquote>

</body>
</html>
```

See Figure 6-1 for a rendering of formatting using the block element.

Many HTML page development tools still use **<blockquote>** to move things around the screen. If you are unconvinced, just try using the indent feature in a WYSIWYG editor; then view the generated HTML. This is an improper use of the tag, which is further complicated by the fact that there is no guarantee how much each application of the element will cause the text to be indented. Further, it doesn't take into account that the default rendering of the tag might be overridden by a style sheet. However, despite these problems this approach is still used and will actually validate!

Another HTML-based approach to control text layout is the use of the **<pre>** tag. As discussed in Chapter 3, any text enclosed by **<pre>** preserves returns, tabs, and spaces. Using **<pre>**, it is possible to force text to lay out the way the page author requires, even forcing the browser to scroll to the right to read text. Generally speaking, the browser changes the typeface of any preformatted text to a fixed-width font such as Courier. This font change might not be desired.

Nonbreaking Spaces

Web browsers are supposed to minimize all forms of white space to a single white space character; this includes spaces, tabs, and returns. Page authors might be frustrated when

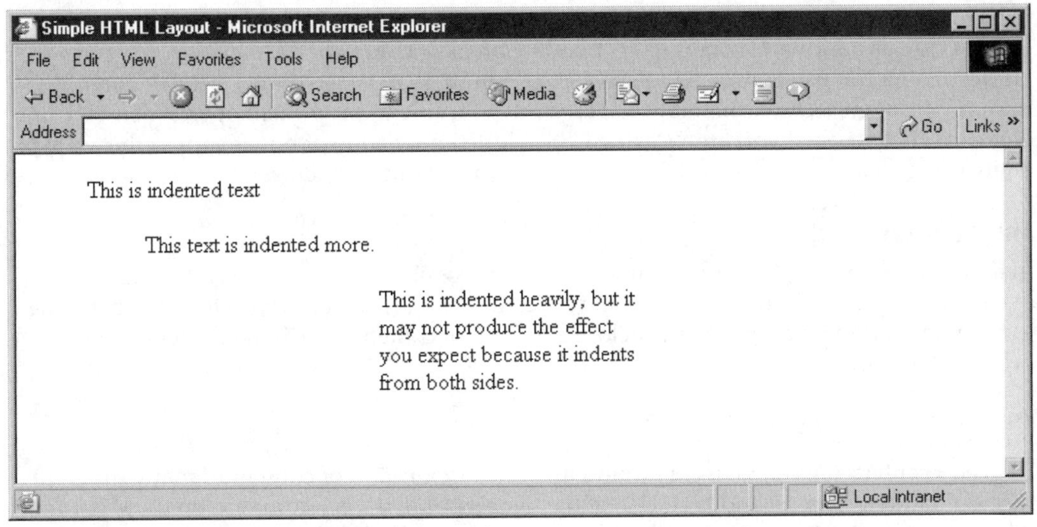

FIGURE 6-1 Text indentation using <blockquote>

attempting to put two spaces between words unless they resort to using the **<pre>** tag. However, using the character entity ** ** or ** ** should insert a nonbreaking space that will not be collapsed by the browser. To enter three spaces between words, use ** ** ** ** or ** **. This leads many people to force text layout like so:

```
          
Now we are ten spaces from the left!
```

Although use of this nonbreaking space is a convenient crutch, it won't work well in all situations, particularly if the user changes the default font in his or her browser. This should make sense to you, particularly if you have tried to align columns of text in a word processor using the spacebar. Things just never quite seem to line up this way. This problem occurs because of the proportional nature of fonts versus the size of the space character. Why would this work any differently on the Web?

Although not perfect for forcing layout, the ** ** entity can be considered the duct tape of the Web. Anyone who has performed a little home repair knows a little duct tape can go a long way; so can ** ** on the Web! Consider, for example, the fact that browsers often will minimize elements that do not appear to be needed or used because there is no content within them. A single character within the element would prevent this minimization, but do you want that character to appear on the screen? Probably not, so in comes the ** ** entity. Although useful with table tags and such, this approach unfortunately is often abused, particularly by WYSIWYG editors. Consider the markup

```
<p> </p>
```

that often is created by a WYSIWYG Web editor after a simple press of the Return key. This particular markup says we have an empty paragraph, but does that really make sense?

In some sense it does, when you think of HTML/XHTML as a structural language. If you view HTML as a formatting language, two line breaks (**

) makes more sense. However, you can use nonbreaking spaces to do more than space things out. For example, the entity is often seen within table cell tags (<td>**) trying to prop them open when they are empty of content. So if you aren't using CSS, a little knowledge of how to apply the ** ** entity can go a long way toward fixing troublesome layout problems.

The <center> Tag

In the early days of the Web, it was difficult, if not impossible, to control screen layout. Netscape eventually introduced a few elements and attribute changes useful for positioning, including the **<center>** tag. This element can enclose any form of content, which then is centered in the browser window:

```
<center>I am centered!</center>
```

The **<center>** tag can be used around an arbitrary amount of content in many different forms, including images and text. Use of the **<center>** tag is very common on the Web, and it has been included in many of the HTML standards including HTML 4 transitional. However, today the element is considered shorthand for **<div align="center">** with both syntax forms superseded by CSS properties.

Alignment Attributes

In addition to **<center>**, there are many tags under older HTML specifications and the transitional XHTML specification that support the **align** attribute. For example, the **div** element, which is used to create a division in a document, might have the **align** attribute set to **left**, **center**, **right**; or, even, **justify**. If the **align** attribute is not set, text generally is aligned to the left when language direction is set to **ltr** (left to right) and to the right when the language direction is set to **rtl** (right to left). Initially, the **justify** attribute did not work in most browsers; now it is supported by the latest versions of the two major browsers. The paragraph (**<p>**) tag; the **<table>** tag; and the headings **<h1>**, **<h2>**, **<h3>**, **<h4>**, **<h5>**, and **<h6>** also support the **align** attribute, with the same basic values and meaning. Note that, as discussed in Chapter 5, the **align** attribute on the **img** element serves a different purpose.

NOTE *Under strict HTML 4 and XHTML, the use of alignment attributes and the* ***center*** *element is deprecated in favor of CSS.*

Word Hinting with <nobr> and <wbr>

Under many browsers, it is possible to control text layout beyond simple alignment. Because font size and browser widths might be different, word wrapping can occur in strange ways. Microsoft and Netscape, as well as many other browsers, support the **<nobr>** and **<wbr>** tags as a way to provide the browser with hints for text layout. While these tags are not standard, they are occasionally still used by Web designers.

The **<nobr>** ("no break") tag makes sure that an enclosed line of text does not wrap to the next line, regardless of browser width. This element is useful for words or phrases that must be kept together on one line. If the line of text is long, it might extend beyond the browser window, obliging the user to scroll in order to view the unbroken text. A simple example of using the **nobr** element is shown here:

```
<nobr>This is a very important long line of text, so it should not
be allowed to break across two lines.</nobr>
```

In contrast to the **nobr** element, which is quite firm in its word wrapping, the **wbr** element allows the page designer to suggest a soft break within text enclosed by the **nobr** element. In essence, the **<wbr>** tag marks a spot where a line break can take place. The element is an advisory one, unlike **
** and **<nobr>**, which force layout. Depending on the situation, the browser may choose to ignore the **<wbr>** element because there is no need for it. The **<wbr>** element is an empty element that does not require a closing tag. The XHTML self-closing syntax is pointless given the fact that like **<nobr>**, **<wbr>** is not part of a W3C HTML or XHTML specification. Here's a simple example showing how **<wbr>** works:

```
<nobr>This is a very important long line of text that should not
break across two lines. If the line must be split, it should
happen here <wbr> and nowhere else.</nobr>
```

A **<wbr>** tag should exist only within a **nobr** element, although it might work outside of it. The basic feature—and a very useful one—of this element is to suggest a line break point.

PART III

NOTE *The* ***<wbr>*** *tag is purposefully not presented in XHTML style syntax with a self-identifying close tag as it is not part of any XHTML specification. However, if you use the* ***<wbr>*** *tag, you can add the close tag if you like (****<wbr />****) although it will not validate either way.*

Text Alignment with Images

As discussed in Chapter 5, the **img** element has an **align** attribute, which helps align text with images or even allows text to flow around images. For example, when **align** is set to a value of **top**, **bottom**, or **middle** and the image is included within a block structure of text, the next line of text would be aligned to the top, middle, or bottom of the image, depending on the value of the attribute. If the attribute were not set, it would default to the bottom. When alignment of the image is set to **left** or **right**, the document text flows around the image on the opposite side. For example, when setting an image tag like **<img src="logo.gif" align="left" />**, the image is aligned to the left and the text flows around to the right. Correspondingly, when using code such as **<img src="logo.gif" align="right" />**, the image is aligned to the right and the text flows around to the left.

An easy way to think of this is to consider an image a rock in a river with the text flowing around it. Align the image to the left and the text flows around to the right. Align the image to the right and text flows to the left. Most browsers also support other values for **align** including **textop**, **baseline**, **absmiddle**, and **absbottom**. Avoid these attributes in most cases because they may not be supported identically across browsers. Furthermore, if you need to control text alignment in relation to images it would be more appropriate to use style sheets. For more information on image alignment, see Chapter 5 as well as the element reference (Appendix A).

Extensions to

Because text might flow in undesirable ways around images, an extension to the **br** element was developed. Under transitional forms of markup, the **br** element takes a **clear** attribute, which can be set to **left**, **right**, **all**, or **none**. By default, the **clear** attribute is set to **none**, which makes the element produce a new line. When an image is aligned to the **left**, it might be useful to return past the image to start a new section of text. Placing another object using **<br clear="left" />** causes the browser to go all the way down a column until the left side of the window is clear. The markup **<br clear="right" />** does the same thing with right-aligned images. When trying to pass multiple images that might be aligned both on the **left** and **right**, use **<br clear="all" />**. The idea of the **clear** attribute for **
** is illustrated here:

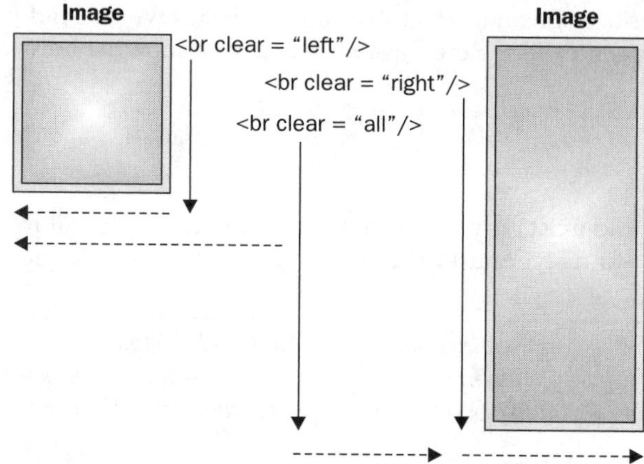

Layout with Invisible Images

You can also push text around a page with HTML/XHTML markup by using an invisible image. This approach is well-known to users of the desktop publishing program QuarkXPress. With this program, users can create invisible regions and run text around them to achieve specific layout effects. You can do this under HTML/XHTML transitional forms by using an invisible image in combination with the **align**, **hspace**, and **vspace** attributes. Given a transparent 1-pixel image or, if you like, "invisible pixel," the designer can perform a variety of interesting tricks. Usually, these images are named something like space.gif, spacer.gif, blank.gif, clear.gif, pixel.gif, or shim.gif. Regardless of how you have named your image, to see it in use, put it at the start of a paragraph and use the attribute **width** to set it to 50 pixels, as shown here:

```
<p><img src="pixel.gif" alt="" width="50" align="left" border="0" />
This is the start of the paragraph.</p>
```

Given this fragment, the first line of the paragraph is indented 50 pixels. The illustration here shows this basic trick with a border on the image turned off and on to show where the invisible pixel is.

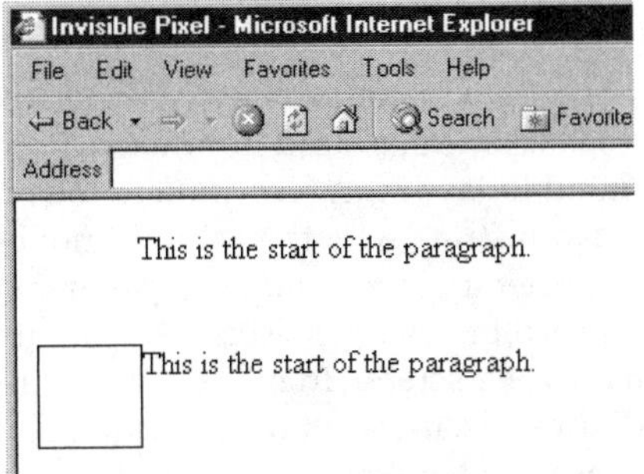

NOTE *While it certainly is very easy to make a transparent pixel, you can have one of your own free of charge from http://www.htmlref.com/examples/chapter6/ pixel.gif. If you find it difficult to save, try http://www.htmlref.com/examples/ chapter6/pixel.html, which provides explicit instructions on how to grab one of these useful images.*

Aside from indentation, you could format text in a variety of ways and with careful use of **hspace** and **vspace** attributes you could even space out lines without using style sheets. Of course, formatting using CSS is so much easier that this really should never be done.

Much larger regions also can be created with an invisible pixel by setting the **height** and **width** attributes of the **img** element and using **align** to flow text around the invisible region. For example, **<img src="pixel.gif" height="100" width="50" align="left" />** could create a large invisible block to run text around.

The pixel trick can be a useful workaround. However, the trick has its failings. Consider what happens when the page is viewed with the images turned off, or the stop button is pressed before the pixel.gif image is loaded. The previous example might look something like this:

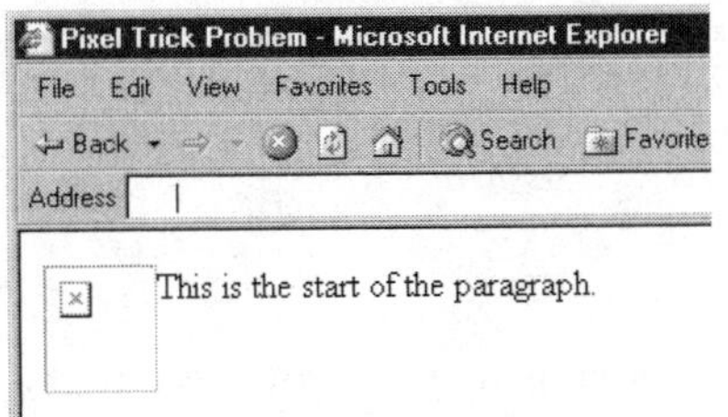

Despite their problems, image layout tricks are still too common on the Web. They are considered so useful that for a while Netscape introduced a special tag called **<spacer>** that mimics much of the functionality of invisible images. We briefly discuss proprietary elements such as spacer, primarily for historical reasons and to convince readers not to use proprietary tags.

NOTE *Pixel GIFs are still useful without resorting to layout tricks such as the ones discussed in this section. Often, such GIFs are used within table cells to keep the cells from collapsing when used for layout. This use of an invisible pixel GIF, often dubbed a "shim," is discussed in the next chapter.*

Proprietary Layout Tags

The 3.*x* and 4.*x* generations of the two major browsers introduced numerous proprietary HTML elements. Some of these became standard but many did not. Most of the HTML elements left behind were related to layout. A few of these tags are briefly mentioned here for historical reasons and to demonstrate why they should not be used.

One relatively common proprietary layout tag is **<spacer>**, supported only by Netscape 3.*x* and 4.*x* browsers. The **<spacer>** tag enables users to create invisible regions to push text and other objects around the browser screen. In many ways, this element is a response to the invisible, single-pixel GIF trick discussed in the previous section. Just to get the flavor of the tag, the following is an example of using **<spacer>** to create an invisible runaround region 150 pixels high and 100 pixels across:

```
... text...
<spacer type="block" height="150" width="100" align="left">
... text...
```

TIP *If you must provide the function of a* **<spacer>** *tag, the invisible GIF trick discussed in the previous section is a much better solution.*

TIP *Interestingly, some older WYSIWYG editors seem to like to use* **<spacer>** *in conjunction with table-based layouts. Designers should avoid its use in all instances and cleanup any occurrences of the tag.*

Another layout tag, **<multicol>**, is also unique to Netscape 3.*x* and 4.*x* browsers. This element allows page designers to specify text in multiple columns, which are rendered with equal width. The basic syntax is summarized here:

```
<multicol cols="number of columns"
          gutter="gutter width in pixels or percentage"
          width="column width in pixels or percentage">

Text to put in column form

</multicol>
```

An example of two-column text using this syntax would be as follows:

```
<multicol cols="2" gutter="50" width="80%">
This only works in Netscape, so don't try this at home!
The rain in Spain falls mainly on the plain. Now is the time
for all good men to come to the aid of the country.

...more text here to create columns...

</multicol>
```

Finally, the much maligned **<layer>** tag can be used only in Netscape 4.*x* browsers to position content at arbitrary positions on the page. For example,

```
<layer name="layer1" bgcolor="#ff0000" left="100" top="100">
   I am positioned!
</layer>
```

would position the text 100 pixels from the top and left of the browser window or enclosing positioned layer. While this seems to provide a powerful facility for layout, the same can be accomplished in CSS in a more cross-platform manner.

All the elements presented here do not degrade gracefully and layouts will fail somewhat catastrophically in nonsupporting browsers. These tags are presented primarily as an example to explain why page designers should avoid the use of proprietary HTML elements when designing pages. Figure 6-2 shows how different a layout may look in a browser that does not support a proprietary tag compared to one that does.

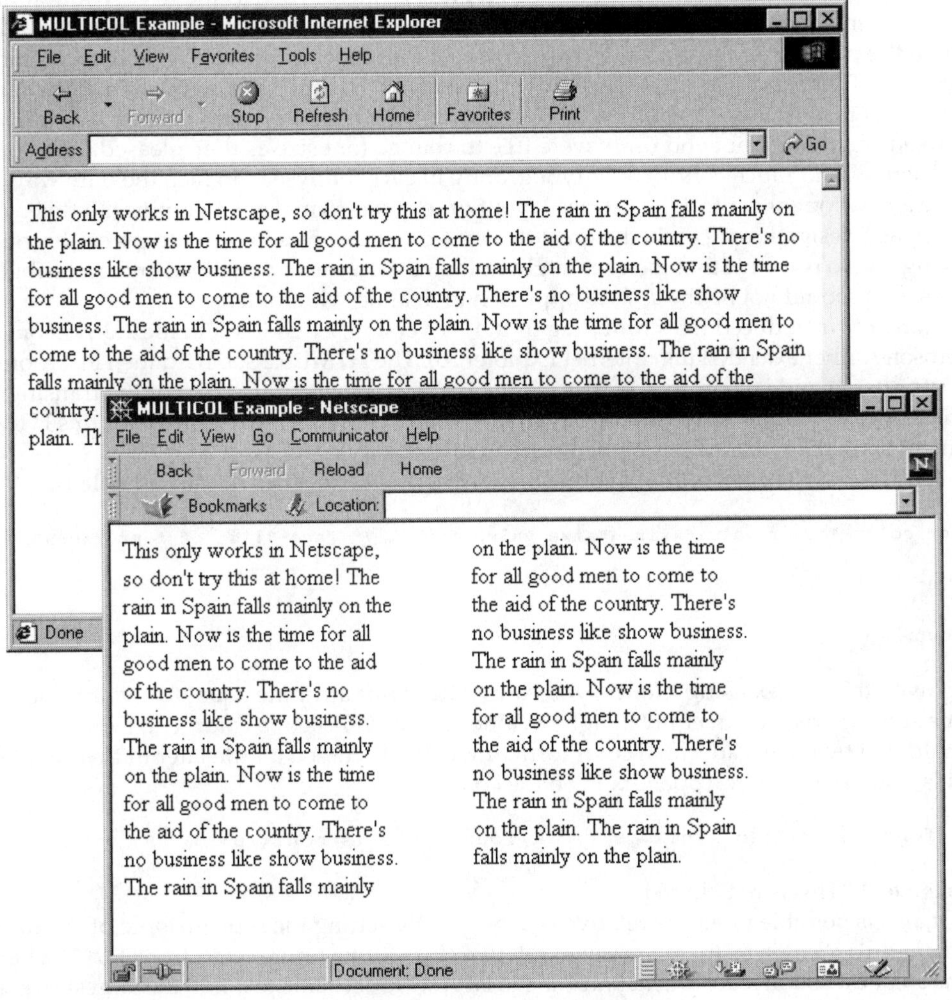

FIGURE 6-2 The <multicol> tag under Internet Explorer and Netscape 4.*x*

Like other browser-specific tags such as **<blink>**, **<marquee>**, and **<bgsound>,** which are discussed in Chapter 9, these proprietary tags really should never be used. Most of what they provide can be accomplished with tables, as discussed in the next chapter, or style sheets, as discussed in Chapter 10. If, however, you are faced with such tags, you can find a complete reference to their syntax in Appendix A. For now, let's move away from the limited layout capabilities of HTML and turn our attention to fonts and then colors and backgrounds.

Fonts

In addition to better support for layout, Web page designers have long desired to be able to specify fonts in their documents. Initially, HTML supported only two fonts, a proportional font and a fixed-width font. Under browsers such as Netscape and Internet Explorer, the proportional font was usually Times or Times New Roman, whereas the fixed-width font was Courier. To set text into Courier, page authors would use the **<tt>** tag. Otherwise, all text on the page generally was in the proportional font unless it was preformatted within a **<pre>** tag. There also was little control over the size of the font, even in relative terms. The font size of the browser generally was 12 point for the variable-width font and 10 point for the fixed-width font, but end users were free to change font size as they pleased.

There wasn't much control over typography in early browsers. In fact, the only way to use a new font or control the precise layout of text was to make it a graphic. To this day, many page designers still embed a great deal of text as graphics in order to precisely control spacing and to use fonts that the user might not have. Because of download and accessibility issues, this should not be the *de facto* approach to dealing with fonts.

Netscape introduced the **<font>** tag in the 1.1 version, extended it in the 2.0 version, and Microsoft further extended it in Internet Explorer 3.0. The HTML 3.2 standard then incorporated the **<font>** tag and it continues to be used by many designers as it is part of the transitional variants of HTML and XHTML. However, like many layout facilities, the use of this HTML element should be phased out in the future in favor of style sheets.

The basic syntax of <**font**> beyond core attributes like **id**, **class**, **style** and **title** is

```
<font color="color value" size="size value from 1-7" face="list of font faces">

styled text here

</font>
```

Given this syntax using **<font>,** you can set the **color** attribute equal to a valid color name such as "red" or an equivalent hex value such as #FF0000 to color text. Don't be intimidated by the hexadecimal color form; it will be discussed a little later in this chapter and is also presented in Appendix E. So the code

```
<p><font color="red">This is red.</font> This is not.</p>
```

sets the text "This is red" in red.

It also is possible to set the relative size of type by setting the **size** attribute of the **font** element. In a Web page, there are seven relative sizes for text numbered from **1** to **7**, where **1** is the smallest text in a document and **7** is the largest. To set some text into the largest size, use

```
<p><font size="7">This is big.</font> This is not.</p>
```

By default, the typical size of text is **3**; this can be overridden with the **basefont** element discussed later in this chapter. If the font size is not known but the text should be made just one size bigger, the author can use an alternative sizing value such as **<font size="+1">** instead of specifying the size directly. The **+** and **-** syntax makes it possible to bring the font size up or down a specified number of settings. The values for this form of the **size** attribute should range from **+1** to **+6** and **-1** to **-6**. It is not possible to specify **<font size="+10">** because there are only seven sizes. If the increase or decrease goes beyond acceptable sizes, the font generally defaults at the largest or smallest size, respectively.

Lastly, the **face** attribute can be set to the name of the font to render the text. So, to render a particular phrase in Verdana, use the following markup:

```
<p><font face="Verdana">This is in Verdana.</font> This is not.</p>
```

The browser then reads this HTML fragment and renders the text in the different font—but only for users who have the font installed on their systems. This raises an interesting problem: What happens if a user doesn't have the font specified? Using the **face** attribute, it is possible to specify a comma-delimited list of fonts to attempt one by one before defaulting to the normal proportional or fixed-width font. The fragment shown here would first try Arial, then Helvetica, and finally Sans-Serif before giving up and using whatever the current browser font is:

```
<p><font face="Arial, Helvetica, Sans-serif">This should be in a
different font</font> than this.</p>
```

Although it is nearly impossible to know what fonts users might have on their systems, the previous example shows how a little guesswork can be applied to take advantage of the **face** attribute. Most Macintosh, Windows, and Unix users have a standard set of fonts. If equivalent fonts are specified, it might be possible to provide similar page renderings across platforms. Table 6-1 shows some of the fonts that can be found on Macintosh, Windows, and Unix systems.

NOTE *Modern browsers generally support default fonts of serif, sans-serif, and monospace as they are included in all CSS-aware browsers. Generally, one of these generic names is given at the end of any font listing.*

TABLE 6-1 Sample System Fonts by Platform Type

Windows	Macintosh	Unix*
Arial	Chicago	Charter
Comic Sans MS	Courier	Clean
Courier New	Geneva	Courier
Impact	Helvetica	Fixed
Times New Roman	Monaco	Helvetica
Symbol	New York	Lucida
Verdana	Palatino	Sans Serif

PART III

TABLE 6-1 Sample System Fonts by Platform Type *(continued)*

Windows	Macintosh	Unix*
Wingdings	Symbol	Serif
	Times	Symbol
		Times
		Utopia

* Unix fonts vary; this is just meant to show most of the common fonts under a standard X-Windows environment.

Given the similarity of these fonts, it generally is safe to use the combinations of font faces shown in this code fragment and achieve approximately the same results across platforms.

```
<p>
<font face="Arial,Helvetica,sans-serif">A sans-serif font</font>
<br />
<font face="Verdana, Arial, Helvetica, sans-serif">
A sans-serif font 2</font>
<br />
<font face="'Times New Roman', Times, serif">A serif font</font>
<br />
<font face="Georgia, Times New Roman, Times, serif">A serif font 2</font>
<br />
<font face="'Courier New',Courier, monospace">A monospaced font</font>
</p>
```

A rendering of these fonts on a Windows system and a Macintosh system is shown here as a comparison.

Fonts on a PC	*Fonts on a Macintosh*
A sans-serif font A sans-serif font 2 A serif font A serif font 2 A mono spaced font	A sans-serif font A sans-serif font 2 A serif font A serif font 2 A mono spaced font

A complete example demonstrating all the **font** element attributes and their use is presented in the following example. A rendering is shown in Figure 6-3.

```
<!DOCTYPE html PUBLIC "-//W3C//DTD XHTML 1.0 Transitional//EN"
 "http://www.w3.org/TR/xhtml1/DTD/xhtml1-transitional.dtd">
<html xmlns="http://www.w3.org/1999/xhtml" lang="en">
<head>
<title>Font Element Demo</title>
<meta http-equiv="content-type" content="text/html; charset=ISO-8859-1" />
</head>
<body>
```

```
<h2 align="center">Font Sizing</h2>

<font size="1">Font size 1</font><br />
<font size="2">Font size 2</font><br />
<font size="3">Font size 3</font><br />
<font size="4">Font size 4</font><br />
<font size="5">Font size 5</font><br />
<font size="6">Font size 6</font><br />
<font size="7">Font size 7</font><br />

This is <font size="+2">+2 from the base size.</font>
Now it is <font size="-1">-1 from base size.</font>

<h2 align="center">Font Color</h2>

<font color="red">Red Text</font><br />
<font color="#ffcc66">Hex #ffcc66 color</font>

<h2 align="center">Font Face</h2>

<font face="Arial">Set font to common fonts like Arial</font><br />
<font face="'Viner Hand ITC'">Take a chance on an unusual
                              font</font><br />
Even set text to dingbat characters
<font face="Webdings">f3khilqm </font><br />

<h2 align="center">Common Font Face Combinations</h2>


<font face="Arial,Helvetica,sans-serif">
Arial,Helvetica,sans-serif</font><br />


<font face="Verdana, Arial, Helvetica, sans-serif">
Verdana, Arial, Helvetica, sans-serif</font><br />


<font face="'Times New Roman',Times,serif">
Times New Roman,Times,serif</font><br />


<font face="Georgia, 'Times New Roman', Times, serif">
Georgia, Times New Roman, Times, serif</font><br />


<font face="'Courier New', Courier, monospace">
Courier New, Courier, monospace</font><br />

<h2 align="center">Combination</h2>

You can <font size="+2" color="red" face="Arial">set all font
attributes at once</font>!

</body>
</html>
```

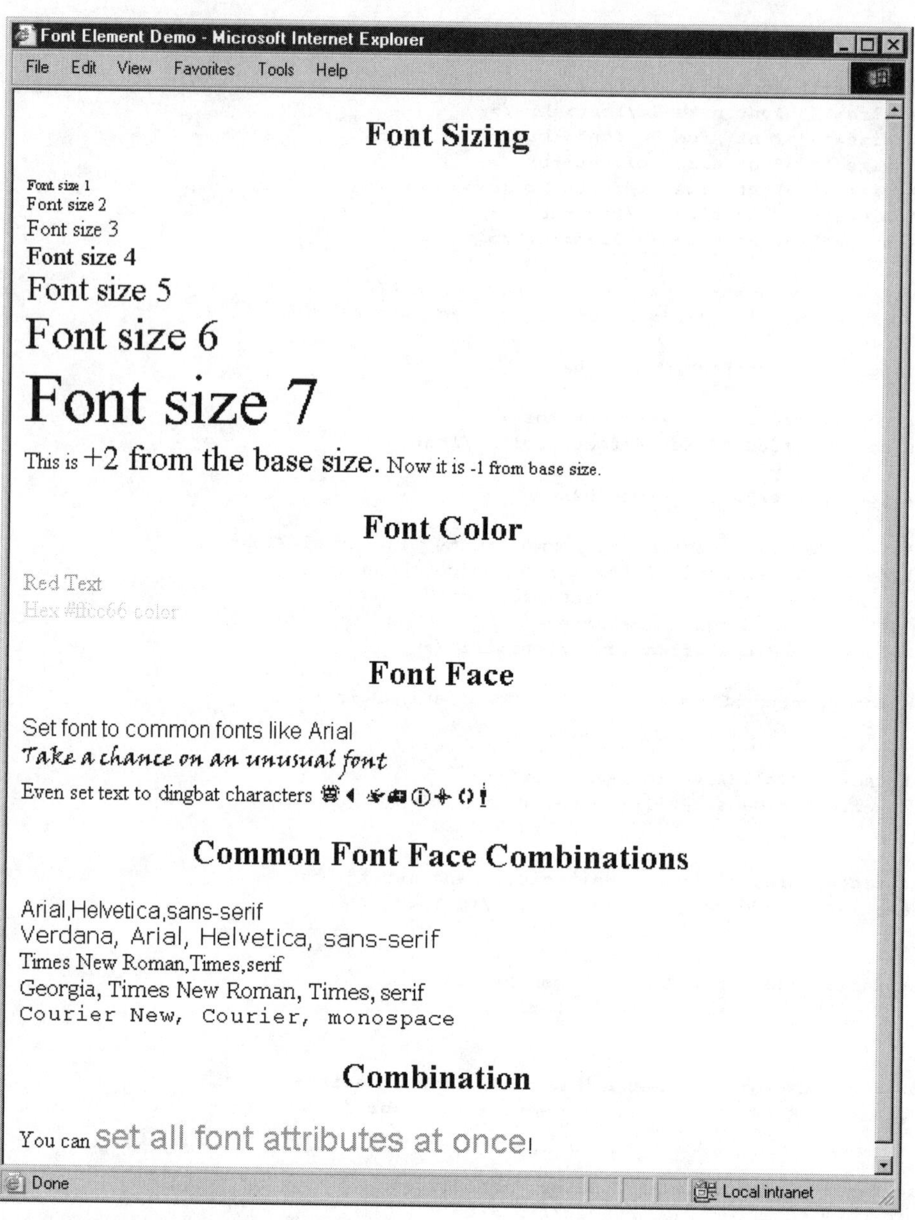

FIGURE 6-3 <font> demonstration

NOTE *The **<font>** tag is deprecated under strict HTML 4 and XHTML in favor of style sheets. However, its use is common and probably will continue for some time.*

Document-Wide Font Settings

In some cases, it might be appropriate to change the font size, color, or face document-wide. To do this, use the **basefont** element in the **head** of the document. The **<basefont>** tag should occur only once in the document and includes major attributes such as **color**, **face**, and **size**. Like the **<font>** tag, the **color** attribute should be set to an RGB hexadecimal equivalent value or color name. The **face** attribute should be set to a font name or comma-delimited list of fonts. Finally, the **size** attribute should be set to a size value between **1** and **7**. To set the font of the document in red Arial or Helvetica with a relative size of 6, use **<basefont color="red" face="Arial, Helvetica" size="6" />** within the **head** element of the document. See Appendix A for more information on **<basefont>**.

NOTE *Like* **<font>**, *the* **<basefont>** *tag is deprecated under strict versions of HTML and XHTML. CSS should always be used for document-level font control if possible.*

Web Fonts

While the common font faces specified in the previous section are safe to use, the typical end user may have many other fonts. For example, users of Microsoft Office also probably have access to fonts such as Algerian, Book Antiqua, Bookman Old Style, Britannic Bold, Desdemona, Garamond, Century Gothic, Haettenschweiller, and many others. Browser applications may even install fonts. For example, since Internet Explorer 4.0, Microsoft has included a font called WebDings, which provides many common icons for use on the page. Some of these icons would be useful for navigation, like arrows, whereas others look like audio or video symbols that could provide an indication of link contents before selection. Just using font sizing, colors, and simple layout, it is possible to make interesting but very browser-specific layouts with WebDings, as shown in Figure 6-4.

```
<!DOCTYPE html PUBLIC "-//W3C//DTD XHTML 1.0 Transitional//EN"
"http://www.w3.org/TR/xhtml1/DTD/xhtml1-transitional.dtd">

<html xmlns="http://www.w3.org/1999/xhtml" lang="en">
<head>
<title>Simple WebDing Demo</title>
<meta http-equiv="content-type" content="text/html; charset=ISO-8859-1" />
</head>
<body bgcolor="blue">
<h1 align="center">WebDing City!</h1>

<font face="WebDings" style="font-size: 64pt;" color="yellow">&#061;</font><br />

<font face="WebDings" style="font-size: 48pt;"
color="white">    &#217;  &#217; </font>

<font face="WebDings" style="font-size: 32pt;" color="Gray">   
&#106;</font>

<br /><br />

<font face="WebDings" style="font-size: 64pt;">
&#067;&#067;&#067;&#067;&#067;&#067;&#077;</font>
```

```
</body>
</html>
```

A common set of icons for the Web actually is not a new idea. The W3C at one point had a working draft covering a predefined set of icon-like symbols, although this does not appear to be gaining any support in the industry. The Microsoft font actually includes many of these symbols, but does not use the same naming convention. It might eventually be possible to include **&audio;** to add an audio icon to a Web page, but for now setting the WebDings value or inserting an image is the best choice.

Downloadable Fonts

Although the Microsoft solution to promote a common set of font faces including dingbats like WebDings helps address the issue of fonts on the Web, it isn't a very flexible approach outside the Windows world. Although many Windows, Macintosh, and Unix systems have similar fonts, consider the situation in which the page author wants to use a customized font. In this case, the page author is typically forced to create a static image of a word or phrase

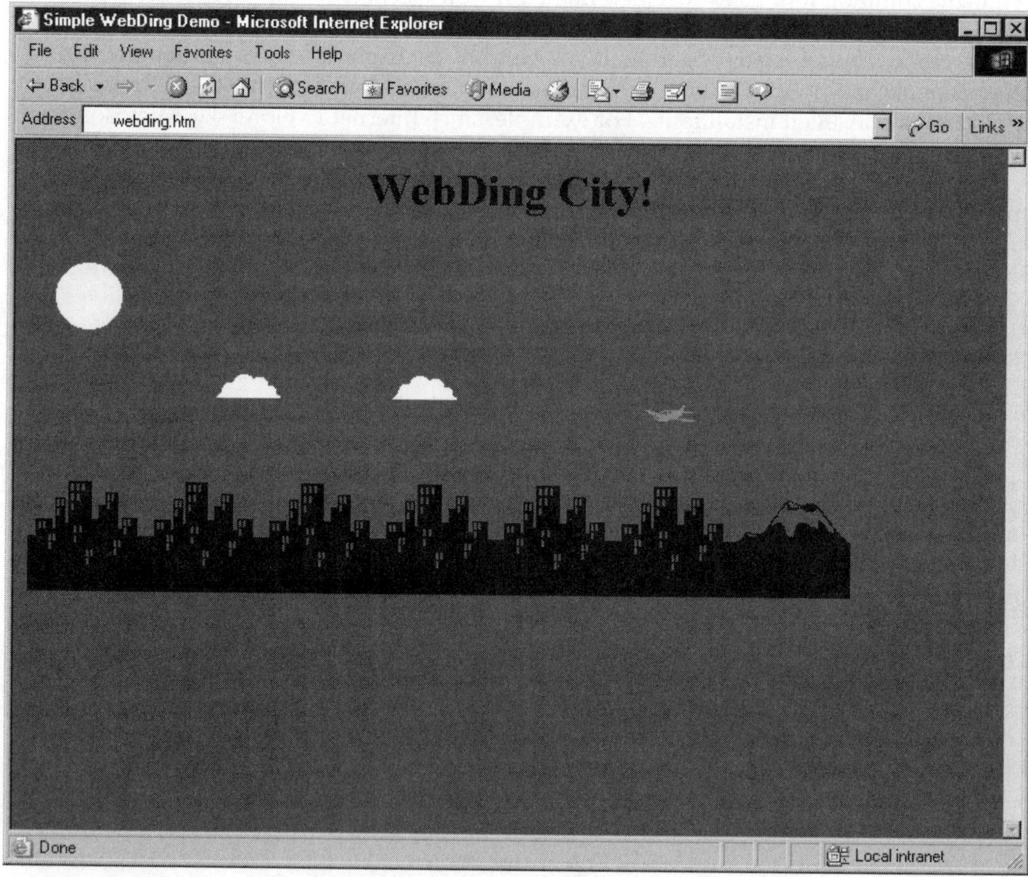

FIGURE 6-4 Example page using Microsoft's WebDings font

in the desired font. While a common practice, this is not really an appropriate approach. Image-based text takes longer to download, is difficult to edit, does not work with search engines unless an **alt** attribute is properly used, doesn't typically scale well with screen resolution, and can't even be copied and pasted by the user.

The best solution for fonts on the Web would be to come up with some cross-platform form of font that could be downloaded to the browser on the fly. Although this sounds easy enough, the problem with downloadable fonts is that they must be highly compact. Page viewers must not be able to steal the font from the page and install it on their own machines. Both of the major browser vendors have supported downloadable fonts at one time or another. Netscape's solution initially used a download font system in Netscape 4.*x* called Dynamic Fonts, based on BitStream's TrueDoc (www.truedoc.com). However, this technology has not been continued in Netscape 6.*x*/7.*x* and while still around is not favored in the developer community even though it has been implemented as an ActiveX control for Internet Explorer. Internet Explorer supports a native browser solution for Web type called OpenType (www.microsoft.com/typography). However, given that the W3C is working on a dynamic font specification, eventually a third approach may arise as well.

PART III

TrueDoc Dynamic Fonts

To use TrueDoc dynamic fonts under older Netscape browsers or, more commonly, to add support for Internet Explorer, the page author simply uses the face attribute of a **<font>** tag, or a style sheet attribute as discussed in Chapter 10, to set the font face. If the user does not have the font installed on his or her system, a downloadable font linked to the page can be fetched and used to render the page. To include a link to a TrueDoc font definition file in Portable Font Resource (PFR) format, use a **<link>** tag and set the **rel** attribute to **fontdef** and the **src** attribute equal to the URL where the font definition file resides. The **<link>** tag must be found within the **head** of the document. An example of how this element would be used is shown here:

```
<!DOCTYPE html PUBLIC "-//W3C//DTD XHTML 1.0 Transitional//EN"
"http://www.w3.org/TR/xhtml1/DTD/xhtml1-transitional.dtd">
<html xmlns="http://www.w3.org/1999/xhtml"  lang="en">
<head>
<title>TrueDoc Font Demo</title>
<meta http-equiv="content-type" content="text/html; charset=ISO-8859-1" />
<script type= "text/javascript"
        src="http://www.truedoc.com/activex/tdserver.js"></script>
<link rel="FONTDEF" src="http://www.truedoc.com/pfrs/Calligraph421.pfr" />
<!-- purposeful validation error because of non-standard link tag usage -->
</head>
<body>
<font face="Calligraph421 BT" size="7">TrueDoc font demo</font>
</body>
</html>
```

In this demo, we point at remote fonts online and require the use of JavaScript for Internet Explorer browsers to download a font player. The demo will work in Netscape 4.*x* and Internet Explorer browsers that download the WebFont player. Other users will see a default font. As you can see, the main obstacle to using dynamic fonts with TrueDoc technology is making the .pfr for the file and making sure the browser can view such a file. Because of the difficulty of making fonts, I resort to using one of a variety of PFR files, which are made available online by BitStream. I also add the freely available script from truedoc.com to address browser issues. However, regardless of this workaround, the technology is simply not well supported beyond the free online fonts and should probably be avoided in favor of the Internet Explorer technology described next.

NOTE *Another drawback to the TrueDoc approach to dynamic fonts is that it might cause screen flashing in versions of Netscape 4.x. This can be disorienting for the user.*

Microsoft's Dynamic Fonts

Microsoft Internet Explorer has provided a way to embed fonts since the 4.*x* generation version of the browser. To include a font, you must first build the page using the **<font>** tag, or style sheet rules that set fonts, as discussed in Chapter 10. When creating your page, don't worry about whether or not the end user has the font installed; it will be downloaded. Next, use Microsoft's Web Embedding Fonts Tool available at www.microsoft.com/typography to analyze the font usage on the page. The program should create an .eot file that contains the embedded fonts. The font use information then will be added to the page in the form of CSS (Cascading Style Sheets) style rules, as shown here:

```
<!DOCTYPE HTML PUBLIC "-//W3C//DTD HTML 4.01 Transitional//EN">
<html>
<head>
<title>Microsoft Font Test</title>
<style type="text/css">
<!--
  @font-face {
    font-family: Ransom;
    font-style:  normal;
    font-weight: normal;
    src: url(http://www.htmlref.com/fonts/ransom.eot);
  }
-->
</style>
</head>
<body>
<font face="ransom" size="6">Example Ransom Note Font</font>
</body>
</html>
```

A possible rendering of font embedding is shown in Figure 6-5.

TIP *Be careful—downloadable fonts can be easily disabled in Internet Explorer depending on the security setting of the browser.*

Like the TrueDoc approach, you first must create a font file and reference it from the file that uses the font. Again, as the example shows, it might be useful to define a fonts directory within your Web site to store font files, similar to storing image files for site use.

FIGURE 6-5 Embedded fonts increase design choices.

The use of the **@font-face** acts as a pseudo-element that allows you to bring any number of fonts into a page. The form of the font embedding supported by Microsoft conforms to the emerging W3C specification for font embedding. Again, for more information on embedded fonts under Internet Explorer, and links to font file creation tools such as WEFT, see the Microsoft Typography site (www.microsoft.com/typography).

It would seem that in order to make fonts cross-platform, it should be possible to provide links to both Microsoft and TrueDoc font technology within the same page. This really adds only one line or a few style rules as the rest of the document would continue to use the same **<font face="">** statements. TrueDoc technology also supports an ActiveX control to allow Internet Explorer users to view their style of embedded fonts. Given the extra download involved, the double font statement approach is preferred. Unfortunately, cross-platform downloadable fonts aren't that easy. Many Macintosh browsers have issues with downloadable font technology and Unix browsers are nearly completely left out. Some server-oriented approaches such as GlyphGate (www.glyphgate.com) have attempted to rectify this issue, but so far, the use of cross-platform fonts on the Web is minimal.

Colors in HTML

Transitional versions of HTML and XHTML support color settings for text as well as for the background of the document, or even individual table cells. With style sheets, you will see that it is also possible to set both foreground and background color for nearly any element. There are 16 widely known color names defined in HTML. These names and their associated hex RGB values are shown in Table 6-2.

To set a particular section of text yellow, simply surround the content with **<font color="yellow">** and **</font>**. Of course, in addition to the simple color names listed in Table 6-2, there are many others, some of which seem to have been introduced by the browser vendors; these are listed in Appendix E. The problem with using browser-defined colors is that they don't always do what they are supposed to do. Even worse, you can invent your own colors. Try setting the following and viewing it under Netscape and Microsoft Internet Explorer:

```
<body bgcolor="html color names are troublesome">
```

TABLE 6-2 Common HTML 4.0 Color Names and Hex Values

Black (#000000)	Green (#008000)
Silver (#C0C0C0)	Lime (#00FF00)
Gray (#808080)	Olive (#808000)
White (#FFFFFF)	Yellow (#FFFF00)
Maroon (#800000)	Navy (#000080)
Red (#FF0000)	Blue (#0000FF)
Purple (#800080)	Teal (#008080)
Fuchsia (#FF00FF)	Aqua (#00FFFF)

This color name is totally invalid, but it still results in a shade of green that is very distinct in each browser. It is possible to make up colors like "chilidog brown" or "stale beer yellow," but this is no more recommended than using the browser-defined color of "dodgerblue." Using hex color values is the preferred way to set colors because some nonstandard color names are not supported correctly across browsers.

Instead of using color names, we ought to use values that represent the color that we want. To understand how to come up with a color value, first consider that a computer displays color using a combination of red, green, and blue. We call this additive color process RGB color. The easiest way to think of RGB color is as a set of three dials that control the amount of red, green, and blue mixed into the final color. Because of the way computers calculate things, the color values range from 0 to 255 in decimal or 00 to FF if we count in hexadecimal like a computer scientist. So a color specified by 0,255,0, or equivalently 00,FF,00, is equivalent to the green dial turned all the way up and the other dials turned off. This is a pure green. Equivalently, FF,00,00 is pure red. Finally, 00,00,FF is pure blue. Obviously, all dials off at 00,00,00 is the absence of color or simply black, whereas all dials on at FF,FF,FF is white. In HTML, we set these hex values using a pound sign and the equivalent RR, GG, and BB values are run together; for example, we could use the hex value #FFFF00 for the **color** attribute instead of the word "yellow."

Rather than becoming an expert at hexadecimal, it is easy to use a Web editor to pick a color or to see Appendix E, which explains the various colors available under HTML. A color reference can be found online at http://www.htmlref.com/colorchart.html.

Color Attributes for body

The **body** element has numerous attributes that you can use to affect the display of content in the body of the document including setting the background color, the color of text, and the color of links. One of the most commonly used **body** element attributes, **bgcolor**, defines the document's background color. Hexadecimal RGB values and color names can be used with **bgcolor** and the four attributes to follow. To create a white background, the attribute can be set to **<body bgcolor="#FFFFFF">** (hexadecimal) or simply **<body bgcolor="white">**. The **text** attribute of the **body** element defines the color of text in the entire document. The attribute takes a color in the form of either a hex code or color name. So **<body bgcolor="white" text="green">** creates a white page with green text. Note that the text color can be overridden in the text by applying the **font** element to selected text with its **color** attribute, as discussed earlier in the chapter.

Aside from the body text, it is also possible to define the color of links by setting the **body** element attributes: **link**, **alink**, and **vlink**. The attribute **link** defines the color of unvisited links in a document. For example, if you've set your background color to black, it might be more useful to use a light link color instead of the standard blue. The **alink attribute** defines the color of the link as it is being clicked. This often happens too quickly to be noticed, but can create a flash effect, if desired. For a more subdued Web experience, it might be better to set the **alink** attribute to match either the **link** attribute or the next one, **vlink**. The **vlink** attribute defines the color of a link after it has been visited, which under many user agents is purple. Many authors wish to set the value of the **vlink** attribute to red, which makes sense given standard color interpretation. So you can create a white page with green text, red links, and fuchsia-colored visited links using the code presented here:

```
<!DOCTYPE html PUBLIC "-//W3C//DTD XHTML 1.0 Transitional//EN"
"http://www.w3.org/TR/xhtml1/DTD/xhtml1-transitional.dtd">
<html xmlns="http://www.w3.org/1999/xhtml" lang="en">
<head>
<title>Colors</title>
<meta http-equiv="content-type" content="text/html; charset=ISO-8859-1" />
</head>
<body bgcolor="#FFFFFF" text="#008000" link="#FF0000"
      vlink="#FF00FF" alink="#FF0000">
  Body content<br />
  <a href="#">Visited Link</a>
  <a href="badlink">Unvisited Link</a>
</body>
</html>
```

Besides setting link state colors, it is possible to set hover colors for links. Although this does require the use of style sheets, it is presented here for completeness. To make the link rollover to a green color, you would use a style sheet like the following:

```
<style type="text/css">
  a:hover {color: green;}
</style>
```

Of course, if you are going to style links with CSS it is probably best to style all states of the link in CSS as well. You can find more information on this in Chapter 10.

Using Color

Page designers should be forewarned not to choose link colors that can confuse their viewers. For example, reversing link colors so that visited links are blue and unvisited links are red could confuse a user. While it is unlikely that a page author would do such a thing, it has been done more than once—particularly in situations where the look and feel is the driving force of the site. Page designers also run into trouble when they set all link values to blue with the belief that users will revisit sections thinking they haven't been there before. While this might make sense from a marketing standpoint, the frustration that results from lost navigation cues overrides any potential benefit from extra visits. Likewise, setting all the link colors to red could create similar trouble because users may think they have seen the site already.

Designers also must be extremely careful to preserve readability when setting text and background colors. Page designers often are tempted to use light colors on light backgrounds or dark colors on dark backgrounds. For example, a gray text on a black background might look cool, but will it look cool on every monitor? If a user's monitor and color settings are much different from your monitor, it will be unreadable. White and black always make a good pairing and red certainly is useful in small doses. The best combination, in terms of contrast, actually is yellow and black, but imagine the headache from reading a page that looks like a road sign. Despite the generally high contrast, designers should be careful of white text on a black background particularly when font sizes are very small or thin font faces are in use.

Background Images

In addition to setting background colors, you also can change the appearance of a Web page by setting a background image using the **background** attribute of the **body** element. The value of **background** should be the URL for a GIF or JPEG file, although in supporting browsers PNG files might also be acceptable. So you might use **<body background="images/tile.gif">** to set the path to a background tile in your site's images directory. The URL is arbitrary; you may store the files wherever, and in fact, you can just as easily include a complete URL to access an image at another site, but this isn't suggested.

Background images will repeat, or *tile,* in the background of a Web page. This can make or break a Web page design. Imagine someone using the **background** attribute to place a 200 × 300 pixel JPEG of a favorite dog on his or her home page. The dog's image would repeat, both vertically and horizontally, in the background of the page. This would make the dog's owner very happy—and make the page very difficult to read! Figure 6-6 shows an example of a bothersome repeating background.

In general, it's a poor design decision to use complex background images. Taking the subtle approach can backfire as well. Some users attempt to create a light background such as a texture or watermark thinking that, like paper, it will create a classy effect. The problem with this is that under many monitors, the image might be difficult to make out at all, or the texture might even slightly blur the text on top of it. Just like setting background colors, the most important consideration is the degree of contrast. Always attempt to keep the foreground and background at a high level of contrast so that users can read the information. What good is an impressive layout if nobody can read it?

If you want a background, you can use image manipulation programs such as Photoshop to create seamless background tiles that are more pleasing to the eye and show no seam. Figure 6-7 illustrates a repeating background tile.

Background images, or tiles, also can be used to create other effects. A single GIF image 5 pixels high and 1,600 pixels wide could be used to create a useful page layout. The first 200 horizontal pixels of the GIF could be color, and the rest could be white. Assuming 1,600 pixels as the maximum width of a browser, this tile would repeat only vertically, thus creating the illusion of a two-tone background. This usage has become very common on the Web. Many sites use the left-hand color for navigation buttons, while the remaining area is used for text, as shown in Figure 6-8. However, to guarantee that content appears on top of the appropriate section of the background image, you need to have precise control over text layout. This calls for tables or CSS.

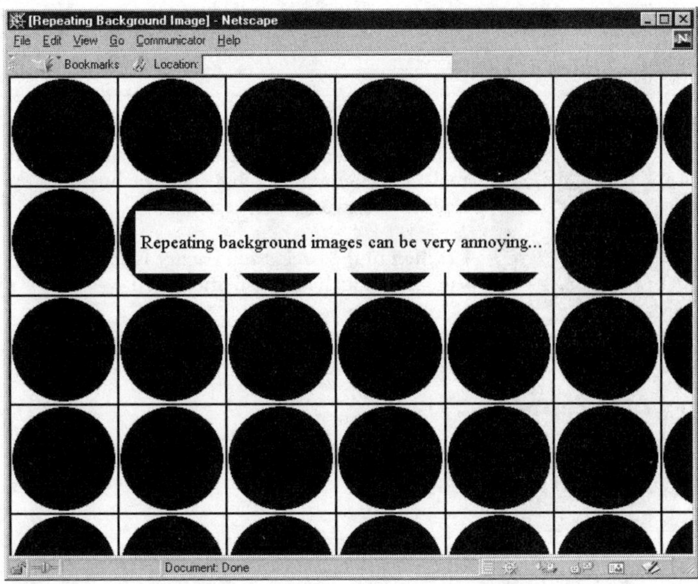

FIGURE 6-6 Repeating background image

Be very careful when segmenting the screen using a background tile. For example, many people are tempted to create page layout with vertical sectioning, as shown in Figure 6-9.

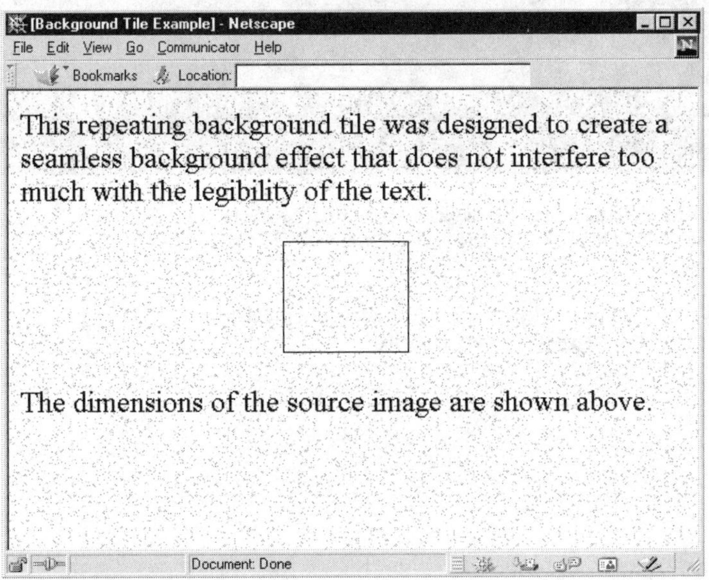

FIGURE 6-7 Background tiles without visible seam

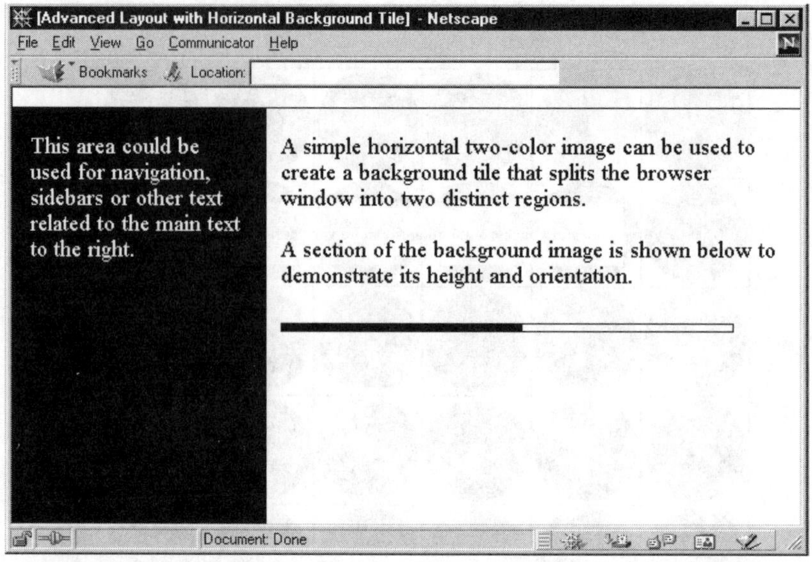

FIGURE 6-8 Sidebar layout using background tile (horizontal GIF)

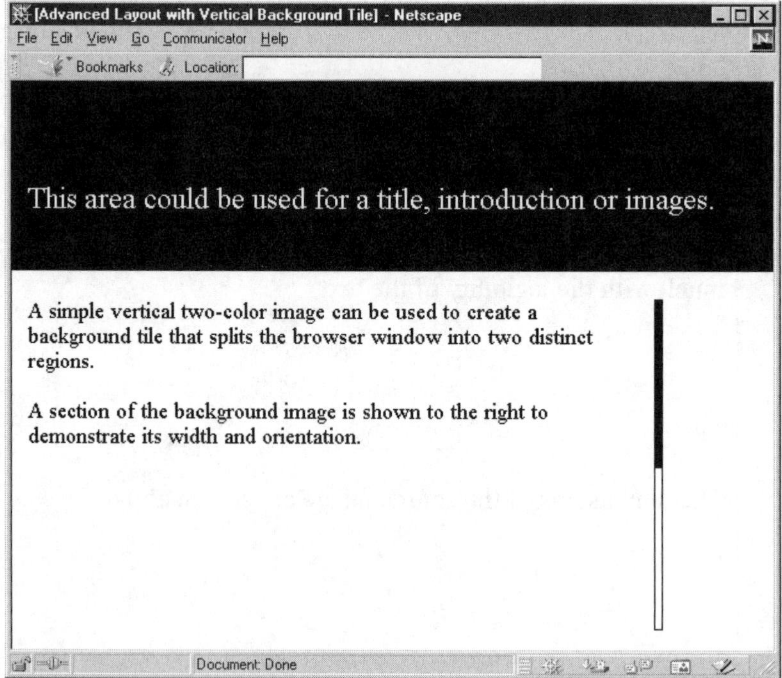

FIGURE 6-9 Layout using background tile (vertical GIF)

However, there is a problem with this layout. Won't the colored bar repeat? Quite possibly, because the length of page content can be hard to determine. Viewers might find the bar repeating over and over with content being lost on top. A solution might be to make the background tile very tall. However, this not only increases file size, but also begs the question of how tall is enough? Because content can vary from page to page and increase or decrease over time, determining the width is next to impossible. It would appear that the same problem would occur with sidebar style tiles. This generally is not the case given that pages usually do not scroll left to right, and monitor resolutions rarely exceed 1,600 pixels. Of course, if they did you could make the image even wider. In either case, the problem of background tile repeats is solved with style sheets that provide the **background-repeat** property to set the direction and frequency of a tile's repeat pattern. This is discussed further in Chapter 10. There are a few other HTML-specific background features touched on briefly here.

NOTE *Another problem with background tiles is that some designers try to minimize file size and download time. For example, a designer can make the background images a single pixel tall; this might cause screen painting problems because the background will have to be tiled as many times as the screen is high in pixels. With a slow video card, this may produce an annoying sweeping effect. To avoid the background painting problem, consider balancing physical file size and download size. So a background image can be 5 or 10 pixels or even taller without really affecting download speed much, but improving painting speed significantly.*

Internet Explorer Background Attributes

Internet Explorer supports a few special attributes for the **body** element that might solve background image and layout problems without resorting to style sheets. The **bgproperties** attribute offers a solution to the problem of scrolling background images. At present, however, it is supported only by Internet Explorer 3.0 and beyond. The attribute **bgproperties="fixed'** for the **<body>** tag will, under Internet Explorer, allow text and images to scroll while the background image accessed with the **background** attribute remains in place. Think of this as a watermark-like effect. It is possible to imitate this action in a cross-browser fashion using the CSS property **background-attachment,** as discussed in Chapter 10.

Controlling Page Margins

Under many browsers, the **body** element includes attributes for setting page margins. Internet Explorer and Netscape take different HTML-based approaches to setting margins. Under Internet Explorer, there are two primary **<body>** attributes that affect margins: **leftmargin** and **topmargin**. Each is set with a pixel value. For example, **leftmargin="25"** creates a margin of 25 pixels between the left edge of the browser window and its content; **topmargin="15"** creates a 15-pixel margin between the top of the browser window and its content, as well as at the bottom if the content extends that far. Under Netscape, use **marginheight** and **marginwidth** and set to similar values like so:

```
<body topmargin="15" leftmargin="15" marginheight="15" marginwidth="15">
```

Note *Microsoft Internet Explorer also supports the use of* **bottommargin** *as well as* **rightmargin** *attributes for the* **body** *element, though they are rarely used. See Appendix A for more information on these and other Internet Explorer proprietary changes.*

Most often, designers want to turn off all margins in order to bleed content, particularly to the edge of the browser screen. In HTML, this could be done using the following attribute values in the **<body>** tag:

```
<body topmargin="0" leftmargin="0" marginheight="0" marginwidth="0">
```

Of course, this approach to layout will be alleviated with style sheets. A simple rule in the **<style>** block found in the **<head>** of a document like so

```
<style type="text/css">
<!--
   body     {margin: 0px;}
-->
</style>
```

would also remove margins and should work under all CSS-compliant browsers. Both could be used just to be sure the margins are removed, even in older browsers.

Although many of the elements and attributes discussed in the last few sections are useful to control the layout, color, and background of a page, many of them are browser-specific or are deprecated under HTML 4 and XHTML, so you won't get cleanly validatable markup using many of these techniques. The goal should be to eventually provide this function solely with CSS. However, until all the problems with style sheets are worked out and browsers are upgraded for backward compatibility, as shown by the previous example, it might be necessary to use both layout forms for some time.

Summary

Designers desperately want pixel-level layout control of Web pages and support for fonts. Although HTML does not provide a great deal of support for layout, it really wasn't meant to. While it is easy to say that people shouldn't use HTML or even XHTML to lay out pages, the fact of the matter is that they wanted, and needed, to do so. In the past, there was no other possibility: CSS simply wasn't available and even now that it is, old habits die hard. The need for improved page design gave rise to the occasional abuse of HTML elements, "hacks" like the invisible pixel trick, and the rise of proprietary tags such as **<spacer>**.

Fortunately, today most of these tricks are no longer necessary and CSS can generally be used for simple layout improvements. However, despite the improvement in layout capabilities, fonts are still an open issue in HTML. Downloadable fonts still haven't hit the mainstream, but hopefully someday better fonts will become a reality on the Web. The next chapter presents tables that make it possible to create fairly precise layouts using HTML. However, it will also reveal that many of the problems raised in this chapter continue with tables, and will only diminish as style sheets continue to become more prevalent.

7

CHAPTER

Tables and Layout

A table is an orderly arrangement of data distributed across a grid of rows and columns similar to a spreadsheet. In printed documents, tables commonly serve a subordinate function, illustrating some point described by accompanying text. Tables still perform this illustrative function in HTML documents. However, because HTML alone does not offer the same layout capacities available to print designers, Web page tables also are commonly used to structure a page for layout. But unlike printed tables, HTML tables can contain information that is *dynamic,* or even interactive, such as the results of a database query. We'll see that even when their impressive layout duties are retired in favor of CSS, tables will still have an important role in the Web developer's toolbox.

Introduction to Tables

In its simplest form, a table places information inside the cells formed by dividing a rectangle into rows and columns. Most cells contain data; some cells, usually on the table's top or side, contain headings. HTML and XHTML represent a basic table using four elements. In markup, a table tag pair, **<table>** … **</table>**, contains an optional **caption** element, followed by one or more rows, **<tr>** … **</tr>**. Each row contains cells holding a heading, **<th>** … **</th>**, or data, **<td>** … **</td>**. However, for most purposes, the following example illustrates a basic table. Note that the only attribute used in this example is **border**, which is used to specify a 1-pixel border so it is clear what the table looks like. The rendering for the simple table under various browsers is shown in Figure 7-1.

```
<!DOCTYPE html PUBLIC "-//W3C//DTD XHTML 1.0 Transitional//EN"
"http://www.w3.org/TR/xhtml1/DTD/xhtml1-transitional.dtd">
<html xmlns="http://www.w3.org/1999/xhtml" lang="en">
<head>
<title>Simple Table Example</title>
<meta http-equiv="content-type" content="text/html; charset=ISO-8859-1" />
</head>
<body>

<table border="1">
<caption>Basic Fruit Comparison Chart</caption>
```

```
<tr>
  <th>Fruit</th>
  <th>Color</th>
</tr>

<tr>
  <td>Apple</td>
  <td>Red</td>
</tr>

<tr>
  <td>Kiwi</td>
  <td>Green</td>
</tr>

<tr>
  <td>Watermelon</td>
  <td>Pink</td>
</tr>
</table>
</body>
</html>
```

A table is made up of rows enclosed within **<tr>** … **</tr>**. The number of rows in the table is determined by the number of occurrences of the **tr** element. What about columns? Generally, the number of columns in a table is determined by the maximum number of data cells in one row indicated by **<td>** … **</td>**, or headings indicated by **<th>** … **</th>** within the table. The headings for the table are set using the **th** element. Generally, the browser renders the style of headings differently, usually centering the contents of the heading and placing the text in bold style. The actual cells of the table are indicated by the **td** element. Both the **td** and **th** elements can enclose an arbitrary amount of data of just about any type. In the previous example, a full paragraph of text could be enclosed in a table cell along with an image, lists, and links. The table might also have a caption enclosed within **<caption>** …

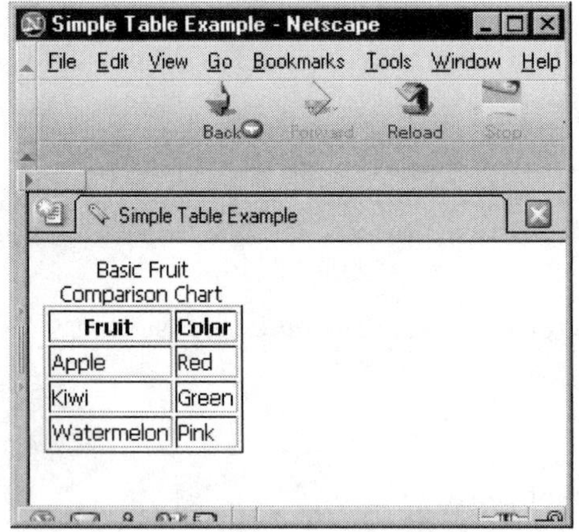

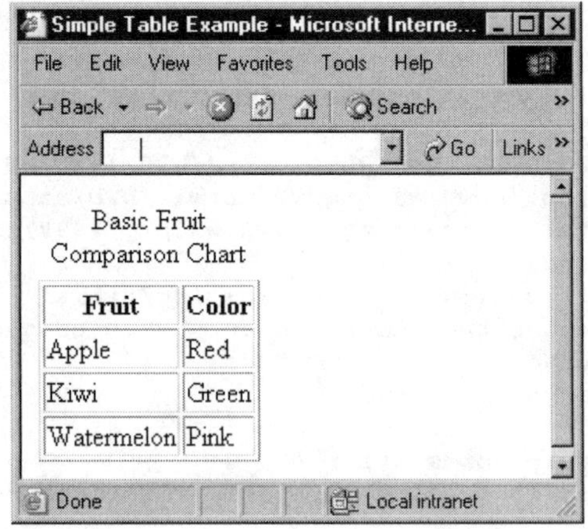

FIGURE 7-1 Browser renderings of a simple example

</caption>, whose contents generally are rendered above or below the table, indicating what the table contains.

NOTE *Under Internet Explorer 4 or better, it is possible to hint to the browser the number of columns used in the table by setting the **cols** attribute. This is used to improve rendering speed, but is nonstandard.*

Technically speaking, under HTML 4 transitional, the closing tags for the **<tr>**, **<th>**, and **<td>** tags are optional. Although this might make for cleaner-looking code in your HTML documents, HTML writers are still encouraged to use the closing tags, as well as indentation. This ensures that table cells and rows are clearly defined, particularly for nested tables. It also helps to avoid problems with versions of Netscape that often "break" tables that don't use closing tags for these elements. And because XHTML, which requires closing tags for all nonempty elements, is the new standard, you should always close table tags.

The rowspan and colspan Attributes

Whereas the preceding example shows that it is possible to create a table with a simple structure, what about when the table cells need to be larger or smaller? The following markup creates tables that are somewhat more complicated. By adding the **rowspan** and **colspan** attributes to the table elements, it is possible to create data cells that span a given number of rows or columns. The rendering of this code appears in Figure 7-2.


```
<!DOCTYPE html PUBLIC "-//W3C//DTD XHTML 1.0 Transitional//EN"
"http://www.w3.org/TR/xhtml1/DTD/xhtml1-transitional.dtd">
<html xmlns="http://www.w3.org/1999/xhtml" lang="en">
<head>
<title>ROWSPAN and COLSPAN</title>
<meta http-equiv="content-type" content="text/html; charset=ISO-8859-1" />
</head>
<body>

<table border="1">
  <caption>ROWSPAN Example</caption>
   <tr>
       <td rowspan="2">Element 1</td>
       <td>Element 2</td>
   </tr>
   <tr>
       <td>Element 3</td>
   </tr>
  </table>

<br /><br />

<table border="1">
  <caption>COLSPAN Example</caption>
    <tr>
       <td colspan="3">Element 1</td>
    </tr>
    <tr>
```

```
        <td>Element 2</td>
        <td>Element 3</td>
        <td>Element 4</td>
    </tr>
</table>

</body>
</html>
```

The basic idea of the **rowspan** and **colspan** attributes for **<td>** and **<th>** is to extend the size of the cells across two or more rows or columns, respectively. To set a cell to span three rows, use **<td rowspan="3">**; to set a heading to span two columns, use **<th colspan="2">**. Setting the value of **colspan** or **rowspan** to more than the number of columns or rows in the table should not extend the size of the table. Be aware, however, that some browsers require precise use of these span attributes. Consider the following markup:

```
<table border="1">
<tr>
    <td>Element 1</td>
    <td>Element 2</td>
    <td rowspan="2">Element 3</td>
</tr>

<tr>
    <td>Element 4</td>
    <td>Element 5</td>
    <td>Element 6</td>
</tr>
</table>
```

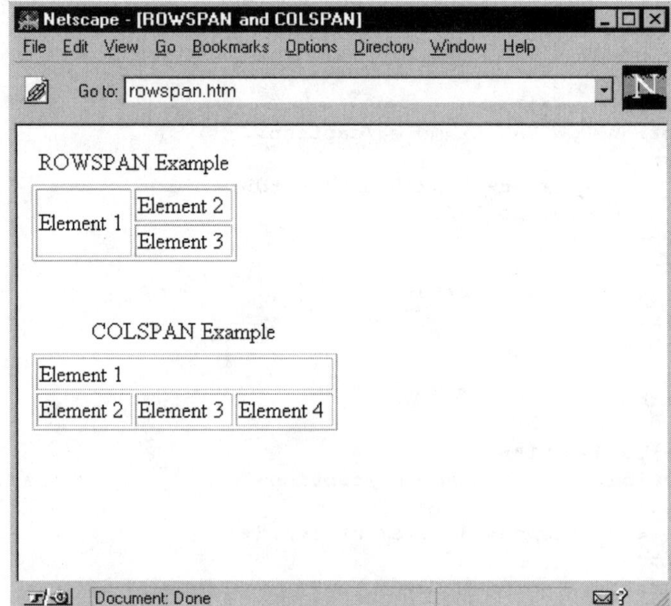

FIGURE 7-2 Rendering of rowspan and colspan

Most browsers will render this code something like this:

Element 1	Element 2	Element 3	
Element 4	Element 5		Element 6

The reason is quite simple: The last data cell in the second row should have been removed to account for the rowspan in cell 3 of the first row, like this:

```
<table border="1">
<tr>
    <td>Element 1</td>
    <td>Element 2</td>
    <td rowspan="2">Element 3</td>
</tr>

<tr>
    <td>Element 4</td>
    <td>Element 5</td>
</tr>
</table>
```


The rendering of the improved markup now works properly:

Element 1	Element 2	Element 3
Element 4	Element 5	

Full Table Example

Aside from being able to span rows and columns, the **table** element, and its enclosed elements **td**, **th**, and **caption**, support a variety of attributes for alignment (**align** and **valign**), sizing (**width**), presentation (**bgcolor** and **background**), and layout (**cellpadding** and **cellspacing**). These attributes will be explained in the next section, but you can probably infer their use by looking at the following example, which shows a more complex kind of table:

```
<!DOCTYPE html PUBLIC "-//W3C//DTD XHTML 1.0 Transitional//EN"
"http://www.w3.org/TR/xhtml1/DTD/xhtml1-transitional.dtd">
<html xmlns="http://www.w3.org/1999/xhtml" lang="en">
<head>
<title>Complex Table Example</title>
<meta http-equiv="content-type" content="text/html; charset=ISO-8859-1" />
</head>
<body>

<table align="left" border="1" width="300" cellspacing="0">
<caption align="bottom">The Super Widget</caption>

<tr>
  <td rowspan="2">
  <img src="widget.gif" alt="super widget" width="100" height="120" />
```

```
   </td>
  <th bgcolor="lightgreen">Specifications</th>
</tr>

<tr>
<td valign="middle" align="left">
    <ul>
      <li>Diameter: 10 cm</li>
      <li>Composition: Kryptonite</li>
      <li>Color: Green</li>
    </ul>
  </td>
</tr>
</table>

<p>Notice how the text of a paragraph can flow around a table
just as it would any other embedded object form. Notice how
the text of a paragraph can flow around a table just as it
would any other embedded object form. Notice how the text
of a paragraph can flow around a table just as it would
any other embedded object form. Notice how the text
of a paragraph can flow around a table just as it would
any other embedded object form. Notice how the text
of a paragraph can flow around a table just as it would
any other embedded object form. Notice how the text
of a paragraph can flow around a table just as it would
any other embedded object form. Notice how the text
of a paragraph can flow around a table just as it would
any other embedded object form. Notice how the text
of a paragraph can flow around a table just as it would
any other embedded object form.</p>

</body>
</html>
```

The rendering of the previous example, as shown in Figure 7-3, suggests that it is possible to place any form of content in a cell including even other tables, although this is not recommended if it can be avoided. Furthermore, it appears we have full control over the individual size of the cells and the table itself. With these features, we now have the facilities required to control layout using a **<table>** tag to create a grid on the page.

Tables for Layout

Tables can be a very important tool for HTML-based page layout. The foundation of graphic design is the ability to spatially arrange visual elements in relation to each other. Tables can be used to define a layout grid for just this purpose. Prior to the advent of style sheets supporting positioning (see Chapter 10), tables were the only reliable way to accomplish this. Even with CSS well supported at the time of this edition's writing, tables still remain the most commonly used technique in Web design.

The key to using a table to create a precise page grid is the use of the **width** attribute. The **width** attribute for the **table** element specifies the width of a table in pixels, or as a

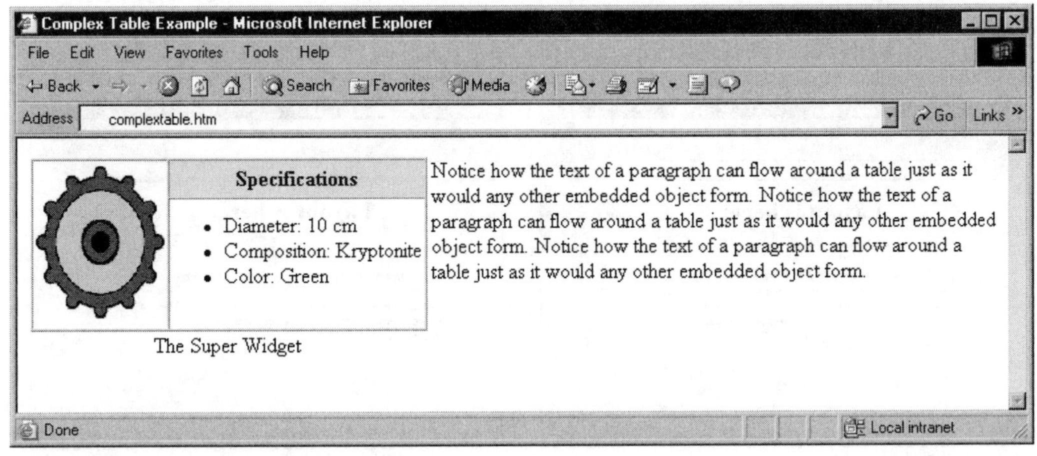

FIGURE 7-3 Advanced table hints at layout possibilities

percentage value such as 80%. It also is possible to set the individual pixel widths of each cell within the table, using a **width** attribute for the **td** or **th** element. Imagine trying to create a 400-pixel column of text down the page with a buffer of 50 pixels on the left and 100 pixels on the right. In HTML before tables, this would be literally impossible without making the text a giant image. With a table, it is easy, as shown by the markup code here:

```
<!DOCTYPE html PUBLIC "-//W3C//DTD XHTML 1.0 Transitional//EN"
"http://www.w3.org/TR/xhtml1/DTD/xhtml1-transitional.dtd">
<html xmlns="http://www.w3.org/1999/xhtml" lang="en">
<head>
<title>Table Layout</title>
<meta http-equiv="content-type" content="text/html; charset=ISO-8859-1" />
</head>
<body>
<table border="0">
<tr>
   <td width="50"> </td>
   <td width="400">
     <h1 align="center">Layout is here!</h1>
     <hr />
     <p>This is a very simple layout that would
      have been nearly impossible to do without tables.
      This is a very simple layout that would
      have been nearly impossible to do without tables.
      This is a very simple layout that would
      have been nearly impossible to do without tables.</p>
   </td>
   <td width="100"> </td>
  </tr>
</table>
</body>
</html>
```

In the preceding code, the **border** value is set to zero. The rendering of the example is shown here, with both the border on and off.

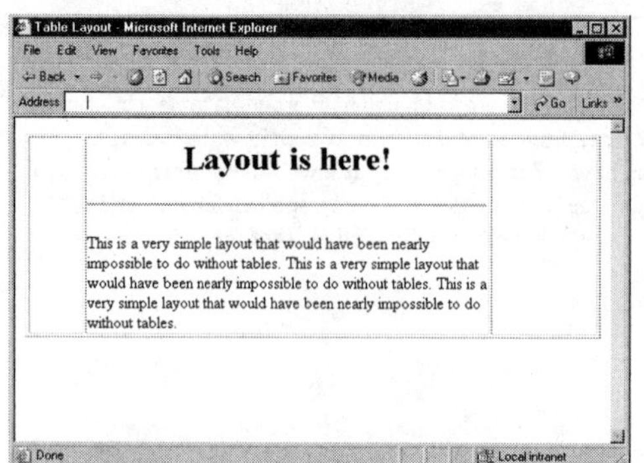

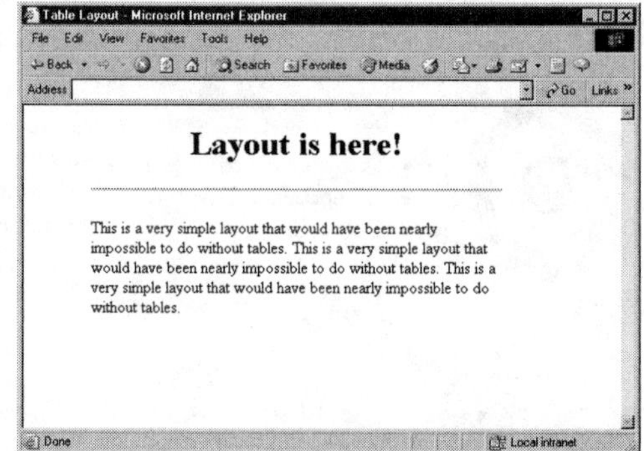

While the border attribute for a **<table>** tag isn't necessary because the browser does not draw a border by default, it is better practice to keep the attribute in, set to zero. The presence of the attribute allows borders to be quickly turned on and off by setting the value to 1 or 0 to check to see what is going on with a particular layout.

Tip *When creating empty table cells, it is a good idea to put a nonbreaking space (** **) or even a clear pixel gif (for example, space.gif) into the cell so it doesn't collapse.*

Besides basic text layout, tables also can be used to provide more precise layout in relation to a background. One popular design concept employs a vertical strip of colored background on the left of the page, which contains navigation controls; the rest of the document contains the main text. Without tables, it is difficult to keep body content off darker regions of a background tile. The following is an example of the markup code to create a two-column design that works on top of a 100-pixel-wide color background:

```
<!DOCTYPE html PUBLIC "-//W3C//DTD XHTML 1.0 Transitional//EN"
"http://www.w3.org/TR/xhtml1/DTD/xhtml1-transitional.dtd">
<html xmlns="http://www.w3.org/1999/xhtml" lang="en">
<head>
<title>Table Layout with Background</title>
<meta http-equiv="content-type" content="text/html; charset=ISO-8859-1" />
</head>
<body background="yellowtile.gif">

<table width="550" cellspacing="0" cellpadding="15">
<tr>
    <td width="100" valign="top">
     <a href="about.html">About</a><br /><br />
     <a href="products.html">Products</a><br /><br />
     <a href="staff.html">Staff</a><br /><br />
     <a href="contact.html">Contact</a><br /><br />
    </td>

    <td width="450">
```

```
      <h1 align="center">Welcome to Demo Company, Inc.</h1>
      <hr />
      <p>This text is positioned over a white background;
        the navigation links are over a colored background.
        This layout combines a table with a background image.
      </p>
     </td>
</tr>
</table>
</body>
</html>
```

The rendering of this layout appears in Figure 7-4. Note how the foreground content (the **<body>** content) is aligned over the **background** image. Another way to achieve such effects is to set the **bgcolor** attribute for the table cells and forego the background image altogether.

```
<table width="550" cellspacing="0" cellpadding="10">
 <tr>
    <td width="100" valign="top" bgcolor="yellow">
      … links here …
    </td>
    <td width="450">
       … content here …
    </td>
 </tr>
</table>
```

PART III

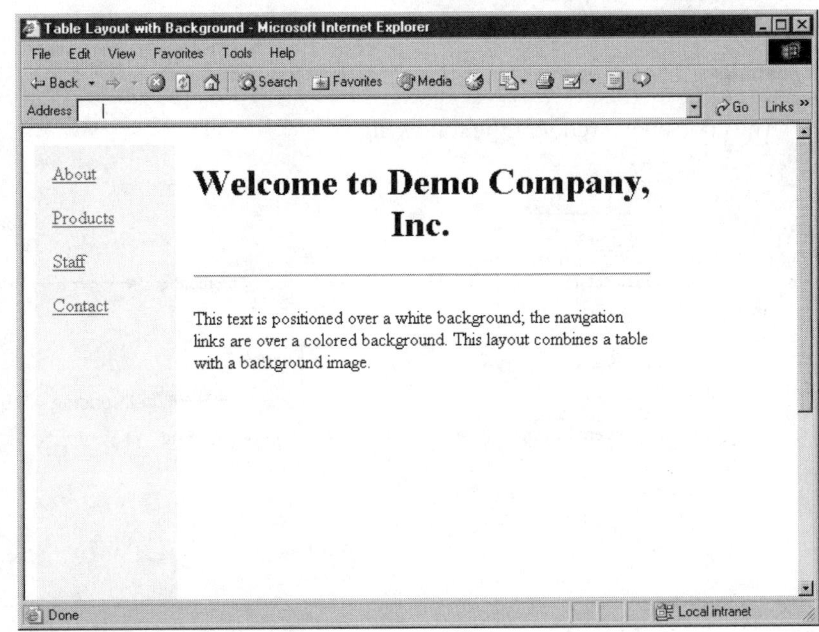

FIGURE 7-4 Rendering of two-column layout

TIP *Often, when setting up table layouts, you will want to control page margins as well. Recall that setting nonstandard **<body>** attributes like so, **<body marginheight="0" marginwidth="0" leftmargin="0" topmargin="0">**, or using the CSS property margin for the **body** element will help rid your page of unsightly gaps.*

cellpadding and cellspacing

The space between cells in a table is controlled by the **cellspacing** attribute for **<table>**. The value is measured in pixels or percentage values. When using tables for layout, cells should jut up next to each other, so this attribute is often set to **0**, as in previous examples. However, it is possible to give space between cells by setting this attribute to a positive integer or percentage value. Similarly, the padding between cell walls and the content they surround is controlled by the **cellpadding** attribute, which is also often set to **0** in tables used for layout. The two approaches are illustrated by this markup:

```
<table border="1" cellspacing="15" cellpadding="40">
<tr>
   <td>Element 1</td>
   <td>Element 2</td>
   <td>Element 3</td>
</tr>
</table>

<br /><br />

<table border="1" cellspacing="0" cellpadding="0">
<tr>
   <td>Element 1</td>
   <td>Element 2</td>
   <td>Element 3</td>
</tr>
</table>
```

The code above renders the following:

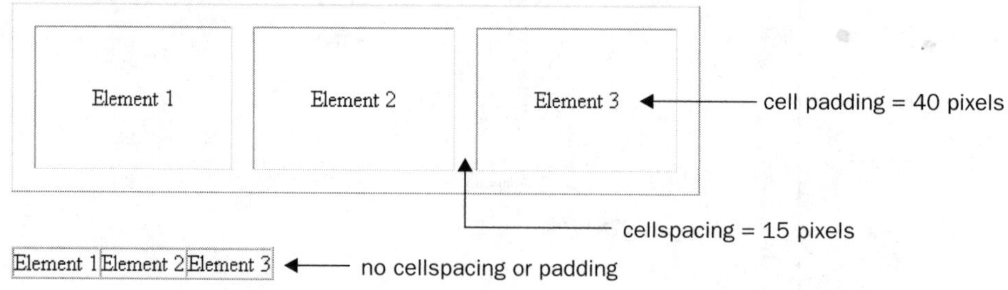

Cell Alignment

Cells defined by **<td>** or **<th>** are generally aligned horizontally by setting the **align** attribute to **left**, **right**, or **center** with **left** being the default. It is also possible to justify their contents by setting the attribute to **justify,** or to align contents on a particular character such as a decimal point using the value **char**. However, aligning on characters is still not that well-supported in browsers. The contents of cells can also be aligned vertically by setting **valign** on **<th>** or **<td>** tags to **top**, **middle**, **bottom** or **baseline**. The following example illustrates the more common uses of these values.

```
<table border="1" cellspacing="0" cellpadding="0" width="100%">
<tr>
   <td align="left">Left</td>
   <td align="center">Center</td>
   <td align="right">Right</td>
</tr>
<tr>
   <td valign="top" height="100">Top</td>
   <td valign="middle">Middle</td>
   <td valign="bottom">Bottom</td>
</tr>
</table>
```

A typical rendering of this markup is shown here.

Left	Center	Right
Top	Middle	Bottom

Colored Tables and Cells

As already mentioned in this chapter, table elements also can be assigned background colors using the **bgcolor** attribute. The **bgcolor** attribute is valid for **<table>**, **<tr>**, **<th>**, and **<td>**.

```
<table border="1" cellspacing="0" cellpadding="8" bgcolor="green">
<tr>
  <th bgcolor="lightblue">lightblue</th>
  <th bgcolor="lightblue">lightblue</th>
  <th bgcolor="lightblue">lightblue</th>
</tr>

<tr bgcolor="orange">
  <td>orange</td>
  <td>orange</td>
  <td>orange</td>
```

```
</tr>

<tr>
  <td bgcolor="red">red</td>
  <td bgcolor="white">white</td>
  <td bgcolor="blue">blue</td>
</tr>

<tr>
  <td>green</td>
  <td>green</td>
  <td>green</td>
</tr>
</table>
```

In this code, the header cells (**th**) in the first row will have a light blue background; all three cells (**td**) in the second row will have an orange background as defined for the entire row (**tr**); the three cells in the third row will have different background colors as defined by the **bgcolor** attribute for each **<td>** tag; and the cells in the last row, which have no background color defined for themselves or their row, will default to the green background color defined in the **<table>** tag.

Recall that the **cellspacing** attribute for **<table>**, which sets how many pixels of space are included between table cells, is set to zero; if it is set to a higher value, the background color will display in the areas between cells in most browsers.

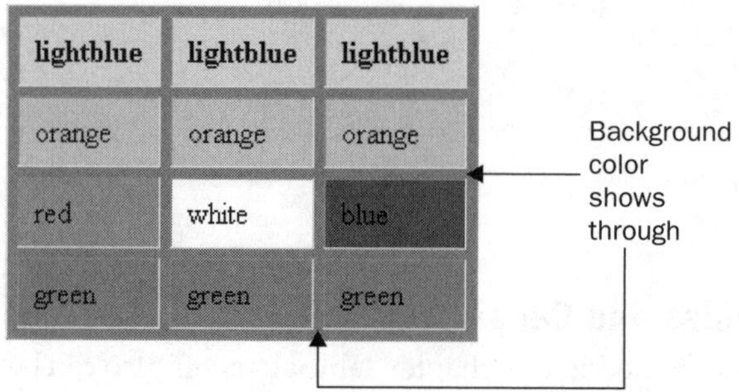

Additional proprietary attributes also have been defined for table border colors. Internet Explorer 4 and higher defines a **bordercolor** attribute for **<table>** as well as for cells. Netscape will recognize the **bordercolor** attribute for **<table>**, but not on the cells. Strict standards-compliant browsers such as Opera 7 will recognize none of these attributes. As an example, the markup

```
<table bordercolor="#ff0000" border="1">
<tr>
  <td bordercolor="#0000ff">Blue Border</td>
  <td>Red Border</td>
</tr>
</table>
```

will render a table with a red border around the entire table and its first cell will have a blue border in Internet Explorer, but not in Netscape.

Internet Explorer 4 and higher also provide two more border color attributes: **bordercolordark** and **bordercolorlight**.

```
<table bordercolorlight="#ff0000" bordercolordark="#0000ff"
       border="4">
<tr>
   <td>Cell</td>
</tr>
</table>
```

Under Internet Explorer, this example will render a two-tone outer border for the table in which the colors simulate a three-dimensional shading, as shown here:

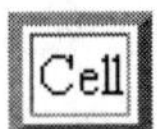

While these proprietary attributes are useful for creating a bevel style effect on a table, the effect is easily accomplished in standard CSS.

Basic HTML initially didn't provide great support for table borders and colors; with all the proprietary extensions and subtle variations, page authors often ended up frustrated. However, sometimes a simple workaround such as using a nested table can solve the problem, albeit messily. Consider the markup here:

```
<table cellspacing="0" cellpadding="0" border="0" width="200">
<tr>
<td bgcolor="#990000">
<!-- begin nested table -->
<table cellspacing="1" cellpadding="3" border="0" width="200">
<tr>
    <td bgcolor="#FFFFFF" width="100">Cell 1</td>
    <td bgcolor="#FFFFFF" width="100">Cell 2</td>
</tr>

<tr>
    <td bgcolor="#FFFFFF" width="100">Cell 3</td>
    <td bgcolor="#FFFFFF" width="100">Cell 4</td>
</tr>
</table>
<!-- end nested table -->
</td>
</tr>
</table>
```

The outer table employs a single table cell with its **bgcolor** set to red. The cells in the nested table have their **bgcolor** set to white. The **cellspacing** for the nested table is set to 1, allowing the black background of the outer table to show through in the spaces between the cells:

Cell 1	Cell 2
Cell 3	Cell 4

Notice 1-pixel-width colored border

This "hack" will work for browsers even as far back as Netscape 3. Still, some care must be taken in using this approach. The two tables must be the same width, or the border effect could be uneven. Given the reliance on tables in layouts, such tricky markup is much more common than readers might imagine.

Background Images in Tables

Using the **background** attribute it is also possible to apply background images to tables and table cells. Defining a table with the code

```
<table width="100%" border="1" cellpadding="0" cellspacing="0"
       background="tabletile.gif">
```

would place a repeating background tile behind the table, as shown here:

Internet Explorer

Netscape 4

Notice that the table on the left is the typical rendering in modern browsers, but beware that the table on the right shows Netscape 4 tiling backgrounds very differently. It is also possible to set table cells (**<td>** and **<th>**), but the tiling effect will be limited to the cell it is defined on, so be careful if you have adjacent cells with different backgrounds.

Applied Layout Using Tables

Now that we understand the basics of using tables for layout, we approach trying to lay pages out using only HTML/XHTML. Don't worry; creating relatively sophisticated layouts with tables doesn't have to be daunting. A little planning and the right tools can go a long way toward achieving a successful layout.

Centered Layout

Let's start first with a very simple design. In this case, we want to create a centered region with content that looks like a printed page on a background color. In this case, we could use a single cell table and set width, alignment, and padding to pull off the design quite easily, as shown here:

```
<!DOCTYPE html PUBLIC "-//W3C//DTD XHTML 1.0 Transitional//EN"
"http://www.w3.org/TR/xhtml1/DTD/xhtml1-transitional.dtd">
<html xmlns="http://www.w3.org/1999/xhtml" lang="en">
<head>
<title>Centered Table</title>
<meta http-equiv="content-type" content="text/html; charset=ISO-8859-1" />
</head>
<body bgcolor="navy">
<table width="80%" align="center" cellpadding="10">
  <tr>
    <td bgcolor="white">
       <h1 align="center">Heading</h1>
```

```
        <hr width="80%" />

        <p>Lorem ipsum dolor sit amet, consectetuer adipiscing elit.
         Nulla nulla. Ut vel magna eu velit tristique tempus. Nunc
         a wisi at ligula euismod tempus. Curabitur vestibulum
         viverra tellus. Phasellus vestibulum. Duis justo...</p>

      … more content …

        </td>
   </tr>
</table>
</body>
</html>
```

A full rendering of the example is shown in Figure 7-5.

To expand upon the previous example, we might want to add in navigation and a site label across the top. That could be done easily with two extra rows of cells and appropriate use of the **colspan** attribute. However, it is not always wise to build complex tables when

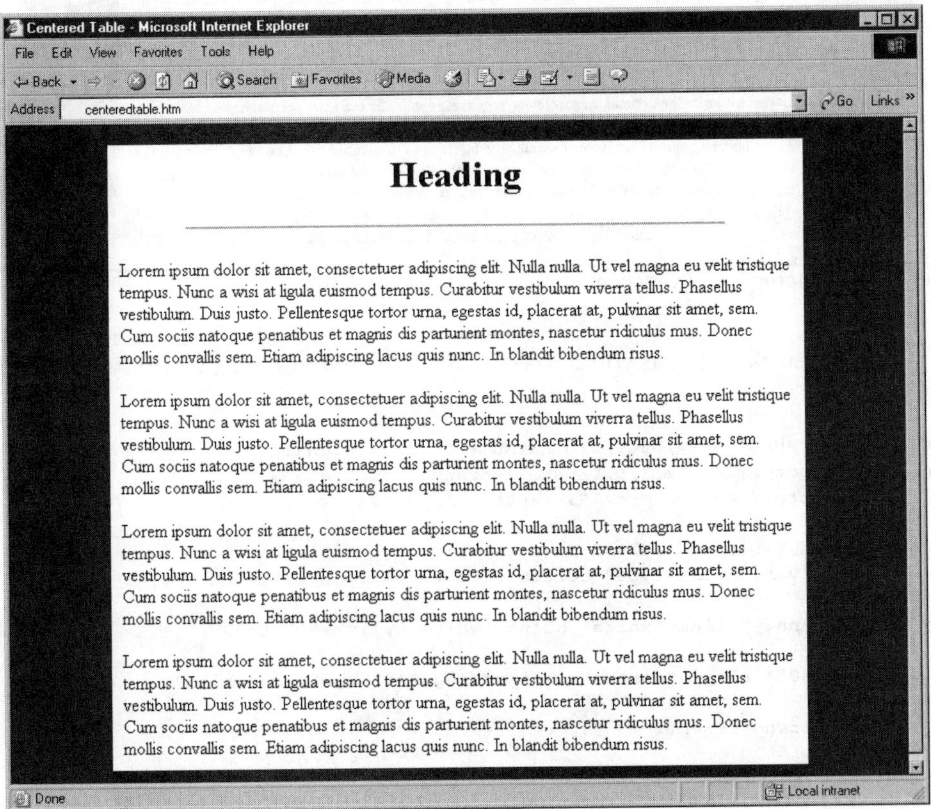

FIGURE 7-5 Centered page using a table

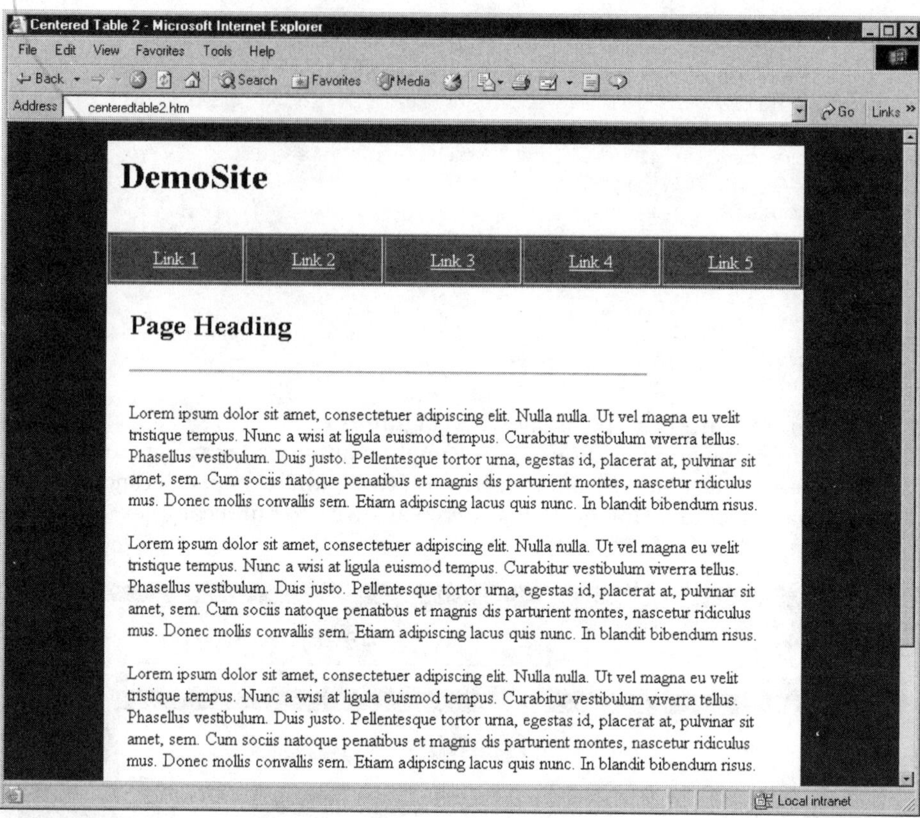

FIGURE 7-6 Centered layout variation

you can simply stack tables, as you can see in the following example, which is presented in Figure 7-6.

```
<!DOCTYPE html PUBLIC "-//W3C//DTD XHTML 1.0 Transitional//EN"
"http://www.w3.org/TR/xhtml1/DTD/xhtml1-transitional.dtd">
<html xmlns="http://www.w3.org/1999/xhtml" lang="en">
<head>
<title>Centered Table 2</title>
<meta http-equiv="content-type" content="text/html; charset=ISO-8859-1" />
</head>
<body bgcolor="navy" link="white" alink="white" vlink="white">

<table width="80%" align="center" cellpadding="10" bgcolor="white">
  <tr>
       <td colspan="5"><h1>DemoSite</h1></td>
  </tr>
</table>

<table width="80%" align="center" cellpadding="10" border="1"
```

```
        bgcolor="maroon">
  <tr>
        <td align="center"><a href="#">Link 1</a></td>
        <td align="center"><a href="#">Link 2</a></td>
        <td align="center"><a href="#">Link 3</a></td>
        <td align="center"><a href="#">Link 4</a></td>
        <td align="center"><a href="#">Link 5</a></td>
  </tr>
</table>

<table width="80%" align="center" cellpadding="20" bgcolor="white">
<tr>
   <td colspan="5" bgcolor="white">
        <h2>Page Heading</h2>
        <hr width="80%" align="left" />

        <p>Lorem ipsum dolor sit amet, consectetuer adipiscing elit.
           Nulla nulla. Ut vel magna eu velit tristique tempus. Nunc
           a wisi at ligula euismod tempus. Curabitur vestibulum
           viverra tellus. Phasellus vestibulum. Duis justo.</p>

      …more content…

        </td>
  </tr>
</table>
</body>
</html>
```


Top-Left-Bottom "TLB" Layout

A modification of the previous layout would provide for secondary navigation on the left of the content as well as backup navigation or extra information at the bottom of the page. This type of template is very commonly used on the Web and is often called a TLB design for "top-left-bottom." A simple example of a TLB template is shown here with a rendering in Figure 7-7.

```
<!DOCTYPE html PUBLIC "-//W3C//DTD XHTML 1.0 Transitional//EN"
"http://www.w3.org/TR/xhtml1/DTD/xhtml1-transitional.dtd">
<html xmlns="http://www.w3.org/1999/xhtml" lang="en">
<head>
<title>TLB Template</title>
<meta http-equiv="content-type" content="text/html; charset=ISO-8859-1" />
</head>
<body bgcolor="#ffffff">

<!--BEGIN: Label or primary nav table -->
<table width="100%" border="0" cellspacing="0" cellpadding="0">
<tr>
   <td width="100%" bgcolor="yellow">
    <h2 align="center">Site Heading and/or Navigation</h2>
   </td>
</tr>
</table>
```

```
<!--END: Label of primary nav table-->



<!--BEGIN: Secondary nav and content -->
<table width="100%" border="0" cellspacing="0" cellpadding="0">
<tr>
   <td width="10" bgcolor="red">   </td>
   <td width="90" valign="top" bgcolor="red">
     <br />
     <a href="#">Link</a><br />
     <a href="#">Link</a><br />
     <a href="#">Link</a><br />
     <a href="#">Link</a><br />
     <a href="#">Link</a><br />
     <a href="#">Link</a><br />
   </td>
   <td width="10" bgcolor="white">   </td>
<td>
     <br />
     <h2>Page Heading</h2>
     <hr />

     <p>Lorem ipsum dolor sit amet, consectetuer adipiscing elit,
        sed diam nonummy nibh euismod tincidunt ut laoreet dolore
        magna aliquam erat volutpat. Ut wisi enim ad minim veniam,
        quis nostrud exerci tation ullamcorper suscipit lobortis
        nisl ut aliquip ex ea commodo consequat.</p>

…more content…

   </td>

   <td width="10" bgcolor="white">   </td>
</tr>
</table>
<!-- END: secondary nav and content -->



<!--BEGIN: footer navigation and legal-->
<div align="center">
<br />
<font size="-2">
   <a href="#">Link</a> |
   <a href="#">Link</a> |
   <a href="#">Link</a> |
   <a href="#">Link</a> |
   <a href="#">Link</a> |
   <a href="#">Link</a>
</font>
<br /><em>&copy;2003 DemoCompany Inc.</em>
</div>
<!-- END: footer nav -->
</body>
</html>
```

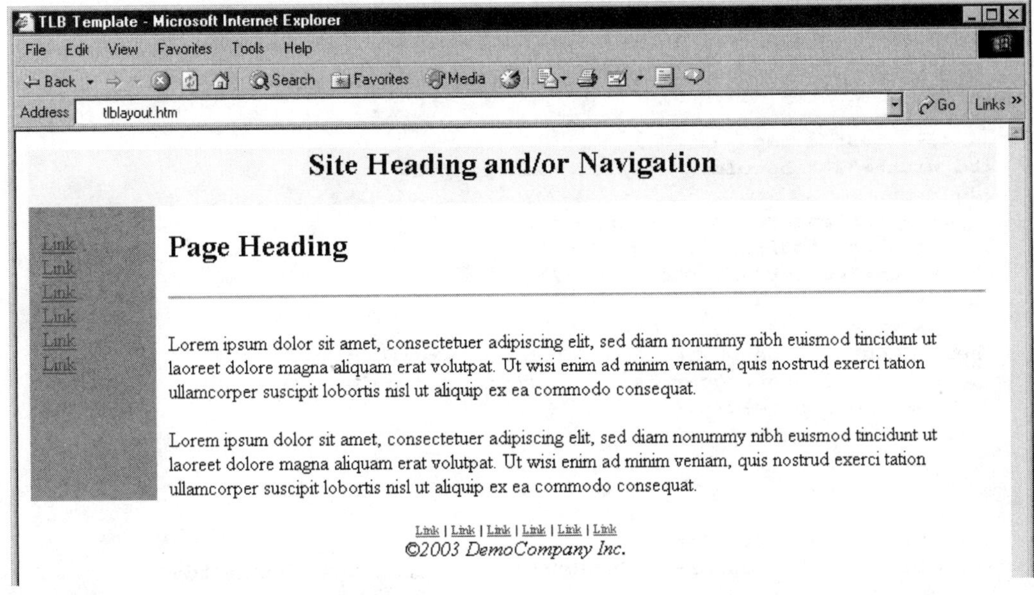

FIGURE 7-7 TLB template example

Stretchable Table Layouts

Another common design is one that stretches to fit the available screen region. The so-called fluid or stretchable design requires that some cells be set with values and others not, to be elastic in response to available screen width. Stretchable designs are particularly common in three-column layouts, as shown in this example:

```
<!DOCTYPE html PUBLIC "-//W3C//DTD XHTML 1.0 Transitional//EN"
"http://www.w3.org/TR/xhtml1/DTD/xhtml1-transitional.dtd">
<html xmlns="http://www.w3.org/1999/xhtml" lang="en">
<head>
<title>Stretch Template</title>
<meta http-equiv="content-type" content="text/html; charset=ISO-8859-1" />
</head>
<body bgcolor="#006699">

     <table border="0" width="100%" cellspacing="0" cellpadding="15">

<tr>

   <!-- just a gap -->
   <td width="20" bgcolor="#006699">   </td>

      <!-- navigation column fixed size -->
   <td width="150" bgcolor="#ffcc00" valign="top">
      <h3 align="center">Navigation</h3>
      <a href="#">Link</a><br />
```

```
        <a href="#">Link</a><br />
        <a href="#">Link</a><br />
        <a href="#">Link</a><br />
    </td>

        <!-- just a gap -->
    <td width="20" bgcolor="#ffffff"> </td>

        <!-- content region variable size -->
    <td bgcolor="#ffffff" valign="top">
    <h2 align="center">Stretch Demo</h2>
    <hr />
        <p>Content goes here. Content goes here. Content goes
     here. Content goes here. Content goes here. Content
     goes here. Content goes here. Content goes here.
     Content goes here.</p>
     </td>


    <!--right column fixed size-->
    <td width="100" bgcolor="#ffcc00">Right column text here</td>

    <!--right margin gap-->
    <td width="20" bgcolor="#006699">  </td>
</tr>
</table>
</body>
</html>
```

The rendering of the stretchable design shown in Figure 7-8 demonstrates one downside of the approach. Without enough content, a stretchable table layout might look rather empty on a very large monitor.

TIP *While a stretchable or fluid design does fit to whatever screen the user wants, it can be rather limiting. Creating stretch points limits the design to simple colors or patterns because the relative areas are elastic and would distort an image placed there.*

Complex Table Layouts

It is also possible to apply tables to layouts in a more complicated fashion. Layouts combining text and images can be created using large graphics that incorporate text, but this approach produces pages that are slow to download. The code example that follows shows a more complicated layout that breaks up an image and reassembles it like a jigsaw puzzle, using

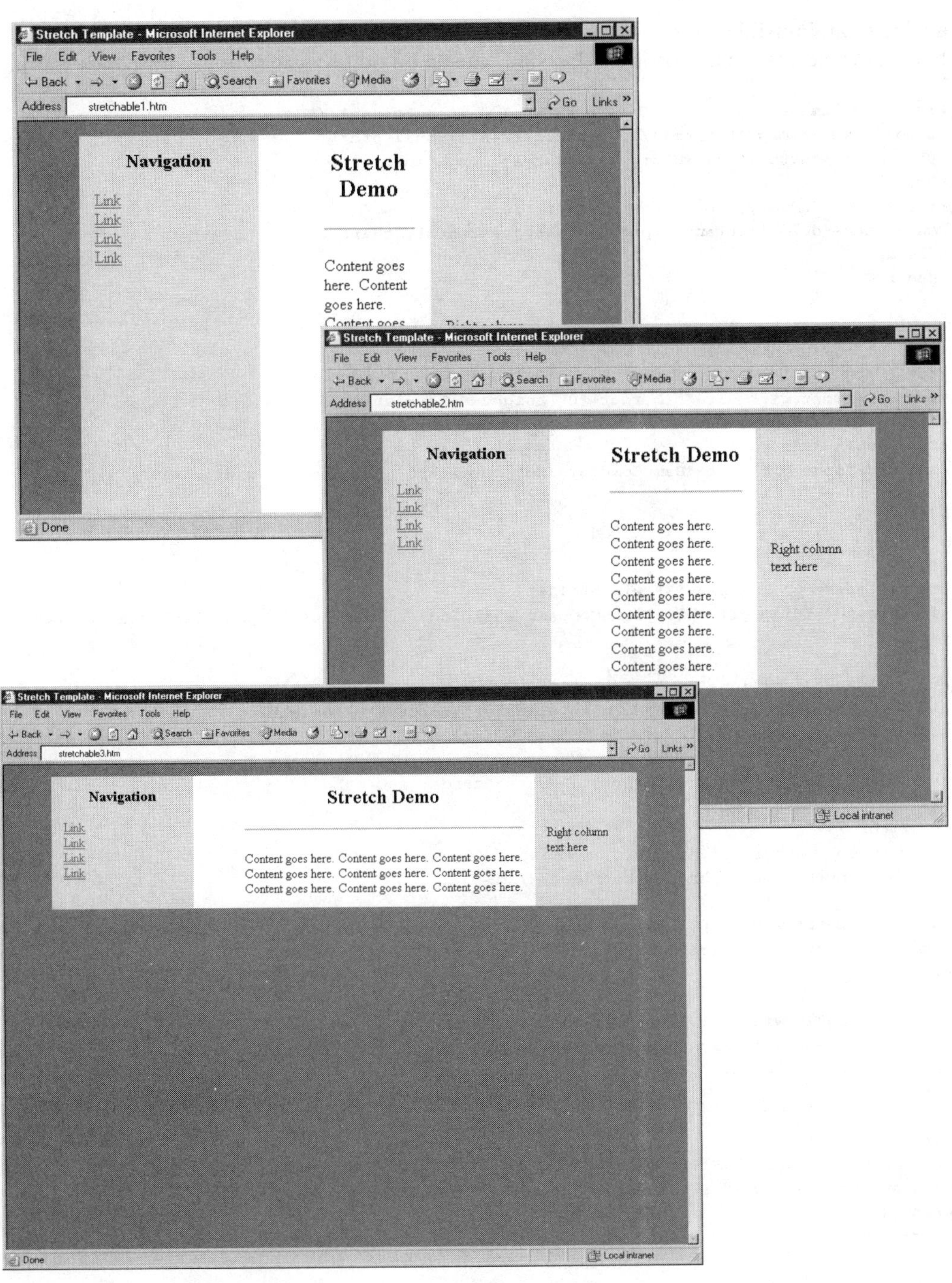

FIGURE 7-8 Stretchable design in action

PART III

a table as an invisible "frame" to hold it in place. Note that anchors have not been applied to the graphic links in this code (widgets.gif, and so on) in order to simplify the code example.

```
<!DOCTYPE html PUBLIC "-//W3C//DTD XHTML 1.0 Transitional//EN"
"http://www.w3.org/TR/xhtml1/DTD/xhtml1-transitional.dtd">
<html xmlns="http://www.w3.org/1999/xhtml" lang="en">
<head>
<title>Demo Company, Inc. Home Page</title>
<meta http-equiv="content-type" content="text/html; charset=ISO-8859-1" />
</head>
<body>

<table border="0" cellpadding="0" cellspacing="0" width="570">
<tr>
<td>
<img src="roof.gif" alt="" border="0" height="45" width="124" />
</td>
<td colspan="4">
<img src="logo.gif" alt="DemoCompany Inc" border="0" height="45" width="446" />
</td>
</tr>

<tr>
<td valign="top" rowspan="7" width="124">
<img src="building.gif" alt="DemoCompany Building" border="0" height="248" width="124" />
</td>

<td rowspan="7" valign="top" width="185">
<img src="headline.gif" alt="We make widgets!" border="0" height="45"
width="185" />
And now, thanks to our merger with Massive Industries, we are now
the world's largest manufacturer of Gadgets&trade; and other
useless products.
<br /><br />
To learn more about our products or our growing monopoly,
click on any of the links to the right.</td>

<td rowspan="3" width="68" valign="top">
<img src="curve.gif" alt="" border="0" height="108" width="68" />
</td>

<td colspan="2" width="193" valign="top">
<img src="blank.gif" alt="" border="0" height="35" width="193" />
</td>
</tr>

<tr>
<td colspan="2" width="193" valign="top">
<img src="widgets.gif" alt="widgets" border="0" height="35" width="193" />
</td>
</tr>

<tr>
<td colspan="2" width="193" valign="top">
<img src="gadgets.gif" alt="gadgets" border="0" height="38" width="193" />
```

```
</td>
</tr>

<tr>
<td colspan="2" rowspan="4" width="136" valign="top">
<img src="gear.gif" alt="" border="0" height="140" width="136" />
</td>
<td valign="top" width="125">
<img src="sales.gif" alt="sales" border="0" height="29" width="125" />
</td>
</tr>

<tr>
<td valign="top" width="125">
<img src="about.gif" alt="about" border="0" height="36" width="125" />
</td>
</tr>

<tr>
<td valign="top" width="125">
<img src="history.gif" alt="history" border="0" height="35" width="125" />
</td>
</tr>

<tr>
<td valign="top" width="125">
<img src="map.gif" alt="map" border="0" height="40" width="125" />
</td>
</tr>

<tr>
<td colspan="2" width="309"> </td>
<td width="68"> </td>
<td width="68"> </td>
<td valign="top" width="125">
<img src="lowcurve.gif" alt="" border="0" height="31" width="125" />
</td>
</tr>
</table>

</body>
</html>
```


When creating a layout like this, it is very important to set the **cellpadding** and **cellspacing** attributes to **0**. Table cell widths should correspond to the width of the image inside the cell, and the width of the table should be the sum of the cells in a table row. It also is important to include the **height** and **width** attributes of the images used. Figure 7-9 shows a browser rendering of this layout, with an overlay to show where the image is broken up.

While the images in the preceding example are all GIFs, JPEGs could also be used. "Photographic" areas of an image should be saved as JPEGs while areas with limited color, such as simple text, should be saved as GIFs. By saving each area in the appropriate format, it is possible to reduce the overall file size and optimize performance. (This is discussed in more detail in Chapter 5.)

FIGURE 7-9 Rendering of layout with "jigsaw"

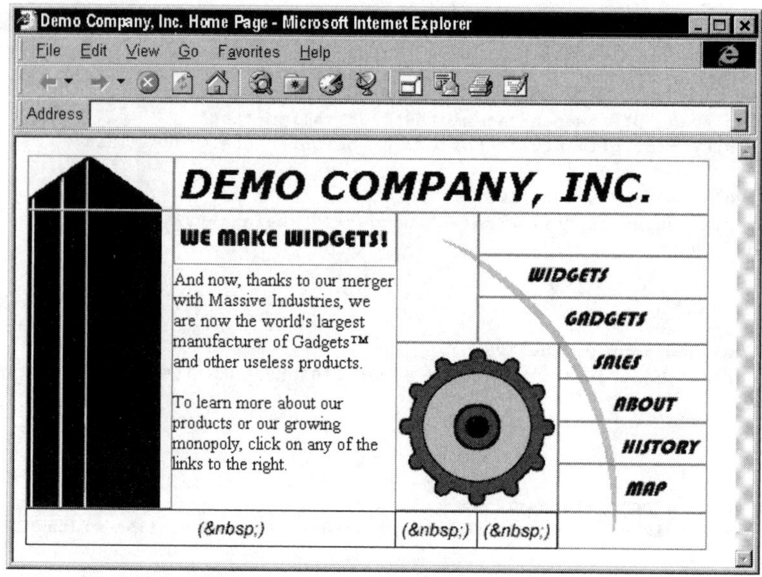

Graphic tools such as Adobe PhotoShop or Macromedia's Fireworks enable Web designers to create a single image layout design, beginning with a file such as a large image that is then sliced up to create an HTML/XHTML layout using a table and pieces of the image converted into GIF and/or JPEG files, as appropriate. The use of such a program is shown in Figure 7-10.

Graphic programs such as Fireworks will not only create markup but even special "shim" images to maintain cell widths and heights throughout the table. Although these tools are certainly very convenient in layout preparation, they often produce overly complicated tables, laden with wildly varying **colspan** and **rowspan** attributes, as suggested by the following grid:

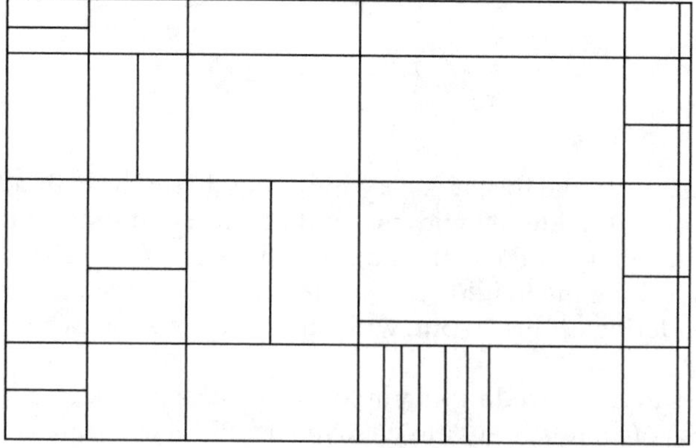

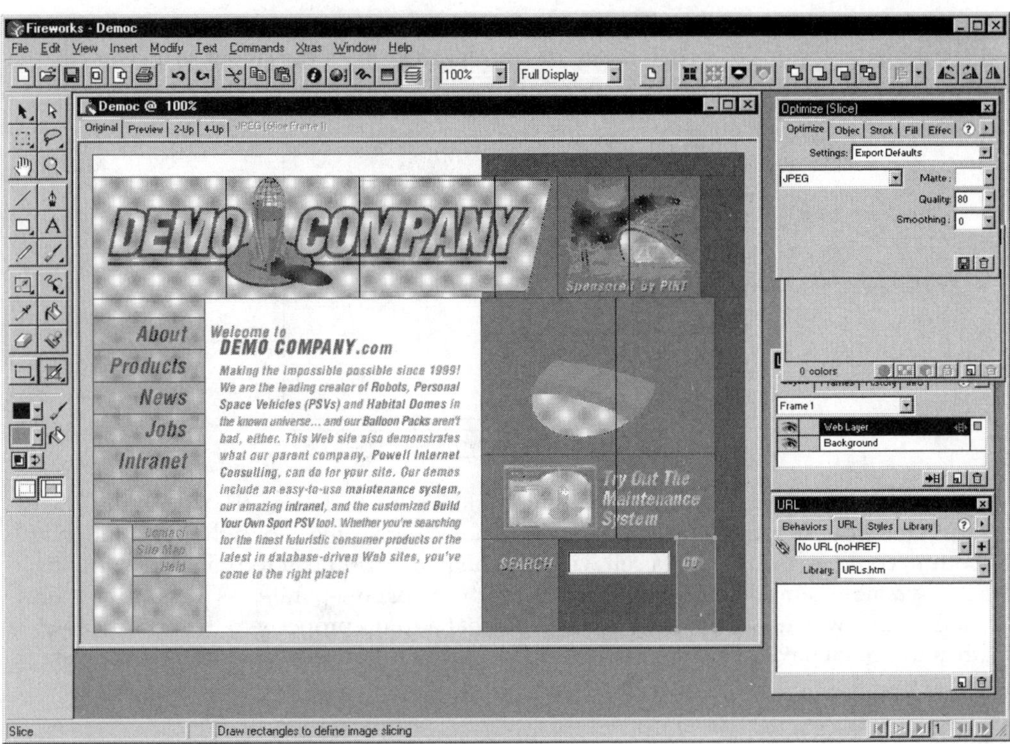

FIGURE 7-10 Slicing visual composite to make a template

Some designers also might generate similar table layouts on their own. Whether using a graphics tool or building such layouts by hand, it is always useful to step back and consider a simpler approach. Consider a basic layout like this:

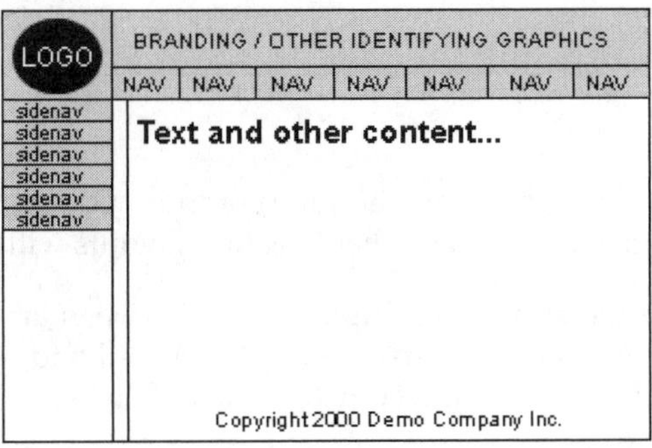

Although it certainly would be possible to create a single table to hold all of the graphic and text elements of this design, it might be simpler to think of the layout as a layer cake, as shown here:

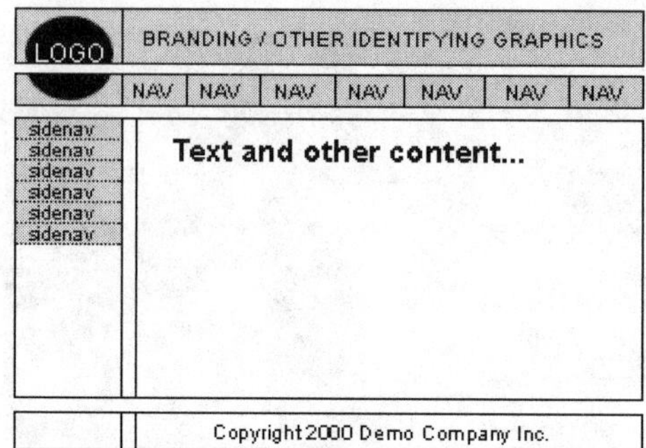

The row featuring the navigation buttons could be one table, and the part of the layout featuring the side navigation could be another one. Whereas the copyright information at the bottom could be included in a cell with the **colspan** attribute, it too could be split off into its own table, simply to keep different parts of the page separate. As long as the tables are all the same width, each has column widths that add up properly to the overall table width, and do not have **
** tags or any other elements between them, they should stack up perfectly.

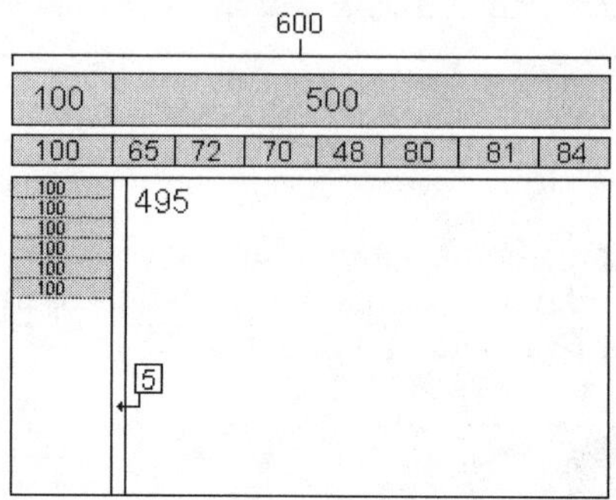

Table Tips

As you saw in the last section, tables can get quite complicated quickly. Here are a few useful rules to make things go smoother when creating layouts with tables.

- Consider using indentation or multiple returns between table rows and cells for easy readability. This is particularly useful if you are hand editing and the extra white space can always be removed before page delivery.
- Always use these three basic attributes with the **table** element: **border**, **cellpadding**, and **cellspacing**. Even if you don't want any of these things, set them to zero; **border** is useful for checking your work, and browsers generally throw in a little bit of unwanted **cellpadding** and **cellspacing** if those attributes are not present.

- Always use the closing tags for every element; this will prevent browser display problems and maintain XHTML compatibility as well.
- Make certain that column widths, as defined by **<th>** or **<td>** cells, add up to the overall defined width of the table. Faulty addition has ruined more than a few seemingly perfect tables.
- Don't forget that use of the **colspan** or **rowspan** attributes in one row will require the removal of some table cells in other rows in the table.
- Certain Microsoft-created attributes, such as **bordercolor**, **bordercolordark**, and **bordercolorlight**, are not suitable for cross-browser usage. Avoid them unless designing for an IE-only environment such as an intranet.
- Try to simplify layouts; don't go crazy with excessive **rowspan** and **colspan** usage when you can stack tables much more simply. It might help to visualize the layout as a layer cake, with a separate table as each layer.
- Don't nest tables deeply. Besides making things overly complicated, you may actually reduce page rendering speed.
- Always comment complex tables so they will make sense to you later. When commenting, at the very least, it is handy to indicate the beginning and end of any table.

  ```
  <!-- begin top nav table -->
     ... table elements ...
  <!-- end top nav table -->
  ```

  If you are nesting tables, be certain to mark them as such.

  ```
  <!-- begin nested table 1 -->
     ... table elements ...
  <!-- end nested table 1 -->
  ```

Use comments to any extent you desire, from comments noting the start of new table rows to comments explaining the purpose of a table cell. As long as your comments are meaningful, it won't hurt to add a few kilobytes to your document size in the interest of good coding practice, and you can always strip these comments out before page delivery.

Advanced Data Tables

So far, the discussion of tables has mentioned five elements: **table**, **caption**, **tr**, **th**, and **td**. These are the most commonly used elements. HTML 4 introduced several new elements that provide increased control over table formatting: **col**, **colgroup**, **thead**, **tfoot**, and **tbody**. A variety of attributes to control table data formatting are also supported in standards-aware browsers.

Rather than the simple structure presented earlier, a full HTML/XHTML table is defined by the specification using the following structure:

- An opening **<table>** tag.
- An optional caption specified by **<caption>** … **</caption>**.
- One or more groups of rows. These might consist of a header section specified by **<thead>**, a footer section specified by **<tfoot>**, and a body section specified by

<tbody>. Although all these elements are optional, the table must contain at least a series of rows specified by **<tr>**. The rows themselves must contain at least one header or data cell, specified by **<th>** and **<td>**, respectively.

- One or more groups of columns specified by **<colgroup>** with individual columns within the group indicated by **<col>**.
- A closing **</table>** tag.

The main difference between strict standards-oriented tables and the more basic table form is that rows and columns can be grouped together. The advantage to grouping is that it conveys structural information about the table that might be useful for rendering the table more quickly or keeping it together when displaying on the screen. For example, specifying the **<thead>** or **<tfoot>** might allow a consistent header or footer to be used across larger tables when they span many screens (or sheets of paper when printed). The use of these elements is mandatory when working with dynamically populated tables that incorporate databinding as introduced by Microsoft and discussed later in this chapter.

The example that follows illustrates the use of the relatively uncommon HTML/XHTML table elements just presented.

```
<!DOCTYPE html PUBLIC "-//W3C//DTD XHTML 1.0 Transitional//EN"
"http://www.w3.org/TR/xhtml1/DTD/xhtml1-transitional.dtd">
<html xmlns="http://www.w3.org/1999/xhtml" lang="en">
<head>
<title>Standard HTML/XHTML Tables</title>
<meta http-equiv="content-type" content="text/html; charset=ISO-8859-1" />
</head>
<body>

<table border="1" frame="box" rules="groups">
<caption>Fun with Food</caption>
<colgroup>
    <col />
</colgroup>

<colgroup>
    <col align="center" />
    <col align="char" char="." charoff="2" />
</colgroup>

<thead>
<tr>
    <th bgcolor="yellow">Fruit</th>
    <th bgcolor="yellow">Color</th>
    <th bgcolor="yellow">Cost per pound</th>
</tr>
</thead>

<tfoot>
<tr>
   <th colspan="3">This has been another fine table example.</th>
</tr>
```

```
</tfoot>

<tbody>
<tr>
    <td>Grapes</td>
    <td>Purple</td>
    <td>$1.45</td>
</tr>

<tr>
    <td>Cherries</td>
    <td>Red</td>
    <td>$1.99</td>
</tr>

<tr>
    <td>Kiwi</td>
    <td>Brown</td>
    <td>$11.50</td>
</tr>
</tbody>

</table>
</body>
</html>
```


The first thing to notice in this code is the use of the **frame** and **rules** attributes for the **<table>** tag. The **frame** attribute specifies which sides of the frame that surrounds the table will be visible. In this example, the value is set to **box**, which means that the frame around the outside of the table is on. Other values for this attribute include **above**, **below**, **hsides**, **vsides**, **lhs**, **rhs**, **void**, and **border**. The meaning of all these values is discussed in the table syntax section of Appendix A.

Do not confuse the idea of the **frame** attribute with that of **rules**. The **rules** attribute defines the rules that might appear between the actual cells in the table. In the example, the value of **rules** is set to **groups**; this displays lines between the row or column groupings of the table. The **rules** attribute also takes a value of **none**, **groups**, **rows**, **cols**, and **all**.

The other major difference in the preceding table example is the inclusion of the **<thead>** and **<tbody>** tags. **<thead>** contains the rows (**<tr>**), headings (**<th>**), and cells (**<td>**) that make up the head of the table. In addition to organization and the application of styles, the advantage of grouping these items is that it might be possible to repeat the elements over multiple pages (under certain browsers). Imagine printing out a large table and having the headers for the rows appear on every page of the printout. This is what **<thead>** might be able to provide. Similarly, the **<tfoot>** tag creates a footer to use in the table, which also might run over multiple pages. Lastly, the **<tbody>** tag indicates the body of the table, which contains the rows and columns that make up the inner part of a table. Whereas there should be only one occurrence of **<thead>** and **<tfoot>**, there can be multiple occurrences of **<tbody>**. Multiple bodies in a document might seem confusing, but these elements are more for grouping purposes than anything else. When a table is specified without **<thead>**, **<tfoot>**, or **<tbody>,** it is assumed to have one body by default.

Notice that one of the **<col>** tags in the example uses the **char** value for **align** in conjunction with the **char** attribute:

```
<col align="char" char="." />
```

This is meant to make the contents of the cells in that column line up with a certain character; in this case, a decimal point. The intended effect would be useful for aligning numbers with decimal points:

Fun with Food

Fruit	Color	Cost per pound
Grapes	Purple	$1.45
Cherries	Red	$1.99
Kiwi	Brown	$11.50
This has been another fine table example.		

Unfortunately, this doesn't seem to work in just any browser:

Fun with Food

Fruit	Color	Cost per pound
Grapes	Purple	$1.45
Cherries	Red	$1.99
Kiwi	Brown	$11.50
This has been another fine table example.		

Although data tables are becoming more difficult to code, you can take heart from the variety of tools that can be used to create them. Most HTML editing tools can easily add the elements needed to make tables; Macromedia Dreamweaver and Homesite offer tools for table creation. This is good, because the combination of standard table elements along with various proprietary extensions introduced by Microsoft results in a dizzying array of elements and attributes for the individual table cells. For those inclined to delve into all the details, the complete syntax for the **table** element and all associated elements can be found in Appendix A.

Databinding: Tables Generated from a Data Source

Tables often contain row after row of identically formatted data that originates in a database. There are two basic methods to create these data-dependent tables. Neither one is ideal:

- If the table data is relatively static, it is common to build a long table by hand or with a tool, individually coding each data cell.
- If the table data is dynamic, it is common to generate the entire page containing the table using a server-side technology such as CGI, ASP, ColdFusion, or PHP as discussed in Chapter 13.

The first approach is difficult for an HTML author. The second, which does not really qualify as HTML authoring, usually requires programming and server access. *Databinding,* while a proprietary client-side browser technology introduced by Microsoft, can be much simpler to use. The basic idea is to dynamically bind HTML elements to data coming from an external source such as a text file, XML file, or database. Although not technically restricted to HTML tables, it does represent a simpler, more powerful approach for generating large data-dependent tables.

In HTML databinding, a data source that provides information is associated with a data consumer that presents it. The data source is a control with some means to access external information that is embedded in an HTML document using the **<object>** tag. This tag is briefly introduced in Chapter 9, and is further explained in Chapter 15. For now, it will be useful to understand that **<object>** adds a small program to the page that can be used to access an external data source. The document also contains a data consumer, an HTML element that uses special attributes to ask the ActiveX control for data that the element subsequently displays. Data consumers come in two sorts: those that present single data values, and those that present tabular data. Tables obviously fall into the latter category.

Creating an HTML table using databinding is a very simple process. It is necessary to define only one table row. The rest are generated automatically according to the template defined by the first row. Think of each row in a tabular data set as corresponding to a database record, and each column as corresponding to a database field. A template table row is defined in HTML that associates **<td>** or **<th>** tags with field names in the data set. A table will subsequently be generated with one row for each record in the data set, and with cell values filled in from the appropriate record fields. The data source control might support processing capabilities such as sorting or filtering the data set. If so, the table can be dynamically regenerated on the client side in response to updated information from the data source. For example, a data source might contain a tabular data set for product price information. One field might contain the name of the product and another its price. By default, a table could present this information sorted alphabetically by product name. In response to a button on an HTML page, the data source could sort the data set by price. The table that displays the information would be dynamically regenerated.

To better understand the idea of databinding, consider the following simple example. An external data file contains two or more columns of comma-delimited data. The first line contains the names of the data set fields corresponding to the columns. The following lines contain the actual data for the appropriate fields. The sample external data file called alphabet.txt is shown here:

```
Letter, Thing
A, Apple
B, Boy
C, Cat
D, Dog
E, Elephant
F, Fox
G, Girl
H, Hat
```

To access the data, an HTML document references an object for a data source control and a related table definition. The following is an example of how this would be accomplished:

```
<!DOCTYPE html PUBLIC "-//W3C//DTD XHTML 1.0 Transitional//EN"
"http://www.w3.org/TR/xhtml1/DTD/xhtml1-transitional.dtd">
<html xmlns="http://www.w3.org/1999/xhtml" lang="en">
<head>
<title>Data Binding Example</title>
<meta http-equiv="content-type" content="text/html; charset=ISO-8859-1" />
<!--   validation not possible due to datasrc and datfld attributes -->
</head>
<body>
<object id="alphabet"
        classid="clsid:333C7BC4-460F-11D0-BC04-0080C7055A83">
    <param name="DataURL" value="alphabet.txt" />
    <param name="UseHeader" value="True" />
</object>

<table datasrc="#alphabet" border="1">
<thead>
    <tr bgcolor="yellow">
        <th>Letter</th>
        <th>Reminder</th>
    </tr>
</thead>
<tbody>
    <tr align="center">
        <td><span datafld="Letter"></span></td>
        <td><span datafld="Thing"></span></td>
    </tr>
</tbody>
</table>
</body>
</html>
```

This HTML code generates a table from the file alphabet.txt in which each table row contains a letter of the alphabet and the name of a thing that can remind the reader of that letter. The rendering of this example under Internet Explorer is shown in Figure 7-11.

Let us examine a little more closely the pieces needed to make this databinding example work. First, the data source uses the Tabular Data Control (TDC) object: an ActiveX control provided by Microsoft and identified by the lengthy class identifier. This particular control locates and manipulates text data files in a tabular format. Other controls supporting databinding could have been used instead. These can support different data access capabilities such as access to remote relational databases. The Microsoft ActiveX Data Objects control (ADO), however, is a representative example. The TDC supports several parameters, two of which are used in this example. The **"DataURL"** parameter tells the TDC the name and location of the data file it is to use. In this case, because only a filename is provided, the TDC looks in the same directory containing the Web page. By default, the TDC treats every line in a data file as data. The **"UseHeader"** parameter tells the TDC that the first line in the data file does not contain data but rather the names of data fields.

As a data consumer, the **table** element uses its **datasrc** attribute to connect to a data source. Note in the example how this attribute is set to the name of the **<object>** tag invoking the data source control. Like anything referenced by an **id**, the object name must be preceded

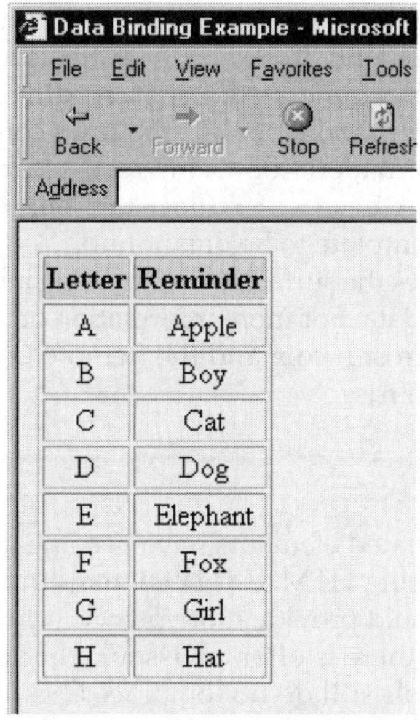

FIGURE 7-11 Databinding example under Internet Explorer

by the # symbol and the **<object>** tag must declare a name using the **id** attribute in order to be accessed by a data consumer. In summary, the **datasrc** attribute identifies a data source to be used in generating a table.

The next step is to associate cells in the template table row with particular fields in the data set. This is done using the **datafld** attribute of appropriate elements. It contains the name of the field in the data set that its element is to be bound to. If data set–specific names are not defined, fields can be identified using default positional names: "Column1", "Column2", and so forth. The **<td>** tag, commonly used for cell data, does not support the **datafld** attribute. To bind a field to a table cell, the **<td>** tag needs to contain one of the elements that supports **datafld**. The tags that make the most sense in the context of a table are **<span>**, **<div>**, **<object>**, and **<img>**. The latter two tags illustrate that databinding is not confined to textual data. For example, a column of images can be created by using a tag declaration such as **<img datafld="Picture">** inside a table cell. Note that the usual **src** attribute would not be required. Instead, the **datafld** attribute identifies a field inside the data set that contains a valid image filename, such as mypict.gif, and binds the image to that value.

Microsoft provides one additional attribute, **datapagesize**, which can be used to limit the number of records displayed from the datasource document. For example, if the **<table>** tag in the preceding example were revised to read

```
<table datasrc="#alphabet" border="1" datapagesize="3">
```

the rendering of the table would display only the first three rows (A, B, and C) of the information in alphabet.txt.

If a table does not explicitly declare header or footer section elements, then implicitly all table content is in the body section. In static tables, this usually does not have visual consequences, but it does in tables generated by databinding. All body rows are included in the template for table row generation, not just the rows containing databound fields. To prevent header or footer information from being repeated for every row in the table, it is necessary to enclose it with the **<thead>** or **<tfoot>** tag. The **<tbody>** tag then can be used to signal the beginning of the template to be databound.

Such a brief example scratches the surface of databinding and merely shows the importance of tables in relation to dynamic data. For more information on databinding, visit the Microsoft MSDN site at http://msdn.microsoft.com and the Remote Data Service site at http://www.microsoft.com/data/ado/rds/.

Summary

The **table** element and its associated elements have become the most commonly used means of creating Web page layouts using HTML/XHTML markup. Although positioning through style sheets (see Chapter 10) should provide more precise layout capacities, browser support is still somewhat inconsistent, there is often an issue of backward compatibility, and developers and Web design tools still do not embrace CSS fully. For better or worse, for many developers tables are still the best way to create layouts that work across multiple browsers, especially when considering older browsers. Even if tables lose their layout duties, they are very useful; remember, they are meant to present tabular data.

CHAPTER 8

Frames

Tables and the other HTML techniques introduced in the previous chapters provide a significant improvement in Web page layout. Many designers want even more design facilities, including multiple windows. Such expectations aren't unreasonable because these features are common in computer interfaces. Such power comes at a price, however. Frames seem to provide significant layout flexibility, but when misused, they can confuse users—or even lock them out of a site completely. While some usability pundits have given frames a bad reputation, don't let this keep you from using them. When properly used, frames have a place in the Web designer's arsenal.

Frames

A framed document divides a browser window into multiple panes, or smaller window frames. Each frame can contain a different document. The benefits of this approach are obvious: users can view information in one frame while keeping another frame open for reference instead of moving back and forth between pages. The contents of one frame can be manipulated, or *linked*, to the contents of another. This enables designers to build sophisticated interfaces. For example, one frame can contain links that produce a result in another frame. An example of such an interface is shown in Figure 8-1.

Frames offer many useful navigation possibilities such as a table of contents, site index, and lists of links. Frames also offer *fixed-screen navigation*—whereby site navigation buttons stay onscreen throughout a visit regardless of the size of the document. The lack of scrolling and the minimization of screen refresh afforded by framed documents can provide great advantages over the single-window approach. On the other hand, framed pages can be difficult to deal with. Frame sites confuse many users because it's not always clear what parts of a page will update when a button is pressed. Furthermore, frames tend to cause other usability problems, such as hiding the current URL, causing printing and bookmarking difficulty, excluding some search engines, and taking up valuable screen real estate with scrollbars and borders.

Regardless of these potential problems, many site designers rushed to develop framed pages as soon as frames were introduced. They removed them just as quickly, however, due to navigational problems and user complaints. Fortunately, today many of the problems associated with frames have been fixed at the browser level, and users have become more comfortable understanding and working with frames. Used properly and in the right

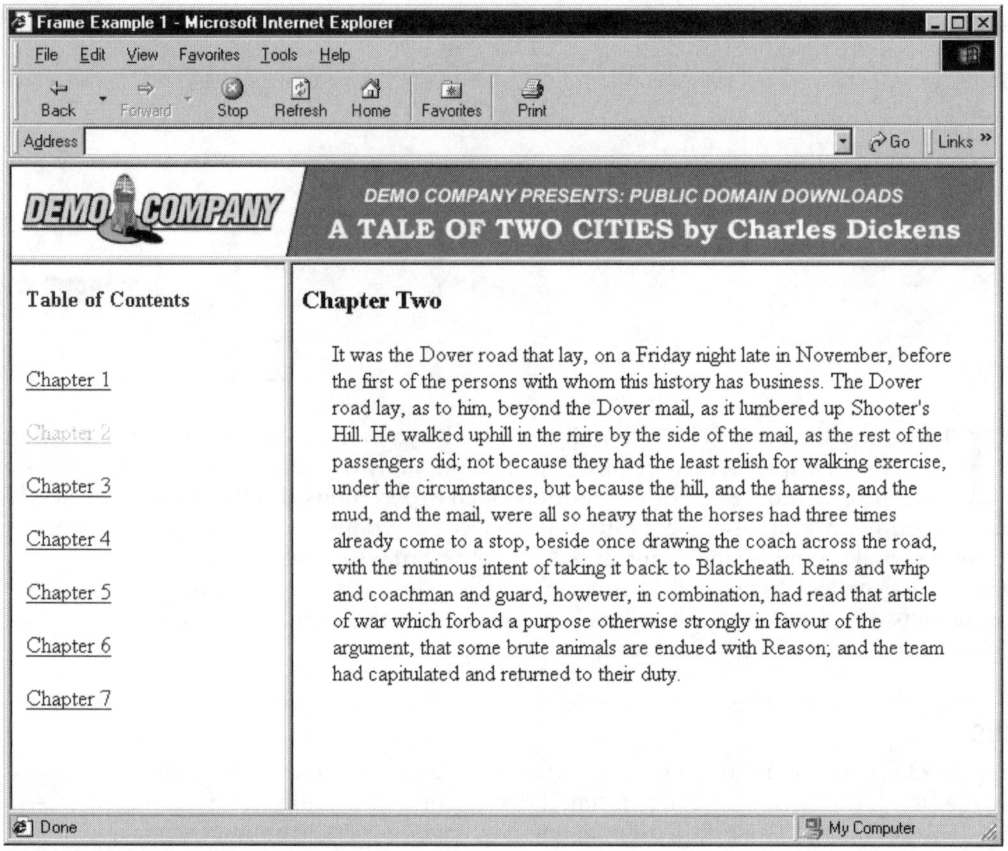

FIGURE 8-1 Example frame interface

situation, frames are important tools in the Web designer's toolbox. Frame-phobic Web designers should consider that frames are no longer considered proprietary browser extensions and are included in the HTML and XHTML standards.

Overview of Frames

A *frame* is an independent scrolling region, or window, of a Web page. Every Web page can be divided into many individual frames, which can even be nested within other frames. Of course, fixed screen sizes limit how many frames can realistically be used simultaneously. Each frame in a window can be separated from the others with a border; in this way, a framed document might resemble a table. However, frames aren't a fancy form of tables. Each separate frame can contain a different document, referenced by a unique URL. Because the documents included in a framed region can be much larger than the space available onscreen, each frame can provide a scrollbar or other controls to manipulate the size of the frame. Individual frames usually are named so that they can be referenced through links or scripting, allowing the contents of one frame to affect the contents of another. This referencing capability is a major difference between tables and frames. Frames provide layout facilities and, potentially, navigation.

Simple Frame Example

The first thing to remember about a framed page is that the screen is composed of several documents. To illustrate, a page with two frames actually involves three files:

- The framing document that defines the framing relationship
- The file that contains the contents of frame one
- The file that contains the contents of frame two

Consider the simple two-frame document shown in Figure 8-2. The first frame, on the left, covers about 20 percent of the screen and contains a list of links contained in a file called links.html. The larger column on the right, which takes up the other 80 percent of the screen, displays content initially referenced in a file called display.html. The actual document that sets up the framing relationship is called basicframes.html.

The framing document (basicframes.html) has a slightly different structure than a typical HTML or XHTML file. Specifically, it uses a **<frameset>** tag instead of a **<body>** tag. Because of this you will notice that a frameset document actually uses a totally different doctype statement, which references a frameset DTD. Within the framing document, the **frameset** element defines the set of frames that makes up the document. The major attributes of this element are **rows** and **cols**. In this example, two columns take up set percentages of the total screen, so the code reads **<frameset cols="20%, 80%">**. Setting up something like **<frameset rows="10%, 80%, 10%">**, which sets up three rows across the screen taking up 10 percent, 80 percent, and 10 percent of the screen respectively, would be just as easy. Within the **frameset** element, individual **<frame>** tags are used to specify the documents that are placed within the rows or columns defined by the **frameset** element. The basic syntax of the **<frame>** tag is **<frame src="*URL of framed document*" name="*unique frame name*" id="*unique frame name*">.** Notice once again the use of both a **name** attribute for older browser support and an **id** attribute for newer browsers. The following is a simple example of a basic framing document:

```
<!DOCTYPE html PUBLIC "-//W3C//DTD XHTML 1.0 Frameset//EN"
"http://www.w3.org/TR/xhtml1/DTD/xhtml1-frameset.dtd">
<html xmlns="http://www.w3.org/1999/xhtml" lang="en">
<head>
<title>Frame Example 1</title>
<meta http-equiv="content-type" content="text/html; charset=ISO-8859-1" />
</head>
<frameset cols="20%, 80%">
<frame src="links.html" name="links" id="links" />
<frame src="display.html" name="display" id="display" />
<noframes>
   <body>
     <p>This document uses frames.
      Please follow this link to a
     <a href="noframes.html">no frames</a>
      version.</p>
```

PART III

```
  </body>
</noframes>
</frameset>
</html>
```

In the preceding example, the file links.html would be placed in the frame column comprising 20 percent of the screen, and the file display.html would be placed in the 80 percent column. Always make sure to consider the order of the **<frame>** tags, as their positions should be relative to the rows or columns defined in the nearest enclosing **<frameset>** tag. Once the framing document is set up, you then have to populate the individual frames using the **<frame>** tags. The **src** attribute is set to the URL of the document to load in the particular frame. For a complete example, the contents of links.html and display.html are presented here:

File: links.html

```
<!DOCTYPE html PUBLIC "-//W3C//DTD XHTML 1.0 Transitional//EN"
"http://www.w3.org/TR/xhtml1/DTD/xhtml1-transitional.dtd">
<html xmlns="http://www.w3.org/1999/xhtml" lang="en">
<head>
<title>Links</title>
<meta http-equiv="content-type" content="text/html; charset=ISO-8859-1" />
</head>
<body>
<h2>Links</h2>
<hr />
<a href="http://www.democompany.com" target="display">Demo Company</a>
</body>
</html>
```

File: display.html

```
<!DOCTYPE html PUBLIC "-//W3C//DTD XHTML 1.0 Transitional//EN"
"http://www.w3.org/TR/xhtml1/DTD/xhtml1-transitional.dtd">
<html xmlns="http://www.w3.org/1999/xhtml">
<head>
<title>Display</title>
<meta http-equiv="content-type" content="text/html; charset=ISO-8859-1" />
</head>
<body>
<h2>Display</h2>
<hr />
<p>Contents of second frame and link clicks will be displayed here.</p>
</body>
</html>
```

Putting all three files in the same directory and loading the framed document (basicframes.htm) into a browser should produce a rendering similar to the one shown in Figure 8-2. (Online, see http://www.htmlref.com/examples/chapter8/basicframes.html.)

The Use of <noframes>

The **<noframes>** tag should contain the markup and text to be displayed when a browser that doesn't support frames accesses the Web page. The **<noframes>** tag should be found

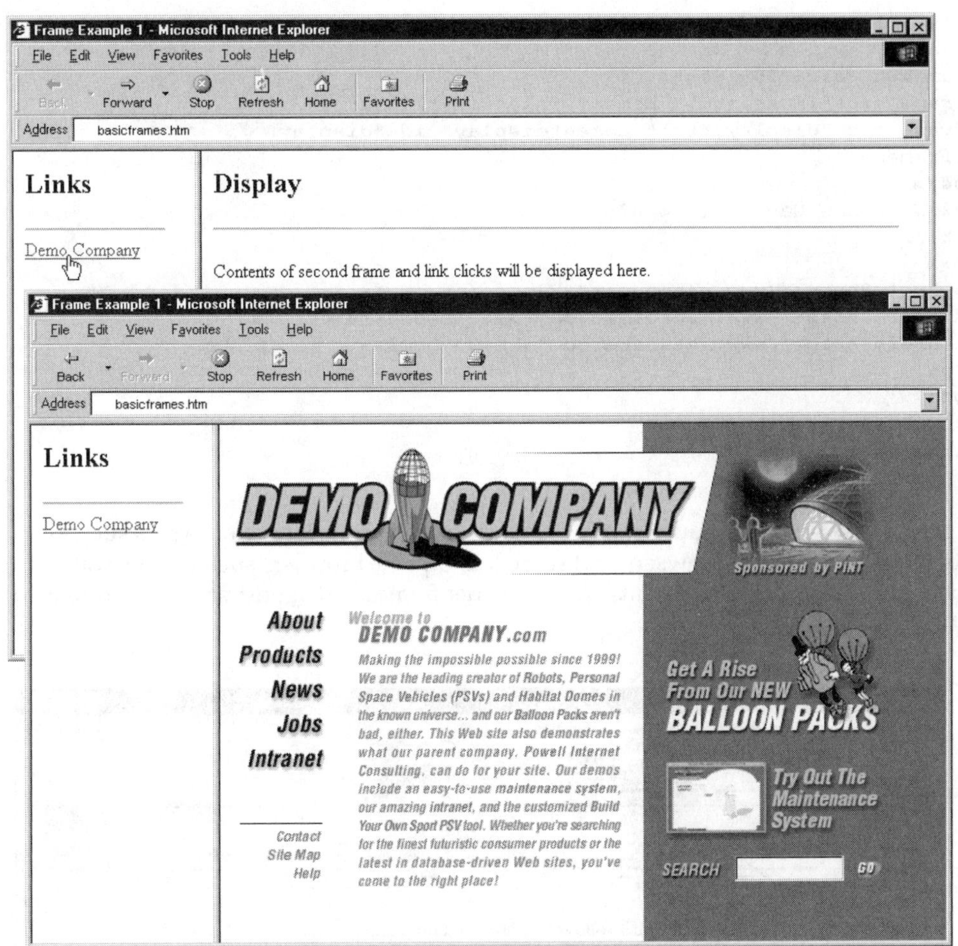

FIGURE 8-2 Simple two-frame example in Internet Explorer

PART III

only within the **frameset** element. Nevertheless, **<noframes>** is often found directly outside the **frameset** element. Because of the permissive nature of browsers, this tends to be interpreted correctly. Also, for XHTML compliance, the **noframes** element should contain a **body** element and a correctly formed HTML document within it; HTML 4 does not require a body tag within **noframes**.

The following example provides the links that occur in the links frame for browsers that don't support frames:

```
<!DOCTYPE html PUBLIC "-//W3C//DTD XHTML 1.0 Frameset//EN"
"http://www.w3.org/TR/xhtml1/DTD/xhtml1-frameset.dtd">
<html xmlns="http://www.w3.org/1999/xhtml" lang="en">
<head>
<title>Simple Noframes Example</title>
```

```
<meta http-equiv="content-type" content="text/html; charset=ISO-8859-1" />
</head>
<frameset cols="20%,80%">
 <frame src="links.html" name="links" id="links" />
 <frame src="display.html" name="display" id="display" />
<noframes>
<body>
 <h2>No Frame Navigation</h2>
 <hr />
 <p>
 <a href="http://www.yahoo.com">Yahoo</a><br />
 <a href="http://www.microsoft.com">Microsoft</a><br />
 <a href="http://www.netscape.com">Netscape</a>
 </p>
</body>
</noframes>
</frameset>
</html>
```

Most browsers today support frames. Of course, extreme legacy browsers such as Netscape 1.*x* generation browsers and some less capable browsers such as those on cell phones or personal digital assistants will not render frames. A demonstration of **<noframes>** is shown in Figure 8-3.

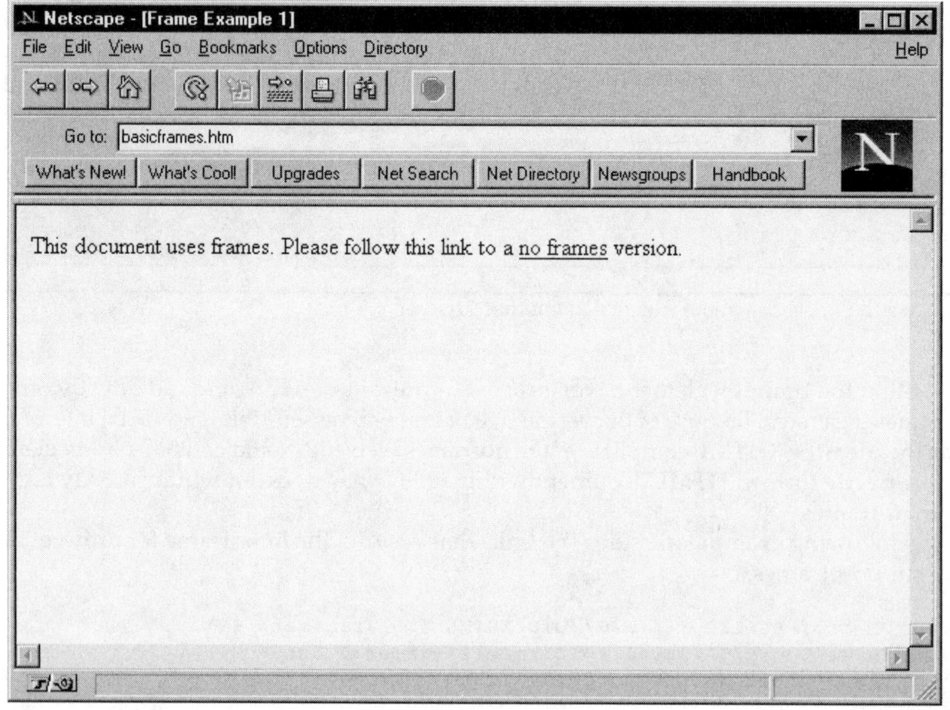

FIGURE 8-3 Legacy browsers might lack support for frames.

Although it seems more and more pointless to support rarely used legacy browsers, today's restricted browsers such as PDA-based browsers or digital cell phone browsers often have problems with frames due to limited screen region or memory. Furthermore, many search engine indexing spiders do not fully support frames. Because of this, **<noframes>** really should be used. Although putting a second copy of site content within **<noframes>** makes the site usable across browsers, you must then update two copies of the same content. Because of this, many designers simply put a statement in the **noframes** element that indicates that the site requires a frame-supporting browser for viewing. This doesn't make the site very accessible, but it does provide some feedback to users and cuts down on content duplication.

Frame Targeting

When you use frames, it is often beneficial to make the links in one frame target another frame. When a user clicks a link in one framed document, the requested page should load in another frame. In the simple frame example in the preceding section, you might want to have the links in the frame named links target the frame named display. Link targeting has two steps:

1. Ensure frame naming by setting the **name** and **id** attributes in each **<frame>** tag to a unique value. While the specification encourages the use of the **id** attribute for naming frames, practice shows that frame targeting in browsers is still generally accomplished using the **name** attribute and not the **id** attribute, which is used mostly for scripting and style sheet access even in modern browsers. For the sake of safety, designers should consider setting both **id** and **name** in a **<frame>** tag to the same value.
2. Use the **target** attribute in an **<a>** tag to set the target for the anchor. For example, a link such as **<a href="http://www.yahoo.com" target="display">** loads the site specified by the **href** into the window called "display," if such a frame exists. If the target specified by the name doesn't exist, the link typically spawns a new window.

You can name your frames anything you like. A simple short word without special characters is the best approach, such as window1, frame3, displayregion, or similar value. Designers also should be wary of using special characters or spaces in the frame name, as they could cause problems. Some values for the **target** attribute could also have special meanings, and should never be used as a frame name. These values and their meanings are summarized in Table 8-1.

Setting the **target** attribute of the links within a site to **_top** ensures that any frames being used are removed after a link is followed. Regardless of your use of frames, using

TABLE 8-1 Reserved target Values

Value	Meaning
_blank	Load the page into a new, generally unnamed, window.
_self	Load the page over the current frame.
_parent	Load the link over the parent frame.
_top	Load the link over all the frames in the window.

the **_top** value for the **target** attribute in links in your site might be beneficial. Sites often frame external links in an attempt to "capture" the user. Because this can limit layout or be undesirable in other ways, site designers often use scripts or simply set target attributes on all site links to **_top** to break out of any enclosing frames.

The **_blank** value for **target** is also useful because it opens another window in which to display the link. The only problem with this action is that the window might tile directly on top of the previous browser window, and the user might not know that multiple windows are open. With JavaScript, as discussed in Chapter 14, it is possible to size and position windows that are opened.

The **_parent** value isn't encountered often because it is useful only when frames are nested to a great degree. The **_parent** value enables you to overwrite the parent frame that contains the nested frame without destroying any frames that the parent might be nested within.

The **_self** value for **target**, which loads a page over its current frame, duplicates the typical default action for most browsers.

NOTE *The HTML and XHTML specifications discourage frame names beginning with an underscore because they might be reserved for values such as **_top**.*

The following is an alternative for the file links.html presented previously. This document uses frame targeting with the names defined in the previous simple frame example. Use it in place of the previous links.html file and load the frameset file to test the target attribute for the **<a>** tag. (Online, see http://www.htmlref.com/examples/chapter8/frametargetting.html, which references this code in the file linktargets.html.)

```
<!DOCTYPE html PUBLIC "-//W3C//DTD XHTML 1.0 Transitional//EN"
"http://www.w3.org/TR/xhtml1/DTD/xhtml1-transitional.dtd">
<html xmlns="http://www.w3.org/1999/xhtml" lang="en">
<head>
<title>Link Targeting</title>
<meta http-equiv="content-type" content="text/html; charset=ISO-8859-1" />
</head>
<body>
<h2 align="center">Test Links</h2>
<hr />
<ul>
<li><a href="http://www.yahoo.com" target="display">
   Yahoo in frame named display</a></li>
<li><a href="http://www.aol.com" target="_blank">
   AOL in new window</a></li>
<li><a href="http://www.msn.com" target="_self">
   MSN in this frame</a></li>
<li><a href="http://www.excite.com" target="_top">
   Excite over whole window</a></li>
<li><a href="http://www.google.com" target="_parent">
   Google over the parent window (should be whole window)</a></li>
<li><a href="http://www.democompany.com" target="mysterywindow">
   DemoCompany in a window that hasn't been named</a></li>
</ul>
</body>
</html>
```

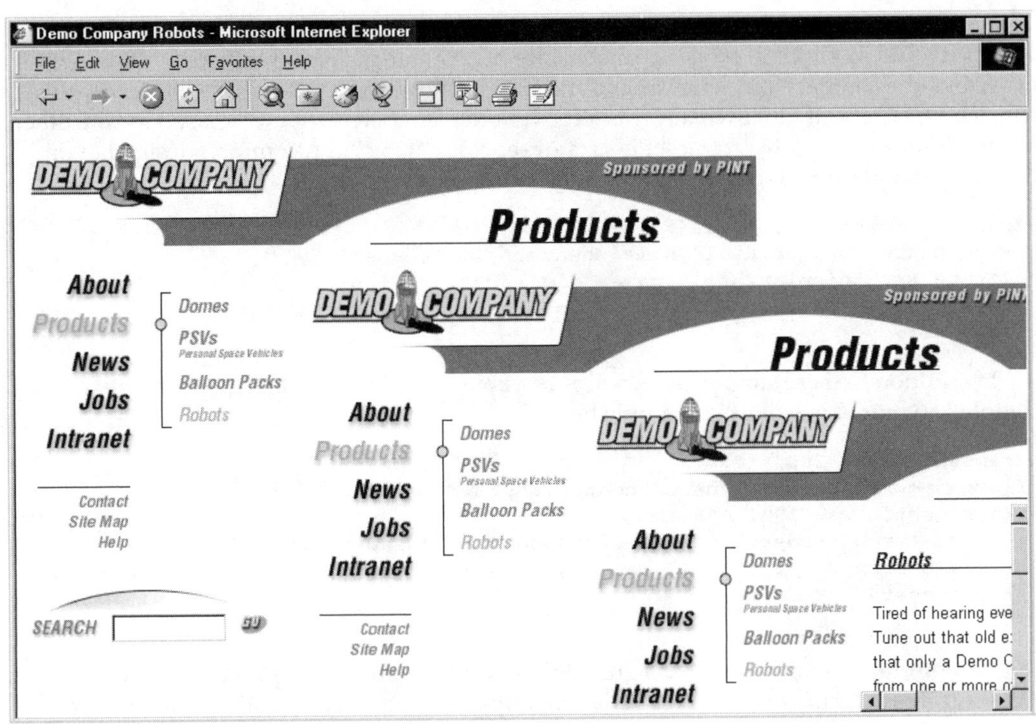

FIGURE 8-4 Frames within frames problem

As shown in the example, when referencing a nonexistent window such as "mysterywindow" the browser generally creates a brand-new window.

As long as you keep names consistent and frame layouts relatively basic, window targeting is fairly straightforward. However, sloppy coding can lead to a problem in which frames keep nesting inside of one another, as shown in Figure 8-4; authors should test links in a framed site thoroughly.

Frame Layouts

You can use frames to structure a page in a variety of ways. First consider that it is possible to use not only percentage values for frame sizing, but pixels and wildcard values. The **rows** and **cols** attributes also can be set to pixel values so that **<frameset cols="200,400">** defines a column 200 pixels wide, followed by a column 400 pixels wide. If the screen is smaller than 600 pixels, the contents might be clipped, or excessive scrolling might be required. If the screen is much larger, there might be a great deal of empty screen space. Because it is difficult to determine the exact size of the screen, it could be dangerous to set these attributes to exact values.

In general, you want to combine absolute pixel sizes with some more flexible measurements such as percentages or wildcards. If you know that the controls frame contains graphic buttons that are 150 pixels wide, consider setting the size of the first frame to 175 pixels to fit the graphic plus some white space. If the frame were any smaller than this size, the graphic would be clipped, so using an absolute pixel value makes sense when you know the size of the contents. But what should the size of the other frame be? Use the wildcard character (*) to specify that whatever is left over after 175 pixels should be used for the other frame. The code for such a frameset is **<frameset cols="175,*">**. A common design beyond the two-column frame is a three-row, header-footer frameset.

```
<frameset rows="100, *, 50">
  <frame src="header.html" name="header" id="header" />
  <frame src="display.html" name="display" id="display" />
  <frame src="footer.html" name="footer" id="footer" />
</frameset>
```

In addition to these simple layouts, it is possible to nest framesets together to create complex layouts. Consider the example here:

```
<frameset cols="200, *">
<frame src="links.html" name="controls" id="controls" />
  <frameset rows="100, *">
   <frame src="header.html" name="header" id="header" />
   <frame src="display.html" name="display" id="display" />
  </frameset>
</frameset>
```

This produces a three-frame design with the second column composed of two rows. An example rendering of such a frame layout appears in Figure 8-5 (online, see http://www.htmlref.com/examples/chapter8/nestedframes.html).

This sort of layout also can be accomplished by using the **<frame>** tags to reference documents containing additional **frameset** elements, although if carried too far this can lead to overly complicated page renderings. Even more complex designs, such as a fixed framed region in the middle of the screen, are possible with nesting. Consider the markup presented here, which could produce a result similar to the one shown in Figure 8-6. It also can be viewed online at http://www.htmlref.com/examples/chapter8/fixedframes.html.

```
<!DOCTYPE html PUBLIC "-//W3C//DTD XHTML 1.0 Frameset//EN"
"http://www.w3.org/TR/xhtml1/DTD/xhtml1-frameset.dtd">
<html xmlns="http://www.w3.org/1999/xhtml" lang="en">
<head>
<title>Frame Example 3</title>
<meta http-equiv="content-type" content="text/html; charset=ISO-8859-1" />
</head>
<frameset rows="100, *, 100">
  <frame src="blue.html" name="top" id="top" />
  <frameset cols="100,*,100">
   <frame src="blue.html" name="left" id="left" />
   <frame src="center.html" name="center" id="center" />
   <frame src="blue.html" name="right" id="right" />
  </frameset>
<frame src="blue.html" name="bottom" id="bottom" />
</frameset>
</html>
```

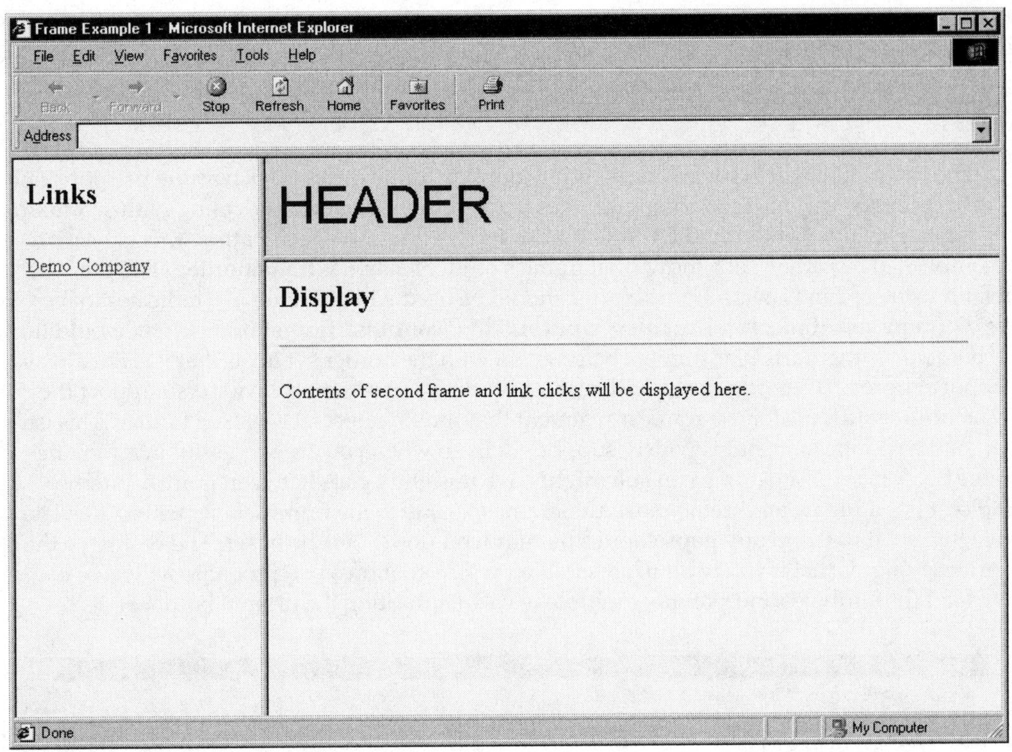

FIGURE 8-5 Nested frame design

The corresponding files blue.html and center.html are shown here for completeness:

File: blue.html

```
<!DOCTYPE html PUBLIC "-//W3C//DTD XHTML 1.0 Transitional//EN"
"http://www.w3.org/TR/xhtml1/DTD/xhtml1-transitional.dtd">
<html xmlns="http://www.w3.org/1999/xhtml" lang="en">
<head>
<title>Blue</title>
<meta http-equiv="content-type" content="text/html; charset=ISO-8859-1" />
</head>
<body bgcolor="blue">
  <!-- just a blank document -->
</body>
</html>
```

File: center.html

```
<!DOCTYPE html PUBLIC "-//W3C//DTD XHTML 1.0 Transitional//EN" "http://
www.w3.org/TR/xhtml1/DTD/xhtml1-transitional.dtd">
<html xmlns="http://www.w3.org/1999/xhtml" lang="en">
<head>
<title>Center</title>
<meta http-equiv="content-type" content="text/html; charset=ISO-8859-1" />
```

```
</head>
<body bgcolor="white">
  <h2 align="center">Frame Fun!</h2>
</body>
</html>
```

The main challenge when working with complex frame designs such as the previous one is to account for various rendering problems across browsers, such as dealing with scrolling.

First, consider removing the frame borders. According to specification, this is best accomplished by setting each individual frame's border using the **frameborder** attribute. The default value of **1** indicates a frame border should be used while a value of **0** indicates to remove it. So **<frame src="links.html" name="controls" id="controls" frameborder="0">** would turn off borders for this particular frame. The problem with the border syntax is that it is not always supported properly, particularly under older browsers. Also, most browsers support the **frameborder** attribute for the **frameset** element that should affect all enclosed frames. This isn't part of the specification, but is widely supported. Even when you are successful in removing frame borders in all situations you still might have unsightly gaps between frames. Internet Explorer has added a proprietary attribute, **framespacing,** to the **frameset** element to alleviate this. Just set it to **0** and any gaps should be removed under this browser. The reality of the border settings is that if you want to cover all browser situations, you probably will have to overload the attributes and provide multiple ways of indicating the desired border style.

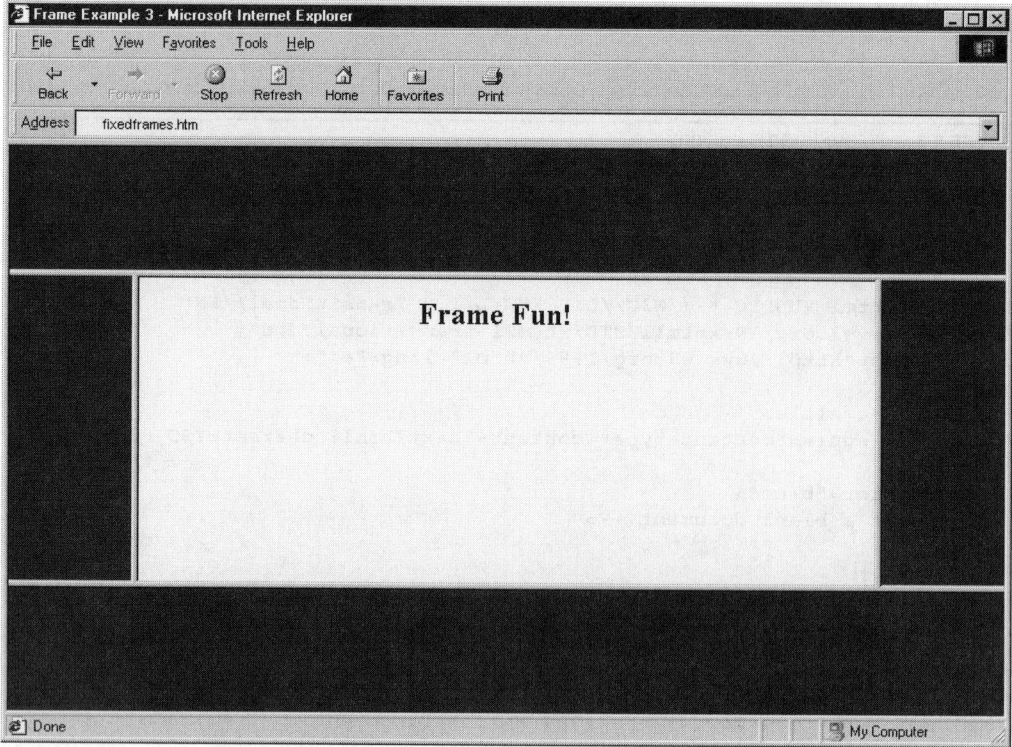

FIGURE 8-6 Fixed window frame design

If borders are left on, you might want to turn off scrolling or even indicate that the frame should not be resized. To set scrolling on a frame, use the **scrolling** attribute on a **<frame>** tag; by default, the value of this attribute is **auto**, which adds scrollbars as needed. However, setting the value to **yes** or **no** will explicitly indicate the presence or lack of scrollbars regardless of the content within the frame. The presence of the **noresize** attribute indicates that the user cannot resize a frame. The example here shows a frame with scrolling off and no resizing:

```
<frame src="test.html" name="frame1" id="frame1" border="0" noresize="noresize"
scrolling="no" />
```

NOTE *Given the XHTML requirement for all attributes to have values, the* ***noresize*** *attribute is set to the value of* ***noresize****.*

Always remember that turning off resizing or limiting scrolling could lead to trouble if the user doesn't have a screen that fits the framed content!

The last common attributes to consider for frame layouts are **marginheight** and **marginwidth**. These attributes are used to control the distance between the frame and its contents. Very often designers will set these values to **0** to achieve the effect of bleeding framed content right to the edge of the frame.

```
<frame src="blue.html" name="right" id="right" marginwidth="0" marginheight="0" />
```

The **frame** and **frameset** elements take a few other attributes beyond the ones previously discussed and the core attributes **id**, **class**, **style**, and **title**. Many browsers—notably Internet Explorer—provide numerous proprietary extensions including the use of transparency and color settings for borders. Interested readers should see Appendix A for complete syntax on these attributes. The next section discusses inline or floating frames, which would have made the previously presented nested frame example quite easy.

Floating Frames

Up to this point, all the frames shown have been attached to the sides of the browser (left, right, top, or bottom). Another form of frame, known as a *floating frame* but more appropriately called an *inline frame,* was initially introduced by Microsoft but has been incorporated into the HTML and XHTML standards. The idea of the floating frame is to create an inline framed region, or window, that acts similarly to any other embedded object, insofar as text can be flowed around it. An inline frame is defined by the **iframe** element and can occur anywhere within the **<body>** of an HTML document. Compare this to the **frame** element that should occur only within the **frameset** element.

The major attributes to set for an **<iframe>** tag include **src**, **height**, and **width**. The **src** is set to the URL of the file to load, while the **height** and **width** are set either to the pixel or percentage value of the screen that the floating frame region should consume. Like an **<img>** tag, floating frames support the **align** attribute for basic positioning within the flow of text. Like standard frames, the **iframe** element also supports **marginheight** and **marginwidth** attributes to control the margins on framed content. Internet Explorer supports the addition of the **hspace** and **vspace** attributes as well, although the HTML and XHTML specification does not. In general, like most elements, more complex presentation should be handled by CSS rules, as discussed in Chapters 10 and 11.

Note that, unlike the empty **frame** element, the **iframe** element has a closing tag. The tag pair **<iframe>** and **</iframe>** should contain any HTML markup code and text that is supposed to be displayed in browsers that don't support floating frames—thus the concept of **<noframes>** is provided in the tag itself. A simple example of floating frames is shown here:

```
<!DOCTYPE html PUBLIC "-//W3C//DTD XHTML 1.0 Transitional//EN"
"http://www.w3.org/TR/xhtml1/DTD/xhtml1-transitional.dtd">
<html xmlns="http://www.w3.org/1999/xhtml" lang="en">
<head>
<title>Floating Frame Example</title>
<meta http-equiv="content-type" content="text/html; charset=ISO-8859-1" />
</head>
<body>
<h1 align="center">Floating Frame Example</h1>
<iframe src="file1.html" name="iframe1" id="iframe1" width="350"
height="200" align="left">
There would be a floating frame here if your browser supported it.
</iframe>

<p>This is a simple example of how floating frames are used. Notice
that in many ways the floating frame acts very similar to an inline
image. Floating frames act like embedded objects in many ways.</p>
</body>
</html>
```

NOTE *Because the **iframe** element occurs within the **<body>** of a document, the actual doctype used with a document using an **iframe** is the standard one and not the frameset doctype.*

The rendering of this example code is shown in Figure 8-7. Note how the Netscape 4.*x* generation browser does not support the **iframe** element, but renders the enclosed text instead, whereas browsers such as Internet Explorer 6 and Netscape 7 render the floating frame (see http://www.htmlref.com/examples/chapter8/iframe.html).

Like other frames it is possible to target an inline frame using the target attribute of the **a** element. Given the previous example, a link such as

```
<a href="http://www.democompany.com" target="iframe1">Load in iframe</a>
```

would have loaded the retrieved file within the inline frame. Unfortunately, a troublesome side effect can occur for those browsers such as Netscape 2.*x*, 3.*x*, and 4.*x* as well as early versions of Opera, which support link targeting but not the **iframe** element. In this situation, the link will still render and open a new window, which is what would normally happen if you set a link target to a non-existent window.

The syntax for **iframe** is strikingly similar to the **img** element as well as to other elements, such as **object**, that are used to insert other forms of content inline. The complete syntax of the **iframe** element is provided in Appendix A.

Using Frames

One of the biggest problems with frames is that they initially were used simply because they existed. Framed documents can provide considerable benefit, but at a price. A potential benefit of frames is that they allow content to be fixed onscreen, although CSS will eventually provide this effect in compliant browsers. As demonstrated in previous examples, one frame can

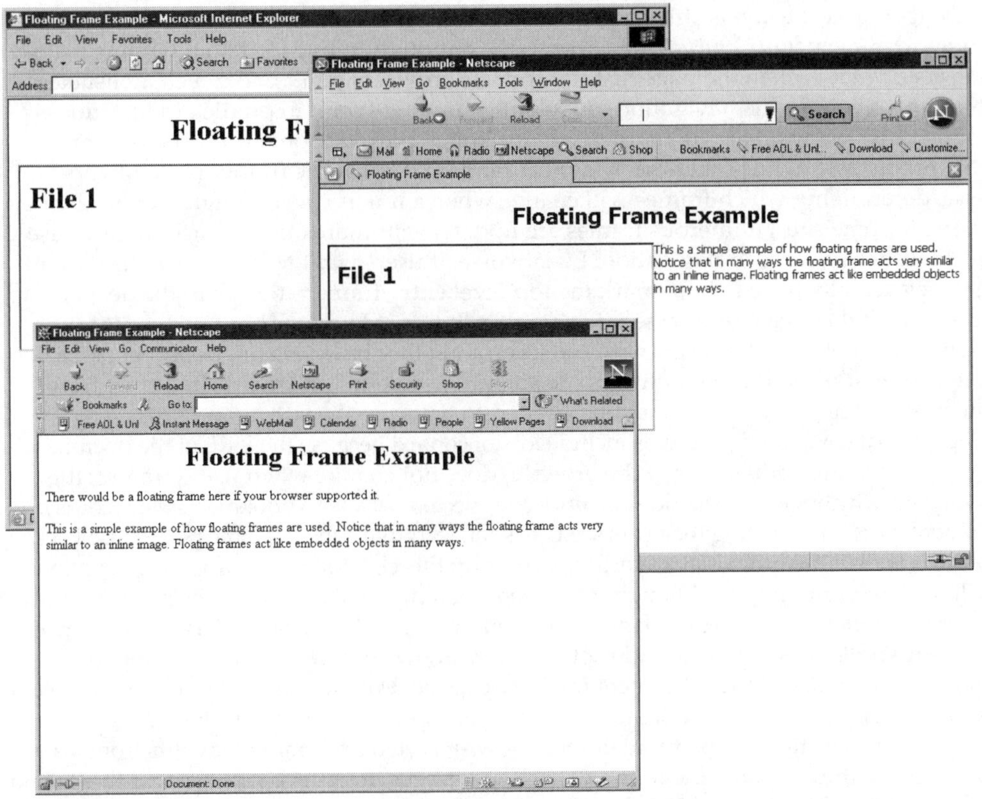

FIGURE 8-7 Rendering of <iframe> example

contain navigation, while the other frame contains the actual information. Keeping navigation onscreen provides a convenient way to navigate the body of information. Furthermore, if one frame has fixed navigation, the user might perceive the Web interface to be more responsive because only part of the screen needs to update between selections. In addition to this benefit, frames enable the designer to present two or more documents simultaneously, which is useful for comparison. Despite their wonderful benefits, however, frames have their costs, as explained in the next section.

Frame Problems

Many usability experts are extremely critical of frames. Given the current implementation of frames, and the many designers who don't understand the potential drawbacks of framed documents, the statement often attributed to usability expert Jakob Nielsen that "frames can give designers more rope to hang themselves with" has some truth to it. However, browser vendors are addressing many of the problems of frames. With luck, designers will learn to use frames only when they provide added benefit.

The problems with frames are numerous, and include problems with design, navigation, bookmarking, URL context, search engine compatibility, and printing.

Navigation confusion is still a big issue when using frames. Under Netscape 2, the first browser to implement frames, the browser Back button didn't go back in the frame history, but instead went back in the page history. Today's browsers don't make such a mistake but frames still make the navigation model much more difficult to predict. In fact, does the user really know what will happen when a link is clicked? Some frame layouts are highly predictable, while others seem almost random. Unless the framing is kept very simple, determining which frames will change when a link is clicked might not be obvious to users. In some sites, numerous frames are updated simultaneously, which might cause users to lose their sense of navigation. Even worse, if users want to bookmark the current page, they actually have to bookmark the top-level entry frame rather than the deeper level to which they have progressed. Fortunately, Internet Explorer has fixed most frame bookmarking problems, but users with Netscape and other browsers might find bookmarking framed content difficult. Even if users are somehow able to bookmark the actual frame content, they could lose any navigation needed to navigate the site upon return.

Additional navigation problems include loss of context because the URL of the document, as displayed in the address bar of the browser, does not change when using frames; this accounts for why bookmarking doesn't work as expected because a bookmark just records a document's URL. Not letting the users see URLs can lead to trouble as some people use URLs as a way to orient themselves at a site; frames give up this clue to location. In many situations, it is difficult to print frames. Although the contents of individual frames can be printed, printing an entire document consisting of many frames can cause problems, particularly if the framed document scrolls. The newer versions of browsers allow complete frame printing, but page authors should understand that content might be clipped. With frames and resolution problems it is no wonder that many site designers have adopted special print-specific Web pages.

Finally, search engines and more limited browsers often find framed layouts troublesome. In some cases, they are not able to travel to deeper pages in a site, particularly if there is no **<noframes>** tag. This issue alone could keep developers from using frames on a public site.

Site designers should thoroughly consider these limitations before rushing to use frames, particularly when similar layout effects might be achieved using style sheets without such problems. While none of the frame problems are insurmountable, designers should approach the technology with caution, and not just use it to show off their technical prowess. Readers looking for more details on dealing with frames should reference Chapter 8 in the companion book *Web Design: The Complete Reference, Second Edition* (Osborne 2002), also by the same author, as it provides many techniques for dynamic frame building, bookmarking fixes, and frame busting.

Summary

Web page layout using HTML tags is really not appropriate, but until the rise of CSS, frames were often used as both navigational and presentational elements. While frames can provide great power in making sophisticated layouts, it comes with a great price. Navigational confusion, printing mishaps, and design problems can all result from the misuse of frames. However, when frames are used properly (for example, to provide a fixed table of contents or navigation aid), they are a valuable addition to the page designer's arsenal. Because of their power and popularity, frames finally are included in the HTML and XHTML specifications, so you shouldn't have to worry about their future use. Although frames can be used to create impressive and dynamic layouts, similar effects can be achieved using less troubling technology—particularly style sheets, which are discussed in Chapters 10 and 11.

CHAPTER 9

Multimedia

One of the innovations that led to the development of the modern Web was the Mosaic browser's introduction of images in 1993—but this was just the first step toward the dream of a multimedia Web. These days, the Web can bring a variety of media forms—including sound, video, and animation—right to your browser or desktop. The last several years have seen a number of changes in this area of the Web, particularly where music distribution is concerned. This chapter looks at some of the latest, most popular technologies for Web multimedia, and how to include them in Web pages.

Audio

Few things are as persuasive as sound. Just try watching television with the volume muted; it's not terribly interesting. Sound is a vital element of true multimedia Web pages—but how should sound be used? What Web audio technology is appropriate for the job? Simply adding a MIDI file to a site to provide continuous background sound may turn your page into the online equivalent of an in-store electronic organ demonstration. Audio support on the Web has seen a lot of changes in the past few years, and the emphasis has shifted greatly from playing music in Web pages to using external applications and stand-alone devices such as MP3 players, and independent, browser-enabled programs such as RealPlayer and RealJukebox. This section begins with a quick survey of sound and compression basics, reviews some older formats and approaches such as MIDI, and concludes with a look at MP3's impact and the current state of streaming audio as demonstrated by RealAudio. URLs in the text provide pointers to sites where you can learn more about these technologies.

Digital Sound Basics

Digital sound is measured by the frequency of *sampling*, or how many times the sound is digitized during a specific time period. Sampling frequencies are specified in kilohertz (KHz), which indicate the sound sampling rate per second. CD-quality sound is approximately 44.1 KHz, or 44,100 samples every second. For stereo, two channels are required, each at 16 bits; at 16 bits per sample, that yields 1,411,200 bits of data for each second of CD-quality sound. Like any other data, the bits of data on a CD could be delivered over the Internet, creating high-quality music at the end user's demand. In reality, transmitting this amount of data would take nearly a T1 connection's bandwidth. Obviously, this type of *sustained* and *guaranteed* bandwidth is not available to the average home Web user. Even if it were, we may find that bandwidth across the Internet at large may not allow end-to-end throughput for thousands or millions of users simultaneously.

Given the cost of raw delivery, another approach is to lower the sampling rate when creating digital sound for Web use. A sampling rate of 8 KHz in mono might produce acceptable playback results for simple applications, such as speech, particularly considering that playback hardware often consists of a combination of a basic sound card and low quality speakers. Low-quality audio requires a mere 64,000 bits of data per second, but the end user may still have to wait to download the sound. For modem users, even in the best of conditions, each second of low-quality sound takes a few seconds to be delivered, making continuous sound unrealistic.

Audio File Formats and Compression

Like graphics files, audio files can be compressed to reduce the amount of data being sent. The software on the serving side compresses the data, which is decompressed and played back on the receiving end. The compression/decompression software is known together as a *codec*. Just like image formats, audio compression methods are either lossy or lossless. *Lossy* data compression doesn't perfectly represent what was compressed, but is close enough, given the size savings. Because *lossless* compression techniques guarantee that what goes in one end comes out the other, most techniques can't compress files to any significant degree. Compression always involves a tradeoff between sound quality and file size; larger file sizes mean longer download times.

Downloading and Playing Audio

Early approaches to delivering sound via the Internet followed the "download and play" model, using formats such as WAV (waveform) files and AU (Sparc-audio, or u-law, format). In this scenario, users typically download sounds completely before they can play them. This takes up valuable hard drive space, even if a user wants to hear only the first few seconds of a file. Sounds must be degraded significantly in this situation, which might not be acceptable for content that requires flawless playback. Even at very low sampling rates, these sounds must be fairly short to spare impatient users the agony of prolonged download times. Download time can be reduced by creating smaller audio files, which only accentuates the drawbacks of this method.

Various older formats, such as AU and AIFF, are still in use on the Web, but are becoming less commonplace. One format that remains somewhat popular for this purpose is MIDI (Musical Instrument Digital Interface), which is often used with the Microsoft-specific **<bgsound>** tag discussed later in this chapter in the section "Audio Inclusion Basics." Netscape's LiveAudio technology once could be used to create a similar effect in conjunction with the **<embed>** tag, but LiveAudio now seems to have been dropped from more recent versions of Netscape and lacked cross-browser viability in any case. Most importantly, MIDI is not actually a digitized audio format, but represents notes and other information so that music can be synthesized. It can be a powerful tool for musicians when used with synthesizers and other electronic instruments, but MIDI files played back via PC sound cards often sound like cheap, synthesized music, which is more a reflection of the playback hardware than the protocol itself. Table 9-1 shows some of the older formats that might still be encountered on the Web.

TABLE 9-1 Older Internet Sound Formats

File Format	Description
WAV	Waveform (or simply *wave*) files are the most common sound format on Windows platforms. WAVs can also be played on Macs and other systems with player software.
AU	Sparc-audio, or u-law format, is one of the oldest Internet sound formats. A player for nearly every platform is available.
AIFF	Audio Interchange File Format is very common on Macs. Widely used in multimedia applications, it is not very common on the Web.
MIDI	Musical Instrument Digital Interface format is not a digitized audio format. It represents notes and other information so that music can be synthesized. MIDI is well-supported and files are very small, but it is useful only for certain applications because its reproduction quality is often limited by PC playback hardware.

While many of the file formats listed in Table 9-1 may linger on the Web for quite some time to come, MP3 (MPEG Level 3) is really the only choice for high-quality, sampled audio playback. Not surprisingly, MP3 is the most popular form of audio file on the Web today.

MP3

MP3 is one of the formats for audio and video developed by MPEG (Moving Picture Experts Group) for transmission over the Web. MPEG Level 3 is an audio format that generally compresses CD-quality sound by a factor of about 10–12 times, using techniques that were designed to take human audio perception into account, in order to minimize inaudible or unimportant frequencies and optimize the rest. Thus, a typical MP3 file (named for the format's file extension .mp3) of an average-length song weighs in at about 3MB, as opposed to the more than 30MB required for that same song on a compact disc.

In the last couple of years, this format has really taken off. The reason is simple: it provides high-quality audio that is not just suited for use on the Web, but in the real world as well, thanks to the increased availability of affordable CD copying devices, or burners. Music tracks from CDs can be converted to MP3 files, uploaded and downloaded across the Web, decompressed into CD-quality files, loaded onto MP3 players, or even burned to compact disc by anyone with a computer, a CD burner, and the right software. The grass-roots surge in MP3's popularity has, of course, generated considerable controversy. Regardless of the legal take on the various MP3-related battles, one thing is certain: the format has a very broad user base and will be around for quite some time.

Audio Inclusion Basics

Including download-and-play audio samples such as MP3 files in a Web page is simply a matter of using the anchor tag, **<a>**, to link to it. For example,

```
<a href="thememusic.mp3">Demo Company Theme Music</a><br />
<a href="theme.midi">Theme Music 2</a><br />
<a href="robotsound.wav">Robots in Action</a><br />
```

Assuming that users have the appropriate playback hardware and software when they click the link, the sound should be downloaded and then played. If they don't have the appropriate software, nothing may happen either.

NOTE *There may be a problem that a Web server is not set up properly to deliver the associated sound files. If files play properly locally but seem to be downloaded as text or always prompt as an unknown type, you might have a problem with your Web server.*

Even when everything is set up properly, it is a very good idea to let users know what they are getting into by indicating the file size, file type, and the fact that the object is a music file. For example,

```
<a href="robotsound.wav" title="Play robot sound in Wav Format (10K)">
<img src="speaker.gif" alt="" height="10" width="10" border="0" />
Robots in Action</a> [wav format / 10k]
```

might look something like this:

Robots in Action [wav format / 10k]

If you are using an MP3 file, you may desire to make it play as it downloads or streams. It is actually quite easy to do this. Instead of a link to a file like thememusic.mp3, link to a small text file called thememusic.m3u. In that text file, put a single line of text indicating a URL to the actual MP3 file like http://www.*yourservername*.com/music/thememusic.mp3. Then just link to the m3u like so

```
<a href="thememusic.m3u">Demo Company Theme Music</a><br />
```

and you will have sound that should play as it downloads! However, even though this idea is much easier than complex streaming technologies discussed later, you still might want to embed a sound file directly within a page. There are a variety of ways to do this, the easiest being Microsoft's proprietary **<bgsound>** tag.

Microsoft's <bgsound>

Microsoft Internet Explorer 2 and later supports WAV and MIDI files directly using a **<bgsound>** tag, which plays a sound in the background after it is loaded. The tag takes an **src** attribute that is set to the URL of the sound file to play. The sound file must be in the appropriate format, either WAV or MIDI. A **loop** attribute, which can be set to an integer value indicating how many times the sound should play, is also available. The **loop** attribute can also be set to the value **infinite** to keep playing over and over. To play a sound called test.wav two times under Internet Explorer, for example, you could write **<bgsound src="test.wav" loop="2">**. Because the element is empty, there is, of course, no close tag. While it could be written to be XHTML-compliant as **<bgsound src="test.wav" loop="2" / >**, the value of doing so is limited considering this is a completely Internet Explorer proprietary element that won't validate. Volume can be controlled through the **volume** attribute, which has a value from –10,000 to 0, with 0 being full natural sound volume and -10,000 being volume off. While this range may seem unusual, it does work. The tag should occur within the body of a document. A complete tag example might look like this:

```
<bgsound src="boing.wav" loop=3" volume="0" />
```

TIP *With **<bgsound>**, the user has no direct control over the volume or the playback of the sound, which may be annoying, so use sound carefully.*

RealAudio

Download and play formats such as MP3 and even WAV are popular because they allow the transfer of high-quality audio files across the Internet—but they were not really designed with the delivery demands of the Internet in mind. However, there is a strong desire, both among content creators and end users, to use the Web as a broadcast medium. The key to Webcasting is something called *streaming*. One of the most popular means of streaming audio is the RealAudio format developed by RealNetworks (www.realnetworks.com), which allows for the transmission of audio programming at a number of different speeds—and even at multiple speeds, depending on the end user's requirements. But before we explore what can be done with RealAudio, it might be useful to take a closer look at streaming itself.

What is streaming? First of all, consider that a 28.8 Kbps modem user receives approximately 2K of data per second. If one second of sound could be represented in 2K, and the data could get to the end user at a rate of 2K every second, the data would effectively *stream*, or play in real time. Streaming seems to make a whole lot of sense. Why wait for an hour-long speech to download before playing when you care only about the current second of data being listened to? Streamed data doesn't take up hard drive space, and it opens up random access to any position in an audio file. However, streaming audio has a few potential serious drawbacks. First, to compress audio far enough for streaming, you have to sacrifice a certain degree of sound quality. Second, the Internet protocols themselves do not readily support the requirements of streaming. However, despite these problems, streaming music can be very effective and works more often than not.

The first—and still the most popular—approach to streaming audio was developed by RealNetworks. RealAudio uses a special server to send continuous audio data to a browser helper application, Netscape plug-in, ActiveX control, or RealNetworks' own freestanding RealOne Player. With players available for all major platforms, RealAudio is the most common streaming audio format on the Internet. Putting data in RealAudio format is fairly easy if the files exist in WAV or other common audio formats. Simply use the RealAudio production tools, which can be downloaded from RealNetworks, and the data is ready to publish. But despite RealAudio's wide support, it has certain drawbacks, which mostly revolve around the use of a special server.

Streaming servers can provide a higher degree of control. For example, they can limit or control the number of audio streams delivered and allow for easy access to specified points in an audio stream. With simpler "serverless" audio-streaming solutions, the virtual Fast Forward button provided by random access is sacrificed. Some sophisticated servers could potentially upgrade data quality as bandwidth becomes available. Less complex systems give the same quality of data regardless of the end-to-end access speed. Server-based systems are expensive and require computing resources beyond the basic Web server. RealAudio-based streaming audio servers have a per-stream cost for high-end sites that keeps some users from adopting this solution. Fortunately, entry-level RealAudio systems with a few streams are still free or very inexpensive, and RealAudio can also be streamed directly off an ordinary Web server, with certain limitations. Already, many organizations are using the RealAudio platform, which is a testament to the quality of the system.

RealAudio Basics

The first step in producing RealAudio content for the Web is to convert your existing audio files into RealAudio format, which is easy to do with the RealProducer program.

NOTE *At the time of this writing, a free version of RealProducer is available for download from www.realnetworks.com/products/.*

The second step is to link to the RealAudio content from a Web page by using the **<a>** tag, but there is a small nuance as you do not link directly to the .rm file created with a program like RealProducer but to a text file ending in the extension .ram:

```
<a href="http://www.htmlref.com/audio/robotdrone.ram">
Hear our happy robots drone!</a>
```

This simple text file only needs to contain the URL of the .rm file you want to play:

```
http://www.htmlref.com/audio/robotdrone.rm
```

Assuming that the user has RealPlayer installed on the system being used, this will cause the RealPlayer program to pop open and begin playing the .rm file, as shown in Figure 9-1. RealAudio content can be played off any ordinary Web server, but content developers planning to reach a wide audience would be advised to look into the various RealServer packages available, which offer various levels of multiple stream support.

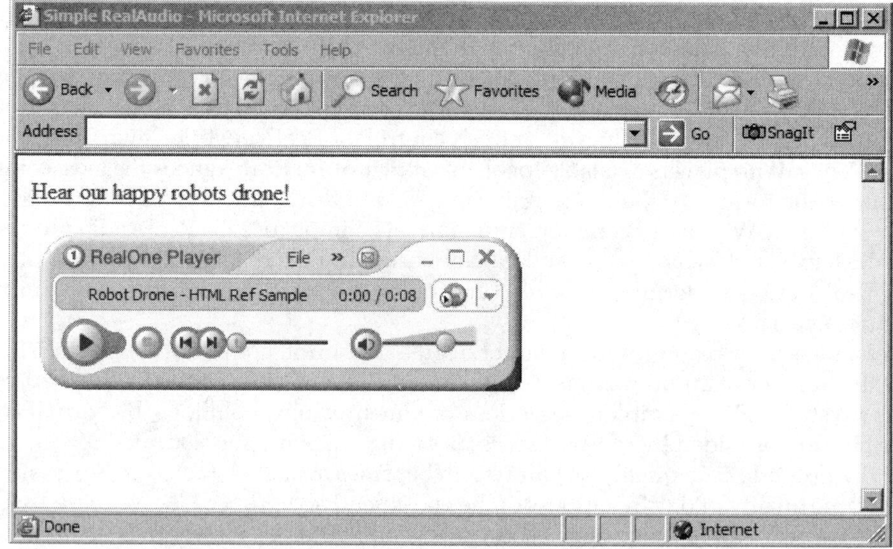

FIGURE 9-1 RealAudio's RealPlayer

More complicated audio presentations that play a sequence of audio clips can be created by linking the .ram file to another file written in *Synchronized Media Integration Language* (SMIL), which should have the file extension .smil. SMIL can also be used to integrate video, text, and animations with your audio presentation.

Embedding RealAudio

RealAudio can also be embedded in a Web page using an **<object>** or **<embed>** tag. To use the **<embed>** tag, use a code fragment like this:

```
<embed src="http://www.htmlref.com/audio/robotdrone.rpm"
      nojava="true" height="100" width="250" autostart="false">
```

Note that the file referenced ends in the extension .rpm, not .ram. This is the file type used in place of a .ram file when embedding RealPlayer in a Web browser. The .rpm file itself is just like the .ram file; it contains nothing more than the URL for the .rm file, but tells the browser to display the player inside the browser window rather than spawning the RealPlayer application in its own window, shown here in Netscape 7.

The **autostart** attribute determines whether the audio clip plays as soon as the page is loaded; if it is set to **autostart="true"**, the clip will start right away. When it is set to **autostart="false"** or omitted entirely, the audio clip will not start until the user clicks the Play button.

NOTE *Referencing the .rm directly is also possible and generally appears to work in modern editions of RealPlayer.*

It's possible that a user may not have a plug-in capability, so you may want to have a fallback with a link to the .ram file like so:

```
<embed src="http://www.htmlref.com/audio/robotdrone.rpm"
      nojava="true" height="100" width="250" autostart="false">
<noembed>
<a href="http://www.htmlref.com/audio/robotdrone.ram">
Hear our happy robots drone! (RealPlayer File)</a>
</noembed>
</embed>
```

To use the **<object>** tag, the code would look something like this:

```
<object id="robotdrone"
        classid="clsid:CFCDAA03-8BE4-11cf-B84B-0020AFBBCCFA"
        width="75" height="30">
<param name="src"
```

```
 value="http://www.democompany.com/audio/robotdrone.rpm" />
<param name="controls" value="PlayButton" />
</object>
```

Again, the file referenced is an .rpm file. The id value can be set to any allowed value; however, the value shown for the **classid** attribute should always be **clsid:CFCDAA03-8BE4-11cf-B84B-0020AFBBCCFA**, as this identifies the RealAudio plug-in. The first parameter defined by a **<param>** tag is named **src** and has a **value** of the URL of the .rpm file. The second **<param>** tag sets what controls are displayed. In this case, it takes the **PlayButton** value, which displays a Play / Pause button, as shown here, in Internet Explorer.

TIP *Because of cross-browser support issues, it might be sensible to avoid embedding RealAudio, and to simply rely on the RealPlayer program itself, which many users already are comfortable using.*

While it is not within the scope of this book to go into great detail about RealAudio, this discussion should give you a brief glimpse of what can be done with this technology. For more specific information about how to use RealAudio technology, please see the RealNetwork's Web site.

WindowsMedia Audio

Needless to say, Microsoft has its own version of streaming media in the marketplace. After long consideration, they even went and named it WindowsMedia (windowsmedia.com). WindowsMedia supports the Microsoft-proprietary format known as Advanced Streaming Format (.asf). WAV files and MP3 files can be converted to this format using a tool named Windows Media Encoder. The technique for linking to an .asf file is similar to that used with RealMedia. In this case, simply link to a text file that ends with the extension .asx.

```
<a href="robotdrone.asx">Hear our happy robots drone!</a>
```

The format of the .asx file should be like this:

```
<ASX version="3.0">
   <ENTRY>
      <REF href="robotdrone.asf" />
   </ENTRY>
</ASX>
```

Clicking the link to the .asx file causes the WindowsMedia Player to open and play the audio file. Again, since we understand the flavor of how audio is accessed from an HTML document, we leave the research of the specifics up to the adventurous readers as the details required to create such media is well beyond the scope of this book and even the markup syntax required has invariably changed.

Video

The "holy grail" of Internet multimedia is high-quality, 30-frames-per-second real-time video. The use of video on Web pages has expanded considerably in the past few years, with online movie trailers becoming commonplace along with streaming clips on major news sites. However, providing video clips on the Internet is no small feat when you consider the amount of data being transferred.

Digital video is measured by the number of frames per second of video and by the size and resolution of these frames. The total size requirement for video is huge, particularly if you want NTSC (TV quality) video. A 640x480 image with 24 bits of data representation for color and a frame rate of 30 frames per second takes up a staggering 27 megabits per second—and that's without sound. Add CD-quality audio—1,411,200 bits of data for each second of data—and the file size increases proportionately. In theory, the bits of data necessary to deliver TV-quality video could be transmitted over the Internet, creating the long-sought-after interactive TV. Today, transmitting this amount of data generally isn't feasible, even after compression.

Like audio files, video files can be compressed to reduce the amount of data being sent. Because of the degree of compression required by video, most video codecs use a lossy approach that involves a trade-off between picture/sound quality and file size, with larger file sizes obviously resulting in longer download times.

As with audio, simple online video delivery follows the download-and-play model, whereby users must download video clips completely before they can play them. Table 9-2 lists the most common downloadable video formats likely to be encountered on the Web.

The file format usually determines which compression technique is used. However, some file formats, such as QuickTime, allow different codecs to be selected. In some ways, this makes QuickTime the most flexible video format. As with audio, to choose a particular video format, you must consider the needs of the audience as well as the need for streaming or downloading the content.

Video Inclusion Basics

Including download and play video samples such as an AVI file in a Web page is simply a matter of using the anchor tag, **<a>**, to link to it. For example,

```
<a href="movie.avi">Demo Company History</a><br />
```

TABLE 9-2 Common Internet Video Formats

Video Format	Description
AVI	Audio Video Interleave; the Windows file format for digital video and audio is very common and easy to specify. The file size of AVI is significant.
QuickTime	The file extension MOV indicates the use of Apple's QuickTime format. Probably the most common digital video format, it continues its popularity on the Internet. QuickTime has a strong following in the multimedia development community. Various codecs and technology enhancements make QuickTime a strong digital video solution that may work in conjunction with MPEG.
MPEG	Motion Picture Experts Group video format is generally considered the standard format for digital video.

As with audio, if the user has the appropriate playback hardware and software when they click the link, the video should be downloaded and then played. Of course, if they don't have the appropriate software nothing will happen.

As with audio, it is a very good idea to indicate that the file to be viewed is a video.

```
<a href="movie.avi"><img src="tv.gif" alt="" height="10" width="10" />Robots
in Action</a> [AVI format / 1200k]
```

The next section shows a simple way to include an AVI file under Internet Explorer.

Using the <img> Tag with the dynsrc Attribute Under Internet Explorer

The **dynsrc** attribute for the **<img>** tag originated in Internet Explorer 2 and allowed AVI files to be played within a Web page. Although the syntax is currently maintained for backward compatibility, using the **object** or **embed** elements is preferable. Originally, the **dynsrc** attribute supported only AVI files, but testing shows that any ActiveMovie-supported data can be included with this syntax. The basic attributes for **<img>** are all valid; however, the following additions are also available:

- The **dynsrc** attribute should be set to the URL, either relative or absolute, of the content to play.

  ```
  dynsrc="URL of active content"
  ```

- If the **controls** attribute is present, controls are presented below the content, if possible. The attribute does not need a value.

  ```
  controls
  ```

- The **loop** attribute is used to set the number of times to loop the included content. When set to a positive integer, the content loops the specified number of times. When set to **-1** or the keyword **infinite**, the content loops continuously.

  ```
  loop="value"
  ```

- This attribute is used with **dynsrc** to specify how the content should be played. Setting the value to **fileopen** plays the content as soon as the data file has finished opening. Setting the value equal to **mouseover** delays playing the content until the mouse is positioned over it. The default action for active content is **fileopen**.

  ```
  start="fileopen | mouseover"
  ```

The following is an example of using the **dynsrc** attribute with the image element for an AVI movie:

```
<img src="samplemovie.gif" dynsrc="samplemovie.avi" alt=""
     controls="controls" align="left" vspace="20" />
```

In terms of browser support, it is difficult to come up with a best bet for simple Web video. AVI might appear to be easy to use, but the size and quality of AVI video files makes the format far from ideal. Furthermore, the format isn't necessarily supported natively by all browsers on all operating systems. As an alternative, you might consider QuickTime, though it too has issues and is presented primarily to show readers the flavor of how download-and-play video can be included in a page.

QuickTime

The QuickTime format was designed by Apple to provide the framework for the synchronization of time-based data in a variety of formats, including video, sound, MIDI, and even text. Although it was developed by Apple, it is now supported on PC platforms as well. An interesting aspect of QuickTime is that it can work with different video compression codecs, such as Cinepack, Indeo, MPEG, and even exotic fractal compression codecs. By itself, QuickTime with standard Cinepack encoding lacks the small file size of MPEG or proprietary video files, but the quality of QuickTime files is high. Creating or editing QuickTime files is relatively easy using tools such as the popular Adobe Premiere package.

NOTE *Windows users are required to install QuickTime services for their operating system.*

The basic syntax for the nonstandard **<embed>** tag using the QuickTime plug-in is as follows:

```
<embed src="URL of QuickTime object"
       align="top | bottom | center | baseline | left |
              right | texttop | middle | absmiddle | absbottom"
       autoplay="true | false"
       cache="true | false"
       controller="true | false"
       height="pixels or percentage"
       hidden
       href="URL of page to load"
       hspace="pixels"
       loop="true | false | palindrome"
       playeveryframe="true | false"
       pluginspage="URL of page with plug-in information"
       scale="tofit | aspect | number"
       target="valid frame name"
       volume="0 - 100"
       vspace="pixels"
       width="pixels or percentage">
```

The following lists and describes the key attributes in the preceding syntax:

- **src** Required, and should be set to the URL of a valid QuickTime file.
- **align** Acts like the same attribute for the **img** element and accepts the same values.
- **autoplay** May be set to **true** or **false** (default); indicates whether the movie should be played as soon as possible.
- **cache** May be set to **true** or **false**. A **cache** value of **true** causes the browser to treat the information just like other information and keep it in a local disk cache so that it does not need to be downloaded again. When set to **false**, the movie must be downloaded again.
- **controller** May be set to **true** or **false**; determines whether the movie controller is visible. The controller provides standard stop, play, pause, rewind, frame selection, and volume controls. The controller is 24-pixels high, so the **height** value should be set to account for this. By default, the value of **controller** is set to **true**.

- **height** Set like the **width** attribute, with a pixel value or percentage. The value specifies the **height** of the object and is cropped or expanded in the same method as **width**. For example, if a supplied height is greater than the movie's height, the movie is centered within this height. If the value is smaller, the object is cropped. Avoid values of **0** or **1** for the **height** attribute because they may cause unpredictable results. Be aware that controls for the movie are 24 pixels high, which must be added to the **height** value for the object to display properly.
- **hidden** Takes no parameters and its presence determines whether the movie should be visible. By default, the **hidden** value is **off**. In most cases, this is not an appropriate attribute to use. However, if a sound-only movie is being inserted, this can provide a background sound-like function, assuming that **autoplay** has been set to **true**.
- **href** Indicates the URL of a page to load when the movie is clicked. The meaning of this attribute is somewhat troublesome if the **controller** attribute is set to **false**. The problem revolves around the click having two meanings: one to start the movie and the other to go to the page. Page authors should either use the Autoplay feature or provide controls when using this attribute.
- **hspace** Sets the horizontal pixel buffer for the plug-in and acts the same way as the **hspace** attribute for the **img** element.
- **loop** Indicates whether the movie should play in a looped fashion. Setting the attribute to **true** loops the movie until the user stops it. The default value is **false**. When the **loop** value is set to **palindrome**, the movie loops back and forth. Setting this value produces interesting effects with movies, and even reverses the soundtrack.
- **playeveryframe** May be set to either **true** or **false**. When set to **true**, instructs the plug-in to play every frame, even if it requires the movie to play at a slower rate. This is appropriate in case the processor drops frames that may be valuable. Setting this value to **true** is not advisable for movies with audio tracks; it has the side effect of turning off the sound.
- **pluginspage** Sets the URL of the page that contains information about the required plug-in and how it can be downloaded and installed, if it is not currently installed. This feature is supported by Netscape; it is also documented to work under Internet Explorer. Be careful when using this attribute. It generally should be set to www.apple.com/quicktime, unless special instructions are included in addition to standard QuickTime information.
- **scale** Takes a value of **tofit**, **aspect**, or a number corresponding to the desired scaling factor, such as **1.5**. The default **scale** value is **1**, which is a normally scaled movie. Setting the attribute to **aspect** scales the movie to fit the bounding box set by the **height** and **width** attributes. A value of **tofit** scales the movie to fit the **height** and **width** attribute, with no regard to aspect ratio. Be careful when scaling movies because it may degrade the playback performance and image quality.
- **target** Used in conjunction with the **href** attribute to set the name of a frame into which to load the page indicated by the **href** attribute. The normal reserved frame names, such as _blank, as well as explicitly named frames are available as valid targets. More information on frames can be found in Chapter 8.

- **volume** May be set to a value from **0–100**. The higher the value, the louder the audio track on the QuickTime movie. A value of **0** effectively mutes the soundtrack, whereas **100** sets the volume at the maximum level. If the attribute is not set, the default is **100**. This is a newer attribute and will not be supported under older versions of the QuickTime plug-in.
- **vspace** Set to the number of vertical pixels to buffer between the embedded object and surrounding content. Used in the same way as the corresponding attribute for the **img** element.
- **width** Set to a pixel value or percentage. Be aware that the plug-in may not necessarily stretch the video image to take up the space. As mentioned previously, setting the **scale** attribute to **aspect** scales the movie to fit the bounding box set by the **height** and **width** attributes. If the value supplied for the object width is smaller than the object's true width, it is cropped to fit the dimensions provided. The **width** value must be set, unless the **hidden** attribute is used. Be careful when using small widths, such as 0 or 1 pixels, because this can cause problems.

The following example illustrates only the most basic use of the QuickTime plug-in:

```
<embed src="quicktime.mov" width="180" height="178"
       autoplay="true" align="left" hspace="12" vspace="20">
</embed>
```

In this case, you can see the use of the Netscape **<embed>** style syntax. You can also use the **<object>** style syntax like so:

```
<object classid="clsid:02BF25D5-8C17-4B23-BC80-D3488ABDDC6B"
width="240" height="152" codebase="http://www.apple.com/
qtactivex/qtplugin.cab#version=6,0,2,0">

  <param name="type" value="video/quicktime" />
  <param name="autoplay" value="true" />
  <param name="src" value="quicktime.mov" />

</object>
```

Combining the two is also possible so that you provide something for everybody. You can even add a **<noembed>** in and provide a fallback position for browsers without video support. Of course, this is somewhat simplistic and does not work properly. The reality is that browser detection and the use of JavaScript are generally required for careful browser and plug-in sensing.

```
<object classid="clsid:02BF25D5-8C17-4B23-BC80-D3488ABDDC6B"
width="240" height="152" codebase="http://www.apple.com/
qtactivex/qtplugin.cab#version=6,0,2,0">
  <param name="type" value="video/quicktime" />
  <param name="autoplay" value="true" />
  <param name="src" value="quicktime.mov" />
```

```
<embed src="quicktime.mov" width="180" height="178"
       autoplay="true" align="left" hspace="12" vspace="20">
</embed>
<noembed>
  <a href="http://www.apple.com/quicktime">Download Quicktime</a>
</noembed>

</object>
```

Interested readers are directed to Apple's QuickTime site (www.apple.com/quicktime) for more information about using QuickTime video on the Web.

Streaming Video Choices

In addition to QuickTime, two other video choices are very commonly used online: RealVideo and WindowsMedia. Both are primarily streaming technologies. Generally, videos in either format are viewed in secondary windows rather than directly within a Web page. The general approach to their use is almost identical to audio files with either links to launch a file in an external player or a special launch file to display the content within a page. However, rather than cover the syntax, which changes extremely rapidly, readers should check the specific details of each technology at www.realnetworks.com/resources and www.microsoft.com/windows/windowsmedia.

Animation

Sometimes full-blown video is a little overboard; in fact, just a little animation can spice up a Web page a great deal. Animation on the Web is used for many things: active logos, animated icons, demonstrations, and short cartoons. There are a variety of animation technologies available to Web designers. Some of the most common animation approaches include animated GIFs, Flash, and DHTML animations. Other animation possibilities also exist. Most notably, Java-based animations and older animation techniques such as server push are still possible, but the field has narrowed significantly. Very few older or proprietary animation formats are actually worth exploring, but a few of the browser-specific forms of animation like Microsoft's **<marquee>** tag live on.

<blink>

The much maligned **<blink>** tag was initially introduced to the Web by Netscape. Its simple goal is to make text blink, as shown here:

```
<blink>Buy now!</blink>
```

It has no significant attributes and is primarily supported only in versions of the Netscape browser and is not part of any HTML or XHTML standard. Interestingly enough, despite all the fuss about blinking text, it is actually part of the CSS2 specification, though it is actually not required to be supported by CSS2-conformant browsers. So if you want blinking text that validates, try something like the following:

```
<span style="text-decoration: blink;">Buy Now!</span>
```

Text Animation with <marquee>

One approach to adding new support for multimedia is to add new elements and build in support to the browser for the object. This approach used to be very popular with browser vendors and is partially responsible for the proliferation of browser-specific tags. **<marquee>** is one example of a multimedia-like tag that is fairly common on the Web. Although **<marquee>** isn't an embedded binary object, it tends to act like one in its support for **hspace**, **vspace**, **height**, and **width** attributes. In the proprietary HTML extension wars, Microsoft is the culprit for introducing the dreaded **<marquee>** tag, which is certainly as annoying as **<blink>**. Thanks to **<marquee>**, HTML authors now can create messages that scroll and slide across a viewer's screen in a variety of different ways. Like Netscape's **<blink>** tag, **<marquee>** degrades fairly well and can be used by HTML authors who understand the ramifications of using such proprietary tags. However, the bottom line is that, in good conscience, authors shouldn't recommend more than very occasional use of the **<marquee>** tag.

While initially supported only by Internet Explorer and some second-tier browsers such as MSN TV, **<marquee>** is now even supported in Mozilla-based browsers like Netscape 7, making it somewhat of a de facto standard even if it won't validate. Using the element is simple; just enclose some text in it and it is transformed into a scrolling ticker tape, similar to the one found at Times Square. A very simple continuous marquee could be set with the following markup fragment:

PART III

```
<marquee>
Welcome to Demo Company, Inc. -- the biggest fake company in the world!
</marquee>
```

Under browsers that support the **<marquee>** tag, the enclosed text scrolls repeatedly from right to left. Under browsers that don't support **<marquee>**, the text is displayed simply as plain text because the user agent should safely ignore the tag.

The following is a more complex example that illustrates some of the more common attributes supported by **<marquee>**; the rendering is shown in Figure 9-2:

```
<!DOCTYPE html PUBLIC "-//W3C//DTD XHTML 1.0 Transitional//EN"
"http://www.w3.org/TR/xhtml1/DTD/xhtml1-transitional.dtd">
<html xmlns="http://www.w3.org/1999/xhtml"> lang="en"
<head>
<title>Marquee Demo</title>
<meta http-equiv="content-type" content="text/html; charset=ISO-8859-1" />
</head>
<body>
<!-- Warning: example will not validate on purpose -->
<div align="center">
<marquee bgcolor="yellow"
         behavior="alternate"
         direction="right"
         loop="6"
         scrollamount="1"
         scrolldelay="40"
         title="Silly tags aren't just for Netscape anymore."
         width="80%">
```

```
Welcome to Demo Company, the biggest fake company of them all! </marquee>
</div>
</body>
</html>
```

NOTE *While Mozilla-based browsers support* ***<marquee>****, they do not support all of its attributes, such as* ***scrolldelay****,* ***direction****, and so on.*

Changing the attributes in this example will adjust the presentation of the marquee. For example, the **behavior** attribute may be set to **alternate**, **scroll**, or **slide**. This attribute determines how the scrolling text behaves. By default, a marquee scrolls text from right to left, unless the **direction** is set. The scrolled text, if it is looped, must first disappear before reappearing on the other side. When the attribute is set to **alternate**, the text bounces across the scroll region. When the attribute is set to **slide**, the text slides into position and stays put once onscreen.

The **direction** attribute is used to set the direction in which the scrolled text moves. The allowed values for this attribute are **down**, **left**, **right**, and **up**.

The **loop** attribute is used to set the number of times that the message loops in the scroll region. By default, unless the **behavior** is set to **slide**, a marquee scrolls forever. The value of the **loop** attribute should be a positive integer.

Setting **scrollamount** to a particular number of pixels allows the smoothness of the scroll to be controlled. The value of the **scrollamount** attribute is set to the number of pixels between each drawing of the scrolled message in the display area. The larger the value in pixels, the less smooth the scroll.

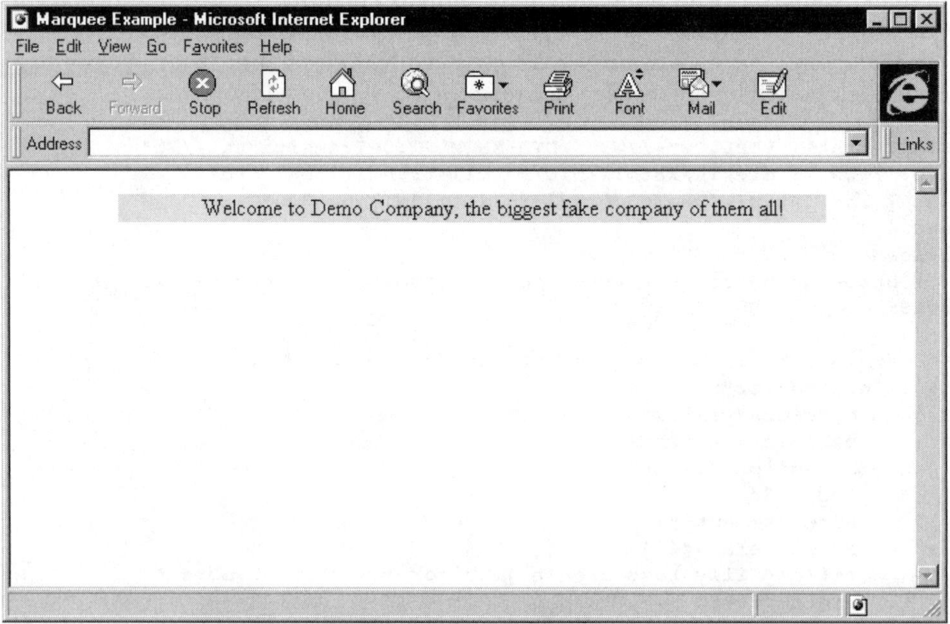

FIGURE 9-2 Rendering of the <marquee> example under Internet Explorer

The **scrolldelay** attribute is used to set the number of milliseconds between each rendering of the scrolled message. A higher value for this attribute slows the scrolling. A reasonable value for this attribute is **50** or greater. Lower values for **scrolldelay** tend to produce marquees that are very difficult to read.

Lastly, because the **<marquee>** tag represents a rectangular region, just like an image (or, for that matter, any binary included object), it has attributes such as **align**, **hspace**, **vspace**, **height**, and **width**. Appendix A provides a complete discussion of the **<marquee>** tag and its numerous attributes.

Animated GIFs

Animated GIFs are the simplest form of animation and are supported natively by most browsers. Looping and minimal timing information can be set in an animated GIF, but complex animation is beyond this format's capabilities.

The GIF89a format also supports animation. It works by stacking GIF after GIF in a manner similar to a flip book to create the animation. The animation extension also allows timing and looping information to be added to the image. Animated GIFs are one of the most popular ways to add simple animation to a Web page because nearly every browser supports them. Browsers that do not support the animated GIF format generally display the first frame of the animation in its place. Including a GIF animation is simply just a matter of referencing it like a normal image, as shown here:

```
<img src="animation.gif" width="100" height="100" border="0"
     alt="DemoCompany" />
```

Although plug-ins or other browser facilities are not required with animated GIFs, authors should not rush out to use animation on their pages. Excessive animations can be distracting for the user and are often inefficient to download. Because the animation is basically image after image, the file size is the total of all the images within the animation combined and can result in a much larger image than the user is willing to wait for. Thus, it is very important to make sure that every frame of the animation is compressed as much as possible. One approach to combat file bloat is to optimize the image by replacing only the moving parts of an individual animation frame. For more about this subject, see Chapter 5.

Flash

Macromedia Flash (www.macromedia.com/flash) is the leading format for sophisticated Web-based animations. Flash files are very compact. The key to Flash's small size is the fact that it is vector-based. Anyone who has worked with Illustrator, or another vector-based graphics program such as Freehand, knows what this means. While a graphics editing program such as Photoshop produces images like GIF and JPEG that are essentially comprised of a mosaic of pixels, vector-based images use mathematically defined curves (Bezier curves, to get technical) to define images. Computers read this mathematical information and create the image on the monitor screen. A 100x100 pixel square with a 2-pixel red border would be defined mathematically, not by a collection of colored dots. If a Web browser could process images in this fashion, it would be feasible to scale images effectively on the Web. By changing the part of the equation—defining the height and width of the square—the browser could increase its size without impacting any other aspect of the image, thus removing the distortion problems you get if you resize a GIF or JPEG using HTML. Unfortunately, most browsers do not support this image type yet, although a format called *Scalable Vector Graphics* (SVG) may someday be natively supported by browsers and Microsoft already supports a simple format called *Vector Markup Language* (VML) in Internet Explorer. For the most part, however, designers are still dependent upon plug-ins to display vector-based formats.

Flash is primarily used to create animations. This requires the Flash player plug-in, but the end result is worth it. A Flash animation (file extension .swf) is superior to an animated GIF in several ways. It can contain a great deal more information than a GIF, allowing more sophisticated and complex effects. The image is scalable and can expand or contract to fit a relative display region, thus becoming larger on top-of-the-line monitors, yet can scale down to fit reasonably comfortably within low-end displays. Often, .swf files can be smaller in kilobyte size than a comparable GIF animation—particularly in larger, more detailed images. Yet the technology far exceeds what is provided by simple animated GIFs. Flash files support a JavaScript-based programming language called ActionScript, which can be used to create games and even rich Internet applications. While the discussion is well beyond the scope of this book, creation of Flash files is not really difficult and can be accomplished with Macromedia's Flash software (www.macromedia.com/flash) or a third-party program such as SWiSH (www.swishzone.com/).

Once you assemble an animation and save it as an SWF file, it's fairly simple to reference it from a Web page. To reference a Flash file, you can use the **<embed>** syntax to reference the Flash player plug-in for Netscape. For example,

```
<embed src="test.swf"
       id="flash1" name="flash1"
       width="320" height="240"
       quality="autohigh" bgcolor="#ffffff"
       type="application/x-shockwave-flash"
       pluginspage="http://www.macromedia.com/go/getflashplayer">

<noembed>
  <img src="test.gif" alt="" height="250" width="320" />
</noembed>
</embed>
```

Note the use of the **<noembed>** tag to provide an alternative file—such as an animated GIF file—in case Flash is not supported.

You also can use the **<object>** syntax to reference an Internet Explorer ActiveX control, as follows:

```
<object classid="clsid:D27CDB6E-AE6D-11cf-96B8-444553540000"
        codebase="http://download.macromedia.com/
        pub/shockwave/cabs/flash/swflash.cab#version=6,0,0,0"
        id="flash1" name="flash1"
        width="320" height="240">

    <param name="movie" value="test.swf" />
    <param name="quality" value="high" />

    <img src="test.gif" alt=""  width="320" height="240" />

</object>
```

Lastly, you could combine all the formats together to deal with all possible situations, as shown here:

```
<object classid="clsid:D27CDB6E-AE6D-11cf-96B8-444553540000"
        codebase="http://download.macromedia.com/
        pub/shockwave/cabs/flash/swflash.cab#version=6,0,0,0"
        id="flash1" name="flash1"
        width="320" height="240">

   <param name="movie" value="test.swf" />
   <param name="quality" value="high" />

<embed src="test.swf"
       id="flash1" name="flash1"
       width="320" height="240"
       quality="autohigh" bgcolor="#ffffff"
       type="application/x-shockwave-flash"
       pluginspage="http://www.macromedia.com/go/getflashplayer">

<noembed>
  <img src="test.gif" alt="" height="250" width="320" />
</noembed>
</embed>


</object>
```

NOTE *The* **<embed>** *syntax is nonstandard and therefore won't validate but really must be used for older Netscape and Opera browser support.*

Given the complexity of the tag syntax for including Flash files in a document, it is best to let the Flash tool generate the base markup and modify it, or to use a Macromedia Web editing program such as Dreamweaver, which can create it directly.

PDF Format

While so far this chapter has focused on dynamic multimedia such as sound, video, and animation, one more aspect of Web multimedia is worth considering: print. It has long been difficult to get a Web page to print out exactly the way it appears onscreen. Improved browser support of CSS promises greater control in this department, as discussed in the next chapter, but the simple truth of the matter remains that Web pages do not offer the range of layout control available in a print-oriented program like Quark, or even Microsoft Word. And while it is possible to view Word documents in a Web browser, their file size makes them a poor choice for online viewing. Fortunately, Adobe's Acrobat technology offers a viable approach to the online distribution of electronic documentation.

Originally proposed to help implement the mythical ideal of the "paperless office," Acrobat has matured into a product with uses both on and off the Web. Adobe Acrobat provides the capability to deliver an electronic document to an end user without requiring the reader to have the authoring environment to open the file. Visually, Acrobat preserves the exact look and feel of the document, both onscreen and in print. For design-oriented Web publishers, Acrobat provides a highly motivating presentation alternative that easily surpasses HTML's relatively simplistic and imprecise layout features, as shown in Figure 9-3.

Acrobat files are created by using a combination of traditional text authoring tools (word processors and desktop publishing software) and special Acrobat authoring software (Adobe Exchange or Distiller). The files are then saved in a file format aptly named *Portable Document Format* (PDF). PDF files are small, self-contained documents that can be transported in a variety of ways: via diskette, CD-ROM, or network. The end user then reads the files by using special Adobe Acrobat Reader software. Thus, by its very nature, Acrobat reader technology must be cross-platform. Versions of the Acrobat Reader software are currently available for the following operating systems: Microsoft Windows variants; Macintosh OS; Linux; Sun Microsystems' Sun SPARC Solaris and SunOS; Hewlett-Packard's HP-UX; Silicon Graphic's IRIX; IBM's AIX and OS/2; and Digital's VMS.

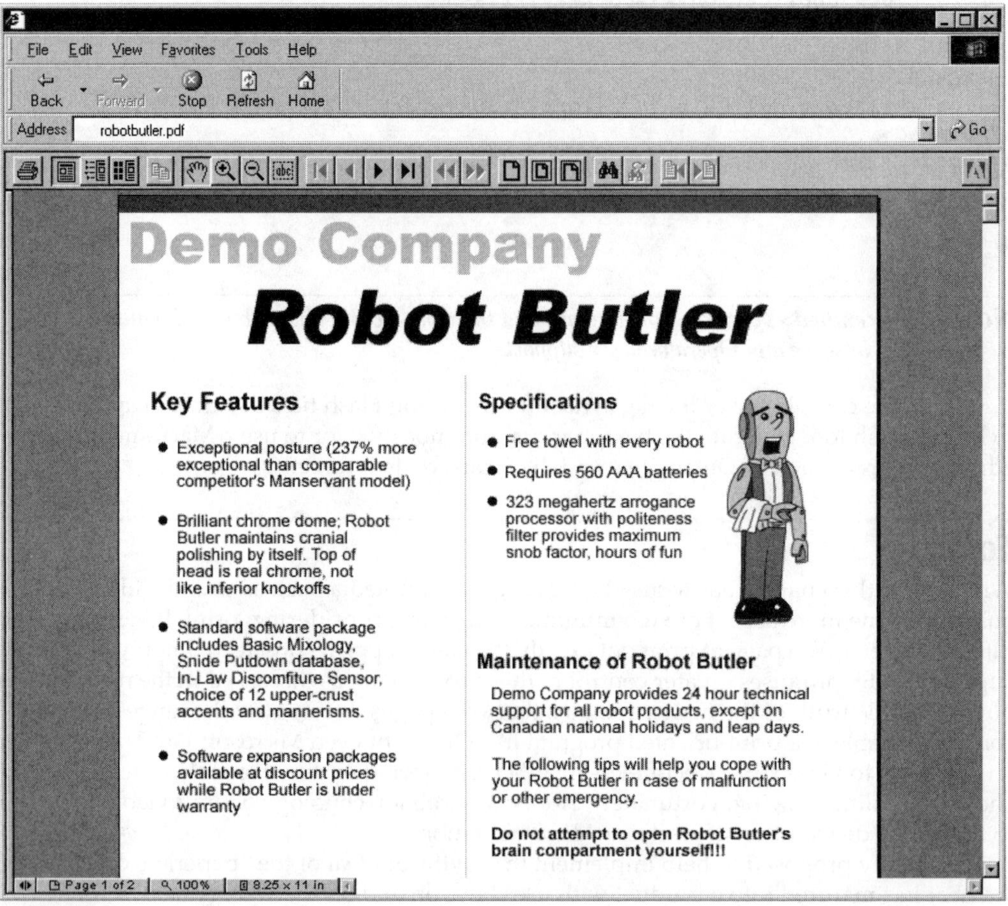

FIGURE 9-3 Sample Acrobat document

Inserting an Acrobat file in a Web page is as simple as linking to the document with the <a> tag. For example,

```
<a href="document.pdf">Demo Company Data sheet
  (Acrobat PDF Format, 55Kb)</a>
```

If a PDF is used, make sure to let users know what it is with an appropriately named link or PDF icon. It is a good idea to indicate the file size of a linked PDF. It might also be useful to the user to know the last time the document was modified. Lastly, make sure to provide information on where to obtain the Acrobat reader for users who may not have it. All these ideas are illustrated here.

The 2001 Annual Report is also available as a PDF (Portable Document Format) file which requires the free Acrobat Reader available from Adobe.

For more information about Acrobat and more details on how Acrobat might be included in a Web page, visit Adobe's Web site at www.adobe.com/acrobat.

Summary

The previous edition of this book suggested that the future of audio on the Internet would be in integration. In a sense, this has proven to be true—but not in the sense expected. The real trend seems to have been toward Web pages that trigger the launch of freestanding programs that can play downloaded files (MP3) or streaming audio (RealAudio), and the development of programs like RealPlayer and WindowsMedia Player that can play a wide variety of file formats. Where online video is concerned, many of the same developments apply. Embedded QuickTime movie trailers may have become a commonplace promotional tool on the Web, but the emphasis has largely shifted away from video clips in Web pages to clips displayed in external players such as RealPlayer or WindowsMedia Player. The rise of vector-based formats like Flash opens the door to more extensive use of animation in Web pages, while animated GIFs still provide a viable, if less powerful, backup where Flash is not supported. For many developers, Flash even seems to offer the layout control so lacking in HTML. Yet do not forgo the use of markup technologies for a binary form like Flash; the cost and flexibility of text makes it very compelling. As discussed in the next chapter, with the rise of cascading style sheets (CSS), the layout complaints associated with HTML and XHTML should come to an end.

CHAPTER 10

CSS1

HTML is a poor language for page formatting, but this isn't a failing of the technology. As mentioned throughout this book, HTML elements are not supposed to be used to represent layout. Even so, people typically use HTML and even XHTML as a visual design environment, tending to think visually, rather than organizationally, when building Web pages. Why? Well, not very many choices were available in the past. Everybody wanted the same thing—a high degree of control over the layout of their Web pages. Until recently, this control required using tables, markup tricks, and images for layout, or embedding a binary format, such as Flash, in a page. These solutions generally were unsatisfactory.

A better solution has emerged—cascading style sheets (CSS). Style sheets offer what designers have been clamoring for over the years: more control over layout. An early problem with CSS adoption was that older versions of Netscape and Microsoft Internet Explorer fell short in some areas of CSS1 (the first specification) support. Newer versions of the browsers are nearly complete in their support of CSS1 and now large portions of the CSS2 specification are even implemented. Yet even as CSS becomes more commonplace, other issues remain. Bugs are commonplace, large portions of CSS2 remain unsupported, developer education and uptake is inconsistent, and proprietary extensions to style sheets are even being introduced by browser vendors. It seems the more things change the more they stay the same regardless of the technology in use.

Style Sheet Basics

A style sheet associates look or formatting to a particular piece of content in a document. In the case of CSS, style sheets rely on an underlying markup structure, such as XHTML. They are not a replacement for markup. Without a binding to an element, a style really doesn't mean anything. The purpose of a style sheet is to create a presentation for a particular element or set of elements. Binding an element to a style specification is very simple; it consists of a *selector*—in this case, simply the element name—followed by its associated style information (called *rules*) within curly braces. The rules are composed of property names and property values separated by colons with each rule in turn being separated by a semicolon. The basic syntax is as follows:

```
selector {property1 : value1; … propertyN : valueN;}
```

Given this syntax, suppose that you want to bind a style rule to all **h1** elements so that they appear as 28-point text. The following rule would result in the desired display:

```
h1  {font-size:  28pt;}
```

Additional rules such as setting the color of the **h1** elements to red or the font face to Impact also could be added simply by separating each style property with a semicolon:

```
h1  {font-size: 28pt; color: red; font-family: Impact;}
```

NOTE *The final rule in a list of style properties does not require the semicolon. However, for good measure and easy insertion of future style rules, page authors should always use semicolons between every style property.*

In general, you will find that CSS property names are separated by dashes when they are multiple words—for example, font-face, font-size, line-height, and so on.

As rules are added, you may take advantage of the fact that CSS is not terribly whitespace sensitive, so

```
h1 {font-size: 28pt;color: red;font-family:Impact;}
```

should render the same as

```
h1 {font-size: 28pt;
    color: red;
    font-family: Impact;}
```

This may allow you to improve your rules for readability or crunch them for delivery. You may also add comments using /* */ like so:

```
/* first CSS rule below */
h1 {font-size: 28pt; color: red; font-family: Impact;}
```

Lastly, under most browsers property names and selectors are not case sensitive, so

```
h1 {FONT-SIZE: 28pt; COLOR: red; FONT-FAMILY: Impact;}
```

could also be used although it isn't encouraged. However, be careful with changing the selector case. While **H1** might work just as well as **h1** in most browsers, you are binding to a tag in a markup language where case may actually matter.

To make the style rule useful, it must be bound to an actual document. There are numerous ways to add style to a document, either using an external style sheet referenced by a **<link>** tag, a document-wide style sheet specified by the **<style>** tag, or using inline styles with the **style** attribute common to most HTML elements. All these methods will be discussed in the next section. For the purpose of this demo, we'll use a document-wide style, as defined with the **<style>** tag found in the **<head>** element of an HTML/XHTML document:

```
<!DOCTYPE html PUBLIC "-//W3C//DTD XHTML 1.0 Transitional//EN"
"http://www.w3.org/TR/xhtml1/DTD/xhtml1-transitional.dtd">
```

```
<html xmlns="http://www.w3.org/1999/xhtml" lang="en">
<head>
<title>First CSS Example</title>
<meta http-equiv="content-type" content="text/html; charset=ISO-8859-1" />

<style type="text/css">
  h1   {font-size: 28pt; font-family: Impact; color: red;}
</style>

</head>
<body>
<h1>New and Improved Markup with CSS Style!</h1>
</body>
</html>
```

CSS provides a powerful set of properties for manipulating the look of HTML elements. Notice even with this simple example the rendering difference between a style sheet–capable and non-style-sheet-supporting browser, as shown in Figure 10-1.

Adding Style to a Document

Style information can be included in an HTML document in any one of three basic ways:

- Use an outside style sheet, either by importing it or by linking to it.
- Embed a document-wide style in the **head** element of the document.
- Provide an inline style using the **style** attribute exactly where the style needs to be applied.

Each of these style sheet approaches has its own pros and cons, as listed in Table 10-1.

CSS On

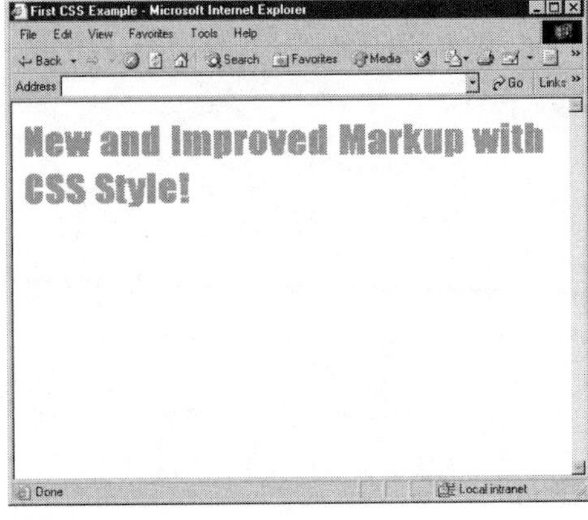

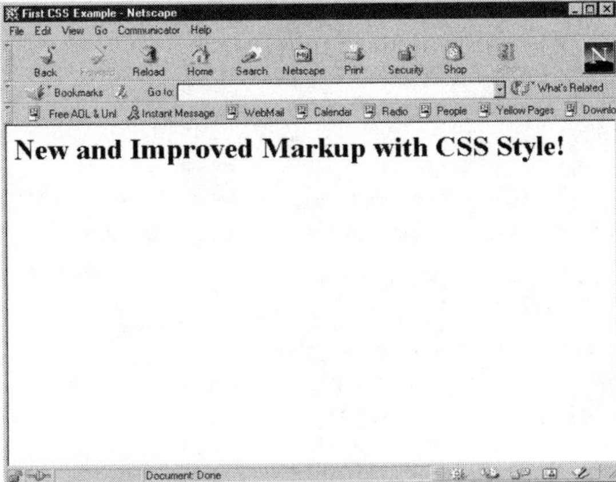

FIGURE 10-1 CSS versus no CSS rendering

	External Style Sheets	Document-Wide Style	Inline Style
Syntax	<link rel="stylesheet " href="main.css" />	<style type="text/css"> body {color: red;} </style>	<p style="color:red; ">Test </p>
Pros	-Can set style for many documents with one style sheet. –Style information cached by the browser.	–Can easily control style document by document. –No additional page requests for style information.	–Can easily control style to a single character instance. –Overrides any external or document styles.
Cons	–Require extra download time for the style sheet, which might delay page rendering or, in the case of import, cause a rendering "flash."	–Need to reapply style information for other documents.	–Need to reapply style information throughout the document and outside documents. –Bound too closely to markup—difficult to update.

TABLE 10-1 Comparison of Style Sheet Approaches

Linking to a Style Sheet

An external style sheet is simply a plain text file containing the style specifications for HTML tags or classes. The common extension indicating that the document provides style sheet information is .css, for Cascading Style Sheets.

NOTE *The file extension .jss was used to indicate Netscape's JavaScript Style Sheets (JSSS), which provided the base functions of CSS but in an unusual Netscape 4.x-specific fashion. Page designers should always avoid the .jss style approach as it is no longer supported.*

The following CSS rules can be found in a file called sitestyle.css, which defines a style sheet used site wide:

```
body        {font-size: 10pt;
             font-family: Serif;
             color: black;
             background-color: white;}

h1          {font-size: 24pt;
             font-family: Sans-Serif;
             color: black;
             text-align: center;}

p           {text-indent: 0.5in;
             margin-left: 50px;
             margin-right: 50px;}
```

```
a:link     {color: blue; text-decoration: none;}
a:visited  {color: red; text-decoration: none;}
a:active   {color: red; text-decoration: none;}
a:hover    {color: red; text-decoration: underline;}
```

NOTE *The pseudoclasses, a:link, a:visited, a:active, and a:hover are selectors that are associated with the various states of a link. These selectors are discussed later in this chapter.*

An XHTML or HTML file that uses this style sheet could reference it by using a **<link>** tag within the **head** element of the document. Recall from Chapter 4 that the **link** element isn't exclusive to style sheets and has a variety of possible relationship settings that can be set with the **rel** attribute. The following is an example of how style sheet linking is used:

```
<!DOCTYPE html PUBLIC "-//W3C//DTD XHTML 1.0 Transitional//EN"
"http://www.w3.org/TR/xhtml1/DTD/xhtml1-transitional.dtd">
<html xmlns="http://www.w3.org/1999/xhtml" lang="en">
<head>
<title>Style Sheet Linking Example</title>
<meta http-equiv="content-type" content="text/html; charset=ISO-8859-1" />
<link rel="stylesheet" href="sitestyle.css" type="text/css" />
</head>
<body>
<h1>HTML with Style</h1>
<p>Cascading Style Sheets 1 as defined by the
<a href="http://www.w3.org">W3C</a> provides
powerful page layout facilities.</p>

</body>
</html>
```

In this example, the relationship for the **link** element as indicated by the **rel** attribute is set to **stylesheet**; then, the **href** attribute is used to indicate the URL of the style sheet to use. In this case, the style sheet resides in the same directory as the referencing file and is known as **sitestyle.css**. However, it would be wise to collect all style sheets in a special styles directory usually named "styles" or "css." Given that we are setting a URL here, it is of course possible to reference a remote style sheet using a full URL such as http://www.htmlref.com/styles/remotestyle.css. Note that linking to an external style sheet has the same problems as linking to an external object insofar as the object may no longer be available or the speed of acquiring that object could inhibit performance of the page.

The last thing to note in the linked style sheet example is the use of the **type** attribute in the **link** element, which is set to the MIME type **"text/css"**. This value indicates that the linked style sheet is a cascading style sheet (CSS). However, CSS is not the only format we could use. If you want to avoid having to use the **type** attribute, you may want to set a default style sheet language in the **head** element of the document by using the **<meta>** tag shown here:

```
<meta http-equiv="Content-Style-Type" content="text/css" />
```

As it stands, by default, most browsers assume that CSS is being used; the **type** setting may have little effect, regardless of how it is applied.

Embedding and Importing Style Sheets

The second way to include a style sheet is to embed it. When you embed a style sheet, you write the style rules directly within the HTML/XHTML document. You could separate the style rules into another file and then import these rules, or you could type them directly into the document. Either possibility involves using a **<style>** tag within the **head** of the document. The basic syntax of the **<style>** tag is as follows:

```
<style type="text/css" media="all | print | screen" >

style rules here

</style>
```

Here, the **type** attribute again is used to indicate the MIME type of the enclosed style sheet. Because this is almost always CSS, it is often omitted as browsers infer this. The **media** attribute indicates the media for which the style sheet applies. By default, the style sheet is applied to all media so most developers omit this attribute as well. However, it is possible to define style sheets that are applied only to a particular output medium. The most common values are **print** and **screen**, which indicate rules applied only to the page when it is printed or correspondingly shown onscreen. Other values are possible for the media attribute but are as of yet not supported. Within the style block, style sheet rules are included. It is important to note that effectively once within the **<style>** tag the rules of HTML/XHTML do not necessarily apply. The **<style>** tag defines an island of CSS within an ocean of markup. The two technologies are intertwined but have their own distinct characteristics.

One concern when including style sheets within an HTML/XHTML document is that not all browsers, particularly older ones, understand style sheets. Given the possibility that a browser will render the content of an unknown tag as text on the screen, you might want to mask the CSS from noncompliant browsers. To avoid such a problem, comment out the style information by using an HTML comment, such as **<!-- -->**. A complete example of a document-wide style sheet, including hiding rules from older browsers, is shown here:

```
<!DOCTYPE html PUBLIC "-//W3C//DTD XHTML 1.0 Transitional//EN"
"http://www.w3.org/TR/xhtml1/DTD/xhtml1-transitional.dtd">
<html xmlns="http://www.w3.org/1999/xhtml" lang="en">
<head>
<title>Document Wide Style Sheet Example</title>
<meta http-equiv="content-type" content="text/html; charset=ISO-8859-1" />
<style type="text/css">
<!--
/* Simple Document Wide CSS rules */

body        {font-size: 10pt;
             font-family: Serif;
             color: black;
             background-color: white;}
```

```
h1          {font-size: 24pt;
             font-family: Sans-Serif;
             color: black;
             text-align: center;}
p           {text-indent: 0.5in;
             margin-left: 50px;
             margin-right: 50px;}
a:link      {color: blue; text-decoration: none;}
a:visited   {color: red; text-decoration: none;}
a:active    {color: red; text-decoration: none;}
a:hover     {color: red; text-decoration: underline;}
-->
</style>
</head>
<body>
<h1>HTML with Style</h1>
<p>Cascading Style Sheets 1 as defined by the
<a href="http://www.w3.org">W3C</a> provides
powerful page layout facilities.</p>
</body>
</html>
```

PART III

NOTE *The preceding example shows the use of CSS comments as designated by /* and */, which can be used to leave comments about complex or confusing CSS usage.*

You can have multiple occurrences of the **style** element within the head of the document, and you can even import some styles, link to some style rules, and specify some styles directly. Dividing style information into multiple sections and forms might be very useful, but a way must exist to determine which style rules apply. This is the idea of the cascade, which is discussed in more detail later in the chapter.

Another way to use document-wide style rules rather than type the properties directly within a **<style>** tag is to import them. The idea is somewhat similar to linking. An external style sheet is still referenced, but in this case, the reference is similar to a macro or inline expansion. The syntax for the rule for importing a style sheet is **@import**, followed by the keyword **url** and the actual URL of the style sheet to include. This rule must be included within a **<style>** tag; it has no meaning outside that element, as compared to the linked style sheet. An example of how to import a style sheet is shown here:

```
<!DOCTYPE html PUBLIC "-//W3C//DTD XHTML 1.0 Transitional//EN"
"http://www.w3.org/TR/xhtml1/DTD/xhtml1-transitional.dtd">
<html xmlns="http://www.w3.org/1999/xhtml" lang="en">
<head>
<title>Imported Style Sheet Example</title>
<meta http-equiv="content-type" content="text/html; charset=ISO-8859-1" />
<style type="text/css">
<!--
@import url(corerules.css);
@import url(linkrules.css);

/* a rule specific to this document */
```

```
h1          {font-size: 24pt;
             font-family: Sans-Serif;
             color: black;
             text-align: center;}
-->
</style>
</head>
<body>
<h1>HTML with Style</h1>
<p>Cascading Style Sheets 1 as defined by the
<a href="http://www.w3.org">W3C</a> provides
powerful page layout facilities.</p>
</body>
</html>
```

In the preceding example, we could include rules for **body** and **p** in the file corestyles.css, whereas the rules affecting the **a** element could be included via the document linkstyles.css. A special rule for the **h1** element, used in this document alone, is placed within the style block to give the reader some sense of how the **@import** feature is used to organize the various parts of a complete style rule. (All **@import** directives should always come before all other style rules.) Although imported style sheets might seem to provide a great advantage for organizing style information, their use currently is limited by the fact that some older CSS-aware browsers such as Netscape 4.*x* do not support this style sheet inclusion form properly. Furthermore, using **@import** can cause an annoying flashing effect on browsers as they load and apply the style. Page designers should stick to the external style sheet reference by a **<link>** tag.

NOTE *Because Netscape 4.x generation browsers ignore* ***@import*** *directives, they are often used to hide complex CSS rules from the browser. In some sense, this is a simplistic form of browser detection. The developer puts modern CSS rules in an* ***@import*** *CSS file and leaves the older rules in the main* ***<style>*** *block. However, this is a misuse of the directive and scripting really would be appropriate for such logic.*

Using Inline Style

In addition to using a style sheet for the whole document, you can add style information directly in a single element. Suppose you want to set one particular **<h1>** tag to render in 48-point, green, Arial font. You could quickly apply the style to only the tag in question using its **style** attribute. Recall that **style** is one of the core HTML attributes besides **class**, **id**, and **title** that can be used within nearly any HTML element. For example, the following example shows how style rules could be applied to a particular **<h1>** tag:

```
<h1 style="font-size: 48pt; font-family: Arial; color: green;">CSS1 Inline</h1>
```

This sort of style information doesn't need to be hidden from a browser that isn't style sheet-aware because browsers ignore any attributes that they don't understand.

Although inline style seems an easy route to using CSS, it does have some significant problems. The main problem is that inline rules are bound very closely to a tag. If you want to affect more than one **<h1>**, as shown in the previous example, you would have to copy-paste the **style** attribute into every other **<h1>** tag. The separation of markup from CSS presentation is just not where it should be. However, for quick and dirty application of CSS rules this might be appropriate, particularly for testing things out.

CSS and HTML Elements

One potential problem with style sheets and HTML is that the default rendering of an HTML element might get in the way. For example, consider applying a style rule to a **<strong>** tag like so:

```
<strong style="color: red;">I am strong!</strong>
```

Whereas this will put the text contents in red, it will also probably be bold because that is the typical rendering of this HTML element. Designers have to consider these default renderings as rules are added; a careless document author can create a potentially confusing use of HTML pretty easily using style sheets, as shown in the next example, which makes a **<b>** tag render like an **<i>** tag.

```
<!DOCTYPE html PUBLIC "-//W3C//DTD XHTML 1.0 Transitional//EN"
"http://www.w3.org/TR/xhtml1/DTD/xhtml1-transitional.dtd">
<html xmlns="http://www.w3.org/1999/xhtml" lang="en">
<head>
<title>HTML Presentation Override</title>
<meta http-equiv="content-type" content="text/html; charset=ISO-8859-1" />
<style type="text/css">
<!--
   b   {font-style: italic; font-weight: normal;}
-->
</style>
</head>
<body>
<b>What am I?</b>
</body>
</html>
```

Given the physical nature of some HTML tags, it should be obvious now why some have been deprecated and others have become more useful with the rise of style sheets. When using an **<em>** tag, it means simply that something is emphasized, not that it is italic. Setting this tag to render any way the developer wants will help prevent any confusion for later viewers of the markup. All the logical tags should enjoy a similar benefit; the next two in particular are quite useful.

<div> and <span> Revisited

When using style sheets and trying to avoid the default rendering of HTML elements, document authors will find the use of the **div** and **span** elements indispensable. Recall from Chapter 3 that the **div** element and **span** are block and inline elements, respectively, that have no particular rendering. You might call them generic tags. Because these tags don't have any predefined meaning or rendering, they are very useful for arbitrary style duties. For example, using a **<div>** tag you can apply a style to a certain section or division of a document very easily:

```
<div style="background-color: yellow; font-weight: bold; color: black;">

<p>Style sheets separate the structure of a document from its
presentation. Dividing layout and presentation has many
theoretical benefits and can provide for flexible documents
that display equally well on large graphically rich systems
and palmtop computers.</p>

<p>This is another paragraph describing the wonderful benefits of
style sheets</p>

</div>
```

A block element **div** should induce a return however, so if you want to provide style information solely for a few words, or even a few letters, the best approach is to use the **span** element, which as an inline element does not induce a return. For example, notice how a **<span>** tag is used to call attention to a particular section of text:

```
<p>Calling out <span style="background-color: yellow; font-weight: bold;
color: black;">special sections of text</span> isn't hard with
span</p>
```

Selectors

As shown in the previous sections, the simplest rules can be applied to all occurrences of a particular tag such as **<p>**. For example, consider setting the line spacing for all paragraphs using a rule such as the following:

```
p  {line-height: 150%;}
```

While some XHTML elements have a default rendering that is expected, you can also use the elements **div** and **span**, which have no predefined presentation. Beyond this caveat, designers are free to use style properties with nearly every XHTML display element, including the **body** element itself. For example, a rule such as

```
body {background-color: black;}
```

would set the background color of the entire document to black. To decrease the amount of typing for setting rules for multiple tags, it is possible to group them with commas. For example, if you want the tags **<h1>**, **<h2>**, and **<h3>** to have the same basic background and color, you could apply the following rule:

```
h1, h2, h3  {background: yellow; color: black;}
```

If it turns out that each particular heading should have a different size, you can then add that characteristic by adding other rules:

```
h1   {font-size: 200%;}
h2   {font-size: 150%;}
h3   {font-size: 125%;}
```

When the grouping rule and the other rules are encountered, they are combined. The resulting rules create the whole style. Although associating all elements with a certain look is useful, in reality page designers probably will want to create very specific rules that are applied only to certain elements in a document or that can be combined to form more complex rules.

id Rules

Without inline styles, how can a particular style be applied to one particular **<h1>** tag, or to only a select few particular **<h1>** tags? The solutions to these problems are the **class** and **id** attributes. As discussed in Chapter 3, you can name a particular tag with the **id** attribute so that it can be made a destination for a link. For example,

```
<h1 id="FirstHeading">Welcome to Demo Company, Inc.</h1>
```

assigns a name of **"FirstHeading"** to this **<h1>** tag. One possible use of this, as discussed in Chapter 4, is for this item to be linked to, like so:

```
<a href="#FirstHeading">Go to Heading 1</a>
```

However, another possible use of the name for an element is to reference it from a style rule. For example, a CSS rule such as

```
#FirstHeading {background-color: green;}
```

would apply a green background to the element with its **id** attribute set to **FirstHeading**.

The following markup shows how a green background is applied to the **<p>** tag with the **id** value of **"SecondParagraph"**, whereas no style is applied to the other paragraphs:

```
<!DOCTYPE html PUBLIC "-//W3C//DTD XHTML 1.0 Transitional//EN"
"http://www.w3.org/TR/xhtml1/DTD/xhtml1-transitional.dtd">
<html xmlns="http://www.w3.org/1999/xhtml" lang="en">
<head>
<title>ID Rule Example</title>
<meta http-equiv="content-type" content="text/html; charset=ISO-8859-1" />
<style type="text/css">
<!--
 #SecondParagraph   {background-color: green;}
-->
</style>
</head>
<body>
<p>This is the first paragraph.</p>
<p id="SecondParagraph">This is the second paragraph.</p>
<p>This is the third paragraph.</p>
</body>
</html>
```

As a core attribute, the **id** attribute is common to nearly all XHTML/HTML elements. However, given widespread use of **id** attributes, page authors need to be very careful to ensure that HTML elements are named uniquely. Developers must not name two elements the same name using the **id** attribute. If two of the paragraphs have **id="secondparagraph"**, what will happen? In the case of most browsers, both paragraphs should show up green. However, this is such sloppy style that it generally will result in significant errors once scripting is added to the document. Furthermore, the document will not validate with such mistakes. If multiple elements should be affected in a similar way, use a class rule instead.

class Rules

The **class** attribute is used to define the name(s) of the class(es) to which a particular tag belongs. Unlike **id** values, **class** values don't have to be unique as many elements can be members of the same class. In fact, elements don't even have to be of the same type to be in a common class. Writing rules for classes is easy: simply specify the class name of your own choosing such as "nature," with a period before it as the selector:

```
.nature {color: green;}
```

The use of **class** is illustrated here:

```
<!DOCTYPE html PUBLIC "-//W3C//DTD XHTML 1.0 Transitional//EN"
"http://www.w3.org/TR/xhtml1/DTD/xhtml1-transitional.dtd">
<html xmlns="http://www.w3.org/1999/xhtml" lang="en">
<head>
<title>Class Example</title>
<meta http-equiv="content-type" content="text/html; charset=ISO-8859-1" />
<style type="text/css">
<!--
 .veryimportant  {background-color: yellow;}
-->
</style>
</head>
<body>
<h1 class="veryimportant">Example</h1>
<p class="veryimportant">This is the first paragraph.</p>
<p>This is the second paragraph.</p>
<p class="veryimportant">This is the third paragraph.</p>
</body>
</html>
```

The previous example has three elements, each of which has its **class** attribute set to **veryimportant**. According to the style sheet information, all members of the **veryimportant** class, as indicated by the period, have a yellow background color.

Other variations on class rules are possible. For example, setting all **h1** elements of the class **veryimportant** to have a background color of orange could be written like this:

```
h1.veryimportant {background-color: orange;}
```

It is also possible to combine classes together directly. For example, consider the following rule:

```
h1.veryimportant.stuff {background-color: green;}
```

This would match only **<h1>** tags with **class** attribute values including **veryimportant** and **stuff**. Given these rules, the following tags with **class** attributes would be affected in the various ways indicated.

```
<h1 class="veryimportant">Has an orange background</h1>

<h1 class="veryimportant stuff">Has a green background</h1>

<h1 class="veryimportant heading stuff">Probably has a green background</h1>

<h1 class="stuff">Has the default background unless class rule for stuff set</h1>
```

Notice that the rule for green background matches any <**h1**> tag that includes the values **veryimportant** and **stuff** but not necessarily uniquely or in order. The following is a complete example showing multiple class rules working together:

```
<!DOCTYPE html PUBLIC "-//W3C//DTD XHTML 1.0 Transitional//EN"
"http://www.w3.org/TR/xhtml1/DTD/xhtml1-transitional.dtd">
<html xmlns="http://www.w3.org/1999/xhtml" lang="en">
<head>
<title>Multiple Classes Example</title>
<meta http-equiv="content-type" content="text/html; charset=ISO-8859-1" />
<style type="text/css">
<!--
 .heading                        {font-family: Impact, Sans-Serif;}
 .veryimportant                  {background-color: yellow;}
 .stuff                          {color: red;}
 .veryimportant.stuff            {font-style: italic;}
 .veryimportant.example.stuff {text-decoration: underline;}
-->
</style>
</head>
<body>

<h1 class="veryimportant heading stuff">Heading (yellow background, red text,
italic, and Impact)</h1>

<p class="veryimportant">This is the first paragraph. (yellow background, black
text)</p>

<p class="stuff">This is the second paragraph. (red text, default background)</p>

<p class="veryimportant stuff">This is the third paragraph. (yellow background, red
text, italic)</p>

</body>
</html>
```

As these examples have shown, classes can be used to significantly reduce the number of style rules necessary in a document.

Pseudoclasses

A special predefined class grouping, called *pseudoclasses*, is used in CSS to deal with special situations such as the first letter or line of information, the focus of the cursor, the states of links, and so on. These selectors are pseudoclasses because they deal with style information for content, which may change depending on user activity, screen size, or other factors. Let's focus first on the more common pseudoclass and then present the less common ones that are not as well-supported in browsers.

Recall that a hypertext link has three primary states in HTML—unvisited, visited, and active—in which the link text color is blue, purple, and red, respectively. In HTML, it is possible to control the color of these link states through the **link**, **vlink**, and **alink** attributes for the **<body>** element. In CSS, the presentation of link states is controlled through the pseudoclass selectors **a:link**, **a:visited**, and **a:active**. CSS2 also adds **a:hover** for the mouse hovering over a link and is one of the most commonly supported CSS2 features in browsers. Another pseudoclass **:focus** is added by CSS2 and would be selected when the link gains focus—generally through keyboard navigation. Unfortunately, **:focus** is not nearly as well-supported in browsers as **:hover**. An example showing how these link pseudoclass selectors are used is shown here:

```
<!DOCTYPE html PUBLIC "-//W3C//DTD XHTML 1.0 Transitional//EN"
"http://www.w3.org/TR/xhtml1/DTD/xhtml1-transitional.dtd">
<html xmlns="http://www.w3.org/1999/xhtml" lang="en">
<head>
<title>Link Pseudo-Class Example</title>
<meta http-equiv="content-type" content="text/html; charset=ISO-8859-1" />
<style type="text/css">
<!--
a:link      {color: blue; text-decoration: none;}
a:active    {color: red; background-color: #FFFFCC;}
a:visited   {color: purple; text-decoration: none;}
a:hover     {color: red; text-decoration: underline;}
a:focus     {border-style: dashed; border-width: 1px;
             background-color: #FFA500;}
-->
</style>
</head>
<body>
<a href="http://www.htmlref.com">HTML: The Complete Reference</a>
</body>
</html>
```

Although the CSS rules associated with the states of a link can be used to change the link's appearance in dramatic ways, designers are encouraged to limit changes to improve usability. Also note that size changes and other significant differences in link presentation can result in undesirable screen refreshes as the document reloads. For example, with a rule such as

```
a:hover {font-size: larger;}
```

you may notice text lines shifting up and down as you roll over links. The hover and focus pseudoclasses are discussed later in the chapter when CSS2 is covered.

Pseudo-Elements

Another form of selector similar to pseudoclasses in terms of syntax is called a pseudo-element. Under CSS1, two pseudo-elements exist: **:first-letter** and **:first-line**. These selectors are used along with common block-level text elements such as **p** to affect the presentation of the first letter or first line of enclosed text. A short example illustrating their use is presented here:

```
<!DOCTYPE html PUBLIC "-//W3C//DTD XHTML 1.0 Transitional//EN"
"http://www.w3.org/TR/xhtml1/DTD/xhtml1-transitional.dtd">
<html xmlns="http://www.w3.org/1999/xhtml" lang="en">
<head>
<title>First Line and Letter</title>
<meta http-equiv="content-type" content="text/html; charset=ISO-8859-1" />
<style type="text/css">
<!--
p:first-line     {background-color: yellow;}
p:first-letter   {color: red; font-size: 150%;}
-->
</style>
</head>
<body>
<p>CSS selectors can be used to select elements in a variety
of interesting ways. This is some text to fill up the paragraph.
This is only text to fill up this paragraph. This should be
enough text to make this paragraph.</p>

<p>CSS selectors can be used to select elements in a variety
of interesting ways. This is some text to fill up the paragraph.
This is only text to fill up this paragraph. This should be
enough text to make this paragraph.</p>
</body>
</html>
```

Figure 10-2 shows two renderings of this example to demonstrate how the text affected by the rule varies depending on the text flow. Pseudoclasses and elements hint at a much more complex set of CSS rules that are invoked depending on where an element appears in a document.

Contextual Selection

Although the **class** and **id** attributes provide a great deal of flexibility for creating style rules, many other types of rules of equal value exist. For example, it might be useful to specify that all **<strong>** tags that occur within a **<p>** tag get treated in a certain way, as compared to the same elements occurring elsewhere within the document. To create such a rule, you must use *contextual selection*. Contextual selectors are created by showing the order in which the tags must be nested for the rule to be applied. The nesting order is indicated by a space between each selector. For example, given the rule

```
p strong {background-color: yellow;}
```

PART III

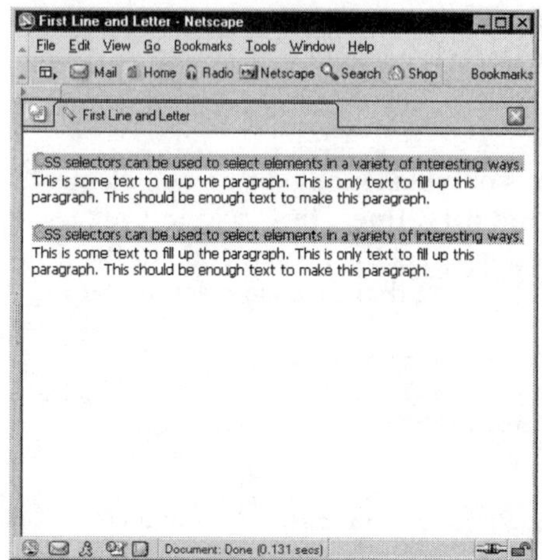

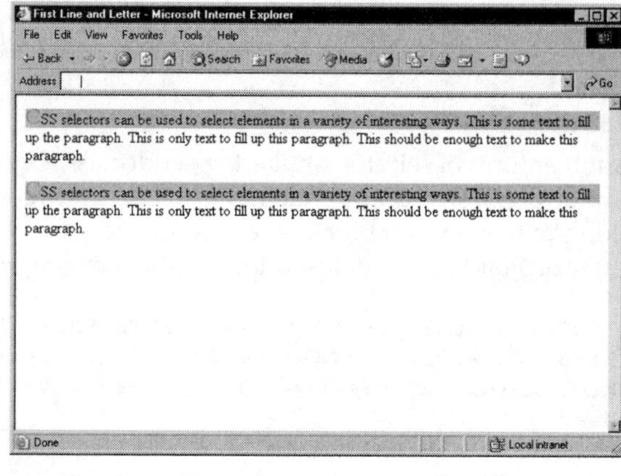

FIGURE 10-2 Pseudo-elements vary their application

all occurrences of the **strong** element within a **p** element have a yellow background. Other occurrences of **strong** might not necessarily have the yellow background. However, contextual selection does not require a direct parent-child relationship with elements. For example, with the rule in the preceding example, you would find that given

```
<p>This <span>is not <strong>directly</strong>within</span>
the paragraph.</p>
```

the nested <**strong**> tag will still have a yellow background even though it is not directly within the <**p**> tag. What you are seeing here is that the rule really says that all <**strong**> tags that are "descendents" of a <**p**> tag are given a yellow background. It is possible to use a more specific CSS2 rule like

```
p > strong {background-color: yellow;}
```

to specify only <**strong**> tags that are directly within <**p**> tags are styled. This is discussed later in the section "CSS2 Selectors." For now, Table 10-2 summarizes the basic selectors found in CSS1.

With these more advanced rules, it becomes clear that precise understanding of the document structure is very important to the correct application of style sheets.

Document Structure and Inheritance

XHTML documents have an implicit structure. They all have a root <**html**> tag. Within this, we find the **head** and **body** elements or, in the case of framed documents, <**head**> and <**frameset**> tags. We dub these tags "children" and the <**html**> tag would be the parent. We then find that children in turn contain other tags. For example, we might find a <**title**> tag within the **head** and a <**p**> tag within the **body**. The structure of the document looks

Selector	Description	Example
element	Selects all elements of the name specified in the rule.	h1 {color: red;} /* makes all h1 tags red */
#id	Selects any tag with an **id** attribute set.	#test {color: green;} /* makes a tag with id='test' green */
.class	Selects any tag with the specified class value.	.note {color: yellow;} /* makes all tags with class='note' yellow */
element.class	Selects the specified elements with a particular class value.	h1.note {text-decoration: underline;} /* underlines all H1 tags with class='note' */
Grouping	Applies the same rules to a group of tags.	h1,h2,h3 {background-color: orange;} /* sets the background color of all h1, h2, and h3 elements to orange */
Contextual	Selects descendent tags.	p strong {color: purple;} /* sets all strong tags that are descendents of p tags purple */
:first-line	Selects the first line of an element.	p:first-line {color: red;} /* makes the first lines of paragraph red */
:first-letter	Selects the first letter of an element.	p:first-letter {font-size: larger;} /* makes the first letter of a paragraph larger */
a:link	Specifies the unvisited link.	a:link {font-weight: bold;} /* makes unvisited links bold */
a:active	Specifies the link as it is being pressed.	a:active {color: red;} /* makes links red as they are pressed */
a:visited	Specifies the link after being pressed.	a:visited {text-decoration: line-through;} /* puts a line through visited links */

TABLE 10-2 CSS1 Selector Summary

somewhat like a family tree. For example, the document shown here would have a tree structure like the one shown in Figure 10-3:

```
<!DOCTYPE html PUBLIC "-//W3C//DTD XHTML 1.0 Transitional//EN"
"http://www.w3.org/TR/xhtml1/DTD/xhtml1-transitional.dtd">
<html xmlns="http://www.w3.org/1999/xhtml" lang="en">
<head>
<title>Test File</title>
</head>
<body>
<h1>Test</h1>
<p>This is a <b>Test</b></p>
</body>
</html>
```

PART III

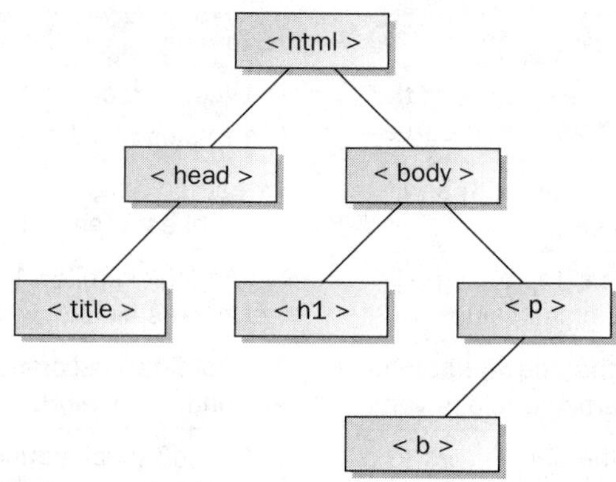

FIGURE 10-3 Simple document parse tree

In the example parse tree, note how the **<b>** tag is a child of the **<p>** tag, which is in the **<body>**, which is in the **<html>** tag. What happens if you set a style rule to **p** elements like so:

```
p {color: red;}
```

Would the contents of the **<b>** tag enclosed in the **<p>** tag also be red? The answer is yes, because the color is inherited from the parent element. Whereas most elements can inherit the style features of their parents, some style properties do not inherit. For example, consider setting the **border** property of the paragraph like so:

```
p {border: solid;}
```

If the enclosed **<b>** tag from the previous example inherited the border, you would expect to see something like this:

This is regular text of the paragraph within a border.
This is bold text and should not be within a border because the bold element does not inherit the border.
Here is a little more paragraph text.

However, this does not happen and the border is limited just to the paragraph itself. As the various CSS properties are introduced later in the chapter, important non-inheriting properties will be pointed out.

Assuming that a property does inherit, it is still possible to override the inheritance of a property. For example, consider the following two rules:

```
p   {color: red; font-size: 14pt;}
b   {color: yellow;}
```

In this case, the color of the text within the **<b>** tag would be yellow and in 14 point. Both of the properties were inherited, but the color property was overridden by the color rule for the **<b>** tag, which is more specific.

The combination of multiple rules with elements inheriting some properties and overriding others is the idea of the *cascade* that CSS is named for. The general idea of the cascade, in effect, is that it provides a system to sort out which rules apply to a document that has many style sheets. For example, a rule for a specific **<p>** tag marked with an **id** attribute is more powerful than a class rule applied to **<p>**, which in turn is more powerful than a rule for the **p** element itself. Inline styles set with a style attribute are more important than a document-wide style or linked style. An easy way to think about which rule wins is to follow these helpful rules of thumb:

- The more specific the rule, the more powerful.
- The closer to the tag the rule, the more powerful.

So with these rules, we see that id rules are more specific than class rules and thus will override them. Inline styles are closer to tags than document-wide or external style rules and thus take precedence, and so on.

TIP *There is an actual process to determine the specificity of a particular rule versus another by assigning numeric values to each rule, but if a designer requires such a careful analysis of the style rules to determine an end result, the style sheet is simply too complex.*

!important Override

If a particular rule should *never* be overridden by another rule, the **!important** indication should be used. For a rule never to be ignored, insert the indication **!important** just before the semicolon of the rule. For example, to always set all paragraphs to red text you might use the following:

```
p {color: red !important; font-size: 12pt;}
```

Later on you might have a paragraph with an inline style such as this:

```
<p style="color: green; font-size: 24pt;">
```

In this paragraph, the text would still be red due to the inclusion of the **!important** indicator, although it would be larger because that rule was overridden as expected. A full example is shown here:

```
<!DOCTYPE html PUBLIC "-//W3C//DTD XHTML 1.0 Transitional//EN"
"http://www.w3.org/TR/xhtml1/DTD/xhtml1-transitional.dtd">
<html xmlns="http://www.w3.org/1999/xhtml" lang="en">
<head>
<title>Important Override</title>
<meta http-equiv="content-type" content="text/html; charset=ISO-8859-1" />
<style type="text/css">
<!--
p {color: red !important; font-size: 12pt;}
-->
</style>
```

```
</head>
<body>
<p>A regular paragraph.</p>
<p style="color: green; font-size: 24pt;">This paragraph has
inline style for green text that is overridden.</p>
<p style="color: green !important; font-size: 24pt;">This inline
rule !important overrides the other rule.</p>
</body>
</html>
```

When using the **!important** indicator, make sure to always put it at the end of a rule; otherwise, it will be ignored.

TIP *Many older CSS-aware browsers do not support the **!important** declaration properly.*

NOTE *Using **!important** to force a style can cause trouble with user-defined style sheets, so use this directive with caution.*

Now that we've covered the basics of style sheet rules, it is time to turn our attention to the various style sheet properties. Before doing so, the next section shows a brief example using many of the ideas presented in the last few sections.

Complete Style Sheet Example

The example shown here uses two forms of style: document-wide and inline. The example also illustrates the use of the **class** and **id** attributes and the appropriate use of HTML elements with CSS properties. Most of the properties should make sense, particularly after seeing the rendering. If you don't get it, don't worry; basic CSS properties and examples are covered later in the chapter.

```
<!DOCTYPE html PUBLIC "-//W3C//DTD XHTML 1.0 Transitional//EN"
"http://www.w3.org/TR/xhtml1/DTD/xhtml1-transitional.dtd">
<html xmlns="http://www.w3.org/1999/xhtml" lang="en">
<head>
<title>Simple CSS Example</title>
<meta http-equiv="content-type" content="text/html; charset=ISO-8859-1" />
<style type="text/css">
<!--
body      {background-color: black;}

div.page  {background-color: #FFD040;
           color: black;
           margin: 50px 10px 50px 10px;
           padding: 10px 10px;
           width: 90%; height: 90%;}

h1        {font-size: 24pt;
           font-family: Comic Sans Ms, Cursive;
           text-align: center;}
```

```
.blackonwhite {color: black; background-color: white;}

.whiteonblack {color: white; background-color: black;}

p           {font-family: Arial, Sans-serif;
             font-size: 16pt;
             line-height: 200%;
             text-align: justify;
             text-indent: 20px;}

.newstyle  {color: blue; font-family: Arial; font-style: oblique;}

.bigsize   {font-size: x-large;}

#letterspace   {letter-spacing: 15pt;}
-->
</style>
</head>
<body>
<div class="page">
<h1><span class="blackonwhite">CSS</span>
    <span class="whiteonblack">Fun</span>
</h1>
<hr />
<p> With style sheets, you will be able to control the presentation
of Web pages with greater precision. Style sheets can be used to
set everything from <span class="newstyle">font styles</span> and
<span class="bigsize">sizes</span> to <span id="letterspace">letter
spacing</span> and line heights.</p>
</div>
</body>
</html>
```

Figure 10-4 shows how the preceding CSS example is rendered by Internet Explorer 6, Netscape 7, Netscape 4.*x* and Opera 7.*x*. Notice that the renderings, while almost the same, have some subtle variations and under some older browsers such as Netscape 4.*x*, significant rendering problems might occur. Designers are cautioned to keep compatibility well in mind as they apply style sheets to their pages.

CSS1 Properties

Now that you've seen *how* rules are formed in style sheets , what *are* the various properties that can be set? CSS1 defines more than 50 different properties and values. CSS2 defines quite a few more and the browser vendors are busy inventing new ones all the time. This section covers the standard CSS1 properties as defined by the W3C, which can be found at http://www.w3.org/TR/REC-CSS1. Although the CSS1 specification was defined well over five years ago and *should* work in all browsers, some properties might not work in your browser. CSS2 (http://www.w3.org/TR/REC-CSS2/) is less supported than CSS1, so let's leave the discussion of it until the next chapter. Although CSS promises a lot more flexibility than HTML-based formatting, it still seems that there are issues regarding lack

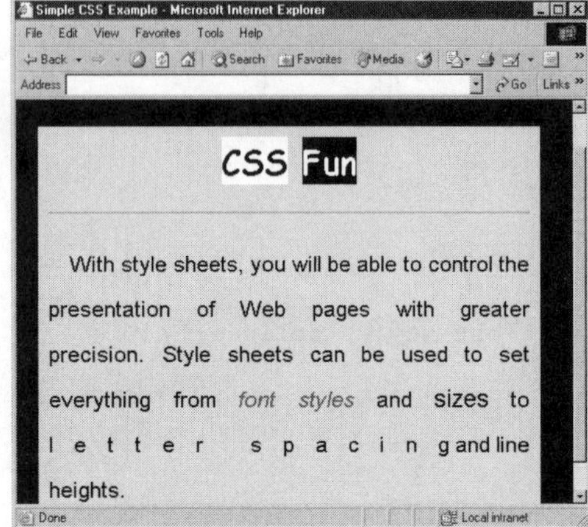

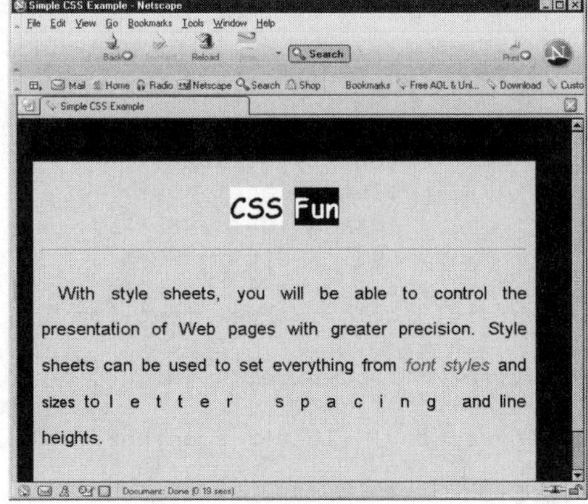

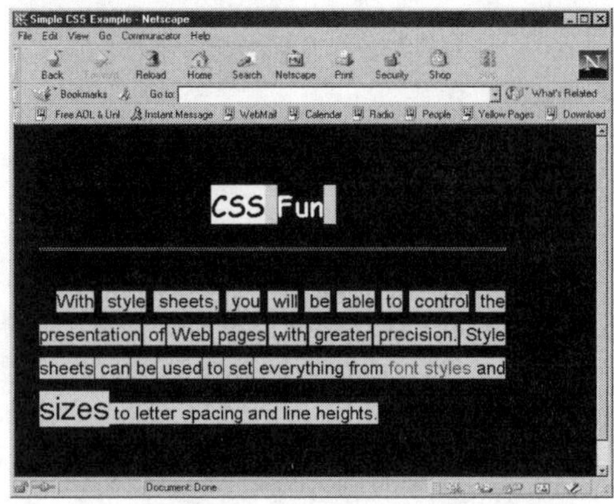

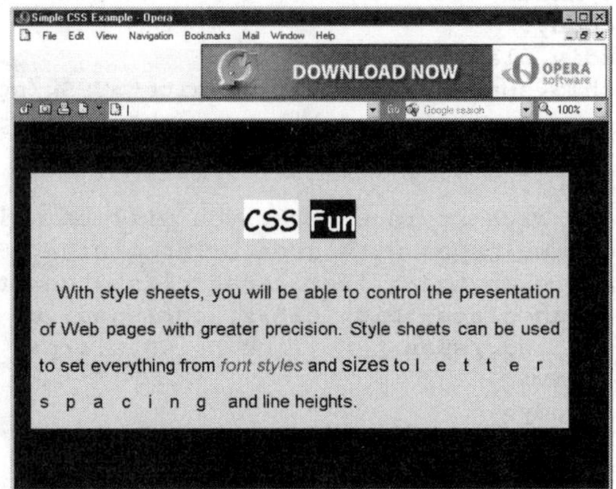

FIGURE 10-4 Browser renderings of the CSS example

of support across browsers and rendering differences. Before turning our attention to the various style properties, it is important to discuss units of measure under CSS.

CSS Measurements

When you manipulate text and other objects with a style sheet, you often must specify a length or size. CSS supports a variety of measurement forms. The CSS1 specification supports traditional English measurements such as inches (**in**) as well metric values in centimeters (**cm**), or millimeters (**mm**). All are demonstrated here with a simple **text-indent** property that can be applied to four paragraph elements with different **id** attribute values:

```
#para1    {text-indent: 1in;}
#para2    {text-indent: 10mm;}
#para3    {text-indent: 0.5cm;}
#para4    {text-indent: -0.75cm;}
```

Notice that it is possible to set values in CSS as both positive and negative integer values as well as decimal values. Of course, negative values may result in somewhat unexpected results.

It also is possible to specify units in publishing length units such as the familiar point size (**pt**) as well as picas (**pc**). For the curious, points relate to inches in that 72 points equals 1 inch, whereas a pica is equivalent to 12 points; thus, there are 6 picas per inch.

```
p.big           {font-size: 64pt;}
.verysmall      {font-size: 6pt;}
#picameasure    {line-height: 2pc;}
```

Interestingly, despite the comfort many designers may have with points as an absolute measurement of text, 12pt will not necessarily be the same on a PC screen as on a Macintosh screen because of the way point size is calculated onscreen on the Web. Pixels do not necessarily correspond to points. On some systems, the resolution is 72 pixels per inch, and thus pixels and points are equivalent. On other systems, you may have 92, 96, or even more pixels per inch; in this situation, one pixel does not equal one point. Because pixels per inch can vary so greatly, designers looking for more exacting measurements might instead opt for pixels (**px**).

```
.bypixel    {font-size: 40px;}
```


Pixels certainly aren't the best measurement form because you may run into problems depending on the user's screen size and the dot pitch of the user's monitor. It just doesn't seem to be that the Web supports absolutes, especially considering that each person's viewing environment is different. Rather than fight this, Web-aware designers often opt for relative units like em-height units (**em**), x-height units (**ex**), and percentage values (**%**). The relative units can be difficult for designers to figure out. The **em** unit is equivalent to the size of a given font. So if you assign a font to 12pt, each "**em**" unit would be 12pt; thus, 2em would be 24pt. Consider the following markup:

```
<div style="font-size: 12pt; text-indent: 1em;">Em example
with font-size at 12pt.</div>

<div style="font-size: 24pt; text-indent: 1em;">Same example
with font-size at 24pt.</div>
```

whose rendering is shown here:

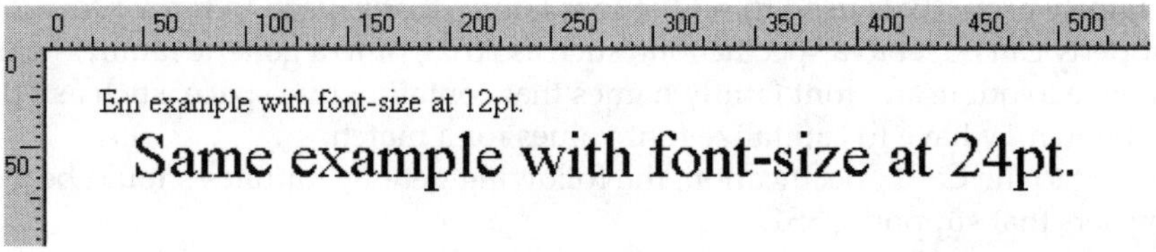

Notice that in the rendering, the second example is indented roughly twice as far as the first based upon the value of the em unit, which is calculated on the font size. Although the value of the em unit might not seem obvious, consider that it can be used to adjust all content relative to a base font measurement. This measurement really lends itself well to a scaling layout in which a user may adjust their fonts.

Slightly easier to understand compared to em, the x-height measurement (**ex**) is used in typography to describe the height of the lowercase x character in a particular font. When setting font sizes and line spacing, it is important to consider the x-height of the font in use. In fact, even when fonts are the same point size, they can be much larger or smaller based upon their x-height, as shown here:

Arial-x Courier-x Times-x

A simple use of x-height measurements (**ex**) would be to specify the line-height relative to a font's x-height.

```
p {line-height: 2.5ex;}
```

Like **em**, the percentage value can be useful when measuring things in CSS, as shown here:

```
b {font-size: 80%;}  /* 80% of the parent element's font */
```

Although page designers who are used to electronic layout tools probably will stick to the measurements most familiar to them, such as points or pixels, the use of relative measurements does make a great deal of sense when trying to create style sheets that work under a variety of conditions.

TIP *Many older CSS1 supporting browsers could have problems with relative measurements such as* ***em*** *and* ***ex****, as well as negative values for measurements.*

Font Properties

CSS1 provides numerous font-oriented properties to set the family, style, size, and variations of the font used within a Web page. In addition to font properties, you also can combine these rules with rules for color, background, margin, and spacing to create a variety of interesting typographic effects.

font-family

The **font-family** property is used to set the font family that is used to render text. The **font-family** property can be set to a specific font, such as Arial, or to a generic family, such as sans-serif. You have to quote any font family names that contain white space, such as **"Britannic Bold"**, and you may have to capitalize font values for a match.

According to the CSS1 specification, the following generic families should be available on all browsers that support CSS1:

- **serif** (e.g., Times)
- **sans-serif** (e.g., Helvetica)
- **cursive** (e.g., Zapf-Chancery)

- **fantasy** (e.g., Western)
- **monospace** (e.g., Courier)

These default fonts as rendered by Internet Explorer, Mozilla, and Opera are shown here:

Internet Explorer | Mozilla | Opera

```
<!DOCTYPE html PUBLIC "-//W3C//DTD XHTML 1.0 Transitional//EN"
"http://www.w3.org/TR/xhtml1/DTD/xhtml1-transitional.dtd">
<html xmlns="http://www.w3.org/1999/xhtml" lang="en">
<head>
<title>CSS Built-in Fonts</title>
<meta http-equiv="content-type" content="text/html; charset=ISO-8859-1" />
<style type="text/css">
<!--
   body {font-size: xx-large;}
-->
</style>
</head>
<body>

<div style="font-family: serif;">serif</div>
<div style="font-family: sans-serif;">sans-serif</div>
<div style="font-family: cursive;">cursive</div>
<div style="font-family: fantasy;">fantasy</div>
<div style="font-family: monospace;">monospace</div>

</body>
</html>
```

Like the **<font>** tag, when setting the **font-family** in CSS, you can provide a prioritized list of names, separated by commas, that will be checked in order. Remember to always provide a backup generic font family, as defined in CSS, at the end of the **font-family** list in case the user's browser doesn't support the fonts suggested. To set a document-wide font, use a rule such as the following for the **body** element:

```
body   {font-family: Futura, Arial, Helvetica, sans-serif;}
```

Whereas the **font-family** property allows both specific and generic CSS1 fonts to be specified, the only way to guarantee that a font is on a user's system is to use a downloadable font, which is discussed at the conclusion of the next chapter.

font-size

The **font-size** property is used to set the relative or physical size of the font used. The value for the property can be a value that is mapped to a physical point size or to a relative word describing the size. Keyword size values include **xx-small**, **x-small**, **small**, **medium**, **large**, **x-large**, and **xx-large**, or a relative word, such as **larger** or **smaller**. Physical sizes also might include examples, such as **48pt**, **2cm**, **12px**, or **.25in**. Relative measurements including percentage values, such as **150%**, also are valid for sizing. However, negative percentages or point sizes are not allowed. A few example rules are shown here:

```
p         {font-size: 18pt;}
strong    {font-size: larger;}
.double   {font-size: 200%;}
```

One suggestion with the **font-size** property is to avoid setting point sizes, where possible, because users who can't see well might have a hard time adjusting size. On certain monitors, a 10-point font might look fine, but on others, it might be microscopic. If you use exact point size, remember to err in favor of readability and increase size.

font-style

The **font-style** property is used to specify **normal**, **italic**, or **oblique** font style for the font being used. A value of **italic** should select an italic version of a font, whereas a value of **oblique** might simply slant the font. In many cases, a value of **italic** or **oblique** results in the same exact rendering. A value of **normal** produces text that is in the Roman style—straight up and down. Usually, this would be used to override an inherited italic style. A few examples are shown here:

```
h1          {font-style: oblique;}
.firstuse   {font-style: italic;}
em          {font-style: normal;}
```

font-weight

The **font-weight** property selects the weight, or darkness, of the font. Values for the property range from **100** to **900**, in increments of 100. Keywords also are supported, including **normal**, **bold**, **bolder**, and **lighter**, which are used to set relative weights. Keywords such as **extra-light**, **light**, **demi-light**, **medium**, **demi-bold**, **bold**, and **extra-bold**, which correspond to the **100** to **900** values, are also provided. A few examples are shown here:

```
.important  {font-weight: bolder;}
h1          {font-weight: 900;}
p.special   {font-weight: extra-bold;}
```

Typically, the value **bold** is the same as **700**, and the **normal** font value is **400**.

NOTE *Most browsers have trouble rendering different font weights onscreen beyond bold and normal. However, you may find that print output does respect weights.*

font-variant

The **font-variant** property is used to select a variation of the specified (or default) font family. The only current variant supported with this property is **small-caps**, which displays text as small uppercase letters, and **normal**, which displays text in the normal style. Interestingly, small-cap text is often used in legal documents such as user software agreements, where all capitals show the importance, but the text is small so you won't read it. A simple rule is shown here:

```
em   {font-variant: small-caps;}
```

font

The **font** property provides a concise way to specify all the font properties with one style rule. One attribute that is included within **font** is **line-height**, which specifies the distance between two lines of text. Each font attribute can be indicated on the line, separated by spaces, except for **line-height**, which is used with **font-size** and separated by a slash. This use of the size of a font followed by the height between lines of text is a common typographic measurement convention that is preserved in CSS. The general form of the font rule is shown here:

```
font: font-style font-variant font-weight font-size/line-height font-family
```

The following is an example of using a compact font rule:

```
p   {font:italic small-caps 600 18pt/24pt "Arial, Helvetica";}
```

The shorthand notation does not require all the properties to be present, so the next example is just as valid as the complete notation:

```
p   {font: italic 18pt/24pt;}
```

However, the ordering is important so be careful with this shorthand form.

TIP *When developing style sheets, you may want to use the specific rules at first and then combine them into shorthand rules once they work appropriately.*

The following is a complete style sheet example that uses all the font rules:

```
<!DOCTYPE html PUBLIC "-//W3C//DTD XHTML 1.0 Transitional//EN"
"http://www.w3.org/TR/xhtml1/DTD/xhtml1-transitional.dtd">
<html xmlns="http://www.w3.org/1999/xhtml" lang="en">
<head>
<title>CSS1 Font Properties Example</title>
<meta http-equiv="content-type" content="text/html; charset=ISO-8859-1" />
<style type="text/css">
<!--
 body          {font-size: 14pt;}
.serif         {font-family: serif;}
.sans-serif    {font-family: sans-serif;}
.cursive       {font-family: cursive;}
.fantasy       {font-family: fantasy;}
.comic         {font-family: Comic Sans MS;}
.xx-small      {font-size: xx-small;}
.x-small       {font-size: x-small;}
```

```
.small          {font-size: small;}
.medium         {font-size: medium;}
.large          {font-size: large;}
.x-large        {font-size: x-large;}
.xx-large       {font-size: xx-large;}
.smaller        {font-size: smaller;}
.larger         {font-size: larger;}
.points         {font-size: 18pt;}
.percentage     {font-size: 200%;}
.italic         {font-style: italic;}
.oblique        {font-style: oblique;}
.weight         {font-weight: 900;}
.smallcaps      {font-variant: small-caps;}
-->
</style>
</head>
<body>

<h2>Font Family</h2>
This text is in <span class="serif">Serif.</span><br />
This text is in <span class="sans-serif">Sans-Serif.</span><br />
This text is in <span class="cursive">Cursive.</span><br />
This text is in <span class="fantasy">Fantasy.</span><br />
Actual fonts can be specified like
<span class="comic">Comic Sans MS</span><br />

<h2>Font Sizing</h2>

This is <span class="xx-small">xx-small text.</span><br />
This is <span class="x-small">x-small text.</span><br />
This is <span class="small">small text.</span><br />
This is <span class="medium">medium text.</span><br />
This is <span class="large">large text.</span><br />
This is <span class="x-large">x-large text.</span><br />
This is <span class="xx-large">xx-large text.</span><br />
This is <span class="smaller">smaller text</span> than the rest.<br />
This is <span class="larger">larger text</span> than the rest.<br />
This is <span class="points">exactly 18 point text.</span><br />
This is <span class="percentage">200% larger text.</span><br />

<h2>Font Style, Weight, and Variant</h2>

This text is <span class="italic">italic.</span><br />
This text is <span class="oblique">oblique.</span><br />
This text is <span class="weight">bold.</span><br />
This text is in <span class="smallcaps">smallcaps.</span><br />
</body>
</html>
```

A rendering of the font example is shown in Figure 10-5. Note that in your browser, there may be slight rendering differences, particularly with named sizes.

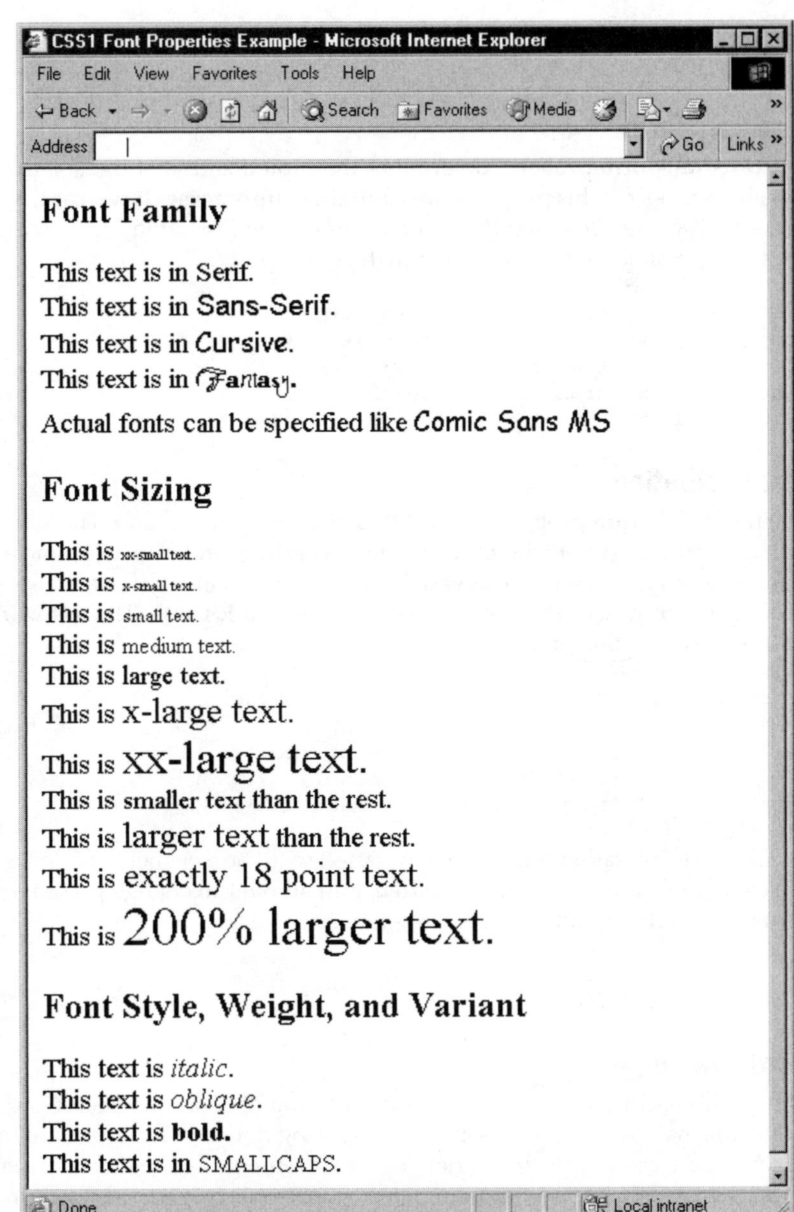

FIGURE 10-5 Rendering of font example under Internet Explorer

Text Properties

Text properties are used to affect the presentation, spacing, and layout of text. The basic properties enable the page designer to set text presentation such as decoration, indentation, word spacing, letter spacing, spacing between lines, horizontal and vertical text alignment, and the control of white space. Let's begin our discussion of these properties with a relatively unused CSS text property, **text-transform**, which enables designers to transform text case.

text-transform

The **text-transform** property determines the capitalization of the text that it affects. The possible values for this property are **capitalize**, **uppercase**, **lowercase,** and **none**, which is the default value. Note that the value **capitalize** will result in capitalizing every word. Here are some possible uses of the **text-transform** property:

```
p        {text-transform: capitalize;}
.upper   {text-transform: uppercase;}
.lower   {text-transform: lower;}
p.none   {text-transform: none;}
/* override the capitalize for some p tags */
```

text-decoration

The **text-decoration** property is used to define an effect on text. The standard values for this property include **line-through**, **overline**, **underline**, and **none**. The meaning of these values should be obvious, except for **overline**, which just creates a line above text. Some versions of Netscape browsers also have support for the **blink** value. The following examples show possible uses for this property:

```
.struck        {text-decoration: line-through;}
span.special   {text-decoration: blink;}  /* browser specific */
h1             {text-decoration: overline;}
a              {text-decoration: none;}
#author        {text-decoration: underline;}
```

The **text-decoration** property often is used with the **a** element and link state pseudoclasses, which include **a:link**, **a:active**, **a:visited,** and **a:hover** to change presentation, in particular turning underlining off or on, as shown here:

```
a        {text-decoration: none;}
a:hover  {text-decoration: underline;}
```

word-spacing

The **word-spacing** property specifies the amount of space between words. The default value, **normal**, uses the browser's word-spacing default. Designers are free to specify the distance between words in a variety of measurements as previously discussed, including inches (**in**), centimeters (**cm**), millimeters (**mm**), points (**pt**), picas (**pc**), the em (**em**) measurement, x-height (**ex**), and pixels (**px**). A few examples are shown here:

```
body    {word-spacing: 10pt;}
p       {font-size: 18pt; word-spacing: 1em;}
```

NOTE *This property is poorly supported, particularly in older CSS-aware browsers.*

letter-spacing

The **letter-spacing** property specifies the amount of space between letters. The default value, **normal**, uses the browser's letter-spacing default. Like the **word-spacing** property, a variety of measurements can be used to set word spacing, from pixels to em values. A few examples of this property are shown here:

```
p        {letter-spacing: 0.2em;}
body     {letter-spacing: 2px;}
.wide    {letter-spacing: 10pt;}
#Fun     {letter-spacing: 2cm;}
```

vertical-align

The **vertical-align** property controls the vertical positioning of text and images with respect to the baseline currently in effect. The possible values for the **vertical-align** property include **baseline**, **sub**, **super**, **top**, **text-top**, **middle**, **bottom**, **text-bottom**, and percentage values. Compare these values with the **align** attribute for the **img** element, as well as alignment options for table cells, and you should see a similarity. However, the flexibility of vertical alignment provided by style sheets enables designers to set element values on individual characters. When not specified, the default value of **vertical-align** is **baseline**. Here are a few examples:

```
p               {vertical-align: text-top;}
.superscript    {vertical-align: super; font-size: smaller;}
.subscript      {vertical-align: sub; font-size: 75%;}
```

Notice in the preceding example how **vertical-align** can be used with other properties to create an interesting contextual class such as **.superscript**. Given this flexibility, it is obvious why presentational tags such as **<sub>** and **<sup>** could be deprecated from strict variants of HTML and XHTML.

NOTE *According to CSS1 specification, the* ***vertical-align*** *property is not inherited by enclosed elements, but testing reveals this not to be the case in most browsers.*

text-align

The **text-align** property determines how text in a block-level element, such as a **<p>** tag, is horizontally aligned. The allowed values for this property are **left,** which is the default, **right**, **center**, and **justify**. This property is used only on block level elements such as **p** in a similar manner to the **align** attributes from HTML. Be aware that setting a value of **justify** may not produce an eye-pleasing result when the font is very large as it might show the added spaces. A few examples are shown here:

```
p          {text-align: justify;}
div        {text-align: center;}
.goright   {text-align: right;}
```

text-indent

The **text-indent** property sets the indentation for text in the first line of a block-level element such as **p**. Its value can be given either as a length value (**.5cm**, **15px**, **12pt**, and so on) or as a percentage of the width of the block, such as **10%**. The default value for the property is **0**, which indicates no indentation. A few examples of how **text-indent** might be used are shown here:

```
p          {text-indent: 2em;}
p.heavy    {text-indent: 150px;}
```

One interesting effect is the use of negative values to create a hanging indent, wherein the text within the block element expands outside of the box defined by the tag. The following rule creates a paragraph with a yellow background with a hanging indent 10 pixels to the left of the paragraph block:

```
p   {text-indent: -10px; background-color: yellow;}
```

Combining the hanging indent with a large first letter using the pseudoclass **:first-letter** for the paragraph element creates an interesting initial-cap effect.

line-height

The **line-height** property sets the height between lines in a block-level element, such as a paragraph. The basic idea is to set the line spacing, known typographically as *leading*. The value of the attribute can be specified as a number of lines (**1.4**), a length (**14pt**), or as a percentage of the line height (**200%**). So, double spacing could be written as

```
p.double       {line-height: 2;}
```

as well as

```
p.double2      {line-height: 200%;}
```

Other examples of using **line-height** are shown here:

```
p              {font-size: 12pt; line-height: 18pt;}
p.carson       {font-size: 24pt; line-height: 6pt;}
```

Notice in the second example how the **line-height** property is much smaller than the **font-size** property. A browser generally should render the text on top of the other text, creating a hard-to-read, but potentially "cool" effect.

white-space

The **white-space** property controls how spaces, tabs, and newline characters are handled in an element. The default value, **normal**, collapses white space characters into a single space and automatically wraps lines, just as in an HTML/XHTML document. When a value of **pre** is used for the property, white-space formatting is preserved, similar to how the **<pre>** tag works in XHTML. The **nowrap** value prevents lines from wrapping if they exceed the element's content width. This example shows how the **white-space** property would be used to simulate the **<pre>** element:

```
p.pre   {white-space: pre;}
.nowrap {white-space: nowrap;}
```

NOTE *The* ***white-space*** *property is not supported well by older CSS-aware browsers.*

A complete example showing the HTML and cascading style sheet markup for text properties previously presented is shown here:

```
<!DOCTYPE html PUBLIC "-//W3C//DTD XHTML 1.0 Transitional//EN"
"http://www.w3.org/TR/xhtml1/DTD/xhtml1-transitional.dtd">
<html xmlns="http://www.w3.org/1999/xhtml" lang="en">
<head>
<title>CSS Text Properties Example</title>
<meta http-equiv="content-type" content="text/html; charset=ISO-8859-1" />
<style type="text/css">
<!--
/* letter and word spacing */
.letterspaced  {letter-spacing: 10pt;}
.wordspaced    {word-spacing: 20px;}

/* vertical alignment examples */
.sub           {vertical-align: sub;}
.super         {vertical-align: super;}

/* text alignment properties */
.right         {text-align: right;}
.left          {text-align: left;}
.justify       {text-align: justify;}
.center        {text-align: center;}

/* indentation and line-height examples */

p.indent       {text-indent: 20px;
                line-height: 200%;}
p.negindent    {text-indent: -10px;
                background-color: yellow;}
#bigchar       {background-color: red;
                color: white;
                font-size: 28pt;
                font-family: Impact;}
p.carson       {font-size: 12pt;
                font-family: Courier;
                letter-spacing: 4pt;
                line-height: 5pt;}
/* text transformation properties */
.uppercase     {text-transform: uppercase;}
.lowercase     {text-transform: lowercase;}
.capitalize    {text-transform: capitalize;}
```

```
/* text-decoration properties */

.underline      {text-decoration: underline;}
.blink          {text-decoration: blink;}
.line-through   {text-decoration: line-through;}
.overline       {text-decoration: overline;}

/* white space control */

.normal         {white-space: normal;}
.pre            {white-space: pre;}
.nowrap         {white-space: nowrap;}
-->
</style>
</head>
<body>
<h2>Letter Spacing and Vertical Alignment</h2>

<p>This is a paragraph of text.
<span class="letterspaced">Spacing letters is possible</span>
and so <span class="wordspaced">should word spacing.
Alas, it is not always supported!</span></p>
<p>Vertical alignment can be used to make
<span class="sub">Subscript</span> and
<span class="super">Superscript</span> text, but the
common use of the property is for aligning text next to images.</p>

<h2>Alignment</h2>

<p class="left">Align a paragraph to the left as normal.</p>

<p class="right">Align paragraphs to the right as we did in HTML.</p>

<p class="justify">You can even set the justification of text so
that it is aligned on both the left and the right side. You need
to be careful with this so that you don't get rivers of white space
running through your paragraphs.</p>

<p class="center">Text can of course also be centered.</p>

<h2>Indentation and Line Height</h2>

<p class="indent">With style sheets it is possible to set
indentation as well as line height. Now double spacing is a
reality. This is just dummy text to show the effects of the
indentation and spacing. This is just dummy text to show the
effects of the indentation and spacing.</p>

<p class="negindent"><span id="bigchar">T</span>his is another
paragraph that has negative indenting. Notice how you can pull
a character outside the paragraph for interesting effects. This
is just dummy text to show the effect of the indent. This is
just dummy text to show the effect of the indent.</p>
```

```
<h2>Surf Gun</h2>

<p class="carson">Don't get carried away with your newfound
powers. You may be tempted to show how cool you can be using
text on top of other text. While this may be good for certain
situations, it may also confuse the viewer.</p>

<h2>Text Transformation</h2>

<p>The next bit of text is transformed <span class="uppercase">to all
uppercase.</span>
<br /> The next bit of text is transformed<span class="lowercase">To All
Lowercase.</span>
<br /><span class="capitalize">This text is all capitalized. It doesn't
do what you think, does it?</span></p>

<h2>Text Decoration</h2>

This text should <span class="blink">blink under Netscape.</span>
<br /><br />

This text should be <span class="underline">underlined.</span>
<br /><br />

This text should be <span class="line-through">struck.</span>
<br /><br />

This text should be <span class="overline">overline.</span>
<br /><br />

<h2>White Space Control</h2>
<p class="normal">This text controls space normally like
  HTML; it condenses               all spaces and
            returns to a single character.</p>
<p class="pre">This paragraph
     preserves any   S  P  E  C  I  A  L   spacing.</p>
<p class="nowrap">This paragraph does not wrap at all and
keeps going and going and going and going to the right
until I stop typing.</p>
</body>
</html>
```

The rendering of the text properties example is shown in Figure 10-6.

List Properties

As discussed in Chapter 3, XHTML supports three major forms of lists: ordered lists, unordered lists, and definition lists. HTML traditionally also has supported other forms of lists that were more compact or formatted differently, but browser support has been spotty. CSS1 provides some list manipulation, including three style properties that can be set for lists: **list-style-type**, **list-style-image**, and **list-style-position**. A general property, **list-style**, provides a shorthand notation to set all three properties at once.

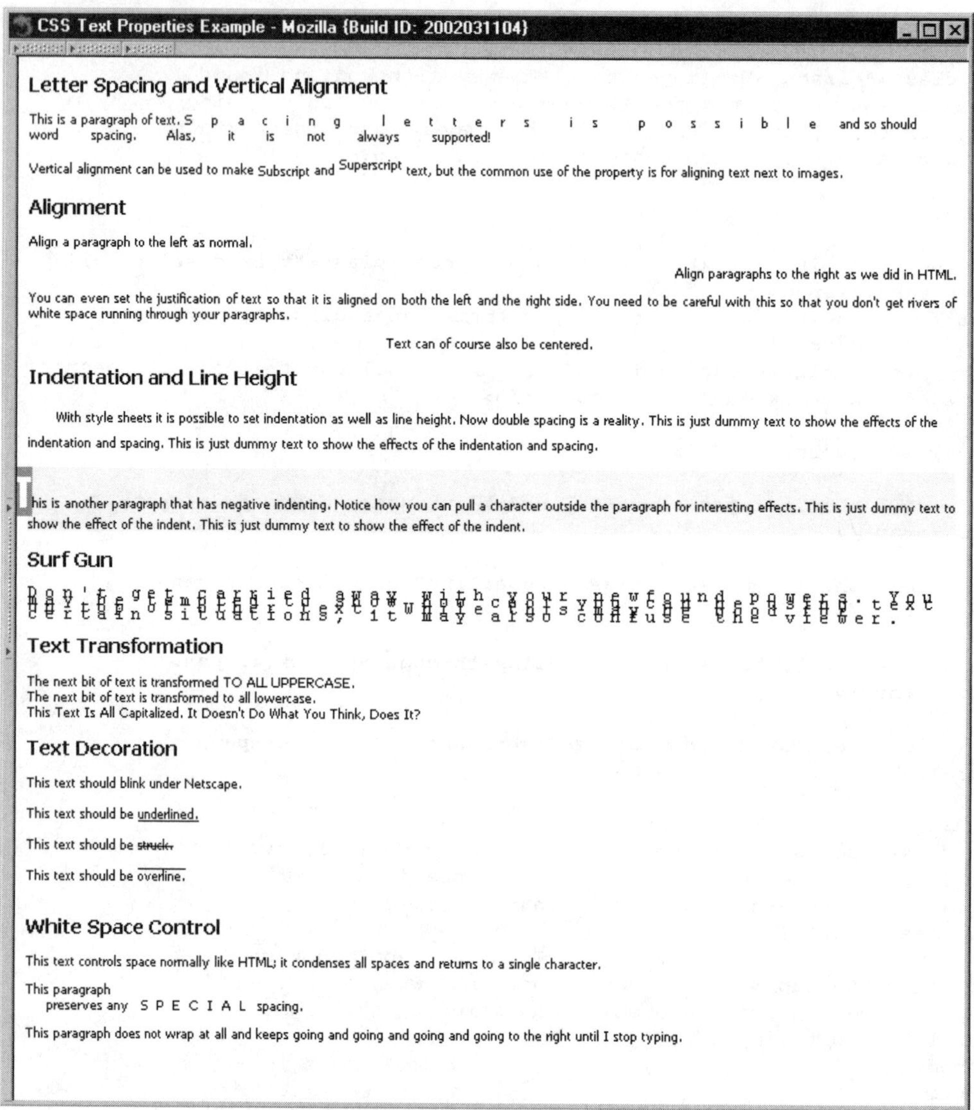

FIGURE 10-6 Rendering of text properties under Mozilla

list-style-type

The items in ordered or unordered lists are labeled with a numeric value or a bullet, depending on the list form. These list labels can be set under CSS1 by using the **list-style-type** property. Five values are appropriate for ordered lists: **decimal**, **lower-roman**, **upper-roman**, **lower-alpha**, and **upper-alpha**. Three values are appropriate for unordered lists: **disc**, **circle**, and **square**. The value **none** prevents a label from displaying. These values are similar to the **type** attribute for the list elements in HTML. Setting the following:

```
ol   {list-style-type: upper-roman;}
```

is equivalent to **<ol type="i">**, whereas the following is equivalent to **<ul type="square">**:

```
ul   {list-style-type: square;}
```

Nested lists can be controlled by using contextual selection rules. For example, to set an outer order list to uppercase Roman numerals, an inner list to lowercase Roman numerals, and a further embedded list to lowercase letters, use the following rules:

```
ol          {list-style-type: upper-roman;}
ol ol       {list-style-type: lower-roman;}
ol ol ol    {list-style-type: lower-alpha;}
```

The **list-style-type** property also can be associated with the **<li>** element, but be aware that setting individual list elements to a particular style may require the use of the **id** attribute, or even inline styles.

One caveat with list styles is that it is very possible to change the meaning of a list tag. For example, consider the rules here:

```
ol   {list-style-type: square;}
ul   {list-style-type: upper-roman;}
```

In this case, we have created ordered lists that have bullets and unordered lists are numbered! Use your CSS power wisely or you'll end up with confusing markup.

list-style-image

The **list-style-type** property provides little different functionality from HTML lists, but the **list-style-image** property can assign a graphic image to a list label; this is awkward to do under plain XHTML. The value of the property is either the URL of the image to use as a bullet or the keyword **none**. So, to use small flags with your list, create an appropriate graphics file and use a rule such as this:

```
ul   {list-style-image: url(flag.gif);}
```

Notice the use of the keyword **url** within which you set a URL either absolute or relative to the image to use. You can use quotes, either double or single, around the value, but it is not required.

list-style-position

Display elements in cascading style sheets are treated as existing inside a rectangular box. Unlike other elements, the labels for list items can exist outside and to the left of the list element's box. The **list-style-position** property controls where a list item's label is displayed in relation to the element's box. The values allowed for this property are **inside** or **outside**. The **outside** value is the default. The following example tightens up a list by bringing the bullets inside the box for the list:

```
ul.compact  {list-style-position: inside;}
```

list-style

Like other shorthand notations, the **list-style** property allows a list's type, image, or position properties all to be set by a single property. The properties can appear in any order and are determined by value. The following is an example of the shorthand notation that sets an unordered list with a bullet image that appears within the list block:

```
ul.special {list-style: inside url(bullet.gif);}
```

A complete example of list properties is shown here, with a rendering in Figure 10-7:

```
<!DOCTYPE html PUBLIC "-//W3C//DTD XHTML 1.0 Transitional//EN"
"http://www.w3.org/TR/xhtml1/DTD/xhtml1-transitional.dtd">
<html xmlns="http://www.w3.org/1999/xhtml" lang="en">
<head>
<title>List Properties Example</title>
<meta http-equiv="content-type" content="text/html; charset=ISO-8859-1" />
<style type="text/css">
<!--

ul          {list-style-image: url(flag.gif);}

.inside     {background-color: yellow;
             list-style-type: upper-roman;
             list-style-position: inside;}

.outside    {background-color: yellow;
             list-style-type: decimal;
             list-style-position: outside;}

-->
</style>
</head>
<body>
<ul>
  <li>Item a</li>
  <li>Item b</li>
</ul>

<ol class="outside">
  <li>Item a</li>
  <li>Item b</li>
</ol>

<ol class="inside">
  <li>Item a</li>
  <li>Item b</li>
</ol>
</body>
</html>
```

CSS2 provides a wealth of additional settings, as well as control over list number. See the section entitled "CSS2 List Changes" for more information on CSS2-based list properties.

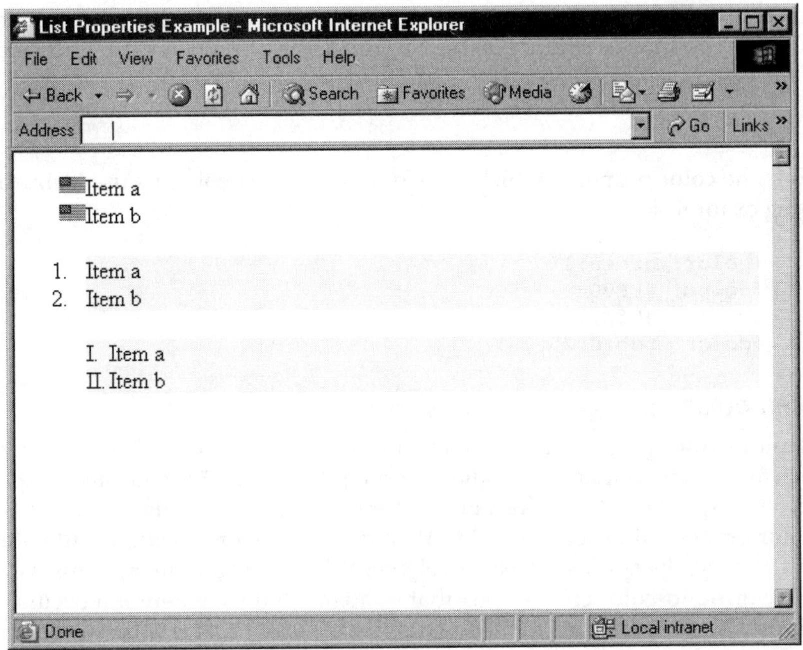

FIGURE 10-7 List properties under Internet Explorer 5

Color and Background Properties

CSS1 supports a variety of properties that can be used to control the colors and backgrounds in a document. With style sheets, you can create arbitrary regions with different background colors and images. In the past, such designs were difficult to accomplish without turning to tables or proprietary HTML extensions.

CSS1 style sheets support three basic forms of color specifications:

- **Color names** The suggested keyword colors supported by browsers are a set of 16 color names taken from the Windows VGA palette. The colors include **Aqua**, **Black**, **Blue**, **Fuchsia**, **Gray**, **Green**, **Lime**, **Maroon**, **Navy**, **Olive**, **Purple**, **Red**, **Silver**, **Teal**, **White**, and **Yellow**. These are the same predefined colors from the XHTML specification.
- **Hexadecimal values** Supports the standard, six-digit color form *#RRGGBB* as used with the **font** and **body** elements. A shortened, three-digit color form, in which R, G, and B are hex digits, also is supported under CSS1. For example, #F00 would represent red. This three-hex color format is less expressive in the range of color it can represent and some older CSS browsers do not support it; thus, its use isn't recommended.
- **RGB values** The RGB format also is specified in the form *rgb(R,G,B)*, whereby the values for R, G, and B range from 0 to 255. This format should be very familiar to users of graphics programs such as Adobe Photoshop. Older CSS-aware browsers

don't support the *rgb(R,G,B)* color format, so use it with caution. However, given this new color measurement, in the future we may find hex values for color a thing of the past.

color

CSS supports the **color** property, which is used to set the text color. Its use is illustrated in the following examples:

```
body        {color: green;}
h1          {color: #FF0088;}
.fun        {color: #0f0;}
#test       {color: rgb(0,255,0);}
```

background-color

The **background-color** property sets an element's background color. The default value is **none**, which allows any underlying content to show through. This state also is specified by the keyword **transparent**. The **background-color** property often is used in conjunction with the **color** property that sets text color. With block elements, **background-color** colors content and *padding,* the space between an element's contents and its margins. With inline elements, **background-color** colors a box that wraps with the element if it occurs over multiple lines. This property takes colors in the same format as the **color** property. A few example rules are shown here:

```
p         {background-color: yellow;}
body      {background-color: #0000FF;}
.fun      {background-color: #F00;}
#test     {background-color: rgb(0,0,0);}
```

The second example is particularly interesting because it sets the background color for the entire document. Given this capability, the **bgcolor** attribute for the **body** element isn't needed.

background-image

The **background-image** property associates a background image with an element. If the image contains transparent regions, underlying content shows through. To prevent this, designers often use the **background-image** property in conjunction with the **background-color** property. The color is rendered beneath the image and provides an opaque background. The **background-image** property requires a URL to select the appropriate image to use as a background within a special url( ) indicator. Background images are limited to whatever image format that the browser supports, generally GIF and JPEG, but increasingly PNG as well. A few examples are shown here, including one that suggests how background colors might show through a transparent hole in a **background-image** tile.

```
#krispy      {background-image: url(donut-tile.gif);
              background-color: white;}
body         {background-image: url(funtile.gif);}
b            {background-image: url(brick.gif);}
div.prison   {background-image: url(bars.gif);}
```

Notice that you can set a background for an inline element, such as **b**, just as easily as you can for larger structures or the whole document, as specified by the **body** element selector.

background-repeat

The **background-repeat** property determines how background images tile in cases where they are smaller than the canvas space used by their associated elements. The default value is **repeat**, which causes the image to tile in both the horizontal and vertical directions. A value of **repeat-x** for the property limits tiling to the horizontal dimension. The **repeat-y** value behaves similarly for the vertical dimension. The **no-repeat** value prevents the image from tiling.

```
p          {background-image: url(donut-tile.gif);
            background-repeat: repeat-x;}
.tileup    {background-image: url(tile.gif);
            background-repeat: repeat-y;}
body       {background-image: url(tile.gif);
            background-repeat: no-repeat;}
```

NOTE *By using the* ***background-repeat*** *property, you can avoid some of the undesirable tiling effects from HTML-based backgrounds. As discussed in Chapter 6, designers often must resort to making very wide or tall background tiles so that users won't notice the repeat. Because the direction of* ***repeat*** *can be controlled, designers can now use much smaller background tiles.*

One unresolved issue with a nonrepeating tile is what happens when the user scrolls the screen: should the background be fixed or scroll offscreen? It turns out that this behavior is specified by the next property, **background-attachment**.

background-attachment

The **background-attachment** property determines whether a background image should scroll as the element content with which it is associated scrolls, or whether the image should stay fixed on the screen while the content scrolls. The default value is **scroll**. The alternate value, **fixed**, can implement a watermark effect, similar to the proprietary attribute **bgproperties** to the **body** element that was introduced by Microsoft. An example of how this can be used is shown here:

```
body    {background-image:url(logo.gif);background-attachment: fixed;}
```

background-position

The **background-position** property specifies how a background image—not a color—is positioned within the canvas space used by its element. There are three ways to specify a position:

- The top-left corner of the image can be specified as an absolute distance; usually in pixels from the origin of the enclosing element.
- The position can be specified as a percentage along the horizontal and vertical dimensions.

- The position can be specified with keywords to describe the horizontal and vertical dimensions. The keywords for the horizontal dimension are **left**, **center**, and **right**. The keywords for the vertical dimension are **top**, **center**, and **bottom**. When keywords are used, the default for an unspecified dimension is assumed to be **center**.

The first example shows how to specify the top-left corner of the background by using an absolute distance 10 pixels from the left and 10 pixels from the enclosing element's origin:

```
p  {background-image: url(picture.gif); background-position: 10px 10px;}
```

Note that this distance is relative to the element's position and not to the document as a whole, unless, of course, the property is being set for the **body** element. If you are a little confused about positioning, don't worry because you will see much more of it in the next chapter. For now let's look at a few more examples. This example shows how to specify a background image position by using percentage values along the horizontal and vertical dimensions:

```
body  {background-image:url(picture.gif);background-position: 20% 40%;}
```

If you forget to specify one percentage value, the other value is assumed to be **50%**.

Specifying an image position by using keywords is an easy way to do simple placement of an image. When you set a value, the keyword pairs have the following meanings:

Keyword Pair	Horizontal Position	Vertical Position
top left	0%	0%
top center	50%	0%
top right	100%	0%
center left	0%	50%
center center	50%	50%
center right	100%	50%
bottom left	0%	100%
bottom center	50%	100%
bottom right	100%	100%

An example of using keywords to position a background image is shown here:

```
body   {background-image: url(picture.gif);
        background-position: center center;}
```

Note that if only one keyword is set, the second keyword defaults to **center**. Thus, in the preceding example, the keyword **center** was needed only once.

background

The **background** property is a comprehensive property that allows any or all of the specific background properties to be set at once, not unlike the shorthand **font** property. Property order does not matter. Any property not specified uses the default value. A few examples are shown here:

```
p          {background: white url(picture.gif) repeat-y center;}
body       {background: url(tile.jpg) top center fixed;}
.bricks    {background: repeat-y top top url(bricks.gif);}
```

The following is a complete example of all the background properties :

```
<!DOCTYPE html PUBLIC "-//W3C//DTD XHTML 1.0 Transitional//EN"
"http://www.w3.org/TR/xhtml1/DTD/xhtml1-transitional.dtd">
<html xmlns="http://www.w3.org/1999/xhtml" lang="en">
<head>
<title>CSS Background Attributes Example</title>
<meta http-equiv="content-type" content="text/html; charset=ISO-8859-1" />
<style type="text/css">
<!--
 body   {background-color: green;}
 p      {background: yellow url(flag.gif) repeat-y fixed 100px;}
 .red   {background-color: red;}
-->
</style>
</head>
<body>
<p>This is a paragraph of text. The left side will probably be hard to
read because it is on top of an image that repeats along the
y-axis. Notice that the area not covered by the background image is
filled with the background color. <span class="red">Backgrounds anywhere!</span>
This is more text just to illustrate the idea. This is even more text. This is
more text just to illustrate the idea. This is even more text. This is more text
just to illustrate the idea. This is even more text. This is more text just to
illustrate the idea. This is even more text. This is more text just to illustrate
the idea. This is even more text.</p>
</body>
</html>
```

Notice that multiple background types with a variety of elements can be included. A similar layout is possible under pure HTML, but the required **table** element would be somewhat complicated. A rendering of the background style sheet example is shown in Figure 10-8.

Box Properties

An important part of mastering CSS layout is understanding the basics of the box model. First consider that XHTML block-level elements, such as **p**, can be thought of as occupying rectangular boxes on the screen. The aspects of boxes that can be controlled with CSS include the following:

- **Margin properties** Determine the distance between edges of an element's box and the edges of adjacent elements.
- **Border properties** Determine the visual characteristics of a border surrounding an element's edges.

PART III

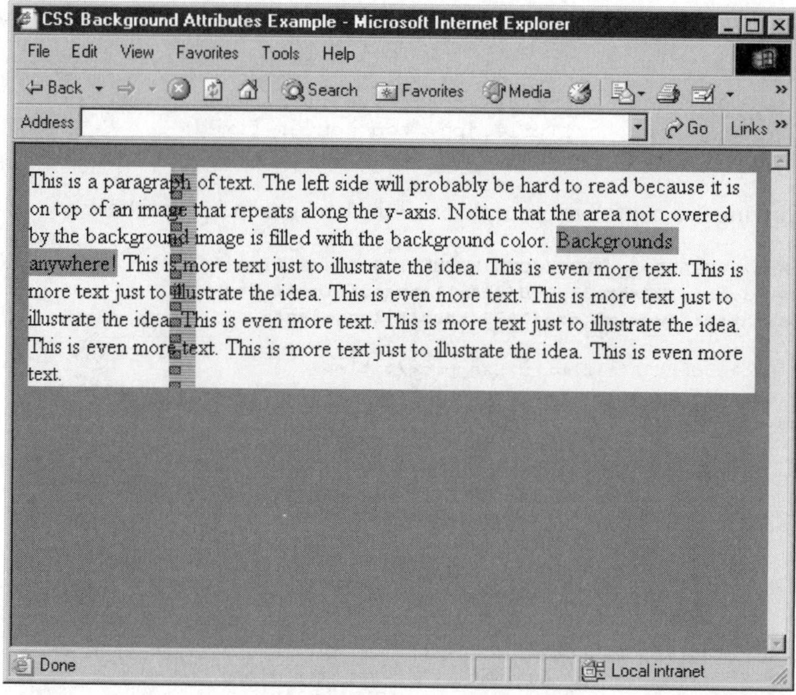

FIGURE 10-8 Rendering of background properties

- **Padding properties** Determine the distance inside an element between its edges and its actual content.
- **Height, width, and positioning properties** Determines the size and position of the box that the element creates.

The relationship of these various box characteristics is illustrated here:

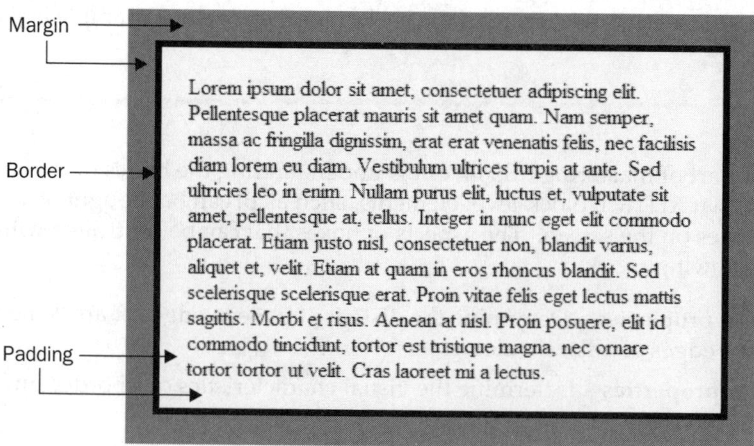

Margin Properties

Four margin properties are available to set each of an element's four margins individually. A fifth **margin** property allows all of the margins to be set together. Individual margins for a block element including the **body** itself can be set by using **margin-top**, **margin-right**, **margin-bottom**, or **margin-left** properties. The values for the margins should be a length (such as **15pt** or **2em**), a percentage value of the block element's width (such as **20%**), or the value **auto**, which attempts to figure out the appropriate margin automatically:

```
body        {margin-top: 20px; margin-bottom: 20px;
             margin-left: 30px; margin-right: 50px;}
p           {margin-bottom: 20mm;}
div.fun     {margin-left: 1.5cm; margin-right: 1.5cm;}
```

One interesting use of margin properties is to set negative margin values. Of course, negative margins could clip the content of the block element in the browser window, if you aren't careful. Try an example such as

```
p   {margin-left: -2em; background-color: green;}
```

to get an idea of how negative margins work.

The last few examples show that you can set one or many margins. To make setting multiple margins even easier, a shorthand notation is available that enables page designers to set all the margins at once. Using the **margin** property, one to four values can be assigned to affect the block element margins. If a single value is specified, it is applied to all four margins. For example,

```
p    {margin: 1.5cm;}
```

sets all the margins equal to 1.5 cm. If multiple values are specified, they are applied in clockwise order: first the top margin, followed by (in order) the right, bottom, and left margins. For example,

```
p    {margin: 10px 5px 15px 5px;}
```

sets the top margin to 10 pixels, the right to 5 pixels, the bottom to 15 pixels, and the left to 5 pixels. If only two or three values are specified in the rule, the missing values are determined from the opposite sides. For example,

```
p    {margin: 10px 5px;}
```

sets the top margin to 10 pixels and the right margin to 5 pixels. The opposite sides, then, are set accordingly, making the bottom margin 10 pixels and the left margin 5 pixels.

A complete example using the margin properties is shown here. Notice that the example uses one negative margin. The background color makes it easier to see the effect.

```
<!DOCTYPE html PUBLIC "-//W3C//DTD XHTML 1.0 Transitional//EN"
"http://www.w3.org/TR/xhtml1/DTD/xhtml1-transitional.dtd">
<html xmlns="http://www.w3.org/1999/xhtml" lang="en">
<head>
```

```
<title>CSS Margin Example</title>
<meta http-equiv="content-type" content="text/html; charset=ISO-8859-1" />
<style type="text/css">
<!--
body     {margin: 0px;}
#one     {background-color: yellow;
          margin: 1cm;}
#two     {background-color: #FFD700;
          margin-top: 1cm;
          margin-bottom: 1cm;
          margin-right: .5cm;
          margin-left: -5px;}
#three   {background-color: #ADFF2F;}
#bigchar {background-color: red;
          color: white;
          font-size: 28pt;
          font-family: Impact;}
-->
</style>
</head>
<body>

<p id="one">This is a paragraph of text that has
margins set for all sides to 1 cm. This is just dummy
text to show the effects of the margins. This is just
dummy text to show the effects of the margins.</p>

<p id="two"><span id="bigchar">T</span>his is another
paragraph that has negative margins on one side. Be
careful not to clip things with negative margins. This
is just dummy text to show the effect of the margins.
This is just dummy text to show the effect of the margin.</p>

<p id="three">This paragraph has the default margins for the page, which
are set to 0. This is just dummy text to show the effects of the margins.
This is just dummy text to show the effects of the margins.
This is just dummy text to show the effects of the margins.
This is just dummy text to show the effects of the margins.</p>

</body>
</html>
```

The rendering of the margin example under Internet Explorer is shown in Figure 10-9.

Border Properties

Elements can be completely or partially surrounded by borders placed between their margins and their padding. The border properties control the edges of block elements by setting whether they should have a border, what the borders look like, their width, their color, and so on. Borders are supposed to work with both block-level and inline elements.

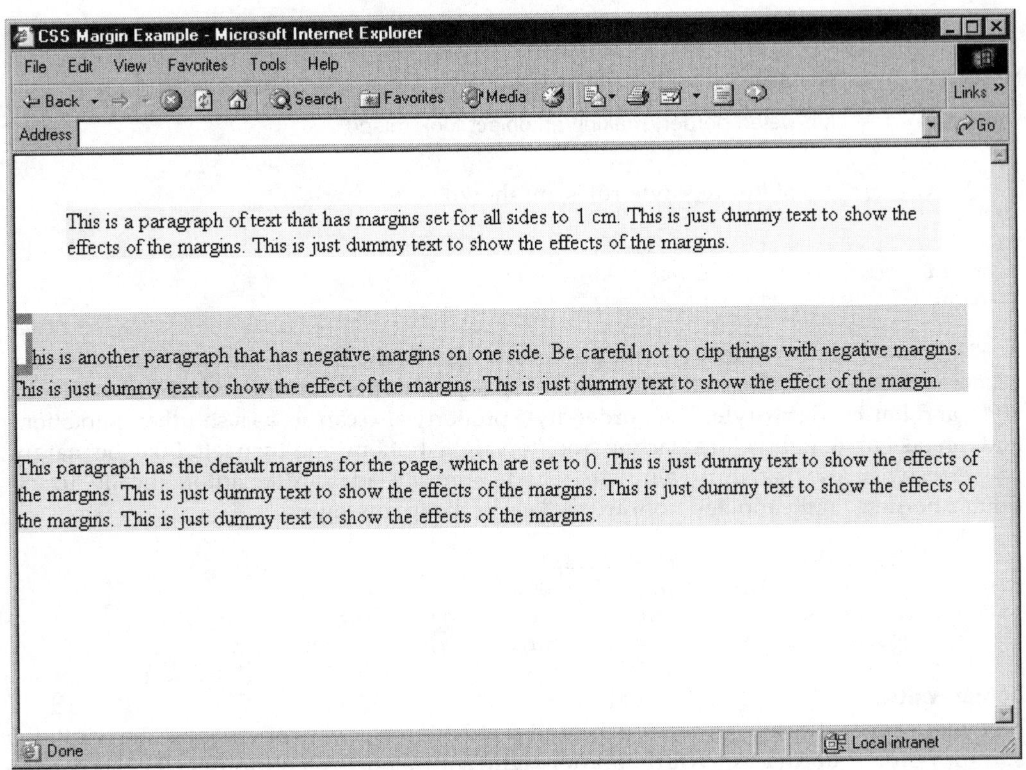

FIGURE 10-9 Margin example under Internet Explorer

However, you will not find that border properties are inherited by enclosed elements when used with block elements.

border-style

The **border-style** property is used to set the appearance of the borders. The default value for the property is **none**, which means no border is drawn, regardless of any other setting. The values for **border-style** include the following:

Value	Intended Rendering
dotted	A dotted border
dashed	A dashed-line border
solid	A normal solid-line border
double	A double-line border
groove	An etched border
ridge	An extruded border

Value	Intended Rendering
inset	An inset border, making an object look like it is set into the page
outset	A beveled border, making an object look raised

A few examples of **border-style** rules are shown here:

```
h1         {border-style: solid;}
p.boxed    {border-style: double;}
.button    {border-style: outset;}
```

The **border-style** property sets the borders for each of the sides of the element. Individual border styles can be controlled with **border-top-style**, **border-bottom-style**, **border-left-style**, and **border-right-style**. The **border-style** property also can act as a shorthand notation and can take up to four values starting from top, right, bottom, and then left. Like the **margin** property, when less than four values are set, the opposite sides are set automatically. To set double borders on the top and bottom, use one of the following rules:

```
p        {border-style: double none;}
p.one    {border-style: double none double none;}
p.two    {border-top-style: double; border-bottom-style: double;
          border-left-style: none; border-right-style: none;}
```

border-width

Numerous properties are used to set the width of borders. Four properties set the width for specific borders: **border-top-width**, **border-right-width**, **border-bottom-width**, and **border-left-width**. Similar to the **border-style** property, the **border-width** property sets all four borders at once and takes from one to four values. Multiple values are applied to borders in a clockwise order: top, right, bottom, left. If only two or three values are used, the missing values are determined from the opposite sides, just as with margins and border styles. Border width can be specified by using the keywords **thin**, **medium**, and **thick** to indicate the given relative sizes for the border, or by using an absolute length measurement such as 10 pixels. The following examples illustrate how border widths can be set:

```
p                {border-style: solid; border-width: 10px;}
p.double         {border-style: double; border-width: thick;}
p.thickandthin   {border-style: solid; border-width: thick thin;}
.fun             {border-style: double none; border-width: thick;}
```

border-color

Borders can be assigned a color by using the **border-color** property. Border colors are specified using standard CSS color values. The **border-color** property sets all four borders and takes from one to four values. Once again, multiple values are applied to borders in a clockwise order: top, right, bottom, left. If only two or three values are used, the missing values are determined from the opposite sides. As with border widths and styles, you can set a color value for each border side individually using **border-top-color**, **border-right-color**, **border-bottom-color**, and **border-left-color**. The following examples illustrate the basic ways to set a border's colors:

```
p         {border-style: solid; border-color: green;}
p.all     {border-style: solid; border-top-color: green;
           border-right-color: #FF0000;
           border-bottom-color: yellow;
           border-left-color: blue;}
```

Border Shorthand

Several border properties allow any combination of width, color, and style information to be set in a single property. The **border-top**, **border-right**, **border-bottom**, and **border-left** properties support this for their respective borders. For example, to set the top border or paragraph elements to be red, double-line style, and 20 pixels thick, use the following:

```
p  {border-top: double 20px red;}
```

The order of the property values to set the style, width, and color may seem arbitrary, but according to the specification, designers probably should set the style, then the width, followed by the color. Multiple properties can be combined in one rule to set the borders differently, as shown in the following example:

```
#RainbowBox {background-color: yellow;
             border-top: solid 20px red;
             border-right: double 10px blue;
             border-bottom: solid 20px green;
             border-left: dashed 10px orange;}
```

Aside from a shorthand notation for each individual border side, you can use a shorthand notation for all sides by using the **border** property. For example, to set all borders of a paragraph to be red, double-line style, and 20 pixels thick, use the following:

```
p   {border: double 20px red;}
```

Note that it is impossible to set the individual border sides with this shorthand notation. The actual properties to set the various borders must be used, such as **border-top** or, even more specifically, **border-top-style**.

The following brief example shows all the border properties used so far. Notice that both compact and explicit notations are used in the example.

```
<!DOCTYPE html PUBLIC "-//W3C//DTD XHTML 1.0 Transitional//EN"
"http://www.w3.org/TR/xhtml1/DTD/xhtml1-transitional.dtd">
<html xmlns="http://www.w3.org/1999/xhtml" lang="en">
<head>
<title>CSS1 Border Example</title>
<meta http-equiv="content-type" content="text/html; charset=ISO-8859-1" />
<style type="text/css">
<!--
#outer {background-color: orange;
        border-style: solid;
        border-width: 5px;
        padding: 10px 10px;}

#one   {background-color: yellow;
```

PART III

```
          border-style: double;
          border-width: medium;}

#two     {background-color: yellow;
          border-style: double solid;
          border-color: red green purple blue;
          border-width: thin medium thick .25cm;}
-->
</style>
</head>
<body>
<div id="outer">
<p id="one">This is a paragraph of text that has a
red double border around it. Notice how the text
creeps up on the edges. Padding values will help you
avoid this problem.</p>

<p id="two">This is another paragraph that has its
borders set in a very bizarre way!</p>

Notice that the paragraph blocks can be within a large
boxed block structure.
</div>
</body>
</html>
```

The rendering of the border property example under Internet Explorer is shown in Figure 10-10.

Padding Properties

The space between an element's border and its content can be specified by using the padding properties. An element's four padding regions can be set by using the **padding-top**, **padding-right**, **padding-bottom**, and **padding-left** properties. As with borders and margins, you can use a shorthand notation property, called **padding**, to set the padding for all sides at once. This example illustrates some basic uses of padding properties:

```
div {padding-top: 1cm;}
p   {border-style: solid; padding-left: 20mm; padding-right: 50mm;}
```

The shorthand notation property **padding** allows a single property assignment to specify all four padding regions. It can take from one to four values. A single value is applied to all four padding areas. Multiple values are applied to padding regions in the usual clockwise order: top, right, bottom, left. If only two or three values are used, the missing values are determined from the opposite sides. So,

```
div   {border-style: solid; padding: 1cm;}
```

sets a region with a solid border, but with contents padded 1 cm from the border on all sides. And

```
p   {padding: 2mm 4mm;}
```

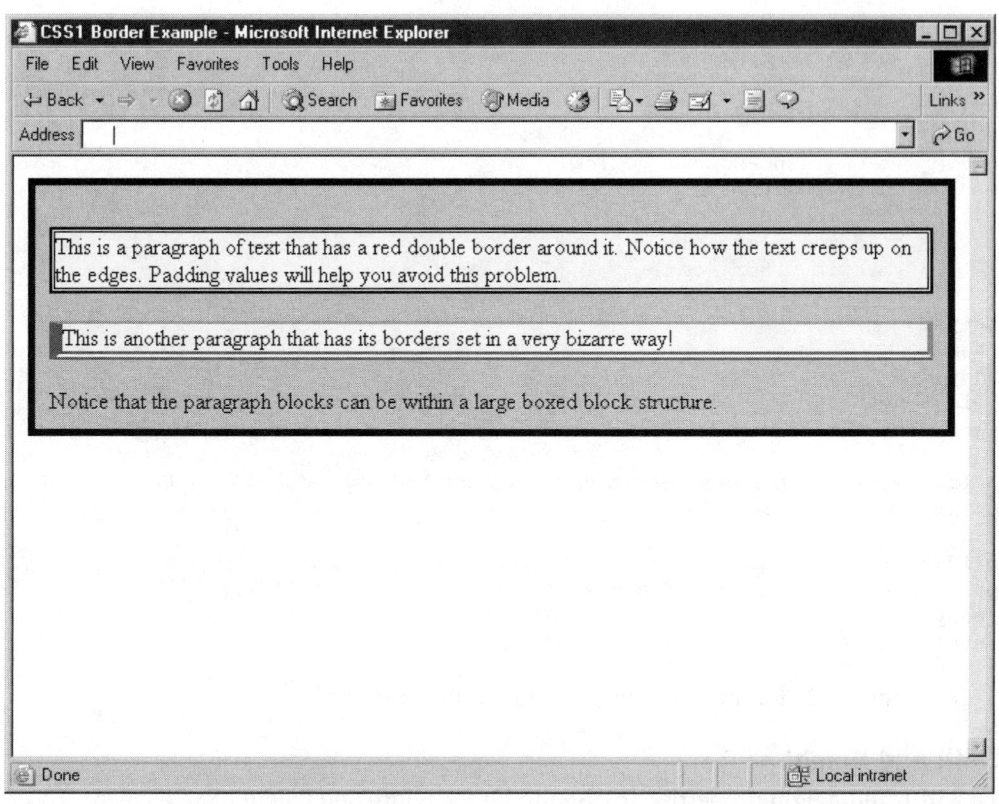

FIGURE 10-10 CSS border properties rendering

sets padding on the top and bottom to 2 mm and the right and left to 4 mm for all paragraphs. The following is an example showing padding and borders to help you better understand padding values:

```
<!DOCTYPE html PUBLIC "-//W3C//DTD XHTML 1.0 Transitional//EN"
"http://www.w3.org/TR/xhtml1/DTD/xhtml1-transitional.dtd">
<html xmlns="http://www.w3.org/1999/xhtml" lang="en">
<head>
<title>CSS1 Padding Example</title>
<meta http-equiv="content-type" content="text/html; charset=ISO-8859-1" />
<styletype="text/CSS">
<!--
#one     {background-color: yellow;
          border-style: double;
          border-width: medium;
          padding-left: 1cm;
          padding-right: .5cm;}

#two     {background-color: yellow;
```

```
         border-style: double;
         border-width: medium;
         padding-top: 1cm;
         padding-bottom: 1cm;}

#three  {background-color: yellow;
         border-style: double;
         border-width: medium;
         padding: 1cm 1cm;
         margin: .5cm 4cm;}
-->
</style>
</head>
<body>
<p id="one">This paragraph of text has padding on the left and
right, but not on the top and bottom.</p>

<p id="two">This paragraph has padding, but this time only on the
top and bottom.</p>

<p id="three">Be careful when using margins. They don't necessarily
apply to the text within the box, but to the box itself.</p>
</body>
</html>
```

See Figure 10-11 for the rendering of the padding example.

Width and Height

The **width** and **height** properties are used to set the width and height of an element. The values for these properties can be either an absolute unit, usually pixels (for example, 300px), or a relative unit, often a percentage value (for example, 50%). Relative to what, you may wonder. Relative units are related to the size of the containing element. For example, for tags directly in the **body** element, the width would be directly related to the browser window width. In the case of other elements, their width would be used as the 100% measurement, which may be much less than the full browser width. The following example demonstrates the difference in the sizing of a paragraph with and without height and width set. A rendering is shown in Figure 10-12.

```
<!DOCTYPE html PUBLIC "-//W3C//DTD XHTML 1.0 Transitional//EN"
"http://www.w3.org/TR/xhtml1/DTD/xhtml1-transitional.dtd">
<html xmlns="http://www.w3.org/1999/xhtml" lang="en">
<head>
<title>CSS Padding Example</title>
<meta http-equiv="content-type" content="text/html; charset=ISO-8859-1" />
<style type="text/css">
<!--
p {border: solid 5px;
   padding: 10px;
   background-color: yellow;
   color: black;}
```

```
#p1  {width: 200px; height: 300px;}
-->
</style>
</head>
<body>
<p id="p1">This is a paragraph with height and width.</p>
<p>Just a regular paragraph without height and width.</p>
</body>
</html>
```

Under strict CSS1, the most legitimate use of the **height** and **width** properties is setting the dimensions of included objects such as images. We will see even more use of them when positioning content regions, which is discussed in the next chapter. In either case, when sizing regions you must carefully consider one issue —what happens when the size of an object is smaller than the contained content? The **overflow** property from CSS2 discussed in the next chapter should really help then.

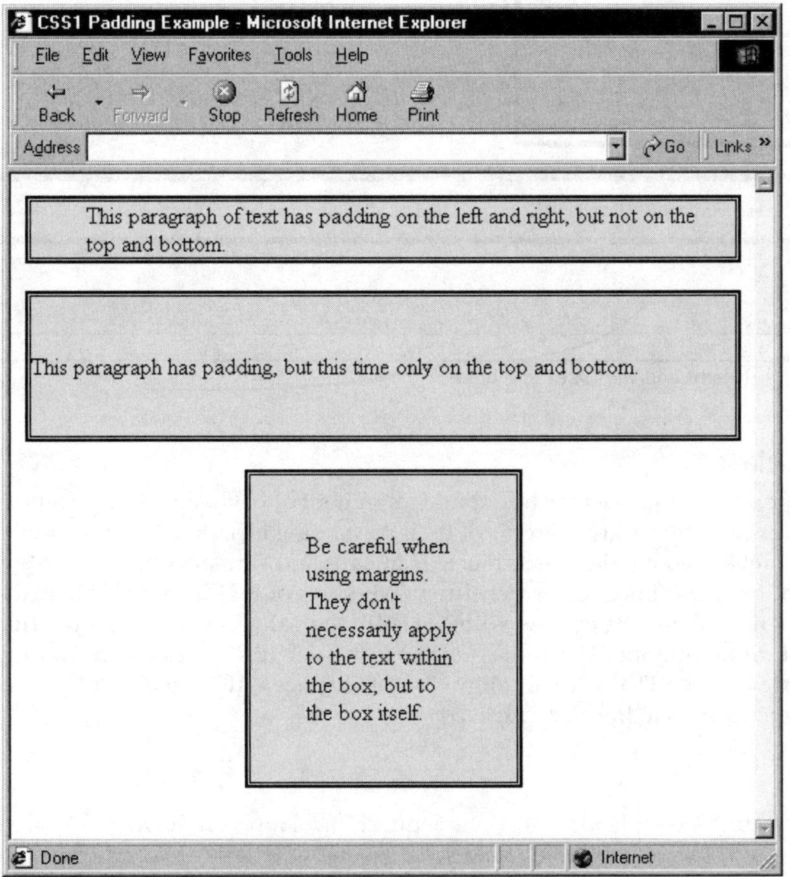

FIGURE 10-11 Rendering of padding example

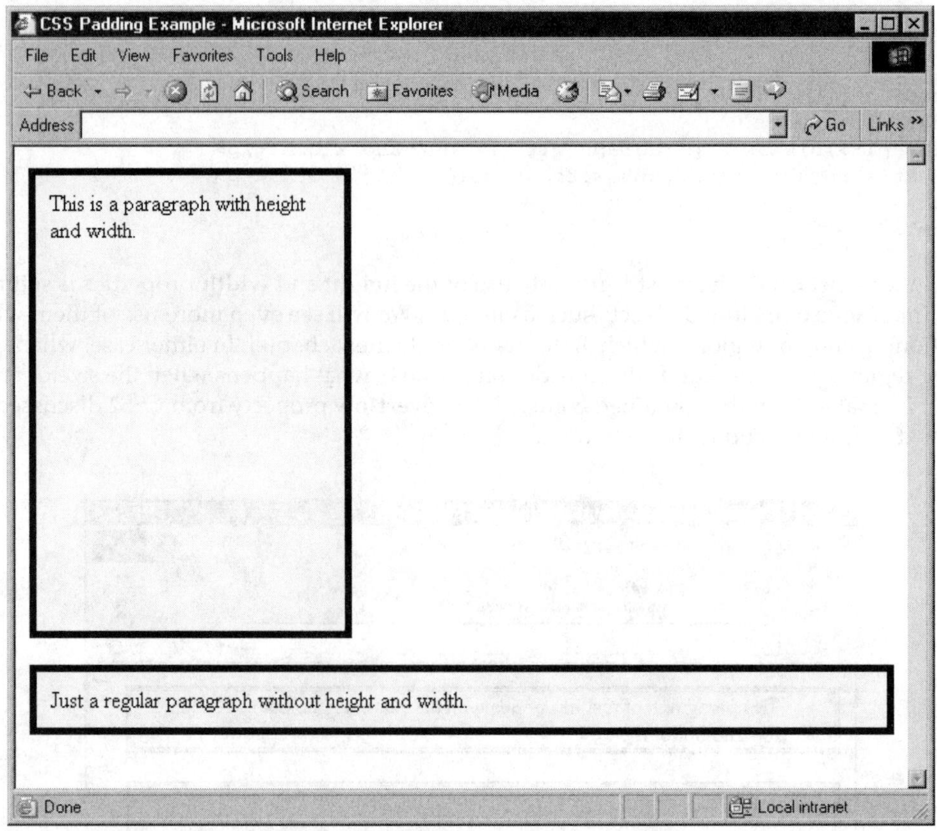

FIGURE 10-12 Height and width set and unset

float and clear

The **float** property influences the horizontal alignment of elements. It causes them to "float" toward either the left or right margins of their containing element. This is especially useful for placing embedded media objects (such as images and similar support) into a Web page. Similar floating capabilities under transitional versions of HTML or XHTML can be found with the **align** attribute settings. As with XHTML, the values available for the **float** property include **left**, **right**, or **none**. The value of **none** is the default. To imitate the markup **<img id="logo" src="logo.gif" alt="logo" align="right" hspace="10" vspace="10" />**, apply a style sheet rule such as this to the element:

```
#logo {float: right;}
```

The preceding example may raise a few questions. How can the **hspace** and **vspace** attributes from HTML be imitated using style sheets? You have a great deal of control over the border, margin, padding, height, and width of any object, so you shouldn't have difficulty achieving the layout that you want by setting padding to 10px all around the image. One thing that may not be obvious is how to clear the content that may flow around an object.

The use of floating elements creates the need to position vertically those elements that immediately follow them in an HTML document. Should the content flow continue at the floating element's side or after its bottom? If floating elements are defined on the right and left margins of the page, should content flow continue between them, after the bottom of the left element, the right element, or whichever is larger? The **clear** property allows this to be specified. A value of **left** for the property clears floating objects to the left, a value of **right** clears floating objects to the right, and the **both** value clears whichever is larger. The default value is **none**. Notice that this is extremely similar to the use of the **clear** attribute with the **
** tag in transitional XHTML. The following code example demonstrates the use of the **clear** and **float** properties in a rather unusual manner. Instead of floating an image, we'll float a paragraph of text to one side of the screen and text around it.

```
<!DOCTYPE html PUBLIC "-//W3C//DTD XHTML 1.0 Transitional//EN"
"http://www.w3.org/TR/xhtml1/DTD/xhtml1-transitional.dtd">
<html xmlns="http://www.w3.org/1999/xhtml" lang="en">
<head>
<title>Float and Clear Control under CSS</title>
<meta http-equiv="content-type" content="text/html; charset=ISO-8859-1" />
<style type="text/css">
<!--
 p.aligned-right {border-style: solid;
                  border-width: 1px;
                  height: 100px;
                  width: 100px;
                  background-color: yellow;
                  float: right;}
 .clearright {clear:right;}
-->
</style>
</head>
<body>
<div>This is some dummy text.

<p class="aligned-right">
A floating region
</p>

Here is some more text. It should keep going next to the
paragraph for a while. Here is some more text. It should
keep going next to the paragraph for a while.
<br class="clearright" />
This text should appear after the floating section.
</div>
</body>
</html>
```

PART III

The rendering of the image alignment and text flow should look something like this:

This is some dummy text. Here is some more text. It should keep going next to the paragraph for a while. Here is some more text. It should keep going next to the paragraph for a while.

A floating region

This text should appear after the floating section.

The previous section has hinted at the great deal of control that CSS affords a designer. Perfect pixel-level positioning of objects is just a moment away, but before getting to what appears to be a designer's nirvana, let's see how we can change the very core meaning of an XHTML element using CSS.

Display Properties

Cascading style sheets contain several classification properties that determine the display classification of an element. Is it a block-level element or an inline element? The CSS1 model recognizes three types of displayed elements: block elements, inline elements, and lists. As you'll see, the CSS2 specification adds even more. The **display** property allows an element's display type to be changed to one of four values: **block**, **inline**, **list-item**, and **none**. A value of **none** causes an element to not display or use canvas space. This differs from the property setting **visibility**, to be discussed in the next section, which also prevents an element from displaying, but does typically reserve canvas space. To turn off a paragraph, try a rule such as the following:

```
p.remove    {display: none;}
```

Aside from turning off elements, the browser should be able to turn a block element (such as a paragraph) into an inline element, thus keeping it from adding a new line. For example, the following would change the form of all paragraphs in the document; overriding the known action if the element is not suggested:

```
p   {display: inline;}
```

Browsers might be able to turn an inline element into a block thus causing a return, like so:

```
em   {display: block;}
```

You also can coerce an element to act somewhat like a list by casting it with the display property, as shown here:

```
b   { display: list-item;}
```

A complete example is shown here:

```
<!DOCTYPE html PUBLIC "-//W3C//DTD XHTML 1.0 Transitional//EN"
"http://www.w3.org/TR/xhtml1/DTD/xhtml1-transitional.dtd">
<html xmlns="http://www.w3.org/1999/xhtml" lang="en">
<head>
<title>Basic Display Example</title>
<meta http-equiv="content-type" content="text/html; charset=ISO-8859-1" />
<style type="text/css">
<!--
  p   {border-style: solid; border-width: 1px;
       margin: 2px;
       background-color: yellow;
       display: inline;}

  #p2 {display: none;}
  em  {display: block;}

-->
</style>
</head>
<body>
<p>Paragraph 1</p>
<p id="p2">Paragraph 2</p>
<p>Paragraph 3</p>

Here is an <em>em tag.</em> Another <em>em tag.</em>
</body>
</html>
```

Notice in the rendering of the example presented here that the tags act not as you would expect them to in XHTML, but are overridden by the display property.

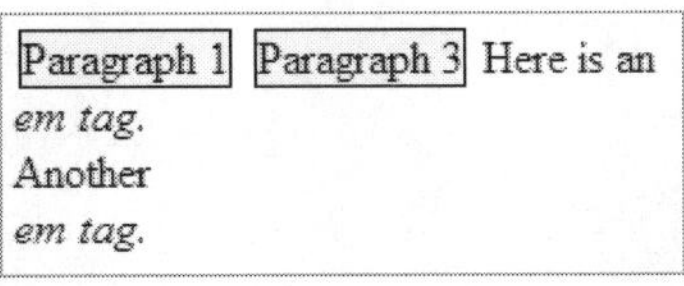

In only a very few cases, other than setting display to **none**, does overriding the meaning of an XHTML element make sense. However, when inventing your own elements using XML, as discussed in Chapter 18, the **display** property becomes invaluable.

Summary

Cascading style sheets provide better control over the look and feel of Web pages. Style sheets aren't just useful for making attractive pages. By dividing structure and style, they make documents simpler and easier to manipulate. The CSS1 specification provides many valuable layout properties for manipulating text, colors, lists, margins, borders, backgrounds, and a few other features. However, the technology should not be considered a replacement for markup. First, CSS relies greatly on correct HTML/XHTML markup as well as proper naming of tags. Second, CSS1 just doesn't quite provide everything needed. Tables are still required to create page grids and layout the basic page structure. The introduction of CSS-based positioning and related properties should solve that problem and is introduced in the next chapter.

CHAPTER 11

CSS2

The CSS1 specification provides a great deal of support for text, colors, backgrounds, borders, and other basic visual elements. However, using only CSS1, Web designers would still have to rely on table-oriented markup to lay out a page grid. Besides being messy, this doesn't help to separate page structure from page presentation. With CSS-based positioning—initially introduced as CSS-P and then rolled into CSS2—we now have all the tools we need to eliminate markup as our primary page design technology. Despite the essential nature of CSS2's facilities, CSS2 is presented as a distinct chapter because support for it is inconsistent even in modern browsers.

The Rise of CSS2

The W3C finalized the CSS2 specification on May 12, 1998. The complete specification can be viewed online at http://www.w3.org/TR/REC-CSS2/. While more and more browsers are supporting features of CSS2, there are many holes in their implementations with one major exception: positioning. Fortunately, this is one of the most useful properties, so designers often overlook all the other holes in their browser's implementation of the specification. As you read through this chapter, make sure to note carefully the features that are probably not supported and try the examples in your browser before assuming they work for every user. Let's begin the discussion of CSS2 with selectors.

CSS2 Selectors

CSS2 provides a much richer set of selectors than CSS1. Most of these selectors can be used to reduce the reliance on **id** and **class** attributes instead of relying on the context of an element's use in a document. The first selector is the wildcard selector designated by the asterisk (*). This selector matches any element, so a rule such as

```
* {color: red;}
```

would set the contents of any element red. This wildcard selector is more useful when creating a contextual rule. For example, consider the following rule, which says that anytime a **<span>** tag is found inside of any element within a **<div>**, its background should be made yellow:

```
div * span  {background-color: yellow;}
```

Using the child selector specified by the greater than symbol (>), it is possible in CSS2 to define a rule that matches only elements that are directly enclosed within another element. Consider the following rule:

```
body > p  {background-color: yellow;}
```

This rule indicates that only **<p>** tags directly within the **<body>** have a yellow background. The following example shows the effect of a child selector rule:

```
<!DOCTYPE html PUBLIC "-//W3C//DTD XHTML 1.0 Transitional//EN"
"http://www.w3.org/TR/xhtml1/DTD/xhtml1-transitional.dtd">
<html xmlns="http://www.w3.org/1999/xhtml" lang="en">
<head>
<title>CSS2 Child Selector</title>
<meta http-equiv="content-type" content="text/html; charset=ISO-8859-1" />
<style type="text/css">
<!--
body > p  {background-color: yellow;}
-->
</style>
</head>
<body>
<div><p>This paragraph is not yellow.</p></div>
<p>While this one is yellow. </p>
</body>
</html>
```

A similar rule called the *adjacent-sibling selector* is specified using the plus sign (+) and is used to select elements that would be siblings of each other. For example, consider the following rule:

```
h1 + p {color: red;}
```

This states that all paragraph elements that are directly after an **<h1>** are red, as demonstrated by this markup:

```
<h1>Heading Level 1</h1>
<p>I am red!</p>
<p>I am not!</p>
```

A very interesting new CSS2 selector allows designers to match attributes. For example, a rule such as

```
a[href] {background-color: yellow;}
```

would match all **<a>** tags that simply have the **href** attribute, whereas a rule such as

```
a[href="http://www.htmlref.com"] {font-weight: bold;}
```

would match only those **<a>** tags that have an **href** value set to the book's support site URL. Under CSS2, it also should be possible to match multiple attribute values or even pieces of the attribute values.

For example, to match a value in a space-separated list, you might use a rule like this:

```
p[title~="Test match"] {font-style:italic;}
```

To match an attribute value separated by dashes, which is common in language values (for example, en-uk, en-us, and so on), use a rule like this:

```
p [lang|="en"] {color:red;} /* English text in red */
```

You can even match multiple attribute aspects at once. Consider the following:

```
p[title="Test Selector"][lang|="en"] {border-style: dashed;
                                      border-width: 1px;}
```

A special form of attribute selectors focuses on the **lang** attribute, allowing designers to set rules to quickly pick out one language or another in a document. The example that follows demonstrates setting French text in blue and English text in red:

```
<!DOCTYPE html PUBLIC "-//W3C//DTD XHTML 1.0 Transitional//EN"
"http://www.w3.org/TR/xhtml1/DTD/xhtml1-transitional.dtd">
<html xmlns="http://www.w3.org/1999/xhtml" lang="en">
<head>
<title>Simple Language Selection</title>
<meta http-equiv="content-type" content="text/html; charset=ISO-8859-1" />
<style type="text/css">
<!--
  *:lang(fr) {color: blue;}
  *:lang(en) {color: red;}
-->
</style>
</head>
<body>

<p lang="en">Howdy partner, this is some wild west English in red.</p>
<p lang="fr">C'est francais et bleu!</p>
<p lang="en-uk">Jolly good old chap, this is English too so it's red.</p>
<p>Document default is English so I am red as well.</p>
</body>
</html>
```

While attribute selectors seem very interesting, they are not implemented in Internet Explorer 6 and they still have some bugs even in those browsers that support them.

CSS2 Pseudoclasses

CSS2 also supports a variety of new pseudo-elements, including **:first-child**, **:focus**, **:hover**, and **:lang**. The **:first-child** selector is used to find only the first child of a parent element. This example illustrates how **first-child** is interpreted; notice how the **<p>** tag varies in color depending on its position in the document tree:

```
<!DOCTYPE html PUBLIC "-//W3C//DTD XHTML 1.0 Transitional//EN"
"http://www.w3.org/TR/xhtml1/DTD/xhtml1-transitional.dtd">
```

```
<html xmlns="http://www.w3.org/1999/xhtml" lang="en">
<head>
<title>First Child Pseudo-Selector</title>
<meta http-equiv="content-type" content="text/html; charset=ISO-8859-1" />
<style type="text/css">
<!--
     p:first-child { color: red;}
-->
</style>
</head>
<body>
<p>I should be red because I am the first child in the body.</p>
<p>I should not be red because I am the second child in the body.</p>
<div>
   <p>I should be red because I am the first child of div.</p>
   <p>Second child of div, thus not red.</p>
</div>
</body>
</html>
```

As discussed in the previous chapter, the **:focus** pseudoclass is used to apply a rule to an element only when that element has focus. Typically, form fields can accept keyboard input and thus can gain focus. So to set any text input field to have a yellow background color when it gains focus, you would use a rule such as the following:

```
input:focus {background-color: yellow;}
```

The **:hover** pseudoclass, presented in the last chapter, is already well-supported and is used primarily to change the appearance of links when the user's pointer is hovering over them. Consider the following:

```
a {text-decoration: none;}
a:hover {text-decoration: underline;}
```

However, it is possible to apply this pseudoclass to just about any element, so a rule such as

```
p:hover {background-color: yellow;}
```

is perfectly valid, although it produces a potentially annoying effect. The following is a complete example showing how these might be applied:

```
<!DOCTYPE html PUBLIC "-//W3C//DTD XHTML 1.0 Transitional//EN"
"http://www.w3.org/TR/xhtml1/DTD/xhtml1-transitional.dtd">
<html xmlns="http://www.w3.org/1999/xhtml" lang="en">
<head>
<title>Hover and Focus Pseudo-Class Example</title>
<meta http-equiv="content-type" content="text/html; charset=ISO-8859-1" />
<style type="text/css" media="all">
<!--

p:hover    {border-style: dashed; background-color: yellow;}
```

```
input:hover      {background-color: yellow; }
input:focus      {background-color: #FFA500;}
-->
</style>
</head>
<body>
<p>Roll over me.</p>
<p>Now roll over me.</p>
<div>I won't do anything.<br /></div>

<form action="#">
   <input type="text" size="40" value="Hover and then click into this field" />
</form>
</body>
</html>
```

NOTE *At the time of this writing, the preceding example only works in Mozilla or Opera-based browsers.*

CSS2 Pseudo-Elements

A few other pseudo-elements, including **:before** and **:after**, can be used to specify content placed before and after an element, respectively. Most often, they are combined with the CSS2 property **content,** which is used to insert content. You can use these two pseudo-selectors, for example, to create special start- and end-of-section indicators. Consider the following:

```
div:before {content: url(sectionstart.gif);}
div:after  {content: url(sectionend.gif);}
```

The **content** property can be used to specify objects like images as indicated by the preceding example, but it also can specify regular text content; for example,

```
p.warn:before {content: "Warning!";}
```

will print the word "Warning!" before every paragraph in class **warn**. This pseudo-element is commonly used to include quotation marks so there are built-in values of **open-quote**, **close-quote**, **no-open-quote**, and **no-close-quote**, which can be used to control the insertion of quotation marks in a document, as shown by this example:

```
blockquote:before {content: open-quote;}
blockquote:after {content: close-quote;}
```

The following example demonstrates a variety of possible uses of these pseudo-elements.

```
<!DOCTYPE html PUBLIC "-//W3C//DTD XHTML 1.0 Transitional//EN"
"http://www.w3.org/TR/xhtml1/DTD/xhtml1-transitional.dtd">
<html xmlns="http://www.w3.org/1999/xhtml" lang="en">
<head>
<title>Before and After Pseudo Selectors</title>
<meta http-equiv="content-type" content="text/html; charset=ISO-8859-1" />
<style type="text/css">
```

PART III

```
<!--
   a {text-decoration: none;}
   a:hover {color: red; }
   .external:after {content: url('newwindow.gif'); margin-left: .2em;}
   .warning:before {content: "Warning!";
                    background-color: yellow;
                    border-style: dashed; border-width: 1px;
                    margin-right: 1em;}
   .warning:after {content: "**";
                   background-color: yellow;
                   border-style: dashed; border-width: 1px;
                   margin-left: 1em;}
   blockquote:before {content: open-quote;}
   blockquote:after {content: close-quote;}
-->
</style>
</head>
<body>
<a href="#">local link</a><br />
<a href="http://www.htmlref.com" class="external">external link</a>

<br /><br />

<div class="warning">This is dangerous XHTML example text.
Be careful, you may suffer boredom typing in a bunch of fake
text just to make this example work. Don't worry, almost done.
Finally!</div>

<blockquote>
I am a blockquote.  To be or not to be a blockquote, that is the overused
quotation style question.
</blockquote>
</body>
</html>
```

A rendering in Mozilla shows how these rules would work, as Internet Explorer 6 is unable to render the example.

CSS Properties

CSS2 introduces numerous properties—the most important of these are related to positioning. Let's begin the section with a discussion of the properties well-supported by browsers. As the section progresses, we'll move on to the less commonly supported properties, so be careful.

Positioning and Sizing of Regions

Positioning originally was developed as a separate specification called CSS-P, which has now been incorporated into the CSS2 specification. Even before finalization of CSS2, the major browsers supported style sheet–based positioning. When combined with elements such as **<div>**, the functionality of Netscape's proprietary **layer** element can be achieved with style sheets.

The first and most important property to discuss is the **position** property, which has the following values:

- **static** Places elements according to the natural order in which they occur in a document (the default).
- **absolute** Places elements at an absolute position away from an enclosing element. Typically, absolute positioning uses the upper-left corner of the browser as the origin, but if positioned objects are within positioned regions themselves, their origin is the top-left most coordinate of their container.
- **relative** Makes the element's position relative to its natural position in document flow. This can be confusing, so most designers tend to use absolute values.
- **fixed** Acts like **absolute**, but does not allow the object to move offscreen. This value allows the designer to peg an object's position similar to using a frame.
- **inherit** Sets the positioning relative to the enclosing parent.

Generally, after you specify how to position the region (**absolute**, **relative, or fixed**), the actual location of positioned elements should be specified by using their top-left corner. The position usually is set with the **left** and **top** style properties. The coordinate system for positioned elements uses the upper-left corner of the enclosing object as the origin point, 0, 0. Often, if the tag is directly enclosed in the **<body>**, the origin will be the upper-left-hand portion of the screen, but it might not necessarily be if you consider positioned elements that contain other positioned elements. Values for the *x* coordinate increase to the right; *y* values increase going down from a positioned origin. A value such as **10,100** would be 10 units to the right and 100 units down from the origin. Values can be specified as a length in a valid CSS measurement (such as pixels) or as a percentage of the containing object's (parent's) dimension. You may find that elements contain other elements, so 0,0 isn't always the upper-left corner of the browser. Note that it also is possible to set the **bottom** and **right** values for an object, but that not all positioning-aware browsers, notably Netscape 4.*x*, support these properties; thus, it is best to stick to **top** and **left** for describing an object's location. After you position the region, you may want to set its size. By default, the **height** and **width** of the positioned region are set to fit the enclosed content, but the **height** and **width** properties, as discussed early in the chapter, can be used to specify the region's size.

The following example uses an inline style to set a **<div>** tag to be 120 pixels from the left and 50 pixels down from the top-left corner of the browser, assuming it is not enclosed in any other positioned elements:

```
<div style="position:absolute;
     left: 120px;  top: 50px;
     height: 100px; width: 150px;
```

```
     background-color: yellow;">
At last, absolute positioning!
</div>
```

Before you rush off and position elements all over the screen, be aware of the nuances of nested items. For example, look at the following markup. Notice how the position of the second area is relative to the first. If you read the coordinate values numerically, the inner area should be positioned to the left and above where it shows onscreen. Remember, the coordinates are relative to the containing box.

```
<!DOCTYPE html PUBLIC "-//W3C//DTD XHTML 1.0 Transitional//EN"
"http://www.w3.org/TR/xhtml1/DTD/xhtml1-transitional.dtd">
<html xmlns="http://www.w3.org/1999/xhtml" lang="en">
<head>
<title>Positioning Items</title>
<meta http-equiv="content-type" content="text/html; charset=ISO-8859-1" />
<style type="text/css">
<!--
#outer  {position: absolute;
         left: 100px; top: 50px;
         height: 400px; width: 150px;
         background-color: yellow;}

#inner  {position: absolute;
         left: 75px; top: 50px;
         height: 30px; width: 40px;
         background-color: #FFA500;}

#outer2  {position: absolute;
         left: 90%;
         height: 100px; width: 10%;
         background-color: green;
         color: white;}

#outer3  {position: absolute;
         bottom: 10px; right: 150px;
         height: 100px; width: 100px;
         background-color: purple;
         color: white;}
-->
</style>
</head>
<body>
<div id="outer">
This is the outer part of the nest.

<span id="inner">This is the inner part of the nest.</span>
</div>

<div id="outer2">Way to the far right at the top</div>

<div id="outer3">Using the bottom and right properties</div>
```

```
</body>
</html>
```

The rendering of this example is shown in Figure 11-1.

Setting the **fixed** value for the **position** property is similar to the previous positioning example. Consider the following markup:

```
<div style="position: fixed; top: 0px; left: 0px;
background-color: blue; color: yellow;">DemoCompany, Inc.</div>
```

In a browser that supported the **fixed** property, this header text would stay in the upper-left corner of the screen regardless of scrolling at all times. We could use this property to keep navigation pegged onscreen without employing HTML's much maligned **frame**. Unfortunately, this feature is not supported in Internet Explorer even as of the 6.0 release.

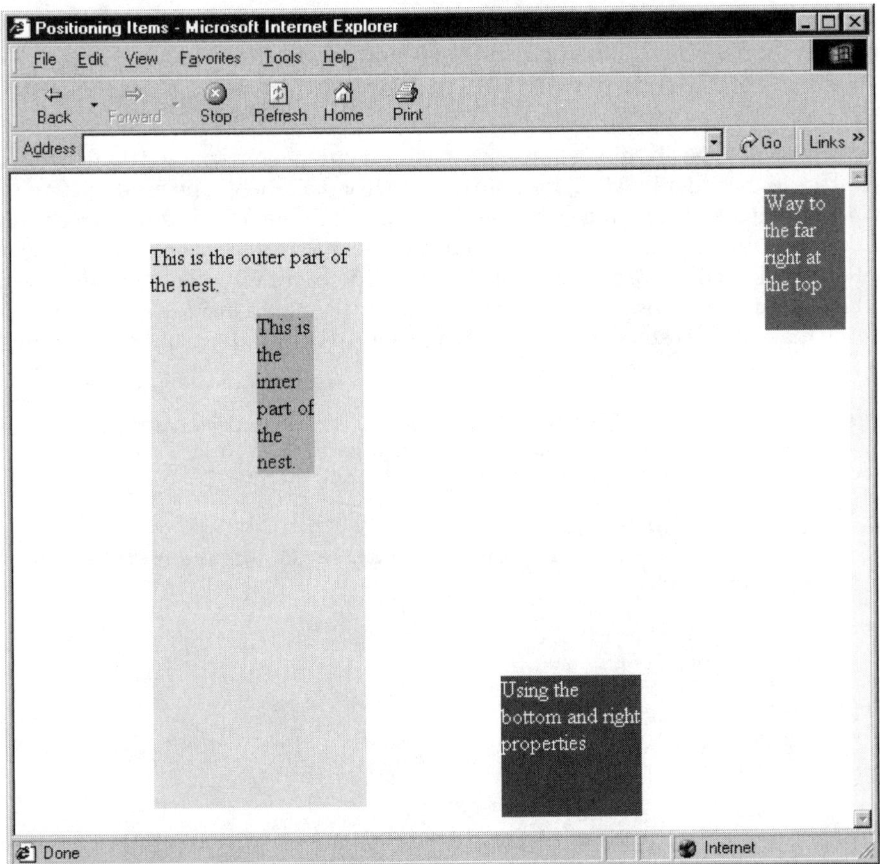

FIGURE 11-1 Rendering of positioned objects under Internet Explorer

The last value for the **position** property is **relative**. This value is used when you want to position an object relative to its current position in the document flow. This is best illustrated by example; consider the markup here:

```
<p style="background-color: #FFA500;">This is a test of <span style="position:
 relative; top: 10px; left: 20px; background-color: yellow;">relative
positioning.</span> This is only a test.</p>
```

The **<span>** tag in this example surrounds text that is dropped down 10 pixels from the top and 20 pixels from the left of the point at which the text normally would fall, as shown here:

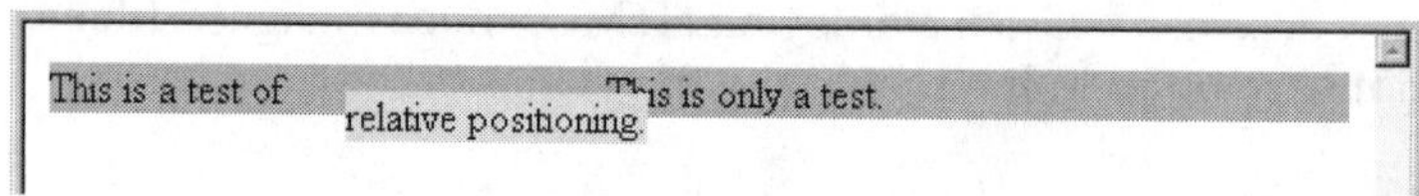

Notice that in this example text overlaps other text, showing that objects can stack on top of one another, and revealing the **z-index** property available to us.

z-index

Absolute and relative positioning allow elements' content to overlap. By default, overlapping elements stack in the order in which they are defined in a document. The most recent elements go on top. This default order can be redefined by using an element's **z-index** property. Absolute- or relative-positioned elements define a **z-index** context for the elements that they contain. The containing element has an index of **0**; the index increases with higher numbers stacked on top of lower numbers. The following example forces all images inside a container to overlap. Notice how the elements stack in the specified order set by **z-index** rather than in the order defined by the markup:

```
<!DOCTYPE html PUBLIC "-//W3C//DTD XHTML 1.0 Transitional//EN"
"http://www.w3.org/TR/xhtml1/DTD/xhtml1-transitional.dtd">
<html xmlns="http://www.w3.org/1999/xhtml" lang="en">
<head>
<title>Z-index Example</title>
<meta http-equiv="content-type" content="text/html; charset=ISO-8859-1" />
<style type="text/css">
<!--
div.S1     {position: absolute;
            top: 20px; left: 20px;
            height: 50px; width: 50px;
            color: white;
            background-color: blue;
            z-index: 2;}

div.S2     {position: absolute;
            top: 30px; left: 30px;
            height: 25px; width: 100px;
            background-color: #FFA500;
            z-index: 1;}
```

```
div.S3  {position: absolute;
         top: 40px; left: 40px;
         height: 25px; width: 25px;
         background-color: yellow;
         z-index: 3;}
-->
</style>
</head>
<body>
<div class="S1">This is section one.</div>

<div class="S2">This is section two.</div>

<div class="S3">This is section three.</div>
</body>
</html>
```

The rendering of this example is shown in Figure 11-2.

TIP *It is a good idea not to number z-index values contiguously. Consider using gaps of 5 between layered regions, which allows you to easily insert objects in between later.*

visibility Property

The **visibility** property determines whether an element is visible. The values for the property are **hidden**, **visible**, or **inherit**. The **inherit** value means that a property inherits its visibility state from the element that contains it. If an element is **hidden**, it still occupies the full

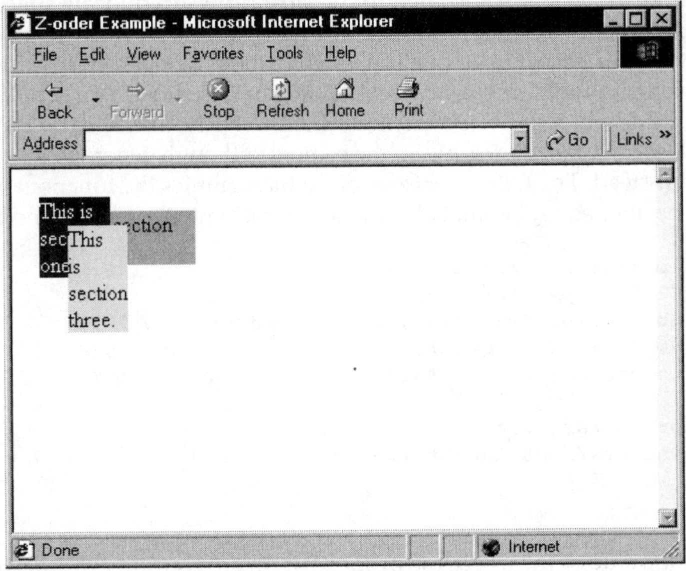

FIGURE 11-2 Rendering of z-index example

canvas space, but is rendered as transparent. This simple example shows how the item is made invisible, but is not removed:

```
<p>This is a <em style="visibility: hidden;">test</em> of the
visibility property.</p>
```

The rendering here shows how the word "test" still takes up space, but isn't visible.

You can of course hide any region, positioned or not. Although the contents might take up canvas space, if you place the object under other objects using the **z-index**, the viewer will be none the wiser. When combined with scripting, it is possible to hide and reveal regions easily for an interesting dynamic effect. This effect and others are possible using the powerful combination of HTML, CSS, and JavaScript, often dubbed Dynamic HTML, as discussed in Chapter 14.

Content Overflow Properties

An important issue to consider with positioned objects is what to do when the element's content is greater than the space allocated for it. Most browsers allocate space for content, unless size is set explicitly or a clipping region is set. The **overflow** property determines how an element should handle the situation when content doesn't fit. A value of **hidden** for the property clips content to the size defined for the container. The **scroll** value allows content to scroll using a browser-dependent mechanism such as scrollbars. The default value is **none**, which does nothing and might clip the content, although generally the browser makes the region larger instead. The following example, which mimics the functionality of a floating frame, creates a positioned region that allows scrolling if content goes beyond its defined size:

```
<div style="  position:absolute;
              left:20px; top:20px;
              border-style: solid; border-width: 1px;
              width:100px; height:100px;
              overflow: scroll;">

This<br />is<br />a<br />case<br />of<br />
lines<br />going<br />outside<br />the<br />box,
which may be clipped.
</div>
```

Try setting the value of the **overflow** property in the preceding example to **hidden** and notice that the content is truncated. The following shows the likely rendering of both cases.

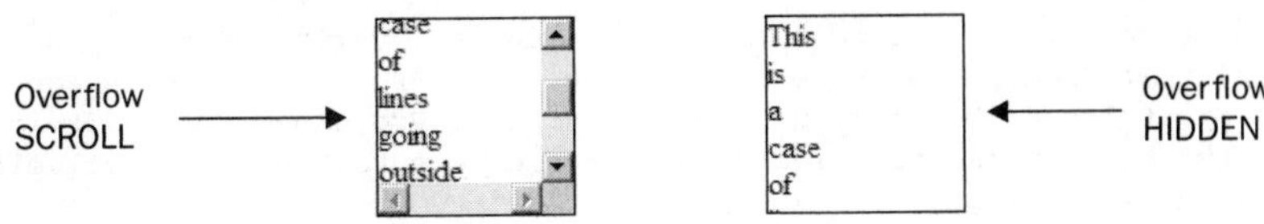

Max and Min Height and Width

As boxes are expanded and contracted, their sizes often become too large or too small to be useful for the content they are containing. CSS2 adds properties to set boundaries on the size of boxes. These properties are particularly useful when a region's **height** and **width** are set to a relative unit such as % where dimensions may change radically with content and window sizing.

The **max-width** and **max-height** properties can be set to indicate how large a region can grow when the browser is resized. The **min-width** and **min-height** are used to limit how far down a region can shrink. The **min-width** and **max-width** values tend to be the most useful in Web design. Unfortunately, browsers are somewhat inconsistent in their support for these very useful properties. The following example should give you a test of what to expect if your browser does support them:

```
<!DOCTYPE html PUBLIC "-//W3C//DTD XHTML 1.0 Transitional//EN"
"http://www.w3.org/TR/xhtml1/DTD/xhtml1-transitional.dtd">
<html xmlns="http://www.w3.org/1999/xhtml" lang="en">
<head>
<title>Max-Min Height and Width</title>
<meta http-equiv="content-type" content="text/html; charset=ISO-8859-1" />
<style type="text/css">
<!--
 #div1 {width: 50%;
        max-width: 300px;
        min-width: 150px;
        height: 50%;
        max-height: 500px;
        min-height: 100px;
        background-color: yellow;
        border-style: solid;
        border-width: 1px;
        overflow: hidden;}

 h1    {text-align: center;}
-->
</style>
</head>
<body>
<div id="div1">

<h1>Div 1</h1>

<p>Lorem ipsum dolor sit amet, consectetuer adipiscing elit. Pellentesque
   placerat mauris sit amet quam. Nam semper, massa ac fringilla dignissim, erat
   erat venenatis felis, nec facilisis diam lorem eu diam. Vestibulum ultrices turpis
   at ante. Sed ultricies leo in enim. Nullam purus elit, luctus et, vulputate sit
   amet, pellentesque at, tellus. Integer in nunc eget elit commodo placerat. Etiam
```

```
justo nisl, consectetuer non, blandit varius, aliquet et, velit. Etiam at quam in
eros rhoncus blandit. Sed scelerisque scelerisque erat. Proin vitae felis eget
lectus mattis sagittis. Morbi et risus. Aenean at nisl. Proin posuere, elit id
commodo tincidunt, tortor est tristique magna, nec ornare tortor tortor ut velit.
Cras laoreet mi a lectus.</p>

</div>
</body>
</html>
```

Clipping Regions

Sometimes it may be desirable to clip content. For elements whose position type is **absolute**, a *clipping rectangle* defines the subset of the content rectangle that actually is shown. The property **clip** can be used to set the coordinates of the clipping rectangle that houses the content. The form of the property is

```
clip: rect(top right bottom left)
```

where *top*, *right*, *bottom*, and *left* are the coordinate values that set the clipping region:

```
<div style="background-color: green;
     height: 140px; width: 140px;
     position: absolute; left: 10px;">

<div style="position:absolute;
     background-color: #FFA500;
     left:20px; top:20px;
     width:140px; height:140px;
     border-style: solid; border-width: 1px;
     clip: rect(10px 90px 90px 10px);" >

With clipping

</div>

</div>
```

The clipping region is obvious when compared with the same example without the clipping rectangle, as shown here:

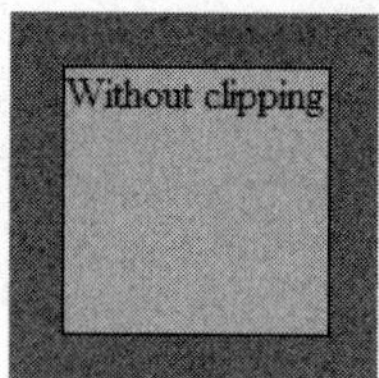

Now that you've seen the most commonly used aspect of CSS2, let's turn our attention to the other features that the specification introduces. Unfortunately, many of these features are not yet supported by Internet Explorer.

CSS2 Text and Font Improvements

CSS2 introduces a variety of font properties. For example, **font-stretch** is used to stretch or condense a font and takes values of **ultra-condensed**, **extra-condensed**, **condensed**, **semi-condensed**, **normal**, **semi-expanded**, **expanded**, **extra-expanded**, and **ultra-expanded**. The property also can take a relative value of **wider** or **narrower** to modify the appearance of text relative to a parent font. A few examples of its use are shown here:

```
.narrow          {font-stretch: narrower;}
#arialstretch    {font-family: Arial; font-stretch: ultra-expanded;}
```

CSS2 also introduces the **font-size-adjust** property. This property is used for scaled fonts to make sure that text takes up the same amount of room regardless of the availability of a particular font or not. The use of this property so far is not supported by any browsers and its exact usage is not well-defined.

The last interesting text change made in CSS2 is to support shadows on text using the **text-shadow** property. To specify a shadow for text, you must define the offset of the shadow, vertically as well as horizontally, and optionally set the blur radius and the color of the shadow. Positive horizontal offsets mean the offset is to the right, and negative values indicate the shadow falls to the left. Positive vertical offsets mean the offset is below, and negative above the text. A simple example setting the shadow for **h1** elements is shown here:

```
h1 {color: #CC0000; text-shadow: 0.2em 0.2em blue;}
```

Of course, at the time of this writing no browser yet supports this property. However, readers are warned that the shadows are fast approaching and ready to storm Web page design quicker than a **<blink>** tag. In short: when this property works, please don't abuse it.

CSS2 List Changes

A minor change made by CSS2 is the support of new values for the **list-style-type** property. Now the property supports a value of **decimal-leading-zero**, which creates numbers that are padded with zeros to be equivalent to the largest number in the list. For example, when using a value of **decimal-leading-zero** for the **list-style-type** property, the first item in a list between 10 and 99 would be 01, in a list from 100 to 999 would be 001, and so on. Other values include **lower-greek** and **upper-greek**, which count an ordered list in lowercase and uppercase Greek symbols, respectively, and **lower-latin** and **upper-latin**, which are the same as the normal lower and upper alphabetical. A variety of values to indicate foreign language counting systems also are supported under CSS2: **hebrew**, **armenian**, **georgian**, **cjk-ideographic**, **katakana**, **hiragana-iroha**, and **katakana-iroha**.

Automatic Numbering of Objects

CSS2 returns HTML elements such as lists and headings to their true logical nature with the introduction of automatic numbering. Using the **counter**, **counter-increment**, and **counter-reset** properties you can automatically number sections of an HTML document using a CSS2 rule. For example, we could number all **<h1>** tags with a counter using the **:before** pseudo-element, like so:

```
h1:before {content: "Section" counter(section); counter-increment: section;}
```

It would be possible to run multiple counters at once to create an outline numbering style and even create lists that count in steps or backward. This simple example shows the application of counters for a document numbering:

```
<!DOCTYPE html PUBLIC "-//W3C//DTD XHTML 1.0 Transitional//EN"
"http://www.w3.org/TR/xhtml1/DTD/xhtml1-transitional.dtd">
<html xmlns="http://www.w3.org/1999/xhtml" lang="en">
<head>
<title>CSS2 Counter Example</title>
<meta http-equiv="content-type" content="text/html; charset=ISO-8859-1" />
<style type="text/css">
<!--
p  {counter-increment: par-num;}
h1 {counter-reset: par-num;}
p:before {content: counter(par-num, upper-roman) ". ";}
-->
</style>
</head>
<body>

<!-- currently only works in Opera 7 -->

<h1>Heading</h1>
<p>This is a paragraph.</p>
<p>This is a paragraph.</p>
<p>This is a paragraph.</p>
<p>This is a paragraph.</p>

<h1>Heading</h1>
<p>This is a paragraph.</p>
<p>This is a paragraph.</p>
<p>This is a paragraph.</p>

</body>
</html>
```

At the time of this edition's writing, the only browser supporting this property was Opera 7. A rendering is provided to give an idea of its probable look in other browsers once implemented.

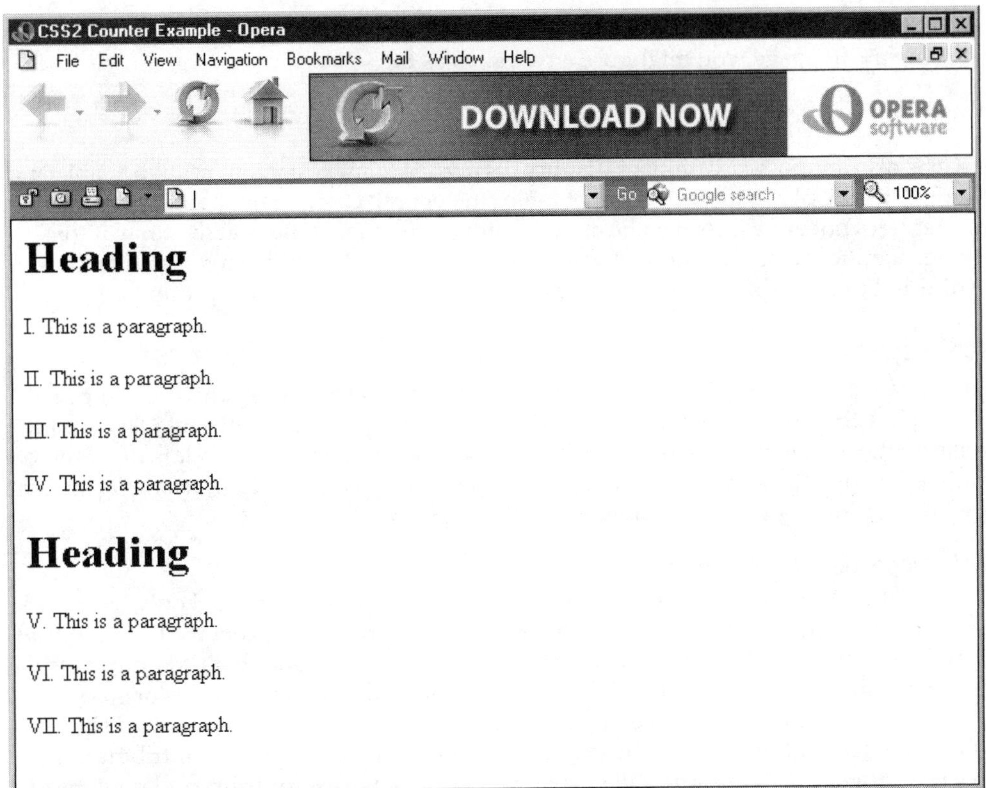

Display Property Changes

Under CSS2, the **display** property supports a variety of values. For example, a **display** property value of **compact** is used to position enclosed text in the margin of a following block element. A value of **run-in** also is supported for the **display** property. This should allow a block-level element such as a heading to be run in or combined with the next block-level element. For example, consider the markup here,

```
<h1 style="display: run-in;">Heading 1</h1>
<p>This paragraph should have the heading run right
into its first line.</p>
```

which should result in the large **<h1>** text appearing as part of the first line of the paragraph. Using **display**, it is also possible to set an item as the type marker. A marker indicates that the contents should be treated like a list marker. For example, you can use a bullet, picture, or other form of indication to bring attention to some content. You can control the position of the marker used by setting the **marker-offset** value. Note that the **marker** value for **display** is not limited to list items; it can be used to indicate a marker for anything. For example, if you wanted to indicate a particular paragraph as a new piece of text using a GIF image, you might use a rule such as the following:

```
#new:before   {display: marker; content: url(new.gif); marker-offset: 1.5em;}
```

CSS2 also supports a variety of **display** properties to make content act like a table and to control the display and formatting of tables in general. Once again, because the major browser does not appear to even be close to supporting these values at the time of this writing, significant discussion is left for a future edition of this book. Interested readers are directed to the CSS2 specification for further details on the **display** property.

Media Types

A significant goal of CSS2 is to support other output media forms beyond the computer screen. The CSS2 specification defines numerous media types, listed in Table 11-1. Today, primarily the values **all**, **screen**, and **print** are used, so until browser vendors or developers of other user agents begin to support these media types, these definitions might have no meaning outside of the specification.

Media-Dependent Style Sheets

Under the CSS2 specification, certain style sheet properties are supported only by specific media types. In other cases, more than one media type supports a property, but might call for different values, such as when font-related properties are used for both computer display and for printing, two different media that might require different font styles or sizes. CSS2 provides two main ways to define media types for style sheets. The first method simply uses the media attribute for the <**link**> tag to define the media type. This attribute enables the page designer to define one style for computer screens, one for print, and perhaps one

TABLE 11-1 Media Types Defined Under CSS2

Media Type	Definition
all	For use with all devices
aural	For use with speech synthesizers
Braille	For use with tactile Braille devices
embossed	For use with Braille printers
handheld	For use with handheld devices
print	For use with printed material and documents viewed onscreen in print preview mode
projection	For use with projected media (direct computer-to-projector presentations), or printing transparencies for projection
screen	For use with color computer screens
tty	For use with low-resolution teletypes, terminals, or other devices with limited display capabilities
tv	For use with television-type devices

for personal digital assistants (PDAs). For example, a document could include two links, one for screen and one for print, as shown here:

```
<link rel="stylesheet" href="screenstyle.css" media="screen"
      type="text/css" />

<link rel="stylesheet" href="printstyle.css" media="print"
      type="text/css" />
```

Multiple values also can be set for the attribute. These should be separated by commas, to show that the style can apply to many media forms; for example, **media="screen, print"**. The default value for media is **all** and is applied if the attribute is not used. Currently, the main use of this attribute is to specify one style sheet for printing and one for viewing onscreen, as demonstrated here:

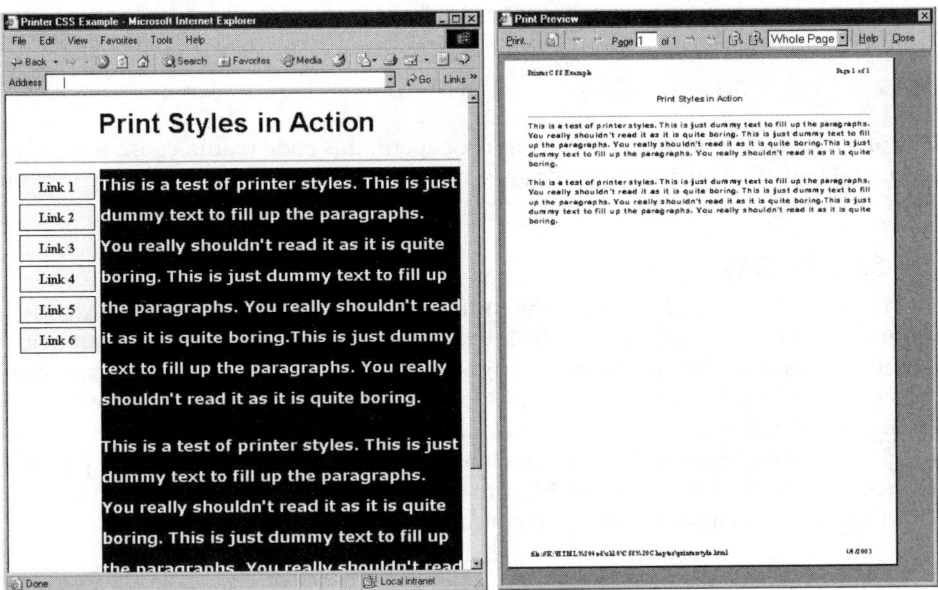

Most of the browsers now support this, which should render the concept of a special "print format" link obsolete someday.

The **@import** rule has already been discussed in the previous chapter (refer to "Embedding and Importing Style Sheets"). Defining a media type under CSS2 simply requires the addition of an appropriate media type after defining the URL with the **@import** rule, as shown in this code fragment:

```
@import url("Braille.css") Braille;
```

The **@media** rule is used to define style rules for multiple media types in a single style sheet. For example, you might want to have a document display in a large sans serif font when viewed on a monitor, but display in a smaller serif font when printed. Multiple media types should be separated by commas, as shown in the following code fragment:

```
<style type="text/css">
<!--
@media screen {body
                 {font-family: sans-serif;
                  font-size: 18 pt;}
               }

@media print {body
               {font-family: serif;
                font-size: 9 pt;}
             }

@media screen, print {body
                       {line-height: 150%;}
                     }
-->
</style>
```

If implemented by a browser or another user agent, this code would cause the body of the document to display in an 18-point sans serif font on a computer monitor, to print out as a 9-point serif font, and to have a line height of 150 percent in both media.

Printer Specific CSS

As shown by the CSS2 specification, in the future, style sheets certainly will be extended to support more printing capabilities. Most of the browsers have begun to support printer style sheets and Microsoft has provided the **page-break-before** property and **page-break-after** property since Internet Explorer 4. These properties can be used to set a page break on the printer. By using these properties, you can set the printer to go to a new page before or after a particular element. The default value for either of the properties is **auto**. Other possible values include **always**, **left**, and **right**. Most likely, the value **always** will be used to tell the printer to always insert a page break. Imagine a rule such as this:

```
br.newpage   {page-break-after: always;}
```

Adding this rule would always cause a page break wherever the rule is inserted into a document.

Alternative Styles and User Styles

The opportunity to have different looks for different situations is an aspect often mentioned about CSS but rarely seen. The easiest way to see this is through alternative style sheets. In supporting browsers, it is possible to then change the look of a page by selecting an alternative style. To insert different styles, use the **<link>** tag and set the **rel** attribute equal to "**alternate stylesheet**." You will also need to set the **title** attribute for the tag so the browser can present a choice for the user. Three examples are shown here.

```
<link rel="stylesheet" href="standard.css" title="standard" />
<link rel="alternate stylesheet" href="orange.css" title="halloween" />
<link rel="alternate stylesheet" href="greenandred.css" title="xmas" />
```

A browser that supports the selection of alternative style sheets, such as Mozilla, would then present the possibility of choosing a different look to the user, as shown under the menu selection here:

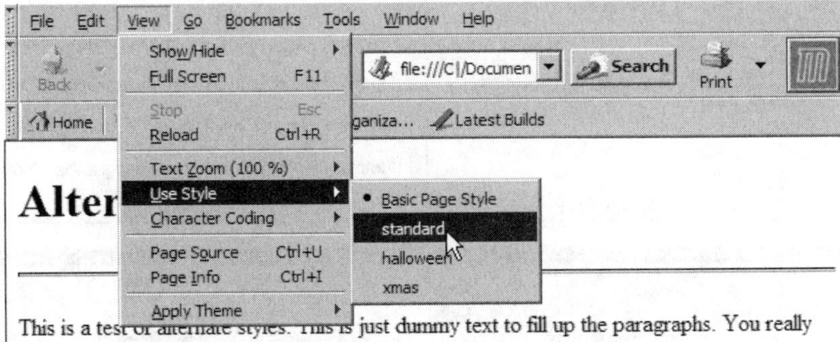

The looks created with alternative style sheets might be radically different, as shown in Figure 11-3.

It is also possible for the user to set his or her own style sheet to use. Most often, this is done to create a look that is easier for the user to read. Under Internet Explorer, users have the option of setting their own style sheet, as shown here:

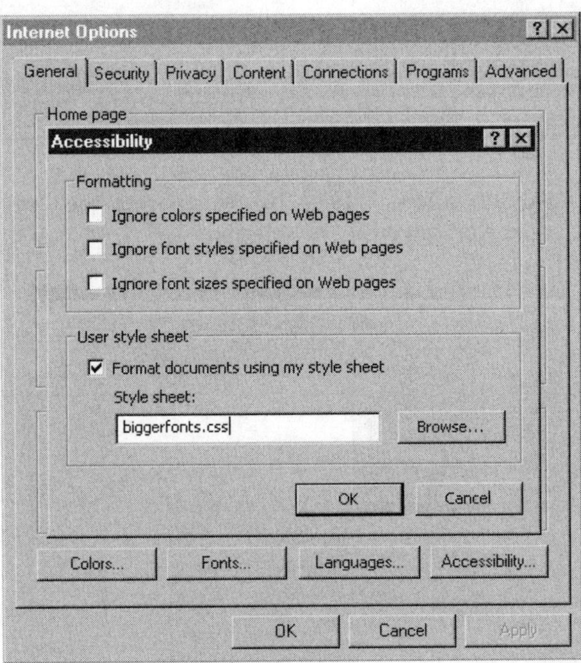

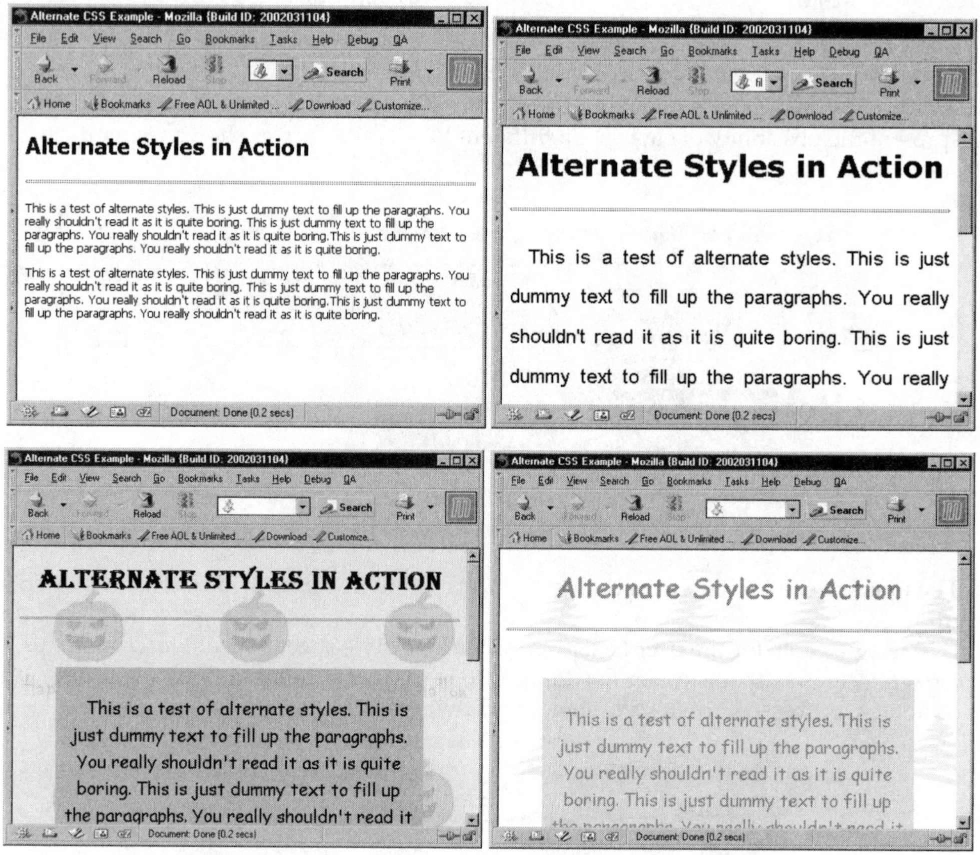

FIGURE 11-3 Drastic look changes per style sheet

Given the need to provide different styles for special users, the Opera browser even includes built-in user styles that can easily be selected.

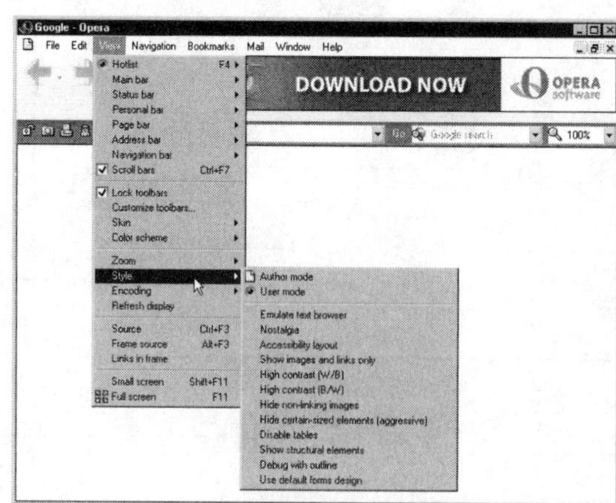

Opera's user styles can be applied to arbitrary Web pages to improve usability or to inspect site construction. For example, consider Google in a "text only" mode under Opera, as shown here:

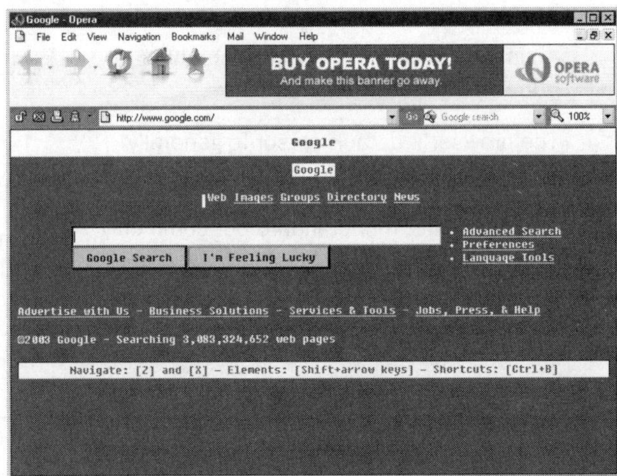

While user styles let the user be in control of the viewing experience, many designers are uncomfortable with this. Some try to use fixed sizes and positioning or even resort to **!important** overrides to make sure their designs stay the same. The Web is not print, however, and forcing strict designs on users will not always meet with success. Furthermore, forcing appearance may not be in the best interest of usability. For example, if you force a particular layout of font size, what happens to the user with poor eyesight who really needs to adjust fonts in order to read the page?

User Interface Changes

The CSS2 specification also promises more options for user interfaces, enabling page designers to implement various contextual display options for cursors, colors, and fonts, many of which can be set to match the end user's system settings.

cursor

The **cursor** property determines how the cursor displays when passed over the affected element. The **auto** value leaves the display to be determined by the user agent, so the cursor will display according to either the browser default settings or the user settings. The **crosshair** value renders the cursor as a simple cross, whereas **default** displays the system's default cursor (usually an arrow). Various other values listed in the CSS2 specification can indicate that something is a link (**pointer**), that text can be selected (**text**), that something can be resized in various directions (**e-resize**, **ne-resize**, **nw-resize**, **n-resize**, **se-resize**, **sw-resize**, **s-resize**, **w-resize**), or that the user must wait while a program is busy (**wait**). Table 11-2 details the cursors supported in CSS2.

In addition to the built-in cursor forms, one value, **uri**, can be used to reference a cursor source; multiple cursor sources can be listed, as shown in this example from the CSS2 specification:

```
p { cursor:url("mything.cur"), url("second.cur"), text; }
```

CSS Cursor Property Values	Description	Typical Rendering
auto	The browser determines the cursor to display based on the current context.	N/A
crosshair	A simple crosshair generally resembles a plus symbol.	
default	The browser's default cursor is generally an arrow.	
hand	A hand pointer (nonstandard but commonly supported).	
move	This indicates something is to be moved; usually rendered as four arrows together.	
e-resize	This indicates resizing as a double arrow pointing east-west (left-right).	
ne-resize	This indicates resizing as a double arrow pointing northeast-southwest.	
nw-resize	This indicates resizing as a double arrow pointing northwest-southeast.	
n-resize	This indicates resizing as a double arrow pointing north-south.	
pointer	Sets the cursor as the pointer, typically a hand.	
se-resize	This indicates resizing as a double arrow pointing southeast-northwest.	
sw-resize	This indicates resizing as a double arrow pointing southwest-northeast.	
s-resize	This indicates resizing as a double arrow pointing north-south.	
w-resize	This indicates resizing as a double arrow pointing west-east.	
text	This indicates text that may be selected or entered; generally rendered as an I-bar.	

TABLE 11-2 CSS2 Cursor Properties

CSS Cursor Property Values	Description	Typical Rendering
wait	This indicates that the page is busy; generally rendered as an hourglass.	
help	This indicates that Help is available; the cursor is generally rendered as an arrow and a question mark.	

TABLE 11-2 CSS2 Cursor Properties *(continued)*

As with fonts, the user agent should attempt to render the first cursor listed, try the second one if necessary, and ultimately default to the generic cursor value listed last. Internet Explorer 6 started custom cursor support, but even though it has not been widely implemented, a variety of JavaScript tricks are often employed to imitate this CSS2 property.

Integrating Colors with User Preferences

Under CSS2, authors will be able to provide color values that match pre-existing settings on the end user's system. This can be particularly useful in providing pages that are set to accommodate a user's visual impairment or other disability. These values can be used with any CSS color properties (**color**, **background-color**, and so on). The CSS2 specification recommends using the mixed-case format of the values shown in Table 11-3, even though they are not, in fact, casesensitive.

Color Value	Intended Rendering
ActiveBorder	Color of user's active window border setting
ActiveCaption	Color of user's active window caption setting
AppWorkspace	Background color of user's multiple document interface setting
Background	Color of user's desktop background setting
ButtonFace	Face color of user's 3-D display elements setting
ButtonHighlight	Highlight color of user's 3-D display elements setting
ButtonShadow	Shadow color of user's 3-D display elements setting
ButtonText	Color of user's push-button text setting
CaptionText	Color of user's text settings for captions, size box, and scrollbar arrow box
GrayText	Color of user's disabled text setting; if system doesn't display gray, defaults to black
Highlight	Background color of user's control-selected items setting
HighlightText	Text color of user's control-selected items setting

TABLE 11-3 User Color Preferences Under CSS2

Color Value	Intended Rendering
InactiveBorder	Color of user's inactive window border setting
InactiveCaption	Color of user's inactive window caption setting
InactiveCaptionText	Text color of user's inactive caption setting
InfoBackground	Background color of user's Tooltip control setting
InfoText	Text color of user's Tooltip control setting
Menu	Color of user's menu background setting
MenuText	Text color of user's menus setting
Scrollbar	Color of user's scrollbar setting (gray area)
ThreeDDarkShadow	Dark-shadow color of user's setting for edges of 3-D display elements
ThreeDFace	Face color of user's for 3-D display elements setting
ThreeDHighlight	Highlight color of user's 3-D display elements setting
ThreeDLightShadow	Light-shadow color of user's setting for edges of 3-D display elements
ThreeDShadow	Dark-shadow color of user's setting for 3-D display elements
Window	Background color of user's window setting
WindowFrame	Frame color of user's window setting
WindowText	Text color of user's window setting

TABLE 11-3 User Color Preferences Under CSS2 *(continued)*

The following code fragment shows how these values could be used to make a paragraph display with the same foreground and background colors as the user's system:

```
p { color: WindowText; background-color: Window;}
```

Integrating Fonts with User Preferences

Under CSS2, designers will have the option of coordinating fonts with the fonts defined by the end user's system. According to specification, these system font values can be used only with the shorthand **font** property—*not* with **font-family**. However, browser implementation might be more flexible. Table 11-4 lists these values and their related system font values.

Thus, to make level-three headers in a document display in the same font as a user's system uses to display window status bars, you would use the following code fragment in a style sheet:

```
h3 {font: status-bar;}
```

Outline Properties

Outlines are a new CSS2 feature that resemble borders but take up no additional space, and can be set to a shape different from that of the image, form field, or other element to which

Font Value	System Font Referenced
caption	System font used to caption buttons and other controls
icon	System font used to label icons
menu	System font used for drop-down menus and menu lists
message-box	System font used in dialog boxes
small-caption	System font used for labeling small controls
status-bar	System font used in window status bars

TABLE 11-4 Using CSS2 to Match an End-User's System Fonts

they are applied. Outlines are drawn over an item, rather than around it, thus causing no reflow. Outlines can be used dynamically, to indicate what element in a page has focus. Outline properties include **outline-width**, **outline-style**, **outline-color**, and the shorthand property **outline**. Table 11-5 lists the values associated with these properties.

Consider the following rule that would outline paragraphs with a dashed line when they are hovered over:

```
p:hover  {outline-style: dashed;}
```

According to the specification, unlike the **border** property, outlined elements do not necessarily draw as a box. However, under Opera 7, which is the only browser that currently supports outlines, the rendering seems no different from a border. CSS2 has also incorporated support for audio renderings of pages but as exciting as it may sound, it can be very difficult to describe and demonstrate.

CSS2 Aural Improvements

The CSS2 specification contains numerous properties designed to provide aural rendering of Web documents. Although not widely implemented, these properties represent one of the most forward-looking aspects of CSS2, targeted primarily for the sight-impaired, but offering expanded media possibilities for the Web, as well. While the use of a speech-based interface might seem like science fiction to some readers, the advances made in both speech synthesis and speech recognition suggest that practical use of this technology is not really that far away. This is a brief summary of the aural properties defined in CSS2. Again, these

Outline Property	Values Accepted
outline-width	Same values as **border-width**
outline-style	Same values as **border-style**, except **hidden**
outline-color	All color values, including **invert**
outline	Sets all three values

TABLE 11-5 CSS2 Outline Properties and Values

properties haven't been broadly implemented, so any references to them in the present tense are based on their definition within the CSS2 specification, not on their actual use.

Basically, aural style sheets allow synthetic speech sources to be associated with paragraphs and other elements. Timing and the spatial relationships between sounds also will be subject to control by style sheets. Presumably, various synthetic voices will function in a way analogous to fonts on a computer screen; different "voices" can be assigned to different elements or classes of elements, or the qualities of any given voice can be altered to suit an element (more emphasis for headers, and so forth).

speech-rate

The **speech-rate** property is used to determine the rate of speech. Values include numeric values, **x-slow**, **slow**, **medium**, **fast**, **x-fast**, **faster**, **slower**, and **inherit**. Numeric values determine the number of words spoken per minute (wpm). Speeds range from 80 wpm for the value **x-slow**, to 500 wpm for the value **x-fast**. The relative value **faster** increases the speech rate by 40 wpm, while **slower** reduces it by 40 wpm. The default value is **medium**. The value **inherit** also can be used with this property.

voice-family

The **voice-family** property works much like the **font-family** property insofar as it can be set to reference a specific voice "font," generic voice "fonts," or a combination thereof, using a comma-separated list. A sample might look like this:

```
p.voiceone {voice-family: "bill gates", executive, male;}
p.voicetwo {voice-family: "jewel", singer, female;}
```

In this hypothetical example, the first voice name is a specific voice based on a public figure, the second is a specific voice meant to suggest a similar character, and the final voice is a generic voice. According to the CSS2 specification, names can be quoted, and should be quoted if they contain white space. The value **inherit** also can be used with this property.

pitch

The **pitch** property defines the average pitch of a voice. Values include numeric values, which determine the voice's frequency in hertz, as well as **x-low**, **low**, **medium**, **high**, and **inherit**. The default value is **medium**. The values **x-low** through **high** are dependent on the pitch of the voice family in use (as determined by the **voice-family** property). The value **inherit** also can be used with this property.

pitch-range

The **pitch-range** property determines the range of pitch variation of a voice's average pitch, as defined through the **voice-family** and **pitch** properties. Values are either inherited (**inherit**) or defined by a numeric value between **0** and **100**. The value **0** produces no pitch variation; **50** approximates normal pitch variation, and **100** produces an exaggerated pitch range. The value **inherit** also can be used with this property.

stress

The **stress** property assigns stress, or peaks, in a voice's intonation. Used in conjunction with **pitch-range**, this might allow the creation of more detailed vocal ranges. The rendering of numeric values might be dependent on the voice's gender and the language spoken. Values are numeric, ranging from **0** to **100**; the default value is **50**. The value **inherit** also can be used with this property.

richness

The **richness** property determines the richness of a voice. Numeric values range from **0** to **100**, with a default value of **50**. The higher the number, the more the voice carries. The value **inherit** also can be used with this property.

volume

The **volume** property determines the average volume of a voice. Numeric values range from **0** to **100**. A value of **0** produces the lowest audible volume, and **100** the loudest comfortable volume. Values also can be set to a percentage of the inherited volume. Other values include **silent** (no sound), **x-soft** (equivalent to **0**), **soft** (equivalent to **25**), **medium** (equivalent to **50**), **loud** (equivalent to **75**), and **x-loud** (equivalent to **100**). The only other value is **inherit**. These values will depend largely on the speech-rendering system used, and on user settings such as speaker volume.

speak

The **speak** property determines whether text is spoken, and how. The value **none** prevents text from being spoken. The default value **normal** renders text in a "normal" speaking voice, as determined by other properties and the user agent. The value **spell-out** causes the user agent to speak text as individual letters, useful when dealing with acronyms. The only other value is **inherit**.

pause-before

The **pause-before** property defines a pause to take place before an element's content is spoken. Values can be expressed as time, measured in seconds (default) or milliseconds (**ms**), or as a percentage. Percentages define pause length in relation to the average length of a word, as determined by the **speech-rate** property. (For a **speech-rate** of **100wpm**, each word takes an average time of 600 milliseconds; a **pause-before** value of **100%** creates a pause of 600 ms, while a value of **50%** creates a pause of 300 ms.) The CSS2 specification recommends the use of relative (percentage) units. This property is not inherited.

pause-after

The **pause-after** property defines a pause to take place before an element's content is spoken. Values can be expressed as time, measured in seconds (default) or milliseconds (**ms**), or as a percentage. Percentages define pause length in relation to the average length of a word, as determined by the **speech-rate** property. (For a **speech-rate** of **100wpm**, each word takes an average time of 600 milliseconds; a **pause-after** value of **100%** creates a pause of 600 ms, and a value of **50%** creates a 300 ms pause.) The CSS2 specification recommends the use of relative (percentage) units. This property is not inherited.

pause

The **pause** property is a shorthand notation for the **pause-before** and **pause-after** properties just discussed. A style rule of

```
p {pause: 12ms;}
```

creates a 12-second pause before and after rendering an element; a style rule of

```
p {pause: 12ms 20ms;}
```

creates a 12-second pause before the element and a 20-second pause after it.

cue-before

The **cue-before** property sets an "audio icon" to be played before an element. One example might be a musical tone at the start of a paragraph, or a voice stating "begin paragraph." In some sense, this might be similar to the page-turning noise that often is used in children's books with an accompanying tape, record, or CD; this would serve as an attention cue for the listener. The value can be set to the URL of an audio file, as shown here:

```
p {cue-before: url("ding.wav");}
```

This would play the sound file ding.wav just before speaking the contents of the paragraph. The value of the property also can be set to **none**. If a URL is used that doesn't reference a viable audio file, the property renders as if the value were **none**. The CSS2 specification recommends that user agents reference a default sound file if the file referenced is not valid. This property is not inherited, but the value can be set to inherit from a parent element.

cue-after

The **cue-after** property sets an "audio icon" to be played after an element. Values are the same as for **cue-before**:

```
p {cue-after: url("ding.wav");}
```

cue

The **cue** property provides shorthand notation for **cue-before** and **cue-after**. A single value sets both properties to the same value; the properties also can be set separately:

```
p {cue: url("ding.wav");}
```

play-during

The **play-during** property allows a background sound (music, sound effects, and such) to play while an element is being rendered. The sound is determined by the URI of an audio file. Additional values include the following:

- **mix** Causes the sound set by a parent element's **play-during** property to continue playing while the child element is being spoken; otherwise, the sound determined by the child element's **play-during** property plays.
- **repeat** Causes the sound to repeat if its duration is less than the time needed to render the element's content; if the rendering time of content is shorter than the sound file's duration, the sound is clipped.
- **auto** Causes the parent element's sound to keep on playing.

- **none** Terminates the parent element's background sound until the child element is finished rendering, at which time it should resume. The **play-during** property is not inherited unless the value is set to **inherit**.
- **inherit** Causes the parent element's background sound to start over for the child element, rather than continue to play as determined by the **mix** and **auto** values.

azimuth

The **azimuth** property determines the horizontal location of a sound. How this renders will depend largely on the user agent and the audio system used with it. Values can be set to specific angles based on the concept of 360-degree surround sound. A value of **0deg** places a sound dead center, as if originating directly in front of the listener. A value of **180deg** places a sound directly behind a listener; **90deg** indicates dead right, while **270deg** or **-90deg** indicates dead left. Named values include **left-side** (270 degrees); **far-left**, **left**, **center-left**, **center** (0 degrees); **center-right**, **right**, **far-right**, and **right-side** (90 degrees). The default value is **center**. The relative value **leftward** moves the sound 20 degrees counterclockwise, and **rightward** moves it 20 degrees clockwise. The CSS2 specification notes that these values indicate a desired result, but how this will work must be determined by user agents. The **azimuth** property is inherited.

elevation

The **elevation** property determines the vertical location of a sound relative to the listener. Angle values range from **90deg** (directly above) to **-90deg** (directly below). A value of **0deg** locates the sound on the same level as the listener. Named values include **above** (90 degrees), **level** (0 degrees), and **below** (-90 degrees). The relative value **higher** adds 10 degrees of elevation, whereas **lower** subtracts 10 degrees. The **elevation** property is inherited.

speak-punctuation

The **speak-punctuation** property gives the option of having punctuation rendered as speech. The value **code** causes punctuation to render as literal speech (in other words, "," is spoken as "comma," "?" as "question mark," and so forth). A value of **none** (default) prevents punctuation from being spoken, presumably to be rendered as it would be in ordinary speech (short and long pause, proper inflection of questions, and so on). The only other value is **inherit**. The **speak-punctuation** property is inherited.

speak-numeral

The **speak-numeral** property provides two options for the rendering of numbers. The value **digits** causes numbers to render as a sequence of digits (**1001** renders as one, zero, zero, one). A value of **continuous** (default) causes numbers to render as complete numbers (**1001** renders as one thousand and one). The only other value is **inherit**. The **speak-numeral** property is inherited.

speak-header

The **speak-header** property provides options for speech rendering of table headers relative to table data. Values include **once**, **always**, and **inherit**. The value **once** causes the content of a table header to be spoken once before the content of all associated table cells is rendered ("Animal: dog, cat, cow…"). The value **always** causes the table header content to render before each associated table cell is rendered ("Animal: dog; Animal: cat; Animal: cow…"). The **speak-header** property is inherited.

This is just a brief overview of many of the defined aural properties under CSS2. Although the exact syntax is well-defined in the CSS2 specification, at the time of this writing, so few browsers actually support this technology for testing purposes that the actual syntax might vary once finally implemented.

CSS3: Someday?

Already, significant work is being performed on defining CSS Level 3—despite the fact that no browsers have been implemented that cover CSS2 completely and some browsers still have problems with areas of CSS1 for that matter. Readers interested in following the current progress of CSS3 should visit the W3C site's section on CSS (http://www.w3.org/Style/CSS/). A quick perusal of the current activities at the time of this edition's writing indicates that CSS3 will break the CSS specification up into modules so that it can be more easily adapted to suit a variety of situations. CSS3 also promises changes to add support for international languages, ruby text, and vertically flowing text, and to improve support for tables, print output, color correction, downloadable fonts, and integration with other technologies such as Scalable Vector Graphics (SVG), MathML, or SMIL (Synchronized Multimedia Interchange Language). CSS3 will also address the increased integration between XHTML, style sheets, and scripting languages through ideas like BECSS (Behavioral Extensions to CSS).

If you look at the working drafts that are close to recommendation stage at the time of this edition's writing, it is obvious that CSS3 will add a richness that makes CSS2 look somewhat simple. For example, no longer will you be limited to select the first-child or basic siblings in a tree structure, but arbitrary children can be specified. Attribute selectors become even richer in pattern matching capabilities and selectors can also examine the enclosed content in a tag. The CSS3 text specification promises improved layout even providing the ability to fully control kerning in a document. All the details that print designers would want, down to the tiny details of controlling the type of underline style and color, are promised by CSS3. But don't hold your breath for these features; they are probably a long way off. Interestingly some of the more important features may see the light of day first as browser-specific extensions. The next section covers some properties that are implemented by browser vendors, but that may or may not be part of any eventual CSS specification.

Microsoft-Specific Style Sheet Properties Sampler

Browser vendors are already making new additions to cascading style sheets, Microsoft being the most notable extender of the specification. Undoubtedly, these additions are just the beginning of a slew of new proprietary changes introduced into style sheets. Before we get started, an important note: the DTD statement used can be very important when trying proprietary extensions. In a strict rendering mode, Internet Explorer may not respect its own extensions. You may have to remove your DTD statement to get the browser into quirk mode to render the examples.

The first example of browser specific CSS is the **zoom** property, which can be used to scale content. The **zoom** property takes either a percentage value, a floating point number indicating a magnification scale such as 2.0 for twice as big or 0.5 for half-size, or the keyword **normal** indicating an object's normal magnification. For example, to zoom objects in a class named twotimes, use a CSS rule such as

```
.twotimes   {zoom: 200%;}
```

Although setting a zoom property might not make much sense with a static rule, when combined with scripting it can create an interesting possibility of zooming images or text based on response to user events. For example, try this

```
<p onmouseover="this.style.zoom='200%'"
   onmouseout="this.style.zoom='normal'">
Roll your mouse over me and watch me zoom!</p>
```

under Internet Explorer 5.5 or better to see a possibility of how the **zoom** property can be used.

An interesting collection of CSS property extensions is supported by Microsoft Internet Explorer 5.5 and higher and can be used to control the appearance of scrollbars for the entire window, as set by a rule on the **body** element and for the **textarea** element as well. These properties include **scrollbar-3d-light-color**, **scrollbar-arrow-color**, **scrollbar-base-color**, **scrollbar-dark-shadow-color**, **scrollbar-face-color**, **scrollbar-highlight-color**, and **scrollbar-shadow-color**. Each of these properties takes a color value defined in CSS in any form. A simple rule showing how to change your document's scrollbars to red is shown here:

```
body {scrollbar-face-color: red;}
```

Aside from cosmetic improvements to screen presentation, Microsoft has introduced a variety of style sheet extensions for supporting foreign language display, probably the most interesting being the **writing-mode** property. With this property, it is possible to make text flow up and down or right to left, which is very useful in languages such as Japanese. The following markup demonstrates how this property is used:

```
<div style="writing-mode:tb-rl">Up and down text.
<span style="writing-mode:lr-tb; color: red;">Left and
   right.</span>
More up and down.
<span style="writing-mode:lr-tb; color: green;">Back to
   left and right.</span>
</div>
```

This markup produces an interesting layout under Internet Explorer 5.5 or better, as shown here:

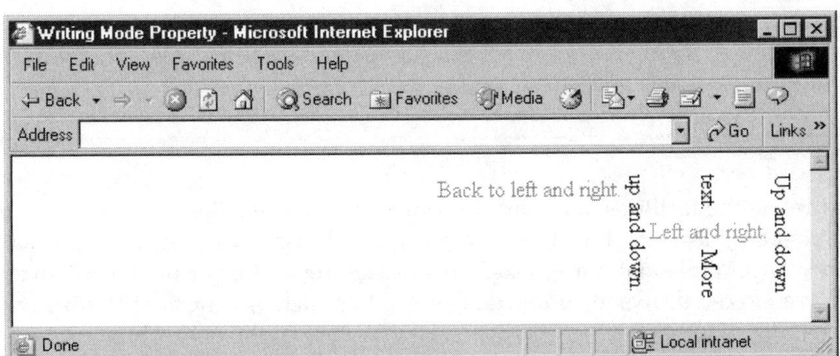

Although this is a property extension, it would be useful to render some languages like Japanese, and something similar to this property probably will wind up in CSS3.

There are a variety of other extensions to CSS introduced by Microsoft, most notably multimedia filters that can be used to change the appearance of objects and even control the loading and unloading of pages. The reality is that these properties have bugs and the syntax is not stable, having changed dramatically between releases of the Internet Explorer browsers. Furthermore, under the browser's own strict rendering mode, they may not even work! Given such limitations, designers are not encouraged to use these properties. For definitive information on the latest style sheet extensions, check Microsoft's developer information for Internet Explorer at http://www.msdn.microsoft.com/.

Downloadable Fonts

The last requirement for perfect layout control would be the inclusion of dynamic fonts. Although the CSS specifications are still working this out, the browser vendors have gone ahead and provided downloadable fonts since their 4.*x* releases. However, today only Internet Explorer continues to support downloadable fonts natively. As you may recall from the discussion of dynamic font technology in Chapter 6, fonts can be embedded in a Web page. They are best referenced using style sheet syntax.

To embed fonts in a Web document under Microsoft Internet Explorer, use the **@font-face** property. This property allows the designer to specify fonts in the document that might not be available on the viewer's system. To embed a font, first specify the **font-family** property. Then, specify the **src** property and set it equal to the URL of an embedded OpenType file, which should have an .eot extension. When the file is downloaded, it is converted to a TrueType font and then displayed on the screen. By putting a rule such as the following in the style sheet, the font named GhostTown can be used elsewhere on the page by using the **font-family** property:

```
@font-face {font-family:GhostTown;
            src:url(http://www.democompany.com/fonts/ghost.eot);}
```

You may wonder how to create a special embedded font file. The designer has to run the font through a tool to create the font definition file and then place that file on the Web server. The designer or someone else on the project may also have to make changes to the Web server so that the file is delivered correctly. See the Microsoft Typography Web site at http://www.microsoft.com/typography/ for information about the embedded font creation tool WEFT and other deployment issues.

NOTE *The Microsoft style of adding an* ***src*** *rule for* ***@font-face*** *is the proposed solution from the W3C and eventually may become standard.*

Summary

CSS2 provides all the facilities necessary to completely remove the last vestiges of HTML/XHTML table-based layout. Unfortunately, the standard isn't fully supported even by many modern browsers. While major areas such as positioning and layering of content are well-supported even in old browsers, important properties such as **min-height**, **min-width**,

max-height, and **max-width** are not. Even more troubling is that without full CSS2 support the browser vendors have already started to introduce proprietary features. It would seem that the more things change, the more they stay the same. Eventually, most of these issues will become less troubling, but by that point, you may be asking: why just strive for a print-style layout when fully programmed pages are possible? The next chapter begins to address the transition from static Web pages to programmed pages, beginning with forms.

IV

PART

Interactivity

CHAPTER 12

Forms

Up to this point, the discussion has focused on the Web as a static publishing environment. But Web sites also can be thought of as software because users can perform tasks and interact with content in ways that are beyond the capabilities of print. While links provide basic ability for users to make choices, fill-out forms enable users to submit information that can be used to create an interactive environment ranging from an order entry system to a dynamically created Web site. Today, forms are commonplace on the Web and mastery over their syntax is required to build a modern site.

How Are Forms Used?

There are many types of fill-in forms on the Web. The most common ones include comment response forms, order entry forms, subscription forms, registration forms, and so on. For example:

- A comment response form generally is used to collect comments from Web site viewers and elicit suggestions for improvement.
- Order entry forms provide a way for viewers to order goods from online stores. Order entry forms typically require the user to provide an address, credit card number, and other information necessary to facilitate online commerce.
- Registration forms are used to collect information about a user and often are tied to an authentication system, which limits access to the site.
- Forms often are used to access database-hosted information—for example, looking up information in a catalog or performing a search.

There are many other examples of how forms are used on the Web. The point here is to illustrate the kind of interactivity provided by forms.

Form Preliminaries

Creating forms is easy. Just add a **<form>** tag and associated tags for the various needed form fields to the document. You'll learn more about that in the next section, but first, let's consider how the content of a form is processed once the user submits the information. The answer isn't that complicated if we start from the big picture. After a form is filled in, the specified data is associated with various form field names and sent somewhere (as specified by a URL). Generally, the data is sent to a program on a remote Web server that parses the submitted information and acts upon it. Often, Common Gateway Interface (CGI) programs handle the incoming form-submitted data. However, it is also possible such form handling programs can be written in server-side scripting solutions such as ASP, ColdFusion or PHP, or even complex server modules such as ISAPI programs. Regardless of the technology used, some server-hosted program will receive the data, parse it, use the data, and then respond. A basic overview of how the relationship works is shown in Figure 12-1.

The point here isn't to get into the complications of how to make a server-side program handle form-submitted data, just to understand that the form itself is only part of the equation. There still must be some way to make the form do something, but this might not be your responsibility. It is usually a good idea for team members to focus individually on certain specific aspects of a Web site. For example, does the person who creates the IRS tax form know how the program that calculates things works? Why should you worry about how the server-side program or CGI for the database query form you created is written? You shouldn't, yet this division of labor far too often is missing in Web projects. The people who build the back end of the Web site that the form interacts with probably aren't the best ones to code the form. Conversely, the person who codes the form isn't necessarily always the best person to write the back-end program. Think about how the form works in the grand scheme of things, but worry most about making your end of the site work. Yet if you do want to delve into server-side programming, readers should take a look at the next chapter, which discusses server programming in more depth. For now, we'll focus solely on making the form work in the browser.

The <form> Tag

A form in HTML is contained within a **form** element. The form itself contains regular text, other HTML/XHTML elements such as tables, and form elements such as check boxes, pull-down menus, and text fields. The W3C specification calls these form elements *controls*. This is somewhat confusing because Microsoft also refers to ActiveX objects as controls. To

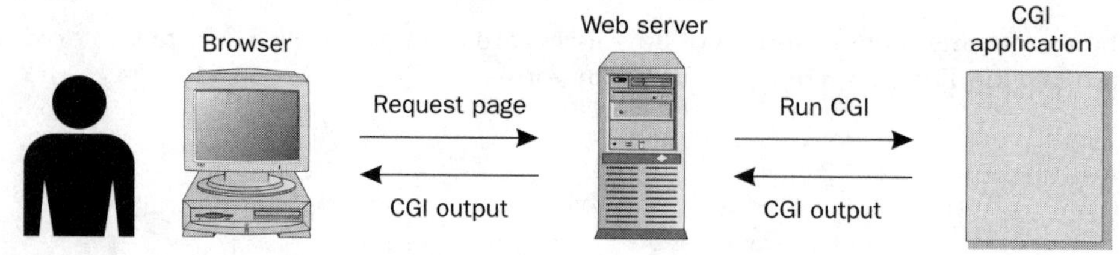

FIGURE 12-1 Form interaction interview

avoid confusion and to follow the common industry jargon, form elements are referred to as "form fields."

In a form, a variety of fields can be inserted. Each field will be named by setting a value with its **name** attribute in traditional HTML or its **id** attribute in HTML 4 and XHTML. For backwards compatibility, typically both attributes are used. Once a user has finished filling out the form and the Submit button is pressed, the contents of each field is related to its name in the form of a name-value pair (for example, username=Thomas) and is typically sent to a server-based program such as a CGI script for processing. However, the contents of a form might even be mailed to a user for further inspection.

Given this basic overview, in order to make the form work, you must specify two things in the **<form>** tag: the address of the program that will handle the form contents using **action** and the method by which the form data will be passed using the **method** attribute. The **name** and **id** attributes might also be useful to set a name for the form so it can later be manipulated by a scripting language such as JavaScript. Finally, in some cases you might have to specify how the form will be encoded using the **enctype** attribute.

The action Attribute

How a form is to be handled is set using the **action** attribute for the form element. The **action** attribute usually is set to a URL of the program that will handle the form data. This URL will usually point to a CGI script to decode the form results. For example, the code

```
<form action="http://www.democompany.com/cgi-bin/post-query.pl"
      method="post">
```

would be for a script called post-query.pl in the cgi-bin directory on the server www.democompany.com. It also is possible to use a relative URL for the **action** attribute if the form is delivered by the same server that houses the form-handling program:

```
<form action="../cgi-bin/post-query.pl" method="post">
```

Setting the **action** immediately begs this question: What program should the data be passed to? Generally, you or someone at your company will have a program set up to handle the form data. If a hosting vendor is used, there may even be canned programs to handle the contents of the form. However, what happens if there is no way to use a remotely hosted program? It is possible to create a "poor man's" form using the mailto URL. Remember that the **action** attribute is set to a URL. Thus, in some cases a **form** element such as

```
<form action="mailto:formtest@democompany.com" method="post"
      enctype="text/plain">
```

will work. It is even possible to use an extended form of mailto URL, which is supported by some browsers such as most versions of Netscape and newer versions of Internet Explorer. For example,

```
<form action="mailto:formtest@democompany.com?
Subject="Comment%20Form%20Result" method="post"
      enctype="text/plain">
```

NOTE *The %20 is simply the encoding of the space character.*

Although the mailto URL style form seems the best way to do things, not all browsers support this properly and many users may not have their e-mail environment set up in such a way to allow this. Even if the browser supports the mailto style, the data should always be passed using the **post** method. It also might be useful to encode the data differently by setting it to use text/plain encoding rather than the default style, which is a cryptic encoding style similar to how URLs look. The next section will discuss the methods and the encoding type.

The method Attribute

It also is necessary to specify how the form will be submitted to the address specified by the **action** attribute. How data will be submitted is handled by the **method** attribute. There are two acceptable values for the **method** attribute: **get** and **post**. These are the HTTP methods that a browser uses to "talk" to a server. You'll find out more about that in a moment, as well as in Chapter 13. Note that if the **method** attribute remains unspecified, most browsers should default to the **get** method. Although much of the following discussion is more applicable to the people writing the programs that handle form data, it is important to understand the basic idea of each method.

NOTE *When discussing the HTTP methods, we ought to refer to them in uppercase as GET and POST, as defined by the HTTP specification. While traditional HTML tended to refer to the **method** attribute allowed values in the same manner, XHTML requires that **get** and **post** always be lowercase despite this not matching the HTTP specification. I will use the lowercase syntax throughout this discussion given the focus on markup rather than HTTP.*

The get Method

The HTTP **get** method generally is the default method for browsers to submit information. In fact, HTML documents generally are retrieved by requesting a single URL from a Web server using the **get** method, which is part of the HTTP protocol. When you type a URL such as http://www.democompany.com/staff/thomas.html into your Web browser, it is translated into a valid HTTP **get** request like this:

```
GET /staff/thomas.html HTTP/1.1
```

This request is then sent to the server www.democompany.com. What this request says, essentially, is "Get me the file thomas.html in the staff directory. I am speaking the 1.1 dialect of HTTP." How does this relate to forms? You really aren't getting a file *per se* when you submit a form, are you? In reality, you are running a program to handle the form data. For example, the **action** value might specify a URL such as http://www.democompany.com/cgi-bin/comment.exe, which is the address of a program that can parse your comment form. So wouldn't the HTTP request be something like the one shown here?

```
GET /cgi-bin/comment.exe HTTP/1.1
```

Almost, but you also need to pass the form data along with the name of the program to run. To do this, all the information from the form is appended onto the end of the URL being requested. This produces a very long URL with the actual data in it, as shown here:

```
http://www.democompany.com/cgi-bin/comments.exe?
Name=Matthew+Foley&Age=32&Sex=male
```

The **get** method isn't very secure because the data input appears in the URL. Furthermore, there is a limitation to just how much data can be passed with the **get** method. It would be impossible to append a 10,000-word essay to the end of a URL, as most servers limit a URL to around two thousand characters. Interestingly, under the HTML specification, the **get** method has been deprecated. Despite the fact that **get** is not recommended, it still is the default method when the **method** attribute is not specified, and it continues to be used heavily on the Web.

With these potential problems, why use **get**? First, **get** is easy to deal with. An example URL like the following should make it obvious that the Name field is set to Matthew Foley, the Age is 32, and the Sex is male:

```
http://www.democompany.com/cgi-bin/
comments.exe?Name=Matthew+Foley&Age=32&Sex=male
```

Form field names are set to values that generally are encoded with plus signs instead of spaces. Non-alphanumeric characters are replaced by "%*nn*" where *nn* is the hexadecimal ASCII code for the character, which turns out to be exactly the same as the URL encoding described in Chapter 4. The individual form field values are separated by ampersands. It would be trivial to write a parsing program to recover data out of this form, but it probably is better to use one of the many existing libraries to decode submitted data.

The other HTTP method, **post**, is just as easy, so simplicity of parsing should not be a motivating reason to use **get**. Perhaps the best reason to use **get** is that it comes in the form of a URL, so it can be bookmarked or set as a link. The **get** method is used properly in search engines. When a user submits a query to a search engine, the engine runs the query and then returns page upon page of results. It is possible to bookmark the query results and rerun the query later. It also is possible to create anchors that fire off canned server-side programs. This is particularly useful in certain varieties of dynamic Web sites. For example, the link shown next fires off a server-side program written in the ColdFusion Markup language (CFM) and passes it a value setting—setting the ExecutiveID to 1.

```
<a href="displaybio.cfm?Id=1">Joe Somolovich</a>
```

The query is built into the link; when the link is clicked, the server-side program accesses the appropriate database of executives and brings up information about Joe Somolovich.

Although the **get** method is far from perfect, there are numerous situations in which it makes a great deal of sense. It is unlikely that **get** will be truly deprecated for quite some time, if ever.

The post Method

In situations where a large amount of information must be passed back, the **post** method is more appropriate than **get**. The **post** method transmits all form input information as a data stream immediately after the requested URL. In other words, once the server has received a request from a form using **post**, it knows to continue "listening" for the rest of the information. The **get** method comes with the data to use right in the URL request. The encoding of the form data is handled in the same general way as the **get** method by default; spaces become plus signs and other characters are encoded in the URL fashion. A sample form might send data that would look like the following:

```
Name=Jane+Smith&Age=30&Sex=female
```

Like data transmitted using the **get** method, the data will still have to be broken up to be used by the handling program. The benefit of using the **post** method is that a large amount of data can be submitted this way because the form contents are not in the URL. It is even possible to send the contents of files using this method. In the **post** example, the encoding of the form data is the same as **get**, although it is possible to change the encoding method using the **enctype** attribute.

NOTE *One potential downside of the **post** method is that pages generated by data submitted via **post** cannot be bookmarked. You may have noticed that the preservation of **post** data is such a challenge that browsers will even try to assist users with automatic reposting of form data.*

The enctype Attribute

When data is passed from a form to a Web server, it typically is encoded just like a URL, as discussed in Chapter 4. In this encoding, spaces are replaced by the "+" symbol and non-alphanumeric characters are replaced by "%*nn*", where *nn* is the hexadecimal ASCII code for the character. The form of this is described in the special MIME file format *application/x-www-form-urlencoded*. By default, all form data is submitted in this form. It is possible, however, to set the encoding method for form data by setting the **enctype** attribute. When using a mailto URL in the **action** attribute, the encoding type of *text/plain* might be more desirable. The result would look like the example shown here:

```
First Name=Joe
Last Name=Smith
Sex=Male
Submit=Send it
```

Each form field is on a line of its own. Even with this encoding form, non-alphanumeric characters can be encoded in the hexadecimal form.

Another form of encoding is also important: **multipart/form-data**. When passing files back using a form, it is important to designate where each file begins and ends. A value of **multipart/form-data** for the **enctype** is used to indicate this style. In this encoding, spaces and non-alphanumeric characters are preserved; data elements are separated by special delimiter lines. The following file fragment shows the submission of a form with **multipart/form-data** encoding, including the contents of the attached files:

```
Content-type: multipart/form-data;
boundary=---------------------------2988412654262
Content-Length: 5289
```

```
------------------------------2988412654262
Content-Disposition: form-data; name="firstname"
Joe
------------------------------2988412654262
Content-Disposition: form-data; name="lastname"
Smith
------------------------------2988412654262
Content-Disposition: form-data; name="myfile";
filename="C:\WINNT\PROFILES\ADMINISTRATOR\DESKTOP\TEST.HTML"
Content-Type: text/html
<html><head><title>Test File</title></head>
<body><h1>Test File</h1></body></html>
----------------------------------------
8/12/97 4:47:45 PM--SF_NOTIFY_PREPROC_HEADERS
URL=/programs/postit.cfm?
----------------------------------------
8/12/97 4:47:45 PM--SF_NOTIFY_URL_MAP
URL=/programs/postit.cfm
Physical Path=C:\InetPub\wwwroot\programs\postit.cfm
----------------------------------------
```

Simple Form Example

Given that we have some place to send form data, as specified by the **action** attribute and **method** (either **get** or **post**), we can write a simple stub example for a form, as shown here:

```
<!DOCTYPE html PUBLIC "-//W3C//DTD XHTML 1.0 Transitional//EN"
"http://www.w3.org/TR/xhtml1/DTD/xhtml1-transitional.dtd">
<html xmlns="http://www.w3.org/1999/xhtml" lang="en">
<head>
<title>Form Template</title>
<meta http-equiv="content-type" content="text/html; charset=ISO-8859-1" />
</head>
<body>
<form action="insert URL to server-side program here" method="post"
      name="form1" id="form1">
<!-- Form fields and other standard XHTML markup and text  -->

</form>
</body>
</html>
```

Although this syntax is adequate to build the form framework in most cases, there are other attributes for the **form** element that might be useful for frame targeting, scripting, and style sheets; these are described in Appendix A.

The name and id Attributes

Before presenting all the form fields, it's important to understand the issues surrounding the **name** and **id** attributes. Both of these attributes are used to name the **<form>** tag itself and the individual fields within it. Traditionally, only the **name** attribute was supported and was used both for the name-value pairs submitted to the server as well as for scripting. With HTML 4 and XHTML, the **id** attribute is also used. The main duty of **id** is for CSS and JavaScript usage, while **name** is used for both server-side programming and JavaScript. Given the overlap, page authors often set **name** and **id** to the same value where possible. In most cases, they are exactly the same but there are some troubling inconsistencies. For example, for fields such as check boxes and radio buttons, the values may actually have to be different. This important difference will be presented in detail when those fields are discussed.

NOTE *Interestingly enough, under the strict variant of XHTML, the attribute* ***name*** *on the* ***form*** *element is deprecated, but current browser support suggests to ignore the validation error as the form may not be scriptable under some browsers without* ***name****.*

Form Field Elements

A form is made up of *fields* as well as the markup necessary to structure the form and potentially control its presentation. Form fields include text fields, password fields, multiple-line text fields, pop-up menus, scrolled lists, radio buttons, check boxes, and buttons. Hidden form fields are also possible. In the following sections, we explore the common form fields one by one. Newer and less common form items such as **<button>**, **<label>**, **<fieldset>**, and **<legend>** are discussed later in the section "Other Form Elements."

Text Fields

Single-line text entry fields are specified using the **input** element and are useful for collecting small bits of data such as a user's name, address, e-mail address, and so on. It also is possible to specify a multiple-line text field using the **textarea** element, but for now let's focus on the simplest form of text entry. To set a text entry control, use the **<input>** tag and set the **type** attribute equal to **text,** as shown here, for traditional HTML:

```
<input type="text" name="UserName" id="UserName">
```

In XHTML syntax, because this is an empty element we would write the following:

```
<input type="text" name="UserName" id="UserName" />
```

The rest of the discussion will utilize XHTML syntax, but all examples could easily be modified back to HTML 4.

All form elements should be named by setting the **name** attribute to some unique value. In the previous example, the **name** attribute was set to "UserName" in order to indicate that the field is used to collect a user's name on an order form. Remember to pick a name that makes sense and is unique to the form. The name will be used when the form is submitted, as well as for manipulation by scripting languages. You should also set the **id** attribute to the same value as **name** for use in CSS and scripting, but a few areas like radio buttons will vary from this rule of thumb. This will be discussed more in an upcoming section.

The last example does not specify the size of the field nor the maximum number of characters that can be entered into the field. By default, unless specified this field generally will be a width of 20 characters, although browsers might not necessarily follow this typical situation. To set the size of the field in characters, use the **size** attribute. For example,

```
<input type="text" name="UserName" id="UserName" size="40" />
```

The value of the **size** field for an **<input>** tag is the number of characters to be displayed. It is possible for the user to type more characters than this value. The text will just scroll by. If you want to limit the size of the field, you need to set the value of the **maxlength** attribute to the maximum number of characters allowed in the field. The browser will keep the user from typing more than the number of characters specified. Browser feedback can include beeping or can just overstrike the last character. To set a text field that shows 30 characters but has a maximum of 60 characters that can be entered, you can use the following:

```
<input type="text" name="UserName" id="UserName" size="30" maxlength="60" />
```

The final attribute that is useful to set with a text entry field is the **value** attribute. With this attribute, you can specify the default text you want to appear in the field when the form is first loaded. For example, in the following code fragment, a value of **"Enter your name here"** is provided as a prompt to the user to fill in the field properly:

```
<input type="text" name="UserName" id="UserName" size="30" maxlength="60"
      value="Enter your name here" />
```

A very simple example of the basic text field is shown here, complete with a Submit button, the purpose of which is to send a form in:

```
<!DOCTYPE html PUBLIC "-//W3C//DTD XHTML 1.0 Transitional//EN"
"http://www.w3.org/TR/xhtml1/DTD/xhtml1-transitional.dtd">
<html xmlns="http://www.w3.org/1999/xhtml" lang="en">
<head>
<title>Text Field Example</title>
<meta http-equiv="content-type" content="text/html; charset=ISO-8859-1" />
</head>
<body>
<h1 align="center">Text Field Example</h1>
<hr />
<form action="http://www.htmlref.com/scripts/formecho.php"
     method="post" name="form1" id="form1">
<strong>Customer Name:</strong>
<input type="text" name="UserName" id="UserName" size="25" maxlength="35" />
<input type="submit" value="Submit" />
</form>
</body>
</html>
```

A rendering of the previous example is shown in Figure 12-2.

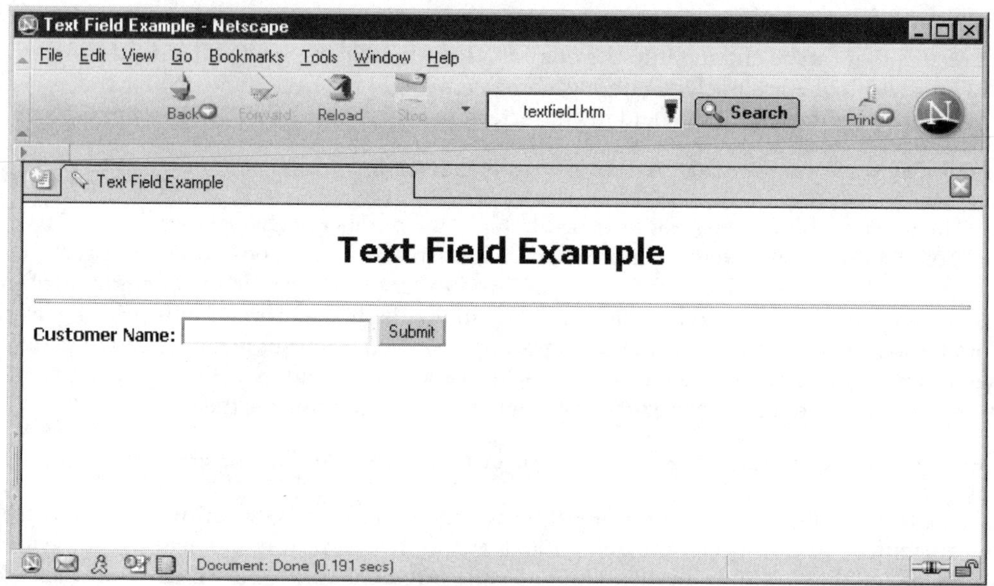

FIGURE 12-2 Text field rendering under Netscape

Password Fields

The password form field is the same as the simple text entry field, except that the input to the field is not echoed when typed. In many cases, the browser may render each character as an asterisk or dot to avoid people seeing the password being entered, as shown here:

Customer Name: Bob Smith
Customer ID: *******

Customer Name: Bob Smith
Customer ID: *******

Customer Name: Bob Smith
Customer ID: •••••••

Not echoing the password onscreen is appropriate. It discourages the idea of "shoulder surfing" in which an unscrupulous user looks on your screen to see what secret data you input. To set a password form control, use the **<input>** tag again but this time set the **type** attribute equal to **password**. As with the text field, it is possible to specify the size of the field in characters with **size** and the maximum entry in characters with **maxlength**. In the case of the password field, it is probably wise to limit its length so users don't become confused about how many characters they have entered.

The password form is very similar to the single-line text entry field. However, setting a default value for the password field with the **value** attribute doesn't make much sense because the user can see it by viewing the HTML source of the document. Of course, the **name** and **id** attributes should also be used on this form field. A complete example of the password field's use within the form is shown here:

```
<!DOCTYPE html PUBLIC "-//W3C//DTD XHTML 1.0 Transitional//EN"
"http://www.w3.org/TR/xhtml1/DTD/xhtml1-transitional.dtd">
<html xmlns="http://www.w3.org/1999/xhtml" lang="en">
<head>
<title>Password Field Example</title>
<meta http-equiv="content-type" content="text/html; charset=ISO-8859-1" />
</head>
<body>
<h1 align="center">Password Field Example</h1>
<hr />
<form action="http://www.htmlref.com/scripts/formecho.php"
      method="post" name="form1" id="form1">
<strong>Password:</strong>
<input type="password" name="Pass" id="Pass" size="10" maxlength="10" />
<br />
<input type="submit" value="Submit" />
</form>
</body>
</html>
```

NOTE *Don't assume that password fields are secure. The data is not encoded in any way that is difficult to figure out. Sensitive data must be transmitted using an SSL (Secure Sockets Layer) connection as designated by the https communication protocol.*

Multiple-Line Text Input

When it is necessary to enter more than one line of text in a form field, the **input** element must be abandoned in favor of the **textarea** element. Like the text input field, there are similar attributes to control the display size of the data entry area as well as the default value and the name of the control. For example, to set the number of rows in the text entry area, set the **rows** attribute equal to the number of rows desired. To set the number of characters per line, set the **cols** attribute. So, to define a text area of five rows of 80 characters each, use the following:

```
<textarea rows="5" cols="80" name="CommentBox" id="CommentBox">
</textarea>
```

Because there can be many lines of text within a **<textarea>** tag, it is not possible to set the default text for the area using the **value** attribute. Instead, place the default text between the **<textarea>** and **</textarea>** tags:

```
<textarea rows="5" cols="80" name="CommentBox" id="CommentBox">
Please fill in your comments here.
</textarea>
```

PART IV

The information enclosed within a **<textarea>** tag must be plain text and should not include any HTML markup. In fact, the default text in a **<textarea>** tag preserves all the spaces, returns, and other special characters. Markup included within the form control will not be interpreted. A complete example of a multiple-line text field is shown here:

```
<!DOCTYPE html PUBLIC "-//W3C//DTD XHTML 1.0 Transitional//EN"
"http://www.w3.org/TR/xhtml1/DTD/xhtml1-transitional.dtd">
<html xmlns="http://www.w3.org/1999/xhtml" lang="en">
<head>
<title>Textarea Example</title>
<meta http-equiv="content-type" content="text/html; charset=ISO-8859-1" />
</head>
<body>
<h1 align="center">Textarea Example</h1>
<hr />
<form action="http://www.htmlref.com/scripts/formecho.php"
      method="post" name="form1" id="form1">
<strong>Comments:</strong><br />
<textarea name="Comments" id="Comments" rows="8" cols="40">

Your comments go
here.
</textarea><br />
<input type="submit" value="Submit" />
</form>
</body>
</html>
```

The rendering of the preceding example is shown in Figure 12-3.

When typing text into a multiline field, wrapping must be considered. By default, most browsers will wrap text, but versions 4.0 and previous of Netscape will not. To address this, you can use the nonstandard **wrap** attribute for the **<textarea>** tag. The values for this attribute are **off**, **hard**, and **soft**. A value of **off** disables word wrapping in the form control. Any text the user enters is displayed exactly as is, although the user may insert hard returns of his or her own. A value of **hard** allows word wrapping, and the actual break points are included when the form is submitted. A value of **soft** allows word wrapping in the form control, but the line breaks are not sent with the form's contents. A value of **soft** is the default in Internet Explorer, but should always be explicitly set to make sure that other browsers such as Netscape wrap text properly. The modern implementations of browsers (including Netscape) do not have this problem, so this attribute should be avoided, particularly because it is not part of the XHTML standard.

One interesting omission with the **textarea** element is that there is no attribute to limit the amount of content that can be entered into the field. This really is a glaring omission from HTML/XHTML. Fortunately, using JavaScript you can address the lack of a **maxlength** attribute and limit a user from entering more data, assuming they have a script-enabled browser.

Pull-Down Menus

A pull-down menu enables the user to select one choice out of many possible choices. One nice aspect of pull-down menus is that all choices do not have to be seen on the screen and

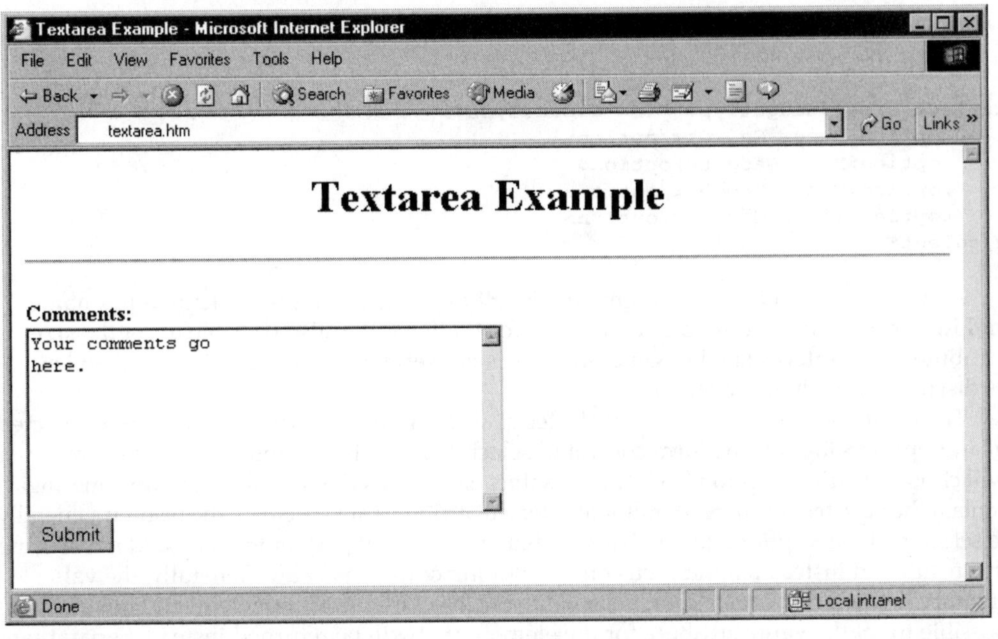

FIGURE 12-3 Rendering of <textarea> example under Internet Explorer

are generally are hidden. The following illustration shows the rendering of a pull-down menu under different browsers:

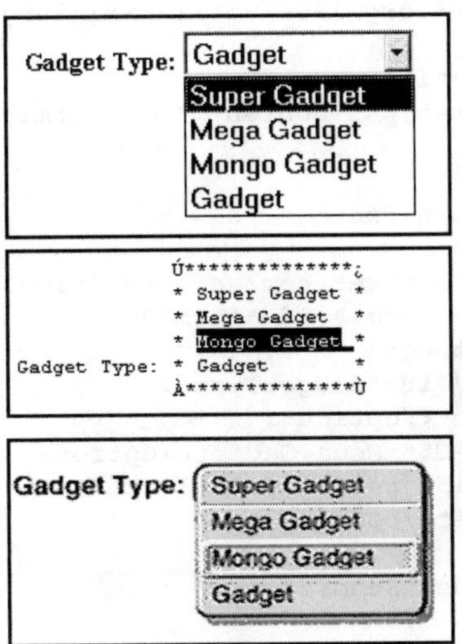

To create a pull-down menu, use the **<select>** tag. The tag should contain one or more occurrences of the **option** element. Each **<option>** tag specifies a menu choice. In many ways, the structure of a pull-down menu looks similar to a list structure, as shown in the following code fragment:

```
<select name="GadgetType" id="GadgetType">
    <option>Super Gadget</option>
    <option>Mega Gadget</option>
    <option>Mongo Gadget</option>
    <option>Plain Gadget</option>
</select>
```

As you can see in the code fragment, like all form fields the **select** element has **name** and **id** attributes used to set a unique name for the field. It is also possible to set the **size** attribute on a **<select>** tag, but generally this is not set unless the menu is a scrolled list, as discussed later in this chapter.

The **option** element has a few attributes as well. An occurrence of the attribute **selected** in an **<option>** tag sets the form control to select this item by default. Otherwise, a browser will choose the first **<option>** within the **select** element as the default if no **<option>** tags contain the **selected** attribute. If multiple **selected** attributes are specified, the result is generally to select the final **<option>** tag with a **selected** attribute, but page authors should not assume this result and instead should focus on developing correct markup. Generally, the value submitted when the form is sent is the value enclosed by the **option** element. However, it is possible to set the **value** attribute for the element that will be returned instead. Separating the text of the option from the submitted value is often a good idea so you can have a descriptive message for the user and a short data item for transmission. A complete example of a simple pull-down menu is shown here:

```
<!DOCTYPE html PUBLIC "-//W3C//DTD XHTML 1.0 Transitional//EN"
"http://www.w3.org/TR/xhtml1/DTD/xhtml1-transitional.dtd">
<html xmlns="http://www.w3.org/1999/xhtml" xml:lang="en" lang="en">
<head>
<title>Pulldown Example</title>
<meta http-equiv="content-type" content="text/html; charset=ISO-8859-1" />
</head>
<body>
<h1 align="center">Pulldown Example</h1>
<hr />
<form action="http://www.htmlref.com/scripts/formecho.php"
      method="post" name="form1" id="form1">
<strong>Gadget Type:</strong>
<select name="GadgetType" id="GadgetType">
      <option>Super Gadget</option>
      <option value="MEG-G5">Mega Gadget</option>
      <option value="MO-45" selected="selected">Mongo Gadget</option>
      <option>Plain Gadget</option>
</select><br />
<input type="submit" value="Submit" />
</form>
</body>
</html>
```

<optgroup>

HTML 4 introduced a variation to pull-down menus that is not often seen, the **optgroup** element. The goal of an **<optgroup>** tag is to create menu categories. It was initially designed to allow for cascading style menus, but it doesn't quite support that functionality. Although initially not well-supported by browsers, today's modern browsers do recognize **<optgroup>**. This simple example shows how **<optgroup>** might be used:

```
<select name="GadgetType" id="GadgetType">
     <optgroup label="S* Gadgets">
        <option value="SG-01">Super Gadget</option>
     </optgroup>
     <optgroup label="M* Gadgets">
        <option value="MEG-G5">Mega Gadget</option>
        <option value="MO-45">Mongo Gadget</option>
     </optgroup>
     <option selected="selected">Gadget</option>
</select>
```

Example renderings here under today's browsers show **<optgroup>** is useful.

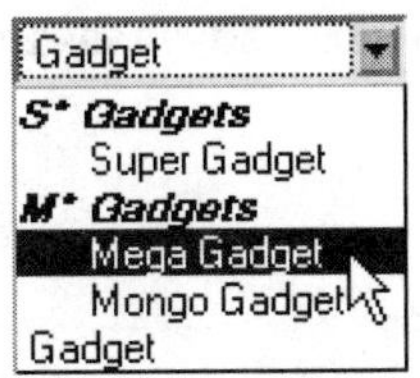

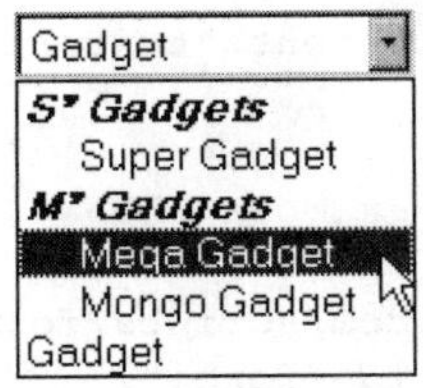

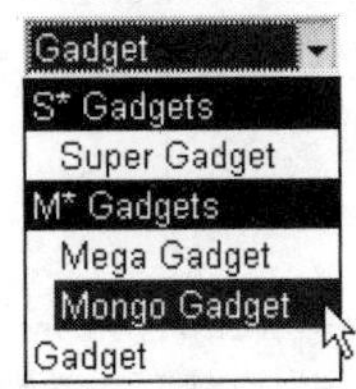

Even if browsers do not support **<optgroup>**, its use is relatively harmless because most browsers will just ignore it and render the list normally. The complete syntax for this element can be found in Appendix A.

Scrolled Lists

The **select** element also might contain the **size** attribute, which is used to specify the number of items showing on the screen at once. The default value for this attribute is 1, which specifies a normal pull-down menu. Setting the size attribute to a value of two or more creates a list in a window of the specified number of rows, as shown here:

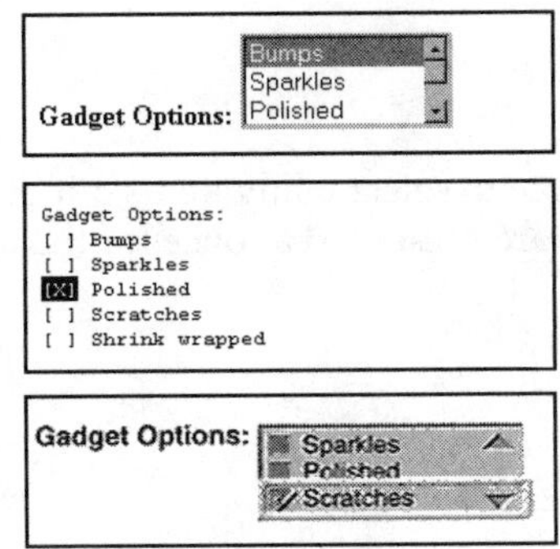

In the default case, scrolled lists act just like pull-down menus. However, if a **<select>** tag contains the attribute **multiple**, it becomes possible to select more than one entry. How multiple items are selected depends on the browser, but generally, it requires holding down some modifier key such as CTRL, COMMAND, or SHIFT and selecting the appropriate items with the mouse.

NOTE *Many novice users have a hard time with the scrolled list control and multiple entries. Depending on your site's target audience and size, it might be wise to provide instructions near the control to assist the user.*

Because it is possible to select more than one entry in a scrolled list when the multiple option is applied, it is possible to use the **selected** attribute multiple times in the enclosed **option** elements. A complete example illustrating how the scrolled list is used is shown here:

```
<!DOCTYPE html PUBLIC "-//W3C//DTD XHTML 1.0 Transitional//EN"
"http://www.w3.org/TR/xhtml1/DTD/xhtml1-transitional.dtd">
<html xmlns="http://www.w3.org/1999/xhtml" xml:lang="en" lang="en">
<head>
<title>Scrolled List Example</title>
<meta http-equiv="content-type" content="text/html; charset=ISO-8859-1" />
</head>
<body>
<h1 align="center">Scrolled List Example</h1>
<hr />
<form action="http://www.htmlref.com/scripts/formecho.php"
      method="post" name="form1" id="form1">
<strong>Gadget Options:</strong><br />
<select name="GadgetOptions" id="GadgetOptions"
        multiple="multiple" size="3">
  <option selected="selected" value="Hit with hammer">Bumps</option>
  <option value="Add glitter">Sparkles</option>
  <option selected="selected" value="Buff it">Polished</option>
  <option>Scratches</option>
  <option>Shrink wrapped</option>
</select><br />
<input type="submit" value="Submit" />
</form>
</body>
</html>
```

Check Boxes

With the scrolled list, it is possible to select many items out of a large group of items. Unfortunately, not all the items are presented at once for the user to choose. If there are a few options to select from that are not mutually exclusive, it probably is better to use a group of check boxes that the user can check off.

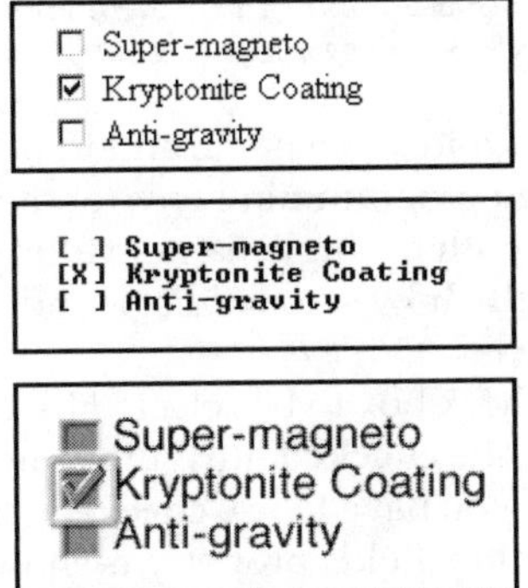

Check boxes are best used to toggle choices on and off. Although it is possible to have multiple numbers of check boxes and let the user select as many as he or she wants, if there are too many it can be difficult to deal with because they take up so much screen real estate, so don't forget about scrolled lists.

To create a check box, use an **<input>** tag and set the **type** attribute equal to **checkbox**. The check box also should be named by setting the **name** and **id** attributes. For example, to create a check box asking if a user wants cheese, use some markup like the following:

```
Cheese: <input type="checkbox" name="Cheese" id="Cheese" />
```

In this example, the label to the left is arbitrary. It could be to the right as well. The label could say "Put cheese on it," but there will be no indication of this label to the receiving program. In this simple example, if the check box is selected, a value of **Cheese=on** will be transmitted to the server. Setting a value for the check box might make more sense. Values to be transmitted instead of the default value can be set with the **value** attribute. The code

```
Cheese: <input type="checkbox" name="Extras" id="Extras" value="Cheese" />
```

would send a response such as **Extras=Cheese** to the server. Under traditional HTML, it was possible to have multiple check box controls with the same name. For example, the HTML 4 markup

```
Cheese: <input type="checkbox" name="Extras" id="Extras" value="Cheese">
Pickles: <input type="checkbox" name="Extras" id="Extras" value="Pickles">
```

would send multiple entries such as the following to the server when both extras were selected:

```
Extras=Cheese&Extras=Pickles
```

However, under XHTML you should have unique **id** attributes everywhere, so you would write:

```
Cheese: <input type="checkbox" name="Extras" id="cheese" value="Cheese" />
Pickles: <input type="checkbox" name="Extras" id="pickles" value="Pickles" />
```

However, another reason to avoid same name and id on multiple check boxes besides standards issues is that some Web programming environments will also make it difficult to parse incoming query strings with multiple name/value pairs with the same name. Interestingly enough, this is exactly how scrolled lists send in data, so yet another reason to avoid that construct.

Lastly, it is possible to set a check box to be selected by default by using the **checked** attribute within an **<input>** tag. The **checked** attribute requires no value under traditional HTML. However, under XHTML you have to use **checked="checked"** to be perfectly correct. A complete example using check box fields properly is shown here:

```
<!DOCTYPE html PUBLIC "-//W3C//DTD XHTML 1.0 Transitional//EN"
"http://www.w3.org/TR/xhtml1/DTD/xhtml1-transitional.dtd">
<html xmlns="http://www.w3.org/1999/xhtml" lang="en">
<head>
<title>Checkbox Example</title>
<meta http-equiv="content-type" content="text/html; charset=ISO-8859-1" />
</head>
<body>
<h1 align="center">Checkbox Example</h1>
<hr />
<form action="http://www.htmlref.com/scripts/formecho.php"
      method="post" name="form1" id="form1">
<strong>Gadget Bonus Options:</strong><br />
Super-magneto:
<input type="checkbox" name="mag" id="mag" value="Magnetize" /><br />
Kryptonite Coating:
<input type="checkbox" name="krypto" id="krypto"
       value="Anti-Superman" checked="checked" /><br />
Anti-gravity:
<input type="checkbox" name="antigrav" id="antigrav"
        value="Anti-gravity" /><br />
<input type="submit" value="Submit" />
</form>
</body>
</html>
```

Radio Buttons

Radio buttons use a similar notation to check boxes, but only one option may be chosen among many. This is an especially good option for choices that don't make sense when selected together. In this sense, radio buttons are like pull-down menus that allow only one choice. The main difference is that all options are shown at once with radio buttons. Possible renderings of the radio button form control are shown here:

Gadget Color:
Groovy Green: ○ Rocket Red: ◉ Yipee! Yellow: ○

Gadget Color:
Groovy Green: ( ) Rocket Red: (*) Yipee! Yellow: ( )

Gadget Color:
Groovy Green: Rocket Red: Yipee! Yellow:

Like check boxes, this form field uses the standard **<input type=“”>** format. In this case, set **type** equal to **radio**. Setting the **name** attribute is very important in the case of radio buttons because it groups together controls that share the radio functionality. The radio functionality says that when an item is selected, it deselects the previously pressed item. If the names are not the same, the radio group will not work. Be careful when naming radio fields. Although you should set the **name** attribute the same for all buttons in a group, radio buttons must not have the same **id** attribute under XHTML, similar to the situation with check boxes. In short, radio groups need the same **name** attribute value, but different **id** values.

When working with radio buttons, the **value** attribute must also be carefully considered. It is important to set each individual radio button to a different value entry. Otherwise, it will be impossible to decipher which button was selected. Like check boxes, the occurrence of the **selected** attribute in an **<input>** tag will preselect the item. Only one item may be selected as a default out of a radio group. If the **selected** attribute does not occur, the browser typically will not display any items as selected. A complete example using radio buttons is shown here:

```
<!DOCTYPE html PUBLIC "-//W3C//DTD XHTML 1.0 Transitional//EN"
"http://www.w3.org/TR/xhtml1/DTD/xhtml1-transitional.dtd">
<html xmlns="http://www.w3.org/1999/xhtml" lang="en">
<head>
<title>Radio Button Example</title>
<meta http-equiv="content-type" content="text/html; charset=ISO-8859-1" />
</head>
<body>
<h1 align="center">Radio Button Example</h1>
<hr />
<form action="http://www.htmlref.com/scripts/formecho.php"
      method="post" name="form1" id="form1">
<strong>Gadget Color:</strong><br />
Groovy Green: <input type="radio" name="Color" id="radio1" value="Green" />
Rocket Red: <input type="radio" name="Color" id="radio2"
                  value="Red" checked="checked" />
Yipee! Yellow: <input type="radio" name="Color" id="radio3"
                     value="Yellow" />
<br />
<input type="submit" value="Submit" />
</form>
</body>
</html>
```

Reset and Submit Buttons

Once a form has been filled in, there must be a way to send it on its way, whether it is submitted to a program for processing or simply mailed to an e-mail address. The **input** element has two values, **reset** and **submit**, for the **type** attribute for accomplishing this. Setting the **type** attribute for an **<input>** tag to **reset** creates a button that allows the user to clear or set to default all the form fields at once. Setting the **type** attribute for **<input>** to **submit** creates a button that triggers the browser to send the contents of the form to the address specified in the **action** attribute of the enclosing **form** element. Common renderings of the Submit and Reset form buttons are shown here:

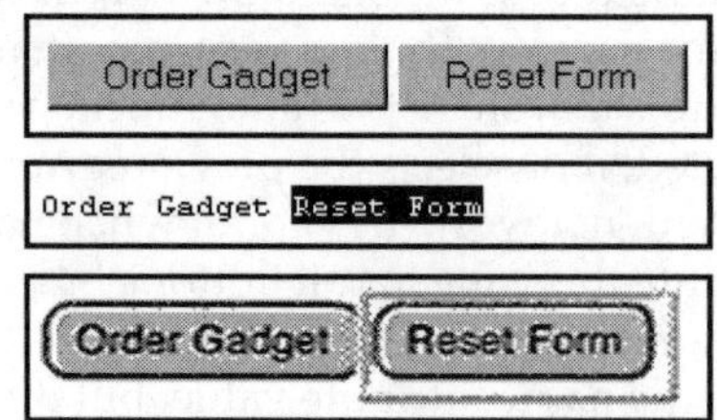

The buttons have two important attributes: **value** and **name**. The **value** attribute sets both the value of the button transmitted to the server and the text wording on the button. The **name** value associates an identifier with the form field for submission. Of course, **id** can be used as well for setting a name, but it is typically more related to style sheets. A complete example showing a small form with Submit and Reset buttons is shown here:

```
<!DOCTYPE html PUBLIC "-//W3C//DTD XHTML 1.0 Transitional//EN"
"http://www.w3.org/TR/xhtml1/DTD/xhtml1-transitional.dtd">
<html xmlns="http://www.w3.org/1999/xhtml" lang="en">
<head>
<title>Reset and Submit Example</title>
<meta http-equiv="content-type" content="text/html; charset=ISO-8859-1" />
</head>
<body>
<h1 align="center">Gadget Order Form</h1>
<hr />
<form action="http://www.htmlref.com/scripts/formecho.php"
     method="post" name="form1" id="form1">
<strong>Customer Name:</strong>
<input type="text" name="UserName" id="UserName" size="25"
     maxlength="35" />
<br />
<strong>Password:</strong>
<input type="password" name="Pass" id="Pass" size="10" maxlength="10" />
<br />
<strong>Gadget Type:</strong>
<select name="GadgetType" id="GadgetType">
      <option value="SG-01">Super Gadget</option>
      <option value="MEG-G5">Mega Gadget</option>
      <option value="MO-45">Mongo Gadget</option>
      <option selected="selected">Gadget</option>
```

```
</select>
<br /><br />
<input type="submit" value="Order Gadget" />
<input type="reset" value="Reset Form" />
</form>
</body>
</html>
```

Because the Submit and Reset buttons cause an action, either form submission or field reset, it may not be obvious why the **name** field can be useful. Although having multiple Reset buttons might not be so useful, multiple Submit buttons are useful because the value of the button is sent to the address specified in the **form** element's **action** attribute. One possible use might be to have three Submit buttons: one for add, one for delete, and one for update.

```
<input type="submit" value="Place Order" name="Add" />
<input type="submit" value="Delete Order" name="Delete" />
<input type="submit" value="Update Order" name="Update" />
<input type="reset" value="Reset Form" name="ResetButton" />
```

When the form is submitted, the name and value of the button is sent to the form-handling program, which will decide what to do with the submitted data based upon its contents. This use of a Submit button hints at a more generalized form of button, which will be discussed in the next section.

NOTE *If you have two buttons next to each other, it is useful to separate the two with a nonbreaking space (** **). Otherwise, the buttons probably will render too closely together. Another approach would be to use a small table around the buttons and provide some cell padding or a blank cell between the buttons. CSS could also be used with form elements to avoid using HTML for presentation and is the preferred method for layout. However, some browsers have problems with CSS formatting with form fields, particularly when they are positioned, and you may see that form fields, noticeably pull-down menus, may have higher z-index values than other page objects regardless of your layout efforts.*

PART IV

Additional <input> Types

There are a few types of **input** elements that have not been discussed. These elements hint at the potential complexity of using forms. Some of these elements, particularly the file selection form element, are not supported in very old browsers.

Hidden Text and Its Uses

The usefulness of this field is not always obvious to the new user. By setting the **type** attribute of the **input** element to a value of **hidden**, it is possible to transmit default or previously specified text that is hidden from the user to the handling program. For example, if there were many versions of the same form all over a Web site, the hidden text could be used to specify where the form came from, as shown here:

```
<input type="hidden" name="SubmittingFormName" id="SubmittingFormName"
       value="Form1" />
```

While this last example seems rather contrived, there actually is a very important use for hidden form controls.

When filling in forms, you may need to remember information the user entered from one form to the next. Imagine a form in which the user fills in his or her personal information on one page and the ordering information on the next page. How will the two pages be related to each other? This presents the state-loss problem. The protocols of the Web, primarily HTTP, do not support a "memory." In other words, they don't preserve state. One way to get around this is to use hidden text. Imagine that, in the last example, the personal information is passed to the next page by dynamically embedding it in the ordering page as hidden text. Then state has been preserved—or has it? When users are finished ordering, they submit the whole form at once as a complete transaction. The use of hidden text to get around the state-loss problem is illustrated in Figure 12-4.

While hidden form data seems very useful, there are significant issues to consider. First, consider that nefarious users might be able to determine the internal workings of your system or even falsify requests that include control information in the hidden fields. Not to alarm

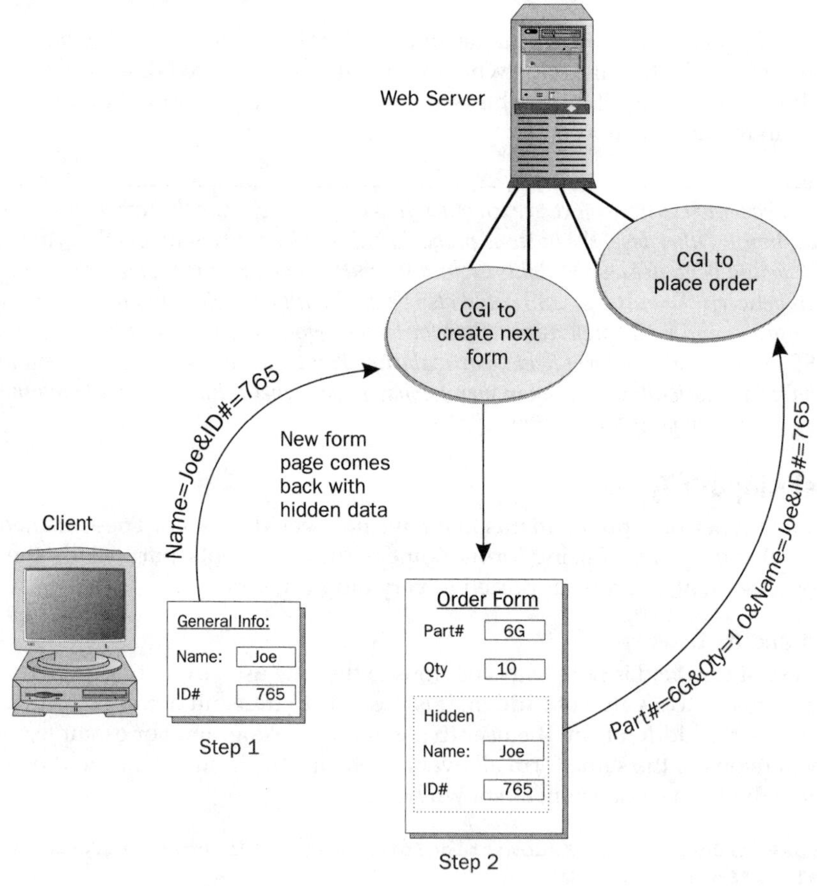

FIGURE 12-4 Using hidden form fields to preserve state

page designers, but do consider that to see hidden form fields, all the user has to do is view the page source! Furthermore, even the casual hacker can modify such values. Because of the security implications of hidden form data, using it to control things such as shopping carts or other server-side activity is potentially extremely dangerous. Fortunately, there are other approaches to saving state, including extended path information and cookies. These ideas will be briefly discussed in the next chapter.

Image Type

One form of the **input** element that is somewhat strange is the image type, as specified by setting **type="image"**. This form of an **<input>** tag creates a graphical version of the Submit button, which not only submits the form but transmits coordinate information about where the user clicked in the image. The image is specified by the **src** attribute. Many of the attributes used for the **img** element might be valid for this form of **<input>** as well. The specification defines **alt** and **align**. Other attributes such as **border**, **hspace**, or **vspace** may or may not be supported by browsers. Like all other forms of **<input>**, the **name** attribute is a very important part of how the coordinate information is transmitted. The example use of **<input>** shown next could be used to insert a map of the United States, allowing users to click on the regional office where they want to submit their order forms.

```
<input type="image" src="usamap.gif" name="Sales" alt="Sales Region Map" />
```

When clicked, the form values would be submitted along with two extra values, **Sales.*x*** and **Sales.*y***. **Sales.*x*** and **Sales.*y*** would be set equal to the *x* and *y* coordinates of where the image was clicked. The *x* and *y* coordinates are relative to the image with an origin in the upper left-hand corner of the image. You might notice a similarity to image maps. Indeed, much of the functionality of this form control could be imitated with a client-side image map in conjunction with some scripting code. A future extension to this form of the **input** element would be to make it less server-side dependent, possibly even allowing the page author to set a map name to decode coordinates or set function. Except for specialized needs, page designers probably should look to provide the functionality of the image form control in some other way.

File Form Control

A newer addition to the **input** element that now is part of the HTML and XHTML specifications is the capability to set the **type** attribute to **file**. This form control is used for file uploading. The field generally consists of a text entry box for a filename that can be manipulated with the **size** and **maxlength** attributes, as well as a button immediately to the right of the field, which usually is labeled "Browse." Pressing the Browse button enables the user to browse the local system to find a file to specify for upload. The logistics of how a file is selected depends on the user agent.

Following is an example of the syntax of the file form control, in which the **enctype** value has been set to **multipart/form-data** to allow the file to be attached to the uploaded form:

```
<!DOCTYPE html PUBLIC "-//W3C//DTD XHTML 1.0 Transitional//EN"
"http://www.w3.org/TR/xhtml1/DTD/xhtml1-transitional.dtd">
<html xmlns="http://www.w3.org/1999/xhtml" xml:lang="en" lang="en">
<head>
<title>File Upload Test</title>
```

```
<meta http-equiv="content-type" content="text/html; charset=ISO-8859-1" />
</head>
<body>
<h1 align="center">File Upload System </h1>
<hr />
<form action="http://www.htmlref.com/scripts/fileupload.php" method="post"
      enctype="multipart/form-data" name="form1" id="form1">
<strong>File Description:</strong><br />
<input type="text" name="Description" id="Description" size="50"
      maxlength="100" />
<br /><br />
<strong>Specify File to Post:</strong><br />
<input type="file" name="FileName" id="FileName" />
<hr />
<input type="submit" value="Send it" name="SubmitButton"
      id="SubmitButton" />
<input type="reset" value="Reset Form" />
</form>
</body>
</html>
```

A rendering of this example is shown in Figure 12-5.

Although it is possible to set the **size** and **maxlength** values of the **<input type="file">** element, this is not suggested because the path name might be larger than the size specified. (This depends on how the user has set up his or her system.)

The HTML specification also specifies the **accept** attribute for the **<input type="file" />** tag, which can be used to specify a comma-separated list of MIME types that the server receiving the contents of the form will know how to handle properly. Browsers could use this attribute to keep users from uploading files that are unacceptable to a server (for example, executable files). It is not known whether browsers actually pay any attention to this attribute.

Note *The file form control is not supported by all browsers, particularly older versions.*

Generalized Buttons

One last form of the **input** element, hinted at earlier, is the generalized button. By using **<input type="button" />**, it is possible to create a button in the style of the Submit or Reset buttons, but that has no predetermined actions. Inserting something like the following doesn't really do much:

```
<input type="button" value="Press Me!" />
```

If you click the rendering of this button, no action is triggered, and no value will be submitted. So what's the point? By using a scripting language, it is possible to tie an event to the button and create an action. For example,

```
<input type="button" value="Press Me!"
      onclick="alert('Hello from JavaScript');" />
```

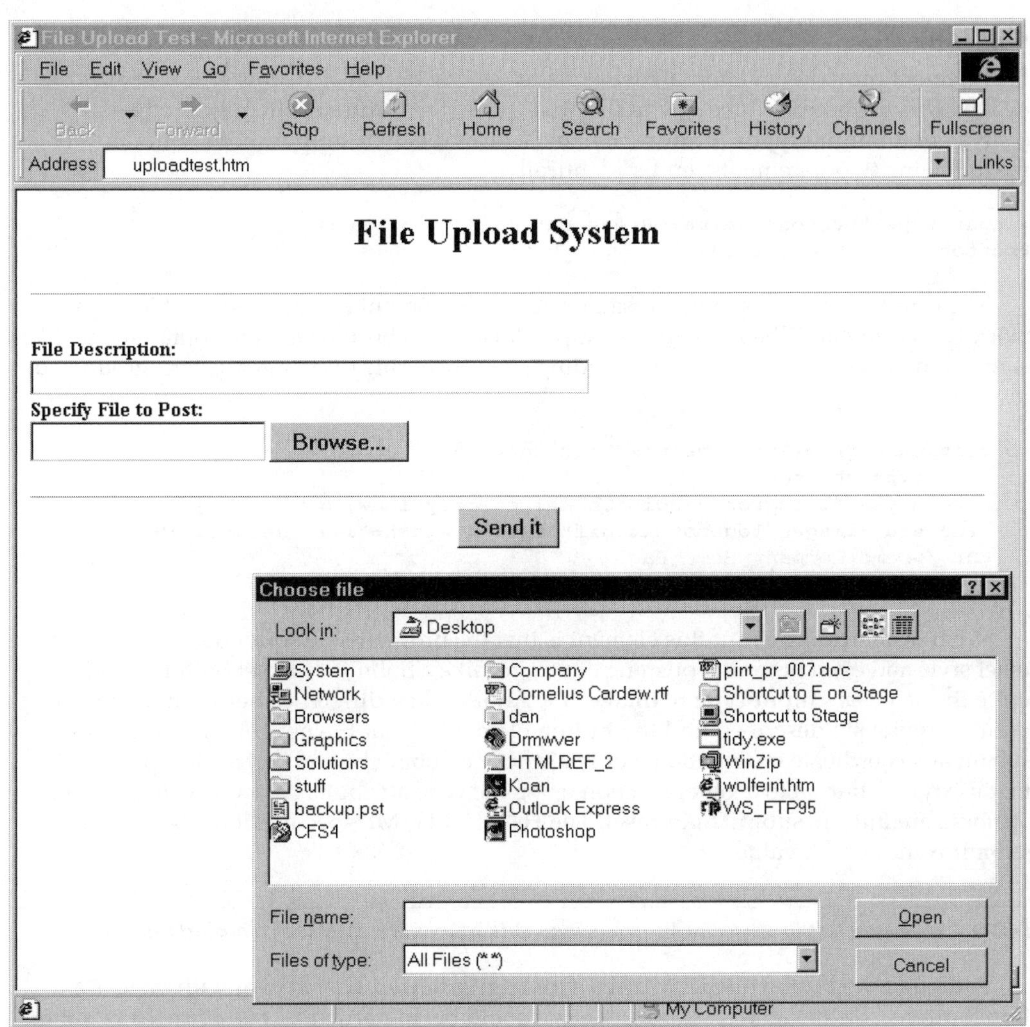

FIGURE 12-5 File form control rendering with browser dialog box

In Chapter 14, you'll see how forms can be tied to scripting languages to create powerful interactive documents.

Other Form Elements

HTML 4.0 initially added several form-related tags and attributes beyond those commonly used by Web developers. These are intended to address limitations in the current forms and to make them more interactive. While initially not supported, today most of these elements are supported in browsers and are included in the XHTML specification.

<button>

This element provides an alternate way to add generic buttons to forms. The text enclosed by the tag is the button's label. In its simplest usage, the **button** element is functionally equivalent to **<input type="button">**. In most browsers that support both button forms, the following two statements render identically:

```
<input type="button" value="Press Me" />
<button>Press Me</button>
```

The **<button>** usage is more versatile because its content can include most inline and block-level elements. The following example illustrates a button element containing text, an embedded image, and the use of a cascading style sheet rule to change the background and text color.

```
<button name="HomePage" value="Test Button"
        type="button"
        style="background-color:blue; color:yellow;">
   <img src="images/logonotext.gif" alt="" width="141" height="197" />
   <br />Demo Company Home Page
</button>
```

What is interesting about this element is that the browser should render the button in a relief style and even present a pushing effect, just like a Submit or Reset button, so it is not quite the same as **<input type ="image" />**. Another key difference between the image button previously described and the **button** element is that the new element does not submit any coordinate information, nor is it strictly a Submit button. In fact, it is possible to tie this style of button to a general action using the **type** attribute. Allowed values for this attribute are **button**, **submit**, and **reset**. The HTML/XHTML specification suggests that **submit** is the default value.

NOTE *It is incorrect to associate an image map with any image enclosed by a* **<button>** *tag.*

Although the **button** element seems a more generalized way to deal with images as form buttons, it is not as well-supported as it could be. In particular, older browsers might require an alternative approach.

Labels

Another new form element initially introduced in HTML 4.0 is the **label** element. One use of this tag is to better support speech-based browsers that can read descriptions next to form fields. However, a more common use of the **label** element is to associate the labeling text of form controls with the actual controls they describe.

A **<label>** tag can be associated with a form control by enclosing it as shown here:

```
<label>First Name:
    <input type="text" name="FirstName" id="FirstName" size="20" maxlength="30" />
</label>
```

A **<label>** tag also can be associated with a control by referring to the control's **id** with the **for** attribute. In this usage, the label does not need to enclose the control. This allows labels to be positioned in tables with their own cells. It is common to use tables to make better-looking forms. Far too often, form elements snake down a page and are not aligned very well. The following code fragment illustrates how a **<label>** tag with the **for** attribute would be used.

```
<table>
   <tr>
      <td align="right">
         <label for="CustName">Customer Name:</label>
      <td align="left">
         <input type="text" name="CustName" id="CustName" size="25"
                maxlength="35" />
   </tr>
</table>
```

The **label** element also supports the **id**, **class**, **style**, **title**, **lang**, and **dir** attributes as well as numerous event handlers. These are used in the same way as on any other HTML element. In particular, consider the use of **label** within style sheets to set the look of all form labels at once or in a group. The **disabled** and **accesskey** also are supported attributes for this element; these are discussed later in the chapter in the section on form accessibility enhancements.

NOTE *Many browsers allow you to click on text enclosed within a* ***label*** *and have the associated field automatically focused. For this small usability improvement alone, page designers are encouraged to strongly consider using* ***<label>*** *tags.*

<fieldset>

The **fieldset** element groups related form elements in much the same way the **<div>** element groups general body content. Like a **<div>** tag, a **<fieldset>** tag can be especially useful in conjunction with CSS to apply look or positioning information to a group of form fields at once. The **fieldset** element also can have an associated **legend** element to describe the enclosed items. The **fieldset** element itself has no special attributes aside from those core attributes common to all elements. However, the **legend** element does support the **align** attribute, which can be used to specify where the description will be rendered in relation to the group of form items; its values are **top** (the default value), **bottom**, **left**, or **right**. The example here illustrates how **<fieldset>** and **<legend>** tags are used:

```
<!DOCTYPE html PUBLIC "-//W3C//DTD XHTML 1.0 Transitional//EN"
"http://www.w3.org/TR/xhtml1/DTD/xhtml1-transitional.dtd">
<html xmlns="http://www.w3.org/1999/xhtml" xml:lang="en" lang="en">
<head>
<title>Fieldset and Legend Example</title>
<meta http-equiv="content-type" content="text/html; charset=ISO-8859-1" />
</head>
<body>
<form action="http://www.htmlref.com/scripts/scriptecho.php" method="post"
```

```
      name="form1" id="form1">
<fieldset>
<legend>Customer Identification</legend>
<br />
<label>Customer Name:
<input type="text" name="CustomerName" id="CustomerName" size="25" />
</label>
<br /><br />
<label>Password:
<input type="password" name="CustomerID" id="CustomerID" size="8"
       maxlength="8" />
</label>
</fieldset>
<br />
<input type="submit" value="Send" />
<input type="reset" value="Reset Form" name="reset">
</form>
</body>
</html>
```

The HTML/XHTML specification recommends that content within a **fieldset** element be enclosed by a box. An example rendering as supported by Internet Explorer is shown in Figure 12-6.

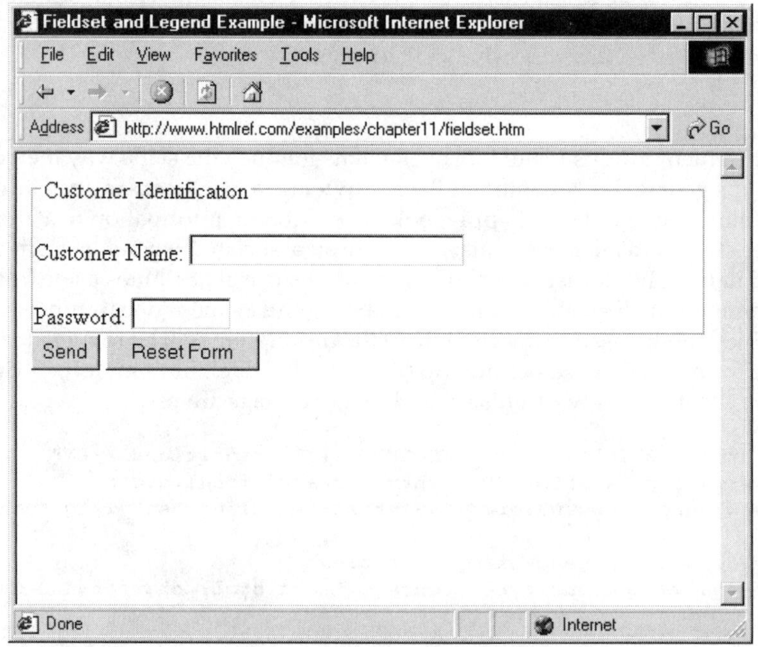

FIGURE 12-6 **<fieldset>** and **<legend>** rendering under Internet Explorer

Form Accessibility Enhancements

One of the most important changes made to forms under HTML 4 and preserved in XHTML is the improved support for accessibility. Some of the accessibility improvements provide more assistance to users who use the keyboard, while others are useful for all comers. Many of the more obscure HTML form elements such as **fieldset** or **label** are also concerned primarily with accessibility. We survey a few more of the improvements made in HTML 4 and XHTML in this section.

Keyboard Improvements for Forms

The **accesskey** attribute for form fields is an important accessibility improvement. Setting the value of the key to a character creates an accelerator key that can activate the form control associated with the element. Generally, the key must be pressed in combination with the ALT or OPTION key to activate the field. An example of how this attribute might be used is shown in the following code:

```
<label>Customer <u>N</u>ame:
   <input type="text" accesskey="N" size="25" />
</label>
```

Notice how a **<u>** tag is used to highlight the letter that will activate the field. This is the common practice to indicate accelerator keys in a Windows GUI. A more CSS-aware approach to indicating accesskey bindings is shown here:

```
<label>Customer <span class="accesskeyindication">N</span>ame:
   <input type="text" accesskey="N" size="25" />
</label>
```

From this, you would set the class to indicate the accesskeyindication in whatever manner you wanted. Interestingly enough, neither method should be required because according to the HTML 4 specification, browsers should provide their own form of highlighting for an access key, but in reality this isn't very common.

The HTML and XHTML standard defines the **accesskey** attribute for the **<label>**, **<input>**, **<legend>**, and **<button>** tags, although in various versions it leaves off support for **<select>** and **<textarea>**. Microsoft supports this attribute for the **<select>** and **<textarea>** tags. It seems likely that eventually this will be rolled into future specifications.

While the **accesskey** attribute can improve a form by making it more keyboard access–friendly, there are certain letters to avoid because they map to browser functions in the two major browsers, as shown in Table 12-1.

Another accessibility improvement initially introduced in HTML 4.0 is the use of the **tabindex** attribute for links and form-related elements. This attribute allows the tab order between fields to be defined. In general, elements with **tabindex** values greater than zero are selected in increasing order. Any elements with a **tabindex** of **0** are selected in the order they are encountered after the rest of the tabbing controls have been exhausted. Fields with negative **tabindex** values should be left out of the tabbing order. If a browser supports tabbing through form fields, it is usually by the order in which they are defined, which is often similar to the desired tabbing order. The next markup fragment demonstrates

TABLE 12-1 Browser Reserved Accelerator Keys

Key	Description
F	File menu
E	Edit menu
V	View menu
N	Navigation menu (Opera 6)
G	Go menu (Netscape/Mozilla), Messaging menu (Opera 6)
B	Bookmarks menu (Netscape/Mozilla only)
A	Favorites menu (Internet Explorer Only)
T	Tools or Tasks menu
M	E-mail menu (Opera 6)
S	Search menu (Netscape 6), News menu (Opera 6)
W	Window menu (Netscape 7/Mozilla)
A	Favorites menu (Internet Explorer Only)
H	Help

tabindex as the last field gets selected first, then the first, and then the second field is completely skipped over.

TIP *Page designers are encouraged to set **accesskey** and **tabindex** attributes to their documents immediately; they will have no harmful side effects in older browsers, which will simply ignore them.*

```
<form action="#" method="get">
Field 1: <input type="text" tabindex="2" /><br />
Field 2: <input type="text" tabindex="-1" /><br />
Field 3: <input type="text" tabindex="1" /><br />
</form>
```

NOTE *Be careful when setting the **tabindex** value with radio buttons, as the browser might use arrow keys to move among a group of radio buttons rather than the* TAB *key.*

Tooltips and Form Fields

Another accessibility improvement is the use of the **title** attribute to give users a hint about how to use a form field. Consider this markup:

```
<label>
Phone Number:
<input type="text" size="10" name="phone" id="phone"
       title="Please enter your phone number here without dashes." />
</label>
```

This is fairly well-supported in most browsers that will be encountered; the following rendering is in the Netscape 4.7 browser.

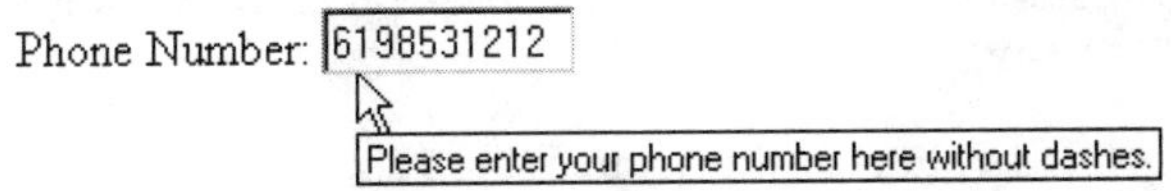

Be careful not to put critical information in a Tooltip, in case the user has a browser that doesn't display them. JavaScript can be used in some browsers to simulate a Tooltip, or to display similar information in the browser's status bar.

Browser-Specific Form Accessibility Improvements

One of the primary proprietary form improvements introduced initially by Internet Explorer 5 is a feature called AutoComplete. The concept of AutoComplete is to help users fill out forms by providing a pick list of previously used values for similar form names, or even relating the information in their personal data profile or vCard to form fields. To enable the AutoComplete feature for forms in IE 5 or later, select Internet Options on the Tools menu, select the Content tab, and then click the AutoComplete button. You might also want to fill out your personal information by selecting the My Profile button on the same dialog box. Once you have enabled AutoComplete, the browser should provide a pick list for text fields when you either press the down arrow key or the characters you are typing match a previously entered value for a similar field, as shown here:

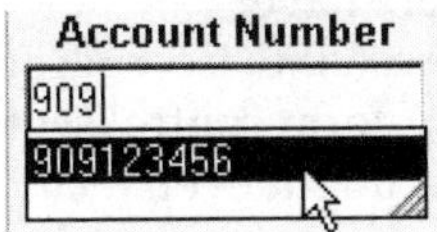

From an HTML perspective, a few things are important to know. First, some people might want to disable AutoComplete. You can set an attribute called **autocomplete** to off in either the **<form>** or the **<input>** tag:

```
<form autocomplete="off"> ... </form>
```

or

```
<input type="password" autocomplete="off" name="secretcodeword"
      id="secretcodeword" />
```

Notice in the previous example that you may want to turn off **autocomplete** for sensitive fields.

Finally, document authors may want to use the **vcard_name** attribute within the **<input>** tag to suggest to Internet Explorer to use data from a person's personal profile for basic fields such as name, address, city, state, zip, and so on. For example, to allow someone to automatically fill in form data from their vCard you might have **<input>** tags like this:

```
<input type="text" name="company" vcard_name="vCard.Company"
      id="vCard.Company" />
```

A complete list of vCard values is shown in Table 12-2.

For more information on proprietary features of Internet Explorer such as AutoComplete, interested readers should visit http://msdn.microsoft.com.

NOTE *Opera and Mozilla-based browsers such as Netscape 6 or better have form autocompleting systems, but their integration with vCards and control from a Web page are not as complete nor as well-documented as Internet Explorer. Interested readers should see the* ***www.mozilla.org*** *or* ***www.opera.com*** *sites for more information.*

Miscellaneous Form Field Attributes

The HTML 4 specification added two other attributes to certain form controls: **disabled** and **readonly**. When the **disabled** attribute is present in a form control element, it turns off the field. Disabled elements will not be submitted, nor may they receive any focus from the keyboard or mouse. The browser might also gray out the disabled form. The point of the **disabled** attribute might not be obvious, but imagine being able to disable the form submission button until the appropriate fields have been filled in. Of course, the capability to dynamically turn the **disabled** attribute for a form control on or off requires scripting support that not all browsers have.

When the **readonly** attribute is present in a form control element, it prevents the control's value from being changed. A form control set to **readonly** can be selected by the user but cannot be changed. Selection might even include the form control in the tabbing order. Unlike disabled controls, the values of read-only controls are submitted with the

vCard.Cellular	vCard.Company	vCard.Department
vCard.DisplayName	vCard.Email	vCard.FirstName
vCard.Gender	vCard.Home.City	vCard.Home.Country
vCard.Home.Fax	vCard.Home.Phone	vCard.Home.State
vCard.Home.StreetAddress	vCard.Home.Zipcode	vCard.Homepage
vCard.JobTitle	vCard.LastName	vCard.MiddleName
vCard.Notes	vCard.Office	vCard.Pager
vCard.Business.City	vCard.Business.Country	vCard.Business.Fax
vCard.Business.Phone	vCard.Business.State	vCard.Business.StreetAddress
vCard.Business.URL	vCard.Business.Zipcode	

TABLE 12-2 vCard Attribute Values

form. You can think of a read-only form control as a visible form of**<input type="hidden">**. According to the HTML specification, the **readonly** attribute is defined for the **<input type="text">**, **<input type="password">**, and **<textarea>** tags, but in practice many browsers support the other fields such as pull-downs, radios, and check boxes. Like a disabled form control, read-only controls can be changed only through the use of a script.

Form Presentation

Unfortunately, often on the Web, little attention seems to be paid to making logical or even presentable forms. For example, take a look at the form in Figure 12-7; notice that nothing is grouped or lined up.

Form Presentation with HTML

Form designers are reminded that other HTML markup elements can be used within forms, so there is no excuse for having a poorly laid-out form. For example, a form can be vastly

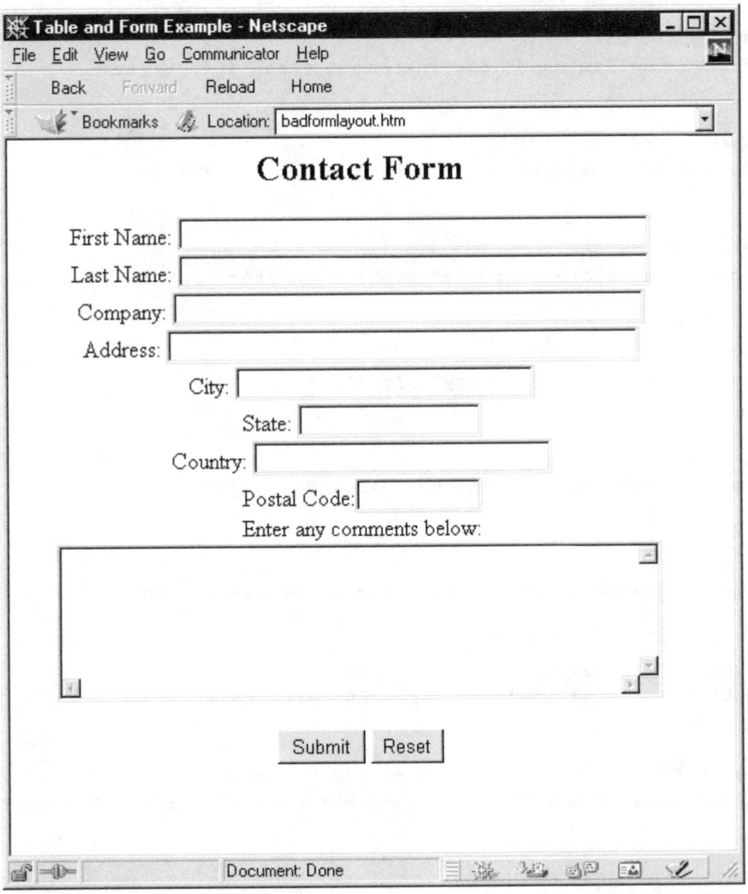

FIGURE 12-7 Example of a poorly laid-out form

improved by using a table, as shown in Figure 12-8. The markup for the form using a table is shown here:

```
<!DOCTYPE html PUBLIC "-//W3C//DTD XHTML 1.0 Transitional//EN"
"http://www.w3.org/TR/xhtml1/DTD/xhtml1-transitional.dtd">
<html xmlns="http://www.w3.org/1999/xhtml" lang="en" >
<head>
<title>Form Layout with HTML Example</title>
<meta http-equiv="content-type" content="text/html; charset=ISO-8859-1" />
</head>
<body>
<h2>Contact Form</h2>
<form action="http://www.htmlref.com/scripts/formecho.php"
      method="post" name="form1" id="form1">
<table border="1">
  <tr>
    <td>First Name:</td>
    <td><input name="firstname" id="firstname" size="40" /></td>
  </tr>
  <tr>
    <td>Last Name:</td>
    <td><input name="lastname" id="lastname" size="40" /></td>
  </tr>
  <tr>
    <td>Company:</td>
    <td><input name="company" id="company" size="40" /></td>
  </tr>
  <tr>
    <td>Address:</td>
    <td><input name="address" id="address" size="40" /></td>
  </tr>
  <tr>
    <td>City:</td>
    <td><input name="city" id="city" size="25" /></td>
  </tr>
  <tr>
    <td>State:</td>
    <td><input name="state" id="state" size="2" /></td>
  </tr>
  <tr>
    <td>Country:</td>
    <td><input name="country" id="country" size="25" /></td>
  </tr>
  <tr>
    <td>Postal Code:</td>
    <td><input name="zip" id="zip" size="10" /></td>
  </tr>
  <tr>
    <td colspan="2"><br />Enter any comments below:<br />
      <textarea name="comments" id="comments" rows="5" cols="50"></textarea></td>
```

```
  </tr>
  <tr>
    <td colspan="2" align="center"><br />
      <input type="submit" value="Submit" />
      <input type="reset" value="Reset" /><br /><br />
    </td>
  </tr>
</table>
</form>
</body>
</html>
```

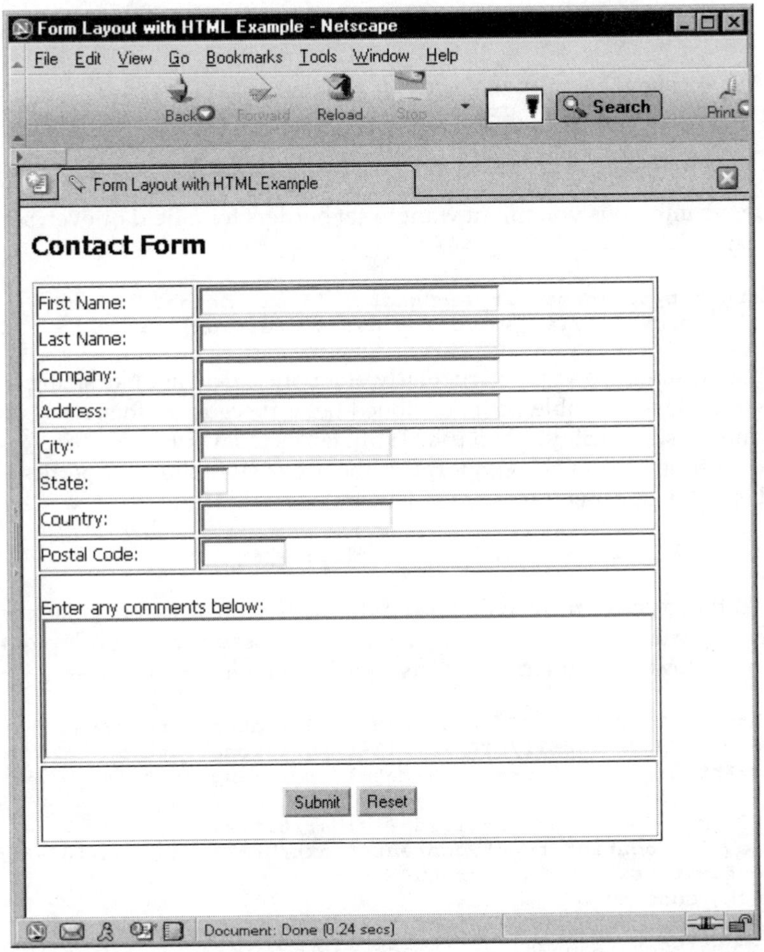

FIGURE 12-8 Form layout improved with a table

Form Presentation and CSS

Obviously, CSS would be more suitable for controlling the look and feel of a form. As expected, under HTML and XHTML both the **form** element and the various fields defined by **input**, **select**, and so on support the **class**, **id**, and **style** attributes to allow access from style sheets. Simple control of look and feel such as font or color is straightforward using CSS, as you can see in the following example:

```
<form>
   <input type="text" value="but this text is blue"
          style="font-family: Arial; color: blue;
                 font-size: 12px; background-color: lightblue;">

   <br /><br />

   <input type="submit" value="Submit" style="color: white;
          background-color: green; font-weight: bold; font-size: 22px;">

</form>
```

Getting more ambitious you might want to set borders for a field or even set their dimensions using CSS.

```
Field 1: <input type="text" style="width: 150px; height: 35px;
             border-style: solid; border-width: 1px; ">
```

Unfortunately, some browsers, particularly older ones, may not like sizing fields and many browsers still have trouble with positioned fields. Because of this, some designers stick with standard size attributes and use HTML tables to layout forms.

A very interesting use of CSS with forms is the use of style sheet properties to indicate when a field is selected, using the pseudo-element focus:

```
input:focus {background-color: black; color: white;}
```

A text field that receives focus will thus render with white text and a black background. A complete example using this CSS property, which also uses a background color to indicate required fields, follows; its rendering in Netscape 7 is shown in Figure 12-9.

```
<!DOCTYPE html PUBLIC "-//W3C//DTD XHTML 1.0 Transitional//EN"
"http://www.w3.org/TR/xhtml1/DTD/xhtml1-transitional.dtd">
<html xmlns="http://www.w3.org/1999/xhtml" xml:lang="en" lang="en" >
<head>
<title>CSS Forms: Focus and Required Fields</title>
<meta http-equiv="content-type" content="text/html; charset=ISO-8859-1" />
<style type="text/css" media="screen">
   body {background-color: white;}
   input.required {background-color: #f3a36d;}
   input:focus {background-color: black; color: white;}
   label {font-weight: bold;}
   label.required {color: red;}
</style>
</head>
<body>
```

```
<form action="http://www.htmlref.com/scripts/formecho.php"
method="post">

<label class="required">Name:

<input type="text" name="name" id="name" size="30" maxlength="50"
      class="required" /> (*)</label>
<br /><br />

<label>Company:
<input type="text" name="company" id="company" size="30" maxlength="50" />

</label>

<br /><br />
<label class="required">E-mail:
<input type="text" name="email" id="email" size="50" maxlength="100"
      class="required" /> (*)</label>
<br /><br />

<input type="submit" value="Submit">
<input type="reset" value="Clear">
</form>
<strong>* = Required Field</strong>
</body>
</html>
```

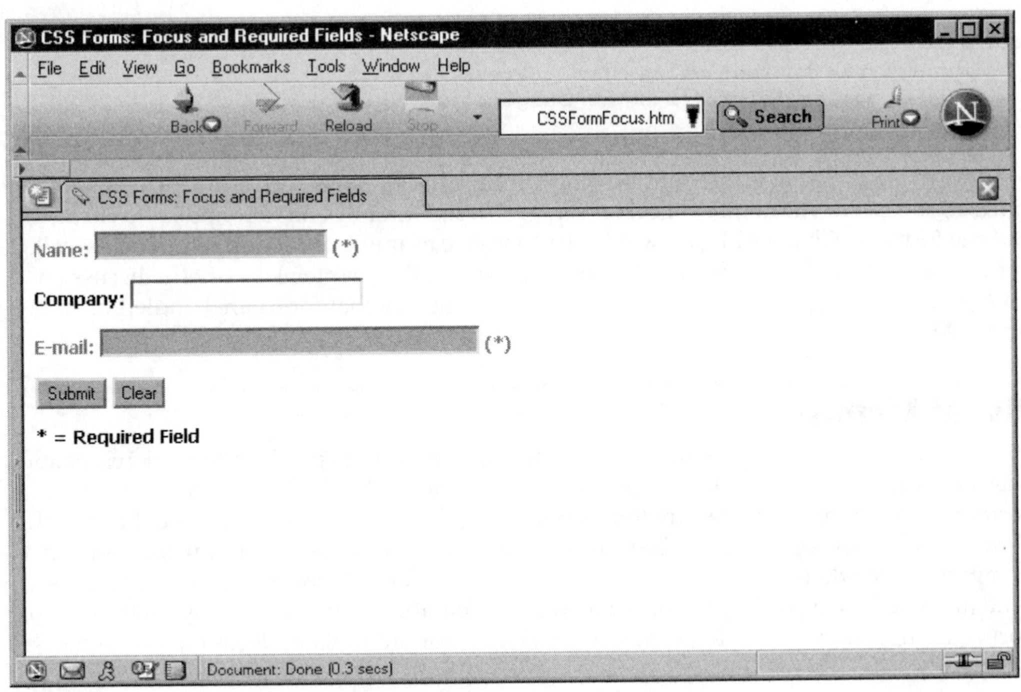

FIGURE 12-9 Using a CSS to indicate field focus

Of course, under many browsers advanced aspects of CSS are poorly supported; for example, the **input:focus** pseudo-element still primarily works only in Mozilla browsers at the time of this edition's writing. Until these issues are cleared up for commonly used browsers, page authors should carefully explore the use of style sheets with form elements before using them.

Forms and Scripting

As presented here, forms really don't finish the job. It is easy to create a form that asks users for their name and the number of gadgets they want to order. It also is easy to write a server-side program (assuming you're a programmer) that can take submitted form data and do something with it. However, it is not easy to make sure that the submitted data is correct. Why should you let the user enter a quantity of –10 (negative ten) gadgets in the form and submit it when that is obviously wrong? Sure, the server-side program could catch this, but it's best to try to catch this at the browser level before submitting the form for processing. This is one of the main reasons for client-side scripting. Of course, you'll probably end up having to do both client- as well as server-side validation just to be on the safe side.

Starting with Netscape 2.0 and continuing until today, it has been possible to use a scripting language such as JavaScript to associate scripts with user-generated events in a browser. To handle events for a form control, set an event handler using an attribute that corresponds to the name of the event. If you want to trigger a script when a button is pressed, you could insert some script code associated with the event attribute, as shown in the following dummy form:

```
<form>
   <input type="button" value="Don't Press Me!"
          onclick="alert('Danger! Danger!');" />
</form>
```

Events are added to form controls using attribute declarations such as **onclick**, **onsubmit**, **onreset**, and so on. The number of events has grown significantly and now applies to elements outside forms. In Chapter 14, you will find a complete example of checking form fields, called form validation, using JavaScript. Before wrapping up the chapter, let's briefly discuss an emerging technology that may completely change the way that forms are handled in Web sites—XForms.

The Rise of XForms?

HTML forms have certainly begun to show their age. In order to get them to work reasonably, they are often augmented with a significant amount of JavaScript. Most of the time, such script is used simply to make sure that simple data filters are applied to form fields. HTML forms are also not well-suited to be transformed into other display environments beyond a computer even when all accessibility additions such as label, fieldset, and so on are in use. And just as CSS solved the problem of mixing presentation with our markup, in the case of forms, we now have mixed logic into the markup. Shouldn't this be decoupled from the markup as well? The new XForms specification (http://www.w3.org/MarkUp/Forms/) addresses all these issues and more, and under XHTML 2 and beyond, XForms should replace traditional HTML form elements. However, despite all this, so far their use is limited only to those environments with heavy investment in XML and even then their use is questionable, given that no major browser is supporting them as of yet.

Summary

Forms provide a basic interface for adding interactivity to a Web site. HTML and XHTML support traditional graphical user interface controls such as check boxes, radio buttons, pull-down menus, scrolled lists, multi- and single-line text areas, and buttons. These fields can be used to build a form that can be submitted to a server-side program for processing. While making a rudimentary form isn't terribly difficult, laying out the form often is overlooked. Using tables and improved grouping tags such as **<label>**, **<fieldset>**, and **<legend>** can improve a form dramatically. Accessibility features initially introduced by HTML 4.0, such as accelerator keys and tabbing order specification, also can improve how a form is used. Even browser extensions often frowned upon can improve form use. While next generation forms also are in the works, for now designers should be content with the standard form features offered in HTML and XHTML.

CHAPTER 13

Introduction to Server-Side Programming

The last chapter hinted at the move from static Web pages to a more dynamic paradigm. The Web is undergoing a shift from a page-oriented view of the world to a more program-oriented view. The Web uses a client-server programming model in which some programming logic is executed by the client user agent—usually a Web browser—and some executed on the Web server. This chapter begins with an introduction to Web programming technologies as they relate to HTML/XHTML and focuses on server-side programming. The following chapters will continue the discussion, but with a focus on client-side scripting technologies and object technologies.

Overview of Client/Server Programming on the Web

When it comes right down to it, the Web is just a form of client/server interaction. Typically, Web browsers make requests of Web servers to return a file that is sent back and displayed in the browser. In this basic scenario, a Web server simply acts as a file or server that delivers files or associated error messages, usually in HTML or XHTML format, to a Web browser, as shown here:

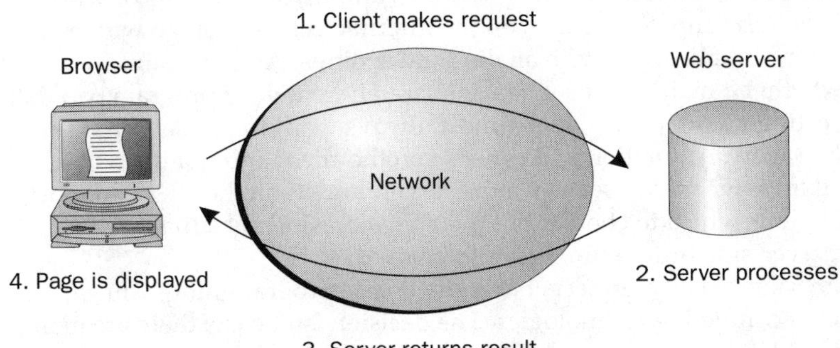

As introduced in the last chapter, thinking about the Web as a static medium is somewhat limiting, and does not enable you to take advantage of the potential for interactivity. The most basic form of interactivity on the Web, beyond link selection, is filling out a form to be processed by a program running on a Web server. The way a user interacts with a server-side program is relatively easy to describe. First, the user requests a dynamic page or fills out a form to perform a task, such as ordering a product. The request is sent to the Web server via HTTP (Hypertext Transfer Protocol), which runs a server-side program CGI program, that then outputs information (generally HTML or XHTML) to return to the Web browser. This process is shown here:

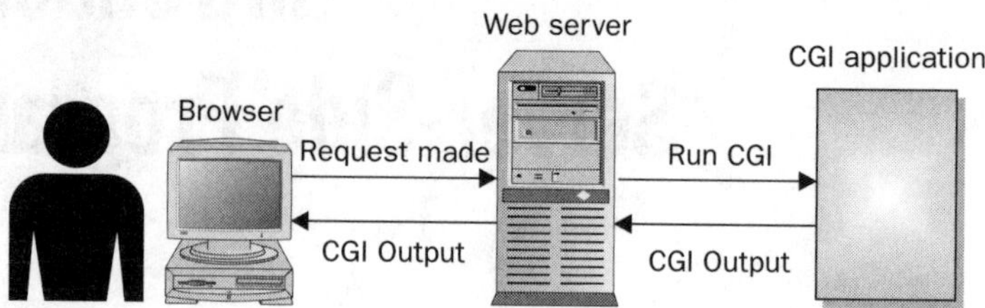

When described this way, the Web begins to look more and more like a client/server application environment.

Given the previous diagram, you might have two questions. First, where should the programming happen? And second, what technology should it use? On the early Web, the browser tended to do very little computing. It was responsible only for rendering pages on the screen. Now, with the rise of client-side technologies such as JavaScript, plug-ins, ActiveX, and Java applets, it is possible to perform a great deal of computation from within the browser. Put all the pressure on the server, and it may get bogged down, or the user may get frustrated with poor responsiveness. Yet doing most of the computing on the client side may result in compatibility problems given the wide range of browsers out there.

The best solution is a mixture: some things are better suited for the client while others are better suited for the server. For example, it makes sense to use a client-side scripting language such as JavaScript to check the contents of a form before it is submitted to a server-side program, rather than have the server-based program check the data and have to round-trip over the network just to deliver an error message. However, you still would want to check the data at the server side for users who are running older clients or who have turned off client-side scripting. Remember, on the Internet things often go wrong, and users don't always have the best browser with all the right settings. And, of course, you still would want to check whether a malicious user has deliberately sent your program bad data. Yet in the case of connecting to a database, you almost always want to use server-side technology to improve security. Animation makes sense on the client and not the server, while sending an e-mail message makes sense via the server more than the client. In most situations, it is pretty obvious which to choose, but there are occasionally situations in which both client and server-side programming could be used.

Now that we see the balance between server and client-side programming, you still must choose among many competing technologies. The decision isn't easy; there are many choices, as listed in Table 13-1.

TABLE 13-1 Web Programming Technology Choices

Client-Side	Server-Side
Helper programs	CGI programs
Browser objects Netscape plug-ins ActiveX cntrols Java applets	Web server API programs Apache modules Java servlets
Client-side scripting JavaScript VBScript	Server-side scripting Server-side Includes (.shtml) ASP or ASP.NET (.asp/.aspx) ColdFusion (.cfm/.cfmx) PHP (.php) Java Server Pages (.jsp)

What's interesting about the numerous technologies available for Web programming is that developers often focus too much on one technology or one side of the equation (client or server) rather than thinking about how the applications they are trying to build will work. This limited focus should be avoided at all costs, if possible, to ensure that you find the correct mix of technologies. This chapter looks at the server side of the equation; subsequent chapters focus on the client side.

Server-Side Programming

When adding interactivity to a Web page, it often makes sense to add a majority of the functionality on the server side unless the interactivity is purely client-side in nature, such as animation or user interface related issues. There are two basic reasons for doing this. First, the server side is the only part of the equation that can be completely controlled. If you only rely on the browser to render HTML pages, life is relatively simple. If you assume that users have JavaScript, Java, or a particular plug-in, things become less predictable. Given that most modern browsers come with many of these technologies, this might seem unlikely. However, the reality is that there are just too many variables and too many bugs. Users often turn off support for Java, JavaScript, or ActiveX due to fear of security breaches. Even when turned on, these technologies aren't as reliable as we might like. For example, JavaScript comes in numerous flavors, all with their own subtle and not-so-subtle differences, including feature disparity and bugs. It is no wonder we would want to move computation to the server, where these issues are more controllable.

While server-side computing provides safety and control, it relies greatly on server resources. In many Web sites, the server is required to do all the computation, from database access to building dynamic pages. In such a scenario, the browser is responsible for only basic page rendering and simple data collection tasks such as form entry. The downside to such heavy reliance on the server is that it is the critical part of the interactivity. If the server becomes overloaded or the network connection to the server is clogged, the result might be an unresponsive site and a disappointed user. Although control is gained with server-side programming, it is exchanged for speed and scalability.

For now, let's put the theory aside and turn our discussion to the various approaches to server-based interactivity. Let's start first with CGI programs and use them to explain the fundamentals of how any server-side technology interacts with a Web browser, markup, and related Web technologies.

Common Gateway Interface (CGI)

The oldest and still a very common way to add interactivity to a Web page is through a CGI program. *Common Gateway Interface* (CGI) is a protocol standard that specifies how information can be passed from a Web page through a Web server, to a program, and back from the program to a browser in the proper format. Unfortunately, many people confuse the actual program that does a particular task with the CGI protocol. In reality, the program is just a program. It just happens to be a CGI program because it was written to pass information back and forth using the CGI specification. Furthermore, CGI programs can be written in any language the server can execute; whereas Perl most commonly is associated with CGI, there is no reason that C, C++, Pascal, Visual Basic, or even FORTRAN couldn't be used to create a CGI program.

It is possible to create anything with CGI. Some common CGI applications include:

- Form processing
- Database access
- Security and authentication systems
- Browser-specific page delivery
- Banner ad serving
- Guest books
- Threaded discussion
- Games

Later on in the section, we'll take a look at how such programs can be built from scratch, or even downloaded from various Web sites for little or no cost. Regardless of how we end up obtaining our server-side programs, it is important to understand at least in general how they work.

Browser-Server Interaction Close-up

As an overview of how the browser and server exchange information, consider the various steps that happen when interacting with a user providing data through a form fill-out.

1. The user submits a form.
2. The form is sent to the server using HTTP and eventually to the CGI program using the following steps:
    a) The server determines whether the request is a document or program request by examining execution settings and path.

b) The server locates the program (often in the cgi-bin directory on the server) and determines if the program can be executed.

c) The server starts the program and sends the user submitted data and any extra information from the environment to the CGI program.

d) The program runs.

e) The server waits for the program to exit and potentially produce any output (optional).

3. The CGI program finishes processing data and responds to the server with a result or error message, although it may also send nothing back at all.
4. The Web server passes any response back to the browser via HTTP.
5. The browser reads the incoming data stream and determines how to render any returned data, usually by examining the MIME type found in the Content-type response header.

NOTE *Server launching of the program (Step 2c) is operating system–dependent and may require starting a new process, which could be slow, thus contributing to CGI's reputation for being slow.*

It appears that a key aspect of understanding how server-side programs like CGIs work is understanding how the HTTP protocol works.

Example HTTP Dialog

Web browsers and servers communicate using the Hypertext Transfer Protocol (HTTP), which is described thoroughly in Chapter 16. The protocol is a simple request response protocol in which a browser requests a resource from a server and the server responds with either an error message like a 404 or a success code and some data. To demonstrate this discussion, we can use a telnet program or other utility to manually talk to a Web server. To do this, use a telnet program to access a Web server and set the port number to 80, which is the default TCP port number for a Web server. In UNIX, Linux, or Max OS X–based systems, you can type at a command prompt:

```
telnet www.democompany.com 80
```

You could use a graphical telnet application such as the built-in one for Windows. Just make sure to set the port value to 80 in a similar fashion to the dialog shown here:

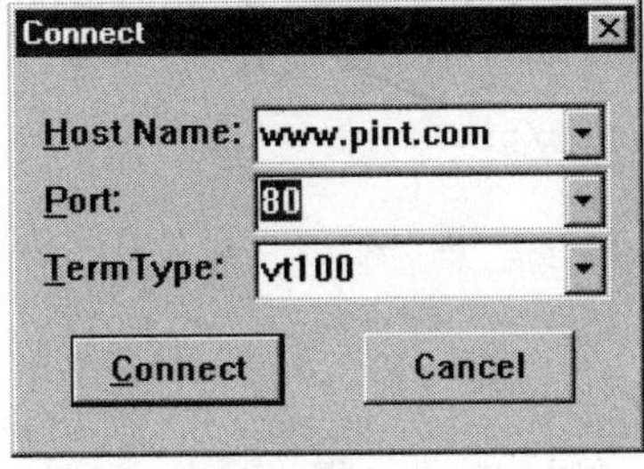

PART IV

In some Windows environments, you may have a command prompt instead, which would look something like this:

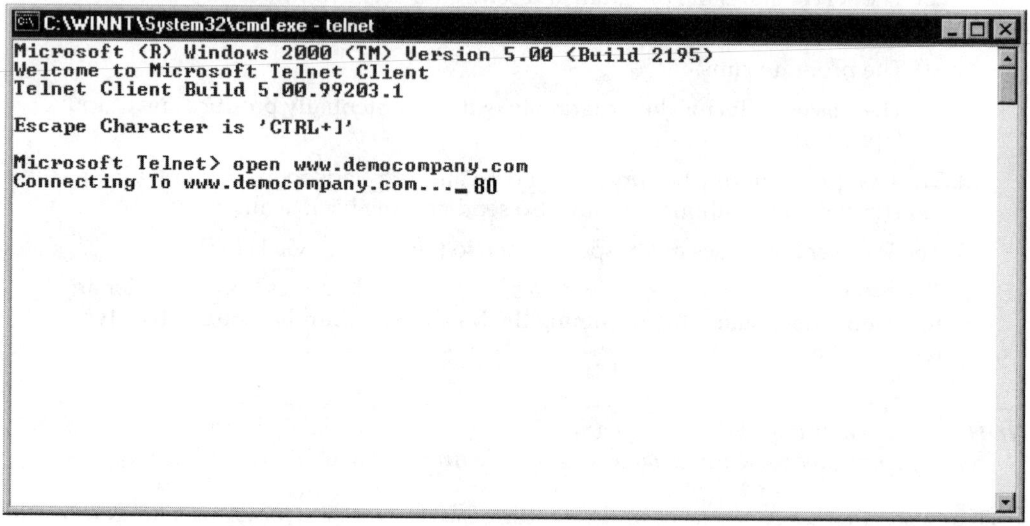

```
C:\WINNT\System32\cmd.exe - telnet
Microsoft (R) Windows 2000 (TM) Version 5.00 (Build 2195)
Welcome to Microsoft Telnet Client
Telnet Client Build 5.00.99203.1

Escape Character is 'CTRL+]'

Microsoft Telnet> open www.democompany.com
Connecting To www.democompany.com..._ 80
```

Once connected to the Web server you will get little feedback, but type in the proper HTTP request. A simple request would be

```
GET / HTTP/1.1
Host: www.democompany.com
```

Then press ENTER twice to send a blank line, without which the operation won't work.

Once the server processes the request, the result should look something like the listing shown here:

```
HTTP/1.1 200 OK
Server: Microsoft-IIS/5.0
Date: Sun, 06 Jul 2003 20:28:51 GMT
Content-type: text/html
Content-length: 1200

<!DOCTYPE html PUBLIC "-//W3C//DTD XHTML 1.0 Transitional//EN"
 "http://www.w3.org/TR/xhtml1/DTD/xhtml1-transitional.dtd">
<html xmlns="http://www.w3.org/1999/xhtml" lang="en">
<head>
<title>Sample XHTML Document</title>
</head>
<body>
...content...
</body>
```

If a Web browser were reading this data stream, it would read the **Content-type** line, and then determine what to do with the data. Browsers have a mapping that takes a MIME type and then determines what to do with it. Figure 13-1 shows the mapping file from Netscape Navigator.

Notice in the preceding code that the content type is **text/html**. This has the action of a browser, which would render the HTML within the browser window. Remember that Web servers can serve just about any type of data and pass that data to a plug-in or helper, or query the user to save the file.

NOTE *MIME stands for Multipurpose Internet Mail Extension and was originally developed to sort out the various multimedia enclosures that could occur in an e-mail message. However, today these content stamps are used for purposes well beyond e-mail and, as you have seen, are used to tell Web browsers what kind of data they are receiving so they can figure out how they might process it.*

CGI Output: MIME Types

Given that you now have seen the manual execution of an HTTP request, what is important to the Web browser? The simple answer is the MIME type and its associated data. In most cases, the pages being delivered are HTML-based, so the MIME type should be text/html. With this idea in mind, it should be easy to write a CGI program that generates an HTML page. To do this, you need to print out the MIME type indication **Content-type: text/html**, followed by the appropriate page markup and content.

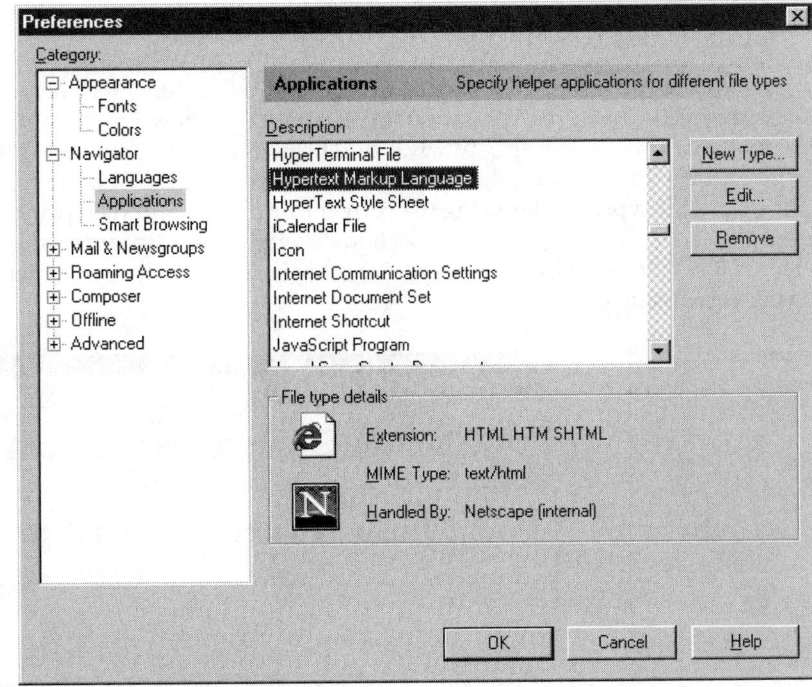

FIGURE 13-1 Sample MIME mapping dialog box under Netscape

NOTE *A significant debate rages about the use of* ***text/html*** *versus the more standards oriented* ***application/xhtml+xml***, ***text/xml*** *or* ***application/xml*** *MIME types, particularly when the content is server-generated. Given the inconsistent support by browsers at the time of this edition's writing, it is still the best idea to stick with MIME types of just text/html. Let's hope this changes soon, but for now better safe than sorry.*

The following small Perl program shows how this might be done; any language, including C, Pascal, or BASIC, could also be used to create such an example:

```
#!/usr/bin/perl
# Note the path to Perl may vary.
#
print "Content-type: text/html\n\n";

print "<html>\n<head><title>From CGI</title></head>\n";
print "<body>\n<h1>\n";
print "Wow! I was created by a CGI program!!";
print "</h1>\n </body>\n</html>";
```

Notice in the preceding example that it is very important to note the two line feeds in the first print statement. The blank line after the content-type line indicates the program is done sending headers and without the two returns the example will not work. The Web server itself will take care of sending any appropriate response codes and other headers.

NOTE *The other newline characters* ***\n*** *are used primarily for formatting. If you view source on the resulting page generated by the CGI script, you will see many of the newlines are just used to make the markup halfway readable.*

If this example were typed and set to run on a Perl-capable Web server, it could be accessed directly by a user to print out the simple page shown in Figure 13-2. To see the program in action, go to http://www.htmlref.com/examples/chapter13/firstcgi.cgi.

To create a document on the fly, you have to print a group of headers with special focus on the **Content-type:** header using the correct MIME type and then print out the tags and content that compose the page. This section covered returning information from the server, which is just half of the CGI equation. The following section discusses getting information to your server-side program.

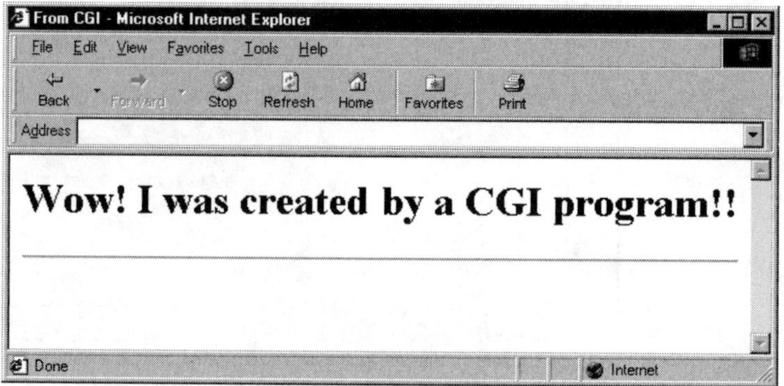

FIGURE 13-2 Output of simple CGI program

CGI Input: Environment Variables

While the primary way to get information to a server-side program like CGI is to use a form, there is also useful information that can be garnered from the environment in which the transaction took place. An example of this information called *environment variables* includes the type of browser making the request, the time of day, the language being used, and so on. This information can be particularly useful for a server-side program to decide what kind of pages to prepare for a visitor. A list of the most common environment variables is provided in Table 13-2.

Variable Name	Description
SERVER_NAME	The domain name or IP address of the Web server running the CGI program.
SERVER_SOFTWARE	Information about the Web server, typically the name and version number of the software; for example, Netscape-Commerce/1.12.
SERVER_PROTOCOL	The version number of the HTTP protocol being used in the request; for example, HTTP/1.1.
SERVER_PORT	The port on which the Web server is running, typically 80.
REQUEST_METHOD	The method by which the information is being passed, either in **GET** or **POST**.
CONTENT_TYPE	For queries that have attached information, because they use the **POST** or **PUT** method; contains the content type of the passed data in MIME format.
CONTENT_LENGTH	The length of any passed content (**POST** or **PUT**) as given by the client, typically as length in bytes.
PATH_INFO	Any extra path information passed in with the file request. This usually would be associated with the **GET** request.
SCRIPT_NAME	The relative path to the script that is running.
QUERY_STRING	Query information passed to the program.
DOCUMENT_ROOT	The document root of the Web server.
REMOTE_USER	If the server supports user authentication and the script is protected, this variable holds the user name that the user has authenticated.
AUTH_TYPE	This variable is set to the authentication method used to validate the user if the script being run is protected.
REMOTE_IDENT	If the Web server supports RFC 931–based identification, this variable will be set to the remote user name retrieved from the server. This is rarely used.
REMOTE_HOST	The remote host name of the browser passing information to the server; for example, sun1.bigcompany.com.

TABLE 13-2 Common CGI Variables

Variable Name	Description
REMOTE_ADDR	The IP address of the browser making the request.
HTTP_ACCEPT	A list of MIME types the browser can accept. Modern browsers may send ratings indicating the preferred type of content desired.
HTTP_ACCEPT_ENCODING	Indicates the forms of compression the browser can handle, if any.
HTTP_ACCEPT_LANGUAGE	Indicates the type of spoken language the browser is set to by default.
HTTP_USER_AGENT	A code indicating the type of browser making the request.
HTTP_REFERER	The URL of the linking document (the document that is linked to the CGI being run). If the user types in the address of the program directly, the **HTTP_REFERER** value will be unset.

TABLE 13-2 Common CGI Variables *(continued)*

Figure 13-3 shows the results of a CGI program that prints out the environment information. Try to execute the program at http://www.htmlref.com/examples/chapter13/printenv.cgi to see if the results are different.

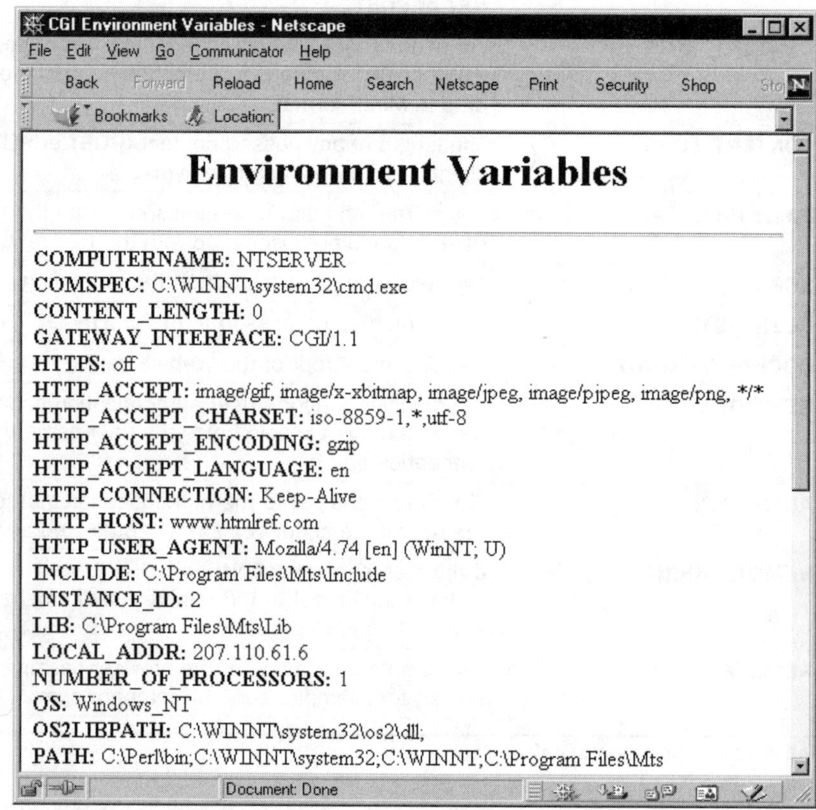

FIGURE 13-3 CGI environment variables example

The following is the Perl code for the result in Figure 13-3:

```
#!/usr/bin/perl

&print_HTTP_header;
&print_head;
&print_body;
&print_tail;

# print the HTTP Content-type header

sub print_HTTP_header {
    print "Content-type: text/html\n\n";
}

#Print the start of the HTML file

sub print_head {
    print <<END;

<!DOCTYPE html PUBLIC "-//W3C//DTD XHTML 1.0 Transitional//EN"
 "http://www.w3.org/TR/xhtml1/DTD/xhtml1-transitional.dtd">
<html xmlns="http://www.w3.org/1999/xhtml" lang="en">
<head>
<title>CGI Environment Variables</title>
<meta http-equiv="content-type" content="text/html; charset=ISO-8859-1" />
</head>

<body>
<h1 align="center">Environment Variables</h1>
<hr />
END
}

#Loop through the environment variable

#associative array and print out its values.

sub print_body {
    foreach $variable (sort keys %ENV) {
        print "<b>$variable:</b> $ENV{$variable}<br />\n";
    }

}

#Print the close of the HTML file

sub print_tail {
        print <<END;
</body>
</html>
END
}
```

Notice that the code is written to make the printing of the appropriate headers, the start of the HTML file, the results, and the close of the file more straightforward. Fortunately, code libraries, which do much of the work of CGI, are commonly available.

CGI Input: Form Data

Forms are a good way to collect user input such as survey results or comments. They also can start database queries or launch programs. Creating forms was discussed in the previous chapter. For a quick refresher on form syntax, take a look at the following example:

```
<!DOCTYPE html PUBLIC "-//W3C//DTD XHTML 1.0 Transitional//EN"
 "http://www.w3.org/TR/xhtml1/DTD/xhtml1-transitional.dtd">
<html xmlns="http://www.w3.org/1999/xhtml" lang="en">
<head>
<title>Meet and Greet</title>
<meta http-equiv="content-type" content="text/html; charset=ISO-8859-1" />
</head>
<body>
<h1 align="center">Welcome to CGI!</h1>
<hr />

<form method="post" action="http://www.htmlref.com/cgi-bin/hello.pl">
<b>What's your name?</b>
<input type="text" name="username" size="25" />
<input type="submit" value="Hi I am..." />
</form>

</body>
</html>
```

The previous example will greet the user by whatever name he or she types in. The example can be found at http://www.htmlref.com/examples/chapter13/postwelcome.html.

The **<form>** tag is the key to this example because it has an action to perform (as indicated by the **action** attribute when the form is submitted). The action is to launch a CGI program indicated by the URL value of the **action** attribute; in this case, www.htmlref.com/cgi-bin/hello.pl. The **<form>** tag has another attribute, **method**, which indicates how information will be passed to the receiving CGI program; in this case, **post**. Recall from the previous chapter that there are two basic methods to pass data in through a form: **get** and **post**. To see the preceding example in action using **get** instead of **post**, view http://www.htmlref.com/examples/chapter13/getwelcome.html. The **get** method appends information on the end of the submitting URL, so the URL accessed through getwelcome.html might be something like this:

```
http://www.htmlref.com/cgi-bin/hello.pl?username=Joe+Smith
```

The data sent will be encoded; the string might have all spaces turned into + signs, and special characters might be encoded as *%nn* hex character values. The various form element names will be sent to the CGI program as name/value pairs such as **username=Joe** separated by ampersands. For example, if the previous example had other fields in the form named **age** and **sex**, you might see a **get** query string like the following:

```
http://www.htmlref.com/cgi-bin/hello.pl?username=Joe+Smith&
age=32&sex=male
```

Submitting data with the **get** method does have drawbacks. First, you are limited to the amount of data that can be submitted. A limit of either 1,024 or 2,048 bytes is commonly encountered with query strings in URLs. Also, because request strings from a **get** method are simply URLs, they are often open to easy manipulation by the curious or malicious user. Finally, they don't look terribly user-friendly.

However, the **get** method does have its advantages. First, it is easy to understand and experiment with. Second, it provides the possibility for canned queries because the value of fields can be placed in the URL itself. This allows the query to be linked to via a URL. It's also very important to note that because you are storing data in the URL, **get** queries can be bookmarked, unlike posted data.

In contrast to the data-limited **get** method is the **post** method, which sends the form data to the server as a separate data stream following the request. This data stream consists of many lines, such as **username=Joe%20Smith**, that are the various name value pairs created by the form entry made by the user. If you look at posted data, you'll observe it is encoded in pretty much the same manner as a **get** request. However, data sent using **post** can be much larger than what is allowed in a **get** request, although it is not possible to bookmark a **post** request. The common "Repost form data?" message from a browser is the result of not being able to easily save posted data.

Regardless of the method used to send data, once received by the server-side program, the information needs to be parsed for later processing. Given the simplicity of how form data is encoded, a skilled programmer easily could determine how to parse data and access the values. However, instead of doing that work ourselves, we might instead rely on a CGI library (like cgi-lib.pl). The following code is a simple example that we have been using to echo back the form data sent in from the user. Notice that the reading and splitting of the data submitted requires only the statement &ReadParse.

```
#! /usr/bin/perl

require ("cgi-lib.pl");

&ReadParse;
$name = $in{"username"};

print "Content-type: text/html\n\n";

print "<html><head><title>";
print "Hello from CGI</title></head><body>";
print "<h1>Hello $name!</h1> <br/>";
print "</body></html>";
```

The preceding examples might seem to suggest that writing CGI programs is trivial. This is true if data is only to be read in and written out. In fact, this part of CGI is so mechanical that page designers are discouraged from attempting to parse the data themselves. There are many scripting libraries available for Perl. These include cgic (http://www.boutell.com/cgic/) for ANSI C programs, cgi++ (http://www.webthing.com/cgiplusplus/) for C++, the CGI module (http://www.python.org/doc/lib/module-cgi.html)

for Python, and CGI.pm (http://stein.cshl.org/WWW/software/CGI/cgi_docs.html) for Perl. These libraries, and others available on the Internet, make the reading of environment variables and parsing of encoded form data a simple process. However, you'll see later in the chapter that it is even easier in a server-side scripting language such as PHP.

The difficult part of CGI isn't the input and output of data; it's the logic of the code itself. Given that the CGI program can be written in nearly any language, Web programmers might wonder what language to use. Performance and ease of string handling are important criteria for selecting a language for CGI programming. Performance-wise, compiled CGI programs typically will have better performance than interpreted programs written in a scripting language such as Perl. However, it probably is easier to write a simple CGI program in a scripting language such as Perl and then use a form of compiled Perl or the mod_perl module to get most of the performance gains of compilation with the ease of a scripting language.

Some programming languages might have better interfaces to Web servers and HTTP than others. For example, Perl has a great number of CGI libraries and operating system facilities readily available. Because much of CGI is about reading and writing text data, ease of string handling also might be a big consideration in selecting the language. The bottom line is that the choice of scripting language mainly depends on the server the script must run on and the programmer's preference. It is even possible to use an old version of FORTRAN or some obscure language to write a CGI program, although it would be easier to pick a language that works well with the Web server and use it to access some other program. CGI lives up to its name as a gateway.

Table 13-3 lists the common languages for CGI coding based on the Web server's operating system. Notice that Perl is common to most of the platforms, due to its ease of use and long-standing use on the Web.

NOTE *Writing CGI programs in a UNIX shell scripting language such as csh, ksh or sh can pose serious security risks and should be avoided.*

Don't rush around getting ready to code your own form handlers. Consider how many other people in the world need to access a database or e-mail a form. Given these common needs, it might be better to borrow or buy a canned CGI solution than to build a new one.

Buying or Borrowing CGI Programs

Most CGI programs are similar to one another. There are many shareware, freeware, and commercial packages available to do most of the common Web tasks. Matt's Script Archive (www.scriptarchive.com) and the CGI Resource Index (www.cgi-resources.com) are good

Web Server Operating System	Common CGI Languages
UNIX	Perl, C, C++, Java, Shell script languages (csh, ksh, sh), Python
Windows	Visual Basic, C, C++, Perl, Python
Macintosh	AppleScript, Perl, C, C++, Python

TABLE 13-3 Common CGI Language Choices

places to start looking for these. There are many scripts for form parsing, bulletin boards, counters, and countless other things available free of charge on the Internet. There are also compiled commercial CGI programs made to perform a particular task. Site developers are urged to consider the cost of developing custom solutions versus buying canned solutions, particularly when time is an important consideration in building the site.

Server Modules: Apache Modules, ISAPI, and Others

One serious problem with CGI programs is performance. There are two reasons that CGI programs can be slow. First of all, the launch of the CGI program by the Web server can itself be slow. Then, once launched, the program might run relatively slowly because it is written in an interpreted language such as Perl. Solving the second problem is easy: simply rewrite the program in a compiled language such as C. Performance should quickly improve. What about the launch problem? One approach would be to pre-launch the main CGI program so that it is running all the time, and have smaller CGI programs launch when needed. Although this would help, the server still would have to communicate with an external program, which does incur a performance penalty because the operating system must switch between programs.

If speed is really an all-consuming issue, it would be best for the CGI to be native to the Web server itself. This is the idea behind a Web server API module. The basic idea is that the server-side program is written to be a component of a Web server. There are many types of server modules and they are typically associated with a particular server. For example, on the Microsoft Web server IIS, Internet Server Application Programming Interface (ISAPI) programs can be written to extend the server. On the older Netscape server, NSAPI programs could be written. Apache servers have Apache modules. Servers with Java capability would use Java servlets, and so on. Collectively, we will refer to these server programs simply as server modules.

A server module is an extension for a particular Web server that is typically written in C or C++ and conforms to a particular server application programming interface (API). Obviously, given the various server-specific details and the need for a language like C or C++, writing a server module is much more difficult than writing a simple CGI program. There are other drawbacks as well. For example, a misbehaving server module can bring a whole server down. Developers who write a server module–based solution also might be stuck using a particular server platform, whereas CGI programs generally are portable from server to server. Regardless of their drawbacks, server modules have the advantage of speed and the capability to share data across sessions and users very easily. With this power, many third-party developers have created server extensions to extend a Web server. A list of Apache modules can be found at http://modules.apache.org/, while ISAPI filters and extensions can be found at http://www.iismodules.com.

Although most developers are about as likely to write custom server modules as they are to write browser plug-ins, the technology has enabled the creation of server-side scripting technology, which is useful to almost every Web page developer.

Server-Side Scripting

CGI and server modules can be complex; however, adding interactivity to a site does not always have to be difficult. Another form of server-based programming, generically termed *server-side scripting*, provides much of the sophistication of general CGI with the ease of HTML. The idea of server-side scripts is simple. First, create a page using standard HTML or XHTML. Then, add special new elements or code directives to indicate what to do in particular cases. For example, imagine if you wanted to print out different markup for Netscape users, Microsoft Internet Explorer, and other browser users. You could add some logic to your HTML/XHTML document like this:

```
$if browser = Netscape
     <blink>Hey Netscape User!</blink>
$else if browser = IE
      <marquee>Hello Microsoft User!</marquee>
$else
      <h1>Hello User!</h1>
$endif
```

To indicate that the file includes a server-side script that needs to be executed before delivery, you would name it with some special extension indicating the type of language (for example, .php, .cfm, .asp). Finally, when the user requests the page, the server will then parse the page and output only the appropriate markup depending on the particular browser being used. This, of course, is a completely fictitious server-side scripting language but it serves to illustrate how all of them fundamentally work. An overview of server-parsed script solutions is shown in Figure 13-4.

Although server-side scripts are very easy for people to deal with, they can put a significant load on the server and might be unnecessarily parsed over and over again. The next few sections describe a few common parsed HTML technologies used on the Web: server-side includes (SSI), PHP, ColdFusion, and Active Server Pages (ASP).

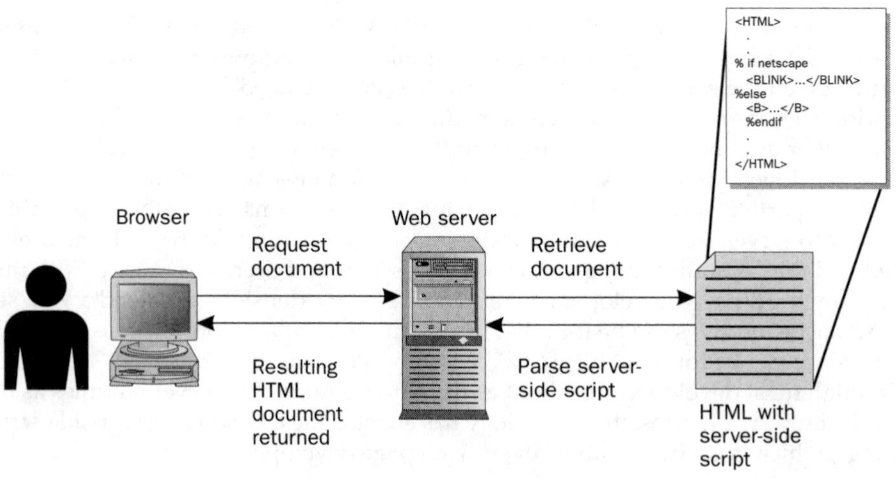

FIGURE 13-4 Overview of parsed HTML solutions

Server-Side Includes (SSI)

Server-side includes (SSI) are the simplest form of parsed HTML. SSIs are short directives you can embed in an HTML document to indicate files to be read and included in the final output. This might be useful if the designer wants to make one file with footer information, such as an address and copyright, and then append it to all pages dynamically. To do this, create a file called footer.html and then include it dynamically using SSI. The contents of footer.html might look something like this:

```
<hr noshade="noshade" />
<div align="center">
<font size="-1">
Copyright 2003, Demo Company Inc.<br />
</font>
</div>
```

To include this file in another file, you would need an SSI directive like this:

```
<!--#include file="footer.html" -->
```

Notice that this is just a special form of an HTML comment with a command **#include** and a parameter file, which is set to the file you want to include. To indicate to the server that the page contains SSI commands, use the .shtml extension. If the server is properly configured, it should pick up the file and execute it before sending the result. Aside from including external files, SSI also can be used to show the results of programs, including CGI programs. Thus, it can provide a way to query databases and make a page counter, among other things.

While SSI looks appealing, it has two potential problems: security and performance. The security problem results from SSI's capability to easily execute a program on the server. With this feature, security breaches are possible. For example, it might be possible to insert a command to launch a remote session. Even if security isn't a big issue, depending on how SSI and the Web server are configured, the executing command could have a great deal of permissions and be able to remove values. Web administrators are advised to limit use of scripting with SSI.

The other problem with SSI, performance, is typical of any server-parsed scripting solution. Because all SSI files have to be parsed, they can cause a performance hit. If a site has serious performance requirements, SSI-driven pages might be inappropriate. Fortunately, it is possible to limit its uses by having only certain files, for example those ending in .shtml, parsed by the server. When used in a limited fashion, SSI can provide powerful features that are within the technical ability of any HTML writer. However, SSI is limited in what it can do. Page designers might find other server-side scripting solutions, such as PHP, ColdFusion, or ASP, more appropriate.

TIP *Nearly every Web server should have SSI capability directly, but it is often not enabled by default. For more information on enabling SSI, see your Web server software's documentation.*

PHP

PHP (www.php.net) is a very powerful and easy-to-use open source server-side scripting environment. While initially developed for the Linux/UNIX community, PHP can also be found on Windows server platforms. The reason for the widespread adoption of PHP is the simplicity of the language. For example, consider the simplest "hello world" example here:

```
<!DOCTYPE html PUBLIC "-//W3C//DTD XHTML 1.0 Transitional//EN"
 "http://www.w3.org/TR/xhtml1/DTD/xhtml1-transitional.dtd">
<html xmlns="http://www.w3.org/1999/xhtml" lang="en">
<head>
<title>PHP Hello World</title>
<meta http-equiv="content-type" content="text/html; charset=ISO-8859-1" />
</head>
<body>
<?php
  print("Hello world from PHP!");
?>
</body>
</html>
```

In this example, the PHP code is delimited by **<?php** and **?>**. The code simply outputs the text "Hello world from PHP!". If the file was saved as hello.php and uploaded to a PHP aware server, it would execute when requested, resulting in a seemingly static HTML page. This example can be found at http://www.htmlref.com/examples/chapter13/helloworld.php.

Obviously, you might like to do something a little more complicated than the previous example to get the flavor of PHP. Consider the form echo example presented earlier in the chapter; you could use that form but have it post to a PHP program (sayhello.php) instead, as shown here:

```
<form method="post"
 action="http://www.htmlref.com/examples/chapter13/sayhello.php">
<b>What's your name?</b>
<input type="text" name="username" size="25" />
<input type="submit" value="Hi I am..." />
</form>
```

The PHP template (sayhello.php) to handle the form would simply be as follows:

```
<!DOCTYPE html PUBLIC "-//W3C//DTD XHTML 1.0 Transitional//EN"
 "http://www.w3.org/TR/xhtml1/DTD/xhtml1-transitional.dtd">
<html xmlns="http://www.w3.org/1999/xhtml" lang="en">
<head>
<title>Hello from PHP</title>
<meta http-equiv="content-type" content="text/html; charset=ISO-8859-1" />
</head>
<body>
<h1 align="center">Hello from PHP!</h1>
<hr />
<h1>Hello
<?php
print($POST["username"])
```

```
?>
</h1>
</body>
</html>
```

This example is even simpler than the CGI program using a library, and all that was necessary was to print out the posted value from the previous form by referencing the **$_POST** variables array. Setting your PHP installation to allow global variables you might even avoid that and simply have **print($username)**. It should be obvious that the beauty of PHP is its simplicity. It also seems easier for those comfortable with markup to put code in their markup rather than markup in their code as in the case of Perl or other technologies. As an example of script in markup or markup in script, compare the earlier example to print environment variables in Perl with a much shorter and cleaner version in PHP:

```
<!DOCTYPE html PUBLIC "-//W3C//DTD XHTML 1.0 Transitional//EN"
 "http://www.w3.org/TR/xhtml1/DTD/xhtml1-transitional.dtd">
<html xmlns="http://www.w3.org/1999/xhtml" lang="en">
<head>
<title>PHP Hello World</title>
<meta http-equiv="content-type" content="text/html; charset=ISO-8859-1" />
</head>
<body>
<?php

 echo "<b>Environment Variables from \$HTTP_ENV_VARS</b><br /><br />";
 reset($HTTP_ENV_VARS);
 while (list ($key, $val) = each ($HTTP_ENV_VARS))
  {
   print $key . " = " . $val . "<br />";
  }
?>
</body>
</html>
```

While offering only a taste of PHP, this discussion should convince readers to visit a site such as http://php.resourceindex.com/ or the primary site www.php.net to find out more information about this popular server-side scripting technology.

TIP *On Linux distributions with Apache, PHP may be preinstalled; otherwise, you will most likely have to install, or at the least enable, a PHP module on your Web server. See www.php.net for information on how to download and install PHP for your Web server.*

ColdFusion

Another popular server-scripting solution is Macromedia's ColdFusion (www.macromedia.com). Like PHP, ColdFusion focuses on helping developers build dynamic, database-driven Web site applications with an easy-to-use, server-side markup language similar to HTML. Getting started with ColdFusion requires learning a few new markup tags that look like HTML but make up what is called ColdFusion Markup Language (CFML). Because one of its primary functions is database access, ColdFusion uses the Open Database

Connectivity (ODBC) standard to connect to popular database servers such as Microsoft SQL Server, Access, Sybase, Oracle, and others. ColdFusion is not dependent on a particular database or Web server, and it works well on a variety of Windows-based servers as well as Solaris and Linux. While ColdFusion is not open source nor a W3C-defined standard, it is widely used. It is presented here to illustrate another example of parsed HTML and demonstrate a simple database-driven page.

Like PHP, Web applications built with ColdFusion use dynamic pages composed of a mixture of code and HTML markup, but in the case of ColdFusion, the code is represented in tags. When the page is requested, the ColdFusion application running on the server preprocesses the page, interacts with a database or other server-side technologies, and returns a dynamically generated HTML page. It probably is better to refer to ColdFusion-enabled pages as templates because the actual page output varies.

The following discusses how to use CFML to select and output data in a dynamic Web page. This section shows how to use a number of CFML tags to query data from a database, take the results of the query, and populate a Web page.

A database is simply a collection of data that is organized in a regular fashion, typically in the form of a table. Imagine you want to create a Web site to post the various job openings in your company. The first thing you need to do is decide what information is relevant: position number, job title, location, brief job description, hiring manager, and posting date. This information could be organized in the form of a database table, called Positions, as shown in Table 13-4.

The example is populated with some simple data, but how can the data be retrieved to be displayed in a Web page automatically?

PositionNum	JobTitle	Location	Description	Hiring Manager	PostDate
343	Gadget Sales	Austin	This position requires an aggressive salesperson to sell gadgets to guys and gals.	M. Spacely	01/20/00
525	Office Manager	San Jose	Responsible for running the entire office single-handedly.	P. Mohta	01/24/00
2585	President	San Diego	Figurehead position, requires daily golf games and nightly poker parties.	T. Powell	01/30/00
3950	Groundskeeper	San Diego	Must like outdoor work and long hours in the sun with no sunscreen.	J. Tam	01/30/00
1275	HTML Hacker	Seattle	Must be able to recite HTML specifications by heart and code HTML by hand. Long hours, low pay.	D. Whitworth	01/27/00
2015	Game Tester	Los Angeles	Must be able to play games all day long; poor posture and junk food diet essential.	J. Daffyd	01/18/00

TABLE 13-4 Simple Database Table Called "Positions"

The first step is to define a database query using Structured Query Language (SQL). SQL is the language used to retrieve or modify data from the tables in a database. The language is relatively simple, at least as far as mastering the basics. If you were interested in making a query to the database table called Positions, you would use a SQL statement like this:

```
SELECT * FROM Positions
```

This query simply says to select all items indicated by the wildcard (*) in the table called Positions. If you want only to list all the positions in Austin, you could qualify the query by adding a **WHERE** modifier, indicating you only want entries for which the location is Austin.

```
SELECT * FROM Positions WHERE Location="Austin"
```

Using the **WHERE** modifier, it is possible to create complex queries. For example, you could query all jobs in Austin, or in Los Angeles, where the position is Game Tester:

```
SELECT *
      FROM Positions
      WHERE ((Location="Austin" OR
             (Location="Los Angeles") AND
             (Position="Game Tester"))
```

This brief discussion should reveal the flavor of SQL. Although the basic language is simple, queries can be more complicated. A full discussion of SQL is well beyond the scope of this book. For the sake of this discussion, only simple queries are used in the examples.

To pull data out of the database, write a SQL query, and then place it within a **<CFQUERY>** element. The following example illustrates the use of **<CFQUERY>**. A select SQL query called **ListJobs**, as specified by the **NAME** attribute, will query a database and retrieve all the records in the Positions table. The syntax for this example is shown here:

```
<CFQUERY NAME="ListJobs"
         DATASOURCE="CompanyDataBase">
SELECT * FROM Positions
</CFQUERY>
```

Notice that the **DATASOURCE** attribute is set equal to CompanyDataBase, which is the ODBC data source that contains a database called Company, which contains the Positions table from which data is pulled.

NOTE *Open Database Connectivity (ODBC) is a standardized way to access data from a variety of different databases. ODBC provides a layer of abstraction that protects the developer from having to learn the particulars of a specific database system. To query the Positions table, your server might connect to a simple Microsoft Access database or a powerful Oracle system. To access a database, a developer needs to set up an ODBC data source. This requires that developer to select an ODBC driver, name the data source, and configure any specific settings for the database. A complete discussion of how to set up ODBC drivers and configure data sources can be found in the documentation for ColdFusion.*

Aside from **NAME** and **DATASOURCE**, the **<CFQUERY>** element has a variety of attributes, but these are all that are necessary for most simple queries.

Using the **<CFOUTPUT>** tag, it is possible to display the data retrieved from a previously defined **<CFQUERY>** tag. For example, in order to output the query called ListJobs, you would use a code fragment, as shown here:

```
<CFOUTPUT QUERY="ListJobs">

      <hr noshade="noshade"><br />
      Position Number: #PositionNum#<br /><br />
      Title: #JobTitle#<br /><br />
      Location: #Location#<br /><br />
      Description: #Description#

</CFOUTPUT>
```

Notice the use of the # symbols throughout this code fragment. These values are used to delimit the areas in which you wish to place the data from the database. For example, **#PositionNum#** will be populated with data from the column **PositionNum**, while **#JobTitle#** will get the values for the **JobTitle** column in the database. Notice also that normal HTML markup can be used within the query.

By putting both the **<CFQUERY>** and the **<CFOUTPUT>** tags together in a complete CFML template file, which you could call listjobs.cfm, and putting this on a server that understands ColdFusion, you could create a dynamically generated page. The following is a complete example showing the two primary ColdFusion elements:

```
<!DOCTYPE html PUBLIC "-//W3C//DTD XHTML 1.0 Transitional//EN"
 "http://www.w3.org/TR/xhtml1/DTD/xhtml1-transitional.dtd">
<html xmlns="http://www.w3.org/1999/xhtml" lang="en">

<!-- SQL statement to select jobs available from the database-->
<CFQUERY NAME="ListJobs" DATASOURCE="CompanyDataBase">
SELECT * from Positions
</CFQUERY>

<head>
<title>Demo Company Job Listings</title>
<meta http-equiv="content-type" content="text/html; charset=ISO-8859-1" />
</head>
<body>
<h2 align="center">Job Listings</h2>
<hr />
<CFOUTPUT QUERY="ListJobs">
      <hr noshade="noshade"><br />
      Position Number: #PositionNum#<br /><br />
      Title: #JobTitle#<br /><br />
      Location: #Location#<br /><br />
      Description: #Description#
</CFOUTPUT>
```

```
<hr />

<address>
Demo Company, Inc. &copy; 2003
</address>
</body>
</html>
```

Figure 13-5 shows a ColdFusion dynamically generated page under Netscape. Of course, like any server-side language, there are generally no browser-side requirements. In other words, this application would work equally well under Internet Explorer, Lynx, MSN TV, or any other browser.

The preceding discussion is just a sample of what ColdFusion can do. It is meant only to illustrate what a server-side HTML language can do. For more detailed information on the

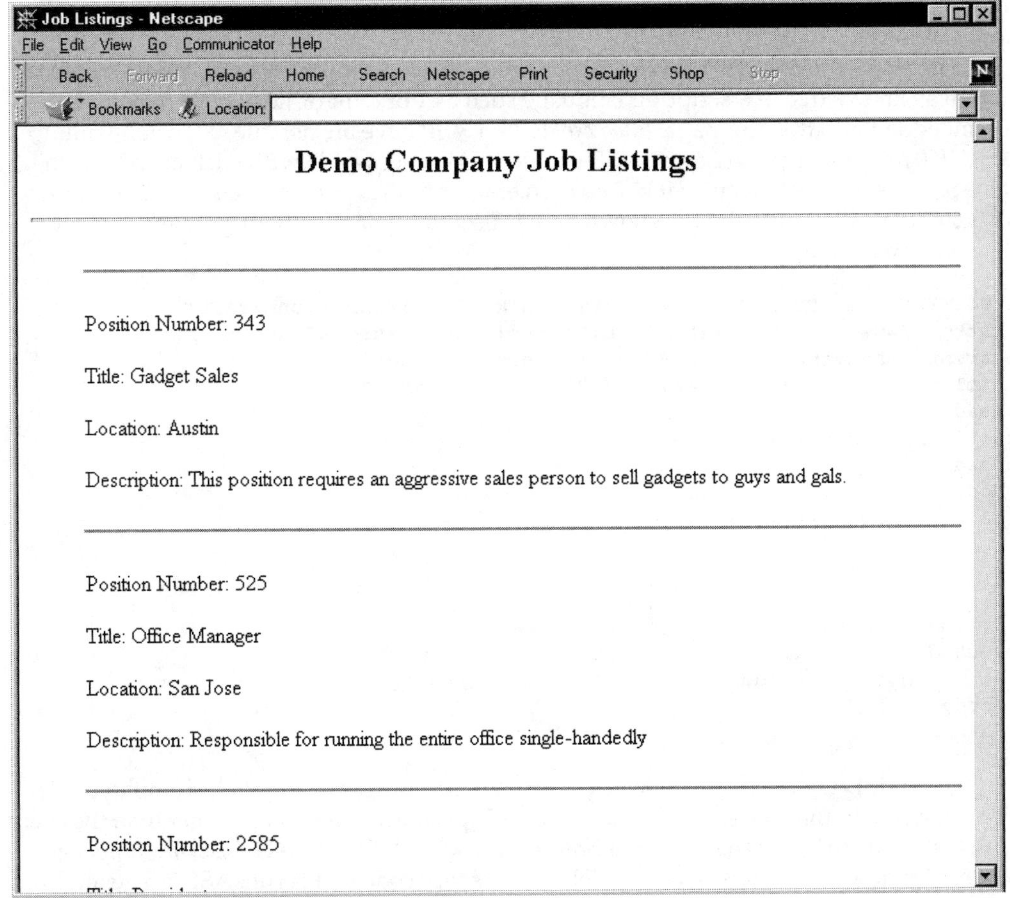

FIGURE 13-5 ColdFusion output under Netscape

syntax of ColdFusion, as well as examples of its use, see the ColdFusion Language Reference at Macromedia (www.macromedia.com/software/coldfusion). Whereas ColdFusion seems somewhat specific to database access, there are other server-side parsed HTML solutions, such as Microsoft's ASP, which might appear to provide more general functionality.

Active Server Pages (ASP) and ASP.NET

Microsoft's ASP is a server-side scripting environment primarily for the Microsoft Internet Information Server (IIS) Web server. A newer version called ASP.NET brings even more power to ASP programmers but with significantly more complexity. With either ASP or ASP.NET, it is possible to combine HTML, scripting code, and server-side ActiveX components to create dynamic Web applications. The ability to write scripts in standard scripting languages such as VBScript, JavaScript, or other scripting languages such as Perl, enables developers to create applications with almost any type of functionality. This makes the ASP/ASP.NET approach to server-side scripting very generalized for a broad range of applications.

To get started using ASP, the developer needs to have a working knowledge of HTML, as well as knowledge of a scripting language such as VBScript or JavaScript, which will be embedded into the ASP page. Files created for ASP have an .asp file extension while ASP.NET files use .aspx. When an ASP-enabled server sees a file with such an extension, the ASP-aware server executes it before delivering it to the user. For example, the simple VBScript embedded into the file shown here is used to dynamically display the current date on a Web page:

```
<!DOCTYPE html PUBLIC "-//W3C//DTD XHTML 1.0 Transitional//EN"
 "http://www.w3.org/TR/xhtml1/DTD/xhtml1-transitional.dtd">
<script language="VBScript" runat="Server"></script>
<html xmlns="http://www.w3.org/1999/xhtml" lang="en">
<head>
<title>ASP Example</title>
</head>
<body>
<h1>Breaking News</h1>

<% = date() %>

<p>Today the stock of a major software company
reached an all time high, making the Demo Company CEO
the world's first and only trillionaire.</p>
</body>
</html>
```

The **<script>** tag is used to indicate the primary scripting language being employed. This element also tells the Web server to execute the script code on the server rather than the client with the **runat** attribute. This can be abbreviated as **<%@ LANGUAGE=*<script_language>* %>**. Notice how the <% %> is used to delimit the script code that is run. ASP is a generalized technology that can use nearly any scripting language and objects the developer may want. Think of ASP as more of a framework than a language like PHP or ColdFusion.

As a more meaningful example of ASP, let's look at database access similar to the previous ColdFusion example. As in the previous example, let's access the Positions database described earlier in the chapter. The first step in this example is to create an instance of the database component by adding the following line to an ASP file, which might be named example.asp:

```
<object runat="Server" id="Conn" progid="ADODB.Connection">
</object>
```

or more appropriately, just use a simple statement like the following:

```
<%
Set Conn = Server.CreateObject("ADODB.Connection")
%>
```

This statement creates an instance of a database access object called **Conn** that can be used with a server-side script.

Later on, the file will open a connection to the database and execute a SQL command to select job positions and return a set of records. The small code fragment shown next does this. The code is enclosed within <% and %> so that the server knows to execute this rather than display it on the screen:

```
<%
     Conn.Open ODBCPositions
     SQL = "SELECT * FROM Positions"
     SET RS = Conn.Execute(SQL)
     Do While Not RS.EOF
%>
```

The code between the <% %> statements is VBScript, which is interpreted by the Web server when this page is requested. The Do While statement is a standard VBScript looping statement, which is used here to loop through the record set until an end of file (EOF) marker is reached, signifying the end of the records. While looping through each record, the output is displayed in the context of regular HTML code, such as displaying the Job Department field in a table cell:

```
<td>
<% = RS("JobDepartment") %>
</td>
```

Putting all of this together in a file called example.asp provides a complete ASP database access example:

```
<%@ LANGUAGE = VBScript %>
<!DOCTYPE html PUBLIC "-//W3C//DTD XHTML 1.0 Transitional//EN"
 "http://www.w3.org/TR/xhtml1/DTD/xhtml1-transitional.dtd">
<html xmlns="http://www.w3.org/1999/xhtml" lang="en">
<head>
<title>Job Openings</title>
<meta http-equiv="content-type" content="text/html; charset=ISO-8859-1" />
```

```
</head>
<body>
<h2 align="center">Open Positions</h2>
<br /><br />
<table width="100%" border="1" cellspacing="0" cellpadding="4">
<tr>
<th>Position Number</th>
<th>Location</th>
<th>Description</th>
<th>Hiring Manager</th>
<th>Date Posted</th>
</tr>

<!--
      Open Database Connection
      Execute SQL query statement
      Set RS variable to store results of query
      Loop through records while still records to process
-->
<%
     Set Conn = Server.CreateObject("ADODB.Connection")
    Conn.Open ODBCPositions
    SQL = "SELECT JobTitle, Location, Description, HiringManager,
PostDate FROM Positions"
     Set RS = Conn.Execute(SQL)
     Do While Not RS.EOF
%>

<!-- Display database fields in table cells -->
<tr>
    <td>
    <% = RS("JobTitle") %>
    </td>
    <td>
    <% = RS("Location") %>
    </td>
    <td>
    <% = RS("Description") %>
    </td>
    <td>
    <% = RS("Hiring Manager") %>
    </td>
    <td>
    <% = RS("Post Date") %>
    </td>
</tr>

<!-- Move to next record and continue loop -->

<%
   RS.MoveNext
   Loop
```

```
%>

</table>
</body>
</html>
```

From this example, you can see that ASP is more complicated than PHP or ColdFusion, but it is also more like traditional programming environments. If you then add in the new .NET architecture with its objects, form controls, and support for Web services you have a very powerful programming framework indeed. More information about ASP and ASP.NET can be found at www.asp101.com and www.asp.net.

Choosing a Server-Side Scripting Language

When it comes right down to it, the differences between the various server-scripting languages such as PHP, ColdFusion, and ASP are somewhat cosmetic. The syntax seems to be the main distinguishing factor for some developers. Developers with a programming background may find ASP comfortable, whereas skilled markup authors may find ColdFusion or PHP friendlier. Java developers might like Java Server Pages (JSP) while others might like Python or even Perl. Yet, in the end, all these server-parsed scripting technologies suffer from speed problems when compared to server-side modules. Furthermore, some of these technologies bring such significant complexity that the real benefit of using a scripting language is often lost. Cost is often mentioned as a selection criterion for choosing a server-side programming environment. ASP and PHP are considered free while others like ColdFusion or JSP typically do have some up-front server costs. However, total cost might include operating system costs, setup time, or increased development efforts. Choosing one language over another is rarely simple and often too religious for some Web developers. In short, it's important to keep an open mind when picking a server-side scripting language.

Summary

Server-side programming is one way to add interactivity to a Web page. CGI was the traditional way to do this. Writing a CGI program isn't difficult if you use libraries, but the price you pay for ease is often speed. Because so many CGI programs are very similar, some are rewritten as faster server-side modules such as ISAPI and Apache modules. Although writing a custom server module tends to be beyond the expertise of most developers, it is easy to buy one to solve a common problem such as database access. Today, most Web servers support a form of server-side scripting such as SSIs, PHP, ColdFusion, or ASP. All of the technologies provide a relatively easy way for Web developers to add basic interactivity to their Web pages. While server-side technologies provide a great deal of power for the Web developer, they are only half the picture. It is also possible to add interactivity using a client-side technology such as JavaScript or Java. The subsequent chapters discuss these technologies and their intersection with HTML/XHTML and CSS.

CHAPTER 14

JavaScript and DHTML

Adding interactivity to a Web site is not limited to server-side programs. The client side of the Web—the browser—generally can execute code in the form of scripting or embedded programmed objects. For Web developers, often the easiest way to begin adding dynamic aspects to a Web page is through client-side scripting, primarily using JavaScript. In the case of JavaScript, code is either directly inserted into or referenced from an HTML/XHTML document, and is executed when the page is loaded by the browser. This chapter discusses the intersection between scripting and markup, but does not attempt to teach scripting techniques in depth. In-depth coverage of JavaScript can be found in the companion book *JavaScript: The Complete Reference* (Powell & Schneider, Osborne, 2001). However, we will present the material required for developers to incorporate canned script code properly and to appreciate the important role JavaScript will play in Web pages in the future as markup, style sheets, and scripting intersect in the Document Object Model (DOM).

JavaScript

The most popular client-side scripting language on the Web is JavaScript, a scripting language originally developed by Netscape. Microsoft also supports JavaScript in the form of JScript, a JavaScript clone used in Internet Explorer. The language was turned over to the international standards body *European Computer Manufacturers Association* (ECMA), which announced during the summer of 1997 the approval of ECMA-262, or ECMAScript, as a cross-platform Internet standard for scripting. Many browser vendors comply with the ECMAScript specification, but users and vendors alike commonly use the widely recognized JavaScript name.

JavaScript will seem very familiar to programmers. The syntax of JavaScript is fairly similar to C or Java with Perl-style regular expression handling. However, unlike Java, the language does not force users to develop in such a style and retains features (such as weak typing) that are common to simple scripting languages. The following is a simple example of JavaScript code that is used to greet the user; a rendering of the script in action is shown in Figure 14-1.

```
<!DOCTYPE html PUBLIC "-//W3C//DTD XHTML 1.0 Transitional//EN"
"http://www.w3.org/TR/xhtml1/DTD/xhtml1-transitional.dtd">
<html xmlns="http://www.w3.org/1999/xhtml" lang="en">
```

```
<head>
<title>First JavaScript Example</title>
<meta http-equiv="content-type" content="text/html; charset=ISO-8859-1" />
<script type="text/javascript">
<!--

function greet()
 {
    alert("Hello user! Welcome to JavaScript.");
 }
//-->

</script>
</head>
<body>
<h1 align="center">First JavaScript Example</h1>
<div align="center">
<form action="#">
<input type="button" value="Press Me" onclick="greet()" />
</form>
</div>
</body>
</html>
```

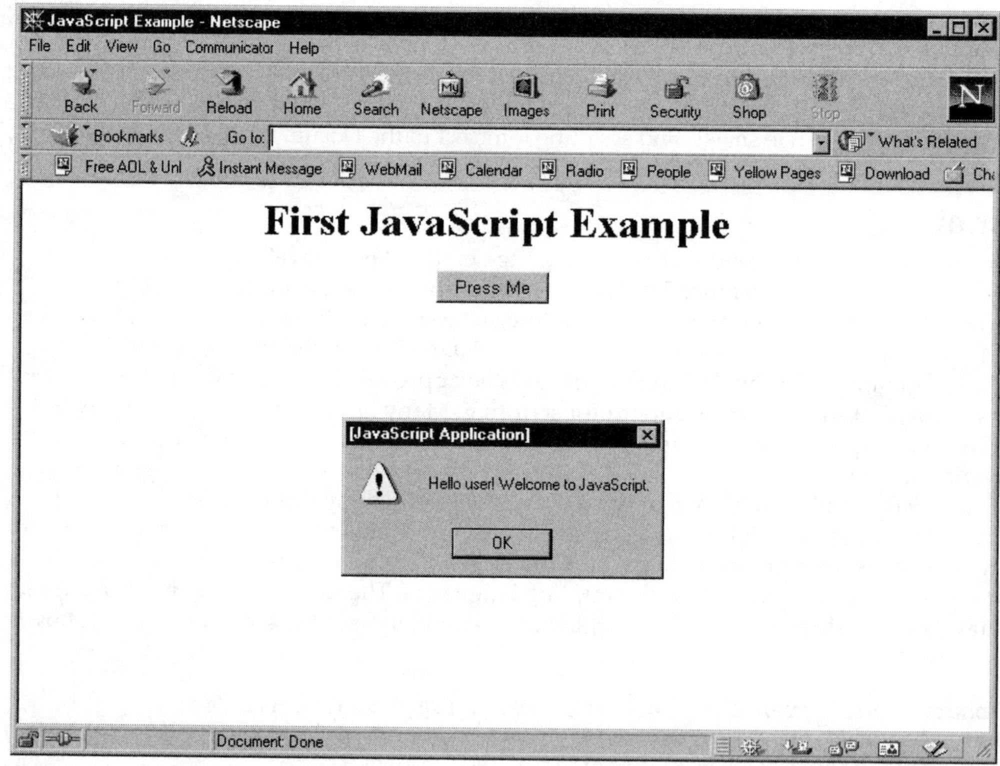

FIGURE 14-1 JavaScript says hello

This example demonstrates a simple JavaScript function c[illegible]hich is triggered by a user's button press. The event handler attrib[illegible] to tie the markup to the JavaScript that is contained in the head [illegible]e **script** element. Although this example is very simple, rememb[illegible]ample; this is a real programming language that has many nuanc[illegible]er in this chapter.

VBScript

Visual Basic Scripting Edition, generally called VBScript, is a subse[illegible] Basic language. Because of its Visual Basic heritage, in some ways V[illegible] better defined and seems to have a more stable specification than Java[illegible] less prevalent than JavaScript on the Internet, largely because VBScript [illegible] in only Internet Explorer browsers. The language can be used to provide the [illegible] as JavaScript, and is just as capable as accessing the various objects that co[illegible] page (termed a browser's *Object Model*). Given its Internet Explorer limitatio[illegible] to use VBScript as a cross-platform scripting solution. However, used in a mo[illegible] environment, such as an intranet, VBScript might just be what the Microsoft-oriente[illegible]per needs. The following is a sample of VBScript to give you a flavor of its syntax; thi[illegible]xample has the same functionality as the JavaScript example given previously:

```
<!DOCTYPE html PUBLIC "-//W3C//DTD XHTML 1.0 Transitional//EN"
"http://www.w3.org/TR/xhtml1/DTD/xhtml1-transitional.dtd">
<html xmlns="http://www.w3.org/1999/xhtml" lang="en">
<head>
<title>VBScript Example</title>
<meta http-equiv="content-type" content="text/html; charset=ISO-8859-1" />
<script type="text/vbscript">
<!--
Sub greet_OnClick
      MsgBox "Hello user! Welcome to VBScript."
End Sub
-->
</script>
</head>
<body>
<h1 align="center">First VBScript Example</h1>
<div align="center">
<form action="#">
<input type="button" value="Press Me" name="greet" />
</form>
</div>
</body>
</html>
```

This is a simple example of how VBScript can be included in an XHTML file and should produce a rendering similar to the one shown in Figure 14-2.

As in the first example, the form button named "greet" triggers an alert box that greets the user. Notice that rather than using an explicit XHTML attribute such as **onclick**, as was used in the JavaScript example, the VBScript example names the subroutine in a certain way

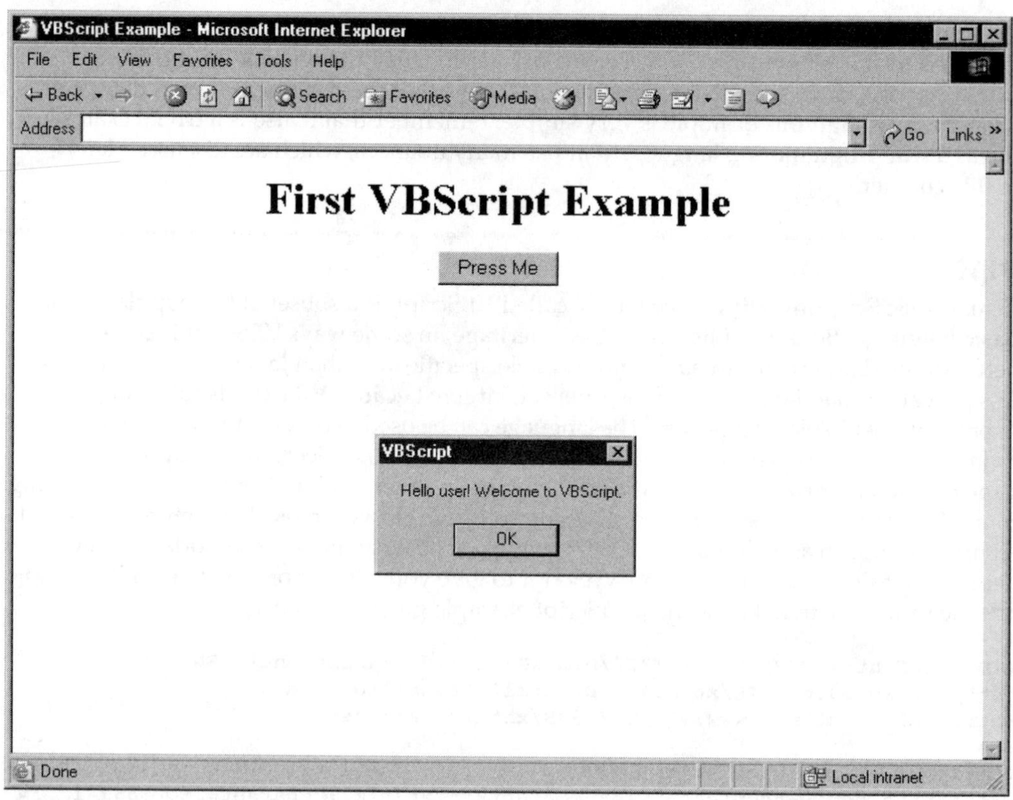

FIGURE 14-2 VBScript says hello

to associate it with the button event; in this case, **greet_OnClick**. Other differences with the VBScript example include the use of the **MsgBox** function to create the alert window, as well as syntactical differences such as the use of parentheses. Readers familiar with Visual Basic should find this example very easy because this language is just a subset of Visual Basic proper.

Once again, though, as a client-side technology, VBScript is not really very useful because it is limited to Internet Explorer. Relying on VBScript locks out others such as Netscape, Opera, or Safari users, which is unacceptable for a public Web site. Because of this, VBScript often is limited to being used within a Microsoft-oriented intranet or on the server side, in the form of Active Server Page code (as discussed in Chapter 13). No further discussion of VBScript occurs during this client-side discussion. However, readers interested in more information about the syntax of VBScript, as well as examples, are encouraged to visit Microsoft's scripting site (http://msdn.microsoft.com/scripting/).

Including Scripts in an XHTML Document

As suggested by the introductory examples, the primary way to include scripts—written in any language—in a Web page is through the use of the **<script>** tag. There are actually four ways to include script code in a document:

- Within a **<script>** tag
- As a linked .js file indicated by the **src** attribute of a **<script>** tag
- Within an event handler attribute such as **onclick**
- Via the pseudo-URL **javascript:** syntax referenced by a link

The syntax of each of these approaches is presented in the following sections with simple examples.

The <script> Tag

The **script** element is used to section off any script included directly within a Web page. Within the element should be scripting statements in the particular language used. Any script code is executed by the browser and the results are then output to the document. If the output contains markup, CSS, or even more script code, it is then parsed further by the browser. For example, consider the short markup and script fragment here that might be found in a document body:

```
<h2>Before the JavaScript</h2>
<script type="text/javascript">
   document.write("Hello world from <b>Javascript</b>.");
</script>
<h2>After the Javascript</h2>
```

This would produce a heading of text, the short greeting from JavaScript, and then the second heading. Notice that the text generated by JavaScript includes the **<b>** tag, which then would be interpreted by the browser before final display. A more telling example shows how the browser executes a few statements at a time:

```
<h2>Heading 1</h2>
<script type="text/javascript">
   alert("Script 1");
</script>
<h2>Heading 2</h2>
<script type="text/javascript">
   alert("Script 2");
</script>
<h2>Heading 3</h2>
<script type="text/javascript">
   alert("Script 3");
</script>
<h2>Done!</h2>
```

In this example, the browser will output a statement and then an alert allowing you to witness the incremental display and parse of the page.

The **<script>** tag can occur in either the **head** or the **body** elements numerous times. Because a document is read from top to bottom, many scripts will be found in the head; these must be read before the page is loaded. Programmers will find scripts in the head of the document useful to declare and initialize variables and set up functions for later use. For example, the following example sets up a function that can be triggered later on in the document:

```
<!DOCTYPE html PUBLIC "-//W3C//DTD XHTML 1.0 Transitional//EN"
"http://www.w3.org/TR/xhtml1/DTD/xhtml1-transitional.dtd">
<html xmlns="http://www.w3.org/1999/xhtml" lang="en">
<head>
<title>JavaScript Example</title>
<meta http-equiv="content-type" content="text/html; charset=ISO-8859-1" />
<script type="text/javascript">
 function greet()
  {
    alert("Hello user! Welcome to JavaScript.");
  }
</script>
</head>
<body>

  markup and JavaScript that may eventually trigger script
found in the head of the document

</body>
</html>
```

In this particular example, the script in the head is only a function definition. It won't necessarily be executed unless you call it down in the **<body>** of the document. Later on in the page, you could have a special script block such as

```
<script type="text/javascript">
   greet();
</script>
```

which could invoke the short script defined in the **<head>** of the document.

Hiding Script

When using script markup within a document, you may have to address what to do when a browser doesn't support scripting. Traditionally when a browser encounters an element it doesn't support it simply skips it and prints out the contents within the element as plain text. A non-JavaScript-aware browser encountering an example such as

```
<script type="text/javascript">
         alert("I am a script.");
</script>
```

literally would print **alert("I am a script.");** rather than running the script first. In order to avoid this undesirable situation, you should attempt to hide the script code from older browsers using comments, in a fashion similar to the technique for hiding style sheets. An example of commenting on JavaScript is shown here:

```
<script type="text/javascript">
<!--
```

```
alert("I am a script.");
//-->
</script>
```

Notice how the HTML comment starts the exclusion of JavaScript, but **//-->** is used to close the comment. This is because JavaScript interprets lines with **//** as comments and does not attempt to run **-->** as a command.

NOTE *Other scripting languages such as VBScript may have different commenting styles for hiding the script code from older browsers.*

XHTML has a slightly different issue with the **script** element. Given that XHTML is an XML-based language, many of the characters found in a JavaScript, such as > or &, have special meaning so there could be trouble with the previous approach. According to the strict XHTML specification, you also are supposed to hide the contents of the script from the XHTML-enforcing browser using the following technique:

```
<script type="text/javascript">
<![CDATA[
  ..script here ..
]]>
</script>
```

Of course, this approach does not work in any but the strictest XML enforcing browsers, so authors will have to instead use linked scripts, traditional comment blocks, or simply ignore the problem. This is not the optimal solution to say the least, but it is typical of the compromises often made in Web development.

<noscript>

Like other elements that reference technologies beyond basic markup, the **script** element supports a special element to deal with browsers that don't execute a script. The **<noscript>** tag is used to enclose alternative text and markup for browsers that don't interpret a script. Furthermore, users can turn off support for a scripting language in their browsers. The **<noscript>** content renders onscreen, as shown in the following example, if the user has turned off scripting support or is using a browser that doesn't understand JavaScript:

```
<!DOCTYPE html PUBLIC "-//W3C//DTD XHTML 1.0 Transitional//EN"
"http://www.w3.org/TR/xhtml1/DTD/xhtml1-transitional.dtd">
<html xmlns="http://www.w3.org/1999/xhtml" lang="en">
<head>
<title>JavaScript and noscript</title>
<meta http-equiv="content-type" content="text/html; charset=ISO-8859-1" />
</head>
<body>
<script type="text/javascript">
<!--
 document.write('JavaScript is on');
//-->
</script>
<noscript>
```

```
<b>This page requires JavaScript. Please turn on JavaScript if you
   have it and reload this page!</b>
</noscript>
</body>
</html>
```

NOTE *It is possible to turn off JavaScript support in a browser rather easily by setting your preferences. This browser modification is performed by users primarily for security reasons, because there are many privacy exploits related to JavaScript usage.*

Specifying the Scripting Language

By default, most browsers assume that the script language being used is JavaScript. As the previous examples have shown, the **type** attribute is used to indicate the MIME type of the script to run; for example, **text/javascript**. However, this indication of scripting dialect, while a specified standard, might not provide the flexibility provided by the nonstandard **language** attribute. For example, consider that not all versions of JavaScript support the same features. The **language** attribute can be used to indicate the version of JavaScript being used. The attribute can be set to "JavaScript1.1" or "JavaScript1.2" rather than simply "JavaScript". Only browsers that understand the particular dialect of JavaScript will execute the enclosed script code. To deal with this, you can make a fall-back situation with multiple versions of similar code, as shown here:

```
<script language="JavaScript">
 Traditional JavaScript version
</script>

<script language="JavaScript1.1">
 JavaScript 1.1 version
</script>

<script language="JavaScript1.2">
  JavaScript1.2 version
</script>

<script language="JavaScript1.5">
  JavaScript1.5 version
</script>
```

In the previous example, the browser will execute each script block in order and skip any versions of the language attribute it doesn't understand. This would allow the developer to put different versions of code in different blocks. One caveat to consider with the **language** attribute is that because a browser will ignore any element with any unknown language, a simple typo such as **<script language="javascipt">** will cause the entire script to be skipped. Furthermore, while commonly used and more useful than the **type** attribute, markup using the **language** attribute will of course not validate.

Linked Scripts

While it is easy to put scripts directly in a document, it probably is better to separate them out in an external file and link to them, similar to linked style sheets. You can place the script code in a separate file and use the **src** attribute to specify the URL of the script to include. For example,

```
<script src="/scripts/myscript.js" type="text/javascript"></script>
```

loads a script called myscript.js, specified by the URL for the **src** attribute. The external file would contain only JavaScript and no HTML/XHTML markup, not even a **<script>** tag. For example, using the previous example, you would have

```
function greet()
{
    alert("Hello user! Welcome to JavaScript.");
}
```

in the file myscript.js.

One major advantage of external scripts is that a browser can cache the script file locally. If the same script code is used over and over again, the files that reference it require only another **<script>** tag and can reuse the cached copy. Considering how much script code is inserted in many pages, this could improve site efficiency. Furthermore, using an included script also keeps markup, script, and style elements separate.

Although external scripts seem the way to go, they do have problems. The most troubling issue has to do with load order. Given that each .js file is a separate request, some code may be downloaded and executed before related code is. This multirequest can lead to transitory network-related scripting errors, which can be very hard to pin down. There are other issues with compatibility with external scripts. Even today's modern browsers have occasional problems with certain constructs in external scripts and very old browser implementations of JavaScript—notably Netscape 2.0 and early versions of Internet Explorer 3.0—do not support external scripts at all. However, today these browser problems are rarely an issue, and linked scripts should be employed whenever possible.

PART IV

Event Handler Attributes

Script code can also be added to XHTML documents through special attributes called *event handlers*. What are events? Events occur as the result of a user action or, potentially, an external event, such as a page loading. Examples of events include a user clicking a button, pressing a key, scrolling a window, or even simply moving the mouse around the screen. XHTML provides a way to bind a script to the occurrence of a particular event, through an *event handler attribute*. This is the name of the event, prefixed by the word "on": for example, **onclick**. The following code shows how the **onclick** event handler attribute is used to bind a script to a button click occurrence:

```
<form action="#">
<input type="button" onclick="alert('This is JavaScript');"
       value="Press Me" />
</form>
```

Under standard HTML and XHTML, event handler attributes can be added to quite a number of elements, some of which may be unexpected. Consider the following:

```
<p onclick="alert('Under HTML 4 and XHTML you can!');">Can you click me?</p>
```

The core event model introduced in HTML 4 and supported in XHTML includes **onclick, ondblclick, onkeydown, onkeypress, onkeyup, onmousedown, onmousemove, onmouseout, onmouseover**, and **onmouseup**. These core events are defined for nearly all markup elements in which the element is displayed onscreen. The specific elements and their events are discussed in Appendix A. Be careful, however, because some browsers, particularly slightly older ones, do not support core events on every element. In reality, it often doesn't make sense to associate events with some elements anyway.

In addition to the core events, certain elements have their own special events. For example, the **body** and **frameset** elements have an event for loading (**onload**) and unloading pages (**onunload**). In the case of the **frameset** element, the load and unload events don't fire until all the frames have been loaded or unloaded, respectively. The **<form>** tag also has two special events that typically are triggered when the user clicks the Submit or Reset button for a form. These events are **onsubmit** and **onreset**. For form text fields set with the **<input>** tag, you can catch the focus and blur events with **onfocus** and **onblur**. These events fire when the user accesses the field and moves on to another one. You also can watch for the select event with **onselect**, which is triggered when a user selects some text, as well as the change event (**onchange**), which is triggered when a form field's value changes and loses focus. Table 14-1 summarizes the main events supported by HTML and XHTML and their associated elements.

Event Attribute	Event Description	Elements Allowed Under XHTML
onblur	A blur event occurs when a form field loses focus, typically meaning that the user has entered into another form field either typically by clicking the mouse on it, or by tabbing to it.	**a** **area** **button** **input** **label** **select** **textarea**
onchange	A change event signals both that the form field has lost user focus and that its value has been modified during its last access.	**input** **select** **textarea**
onclick	Indicates that the element has been clicked.	Most elements
ondblclick	Indicates that the element has been double-clicked.	Most elements

TABLE 14-1 Events Defined in HTML 4 and XHTML

Event Attribute	Event Description	Elements Allowed Under XHTML
onfocus	The focus event describes when a form field has received focus, namely that it has been selected for manipulation or data entry.	**a** **area** **button** **input** **label** **select** **textarea**
onkeydown	Indicates that a key is being pressed down.	Most elements
onkeypress	Describes the event of a key being pressed and released.	Most elements
onkeyup	Indicates that a key is being released.	Most elements
onload	Indicates the event that occurs when a window or frame finishes loading a document.	**body** **frameset**
onmousedown	Indicates the press of a mouse button.	Most elements
onmousemove	Indicates that the mouse has moved.	Most elements
onmouseout	Indicates that the mouse has moved away from an element.	Most elements
onmouseover	Indicates that the mouse has moved over an element.	Most elements
onmouseup	Indicates the release of a mouse button.	Most elements
onreset	Indicates that the form fields are to be cleared as indicated by the click of a Reset button.	**form**
onselect	Indicates the selection of text by the user, typically by highlighting the text.	**input** **textarea**
onsubmit	Indicates a form submission by the clicking of a Submit button.	**form**
onunload	Indicates that the browser is leaving the current document and unloading it from the window or frame.	**body** **frameset**

TABLE 14-1 Events Defined in HTML 4 and XHTML *(continued)*

The following markup illustrates simple use of the core event attributes with form elements and links:

```
<!DOCTYPE html PUBLIC "-//W3C//DTD XHTML 1.0 Transitional//EN"
"http://www.w3.org/TR/xhtml1/DTD/xhtml1-transitional.dtd">
```

```
<html xmlns="http://www.w3.org/1999/xhtml" lang="en">
<head>
<title>Core Events</title>
<meta http-equiv="content-type" content="text/html; charset=ISO-8859-1" />
</head>
<body onload='alert("Event demo loaded");'
      onunload='alert("Leaving demo");'>

<h1 align="center">Core Events</h1>
<form action="#" onreset='alert("Form reset");'
      onsubmit='alert("Form submit");return false;'>

<ul>
<li>onblur: <input type="text" value="Click into field and then leave"
                   size="40" onblur='alert("Lost focus");' />
<br /><br /></li>

<li>onclick: <input type="button" value="Click Me"
                    onclick='alert("Button click");' /><br /><br /></li>

<li>onchange: <input type="text" value="Change this text then leave"
                     size="40" onchange='alert("Changed");' />
<br /><br /></li>

<li>ondblclick: <input type="button" value="Double-click Me"
                       ondblclick='alert("Button double-clicked");' />
<br /><br /></li>

<li>onfocus: <input type="text" value="Click into field"
                    onfocus='alert("Gained focus");' /><br /><br /></li>

<li>onkeydown: <input type="text"
                      value="Press key and release slowly here" size="40"
                      onkeydown='alert("Key down");' /><br /><br /></li>

<li>onkeypress: <input type="text" value="Type here" size="40"
                       onkeypress='alert("Key pressed");' />
<br /><br /></li>

<li>onkeyup: <input type="text" value="Type and release" size="40"
                    onkeyup='alert("Key up");' /><br /><br /></li>

<li>onload:   Alert presented on initial document load.<br /><br /></li>

<li>onmousedown: <input type="button" value="Click and hold"
                        onmousedown='alert("Mouse down");' />
<br /><br /></li>

<li>onmousemove: Move mouse over this
<a href="#" onmousemove='alert("Mouse moved");'>link</a><br /><br /></li>

<li>onmouseout: Position
mouse <a href="#" onmouseout='alert("Mouse out");'>here</a>
and now leave.<br /><br /></li>
```

```
<li>onmouseover: Position mouse over this
<a href=""onmouseover='alert("Mouse over");'>link</a><br /><br /></li>

<li>onmouseup: <input type="button" value="Click and release"
                      onmouseup='alert("Mouse up");' /><br /><br /></li>

<li>onreset: <input type="reset" value="Reset Demo" /><br /><br /></li>

<li>onselect: <input type="text" value="Select this text" size="40"
                     onselect='alert("Selected");' /><br /><br /></li>

<li>onsubmit: <input type="submit" value="Test Submit" /><br /><br /></li>

<li>onunload: Try to leave document by following this
<a href="http://www.yahoo.com">link</a>.<br /><br /></li>

</ul>
</form>
</body>
</html>
```

Whereas HTML and XHTML specifies numerous events, Netscape and Internet Explorer support many more events beyond the core set. A more detailed discussion of the various events unique to browsers can be found in Appendix A.

The javascript: URL

Most JavaScript-aware browsers introduced the use of a new URL style in the form of **javascript:**, which can be used with links. For example,

```
<a href="javascript:alert('Danger! JavaScript ahead!');">
Click for script</a>
```

creates a link that, when clicked, executes the specified JavaScript code. Although this pseudo-URL form is commonly used in many scripts, it does have a downside in that the link will not function at all when scripting is turned off. Designers should at minimum make sure to include a **<noscript>** tag to warn users of this situation or to avoid the use of pseudo-URL script triggers. A better solution would be to avoid using the **javascript:** pseudo-URL, as demonstrated here:

```
<a href="errors/noscript.html"
   onclick="alert('Danger! JavaScript ahead!');return false;">
Click for script</a>
```

In this situation, notice that with the scripting on, the alert is displayed and then the link load is canceled by returning a false value. Some events such as link loads, right-clicks, and form submissions can be controlled by returning a value to the handler. You'll see this used later on with form validation. In this particular case, you see that by providing both an event handler approach and a set URL, you handle all user cases. With the scripting off, the link could be directed to send the user to an error page, as shown in the previous code listing, or to an alternative version of the content.

JavaScript Language Overview

Readers familiar with programming should be able to inspect an existing JavaScript program with little trouble. A quick overview of the language to orient a reader familiar with programming is presented here. However, readers new to programming or looking for a detailed explanation are encouraged to learn JavaScript from any of the numerous online tutorials or books available, and might want to skip directly to the section "Common Scripts" to find a few useful copy-pasteable scripts.

As a programming language, JavaScript itself is not terribly difficult to learn. It shares syntax similarities with C, Perl, and Java and has only a few commands. As a language, it has only a few basic types: numbers such as 3, -45, 56.78; strings such as "Hello" and "Thomas Powell"; and the Boolean values true and false. The language also supports a few more complex data types such as arrays and objects that should be familiar to anyone who has programmed before.

Variables in JavaScript can be declared at any time. For example,

```
var x = 5;
```

would set a variable named *x* to a number and

```
var today="Wednesday";
```

sets the variable *today* to the string "Wednesday". As a loosely typed language, it is possible to set variables to other types at any time, so a statement such as

```
today = x;
```

is perfectly legal and just changes the value of *today* to a number value of 5.

NOTE *Although loosely typed languages such as JavaScript ease a burden on the programmer for keeping track of what type of data is variable, they also tend to introduce significant run time errors as a result of sloppy programming.*

JavaScript is a case-sensitive language, so invoking the built-in alert method with a call such as **alert('hello');** is okay, whereas **Alert('hello');** is not. Note that most objects, properties, and methods in JavaScript should initially be lowercase with other words in the string capitalized. For example, **alert()** is all lowercase but **document.lastModified** does have the second part of the property initially capitalized. This follows the casing scheme found in many other languages. Remember that JavaScript is case sensitive while HTML is not. Of course, with the rise of XHTML, you will always want to use lowercase in HTML.

Statements in JavaScript are terminated with semicolons (;) or the return character, so

```
alert("hi");
alert("there");
```

is equivalent to

```
alert("hi")
alert("there")
```

However, if you remove the return in the second example, an error will occur, whereas putting two statements on the same line with semicolons between, as in

```
alert("hi"); alert("there");
```

is perfectly fine.

JavaScript has a simple set of operators including basic arithmetic (+,-, /, *), Boolean comparisons (>, <, >=, <=, !, and = =), string operators, and so on.

The statements of the language include conditional statements using an **if-else** syntax. Consider the following script, which alerts the user based on the value of the variable *x*.

```
x=5;
if (x > 4)
  alert('Greater than 4');
else
   alert('Less than or equal to 4');
```

More complex types of conditions also can be handled using a **switch** statement, whose syntax is similar to the C programming language. For example, rather than using a multitude of **if** statements, you could use a single **switch** with multiple **case** statements, as shown here:

```
var x=3;
switch (x)
{
  case 1: alert('x is 1');
          break;
  case 2: alert('x is 2');
          break;
  case 3: alert('x is 3');
          break;
  case 4: alert('x is 4');
          break;
  default: alert('x is not 1, 2, 3 or 4');
}
```

In the previous example, the value of *x* would determine which message was printed by comparing the value of the variable to the various **case** statements. If no match were found, the **default** statement would be executed. The **break** statement is also used commonly within **switch** to exit the statement once the appropriate choice is found. However, the **break** statement's use is also commonly associated with loops, which are discussed next.

Loops are primarily specified with **while** or **for**. Consider the short script here that alerts the user three times:

```
x=1;
while (x < 4)
{
 alert(x);
 x++;
}
```

This also could be written as a **for** loop like so:

```
for (var x = 1; x < 4; x++)
{
     alert(x);
}
```

Like most modern program languages, it is possible to abort a loop or modify the number of loop iterations using the **break** and **continue** statements.

The language also supports the use of functions. For example, you could define a function called sayHi that you use over and over in the document:

```
function sayHi( )
{
 alert('hi');
}
```

This function could be called at any time with a simple call such as **sayHi( )**. Good programming practice suggests that developers try to encapsulate commonly used code in functions.

TIP *For more information on core JavaScript, visit Netscape's developer site at http://developer.netscape.com/. Information about Microsoft's implementation of JavaScript, called JScript, can be found at http://msdn.microsoft.com/scripting/.*

While I have glossed over a great deal of issues including regular expressions, weak typing, functions, variable scope, and so on, the point to take home is simply that the JavaScript language itself is relatively simple for an experienced programmer to learn. The key to doing anything terribly useful with the language, however, is figuring out how to access the built-in objects of the browser as well as the objects related to the markup of an HTML or XHTML document. It is, in fact, the relationship of markup to JavaScript objects, dubbed the Document Object Model, that is the key to understanding the true power of scripting.

JavaScript Object Models

Every Web document is made up of a variety of text intermixed with tags such as **<a>**, **<img>**, and **<form>**. A page might be composed of three image elements, two paragraphs, an unordered list, and the text within these elements. The *Document Object Model* (DOM) describes each document as a collection of individual objects such as images, paragraphs, and forms, all the way down to the individual fragments of text. As a browser parses a particular HTML/XHTML document, it creates corresponding scripting objects for each tag encountered. The properties of these objects are determined by the attributes of the encountered markup. For example, the paragraph tag **<p>** has an **align** attribute that can be set to **left**, **right**, or **center**. In the object model, the **HTMLParagraphElement** object is defined to model the **<p>** tag and it has an *align* property that corresponds to the tag's **align** attribute. An object can have methods that are associated with it, and events that can occur and affect it. An image tag can have an **onmouseover** event that is triggered when a user places the cursor over the image. A form can have a **submit()** method that can be used to trigger the submission of the form and its contents to a server-side program.

The best way to explain the idea of an object model is by an example. Look at the simple markup example here:

```
<!DOCTYPE html PUBLIC "-//W3C//DTD XHTML 1.0 Transitional//EN"
"http://www.w3.org/TR/xhtml1/DTD/xhtml1-transitional.dtd">
<html xmlns="http://www.w3.org/1999/xhtml" lang="en">
<head>
<title>Demo Company</title>
</head>
<body bgcolor="white">
<h1 align="center">Demo Company</h1>
<hr />
<p id="para1">This is a paragraph of text.</p>
<ul>
   <li><a href="about.htm">About</a></li>
   <li><a href="products.htm">Products</a></li>
</ul>
</body>
</html>
```

This file could be modeled as a parse tree, as shown in Figure 14-3. The structured breakdown of markup elements and how they enclose one another should be familiar even from the first chapter of this book.

The concept of an object model like the DOM is that there is a rigid structure defined to access the various markup elements and text items that make up a document using a scripting language. This model starts from the browser window itself. A typical window contains either a document or a collection of frames (basically windows), which in turn contains documents. Within a document is a collection of markup elements. Some of these

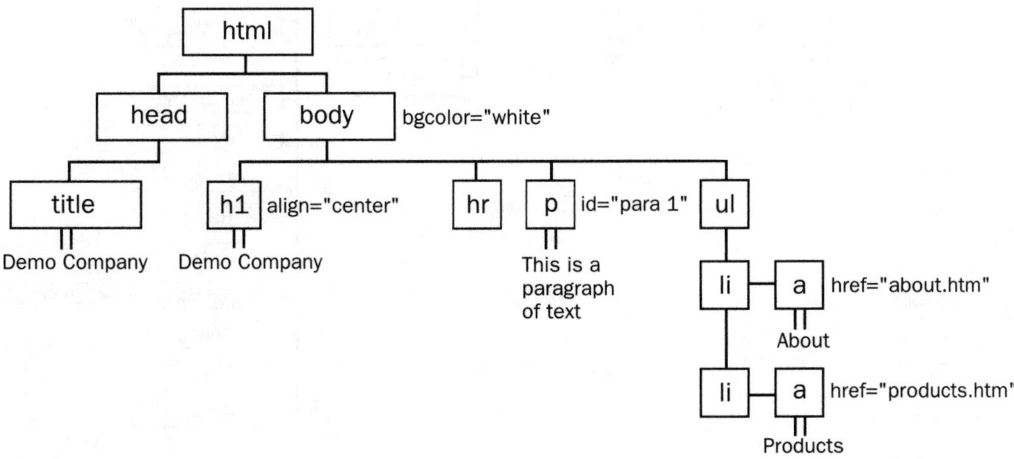

FIGURE 14-3 Parse tree for example HTML

elements, particularly forms, contain even more elements, some might contain text, and others contain both text and markup. The key to accessing the elements in a document is to understand the hierarchy and make sure to name the various elements in the page using either the **id** or the **name** attribute, or for maximum compatibility, both.

Since Netscape 2, the browser, window, document, and document contents—forms, images, links, and so on—have been modeled as a collection of objects. As mentioned previously, this is generically referred to as an object model or, more precisely, a document object model (DOM). Both of the major browsers support the DOM idea, but over the years each has supported different naming conventions and a different degree of exposure. For example, under Netscape 3, only particular items—form elements, links, and so on—are accessible for scripting. Figure 14-4 illustrates the object model for Netscape 3 and Internet Explorer 3.

Objects in the Netscape 3 object hierarchy provide access not only to page elements such as links, anchors, frames, and forms, but to things such as the browser's name, history, plug-ins, and Java classes associated with the current window.

With the introduction of Netscape 4, more elements, such as the nonstandard HTML element **layer**, became accessible. Under Internet Explorer 4, all page elements are scriptable through the **document.all** collection. Figure 14-5 shows an expanded object model for this troubling browser generation, which was characterized by the idea of *DHTML* (Dynamic

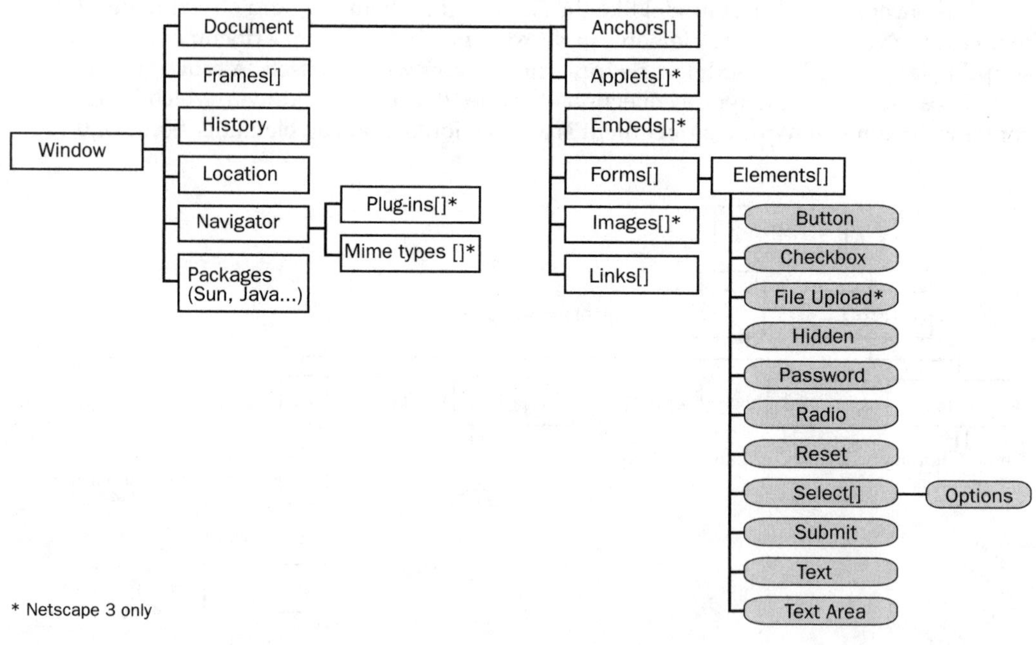

FIGURE 14-4 Object model for Netscape 3 and Internet Explorer 3 browsers

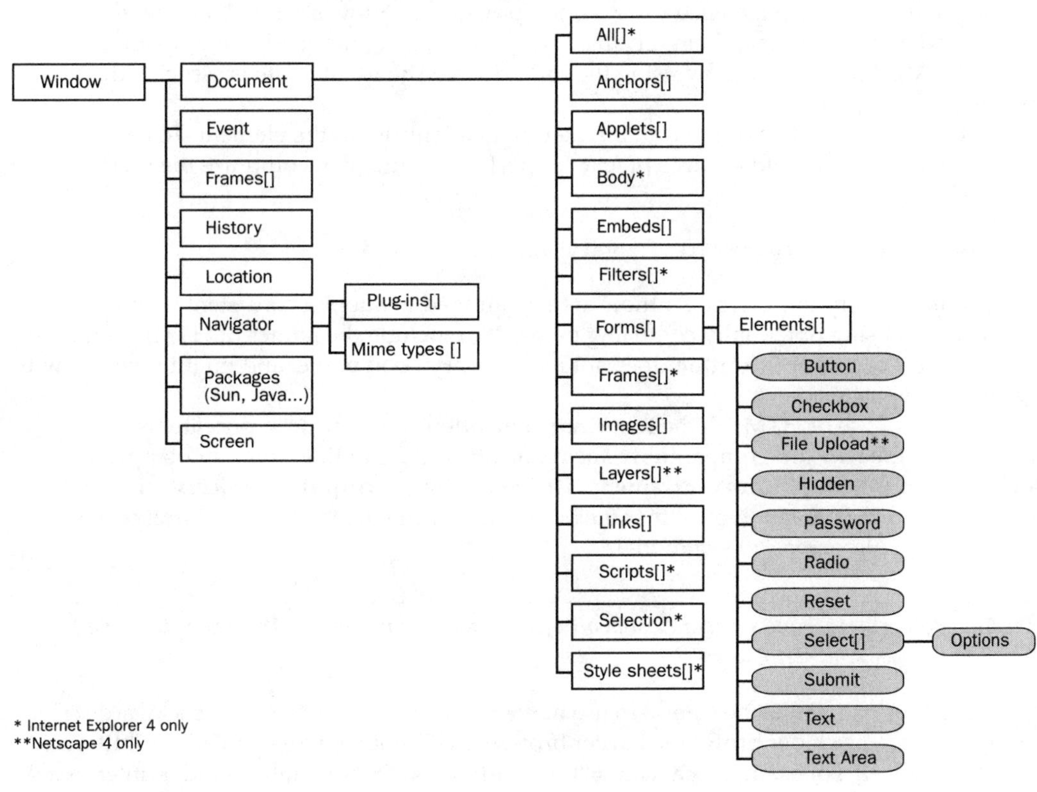

FIGURE 14-5 Expanded object model for 4.x generation browsers

HTML). The problem with these second generation object models is that there are many differences between the two browsers, so note in Figure 14-5 the numerous items that are available under only one browser or another. While the future should eliminate such inconsistencies, these models serve to illustrate the significant differences in JavaScript between browsers.

Because of the significant difference in the object models supported by each browser, it can be challenging to write script code that works in both browsers. Fortunately, the W3C is working on standardizing the access to page content via the standard DOM. You'll see this later, but for now let's turn our attention to how to access page objects regardless of the object model supported.

Markup Elements and Scripting Access

Markup elements in a page need to be named properly to allow scripting languages to easily read and manipulate them. The basic way to attach a unique identifier to an element under HTML 4 or XHTML is by using the **id** attribute. The **id** attribute is associated with nearly every element.

The point of the **id** attribute is to bind a unique identifier to the element. To name a particular enclosed bolded piece of text "SuperImportant," you could use the markup shown here:

```
<b id="SuperImportant">This is very important.</b>
```

Naming is very important. Authors are encouraged to adopt a consistent naming style and to avoid using potentially confusing names that include the names of HTML elements themselves. For example, **button** does not make a very good name, and might interfere with scripting language access.

Before the rise of HTML 4, the **name** attribute often was used to expose items to scripting. For backward compatibility, the **name** attribute is defined for **<a>**, **<applet>**, **<button>**, **<embed>**, **<form>**, **<frame>**, **<iframe>**, **<img>**, **<input>**, **<object>**, **<map>**, **<select>**, and **<textarea>**. Notice that the occurrence of the **name** attribute corresponds closely to the Netscape 3 object model.

NOTE *Both **<meta>** and **<param>** support attributes called **name**, but these have totally different meanings beyond script access.*

Page developers must be careful to use **name** where necessary to ensure backward script compatibility with older browsers. Earlier browsers will not recognize the **id** attribute, so use **name** as well. For example, **<a name="link1" id="link1">** hopefully would be interpreted both by older script-aware browsers as well as by the latest standards-supporting browser.

NOTE *There are some statements in standards documentation that suggest that it is not a good idea to set the **name** and **id** attributes the same, but practice shows this appears to be the only way to ensure backward browser compatibility.*

When documents are well formed, in the sense that tags are used and named properly, scripting languages such as JavaScript can be used to read and manipulate the various objects in a page. The object models previously mentioned define a special set of reserved names that use this notation to allow scripting languages such as JavaScript to refer to entities in the browser and the document, including form elements. The basic notation uses a series of object and property names separated by dots. For example, to access the form defined by

```
<form action="#" name="myform" id="myform">
 <input type="text" name="username" id="username" />
</form>
```

with a scripting language, use either **window.document.myform** or simply **document.myform** because the current **window** can be assumed. The field and its value can be accessed in a similar fashion. To access the text field, use **document.myform.username**. To access the actual value of the username field, access the value property using **document.myform.username.value.**

NOTE *Under Internet Explorer, it may be possible to use a shorthand notation such as* ***myform.username.value****, but this will cause problems in other browsers.*

NOTE *In addition to proper naming, when adding scripting to a page the HTML should always be well formed. Simple things—for example, crossed elements such as* **<b><i>***Test***</b></i>***— might cause a problem with a scripting language. This has to do with the manipulation of the text within the elements. Page authors should consider it extremely dangerous to manipulate poorly formed markup with scripts.*

The following example shows how the content of a form field is accessed and displayed dynamically in an alert window by referencing the fields by name.

```
<!DOCTYPE html PUBLIC "-//W3C//DTD XHTML 1.0 Transitional//EN"
"http://www.w3.org/TR/xhtml1/DTD/xhtml1-transitional.dtd">
<html xmlns="http://www.w3.org/1999/xhtml" lang="en">
<head>
<title>Meet and Greet</title>
<meta http-equiv="content-type" content="text/html; charset=ISO-8859-1" />
<script type="text/javascript">
<!--
function sayHello()
{
 var theirname;

 theirname=document.myform.username.value;
 if (theirname != "")
  alert("Hello "+theirname+"!");
 else
  alert("Don't be shy.");
}
// -->
</script>
</head>
<body>
<form action="#" name="myform" id="myform">
<b>What's your name?</b>
<input type="text" name="username" id="username"  size="20" />
<input type="button" value="Greet" onclick="sayHello();" />
</form>
</body>
</html>
```

It also is possible to refer to elements such as forms and form elements without assigning them a name using an array notation. For example, forms can be referred to by a **forms[ ]** array with the numbers beginning at 0. Elements within a form can be referred to by an

elements[ ] array that also begins at 0. The previous example contains only one form and one field, so the syntax **document.forms[0].elements[0].value** is the same as **document.myform.username.value**. Note that it generally is better to name elements than to access them through their position in a page because any additions or movement of the markup elements within the page could potentially break the script.

Aside from reading the contents of an element with JavaScript, it is also possible, in some cases, to update the contents of certain elements such as form fields. The following example code shows how this might be done:

```
<!DOCTYPE html PUBLIC "-//W3C//DTD XHTML 1.0 Transitional//EN"
"http://www.w3.org/TR/xhtml1/DTD/xhtml1-transitional.dtd">
<html xmlns="http://www.w3.org/1999/xhtml" lang="en">
<head>
<title>Meet and Greet 2</title>
<meta http-equiv="content-type" content="text/html; charset=ISO-8859-1" />
<script type="text/javascript">
<!--
function sayHello()
{
 var theirname;

 theirname = document.myform.username.value;
 if (theirname != "")
  document.myform.response.value="Hello "+theirname+"!";
 else
  document.myform.response.value="Don't be shy.";
}
// -->
</script>
</head>
<body>
<form action="#" name="myform" id="myform">
<b>What's your name?</b>
<input type="text" name="username" id="username"  size="20" />
<br /><br />
<b>Greeting:</b>
<input type="text" name="response" id="response" size="40" />
<br /><br />
<input type="button" value="Greet" onclick="sayHello();" />
</form>
</body>
</html>
```

If you look at Figure 14-4, you'll notice that under Netscape 3 and Internet Explorer 3, only some objects in a page are changeable, notably form elements. Starting with Internet Explorer 4, everything in a page can be modified right down to the very text and markup itself. This is the real idea of Dynamic HTML and is discussed next.

Dynamic HTML

The previous examples have shown script interaction with HTML elements in the traditional fashion, manipulating form elements. However, with the rise of the 4.*x* generation of browsers, a new concept called Dynamic HTML or DHTML was introduced. DHTML describes the ability to dynamically manipulate the page elements, potentially changing the document's structure in a significant way. In its most obvious form, DHTML is an HTML document that displays dynamic characteristics such as movement or the showing or hiding of page content. These sophisticated features are made possible through the intersection of HTML, CSS, and JavaScript. So in some sense, the idea of DHTML can be summarized in the formula

DHTML = HTML + CSS + JavaScript

In the case of DHTML, we generally assume that all page content from form fields to bold tags can be modified. For example, consider if you had a paragraph in HTML like so:

```
<p id="para1">This is a test</p>
```

It could be referenced under Internet Explorer 4 or later DHTML style object mode using **window.document.all['para1'], document.all['para1']** or simply **para1**. The simple example that follows moves the paragraph around the page by changing the **align** attribute of the paragraph tag through its corresponding **align** property:

```
<!DOCTYPE html PUBLIC "-//W3C//DTD XHTML 1.0 Transitional//EN"
"http://www.w3.org/TR/xhtml1/DTD/xhtml1-transitional.dtd">
<html xmlns="http://www.w3.org/1999/xhtml" lang="en">
<head>
<title>The Dynamic Paragraph: DHTML Style</title>
<meta http-equiv="content-type" content="text/html; charset=ISO-8859-1" />
</head>
<body>
<h1 align="center">The Dynamic Paragraph</h1>
<hr />
<p id="para1">I am a dynamic paragraph. Watch me dance!</p>
<hr />
<form action="#">
<input type="button" value="Right" onclick="para1.align='right';" />
<input type="button" value="Left" onclick="para1.align='left';" />
<input type="button" value="Center" onclick="para1.align='center';" />
</form>
</body>
</html>
```

We can even consider modifying the content. For example, consider adding the button here,

```
<input type="button" value="Change" onclick="para1.innerText='Changed!';" />
```

which modifies the actual contents of the paragraph tag.

While the Dynamic HTML approach is quite powerful, it suffers from extreme compatibility problems. Other browsers may not expose all the same objects and even when they do, their syntax is not always the same, which can cause developers great annoyance.

The Standard DOM

The W3C standard Document Object Model or DOM should alleviate many of the incompatibilities of the DHTML approach to JavaScript and allow a developer to access the contents of a document in a standard fashion. There will be many levels of the DOM. Level 0 will preserve much of what is considered to be standard JavaScript—that which is supported by Netscape 3—and Level 1 and Level 2 will allow access to HTML elements and style sheet properties. Today, we can count on support for most of DOM Level 1 and 2 in Internet Explorer browsers and the complete DOM Level 1 and 2 specifications in Mozilla/Netscape and Opera browsers.

To access an element using the DOM, you use the **getElementById** method and specify the **id** attribute value of the object you desire to access. For example, you can access the element using **getElementById('para1')**. Once the object is returned, you can modify its attributes so **getElementById('para1').align** would access the align attribute the same way Internet Explorer used **para1.align**. The following example, which works under Internet Explorer 5 and greater, Netscape 6 and greater, as well as any DOM-compliant browser, is equivalent to the last one and illustrates a standard manipulation of markup using JavaScript:

```
<!DOCTYPE html PUBLIC "-//W3C//DTD XHTML 1.0 Transitional//EN"
"http://www.w3.org/TR/xhtml1/DTD/xhtml1-transitional.dtd">
<html xmlns="http://www.w3.org/1999/xhtml" lang="en">
<head>
<title>The Dynamic Paragraph: DOM Style</title>
<meta http-equiv="content-type" content="text/html; charset=ISO-8859-1" />
</head>
<body>
<h1 align="center">The Dynamic Paragraph</h1>
<hr />
<p id="para1">I am a dynamic paragraph. Watch me dance!</p>
<hr />
<form action="#">
<input type="button" value="Right"
onclick="getElementById('para1').align='right';" />
<input type="button" value="Left"
       onclick="getElementById('para1').align='left';" />
<input type="button" value="Center"
onclick="getElementById('para1').align='center';" />
</form>
</body>
</html>
```

In the previous example, every time the user clicks on the spanned text, the actual value of the **align** attribute for the **<p>** tag is manipulated. Of course, if you view the source of the page you won't notice anything, but this is basically what is happening.

The DOM allows not only manipulation of the existing tags within a document, but allows you to change the contents of tags or even add new tags dynamically. For example, the following markup shows how data can be added to a page:

```
<!DOCTYPE html PUBLIC "-//W3C//DTD XHTML 1.0 Transitional//EN"
"http://www.w3.org/TR/xhtml1/DTD/xhtml1-transitional.dtd">
<html xmlns="http://www.w3.org/1999/xhtml" lang="en">
<head>
<title>Dynamic Page Demo</title>
<meta http-equiv="content-type" content="text/html; charset=ISO-8859-1" />
<script type="text/javascript">
<!--
function addText()
{
 var theString,theElement,insertSpot;
 /* create the string */
 var theString = document.createTextNode(document.testform.newtext.value);

 /* create the br element */
 theElement = document.createElement("br");

 /* find the div tag and add the string and br */
 insertSpot = document.getElementById("div1");
 insertSpot.appendChild(theString);
 insertSpot.appendChild(theElement);
}
//-->
</script>
</head>
<body>
<div id="div1">This is some text.</div>
<hr />
<form action="#" name="testform" id="testform">
New text: <input type="text" name="newtext" id="newtext" />
<input type="button" value="Add" onclick="addText()" />
</form>
</body>
</html>
```

NOTE *In this example, it looks clumsy to create individual elements and text fragments and join them together. The DHTML object model introduced by Internet Explorer relied on* ***innerHTML*** *attributes of an HTML tag such as* ***<div>*** *to perform the same task. While not part of the DOM standard, many browsers support it and developers seem to prefer the simpler syntax.*

The previous example shows that with the DOM it is possible to manipulate the very parse tree of an HTML document. Adding elements, deleting elements, and moving elements around the document are all possible using JavaScript and the DOM. Now, if you combine the capability to interact with CSS properties, you can create the interesting effects that many people associate with DHTML.

PART IV

Scripting and CSS

Microsoft Internet Explorer 4 was the first browser to demonstrate how style sheets could be manipulated using scripting language. The small markup fragment that follows shows how events can be tied with style changes to make text that changes color or size in response to a mouse event. In this situation, you change the style property and set its **color** and **font-size** CSS properties using the **color** and **fontSize** JavaScript properties for the tag.

```
<span id="testspan" onmouseover="testspan.style.color='#FF0000';"
      onmouseout="testspan.style.color='#0000FF';"
      onclick="testspan.style.fontSize='larger';">Click Me!</span>
```

In the 4.*x* generation DHTML style approach, Netscape and Microsoft support scripting access for style sheets. Of course, the variations between the two browsers are significant. You should use DOM style interaction to make changes, like so:

```
<span id="testspan"
onmouseover="document.getElementById('testspan').style.color='red';"
onmouseout="document.getElementById('testspan').style.color='blue';"
onclick="document.getElementById('testspan').style.fontSize='larger';">
Click Me!</span>
```

To simplify the example, we might rely on JavaScript special scripting keyword **this** as a shortcut reference to the current element.

```
<span onmouseover="this.style.color='red';"
      onmouseout="this.style.color='blue';"
      onclick="this.style.fontSize='larger';">
Click Me!</span>
```

Access to CSS via JavaScript is quite elegant under the DOM. If a tag has a style sheet with properties such as **font-style**, **font-size**, and **border-width,** you can access them using properties of the **Style** object named **fontStyle**, **fontSize**, and **borderWidth**. In nearly all cases, it is a matter of removing the dash in the property name and changing the case of the second and following words in a property to access its equivalent JavaScript property. The following example illustrates how CSS can be manipulated with the DOM:

```
<!DOCTYPE html PUBLIC "-//W3C//DTD XHTML 1.0 Transitional//EN"
"http://www.w3.org/TR/xhtml1/DTD/xhtml1-transitional.dtd">
<html xmlns="http://www.w3.org/1999/xhtml" lang="en">
<head>
<title>CSS via the DOM Demo</title>
<meta http-equiv="content-type" content="text/html; charset=ISO-8859-1" />
<style type="text/css">
#d1 {
      font-style: italic;
      font-size: 36pt;
      border-style: solid;
      border-width: 1px;
      width:80%;
      text-align: center;
```

```
     }
</style>
<script type="text/javascript">
<!--
function changeStyle()
{
 var theElement = document.getElementById('d1');

 theElement.style.fontStyle='normal';
 theElement.style.fontSize='12pt';
 theElement.style.borderStyle='dashed';
 theElement.style.borderWidth='3px';
 theElement.style.backgroundColor='yellow';
 theElement.style.textAlign='left';
}

function show()
{
 var theElement = document.getElementById('d1');
 theElement.style.visibility='visible';
}

function hide()
{
 var theElement = document.getElementById('d1');
 theElement.style.visibility='hidden';
}
//-->
</script>
</head>
<body>

<div id="d1">CSS Test</div>
<hr />
<form action="#">
     <input type="button" value="change" onclick="changeStyle();" />
     <input type="button" value="hide" onclick="hide();" />
     <input type="button" value="show" onclick="show();" />
</form>
</body>
</html>
```

While the DOM promises an ease of advanced scripting, so far problems still exist. Cross-browser JavaScript often requires multiple versions of the same code to address all the variations in browsers.

Cross-Browser JavaScript

Traditionally, browsers have differed significantly on how style sheets can be accessed and the degree to which they can be manipulated. For example, under Netscape 4 the only style sheet properties that can be changed after the document has loaded are the absolute positioning properties **left**, **top**, **z-index**, and **visibility**. Add the fact that the standard DOM access is totally different from the way that Microsoft or Netscape tend to reference things in their 4.*x* generation browsers and you'll soon come to know that writing cross-browser scripts can be a real chore. However, it is possible to come up with scripts that take everything into account. For example, the script that follows can move and change the visibility of objects in just about any 4.*x* generation browser and beyond:

```
<!DOCTYPE html PUBLIC "-//W3C//DTD XHTML 1.0 Transitional//EN"
"http://www.w3.org/TR/xhtml1/DTD/xhtml1-transitional.dtd">
<html xmlns="http://www.w3.org/1999/xhtml" lang="en">
<head>
<title>Cross Browser Layer Visibility / Placement Routines</title>
<meta http-equiv="content-type" content="text/html; charset=ISO-8859-1" />
<style type="text/css">
<!--

  #test { position:absolute;
          top:20px;
          left:300px;
          background-color: yellow;
         }
-->
</style>
<script type="text/javascript">
<!--

/* test for objects */
(document.layers) ? layerobject=true : layerobject=false;
(document.all) ? allobject = true: allobject = false;
(document.getElementById) ? dom = true : dom = false;

function changeVisibility(id,action)
{
 switch (action)
{
  case "show":
     if (layerobject)
          document.layers[''+id+''].visibility = "show";
       else if (allobject)
           document.all[''+id+''].style.visibility = "visible";
       else if (dom)
           document.getElementById(''+id+'').style.visibility = "visible";
      break;

  case "hide":
     if (layerobject)
             document.layers[''+id+''].visibility = "hide";
        else if (allobject)
            document.all[''+id+''].style.visibility = "hidden";

        else if (dom)
            document.getElementById(''+id+'').style.visibility = "hidden";
     break;
  default:return;
 }
```

```
 return;
}
function changePosition(id,x,y)
{
  if (layerobject)
   {
    document.layers[''+id+''].left = x;
    document.layers[''+id+''].top = y;
   }
  else if (allobject)
      {
         document.all[''+id+''].style.left=x;
         document.all[''+id+''].style.top=y;
       }
  else if (dom)
      {
         document.getElementById(''+id+'').style.left=x+"px";
         document.getElementById(''+id+'').style.top=y+"px";
        }
  return;
}
//-->
</script>
</head>
<body>
<div id="test">This is a test division</div>

<form action="#" name="testform" id="testform">
<input type="button" value="show" onclick="changeVisibility('test','show');" />
<input type="button" value="hide" onclick="changeVisibility('test','hide');" />
<br /><br />

X:
<input type="text" name="xcoord" id="xcoord" size="4" maxlength="4" value="100" />

Y:
<input type="text" name="ycoord" id="ycoord" size="4" maxlength="4" value="100" />

<input type="button" value="move"
onclick="changePosition('test',document.testform.xcoord.value,document.testform.yco
ord.value);" />
</form>
</body>
</html>
```

Even with the standard DOM, the implementations vary, so developers often rely on cross-browser libraries such as CBE (www.cross-browser.com) and DomAPI (www.domapi.com) to address subtle differences in JavaScript object models.

Although this has been only a brief introduction to scripting and the ideas of the JavaScript and the DOM, it should reveal that to be a seasoned, competent client-side Web developer in the future, you will be required to know HTML/XHTML, CSS, and JavaScript in a very deep way. Readers are encouraged to learn these technologies in that order as they build one upon another.

Common Scripts

Before concluding the chapter, let's see a few examples of the useful scripts commonly found on the Web. The scripts here are provided only with modest explanation on their use. However, even JavaScript novices should be able to use them by copying them into their pages with little or no modification. Other copy-paste scripts can be found online at sites such as www.webreference.com/js and www.dynamicdrive.com.

Last Modification Date

A common use of script is to add small bits of content or HTML to a page dynamically. For example, consider the need to write a last modification date to the bottom of every document in a Web site. Using a short JavaScript at the bottom of a page could be quite easy, as illustrated here:

```
<!DOCTYPE html PUBLIC "-//W3C//DTD XHTML 1.0 Transitional//EN"
"http://www.w3.org/TR/xhtml1/DTD/xhtml1-transitional.dtd">
<html xmlns="http://www.w3.org/1999/xhtml" lang="en">
<head>
<title>Last Modified Example</title>
<meta http-equiv="content-type" content="text/html; charset=ISO-8859-1" />
</head>
<body>
...Page Content here...
<hr />
<div align="center">
<small>
&copy; 2003, Demo Company Inc.<br />

<script type="text/javascript">
<!--
  document.write("Document last modified: "+document.lastModified);
//-->
</script>
</small>
</div>
</body>
</html>
```

Using this script is quite easy: just take the script element and its contents and copy-paste it where you like in your document, and put markup elements around it or within the quotes for formatting.

Conditional Markup Inclusion

JavaScript is commonly used to add markup to a page in a conditional fashion. It is possible, using JavaScript, to detect the version of the browser in use and then produce some markup that fits. Consider the following example that produces a page with a **<blink>** tag if Netscape is detected or a **<marquee>** tag if Internet Explorer is in use:

```
<!DOCTYPE html PUBLIC "-//W3C//DTD XHTML 1.0 Transitional//EN"
"http://www.w3.org/TR/xhtml1/DTD/xhtml1-transitional.dtd">
```

```
<html xmlns="http://www.w3.org/1999/xhtml" lang="en">
<head>
<title>Browser Detect Example</title>
<meta http-equiv="content-type" content="text/html; charset=ISO-8859-1" />
</head>
<body>
<script type="text/javascript">
<!--
  var useragent=navigator.userAgent.toLowerCase();
   var is_nav=((useragent.indexOf('mozilla')!=-1));
   var is_ie=(useragent.indexOf("msie") != -1);
   if (is_nav && !is_ie)
      document.write("<blink>Netscape should blink</blink>");
   else if (is_ie)
       document.write("<marquee>IE loves the marquee</marquee>");
   else
      document.write("<strong>Strong for the unknown browser</strong>");
//-->
</script>
</body>
</html>
```

Detection is not limited to a particular browser type, but to individual versions or even the support of a particular technology or plug-in. Readers interested in conditional page generation should review http://devedge.netscape.com/viewsource/2002/browser-detection/ or turn to a server-side tool such as BrowserHawk (www.browserhawk.com) rather than rolling their own detection routines.

Pull-down Menu Navigation

A common use of JavaScript is for navigation systems. Designers recently have begun to rely more and more on pull-down menu systems within a site for navigation to frequently accessed areas. The following example shows the use of JavaScript:

```
<!DOCTYPE html PUBLIC "-//W3C//DTD XHTML 1.0 Transitional//EN"
"http://www.w3.org/TR/xhtml1/DTD/xhtml1-transitional.dtd">
<html xmlns="http://www.w3.org/1999/xhtml" lang="en">
<head>
<title>Select Navigation</title>
<meta http-equiv="content-type" content="text/html; charset=ISO-8859-1" />
<style type="text/css">
<!--
   .nochoice    {color: black;}
   .choice      {color: blue;}
-->
</style>
<script type="text/javascript">
<!--
function redirect(pulldown)
{
  newlocation = pulldown[pulldown.selectedIndex].value;
  if (newlocation != "")
```

```
    self.location = newlocation;
}

function resetIfBlank(pulldown)
{
  possiblenewlocation = pulldown[pulldown.selectedIndex].value;
  if (possiblenewlocation == "")
    pulldown.selectedIndex = 0; /* reset to start since no movement */
}
//-->
</script>
</head>
<body>
<form action="#" name="navForm" id="navForm">
<b>Favorite Sites:</b>

<select name="menu" id="menu" onchange="resetIfBlank(this);">

<option value="" class="nochoice" selected="selected">Choose your site
</option>
<option value="" class="nochoice"></option>
<option value="" class="nochoice">Search Sites</option>
<option value="" class="nochoice">----------------------------</option>
<option value="http://www.yahoo.com" class="choice">Yahoo! </option>
<option value="http://www.msn.com" class="choice">MSN</option>
<option value="http://www.google.com" class="choice">Google</option>
<option value="" class="nochoice"></option>
<option value="" class="nochoice">Demos</option>
<option value="" class="nochoice">----------------------------</option>
<option value="http://www.democompany.com" class="choice">Demo Company
</option>

</select>

<input type="button" value="go"
       onclick="redirect(document.navForm.menu);" />
</form>

<script type="text/javascript">
<!--
  document.navForm.menu.selectedIndex = 0;
//-->
</script>
</body>
</html>
```

Adding more choices to the menu is simply a matter of setting an **<option>** tag's **class** to "choice" and its **value** attribute to the URL of the document to load. Readers can remove the style sheet and **class** attributes if there is no interest in making choices and labels look different.

Note that this example requires the use of a button press to trigger a page load. However, it is easy enough to modify the script to make the menu trigger as soon as a choice is made.

Change the **<select>** tag to trigger the redirect function using the **onchange** event handler, as shown here:

```
<select name="menu" onchange="redirect(document.navForm.menu);">
```

Readers should note that the use of pull-down navigation with such "hair triggers" does introduce some usability problems.

Rollover Buttons

JavaScript is also commonly used for page embellishment. One of the most common embellishments is the inclusion of rollover buttons, a JavaScript feature that has been available since Netscape 3. A *rollover button* is a button that becomes active when the user positions the mouse over it. The button also can have a special activation state when it is pressed. To create a rollover button, you first will need at least two, perhaps even three images, to represent each of the button's states—inactive, active, and unavailable. A sample set of rollover images is shown here:

To add this rollover image to the page, simply use the **<img>** tag like another image. The idea is to swap the image out when the mouse passes over the image and switch back to the original image when the mouse leaves the image. By literally swapping the value of the **src** attribute when the mouse is over the image, you can achieve the rollover effect. Assuming you have two images, buttonon.gif and buttonoff.gif, this in essence is what the following script, which should work in nearly any browser, would do:

```
<!DOCTYPE html PUBLIC "-//W3C//DTD XHTML 1.0 Transitional//EN"
"http://www.w3.org/TR/xhtml1/DTD/xhtml1-transitional.dtd">
<html xmlns="http://www.w3.org/1999/xhtml" lang="en">
<head>
<title>Rollover Script</title>
<meta http-equiv="content-type" content="text/html; charset=ISO-8859-1" />
<script type="text/javascript">
<!--
/* check to ensure rollovers are supported in browser */
if (document.images)
{
 /* preload the images */
 buttonoff = new Image();
 buttonoff.src = "buttonoff.gif";
 buttonon = new Image();
 buttonon.src = "buttonon.gif";
}


/* function to set image to on state */
```

PART IV

```
function On(imageName)
{
 if (document.images)
  {
    document[imageName].src = eval(imageName+"on.src");
  }
}


/* function to reset image back to off state */
function Off(imageName)
{
 if (document.images)
   {
    document[imageName].src = eval(imageName+"off.src");
   }
}
//-->
</script>
</head>
<body>
<h1 align="center">Rollover Fun</h1>
<hr />
<a href="http://www.democompany.com" onmouseover="On('button');"
   onmouseout = "Off('button');">
<img src="buttonoff.gif" alt="DemoCompany" name="button"
     width="90" height="20" border="0" /></a>
</body>
</html>
```

Let's take a look at how the code works. The first section of the JavaScript checks to make sure the browser supports the images part of the document object model. This capability is required if rollover buttons are to work. If the browser supports this feature, the images are loaded in and assigned names. Once the page is loaded, the user can move the mouse over the image. The link, as indicated by the **<a>** tag, has two event handlers: one for the mouse passing over the image (**onmouseover**) and one for the mouse leaving the image (**onmouseout**). These handlers call our defined **On()** and **Off()** JavaScript functions, respectively. The function **On()** simply sets the **src** of the **<img>** tag to the name of the image passed to it and appends **on.src**, which changes the image to the on state. The function **Off()** does the opposite by setting the **src** equal to the image name with **off.src** appended to it. The key to adding more rollover images is adjusting their names carefully. For example, if you wanted to add another button called **button1.gif**, you add the following code to the **<script>** tag within the first if statement:

```
button1off = new Image();
button1off.src = "button1off.gif";
button1on = new Image();
buttonon1.src = "button1on.gif";
```

and the following code later on in the document:

```
<a href="URL to load " onmouseover="On('button1')"
   onmouseout = "Off('button1')">
<img src="buttonoff1.gif" alt="button 1" name="button1" width="90"
     height="20" border="0" /></a>
```

Of course, the URL height, width, and even image name can vary from rollover image to rollover image. Make especially sure to name objects uniquely and consistently and set the **name** attribute for the **<img>** tag properly. Because rollovers are so common on Web sites, there are many sites, such as http://www.webreference.com/js, that offer rollover tutorials. Tools such as Macromedia's Dreamweaver also can create the code instantly when provided with two images.

TIP *Given the penalty of downloading multiple images, it is a good idea to phase out JavaScript-based image rollovers for light-weight CSS text rollovers using the* ***:hover*** *pseudo property discussed in Chapters 10 and 11.*

Form Validation

Form validation, the final example of script usage, probably is the most important use of scripting on the Web. Interestingly enough, it was the original reason JavaScript was developed. JavaScript form validation is the process of checking the validity of user-supplied data in an XHTML form before it is submitted to a server-side program such as a CGI program. By checking data before it is sent to a server, you can avoid a lot of user frustration, and reduce communication time between the Web browser and the server.

Because it is easy enough in JavaScript to look at a field's value, suppose that you want to make sure that the user enters something in the field before submitting a form. Consider the example here, which looks at the contents of a field and makes sure it isn't blank before allowing submission:

```
<!DOCTYPE html PUBLIC "-//W3C//DTD XHTML 1.0 Transitional//EN"
"http://www.w3.org/TR/xhtml1/DTD/xhtml1-transitional.dtd">
<html xmlns="http://www.w3.org/1999/xhtml" lang="en">
<head>
<title>Overly Simple Form Validation </title>
<meta http-equiv="content-type" content="text/html; charset=ISO-8859-1" />
<script type="text/javascript">
<!--
function validate()
 {
  if (document.myform.username.value == "")
   {
    alert('Please enter your name');
    return false;
   }
  else
   return true;
 }
// -->
</script>
</head>
```

PART IV

```
<body>
<form name="myform" id="myform" action="http://www.htmlref.com"
     method="get" onsubmit="return validate();">
<b>Name:</b>
<input type="text" name="username" id="username"
      size="25" maxlength="25" />
<br /><br />
<input type="submit" value="Submit" />
</form>
</body>
</html>
```

In this example, the function **validate()** is called and the contents of the field **username** is checked to see whether it is blank or contains information. If the field is left blank when the user clicks the button, the user is told to complete the field and a **false** value is returned. Otherwise, a return value of **true** is set and the submission is allowed to continue. The return value is related to the call via the HTML event handler attribute **onsubmit**, which is triggered when the user clicks the Submit button. The submission will occur unless the event returns a **false** value. Notice how the validation function **validate()** returns a **true** or **false** value, based upon the user's input. Expanding this example to check more fields is not difficult.

The next example can be configured to check arbitrary fields for blank entries, valid e-mail addresses, or numeric only values. At the start of the script that follows, notice the **validations[ ]** array. To modify the script, just set the value of the array entries to the name of your fields and a validation string of either **notblank**, **validemail**, or **isnumber**. So, if you had a field named myAge in a form named form1, you would use

```
validations[0] = ["document.form1.myAge", "isnumber"];
```

For every field in your form, you would increment the value in the **validations[ ]** array and add a new value pair consisting of the object path to the field to check the validation string.

```
<!DOCTYPE html PUBLIC "-//W3C//DTD XHTML 1.0 Transitional//EN"
"http://www.w3.org/TR/xhtml1/DTD/xhtml1-transitional.dtd">
<html xmlns="http://www.w3.org/1999/xhtml" lang="en">
<head>
<title>Form Check</title>
<meta http-equiv="content-type" content="text/html; charset=ISO-8859-1" />
<script type="text/javascript">
<!--
var whitespace = " \t\n\r";
/* Define validations to run */

validations = new Array();
validations[0] = ["document.myform.username", "notblank"];
validations[1] = ["document.myform.useremail", "validemail"];
validations[2] = ["document.myform.favoritenumber", "isnumber"];
function isEmpty(s)
{
   var i;
   if((s == null) || (s.length == 0))
```

```
        return true;
    // Search string looking for characters that are not whitespace
     for (i = 0; i < s.length; i++)
     {
         var c = s.charAt(i);
         if (whitespace.indexOf(c) == -1)
               return false;
     }
     // All characters are whitespace.
     return true;
}

function isEmail(field)
{
  var positionOfAt;
  var s = field.value;
  if (isEmpty(s))
   {
       alert("Email may not be empty");
       field.focus();
       return false;
   }
  positionOfAt = s.indexOf('@',1);
  if ( ( positionOfAt == -1) || (positionOfAt == (s.length-1))  )
   {
    alert("E-mail not in valid form!");
    field.focus();
    return false;
   }
   return true;
}

function isDigit(c)
{
 return ((c >= "0") && (c <= "9"))
}

function isInteger(field)
{
  var i, c;
  var s = field.value;
  if (isEmpty(s))
   {
    alert("Field cannot be empty");
    field.focus();
    return false;
   }
 for (i = 0; i < s.length; i++)
  { // Check if current character is number.
   c = s.charAt(i);
   if (!isDigit(c))
    {
      alert("Field must contain only digits");
```

PART IV

```
        field.focus();
        return false;
      }
    }

  return true;
 }

 function validate()
 {
  var i;
  var checkToMake;
  var field;

  for (i = 0; i < validations.length; i++)
    {
      checkToMake = validations[i][1];
      field = eval(validations[i][0]);
      switch (checkToMake)
       {
        case 'notblank': if (isEmpty(field.value))
                          {
                           alert("Field may not be empty");
                            field.focus();
                           return false;
                          }
                        break;
          case 'validemail' : if (!isEmail(field))
                                return false;
                                break;
          case 'isnumber' : if (!isInteger(field))
                              return false;
        }
   }
   return true;
}
//-->
</script>
</head>
<body>
<form name="myform" id="myform" method="get"
      action="http://www.htmlref.com"
      onsubmit="return validate();">
Username: <input type="text" name="username" id="username" size="30" />
<br />
Email: <input type="text" name="useremail" id="useremail" size="30"
maxlength="30" /><br />
Favorite number: <input type="text" name="favoritenumber"
id="favoritenumber" size="10" maxlength="10" /><br />
<input type="submit" value="Submit" />
</form>
</body>
</html>
```

The previous discussion is meant to serve only as a basic introduction to form validation. It is easy enough to add more fields to the example and even check for other types of data. However, even if you are an experienced programmer, it is not suggested that you go out and attempt to create your own validation scripts for e-mail addresses, credit card numbers, zip codes, and so on. Many libraries already exist that perform these tasks; these libraries are available from JavaScript archive sites as well as from Netscape's original form validation library, located at http://developer.netscape.com/docs/examples/javascript/formval/overview.html.

Summary

Client-side technologies are a very important component of Web sites. The evolution of scripting technologies has offloaded some of the processing that traditionally occurred on the server. For example, validating form field entries by using JavaScript or VBScript on the client side makes more sense than relegating this processing to the server. Script can be integrated in markup using the **script** element as well as event handler attributes such as **onclick**. Just as developers should avoid mixing style and structure, they should also try to separate out the logic of a page in an external script wherever possible. Yet even with such separation, the paths of XHTML, CSS, and JavaScript are very intertwined. At its core, scripting is used to manipulate markup through the document object mode. The reliance between the technologies is great given that when markup is not well-formed the script may fail. However, if all the components of a page are working together correctly, pages can come to life bringing significant meaning to the idea of DHTML.

15

CHAPTER

Plug-ins, ActiveX Controls, and Java Applets

In the last chapter, we saw how scripts can be added to XHTML documents. Scripts can manipulate a variety of form elements and, in the case of so-called Dynamic HTML, the page elements themselves. Scripts also are used to access embedded binary objects. As discussed in Chapter 9, embedded objects can be used to bring multimedia, such as sounds and movies, to the Web. They also can be used to add small executable programs to a page. Binary objects come in many forms, including Netscape plug-ins, Microsoft ActiveX controls, and Java applets. Each of these requires special markup. In the future, all included media types will be added with the **object** element. However, until such standardization is universally supported, it is useful to study each individual technology with particular emphasis on how it can intersect with markup.

Scripting, Programming, and Objects

You might wonder why this chapter is separate from the last one. With both scripts and embedded objects, the interactivity takes place on the client side. What's the difference? Why distinguish between scripting and objects? Remember the point of Web client-side scripting—small bits of interpreted code used to add a bit of functionality to a page or fill the gaps in an application. Scripting is *not* necessarily as complex or general as programming, although it often seems as if it is. Programming is more generalized than scripting; programming enables you to create just about anything that you can imagine, although it tends to be more complex in some sense than scripting. Think about checking the data fields of a form; you need only a few lines of JavaScript to make sure the fields are filled. Now consider trying to create something sophisticated, such as a full-blown video game within a Web page. This takes more than a few lines of JavaScript code, and probably should be programmed in a language such as Java, C/C++, or Visual Basic. In fact, building objects is not trivial. It can require significant knowledge of programming. Fortunately for most casual Web page designers, putting together a custom object probably isn't necessary as existing components can be used. This chapter discusses each of the object technologies, as well as how such objects can be inserted into a Web page in conjunction with HTML/XHTML markup and scripting.

Plug-ins

Plug-ins such as the Flash player, QuickTime player, and others, are small helper programs (components) that extend the browser to support new functionality. Plug-ins are primarily a Netscape technology and have been around since Netscape Navigator 2. They are supported by some other browsers, notably Opera (www.opera.com). The **embed** element used to reference plug-ins is also supported under Internet Explorer, although it does result in the launch of an ActiveX control (a similar Microsoft technology discussed later in the chapter). Although plug-ins can go a long way toward extending the possible capabilities of a browser, the technology does have its drawbacks. Users must locate and download plug-ins, install them, and occasionally even restart their browsers. Many users find this rather complicated. Beginning with Netscape 4.*x*, some installation relief was found with somewhat self-installing plug-ins and other features, but plug-ins can still be occasionally troublesome for users. To further combat this problem, many of the most commonly requested plug-ins, such as Macromedia's Flash, are being included as a standard feature with Netscape and other browsers. However, even if installation were not such a problem, plug-ins are not available on every machine; an executable program, or *binary,* must be created for each particular operating system. Because of this machine-specific approach, many plug-ins work only on Windows-based systems. A decreasing number of plug-ins work on Macintosh and even less on Linux or UNIX. Finally, each plug-in installed on a system is a persistent extension to the browser, and takes up memory and disk space.

The benefit of plug-ins is that they can be well integrated into Web pages. You include them by using the **<embed>** or **<object>** tags. Typically, the **<embed>** syntax is used, but the **<object>** syntax is the preferred method because it is part of the XHTML specification and will, therefore, validate. Eventually, **<object>** will supplant **<embed>** completely, but for now it is very common in Web pages. In general, the **embed** element takes a **src** attribute to specify the URL of the included binary object. The **height** and **width** attributes often are used to indicate the pixel dimensions of the included object, if it is visible. To embed a short Audio Video Interleaved (AVI) format movie called welcome.avi that can be viewed by a video plug-in such as those generally installed with many browsers, use the following markup fragment:

```
<embed src="welcome.avi" height="100" width="100"></embed>
```

The **<embed>** tag displays the plug-in (in this case a movie) as part of the HTML/ XHTML document.

A browser can have many plug-ins installed. To check which plug-ins are installed in Netscape, the user can enter a strange URL, such as **about:plugins**, or look under the browser's Help menu for the option "About Plug-ins." The browser will show a list of plug-ins that are installed, the associated MIME type that will invoke each plug-in, and information as to whether that plug-in is enabled. Figure 15-1 shows an example of the plug-in information page.

<embed> Syntax

The primary way to load plug-ins for Netscape browsers is to use the nonstandard **<embed>** tag. It is preferable to use the **object** element, which is part of the HTML and XHTML specification, but **<object>** does not always work well, particularly in older

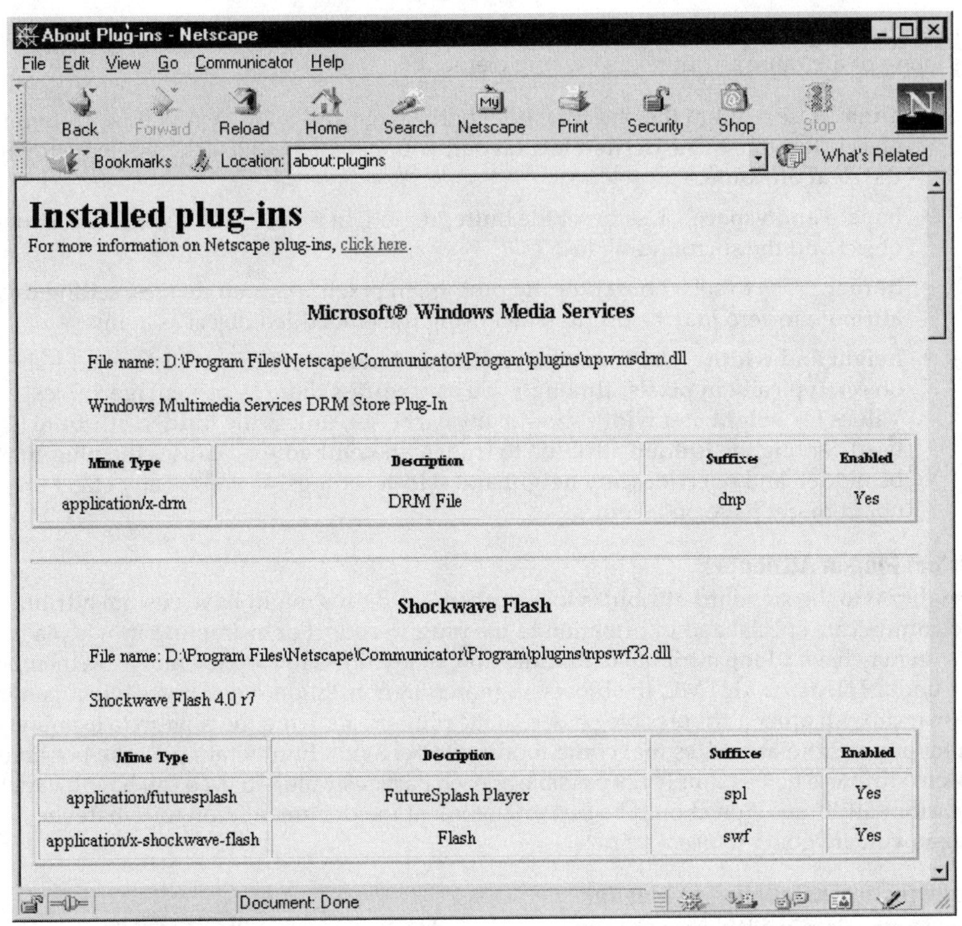

FIGURE 15-1 About Plug-ins listing

browsers. Furthermore, many developers and editors seem stuck on the **<embed>** syntax. For backward compatibility, you might have to use both forms, as shown later in this chapter. You can find the general syntax of an **<embed>** tag in the element reference in Appendix A.

The most important attribute for an **<embed>** tag probably is **src**, which is set to the URL of the data object that is to be passed to the plug-in and embedded in the page. The browser generally determines the MIME type of the file—and thus the plug-in to pass the data to—by the filename suffix. For example, a file such as test1.dcr would be mapped to a MIME type of application/x-director and passed to a Shockwave for Director plug-in. In some cases, however, the plug-in to use with a particular **<embed>** tag is not obvious. The plug-in might not need to use an **src** attribute if it reads all of its data at run time or doesn't need any external data.

Because plug-ins are rectangular, embedded objects similar to images, the **embed** element has many of the same attributes as the **img** element:

- **align** Use to align the object relative to the page and allow text to flow around the object. To achieve the desired text layout, you may have to use the **br** element with the **clear** attribute.
- **hspace** and **vspace** Use to set the buffer region, in pixels, between the embedded object and the surrounding text.
- **border** Use to set a border for the plug-in, in pixels. As with images, setting this attribute to zero may be useful when using the embedded object as a link.
- **height** and **width** Use to set the vertical and horizontal size of the embedded object, typically in pixels, although you can express them as percentage values. Values for **height** and **width** should always be set, unless the **hidden** attribute is used. Setting the **hidden** attribute to **true** in an **<embed>** tag causes the plug-in to be hidden and overrides any **height** and **width** settings, as well as any effect the object might have on layout.

Custom Plug-in Attributes

In addition to the standard attributes for **<embed>**, plug-ins might have custom attributes to communicate specialized information to the plug-in code. For example, a movie player plug-in may have a **loop** attribute to indicate how many times to loop the movie. Remember that under HTML or XHTML, the browser ignores all nonstandard attributes when parsing the markup. All other attributes are passed to the plug-in, allowing the plug-in to examine the list for any custom attributes that could modify its behavior. Enumerating all the possible custom attributes here is simply not possible as each particular plug-in used can have a variety of custom attributes. You should be certain to look at the documentation for whatever plug-in you are going to use.

Attributes for Installation of Plug-ins

If embedded data in a Web page has no associated plug-in, the user will need to install a plug-in to address it. However, making users figure out which plug-in to install isn't a very good idea; instead, set the **pluginspage** attribute equal to a URL that indicates the instructions for installing the needed plug-in. This way, if the browser encounters an **embed** element that it can't handle, it visits the specified page and provides information on how to download and install the plug-in. Starting with Netscape 4, however, this attribute automatically points to a special Netscape plug-in finder page.

Netscape 4 and beyond simplify the plug-in installation process by introducing the JAR Installation Manager (JIM), which is used to install Java Archive files (JARs). JAR files are a collection of files, including plug-ins, which can be automatically downloaded and installed. Set the **pluginurl** attribute for an **<embed>** tag to the URL of a JAR file containing the plug-in that is needed. If the user doesn't have the appropriate plug-in already installed, the browser invokes JIM with the specified JAR file and begins the download and installation process. The user has control over this process. The downloaded objects can be signed—a type of authentication—to help users avoid downloading malicious code. Figure 15-2 shows a sample JIM window under Netscape 4.

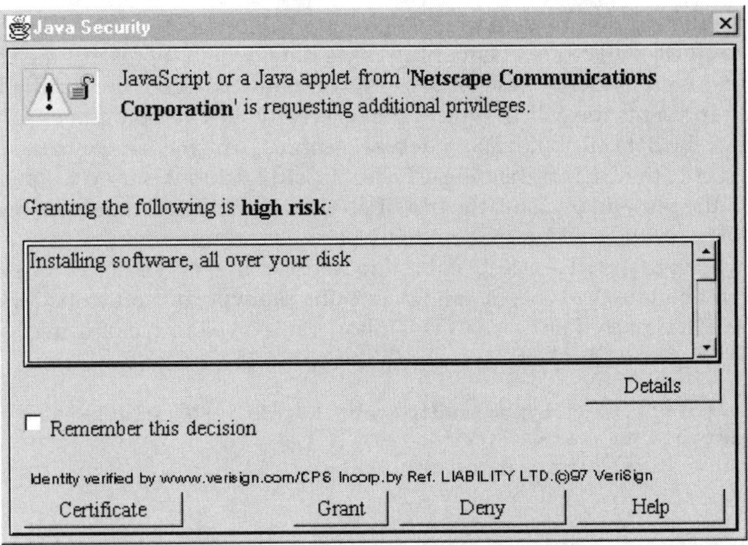

FIGURE 15-2 JIM window under Netscape 4

In Netscape 4 or greater, the **pluginurl** attribute takes precedence over **pluginspage**. However, if neither attribute is used, the Netscape browser should default to a plug-in finder page.

<noembed>

Some browsers don't understand Netscape's plug-in architecture, or even the **<embed>** tag. Rather than lock out these browsers from a Web page, the **<noembed>** tag enables you to provide some alternative text or marked-up content. In the following short example, an AVI video is embedded in the page. The **<noembed>** tag contains an image, which in turn has an alternative text reading set with the **alt** attribute. Note how the example degrades from a very sophisticated setting all the way down to a text-only environment:

```
<embed src="welcome.avi" height="100" width="100" />
<noembed>
   <img src="welcome.gif" alt="Welcome to Demo Company, Inc." />
</noembed>
```

One potential problem with the **<noembed>** approach occurs when a browser supports plug-ins but lacks the specific plug-in to deal with the included binary object. In this case, the user is presented with a broken puzzle-piece icon or a similar icon, and then is directed to a page to download the missing plug-in. As discussed previously, you should always set the **pluginurl** or **pluginspage** attribute to start the user on the process of getting the plug-in needed to view the content.

<object> Syntax for Plug-ins

The **<object>** tag can also be used to include a variety of object types in a Web page, including Netscape plug-ins. Like an **<embed>** tag, an **<object>** tag's attributes determine the type of object to include, as well as the type and location of the plug-in. The primary attribute for **<object>** when referencing plug-ins is **data,** which represents the URL of the object's data and is equivalent to the **src** attribute of **<embed>**. Like the **<embed>** tag, the **type** attribute represents the MIME type of the object's data. This sometimes can be inferred from the value of the **data** attribute. The **codebase** attribute, which is similar to the **pluginspage** attribute, represents the URL of the plug-in. The **classid** attribute is used to specify the URL to use to install the plug-in, by using the JIM. If no **classid** attribute is specified and the object can't be handled, the object is ignored, and any nested markup is displayed as an alternative rendering. The **id** attribute is used to set the name of the object for scripting. If the browser can't handle the type, or can't determine the type, it can't embed the object. Subsequent HTML is parsed as normal. The following is an example of using Netscape's old LiveAudio plug-in under Netscape 4 with the **<object>** syntax:

```
<object data="click.wav" type="audio/wav" height="60" width="144"
        autostart="false">
   <b>Sorry, no LiveAudio installed...</b>
</object>
```

Page authors should be cautious when referencing plug-ins with an **<object>** tag because compatibility issues with Microsoft Internet Explorer can arise. For the complete syntax of the **object** element, refer to the element reference in Appendix A.

Scripting and Plug-ins

Plug-ins can be accessed from a scripting language. Each plug-in used in a document can be referenced in Netscape's browsers as an element of the JavaScript **embeds[ ]** collection, which is part of the document object, as discussed in the previous chapter. Under Netscape, you can determine which plug-ins are available in the browser by using the **plugins[ ]** collection, which is part of the navigator object in JavaScript. The following markup displays the plug-ins that are installed in a Netscape browser:

```
<!DOCTYPE html PUBLIC "-//W3C//DTD XHTML 1.0 Transitional//EN"
"http://www.w3.org/TR/xhtml1/DTD/xhtml1-transitional.dtd">
<html xmlns="http://www.w3.org/1999/xhtml" lang="en">
<head>
<title>Print Plug-ins</title>
<meta http-equiv="content-type" content="text/html; charset=ISO-8859-1" />
</head>
<body>
<h2 align="center">Plug-ins Installed</h2>
<hr />
<script type="text/javascript">
<!--
if (navigator.appName == "Microsoft Internet Explorer")
 document.write("Plug-ins[] collection not supported under IE");
else
 {
   var num_plugins = navigator.plugins.length;
   for (var count=0; count < num_plugins; count++)
     document.write(navigator.plugins[count].name + "<br />");
```

```
 }
//-->
</script>
</body>
</html>
```

Note that this example will not display the plug-ins under Internet Explorer because IE doesn't support the **plugins[ ]** collection. Under Netscape, however, you can use some simple if-then logic in JavaScript to determine which markup to output depending on if a particular plug-in is loaded in the browser or not.

Once plug-ins are used in a page, they always should be named using the **name** and **id** attributes so they can be accessed easily from JavaScript. For example, the markup

```
<embed src="welcome.avi" name="welcomemovie" id="welcomemovie"
height="100" width="100"></embed>
```

gives this instance of the LiveVideo plug-in the name WelcomeMovie. After the plug-in is named, it can be accessed from JavaScript as **document.welcomemovie**. If it is the second plug-in in the page, it also could be referenced as **document.embeds[1]**. Why not "index 2"? Arrays in JavaScript, which is how collections are implemented, start numbering at zero, so **document.embeds[0]** references the first plug-in, **document.embeds[1]** references the second plug-in, and so on.

After you name an occurrence of a plug-in in a page, you might be able to manipulate the plug-in's actions even after you load the page. Netscape browsers, starting with the 3.*x* generation, include a technology called *LiveConnect* that enables JavaScript to communicate with Java applets and plug-ins. However, only plug-ins written to support LiveConnect can be manipulated using JavaScript. Fortunately, many plug-ins such as Macromedia Flash support LiveConnect. This simple example shows how LiveConnect works by using form buttons to start and stop the playing of a Flash movie in a page using JavaScript:

PART IV

```
<!DOCTYPE html PUBLIC "-//W3C//DTD XHTML 1.0 Transitional//EN"
"http://www.w3.org/TR/xhtml1/DTD/xhtml1-transitional.dtd">
<html xmlns="http://www.w3.org/1999/xhtml" lang="en">
<head>
<title>Flash JavaScript Control Example</title>
<meta http-equiv="content-type" content="text/html; charset=ISO-8859-1" />
<script type="text/javascript">
<!--

var loaded=false;
function playFlash(id)
{
 var flashFile = eval("window.document."+id);
  if (!loaded)
   {
    while (!loaded)
     {
       if (flashFile.PercentLoaded() == 100)
        {
          flashFile.Play();
          loaded = true;
         }
```

```
      }
    }
   else
    flashFile.Play();
}

function stopFlash(id)
{
  var flashFile = eval("window.document."+id);
  flashFile.StopPlay();
}
//-->
</script>
</head>
<body>
<h2 align="center">Plug-in and JavaScript Interaction</h2>
<embed src="example.swf" quality="high"
       pluginspage="http://www.macromedia.com/go/getflashplayer"
       type="application/x-shockwave-flash"
       width="400" height="250"
       id="example" name="example"
       swliveconnect="true">
  <noembed>
      You need Flash and Netscape for this demo
  </noembed>
</embed>
<hr />
<form action="#">
<input type="button" name="Button1" value="Start Flash" onclick="playFlash('example');" />
<input type="button" name="Button2" value="Stop Flash" onclick="stopFlash('example');" />
</form>
</body>
</html>
```

NOTE *The **swliveconnect="true"** attribute is very important and will ensure that this example works. Without this attribute, the demo should not work. Even so, the preceding example is very specific to Netscape and it may not work even in some Mozilla variants. Also, it might work under Internet Explorer, but there is no guarantee of this. Furthermore, the implementation of LiveConnect is buggy and might not work under all versions of Navigator. Still, the example illustrates the basics of a script talking to a plug-in.*

Tying together plug-ins by using a scripting language in conjunction with LiveConnect hints at the power of such component models as Netscape's plug-ins. However, Netscape plug-ins often are passed over in favor of ActiveX or Java applets for general programming tasks, and plug-ins often are regulated to handling new media forms as this example just demonstrated.

ActiveX Controls

ActiveX (http://www.microsoft.com/com/tech/activex.asp), which is the Internet portion of the Component Object Model (COM), is Microsoft's component technology for creating small components, or *controls*, within a Web page. It is intended to distribute these controls via the Internet to add new functionality to browsers such as Internet Explorer. ActiveX controls are more similar to generalized programmed components than plug-ins because they can reside beyond the browser within container programs such as Microsoft Office. ActiveX controls are similar to Netscape plug-ins insofar as they are persistent and machine specific. Although this makes resource use a problem, installation is not an issue: the components download and install automatically.

Security is a big concern for ActiveX controls. Because these small pieces of code could potentially have full access to a user's system, they could cause serious damage. This capability, combined with automatic installation, creates a serious problem with ActiveX. End users might be quick to click a button to install new functionality, only to accidentally get their hard drives erased. To address this problem, Microsoft provides authentication information to indicate who wrote a control, in the form of code signing and a certificate, as shown in Figure 15-3.

Certificates provide only some indication that the control creator is reputable; they do nothing to prevent a control from actually doing something malicious. Safe Web browsing should be practiced by accepting controls only from reputable sources.

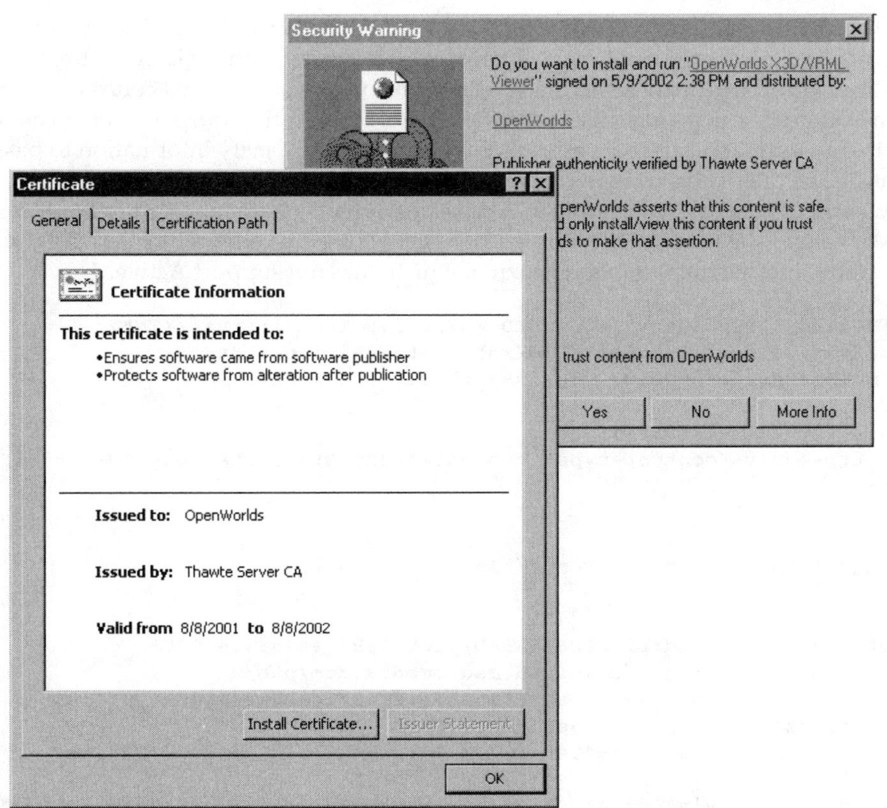

FIGURE 15-3 ActiveX signed-code certificate

Adding Controls to Web Pages

Adding an ActiveX control to a Web page requires the use of the **<object>** tag. The basic form of <**object**> for an ActiveX control is as follows:

```
<object classid="CLSID:class-identifier"
        height="pixels or percentage"
        width="pixels or percentage"
        id="unique identifier">

Parameters and alternative text rendering

</object>
```

When you insert ActiveX controls, **classid** is the most important attribute for an **<object>** tag. The value of **classid** identifies the object to include. Each ActiveX control has a class identifier of the form "**CLSID**: *class-identifier*," where the value for *class-identifier* is a complex string, such as the following, which uniquely identifies the control:

```
D27CDB6E-AE6D-11cf-96B8-444553540000
```

This is the identifier for the ActiveX implementation of the Flash Player. The other important attributes for the basic form of **<object>** when used with ActiveX controls include **height** and **width**, which are set to the pixel dimensions of the included control, and **id**, which associates a unique identifier with the control for scripting purposes. Between the **<object>** and **</object>** tags are various **<param>** tags that specify information to pass to the control, and alternative content and markup that displays in non-ActiveX-aware browsers. The following is a complete example that uses an **<object>** tag to insert an ActiveX control into a Web page. The markup specifies a Flash file. Figure 15-4 shows the rendering of the control under Internet Explorer and Mozilla, which does not support ActiveX.

```
<!DOCTYPE html PUBLIC "-//W3C//DTD XHTML 1.0 Transitional//EN"
"http://www.w3.org/TR/xhtml1/DTD/xhtml1-transitional.dtd">
<html xmlns="http://www.w3.org/1999/xhtml" lang="en">
<head>
<title>ActiveX Test</title>
<meta http-equiv="content-type" content="text/html; charset=ISO-8859-1" />
</head>
<body>

<h1 align="center">ActiveX Demo</h1>
<hr />

<object classid="clsid:D27CDB6E-AE6D-11cf-96B8-444553540000"
        codebase="http://download.macromedia.com/pub/
                  shockwave/cabs/flash/swflash.cab#version=6,0,0,0"
        id="flash1" name="flash1"
        width="320" height="240">

   <param name="movie" value="http://www.htmlref.com/flash/example.swf" />
   <param name="quality" value="high" />
```

```
    <b>Hello World for you non-ActiveX users!</b>

</object>
</body>
</html>
```

After you look at the previous markup, you may have questions about how to determine the **classid** value for the control and the associated **<param>** values that can be set. However, providing a chart for all the controls and their associated identifiers isn't necessary. Many Web development tools, including Macromedia Dreamweaver and Microsoft Visual Studio

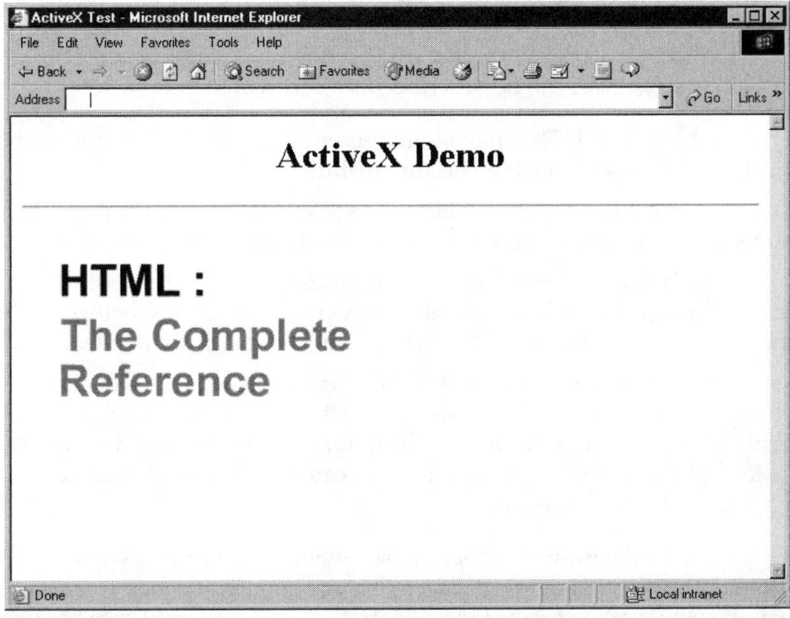

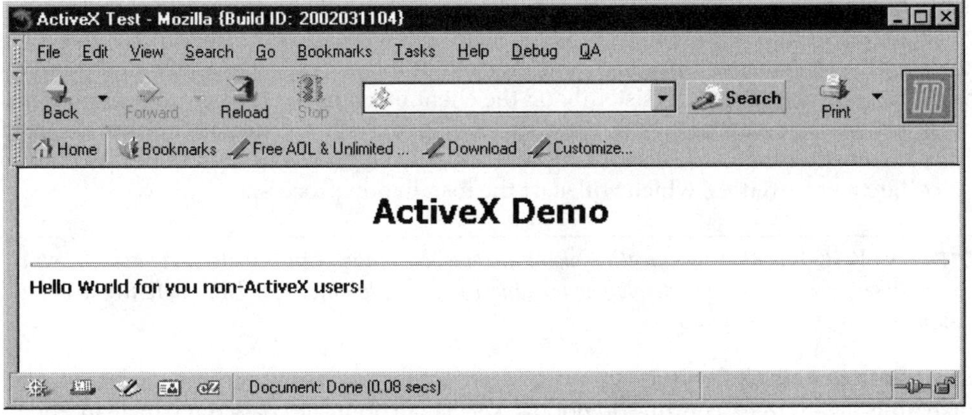

FIGURE 15-4 Rendering of ActiveX control under Internet Explorer and Mozilla

support the automated insertion of controls into a page, as well as configuration of the various control properties. If you are required to insert one by hand, hopefully the vendor of the control has provided documentation that you can consult to find the appropriate **classid**.

Installing ActiveX Controls

As mentioned previously, the most important attribute in the **<object>** syntax probably is **classid**, which is used to identify the particular object to include. For example, the syntax "CLSID:class-identifier" is for registered ActiveX controls. Generally, however, when the **object** element supports other included items well, **classid** might be set to other forms, such as "java: Blink.class," as discussed later in the chapter. Explorer also allows the use of the **code** attribute for the **<object>** tag; **code** is used to set the URL of the Java class file to include.

ActiveX and plug-ins are similar in the sense that both are persistent, platform-specific components. ActiveX controls, however, are easy to download and install. This installation, or running of ActiveX controls, can be described as a series of steps:

1. The browser loads an HTML page that references an ActiveX control with the **<object>** tag and its associated **classid** attribute.
2. The browser checks the system registry to see whether the control specified by the **classid** value is installed; this control takes the form "CLSID: some-id-number."
3. If the control is installed, the browser compares the **codebase** version attribute stored in the registry against the **codebase** version attribute specified in the tag. If a newer version is specified in the page, a newer control is needed.
4. If the control is not installed or a newer control is needed, the value of the **codebase** attribute is used to determine the location of the control to download. The **codetype** attribute also can be used to set the MIME type of the object to download. Most inclusions of ActiveX controls avoid this because it tends to default to the MIME type application/octet-stream.

For security reasons, the browser checks to see whether the code is signed before the download and installation begins. If the code is not signed, the user is warned. If the code is signed, the user may be presented with an Authenticode certificate bearing the identity of the author of the control. Based on these criteria, the user can allow or deny the installation of the control on his or her system. If the user accepts the control, it is automatically downloaded, installed, and invoked in the page for its specific function. Finally, the control is stored persistently on the client machine for further invocation. This process can be avoided when the **declare** attribute is present. The **declare** attribute is used to indicate whether the **<object>** is being defined only and not actually instantiated until later **<object>** occurrences, which will start the installation process.

NOTE *The W3C HTML 4 specification also indicates use of the* ***standby*** *attribute, which can be used to specify a message to display as the object is being downloaded. This currently is not supported by most browsers.*

Passing Data to ActiveX Controls

Unlike plug-ins, ActiveX controls do not use special attributes to pass data. Instead, they use a completely different element, called **param**, which is enclosed within an **<object>** tag. You can pass parameters to a control by using **<param>** tags, as shown here:

```
<object classid="CLSID:control-classid-here"
        id="label1" height="65" width="325">
   <param name="Caption" value="Hello World" />
   <param name="FontName" value="Arial" />
   <param name="FontSize" value="36" />

</object>
```

In this case, the **Caption** parameter is set to Hello World, the **FontName** parameter is set to Arial, and the **FontSize** parameter is set to 36 points. This is just a generic example to illustrate the idea; the previous example with Flash illustrated setting the source of the *movie* and its *quality* via **<param>** tags.

ActiveX Controls and Scripting

Similar to plug-ins, you can control ActiveX controls by using a scripting language such as JavaScript or VBScript. Before a control can be scripted, however, it must be named by using the **id** attribute. After it is named, scripting code for a particular event can be set for the control so that it can respond to events such as user clicks or mouse movements. The following simple example shows the previous Flash demo using ActiveX style **<object>** syntax with only minor modifications to the script to make it more like traditional Explorer JavaScript syntax:

```
<!DOCTYPE html PUBLIC "-//W3C//DTD XHTML 1.0 Transitional//EN"
"http://www.w3.org/TR/xhtml1/DTD/xhtml1-transitional.dtd">
<html xmlns="http://www.w3.org/1999/xhtml" lang="en">
<head>
<title>Flash JavaScript Control Example</title>
<meta http-equiv="content-type" content="text/html; charset=ISO-8859-1" />
<script type="text/javascript">
<!--
var loaded=false;

function playFlash(id)
{
  var flashFile = eval("window.document.all."+id);
  if (!loaded)
     {
       while (!loaded)
      {
        if (flashFile.PercentLoaded() == 100)
        {
          flashFile.Play();
          loaded = true;
        }
      }
     }
   else
     flashFile.Play();
}

function stopFlash(id)
{
  var flashFile = eval("window.document.all."+id);
  flashFile.StopPlay();
```

PART IV

```
}
//-->
</script>
</head>
<body>
<h2 align="center">Plug-in and JavaScript Interaction</h2>

<object classid="clsid:D27CDB6E-AE6D-11cf-96B8-444553540000"
        codebase="http://download.macromedia.com/pub/shockwave
                  /cabs/flash/swflash.cab#version=6,0,0,0"
        id="example" name="example"
        width="320" height="240">

   <param name="movie" value="http://www.htmlref.com/flash/example.swf" />
   <param name="quality" value="high" />
   <param name="swliveconnect" value="true" />

   <b>Hello World for you non-ActiveX users!</b>

</object>

<form action="#">
<input type="button" name="Button1" value="Start Flash" onclick="playFlash('example');" />
<input type="button" name="Button2" value="Stop Flash" onclick="stopFlash('example');" />
</form>
</body>
</html>
```

NOTE *This example won't work in anything other than Internet Explorer 3 or better running on a Windows-based system.*

Using ActiveX

Developers can access an abundance of available controls for various purposes. Today, most of the controls used are for playing media such as Flash movies or wrap-around images. While Microsoft used to include a variety of controls with its applications, including Internet Explorer, most of these are being phased out in favor of technologies that are part of the .NET framework. Yet despite this, ActiveX still survives and some developers even write their own browser controls and helper objects in Visual Basic, C++, and other high-level languages. ActiveX and related technologies are part of a larger Microsoft development framework that has undergone numerous name changes over the years and at the time of this writing is known as the .NET platform. Even that might change by the time you read this, so for the very latest information on development for the Microsoft platform, see http://msdn.microsoft.com.

Java Applets

Whereas both Microsoft's ActiveX and Netscape's plug-ins are platform and browser specific, Sun Microsystems' Java technology (http://java.sun.com) aimed to provide a platform-neutral development language, allowing programs to be written once and deployed on any machine, browser, or operating system that supports the Java virtual machine (JVM). Java uses small Java programs, called *applets*, that were first introduced by Sun's HotJava browser. Today, applets are supported by most Web browsers, including Netscape Navigator and Microsoft Internet Explorer. Of course, the nirvana of perfect cross-platform development never really materialized. Many versions of the Windows operating system do not ship with Java virtual machines and the technology never really took off in public Web sites. However, they are still used and Java applets continue to play an important role even in client-side development, particularly within controlled environments such as intranets.

Applets are written in the Java language and compiled to a machine-independent byte-code, which is downloaded automatically to the Java-capable browser and run within the browser environment. But even with a fast processor, the end system might appear to run the byte-code slowly compared to a natively compiled application because the byte code must be interpreted by the Java Virtual Machine. Even with recent Just-In-Time (JIT) compilers in newer browsers, Java often doesn't deliver performance equal to natively compiled applications upon startup. Once running, Java applets and applications perform well. However, even if compilation weren't an issue, current Java applets generally aren't persistent; they may have to be downloaded again in the future. Java-enabled browsers act like thin-client applications because they add code only when they need it. In this sense, the browser doesn't become bloated with added features, but expands and contracts upon use.

Security in Java has been considered from the outset. Because programs are downloaded and run automatically, a malicious program could be downloaded and run without the user being able to stop it. Under the first implementation of the technology, Java applets had little access to resources outside the browser's environment. Within Web pages, applets can't write to local disks or perform other harmful functions. This framework has been referred to as the *Java sandbox*. Developers who want to provide Java functions outside of the sandbox must write Java applications, which run as separate applications from browsers. Other Internet programming technologies (for example, ActiveX) provide little or no safety from damaging programs.

Oddly, Java developers often want to add just these types of insecure features, as well as such powerful features as persistence and inter-object communication. In fact, under new browsers, extended access can be requested for signed Java applets. (A *signed applet* enables users to determine who authored its code, and to accept or reject the applet accordingly.) Java applets can securely request limited disk access, limited disk access and network usage, limited disk read access and unlimited disk write access, and unrestricted access. Users downloading an applet that is requesting any enhanced privileges are presented with a dialog box that outlines the requested access and presents the applet's credentials in the form of its digital signature. The user then can approve or reject the applet's request. If the user doesn't approve the request, the applet can continue to run, but it can't perform the denied actions.

Java code looks very much like C++. The following code fragment shows a simple example of a Java applet:

```
import java.applet.Applet;
import java.awt.Graphics;

public class helloworld extends Applet
{
```

```
    public void paint(Graphics g)
     {
        g.drawString("Hello World", 50, 25);
     }
}
```

You can save this previous example into a file named helloworld.java and then send the code through a Java compiler (such as JavaSoft's javac) to produce a class file called helloworld.class, which can be used on a Web page to display the phrase "Hello World." You can use an **<applet>** tag to add a Java applet to a Web page. As with the **<embed>** tag, you must indicate the object to add. In this case, use the **code** attribute to indicate the URL of the Java class file to load. Because this is an included object, the **height** and **width** attributes should also be set. The following example includes the HelloWorld applet in a Web page. Figure 15-5 shows the rendering of the Java example under Netscape 4 with Java turned on and Java turned off.

```
<!DOCTYPE html PUBLIC "-//W3C//DTD XHTML 1.0 Transitional//EN"
"http://www.w3.org/TR/xhtml1/DTD/xhtml1-transitional.dtd">
<html xmlns="http://www.w3.org/1999/xhtml" lang="en">
<head>
<title>Java Hello World</title>
<meta http-equiv="content-type" content="text/html; charset=ISO-8859-1" />
</head>
<body>
<h1 align="center">Java Applet Demo</h1>
<hr />
<applet code="helloworld.class"
        height="50" width="175">

 <h1>Hello World for you non-Java-aware browsers</h1>

</applet>
</body>
</html>
```

In the preceding code example, between **<applet>** and **</applet>** is an alternative rendering for browsers that don't support Java or the **applet** element, or that have Java support disabled.

<applet> Syntax

Because Java applets are included objects, just like Netscape plug-ins, the syntax for the **applet** element is similar to the **embed** element, particularly for things such as alignment and sizing. The complete syntax for **<applet>** is shown in the element reference in Appendix A.

The most important attribute for the **applet** element probably is **code**, which is set to the URL of the Java class to load into the page. The **codebase** attribute can be set to the URL of the directory that contains the Java classes; otherwise, the current document's URL is used for any relative URLs.

Because Java applets are rectangular, embedded objects similar to images or plug-ins, an **<applet>** tag has many of the same attributes as images and plug-ins, including **align**, **height**, **width**, **hspace**, and **vspace**.

FIGURE 15-5 Java example under Netscape 4 with Java turned on and off

The **archive** attribute can be used to include many classes into a single archive file, which then can be downloaded to the local disk. The file specified by the **archive** attribute can be a compressed ZIP file (.zip) or a Java Archive (.jar), which can be made with a JAR packaging utility. For example,

```
<applet archive="bunchofclasses.zip"
        code="sampleApp.class"
        width="560"
        height="270">
</applet>
```

downloads all the classes in bunchofclasses.zip. After the file is downloaded, the **code** attribute is examined and the archive is checked to see whether sampleApp.class exists there. If not, it is fetched from the network. Due to the expense of fetching many class files by using HTTP, ideally, you should attempt to archive all potentially used classes and send them simultaneously. You also can derive some caching benefit by using the **archive** attribute because it keeps class files in the user's cache or a temporary directory. According to the HTML specification, the **archive** attribute can take a comma-separated list of archive files.

Passing Data to Java Applets

Unlike plug-ins, Java applets don't use special attributes to pass data. Instead, like ActiveX control's syntax, they use a different tag called **<param>**, which is enclosed within an **<applet>** tag, as the way to pass on information. You could extend the HelloWorld applet to allow the message output to be modified by using the **<param>** tag to pass in a message, as shown here:

```
<applet code="helloworld.class" width="50" height="175">

<param name="Message" value="Hello World in Java!" />

<h1>Hello World for you non-Java-aware browsers</h1>

</applet>
```

The following is the basic transitional XHTML syntax for **<param>**. Note that it is the same for Java applets and ActiveX controls:

```
<param name="Object property name"
       value="Value to pass in with object name"
       valuetype="DATA | REF | OBJECT"
       type="MIME Type"
       id="document-wide unique id" />
```

The **name** attribute for **<param>** is used to specify the name of the object property that is being set; in the preceding example, the name is "Message." If you are using a pre-made Java applet, the various property names should be specified in the documentation for the applet. The actual value to be assigned to the property is set by the **value** attribute. The **valuetype** attribute specifies the meaning of the **value** attribute. The data passed to an attribute typically takes the form of a string. Setting the **valuetype** attribute to **data** results in the default action. Setting **valuetype** to **ref** indicates that the data assigned to the **value** attribute is a URL that references an external file to load for the attribute. The last value for **valuetype is object**, which indicates that **value** is set to the name of an applet or object located somewhere else within the document. The data in the applet or object can be referenced to allow objects to "talk" to each other.

The **param** elements for a particular Java applet occur within the **<applet>** tag; a Java applet can have many **param** elements. The **applet** element also can enclose regular XHTML markup and other textual content that provides an alternative rendering for non-Java-capable browsers. When alternative content is found within the **<applet>**, the **<param>** tags should be placed before the other content. Note that you also can set the **alt** attribute for the **applet** element to provide a short description. Authors should use the text contained within the element as the alternative text, and not the **alt** attribute.

Java Applets and Scripting

Java applets can control scripts in a Web page. Supposedly, the inclusion of the **mayscript** attribute in an **<applet>** tag permits the applet to access JavaScript. When dealing with applets retrieved from other sources, you can use the **mayscript** attribute to prevent the applet from accessing JavaScript without the user's knowledge. If an applet attempts to access JavaScript when this attribute has not been specified, a run-time exception should occur. In practice, however, it appears that browsers do not necessarily care about the absence of **mayscript**.

Probably more interesting for page designers is the fact that scripts can control or even modify Java applets that are embedded in a page. For the applet to be accessed, it should be named using the **name** attribute as well as the **id** attribute. Providing a unique name for the applet allows scripts to access the applet and its public interfaces. The name also can be used by other applets to allow the applets to communicate with each other. JavaScript in Netscape 3 and above, as well as in Internet Explorer 4 and above, allows access to the applets in a page via the **applets[ ]** collection, which is a property of the document object. When an applet is named, it can be accessed through JavaScript as **document.*appletname***, such as **document.myApplet**, or through the array of applets in the document such as **document.applets[0]** or **document.applets["myApplet"]**. If the Java applet has public properties exposed, they can be modified from a script in a Web page. The following simple

Java code takes the "Hello World" example from earlier in the chapter and expands it with a **setMessage** method, which can be used to change the message displayed in the applet:

```
import java.applet.Applet;
import java.awt.Graphics;
public class newhelloworld extends Applet
{
    String theMessage;

    public void init()
     {
       theMessage = new String("Hello World");
     }
    public void paint(Graphics g)
     {
        g.drawString(theMessage, 50, 25);
     }
    public void setMessage(String message)
     {
       theMessage = message;
       repaint();
     }
}
```

If this Java code is compiled into a class file as explained earlier, it can be included in a Web page and accessed via JavaScript, as shown next. The following example markup shows how a form could be used to collect data from the user and update the applet in real time:

```
<!DOCTYPE html PUBLIC "-//W3C//DTD XHTML 1.0 Transitional//EN"
"http://www.w3.org/TR/xhtml1/DTD/xhtml1-transitional.dtd">
<html xmlns="http://www.w3.org/1999/xhtml" lang="en">
<head>
<title>Java and Scripting Demo</title>
<meta http-equiv="content-type" content="text/html; charset=ISO-8859-1" />
<script type="text/javascript">
<!--
function setMessage()
{
  var message = document.TestForm.NewMessage.value;
  document.NewHello.setMessage(message);
}
//-->
</script>
</head>
<body>
<h1 align="center">Java and Scripting Demo</h1>
<hr />

<applet code="newhelloworld.class"
        name="NewHello"
        height="50" width="175">
```

```
  <h1>You need Java for this example.</h1>
</applet>

<br /><br />

<form action="#" name="TestForm" id="TestForm">
  <input type="text" size="15" maxlength="15" name="NewMessage" />
  <input type="button" value="Set Message" onclick="setMessage()" />
</form>
</body>
</html>
```

<object> Syntax for Java Applets

The strict variants of HTML and XHTML indicate that the **applet** element has been deprecated and that **object** should be used instead. The following is the most basic XHTML syntax for inserting an object, such as a Java applet:

```
<object classid="URL of object to include"
        height="pixels or percentage"
        width="pixels or percentage">

  Parameters and alternative text

</object>
```

For the complete **<object>** syntax, see the element reference in Appendix A.

Notice that the **classid** attribute is used to specify the URL of the object to include. In the case of Java applets, you should use **java:**. For ActiveX controls, use **clsid:**. The following example rewrites the first simple Java applet example to use **<object>** and to work under strict XHTML:

```
<!DOCTYPE html PUBLIC "-//W3C//DTD XHTML 1.0 Strict//EN"
"http://www.w3.org/TR/xhtml1/DTD/xhtml1-strict.dtd">
<html xmlns="http://www.w3.org/1999/xhtml" lang="en">
<head>
<title>Java Hello World</title>
<meta http-equiv="content-type" content="text/html; charset=ISO-8859-1" />
</head>
<body>
<h1>Java Applet Demo</h1>
<hr />
<div>

<object classid="java:helloworld.class"
        height="50" width="175">

  <h1>Hello World for you non-Java-aware browsers</h1>
</object>

</div>
```

```
</body>
</html>
```

Because of the fragmentation of the Java community, Sun has made some attempts to bring together the syntax of Java applets using a Java plug-in. The specific syntax for this plug-in under Netscape and Internet Explorer includes both **<object>** and **<embed>** forms. Readers interested in this syntax for applet inclusion should go straight to Sun's Java support site for the latest syntax (http://java.sun.com) because the syntax continues to change.

Cross-Platform <object> Syntax Today and Tomorrow

Although the whole point of Java applets is to deal with cross-platform compatibility issues, Microsoft ActiveX controls and Netscape plug-ins are extremely platform- and browser-dependent. While this might suggest that using Java applets would be the way to go, in many cases, it is more likely that ActiveX controls and Netscape plug-ins can be referenced side-by-side in a Web page before Java applets are even considered. For example, consider the **<object>** syntax, **<embed>** syntax, and **<noembed>** syntax combined in the following way:

```
<object classid="XXX" id="object1" name="object1"
        height="100" width="100">
    <param name="sample param" value="sample" />
    <!--   other param elements here -->
    <embed src="XXX" id="plug1" name="plug1" height="100" width="100">
          <noembed>
            Sorry, your browser supports neither ActiveX nor plug-ins.
          </noembed>
    </embed>
</object>
```

In this case, the ActiveX control is tried first, then the plug-in, and finally the content within the **<noembed>** would be used if none of the other worked. Other methods for addressing cross platform issues might include using JavaScript to detect what browser is being run and then outputting the appropriate markup to reference an ActiveX control, Java applet, or maybe even some other alternative form. The point is that it is possible with some careful thought to cover all the possible situations and until the syntax and technology for including objects is straightened out, this is the only reasonable approach to handling cross-browser issues, short of locking out users from a page or falling back to less interactive or less motivating technology.

Although the future of cross-browser object support sounds enticing, it has yet to materialize. For example, according to the strict versions of XHTML including the upcoming XHTML 2.0, **<object>** will be the main way to add any form of object to a Web page, whether it's an image, image map, sound, video, ActiveX control, Java applet, or anything else. This approach seems appropriate, but before rushing out to use **<object>**, understand the ramifications—little backwards compatibility.

Even today, while standardized, the syntax is not consistently supported. For example, according to even the HTML 4 specification, the **object** element can be used to include markup from another file by using the **data** attribute. Imagine specifying a header file called header.html with the contents shown here:

```
<h1 style="text-align: center; background-color: #FFA500;">
I am an included heading!</h1>
```

This file then could be included in a Web page by using an **<object>** tag, like so:

```
<object data="header.html">
Header not included
</object>
```

This example should pull in the contents of the file header.htm in browsers that support this feature, and display "Header not included" in all others. The example here demonstrates this in use:

```
<!DOCTYPE html PUBLIC "-//W3C//DTD XHTML 1.0 Transitional//EN"
"http://www.w3.org/TR/xhtml1/DTD/xhtml1-transitional.dtd">
<html xmlns="http://www.w3.org/1999/xhtml" lang="en">
<head>
<title>Object Inclusion Test</title>
</head>
<body>

<div style="background-color: yellow; border-style: solid;
text-align: center; margin: 5px;"> Before Object </div>

<object data="header.html" style="width: 100%;
border-style: dashed; border-width: 1px;">
Header not included
</object>

<div style="background-color: yellow; border-style: solid;
text-align: center; margin: 5px;">  After Object </div>

</body>
</html>
```

A rendering of Internet Explorer 6 and Mozilla shown in Figure 15-6 demonstrates the drastic difference in browsers that do and do not support the full **<object>** syntax.

Eventually, **<object>** will be used in a generalized sense and maybe object technologies will be supported through very simple markup. For now, you should carefully use the **applet**, **embed,** and **object** elements to include components and media objects other than images in pages along with any required scripting to avoid locking users out of viewing your Web page.

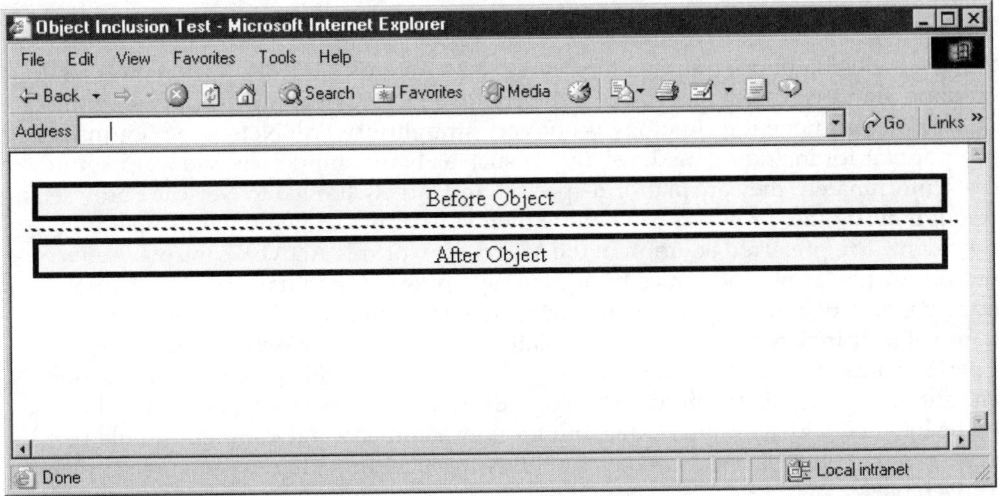

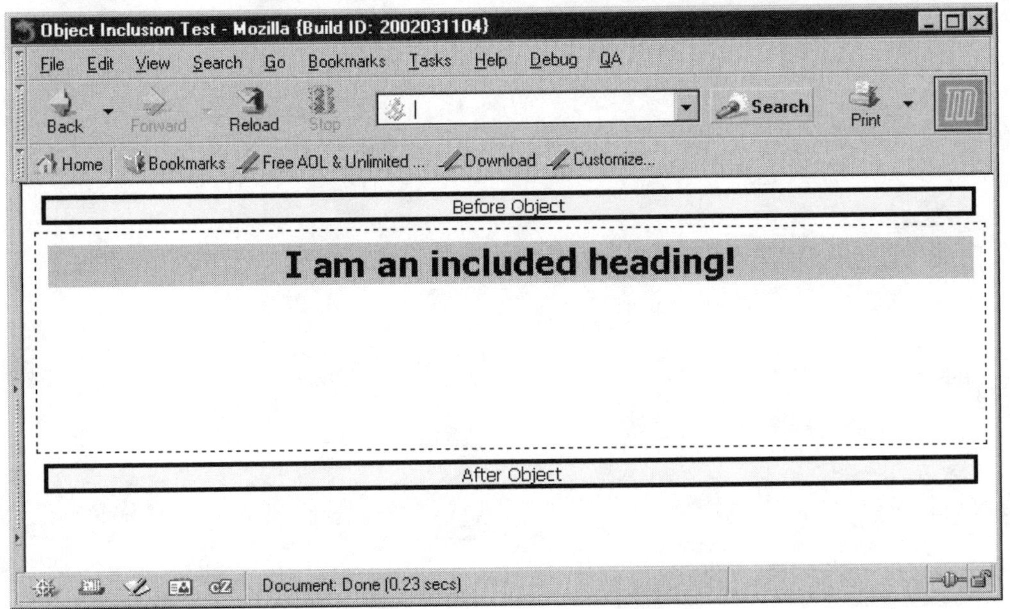

FIGURE 15-6 <object> for file inclusion in Internet Explorer and Mozilla

Summary

With the inclusion of programmed objects such as ActiveX controls, Java applets, and Netscape plug-ins, Web pages can become complex, living documents. Choosing the appropriate component technology is not very straightforward. Netscape plug-ins are very popular for including media elements such as Flash animations, video, or sound files. Unfortunately, they are platform-specific, and largely limited to Netscape browsers, although most other browsers can handle their syntax and come up with something equivalent. The preferred solution in the Microsoft world is ActiveX controls. ActiveX controls are just as platform-specific as Netscape plug-ins, and have some potential security issues. Solving the cross-platform problem requires complex page scripting or the use of Java applets that provide cross-platform object support, typically at the expense of performance. Either way, the page rendering should degrade gracefully if the user can't support the particular object technology. Eventually, the syntax for all included media will be handled with an **<object>** tag, but for now, **<embed>** and **<applet>** should be used as well to provide backward compatibility for including plug-ins and Java applets in a Web page.

V

PART

Site Delivery and Management

CHAPTER 16

HTTP and Site Delivery

As you develop your Web pages, it's important to consider how to deliver them to the user. Even if developers master the creation of Web pages using HTML/XHTML, CSS, JavaScript and so on, they can still fall flat on their faces if they don't pay careful attention to how they deliver the pages to the user. As far as the viewer of a page is concerned, the Web is one big system. If a page is slow because of a server, the user still views the site in a negative light no matter how correctly implemented the markup or other technology used might be, and in spite of how compelling the content or inspiring the design. Leaving important site delivery considerations until the very end of Web projects is a surefire way to improve the chances the site will fail.

The Importance of Delivery

Unfortunately, delivery issues often are only contemplated after a Web site has been designed and built. In many cases, the budget for the site doesn't significantly consider delivery costs, so corners are cut. This is like spending big money to design and print a corporate brochure, only to have it delivered by third-class postal mail because no funds were left after design and printing. The effect of the brochure would be severely diminished by its slow arrival. Delivery of Web sites is even more critical, particularly given the rise of task-oriented Web sites or e-commerce sites, in which any delay can mean the difference between a successful sale and a lost one.

Although designers might admit that users don't like slow sites, they tend to focus only on a few aspects of what makes a site slow. Consider that users will not be able to distinguish which aspect of site delivery is causing a page to load slowly. They are going to view it as a slow site, whether or not the graphics were optimized properly. Too much emphasis on optimizing file size, and not enough attention to servers, network choice, and even the characteristics of the medium itself, is a common mistake made by Web site designers. Consider all the possible reasons a site might be slow, as illustrated in Figure 16-1.

Although there are numerous potential problems to consider when delivering a site, the one inescapable fact is that, eventually, data will have to be transferred. Whether you download now or download later, you eventually have to do it. From the user's perspective, how much data is downloaded doesn't really matter; it only matters how responsive the site is. The user only counts the seconds on his or her watch, not the number of bytes delivered. How much data

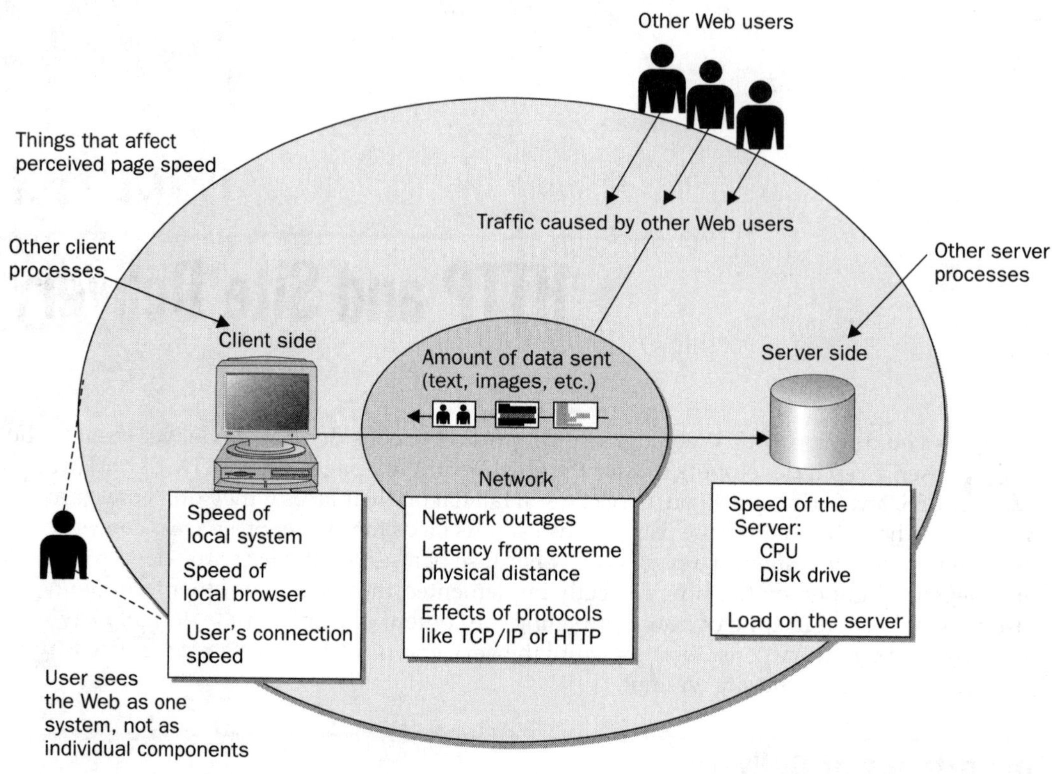

FIGURE 16-1 User does not see components affecting Web site delivery speed

comes down doesn't matter to the end user. Furthermore, if you are using huge graphics by downloading them during the idle moments, the user certainly won't care.

The bottom line is keeping the user happy. If your design requires a great deal of bandwidth, has many individual requests, or requires real-time delivery, you might have to shelve it. Always respect the medium of the Web. Just as a print designer understands that ink might bleed through paper, Web designers should understand the nature of the network and servers used to deliver their creations.

How to Deliver Web Sites

There are two basic choices for publishing your Web site on the public Internet: doing it yourself or outsourcing. Doing it yourself requires having a dedicated connection to the Internet and running your own server, whereas outsourcing involves renting physical space, bandwidth, or services on an existing Web server from an outside vendor.

Running your own Web server and connection to the Internet might seem like the way to go, but it can be quite expensive. A common dedicated connection such as a T1 to the Internet can cost thousands of dollars a year. When factoring in labor, server, facilities, and other expenses, the total cost is significant. Often, many of these facilities are already available within the organization and should be used. Yet, using someone else's server might be the

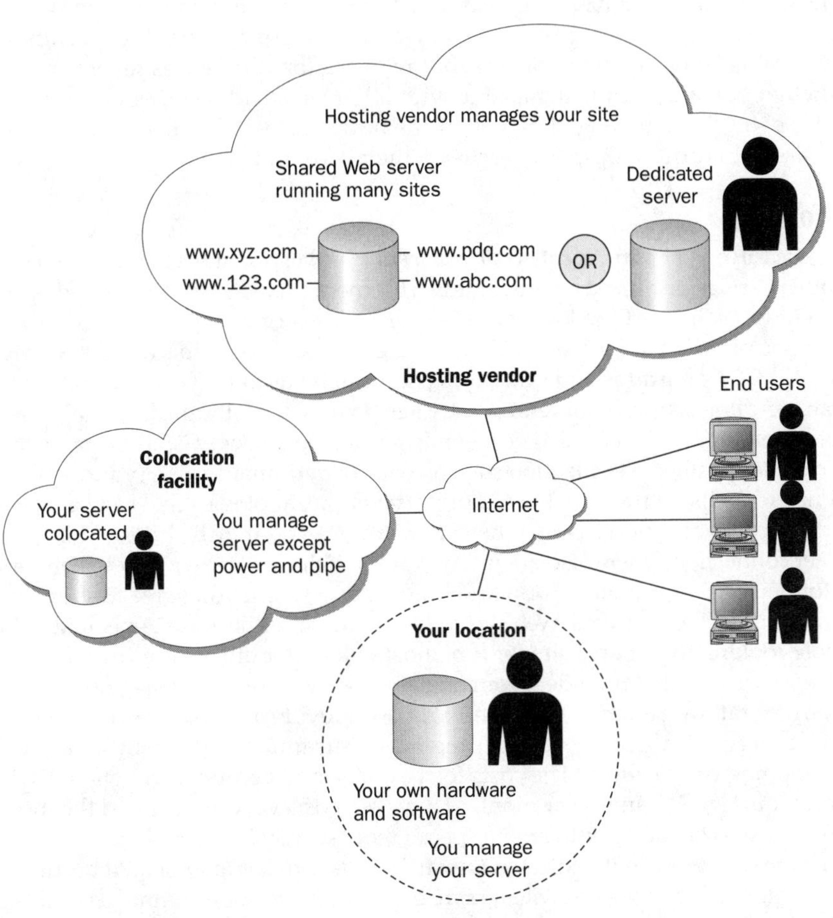

FIGURE 16-2 Hosting choices overview

only choice for people who want to publish Web documents but can't afford a huge fee. Even firms that have a capable staff should consider outsourcing, as it provides many benefits. Figure 16-2 gives a basic overview of the major hosting approaches.

Outsourcing Web Hosting

As Web sites become more critical to the information infrastructure of companies, there is a growing need to provide high-quality, high-availability solutions. For example, a business selling something only online can't afford to have its site go down if at all possible. The serving of a site to an e-business is as critical as power and telephone services would be to a traditional business. This trend might be termed the "utilization" of the Web, as some might consider the health and delivery of their Web site as important as utilities such as power, phone, or water. Firms quickly discover that it is, in fact, quite expensive for companies to develop in-house the talents and facilities to run a mission-critical Web site. Similarly, a small firm typically does not have the resources to build and maintain a basic Web server facility. For these reasons, many firms have decided to outsource their Web facilities. Web server outsourcing comes in many flavors, but many of the differences revolve around two factors: whether you are sharing a machine with other sites and whether or not the machine being used is owned and managed by you or the outsource vendor. Each type of service will be discussed in turn, with special focus on their pros and cons.

Shared Hosting

The most basic form of hosting is called *shared hosting* and can range from free Web space added to other services, or in exchange for advertisement placement, to high-end application service providers (ASPs). At the low end, many Internet service providers will provide a directory on one of their Web servers with a few megabytes of disk space and possibly access to a few shared CGI programs and other tools that can be used on your Web site, such as simple form handling scripts, counters, or message boards. Usually, the URL for a site such as this is of the form http://www.isp.net/~enduser or http://www.isp.net/enduser. The hosting service lacks any customization such as your own domain name (yourname.com), and may impose limits on traffic delivered or particular technologies that can be used. The upside to these types of services is that they often are free and may be included in the cost of your Internet connection. There also are many vendors who will provide free Web serving in exchange for personal information for marketing purposes, or if you agree to show banner advertisements they book on your Web site. Whereas these services are appealing to home users or those looking to put up a site for fun, most will prefer other forms of shared hosting.

Shared host services that provide a domain name (www.yourname.com), often called a *virtual server*, generally are not free. These services also provide improved development facilities such as your own cgi-bin directory, statistics reports on site traffic, and other useful features, including shopping cart facilities. The costs for virtual server accounts on a shared system usually start around $20 or more per month. However, costs vary greatly and the more bandwidth your site consumes or the more special requests you have, the higher the possible cost—even if the machine is not dedicated to you. In fact, with complex shared hosting services, in which you might have access to content management systems or e-commerce facilities, the cost can literally skyrocket to hundreds or even thousands of dollars per month.

The major downside of shared Web hosting is that it involves using the shared server facilities of a hosting vendor. This means that the site will share Web server resources and bandwidth with other hosted sites. Server responsiveness can be significantly affected because of other hosted Web sites, particularly if those sites become popular. Furthermore, many customers are wary of sharing a server with others because security often cannot be guaranteed on these shared systems. Despite its drawbacks, shared hosting is very popular—mainly due to price.

Dedicated Hosting

As a result of the security and control issues with a shared server, many people opt to use a dedicated server. Dedicated servers are advantageous because you can customize your server with whatever tools or programs you like, and they are not affected by other sites as much. However, the trade-off is cost. Dedicated servers tend to be more expensive.

There are two forms of dedicated server hosting. In the first, the outsource vendor owns and maintains the equipment. This is called *fully managed* or *dedicated hosting*. In the other, you own and may even be responsible for maintaining your server. This usually is called *colocation*. With colocation, the vendor provides space at its facility, electrical power, a network connection, a certain amount of bandwidth, and very limited system management for your server (such as rebooting it if it crashes or maybe doing tape backups). Colocation generally is cheaper than fully managed services, but for those who don't want to be bothered with the details of Web site delivery, colocation is not as great a deal as it might seem. The extra money paid for a fully managed service seems to be appreciated only when a machine fails in the middle of the night.

Dedicated hosting solutions are very attractive to those who want control, security, and power, but don't want to deal with many of the day-to-day issues of running a Web server. The major downside of these solutions is price. Services-provided top-tier hosting vendors might run many thousands of dollars per month based on the equipment and bandwidth required as well as any services added, such as security monitoring or sophisticated hosting requirements such as mirroring a site at multiple locations. However, if a business really relies on robust, fast Web site delivery, many of these vendors are a bargain even at what appears to be a high price. Consider the actual cost of maintaining a telephone company–grade equipment room filled with servers connected to numerous Internet providers being monitored twenty-four hours a day, seven days a week by capable system and network administrators, and you'll see that the cost might be well worth it. Consider that some of the largest content, search engine, and e-commerce sites don't run their own servers and you'll see that considering an outside hosting vendor is a good idea.

Companies looking to save money on Web delivery may find outsourcing very attractive, but some flexibility and security may have to be sacrificed. With less experienced hosting companies, this lack of control can be disastrous, resulting in hidden costs or problems with reliability. Those who want more control over their Web services should consider colocation or running their own servers locally. Of course, running your own servers introduces the potential headaches involved with setting up and administering your Web server continuously, which even for small sites might be a significant amount of work.

TIP *A directory of commercial hosting vendors can be found at http://www.webhostlist.com.*

Web Servers

If you decide to run your Web server, it is important to consider how they work. To many, Web servers seem mystical. In reality, a Web server is just a computer running a piece of software that fulfills HTTP requests made by browsers. In the simplest sense, a Web server is just a file server, and a very slow one at times. Consider the operation of a Web server resulting from a user requesting a file, as shown in Figure 16-3. Basically, a user just requests a file and the server either delivers it back or issues some error message, such as the ubiquitous 404 not found message.

However, a Web server isn't just a file server because it also can run programs and deliver results. In this sense, Web servers also can be considered application servers—if occasionally simple or slow ones.

Web Server Components

A Web server is composed of both hardware and software. The primary operation of a Web server is to copy the many (generally small) files making up a Web page from disk to network as fast as possible for numerous simultaneous users. A secondary mission is to run

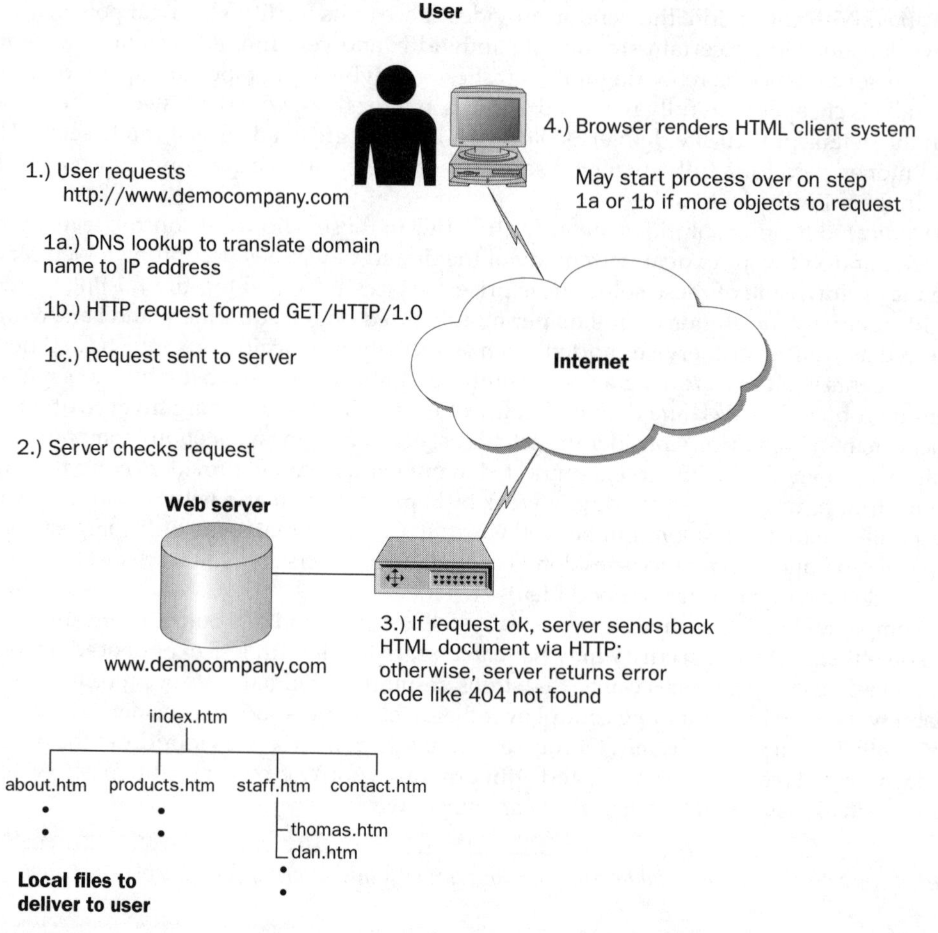
User
4.) Browser renders HTML client system
May start process over on step 1a or 1b if more objects to request
1.) User requests http://www.democompany.com
1a.) DNS lookup to translate domain name to IP address
1b.) HTTP request formed GET/HTTP/1.0
1c.) Request sent to server
Internet
2.) Server checks request
Web server
www.democompany.com
3.) If request ok, server sends back HTML document via HTTP; otherwise, server returns error code like 404 not found
index.htm
about.htm
products.htm
staff.htm
contact.htm
thomas.htm
dan.htm
Local files to deliver to user

FIGURE 16-3 Web server operation overview

programs for numerous individuals and deliver the results as fast as possible. Given these requirements, consider the hardware components of a Web server shown in Table 16-1.

In addition to getting the best hardware you can afford, it is important to consider that the operating system running on the hardware and the available server and development software options are going to have a great effect on the speed of the Web server. In general, given that Web servers have to deal with multiple requests simultaneously and need a rich set of development options, most developers tend to use either Windows NT/2000/2003 or some variant of UNIX, including Linux, for their operating system. Table 16-2 presents the major operating system choices as well as some of the issues in using them for Web serving.

While Table 16-2 presents a good overview of some of the issues faced when choosing one operating system over another for a Web server, the decision may often be based on familiarity or personal taste. While one person may argue about the merits of UNIX or Linux, introducing such a server into an environment with heavy Windows investment would be foolish. The bottom line is to always remember suitability and total cost over time.

Hardware Component	Considerations
Processor	While a fast processor seems key to a fast Web server, the reality is that computational requirements of a Web server are limited. Multiple processors may be more useful than a single fast processor when dealing with numerous requests made on a server.
Memory	A Web server may need a large amount of RAM to hold numerous individual processes running server-side programs for users or fulfilling file requests. Furthermore, memory is useful for caching commonly requested content.
Bus	Web data will constantly move from disk to memory to network. Don't limit the data path with a slow bus.
Disk drive	Because a Web server's primary task is delivering files to a user, a high-speed disk drive that is kept optimized is a primary goal. Spend extra on drives with high-speed adapters.
Network interface	Once files are retrieved from disk, they are delivered back to the user via the network. Don't limit a server by its network interface card. For high-volume servers, multiple network interfaces may be mandatory.
Other	Most other aspects of a Web server have little bearing on the delivery of a site. However, some peripherals such as tape drives or other backup storage facilities are mandatory for site maintenance.

TABLE 16-1 Web Server Hardware Issues

Operating System	Pros	Cons
UNIX	-Tends to run on fast hardware such as UltraSparc systems. -Very flexible development environment. -High-end applications and servers are available.	-Can be complicated to use and difficult to set up and maintain. -Labor costs may be high. -Buy-in costs for hardware and software are relatively high.
Windows NT/ 2000/2003	-Runs on a wide range of hardware. -Many servers and development tools available. -Basic administration is simple.	-May require multiple servers for high-volume sites. -Advanced administration may rival -UNIX in difficulty. -Guaranteeing server stability and security can be troublesome.
Linux	-Available on low-end equipment. -Cost is low. -Many servers and development tools available.	-Like standard UNIX, can be complicated to use and difficult to maintain. -Lacks some commercial software support.

TABLE 16-2 Operating Systems and Web Serving Considerations

Operating System	Pros	Cons
Windows 98/ ME/XP	-Easy to run. -Low equipment costs. -Inexpensive software.	-Not as robust as NT or UNIX for server applications. -Selection of Web software is limited, compared to Windows Server or UNIX variants. -Similar security and stability issues like Windows server environments.
Macintosh	-Easy to run and administer. -Relatively low equipment costs. -Inexpensive software.	-Traditional Macintosh OS is not suitable for Web serving, though the UNIX-based OS X is very well-suited for it. -Selection of Web software is limited, but is growing fast given OS X's UNIX core. -Traditional Mac OS not as robust as -NT or UNIX for serving, but Mac OS X very stable.

TABLE 16-2 Operating Systems and Web Serving Considerations *(continued)*

A relatively low-traffic site for a school might do well on an older Macintosh. A Windows system might make a great departmental server in a corporation that favors Windows systems. A Linux system might appeal to a technical-minded individual looking to avoid spending money on hardware and software, and a high-end Sun server running Solaris might be appropriate for a large e-commerce venture. Some sites may find that a server-appliance that does not directly expose operating system issues may also be appropriate if maintenance is a significant concern. The point is always to choose an operating system for a server based on the practicality of performance, development, and long-term maintenance characteristics of the OS.

Web Server Software

Once the hardware and operating system are selected, it is time to consider which Web server package to use. A few years ago, there were only two major Web servers available: NCSA's httpd server for UNIX and CERN's httpd server for UNIX, both free servers that required a fairly substantial knowledge of UNIX and programming. Today, there are dozens of different Web servers—both commercial and freeware—available on a variety of machines. Rather than considering all Web servers in your decision, it might be wise to look at the most common Web servers used. On the basis of surveys and analysis of reachable servers on the Internet (www.netcraft.com), the following are considered to be some of the most common Web servers used, though their exact market percentage is a topic of hot debate.

Apache	Zeus
Microsoft's IIS	WebStar
Sun servers (formerly IPlanet and Netscape)	Domino

A discussion of each of the popular Web servers follows. This should by no means be considered as approval of these products, but rather just a synopsis of each product highlighting some of its known characteristics.

TIP *Serverwatch (www.serverwatch.com) provides links and reviews of most of the popular Web servers available.*

Apache (http://www.apache.org/)

A descendant of NCSA's httpd server, Apache is probably the most popular Web server on the Internet, at least as far as public Web sites are concerned. Apache's popularity stems from the fact that it is free and fast. It is also very powerful, supporting features like HTTP 1.1, extended server-side includes (SSIs), a module architecture similar to NSAPI/ISAPI, and numerous free modules that perform functions such as content negotiation, text compression, spell checking, and much more. However, Apache is not for everyone. The main issue with Apache is that it isn't a commercial package. Some firms are hesitant to run their mission-critical systems on a user-supported product. However, as with operating systems like Linux, various third parties offer commercial implementations of Apache or sell support for the free version. Another potential limiting factor for Apache is that the system currently is mainly for UNIX or Linux system variants including Mac OS X. Although there is a port of Apache to Windows 32-bit systems, the server was initially built for popular UNIX and Linux variants. The lack of heavy Windows support may limit the use of Apache within many Microsoft-centric enterprises, but the Apache 2.0 release aims to change that. However, given the development integration Microsoft IIS provides, it may be a hard sell to the Windows crowd. Probably the most troublesome aspect of Apache for some developers is that it may require modification of configuration files or even compilation in order to install properly. If you like to tinker or desire speed, have a UNIX or Linux system, or don't have a lot of money, then Apache might just be for you. You'll be in good company; some of the largest Web sites on the Internet swear by this server.

NOTE *For Web trivia buffs, the name "Apache" is derived from the description of the software as a patched version of NCSA. Think "a patchy NCSA server."*

Microsoft Internet Information Services (http://www.microsoft.com/iis/)

IIS is Microsoft's server for Windows NT/2000/XP/2003. Other Windows variants also support a similar but much less powerful version of IIS called the Personal Web Server (PWS). While PWS is certainly popular, of the two, most organizations favor IIS. One very important aspect of IIS is that it is very tightly integrated with the Windows environment. In fact, today it is hard to distinguish IIS as a stand-alone service within Windows 2000. Unfortunately, being so Windows-specific is also one of the main problems with IIS. The tight integration has lead to numerous security exploits in IIS and the operating system has not proved to be quite as scalable as some UNIX-based servers. With new Microsoft clustering technologies and integration with a transaction processor, this scalability problem is likely to change. Microsoft also promises great improvements in security, which would certainly be welcome. However, for an intranet environment—particularly one with heavy Microsoft investment—it is difficult to beat the features offered by IIS, particularly its Active Server Pages and .NET development platform and its integration with other Microsoft technologies and products. The price for IIS is currently a major positive point for the software—it's freely bundled with the operating system.

Sun (Servers formerly known as iPlanet or Netscape) (http://www.sun.com/software/)

Sun servers, born from the iPlanet joint venture between Sun and Netscape after the merger between Netscape and AOL, constitute a large number of Web servers. These servers continue a long history started by Netscape of supporting high-end Web and application servers running on most major variants of UNIX (Solaris, SunOS, AIX, HP-UX, Digital UNIX, and IRIX) as well as on Windows. The servers are well developed, as they represent more than four generations of software releases. The servers are also very developer friendly and powerful, with support for databases and directory services, content management, HTTP 1.1, and a variety of other features. Given Sun's involvement, a focus on Java is core to the server offering. If you are in a cross-platform or UNIX environment and you are looking for commercial-quality Web serving solutions, then consider using these servers.

4D WebStar (http://www.webstar.com/)

Initially a popular Web server for the Macintosh originally based on MacHTTPD, WebStar integrates well with the traditional Macintosh interface. The server has solid security features and supports both native Macintosh technologies as well as UNIX-style CGI programs, PHP, a Java virtual machine for server-side Java, and extended SSI. The performance of most Macintosh Web servers has often left much to be desired, though it is improving and is probably more than adequate for intranets or small Web sites. Today, in an OS X environment most folks use the Apache server, which is included in the OS X distribution.

Lotus Domino (http://www.lotus.com/domino)

Domino is an example of the collision between traditional Web serving and messaging and groupware. Domino runs on Windows NT, variants of UNIX, and even large IBM systems such as AS/400s. It is often used in corporate intranet and extranet environments where workflow and integration with messaging and backend systems may be more important than raw Web serving performance.

Zeus (http://www.zeus.com)

Finally, we have Zeus as a contender for the fastest Web server. This server is becoming popular with extremely high volume Web sites. The Zeus server does not lack development capabilities, as it provides not only Java compatibility but supports both IIS's ISAPI interface and the NSAPI interface introduced on Netscape Enterprise servers.

Making the Choice

There are numerous Web server software choices. Remember that different packages will have different performance characteristics. Using the same hardware, one Web server software package may far outperform another. When planning to build a Web server, start either from the hardware and build up or from the particular software and build down, picking the best possible hardware compatible with the selected server. If you make good software and hardware choices, the performance of the site can be significantly improved. Always try to base your choices on usage requirements, such as a target number of simultaneous users or requests per minute or second. However, don't forget that you will have to maintain the site. If you are unfamiliar with UNIX systems and your company uses only Windows servers, your decision is probably already made for you. Once all the requirements of the site have been carefully determined, it is possible to best choose how to serve a site.

How Web Servers Work

When it comes to the physical process of publishing documents, the main issues are whether to run your own server or to host elsewhere in conjunction with Web server software and hardware. However, a deeper understanding of how Web servers do their job is important to understand potential bottlenecks. Recall that, in general, all that a Web server does is listen for requests from browsers or, as they are called more generically, *user agents*. Once the server receives a request, typically to deliver a file, it determines whether it should do it. If so, it copies the file from the disk out to the network. In some cases, the user agent might ask the server to execute a program, but the idea is the same. Eventually, some data is transmitted back to the browser for display. This discussion between the user agent, typically a Web browser, and the server takes place using the HTTP protocol.

HTTP

The Hypertext Transfer Protocol (HTTP) is the basic, underlying, application-level protocol used to facilitate the transmission of data to and from a Web server. HTTP provides a simple, fast way to specify the interaction between client and server. The protocol actually defines how a client must ask for data from the server and how the server returns it. HTTP does not specify how the data actually is transferred; this is up to lower-level network protocols such as TCP.

The first version of HTTP, known as version 0.9, was used as early as 1990. HTTP version 1.0 as defined by RFC 1945, is supported by most servers and clients (Web browsers). However, HTTP 1.0 does not properly handle the effects of hierarchical proxies and caching, or provide features to facilitate virtual hosts. More important, HTTP 1.0 has significant performance problems due to the opening and closing of many connections for a single Web page.

The current version, HTTP 1.1, solves many of the past problems of the protocol. It is supported by version 4–generation Web browsers and up. There still are many limitations to HTTP, however. It is used increasingly in applications that need more sophisticated features, including distributed authoring, collaboration, multimedia support, and remote procedure calls. Various ideas to extend HTTP have been discussed and a generic Extension Framework for HTTP has been introduced by the W3C. Already, some facilities such as client capability detection and privacy negotiation between browser and server have been implemented on top of HTTP, but most of these protocols are still being worked out. For now, HTTP continues to be fairly simple, so this discussion will focus on HTTP 1.0 and 1.1.

HTTP Requests

The process of a Web browser or other user agent—such as Web spider or Robot—requesting a document from a Web (or more correctly HTTP) server is simple, and has been discussed throughout the book. The overall process was diagrammed in Figure 16-3. In the figure, the user first requests a document from a Web server by specifying the URL of the document desired. During this step, a domain name lookup may occur, which translates a machine name such as www.democompany.com to an underlying IP address such as 206.251.142.3. If the domain name lookup fails, an error message such as "No Such Host" or "The server does not have a DNS entry" will be returned. Certain assumptions, such as the default service port to access for HTTP requests (80), also might be made. This is transparent to the user, who simply uses a URL to access a page. Once the server has been located, the browser forms the proper HTTP request and sends the request to the server residing at the address specified by the URL. A typical HTTP request consists of the following:

```
HTTP-Method Identifier HTTP-version
<Optional additional request headers>
```

In this example, the **HTTP-Method** would be **GET** or **POST**. An identifier might correspond to the file desired (for example, /examples/Chapter16/report.htm), and the **HTTP-version** indicates the dialect of HTTP being used, such as HTTP/1.0.

If a user requests a document with the URL http://www.htmlref.com/examples/chapter15/report.htm, the browser might generate a request such as the one shown here to retrieve the object from the server at www.htmlref.com:

```
GET /examples/chapter16/report.htm HTTP/1.0
If-Modified-Since: Tuesday, 15-Aug-00 01:39:39 GMT;
Connection: Keep-Alive
User-Agent: Mozilla/4.02 [en] (X11; I; SunOS 5.4 sun4m)
Accept: image/gif, image/x-xbitmap, image/jpeg, image/pjpeg, */*
Accept-Language: en
Accept-Charset: iso-8859-1,*,utf-8
```

People often ask why the complete URL is not shown in the request. It isn't necessary in most cases, except when using a proxy server. The use of a relative URL in the header is adequate. The server knows where it is; it just needs to know what document to get from its own file tree. In the case of using a proxy server, which requests a document on behalf of a browser, a full URL is passed to it that later is made relative by the proxy. Aside from the simple **GET** method, there are various other methods specified in HTTP. Not all are commonly used. Table 16-3 provides a summary of the HTTP 1.1 request methods.

It is interesting to note that two of the methods (**GET** and **POST**) supported by HTTP are the values of the **form** element's **method** attribute. Recall that this attribute indicates the method in which data is passed from the form to the server-side program. In the case of **GET**, it is passed through the URL because another page is simply being fetched, as a normal **GET** request would do. In the case of a **POST** value, the data of the form is passed behind the scenes to the server program that should return a result page to the browser as well. This is discussed in Chapters 12 and 13 and, as shown by the **form** element, it should become clear that HTML and HTTP do interact in more than a casual way.

HTTP Request Headers

Within an HTTP request, there are a variety of optional fields for creating a complete request. The fields are specified by a header name, a colon and then a value. A user agent generally sends extra header information in a request indicating the type of device making the request (user-agent), the type of data it prefers (accept), what language is in use (accept-language), and so on. The value of this header information should not be understated. With it, your server side programs can detect things such as the browser being used, the particular types of images supported by the browser, the language of the browser such as French, English, or Japanese, and so on. The common request headers and an example for each are shown in Table 16-4.

Method	Description
GET	Returns the object specified by the identifier. Notice that it also is one of the values of the **method** attribute for the **form** element.
HEAD	Returns information about the object specified by the identifier, such as last modification data, but does not return the actual object.
OPTIONS	Returns information about the capabilities supported by a server if no location is specified, or the possible methods that can be applied to the specified object.
POST	Sends information to the address indicated by the identifier; generally used to transmit information from a form using the **method="POST"** attribute of the **form** element to a server-based CGI program.
PUT	Sends data to the server and writes it to the address specified by the identifier overwriting previous content, in basic form. This method can be used for file upload.
DELETE	Removes the file specified by the identifier; generally disallowed for security reasons.
TRACE	Provides diagnostic information by allowing the client to see what is being received on the server.

TABLE 16-3 Summary of HTTP 1.1 Request Methods

Request Header	Description	Example
Accept: *MIME-type/ MIME-subtype*	Indicates the data types accepted by the browser. An entry of */* indicates anything is accepted; however, it is possible to indicate particular content types such as image/jpeg so the server can make a decision on what to return. This facility could be used to introduce a form of content negotiation so that a browser could be served only data it understands or prefers. Apache provides this feature and IIS can be extended to provide this feature as well, but at the time of this edition's writing this concept is not widely understood or implemented by Web developers.	Accept: image/gif, image/x-xbitmap, image/jpeg, image/pjpeg, */*
Accept-Charset: *charset*	Indicates the character set that is accepted by the browser, such as ASCII or foreign character encodings.	Accept-Charset: iso-8859-1,*,utf-8
Accept-Encoding: *encoding-type*	Instructs the server on what type of encoding the browser understands. Typically, this field is used to indicate to the server that compressed data can be handled.	Accept-Encoding: x-compress

TABLE 16-4 HTTP Request Headers

Request Header	Description	Example
Accept-Language: *language-code*	Lists the languages preferred by the browser and could be used by the server to pass back the appropriate language data.	Accept-Language: en
Authorization: *authorization-scheme authorization-data*	This header typically is used to indicate the userid and encrypted password if the user is returning authorization information.	Authorization: user joeblow:testpass
Content-length: *bytes*	Gives the length in bytes of the message being sent to the server, if any. Remember that the browser can upload or pass data using the **PUT** or **POST** method.	Content-length: 1805
Content-type: *MIME-type/ MIME-subtype*	Indicates the MIME type of a message being sent to a server, if any. The value of this field would be particularly important in the case of file upload.	Content-type: text/plain
Date: *date-time*	Indicates the date and time that a request was made in Greenwich Mean Time (GMT). GMT time is mandatory for time consistency, given the worldwide nature of the Web.	Date: Thursday, 15-Jan-98 01:39:39 GMT
Host: *hostname*	Indicates the host and port of the server to which the request is being made. It is extremely important in a server that is running many domain names at once in the form of virtual servers.	Host: www.democompany.com
If-Modified-Since: *date-time*	This field indicates file freshness to improve the efficiency of the **GET** method. When used in conjunction with a **GET** request for a particular file, the requested file is checked to see if it has been modified since the time specified in the field. If the file has not been modified, a "not modified" code (304) is sent to the client so a cached version of the document can be used; otherwise, the file is returned normally.	If-Modified-Since: Thursday, 15-Jan-98 01:39:39 GMT
If-Match: *selector-string*	This field makes a request conditionally only if the items match some selector value passed in. Imagine only using **POST** to add data once it has been moved to a file called olddata.	If-Match: "olddata"
If-None-Match: *selector-string*	This field does the opposite of **If-Match**. The method is conditional only if the selector does not match anything. This might be useful for preventing overwrites of existing files.	If-None-Match: "newfile"

TABLE 16-4 HTTP Request Headers *(continued)*

Request Header	Description	Example
If-Range: *selector*	If a client has a partial copy of an object in its cache and wishes to have an up-to-date copy of the entire object there, it could use the **Range** request header with this conditional **If-Range** modifier to update the file. Modification selection can take place on time as well.	If-Range: Thursday, 15-Jan-98 01:39:39 GMT;
If-Unmodified-Since: *date-time*	If the requested file has not been modified since the specified time, the server should perform the requested method; otherwise, the method should fail.	If-Unmodified-Since: Thursday, 15-Jan-98 01:39:39 GMT
Max-Forwards: *integer*	Indicates the limit of the number of proxies or gateways that can forward the request. Often ignored in practice.	Max-Forwards: 6
MIME-version: *version-number*	This field indicates the MIME protocol version understood by the browser that the server should use when fulfilling requests.	MIME-Version: 1.0
Proxy-Authorization: *authorization information*	Allows the client to identify itself or the user to a proxy that requires authentication.	Proxy-Authorization: joeblow: testpass; Realm: All
Pragma: *server-directive*	Passes information to a server; for example, this field can be used to inform a caching proxy server to fetch a fresh copy of a page.	Pragma: no-cache
Range: *byte-range*	Indicates a request for a particular range of a file such as a certain number of bytes. The example shows a request for the last 500 bytes of a file.	Range: bytes=-500
Referer: *URL*	This field indicates the URL of the document from which the request originates (in other words, the linking document). This value might be empty if the user has entered the URL directly rather than by following a link.	Referer: http://www.democompany.com/reports/index.html
User-Agent: *Agent-code*	This field indicates the type of browser making the request. Very useful for browser detection but may be falsified.	User-Agent: Mozilla/4.0 (compatible; MSIE 5.5; Windows 98)

TABLE 16-4 HTTP Request Headers *(continued)*

PART V

NOTE *The request headers seem very familiar because they constitute the same environment variables that you can access from within a server-side program. Now it should be clear how this information is obtained.*

HTTP Responses

After receiving a request, the Web server attempts to process the request. The result of the request is indicated by a server status line that contains a response code; for example, the ever popular "404 Not Found." The server response status line takes this form:

```
HTTP-version Status-code Reason-String
```

For a successful query, a status line might read as follows:

```
HTTP/1.0    200    OK
```

whereas in the case of an error, the status line might read:

```
HTTP/1.0    404    Not Found
```

The status codes for the emerging HTTP 1.1 standard are shown in Table 16-5.

Status-Code	Reason-String	Description
Informational Codes (Process Continues After This)		
100	Continue	An interim response issued by the server that indicates the request is in progress but has not been rejected or accepted. This status code is in support of the persistent connection idea introduced in HTTP 1.1.
101	Switching Protocols	Can be returned by the server to indicate that a different protocol should be used to improve communication. This could be used to initiate a real-time protocol.
Success Codes (Request Understood and Accepted)		
200	OK	Indicates the successful completion of a request.
201	Created	Indicates the successful completion of a **PUT** request and the creation of the file specified.
202	Accepted	This code indicates that the request has been accepted for processing, but that the processing has not been completed and the request might or might not actually finish properly.
203	Non-Authoritative Information	Indicates a successful request, except that returned information, particularly meta-information about a document, comes from a third source and is unverifiable.
204	No Content	Indicates a successful request, but there is no new data to send to the client.

TABLE 16-5 HTTP 1.1 Status Codes

Status-Code	Reason-String	Description
205	Reset Content	Indicates that the client should reset the page that sent the request (potentially for more input). This could be used on a form page that needs consistent refreshing, rather than reloading as might be used in a chat system.
206	Partial Content	Indicates a successful request for a piece of a larger document or set of documents. This response typically is encountered when media is sent out in a particular order, or byte-served, as with streaming Acrobat files.
Redirection Codes (Further Action Necessary to Complete Request)		
300	Multiple Choices	Indicates that there are many possible representations for the requested information, so the client should use the preferred representation, which might be in the form of a closer server or different data format.
301	Moved Permanently	Requested resource has been assigned a new permanent address and any future references to this resource should be done using one of the returned addresses.
302	Moved Temporarily	Requested resource temporarily resides at a different address. For future requests, the original address should still be used.
303	See Other	Indicates that the requested object can be found at a different address and should be retrieved using a **GET** method on that resource.
304	Not Modified	Issued in response to a conditional **GET**; indicates to the agent to use a local copy from cache or similar action as the request object has not changed.
305	Use Proxy	Indicates that the requested resource must be accessed through the proxy given by the URL in the Location field.
Client Error Codes (Syntax Error or Other Problem Causing Failure)		
400	Bad Request	Indicates that the request could not be understood by the server due to malformed syntax.
401	Unauthorized	Request requires user authentication. The authorization has failed for some reason, so this code is returned.
402	Payment Required	Obviously in support of commerce, this code is currently not well-defined.

TABLE 16-5 HTTP 1.1 Status Codes *(continued)*

Status-Code	Reason-String	Description
403	Forbidden	Request is understood but disallowed and should not be reattempted, compared to the 401 code, which might suggest a reauthentication. A typical response code in response to a query for a directory listing when directory browsing is disallowed.
404	Not Found	Usually issued in response to a typo by the user or a moved resource, as the server can't find anything that matches the request nor any indication that the requested item has been moved.
405	Method Not Allowed	Issued in response to a method request such as **GET**, **POST**, or **PUT** on an object where such a method is not supported. Generally an indication of what methods that are supported will be returned.
406	Not Acceptable	Indicates that the response to the request will not be in one of the content types acceptable by the browser, so why bother doing the request? This is an unlikely response given the */* acceptance issued by most, if not all, browsers.
407	Proxy Authentication Required	Indicates that the proxy server requires some form of authentication to continue. This code is similar to the 401 code.
408	Request Time-out	Indicates that the client did not produce or finish a request within the time that the server was prepared to wait.
409	Conflict	The request could not be completed because of a conflict with the requested resource; for example, the file might be locked.
410	Gone	Indicates that the requested object is no longer available at the server and no forwarding address is known. Search engines might want to add remote references to objects that return this value because it is a permanent condition.
411	Length Required	Indicates that the server refuses to accept the request without a defined Content-Length. This might happen when a file is posted without a length.
412	Precondition Failed	Indicates that a precondition given in one or more of the request header fields, such as **If-Unmodified-Since**, evaluated to false.
413	Request Entity Too Large	Indicates that the server is refusing to return data because the object might be too large or the server might be too loaded to handle the request. The server also might provide information indicating when to try again, if possible, but just as well might terminate any open connections.

TABLE 16-5 HTTP 1.1 Status Codes *(continued)*

Status-Code	Reason-String	Description
414	Request-URI Too Large	Indicates that the Uniform Resource Identifier (URI), generally a URL, in the request field is too long for the server to handle. This is unlikely to occur as browsers probably will not allow such transmissions.
415	Unsupported Media Type	Indicates the server will not perform the request because the media type specified in the message is not supported. This code might be returned when a server receives a file that it is not configured to accept using the **PUT** method.
Server Error Codes (Server Can't Fulfill a Potentially Valid Request)		
500	Internal Server Error	A serious error message indicating that the server encountered an internal error that keeps it from fulfilling the request.
501	Not Implemented	This response is to a request that the server does not support or might be understood but not implemented.
502	Bad Gateway	Indicates that the server acting as a proxy encountered an error from some other gateway and is passing the message along.
503	Service Unavailable	Indicates the server currently is overloaded or is undergoing maintenance. Headers can be sent to indicate when the server will be available.
504	Gateway Time-out	Indicates that the server, when acting as a gateway or proxy, encountered too long a delay from an upstream proxy and decided to time out.
505	HTTP Version not supported	Indicates that the server does not support the HTTP version specified in the request.

TABLE 16-5 HTTP 1.1 Status Codes *(continued)*

PART V

After the status line, the server responds with information about itself and the data being returned. There are various selected response headers, but the most important indicates the type of data in the form of a MIME-type and subtype that will be returned. Like request headers, many of these codes are optional and depend on the status of the request.

An example server response for the request shown earlier in the chapter (see "HTTP Requests") follows:

```
HTTP/1.1 200 OK
Date: Wed, 20 Sep 2000 18:59:54 GMT
Server: Apache/1.3.12 (Unix)
Last-Modified: Fri, 25 Aug 2000 22:19:12 GMT
Accept-Ranges: bytes
Content-Length: 205
```

```
Connection: close
Content-Type: text/html

<!DOCTYPE html PUBLIC "-//W3C//DTD XHTML 1.0 Transitional//EN"
"http://www.w3.org/TR/xhtml1/DTD/xhtml1-transitional.dtd">
<html xmlns="http://www.w3.org/1999/xhtml" lang="en">
<head>
<title>Report 1</title>
<meta http-equiv="content-type" content="text/html; charset=ISO-8859-1" />
</head>
<body>
<h1>Report About Important Things</h1>
<hr />
<p>Here is some information about important things. </p>
</body>
</html>
```

A list of the common server response headers for HTTP 1.1, as well as examples of each, can be found in Table 16-6.

Response Header	Description	Example
Age	Shows the sender's estimate of the amount of time since the response was generated at the origin server. Age values are nonnegative decimal integers, representing time in seconds.	Age: 10
Content-encoding	Indicates the encoding the data returned is in.	Content-encoding: x-compress
Content-language	Indicates the language used for the data returned by the server.	Content-language: en
Content-length	Indicates the number of bytes returned by the server.	Content-length: 205
Content-range	Indicates the range of the data being sent back by the server.	Content-range: -500
Content-type	This probably is the most important field and indicates what type of content is being returned by the server in the form of a MIME type.	Content-type: text/html
Expires	Gives the date/time after which the returned data should be considered stale and should not be returned from a cache.	Expires: Thu, 04 Dec 1997 16:00:00 GMT
Last-modified	The Last-Modified response-header field is used to indicate the date the content returned was last modified. This can be used by caches to decide to keep local copies of objects.	Last-modified: Thursday, 01-Aug-96 10:09:00 GMT
Location	Used to redirect the browser to another page. Occasionally scripts will use this method for browser redirection based on capability.	Location: http://www.democompany.com/products/index.htm

TABLE 16-6 Common HTTP 1.1 Server Response Headers

Response Header	Description	Example
Proxy-authenticate	Included with a 407 (Proxy Authentication Required) response. The value of the field consists of a challenge that indicates the authentication scheme and parameters applicable to the proxy for the request.	Proxy-authenticate: GreenDecoderRing: 0124.
Public	Lists the set of methods supported by the server. The purpose of this field strictly is to inform the browser of the capabilities of the server when new or unusual methods are encountered.	Public: **OPTIONS, MGET, MHEAD, GET, HEAD**
Retry-after	Can be used in conjunction with a 503 (Service Unavailable) response to indicate how long the service is expected to be unavailable to the requesting client. The value of this field can be either an HTTP-date or an integer number of seconds after which to retry.	Retry-after: Fri, 31 Dec 1999 23:59:59 GMT Retry-after: 60
Server	Contains information about the Web software used.	Server: Apache/1.3.12 (Unix)
Warning	Used to carry additional information about the status of a response that might not be found in the status code.	Warning: 10 Response is stale
WWW-authenticate	Included with a 401 (Unauthorized) response message. The field consists of at least one challenge that indicates the authentication scheme and parameters applicable to the request made by the client.	WWW-authenticate: Magic-Key-Challenge= 555121, DecoderRing= Green

TABLE 16-6 Common HTTP 1.1 Server Response Headers *(continued)*

The most important header response field is the Content-type field. The MIME type indicated by this field is a device by which the browser is able to figure out what to do with the data being returned.

MIME

MIME (Multipurpose Internet Mail Extensions) was originally developed as an extension to the Internet mail protocol that allows for the inclusion of multimedia in mail messages. The basic idea of MIME is transmission of text files with headers that indicate binary data that will follow. Each MIME header is composed of two parts that indicate the data type and subtype in the following format:

```
Content-type: type/subtype
```

where *type* can be image, audio, text, video, application, multipart, message, or extension-token; and *subtype* gives the specifics of the content. Some samples are listed here:

```
text/html
application/x-director
application/x-pdf
video/quicktime
video/x-msvideo
image/gif
audio/x-wav
```

In addition to these basic headers, you also can include information such as the character-encoding language. For more information about MIME, refer to RFC 1521, available from many sites including http://www.faqs.org/rfcs/, or the list of registered MIME types at ftp://ftp.isi.edu/in-notes/iana/assignments/media-types/.

When a Web server delivers a file, the header information is intercepted by the browser and questioned. The MIME type, as mentioned earlier, is specified by the Content-type HTTP response field. For example, if a browser receives a basic HTML file, the text/html value in the Content-type header indicates what the browser should do. In most cases, this results in the browser rendering the file in the browser window. To determine what to do with a particular MIME type that has been sent, the browser consults a lookup table mapping MIME types to actions, as shown here:

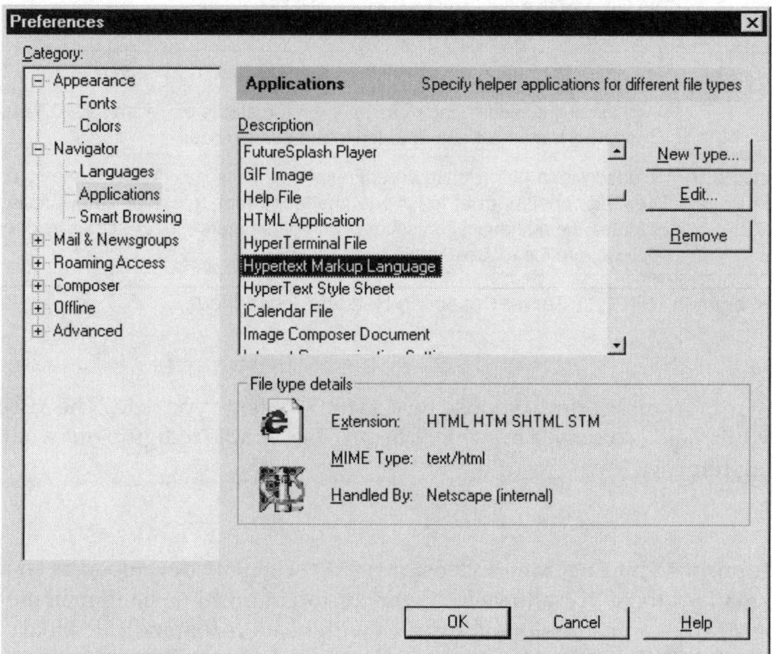

NOTE *A lookup table that maps file extensions to outgoing MIME type headers exists on the server as well.*

Notice that in the example, the type is text/html and the actual HTML document is passed back after all the headers are finished. The dialog indicates that the browser itself will handle the file internally. Also notice that the browser indicates that it recognizes the file extensions .html, .htm, .stm, and .shtml as HTML files. However, other file extensions seem to appear as normal HTML when they are viewed online. The MIME type is the key to why a file with an extension such as .cfm, .asp, .jsp, and so on is treated as HTML by a Web browser when delivered over a network, but if opened from a local disk drive is not read properly. These extensions often are associated with dynamically generated pages that are stamped with the HTML MIME type by the server; when reading off the local drive, the browser relies instead on the file extension such as .htm to determine the contents of a file. If a browser attempts to read a file that it is unsure about, either because of file extension or MIME type, it should respond with a dialog box such as the one shown here, as Netscape does.

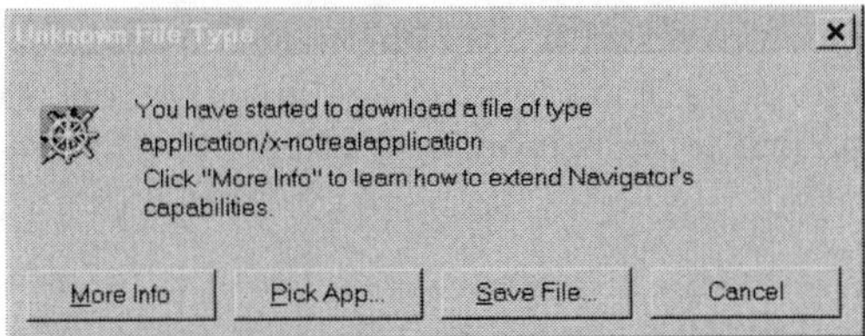

What's very interesting is how Internet Explorer prompts the user to immediately save data if the MIME type is not understood, as shown by this dialog box:

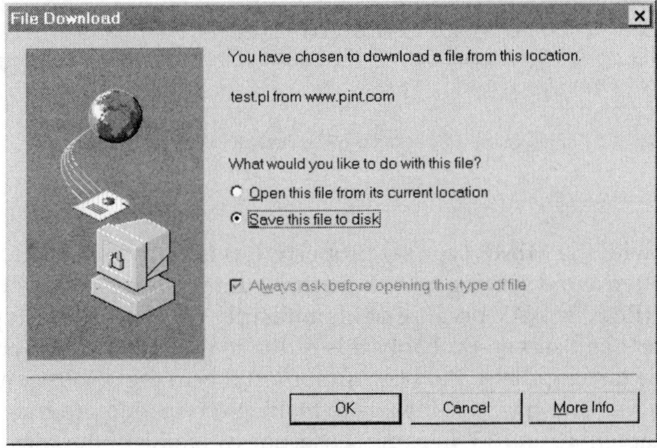

NOTE *It is very easy to install a relationship between a MIME type and a program to handle the data, yet few people seem to add the relationships to directly deal with any form of data served by a Web server.*

Typically, Web pages are delivered properly, so these dialog boxes are not seen. The browser first would read the HTML being delivered and then retrieve any other objects, such as GIF images, sound files, Flash files, Java applets, and so on, that are associated with the page. Each object would result in another request to the server. If the browser encountered something such as

```
<img src="images/logo.gif" alt="demo company" height="100" width="200"
alr="Demo Company" />
```

it would then form a request like the following:

```
GET /images/logo.gif HTTP/1.1
Connection: Keep-Alive
User-Agent: Mozilla/4.0 (compatible; MSIE 5.01;
```

```
                Windows 98)
Accept: application/x-comet, image/gif, image/x-xbitmap,
        image/jpeg, image/pjpeg, */*
Accept-Language: en-us
```

The server then would respond with a similar answer as before, but this time indicating that a MIME type of image/gif is being returned, followed by the appropriate form of binary data to make up an image, as demonstrated here:

```
HTTP/1.1 200 OK
Date: Tue, 18 Jan 2000 04:41:15 GMT
Server: Apache/1.3.4 (Unix)
Last-Modified: Wed, 13 Oct 1999 23:37:38 GMT
Content-Length: 28531
Connection: close
Content-Type: image/gif

GIF87a—  æ÷ÿïÿÿÆï÷÷òÒÖ÷ïïõñî½Öïïïèñ½ïèóÆçã¿ÆçÕ½çç÷áß´µçÞï-çÝç½
Þñ¥çß÷´Þï-ÞÞÖä¥Ü÷œÞÖïºÕç"ÞÏ®ŒÞÕï™×÷"ÖÇµŒÖÆ-„ÖÆ-{ÖÅÓsÖ½-½½¥À½œsÎ½
¥¿¹ kÎÌµ¥¬- yµÏ©¨<¥¥¥ ¡-œ>Œ¥Ã{""‡'
X
< ˆŒŒ{„Œ{j ¢„„s, „'}l {„{s¸fT{{s zjq|~¦eUmogKvŠ ]QljZckZoe
PfegccZccRZcRX
… binary file continues …
```

Consider that with the MIME type set properly, it is literally possible to serve any object. Yet page authors often avoid serving custom forms of data beyond HTML or common media types such as GIF, JPEG, or WAV because of unfamiliarity with the MIME-type configuration possibilities on client and server. Probably this is due to how little is said about MIME when discussing Web site development, but how important it is in the discussion between the browser and the server, and how it is the key to making server-side programs work properly, as discussed in Chapters 12 and 13. In some sense, one can think of the core Web protocols—HTML, HTTP, and MIME—like the world-famous three tenors. People often only remember the first two, but it truly takes three to make it work!

The Realities of Publishing and Maintaining a Web Site

Although understanding how Web servers work and the issues in choosing an in-house or outsourced server appears easy enough, it does not hint at the challenges of actually running a Web site. Far too often, Web professionals are quick to start a Web project but slow to continue it. The fun often is in the development of the site, setting the structure, designing the navigation, creating the look and feel, and then coding the page. But what happens next? The site is released to its intended audience, but you can't abandon it now. Web sites need care and feeding. Depending on the site, there might be daily, weekly, or monthly maintenance to perform. Adding new information, checking for broken links, continually testing under new browsers, upgrading HTML or script code to modern standards, running statistics, and performing various server-related activities such as upgrading software or running backups all are vital tasks. The real work of the site comes after it is released. The site was built for some purpose, and now it is time to fulfill it. The next chapter discusses some of these topics and explains how Web publishing truly is an ongoing process.

Summary

Site development should address the need of hosting pages on a Web server. Developers can choose to host sites on servers within companies; obtain the necessary hardware, software, Internet connection, and labor required to do hosting themselves; or elect to outsource hosting to an ISP or Web hosting company. Because of the costs and complications involved in trying to provide sufficient resources to do your own hosting, it often makes sense to outsource. This approach offers the options of renting space on a shared server or the colocation of a dedicated server at a hosting facility. There is more flexibility in running your own server, rather than being at the mercy of what a shared hosting provider makes available. Running your own server requires selection and evaluation of server software and hosting platform, as well as consideration of performance requirements. In addition to server and hosting choices, an understanding of how Web servers work using the HTTP and MIME protocols can be useful.

17 CHAPTER

Site Management

Even after all the work of building and delivering a Web site, the Web developer's job is not done. Web sites live on and must be maintained to be effective. There are many aspects to Web site maintenance, from adding new content to upgrading a server. This chapter focuses on Web site maintenance issues controlled by or related to markup. A brief discussion about the potential extent of site maintenance duties is presented at the end of the chapter.

Meta-Information

Meta-information is simply information about information. Information on the Web often involves many pieces of associated, descriptive information that isn't always explicitly represented in the resource itself. Examples of meta-information include the creator of a document, the document's subject, the publisher, the creation date, and even the title. When used properly, descriptive meta-information has many benefits. Meta-information can assist in a variety of tasks. For example, it makes the indexing task of search engines easier, and helps filtering software determine the presence of objectionable content. As already discussed, meta-information is related to linking because it helps provide meaning for a document's role in a global or local information space. Meta-information also can provide room for miscellaneous information related to the document. HTML and XHTML's primary support for meta-information is through the **meta** element, which allows authors to add arbitrary forms of meta-data. This tag is found in the **<head>** of an HTML document and generally has **name** and **value** attributes, but an alternative form uses **http-equiv** and **content** attributes.

The name Attribute

A **<meta>** tag that uses the **name** attribute is the easiest to understand. The **name** attribute specifies the type of information. The **content** attribute is set to the content of the meta-information itself. For example, the markup

```
<meta name="Favorite Sandwich" content="Turkey and Swiss" />
```

defines meta-information indicating the document author's favorite lunch. Although metadata can be inserted into a document and list characteristics limited only by an author's imagination, there are some well-understood values that have meaning for Web search tools such as

Google, AltaVista, and so on. Many search robots understand the **author**, **description**, and **keywords** values for the **name** attribute. By setting the **name** and **content** attributes, developers can add meta-information to the head of their documents and improve the indexing of their pages by Web search robots. The following code sets the description of a Web page for a fictitious company:

```
<!DOCTYPE html PUBLIC "-//W3C//DTD XHTML 1.0 Transitional//EN"
"http://www.w3.org/TR/xhtml1/DTD/xhtml1-transitional.dtd">
<html xmlns="http://www.w3.org/1999/xhtml" lang="en">
<head>
<title>Demo Company Home Page</title>
<meta http-equiv="content-type" content="text/html; charset=ISO-8859-1" />
<meta name="author" content="Demo Company, Inc." />
<meta name="description" content="Demo Company, the #1 vendor
of green gadgets on the Web" />
<meta name="keywords" content="Demo Company, green gadgets, gadgets" />
</head>
<body>
. . .Content of the page. . .
</body>
</html>
```

As this example demonstrates, HTML authors can improve the indexing of their pages simply by providing the appropriate keywords in the correct **<meta>** tag format and alerting the search robot to the site's existence. This will be discussed in more depth later in this chapter in the section "Search Engine Promotion." For now, let's turn our attention to the other various uses of the **<meta>** tag.

<meta> and http-equiv

The other form of the **meta** element uses the **http-equiv** attribute, which directly allows the document author to insert HTTP header information. The browser can access this information during read time. The server also can access it when the document is sent, but this is rare. The **http-equiv** attribute is set to a particular HTTP header type, whereas the **content** value is set to the value associated with the header. For example, the markup

```
<meta http-equiv="Expires" content="Wed, 04 Jun 1998 22:34:07 GMT" />
```

placed in the head of a document sets the expiration date to be June 4, 1998. A variety of HTTP headers can be specified by a **<meta>** tag. Of course, you would generally not want to set them in the page but in the actual HTTP headers themselves if you have access to the server. If you don't have access to set this up on your Web server, you may find this form of **<meta>** tag very useful, especially for cache control, client-pull, and site filtering.

Cache Control

Caching on the Web involves keeping a copy of a page or media item either locally on a user's disk drive or up on a proxy server on the network to avoid fetching a brand new copy from a Web site. This is a very good idea because it avoids redundant network traffic. Consider the value of refetching a page over and over and over again for numerous visitors if it is not changing. However good the idea of caching might be, very often browsers or proxy servers cache pages too aggressively, which causes users to inadvertantly view old content. The **<meta>** tag can be used to influence caching by setting expiration dates as well as to provide other cache control information.

There are three **<meta>** tag forms that you can use to control document caching.The first, **Expires**, actually is supposed to specify an expiration date for the Web page. You can set the date for expiration in the past, and the browser or proxy should always ask for a new page. For example, as previously shown, we placed

```
<meta http-equiv="Expires" content="Wed, 04 Jun 1998 22:34:07 GMT" />
```

in the head of a document to set the expiration date to be June 4, 1998. Because this obviously is in the past, it should cause the page to expire. However, it's far easier to set the content attribute value to **0**, which should indicate an expiration time of "now," and therefore cause the browser to ask for a new version of the page every time:

```
<meta http-equiv="Expires" content="0" />
```

Of course, you also can set a real time value in GMT format, as shown in the previous examples, to indicate a page expiration at a future date.

Aside from setting the expiration date, two values for the **http-equiv** attribute—**Pragma** and **Cache-Control**—are specifically designed to prevent (or control) caching, and should take a value of **no-cache**. So, to prevent your page being cached in most browsers, you should use the following lines:

```
<meta http-equiv="Pragma" content="no-cache" />

<meta http-equiv="Cache-Control" content="no-cache" />
```

While cache control is certainly a good idea, far too many sites don't use it or use it too aggressively, thus defeating the value of network caches. Furthermore, some caches on the Web really don't respect the cache control information provided to them. Lastly, the **<meta>** tag simply does not provide developers all that they need. In most cases, the images and other embedded media items are really the items that need cache control information set and these cannot be set using this tag; instead, the server must be configured in such a way as to add these cache control options to each object's response headers.

PART V

Client-Pull

The concept of a page reloading itself or loading another page after a certain period of time is called *client-pull*. For example, you can build an entry page, or *splash page,* that welcomes visitors to a site and then automatically follow with a second page after a certain period of time. The following example **<meta>** tag loads a page called secondpage.htm two seconds after the first page loads:

```
<meta http-equiv="REFRESH" content="2;URL=secondpage.htm" />
```

Using the client-pull form of the **<meta>** tag is easy. Just set the content equal to the desired number of seconds, followed by a semicolon and the URL (full or relative) of the page to load. Note, however, that not all browsers support this form of meta-refresh, so often people add a link to a page that indicates the user should click on the link if a page does not refresh after a certain amount of time. Consider that even modern browsers such as Internet Explorer can set their security preferences to disallow client-pull, so don't assume it is always available.

The **meta** element is very open-ended. The World Wide Web Consortium (W3C) is already developing more sophisticated approaches for representing metadata. The most interesting approach probably is PICS, described next, which provides a standard for site filtering.

Site Filtering with PICS

One major use of meta-information for links and pages is *site filtering*. At its base level, a filter can be used to restrict access to certain files or types of information. As a technology, this sounds rather innocuous, but when extended, site filtering can quickly lead to censorship. Whether filtering information on the Internet is right or wrong is an area of great debate. Obviously, parents and educators are extremely concerned with the availability of pornographic, violent, or other "inappropriate" types of information on the Internet. Deciding what is inappropriate is the key to the censorship problem because definitions of what should be allowed vary from person to person. Regardless of how "inappropriate" is defined, few people would disagree that information considered inappropriate by just about everyone does exist on the Internet. The perceived extent of this information tends to be directly related to a person's belief system. The W3C has proposed the *Platform for Internet Content Selection*, or PICS (http://www.w3.org/pub/WWW/PICS/), as a way to address the problem of content filtering on the Web.

The idea behind PICS is relatively simple. A rated page or site will include a **<meta>** tag within the head of an HTML document. This **<meta>** tag indicates the rating of the particular item. A rating service, which can be any group, organization, or company that provides content ratings, assigns the rating. Rating services include independent, nonprofit groups such as the *Internet Content Rating Association (ICRA)* (http://www.icra.org/webmasters/). The rating label used by a particular rating service must be based on a well-defined set of rules that describes the criteria for rating, the scale of values for each aspect of the rating, and a description of the criteria used in setting a value.

To add rating information to a site or document, a PICS label in the form of a **<meta>** tag must be added to the head of an HTML file. This particular **<meta>** tag must include the URL of the rating service that produced the rating, some information about the rating such as its version, submitter, or date of creation, and the rating itself. Many rating services, such as ICRA allow free self-rating. Filling out a form and answering a few questions about a site's content are all that is required to generate a PICS label.

After you complete and submit the questionnaire, you will receive the appropriate meta-information, which then can be placed in the head of your XHTML documents. An example of a PICS label using the ICRA rating is shown here:

```
<!DOCTYPE html PUBLIC "-//W3C//DTD XHTML 1.0 Transitional//EN"
 "http://www.w3.org/TR/xhtml1/DTD/xhtml1-transitional.dtd">
<html xmlns="http://www.w3.org/1999/xhtml" lang="en">
<head>
<title>PICS Meta Tag Example</title>
```

```
<meta http-equiv="content-type" content="text/html; charset=ISO-8859-1" />
<meta http-equiv="pics-label" content='(pics-1.1
"http://www.icra.org/ratingsv02.html" comment
"ICRAonline EN v2.0" l gen true for
"http://www,htmlref.com" r (nz 1 vz 1 lz 1 oz 1 cz 1)
"http://www.rsac.org/ratingsv01.html" l gen true for
"http://www,htmlref.com" r (n 0 s 0 v 0 l 0))' />

</head>
<body>
<h1 align="center">XHTML: The Complete Reference</h1>
<hr />
<p>There's nothing offensive at this site.</p>
</body>
</html>
```

Under the RSACi rating system, which is now administered by the ICRA, information is rated based on nudity, sex, violence, and language, on a five-category scale from 0 to 4. You can see the questionnaire and get more information at the ICRA Web site (http://www.icra.org/_en/label/extended/).

NOTE *While ICRA has taken over most PICS ratings, the older RSACi style is still used because it is recognized by many filtering devices including Internet Explorer.*

When filtering software reads a file that contains a rating, it determines whether the information should be allowed or denied. Very strict filtering environments might deny all sites that have no rating, so sites with a broad audience are encouraged to use ratings to avoid restricting readership.

Filtering technology that supports PICS is beginning to achieve widespread acceptance and use. Internet Explorer already includes PICS-based rating filtering, as shown in Figure 17-1.

NOTE *The* **<meta>** *tag with PICS information must occur within the head of the document; otherwise, it will not be recognized. However, more than one* **<meta>** *tag may be included within the head so that multiple rating services can be used simultaneously.*

Numerous filtering software packages, such as www.cyberpatrol.com, are extremely popular both with parents and corporate users trying to limit employee Web abuse. Of course, the technology itself can't cure the problem. Trust in a particular ratings system is a major stumbling block in adoption of the filtering idea. Even when trust is gained, if the rating system seems confusing or arbitrary, its value is lowered. In the "real world," Hollywood's MPAA movie rating system has a single value of G, PG, PG-13, R, or NC-17 for each movie. The assignment of a particular movie rating is based on many factors that often seem arbitrary to casual observers. When considering movies, parents might wonder how scenes of a dinosaur ripping a man to shreds merits a PG or PG-13 rating, whereas the use of certain four-letter words indicates an R rating. Certainly similar situations occur on the Web. Because of the imprecise nature of ratings, the topic is a loaded one, both off and on the Web.

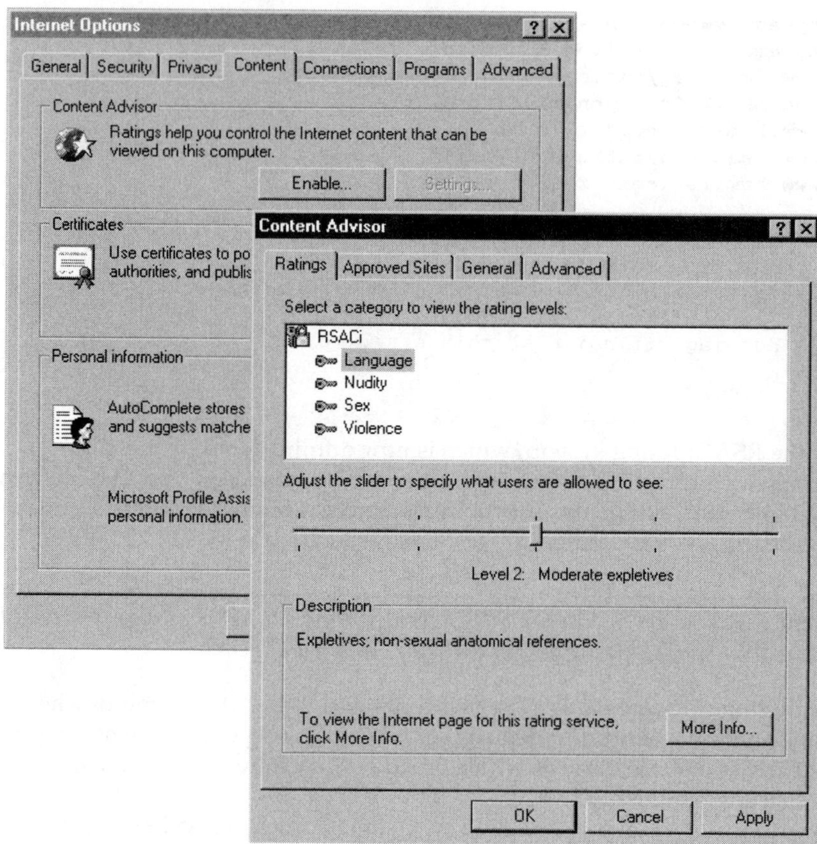

FIGURE 17-1 PICS rating support under Internet Explorer

Beyond simple content rating, some potential benefits of PICS aren't immediately obvious. With PICS-based environments, employers could limit employee access to Web sites that are used for day-to-day business. The idea of PICS can be extended not just to deny or allow information, but to prefer it. Imagine a filtering service for search engines that could return sites that have a particular quality of content or level of accuracy. In the general sense, labels are important because they allow documents to move beyond a mere description of where the document *is* to what the document is *about*.

Search Engine Promotion

Site owners always want to be number one in search engines. Imagine that you are a small travel agent. You probably would love it if people would go to a search engine, type "travel," and have a link to your site show up as the first one. You'd certainly get a large number of visits. Unfortunately, there probably are a lot of other people who would like to be number one, and being ranked 4,036th isn't going be worth much. In fact, if you are outside the first 20 sites or so returned, you probably aren't going to get many hits at all. Because of this, page authors are always trying to determine how search engines categorize pages, and they build their page with keywords in such a way to get a high ranking. In some ways, this idea is similar to how people name their company something like AAA Travel in order to be listed first in the phone book. Unfortunately, consider how many travel agents in the world want their sites to be in the top ten in search engines and you'll see a potential problem. The Web is not as geographically specific as the phone book. Consider if there were a single phone book for the United States. There probably would be dozen of pages filled with companies, all starting with AAA. The Web already has this problem, and that's one of the reasons you get so many results when you run a query for a competitive industry such as discount travel.

The war to be first in the search engine has an obvious final chapter—the rise of pay for position. Consider that the tricks to be at the top of the search engine list have spread rapidly. Even with common search phrases, it is nearly impossible to stay at the top of the list for long because other sites use the same search engine promotion techniques. Already search engines such as Google (www.google.com) and Overture (www.overture.com) are opting to push people who are willing to pay for position to the top of the list. For Google, "pay for play" is limited to special advertising entries, but for Overture, it is in the natural search result. Beyond these approaches, priority placement has long been made for banner ads triggered to correspond to particular search phrases. However, one wonders how long the separation between paid and free search listings will last. Consider that with the phone book, naming your company AAA Travel might put you at the top of the very small line listings, but readers might be overwhelmed with large display ads. It's very likely search engines eventually will adopt at least a variation of the same model. The eventual outcome of the search engine war will almost certainly be a return to traditional models of information retrieval methods used in other advertising forms in which you pay for audience relevancy and position. For now, page authors should consider the failure to take advantage of search engine positioning tricks to be very foolish, regardless of their long-term viability.

NOTE *This is by no means a complete discussion of a topic that changes on a weekly basis. Readers looking for more up-to-date information are directed to the numerous site promotion sites that exist on the Web, especially Search Engine Watch (www.searchenginewatch.com).*

How Search Engines Work

So how do search engines work? First, a large number of pages are gathered from the Web using a process often called *spidering*. Next, the collected pages are indexed to determine what they are about. Finally, a search page is built so that users can enter queries and see what pages are related to their queries. The best analogy for the process is that the search engine collects as big a haystack as possible, then tries to organize the haystack somehow, and finally lets the user try to find the proverbial needle in the resulting haystack of information by entering a query on a search page. Figure 17-2 shows a basic overview of how search engines work.

Adding to the Engines

Getting a site's pages gathered by a search engine is the first step in making a site findable on the Web. The easiest way to do this is simply to tell search engines that your site exists. Most search engines will allow you to add a URL to be indexed. For example, Google allows

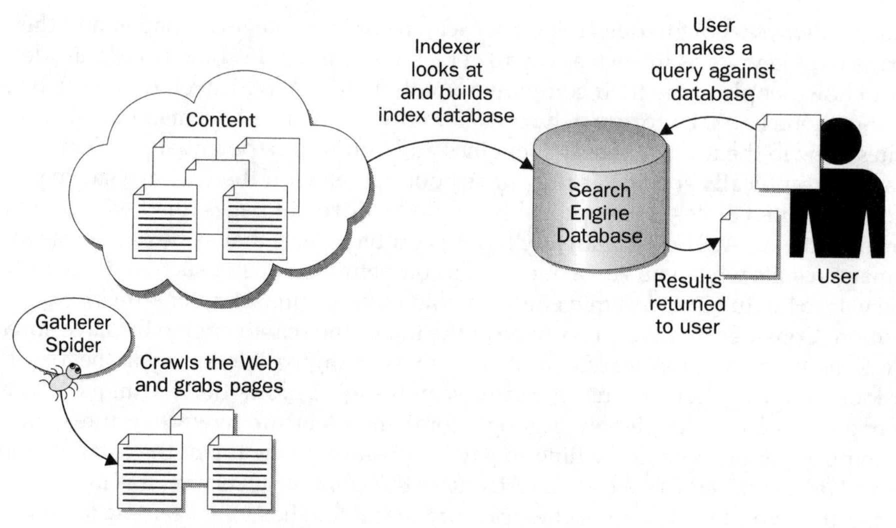

FIGURE 17-2 Overview of search engines

you to add a site for gathering by using a simple form (www.google.com/addurl.html). Of course, adding your site to every single search engine could be a tedious task, so many vendors (www.submit-it.com) are eager to provide developers with a way to bulk submit to numerous search engines. Most Web site promotion software, such as WebPosition Gold (www.webposition.com), also includes automated submission utilities.

You may wonder how many search engines you should submit your site to. Some people favor adding only a few links to the important top ten engines, especially Google, MSN, AltaVista and Yahoo! Numerous studies, as well as this author's experience, suggest that big search sites, particularly Google and Yahoo!, account for most search engine referring traffic. However, some site promotion experts feel this is not correct, and believe it is best to create as many links to sites as possible. In fact, a whole class of link sites called "Free For All" links or FFA sites (not to be confused with anything related to the Future Farmers of America) have sprung up to service people who believe that "all links should lead to me" works. The reality is that most of these link services are pretty much worthless and often generate worthless traffic and spam messages. Further, consider that even if you do get back links and e-mail, it is mostly from people who are doing the same thing you're doing—trying to get links.

Robot Exclusion

Before getting too involved putting yourself in every search engine, consider that it isn't always a good idea to have a robot index your entire site, regardless of whether it is your own internal search engine or a public search engine. First consider that some pages, such as programs in your cgi-bin directory, don't need to be indexed. Second, many pages can be transitory, and having them indexed might result in users seeing 404 errors if they enter from a search engine. Last, you might just not want people to enter on every single page—particularly those deep within a site. So-called "deep linking" can be confusing for users entering from public search engines. Consider that because these users start out deep in a site, they are not exposed to the home or entry page information that often is used to orient site visitors.

Probably the most troublesome aspect of search engines and automated site gathering tools such as offline browsers is that they can be used to stage a denial of service attack on a site. The basic idea of most spiders is to read pages and follow pages as fast as they can. Consider if you tell a spider to crawl a single site as fast as it possibly can. All the requests to the crawled server could very quickly overwhelm it, causing the site to be unable to fulfill requests—thus denying services to legitimate site visitors. Fortunately, most people are not malicious in spidering, but understand that it does happen inadvertently when a spider keeps re-indexing the same dynamically generated page.

Robots.txt

To deal with limiting robot access, the Robot Exclusion protocol was adopted. The basic idea is to use a special file called robots.txt that should be found in the root directory of a Web site. For example, if a spider was indexing http://www.htmlref.com, it would first look for a file at http://www.htmlref.com/robots.txt. If it finds a file, it would analyze the file first before proceeding to index the site.

NOTE *If you have a site such as http://www.bigfakehostingvendor.com/~customer, you will find that many spiders will ignore a robots.txt file with a URL of http://www.bigfakehostingvendor .com/~customer/robots.txt. Unfortunately, you will have to ask the vendor to place an entry for you in their robots.txt file.*

The basic format of the robots.txt file is a listing of the particular spider or user agent you are looking to limit and statements including which directory paths to disallow. You can also specify rules to apply for all user agents using the wildcard *. Consider the following:

```
User-agent: *
Disallow: /cgi-bin/
Disallow: /temp/
Disallow: /archive/
```

In this case, you have denied access for all robots to the cgi-bin directory, the temp directory, and an archive directory—possibly where you would move files that are very old but still might need to be online. You should be very careful with what you put in your robots.txt. Consider the following file:

```
User-agent: *
Disallow: /cgi-bin/
Disallow: /images/
Disallow: /subscribers-only/
Disallow: /resellers.html
```

In this file, a special subscribers-only and resellers file has been disallowed for indexing. However, you have just let people know this is sensitive. For example, if you have content that is hidden unless someone pays to receive a URL via e-mail, you certainly will not want to list it in the robots.txt file. Just letting people know the file or directory exists is a problem.

Consider that malicious visitors actually will look carefully at a robots.txt file to see just what it is you don't want people to see. That's very easy to do; just type in the URL like so: http://www.*companytolookat*.com/robots.txt.

Be aware that the robot exclusion standard assumes that spidering programs will abide by it. A malicious spider will, of course, simply ignore this file, and you might be forced to set up your server to block particular IP addresses or user agents in case someone has decided to attack your site.

Robot Control with <meta>

An alternative method to the robots.txt file that is useful, particularly for those users who have no access to the root directory of their domain, is to use a **<meta>** tag to control indexing. To disallow indexing of a particular page, use a **<meta>** tag such as

```
<meta name="robots" content="noindex" />
```

in the **<head>** of the document. You also can instruct a spider to not follow any links coming out of the page:

```
<meta name="robots" content="noindex, nofollow" />
```

When using this type of exclusion, just make sure not to confuse the robot with contradictory information such as

```
<meta name="robots" content="index, noindex" />
```

or

```
<meta name="robots" content="index, nofollow, follow" />
```

as the spider may either ignore the information entirely or maybe even index anyway. The other downside to the **<meta>** tag approach is that fewer of the public search engines support it than robots.txt.

Optimizing for Search Engines

Optimizing your site for a search engine is not difficult. The first thing to do is to start to think like a search engine—in other words, don't really think at all. Search engines look at pages and make educated guesses about their content by following a set of rules to try to understand what the page is about. For example, search engines look for word frequency, linking information, **<meta>** tags, and a variety of other things. However, when you get right down to it they really can't perfectly tell the difference between a page about the Miami Dolphins football team and a dolphin show in Miami, because search engines generally rely on keyword matching in conjunction with some heuristics such as the placement of words in a page or the number of linking sites. So if a page author knows what a search engine is looking for, it is easy enough to optimize a page for the search engine to rank it highly. The next few sections provide a brief overview of some of the things search engines look for as well as some tricks people have employed to improve their search rankings.

Relevant Text Content

Probably the best ways to get indexed is to have the keywords and phrases actually within the content of the page. Many search engines will look at text within a page, particularly if it is either toward the top of the page or within heading tags such as **<h1>** or **<h2>**. Search engines may also look at the contents of link text. Thus,

```
<a href="specifications.html">Specifications</a>
```

is not as search engine friendly as

```
<a href="specifications.html">Robot Butler Specification</a>
```

One problem with the fact that search engines focus on page text is that often page authors create home pages that are primarily graphic. Search engines might have little more to go on than the **<meta>** tag and page title and thus could rank the page lower. Consider first using the **alt** attribute for the **<img>** tag to provide some extra information; for example,

```
<img src="robot.gif" alt="Butler-1000: Demo Company's industry
leading robot butler"/>
```

Of course, putting the actual text in the page would be better. Some page authors resort to either making text very small or in a color similar to the background—or both—so that users won't see it but search engines will pick it up. For example,

```
<font size="1" color="white">The Demo Company Butler1000 is the
best robot butler. The Demo Company Butler1000 is the best robot
butler. The Demo Company Butler1000 is the best robot butler.</font>
```

Be careful with the small or invisible text trick. Many search engines will consider this to be spamming and might drop the page from the search engine.

Using <meta> for Search Engines

In addition to page content, search engines may look at the **<meta>** tags for keywords and descriptions of a page's content. A **<meta>** tag such as

```
<meta name="Keywords" content="Butler-1000, Robot butler, Robot butler
specifications, where to buy a robot butler, Metallic Man Servant, Demo
Company, robot, butler" />
```

could be used in a Demo Company page about robot butlers. Notice how the content started first with the most specific keywords and phrases and ended with generic keywords. This should play into how most users approach search engines.

Once a search engine looks at the **<meta>** tag, it can rate one site higher than another based upon the frequency of keywords in the **content** attribute. Because of this, some page authors load their **<meta>** tags with redundant keywords:

```
<meta name="Keywords" content=" Robot butler, Robot butler, Robot butler,
Robot butler, Robot butler, Robot butler, Robot butler, Robot butler,
Robot butler, Robot butler" />
```

However, many search engines consider this to be keyword loading and might drop the page from their indexes. If the keyword loading is a little less obvious and combinations of words and phrases are repeated like so

```
<meta name="Keywords" content="Robot butler, Butler-1000, Metallic
Man Servant, Robot butler, Butler-1000, Metallic Man Servant, Robot
butler, Butler-1000, Metallic Man Servant, Robot butler,
Butler-1000, Metallic Man Servant" />
```

the search engine might not consider this improper. An even better approach is to make sure the pattern of repeating words isn't quite as obvious as it varies its order, as shown here:

```
<meta name="Keywords" content="Butler-1000, Robot butler, Metallic
Man Servant, Robot butler, Butler-1000, robot, Robot butler,
Democompany, Metallic Man Servant, Butler-1000, robot, butler,
Robot butler, Butler-1000" />
```

However, be aware that search engines might still notice the heavy use of certain words or phrases and consider this spamming, potentially reducing the page's ranking or dropping it from the index completely.

Search engines also look at the description value for the **<meta>** tag. For example,

```
<meta name="Description" content="The Demo Company Robot Butler is
the most outstanding metallic man servant on the market. The
Butler-1000 comes complete with multiple personalities and voice
modules including the ever-popular faux-British accent." />
```

would be included on the robot butler page and could be examined by the search engine as well as returned by the search engine on the results page. Because it might be output for the user to see, you should provide some valuable information in the description that will help the user determine whether they want to visit your site. Preferably, keep the description to a sentence or two, and at most, three or four sentences.

Titles and File Naming

It's important for search engine ranking to make sure your page has a very good title. For example,

```
<title>Robot Butler</title>
```

is a bad title as far as search engine ranking goes. A better title might be

```
<title>Butler-1000: Specification of Demo Company's Robot Butler,
the leading metallic man servant on the market</title>
```

Remember that people also look at page titles, and they are used for bookmarking, so a really long title might be more for search engines than for users.

The name of a file also can be important for search engines. Rather than naming a file butler.htm, use butler1000-robot-butler.htm. Consider that if you have a good domain name and directory structure, you can create a URL that almost makes sense. Consider, for example, if we named our server democompany.com as well as www.democompany.com. We might have a URL like

```
http://democompany.com/products/robots/butler1000-robot-butler.htm
```

Notice how this almost includes the same information as the title. This provides a secondary benefit of letting the user know where they are, rather than resorting to cryptic URLs such as

```
http://democompany.com/products.asp?prod=robots&mod=butler1000
```

Links and Entry Points

Search engine ranking may also depend on the number of links leaving a page as well as the number of pages that link to a page. Landmark pages such as home pages tend to have a lot of outgoing and incoming links. Search engines would prefer to rank landmark pages highly, so it is important that key pages in your site have links to them from nearly every page. Some search engines also favor sites that have many sites pointing to them. Because of this, people are already starting to create sites solely for the purpose of pointing to other sites.

Another approach to improving search engine ranking is to submit many pages in a site, or even off a site to a search engine. All of these entry pages, often called *doorway pages*, point to important content within your site. Unfortunately for many users, doorway pages are more like decoy pages, as they can be loaded with false content to attract the visitor and nearly always eventually deposit the user at a page they didn't really want to see. The problem with search engine promotion is that the distance from simple logical keyword loading and various tricks is a short one—particularly if page authors are obsessed with top-ten ranking.

Tricky Business

The tricks employed by search engine specialists are numerous and change all the time. Many ideas are simple add-ons to normal Web design techniques. For example, many page authors rely on invisible pixel shims to force layout. Search engine promoters say, "Why not put **alt** attributes on these images to improve things?" Imagine this

```
<img src="pixel.gif" alt="robot butler robot butler robot butler" />
```

all over your page. Then pity the user who pauses on top of one of these invisible pixels only to have a Tooltip pop up screaming about whatever the page is promoting. Spamming pages with invisible text, small text, and multiple images, or just loading the **<meta>** or **<title>** tags, are not the most sophisticated tricks, but they seem to work, at least for some sites.

Other tricks include the infamous "bait and switch," in which a special search engine page is created and then posted to a search engine. Once the ranking is high, the bait page is replaced with a real page built for users. A more complicated version of this is dubbed "cloaking." In the "cloaking" scenario, you write a program that senses when a search engine hits the site and "feeds" the engine the page it wants to see. Like a ravenous dog, it gobbles up the information with no idea it just ate the equivalent of informational pig snouts. As real users hit the site, they aren't served the search engine bait page, but instead get the real site.

Detecting search engines versus regular users isn't terribly difficult because the engines identify themselves and come from consistent IP addresses. In reality, "site cloaking" is just a modified form of browser detection. Search engines can do little to combat this approach because they would have to consider eliminating dynamically built pages—which is impossible given their growing importance—or not informing sites that they are search engines while indexing. A few search engines have already begun to provide a link to a page that shows what was indexed so users can determine if they are being shown something different than what a search engine indexed. Furthermore, if search engines do detect cloaking, it is a pretty sure fire way to get banned from being indexed.

The problem with all the search engine promotion business is that it tempts the page author to stop building pages for users and start building them for search engines. This is just another form of designing more for your own needs than for your users. One of the most interesting aspects about search engines is that many large organizations don't rely greatly on them for driving traffic. In fact, for many corporations, unless you type their name in directly, you'll be hard-pressed to find them in a search engine under generic keywords. Of course, if you try to look for them, they do come up. Despite what appears to be a major oversight by these organizations, these sites continue to get huge amounts of traffic. According to studies such as the GVU Internet Survey, people type in URLs directly quite often. How are they finding out about sites? Always remember that search engines aren't the only way to drive traffic and even when users rely on them significantly they will tend to trust the brands and organizations they are familiar with over the ones they are not.

Managing Web Sites

Once a Web server is installed and successfully delivering content to users, there are a great number of maintenance tasks that should take place. Servers must be continually monitored for availability, performance, and security. Site content must also be checked for accuracy and freshness as content probably will be continually added and deleted. Functional elements of sites beyond simple links also might have to be maintained as bugs might be discovered or new features required by users. Even the introduction of a new browser might require some modification of site code to handle new features or account for rendering or use problems. Finally, as visitors use the site their usage patterns should be analyzed to determine which sections are being used as well as which are not. Usage analysis can lead to further modification of the site.

Given the multitude of tasks involved in Web site maintenance, the line between system, network, and content management blurs fairly often, which can be a problem. Providing 24/7 monitoring of systems, upgrades, usage analysis, testing, and content management of any significantly sized corporate site probably is beyond the means of a single individual— whether they have the title "Webmaster" or not. Readers are encouraged to focus on acquiring enough skills in individual areas as required. Knowledge of server maintenance and management should not be considered a requirement for authoring content for a Web site. However, XHTML document authors probably will be directly involved with link and content management so a more in-depth discussion will be presented here.

Link Maintenance

Even when links are used correctly within a site, they eventually require maintenance as pages are moved around. Commonly, links to external sites will break as other sites move their pages without considering outside linkage. Ferreting out the broken links within a site can be tedious, but doing so should be a top priority. A broken link should be considered a serious problem. Users clicking on a broken link are on the road to nowhere, eventually to receive the now infamous "404 Not Found" message or something similar. Imagine if a menu on a software application triggered a message saying "Sorry, spell check not found." Such oversights would not be tolerated within software and should be considered the same level of problem within a site.

Fortunately, identifying and fixing broken links isn't terribly difficult. Armed with a tool such as Coast WebMaster (www.coast.com), finding broken links is a simpler matter. However, consider that if you have external links within a site, even constant monitoring isn't going to keep broken links out of the site at all times. To account for the unforeseen broken link, consider installing a custom 404 page. Then, put information such as a link to a site map or a method to contact the site's administrator in the custom error page. An example custom 404 page is shown in Figure 17-3.

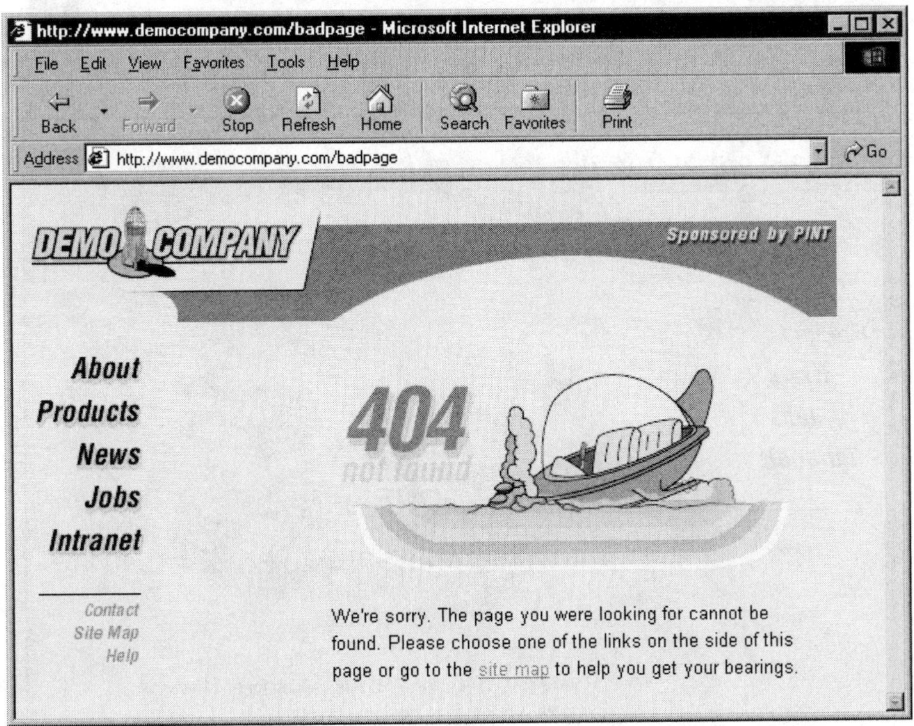

FIGURE 17-3 Custom 404 pages can fit with a site design.

PART V

NOTE *Installation of a custom 404 error page depends on the server being utilized.*

One interesting possibility is to try to address broken links before they happen. For example, if you expect that people may make typos with your domain name or site URLs, create contingency URLs in advance. You can even install a spell-checking system on your server to catch URL typos. For Apache, this is called mod_speling and for IIS, it is called URLSpellcheck (www.urlspellcheck.com).

Redirection Pages

Rather than showing 404 errors, many sites prefer to redirect users to new pages. If the content at a URL such as http://www.democompany.com/robots.html has moved to a new location, it is best to install a page that points people to the new page or even quickly redirects them there. Some site maintainers prefer to send people directly to the new page, whereas others will install a temporary page informing visitors of the page change, like the one shown in Figure 17-4.

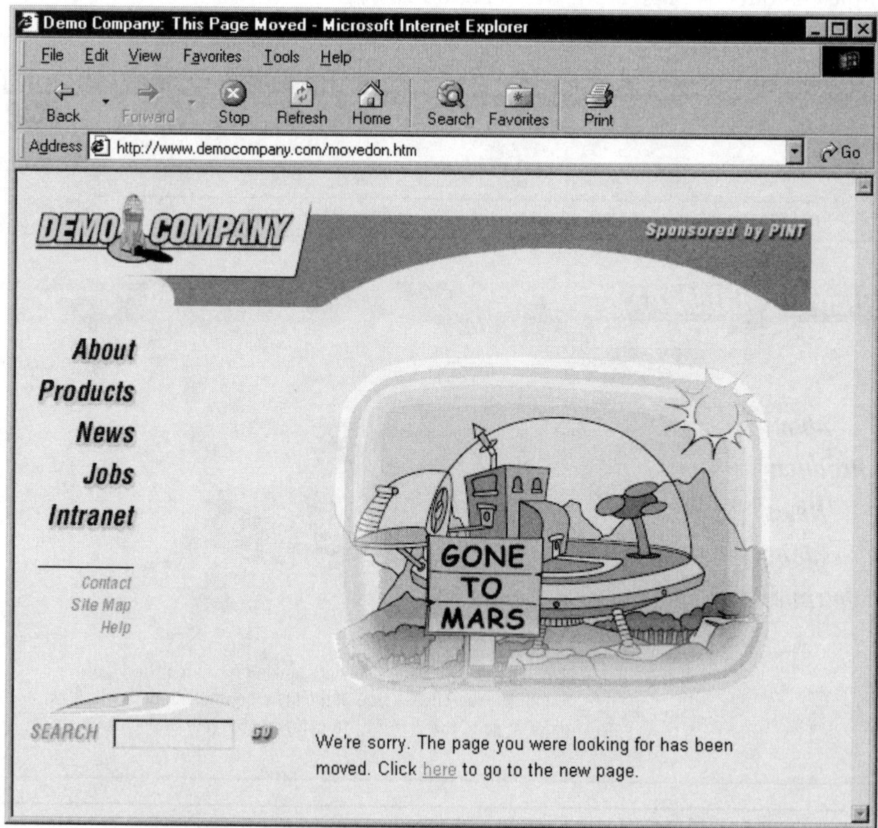

FIGURE 17-4 "Page Moved" example page

Sending people directly to the new page might be seamless, but it does take some control away from the user. For example, if the user requests a particular page on, say, robotic dogs, and a redirect takes them to a different page, they will become very frustrated. Always make sure that the new page is related to the moved page.

Maintaining site links can be a great deal of work. Custom error pages and redirection pages can help, but Web managers will have to be ever vigilant in link monitoring. Good Web sites should make sure to watch log files for referring sites. Furthermore, consider visiting a search engine and doing a reverse search. Specifically, search for sites that link to yours and make sure they are up-to-date on any significant site changes made. Making sure that other sites link to you correctly might be a great deal of work, but it is all part of being a good Web citizen. The next section presents a brief overview of common site content management issues.

Content Management

Maintaining content is just as important as maintaining the server itself. Large sites or those with numerous contributors will quickly degrade if special care is not taken. First, make sure there is a set policy for naming files. For example, consider avoiding using special characters such as underscores (_) in filenames because it will be difficult for users to notice them in the address line of a browser. Instead of robot_butler.htm, consider robot-butler.htm or just robotbutler.htm. However, be careful with using filenames such as RobotButler.html or even capitalizing directories. The domain aspect of a URL is not case sensitive and the user might not be consistent in his or her use of case. Also, some servers such as UNIX systems are case sensitive, whereas others such as NT are not, so moving sites between the systems could be troublesome. Always use lowercase to avoid such problems. Shorter extensions generally are better if you just consider the extra characters to type, as well as the fact that some older systems prefer three-character extensions. However, regardless of your take on .htm versus .html, pick one and be consistent.

If you are really aggressive, it is even possible to remove extensions from your URLs directly. In such a case, you will no longer reference files in links like

```
<a href="products/robot.html">Butler Robot</a>
```

but simply use

```
<a href="products/robot">Butler Robot</a>
```

Even media objects will no longer have extensions, so

```
<img src="/images/logo.gif" alt="logo" />
```

becomes

```
<img src="/images/logo" alt="logo" />
```

There are significant advantages to cleaned URLs without file extensions. They allow you to change the underlying technology at any time. So instead of referencing a GIF image, you are referencing just an image and letting the server and browser decide if a GIF, JPEG, or PNG should be sent. This is called *content negotiation* and is a powerful idea that should see more usage in the next few years.

Regardless of whether you use file extensions or not, consider limiting filename length, or using consistent naming schemes. For example, some files such as press releases may include dates in them. Consider that pr021299.html and pr010500.html could reference press releases on February 12,1999 and January 5, 2000, respectively. Coming up with a reasonable format can really help people find and manage information.

Make sure to use the same care with directories that you do with files. Pick short, easy-to-type and -spell directories in all lowercase letters that lack special characters. Also, consider using common directory names to hold site assets. Table 17-1 details a few common directory names and their usual contents.

Probably the most difficult aspect of dealing with site content is managing all the changes that are made. When many people are working on a site, it is easy for conventions to be overlooked and for simple errors to be introduced. To reduce the possibility that content degrades, first carefully limit who can make changes to a site. Second, resist the desire to fix site problems or add content on a moment's notice. It is far better to make regular updates, such as once a day or once a week. This allows backups to be made and provides a stable base to roll back to in case problems are introduced.

If a site is heavily updated, consider employing a content management tool. A simple source code control system can be used. A source code control system will provide an audit trail and rollback facilities, and will force site contributors to check out pages to make changes to them. More powerful content management systems that include easy-to-use, browser-based front ends, including form-based page editing, can be built or purchased. The Demo Company site (www.democompany.com) itself uses a very simple version of such a tool, as shown in Figure 17-5.

Directory Name	Contents
/cgi-bin	The traditional location for executable programs on a Web server, particularly CGI programs.
/scripts	Contains scripts for the site including JavaScripts, CGI scripts, and server-parsed languages such as Cold Fusion or Active Server pages. Occasionally, the directory might be named after the type of script stored; for example, /js or /javascripts for linked JavaScript files.
/styles or /css	Should contain any linked style sheets used on a site.
/images	Contains all site images, including GIFs, JPEGs, and PNG files.
/video	Contains video assets—primarily non-streamed video clips.
/audio	Contains audio assets—primarily non-streamed audio files.
/pdfs	Contains PDF files such as a library of datasheets.
/download or / binaries	A central location for any programs or software distributions that are to be downloaded from the site.

TABLE 17-1 Common Site Directory Names

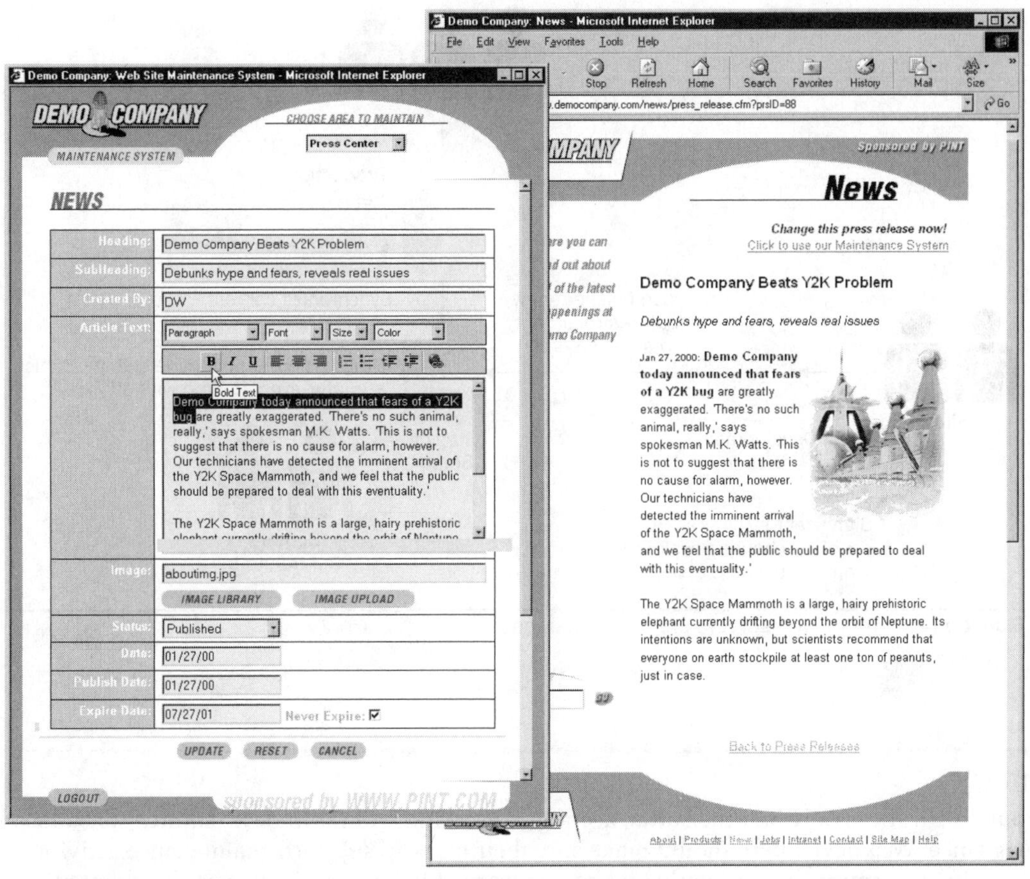

FIGURE 17-5 Demo Company's content management system

Regardless of the methodology used to control the update of a site, one rule cannot be stressed enough: *Never work directly on a live site*. Consider that users might see your changes as they happen, and even see pages in half-finished form. Furthermore, if any serious blunder is made, it may be difficult to recover from if the live site is being edited directly.

Rather than working on a live site, consider using a three-site architecture as illustrated in Figure 17-6. First, set aside a development server where a copy of the site is kept and major changes and programming features can be added and tested. Second, create a staging server with an exact duplicate of the published site. The staging server is where changes are made and tested. Lastly, a production server should be utilized to actually hold the site being delivered. Changes should only be made on the development or staging site, which is later synchronized with the production server.

As Web sites become more and more important to organizations, the care and feeding of sites and servers certainly will be treated with increased seriousness and procedures and policies will be adopted to ensure that changes are made properly.

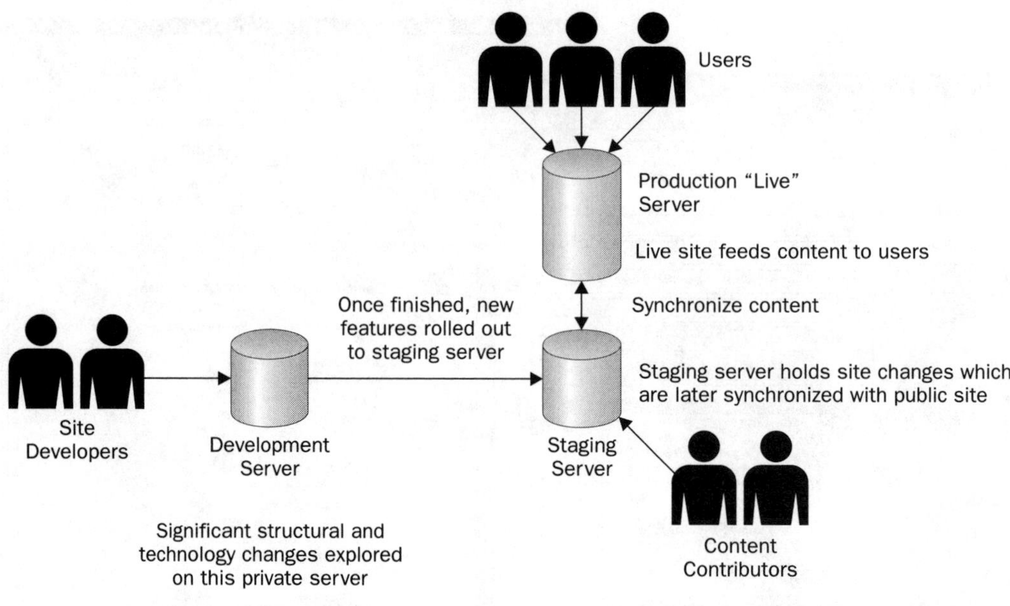

FIGURE 17-6 Three Web servers are better than one

Summary

Building a site is only half the battle; keeping it working and up-to-date requires constant vigilance. Web developers should make sure their markup supports maintenance activities by using the **<meta>** tag properly and being aware of link usage. However, the maintenance requirements of a site will far exceed correct use of XHTML. Monitoring the server, upgrading software, adding content, and analyzing log files can require significant time. In fact, for most sites, maintenance duties may have to be shared among many individuals. As we conclude the book, we turn to the future of markup—XML.

VI

PART

Advanced Topics

18 CHAPTER

XML

With much fanfare, *Extensible Markup Language* (XML) has emerged rapidly as a new approach to delivering structured data over the Web. Numerous languages have been developed using XML. Many are starting to become well-known by average Web developers including RSS (Really Simple Syndication), WML (Wireless Markup Language), SVG (Scalable Vector Graphics), SOAP (Simple Object Access Protocol), and others. Of course XHTML, the topic of much of this book, is probably the most widely understood XML-based language. Yet given the widespread success of traditional HTML, you may wonder, why do we need something else? What does XML really offer the typical Web developer? This chapter attempts to answer that question and explains both the practical uses and the theoretical value of XML.

The Need for XML

The first question that needs to be addressed is why XML is even necessary when HTML is already available. Any technology that is used globally by millions and millions of people must be doing something right. As a general-purpose technology, traditional HTML meets an extraordinarily broad set of user needs. However, it doesn't fit very well with applications that rely upon specialized information, either as data files or as complex, structured documents. This is particularly true for applications such as automated data interchange, which require data to be structured in a consistent and well-formed manner.

As you have seen already, by itself, HTML just can't realistically accommodate the structuring and formatting needs of documents that require more than paragraphs, sections, and lists. HTML can't deal with more complex, application-specific problems because its elements are fixed. The language contains no provision for extending itself; namely, it has no provision for defining new elements. Although browser vendors used to add new elements all the time, any proposed extension now entails lengthy advocacy before the W3C.

Regardless, adding more element types to HTML doesn't make sense at this point. The language is already large enough. It is meant to be a general-purpose language that is capable of handling a large variety of documents. Thus, HTML needs some mechanism so that its general-purpose framework can be augmented to accommodate specialized content. It also needs to be cleaned up syntactically so that the structure of documents can be ensured. Lastly, it needs to continue to move away from a presentation style language and focus on structure. Even with modifications, traditional HTML just isn't capable of these diverse requirements, thus the need for XML.

SGML and XML

The syntax of traditional HTML (2.0, 3.0, 3.2, and 4.0) is defined in SGML (Standard Generalized Markup Language) notation. SGML is a *meta-language,* a language that is used to define other languages. Although HTML is the best-known SGML-defined language, SGML itself has been used successfully to define special document types ranging from aviation maintenance manuals to scholarly texts. SGML is used to define the various elements, attributes, and entities of a markup language and the ways they can be used together. The various rules of the language are represented in a file called a *document type definition* or DTD. We reference the DTD for HTML using a **doctype** statement like this:

```
<!DOCTYPE HTML PUBLIC "-//W3C//DTD HTML 4.01 Transitional//EN"
"http://www.w3.org/TR/html4/loose.dtd">
```

The actual DTD file contains a variety of statements in SGML that define the syntax of HTML. For example, the syntax for a **br** element is defined in SGML by the following:

```
<!ELEMENT BR - O EMPTY                    -- forced line break -->
<!ATTLIST BR
  %coreattrs;                             -- id, class, style, title --
  clear      (left|all|right|none) none -- control of text flow --
  >
```

The SGML syntax indicates that the **br** element is empty; namely, it encloses no content or markup and has the **clear** attribute to control text flow and core attributes **id**, **class**, **style**, and **title**. The rest of the HTML elements are similarly defined. If you are interested in reading the specification directly, you can learn how to read a DTD in Appendix F.

SGML is used to specify languages, and unless you are writing your own language, you probably will not use SGML directly but rather one of its application instance languages like HTML. However, if you are writing your own tags for a specialized application, you might wonder, why not use SGML? While SGML seems like a reasonable candidate to increase HTML's flexibility, as well as being able to scale and represent very complex information structures, it is overly complex at times and wasn't built with today's online applications in mind. The language first appeared in the late 1970s, the golden age of batch processing, and simply wasn't designed to be used in networked, interactive applications.

XML is, in fact, an attempt to define a subset of SGML that is specifically designed for use in a Web context. With XML, we define application languages generally using either a document type definition just like in SGML or a more powerful grammar mechanism called a *schema*. Consider the **doctype** statement for XHTML, which looks very similar to the traditional HTML **doctype**.

```
<!DOCTYPE html PUBLIC "-//W3C//DTD XHTML 1.0 Transitional//EN"
"http://www.w3.org/TR/xhtml1/DTD/xhtml1-transitional.dtd">
```

The only differences we see between the two doctype statements are that the root element **html** is now lowercased and the identifier and URL reference the XHTML transitional specification instead of the HTML transitional specification.

Once you look at the XHTML DTD you'll note that even the syntax of DTDs is extremely similar to the HTML DTD, as demonstrated by the syntax for the br element under the XHTML transitional specification presented here.

```
<!ELEMENT br EMPTY>    <!-- forced line break -->
<!ATTLIST br
       %coreattrs;
       clear      (left|all|right|none) "none"
>
```

Both SGML and XML are meta-languages used to define markup languages. Over the years, various application languages have been defined using each, as shown here:

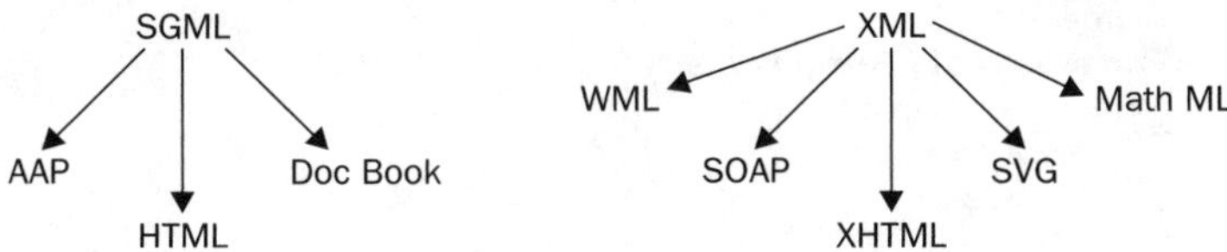

Of course, HTML and XHTML are by far the most popular languages defined with these technologies.

At this point, you might wonder why you should care about XML. You might imagine you won't need to write a language of your own, and if you do you really wouldn't want to learn all that nasty XML syntax anyway. Writing your own language, however, does have advantages for exchanging information with other sites, and the strictness that XML provides actually makes parsing the data much easier. So read on— you'll find out that you can indeed get started with XML with very little difficulty!

Well-Formed XML

Writing simple XML documents is fairly easy. For example, suppose that you have a compelling need to define a document with markup elements to represent a fast-food restaurant's combination meals, which contain a burger, drink, and fries. You might do this because this information will be sent to your suppliers, you might expect to receive electronic orders from customers via e-mail this way, or it might just be a convenient way to store your restaurant's data. Regardless of the reason why, the question is how you can do this in XML. You would simply create a file such as burger.xml that contains the following markup:

```
<?xml version="1.0" encoding="UTF-8" standalone="yes" ?>
<combomeal>
   <burger>
   <name>Tasty Burger</name>
   <bun bread="white">
      <meat />
      <cheese />
      <meat />
   </bun>
   </burger>
   <fries size="large" />
   <drink size="large">
      Cola
   </drink>
</combomeal>
```

A rendering of this example under Internet Explorer is shown in Figure 18-1.

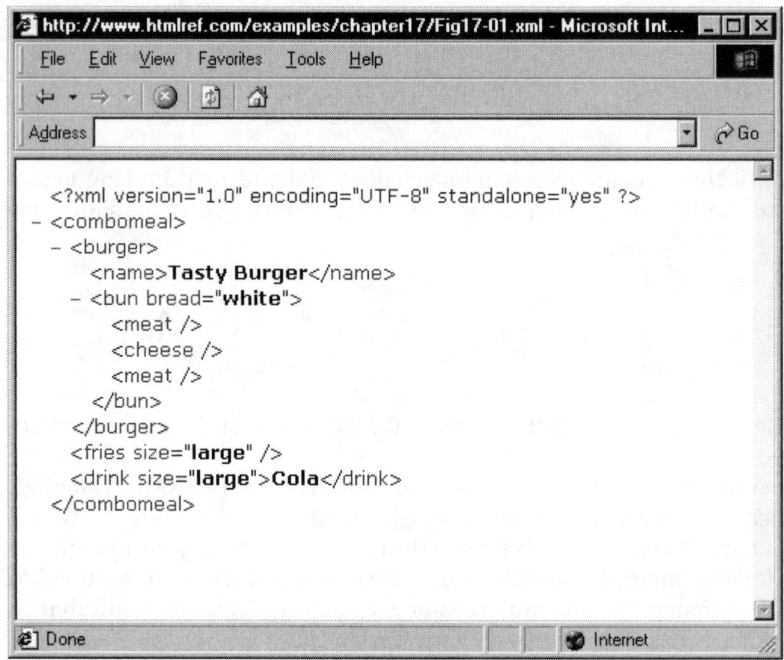

FIGURE 18-1 Well-formed XML under Internet Explorer

Notice that the browser shows a structural representation of the markup, not a screen representation. You'll see how to make this file actually look like something later in the chapter. First, take a look at the document syntax. In many ways, this example "Combo Meal Markup Language" (or CMML, if you like) looks similar to HTML—but how do you know to name the element **<combomeal>** instead of **<mealdeal>** or **<lunchspecial>**? You don't need to know, because the decision is completely up to you. Simply choose any element and attribute names that meaningfully represent the domain that you want to model. Does this mean that XML has no rules? It has rules, but they are few, simple, and relate only to syntax:

- *The document must start with the appropriate XML declaration,* like so:

  ```
  <?xml version="1.0" encoding="UTF-8" standalone="yes" ?>
  ```

  or, more simply, just

  ```
  <?xml version="1.0" ?>
  ```

- *A root element must enclose the entire document.* For example, in the previous example notice how the **<combomeal>** element encloses all other elements. In fact, not only must a root element enclose all other elements, the internal elements should close properly.
- *All elements must be closed.* The following

  ```
  <burger>Tasty
  ```

is not allowed under XML, but

```
<burger>Tasty</burger>
```

would be allowed. Even when elements do not contain content, they must be closed properly, as discussed in the next rule, for a valid XML document.

- *All elements with empty content must be self-identifying, by ending in "/>" just like XHTML.* An empty element is one such as the HTML **
, **<hr>, or **<img src="test.gif">** tags. In XML and XHTML, these would be represented, respectively, as **
, **<hr />, and **<img src="test.gif" />**.
- Just like well-written HTML and XHTML, *all elements must be properly nested.* For example,

```
<outer><inner>ground zero</inner></outer>
```

is correct, whereas this isn't:

```
<outer><inner>ground zero</outer></inner>
```

- *All attribute values must be quoted.* In traditional HTML, quoting is good authoring practice, but it is required only for values that contain characters other than letters (A–Z, a–z), numbers (0–9), hyphens (-), or periods (.). Under XHTML, quoting is required as it is in XML as well. For example,

```
<blastoff count="10" ></blastoff>
```

is correct, whereas this isn't:

```
<blastoff count=10></blastoff>
```

- *All elements must be cased consistently.* If you start a new element such as **<BURGER>**, you must close it as **</BURGER>**, not **</burger>**. Later in the document, if the element is in lowercase, you actually are referring to a new element known as **<burger>**. Attribute names also are case sensitive.
- *A valid XML file may not contain certain characters that have reserved meanings.* These include characters such as **&**, which indicates the beginning of a character entity such as **&**, or **<** , which indicates the start of an element name such as **<sunny>**. These characters must be coded as **&** and **<**, respectively, or can occur in a section marked off as character data. In fact, under a basic stand-alone XML document, this rule is quite restrictive as only **&**, **<**, **>**, **'**, and **"** would be allowed.

A document constructed according to the previous simple rules is known as a *well-formed document*. Take a look in Figure 18-2 at what happens to a document that doesn't follow the well-formed rules presented here.

Markup purists might find the notion of well-formed-ness somewhat troubling. Traditional SGML has no notion of well-formed documents; instead, it uses the notion of *valid* documents—documents that adhere to a formally defined document type definition (DTD). For anything beyond casual applications, defining a DTD and validating documents against that definition are real benefits. XML supports both well-formed and valid documents. The well-formed model that just enforces the basic syntax should encourage those not schooled in the intricacies

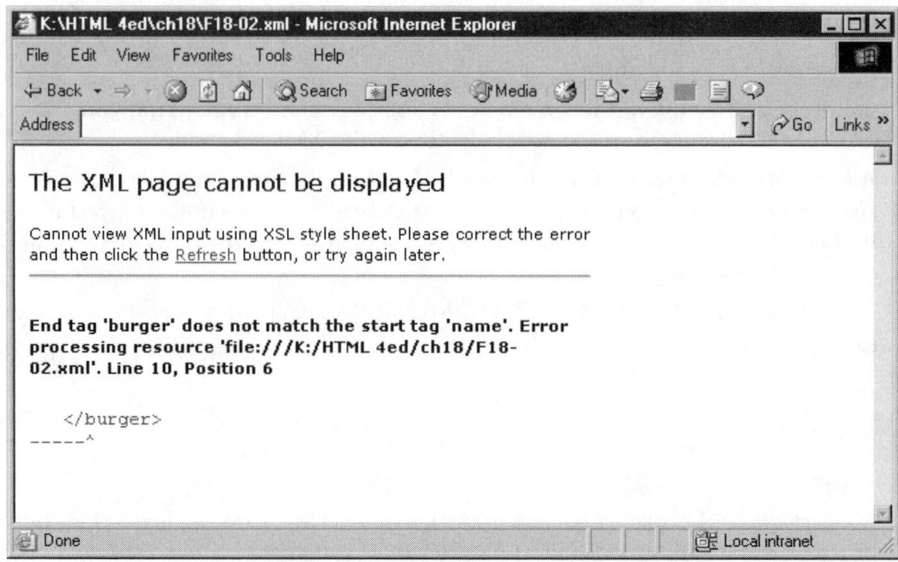

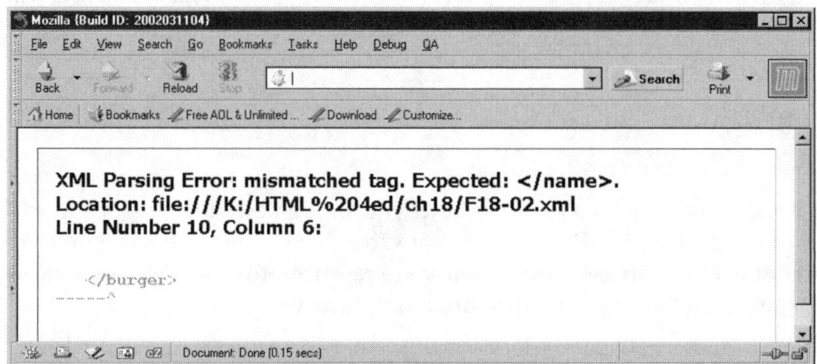

FIGURE 18-2 Documents that aren't well-formed won't render

of language design and syntax to begin authoring XML documents, thus making XML as accessible as traditional HTML has been. However, the valid model is available for applications in which a document's logical structure needs to be verified. This can be very important when we want to bring meaning to a document.

Valid XML

A document that conforms to a DTD is said to be *valid*. Unlike many HTML document authors, SGML and XML document authors normally concern themselves with producing valid documents. With the rise of XML, Web developers can look forward to mastering a new skill: writing DTDs. The following example illustrates how XML might be used to create some structure for the combo meal example. A definition of the sample language to accomplish this task can be found within the document, although this definition can be kept outside the file as well. The burger2.xml file shown here includes both the DTD and an occurrence of a document that conforms to the language in the same document:

```
<?xml version="1.0"?>
<!DOCTYPE combomeal [
<!ENTITY cola "Pepsi">
<!ELEMENT combomeal (burger+, fries+, drink+)>

<!ELEMENT burger (name, bun)>
<!ELEMENT name (#PCDATA)>
<!ELEMENT bun (meat+, cheese+, meat+)>
<!ATTLIST bun
     bread (white | wheat) #REQUIRED
>

<!ELEMENT meat EMPTY>
<!ELEMENT cheese EMPTY>

<!ELEMENT fries EMPTY>
<!ATTLIST fries
     size (small | medium | large) #REQUIRED
>

<!ELEMENT drink (#PCDATA)>
<!ATTLIST drink
     size (small | medium | large) #REQUIRED
>


]>
<!-- the document instance -->
<combomeal>
   <burger>
   <name>Tasty Burger</name>
   <bun bread="white">
      <meat />
      <cheese />
      <meat />
   </bun>
   </burger>
   <fries size="large" />
   <drink size="large">
       &cola;
   </drink>
</combomeal>
```

We could easily have just written the document itself and put the DTD in an external file referencing it using a statement such as

```
<!DOCTYPE combomeal SYSTEM "combomeal.dtd">
```

at the top of the document and the various element, attribute and entity definitions in the external file combomeal.dtd. Regardless of how it is defined and included, the meaning of the defined language is relatively straightforward. A document is enclosed by the **<combomeal>** tag, which in turn contains one or more **<burger>, <fries>,** and **<drink>** tags. Each **<burger>** tag contains a **<name>** and **<bun>**, which in turn contain **<meat />** and **<cheese />** tags. Attributes are defined to indicate the bread type of the bun as well as the size of the fries and drink in the meal. We even define our own custom entity **&cola;** to make it easy to specify and change the type of cola, in this case Pepsi, used in the document.

One interesting aspect of using a DTD with an XML file is that the correctness of the document can be checked. For example, adding nondefined elements or messing up the nesting orders of elements should cause a validating XML parser to reject the document, as shown in Figure 18-3.

NOTE *At the time of this writing, most browser-based XML parsers don't necessarily validate the document, but just check to make sure the document is well-formed. The Internet Explorer browser snapshot was performed using an extension that validates XML documents.*

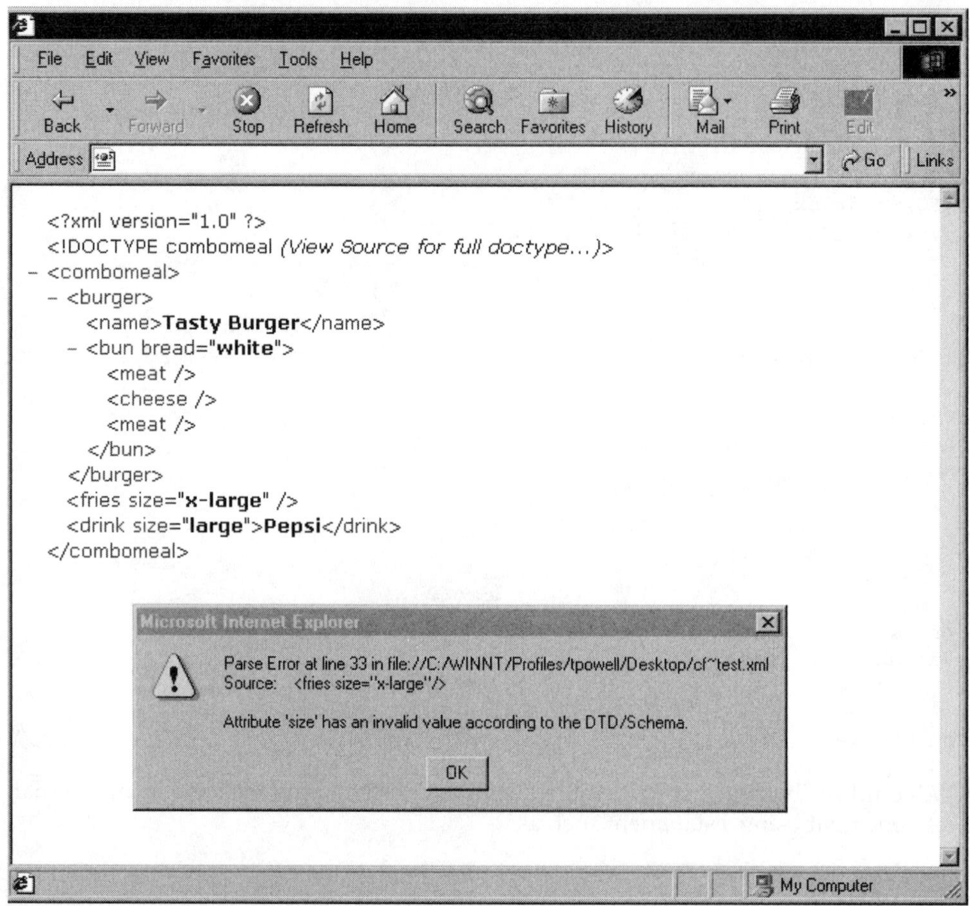

FIGURE 18-3 Validation error message

Writing a DTD might seem like an awful lot of trouble, but without one, the value of XML is limited. If you can guarantee conformance to the specification, you can start to allow automated parsing and exchange of documents. Writing a DTD is going to be a new experience for most Web developers, and not everybody will want to write one. Fortunately, although not apparent from the DTD rules in this brief example, XML significantly reduces the complexity of full SGML. However, regardless of how easy or hard it is to write a language definition, readers might wonder how to present an XML document once it is written.

Displaying XML

Notice that inherently XML documents have no predefined presentation; thus, we must define one. While this may seem like a hassle, it actually is a blessing as it forces the separation of content structure from presentation. Already, many Web developers have embraced the idea of storing Web content in XML format and then transforming it into an appropriate output format such as HTML or XHTML and CSS using *eXtensible Style Sheet Transformations* (XSLT) or some form of server-side programming. It is also possible to render XML natively in most browsers by binding CSS directly to user-defined elements.

Using XSL to Transform XML to HTML

With XSL, you can easily transform and then format an XML document. Various elements and attributes can be matched using XSL, and other markup languages such as HTML or XHTML and then can be output. Let's demonstrate this idea using client-side processed XSL found in most modern browsers. Consider the following simple well-formed XML document called demo.xml:

```
<?xml version="1.0" ?>
<?xml-stylesheet type="text/xsl" href="test.xsl"?>
<example>
  <demo>Look </demo>
  <demo>formatting  </demo>
  <demo> XML </demo>
  <demo>as HTML</demo>
</example>
```

Notice that the second line applies an XSL file called test.xsl to the document. That file will create a simple HTML document and convert each occurrence of the **<demo>** tag to an **<h1>** tag. The XSL template called test.xsl is shown here:

```
<?xml version="1.0"?>
<xsl:stylesheet version="1.0"
                xmlns:xsl="http://www.w3.org/1999/XSL/Transform">
   <xsl:template match="/">
      <html>
      <head>
      <title>XSL Test</title>
      </head>
      <body>

         <xsl:for-each select="example/demo">
          <h1><xsl:value-of select="."/></h1>
         </xsl:for-each>
```

```
      </body>
      </html>

   </xsl:template>
</xsl:stylesheet>
```

NOTE *In order to make the examples in this section work under Internet Explorer 5 or 5.5, use the statement* ***<xsl:stylesheet xmlns:xsl="http://www.w3.org/TR/WD-xsl">*** *to define the XSL version in place of the second line of each XSL document.*

Given the previous example, you could load the main XML document through an XML- and XSL-aware browser such as Internet Explorer. You would then end up with the following markup once the XSL transformation was applied:

```
<html>
<head>
<title>XSL Test</title>
</head>
<body>
<h1>Look</h1>
<h1>formatting</h1>
<h1>XML</h1>
<h1>as HTML</h1>
</body>
</html>
```

The example transformation under Internet Explorer is shown in Figure 18-4.

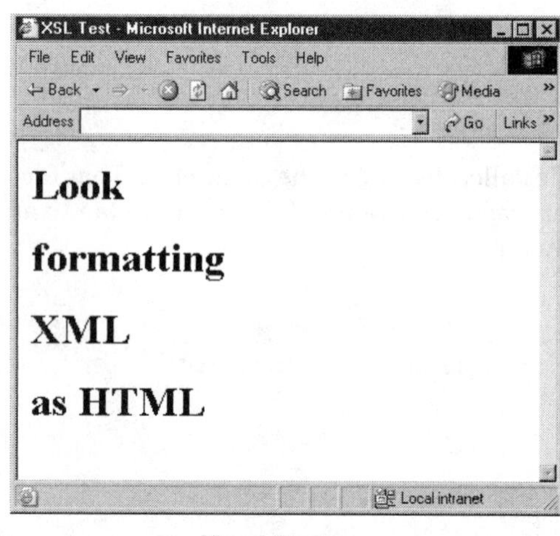

Visual Display

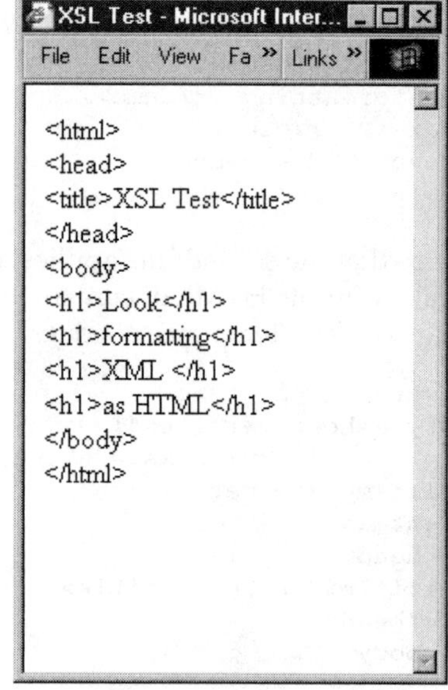

Generated markup from XSLT

FIGURE 18-4 Internet Explorer supports basic XSL

Whereas the preceding example is rather contrived, it is possible to create a much more sophisticated example. For example, given the following XML document representing an employee directory, you might wish to convert it into a traditional HTML table-based layout:

```
<?xml version="1.0" encoding="UTF-8" standalone="yes" ?>
<directory>
<employee>
     <name>Fred Brown</name>
     <title>Widget Washer</title>
     <phone>(543) 555-1212</phone>
     <email>fbrown@democompany.com</email>
</employee>

<employee>
     <name>Cory Richards</name>
     <title>Toxic Waste Manager</title>
     <phone>(543) 555-1213</phone>
     <email>richards@democompany.com</email>
</employee>

<employee>
     <name>Tim Powell</name>
     <title>Big Boss</title>
     <phone>(543) 555-2222</phone>
     <email>tpowell@democompany.com</email>
</employee>

<employee>
     <name>Samantha Jones</name>
     <title>Sales Executive</title>
     <phone>(543) 555-5672</phone>
     <email>jones@democompany.com</email>
</employee>


<employee>
     <name>Eric Roberts</name>
     <title>Director of Technology</title>
     <phone>(543) 567-3456</phone>
     <email>eric@democompany.com</email>
</employee>


<employee>
     <name>Frank Li</name>
     <title>Marketing Manager</title>
     <phone>(123) 456-2222</phone>
     <email>fli@democompany.com</email>
</employee>
</directory>
```

You might consider creating an XHTML table containing each of the individual employee records. For example, an employee represented by

```
<employee>
     <name>Employee's name</name>
     <title>Employee's title</title>
     <phone>Phone number</phone>
     <email>Email address</email>
</employee>
```

might be converted into a table row (**<tr>**), as in the following:

```
<tr>
     <td>Employee's name</td>
     <td>Employee's title</td>
     <td>Phone number</td>
     <td>Email address</td>
</tr>
```

You can use an XSL style sheet to perform such a transformation. The following is an example XSL style sheet (staff.xsl):

```
<?xml version="1.0"?>
<xsl:stylesheet version="1.0"
                xmlns:xsl="http://www.w3.org/1999/XSL/Transform">
<xsl:template match="/">

    <html>
    <head>
    <title>Employee Directory</title>
    </head>
    <body>

    <h1 align="center">DemoCompany Directory</h1>
    <hr/>
    <table width="100%">
       <tr>
         <th>Name</th>
         <th>Title</th>
         <th>Phone</th>
         <th>Email</th>
       </tr>

       <xsl:for-each select="directory/employee">

        <tr>
         <td><xsl:value-of select="name"/></td>
         <td><xsl:value-of select="title"/></td>
         <td><xsl:value-of select="phone"/></td>
         <td><xsl:value-of select="email"/></td>
```

```
         </tr>

        </xsl:for-each>

        </table>
        </body>
        </html>

</xsl:template>

</xsl:stylesheet>
```

You can reference the style sheet from the original XML document, adding this line in the original staff.xml file,

```
<?xml-stylesheet href="staff.xsl" type="text/xsl"?>
```

just below the initial **<?xml?>** declaration. The output of this previous example together with the generated markup created by the browser client-side is shown in Figure 18-5. If

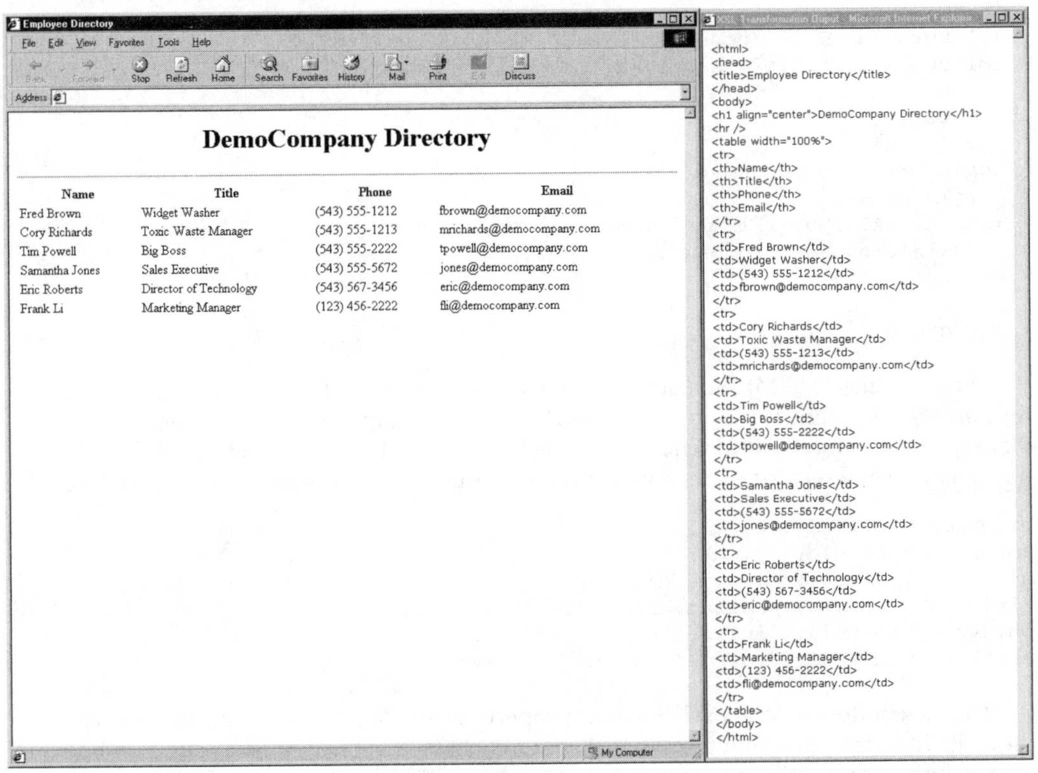

FIGURE 18-5 XML document transformed to HTML tables using XSL

you are worried about browser compatibility, given that not all browsers are aware of XSL, you can just as easily transform this into HTML on the server-side. This is probably a safer way to go for any publicly accessible Web page.

NOTE *XSL transformation can create all sorts of more complex documents complete with embedded JavaScript or style sheets.*

The previous discussion only begins to touch on the richness of XSL, which provides complex pattern matching and basic programming facilities. Readers interested in the latest developments in XSL are directed to the W3C Web site (http://www.w3.org/Style/XSL/) as well as Microsoft's XML site (http://msdn.microsoft.com/xml).

Displaying XML Documents Using CSS

The conversion from XML to HTML seems awkward; it would be preferable to deliver a native XML file and display it. As it turns out, it is also possible in most modern browsers to directly render XML by applying CSS rules immediately to tags. For example, given the following simple XML file, you might apply a set of CSS rules by relating the style sheet using **<?xml-stylesheet href="*URL to style sheet* " type="text/css"?>**, as shown here:

```
<?xml version="1.0" encoding="UTF-8" standalone="yes" ?>
<?xml-stylesheet href="staff.css" type="text/css"?>

<directory>
  <employee>
  <name>Fred Brown</name>
  <title>Widget Washer</title>
  <phone>(543) 555-1212</phone>
  <email>fbrown@democompany.com</email>
</employee>
...
</directory>
```

The CSS rules for XML elements are effectively the same as for HTML or XHTML documents, although they do require knowledge of less commonly used properties such as **display** to create meaningful renderings. The CSS rule for the previously presented XML document is shown here and its output under Internet Explorer is shown in Figure 18-6.

```
directory {display: block;}
employee  {display: block; border: solid;}
name      {display: inline; font-weight: bold; width: 200px;}
title     {display: inline; font-style: italic; width: 200px;}
phone     {display: inline; color: red; width: 150px;}
email     {display: inline; color: blue; width: 100px;}
```

The lack of flow objects in CSS makes properly displaying this XML document very difficult. To format anything meaningful, you may have to go and invent your own line breaks, headings, or other structures. In some sense, CSS relies heavily on XHTML for basic document structure. However, it may be possible instead to simply include such structures from XHTML into your document. The next section explores how you can put XHTML into your XML and vice versa.

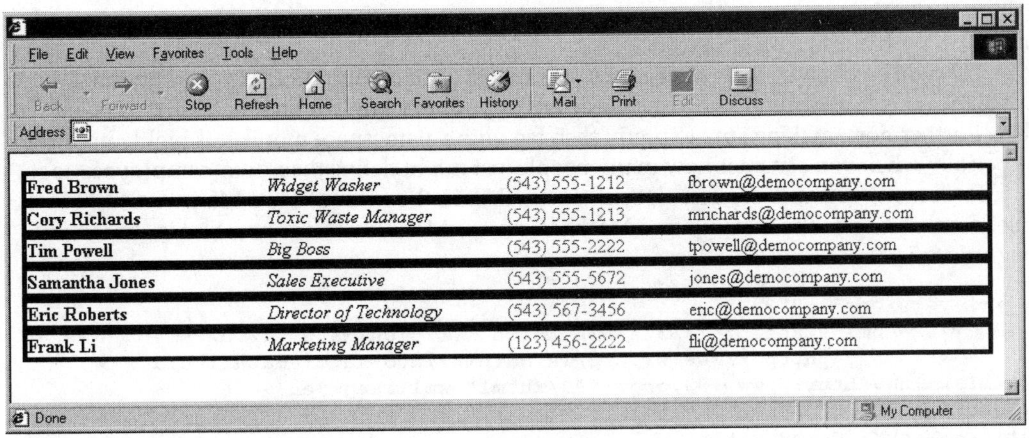
File Edit View Favorites Tools Help
Back Forward Stop Refresh Home Search Favorites History Mail Print Edit Discuss
Address
Fred Brown
Widget Washer
(543) 555-1212
fbrown@democompany.com
Cory Richards
Toxic Waste Manager
(543) 555-1213
mrichards@democompany.com
Tim Powell
Big Boss
(543) 555-2222
tpowell@democompany.com
Samantha Jones
Sales Executive
(543) 555-5672
jones@democompany.com
Eric Roberts
Director of Technology
(543) 567-3456
eric@democompany.com
Frank Li
Marketing Manager
(123) 456-2222
fli@democompany.com
Done
My Computer

FIGURE 18-6 Direct display of XML documents with CSS

Combining XML and XHTML

In the previous example, which tried to render an XML document using CSS, it might have been useful to add a heading and use line breaks more liberally. You could go about inventing your **<h1>** and **
** tags but why do so when you have XHTML to serve you? You can use existing XHTML tags easily if you use the **xmlns** attribute. Consider the following:

```
<directory xmlns:html="http://www.w3.org/1999/xhtml">
… elements and text …
</directory>
```

Within the directory element, you can use XHTML tags freely as long as you prefix them with the namespace moniker **html** we assigned. For example,

```
<?xml version="1.0" encoding="UTF-8" standalone="yes" ?>
<?xml-stylesheet href="staff.css" type="text/css"?>

<directory xmlns:html="http://www.w3.org/1999/xhtml">
<html:h1>Employee Directory</html:h1>
<html:hr />
<employee>
<name>Fred Brown</name>
<title>Widget Washer</title>
<phone>(543) 555-1212</phone>
<email>fbrown@democompany.com</email>
</employee>
<html:br /><html:br />
…
</directory>
```

PART VI

In this case, you could even attach CSS rules to our newly used XHTML elements and come up with a much nicer layout.

It should be obvious that namespaces are not just for including XHTML markup into an XML file. This facility allows you to include any type of markup within any XML document you like. Furthermore, making sure to prefix each tag with a namespace moniker is highly important especially when you consider how many people just might define their own **<employee>** tag!

To demonstrate namespaces, let's include XML in the form of MathML into an XHTML file. A rendering of the markup in a MathML-aware Mozilla variant browser is shown in Figure 18-7.

```
<?xml version="1.0"?>
<!DOCTYPE html PUBLIC "-//W3C//DTD XHTML 1.1 plus MathML 2.0//EN"
               "http://www.w3.org/TR/MathML2/dtd/xhtml-math11-f.dtd">
<html xmlns="http://www.w3.org/1999/xhtml" xml:lang="en">
<head>
<title>MathML Demo</title>
</head>
<body>
<h1 style="text-align:center;">MathML Below</h1>
<hr />
<math mode="display" xmlns="http://www.w3.org/1998/Math/MathML">
  <mrow>
    <mfrac>
      <mrow>
        <mi>x</mi>
        <mo>+</mo>
        <msup>
          <mi>y</mi>
          <mn>2</mn>
        </msup>
      </mrow>

      <mrow>
        <mi>k</mi>
        <mo>+</mo>
        <mn>1</mn>
      </mrow>
    </mfrac>
  </mrow>
</math>

<hr />
</body>
</html>
```

NOTE *This example requires the file to be named as .xml or .xhtml to invoke the strict XML parser on XHTML.*

The previous example should suggest that XHTML may become host to a variety of languages in the future or that it will be hosted in a variety of other XML-based languages. The questions, then, are: Should the XML be within the XHTML/HTML or should the XHTML be inside the XML? While the W3C may lean toward XML hosting XHTML markup

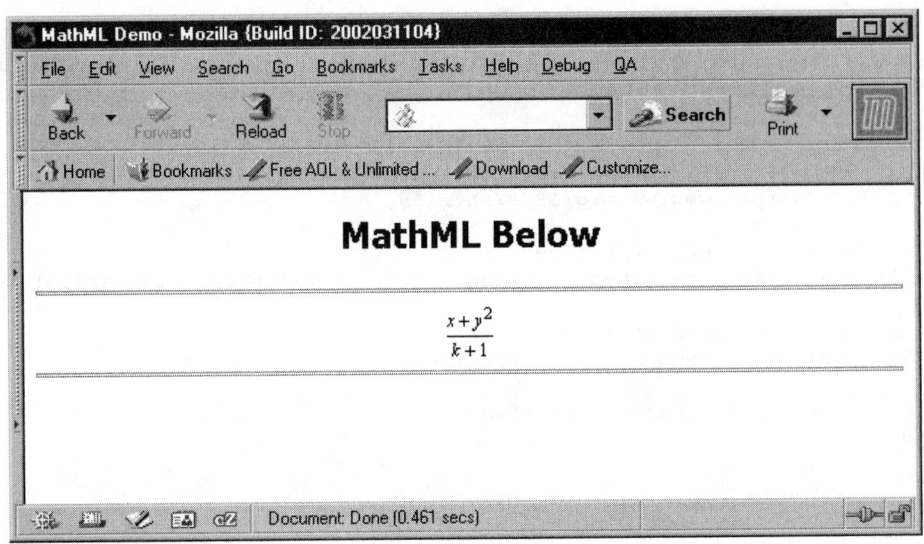

FIGURE 18-7 XHTML with MathML and SVG under Mozilla

given the deployed base of HTML documents, markup authors may be more comfortable with just the opposite.

Internet Explorer XML Data Islands

Because of the common desire, or in many cases *need*, to embed XML data content into an HTML document, Microsoft introduced a special **<xml>** tag in Internet Explorer 4. The **<xml>** tag is used to create a so-called XML data island that can hold XML to be used within the document. Imagine running a query to a database and fetching more data than needed for the page and putting it in an XML data island. You may then allow the user to retrieve new information from the data island without going back to the server. To include XML in an HTML document, you can use the **<xml>** tag and either enclose the content directly within it, like so:

```
...HTML content...

<xml id="myIsland">
  <directory>
  <employee>
    <name>Fred Brown</name>
    <title>Widget Washer</title>
    <phone>(543) 555-1212</phone>
    <email>fbrown@democompany.com</email>
  </employee>
  </directory>
</xml>

...HTML content...
```

or you can reference an external file by specifying its URL: **<xml id="myIsland" src="staff.xml"></xml>**.

Once the XML is included in the document, you can then bind the XML to HTML elements. In the example here, we bind XML data to a table. Notice that you must use fully standard table markup to avoid repeating the headings over and over:

```
<!DOCTYPE html PUBLIC "-//W3C//DTD XHTML 1.0 Transitional//EN"
 "http://www.w3.org/TR/xhtml1/DTD/xhtml1-transitional.dtd">
<html xmlns="http://www.w3.org/1999/xhtml">
<head>
<title>Employee Directory</title>
<meta http-equiv="content-type" content="text/html; charset=ISO-8859-1" />
<body>
<xml id="myIsland" src="staff.xml"></xml>
<h1 align="center">DemoCompany Directory</h1>
<hr/>
<table width="100%" datasrc="#myIsland">
<thead>
       <tr>
          <th>Name</th>
          <th>Title</th>
          <th>Phone</th>
          <th>Email</th>

      </tr>
</thead>
<tbody>
      <tr>
          <td><span datafld="name"></span></td>
          <td><span datafld="title"></span></td>
          <td><span datafld="phone"></span></td>
          <td><span datafld="email"></span></td>
     </tr>
</tbody>
</table>
</body>
</html>
```

NOTE *This example will not validate nor work in other browsers besides Internet Explorer as the* **<xml>** *tag is a proprietary tag.*

The output of the example is as expected and is shown in Figure 18-8.

Once you bind data into a document, you can display it as we did in the previous example, or even use JavaScript and manipulate the contents. Imagine sending the full result of a query to a browser and then allowing the user to sort and page through the data without having to go back to the server. Embedded XML together with JavaScript can make this happen.

Now that you have seen some of the basics of XML, let's consider how the language is actually used on the Web today by discussing some of its application languages.

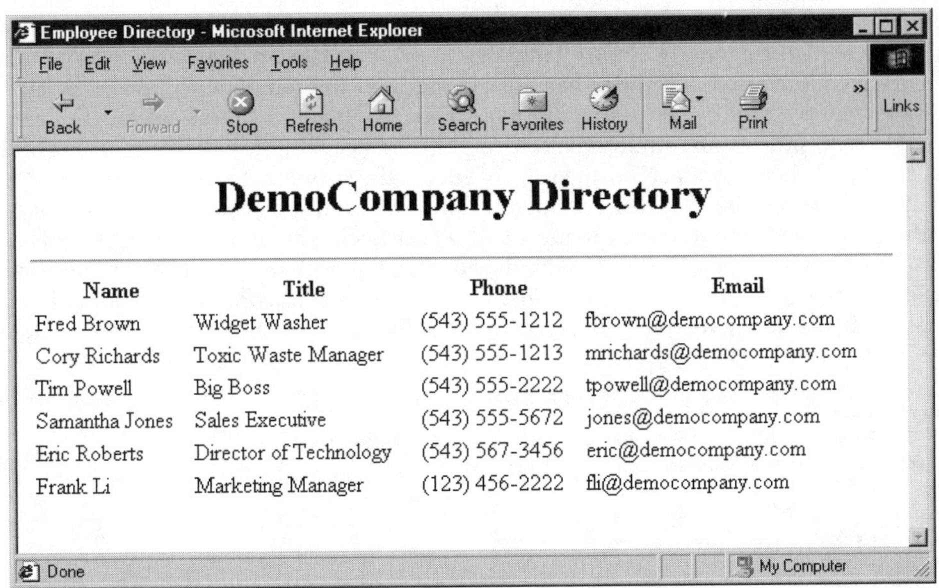

DemoCompany Directory

Name	Title	Phone	Email
Fred Brown	Widget Washer	(543) 555-1212	fbrown@democompany.com
Cory Richards	Toxic Waste Manager	(543) 555-1213	mrichards@democompany.com
Tim Powell	Big Boss	(543) 555-2222	tpowell@democompany.com
Samantha Jones	Sales Executive	(543) 555-5672	jones@democompany.com
Eric Roberts	Director of Technology	(543) 567-3456	eric@democompany.com
Frank Li	Marketing Manager	(123) 456-2222	fli@democompany.com

FIGURE 18-8 With IE's data-binding you can output structured data easily

NOTE *The previous discussion is by no means a complete discussion of XML and related technologies, but just enough for us to have the necessary background to present some use of XML and JavaScript together for those unfamiliar with the basics of XML. Readers looking for more detailed information on XML might consider sites like www.xml101.com and, of course, the W3 XML section (www.w3.org/XML).*

XML Application Languages

What's interesting about XML is how many people do not see that it is the applications and application languages built with it, and not the language itself that is really interesting. It probably is not always in the best interests of Web designers to invent their own XML-based languages, but rather to use a language written using XML. Even with this approach, the Web could spawn thousands of new XML-based languages that many people can't use right away. Always remember that the value of knowing a language generally is proportional to the number of people with whom you can communicate by using the language. The following sections briefly present four XML-based application languages to give you a sense of how this technology is used.

Wireless Markup Language (WML)

The Wireless Markup Language (WML) originally defined by the WAP forum (http://www.wapforum.org) and now being maintained by the Open Mobile Alliance (http://www.openmobilealliance.org)has become a leading standard for wireless Web sites. Initially based on Phone.com's *Handheld Device Markup Language* (HDML), WML aims to be the general-purpose language to present data on devices such as cellular phones. Given that a cellular phone has limited memory, limited network connectivity, a relatively simple user interface that favors content reading and simple selection over data input, and little or no multimedia or programming capabilities, the language is built to be small and speedy. In fact, for the sake of speed, the entire metaphor of pages that is fundamental to Web sites has been removed from WML and replaced with the idea of a *deck* and *cards;* the idea being that each request to a server fetches an entire deck or document and the deck itself contains individual cards. Further, the deck represents a complete idea or task and the cards represent pieces of the task. This is best illustrated by looking at the generic WML document template, which consists of four tags, **<wml>**, **<head>**, **<template>**, and **<card>**, as shown here:

```
<?xml version="1.0"?>
<!DOCTYPE wml PUBLIC "-//WAPFORUM//DTD WML 1.3//EN"
"http://www.wapforum.org/DTD/wml13.dtd">
<wml>
<head>
  head information here
</head>

<template>
  template information here
</template>

<card>
  card contents
</card>
  more cards
</wml>
```

Whereas the document is defined by the **<wml>** tag, the **<head>** contains supplementary information about the document similar to the **<head>** tag in HTML. The **<template>** section, which is optional, contains information that should be applied to multiple cards in the deck. Last, the individual pieces of a deck are defined with the **<card>** tag. Within the **<card>** tag are the various screen elements defined by WML, such as paragraphs, input fields, tables, images, and so on. Given the standard WML template previously shown, the simplest example in WML is presented here:

```
<?xml version="1.0"?>
<!DOCTYPE wml PUBLIC "-//WAPFORUM//DTD WML 1.3//EN"
          "http://www.wapforum.org/DTD/wml13.dtd">
<wml>
<card id="card1" title="First Deck">
<p>Hello WML World!</p>
</card>
</wml>
```

Using a cell phone simulator such as Openwave's Mobile SDK (http://developer.openwave.com) or Nokia's Phone Simulator (http://forum.nokia.com), it is possible to view the likely presentation of this document, as shown in Figure 18-9.

The language itself is relatively simple. Table 18-1 shows most of the elements defined under the WML 1.3 specification. Notice the similarity in elements between WML and HTML, particularly in text formatting.

Despite its apparent similarities to XHTML, WML is very domain-specific; consider that many of its elements and attributes are built to reduce network traffic (as in cache control using **<meta>** and deck size reduction using **<template>**), to improve state management for programming by defining variables with **<setvar>**, and to reduce data input using input masks defined with the mask attribute for **<input>**. XHTML also has a special limited version called the XHTML Mobile profile used on some wireless devices. However, regardless of the eventual dominance of one form of markup or another, WML serves as a good example of how XML can be used to rigorously define a special-purpose language.

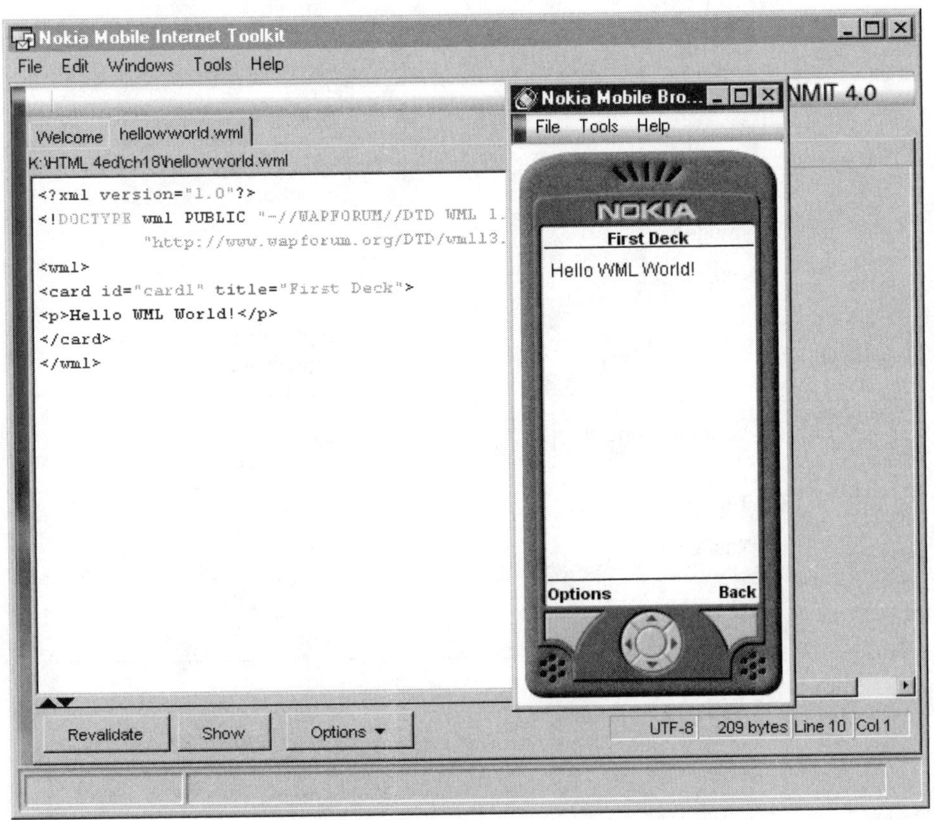

FIGURE 18-9 Hello WML World in Nokia Simulator

TABLE 18-1
WML Elements

Element Category	Sample WML Elements
Deck and card structure	<wml> <card> <template> <head>
Head Information	<access> <meta>
Text Formatting	<p> <b> <i> <u> <em> <strong> <small> <big> <table> <tr> <td>
Links and Anchors	<a> <anchor>
Images	<img>
User Input	<input> <select> <option> <optgroup> <fieldset>
Variable Control	<setvar> <postfield>
Timers	<timer>
Tasks	<go> <prev> <refresh> <noop>
Events	<do> <ontimer> <onenterforward> <onenterbackward> <onpick> <onevent>

SVG

Scalable Vector Graphics (SVG) aims to provide basic drawing and animation facilities specified in an XML format. While not as ubiquitous in use as Flash, SVG is a W3C standard. Furthermore, the language has heavy support from Adobe, so its future, while not certain, seems bright.

The basic structure of an SVG file by itself is shown here:

```
<?xml version="1.0" encoding="ISO-8859-1" standalone="no"?>
<!DOCTYPE svg PUBLIC "-//W3C//DTD SVG 20010904//EN"
     "http://www.w3.org/TR/2001/REC-SVG-20010904/DTD/svg10.dtd">
<svg xmlns="http://www.w3.org/2000/svg">
<!-- SVG content goes here -->
</svg>
```

Given this basic template, you could create a simple example that wraps some text around a circle:

```
<?xml version="1.0" encoding="ISO-8859-1" standalone="no"?>
<!DOCTYPE svg PUBLIC "-//W3C//DTD SVG 20010904//EN"
"http://www.w3.org/TR/2001/REC-SVG-20010904/DTD/svg10.dtd">

<svg xmlns="http://www.w3.org/2000/svg"
    xmlns:xlink="http://www.w3.org/1999/xlink">
<defs>
    <path id="textPath" d="M10 50 C10 0 90 0 90 50"/>
</defs>

<text fill="red" style="font-size: 12pt;">
    <textPath xlink:href="#textPath">Hello SVG World!</textPath>
</text>

<circle cx="50" cy="50" r="20" fill="blue"/>
</svg>
```

Using Adobe's SVG viewer, you might reference your example file, like so:

```
<!DOCTYPE html PUBLIC "-//W3C//DTD XHTML 1.0 Transitional//EN"
 "http://www.w3.org/TR/xhtml1/DTD/xhtml1-transitional.dtd">
<html xmlns="http://www.w3.org/1999/xhtml"> lang="en"
<head>
<title>Hello SVG World</title>
</head>
<body>
 <embed src="helloworld.svg" width="150" height="150"
        type="image/svg+xml" />
</body>
</html>
```

The output of the simple example is shown here:

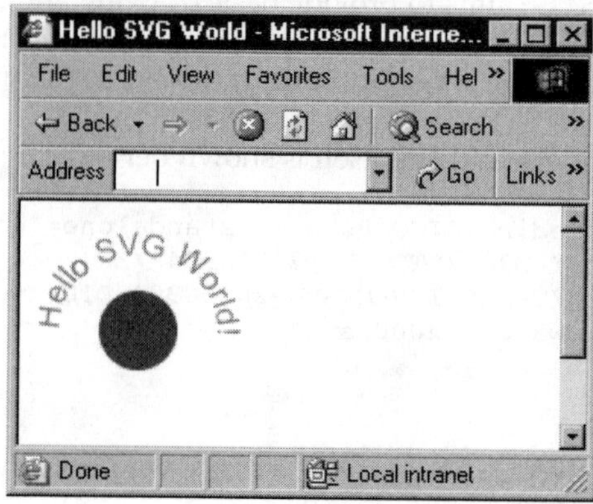

NOTE *The Adobe player requires* **<embed>** *or* **<object>** *tags to reference an external .svg file. A Mozilla (www.mozilla.org/projects/svg/) native SVG implementation allows SVG to be intermixed with XHTML using namespaces. While this syntax may be more standards focused, the Adobe player is the dominant way to view SVG files at the time of this edition's writing.*

The SVG format supports the capability to create arbitrary shapes; style and download fonts; set opacity levels, gradients, and filters; and even animate text and graphics. While it would seem quite a hassle to define graphics in SVG format, using a tool such as Adobe Illustrator, designers can easily export to SVG. The value of saving in the format is significant. Given that it is just text, it is very easy to generate from a server-side program and can be manipulated using client-side JavaScript. Readers looking for interesting demos and more information on SVG should visit Adobe's SVG support area at www.adobe.com/svg.

SOAP

SOAP (Simple Object Access Protocol) is an XML-based language that is used for inter-application communication on the Web. The idea behind SOAP is to allow a browser, server, or other user agent to communicate with a remote resource and potentially run an application or gather data from it in a structured fashion. A SOAP message contains the following elements:

- A required **Envelope** element that identifies the document as a SOAP message.
- An optional **Header** element that contains header information of the message such as application-specific information like authentication, payment, and so on necessary for message.
- A required **Body** element that contains call and/or response information.
- An optional **Fault** element that provides information about errors that occurred while processing the SOAP message.

The following is an example of a SOAP template message:

```
<?xml version="1.0"?>
<soap:Envelope xmlns:soap="http://www.w3.org/2001/12/soap-envelope"
      soap:encodingStyle="http://www.w3.org/2001/12/soap-encoding">
<soap:Header>
  ...header info here...
</soap:Header>

<soap:Body>

  ...the payload here...

  <soap:Fault>
    ... Fault information here...
  </soap:Fault>

</soap:Body>
</soap:Envelope>
```

You can populate your SOAP message and then, using HTTP, send it over the Internet to another site that fulfills your request. In the simple sense, SOAP = HTTP + XML and is used to build a simple remote procedure call system for the Web. The capability to transact and exchange information between sites is the core idea of the much hyped idea of *Web services*. Many interesting possibilities arise from these ideas; for example, consider accessing Google programmatically. An API provided by Google (www.google.com/apis/) makes a simple SOAP demonstration possible. The following is an example SOAP search packet to Google to look for "HTML Complete Reference":

```
<?xml version="1.0" encoding='UTF-8'?>

<SOAP-ENV:Envelope
      xmlns:SOAP-ENV="http://schemas.xmlsoap.org/soap/envelope/"
      xmlns:xsi="http://www.w3.org/1999/XMLSchema-instance"
      xmlns:xsd="http://www.w3.org/1999/XMLSchema">

  <SOAP-ENV:Body>

    <ns1:doGoogleSearch xmlns:ns1="urn:GoogleSearch"
      SOAP-ENV:encodingStyle="http://schemas.xmlsoap.org/soap/encoding/">
      <key xsi:type="xsd:string">00000000000000000000000000000000</key>
      <q xsi:type="xsd:string">HTML The Complete Reference</q>
      <start xsi:type="xsd:int">0</start>
      <maxResults xsi:type="xsd:int">10</maxResults>
      <filter xsi:type="xsd:boolean">true</filter>
      <restrict xsi:type="xsd:string"></restrict>
      <safeSearch xsi:type="xsd:boolean">false</safeSearch>
      <lr xsi:type="xsd:string"></lr>
      <ie xsi:type="xsd:string">latin1</ie>
      <oe xsi:type="xsd:string">latin1</oe>
    </ns1:doGoogleSearch>

  </SOAP-ENV:Body>
</SOAP-ENV:Envelope>
```

NOTE *The Google API license key has been set to all zeros. You must apply to Google to get a key to access their service.*

Next, let's use a simple SOAP client in the form of Netscape 7 with some JavaScript to execute our remote query and display the results in our browser, as shown here:

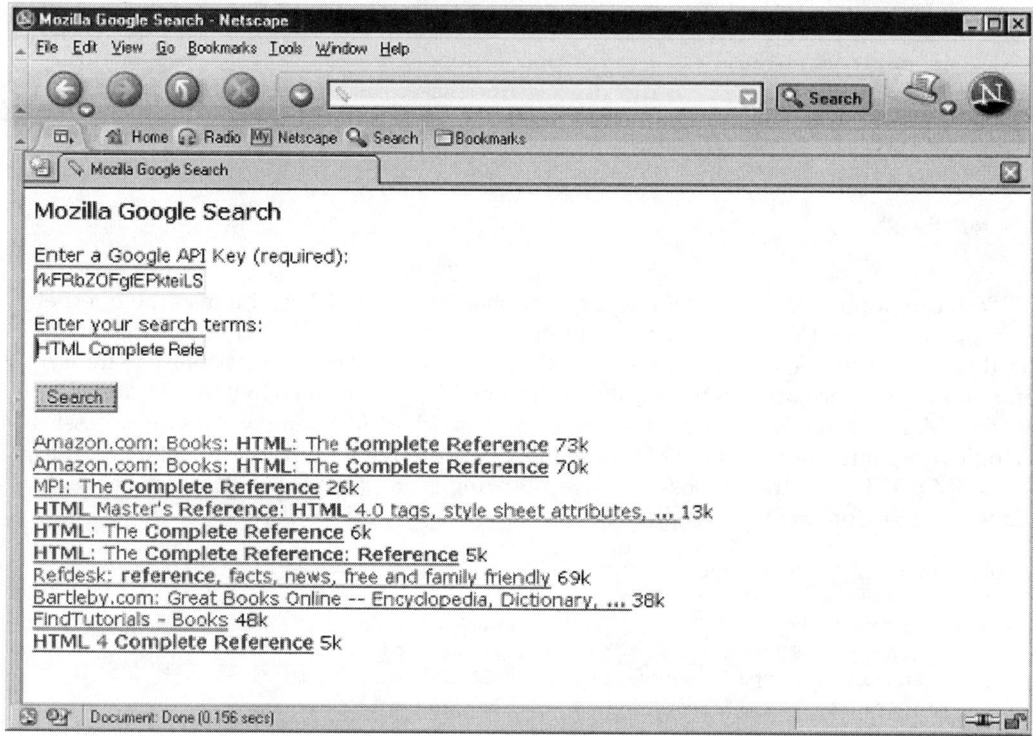

The simple SOAP example presented hints at some of the possibilities when sites begin to exchange information. The next XML application language shows another use of XML exchange on the Web.

RSS

The XML-based RSS (Really Simple Syndication) language is used heavily amongst sites to share headlines and stories. It is quite popular with the Web logger or "blog community" because of its ease of use. A simple example of RSS that would specify some news articles is shown here:

```
<?xml version="1.0" ?>
<!DOCTYPE rss PUBLIC "-//Netscape Communications//DTD RSS 0.91//EN"
"http://my.netscape.com/publish/formats/rss-0.91.dtd">

<rss version="0.91">
<channel>
```

```
<title>HTML Reference News</title>
<link>http://www.htmlref.com/</link>
<description>
A silly example of RSS for HTML The Complete Reference
</description>
<language>en-us</language>

<item>
<title>
Bold tag voted most popular XHTML tag
</title>
<link>
http://www.htmlref.com/fakelink1.html
</link>
<description>
The b tag wins the vote amongst US HTML authors as the most popular tag.
</description>
</item>

<item>
<title>
HTML examples considered hazardous to your health
</title>
<link>
http://www.htmlref.com/fakelink2.html
</link>
<description>
This is another fake story and doesn't have any value.
</description>
</item>

</channel>
</rss>
```

In this example, notice that the **<channel>** tag defines the feed, followed by a **<link>** to the site and a short **<description>**. Each individual news item is enclosed within an **<item>** tag and has a short **<description>** and **<link>** of its own. Given the ease of the format, it is no wonder that RSS has taken off; however, a significant problem with RSS does exist—the human factor. With many different competing variations such as RSS 0.91, RSS 1.0, and RSS 2.0 pushed by different organizations, it is hard to keep everything straight.

The last few sections have given readers a taste of the wide range of XML-based application languages that are possible. Anything from domain-specific languages such as MathML to generic languages such as XHTML can be defined. The possibilities are literally endless, but how XML will actually be used in the larger picture is still anyone's guess.

Predicting the Future of XML

Predicting the future of XML and its effect on HTML is difficult. So far, the uptake of custom XML documents in the public isn't nearly as fast as many of the pundits have suggested, although it has really taken off internally in many organizations. However, even on the Web, XML is starting to catch on, as shown by the uptake of new languages such as WML,

SMIL, SVG, and so on. Data interchange languages such as RSS and SOAP have been particularly interesting to watch develop and show that XML has a significant role to play in data interchange.

XML's potential for success should be no surprise. The technology is simple to describe, yet provides the power to create data that can be passed between programs or people without loss of meaning. With its structure, XML will enable Web-based automation, improved search engines, and a host of motivating e-commerce applications. However, before you get too excited, consider that to achieve the dream of an XML-enabled Web, many diverse groups need to get together and agree on data formats.

Just because XML *could* be used to write a special language to be used to automate data interchange in a particular industry doesn't mean that people *will* accept it. Remember that XML is based on SGML, and SGML has promised similar benefits during its history. Getting groups to agree upon a common data format and actually use it isn't always feasible, given the competitive nature of business. Anyone can define his or her own XML-based language. McDonald's could define FFML (Fast Food Markup Language). But does this mean that Burger King will accept it as standard? With people defining languages for their own special needs, the chaos of the Web could multiply into a markup Tower of Babel.

One thing is certain: HTML in its present form isn't going away any time soon. Simply too many people are writing HTML documents for it to go away overnight. XHTML is indeed the future, but it won't happen all at once. Like it or not, people and many editors just don't seem to follow the rules with HTML. Furthermore, legacy documents written in old style HTML will continue for some time. Already we see that browsers will support some sort of compatibility mode to deal with old HTML markup. Unfortunately, this has already watered down the effect of XHTML in the short term by not encouraging enough people to move to it.

Never underestimate the simplicity of traditional HTML. It might be ill-defined and misused, but it is commonly known and understood. In some sense, HTML is the English of the Web—often poorly spoken but well understood. Unfortunately, following the language analogy might mean that many XML application languages are the equivalent of Esperanto—the supposed well-defined perfect common language—well-designed but not used. To move the Web from an HTML-centered approach to an XML-centered one will take some time.

Summary

This discussion of XML's core syntax and extension only scratches the surface of what remains an emerging technology. The best way to track XML's rapid evolution is to closely monitor the XML activity at the W3C, http://www.w3.org/XML/. The implications of XML are enormous. Just as a metadata definition language, XML has some wonderful uses for extending the Web. Languages such as WML, RSS, SOAP, and SVG show how XML can be used. Other languages certainly are possible, including markup to help search engines to more accurately index Web pages. Like many new, hot technologies, XML will go through a "hype phase" that suggests it is good for everything. However, at least in the short term, XML will augment HTML and address its weaknesses rather than replace it outright. Just as Windows relied on DOS and did not quickly supplant it, the market-driven nature of Web technologies in conjunction with the existing heavy investment in HTML-based information probably will spur an XML evolution rather than XML revolution.

VII

PART

Appendixes

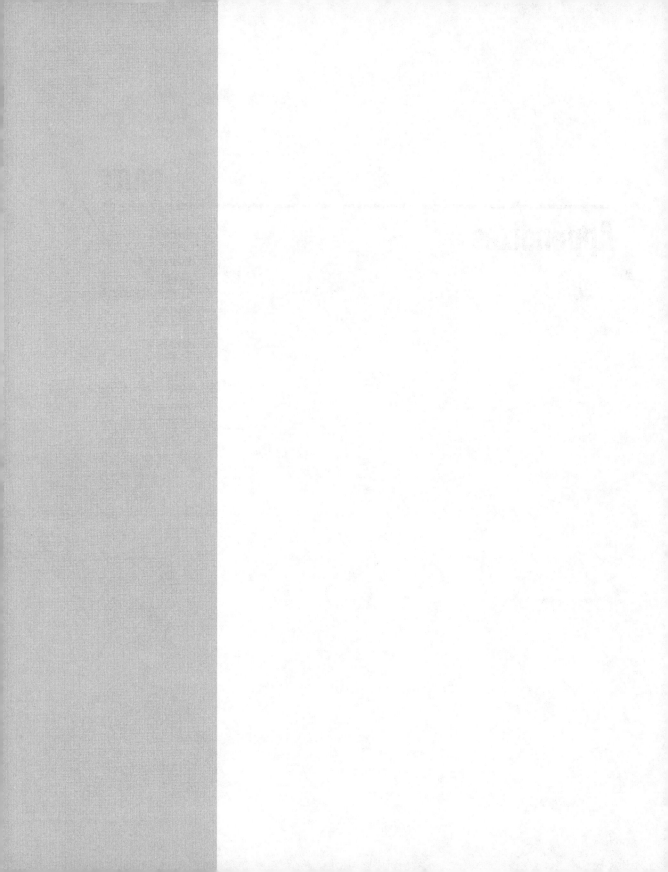

APPENDIX A

HTML and XHTML Element Reference

This appendix provides a complete reference for the elements in the HTML 4.01 and XHTML 1.0 specifications. Elements commonly supported by Internet Explorer, Netscape, and Opera are also presented. Some elements presented here might be deprecated, but they are also included because browser vendors continue to support them or they are still in common use.

Flavors of HTML and XHTML

There are many versions of HTML and XHTML in existence. In the early days, the specification of HTML was somewhat fluid, and browser vendors of all sizes added their own elements. First, the Internet Engineering Task Force (IETF) and later the World Wide Web Consortium (W3C) set standards for HTML, including the following:

- **HTML 2** The basic standard supported by early browsers like Mosaic.
- **HTML 3.0** A standard that was never widely adopted, as it was developed during the time of heavy browser innovation.
- **HTML 3.2** A version of the HTML 3.0 specification that adopted many browser-invented elements and removed nonimplemented HTML 3.0 elements.
- **HTML 4.0 Transitional** The modern version of HTML, complete with frames, scripting, and style sheet support. This version includes presentational elements.
- **HTML 4.0 Strict** A version of HTML that removes most of the presentational features of the language in favor of CSS-based presentation.
- **HTML 4.0 Frameset** A version of HTML that defines support for frames and inline frames.
- **HTML 4.01 Transitional, Strict, and Frameset** A slight bug fix release of the HTML 4 specifications.

Eventually, the rigor of XML was added to HTML, and XHTML 1.0 (http://www.w3.org/TR/xhtml1/) became a W3C recommendation on January 26, 2000. XHTML 1.0 retains a number of deprecated, presentational elements that are still present in the HTML specifications. XHTML 1.0 supports the transitional, strict, and frameset variants of HTML 4. The versions that have begun to follow XHTML 1.0 are not covered in depth in this book, as they are still not widely adopted, and in the case of XHTML 2, not fully defined.

XHTML 1.1

XHTML 1.1 is a stricter specification that, as defined by the W3C, is "a markup language that is rich in structural functionality, but that relies upon style sheets for presentation." XHTML 1.1's other focus is on modularization of XHTML, which makes it easier to define and segment the features supported in the language. XHTML 1.1 has only very basic changes from the strict variant of XHTML. These changes are summarized here:

- On every element supporting the **lang** attribute, the **lang** attribute has been replaced with **xml:lang**.
- The **name** attribute has been removed in favor of **id** on the **a** and **map** elements.
- The ruby-related elements (such as **ruby** and **rt**) have been included for adding small text readings to primarily eastern character-set text.

The XHTML 1.1 specification can be found online at http://www.w3.org/TR/xhtml11/.

XHTML Basic

A pared-down version of XHTML 1.1, called XHTML Basic, is geared toward mobile applications. The specification defines a subset of XHTML, including the following:

- Structure module: **html, head, title, body**
- Text module: **abbr, acronym, address, blockquote, br, cite, code, dfn, div, em, h1, h2, h3, h4, h5, h6, kbd, p, pre, q, samp, span, strong, var**
- Hypertext module: **a**
- List module: **dl, dt, dd, ol, ul, li**
- Basic forms module: **form, input, label, select, option, textarea**
- Basic tables module: **table, caption, tr, td, th**
- Image module: **img**
- Object module: **object, param**
- Metainformation module: **meta**
- Link module: **link**
- Base module: **base**

Of these, the structure, text, hypertext, and list modules are mandatory, but other modules may even be omitted if the device cannot handle them. The XHTML Basic specification can be found at http://www.w3.org/TR/xhtml-basic/.

XHTML 2

The XHTML 2 specification is in progress at the time of this edition's writing and represents a somewhat radical departure from XHTML 1. The goal of XHTML 2 is to make the markup language completely logical and provide no backward compatibility for older versions. Already this approach has been the recipient of significant ire from some developers, particularly those who followed W3C standards for years and who now find that their well-crafted documents may be without an easy upgrade path. A few of the changes XHTML 2 may introduce include the following:

- Some improvement to text direction handling.
- A common **edit** attribute to indicate inserted, deleted, changed, and moved text, and a **datetime** common attribute to indicate when changes were made.

- A change to use **navindex** over **tabindex** for selecting elements using a keyboard or alternative mechanism.
- The ability to make nearly any object a link, and to link content into any object.
- A completely different way to handle events based upon XML Events (http://www.w3.org/TR/xml-events/).
- A new **<h>** tag to be used with a **<section>** tag to better organize documents. The various heading tags like **<h1>** may be deprecated in favor of this new style.
- A line tag **<l>** to define a line of text or computer code. This may remove the need for a **
** tag.
- An exciting new **<nl>** tag that would be used to create navigation lists or menus.
- The removal of **<img>** in favor of **<object>**.
- A **<standby>** tag to help deal with slow loading objects.
- A **<summary>** tag for tables.
- The removal of traditional form-field elements in favor of the richer XForms specification (http://www.w3.org/TR/xforms/)

Beyond this brief description, which may certainly be wrong by the time you read it, little can be said about XHTML 2 with certainty, other than the specification may take quite some time to be finalized, and it will certainly take even more time before the major browsers embrace it. To keep up with the latest XHTML 2 activity, visit http://www.w3.org/TR/xhtml2/.

Core Attributes Reference

The HTML and XHTML specifications provide four main attributes that are common to nearly all elements and have much the same meaning for all elements. These attributes are **class, id, style,** and **title**. Rather than replicating this information throughout the appendix, it is summarized here.

class

This attribute indicates the class or classes that a particular element belongs to. A class name might be used by a style sheet to associate style rules to multiple elements at once. For example, one could associate a special class name called "important" with all elements that should be rendered with a yellow background. Class values are not unique to a particular element, so **<b class="important">** could be used as well as **<p class="important">** in the same document. It also is possible to have multiple values for the **class** attribute separated by white space; **<strong class="important special-font">** would define two classes with the particular **strong** element. Currently, most browsers recognize only one class name for this attribute.

id

This attribute specifies a unique alphanumeric identifier to be associated with an element. Naming an element is important to being able to access it with a style sheet, a link, or a scripting language. Names should be unique to a document and should be meaningful; although **id="x1"** is perfectly valid, **id="Paragraph1"** might be better. Values for the **id** attribute must begin with a letter (A–Z or a–z) and may be followed by any number of letters, digits, hyphens, colons, and periods. Of course it is generally not encouraged to have **id** values with special characters, even if they are allowed.

One potential problem with the **id** attribute is that for some elements, particularly form controls and images, the **name** attribute already serves its function. Values for **name** should not collide with values for **id**, as they share the same naming space. For example, the following would not be allowed:

```
<b id="elementX">This is a test.</b>
<img name="elementX" src="image.gif" />
```

There is some uncertainty about what to do to ensure backward compatibility with browsers that understand **name** but not **id**. Some experts suggest that the following is illegal:

```
<img name="image1" id="image1" src="image.gif" />
```

Because **name** and **id** are naming the same item, there should be no problem; the common browsers do not have an issue with such markup. Complex scripting could be used if you assign two different names for the image, such as

```
<img name="image1name" id="image1id" src="image.gif" />
```

but it might not be necessary.

Page designers are encouraged to pick a naming strategy and use it consistently. Once elements are named, they should be easy to manipulate with a scripting language.

Like the **class** attribute, the **id** attribute is also used by style sheets for accessing a particular element. For example, an element named **Paragraph1** can be referenced by a style rule in a document-wide style by using a fragment identifier:

```
#Paragraph1   {color: blue;}
```

Once an element is named using **id**, it also is a potential destination for an anchor. In the past, an **a** element was used to set a destination; now any element can be a destination. For example,

```
<a href="#firstbolditem">Go to first bold element.</a>
<b id="firstbolditem">This is important.</b>
```

style

This attribute specifies an inline style associated with an element, which determines the rendering of the affected element. Because the **style** attribute allows style rules to be used directly with the element, it gives up much of the benefit of style sheets that divide the presentation of an HTML document from its structure. An example of this attribute's use is shown here:

```
<strong style="font-family: Arial;
font-size: 18pt;">Important text</strong>
```

title

The **title** attribute supplies advisory text that can be rendered as a Tooltip when the mouse is over the element. (Internet Explorer supports this Tooltip display, but Netscape browsers prior to version 6 do not.) In some cases, like the **a** element, the **title** attribute can provide additional help in bookmarking. Like the title for the document itself, **title** attribute values such as advisory information should be short, yet useful. For example, **<p title="paragraph1">** provides little information of value, whereas **<p title="HTML: The Complete Reference Appendix A Paragraph 10">** provides much more detail. When combined with scripting, this attribute can provide facilities for automatic index generation.

Language Attributes Reference

A main goal of the HTML and XHTML specifications is to provide better support for languages besides English. The use of other languages in a Web page might require that text direction be changed from left to right or right to left. Once supporting non-ASCII languages becomes easier, it might be more common to see documents in mixed languages. Thus, there must be a way to indicate the language in use and its formatting. The basic language attributes are summarized here to avoid redundancy.

lang

The **lang** attribute indicates the language being used for the enclosed content. The language is identified using the ISO standard language abbreviations, such as *fr* for French, *en* for English, and so on. RFC 1766 (http://www.ietf.org/rfc/rfc1766.txt?) describes these codes and their formats.

dir

The **dir** attribute sets the text direction as related to the **lang** attribute. The accepted values under the HTML 4.01 specification are **ltr** (left to right) and **rtl** (right to left). It should be possible to override whatever direction a user agent sets by using this attribute with the **bdo** element:

```
<bdo dir="rtl">Napoleon never really said "Able was I ere I saw Elba."</bdo>
```

Internet Explorer 5.5 and higher supports **dir** for the **bdo** element, but Netscape 6 does not. If used with other block-level elements, such as **p** and **div**, the **dir** attribute might produce right-aligned text, but it will not change the actual direction of the text flow.

Common Internet Explorer Attributes Reference

Microsoft introduced a number of new proprietary attributes with the Internet Explorer 4, 5, 5.5, and 6 browsers. These are summarized here to avoid redundancy.

accesskey

Microsoft applied this W3C attribute to a wider variety of elements with the advent of its IE 5.5 browser. The **accesskey** attribute specifies a keyboard navigation accelerator for the element. Pressing ALT or a similar key (depending on the browser and operating system) in association with the specified key selects the anchor element correlated with that key.

contenteditable

This proprietary Microsoft attribute allows users to edit content rendered in Internet Explorer 5.5 or greater. Values are **false**, **true**, and **inherit**. A value of **false** will prevent content from being edited by users; **true** will allow editing. The default value, **inherit**, applies the value of the affected element's parent element.

disabled

Again, Microsoft has applied an existing W3C attribute to a range of elements not associated with it in the W3C specifications. Elements with the **disabled** attribute set may appear faded and will not respond to user input. Values under the Microsoft implementation are **false** and **true**. The default value is **true**, so IE 5.5 and higher will read **disabled** as "on," even without a value set for the attribute.

hidefocus

This proprietary attribute, introduced with Internet Explorer 5.5, hides focus on an element's content. Focus must be applied to the element using the **tabindex** attribute.

language

In the Microsoft implementation, this attribute specifies the scripting language to be used with an associated script bound to the element, typically through an event handler attribute. Possible values might include **javascript**, **jscript**, **vbs**, and **vbscript**. Other values that include the version of the language used, such as **JavaScript1.1**, might also be possible.

tabindex

This attribute uses a number to identify the object's position in the tabbing order for keyboard navigation using the TAB key. While **tabindex** is defined for some elements as part of W3C standards, IE 5.5 added support for this attribute to a wider range of elements. Under IE 5.5 or better, this focus can be disabled with the **hidefocus** attribute.

unselectable

This proprietary Microsoft element can be used to prevent content displayed in Internet Explorer 5.5 from being selected. Testing suggests that this might not work consistently. Values are **off** (selection permitted) and **on** (selection not allowed).

Event Attributes Reference

In preparation for a more dynamic Web, the W3C has defined a set of core events that are associated with nearly every HTML or XHTML element. Most of these events cover simple user interaction, such as the click of a mouse button or a key being pressed. A few elements, such as form controls, have some special events associated with them. For example, form events might indicate that the field has received focus from the user or that the form was submitted. Intrinsic events, such as a document loading and unloading, are also defined. All the W3C-defined events are described in Table A-1.

This event model is far from complete, and it still is not fully supported by some browsers. The event model should be considered a work in progress. It will certainly change as the Document Object Model (DOM) is extended. More information about the DOM can be found at http://www.w3.org/DOM/. Already browser vendors are busy paving the way with their own events.

Event attribute	Event description
onblur	Occurs when an element loses focus, meaning that the user has moved focus to another element, typically either by clicking the mouse or tabbing.
onchange	Signals that the form control has lost user focus and its value has been modified during its last access.
onclick	Indicates that the element has been clicked.
ondblclick	Indicates that the element has been double-clicked.
onfocus	Indicates that an element has received focus; namely, it has been selected for manipulation or data entry.
onkeydown	Indicates that a key is being pressed down with focus on the element.
onkeypress	Describes the event of a key being pressed and released with focus on the element.
onkeyup	Indicates that a key is being released with focus on the element.
onload	Indicates the event of a window or frame set finishing the loading of a document.
onmousedown	Indicates the press of a mouse button with focus on the element.
onmousemove	Indicates that the mouse has moved while over the element.
onmouseout	Indicates that the mouse has moved away from an element.
onmouseover	Indicates that the mouse has moved over an element.
onmouseup	Indicates the release of a mouse button with focus on the element.

TABLE A-1 W3C-Defined Core Events

Event attribute	Event description
onreset	Indicates that the form is being reset, possibly by the click of a reset button.
onselect	Indicates the selection of text by the user, typically by highlighting the desired text.
onsubmit	Indicates a form submission, generally by clicking a submit button.
onunload	Indicates that the browser is leaving the current document and unloading it from the window or frame.

TABLE A-1 W3C-Defined Core Events *(continued)*

Extended Events

Some browsers support events other than those defined in the HTML and XHTML specifications. Microsoft, in particular, has introduced a variety of events to capture more complex mouse actions such as dragging, element events such as the bouncing of **marquee** text, data-binding events signaling the loading of data into an object, and fine-grain event control to catch events just before or after they happen. The basic meaning of the various extended events is briefly summarized in Table A-2.

CAUTION *With events documentation, errors might exist. The event model changes rapidly, and the browser vendors have not stopped innovating in this area. Events were tested by the author for accuracy, but for the most accurate, up-to-date event model for Internet Explorer, visit http://msdn.microsoft.com/.*

Event attribute	Description
onabort	Triggered by the user aborting the image load with a stop button or similar effect.
onactivate	Fires when the object is set as the active element.
onafterprint	Fires after user prints a document or previews a document for printing.
onafterupdate	Fires after the transfer of data from the element to a data provider, namely a data update.
onbeforeactivate	Fires immediately before the object is set as the active element.
onbeforecopy	Fires just before selected content is copied and placed in the user's system clipboard.
onbeforecut	Fires just before selected content is cut from the document and added to the system clipboard.
onbeforedeactivate	Fires immediately before the active element is changed from one object to another.
onbeforeeditfocus	Fires before an object contained in an editable element is focused for editing.
onbeforepaste	Fires before the selected content is pasted into a document.
onbeforeprint	Fires before the user prints a document or previews a document for printing.
onbeforeunload	Fires just prior to a document being unloaded from a window.
onbeforeupdate	Triggered before the transfer of data from the element to the data provider. Might be triggered explicitly, or by a loss of focus or a page unload forcing a data update.
onbounce	Triggered when the bouncing contents of a marquee touch one side or another.
oncontextmenu	Triggered when the user right-clicks (invokes the context menu) on an element.

TABLE A-2 Microsoft's Extended Event Model

Event attribute	Description
oncontrolselect	Fires when the user makes a control selection of the object.
oncopy	Fires on target when selected content is pasted into a document.
oncut	Fires when selected content is cut from a document and added to the system clipboard.
ondataavailable	Fires when data arrives from data sources that transmit information asynchronously.
ondatasetchanged	Triggered when the initial data is made available from a data source or when the data changes.
ondatasetcomplete	Indicates that all the data is available from the data source.
ondeactivate	Fires when the active element is changed to another object.
ondrag	Fires continuously during a drag operation.
ondragend	Fires when the user releases during a drag operation.
ondragenter	Fires when the user drags an object onto a valid drop target.
ondragleave	Fires when the user drags the object off a valid drop target.
ondragover	Fires continuously when the object is over a valid drop target.
ondragstart	Fires when the user begins to drag a highlighted selection.
ondrop	Fires when the mouse is released during a drag-and-drop operation.
onerror	Fires when the loading of a document, particularly the execution of a script, causes an error. Used to trap runtime errors.
onerrorupdate	Fires if a data transfer has been canceled by the onbeforeupdate event handler.
onfilterchange	Fires when a page filter changes state or finishes.
onfinish	Triggered when a looping marquee finishes.
onfocusin	Fires just before an object receives focus.
onfocusout	Fires when an object is losing focus.
onhelp	Triggered when the user presses the F1 key or similar help button in the user agent.
onlayoutcomplete	Fires when the print or print preview process finishes.
onlosecapture	Fires when the object loses mouse capture.
onmouseenter	Fires when the user moves the mouse pointer into the object.
onmouseleave	Fires when the user moves the mouse pointer away from the object.
onmousewheel	Fires when the mouse scroll wheel is used.
onmove	Triggered when the user moves a window.
onmoveend	Fires when an object stops moving.
onmovestart	Fires when an object starts moving.
onpaste	Fires when selected content is pasted into a document.
onpropertychange	Fires when a property changes on an object.
onreadystatechange	Similar to onload. Fires whenever the ready state for an object has changed.
onresize	Triggered whenever an object is resized.

TABLE A-2 Microsoft's Extended Event Model *(continued)*

Event attribute	Description
onresizeend	Fires when the user finishes changing the dimensions of an object.
onresizestart	Fires when the user begins to change the dimensions of an object.
onrowenter	Indicates that a bound data row has changed and new data values are available.
onrowexit	Fires just prior to a bound data-source control changing the current row.
onrowsdelete	Fires when dataset rows are about to be deleted.
onrowsinserted	Fires when dataset rows are inserted.
onscroll	Fires when a scrolling element is repositioned.
onselectionchange	Fires when the selection state of a document changes.
onselectstart	Fires when the user begins to select information by highlighting.
onstart	Fires when a looped marquee begins or starts over.
onstop	Fires when the user clicks the stop button in the browser.
ontimeerror	Fires whenever a time-specific error occurs, usually as a result of setting a property to an invalid value.

TABLE A-2 Microsoft's Extended Event Model *(continued)*

HTML Element Reference

The element entries that follow generally include the following information:

- **Brief summary** Brief summary of the element's purpose
- **Standard syntax** HTML 4.01 or XHTML 1.0 syntax for the element, including attributes and event handlers defined by the W3C specification
- **Attributes defined by browser** Additional syntax defined by different browsers
- **Standard events** Descriptions of event handler attributes for the element
- **Events defined by browser** Additional event attributes introduced primarily by Internet Explorer
- **Examples** Examples using the element
- **Compatibility** The element's general compatibility with HTML and XHTML specifications and browser versions
- **Notes** Additional information about the element

All attributes not defined in a particular listing are common attributes that can be found at the start of the appendix.

NOTE *Listings of attributes and events defined by browser versions assume that these attributes and events generally remain associated with later versions of that browser. For example, attributes defined by Internet Explorer 4 are valid for Internet Explorer 5 and higher, and attributes defined for Netscape 4 remain valid for Netscape 4.5 and higher, up to Netscape 4.8x. Compatibility pre-Opera 4 is not specified.*

TIP *The support site http://www.htmlref.com has this reference online and may have updates or fixes to this information.*

<!-- ... --> (Comment)

This construct encloses text comments that will not be displayed by the browser. No attributes or events are associated with this construct.

Standard Syntax

```
<!-- ... -->
```

Examples

```
<!-- This is an informational comment that can occur
     anywhere in an HTML document. The next few examples
     show how style sheets and scripts are "commented out" to prevent
     older browsers from misinterpreting the content.
-->

<style type="text/css">
<!--
   h1 {color: red; font-size: 40pt;}
-->
</style>
<script type="text/javascript">
<!--
document.write("hello world");
// -->
</script>
```

Compatibility

HTML 2, 3.2, 4, 4.01	Internet Explorer 2, 3, 4, 5, 5.5, 6
XHTML 1.0, 1.1, Basic	Netscape 1,1.1, 2, 3, 4, 4.5–4.8, 6, 7
	Opera 4–7

Notes

- Comments often are used to exclude content from older browsers, particularly those that do not understand client-side scripting or style sheets. Page developers should be careful when commenting HTML markup. Older browsers may or may not render the enclosed content.

<!DOCTYPE> (Document Type Definition)

This SGML construct specifies the document type definition corresponding to the document. There are no attributes or events associated with this element.

Standard Syntax

```
<!DOCTYPE "DTD IDENTIFIER">
```

Examples

```
<!DOCTYPE HTML PUBLIC "-//W3C//DTD HTML 4.01 TRANSITIONAL//EN">

<!DOCTYPE HTML PUBLIC "-//W3C//DTD XHTML 1.0 TRANSITIONAL//EN">

<!DOCTYPE html PUBLIC "-//W3C//DTD XHTML 1.0 Transitional//EN"
"http://www.w3.org/TR/xhtml1/DTD/xhtml1-transitional.dtd">

<!DOCTYPE html PUBLIC "-//W3C//DTD XHTML 1.1//EN" "xhtml11.dtd">
```

Compatibility

HTML 2, 3.2, 4, 4.01	Internet Explorer 2, 3, 4, 5, 5.5, 6
XHTML 1.0, 1.1, Basic	Netscape 1, 2, 3, 4, 4.5–4.8, 6, and 7
	Opera 4–7

Notes

- The **doctype** statement should be used as the first line of all documents.
- Validation programs might use this construct when determining the correctness of an HTML document.
- Modern browsers may determine what rendering mode to use depending on the **doctype** statement. This is dubbed the *doctype switch*. An incorrect **doctype** that does not correspond to appropriate markup usage may result in inaccurate display.

<a> (Anchor)

This element defines a hyperlink, the named target destination for a hyperlink, or both.

Standard Syntax

```
<a
     accesskey="key"
     charset="character code for language of linked
          resource"
     class="class name(s)"
     coords="comma-separated list of numbers"
     dir="ltr | rtl"
     href="url"
     hreflang="language code"
     id="unique alphanumeric identifier"
     lang="language code"
     name="name of target location"
     rel="comma-separated list of relationship values"
     rev="comma-separated list of relationship values"
     shape="default | circle | poly | rect"
     style="style information"
     tabindex="number"
     target="_blank | frame-name | _parent | _self | _top"
          (transitional only)
     title="advisory text"
     type="content type of linked data">

</a>
```

Attributes Defined by Internet Explorer

```
     contenteditable="false | true | inherit" (5.5)
     datafield="name of column supplying bound data" (4)
     datasrc="ID of data source object supplying data" (4)
     disabled="false | true" (5.5)
     hidefocus="true | false" (5.5)
     language="javascript | jscript | vbs | vbscript" (4)
     methods="http-method" (4)
     unselectable="off | on" (5.5)
     urn="URN string" (4)
```

Standard Events

`onclick, ondblclick, onmousedown, onmouseup, onmouseover, onmousemove, onmouseout, onkeypress, onkeydown, onkeyup`

Events Defined by Internet Explorer

`onactivate, onbeforeactivate, onbeforecopy, onbeforecut, onbeforedeactivate, onbeforeeditfocus, onbeforepaste, onblur, oncontextmenu, oncontrolselect, oncopy, oncut, ondeactivate, ondrag, ondragend, ondragenter, ondragleave, ondragover, ondragstart, ondrop, onfocus, onfocusin, onfocusout, onhelp, onlosecapture, onmouseenter, onmouseleave, onmousewheel, onmove, onmoveend, onmovestart, onpaste, onpropertychange, onreadystatechange, onresize, onresizeend, onresizestart, onselectstart, ontimeerror`

Element-Specific Attributes

accesskey This attribute specifies a keyboard navigation accelerator for the element. Pressing ALT or a similar key (depending on the browser and operating system) in association with the specified key selects the anchor element correlated with that key.

charset This attribute defines the character encoding of the linked resource. The value is a space- and/or comma-delimited list of character sets as defined in RFC 2045. The default value is **ISO-8859-1**.

coords For use with object shapes, this attribute uses a comma-separated list of numbers to define the coordinates of the object on the page.

datafld This attribute specifies the column name from the data source object that supplies the bound data. This attribute is specific to Microsoft's data binding.

datasrc This attribute indicates the **id** of the data source object that supplies the data that is bound to this element. This attribute is specific to Microsoft's data binding.

href This is the single required attribute for anchors defining a hypertext source link. It indicates the link target—either a URL or a URL fragment, which is a name preceded by a hash mark (#) specifying an internal target location within the current document. URLs are not restricted to Web-based (http) documents. URLs might use any protocol supported by the browser. For example, file, ftp, and mailto work in most user agents.

hreflang This attribute is used to indicate the language of the linked resource.

methods The value of this attribute provides information about the functions that might be performed on an object. The values generally are given by the HTTP protocol when it is used, but as for the **title** attribute, it might be useful to include advisory information in advance in the link. For example, the browser might choose a different rendering of a link as a function of the methods specified; something that is searchable might get a different icon, or an outside link might render with an indication of leaving the current site. This element is not well understood nor supported, even by the defining browser, Internet Explorer.

name This attribute is required in an anchor defining a target location within a page. A value for **name** is similar to a value for the **id** core attribute, and it should be an alphanumeric identifier unique to the document. Under the HTML and XHTML specifications, **id** and **name** both can be used with an **<a>** tag as long as they have identical values.

rel For anchors containing the **href** attribute, this attribute specifies the relationship of the target object to the link object. The value is a comma-separated list of relationship values. The values and their semantics will be registered by some authority that might have meaning to the document author. The default relationship, if no other is given, is **void**. The **rel** attribute should be used only when the **href** attribute is present.

rev This attribute specifies a reverse link, the inverse relationship of the **rel** attribute. It is useful for indicating where an object came from, such as the author of a document.

shape This attribute is used to define a selectable region for hypertext source links associated with a figure in order to create an image map. The values for the attribute are **circle**, **default**, **polygon**, and **rect**. The format of the **coords** attribute depends on the value of **shape**. For **circle**, the value is *x,y,r*, where *x* and *y* are the pixel coordinates for the center of the circle and *r* is the radius value in pixels. For **rect**, the **coords** attribute should be *x,y,w,h*. The *x,y* values define the upper-left corner of the rectangle, while *w* and *h* define the width and height, respectively. A value of **polygon** for **shape** requires *x1,y1,x2,y2,...* values for **coords**. Each of the *x,y* pairs define a point in the polygon, with successive points being joined by straight lines and the last point joined to the first. The value of **default** for **shape** requires that the entire enclosed area, typically an image, be used.

NOTE *It is advisable to use the **usemap** attribute for the **img** element and the associated **map** element to define hotspots instead of the **shape** attribute.*

tabindex This attribute uses a number to identify the object's position in the tabbing order for keyboard navigation using the TAB key.

target This attribute specifies the target window for a hypertext source link that references frames. The information linked to **target** will be displayed in the named window. Frames and inline frames must be named to be targeted.

There are, however, special name values. These include **_blank**, which indicates a new window; **_parent**, which indicates the parent frame set containing the source link; **_self**, which indicates the frame containing the source link; and **_top**, which indicates the full browser window.

type This attribute specifies the media type in the form of a MIME type for the link target. Generally, this is provided strictly as advisory information; however, in the future a browser might add a small icon for multimedia types. For example, a browser might add a small speaker icon when **type** is set to audio/wav. For a complete list of recognized MIME types, see http://www.w3.org/TR/html4/references.html#ref-MIMETYPES.

urn This supposedly Microsoft-supported attribute relates a uniform resource name (URN) with the link. While it is based on standards work years back, the meaning of URNs is still not well defined, so this attribute is meaningless.

Examples

```
<!-- anchor linking to external file -->
<a href="http://www.democompany.com/">External Link</a>

<!-- anchor linking to file on local file system -->
<a href="file:/c:\html\index.html">local file link</a>

<!-- anchor invoking anonymous FTP -->
<a href="ftp://ftp.democompany.com/freestuff">Anonymous FTP
link</a>

<!-- anchor invoking FTP with password -->
```

```
<a href="ftp://joeuser:secretpassword@democompany.com/path/file">
FTP with password</a>

<!-- anchor invoking mail -->
<a href="mailto:fakeid@democompany.com">Send mail</a>

<!-- anchor used to define target destination within document -->
<a name="jump">Jump target</a>
<!-- anchor linking internally to previous target anchor -->
<a href="#jump">Local jump within document</a>
<!-- anchor linking externally to previous target anchor -->
<a href="http://www.democompany.com/document#jump">
Remote jump within document</a>
```

Compatibility

HTML 2, 3.2, 4, 4.01	Internet Explorer 2, 3, 4, 5, 5.5, 6
XHTML 1.0, 1.1, Basic	Netscape 1, 2, 3, 4, 4.5–4.8, 6, 7
	Opera 4–7

Notes

- The following are reserved browser key bindings for the two major browsers and should not be used as values for **accesskey**: **a**, **c**, **e**, **f**, **g**, **h**, **v**, left arrow, and right arrow.
- HTML 3.2 defines only **name**, **href**, **rel**, **rev**, and **title**.
- The **target** attribute is not defined in browsers that do not support frames, such as Netscape 1 generation browsers. Furthermore, **target** is not allowed under strict variants of XHTML but is limited to frameset or transitional forms.

<abbr> (Abbreviation)

This element allows authors to clearly indicate a sequence of characters that define an abbreviation for a word (such as Mr. instead of Mister, Calif instead of California).

Standard Syntax

```
<abbr
     class="class name(s)"
     dir="ltr | rtl"
     id="unique alphanumeric identifier"
     lang="language code"
     style="style information"
     title="advisory text">

</abbr>
```

Standard Events

```
onclick, ondblclick, onmousedown, onmouseup, onmouseover, onmousemove, onmouseout,
onkeypress, onkeydown, onkeyup
```

Examples

```
<abbr title="California abbreviated">Calif
</abbr>

Isn't <abbr>WWW</abbr> an acronym? Are you sure?
```

Compatibility

HTML 4, 4.01	Netscape 6, 7
XHTML 1.0, 1.1, Basic	Opera 6, 7

Notes

- This tag is commonly confused with **<acronym>**. Debate about just what constitutes an acronym as compared with an abbreviation is common amongst very detail-oriented Web standards experts. In reality, Web developers appear to use the **<acronym>** tag more often than the **<abbr>** tag.
- With the **title** attribute set on this element, Opera and Mozilla may render a dotted underline useful to suggest the Tooltip that might contain a definition for the word.
- Because there is typically no markup-oriented presentation for this element, it is primarily used in conjunction with style sheets and scripts.

<acronym> (Acronym)

This element allows authors to clearly indicate a sequence of characters that compose an acronym (XML, WWW, and so on).

Standard Syntax

```
<acronym
     class="class name(s)"
     dir="ltr | rtl"
     id="unique alphanumeric identifier"
     lang="language code"
     style="style information"
     title="advisory text">

</acronym>
```

Attributes Defined by Internet Explorer

```
     accesskey="key" (5.5)
     contenteditable="false | true | inherit" (5.5)
     disabled="false | true" (5.5)
     hidefocus="true | false" (5.5)
     language="javascript | jscript | vbs | vbscript" (4)
     tabindex="number" (5.5)
     unselectable="off | on" (5.5)
```

Standard Events

```
onclick, ondblclick, onmousedown, onmouseup, onmouseover, onmousemove, onmouseout,
onkeypress, onkeydown, onkeyup
```

Events Defined by Internet Explorer

```
onactivate, onbeforedeactivate, onbeforeeditfocus, onblur, oncontrolselect,
ondeactivate, ondrag, ondragend, ondragenter, ondragleave, ondragover, ondragstart,
ondrop, onfocus, onmouseenter, onmouseleave, onmove, onmoveend, onmovestart,
onreadystatechange, onresizeend, onresizestart, onselectstart, ontimeerror
```

Examples

```
<acronym title="Extensible Markup Language">XML</acronym>
<acronym lang="fr" title="Soci&eacute;t&eacute; Nationale de Chemins de
Fer">SNCF</acronym>
```

Compatibility

HTML 4, 4.01	Internet Explorer 4, 5, 5.5, 6
XHTML 1.0, 1.1, Basic	Netscape 6, 7
	Opera 6, 7

Notes

- **<acronym>** is a new element that is not defined under HTML 2 or 3.2.
- This tag is often confused with **<abbr>**.
- With the **title** attribute set on this element, Opera and Mozilla may render a dotted underline to suggest the Tooltip that might contain a definition for the word.

<address> (Address)

This element marks up text indicating authorship or ownership of information. It generally occurs at the beginning or end of a document.

Standard Syntax

```
<address
     class="class name(s)"
     dir="ltr | rtl"
     id="unique alphanumeric identifier"
     lang="language code"
     style="style information"
     title="advisory text">

</address>
```

Attributes Defined by Internet Explorer

```
     accesskey="key" (5.5)
     contenteditable="inherit | false | true" (5.5)
     disabled="false | true" (5.5)
     hidefocus="true | false" (5.5)
     language="javascript | jscript | vbs | sbscript" (4)
     tabindex="number" (5.5)
     unselectable="off | on" (5.5)
```

Standard Events

```
onclick, ondblclick, onmousedown, onmouseup, onmouseover, onmousemove, onmouseout,
onkeypress, onkeydown, onkeyup
```

Events Defined by Internet Explorer

```
onactivate, onbeforeactivate, onbeforecopy, onbeforecut, onbeforedeactivate,
onbeforeeditfocus, onbeforepaste, onblur, oncontextmenu, oncontrolselect, oncopy, oncut,
ondeactivate, ondrag, ondragend, ondragenter, ondragleave, ondragover, ondragstart,
ondrop, onfocus, onfocusin, onfocusout, onhelp, onlosecapture, onmouseenter,
onmouseleave, onmousewheel, onmove, onmoveend, onmovestart, onpaste, onpropertychange,
onreadystatechange, onresize, onresizeend, onresizestart, onselectstart, ontimeerror
```

Example

```
<address>Big Company, Inc.<br />
2105 Demo Street<br />
San Diego, CA 92109 U.S.A.</address>
```

Compatibility

HTML 2, 3.2, 4, 4.01	Internet Explorer 2, 3, 4, 5, 5.5, 6
XHTML 1.0, 1.1, Basic	Netscape 1, 2, 3, 4, 4.5–4.8, 6, and 7
	Opera 4

Notes

- Under HTML 2.0 and 3.2, there are no attributes for **<address>**.

<applet> (Java Applet)

This element identifies the inclusion of a Java applet. The strict HTML 4.01 definition does not include this element; it has been deprecated in favor of **<object>**.

Standard Syntax (HTML 4.01 Transitional Only)

```
<applet
     align="bottom | left | middle | right | top"
     alt="alternative text"
     archive="URL of archive file"
     class="class name(s)"
     code="URL of Java class file"
     codebase="URL for base referencing"
     height="pixels"
     hspace="pixels"
     id="unique alphanumeric identifier"
     name="unique name for scripting reference"
     object="filename"
     style="style information"
     title="advisory text"
     vspace="pixels"
     width="pixels">

</applet>
```

Attributes Defined by Internet Explorer

```
     accesskey="key" (5.5)
     datafld="name of column supplying bound data" (4)
     datasrc="ID of data source object supplying data" (4)
     hidefocus="true | false" (5.5)
     src="URL" (4)
     tabindex="number" (5.5)
     unselectable="off | on" (5.5)
```

Attributes Defined by Netscape

```
     mayscript (4)
```

Events Defined by Internet Explorer

```
onactivate, onbeforeactivate, onbeforecut, onbeforedeactivate, onbeforeeditfocus,
onbeforepaste, onblur, oncontextmenu, oncontrolselect, oncut, ondataavailable,
ondatasetchanged, ondatasetcomplete, ondeactivate, onfocus, onfocusin, onfocusout,
onhelp, onkeypress, onload, onlosecapture, onmouseenter, onmouseleave, onmousewheel,
onmove, onmoveend, onmovestart, onpaste, onpropertychange, onreadystatechange,
onresize, onresizeend, onresizestart, onrowenter, onrowexit, onrowsdelete,
onrowsinserted, onscroll
```

Element-Specific Attributes

align This attribute is used to position the applet on the page relative to content that might flow around it. The transitional specifications define values of **bottom**, **left**, **middle**, **right**, and **top**, whereas Microsoft and Netscape also might support **absbottom**, **absmiddle**, **baseline**, **center**, and **texttop**.

alt This attribute causes a descriptive text alternative to be displayed in browsers that do not support Java. Page designers should also remember that content enclosed within an **<applet>** tag may also be rendered as alternative text.

archive This attribute refers to an archived or compressed version of the applet and its associated class files, which might help reduce download time.

code This attribute specifies the URL of the applet's class file to be loaded and executed. Applet filenames are identified by a .class filename extension. The URL specified by **code** might be relative to the **codebase** attribute.

codebase This attribute gives the absolute or relative URL of the directory where applets' .class files referenced by the **code** attribute are stored.

datafld This attribute, supported by Internet Explorer 4 and higher, specifies the column name from the data source object that supplies the bound data. This attribute might be used to specify the various **<param>** tags passed to the Java applet.

datasrc Like **datafld**, this attribute is used for data binding under Internet Explorer 4. It indicates the **id** of the data source object that supplies the data that is bound to the **<param>** tags associated with the applet.

height This attribute specifies the height, in pixels, that the applet needs.

hspace This attribute specifies additional horizontal space, in pixels, to be reserved on either side of the applet.

mayscript In the Netscape implementation, this attribute allows access to an applet by programs in a scripting language embedded in the document.

name This attribute assigns a name to the applet so that it can be identified by other resources, particularly scripts.

object This attribute specifies the URL of a serialized representation of an applet.

src As defined for Internet Explorer 4 and higher, this attribute specifies a URL for an associated file for the applet. The meaning and use is unclear and not part of the HTML standard.

vspace This attribute specifies additional vertical space, in pixels, to be reserved above and below the applet.

width This attribute specifies the width, in pixels, that the applet needs.

Example

```
<applet code="game.class" align="left" archive="game.zip"
        height="250" width="350">
   <param name="difficulty" value="easy">
     <b>Sorry, you need Java to play this game.</b>
</applet>
```

Compatibility

HTML 2, 3.2, 4, 4.01 (transitional)	Internet Explorer 4, 5, 5.5, 6
XHTML 1.0 (transitional)	Netscape 2, 3, 4, 4.5–4.8, 6, 7

Notes

- The W3C specification does not encourage the use of **<applet>** and prefers the use of the **<object>** tag. Under the strict definition of HTML 4.01, this element is deprecated.

<area> (Image Map Area)

Defines a hot-spot region on an image, and associates it with a hypertext link. This element is used only within a **<map>** tag.

Standard Syntax

```
<area
     accesskey="character"
     alt="alternative text"
     class="class name(s)"
     coords="comma separated list of values"
     dir="ltr | rtl"
     href="url"
     id="unique alphanumeric identifier"
     lang="language code"
     nohref="nohref"
     shape="circle | default | poly | rect"
     style="style information"
     tabindex="number"
     target="_blank | frame-name | _parent | _self |
             _top" (transitional or frameset only)
     title="advisory text" />
```

Attributes Defined by Internet Explorer

```
     language="javascript | jscript | vbs | vbscript" (4)
     hidefocus="true | false" (5.5)
     unselectable="off | on" (5.5)
```

Standard Events

```
onclick, ondblclick, onmousedown, onmouseup, onmouseover, onmousemove, onmouseout,
onkeypress, onkeydown, onkeyup
```

Events Defined by Internet Explorer

```
onactivate, onbeforeactivate, onbeforecopy, onbeforecut, onbeforedeactivate,
onbeforeeditfocus, onbeforepaste, onblur, oncontextmenu, oncontrolselect, oncopy, oncut,
ondeactivate, ondrag, ondragend, ondragenter, ondragleave, ondragover, ondragstart,
ondrop, onfocus, onfocusin, onfocusout, onhelp, onlosecapture, onmouseenter,
onmouseleave, onmousewheel, onmove, onmoveend, onmovestart, onpaste, onpropertychange,
onreadystatechange, onresizeend, onresizestart, onselectstart, ontimeerror
```

Element-Specific Attributes

accesskey This attribute specifies a keyboard navigation accelerator for the element. Pressing ALT or a similar key in association with the specified character selects the form control correlated with that key sequence. Page designers are forewarned to avoid key sequences already bound to browsers.

alt This attribute contains a text string alternative to display on browsers that cannot display images.

coords This attribute contains a set of values specifying the coordinates of the hot-spot region. The number and meaning of the values depend upon the value specified for the **shape** attribute. For a **rect** or **rectangle** shape, the **coords** value is two *x,y* pairs: **left**, **top**, **right**, and **bottom**. For a **circ** or **circle** shape, the **coords** value is *x,y,r* where *x,y* is a pair specifying the center of the circle and *r* is a value for the radius. For a **poly** or **polygon** shape, the **coords** value is a set of *x,y* pairs for each point in the polygon: *x1,y1,x2,y2,x3,y3,* and so on.

href This attribute specifies the hyperlink target for the area. Its value is a valid URL. Either this attribute or the **nohref** attribute must be present in the element.

name This attribute is used to define a name for the clickable area so that it can be scripted by older browsers.

nohref This attribute indicates that no hyperlink exists for the associated area. Either this attribute or the **href** attribute must be present in the element.

shape This attribute defines the shape of the associated hot spot. HTML 4 defines the values **rect**, which defines a rectangular region; **circle**, which defines a circular region; **poly**, which defines a polygon; and **default**, which indicates the entire region beyond any defined shapes. Many browsers, notably Internet Explorer 4 and higher, support **circ**, **polygon**, and **rectangle** as valid values for **shape**.

tabindex This attribute uses a numeric value to specify the position of the defined area in the browser tabbing order.

target This attribute specifies the target window for hyperlink referencing frames. The value is a frame name or one of several special names. A value of **_blank** indicates a new window. A value of **_parent** indicates the parent frame set containing the source link. A value of **_self** indicates the frame containing the source link. A value of **_top** indicates the full browser window.

Example

```
<map name="primary">
  <area shape="circle" coords="200,250,25" href="another.html" />
  <area shape="default" nohref="nohref" />
</map>
```

Compatibility

HTML 2, 3.2, 4, 4.01	Internet Explorer 2, 3, 4, 5, 5.5, 6
XHTML 1.0, 1.1	Netscape 1, 2, 3, 4, 4.5–4.8, 6, and 7
	Opera 4–7

Notes

- Under the HTML 3.2 and 4.0 specifications, the closing tag **</area>** is forbidden.
- The XHTML 1.0 specification requires a trailing slash: **<area />**.
- The **id**, **class**, and **style** attributes have the same meaning as the core attributes defined in the HTML 4 specification, but only Netscape and Microsoft define them.
- Netscape 1–level browsers do not understand the **target** attribute as it relates to frames.
- HTML 3.2 defines only **alt**, **coords**, **href**, **nohref**, and **shape**.

<b> (Bold)

This element indicates that the enclosed text should be displayed in boldface.

Standard Syntax

```
<b>
     class="class name(s)"
     dir="ltr | rtl"
     id="unique alphanumeric identifier"
     lang="language code"
     style="style information"
     title="advisory text">

</b>
```

Attributes Defined by Internet Explorer

```
     accesskey="key" (5.5)
     contenteditable="false | true | inherit" (5.5)
     disabled="false | true" (5.5)
     hidefocus="true | false" (5.5)
     language="javascript | jscript | vbs | vbscript" (4)
     tabindex="number" (5.5)
     unselectable="off | on" (5.5)
```

Standard Events

```
onclick, ondblclick, onmousedown, onmouseup, onmouseover, onmousemove, onmouseout,
onkeypress, onkeydown, onkeyup
```

Events Defined by Internet Explorer

```
onactivate, onbeforeactivate, onbeforecopy, onbeforecut, onbeforedeactivate,
onbeforeeditfocus, onbeforepaste, onblur, oncontextmenu, oncontrolselect, oncopy,
oncut, ondeactivate, ondrag, ondragend, ondragenter, ondragleave, ondragover,
ondragstart, ondrop, onfocus, onfocusin, onfocusout, onhelp, onlosecapture,
onmouseenter, onmouseleave, onmousewheel, onmove, onmoveend, onmovestart, onpaste,
onpropertychange, onreadystatechange, onresizeend, onresizestart, onselectstart,
ontimeerror
```

Example

```
This text is <b>bold</b> for emphasis.
```

Compatibility

HTML 2, 3.2, 4, 4.01 XHTML 1.0, 1.1	Internet Explorer 2, 3, 4, 5, 5.5, 6 Netscape 1, 2, 3, 4, 4.5–4.8, 6, 7 Opera 4–7

Notes

- HTML 2 and 3.2 do not define any attributes for this element.

<base> (Base URL)

This element specifies the base URL to be used for all relative URLs contained within a document.

Standard Syntax

```
<base
     href="url"
     id="unique alphanumeric identifier"
     target="_blank | frame-name | _parent | _self | top" (transitional only)
/>
```

Events Defined by Internet Explorer

```
onlayoutcomplete, onmouseenter, onmouseleave, onreadystatechange
```

Element-Specific Attributes

href This attribute specifies the base URL to be used throughout the document for relative URL addresses.

target For documents containing frames, this attribute specifies the default target window for every link that does not have an explicit target reference. Aside from named frames, several special values exist. A value of **_blank** indicates a new window. A value of **_parent** indicates the parent frame set containing the source link. A value of **_self** indicates the frame containing the source link. A value of **_top** indicates the full browser window.

Examples

```
<base href="http://www.democompany.com/" />
<base target="_blank" href="http://www.democompany.com/" />
```

Compatibility

HTML 2, 3.2, 4, 4.01	Internet Explorer 2, 3, 4, 5, 5.5, 6
XHTML 1.0, 1.1, Basic	Netscape 1, 2, 3, 4, 4.5–4.8, 6, 7
	Opera 4–7

Notes

- This element should only occur within the **head** element.
- HTML 2.0 and 3.2 define only the **href** attribute.
- XHTML 1.0 requires a trailing slash: **<base />**.

<basefont> (Base Font)

This element establishes a default font size for a document. Font size then can be varied relative to the base font size using the **font** element.

Standard Syntax (Transitional Only)

```
<basefont
     color="color name | #RRGGBB"
     face="font name(s)"
     id="unique alphanumeric identifier"
     size="1-7 | +/-int" />
```

Events Defined by Internet Explorer

```
onlayoutcomplete, onmouseenter, onmouseleave, onreadystatechange
```

Element-Specific Attributes

color This attribute sets the text color using either a named color or a color specified in the hexadecimal *#RRGGBB* format.

face This attribute contains a list of one or more font names. The document text in the default style is rendered in the first font face that the client's browser supports. If no font listed is installed on the local system, the browser typically defaults to the proportional or fixed-width font for that system.

size This attribute specifies the font size as either a numeric or relative value. Numeric values range from **1** to **7** with **1** being the smallest and **3** the default.

Example

```
<basefont color="#ff0000" face="Helvetica" size="+2" />
```

Compatibility

HTML 2, 3.2, 4, 4.01 (transitional)	Internet Explorer 2, 3, 4, 5, 5.5, 6
XHTML 1.0 (transitional)	Netscape 1, 2, 3, 4, 4.5–4.8

Notes

- HTML 3.2 supports the **basefont** element but only with the **size** attribute.
- The strict HTML and XHTML specifications do not support this element.
- Despite being part of transitional standards, some standards-focused browsers like Mozilla and Opera do not support this element.
- This element can be imitated with a CSS rule on the body element.
- XHTML 1.0 requires a trailing slash for this element: **<basefont />**.

<bdo> (Bidirectional Override)

This element is used to override the current directionality of text.

Standard Syntax

```
<bdo
     class="class name(s)"
     dir="ltr | rtl"
     id="unique alphanumeric identifier"
     lang="language code"
     style="style information"
     title="advisory text">

</bdo>
```

Attributes Defined by Internet Explorer

```
accesskey="key" (5.5)
contenteditable="inherit | false | true" (5.5)
disabled="false | true" (5.5)
hidefocus="true | false" (5.5)
language="javascript | jscript | vbs | vbscript | xml" (5.0)
tabindex="number" (5.5)
unselectable="off | on" (5.5)
```

Standard Events

```
onclick, ondblclick, onmousedown, onmouseup, onmouseover, onmousemove, onmouseout,
onkeypress, onkeydown, onkeyup
```

Events Defined by Internet Explorer

```
onactivate, onafterupdate, onbeforeactivate, onbeforecopy, onbeforecut,
onbeforedeactivate, onbeforeeditfocus, onbeforepaste, onbeforeupdate, onblur,
oncellchange, oncontextmenu, oncontrolselect, oncopy, oncut, ondeactivate, ondrag,
ondragend, ondragenter, ondragleave, ondragover, ondragstart, ondrop, onerrorupdate,
onfilterchange, onfocus, onfocusin, onfocusout, onhelp, onlosecapture, onmouseenter,
onmouseleave, onmousewheel, onmove, onmoveend, onmovestart, onpaste, onpropertychange,
onreadystatechange, onresizeend, onresizestart, onscroll, onselectstart
```

Example

```
<!-- Switch text direction -->
<bdo dir="rtl">This text will go right to left if you can
find a browser that supports this element.
</bdo>
```

Compatibility

HTML 4, 4.01	Internet Explorer 5, 5.5, 6
XHTML 1.0, 1.1	Netscape 6, 7
	Opera 7

Notes

- The HTML 4 specification did not specify events for this element; they were added in XHTML. This is most likely an oversight.

<bgsound> (Background Sound)

This Internet Explorer element associates a background sound with a page.

Standard Syntax (Defined by Internet Explorer 4)

```
<bgsound
     balance="number"
     id="unique alphanumeric identifier"
     loop="number"
     src="url of sound file"
     volume="number">
```

Events Defined by Internet Explorer

```
onlayoutcomplete, onmouseenter, onmouseleave, onreadystatechange
```

Element-Specific Attributes

balance This attribute defines a number between –10,000 and +10,000 that determines how the volume will be divided between the speakers.

loop This attribute indicates the number of times a sound is to be played and either has a positive numeric value or **-1** to specify that it will continuously loop. The keyword **infinite** is also supported in many Internet Explorer implementations.

src This attribute specifies the URL of the sound file to be played, which must be one of the following types: .wav, .au, or .mid.

volume This attribute defines a number between –10,000 and 0 that determines the loudness of a page's background sound.

Examples

```
<bgsound src="sound1.mid">
<bgsound src="sound2.au" loop="infinite">
```

Compatibility

No standards	Internet Explorer 2, 3, 4, 5, 5.5, 6

Notes

- Similar functionality can be achieved in some versions of Netscape using the **<embed>** tag to invoke an audio player.
- You can write **bgsound** with a self-closing tag **<bgsound />**. However, since this element is not part of a standard, making it XHTML-like will not make it validate.

<big> (Big Font)

Indicates that the enclosed text should be displayed in a larger font relative to the current font.

Standard Syntax

```
<big
     class="class name(s)"
     dir="ltr | rtl"
     id="unique alphanumeric identifier"
     lang="language code"
     style="style information"
     title="advisory text">

</big>
```

Attributes Defined by Internet Explorer

```
     language="javascript | jscript | vbs | vbscript" (4)
     accesskey="key" (5.5)
     contenteditable="false | true | inherit" (5.5)
     disabled="false | true" (5.5)
     hidefocus="true | false" (5.5)
     tabindex="number" (5.5)
     unselectable="off | on" (5.5)
```

Standard Events

```
onclick, ondblclick, onmousedown, onmouseup, onmouseover, onmousemove, onmouseout,
onkeypress, onkeydown, onkeyup
```

Events Defined by Internet Explorer

```
onactivate, onbeforeactivate, onbeforecopy, onbeforecut, onbeforedeactivate,
onbeforeeditfocus, onbeforepaste, onblur, oncontextmenu, oncontrolselect, oncopy, oncut,
ondeactivate, ondrag, ondragend, ondragenter, ondragleave, ondragover, ondragstart,
ondrop, onfocus, onfocusin, onfocusout, onhelp, onlosecapture, onmouseenter,
```

```
onmouseleave, onmousewheel, onmove, onmoveend, onmovestart, onpaste, onpropertychange,
onreadystatechange, onresizeend, onresizestart, onselectstart, ontimeerror
```

Example

```
This text is regular size. <big>This text is larger.</big>
```

Compatibility

HTML 2, 3.2, 4, 4.01 XHTML 1.0, 1.1, Basic	Internet Explorer 2, 3, 4, 5, 5.5, 6 Netscape 1, 2, 3, 4, 4.5–4.8, 6, 7 Opera 4–7

Notes

- HTML 3.2 does not support any attributes for this element.

<blink> (Blinking Text)

This Netscape-specific element causes the enclosed text to flash slowly.

Syntax (Defined by Netscape)

```
<blink
     class="class name(s)"
     id="unique alphanumeric identifier"
     lang="language code"
     style="style information">

</blink>
```

Example

```
<blink>Annoying, isn't it?</blink>
```

Compatibility

No Standards	Netscape 1, 2, 3, 4–4.7, 6, 7

Notes

- The attributes **class**, **id**, and **style** were added during the Netscape 4 release; **lang** was added from Netscape 6.

<blockquote> (Block Quote)

This block element indicates that the enclosed text is an extended quotation. Usually, this is rendered visually by indentation.

Standard Syntax

```
<blockquote
     cite="url of source information"
     class="class name(s)"
     dir="ltr | rtl"
     id="unique alphanumeric identifier"
     lang="language code"
     style="style information"
     title="advisory text">
```

```
</blockquote>
```

Attributes Defined by Internet Explorer

```
accesskey="key" (5.5)
contenteditable="false | true | inherit" (5.5)
disabled="false | true" (5.5)
hidefocus="true | false" (5.5)
language="javascript | jscript | vbs | vbscript" (4)
tabindex="number" (5.5)
unselectable="off | on" (5.5)
```

Standard Events

```
onclick, ondblclick, onmousedown, onmouseup, onmouseover, onmousemove, onmouseout,
onkeypress, onkeydown, onkeyup
```

Events Defined by Internet Explorer

```
onactivate, onbeforeactivate, onbeforecopy, onbeforecut, onbeforedeactivate,
onbeforeeditfocus, onbeforepaste, onblur, oncontextmenu, oncontrolselect, oncopy, oncut,
ondeactivate, ondrag, ondragend, ondragenter, ondragleave, ondragover, ondragstart,
ondrop, onfocus, onfocusin, onfocusout, onhelp, onlosecapture, onmouseenter,
onmouseleave, onmousewheel, onmove, onmoveend, onmovestart, onpaste, onpropertychange,
onreadystatechange, onresizeend, onresizestart, onselectstart, ontimeerror
```

Element-Specific Attributes

cite The value of this attribute should be a URL for the document in which the information cited can be found.

Example

```
The following paragraph is taken from our March report:
<blockquote cite="marchreport.html"> ... text ...
</blockquote>
```

Compatibility

HTML 2, 3.2, 4, 4.01	Internet Explorer 2, 3, 4, 5, 5.5, 6
XHTML 1.0, 1.1, Basic	Netscape 1, 2, 3, 4, 4.5–4.8, 6, 7
	Opera 4–7

Notes

- HTML 2.0 and 3.2 do not support any attributes for this element.
- Some browsers understand the **<bq>** shorthand notation.

<body> (Document Body)

This element encloses a document's displayable content.

Standard Syntax

```
<body
     alink="color name | #RRGGBB" (transitional only)
     background="url of background image" (transitional only)
     bgcolor="color name | #RRGGBB" (transitional only)
     class="class name(s)"
```

```
     dir="ltr | rtl"
     id="unique alphanumeric identifier"
     lang="language code"
     link="color name | #RRGGBB" (transitional only)
     style="style information"
     text="color name | #RRGGBB" (transitional only)
     title="advisory text"
     vlink="color name | #RRGGBB"> (vlink attribute transitional only)

</body>
```

Attributes Defined by Internet Explorer

```
accesskey="key" (5.5)
bgproperties="fixed" (4)
bottommargin="pixels" (4)
contenteditable="false | true | inherit" (5.5)
disabled="false | true" (5.5)
hidefocus="true | false" (5.5)
language="javascript | jscript | vbs | vbscript" (4)
leftmargin="pixels" (4)
nowrap="false | true" (4)
rightmargin="pixels" (4)
scroll="no | yes" (4)
tabindex="number" (5.5)
topmargin="pixels" (4)
unselectable="off | on" (5.5)
```

Attributes Defined by Netscape

```
marginheight="pixels" (4)
marginwidth="pixels" (4)
```

Standard Events

```
onclick, ondblclick, onload, onmousedown, onmouseup, onmouseover, onmousemove,
onmouseout, onkeypress, onkeydown, onkeyup, onunload
```

Events Defined by Internet Explorer

```
onactivate, onafterprint, onbeforeactivate, onbeforecut, onbeforedeactivate,
onbeforeeditfocus, onbeforepaste, onbeforeprint, onbeforeunload, oncontextmenu,
oncontrolselect, oncut, ondeactivate, ondrag, ondragend, ondragenter, ondragleave,
ondragover, ondragstart, ondrop, onfilterchange, onfocusin, onfocusout, onlosecapture,
onmouseenter, onmouseleave, onmousewheel, onmove, onmoveend, onmovestart, onpaste,
onpropertychange, onreadystatechange, onresizeend, onresizestart, onscroll, onselect,
onselectstart
```

Element-Specific Attributes

alink This attribute sets the color for active links within the document. Active links represent the state of a link as it is being clicked. The value of the attribute can be either a browser-dependent named color or a color specified in the hexadecimal *#RRGGBB* format.

background This attribute contains a URL for an image file, which will be tiled to provide the document background.

bgcolor This attribute sets the background color for the document. Its value can be either a browser-dependent named color or a color specified using the hexadecimal *#RRGGBB* format.

bgproperties This attribute, first introduced in Internet Explorer 2, has one value, **fixed**, which causes the background image to act as a fixed watermark and not to scroll.

bottommargin This attribute specifies the bottom margin for the entire body of the page and overrides the default margin. When set to **0** or "", the bottom margin is the bottom edge of the window or frame the content is displayed in.

leftmargin This Internet Explorer–specific attribute sets the left margin for the page in pixels, overriding the default margin. When set to **0** or "", the left margin is the left edge of the window or the frame.

link This attribute sets the color for hyperlinks within the document that have not yet been visited. Its value can be either a browser-dependent named color or a color specified using the hexadecimal *#RRGGBB* format.

marginheight This Netscape-specific attribute sets the top margin for the document in pixels. If set to **0** or "", the top margin will be exactly on the top edge of the window or frame. It is equivalent to combining the Internet Explorer attributes **bottommargin** and **topmargin**.

marginwidth This Netscape-specific attribute sets the left and right margins for the page in pixels, overriding the default margin. When set to **0** or "", the left margin is the left edge of the window or the frame. It is equivalent to combining the Internet Explorer attributes **leftmargin** and **rightmargin**.

nowrap This Internet Explorer–specific attribute is used to control the wrapping of text body width. If set to **yes**, text should not wrap. The default is **no**. CSS rules should be used instead of this attribute.

rightmargin This attribute, specific to Internet Explorer, sets the right margin for the page in pixels, overriding the default margin. When set to **0** or "", the right margin is the right edge of the window or the frame.

scroll This Internet Explorer attribute turns the scroll bars on or off. The default value is **yes**.

text This attribute sets the text color for the document. Its value can be either a browser-dependent named color or a color specified using the hexadecimal *#RRGGBB* format.

topmargin This Internet Explorer–specific attribute sets the top margin for the document in pixels. If set to **0** or "", the top margin will be exactly on the top edge of the window or frame.

Example

```
<body background="checkered.gif"
      bgcolor="white"
      alink="red"
      link="blue"
      vlink="red"
      text="black"> ... </body>

<body onload="myLoadFunction()"> ... </body>
```

Compatibility

HTML 2, 3.2, 4, 4.01	Internet Explorer 2, 3, 4, 5, 5.5, 6
XHTML 1.0, 1.1, Basic	Netscape 1, 2, 3, 4, 4.5–4.8, 6, 7
	Opera 4–7

Notes

- When defining text colors, it is important to be careful to specify both foreground and background explicitly so that they are not masked out by browser defaults set by the user.
- Under the strict HTML and XHTML definitions, CSS should be used in place of presentation attributes like **alink**, **background**, **bgcolor**, **link**, **text**, and **vlink**.
- This element must be present in all documents except those declaring a frame set.
- Under XHTML 1.0, the closing **</body>** tag is mandatory.

 (Line Break)

This empty element forces a line break.

Standard Syntax

```
<br
     class="class name(s)"
     clear="all | left | none | right" (transitional only)
     id="unique alphanumeric identifier"
     style="style information"
     title="advisory text" />
```

Events Defined by Internet Explorer

```
onlayoutcomplete, onlosecapture, onreadystatechange
```

Element-Specific Attributes

clear This attribute forces the insertion of vertical space so that the tagged text can be positioned with respect to images. A value of **left** clears text that flows around left-aligned images to the next full left margin, a value of **right** clears text that flows around right-aligned images to the next full right margin, and a value of **all** clears text until it can reach both full margins. The default value according to the transitional HTML and XHTML specifications is **none**, but its meaning generally is supported as just introducing a return and nothing more.

Examples

```
This text will be broken here <br />and continued on a new line.

<img src="test.gif" align="right" />
This is the image caption.<br clear="right" />
```

Compatibility

HTML 2, 3.2, 4, 4.01	Internet Explorer 2, 3, 4, 5, 5.5, 6
XHTML 1.0, 1.1, Basic	Netscape 1, 2, 3, 4, 4.5–4.8, 6, 7
	Opera 4–7

Notes

- This is an empty element. A closing tag is illegal under all HTML specifications. For XHTML compatibility, a closing slash is required: **
**.
- Under the strict HTML and XHTML specifications, the **clear** attribute is not valid. The style property **clear** provides the same functionality as the **clear** attribute.

<button> (Form Button)

This element defines a nameable region known as a button, which can be used together with scripts.

Standard Syntax

```
<button
     accesskey="key"
     class="class name(s)"
     dir="ltr | rtl"
     disabled="disabled"
     id="unique alphanumeric identifier"
     lang="language code"
     name="button name"
     style="style information"
     tabindex="number"
     title="advisory text"
     type="button | reset | submit"
     value="button value">

</button>
```

Attributes Defined by Internet Explorer

```
     contenteditable="false | true | inherit" (5.5)
     datafld="name of column supplying bound data" (4)
     dataformatas="html | text" (4)
     datasrc="id of data source object supplying data" (4)
     hidefocus="true | false" (5.5)
     language="javascript | jscript | vbs | vbscript" (4)
     unselectable="on | off" (5.5)
```

Standard Events

```
onclick, ondblclick, onmousedown, onmouseup, onmouseover, onmousemove, onmouseout,
onkeypress, onkeydown, onkeyup
```

Events Defined by Internet Explorer

```
onactivate, onafterupdate, onbeforeactivate, onbeforecut, onbeforedeactivate,
onbeforeeditfocus, onbeforepaste, onbeforeupdate, onblur, oncontextmenu,
oncontrolselect, oncut, ondeactivate, ondragenter, ondragleave, ondragover, ondrop,
onerrorupdate, onfilterchange, onfocus, onfocusin, onfocusout, onhelp, onlosecapture,
onmouseenter, onmouseleave, onmousewheel, onmove, onmoveend, onmovestart, onpaste,
onpropertychange, onreadystatechange, onresize, onresizeend, onresizestart,
onselectstart
```

Element-Specific Attributes

accesskey This attribute specifies a keyboard navigation accelerator for the element. Pressing ALT or a similar key in association with the specified key selects the anchor element correlated with that key.

datafld This Internet Explorer–specific attribute specifies the column name from the data source object that supplies the bound data that defines the information for the **<button>** tag's content.

dataformatas This Internet Explorer–specific attribute indicates whether the bound data is plain text or HTML.

datasrc This Internet Explorer-specific attribute indicates the **id** of the data source object that supplies the data that is bound to the **<button>** tag.

disabled This attribute is used to disable the button.

name This attribute is used to define a name for the button so that it can be scripted by older browsers or used to provide a name for submit buttons when there is more than one in a page.

tabindex This attribute uses a number to identify the object's position in the tabbing order.

type This attribute defines the action of the button. Possible values include **button**, **reset**, and **submit**, which are used to indicate that the button is a plain button, form reset button, or form submission button, respectively. The XHTML specification suggests **submit** is the default, but browsers may not enforce this in practice.

value Defines the value that is sent to the server when the button is clicked. This might be useful when using multiple **submit** buttons that perform different actions to indicate which button was pressed to the handling server-side program.

Examples

```
<button name="Submit"
        value="Submit"
        type="Submit">Submit Request</button>

<button type="button"
        onclick="doSomething()">Click This Button</button>

<button type="button">
<img src="polkadot.gif" alt="Polkadot"></button>
```

Compatibility

HTML 4, 4.01	Internet Explorer 4, 5, 4.5, 5.5, 6
XHTML 1.0, 1.1	Netscape 6, 7
	Opera 5–7

Notes

- It is illegal to associate an image map with an **<img>** tag that appears as the content of a **button** element.
- The HTML 4.01 specification reserves the data-binding attributes **datafld**, **dataformatas**, and **datasrc** for future use. They were dropped from XHTML but Internet Explorer does support them.
- Developers may want to consider using the markup **<input type="submit">** instead of a **<button>** tag for complete browser backward compatibility.

<caption> (Table Caption)

This element is used within the table element to define a caption.

Standard Syntax

```
<caption
     align="bottom | left | right | top" (transitional only)
     class="class name(s)"
     dir="ltr | rtl"
     id="unique alphanumeric identifier"
     lang="language code"
     style="style information"
     title="advisory text">

</caption>
```

Attributes Defined by Internet Explorer

```
     accesskey="key" (5.5)
     contenteditable="false | true | inherit" (5.5)
     hidefocus="true | false" (5.5)
     language="javascript | jscript | vbs | vbscript" (4)
     tabindex="number" (5.5)
     unselectable="on | off" (5.5)
     valign="bottom | top" (4)
```

Standard Events

onclick, ondblclick, onmousedown, onmouseup, onmouseover, onmousemove, onmouseout, onkeypress, onkeydown, onkeyup

Events Defined by Internet Explorer

onactivate, onbeforeactivate, onbeforecopy, onbeforecut, onbeforedeactivate, onbeforeeditfocus, onbeforepaste, onblur, oncontextmenu, oncontrolselect, oncopy, oncut, ondeactivate, ondrag, ondragend, ondragenter, ondragleave, ondragover, ondragstart, ondrop, onfocus, onfocusin, onfocusout, onhelp, onlosecapture, onmouseenter, onmouseleave, onmousewheel, onmove, onmoveend, onmovestart, onpaste, onpropertychange, onreadystatechange, onresizeend, onresizestart, onselectstart, ontimeerror

Element-Specific Attributes

align This attribute specifies the alignment of the caption. HTML 4 defines **bottom**, **left**, **right**, and **top** as legal values. Internet Explorer also supports **center**. Because this does not provide the possibility to combine vertical and horizontal alignments, Microsoft has introduced the **valign** attribute for the **caption** element.

valign This Internet Explorer–specific attribute specifies whether the table caption appears at the **top** or **bottom**. The default is top.

Example

```
<table>
   <caption align="top">Our High-Priced Menu</caption>
      <tr>
          <td>Escargot</td>
          <td>Filet Mignon</td>
          <td>Big Mac</td>
      </tr>
</table>
```

Compatibility

HTML 3.2, 4, 4.01	Internet Explorer 4, 5, 5.5, 6
XHTML 1.0, 1.1, Basic	Netscape 3, 4, 4.5–4.8, 6, 7
	Opera 4–7

Notes

- There should be only one caption per table.
- HTML 3.2 defines only the **align** attribute with values of **bottom** and **top**. No other attributes are defined prior to HTML 4.

<center> (Center Alignment)

This element causes the enclosed content to be centered within the margins currently in effect. Margins are either the default page margins or those imposed by overriding elements, such as tables.

Standard Syntax (Transitional Only)

```
<center
     class="class name(s)"
     dir="ltr | rtl"
     id="unique alphanumeric identifier"
     lang="language code"
     style="style information"
     title="advisory text">

</center>
```

Attributes Defined by Internet Explorer

```
     accesskey="key" (5.5)
     contenteditable="false | true | inherit" (5.5)
     disabled="false | true" (5.5)
     hidefocus="true | false" (5.5)
     language="javascript | jscript | vbs | vbscript" (4)
     tabindex="number" (5.5)
     unselectable="on | off" (5.5)
```

Standard Events

```
onclick, ondblclick, onmousedown, onmouseup, onmouseover, onmousemove, onmouseout,
onkeypress, onkeydown, onkeyup
```

Events Defined by Internet Explorer

```
onactivate, onbeforeactivate, onbeforecopy, onbeforecut, onbeforedeactivate,
onbeforeeditfocus, onbeforepaste, onblur, oncontextmenu, oncontrolselect, oncopy, oncut,
ondeactivate, ondrag, ondragend, ondragenter, ondragleave, ondragover, ondragstart,
ondrop, onfocus, onfocusin, onfocusout, onhelp, onlosecapture, onmouseenter,
onmouseleave, onmousewheel, onmove, onmoveend, onmovestart, onpaste, onpropertychange,
onreadystatechange, onresizeend, onresizestart, onselectstart, ontimeerror
```

Example

```
<center>This is in the center of the page.</center>
```

Compatibility

HTML 3.2, 4, 4.01 (transitional)	Internet Explorer 2, 3, 4, 5, 5.5, 6
XHTML 1.0 (transitional)	Netscape 1, 2, 3, 4, 4.5–4.8, 6, 7
	Opera 4–7

Notes

- The **center** element defined by the W3C is a shorthand notation for **<div align="center">**.
- The strict versions of HTML and XHTML do not include the **center** element, but it is easily imitated with the **text-align** CSS property.
- HTML 3.2 does not support any attributes for this element.

<cite> (Citation)

This element indicates a citation from a book or other published source and usually is rendered in italics by a browser.

Standard Syntax

```
<cite
     class="class name(s)"
     dir="ltr | rtl"
     id="unique alphanumeric identifier"
     lang="language code"
     style="style information"
     title="advisory text">

</cite>
```

Attributes Defined by Internet Explorer

```
     accesskey="key" (5.5)
     contenteditable="false | true | inherit" (5.5)
     disabled="false | true" (5.5)
     hidefocus="true | false" (5.5)
     language="javascript | jscript | vbs | vbscript" (4)
     tabindex="number" (5.5)
     unselectable="on | off" (5.5)
```

Standard Events

```
onclick, ondblclick, onmousedown, onmouseup, onmouseover, onmousemove, onmouseout,
onkeypress, onkeydown, onkeyup
```

Events Defined by Internet Explorer

```
onactivate, onbeforeactivate, onbeforecopy, onbeforecut, onbeforedeactivate,
onbeforeeditfocus, onbeforepaste, onblur, oncontextmenu, oncontrolselect, oncopy, oncut,
ondeactivate, ondrag, ondragend, ondragenter, ondragleave, ondragover, ondragstart,
ondrop, onfocus, onfocusin, onfocusout, onhelp, onlosecapture, onmouseenter,
onmouseleave, onmousewheel, onmove, onmoveend, onmovestart, onpaste, onpropertychange,
onreadystatechange, onresizeend, onresizestart, onselectstart, ontimeerror
```

Example

```
This example is taken from <cite>HTML: The Complete Reference</cite>.
```

Compatibility

HTML 2, 3.2, 4, 4.01 XHTML 1.0, 1.1, Basic	Internet Explorer 2, 3, 4, 5, 5.5, 6 Netscape 1, 2, 3, 4, 4.5–4.8, 6, 7 Opera 4–7

Notes

HTML 2 and 3.2 do not indicate any attributes for this element.

<code> (Code Listing)

This element indicates that the enclosed text is source code in a programming language. Usually, it is rendered in a monospaced font.

Standard Syntax

```
<code
     class="class name(s)"
     dir="ltr | rtl"
     id="unique alphanumeric identifier"
     lang="language code"
     style="style information"
     title="advisory text">

</code>
```

Attributes Defined by Internet Explorer

```
     contenteditable="false | true | inherit" (5.5)
     disabled="false | true" (5.5)
     language="javascript | jscript | vbs | vbscript" (4)
     unselectable="on | off" (5.5)
```

Standard Events

```
onclick, ondblclick, onmousedown, onmouseup, onmouseover, onmousemove, onmouseout,
onkeypress, onkeydown, onkeyup
```

Events Defined by Internet Explorer

```
onactivate, onbeforeactivate, onbeforecopy, onbeforecut, onbeforedeactivate,
onbeforeeditfocus, onbeforepaste, onblur, oncontextmenu, oncontrolselect, oncopy,
oncut, ondeactivate, ondrag, ondragend, ondragenter, ondragleave, ondragover,
ondragstart, ondrop, onfocus, onfocusin, onfocusout, onhelp, onlosecapture,
onmouseenter, onmouseleave, onmousewheel, onmove, onmoveend, onmovestart, onpaste,
onpropertychange, onreadystatechange, onresizeend, onresizestart, onselectstart,
ontimeerror
```

Example

```
To increment a variable called count, use <code> count++ </code>
```

Compatibility

HTML 2, 3.2, 4, 4.01 XHTML 1.0, 1.1, Basic	Internet Explorer 2, 3, 4, 5, 5.5, 6 Netscape 1, 2, 3, 4, 4.5–4.8, 6, 7 Opera 4–7

Notes

- This element is best used for short code fragments because it does not preserve white space.
- HTML 2.0 and 3.2 do not support any attributes for this element.
- Internet Explorer documentation does not list **accesskey** nor **tabindex** for this element, but it is likely an oversight regardless of the value of the attribute for generally nonfocusable elements.

<col> (Table Column)

This element defines a column within a table and is used for grouping and alignment purposes. It generally is found within a **colgroup** element.

Standard Syntax

```
<col
     align="center | char | justify | left | right"
     char="character"
     charoff="number"
     class="class name(s)"
     dir="ltr | rtl"
     id="unique alphanumeric identifier"
     lang="language code"
     span="number"
     style="style information"
     title="advisory text"
     valign="baseline | bottom | middle | top"
     width="column width specification" />
```

Attributes Defined by Internet Explorer

```
     bgcolor="color name | #RRGGBB" (5.5)
```

Standard Events

```
onclick, ondblclick, onmousedown, onmouseup, onmouseover, onmousemove, onmouseout,
onkeypress, onkeydown, onkeyup
```

Events Defined by Internet Explorer

```
onlayoutcomplete, onreadystatechange
```

Element-Specific Attributes

align This attribute specifies horizontal alignment of a cell's contents.

bgcolor This Internet Explorer–specific attribute sets the background color for the column. Its value can be either a browser-dependent named color or a color specified using the hexadecimal *#RRGGBB* format.

char This attribute is used to set the character on which the cells in a column should be aligned. A typical value for this is a period (.) for aligning numbers or monetary values.

charoff This attribute is used to indicate the number of characters by which the column data should be offset from the alignment characters specified by the **char** value.

span When present, this attribute applies the attributes of the **col** element to additional consecutive columns.

valign This attribute specifies the vertical alignment of the text within the cell. Possible values for this attribute are **baseline**, **bottom**, **middle**, and **top**.

width This attribute specifies a default width for each column in the current column group. In addition to the standard pixel and percentage values, this attribute might take the special form **0***, which means that the width of each column in the group should be the minimum width necessary to hold the column's contents.

Example

```
<table border="1" width="400">
<colgroup>
 <col align="center" width="150" />
 <col align="right" />
<tr>
</colgroup>
  <td>This column is aligned to the center.</td>
  <td>This one is aligned to the right.</td>
</tr>
<tr><td>!</td><td>?</td></tr>

<tr><td>!</td><td>?</td></tr>
</table>
```

Compatibility

HTML 4, 4.01	Internet Explorer 4, 5, 5.5, 6
XHTML 1.0, 1.1	Netscape 6, 7
	Opera 7

Notes

- Under XHTML 1.0, **<col>** requires a trailing slash: **<col />**.
- This element should appear within a **colgroup** element, and like that element, it is somewhat of a convenience feature used to set attributes with one or more table columns. In practice, few developers seem to use it.

<colgroup> (Table Column Group)

This element creates an explicit group of table columns to allow group level scripting or formatting.

Standard Syntax

```
<colgroup
     align="center | char | justify | left | right"
     char="character"
     charoff="number"
     class="class name(s)"
     dir="ltr | rtl"
     id="unique alphanumeric identifier"
     lang="language code"
     span="number"
     style="style information"
     title="advisory text"
     valign="baseline | bottom | middle | top"
     width="column width specification">

   col elements only

</colgroup>
```

Attributes Defined by Internet Explorer

```
bgcolor="color name | #RRGGBB" (5.5)
```

Standard Events

```
onclick, ondblclick, onmousedown, onmouseup, onmouseover, onmousemove, onmouseout,
onkeypress, onkeydown, onkeyup
```

Events Defined by Internet Explorer

```
onreadystatechange
```

Element-Specific Attributes

align This attribute specifies horizontal alignment of the contents of the cells in the column group. The values of **center**, **left**, and **right** have obvious meanings. A value of **justify** for the attribute should attempt to justify all the column's contents. A value of **char** attempts to align the contents based on the value of the **char** attribute in conjunction with **charoff**.

bgcolor This Internet Explorer-specific attribute sets the background color for the columns in the column group. Its value can be either a browser-dependent named color or a color specified using the hexadecimal *#RRGGBB* format.

char This attribute is used to set the character on which the cells in a column should be aligned. A typical value for this attribute is a period (.) for aligning numbers or monetary values.

charoff This attribute is used to indicate the number of characters by which the column data should be offset from the alignment characters specified by the **char** value.

span When present, this attribute specifies the default number of columns in this group. Browsers should ignore this attribute if the current column group contains one or more **<col>** tags. The default value of this attribute is **1**.

valign This attribute specifies the vertical alignment of the contents of the cells within the column group.

width This attribute specifies a default width for each column and its cells in the current column group. In addition to the standard pixel and percentage values, this attribute can take the special form **0***, which means that the width of each column in the group should be the minimum width necessary to hold the column's contents.

Examples

```
<colgroup span="2" align="char" char=":" valign="center">
 <col /><col /><col />
</colgroup>

<colgroup style="background-color: green;">
 <col align="left" />
 <col align="center" />
</colgroup>
```

Compatibility

HTML 4, 4.01	Internet Explorer 4, 5, 5.5, 6
XHTML 1.0, 1.1	Netscape 6, 7
	Opera 7

Notes

- Each column group defined by a **<colgroup>** tag can contain zero or more **<col>** tags.
- Under XHTML 1.0, the closing **</colgroup>** tag is mandatory.

<comment> (Comment Information)

This nonstandard element treats enclosed text as comments. This element should not be used.

Syntax Defined by Internet Explorer

```
<comment
     data="URL"   (6)
     id="unique alphanumeric identifier" (4)
     lang="language code" (4)
     title="advisory text"> (4)

</comment>
```

Events Defined by Internet Explorer

```
onpropertychange, onreadystatechange
```

Element-Specific Attributes

data References a URL that contains the comment information.

Example

```
<comment>This is not the proper way to form comments!!!</comment>
```

Compatibility

No standards	Internet Explorer 4, 5, 5.5, 6

Notes

- It is better to use the **<!--. . .-->** syntax for specifying comments.
- Because the **comment** element is not supported by all browsers, commented text done in this fashion will appear in other browsers.

<dd> (Definition in a Definition List)

This element indicates the definition of a term within a list of defined terms (**<dt>**) enclosed by a definition list (**<dl>**).

Standard Syntax

```
<dd
     class="class name(s)"
     dir="ltr | rtl"
     id="unique alphanumeric identifier"
     lang="language code"
     style="style information"
     title="advisory text">

</dd>
```

Attributes Defined by Internet Explorer

```
accesskey="key" (5.5)
contenteditable="false | true | inherit" (5.5)
disabled="false | true" (5.5)
hidefocus="true | false" (5.5)
language="javascript | jscript | vbs | vbscript" (4)
nowrap="no | yes" (4)
tabindex="number" (5.5)
unselectable="on | off" (5.5)
```

Standard Events

onclick, ondblclick, onmousedown, onmouseup, onmouseover, onmousemove, onmouseout, onkeypress, onkeydown, onkeyup

Events Defined by Internet Explorer

onactivate, onbeforeactivate, onbeforecopy, onbeforecut, onbeforedeactivate, onbeforeeditfocus, onbeforepaste, onblur, oncontextmenu, oncontrolselect, oncopy, oncut, ondeactivate, ondrag, ondragend, ondragenter, ondragleave, ondragover, ondragstart, ondrop, onfocus, onfocusin, onfocusout, onhelp, onlosecapture, onmouseenter, onmouseleave, onmousewheel, onmove, onmoveend, onmovestart, onpaste, onpropertychange, onreadystatechange, onresizeend, onresizestart, onselectstart, ontimeerror

Element-Specific Attributes

nowrap This Internet Explorer–specific attribute is used to control the wrapping of text within a **<dd>** tag. If set to **yes**, text should not wrap. The default is **no**. CSS rules should be used instead of this attribute.

Example

```
<dl>
     <dt>DOG</dt>
        <dd>A domesticated animal that craves attention all the time</dd>
     <dt>CAT</dt>
        <dd>An animal that would just as soon ignore you until it
            gets hungry</dd>
</dl>
```

Compatibility

HTML 2, 3.2, 4, 4.01	Internet Explorer 2, 3, 4, 5, 5.5, 6
XHTML 1.0, 1.1, Basic	Netscape 1, 2, 3, 4, 4.5–4.8, 6, 7
	Opera 4–7

Notes

- Under HTML specifications, the closing tag for this element is optional, though it is encouraged when it will help make the list more understandable.
- Under XHTML 1.0, the closing **</dd>** tag is mandatory.
- This element occurs within a list of defined terms enclosed by a **<dl>** tag. Typically associated with it is the term it defines, indicated by the **<dt>** tag that precedes it.
- HTML 2 and 3.2 define no attributes for this element.

<del> (Deleted Text)

This element is used to indicate that text has been deleted from a document. A browser might render deleted text as strikethrough text.

Standard Syntax

```
<del
     cite="url"
     class="class name(s)"
     datetime="date"
     dir="ltr | rtl"
     id="unique alphanumeric identifier"
     lang="language code"
     style="style information"
     title="advisory text">

</del>
```

Attributes Defined by Internet Explorer

```
     accesskey="key" (5.5)
     contenteditable="false | true | inherit" (5.5)
     disabled="false | true" (5.5)
     language="javascript | jscript | vbs | vbscript" (4)
     tabindex="number" (5.5)
     unselectable="on | off" (5.5)
```

Standard Events

```
onclick, ondblclick, onmousedown, onmouseup, onmouseover, onmousemove, onmouseout,
onkeypress, onkeydown, onkeyup
```

Events Defined by Internet Explorer

```
onbeforeeditfocus, onblur, ondrag, ondragend, ondragenter, ondragleave, ondragover,
ondragstart, ondrop, onfocus, onreadystatechange, onselectstart, ontimeerror
```

Element-Specific Attributes

cite The value of this attribute is a URL that designates a source document or message that might give a reason that the information was deleted.

datetime This attribute is used to indicate the date and time the deletion was made. The value of the attribute is a date in a special format as defined by ISO 8601. The basic date format is

```
YYYY-MM-DDThh:mm:ssTZD
```

where the following is true:

```
YYYY=four-digit year such as 1999
  MM=two-digit month (01=January, 02=February, and so on.)
  DD=two-digit day of the month (01 through 31)
  hh=two digit hour (00 to 23) (24-hour clock, not AM or PM)
  mm=two digit minute (00 through 59)
  ss=two digit second (00 through 59)
  TZD=time zone designator
```

The time zone designator is either **Z**, which indicates Universal Time Coordinate or coordinated universal time format (UTC), or ***+hh:mm***, which indicates that the time is a local time that is *hh* hours and *mm* minutes ahead of UTC. Alternatively, the format for the time zone designator could be ***-hh:mm***, which indicates that the local time is behind UTC. Note that the letter "T" actually appears in the string, all digits must be used, and **00** values for minutes and seconds might be required. An example value for the **datetime** attribute might be **1999-10-6T09:15:00-05:00**, which corresponds to October 6, 1999, 9:15 A.M., U.S. Eastern Standard Time.

Example

```
<del cite="http://www.bigcompany.com/changes/oct97.htm"
     datetime="1998-10-06T09:15:00-05:00">
The penalty clause applies to client lateness as well.
</del>
```

Compatibility

HTML 4, 4.01	Internet Explorer 4, 5, 5.5, 6
XHTML 1.0, 1.1	Netscape 6, 7
	Opera 7

Notes

- Browsers can render deleted (**<del>**) text in a different style to show the changes that have been made to the document. Internet Explorer renders the text as strikethrough text. Eventually, a browser could have a way to show a revision history on a document.
- User agents that do not understand **<del>** or **<ins>** will show the information anyway, so there is no harm in adding information—only in deleting it. Because of the fact that **<del>**-enclosed text might show up, it might be wise to comment it out within the element, as shown here:

```
<del>
<!-- This is old information. -->
</del>
```

<dfn> (Definition)

This element encloses the defining instance of a term. It usually is rendered as bold or bold italic text.

Standard Syntax

```
<dfn
     class="class name(s)"
     dir="ltr | rtl"
     id="unique alphanumeric identifier"
     lang="language code"
     style="style information"
     title="advisory text">

</dfn>
```

Attributes Defined by Internet Explorer

```
     accesskey="key" (5.5)
     contenteditable="false | true | inherit" (5.5)
     disabled="false | true" (5.5)
     hidefocus="true | false" (5.5)
     language="javascript | jscript | vbs | vbscript" (4)
     tabindex="number" (5.5)
     unselectable="on | off" (5.5)
```

Standard Events

```
onclick, ondblclick, onmousedown, onmouseup, onmouseover, onmousemove, onmouseout,
onkeypress, onkeydown, onkeyup
```

Events Defined by Internet Explorer

```
onactivate, onbeforeactivate, onbeforecopy, onbeforecut, onbeforedeactivate,
onbeforeeditfocus, onbeforepaste, onblur, oncontextmenu, oncontrolselect, oncopy,
oncut, ondeactivate, ondrag, ondragend, ondragenter, ondragleave, ondragover,
ondragstart, ondrop, onfocus, onfocusin, onfocusout, onhelp, onlosecapture,
onmouseenter, onmouseleave, onmousewheel, onmove, onmoveend, onmovestart, onpaste,
onpropertychange, onreadystatechange, onresize, onresizeend, onresizestart,
onselectstart
```

Example

```
<p>An <dfn>elephant</dfn> is too large to make a viable pet for anyone
poorer than Bill Gates.</p>
```

Compatibility

HTML 2, 3.2, 4, 4.01 XHTML 1.1, Basic	Internet Explorer 2, 3, 4, 5, 5.5, 6 Netscape 6, 7 Opera 4–7

Notes

- HTML 2 and 3.2 defined no attributes for this element.

<dir> (Directory List)

This element encloses a list of brief, unordered items, such as might occur in a menu or directory.

Standard Syntax (Transitional Only—Deprecated)

```
<dir
     class="class name(s)"
     compact="compact"
     dir="ltr | rtl"
     id="unique alphanumeric identifier"
     lang="language code"
     style="style information"
     title="advisory text">

   li elements only

</dir>
```

Attributes Defined by Internet Explorer

```
     accesskey="key" (5.5)
     contenteditable="false | true | inherit" (5.5)
     disabled="false | true" (5.5)
     hidefocus="true | false" (5.5)
     language="javascript | jscript | vbs | vbscript" (4)
     tabindex="number" (5.5)
     unselectable="on | off" (5.5)
```

Standard Events (Deprecated)

```
onclick, ondblclick, onmousedown, onmouseup, onmouseover, onmousemove, onmouseout,
onkeypress, onkeydown, onkeyup
```

Events Defined by Internet Explorer

```
onactivate, onbeforeactivate, onbeforecopy, onbeforecut, onbeforedeactivate,
onbeforeeditfocus, onbeforepaste, onblur, oncontextmenu, oncontrolselect, oncopy, oncut,
ondeactivate, ondrag, ondragend, ondragenter, ondragleave, ondragover, ondragstart,
ondrop, onfocus, onfocusin, onfocusout, onhelp, onlosecapture, onmouseenter,
onmouseleave, onmousewheel, onmove, onmoveend, onmovestart, onpaste, onpropertychange,
onreadystatechange, onresizeend, onresizestart, onselectstart, ontimeerror
```

Element-Specific Attributes

compact This attribute reduces the white space between list items.

Example

```
<dir>
  <li>Header Files</li>
  <li>Code Files</li>
  <li>Comment Files</li>
</dir>
```

Compatibility

HTML 2, 3.2, 4, 4.01 (transitional) XHTML 1.0 (transitional)	Internet Explorer 2, 3, 4, 5, 5.5, 6 Netscape 1, 2, 3, 4, 4.5–4.8, 6, 7 Opera 4–7

Notes

- Because the **<dir>** tag is supposed to be used with short lists, the items in the list should have a maximum width of 20 characters. This is rarely respected.
- The HTML and XHTML strict specifications do not support this element.
- Most browsers will not render the **<dir>** tag any differently from the **ul** element.
- HTML 2 and 3.2 define only the **compact** attribute.
- Most browsers will not render the **compact** list style.
- For XHTML compatibility, the **compact** attribute must have a value: **<dir compact="compact">**.

<div> (Division)

This element indicates a generic block of document content that should be treated as a logical unit and will have no default rendering or meaning.

Standard Syntax

```
<div
     align="center | justify | left | right" (transitional only)
     class="class name(s)"
     dir="ltr | rtl"
     id="unique alphanumeric identifier"
```

```
     lang="language code"
     style="style information"
     title="advisory text">

</div>
```

Attributes Defined by Internet Explorer

```
accesskey="key" (5.5)
contenteditable="false | true | inherit" (5.5)
disabled="false | true" (5.5)
hidefocus="true | false" (5.5)
language="javascript | jscript | vbs | vbscript" (4)
nowrap="no | yes" (4)
tabindex="number" (5.5)
unselectable="on | off" (5.5)
```

Standard Events

onclick, ondblclick, onmousedown, onmouseup, onmouseover, onmousemove, onmouseout, onkeypress, onkeydown, onkeyup

Events Defined by Internet Explorer

onactivate, onbeforeactivate, onbeforecopy, onbeforecut, onbeforedeactivate, onbeforeeditfocus, onbeforepaste, onblur, oncontextmenu, oncontrolselect, oncopy, oncut, ondeactivate, ondrag, ondragend, ondragenter, ondragleave, ondragover, ondragstart, ondrop, onfocus, onfocusin, onfocusout, onhelp, onlosecapture, onmouseenter, onmouseleave, onmousewheel, onmove, onmoveend, onmovestart, onpaste, onpropertychange, onreadystatechange, onresizeend, onresizestart, onselectstart, ontimeerror

Element-Specific Attributes

align This attribute indicates how the tagged text should be horizontally aligned on the page. The default value is **left**.

nowrap This Internet Explorer–specific attribute is used to control the wrapping of text within a **<div>** tag. If set to **yes**, text should not wrap. The default is **no**. CSS rules should be used instead of this attribute.

Examples

```
<div align="justify">
   All text within this division will be justified
</div>
<div class="special" id="div1" style="background: yellow;">
 Divs are useful for setting arbitrary style
</div>
```

Compatibility

HTML 3.2, 4, 4.01	Internet Explorer 2, 3, 4, 5, 5.5, 6
XHTML 1.0, 1.1, Basic	Netscape 2, 3, 4, 4.5–4.8, 6, 7
	Opera 4–7

Notes

- A **<div>** tag is a generic block tag and is very useful for binding scripts or styles to an arbitrary section of a document. It complements **<span>**, which is used inline.

- The HTML 4.01 specification specifies that the **datafld**, **dataformatas**, and **datasrc** attributes are reserved for **<div>** and might be supported in the future. They were removed from XHTML but Internet Explorer supports them for data binding.
- Under the HTML 4.01 strict specification, the **align** attribute is not supported.
- HTML 3.2 supports only the **align** attribute.

<dl> (Definition List)

This element encloses a list of terms and definition pairs. A common use for this element is to implement a glossary.

Standard Syntax

```
<dl
     class="class name(s)"
     compact="compact" (transitional only)
     dir="ltr | rtl"
     id="unique alphanumeric identifier"
     lang="language code"
     style="style information"
     title="advisory text">

   dt and dd elements only

</dl>
```

Attributes Defined by Internet Explorer

```
     accesskey="key" (5.5)
     contenteditable="false | true | inherit" (5.5)
     disabled="false | true" (5.5)
     hidefocus="true | false" (5.5)
     language="javascript | jscript | vbs | vbscript" (4)
     tabindex="number" (5.5)
     unselectable="on | off" (5.5)
```

Standard Events

```
onclick, ondblclick, onmousedown, onmouseup, onmouseover, onmousemove, onmouseout,
onkeypress, onkeydown, onkeyup
```

Events Defined by Internet Explorer

```
onactivate, onbeforeactivate, onbeforecopy, onbeforecut, onbeforedeactivate,
onbeforeeditfocus, onbeforepaste, onblur, oncontextmenu, oncontrolselect, oncopy, oncut,
ondeactivate, ondrag, ondragend, ondragenter, ondragleave, ondragover, ondragstart,
ondrop, onfocus, onfocusin, onfocusout, onhelp, onlosecapture, onmouseenter,
onmouseleave, onmousewheel, onmove, onmoveend, onmovestart, onpaste, onpropertychange,
onreadystatechange, onresizeend, onresizestart, onselectstart, ontimeerror
```

Element-Specific Attributes

compact This attribute reduces the white space between list items.

Example

```
<dl>
   <dt>Cat</dt>
       <dd>A domestic animal that likes fish.</dd>
```

```
   <dt>Skunk</dt>
       <dd>A wild animal that needs deodorant.</dd>
</dl>
```

Compatibility

HTML 2, 3.2, 4, 4.01	Internet Explorer 2, 3, 4, 5, 5.5, 6
XHTML 1.0, 1.1, Basic	Netscape 1, 2, 3, 4, 4.5–4.8, 6, 7
	Opera 4–7

Notes

- The items in the list comprise two parts: the term, indicated by the **dt** element, and its definition, indicated by the **dd** element.
- Some page designers might use a **<dl>** tag or **<ul>** tag to create text indention. Although this is a common practice on the Web, it is not advisable because it confuses the meaning of the element by making it a physical layout device rather than a list.
- HTML 2 and 3.2 support only the **compact** attribute for this element.
- For XHTML compatibility, the **compact** attribute must be expanded: **<dl compact= "compact">** under the transitional form. It is deprecated under the strict specification.

<dt> (Term in a Definition List)

Identifies a definition list term in a list of terms and definitions.

Standard Syntax

```
<dt
     class="class name(s)"
     dir="ltr | rtl"
     id="unique alphanumeric identifier"
     lang="language code"
     style="style information"
     title="advisory text">

</dt>
```

Attributes Defined by Internet Explorer

```
     accesskey="key" (5.5)
     contenteditable="false | true | inherit" (5.5)
     disabled="false | true" (5.5)
     hidefocus="true | false" (5.5)
     language="javascript | jscript | vbs | vbscript" (4)
     nowrap="true | false" (5.5)
     tabindex="number" (5.5)
     unselectable="on | off" (5.5)
```

Standard Events

```
onclick, ondblclick, onmousedown, onmouseup, onmouseover, onmousemove, onmouseout,
onkeypress, onkeydown, onkeyup
```

Events Defined by Internet Explorer

```
onactivate, onbeforeactivate, onbeforecopy, onbeforecut, onbeforedeactivate,
onbeforeeditfocus, onbeforepaste, onblur, oncontextmenu, oncontrolselect, oncopy,
oncut, ondeactivate, ondrag, ondragend, ondragenter, ondragleave, ondragover,
```

```
ondragstart, ondrop, onfocus, onfocusin, onfocusout, onhelp, onlosecapture,
onmouseenter, onmouseleave, onmousewheel, onmove, onmoveend, onmovestart, onpaste,
onpropertychange, onreadystatechange, onresizeend, onresizestart, onselectstart,
ontimeerror
```

Element-Specific Attributes

nowrap This Internet Explorer–specific attribute is used to control the wrapping of text within a **<dt>** tag. If set to **yes**, text should not wrap. The default is **no**. CSS rules should be used instead of this attribute.

Example

```
<dl>
   <dt>Vole</dt>
     <dd>Small creature related to the weasel</dd>
   <dt>Weasel</dt>
     <dd>Small creature related to the vole</dd>
</dl>
```

Compatibility

HTML 2, 3.2, 4, 4.01	Internet Explorer 2, 3, 4, 5, 6
XHTML 1.0, 1.1, Basic	Netscape 1, 2, 3, 4, 4.5–4.8, 6, 7
	Opera 4–7

Notes

- This element occurs within a list of defined terms enclosed by a **<dl>** tag. It generally is used in conjunction with a **<dd>** tag, which indicates its definition. However, **<dt>** tags do not require a one-to-one correspondence with **<dd>** tags.
- The close tag for the element is optional under older versions of HTML but is suggested when it will make things more clear, particularly with multiple-line definitions.
- Under XHTML 1.0, the closing **</dt>** tag is mandatory.
- HTML 2 and 3.2 support no attributes for this element.

<em> (Emphasis)

This element indicates emphasized text, which many browsers will display as italic text.

Standard Syntax

```
<em
     class="class name(s)"
     dir="ltr | rtl"
     id="unique alphanumeric identifier"
     lang="language code"
     style="style information"
     title="advisory text">

</em>
```

Attributes Defined by Internet Explorer

```
     accesskey="key" (5.5)
     contenteditable="false | true | inherit" (5.5)
     disabled="false | true" (5.5)
```

```
hidefocus="true | false" (5.5)
language="javascript | jscript | vbs | vbscript" (4)
tabindex="number" (5.5)
unselectable="on | off" (5.5)
```

Standard Events

onclick, ondblclick, onmousedown, onmouseup, onmouseover, onmousemove, onmouseout, onkeypress, onkeydown, onkeyup

Events Defined by Internet Explorer

onactivate, onbeforeactivate, onbeforecopy, onbeforecut, onbeforedeactivate, onbeforeeditfocus, onbeforepaste, onblur, oncontextmenu, oncontrolselect, oncopy, oncut, ondeactivate, ondrag, ondragend, ondragenter, ondragleave, ondragover, ondragstart, ondrop, onfocus, onfocusin, onfocusout, onhelp, onlosecapture, onmouseenter, onmouseleave, onmousewheel, onmove, onmoveend, onmovestart, onpaste, onpropertychange, onreadystatechange, onresizeend, onresizestart, onselectstart, ontimeerror

Example

```
This is an <em>important point</em> to consider.
```

Compatibility

HTML 2, 3.2, 4, 4.01	Internet Explorer 2, 3, 4, 5, 5.5, 6
XHTML 1.0, 1.1, Basic	Netscape 1, 2, 3, 4, 4.5–4.8, 6, 7
	Opera 4–7

Notes

- As a logical element, **em** is a prime candidate to bind style information to. For example, to define emphasis to mean a larger font size in the Impact font, you might use a CSS rule like the following in a document-wide style sheet:

  ```
  em {font-size: larger; font-family: Impact;}
  ```

- HTML 2 and 3.2 support no attributes for this element.

<embed> (Embedded Object)

This widely supported nonstandard element specifies an object, typically a multimedia element, to be embedded in an HTML document.

Proprietary Syntax (Commonly Supported)

```
<embed
     accesskey="key" (5.5)
     align="absbottom | absmiddle | baseline | bottom |
            left | middle | right | texttop | top" (4)
     alt="alternative text" (4)
     class="class name(s)" (4)
     code="filename" (4)
     codebase="url" (4)
     height="pixels" (4)
     hspace="pixels" (4)
     id="unique alphanumeric identifier" (4)
     language="javascript | jscript | vbs | vbscript | xml" (5.5)
     name="string" (4)
     src="url" (4)
```

```
    style="style information" (4)
    title="advisory text" (4)
    unselectable="on | off" (5.5)
    vspace="pixels" (4)
    width="pixels" (4)>
</embed>
```

Attributes Defined by Netscape

```
    border="pixels" (4)
    hidden="true | false" (4)
    palette="background | foreground" (4)
    pluginspage="url" (4)
    type="mime type" (4)
    units="en | pixels" (4)
```

Events Defined by Internet Explorer

```
onactivate, onbeforeactivate, onbeforecut, onbeforedeactivate, onbeforepaste, onblur,
oncontextmenu, oncontrolselect, oncut, ondeactivate, onfocus, onfocusin, onfocusout,
onhelp, onload, onlosecapture, onmouseenter, onmouseleave, onmousewheel, onmove,
onmoveend, onmovestart, onpaste, onpropertychange, onreadystatechange, onresize,
onresizeend, onresizestart, onscroll
```

Element-Specific Attributes

align This attribute controls the alignment of adjacent text with respect to the embedded object. The default value is **left**.

alt This attribute indicates the text to be displayed if the included object cannot be executed.

border This attribute specifies the size in pixels of the border around the embedded object.

code This attribute specifies the name of the file containing the compiled Java class if the **embed** element is used to include a Java applet. This is a strange alternative form of Java inclusion documented by Microsoft.

codebase This specifies the base URL for the plug-in or potential applet in the case of the alternative form under Internet Explorer.

height This attribute sets the height of the embedded object in pixels.

hidden If this attribute is set to the value **true**, the embedded object is not visible on the page and implicitly has a size of zero.

hspace This attribute specifies, in pixels, the size of the left and right margins between the embedded object and surrounding text.

name This attribute specifies a name for the embedded object, which can be referenced by client-side programs in an embedded scripting language.

palette This attribute is used only on Windows systems to select the color palette used for the plug-in and might be set to **background** or **foreground**. The default is **background**.

pluginspage This attribute contains the URL of instructions for installing the plug-in required to render the embedded object.

src This attribute specifies the URL of source content for the embedded object.

type This attribute specifies the MIME type of the embedded object. It is used by the browser to determine an appropriate plug-in for rendering the object. It can be used instead of the **src** attribute for plug-ins that have no content or that fetch it dynamically.

units This Netscape-specific attribute is used to set the units for measurement for the embedded object either in **en** or in the default, **pixels**.

vspace This attribute specifies, in pixels, the size of the top and bottom margins between the embedded object and surrounding text.

width This attribute sets the width, in pixels, of the embedded object.

Examples

```
<!-- embed without a close tag -->
<embed src="testmovie.mov" height="150" width="150">
<noembed>
  <img src="testgif.gif" height="150" width="150" alt="Test Image">
</noembed>
<!-- embed with a close tag -->
<embed src="testmovie.mov" height="150" width="150">
<noembed>
  <img src="testgif.gif" height="150" width="150" alt="Test Image">
</noembed>
</embed>
```

Compatibility

No standards	Internet Explorer 3, 4, 5, 5.5, 6 Netscape 2, 3, 4–4.7 Opera 4–7

Notes

- It is actually unclear whether or not the close tag for **<embed>** is required. Many sites tend not to use it, and documentation is not consistent. Some people claim that a close tag is required and should surround any alternative content in a **noembed** element; others do not use a close tag. Whatever the case, this element should be phased out in favor of **object**, so this might be a moot issue.
- The **embed** element is not favored by the W3C and is not part of any official HTML or XHTML specification; however, it is very common. The HTML specification says to use the **object** element, which can be used in conjunction with the **embed** element to provide backward compatibility. See Chapter 15 for examples.
- Embedded objects are multimedia content files of arbitrary type that are rendered by browser plug-ins. The **type** attribute uses a file's MIME type to determine an appropriate browser plug-in. Any attributes not defined are treated as object-specific parameters and are passed through to the embedded object. Consult the plug-in or object documentation to determine these. The standard parameters supported by the Microsoft implementation are **height**, **name**, **palette**, **src**, **units**, and **width**.

<fieldset> (Form Field Grouping)

This element allows form designers to group thematically related controls together.

Standard Syntax

```
<fieldset
     class="class name(s)"
     dir="ltr | rtl"
     id="unique alphanumeric identifier"
     lang="language code"
     style="style information"
     title="advisory text">

</fieldset>
```

Attributes Defined by Internet Explorer

```
     accesskey="key" (5.5)
     align="center | left | right" (4)
     contenteditable="false | true | inherit" (5.5)
     datafld="name of column supplying bound data" (4)
     disabled="false | true" (5.5)
     hidefocus="true | false" (5.5)
     language="javascript | jscript | vbs | vbscript" (4)
     tabindex="number" (5.5)
     unselectable="on | off" (5.5)
```

Standard Events

onclick, ondblclick, onmousedown, onmouseup, onmouseover, onmousemove, onmouseout, onkeypress, onkeydown, onkeyup

Events Defined by Internet Explorer

onactivate, onbeforeactivate, onbeforecopy, onbeforecut, onbeforedeactivate, onbeforeeditfocus, onbeforepaste, onblur, oncontextmenu, oncontrolselect, oncopy, oncut, ondeactivate, ondrag, ondragend, ondragenter, ondragleave, ondragover, ondragstart, ondrop, onfocus, onfocusin, onfocusout, onhelp, onlosecapture, onmouseenter, onmouseleave, onmousewheel, onmove, onmoveend, onmovestart, onpaste, onpropertychange, onreadystatechange, onresizeend, onresizestart, onselectstart, ontimeerror

Element-Specific Attributes

align Internet Explorer defines the **align** attribute, which sets how the element and its contents are positioned in a table or the window.

datafld This attribute specifies the column name from the data source object that supplies the bound data. This attribute is specific to Microsoft's data binding.

Example

```
<fieldset>
<legend>Customer Identification</legend>
<br />
<label>Customer Name:
<input type="text" id="CustName" size="25" />
</label>
</fieldset>
```

Compatibility

HTML 4, 4.01	Internet Explorer 4, 5, 5.5, 6
XHTML 1.0, 1.1	Netscape 6, 7
	Opera 4–7

Notes

- Grouping controls makes it easier for users to understand the purposes of the controls while simultaneously facilitating tabbing navigation for visual user agents and speech navigation for speech-oriented user agents. The proper use of this element makes documents more accessible to people with disabilities.
- The caption for a **<fieldset>** tag can be defined by the **legend** element.
- The typical visual rendering of a fieldset is a boxed grouping of form fields with a label defined by the **legend** element.

<font> (Font Definition)

This element allows specification of the size, color, and font of the text it encloses.

Standard Syntax (Transitional Only)

```
<font
     class="class name(s)"
     color="color name | #RRGGBB"
     dir="ltr | rtl"
     face="font name"
     id="unique alphanumeric identifier"
     lang="language code"
     size="1 to 7 | +1 to +6 | -1 to -6"
     style="style information"
     title="advisory text">

</font>
```

Attributes Defined by Internet Explorer

```
     accesskey="key" (5.5)
     contenteditable="false | true | inherit" (5.5)
     disabled="false | true" (5.5)
     hidefocus="true | false" (5.5)
     language="javascript | jscript | vbs | vbscript" (4)
     tabindex="number" (5.5)
     unselectable="on | off"(5.5)
```

Attributes Defined by Netscape

```
     point-size="point size for font" (4)
     weight="100 | 200 | 300 | 400 | 500
             600 | 700 | 800 | 900" (4)
```

Events Defined by Internet Explorer

```
onactivate, onbeforeactivate, onbeforecopy, onbeforecut, onbeforedeactivate,
onbeforeeditfocus, onbeforepaste, onblur, onclick, oncontextmenu, oncontrolselect,
oncopy, oncut, ondeactivate, ondblclick, ondrag, ondragend, ondragenter, ondragleave,
ondragover, ondragstart, ondrop, onfocus, onfocusin, onfocusout, onhelp, onkeydown,
onkeypress, onkeyup, onlosecapture, onmousedown, onmouseenter, onmouseleave,
onmouseout, onmouseover, onmouseup, onmousewheel, onmove, onmoveend, onmovestart,
onpaste, onpropertychange, onreadystatechange, onresizeend, onresizestart,
onselectstart, ontimeerror
```

Element-Specific Attributes

color This attribute sets the text color using either a browser-dependent named color or a color specified in the hexadecimal *#RRGGBB* format.

face This attribute contains a list of one or more font names separated by commas. The user agent looks through the specified font names and renders the text in the first font that is supported.

point-size This Netscape 4–specific attribute specifies the point size of text and is used with downloadable fonts.

size This attribute specifies the font size as either a numeric or relative value. Numeric values range from **1** to **7** with **1** being the smallest and **3** the default. The relative values, **+** and **–**, increment or decrement the font size relative to the current size. The value for increment or decrement should range only from **+1** to **+ 6** or **–1** to **–6**.

weight Under Netscape 4, this attribute specifies the weight of the font, with a value of **100** being lightest and **900** being heaviest.

Example

```
<font color="#FF0000" face="Helvetica, Times Roman" size="+1">
Relatively large red text in Helvetica or Times.
</font>
```

Compatibility

HTML 3.2, 4, 4.01 (transitional)	Internet Explorer 2, 3, 4, 5, 5.5, 6
XHTML 1.0 (transitional)	Netscape 1.1, 2, 3, 4, 4.5–4.8, 6, 7
	Opera 4–7

Notes

- Use of this element is not encouraged, as it is not part of strict HTML and XHTML specifications. Style sheets provide a cleaner way of providing the same functionality when they are supported.
- Interestingly, the transitional specification for some reason does not define core events for this element. In practice, they are supported by major browsers.
- The default text size for a document can be set using the **size** attribute of the **basefont** element.
- The HTML 3.2 specification supports only the **color** and **size** attributes for this element.

<form> (Form for User Input)

The element defines a fill-in form that can contain labels and form controls, such as menus and text entry boxes that might be filled in by a user.

Standard Syntax

```
<form
     accept-charset="list of supported character sets"
     action="url"
     class="class name(s)"
     dir="ltr | rtl"
     enctype="application/x-www-form-urlencoded |
              multipart/form-data | text/plain |
              Media Type as per RFC 2045"
     id="unique alphanumeric identifier"
```

```
      lang="language code"
      method="get | post"
      name="form's name for scripting"
      style="style information"
      target="_blank | frame name | _parent | _self |
             _top" (transitional only)
      title="advisory text">

</form>
```

Attributes Defined by Internet Explorer

```
autocomplete="yes | no" (5.0)
contenteditable="false | true | inherit" (5.5)
disabled="false | true" (5.5)
hidefocus="true | false" (5.5)
language="javascript | jscript | vbs | vbscript" (4)
tabindex="number" (5.5)
unselectable="on | off" (5.5)
```

Standard Events

onclick, ondblclick, onmousedown, onmouseup, onmouseover, onmousemove, onmouseout, onkeypress, onkeydown, onkeyup, onreset, onsubmit

Events Defined by Internet Explorer

onactivate, onbeforeactivate, onbeforecopy, onbeforecut, onbeforedeactivate, onbeforeeditfocus, onbeforepaste, onblur, oncontextmenu, oncontrolselect, oncopy, oncut, ondeactivate, ondrag, ondragend, ondragenter, ondragleave, ondragover, ondragstart, ondrop, onfocus, onfocusin, onfocusout, onhelp, onlosecapture, onmouseenter, onmouseleave, onmousewheel, onmove, onmoveend, onmovestart, onpaste, onpropertychange, onreadystatechange, onresizeend, onresizestart, onselectstart, ontimeerror

Element-Specific Attributes

accept-charset This attribute specifies the list of character encodings for input data that must be accepted by the server processing the form. The value is a space- or comma-delimited list of character sets as defined in RFC 2045. The default value for this attribute is the reserved value **unknown**.

action This attribute contains the URL of the server program that will process the contents of the form. Some browsers also might support a mailto URL, which can mail the results to the specified address.

autocomplete This Microsoft proprietary attribute, introduced in Internet Explorer 5.0, will automatically finish filling in information that the user has previously input into an input field, and which has been encrypted and stored by the browser.

enctype This attribute indicates how form data should be encoded before being sent to the server. The default is **application/x-www-form-urlencoded**. This encoding replaces blank characters in the data with a plus character (+) and all other nonprinting characters with a percent sign (%) followed by the character's ASCII HEX representation. The multipart/form-data option does not perform character conversion and transfers the information as a compound MIME document. This must be used when using **<input-type="file">**. It also might be possible to use another encoding, such as text/plain, to avoid any form of hex encoding; this might be useful with mailed forms.

method This attribute indicates how form information should be transferred to the server. The **get** option appends data to the URL specified by the **action** attribute. This approach gives the best performance but imposes a size limitation determined by the command line length supported by the server. The **post** option transfers data using a HTTP post transaction. This approach is more secure and imposes no data size limitation.

name This attribute specifies a name for the form and can be used by client-side programs to reference form data.

target In documents containing frames, this attribute specifies the target frame that will display the results of a form submission. In addition to named frames, several special values exist. The **_blank** value indicates a new window. The **_parent** value indicates the parent frame set containing the source link. The **_self** value indicates the frame containing the source link. The **_top** value indicates the full browser window.

Example

```
<form action="http://www.bigcompany.com/cgi-bin/processit.exe"
method="post" name="testform" onsubmit="return validate();">
Enter your comments here:<br />
<textarea name="comments" cols="30" rows="8">
</textarea>
<br /><br />
<input type="submit" value="send" />
<input type="reset" value="clear" />
</form>
```

Compatibility

HTML 2, 3.2, 4, 4.01	Internet Explorer 2, 3, 4, 5, 5.5, 6
XHTML 1.0, 1.1, Basic	Netscape 1, 2, 3, 4, 4.5–4.8, 6, 7
	Opera 4–7

Notes

- Form content is defined using the **<button>**, **<input>**, **<select>**, and **<textarea>** tags, as well as other HTML formatting and structuring elements.
- Special grouping elements, such as **fieldset**, **label**, and **legend** are provided to structure form fields, but more often tags like **<div>** and **<table>** are used to improve form layout.
- HTML 2 and 3.2 support only the **action**, **enctype**, and **method** attributes for the **form** element.

<frame> (Window Region)

This element defines a nameable window region, known as a frame, that can independently display its own content.

Standard Syntax

```
<frame
     class="class name(s)"
     frameborder="0 | 1"
     id="unique alphanumeric identifier"
     longdesc="url of description"
     marginheight="pixels"
```

```
marginwidth="pixels"
name="frame name"
noresize="noresize"
scrolling="auto | no | yes"
src="url" of frame contents
style="style information"
title="advisory text">
```

Attributes Defined by Internet Explorer

```
allowtransparency="no | yes" (5.5)
application="no | yes" (5)
bordercolor="color name | #RRGGBB" (4)
datafld="name of column supplying bound data" (4)
datasrc="id of data source object supplying data" (4)
frameborder="no | yes | 0 | 1" (4)
height="pixels" (4)
hidefocus="true | false" (5.5)
lang="language code" (4)
language="javascript | jscript | vbs | vbscript" (4)
security="restricted" (6)
tabindex="number" (5.5)
unselectable="on | off" (5.5)
width="pixels" (4)
```

Events Defined by Internet Explorer

```
onactivate, onafterupdate, onbeforedeactivate, onbeforeupdate, onblur,
oncontrolselect, ondeactivate, onerrorupdate, onfocus, onload, onmove, onmoveend,
onmovestart, onresize, onresizeend, onresizestart
```

Element-Specific Attributes

allowtransparency This Internet Explorer–specific attribute determines whether the **<frame>** is transparent or opaque. The default value is **false**, which means it is opaque.

application This Microsoft-specific attribute is used to indicate whether the content of an **<frame>** is to be considered an HTA application. HTA applications are applications that use HTML, JavaScript, and Internet Explorer, but are not limited to the typical type of security considerations of a Web page. Given its security implications, this attribute should only be set if the developer is familiar with HTAs.

bordercolor This attribute sets the color of the frame's border using either a named color or a color specified in the hexadecimal *#RRGGBB* format.

datafld This Internet Explorer attribute specifies the column name from the data source object that supplies the bound data.

datasrc This Internet Explorer attribute indicates the **id** of the data source object that supplies the data that is bound to this element.

frameborder This attribute determines whether the frame is surrounded by an outlined three-dimensional border. The HTML specification prefers the use of **1** for the frame border on, and **0** for off; most browsers also acknowledge the use of **no** and **yes**.

longdesc This attribute specifies the URL of a document that contains a long description of the frame's content. This attribute should be used in conjunction with the **title** element.

marginheight This attribute sets the height in pixels between the frame's contents and its top and bottom borders.

marginwidth This attribute sets the width in pixels between the frame's contents and its left and right borders.

name This attribute assigns the frame a name so that it can be the target destination of hyperlinks as well as being a possible candidate for manipulation via a script.

noresize This attribute overrides the default ability to resize frames and gives the frame a fixed size.

scrolling This attribute determines whether the frame has scroll bars. A **yes** value forces scroll bars, a **no** value prohibits them, and an **auto** value lets the browser decide. When not specified, the default value of **auto** is used. Authors are recommended to leave the value as **auto**. If you turn off scrolling and the contents end up being too large for the frame (due to rendering differences, window size, and so forth), the user will not be able to scroll to see the rest of the contents. If you turn scrolling on and the contents all fit in the frame, the scroll bars will needlessly consume screen space. With the **auto** value, scroll bars appear only when needed.

security This attribute sets the value indicating whether the source file of a frame has security restrictions applied. The only allowed value is **restricted**.

src This attribute contains the URL of the contents to be displayed in the frame. If it is absent, nothing will be loaded in the frame.

Example

```
<frameset rows="20%,80%">
  <frame src="controls.html" name="controls" noresize="noresize" scrolling="no" />
  <frame src="content.html" />
</frameset>
```

Compatibility

HTML 4, 4.01	Internet Explorer 2, 3, 4, 5, 5.5, 6
XHTML 1.0 (frameset DTD only)	Netscape 2, 3, 4, 4.5–4.8, 6, 7
	Opera 4–7

Notes

- XHTML 1.0 requires a trailing slash for this element: **<frame />**.
- A frame must be declared as part of a frame set by using the **<frameset>** tag, which specifies the frame's relationship to other frames on a page. A frame set occurs in a special HTML document, in which the **frameset** element replaces the **body** element. Another form of frames called *independent frames*, or *floating frames*, also is supported. Floating frames can be directly embedded in a document without belonging to a frame set. These are defined with the **iframe** element.
- Many browsers do not support frames and require the use of the **<noframes>** tag.
- Frames introduce potential navigation difficulties; their use should be limited to instances in which they can be shown to help navigation rather than hinder it. See Chapter 8 for more details.

<frameset> (Frameset Definition)

This element is used to define the organization of a set of independent window regions known as *frames* as defined by the **frame** element. This element replaces the **body** element in framing documents.

Standard Syntax

```
<frameset
     class="class name(s)"
     cols="list of columns"
     id="unique alphanumeric identifier"
     rows="list of rows"
     style="style information"
     title="advisory text">

</frameset>
```

Attributes Defined by Internet Explorer

```
     border="pixels" (4)
     bordercolor="color name | #RRGGBB" (4)
     frameborder="no | yes | 0 | 1" (4)
     framespacing="pixels" (4)
     lang="language code" (4)
     language="javascript | jscript | vbs | vbscript" (4)
     hidefocus="true | false" (5.5)
     tabindex="number" (5.5)
     unselectable="on | off" (5.5)
```

Standard Events

```
onload, onunload
```

Events Defined by Internet Explorer

```
onactivate, onafterprint, onbeforedeactivate, onbeforeprint, onbeforeunload, onblur,
oncontrolselect, ondeactivate, onfocus, onmove, onmoveend, onmovestart, onresizeend,
onresizestart,
```

Element-Specific Attributes

border This attribute sets the width in pixels of frame borders within the frame set. Setting **border="0"** eliminates all frame borders. This attribute is not defined in the HTML or XHTML specification but is widely supported.

bordercolor This attribute sets the color for frame borders within the frame set using either a named color or a color specified in the hexadecimal *#RRGGBB* format.

cols This attribute contains a comma-delimited list that specifies the number and size of columns contained within a set of frames. List items indicate columns from left to right. Column size is specified in three formats, which might be mixed. A column can be assigned a fixed width in pixels. It also can be assigned a percentage of the available width, such as 50%. Finally, a column can be set to expand to fill the available space by setting the value to *, which acts as a wildcard.

frameborder This attribute controls whether or not frame borders should be displayed. Netscape supports **no** and **yes** values. Microsoft uses **1** and **0** as well as **no** and **yes**.

framespacing This attribute indicates the space between frames in pixels.

rows This attribute contains a comma-delimited list that specifies the number and size of rows contained within a set of frames. The number of entries in the list indicates the number of rows. Row size is specified with the same formats used for columns.

Examples

```
<!-- This example defines a frame set of three columns. The middle column
is 50 pixels wide. The first and last columns fill the remaining space.
-->

<frameset cols="*,50,*">
  <frame src="column1.html">
  <frame src="column2.html">
  <frame src="column3.html">
</frameset>

<!-- This example defines a frame set of two columns, one of which is 20%
of the screen, and the other, 80%. -->

<frameset cols="20%, 80%">
<frame src="controls.html">
<frame src="display.html">
</frameset>

<!-- This example defines two rows, one of which is 10% of the screen,
and the other, whatever space is left. -->

<frameset rows="10%, *">
  <frame src="adbanner.html" name="ad_frame">
  <frame src="contents.html" name="content_frame">
</frameset>
```

Compatibility

HTML 4 and 4.01 (frameset DTD)	Internet Explorer 2, 3, 4, 5, 5.5, 6
XHTML 1.0 (frameset DTD)	Netscape 2, 3, 4, 4.5–4.8, 6, 7
	Opera 4–7

Notes

- The content model says that the **<frameset>** tag contains one or more **<frame>** tags, which are used to indicate the framed contents. A **<frameset>** tag also might contain a **<noframes>** tag whose contents will be displayed by browsers that do not support frames.
- The **<frameset>** tag replaces the **<body>** tag in a framing document, as shown here:

```
<!DOCTYPE html PUBLIC "-//W3C//DTD XHTML 1.0 Frameset//EN"
"http://www.w3.org/TR/xhtml1/DTD/xhtml1-frameset.dtd">
<html xmlns="http://www.w3.org/1999/xhtml" lang="en">
<head>
<title>Collection of Frames</title>
<meta http-equiv="content-type" content="text/html; charset=ISO-8859-1" />
</head>
<frameset cols="*,50,*">
  <frame src="column1.htm" name="col1" />
  <frame src="column2.htm" name="col2" />
```

```
  <frame src="column3.htm" name="col3" />
<noframes>
<body>
Please visit our <a href="noframes.html">no frames</a> site.
</body>
</noframes>
</frameset>
</html>
```

<h1> Through <h6> (Headings)

These tags implement six levels of document headings; **<h1>** is the most prominent and **<h6>** is the least prominent.

Standard Syntax

```
<h1
     align="center | justify | left | right"
           (transitional only)
     class="class name(s)"
     dir="ltr | rtl"
     id="unique alphanumeric identifier"
     lang="language code"
     style="style information"
     title="advisory text">

</h1>
```

Attributes Defined by Internet Explorer

```
     accesskey="key" (5.5)
     contenteditable="false | true | inherit" (5.5)
     disabled="false | true" (5.5)
     hidefocus="true | false" (5.5)
     language="javascript | jscript | vbs | vbscript" (4)
     tabindex="number" (5.5)
     unselectable="on | off" (5.5)
```

Standard Events

```
onclick, ondblclick, onkeydown, onkeypress, onkeyup, onmousedown, onmousemove,
onmouseout, onmouseover, onmouseup,
```

Events Defined by Internet Explorer

```
onactivate, onbeforeactivate, onbeforecopy, onbeforecut, onbeforedeactivate,
onbeforeeditfocus, onbeforepaste, onblur, oncontextmenu, oncontrolselect, oncopy,
oncut, ondeactivate, ondrag, ondragend, ondragenter, ondragleave, ondragover,
ondragstart, ondrop, onfocus, onfocusin, onfocusout, onhelp, onlosecapture,
onmouseenter, onmouseleave, onmousewheel, onmove, onmoveend, onmovestart, onpaste,
onpropertychange, onreadystatechange, onresize, onresizeend, onresizestart,
onselectstart, ontimeerror
```

Element-Specific Attributes

align This attribute controls the horizontal alignment of the heading with respect to the page. The default value is **left**.

Example

```
<h1 align="justify">This is a Major Document Heading</h1>
<h2 align="center=">Second heading, aligned to the center</h2>
<h3 align="right">Third heading, aligned to the right</h3>
```

```
<h4>Fourth heading</h4>
<h5 style="font-size: 20pt;">Fifth heading with style information</h5>
<h6>The least important heading</h6>
```

Compatibility

HTML 2, 3.2, 4, 4.01	Internet Explorer 2, 3, 4, 5, 5.5, 6
XHTML 1.0, 1.1, Basic	Netscape 1, 2, 3, 4, 4.5–4.8, 6, 7
	Opera 4–7

Notes

- In most implementations, heading numbers correspond inversely with the six font sizes supported by the **font** element. For example, **<h1>** corresponds to **<font size="6">**. The default font size is **3**. However, this approach to layout is not encouraged, and page designers should consider using styles to set even relative sizes.
- HTML 3.2 supports only the **align** attribute. HTML 2 does not support any attributes for headings.
- The strict definitions of HTML 4 and XHTML do not include support for the **align** attribute. Style sheet properties like **text-align** should be used instead.

<head> (Document Head)

This element indicates the document head that contains descriptive information about the HTML document as well as other supplementary information, such as style rules or scripts.

Standard Syntax

```
<head
     dir="ltr | rtl"
     id="unique alphanumeric identifier"
     lang="language code"
     profile="url">

</head>
```

Attributes Defined by Internet Explorer

```
     class="class name(s)"
```

Events Defined by Internet Explorer

```
onlayoutcomplete, onreadystatechange
```

Element-Specific Attributes

profile This attribute specifies a URL for a meta-information dictionary. The specified profile should indicate the format of allowed metadata and its meaning.

Example

```
<head>
<title>Big Company Home Page</title>
<base href="http://www.bigcompany.com" />
<meta name="Keywords"content="BigCompany, SuperWidget" />
</head>

<head profile="http://www.bigcompany.com/metadict.xml">
```

Compatibility

HTML 2, 3.2, 4, 4.01	Internet Explorer 2, 3, 4, 5, 5.5, 6
XHTML 1.0, 1.1, Basic	Netscape 1, 2, 3, 4, 4.5–4.8, 6, 7
	Opera 4–7

Notes

- The **<head>** tag must contain a **<title>** tag. It also might contain the **<base>**, **<isindex>**, **<link>**, **<meta>**, **<script>**, and **<style>** tags. Internet Explorer 4 supports the inclusion of the **<basefont>** tag in the **<head>**, but **<basefont>** has been deprecated under HTML 4.
- Under the XHTML 1.0 specification, the **head** element no longer can be implied, but must be used in all documents.
- Under XHTML 1.0, the closing **</head>** tag is mandatory.
- The meaning of the **profile** attribute is somewhat unclear, and no browsers appear to support it in any meaningful way.
- Internet Explorer may allow the **<bgsound>** tag within **<head>**.
- HTML 2 and 3.2 support no attributes for this element.

<hr> (Horizontal Rule)

This element is used to insert a horizontal rule to visually separate document sections. Rules usually are rendered as a raised or etched line.

Standard Syntax

```
<hr
     align="center | left | right" (transitional only)
     class="class name(s)"
     dir="ltr | rtl"
     id="unique alphanumeric identifier"
     lang="language code"id="unique alphanumeric identifier"
     noshade="noshade " (transitional only)
     size="pixels" (transitional only)
     style="style information"
     title="advisory information"
     width="percentage | pixels" />  (transitional only)
```

Attributes Defined by Internet Explorer

```
     accesskey="key" (5.5)
     color="color name | #RRGGBB" (4)
     language="javascript | jscript | vbs | vbscript" (4)
     hidefocus="true | false" (5.5)
     tabindex="number" (5.5)
     unselectable="on | off" (5.5)
```

Standard Event Attributes

```
onclick, ondblclick, onkeydown, onkeypress, onkeyup, onmousedown, onmousemove,
onmouseout, onmouseover, onmouseup
```

Events Defined by Internet Explorer

```
onactivate, onbeforeactivate, onbeforecopy, onbeforecut, onbeforedeactivate,
onbeforeeditfocus, onbeforepaste, onblur, oncontextmenu, oncontrolselect, oncopy, oncut,
```

ondeactivate, ondrag, ondragend, ondragenter, ondragleave, ondragover, ondragstart, ondrop, onfocus, onfocusin, onfocusout, onhelp, onlosecapture, onmouseenter, onmouseleave, onmousewheel, onmove, onmoveend, onmovestart, onpaste, onpropertychange, onreadystatechange, onresize, onresizeend, onresizestart, onselectstart, ontimeerror

Element-Specific Attributes

align This attribute controls the horizontal alignment of the rule with respect to the page. The default value is **left**.

color This attribute sets the rule color using either a named color or a color specified in the hexadecimal *#RRGGBB* format. This attribute currently is supported only by Internet Explorer.

noshade This attribute causes the rule to be rendered as a solid bar without shading.

size This attribute indicates the height in pixels of the rule.

width This attribute indicates how wide the rule should be, specified either in pixels or as a percent of screen width, such as 80%.

Examples

```
<hr align="left" noshade="noshade" size="1" width="420" />

<hr align="center" width="100%" size="3" color="#000000" />
```

Compatibility

HTML 2, 3.2, 4, 4.01	Internet Explorer 2, 3, 4, 5, 5.5, 6
XHTML 1.0, 1.1	Netscape 1, 2, 3, 4–4.7, 6, 7
	Opera 4–7

Notes

- The HTML 4.01 strict specification removes support for the **align**, **noshade**, **size**, and **width** attributes for horizontal rules. These effects are possible using style sheets.
- XHTML 1.0 requires a trailing slash for this element: **<hr />**.

<html> (HTML Document)

This element identifies an HTML or XHTML document.

Standard Syntax

```
<html
     dir="ltr | rtl"
     id="unique alphanumeric identifier"
     lang="language code"
     xmlns="http://www.w3.org/1999/xhtml>

</html>
```

Attributes Defined by Internet Explorer

```
     class="class name(s)" (4)
     scroll="yes | no | auto" (6)
```

Events Defined by Internet Explorer

```
onlayoutcomplete, onmouseenter, onmouseleave, onreadystatechange
```

Element-Specific Attributes

scroll This attribute is used to set whether scroll bars should show for the document or not. The default value of **auto** puts in scroll bars as needed. This attribute, while documented by Microsoft, does not appear to work properly and should be avoided.

xmlns This attribute declares a namespace for XML-based custom tags in the document. For XHTML, this value is always http://www.w3.org/1999/xhtml.

Example

```
<!DOCTYPE html PUBLIC "-//W3C//DTD XHTML 1.0 Transitional//EN"
      "http://www.w3.org/TR/xhtml1/DTD/xhtml1-transitional.dtd">
<html xmlns="http://www.w3.org/1999/xhtml" lang="en">
<head>
<title>Minimal Document</title>
<meta http-equiv="content-type" content="text/html; charset=ISO-8859-1" />
</head>
<body>
<p>Hello world!</p>
</body>
</html>
```

Compatibility

HTML 2, 3.2, 4, 4.01	Internet Explorer 2, 3, 4, 5, 5.5, 6
XHTML 1.0, 1.1, Basic	Netscape 1, 1.1 , 2, 3, 4, 4.5–4.8, 6, 7
	Opera 4–7

Notes

- The **html** element is the first element in a document. Except for comments, the only tags it directly contains are **<head>** followed by either **<body>** or **<frameset>**.
- Because it is the outermost tag in a document, the **html** element is called the root element.
- Under the XHTML 1.0 specification, **<html>** can no longer be implied.
- The **<html>** tag and its closing tag **</html>** are both mandatory under XHTML.
- Under HTML 4 transitional, a **version** attribute is supported.

<i> (Italic)

Indicates that the enclosed text should be displayed in an italic typeface.

Standard Syntax

```
<i
     class="class name(s)"
     dir="ltr | rtl"
     id="unique alphanumeric identifier"
     lang="language code"
     style="style information"
     title="advisory text">

</i>
```

Attributes Defined by Internet Explorer

```
accesskey="key" (5.5)
contenteditable="false | true | inherit" (5.5)
disabled="false | true" (5.5)
hidefocus="true | false" (5.5)
language="javascript | jscript | vbs | vbscript" (4)
tabindex="number" (5.5)
unselectable="off | on" (5.5)
```

Standard Event Attributes

onclick, ondblclick, onkeydown, onkeypress, onkeyup, onmousedown, onmousemove, onmouseout, onmouseover, onmouseup

Events Defined by Internet Explorer

onactivate, onbeforeactivate, onbeforecopy, onbeforecut, onbeforedeactivate, onbeforeeditfocus, onbeforepaste, onblur, oncontextmenu, oncontrolselect, oncopy, oncut, ondeactivate, ondrag, ondragend, ondragenter, ondragleave, ondragover, ondragstart, ondrop, onfocus, onfocusin, onfocusout, onhelp, onlosecapture, onmouseenter, onmouseleave, onmousewheel, onmove, onmoveend, onmovestart, onpaste, onpropertychange, onreadystatechange, onresize, onresizeend, onresizestart, onselectstart, ontimeerror

Examples

```
Here is some <i>italicized</i> text.
This is also <i style="color:red;" id="myItalic">italic</i>.
```

Compatibility

HTML 2, 3.2, 4, 4.01	Internet Explorer 4, 5, 5.5, 6
XHTML 1.0, 1.1, Basic	Netscape 4, 4.5–4.8, 6, 7
	Opera 4–7

<iframe> (Floating Frame)

This element indicates a floating frame, an independently controllable content region that can be embedded in a page.

Standard Syntax (Transitional and Frameset Only)

```
<iframe
     align="bottom | left | middle | right | top"
     class="class name(s)"
     dir="ltr | rtl"
     frameborder="1 | 0"
     height="percentage | pixels"
     id="unique alphanumeric identifier"
     lang="language code"
     longdesc="url of description"
     marginheight="pixels"
     marginwidth="pixels"
     name="string"
     scrolling="auto | no | yes"
     src="url of frame contents"
     style="style information"
     title="advisory text"
     width="percentage | pixels">

</iframe>
```

Attributes Defined by Internet Explorer

```
allowtransparency="false | true" (5.5)
application="yes" (5)
border="pixels" (4)
bordercolor="color name | #RRGGBB" (4)
datafld="name of column supplying bound data" (4)
datasrc="id of data source object supplying data" (4)
frameborder="no | yes | 0 | 1" (4)
hidefocus="true | false" (5.5)
hspace="pixels" (4)
language="javascript | jscript | vbs | vbscript" (4)
security="restricted" (6)
tabindex="number" (5.5)
unselectable="on | off" (5.5)
vspace="pixels" (4)
```

Standard Event Attributes

```
onclick, ondblclick, onkeydown, onkeypress, onkeyup, onmousedown, onmousemove,
onmouseout, onmouseover, onmouseup
```

Events Defined by Internet Explorer

```
onactivate, onafterupdate, onbeforedeactivate, onbeforeupdate, onblur,
oncontrolselect, ondeactivate, onerrorupdate, onfocus, onload, onmove, onmoveend,
onmovestart, onreadystatechange, onresizeend, onresizestart, ontimeerror
```

Element-Specific Attributes

align This attribute controls the horizontal alignment of the floating frame with respect to the page. The default is **left**.

allowtransparency This Internet Explorer–specific attribute determines whether the **<iframe>** is transparent or opaque. The default value is **false**, which means it is opaque.

application This Microsoft-specific attribute is used to indicate whether the contents of an **<iframe>** are to be considered an HTA application. HTA applications are applications that use HTML, JavaScript, and Internet Explorer, but are not limited to the typical type of security considerations of a Web page. Given its security implications, this attribute should only be set if the developer is familiar with HTAs.

border This attribute specifies the thickness of the border in pixels.

bordercolor This attribute specifies the color of the border.

datafld This attribute specifies the column name from the data source object that supplies the bound data.

datasrc This attribute indicates the **id** of the data source object that supplies the data that is bound to this element.

frameborder This attribute determines whether the **iframe** is surrounded by a border. The HTML 4 specification defines **0** to be off and **1** to be on. The default value is **1**. Internet Explorer also defines the values **no** and **yes**.

framespacing This attribute creates additional space between the frames.

height This attribute sets the floating frame's height in pixels.

hspace This attribute specifies horizontal padding between the **iframe** and any contents that may flow around it.

longdesc This attribute specifies the URL of a document that contains a long description of the frame's contents.

marginheight This attribute sets the height in pixels between the floating frame's content and its top and bottom borders.

marginwidth This attribute sets the width in pixels between the floating frame's content and its left and right borders.

name This attribute assigns the floating frame a name so that it can be the target destination of hyperlinks.

scrolling This attribute determines whether the frame has scroll bars. A **yes** value forces scroll bars; a **no** value prohibits them. The default value is **auto**.

security This attribute sets the value indicating whether the source file of an **iframe** has security restrictions applied. The only allowed value is **restricted**.

src This attribute contains the URL of the content to be displayed in the floating frame. If absent, the frame is blank.

vspace This attribute specifies vertical padding between an **iframe** and any content that may flow around it.

width This attribute sets the floating frame's width in pixels.

Example

```
<iframe src="http://www.democompany.com" height="150" width="200"
        name="FloatingFrame1">
Sorry, your browser doesn't support inline frames.
</iframe>
```

Compatibility

HTML 4 (transitional)	Internet Explorer 3, 4, 5, 5.5, 6
XHTML 1.0 (transitional or frameset)	Netscape 6, 7
	Opera 5–7

Notes

- Under the HTML 4 strict specification, the **iframe** element is not defined. However, under XHTML transitional and XHTML frameset, **iframe** is allowed. XHTML 1.1 does not allow it either. Floating frames can be somewhat imitated using the **div** element and CSS positioning facilities.
- When a browser does not understand an **<iframe>** tag, it displays the text included within it as an alternate rendering.

<ilayer> (Inflow Layer)

This Netscape 4–specific element allows the definition of overlapping content layers that can be positioned, hidden or shown, rendered transparent or opaque, reordered front to back, and nested. An *inflow layer* is a layer with a relative position that appears where it would naturally occur in the document, in contrast to a *general layer*, which might be positioned absolutely, regardless of its location in a document. The functionality of layers is available using CSS positioning, and page developers are advised not to use this element.

Syntax (Netscape 4 Only)

```
<ilayer
     above="layer"
     background="url of image"
     below="layer"
     bgcolor="color name | #RRGGBB"
     class="class name(s)"
     clip="x1, y1, x2, y2"
     height="percentage | pixels"
     id="unique alphanumeric identifier"
     left="pixels"
     name="string"
     pagex="pixels"
     pagey="pixels"
     src="url of layer contents"
     style="style information"
     top="pixels"
     visibility="hide | inherit | show"
     width="percentage | pixels"
     z-index="number">

</ilayer>
```

Element-Specific Attributes

above This attribute contains the name of the layer to be rendered above the current layer.

background This attribute contains the URL of a background image for the layer.

below This attribute contains the name of the layer to be rendered below the current layer.

bgcolor This attribute specifies a layer's background color. Its value can be either a named color or a color specified in the hexadecimal *#RRGGBB* format.

clip This attribute specifies the clipping region or viewable area of the layer. All layer content outside that rectangle will be rendered as transparent. The **clip** rectangle is defined by two *x,y* pairs: top *x*, left *y*, bottom *x*, and right *y*. Coordinates are relative to the layer's origin point, **0,0**, in its top-left corner.

height This attribute specifies the height of a layer in pixels or percentage values.

left This attribute specifies, in pixels, the horizontal offset of the layer. The offset is relative to its parent layer if it has one or to the left page margin if it does not.

name This attribute assigns the layer a name that can be referenced by programs in a client-side scripting language. The **id** attribute also can be used.

pagex This attribute specifies the horizontal position of the layer relative to the browser window.

pagey This attribute specifies the vertical position of the layer relative to the browser window.

src This attribute is used to set the URL of a file that contains the content to be loaded into the layer.

style This attribute specifies an inline style for the layer.

top This attribute specifies, in pixels, the top offset of the layer. The offset is relative to its parent layer if it has one or the top page margin if it does not.

visibility This attribute specifies whether a layer is hidden, shown, or inherits its visibility from the layer that includes it.

width This attribute specifies a layer's width in pixels.

z-index This attribute specifies a layer's stacking order relative to other layers. Position is specified with positive integers, with **1** indicating the bottommost layer.

Example

```
<p>Content comes before.</p>
<ilayer name="background" bgcolor="green">
  <p>Layered information goes here.</p>
</ilayer>
<p>Content comes after.</p>
```

Compatibility

No standards	Netscape 4, 4.5–4.8

Notes

- Page developers are strongly encouraged not to use this element. Netscape dropped this element for browser versions 6.0 and higher. Its inclusion in this book is for support of existing documents only.

<img> (Image)

This element indicates a media object to be included in an HTML document. Usually, the object is a graphic image, but some implementations support movies and animations.

Standard Syntax

```
<img
     align="bottom | left | middle | right | top" (transitional only)
     alt="alternative text"
     border="pixels" (transitional only)
     class="class name(s)"
     dir="ltr | rtl"
     height="pixels"
     hspace="pixels" (transitional only)
     id="unique alphanumeric identifier"
     ismap="ismap"
     lang="language code"
     longdesc="url of description file"
     name="unique alphanumeric identifier"
     src="url of image"
     style="style information"
     title="advisory text"
     usemap="url of map file"
     vspace="pixels" (transitional only)
     width="pixels" />
```

Attributes Defined by Internet Explorer

```
accesskey="key" (5.5)
align="absbottom | absmiddle | baseline | texttop" (4)
datafld="name of column supplying bound data" (4)
datasrc="id of data source object supplying data" (4)
dynsrc="url of movie" (4)
galleryimg="yes | no | true | false" (6)
hidefocus="true | false" (5.5)
language="javascript | jscript | vbs | vbscript" (4)
loop="infinite | number" (4)
lowsrc="url of low-resolution image" (4)
tabindex="number" (5.5)
unselectable="on | off" (5.5)
```

Standard Events

onclick, ondblclick, onkeydown, onkeypress, onkeyup, onmousedown, onmousemove, onmouseout, onmouseover, onmouseup

Events Defined by Internet Explorer

onabort, onactivate, onafterupdate, onbeforeactivate, onbeforecopy, onbeforecut, onbeforedeactivate, onbeforeeditfocus, onbeforepaste, onblur, oncontextmenu, oncontrolselect, oncopy, oncut, ondeactivate, ondrag, ondragend, ondragenter, ondragleave, ondragover, ondragstart, ondrop, onerrorupdate, onfilterchange, onfocus, onfocusin, onfocusout, onhelp, onload, onlosecapture, onmouseenter, onmouseleave, onmousewheel, onmove, onmoveend, onmovestart, onpaste, onpropertychange, onreadystatechange, onresize, onresizeend, onresizestart, onselectstart, ontimeerror

Element-Specific Attributes

align This attribute controls the horizontal alignment of the image with respect to the page. The default value is **left**. Netscape and Internet Explorer implementations support the **absbottom**, **absmiddle**, **baseline**, and **texttop** values. This attribute is deprecated under strict variants of HTML and XHTML.

alt This attribute contains a string to be displayed instead of the image for browsers that cannot display images.

border This attribute indicates the width, in pixels, of the border surrounding the image.

datafld This attribute specifies the column name from the data source object that supplies the bound data. In this situation, the bound data is used to set the **src** of an **<img>** tag.

datasrc This attribute indicates the **id** of the data source object that supplies the data that is bound to this **<img>** tag.

dynsrc In the Microsoft implementation, this attribute indicates the URL of a movie file and is used instead of the **src** attribute.

galleryimg This Microsoft attribute is used to control whether the gallery image menu should appear when the mouse pointer hovers over an image. The default value is **true** or **yes**. A value of **no** or **false** suppresses the menu. A meta tag like **<meta http-equiv="imagetoolbar" content="no" />** can be used to suppress the image toolbar document wide.

height This attribute indicates the height, in pixels or percentage of the screen, of the image.

hspace This attribute indicates the horizontal space, in pixels, between the image and surrounding text.

ismap This attribute indicates that the image is a server-side image map. User mouse actions over the image are sent to the server for processing.

longdesc This attribute specifies the URL of a document that contains a long description of the image. This attribute is used as a complement to the **alt** attribute.

loop In the Microsoft implementation, this attribute is used with the **dynsrc** attribute to cause a movie to loop. Its value is either a numeric loop count or the keyword **infinite**. Later versions of Internet Explorer suggest using **-1** to suggest infinite.

lowsrc This nonstandard attribute supported in most browsers contains the URL of an image to be initially loaded. Typically, the **lowsrc** image is a low-resolution or black-and-white image that provides a quick preview of the image to follow. Once the primary image is loaded, it replaces the **lowsrc** image.

name This common attribute is used to bind a name to the image. Older browsers understand the **name** field, and in conjunction with scripting languages, it is possible to manipulate images by their defined names to create effects such as "rollover" buttons. While under future versions of HTML and XHTML the **id** attribute specifies element identifiers, **name** can still be used for backward compatibility.

src This attribute indicates the URL of an image file to be displayed.

usemap This attribute makes the image support client-side image mapping. Its argument is a URL specifying the map file, which associates image regions with hyperlinks.

vspace This attribute indicates the vertical space in pixels between the image and surrounding text.

width This attribute indicates the width in pixels of the image.

Examples

```
<img src="mikka.jpg" lowsrc="mikkabw.jpg" alt="Grand Prix Driver"
     height="320" width="150" />

<img src="hugeimagemap.gif" usemap="#mainmap" border="0" height="200"
     width="200" alt="Image Map Here" />

<a href="home.htm"><img src="homebutton.gif" width="50" height="20"
   alt="Link to Home Page" /></a>
```

Compatibility

HTML 2, 3.2, 4, 4.01 XHTML 1.0, 1.1, Basic	Internet Explorer 2, 3, 4, 5, 5.5, 6 Netscape 1, 1.1, 2, 3, 4, 4.5–4.8, 6, 7 Opera 4–7

Notes

- Typically, when you use the **usemap** attribute, the URL is a fragment, such as #map1, rather than a full URL. Some browsers do not support external client-side map files.
- Under the strict HTML and XHTML definitions, the **<img>** tag does not support **align**, **border**, **height**, **hspace**, **vspace**, and **width**. The functionality of these attributes should be possible using style sheet rules.

- Whereas the HTML 4 specification reserves data-binding attributes such as **datafld** or **datasrc**, it is not specified for **<img>**, although Internet Explorer provides support for these attributes.
- XHTML 1.0 requires a trailing slash for this element: **<img />**.
- Under future versions of XHTML such as 2, **<img>** may be dropped in favor of **<object>**.

<input> (Input Form Control)

This element specifies an input control for a form. The type of input is set by the **type** attribute and can be a variety of different types, including single-line text field, password field, hidden, check box, radio button, or push button.

Standard Syntax

```
<input
     accept="MIME types"
     accesskey="character"
     align="bottom | left | middle | right | top" (transitional only)
     alt="text"
     checked="checked"
     class="class name(s)"
     dir="ltr | rtl"
     disabled="disabled"
     id="unique alphanumeric identifier"
     lang="language code"
     maxlength="maximum field size"
     name="field name"
     readonly="readonly"
     size="field size"
     src="url of image file"
     style="style information"
     tabindex="number"
     title="advisory text"
     type="button | checkbox | file | hidden | image |
           password | radio | reset | submit | text"
     usemap="url of map file"
     value="field value" />
```

Standard Event Attributes

```
onchange, onclick, ondblclick, onkeydown, onkeypress, onkeyup, onmousedown,
onmousemove, onmouseout, onmouseover, onmouseup, onselect
```

Attributes Defined by Internet Explorer

```
     autocomplete="off | on" (5) (password, text types only)
     dynsrc="url of movie" (3) (image type only)
     language="javascript | jscript | vbs | vbscript" (4)
     disabled="false | true" (4) (all types except for hidden)
     hidefocus="true | false" (5.5)
     hspace="pixels or percentage" (3)
     loop="number" (4) (image type only)
     lowsrc="url of low-resolution image" (4) (image type only)
     unselectable="off | on" (5.5)
     vspace="pixels or percentage" (3) (image type only)
```

Events Defined by Internet Explorer

```
onactivate, onafterupdate (checkbox, hidden, password, radio, text), onbeforeactivate
(all types except for hidden), onbeforecut (all types except for hidden),
onbeforedeactivate, onbeforeeditfocus, onbeforepaste (all types except for hidden),
onbeforeupdate (checkbox, hidden, password, radio, text), onblur (all types except
for hidden), oncontextmenu (all types except for hidden), oncontrolselect, oncut
(all types except for hidden), ondeactivate, ondrag (all types except for hidden),
ondragend (all types except for hidden), ondragenter (all types except for hidden),
ondragleave (all types except for hidden), ondragover (all types except for hidden),
ondragstart (all types except for hidden), ondrop (all types except for hidden),
onerrorupdate (checkbox, hidden, password, radio, text), onfilterchange (all types
except for hidden), onfocus, onfocusin (all types except for hidden), onfocusout
(all types except for hidden), onhelp (all types except for hidden), onlosecapture,
onmouseenter (all types except for hidden), onmouseleave (all types except for
hidden), onmousewheel (all types except for hidden), onmove, onmoveend, onmovestart,
onpaste (all types except for hidden), onpropertychange, onreadystatechange, onresize
(button, file, image, password, reset, submit, text), onresizeend, onresizestart,
onselectstart (all types except for hidden), ontimeerror
```

Element-Specific Attributes

accept This attribute is used to list the MIME types accepted for file uploads when using a file upload control (**<input type="file">**).

accesskey This attribute specifies a keyboard navigation accelerator for the element. Pressing ALT or a similar key in association with the specified character selects the form control correlated with that key sequence. Page designers are forewarned to avoid key sequences already bound to browsers.

align With image form controls (**type="image"**), this attribute aligns the image with respect to surrounding text. The HTML 4.01 transitional specification defines **bottom**, **left**, **middle**, **right**, and **top** as allowable values. Netscape and Microsoft browsers might also allow the use of attribute values such as **absbottom** or **absmiddle.** Like other presentation-specific aspects of HTML, the **align** attribute is dropped under the strict HTML 4.01 specification.

alt This attribute is used to display an alternative description of image buttons for text-only browsers. The meaning of **alt** for forms of **<input>** beyond **type="image"** is unclear.

autocomplete This Microsoft-specific attribute is used to indicate whether the form field should be automatically filled in or not. The default value is **no**.

checked The **checked** attribute should be used only for check box (**type="checkbox"**) and radio (**type="radio"**) form controls. The presence of this attribute indicates that the control should be displayed in its checked state.

disabled This attribute is used to turn off a form control. Elements will not be submitted, nor will they receive any focus from the keyboard or mouse. Disabled form controls will not be part of the tabbing order. The browser also might gray out the form that is disabled, in order to indicate to the user that the form control is inactive. This attribute requires no value.

dynsrc In the Microsoft implementation, this attribute indicates the URL of a movie file and is used instead of the **src** attribute for **<input type="image">**.

loop In the Microsoft implementation, this attribute is used with **<input type="image">** and the **dynsrc** attribute to cause a movie to loop. Its value is either a numeric loop count or the keyword **infinite**. Later versions of Internet Explorer suggest using **-1** to suggest infinite.

hspace This Internet Explorer-specific attribute indicates the horizontal space in pixels between the image and surrounding text when using **<input type="image">**.

lowsrc This Microsoft-supported attribute contains the URL of an image to be initially loaded when using **<input type="image">**. Typically, the **lowsrc** image is a low-resolution or black-and-white image that provides a quick preview of the image to follow. Once the primary image is loaded, it replaces the **lowsrc** image.

maxlength This attribute indicates the maximum content length that can be entered in a text form control (**type="text"**). The maximum number of characters allowed differs from the visible dimension of the form control, which is set with the **size** attribute.

name This attribute allows a form control to be assigned a name so that it can be referenced by a scripting language. **Name** is supported by older browsers, such as Netscape 2–generation browsers, but the W3C encourages the use of the **id** attribute. For compatibility purposes, both might have to be used.

readonly This attribute prevents the form control's value from being changed. Form controls with this attribute set might receive focus from the user but might not be modified. Because it receives focus, a **readonly** form control will be part of the form's tabbing order. The control's value will be sent on form submission. This attribute can be used only with **<input>** when **type** is set to **text** or **password**. The attribute also is used with the **textarea** element.

size This attribute indicates the visible dimension, in characters, of a text form control (**type="text"**). This differs from the maximum length of content, which can be entered in a form control set by the **maxlength** attribute.

src This attribute is used with image form controls (**type="image"**) to specify the URL of the image file to load.

tabindex This attribute takes a numeric value that indicates the position of the form control in the tabbing index for the form. Tabbing proceeds from the lowest positive **tabindex** value to the highest. Negative values for **tabindex** will leave the form control out of the tabbing order. When tabbing is not explicitly set, the browser tabs through items in the order they are encountered. Disabled form fields will not be part of the tabbing index, although read-only controls will be.

type This attribute specifies the type of the form control. A value of **button** indicates a general-purpose button with no well-defined meaning. However, an action can be associated with the button by using an event handler attribute, such as **onclick**. A value of **checkbox** indicates a check box control. Check box form controls have a checked and unchecked setting, but even if these controls are grouped together, they allow a user to select multiple check boxes at once. In contrast, a value of **radio** indicates a radio button control. When grouped, radio buttons allow only one of the many choices to be selected at a given time.

A form control type of **hidden** indicates a field that is not visible to the viewer but is used to store information. A hidden form control often is used to preserve state information between pages.

A value of **file** for the **type** attribute indicates a control that allows the viewer to upload a file to a server. The filename can be entered in a displayed field, or a user agent might provide a special browse button allowing the user to locate the file. A value of **image** indicates a graphic image form control that a user can click on to invoke an associated action. (Most browsers allow the use of **img**-associated attributes such as **height**, **width**, **hspace**, **vspace**, and **alt** when the **type** value is set to **image**.) A value of **password** for the **type** attribute indicates a password entry field. A password field will not display text entered as it is typed; it might instead show a series of dots.

Note that password-entered data is not transferred to the server in any secure fashion. A value of **reset** for the **type** attribute is used to insert a button that resets all controls within a form to their default values. A value of **submit** inserts a special submission button that, when clicked, sends the contents of the form to the location indicated by the **action** attribute of the enclosing **<form>** tag. Lastly, a value of **text** (the default) for the **type** attribute indicates a single-line text input field.

usemap This HTML 4.0 attribute is used to indicate the map file to be associated with an image when the form control is set with **type="image"**. The value of the attribute should be a URL of a map file, but generally will be in the form of a URL fragment referencing a map file within the current file.

value This attribute has two different uses, depending on the value for the **type** attribute. With data-entry controls (**type="text"** and **type="password"**), this attribute is used to set the default value for the control. When used with check box or radio form controls, this attribute specifies the return value for the control. If not set for these fields, a default value of **on** will be submitted when the control is activated.

vspace This Internet Explorer–specific attribute indicates the vertical space in pixels between the image and surrounding text when using **<input type="image">**.

width This attribute, supported by Internet Explorer, is used to set the size of the form control in pixels.

Examples

```
<form action="#" method="get">
Enter your name: <input type="text" maxlength="35" size="20" /><br />
Enter your password: <input type="password" maxlength="35" size="20" />
<br /><br />
Which is your favorite food?
  <input type="radio" name="favorite" value="Mexican" />Mexican
  <input type="radio" name="favorite" value="Russian" />Russian
  <input type="radio" name="favorite" value="Japanese" />Japanese
  <input type="radio" checked name="favorite" value="Other" />Other
<br/><br />
  <input type="submit" value="Submit" />
  <input type="reset" value="Reset" />
</form>
```

Compatibility

HTML 2, 3.2, 4, 4.01	Internet Explorer 2, 3, 4, 5, 5.5, 6
XHTML 1.0, 1.1, Basic	Netscape 1, 1.1, 2, 3, 4, 4.5–4.8, 6, 7
	Opera 4–7

Notes

- Some documents suggest the use of **type="textarea"**. Even if this strange form is supported, it should be avoided in favor of the **<textarea>** tag, which is common to all browsers.
- The HTML 2.0 and 3.2 specifications support only the **align**, **checked**, **maxlength**, **name**, **size**, **src**, **type**, and **value** attributes for the **input** element.
- The HTML 4.01 specification also reserves the use of the **datafld**, **dataformatas**, and **datasrc** data-binding attributes. They were not included in the XHTML specification but are supported by Internet Explorer.

- Use of **autocomplete** may have security implications. Use with caution.
- Under the strict HTML and XHTML specifications, the **align** attribute is not allowed.
- As an empty element under XHTML, **<input />** requires the trailing slash.

<ins> (Inserted Text)

This element is used to indicate that text has been added to the document.

Standard Syntax

```
<ins
     cite="URL"
     class="class name(s)"
     datetime="date"
     dir="ltr | rtl"
     id="unique alphanumeric identifier"
     lang="language code"
     style="style information"
     title="advisory text">

</ins>
```

Attributes Defined by Internet Explorer

```
     accesskey="key" (5.5)
     contenteditable=" false | true | inherit " (5.5)
     disabled="false | true" (5.5)
     hidefocus="true | false" (5.5)
     language="javascript | jscript | vbs | vbscript" (4)
     tabindex="number"(5.5)
     unselectable="on | off" (5.5)
```

Standard Event Attributes

```
onclick, ondblclick, onkeydown, onkeypress, onkeyup, onmousedown, onmousemove,
onmouseout, onmouseover, onmouseup
```

Events Defined by Internet Explorer

```
onactivate, onbeforedeactivate, onbeforeeditfocus, onblur, oncontrolselect,
ondeactivate, onfocus, onmove, onmoveend, onmovestart, onreadystatechange,
onresizeend, onresizestart, ontimeerror
```

Element-Specific Attributes

cite The value of this attribute is a URL that designates a source document or message for the information inserted. This attribute is intended to point to information explaining why the text was changed.

datetime This attribute is used to indicate the date and time the insertion was made. The value of the attribute is a date in a special format as defined by ISO 8601. The basic date format is

```
yyyy-mm-ddthh:mm:ssTZD
where the following is true:
yyyy=four-digit year such as 1999
mm=two-digit month (01=January, 02=February, and so on)
dd=two-digit day of the month (01 through 31)
hh=two-digit hour (00 to 23) (24-hour clock not AM or PM)
mm=two-digit minute (00 to 59)
ss=two-digit second (00 to 59)
tzd=time zone designator
```

The time zone designator is either **z**, which indicates Universal Time Coordinate, or coordinated universal time format (UTC), or ***+hh:mm***, which indicates that the time is a local time that is *hh* hours and *mm* minutes ahead of UTC. Alternatively, the format for the time zone designator could be ***-hh:mm***, which indicates that the local time is behind UTC. Note that the letter "T" actually appears in the string, all digits must be used, and **00** values for minutes and seconds might be required. An example value for the **datetime** attribute might be **1999-10-6T09:15:00-05:00**, which corresponds to October 6, 1999, 9:15 A.M., U.S. Eastern Standard Time.

Example

```
<ins cite="http://www.bigcompany.com/changes/oct99.html"
     date="1999-10-06T09:15:00-05:00">
The penalty clause applies to client lateness as well.
</ins>
```

Compatibility

HTML 4, 4.01	Internet Explorer 4, 5, 5.5, 6
XHTML 1.0, 1.1	Netscape 6, 7
	Opera 4–7

Notes

- Browsers can render inserted (**<ins>**) or deleted (**<del>**) text in a different style to show the changes that have been made to the document. Eventually, a browser could have a way to show a revision history on a document. User agents that do not understand **<del>** or **<ins>** will show the information anyway, so there is no harm in adding information, only in deleting it.

<isindex> (Index Prompt)

This element indicates that a document has an associated searchable keyword index. When a browser encounters this element, it inserts a query entry field at that point in the document. The viewer can enter query terms to perform a search. This element is deprecated under the strict HTML and XHTML specifications and should not be used.

Standard Syntax (Transitional Only)

```
<isindex
      class="class name(s)"
      dir="ltr | rtl"
      href="url" (nonstandard but common)
      id="unique alphanumeric identifier"
      lang="language code"
      prompt="string"
      style="style information"
      title="advisory text" />
```

Attributes Defined by Internet Explorer

```
accesskey="key" (5.5)
action="URL to send query" (3)
contenteditable=" false | true | inherit" (5.5)
disabled="false | true" (5.5)
hidefocus="true | false" (5.5)
language="javascript | jscript | vbs | vbscript" (4)
tabindex="number" (5.5)
unselectable="on| off" (5.5)
```

Events Defined by Internet Explorer

```
onactivate, onbeforedeactivate, onbeforeeditfocus, onblur, oncontrolselect,
ondeactivate, onfocus, onmove, onmoveend, onmovestart, onreadystatechange, onresize,
onresizeend, onresizestart
```

Element-Specific Attributes

action This attribute specifies the URL of the query action to be executed when the viewer presses the ENTER key. Although this attribute is not defined under any HTML specification, it is common to many browsers, particularly Internet Explorer 3, which defined it.

prompt This attribute allows a custom query prompt to be defined. The default prompt is "This is a searchable index. Enter search keywords."

Examples

```
<isindex action="cgi-bin/search" prompt="Enter search terms" />

<!-- very old HTML style syntax below -->
<base href="cgi-bin/search">
<isindex prompt="Enter search terms" />

<isindex href="cgi-bin/search" prompt="Keywords:" />
```

Compatibility

HTML 2, 3.2, 4, 4.01 (transitional) XHTML 1.0 (transitional)	Internet Explorer 2, 3, 4, 5, 5.5, 6 Netscape 1.1, 2, 3, 4, 4.5–4.8, 6, 7 Opera 4–7

Notes

- Originally, the W3C intended this element to be used in a document's **head**. Browser vendors have relaxed this usage to allow the element in a document's **body**. Early implementations did not support the **action** attribute and used a **<base>** tag or an **href** attribute to specify a search function's URL.
- As an empty element, **<isindex>** requires no closing tag under HTML specifications. However, under the XHTML specification, a trailing slash **<isindex />** is required.
- The HTML 3.2 specification only allows the **prompt** attribute, whereas HTML 2 expected a text description to accompany the search field.
- Netscape 1.1 originated the use of the **prompt** attribute.

<kbd> (Keyboard Input)

This element logically indicates text as keyboard input. A browser generally renders text enclosed by this element in a monospaced font.

Standard Syntax

```
<kbd
     class="class name(s)"
     dir="ltr | rtl"
     id="unique alphanumeric identifier"
     lang="language code"
```

```
     style="style information"
     title="advisory text">

</kbd>
```

Attributes Defined by Internet Explorer

```
     accesskey="key" (5.5)
     contenteditable=" false | true | inherit" (5.5)
     disabled="false | true" (5.5)
     hidefocus="true | false" (5.5)
     language="javascript | jscript | vbs | vbscript" (4)
     tabindex="number" (5.5)
     unselectable="on | off" (5.5)
```

Standard Event Attributes

onclick, ondblclick, onkeydown, onkeypress, onkeyup, onmousedown, onmousemove, onmouseout, onmouseover, onmouseup

Events Defined by Internet Explorer

onactivate, onbeforeactivate, onbeforecut, onbeforedeactivate, onbeforeeditfocus, onbeforepaste, onblur, oncontextmenu, oncontrolselect, oncut, ondeactivate, ondrag, ondragend, ondragenter, ondragleave, ondragover, ondragstart, ondrop, onfocus, onfocusin, onfocusout, onhelp, onlosecapture, onmouseenter, onmouseleave, onmouseup, onmousewheel, onmove, onmoveend, onmovestart, onpaste, onpropertychange, onreadystatechange, onresize, onresizeend, onresizestart, onselectstart, ontimeerror

Example

```
Enter the change directory command at the prompt as shown below:
<br /><br />
<kbd>CD .. </kbd>
```

Compatibility

HTML 2, 3.2, 4, 4.01	Internet Explorer 2, 3, 4, 5, 5.5, 6
XHTML 1.0, 1.1, Basic	Netscape 1, 2, 3, 4–4.7, 6, 7
	Opera 4–7

Notes

- The HTML 2 and 3.2 specifications support no attributes for this element.

<label> (Form Control Label)

This element is used to relate descriptions to form controls.

Standard Syntax

```
<label
     accesskey="key"
     class="class name(s)"
     dir="ltr | rtl"
     for="id of form field"
     id="unique alphanumeric identifier"
     lang="language code"
     style="style information"
     title="advisory text">

</label>
```

Attributes Defined by Internet Explorer

```
contenteditable="false | true | inherit" (5.5)
datafld="column name" (4)
dataformatas="html | text" (4)
datasrc="data source id" (4)
disabled="false | true" (5.5)
hidefocus="true | false" (5.5)
language="javascript | jscript | vbs | vbscript" (4)
tabindex="number" (5.5)
unselectable="on | off" (5.5)
```

Standard Event Attributes

onblur, onclick, ondblclick, onfocus, onkeydown, onkeypress, onkeyup, onmousedown, onmousemove, onmouseout, onmouseover, onmouseup

Events Defined by Internet Explorer

onactivate, onafterupdate, onbeforeactivate, onbeforecopy, onbeforecut, onbeforedeactivate, onbeforeeditfocus, onbeforepaste, onbeforeupdate, onblur, oncontextmenu, oncontrolselect, oncut, ondeactivate, ondrag, ondragend, ondragenter, ondragleave, ondragover, ondragstart, ondrop, onerrorupdate, onfocus, onfocusin, onfocusout, onhelp, onlosecapture, onmouseenter, onmouseleave, onmouseup, onmousewheel, onmove, onmoveend, onmovestart, onpaste, onpropertychange, onreadystatechange, onresize, onresizeend, onresizestart, onselectstart

Element-Specific Attributes

accesskey This attribute specifies a keyboard navigation accelerator for the element. Pressing ALT or a similar key in association with the specified key selects the anchor element correlated with that key.

datafld This attribute is used to indicate the column name in the data source that is bound to the content of a **<label>** tag.

dataformatas This attribute indicates whether the bound data is plain text (**text**) or HTML (**html**). The data bound with **<label>** is used to set the content of the label.

datasrc The value of this attribute is an identifier indicating the data source to pull data from.

for This attribute specifies the **id** for the form control element the label references. This is optional when the label encloses the form control it is bound to. In many cases, particularly when a table is used to structure the form, a **<label>** tag will not be able to enclose the associated form control, so the **for** attribute should be used. This attribute allows more than one label to be associated with the same control by creating multiple references.

Examples

```
<form action="#" method="get">
    <label id="usernamelabel">Name
    <input type="text" id="username" name="username" />
    </label>
</form>

<form>
  <table>
    <tr>
      <td><label for="username">Name</label></td>
      <td><input type="text" id="username" name="username"></td>
```

```
    </tr>
  </table>
</form>
```

Compatibility

HTML 4, 4.01, XHTML 1.0, 1.1, Basic	Internet Explorer 4, 5, 5.5, 6 Netscape 6, 7 Opera 4–7

Notes

- Each **<label>** must not contain more than one form field.
- The **label** element should not be nested.

<layer> (Positioned Layer)

This Netscape-specific element allows the definition of overlapping content layers that can be exactly positioned, hidden or shown, rendered transparent or opaque, reordered front to back, and nested. Most of the functionality of layers is available using CSS positioning facilities. Developers are strongly advised not to use the **layer** element.

Syntax (Defined by Netscape 4 Only)

```
<layer
     above="layer name"
     background="URL of background image"
     below="layer name"
     bgcolor="color value"
     class="class name(s)"
     clip="clip region coordinates in x1, y1, x2, y2 form"
     height="percentage | pixels"
     id="unique alphanumeric identifier"
     left="pixels"
     name="string"
     overflow="none | clip"
     pagex="horizontal pixel position of layer"
     pagey="vertical pixel position of layer"
     src="url of layer's contents"
     style="style information"
     title="advisory text"
     top="pixels"
     visibility="hide | inherit | show"
     width="percentage | pixels"
     z-index="number">

</layer>
```

Element-Specific Attributes

above This attribute contains the name of the layer (as set with the **name** attribute) to be rendered directly above the current layer.

background This attribute contains the URL of a background pattern for the layer. Like backgrounds for the document as a whole, the image might tile.

below This attribute specifies the name of the layer to be rendered below the current layer.

bgcolor This attribute specifies a layer's background color. The attribute's value can be either a named color, such as **red**, or a color specified in the hexadecimal *#RRGGBB* format, such as **#FF0000**.

clip This attribute clips a layer's content to a specified rectangle. All layer content outside that rectangle will be rendered transparent. The **clip** rectangle is defined by two *x,y* pairs that correspond to the top *x*, left *y*, bottom *x*, and right *y* coordinate of the rectangle. The coordinates are relative to the layer's origin point, **0,0**, in its top-left corner, and might have nothing to do with the pixel coordinates of the screen.

height This attribute is used to set the height of the layer, either in pixels or as a percentage of the screen or region the layer is contained within.

left This attribute specifies, in pixels, the left offset of the layer. The offset is relative to its parent layer, if it has one, or to the left browser margin if it does not.

name This attribute assigns the layer a name that can be referenced by programs in a client-side scripting language. The **id** attribute also can be used.

overflow This attribute specifies what should happen when the layer's content exceeds its rendering box and clipping area. A value of **none** does not clip the content, while **clip** clips the content to its dimensions or defined clipping area.

pagex This attribute is used to set the horizontal pixel position of the layer relative to the document window rather than any enclosing layer.

pagey This attribute is used to set the vertical pixel position of the layer relative to the document window rather than any enclosing layer.

src This attribute specifies the URL that contains the content to be included in the layer. Using this attribute with an empty element is a good way to preserve layouts under older browsers.

top This attribute specifies, in pixels, the top offset of the layer. The offset is relative to its parent layer if it has one, or to the top browser margin if it is not enclosed in another layer.

visibility This attribute specifies whether a layer is hidden (**hidden**), shown (**show**), or inherits (**inherits**) its visibility from the layer enclosing it.

width This attribute specifies a layer's width in pixels or as a percentage value of the enclosing layer or browser width.

z-index This attribute specifies a layer's stacking order relative to other layers. Position is specified with positive integers, with **1** indicating the bottommost layer.

Examples

```
<layer name="scene" bgcolor="#00FFFF>
  <layer name="Shaq" left="100" top="100">
    <img src="shaq.gif">
  </layer>
  <layer name="Rodman" left="200" top="100"
         visibility="hidden">
    <img src="pinkhair.gif" alt="hair">
  </layer>
</layer>

<!-- The better way to do layers -->
```

```
<layer src="contents.html" left="20" top="20"
       height="80%" width="80%">
</layer>
```

Compatibility

No standards	Netscape 4, 4.5–4.8

Notes

- Because this element is specific to Netscape 4, it should never be used and is discussed only for readers supporting existing **<layer>**-filled pages.
- Applets, plug-ins, and other embedded media forms, generically called *objects,* can be included in a layer; however, they will float to the top of all other layers, even if their containing layer is obscured.

<legend> (Field Legend)

Used to assign a caption to a set of form fields as defined by a **fieldset** element.

Standard Syntax

```
<legend
     accesskey="character"
     align="bottom | left | right | top" (transitional only)
     class="class name(s)"
     dir="ltr | rtl"
     id="unique alphanumeric identifier"
     lang="language code"
     style="style information"
     title="advisory text">

</legend>
```

Attributes Defined by Internet Explorer

```
     align="center" (4)
     contenteditable=" false | true | inherit" (5.5)
     disabled="false | true" (5.5)
     hidefocus="true | false" (5.5)
     language="javascript | jscript | vbs | vbscript" (4)
     tabindex="number" (5.5)
     unselectable="on | off" (5.5)
```

Standard Event Attributes

```
onclick, ondblclick, onkeydown, onkeypress, onkeyup, onmousedown, onmousemove,
onmouseout, onmouseover, onmouseup
```

Events Defined by Internet Explorer

```
onactivate, onafterupdate, onbeforeactivate, onbeforecopy, onbeforecut,
onbeforedeactivate, onbeforeeditfocus, onbeforepaste, onblur, oncontextmenu,
oncontrolselect, oncopy, oncut, ondeactivate, onerrorupdate, onfocus, onfocusin,
onfocusout, onhelp, onlosecapture, onmouseenter, onmouseleave, onmouseup,
onmousewheel, onmove, onmoveend, onmovestart, onpaste, onpropertychange,
onreadystatechange, onresize, onresizeend, onresizestart, ontimeerror
```

Element-Specific Attributes

accesskey This attribute specifies a keyboard navigation accelerator for the element. Pressing ALT or a similar key in association with the specified key selects the form section or the legend itself.

align This attribute indicates where the legend value should be positioned within the border created by a **<fieldset>** tag. The default position for the legend is the upper-left corner. It also is possible to position the legend to the right by setting the attribute to **right**. The specification defines **bottom** and **top**, as well. Microsoft also defines the use of the value **center**.

Example

```
<form action="#" method="get">
 <fieldset>
   <legend align="top">User Information</legend>
   <label>First Name:
   <input type="text" id="firstname" name="firstname" size="20" />
   </label><br />
   <label>Last Name:
   <input type="text" id="lastname" name="lastname" size="20" />
   </label><br />
 </fieldset>
</form>
```

Compatibility

HTML 4, 4.01, XHTML 1.0, 1.1	Internet Explorer 4, 5, 5.5, 6 Netscape 6, 7 Opera 4–7

Notes

- A **<legend>** tag should occur only within a **<fieldset>** tag. There should be only one **legend** per **fieldset** element.
- The **<legend>** tag improves accessibility when the **fieldset** is not rendered visually.
- Some versions of Microsoft documentation show a **valign** attribute for **<legend>** positioning. However, the **valign** attribute does not appear to work consistently and has since been dropped from the official documentation.

<li> (List Item)

This element is used to indicate a list item as contained in an ordered list (**<ol>**), unordered list (**<ul>**), or older list styles such as **<dir>** and **<menu>**.

Standard Syntax

```
<li
     class="class name(s)"
     dir="ltr | rtl"
     id="unique alphanumeric identifier"
     lang="language code"
     style="style information"
     title="advisory text"
     type="circle | disc | square | a | A | i | I | 1"
     value="number"> (value attribute transitional only)

</li>
```

Attributes Defined by Internet Explorer

```
accesskey="key" (5.5)
contenteditable=" false | true | inherit" (5.5)
disabled="false | true" (5.5)
hidefocus="true | false" (5.5)
language="javascript | jscript | vbs | vbscript" (4)
tabindex="number" (5.5)
unselectable="on | off" (5.5)
```

Standard Event Attributes

onclick, ondblclick, onkeydown, onkeypress, onkeyup, onmousedown, onmousemove, onmouseout, onmouseover, onmouseup

Events Defined by Internet Explorer

onactivate, onbeforeactivate, onbeforecopy, onbeforecut, onbeforedeactivate, onbeforeeditfocus, onbeforepaste, onblur, oncontextmenu, oncontrolselect, oncopy, oncut, ondeactivate, ondrag, ondragend, ondragenter, ondragleave, ondragover, ondragstart, ondrop, onfocus, onfocusin, onfocusout, onhelp, onlayoutcomplete, onlosecapture, onmouseenter, onmouseleave, onmouseup, onmousewheel, onmove, onmoveend, onmovestart, onpaste, onpropertychange, onreadystatechange, onresize, onresizeend, onresizestart, onselectstart, ontimeerror

Element-Specific Attributes

type This attribute indicates the bullet type used in unordered lists or the numbering type used in ordered lists. For ordered lists, a value of **a** indicates lowercase letters, **A** indicates uppercase letters, **i** indicates lowercase Roman numerals, **I** indicates uppercase Roman numerals, and **1** indicates numbers. For unordered lists, values are used to specify bullet types. Although the browser is free to set bullet styles, a value of **disc** generally specifies a filled circle, a value of **circle** specifies an empty circle, and a value of **b** specifies a filled square.

value This attribute indicates the current number of items in an ordered list as defined by an **<ol>** tag. Regardless of the value of **type** being used to set Roman numerals or letters, the only allowed value for this attribute is a number. List items that follow will continue numbering from the value set. The **value** attribute has no meaning for unordered lists.

Examples

```
<ul>
   <li type="circle">First list item is a circle</li>
   <li type="square">Second list item is a square</li>
   <li type="disc">Third list item is a disc</li>
</ul>

<ol>
   <li type="i">Roman Numerals</li>
   <li type="a" value="3">Second list item is letter C</li>
   <li type="a">Continue list in lowercase letters</li>
</ol>
```

Compatibility

HTML 2, 3.2, 4, 4.01	Internet Explorer 2, 3, 4, 5, 5.5, 6
XHTML 1.0, 1.1, Basic	Netscape 1, 2, 3, 4–4.7, 6, 7
	Opera 4–7

Notes

- Under the strict HTML and XHTML definitions, the **li** element loses the **type** and **value** attributes, as these presentation styles can be emulated with style sheets.
- Whereas bullet styles can be set explicitly, browsers tend to change styles for bullets when **<ul>** lists are nested. However, ordered lists generally do not change style automatically, nor do they support outline-style numbering (1.1, 1.1.1, and so on).
- The closing tag **</li>** is optional under HTML specifications and is not commonly used. However, it is required under XHTML and should always be used.

<link> (Link to External Files or Set Relationships)

This empty element specifies relationships between the current document and other documents. Possible uses for this element include defining a relational framework for navigation and linking the document to a style sheet.

Standard Syntax

```
<link
     charset="charset list from RFC 2045"
     class="class name(s)"
     dir="ltr | rtl"
     href="URL"
     hreflang="language code"
     id="unique alphanumeric identifier"
     lang="language code"
     media="all | aural | braille | print | projection |
            screen | other"
     rel="relationship value"
     rev="relationship value"
     style="style information"
     target="frame name" (transitional only)
     title="advisory information"
     type="content type" />
```

Common Attributes

```
     disabled="disabled "  (from DOM Level 1)
```

Standard Event Attributes

```
onclick, ondblclick, onkeydown, onkeypress, onkeyup, onmousedown, onmousemove,
onmouseout, onmouseover, onmouseup
```

Events Defined by Internet Explorer

```
onload, onreadystatechange
```

Element-Specific Attributes

charset This attribute specifies the character set used by the linked document. Allowed values for this attribute are character set names, such as EUC-JP, as defined in RFC 2045.

disabled This DOM Level 1 defined attribute is used to disable a link relationship. The presence of the attribute is all that is required to remove a linking relationship. In conjunction with scripting, this attribute could be used to turn on and off various style sheet relationships. It appears to be an oversight in the HTML and XHTML specifications.

href This attribute specifies the URL of the linked resource. A URL might be absolute or relative.

hreflang This attribute is used to indicate the language of the linked resource. See the "Language Attributes Reference" section earlier in this appendix for information on allowed values.

media This attribute specifies the destination medium for any linked style information, as indicated when the **rel** attribute is set to **stylesheet**. The value of the attribute might be a single media descriptor, such as **screen**, or a comma-separated list. Possible values for this attribute include **all**, **aural**, **braille**, **print**, **projection**, and **screen**. Other values also might be defined, depending on the browser. Internet Explorer supports **all**, **print**, and **screen** as values for this attribute.

rel This attribute names a relationship between the linked document and the current document. Possible values for this attribute include **alternate, bookmark**, **chapter**, **contents**, **copyright**, **glossary**, **help**, **index**, **next**, **prev**, **section**, **start**, **stylesheet**, and **subsection**.

The most common use of this attribute is to specify a link to an external style sheet. The **rel** attribute is set to **stylesheet**, and the **href** attribute is set to the URL of an external style sheet to format the page.

rev The value of the **rev** attribute shows the relationship of the current document to the linked document, as defined by the **href** attribute. The attribute thus defines the reverse relationship compared to the value of the **rel** attribute. Values for the **rev** attribute are similar to the possible values for **rel**. They might include **alternate**, **bookmark**, **chapter**, **contents**, **copyright**, **glossary**, **help**, **index**, **next**, **prev**, **section**, **start**, **stylesheet**, and **subsection**.

target The value of the **target** attribute defines the frame or window name that has the defined linking relationship or that will show the rendering of any linked resource.

type This attribute is used to define the type of the content linked to. The value of the attribute should be a MIME type, such as **text/html**, **text/css**, and so on. The common use of this attribute is to define the type of style sheet linked, and the most common current value is **text/css**, which indicates a cascading style sheet format.

Examples

```
<link href="products.html" rel="parent" />

<link href="corpstyle.css" rel="stylesheet" type="text/css" media="all" />

<link href="nextpagetoload.html" rel="next" />
```

Compatibility

HTML 2, 3.2, 4, 4.01	Internet Explorer 3, 4, 5, 5.5, 6
XHTML 1.0, 1.1, Basic	Netscape 4–4.7, 6, 7
	Opera 4–7

Notes

- Under XHTML 1.0, empty elements such as **<link>** require a trailing slash: **<link />**.
- A **<link>** tag can occur only in the **head** element; however, there can be multiple occurrences of **<link>**.
- HTML 3.2 defines only the **href**, **rel**, **rev**, and **title** attributes for the **link** element.

- HTML 2 defines the **href, methods, rel, rev, title,** and **urn** attributes for the **link** element. The **methods** and **urn** attributes were later removed from the specifications.
- The HTML and XHTML specifications define event handlers for the **link** element, but it is unclear how they would be used.

<listing> (Code Listing)

This deprecated element from HTML 2 is used to indicate a code listing; it is no longer part of the HTML standard. Text tends to be rendered in a smaller size within this element. The **pre** element should be used instead of **listing** to indicate preformatted text.

Standard Syntax (HTML 2 Only; Deprecated)

```
<listing>
</listing>
```

Attributes Defined by Internet Explorer

```
accesskey="key" (5.5)
class="class name(s)" (4)
contenteditable=" false | true | inherit" (5.5)
dir="ltr | rtl" (5.5)
disabled="false | true" (5.5)
hidefocus="true | false" (5.5)
id="unique alphanumeric string" (4)
lang="language code" (4)
language="javascript | jscript | vbs | vbscript" (4)
style="style information" (4)
tabindex="number" (5.5)
title="advisory text" (4)
unselectable="on | off" (5.5)
```

Events Defined by Internet Explorer

```
onactivate, onbeforeactivate, onbeforecopy, onbeforecut, onbeforedeactivate,
onbeforeeditfocus, onbeforepaste, onblur, onclick, oncontextmenu, oncontrolselect,
oncopy, oncut, ondblclick, ondeactivate, ondrag, ondragend, ondragenter, ondragleave,
ondragover, ondragstart, ondrop, onfocus, onfocusin, onfocusout, onhelp, onkeydown,
onkeypress, onkeyup, onlosecapture, onmousedown, onmouseenter, onmouseleave,
onmousemove, onmouseout, onmouseover, onmouseup, onmousewheel, onmove, onmoveend,
onmovestart, onpaste, onpropertychange, onreadystatechange, onresize, onresizeend,
onresizestart, onselectstart, ontimeerror
```

Example

```
<listing>
This is a code listing. The preformatted text element &lt;PRE&gt;
should be used instead of this deprecated element.
</listing>
```

Compatibility

HTML 2	Internet Explorer 2, 3, 4, 5, 5.6, 6 Netscape 1, 2, 3, 4–4.7, 6, 7 Opera 6, 7

Notes

- As a deprecated element, this element should not be used. This element is not supported by HTML 4, XHTML 1.0, or 1.1. It is still documented and supported by many browser vendors, however, and does creep into some pages. The **pre** element should be used instead of **<listing>**.
- It appears that Internet Explorer browsers also make text within **<listing>** one size smaller than normal text, probably because the HTML 2 specification suggested that 132 characters fit to a typical line rather than 80.

<map> (Client-Side Image Map)

This element is used to implement client-side image maps. The element is used to define a map that associates locations on an image with a destination URL. Each hot spot or hyperlink mapping is defined by an enclosed **area** element. A map is bound to a particular image through the use of the **usemap** attribute in the **img** element, which is set to the name of the map.

Syntax

```
<map
     class="class name(s)"
     dir="ltr | rtl"
     id="unique alphanumeric identifier"
     lang="language code"
     name="unique alphanumeric identifier"
     style="style information"
     title="advisory text">

</map>
```

Standard Event Attributes

```
onclick, ondblclick, onkeydown, onkeypress, onkeyup, onmousedown, onmousemove,
onmouseout, onmouseover, onmouseup
```

Events Defined by Internet Explorer

```
onbeforeactivate, onbeforecut, onbeforepaste, oncut, ondrag, ondragend, ondragenter,
ondragleave, ondragover, ondragstart, ondrop, onfocusin, onfocusout, onhelp,
onlosecapture, onmouseenter, onmouseleave, onmousewheel, onpaste, onpropertychange,
onreadystatechange, onscroll, onselectstart
```

Element-Specific Attributes

name Like **id**, this attribute is used to define a name associated with the element. In the case of the **map** element, the **name** attribute is the common way to define the name of the image map to be referenced by the **usemap** attribute within an **<img>** tag.

Example

```
<map name="mainmap" id="mainmap">
   <area shape="circle" coords="200,250,25"
         href="file1.html" />
   <area shape="rectangle" coords="50,50,100,100"
         href="file2.html#important" />
   <area shape="default" nohref="nohref" />
</map>
```

Compatibility

HTML 3.2, 4, 4.01	Internet Explorer 2, 3, 4, 5, 5.5, 6
XHTML 1.0, 1.1	Netscape 1, 2, 3, 4–4.7, 6, 7
	Opera 4–7

Notes

- HTML 3.2 supports only the **name** attribute for the **map** element.
- Client-side image maps are not supported under HTML 2. They were first suggested by Spyglass and later incorporated in Netscape and other browsers.

<marquee> (Marquee Display)

This proprietary element specifies a scrolling, sliding, or bouncing text marquee.

Proprietary Syntax (Defined by Internet Explorer)

```
<marquee
     accesskey="key" (5.5)
     behavior="alternate | scroll | slide" (3)
     bgcolor="color name | #RRGGBB" (3)
     class="class name(s)" (4)
     contenteditable=" false | true | inherit" (5.5)
     datafld="column name" (4)
     dataformatas="html | text" (4)
     datasrc="data source id" (4)
     direction="down | left | right | up" (3)
     dir="ltr | rtl" (5.0)
     disabled="false | true" (5.5)
     height="pixels or percentage"
     hidefocus="true | false" (5.5)
     hspace="pixels" (3)
     id="unique alphanumeric identifier" (4)
     lang="language code" (4)
     language="javascript | jscript | vbs | vbscript" (4)
     loop="infinite | number" (3)
     scrollamount="pixels" (3)
     scrolldelay="milliseconds" (3)
     style="style information" (4)
     tabindex="number" (5.5)
     title="advisory text" (4)
     truespeed="false | true" (4)
     unselectable="on | off" (5.5)
     vspace="pixels" (3)
     width="pixels or percentage" (3)
>

</marquee>
```

Events Defined by Internet Explorer

```
onactivate, onafterupdate, onbeforeactivate, onbeforecut, onbeforedeactivate,
onbeforeeditfocus, onbeforepaste, onbeforeupdate, onblur, onbounce, onclick,
oncontextmenu, oncontrolselect, oncut, ondblclick, ondeactivate, ondrag, ondragend,
ondragenter, ondragleave, ondragover, ondragstart, ondrop, onerrorupdate,
onfilterchange, onfinish, onfocus, onfocusin, onfocusout, onhelp, onkeydown,
onkeypress, onkeyup, onlosecapture, onmousedown, onmouseenter, onmouseleave,
onmousemove, onmouseout, onmouseover, onmouseup, onmousewheel, onmove, onmoveend,
```

```
onmovestart, onpaste, onpropertychange, onreadystatechange, onresize, onresizeend,
onresizestart, onscroll,  onselectstart, onstart, ontimeerror, ondeactivate
```

Element-Specific Attributes

behavior This attribute controls the movement of marquee text across the marquee. The **alternate** option causes text to completely cross the marquee field in one direction and then cross in the opposite direction. A value of **scroll** for the attribute causes text to wrap around and start over again. This is the default value for a marquee. A value of **slide** for this attribute causes text to cross the marquee field and stop when its leading character reaches the opposite side.

bgcolor This attribute specifies the marquee's background color. The value for the attribute can either be a color name or a color value defined in the hexadecimal *#RRGGBB* format.

datafld This attribute is used to indicate the column name in the data source that is bound to the **marquee** element.

dataformatas This attribute indicates whether the bound data is plain text (**text**) or HTML (**html**). The data bound with **marquee** is used to set the message that is scrolled.

datasrc The value of this attribute is set to an identifier indicating the data source from which data is to be pulled. Bound data is used to set the message that is scrolled in the **marquee**.

direction This attribute specifies the direction in which the marquee should scroll. The default is **left**. Other possible values for **direction** include **down**, **right**, and **up**.

height This attribute specifies the height of the marquee in pixels or as a percentage of the window.

hspace This attribute indicates the horizontal space in pixels between the marquee and surrounding content.

loop This attribute indicates the number of times the marquee content should loop. By default, a marquee loops infinitely unless the **behavior** attribute is set to **slide**. It also is possible to use a value of **infinite** or **–1** to set the text to loop indefinitely.

scrollamount This attribute specifies the width in pixels between successive displays of the scrolling text in the marquee.

scrolldelay This attribute specifies the delay in milliseconds between successive displays of the text in the marquee.

truespeed When this attribute is present, it indicates that the **scrolldelay** value should be honored for its exact value. If the attribute is not present, any values less than 60 are rounded up to 60 milliseconds.

vspace This attribute indicates the vertical space in pixels between the marquee and surrounding content.

width This attribute specifies the width of the marquee in pixels or as a percentage of the enclosing window.

Examples

```
<marquee behavior="alternate">
SPECIAL VALUE !!! This week only !!!
</marquee>
```

```
<marquee id="marquee1" bgcolor="red" direction="right" height="30"
       width="80%" hspace="10" vspace="10">
The super scroller scrolls again!!
More fun than a barrel of &lt;BLINK&gt; elements.
</marquee>
```

Compatibility

No Standards	Internet Explorer 3, 4, 5, 5.5, 6 Limited functionality in Netscape 6, 7

Notes

- This is primarily a Microsoft-specific element, although a few other browsers, notably MSN TV and later Netscape and Mozilla versions, support it to some degree.

<menu> (Menu List)

This element is used to indicate a short list of items that can occur in a menu of choices.

Syntax (Transitional Only)

```
<menu
     class="class name(s)"
     compact="compact"
     dir="ltr | rtl"
     id="unique alphanumeric string"
     lang="language code"
     style="style information"
     title="advisory text">
</menu>
```

Attributes Defined by Internet Explorer

```
     accesskey="key" (5.5)
     contenteditable=" false | true | inherit" (5.5)
     disabled="false | true" (5.5)
     hidefocus="true | false" (5.5)
     tabindex="number" (5.50
     unselectable="on | off" (5.5)
```

Events Defined by Internet Explorer

```
onactivate, onbeforeactivate, onbeforecopy, onbeforecut, onbeforedeactivate,
onbeforeeditfocus, onbeforepaste, onblur, oncontextmenu, oncontrolselect, oncopy,
oncut, ondeactivate, ondrag, ondragend, ondragenter, ondragleave, ondragover,
ondragstart, ondrop, onfocus, onfocusin, onfocusout, onhelp, onlosecapture,
onmouseenter, onmouseleave, onmousewheel, onmove, onmoveend, onmovestart, onpaste,
onpropertychange, onreadystatechange, onresize, onresizeend, onresizestart,
onselectstart, ontimeerror
```

Element-Specific Attributes

compact This attribute indicates that the list should be rendered in a compact style. Few browsers actually change the rendering of the list regardless of the presence of this attribute. The **compact** attribute requires no value under traditional HTML but should be set to a value of **compact** under XHTML transitional.

Example

```
<h2>Taco List</h2>
  <menu>
    <li>Fish</li>
    <li>Pork</li>
    <li>Beef</li>
    <li>Chicken</li>
  </menu>
```

Compatibility

HTML 2, 3.2, 4, 4.01 (transitional)	Internet Explorer 2, 3, 4, 5, 5.5, 6
XHTML 1.0 (transitional)	Netscape 1, 2, 3, 4, 4.5–4.8, 6, 7
	Opera 4–7

Notes

- Under the strict HTML and XHTML specifications, this element is not defined. Because most browsers simply render this style of list as an unordered list, using the **<ul>** tag instead is preferable.
- The HTML 2.0 and 3.2 specifications support only the **compact** attribute.
- Most browsers tend not to support the **compact** attribute.

<meta> (Meta-Information)

This element specifies general information about a document that can be used in document indexing. It also allows a document to simulate HTTP response headers which are useful for cache control, page ratings, page refresh time, and other useful things.

Standard Syntax

```
<meta
     content="string"
     dir="ltr | rtl"
     http-equiv="http header string"
     id="unique alphanumeric string"
     lang="language code"
     name="name of meta-information"
     scheme="scheme type" />
```

Events Defined by Internet Explorer

```
onlayoutcomplete
```

Element-Specific Attributes

content This attribute contains the actual meta-information. The form of the meta-information varies greatly, depending on the value set for **name**.

http-equiv This attribute binds the meta-information in the **content** attribute to an HTTP response header. If this attribute is present, the **name** attribute should not be used.

lang This attribute is the language code associated with the language used in the **content** attribute.

name This attribute associates a name with the meta-information contained in the **content** attribute. If present, the **http-equiv** attribute should not be used.

scheme The scheme attribute is used to indicate the expected format of the value of the **content** attribute. The particular scheme also can be used in conjunction with the metadata profile, as indicated by the **profile** attribute for the **head** element.

Examples

```
<!-- Use of the meta element to assist document indexing -->
<meta name="keywords" content="html, scripting"
      scheme="Lycos" />

<!-- Use of the meta element to implement client-pull to automatically
     load a page -->
<meta http-equiv="refresh"
      content="3;URL='http://www.pint.com/'" />

<!-- Use of the META element to add rating information -->
<meta http-equiv="PICS-Label" content="(PICS-1.1
                'http://www.rsac.org/ratingsv01.html'
                 1 gen true comment 'RSACi North America
                 Server' by 'webmaster@bigcompany.com'
                 for 'http://www.bigcompany.com' on
                '1999.05.26T13:05-0500'
                 r (n 0 s 0 v 0 1 1))" />
```

Compatibility

HTML 2, 3.2, 4, 4.01	Internet Explorer 2, 3, 4, 5, 5.5, 6
XHTML 1.0, 1.1, Basic	Netscape 1.1, 2, 3, 4, 4.5–4.8, 6, 7
	Opera 4–7

Notes

- The **meta** element can occur only in the **head** element. It can be defined multiple times.
- The **meta** element is an empty element (as defined in the HTML specifications) and does not have a closing tag nor contain any content. However, under XHTML 1.0, empty elements such as **<meta>** require a trailing slash: **<meta />**.
- A common use of the **meta** element is to set information for indexing tools, such as search engines. Common values for the **name** attribute when performing this function include **author**, **description**, and **keywords**; other attributes also might be possible.
- The **http-equiv** attribute is often used to create a document that automatically loads another document after a set time. This is called *client-pull*. An example of a client-pull **meta** element is **<meta http-equiv="refresh" content="10;URL='nextpage.html'" />**. Note that the **content** attribute contains two values. The first is the number of seconds to wait, and the second is the identifier URL and the URL to load after the specified time.
- The **http-equiv** attribute is also used for page ratings, cache control, setting defaults such as language or scripting, and a variety of other tasks. In many cases, it would be better to set these values via the actual HTTP headers rather than via a **<meta>** tag.
- The HTML 2.0 and 3.2 specifications define only the **content**, **http-equiv**, and **name** attributes.

<multicol> (Multiple Column Text)

This Netscape-specific element renders the enclosed content in multiple columns. This element should not be used; a table is a more standard way to render multiple columns of text across browsers.

Proprietary Syntax (Defined by Netscape)

```
<multicol
     class="class name(s)"
     cols="number of columns"
     gutter="pixels"
     id="unique alphanumeric identifier"
     style="style information"
     width="pixels">

</multicol>
```

Element-Specific Attributes

cols This attribute indicates the number of columns in which to display the text. The browser attempts to fill the columns evenly.

gutter This attribute indicates the width in pixels between the columns. The default value for this attribute is **10** pixels.

width This attribute indicates the column width for all columns. The width of each column is set in pixels and is equivalent for all columns in the group. If the attribute is not specified, the width of columns will be determined by taking the available window size, subtracting the number of pixels for the gutter between the columns (as specified by the **gutter** attribute), and evenly dividing the result by the number of columns in the group (as set by the **cols** attribute).

Example

```
<multicol cols="3" gutter="20">
Put a long piece of text here....
</multicol>
```

Compatibility

No standards	Netscape 3, 4, 4.5–4.8

Notes

- Page developers are strongly encouraged not to use this element. Netscape dropped this element for browser versions 6.0 and higher. Its inclusion in this book is for support of existing documents only.

<nobr> (No Breaks)

This proprietary element renders enclosed text without line breaks. Break points for where text may wrap can be inserted using the **wbr** element.

Common Syntax

```
<nobr
     class="class name(s)"
     id="unique alphanumeric identifier"
     style="style information"
```

```
    title="advisory text">

</nobr>
```

Attributes Defined by Internet Explorer

```
    contenteditable=" false | true | inherit " (5.5)
    dir="ltr | rtl" (5.5)
    disabled="false | true" (5.5)
    unselectable="on | off" (5.5)
```

Events Defined by Internet Explorer

```
onbeforeactivate, onbeforecopy, onbeforecut, onbeforeedit, onbeforepaste, oncopy,
oncut, ondrag, ondragend, ondragenter, ondragleave, ondragover, ondragstart,
ondrop, onfocusin, onfocusout, onhelp, onlosecapture, onmouseenter, onmouseleave,
onmousewheel, onpaste, onpropertychange, onreadystatechange, onscroll, onselectstart
```

Examples

```
<nobr>This really long text ... will not be broken.</nobr>

<nobr>With this element it is often important to hint where a line may
be broken using &lt;wbr&gt;.<wbr> This element acts as a soft return.</nobr>
```

Compatibility

No standards	Internet Explorer 2, 3, 4, 5, 5.5, 6 Netscape 1.1, 2, 3, 4–4.7, 7 Opera 4–7

Notes

- While many browsers support this attribute, it is not part of any W3C standard.

<noembed> (No Embedded Media Support)

This Netscape-specific element is used to indicate alternative content to be displayed on browsers that cannot support an embedded media object. It should occur in conjunction with the **embed** element.

Proprietary Syntax (Defined by Netscape)

```
<noembed>
Alternative content for non-embed supporting browsers
</noembed>
```

Element-Specific Attributes

Netscape does not specifically define attributes for this element; however, Netscape documentation suggests that **class**, **id**, **style**, and **title** might be supported for this element.

Example

```
<embed src="trailer.mov" height="150" width="150">
   <noembed>
      <img src="trailer.gif" alt="movie trailer" />
      <br />
   Sorry, this browser is not configured to display video.
   </noembed>
</embed>
```

Compatibility

No standards	Netscape 2, 3, 4–4.7

Notes

- This element will disappear as the **<object>** style of inserting media into a page becomes more common.
- Even if other browsers do not support the tag and render its contents, it works in the manner it was designed.

<noframes> (No Frame Support Content)

This element is used to indicate alternative content to be displayed on browsers that do not support frames.

Standard Syntax

```
<noframes
     class="class name(s)"
     dir="ltr | rtl"
     id="unique alphanumeric identifier"
     lang="language code"
     style="style information"
     title="advisory text">

        Alternative content for non-frame-supporting browsers

</noframes>
```

Events Defined by Internet Explorer

```
onreadystatechange
```

Example

```
<frameset rows="100,*">
  <frame src="controls.html"> name-"frame1" id="frame1"
  <frame src="content.html"> "name=frame2" id="frame2"
    <noframes>
    Sorry, this browser does not support frames.
    </noframes>
</frameset>
```

Compatibility

HTML 4, 4.01 (transitional and frameset) XHTML 1.0 (transitional and frameset)	Internet Explorer 2, 3, 4, 5, 5.5, 6 Netscape 2, 3, 4–4.7, 6, 7 Opera 4–7

Notes

- This element should be used within the scope of the **frameset** element.
- The benefit of events and sophisticated attributes, such as **style**, is unclear for browsers that would use content within **<noframes>**, given that older browsers that don't support frames probably would not support these features.

<noscript> (No Script Support Content)

This element is used to enclose content that should be rendered on browsers that do not support scripting or that have scripting turned off.

Syntax

```
<noscript
     class="class name(s)"
     dir="ltr | rtl"
     id="unique alphanumeric identifier"
     lang="language code"
     style="style information"
     title="advisory text">

        Alternative content for non-script-supporting browsers

</noscript>
```

Events Defined by Internet Explorer

```
onreadystatechange
```

Example

```
<script language="type/javascript">
<!--
window.location="http://www.pint.com";
// -->
</script>
<noscript>
  JavaScript is not supported. Follow this
  <a href="http://www.pint.com">link</a> instead.
</noscript>
```

Compatibility

HTML 4, 4.01	Internet Explorer 3, 4, 5, 5.5, 6
XHTML 1.0, 1.1	Netscape 2, 3, 4, 4.5–4.8, 6, 7
	Opera 4–7

Notes

- Improved functionality for the **noscript** element might come if it is extended to deal with the lack of support for one scripting language or another. Currently, the element is used only to indicate whether any scripting is supported or not.
- Oddly **<noscript>** is not allowed in the head even though **<script>** is.

<object> (Embedded Object)

This element specifies an arbitrary object to be included in an HTML document. Initially, this element was used to insert ActiveX controls, but according to the specification, an object can be any media object, document, applet, ActiveX control, or even image.

Standard Syntax

```
<object
     align="bottom | left | middle | right | top" (transitional only)
     archive="url"
```

```
    border="percentage | pixels" (transitional only)
    class="class name(s)"
    classid="id"
    codebase="URL"
    codetype="MIME Type"
    data="URL of data"
    declare="declare"
    dir="ltr | rtl"
    height="percentage | pixels"
    hspace="percentage | pixels" (transitional only)
    id="unique alphanumeric identifier"
    lang="language code"
    name="unique alphanumeric name"
    standby="standby text string"
    style="style information"
    tabindex="number"
    title="advisory text"
    type="MIME Type"
    usemap="URL"
    vspace="percentage | pixels" (transitional only)
    width="percentage | pixels">

param elements and alternative rendering

</object>
```

Attributes Defined by Internet Explorer

```
accesskey="character" (4)
align="absbottom | absmiddle | baseline | texttop" (4)
code="url" (4)
datafld="column name" (4)
datasrc="id for bound data" (4)
hidefocus="true | false" (5.5)
language="javascript | jscript | vbs | vbscript" (4)
unselectable="on | off" (5.5)
```

Standard Event Attributes

```
onclick, ondblclick, onkeydown, onkeypress, onkeyup, onmousedown, onmousemove,
onmouseout, onmouseover, onmouseup
```

Events Defined by Internet Explorer

```
onactivate, onbeforedeactivate, onbeforeeditfocus, onblur, oncellchange,
oncontrolselect, ondataavailable, ondatasetchanged, ondatasetcomplete, ondeactivate,
ondrag, ondragend, ondragenter, ondragleave, ondragover, ondragstart, ondrop,
onerror, onfocus, onlosecapture, onmove, onmoveend, onmovestart, onpropertychange,
onreadystatechange, onresize, onresizeend, onresizestart, onrowenter, onrowexit,
onrowsdelete, onrowsinserted, onscroll, onselectstart
```

Element-Specific Attributes

align This attribute aligns the object with respect to the surrounding text. The default is **left**. The HTML specification defines **bottom**, **middle**, **right**, and **top**, as well. Browsers might provide an even richer set of alignment values. The behavior of alignment for objects is similar to images. Under the strict HTML and XHTML specifications, the **object** element does not support this attribute.

archive This attribute contains a URL for the location of an archive file. An archive file typically is used to contain multiple object files to improve the efficiency of access.

border This attribute specifies the width of the object's borders in pixels or as a percentage.

classid This attribute contains a URL for an object's implementation. The URL syntax depends upon the object's type. With ActiveX controls, the value of this attribute does not appear to be a URL but something of the form *CLSID: object-id*; for example, **CLSID: 99B42120-6EC7-11CF-A6C7-00AA00A47DD2**.

code Under the old Microsoft implementation, this attribute contains the URL referencing a Java applet class file. The way to access a Java applet under the HTML/XHTML specification is to use **<object classid="java: classname.class">**. The pseudo-URL *java:* is used to indicate a Java applet. Microsoft Internet Explorer 4 and beyond support this style, so **code** should not be used.

codebase This attribute contains a URL to use as a relative base to access the object specified by the **classid** attribute.

codetype This attribute specifies an object's MIME type. Do not confuse this attribute with **type**, which specifies the MIME type of the data the object may use, as defined by the **data** attribute.

data This attribute contains a URL for data required by an object.

datafld This Microsoft-specific attribute is used to indicate the column name in the data source that is bound to the **object** element.

datasrc The value of this Microsoft-specific attribute is set to an identifier indicating the data source to pull data from.

declare This attribute declares an object without instantiating it. This is useful when the object will be a parameter to another object. In traditional HTML, this attribute takes no value; under XHTML, set it equal to **declare**.

height This attribute specifies the height of the object in pixels or as a percentage of the enclosing window.

hspace This attribute indicates the horizontal space, in pixels or percentages, between the object and surrounding content.

name Under the Microsoft definition, this attribute defines the name of the control so scripting can access it. Older HTML specifications suggest that it is a name for form submission, but this meaning is unclear and not supported by browsers.

standby This attribute contains a text message to be displayed while the object is loading.

tabindex This attribute takes a numeric value indicating the position of the object in the tabbing index for the document. Tabbing proceeds from the lowest positive **tabindex** value to the highest. Negative values for **tabindex** will leave the object out of the tabbing order. When tabbing is not explicitly set, the browser can tab through items in the order they are encountered.

type This attribute specifies the MIME type for the object's data. This is different from the **codetype**, which is the MIME type of the object and not of the data it uses.

usemap This attribute contains the URL of the image map to be used with the object. Typically, the URL will be a fragment identifier referencing a **map** element somewhere else within the file. The presence of this attribute indicates that the type of object being included is an image.

vspace This attribute indicates the vertical space, in pixels or percentages, between the object and surrounding text.

width This attribute specifies the width of the object in pixels or as a percentage of the enclosing window or block element.

Examples

```
<object id="IeLabel1" width="325" height="65"
        classid="CLSID:99B42120-6EC7-11CF-A6C7-00AA00A47DD2">
   <param name="_ExtentX" value="6879" />
   <param name ="_ExtentY" value="1376" />
   <param name="Caption" value="Hello World" />
   <param name="Alignment" value="4" />
   <param name="Mode" value="1" />
   <param name="ForeColor" value="#FF0000" />
   <param name="FontName" value="Arial" />
   <param name="FontSize" value="36" />
        <b>Hello World for non-ActiveX users!</b>
</object>

<object classid="java:Blink.class"
        standby="Here it comes"
        height="100" width="300">
   <param name="lbl" value="Java is fun, exciting, and new." />
   <param name="speed" value="2" />
This will display in non-Java-aware or -enabled browsers.
</object>

<object data="pullinthisfile.html">
Data not included!
</object>
```

Compatibility

HTML 4, 4.01	Internet Explorer 3, 4, 5, 5.5, 6, 7
XHTML 1.0, 1.1, Basic	Netscape 4, 4.5–4.8, 6, 7
	Opera 4–7

Notes

- Under the strict HTML and XHTML specifications, the **object** element loses most of its presentation attributes, including **align**, **border**, **height**, **hspace**, **vspace**, and **width**. These attributes are replaced by style sheet rules.
- The HTML 4.01 specification reserves the **datafld**, **dataformatas**, and **datasrc** attributes for future use. However, these attributes were dropped in XHTML, though they are well supported by Internet Explorer 4 and beyond.
- Alternative content should be defined within an **<object>** tag after any enclosed **<param>** tags.
- The **object** element is still mainly used to include multimedia binaries in pages. Although the specification defines that it can load in HTML files and create image maps, not every browser supports this, and few developers are aware of these features. In theory, this very versatile tag should take over duties from the venerable **<img>** tag in future XHTML specifications.
- See Chapter 15 for specific examples of **object** and an expanded discussion.

<ol> (Ordered List)

This element is used to define an ordered or numbered list of items. The numbering style comes in many forms, including letters, Roman numerals, and regular numerals. The individual items within the list are specified by **li** elements included with the **ol** element.

Standard Syntax

```
<ol
     class="class name(s)"
     compact="compact" (transitional only)
     dir="ltr | rtl"
     id="unique alphanumeric identifier"
     lang="language code"
     start="number" (transitional only)
     style="style information"
     title="advisory text"
     type="a | A | i | I | 1"> (type attribute transitional only)

  li elements only

</ol>
```

Attributes Defined by Internet Explorer

```
     accesskey="key" (5.5)
     contenteditable="false | true | inherit" (5.5)
     disabled="false | true" (5.5)
     hidefocus="true | false" (5.5)
     language="javascript | jscript | vbs | vbscript" (4)
     tabindex="number" (5.5)
     unselectable="on | off" (5.5)
```

Standard Event Attributes

```
onclick, ondblclick, onkeydown, onkeypress, onkeyup, onmousedown, onmousemove,
onmouseout, onmouseover, onmouseup
```

Events Defined by Internet Explorer

```
onactivate, onbeforeactivate, onbeforecopy, onbeforecut, onbeforedeactivate,
onbeforeeditfocus, onbeforepaste, onblur, oncontextmenu, oncontrolselect, oncopy,
oncut, ondeactivate, ondrag, ondragend, ondragenter, ondragleave, ondragover,
ondragstart, ondrop, onfocus, onfocusin, onfocusout, onhelp, onlayoutcomplete,
onlosecapture, onmouseenter, onmouseleave, onmousewheel, onmove, onmoveend,
onmovestart, onpaste, onpropertychange, onreadystatechange, onresize, onresizeend,
onresizestart, onselectstart, ontimeerror
```

Element-Specific Attributes

compact This attribute indicates that the list should be rendered in a compact style. Few browsers actually change the rendering of the list regardless of the presence of this attribute. The **compact** attribute requires no value under traditional HTML, but under XHTML should be set to **compact**.

start This attribute specifies the start value for numbering the individual list items. Although the ordering type of list elements might be Roman numerals, such as XXXI, or letters, the value of **start** is always represented as a number. To start numbering elements from the letter "C," use **<ol type="A" start="3">**.

type This attribute indicates the numbering type: **a** indicates lowercase letters, **A** indicates uppercase letters, **i** indicates lowercase Roman numerals, **I** indicates uppercase Roman numerals, and **1** indicates numbers. Type set in an **ol** element is used for the entire list unless a **type** attribute is used within an enclosed **li** element.

Examples

```
<ol type="1">
   <li>First step</li>
   <li>Second step</li>
   <li>Third step</li>
</ol>
<ol compact="compact" type="I" start="30">
   <li>Clause 30</li>
   <li>Clause 31</li>
   <li>Clause 32</li>
</ol>
```

Compatibility

HTML 2, 3.2, 4, 4.01	Internet Explorer 2, 3, 4, 5, 5.5, 6
XHTML 1.0, 1.1, Basic	Netscape 1, 2, 3, 4, 4.5–4.8, 6, 7
	Opera 4–7

Notes

- Under the strict HTML and XHTML specifications, the **ol** element no longer supports the **compact**, **start**, and **type** attributes. These aspects of lists can be controlled with style sheet rules.
- Under the XHTML 1.0 specification, the **compact** attribute no longer can be minimized, but must have a quoted attribute value: **<ol compact="compact">**.
- The HTML 3.2 specification supports only the **compact**, **start**, and **type** attributes.
- The HTML 2.0 specification supports only the **compact** attribute.

<optgroup> (Option Grouping)

This element specifies a grouping of items in a selection list defined by **option** elements so that the menu choices can be presented in a hierarchical menu or similar alternative fashion to improve access through nonvisual browsers.

Standard Syntax

```
<optgroup
     class="class name(s)"
     dir="ltr | rtl"
     disabled="disabled"
     id="unique alphanumeric identifier"
     label="text description"
     lang="language code"
     style="style information"
     title="advisory text">

          option elements

</optgroup>
```

Standard Event Attributes

```
onclick, ondblclick, onkeydown, onkeypress, onkeyup, onmousedown, onmousemove,
onmouseout, onmouseover, onmouseup
```

Element-Specific Attributes

disabled Occurrence of this attribute indicates that the enclosed set of options is disabled.

label This attribute contains a short label that might be more appealing to use when the selection list is rendered as items in a hierarchy.

Example

```
Where would you like to go for your vacation?
<select name="vacation" id="vacation">
  <option id="ch1" value="Hong Kong">Hong Kong</option>
  <optgroup label="South Pacific">
    <option id="ch2" label="Australia" value="Australia">
     Australia</option>
    <option id="ch3" label="Fiji" value="Fiji">
     Wakaya (Fiji Islands)</option>
   <option id="ch4" value="New Zealand">
     New Zealand</option>
  </optgroup>
    <option id="ch5" value="home" selected="selected">Your backyard</option>
</select>
```

Compatibility

HTML 4, 4.01	Internet Explorer 6
XHTML 1.0, 1.1	Netscape 6, 7
	Opera 7

Notes

- This element should occur only within the context of a **select** element.
- Only the most modern browsers present this element in a visually meaningful fashion.

<option> (Option in Selection List)

This element specifies an item in a selection list defined by the **select** element.

Standard Syntax

```
<option
     class="class name(s)"
     dir="ltr | rtl"
     disabled="disabled"
     id="unique alphanumeric identifier"
     label="text description"
     lang="language code"
     selected="selected"
     style="style information"
     title="advisory text"
     value="option value">

</option>
```

Attributes Defined by Internet Explorer

```
language="javascript | jscript | vbs | vbscript" (4)
```

Standard Event Attributes

```
onclick, ondblclick, onkeydown, onkeypress, onkeyup, onmousedown, onmousemove,
onmouseout, onmouseover, onmouseup
```

Events Defined by Internet Explorer

```
onlayoutcomplete, onlosecapture, onpropertychange, onreadystatechange, onselectstart,
ontimeerror
```

Element-Specific Attributes

disabled Presence of this attribute indicates that the particular item is not selectable. Traditional HTML did not require a value for this attribute, but it should be set to **disabled** under XHTML.

label This attribute contains a short label that might be more appealing to use when the selection list is rendered as a hierarchy due to the presence of an **optgroup** element.

selected This attribute indicates that the associated item is the default selection. If not included, the first item in the selection list is the default. If the **select** element enclosing the **option** elements has the **multiple** attribute, the **selected** attribute might occur in multiple entries. Otherwise, it should occur in only one entry. Under XHTML, the value of the selected attribute must be set to **selected**.

value This attribute indicates the value to be included with the form result when the item is selected.

Example

```
Which is your favorite dog?:
<select>
   <option value="Scotty">Angus</option>
   <option value="Golden Retriever">Borrego</option>
   <option value="Choco Lab">Dutch</option>
   <option value="Mini Schnauzer" selected="selected">Tucker</option>
</select>
```

Compatibility

HTML 2, 3.2. 4, 4.01	Internet Explorer 2, 3, 4, 5, 5.5, 6
XHTML 1.0, 1.1, Basic	Netscape 1, 2, 3, 4, 4.5–4.8, 6, 7
	Opera 4–7

Notes

- Under HTML specifications, the closing tag for **<option>** is optional. However, for XHTML compatibility the closing tag **</option>** is required.
- This element should occur only within the context of a **select** element.
- The HTML 2.0 and 3.2 specifications define only the **selected** and **value** attributes for this element.

<p> (Paragraph)

This element is used to define a paragraph of text.

Standard Syntax

```
<p
     align="center | justify | left | right" (transitional only)
     class="class name(s)"
     dir="ltr | rtl"
     id="unique alphanumeric identifier"
     lang="language code"
     style="style information"
     title="advisory text">

</p>
```

Attributes Defined by Internet Explorer

```
     accesskey="key" (5.5)
     contenteditable="false | true | inherit" (5.5)
     disabled="false | true" (5.5)
     hidefocus="true | false" (5.5)
     language="javascript | jscript | vbs | vbscript" (4)
     tabindex="number" (5.5)
     unselectable="on | off" (5.5)
```

Standard Event Attributes

onclick, ondblclick, onkeydown, onkeypress, onkeyup, onmousedown, onmousemove, onmouseout, onmouseover, onmouseup

Events Defined by Internet Explorer

onactivate, onbeforeactivate, onbeforecopy, onbeforecut, onbeforedeactivate, onbeforeeditfocus, onbeforepaste, onblur, oncontextmenu, oncontrolselect, oncopy, oncut, ondeactivate, ondrag, ondragend, ondragenter, ondragleave, ondragover, ondragstart, ondrop, onfocus, onfocusin, onfocusout, onhelp, onlayoutcomplete, onlosecapture, onmouseenter, onmouseleave, onmousewheel, onmove, onmoveend, onmovestart, onpaste, onpropertychange, onreadystatechange, onresize, onresizeend, onresizestart, onselectstart, ontimeerror

Element-Specific Attributes

align This attribute specifies the alignment of text within a paragraph. The default value is **left**. The transitional specification of HTML 4.01 also defines **center**, **justify**, and **right**. However, under the strict HTML and XHTML specifications, text alignment can be handled through a style sheet rule.

Examples

```
<p align="right">A right-aligned paragraph</p>

<p id="para1" class="defaultParagraph"
   title="Introduction Paragraph">
This is the introductory paragraph for a very long paper about nothing.
</p>
```

Compatibility

HTML 2, 3.2, 4, 4.01	Internet Explorer 2, 3, 4, 5, 5.5, 6
XHTML 1.0, 1.1, Basic	Netscape 1, 2, 3, 4, 4.5–4.8, 6, 7
	Opera 4–7

Notes

- Because **p** is a block element browsers typically insert a blank line, but this rendering should not be assumed, given the rise of style sheets.
- Under the strict HTML and XHTML specifications, the **align** attribute is not supported. Alignment of text can instead be accomplished using style sheets.
- The closing tag for the **<p>** tag is optional under the HTML specification; however, under the XHTML 1.0 specification, the closing tag **</p>** is required for XHTML compatibility.
- As a logical element, empty paragraphs are ignored by browsers, so do not try to use multiple **<p>** tags in a row, like **<p><p><p><p>**, to add blank lines to a Web page. This will not work; use the **
** tag instead.
- Remove the empty paragraph **<p> </p>** markup inserted by WYSIWYG editors.
- The HTML 3.2 specification supports only the **align** attribute with values of **center**, **left**, and **right**.
- The HTML 2.0 specification supports no attributes for the **p** element.

<param> (Object Parameter)

This element specifies a parameter to be passed to an embedded object that is specified with the **object** or **applet** elements. This element should occur only within the scope of one of these elements.

Standard Syntax

```
<param
     id="unique alphanumeric identifier"
     name="parameter name"
     type="mime Type"
     value="parameter value"
     valuetype="data | object | ref" />
```

Attributes Defined by Internet Explorer

```
     datafld="column name" (4)
     dataformatas="html | text" (4)
     datasrc="data source id" (4)
```

Element-Specific Attributes

datafld This Internet Explorer–specific attribute is used to indicate the column name in the data source that is bound to the **<param>** tag's value.

dataformatas This Internet Explorer–specific attribute indicates whether the bound data is plain text (**text**) or HTML (**html**).

datasrc The value of this attribute is set to an identifier indicating the data source to pull data from. Bound data is used to set the value of the parameters passed to the object or applet with which this **<param>** tag is associated.

name This attribute contains the parameter's name. The name of the parameter depends on the particular object being inserted into the page, and it is assumed that the object knows how to handle the passed data. Do not confuse the **name** attribute for this element with the **name** attribute used for form elements. In the latter case, the **name** attribute does not have a similar meaning to **id**, but rather specifies the name of the data to be passed to an enclosing **<object>** tag.

type When the **valuetype** attribute is set to **ref**, the **type** attribute can be used to indicate the type of the information to be retrieved. Legal values for this attribute are in the form of MIME types, such as **text/html**.

value This attribute contains the parameter's value. The actual content of this attribute depends on the object and the particular parameter being passed in, as determined by the **name** attribute.

valuetype This attribute specifies the type of the **value** attribute being passed in. Possible values for this attribute include **data**, **object**, and **ref**. A value of **data** specifies that the information passed in through the **value** parameter should be treated just as data. A value of **ref** indicates that the information being passed in is a URL that indicates where the data to be used is located. The information is not retrieved, but the URL is passed to the object, which then can retrieve the information if necessary. The last value of **object** indicates that the value being passed in is the name of an object as set by its **id** attribute. In practice, the **data** attribute is used by default.

Examples

```
<applet code="plot.class">
   <param name="min" value="5" />
   <param name="max" value="30" />
   <param name="ticks" value=".5" />
   <param name="line-style" value="dotted" />
</applet>

<object classid="clsid:D27CDB6E-AE6D-11cf-96B8-444553540000"
        codebase="swflash.cab#version=2,0,0,0"
        height="100" width="100">
   <param id="param1" name="Movie" value="SplashLogo.swf" />
   <param id="param2" name="Play" value="True" />
</object>
```

Compatibility

HTML 3.2, 4, 4.01	Internet Explorer 3, 4, 5, 6
XHTML 1.0, 1.1, Basic	Netscape 4, 4.5–4.8, 6, 7
	Opera 5–7

Notes

- The HTML 3.2 specification supports only the **name** and **value** attributes for this element.
- Under XHTML 1.0, empty elements such as **<param>** require a trailing forward slash: **<param />**.

<plaintext> (Plain Text)

This deprecated element from the HTML 2.0 specification renders the enclosed text as plain text and forces the browser to ignore any enclosed HTML. Typically, information affected by the **<plaintext>** tag is rendered in monospaced font. This element is no longer part of the HTML standard and should never be used.

Syntax (HTML 2; Deprecated Under HTML 4)

```
<plaintext>
```

Attributes Defined by Internet Explorer

```
accesskey="key" (5.5)
class="class name(s)" (4)
contenteditable="false | true | inherit" (5.5)
disabled="false | true" (5.5)
dir="ltr | rtl" (4)
hidefocus="true | false" (5.5)
id="unique alphanumeric identifier" (4)
lang="language code" (4)
language="javascript | jscript | vbs | vbscript" (4)
style="style information" (4)
tabindex="number" (5.5)
title="advisory text" (4)
```

Example

```
<!DOCTYPE html PUBLIC "-//IETF//DTD HTML 2.0//EN">
<html>
<head><title>Plaintext Example</title></head>
<body>
   The rest of this file is in plain text.
   <plaintext>
   Even though this is supposed to be <b>bold</b>, the tags still show.
   There is no way to turn plain text off once it is on. </plaintext>
   does nothing to help. Even </body> and </html> will show up.
```

Compatibility

HTML 2	Internet Explorer 2, 3, 4, 5, 5.5, 6 Netscape 1, 2, 3, 4, 4.5–4.8, 6, 7 Opera 4–7

Notes

- No closing tag for this element is necessary because the browser will ignore all tags after the starting tag.
- This element should not be used. Plain text information can be indicated by a file type, and information can be inserted in a preformatted fashion using the **pre** element.
- Most browsers continue to support this tag despite documentation to the contrary.

<pre> (Preformatted Text)

This element is used to indicate that the enclosed text is preformatted, meaning that spaces, returns, tabs, and other formatting characters are preserved. Browsers will, however, acknowledge most

HTML elements that are found within a **<pre>** tag. Preformatted text generally will be rendered by the browsers in a monospaced font.

Standard Syntax

```
<pre
     class="class name(s)"
     dir="ltr | rtl"
     id="unique alphanumeric value"
     lang="language code"
     style="style information"
     title="advisory text"
     width="number"   (transitional only)
     xml:space="preserve">

</pre>
```

Attributes Defined by Internet Explorer

```
     accesskey="key" (5.5)
     contenteditable="false | true | inherit" (5.5)
     disabled="false | true" (5.5)
     hidefocus="true | false" (5.5)
     language="javascript | jscript | vbs | vbscript" (4)
     tabindex="number" (5.5)
     wrap="soft | hard | off" (4)
```

Standard Event Attributes

```
onclick, ondblclick, onkeydown, onkeypress, onkeyup, onmousedown, onmousemove,
onmouseout, onmouseover, onmouseup
```

Events Defined by Internet Explorer

```
onactivate, onbeforeactivate, onbeforecopy, onbeforecut, onbeforedeactivate,
onbeforeeditfocus, onbeforepaste, onblur, oncontextmenu, oncontrolselect, oncopy,
oncut, ondeactivate, ondrag, ondragend, ondragenter, ondragleave, ondragover,
ondragstart, ondrop, onfocus, onfocusin, onfocusout, onhelp, onlosecapture,
onmouseenter, onmouseleave, onmousewheel, onmove, onmoveend, onmovestart, onpaste,
onpropertychange, onreadystatechange, onresize, onresizeend, onresizestart,
onselectstart, ontimeerror
```

Element-Specific Attributes

width This attribute should be set to the width of the preformatted region. The value of the attribute should be the number of characters to display. In practice, this attribute is not supported and is dropped under the strict HTML 4.01 specification.

wrap In some versions of Microsoft browsers, this attribute controls word wrap behavior within a **<pre>** tag. The default value of **off** for the attribute forces the element not to wrap text, so the author must manually enter line breaks. Values of **hard** or **soft** cause word wrap and set different types of line breaks in the wrapped text. Given the nature of the **pre** element, the value of this attribute is limited.

xml:space This attribute is included from XHTML 1.0 and is used to set whether spaces need to be preserved within the element or whether the default white space handling should be employed. It is curious that an element defined to override traditional white space rules would allow such an attribute, and in practice this attribute is not used by developers.

Example

```
<pre>
   Within PREFORMATTED text      A L L    formatting IS   PRESERVED
   NO  m    a    t    t   e   r how wild it is. Remember that some
   <b>HTML</b> markup is allowed within the &lt;PRE&gt; element.
</pre>
```

Compatibility

HTML 2, 3.2, 4, 4.01	Internet Explorer 2, 3, 4, 5, 5.5, 6
XHTML 1.0, 1.1, Basic	Netscape 1, 2, 3, 4, 4.5–4.8, 6, 7
	Opera 4–7

Notes

- The HTML 4.01 and XHTML 1.0 transitional specifications state that the **applet**, **basefont**, **big**, **font**, **img**, **object**, **small**, **sub**, and **sup** elements should not be used within the **<pre>** tag. The strict HTML and XHTML specifications state that only the **<big>**, **<img>**, **<object>**, **<small>**, **<sub>**, and **<sup>** tags should not be used within the **<pre>** tag. The other excluded elements are missing, as they are deprecated from the strict specification. Although these elements should not be used, it appears that the two most popular browsers will render them anyway.
- The strict HTML and XHTML specifications drop support for the **width** attribute, which was not well-supported anyway.
- The HTML 2.0 and 3.2 specifications support only the **width** attribute for **<pre>**.

<q> (Quote)

This element indicates that the enclosed text is a short inline quotation.

Standard Syntax

```
<q
     cite="url of source"
     class="class name(s)"
     dir="ltr | rtl"
     id="unique alphanumeric string"
     lang="language code"
     style="style information"
     title="advisory text">

</q>
```

Attributes Defined by Internet Explorer

```
     accesskey="key" (5.5)
     contenteditable="false | true | inherit" (5.5)
     disabled="false | true" (5.5)
     hidefocus="true | false" (5.5)
     language="javascript | jscript | vbs | vbscript" (4)
     tabindex="number" (5.5)
```

Standard Event Attributes

```
onclick, ondblclick, onkeydown, onkeypress, onkeyup, onmousedown, onmousemove,
onmouseout, onmouseover, onmouseup
```

Events Defined by Internet Explorer

```
onactivate, onbeforedeactivate, onbeforeeditfocus, onblur, oncontrolselect,
ondeactivate, ondrag, ondragend, ondragenter, ondragleave, ondragover, ondragstart,
ondrop, onfocus, onmouseenter, onmouseleave, onmove, onmoveend, onmovestart,
onreadystatechange, onresizeend, onresizestart, onselectstart, ontimeerror
```

Element-Specific Attributes

cite The value of this attribute is a URL that designates a source document or message for the information quoted. This attribute is intended to point to information explaining the context or the reference for the quote.

Example

```
<q style="color: green;">A few green balls and a rainbow bar will
give you an exciting Web page Christmas Tree!</q>
```

Compatibility

HTML 4, 4.01	Internet Explorer 4, 5, 5.5, 6
XHTML 1.0, 1.1, Basic	Netscape 6, 7
	Opera 4–7

Notes

- This element is intended for short quotations that don't require paragraph breaks, as compared to text that would be contained within **<blockquote>**.
- Some browsers, like Internet Explorer, may not make any sort of style change for quotations, but it is possible to apply a style rule.
- Most modern standards-aware browsers, like Mozilla, Opera, and Safari, should add quotes around text enclosed within the **q** element.

rt (Ruby Text)

This initially Microsoft-specific proprietary element is used within a <**ruby**> tag to create *ruby text*, or annotations or pronunciation guides for words and phrases. The base text should be enclosed in a <**ruby**> tag; the annotation, enclosed in an <**rt**> **tag**, will appear as smaller text above the base text. A variation on this element is defined by XHTML 1.1.

Syntax (Defined by Microsoft)

```
<rt
     accesskey="key" (5)
     class="class name(s)" (5)
     contenteditable="false | true | inherit" (5.5)
     dir="ltr | rtl" (5)
     disabled="false | true" (5.5)
     hidefocus="true | false" (5.5)
     id="unique alphanumeric identifier" (5)
     lang="language code" (5)
     language="javascript | jscript | vbs | vbscript | xml" (5)
```

```
     name="string" (5)
     style="style information" (5)
     tabindex="number" (5)
     title="advisory text" (5)
     unselectable="on | off"> (5)

       ... ruby text ..
</rt>
```

Events Defined by Internet Explorer

```
onactivate, onafterupdate, onbeforeactivate, onbeforecut, onbeforepaste, oncut,
ondrag, ondragend, ondragenter, ondragleave, ondragover, ondragstart, ondrop,
onfocusin, onfocusout, onhelp, onlosecapture, onmouseenter, onmouseleave,
onmousewheel, onpaste, onpropertychange, onreadystatechange, onscroll, onselectstart
```

Example

```
<ruby>Base Text
     <rt>Ruby Text</rt>
</ruby>
```

Compatibility

XHTML 1.1	Internet Explorer 5, 5.5, 6

Notes

- This element works only in Internet Explorer 5.0 and higher.
- The **rt** element must be used within the **ruby** element.
- Microsoft defines **rt** as an inline element that requires no closing tag; however, under the Ruby XHTML specification, it does have a close tag, so it should be used in support of the future standard being widely adopted.
- At the time of this edition's writing in 2003, this element should be used only in an Internet Explorer–exclusive environment because other browsers will not interpret it or the **ruby** element yet, despite the rise of the Ruby module for XHTML 1.1.

ruby

This Microsoft-specific proprietary element is used with the **rt** element to create annotations or pronunciation guides for words and phrases. The base text should be enclosed in a **<ruby>** tag; the annotation, enclosed in a **<rt>** tag, will appear as smaller text above the base text.

Syntax Defined by Microsoft

```
<ruby
     accesskey="key" (5)
     class="class name(s)" (5)
     contenteditable="false | true | inherit" (5.5)
     dir="ltr | rtl" (5)
     disabled="false | true" (5.5)
     hidefocus="true | false" (5.5)
     id="unique alphanumeric identifier" (5)
     lang="language code" (5)
     language="javascript | jscript | vbs | vbscript | xml" (5)
     name="string" (5)
     style="style information" (5)
```

```
     tabindex="number" (5)
     title="advisory text"> (5)

          ... base text ...
        <rt>ruby text</rt>

</ruby>
```

Events Defined by Internet Explorer

```
onactivate, onafterupdate, onbeforeactivate, onbeforecut, onbeforepaste, oncut,
ondrag, ondragend, ondragenter, ondragleave, ondragover, ondragstart, ondrop,
onfocusin, onfocusout, onhelp, onlosecapture, onmouseenter, onmouseleave,
onmousewheel, onpaste, onpropertychange, onreadystatechange, onscroll, onselectstart
```

Element-Specific Attributes

name Sets a name for the ruby base text.

Example

```
<ruby>This is the base text within the ruby element

<rt>This is the ruby text, which should appear in a smaller font
    above the base text in Internet Explorer 5.0 or higher.</rt>

</ruby>

<ruby>Base Text
     <rt>Ruby Text</rt>
</ruby>
```

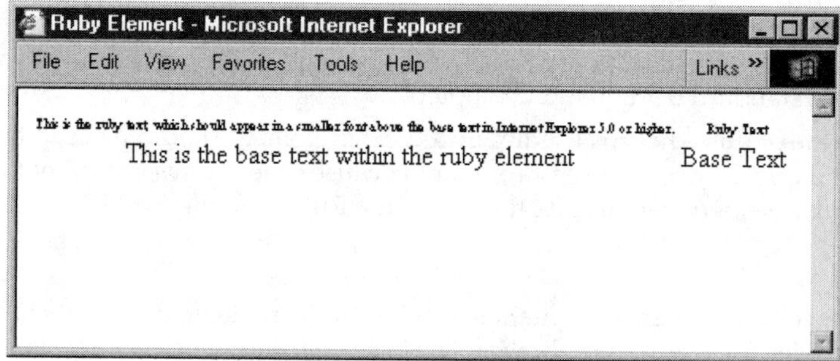

Compatibility

XHTML 1.1 Internet Explorer 5, 5.5, 6

Notes

- This element works only in Internet Explorer 5.0 and higher.
- The **ruby** element must be used in conjunction with the **rt** element; otherwise, it will have no meaning.
- At the time of this edition's writing in 2003, this element should be used only in an Internet Explorer–exclusive environment because other browsers will not interpret it or the **rt** element yet, despite the rise of the Ruby module for XHTML 1.1.

<s> (Strikethrough)

This element renders the enclosed text with a line drawn through it.

Standard Syntax (Transitional Only)

```
<s
     class="class name(s)"
     dir="ltr | rtl"
     id="unique alphanumeric identifier"
     lang="language code"
     style="style information"
     title="advisory text">

</s>
```

Attributes Defined by Internet Explorer

```
     accesskey="key" (5.5)
     contenteditable="false | true | inherit" (5.5)
     disabled="false | true" (5.5)
     hidefocus="true | false" (5.5)
     language="javascript | jscript | vbs | vbscript" (4)
     tabindex="number" (5.5)
     unselectable="off | on" (5.5)
```

Standard Event Attributes

```
onclick, ondblclick, onkeydown, onkeypress, onkeyup, onmousedown, onmousemove,
onmouseout, onmouseover, onmouseup
```

Events Defined by Internet Explorer

```
onactivate, onbeforeactivate, onbeforecopy, onbeforecut, onbeforedeactivate,
onbeforeeditfocus, onbeforepaste, onblur, oncontextmenu, oncontrolselect, oncopy,
oncut, ondeactivate, ondrag, ondragend, ondragenter, ondragleave, ondragover,
ondragstart, ondrop, onfocus, onfocusin, onfocusout, onhelp, onlosecapture,
onmouseenter, onmouseleave, onmousewheel, onmove, onmoveend, onmovestart, onpaste,
onpropertychange, onreadystatechange, onresize, onresizeend, onresizestart,
onselectstart, ontimeerror
```

Examples

```
This line contains a <s>misstake</s>.
<s id="strike1"
   onmouseover="this.style.color='red';"
   onmouseout="this.style.color='black';">Fastball</s>
```

Compatibility

HTML 4, 4.01 transitional XHTML 1.0 transitional	Internet Explorer 2, 3, 4, 5, 5.5, 6 Netscape 3, 4, 4.5–4.8, 6, 7 Opera 4, 5, 6, 7

Notes

- This element should act the same as the **strike** element.
- This HTML 3 element eventually was adopted by Netscape and Microsoft and later was incorporated into the HTML 4.01 transitional specification.

- This element has been deprecated by the W3C. The strict HTML 4.01 specification does not include the **s** element or the **strike** element. It is possible to indicate strikethrough text using a style sheet.

<samp> (Sample Text)

This element is used to indicate sample text. Enclosed text generally is rendered in a monospaced font.

Standard Syntax

```
<samp
     class="class name(s)"
     dir="ltr | rtl"
     id="unique alphanumeric string"
     lang="language code"
     style="style information"
     title="advisory text">

</samp>
```

Attributes Defined by Internet Explorer

```
     accesskey="key" (5.5)
     contenteditable="false | true | inherit" (5.5)
     disabled="false | true"  (5.5)
     hidefocus="true | false" (5.5)
     language="javascript | jscript | vbs | vbscript" (4)
     tabindex="number" (5.5)
     unselectable="off | on" (5.5)
```

Standard Event Attributes

```
onclick, ondblclick, onkeydown, onkeypress, onkeyup, onmousedown, onmousemove,
onmouseout, onmouseover, onmouseup
```

Events Defined by Internet Explorer

```
onactivate, onbeforeactivate, onbeforecopy, onbeforecut, onbeforedeactivate,
onbeforeeditfocus, onbeforepaste, oncontextmenu, oncontrolselect, oncopy, oncut,
ondeactivate, ondrag, ondragend, ondragenter, ondragleave, ondragover, ondragstart,
ondrop, onfocus, onfocusin, onfocusout, onhelp, onlosecapture, onmouseenter,
onmouseleave, onmousewheel, onmove, onmoveend, onmovestart, onpaste, onpropertychange,
onreadystatechange, onresize, onresizeend, onresizestart, onselectstart, ontimeerror
```

Example

```
Use the following salutation in all e-mail messages to the boss:
<samp>Please excuse the interruption, oh exalted manager.</samp>
```

Compatibility

HTML 2, 3.2, 4, 4.01	Internet Explorer 2, 3, 4, 5, 5.5, 6
XHTML 1.0, 1.1, Basic	Netscape 1, 2, 3, 4, 4.5–4.8, 6, 7
	Opera 4, 6, 7

Notes

- As a logical element, **samp** is useful to bind style rules to.
- The HTML 2.0 and 3.2 specifications support no attributes for this element.

<script> (Scripting)

This element encloses statements in a scripting language for client-side processing. Scripting statements can either be included inline or loaded from an external file and might be commented out to avoid execution by nonscripting-aware browsers.

Standard Syntax

```
<script
     charset="character set"
     defer="defer"
     id="unique alphanumeric identifier"
     language="scripting language name"
     src="url of script code"
     type="mime type"
     xml:space="preserve">

</script>
```

Attributes Defined by Internet Explorer

```
     event="event name" (3)
     for="element ID" (3)
```

Events Defined by Internet Explorer

```
onload, onpropertychange, onreadystatechange
```

Element-Specific Attributes

charset This attribute defines the character encoding of the script. The value is a space- and/or comma-delimited list of character sets as defined in RFC 2045. The default value is **ISO-8859-1**.

defer Presence of this attribute indicates that the browser might defer execution of the script enclosed by the **<script>** tag. In practice, deferring code might be more dependent on the position of the **<script>** tag or the contents. Support for this attribute is inconsistent.

event This Microsoft-specific attribute is used to define a particular event that the script should react to. It must be used in conjunction with the **for** attribute. Event names are the same as event handler attributes; for example, **onclick**, **ondblclick**, and so on.

for The **for** attribute is used in Microsoft browsers to define the name or ID of the element to which an event defined by the **event** attribute is related. For example, **<script event="onclick" for="button1" language="vbscript">** defines a VBScript that will execute when a click event is issued for an element named button1.

language This attribute specifies the scripting language being used. The Netscape implementation supports JavaScript. The Microsoft implementation supports JScript (a JavaScript clone) as well as VBScript, which can be indicated by either **vbs** or **vbscript**. IE does recognize the value of "JavaScript" in the **language** attribute, regardless of how they name their scripting language. Other values that include the version of the language used, such as **JavaScript1.1** and **JavaScript1.2**, also might be possible and are useful to exclude browsers from executing script code that is not supported.

src This attribute specifies the URL of a file containing scripting code. Typically, files containing JavaScript code will have a .js extension, and a server will attach the appropriate MIME type; if not, the **type** attribute might be used to explicitly set the content type of the external script file. The **language** attribute also might be helpful in determining this.

type This attribute should be set to the MIME type corresponding to the scripting language used. For JavaScript, for example, this would be **text/javascript**. In practice, the **language** attribute is the more common way to indicate which scripting language is in effect, but the **type** attribute is standard.

xml:space This attribute is included from XHTML 1.0 on, and is used to set whether spaces need to be preserved within the script element or whether the default white space handling should be employed. In practice, this attribute is not used by developers.

Examples

```
<script type="text/javascript">
alert("Hello World !!!");
</script>

<!-- code in external file -->
<script language="JavaScript1.2" src="superrollover.js"></script>
```

Compatibility

HTML 4, 4.01	Internet Explorer 3, 4, 5, 5.5, 6
XHTML 1.0, 1.1	Netscape 2, 3, 4, 4.5–4.8, 6, 7
	Opera 4–7

Notes

- It is common practice to comment out statements enclosed by a **<script>** tag. Without commenting, scripts are displayed as page content by browsers that do not support scripting. The particular comment style might be dependent on the language being used. For example, in JavaScript, use

  ```
  <script type="text/javascript">
  <!--
  JavaScript code here
  // -->
  </script>
  ```

  In VBScript, use

  ```
  <script type="text/vbscript">
  <!--
  VBScript code here
  -->
  </script>
  ```

- The HTML 3.2 specification defined a placeholder **script** element.
- The **event** and **for** attributes are defined under transitional versions of HTML 4.01 but only as reserved values. Later specifications appear to have dropped potential support for them, though they continue to be supported by Internet Explorer.
- Most browsers assume JavaScript when parsing a script element without a set **type** or **language** attribute.
- Refer to the **<noscript>** tag reference in this appendix to see how content might be identified for nonscripting-aware browsers.

<select> (Selection List)

This element defines a selection list within a form. Depending on the form of the selection list, the control allows the user to select one or more list options.

Standard Syntax

```
<select
     class="class name(s)"
     dir="ltr | rtl"
     disabled="disabled"
     id="unique alphanumeric identifier"
     lang="language code"
     multiple="multiple"
     name="unique alphanumeric name"
     size="number"
     style="style information"
     tabindex="number"
     title="advisory text">

  option and optgroup elements only

</select>
```

Attributes Defined by Internet Explorer

```
     accesskey="character"  (4)
     align="absbottom | absmiddle | baseline | bottom |
           left | middle | right | texttop | top" (4)
     datafld="column name" (4)
     datasrc="data source ID" (4)
     hidefocus="true | false" (5.5)
     language="javascript | jscript | vbs | vbscript" (4)
     unselectable="on | off" (5.5)
```

Standard Event Attributes

```
onblur, onchange, onclick, ondblclick, onkeydown, onkeypress, onkeyup, onmousedown,
onmousemove, onmouseout, onmouseover, onmouseup
```

Events Defined by Internet Explorer

```
onactivate, onafterupdate, onbeforeactivate, onbeforecut, onbeforedeactivate,
onbeforeeditfocus, onbeforepaste, onbeforeupdate, oncontextmenu, oncontrolselect,
oncut, ondeactivate, ondragenter, ondragleave, ondragover, ondrop, onerrorupdate,
onfocus, onfocusin, onfocusout, onhelp, onlosecapture, onmouseenter, onmouseleave,
onmousewheel, onmove, onmoveend, onmovestart, onpaste, onpropertychange,
onreadystatechange, onresize, onresizeend, onresizestart, onselectstart
```

Element-Specific Attributes

align This Microsoft-specific attribute controls the alignment of the image with respect to the content on the page. The default value is **left**, but other values such as **absbottom**, **absmiddle**, **baseline**, **bottom**, **middle**, **right**, **texttop**, and **top** also might be supported. The meaning of these values should be similar to those used for inserted objects, such as images.

datafld This Internet Explorer–specific attribute is used to indicate the column name in the data source that is bound to the options in the **select** element.

datasrc The value of this Internet Explorer–specific attribute is set to an identifier indicating the data source that data should be pulled from.

disabled This attribute is used to turn off a form control. Elements will not be submitted nor can they receive any focus from the keyboard or mouse. Disabled form controls will not be part of the tabbing order. The browser also can gray out the form that is disabled in order to indicate to the user that the form control is inactive. This attribute requires no value under traditional HTML, but under XHTML variants should be set to **disabled**.

multiple This attribute allows the selection of multiple items in the selection list. The default is single-item selection. Under XHTML, this attribute must have a value set to **multiple**.

name This attribute allows a form control to be assigned a name so that it can be referenced by a scripting language. **Name** is supported by older browsers, such as Netscape 2–generation browsers, but the W3C encourages the use of the **id** attribute. For compatibility purposes, both might have to be used, though this may cause trouble. See Chapter 12 for implementation issues concerning **name** and **id** collisions.

size This attribute sets the number of visible items in the selection list. When the **multiple** attribute is not present, only one entry should show; however, when **multiple** is present, this attribute is useful for setting the size of the scrolling list box.

tabindex This attribute takes a numeric value indicating the position of the form control in the tabbing index for the form. Tabbing proceeds from the lowest positive **tabindex** value to the highest. Negative values for **tabindex** will leave the form control out of the tabbing order. When tabbing is not explicitly set, the browser might tab through items in the order they are encountered. Form controls that are disabled due to the presence of the **disabled** attribute will not be part of the tabbing index.

Examples

```
Choose your favorite colors:
<select name="colors" multiple="multiple" size="2">
   <option>Red</option>
   <option>Blue</option>
   <option>Green</option>
   <option>Yellow</option>
</select>

Taco Choices:
<select name="tacomenu">
   <option value="SuperChicken">Chicken</option>
   <option value="Baja">Fish</option>
   <option value="RX-Needed">Carnitas</option>
</select>
```

Compatibility

HTML 2, 3.2, 4, 4.01	Internet Explorer 2, 3, 4, 5, 5.5, 6
XHTML 1.0, 1.1, Basic	Netscape 1, 2, 3, 4, 4.5–4.8, 6, 7
	Opera 4–7

Notes

- The HTML 4.01 specification reserves the attributes **datafld** and **datasrc** for future use, but these are removed under XHTML.
- Internet Explorer's variant of the disabled attribute allows values of **true** and **false**, as well as the standard **disabled** value.
- Under traditional HTML, the end tag **</option>** is often omitted.
- Be careful of the **name** and **id** attribute problem that may occur, particularly when setting the **multiple** attribute. It may be better to have separate values.
- The HTML 2.0 and 3.2 specifications define only **multiple**, **name**, and **size** attributes.

<small> (Small Text)

This element renders the enclosed text one font size smaller than a document's base font size, unless it is already set to the smallest size.

Standard Syntax

```
<small
     class="class name(s)"
     dir="ltr | rtl"
     id="unique alphanumeric string"
     lang="language code"
     style="style information"
     title="advisory text">
</small>
```

Attributes Defined by Internet Explorer

```
     accesskey="key" (5.5)
     contenteditable="false | true | inherit" (5.5)
     hidefocus="true | false" (5.5)
     language="javascript | jscript | vbs | vbscript" (4)
     tabindex="number" (5.5)
     unselectable="on | off"
```

Standard Event Attributes

```
onclick, ondblclick, onkeydown, onkeypress, onkeyup, onmousedown, onmousemove,
onmouseout, onmouseover, onmouseup
```

Events Defined by Internet Explorer

```
onactivate, onbeforeactivate, onbeforecopy, onbeforecut, onbeforedeactivate,
onbeforeeditfocus, onbeforepaste, onblur, oncontextmenu, oncontrolselect, oncopy,
oncut, ondeactivate, ondrag, ondragend, ondragenter, ondragleave, ondragover,
ondragstart, ondrop, onfocus, onfocusin, onfocusout, onhelp, onlosecapture,
onmouseenter, onmouseleave, onmousewheel, onmove, onmoveend, onmovestart, onpaste,
onpropertychange, onreadystatechange, onresize, onresizeend, onresizestart,
onselectstart, ontimeerror
```

Examples

```
Here is some <small>small text</small>.
This element can be applied <small><small><small>multiple
times</small></small></small>to make things even smaller.
```

Compatibility

HTML 3.2, 4, 4.01	Internet Explorer 2, 3, 4, 5, 5.5, 6
XHTML 1.0, 1.1	Netscape 2, 3, 4, 4.5–4.8, 6, 7
	Opera 4–7

Notes

- A **<small>** tag can be used multiple times to decrease the size of text to a greater degree. Using more than six **<small>** tags together doesn't make sense because browsers currently only support relative font sizes from **1** to **7**. As style sheets become more common, this element might fall out of favor or be used with measurements in a more logical fashion.
- The default base font size for a document typically is **3**, although it can be changed with the **<basefont>** tag.

<spacer> (Extra Space)

This Netscape proprietary element specifies an invisible region that is useful for page layout.

Proprietary Syntax (Netscape 3 and 4 Only)

```
<spacer
     align="absmiddle | absbottom | baseline | bottom |
             left | middle | right | texttop | top"
     height="pixels"
     size="pixels"
     type="block | horizontal | vertical"
     width="pixels">
```

Element-Specific Attributes

align This attribute specifies the alignment of the spacer with respect to surrounding text. It is used only with spacers with **type="block"**. The default value for the **align** attribute is **bottom**. The meanings of the **align** values are similar to those used with the **img** element.

height This attribute specifies the height of the invisible region in pixels. It is used only with spacers with **type="block"**.

size Used with **type="block"** and **type="horizontal"** spacers, this attribute sets the spacer's width in pixels. Used with a **type="vertical"** spacer, this attribute is used to set the spacer's height.

type This attribute indicates the type of invisible region. A **horizontal** spacer adds horizontal space between words and objects. A **vertical** spacer is used to add space between lines. A **block** spacer defines a general-purpose positioning rectangle, like an invisible image that text can flow around.

width This attribute is used only with the **type="block"** spacer and is used to set the width of the region in pixels.

Examples

```
A line of text with two <spacer type="horizontal" size="20">words
separated by 20 pixels. Here is a line of text.<br>
<spacer type="vertical" size="50">
Here is another line of text with a large space between the two
```

```
lines.<spacer align="left" type="block" height="100" width="100"> This
is a bunch of text that flows around an invisible block region. You
could have easily performed this layout with a table.
```

Compatibility

No standards	Netscape 3, 4, 4.5–4.8

Notes

- This element should not be used. Newer versions of the Netscape browser (6 and 7) have dropped support for this element.
- Some Web editors and slicing tools, particularly older versions of Adobe GoLive (formerly known as CyberStudio), rely on this element. It should be removed from documents, and spacer GIFs or other techniques should be used.

<span> (Text Span)

This element typically is used to group inline text so scripting or style rules can be applied to the content. As it has no preset or rendering meaning, this is the most useful inline element for associating style and script with content.

Syntax

```
<span
     class="class name(s)"
     dir="ltr | rtl"
     id="unique alphanumeric string"
     lang="language code"
     style="style information"
     title="advisory text">

</span>
```

Attributes Defined by Internet Explorer

```
     accesskey="key" (5.5)
     contenteditable="false | true | inherit" (5.5)
     datafld="column name" (4)
     dataformatas="html | text" (4)
     datasrc="data source id" (4)
     hidefocus="true | false" (5.5)
     language="javascript | jscript | vbs | vbscript" (4)
     tabindex="number" (5.5)
     unselectable="on | off" (5.5)
```

Standard Event Attributes

onclick, ondblclick, onkeydown, onkeypress, onkeyup, onmousedown, onmousemove, onmouseout, onmouseover, onmouseup

Events Defined by Internet Explorer

onactivate, onbeforeactivate, onbeforecopy, onbeforecut, onbeforedeactivate, onbeforeeditfocus, onbeforepaste, onblur, oncontextmenu, oncontrolselect, oncopy, oncut, ondeactivate, ondrag, ondragend, ondragenter, ondragleave, ondragover, ondragstart, ondrop, onfocus, onfocusin, onfocusout, onhelp, onlosecapture, onmouseenter, onmouseleave, onmousewheel, onmove, onmoveend, onmovestart, onpaste,

```
onpropertychange, onreadystatechange, onresize, onresizeend, onresizestart,
onselectstart, ontimeerror
```

Examples

```
Here is some <span style="font-size: 14pt; color: purple;">very
strange</span> text.

<span id="toggletext"
      onclick="this.style.color='red';"
      ondblclick="this.style.color='black';">
Click and Double Click Me
</span>
```

Compatibility

HTML 4, 4.01 XHTML 1.0, 1.1, Basic	Internet Explorer 3, 4, 5, 5.5, 6 Netscape 4, 4.5–4.8, 4.7, 6, 7 Opera 4, 5, 6, 7

Notes

- The HTML 4.01 specification reserved the **datafld**, **dataformatas**, and **datasrc** attributes for future use. They were later dropped from XHTML. Internet Explorer 4 and later support these attributes for data binding, as discussed in Chapter 7.
- As a generic element, **span**, like **div**, is useful for binding style to arbitrary content. However, **span** is an inline element and does not cause a return by default like **div**.

<strike> (Strikeout Text)

This element is used to indicate strikethrough text, namely text with a line drawn through it. The **s** element provides shorthand notation for this element.

Syntax (Transitional Only)

```
<strike
     class="class name(s)"
     dir="ltr | rtl"
     id="unique alphanumeric string"
     lang="language code"
     style="style information"
     title="advisory text">

</strike>
```

Attributes Defined by Internet Explorer

```
     accesskey="key" (5.5)
     contenteditable="false | true | inherit" (5.5)
     disabled="false | true" (5.5)
     hidefocus="true | false" (5.5)
     language="javascript | jscript | vbs | vbscript" (4)
     tabindex="number" (5.5)
     unselectable="on | off" (5.5)
```

Standard Event Attributes

```
onclick, ondblclick, onkeydown, onkeypress, onkeyup, onmousedown, onmousemove,
onmouseout, onmouseover, onmouseup
```

Events Defined by Internet Explorer

```
onactivate, onbeforeactivate, onbeforecopy, onbeforecut, onbeforedeactivate,
onbeforeeditfocus, onbeforepaste, onblur, oncontextmenu, oncontrolselect, oncopy,
oncut, ondeactivate, ondrag, ondragend, ondragenter, ondragleave, ondragover,
ondragstart, ondrop, onfocus, onfocusin, onfocusout, onhelp, onlosecapture,
onmouseenter, onmouseleave, onmousewheel, onmove, onmoveend, onmovestart, onpaste,
onpropertychange, onreadystatechange, onresize, onresizeend, onresizestart,
onselectstart, ontimeerror
```

Examples

```
This line contains a spelling <strike>misstake</strike> mistake.
Price: $<strike style="color: red;">5.00</strike>3.00
```

Compatibility

HTML 3.2, 4, 4.01 (transitional) XHTML 1.0 (transitional)	Internet Explorer 2, 3, 4, 5, 5.5, 6 Netscape 3, 4, 4.5–4.8, 6, 7 Opera 4–7

Notes

- This tag should act the same as the **<s>** tag.
- This element has been deprecated by the W3C. The strict HTML and XHTML specifications do not include the **<strike>** tag nor the **<s>** tag as it is possible to indicate strikethrough text using the style sheet property **text-decoration**.

<strong> (Strong Emphasis)

This element indicates strongly emphasized text. It usually is rendered in a bold typeface, but its rendering is not guaranteed, as it is a logical element.

Syntax

```
<strong
     class="class name(s)"
     dir="ltr | rtl"
     id="unique alphanumeric string"
     lang="language code"
     style="style information"
     title="advisory text">

</strong>
```

Attributes Defined by Internet Explorer

```
     accesskey="key" (5.5)
     contenteditable="false | true | inherit" (5.5)
     disabled="false | true" (5.5)
     hidefocus="true | false" (5.5)
     language="javascript | jscript | vbs | vbscript" (4)
     tabindex="number" (5.5)
     unselectable="on | off" (5.5)
```

Standard Event Attributes

```
onclick, ondblclick, onkeydown, onkeypress, onkeyup, onmousedown, onmousemove,
onmouseout, onmouseover, onmouseup
```

Events Defined by Internet Explorer

```
onactivate, onbeforeactivate, onbeforecopy, onbeforecut, onbeforedeactivate,
onbeforeeditfocus, onbeforepaste, onblur, oncontextmenu, oncontrolselect, oncopy,
oncut, ondeactivate, ondrag, ondragend, ondragenter, ondragleave, ondragover,
ondragstart, ondrop, onfocus, onfocusin, onfocusout, onhelp, onlosecapture,
onmouseenter, onmouseleave, onmousewheel, onmove, onmoveend, onmovestart, onpaste,
onpropertychange, onreadystatechange, onresize, onresizeend, onresizestart,
onselectstart, ontimeerror
```

Examples

```
It is really <strong>important</strong> to pay attention.
<strong style="font-family: impact; font-size: 28pt">
Important Info
</strong>
```

Compatibility

HTML 2, 3.2, 4, 4.01	Internet Explorer 2, 3, 4, 5, 5.5, 6
XHTML 1.0, 1.1, Basic	Netscape 1, 2, 3, 4, 4.5–4.8, 6, 7
	Opera 4–7

Notes

- This element generally renders as bold text. As a logical element, however, **strong** is useful to bind style rules to.
- As compared to **b**, this element does have meaning. For example, voice browsers may speak **<strong>** enclosed text in a different voice than text that is enclosed by **<b>**.

<style> (Style Information)

This element is used to surround style sheet rules for a document. This element should be found only in the **head** element. Style rules within a document's **<body>** should be set with the style attribute for a particular element.

Syntax

```
<style
     dir="ltr | rtl"
     id="unique alphanumeric string"
     lang="language code"
     media="all | print | screen | others"
     title="advisory text"
     type="MIME Type"
     xml:space="preserve">

  CSS properties

</style>
```

Common Attributes

```
     disabled="disabled" (DOM Level 1)
```

Events Introduced by Internet Explorer

```
onerror, onreadystatechange
```

Element-Specific Attributes

disabled This initially Microsoft-defined attribute is used to disable a style sheet. The presence of the attribute is all that is required to disable the style sheet. In conjunction with scripting, this attribute could be used to turn on and off various style sheets in a document. While not documented in later versions of Internet Explorer, this attribute is very much supported and used, since it is part of the DOM standard. Internet Explorer may also support values of **true** and **false**.

media This attribute specifies the destination medium for the style information. The value of the attribute can be a single media descriptor, like **screen** or a comma-separated list. Possible values for this attribute include **all**, **aural**, **braille**, **print**, **projection**, **screen**, and **tv**. Other values also might be defined, depending on the browser. Internet Explorer supports **all**, **print**, and **screen** as values for this attribute.

type This attribute is used to define the type of style sheet. The value of the attribute should be the MIME type of the style sheet language used. The most common current value for this attribute is **text/css**, which indicates a cascading style sheet format.

xml:space This attribute is included from XHTML 1.0 and is used to specify whether spaces need to be preserved within the script element or whether the default white space handling should be employed. In practice, this attribute is not used by developers.

Example

```
<!DOCTYPE html PUBLIC "-//W3C//DTD XHTML 1.0 Transitional//EN"
     "http://www.w3.org/TR/xhtml1/DTD/xhtml1-transitional.dtd">
<html xmlns="http://www.w3.org/1999/xhtml">
<head>
<title>Style Sheet Example</title>
<meta http-equiv="content-type" content="text/html; charset=ISO-8859-1" />
<style type="text/css">
   body {background: black; color: white;
         font: 12pt Helvetica;}
   h1 {color: red; font: 14pt Impact;}
</style>
</head>
<body>
<h1>A 14-point red Impact heading on a black
background</h1>
<p>Regular body text, which is 12 point white Helvetica.</p>
</body>
</html>
```

Compatibility

HTML 4, 4.01	Internet Explorer 3, 4, 5, 5.5, 6
XHTML 1.0, 1.1	Netscape 4, 4.5–4.8, 6, 7
	Opera 4–7

Notes

- Style information also can be specified in external style sheets as defined by the **<link>** tag.
- Style information can also be associated with a particular element using the **style** attribute.
- Style rules are often commented out within a **<style>** tag to avoid interpretation by nonconforming browsers. See Chapter 10 for more details on this practice.

```
<style type="text/css">
<!--
   body {background-color: red;
-->
</style>
```

<sub> (Subscript)

This element renders its content as subscripted text.

Syntax

```
<sub
     class="class name(s)"
     dir="ltr | rtl"
     id="unique alphanumeric string"
     lang="language code"
     style="style information"
     title="advisory text">

</sub>
```

Attributes Defined by Internet Explorer

```
     accesskey="key" (5.5)
     contenteditable="false | true | inherit" (5.5)
     disabled="false | true" (5.5)
     hidefocus="true | false" (5.5)
     language="javascript | jscript | vbs | vbscript" (4)
     tabindex="number" (5.5)
     unselectable="on | off" (5.5)
```

Standard Event Attributes

onclick, ondblclick, onkeydown, onkeypress, onkeyup, onmousedown, onmousemove, onmouseout, onmouseover, onmouseup

Events Defined by Internet Explorer

onactivate, onbeforeactivate, onbeforecopy, onbeforecut, onbeforedeactivate, onbeforeeditfocus, onbeforepaste, onblur, oncontextmenu, oncontrolselect, oncopy, oncut, ondeactivate, ondrag, ondragend, ondragenter, ondragleave, ondragover, ondragstart, ondrop, onfocus, onfocusin, onfocusout, onhelp, onlosecapture, onmouseenter, onmouseleave, onmousewheel, onmove, onmoveend, onmovestart, onpaste, onpropertychange, onreadystatechange, onresize, onresizeend, onresizestart, onselectstart, ontimeerror

Examples

```
Here is some <sub>subscripted</sub> text.
The secret formula is X<sub><small>2</small></sub>
```

Compatibility

HTML 3.2, 4, 4.01	Internet Explorer 2, 3, 4, 5, 5.5, 6
XHTML 1.0	Netscape 2, 3, 4, 4.5–4.8, 6, 7
	Opera 4–7

Notes

- The HTML 3.2 specification supports no attribute for **<sub>**.
- The **<sub>** tag is removed from XHTML 1.1 since it can be created using the CSS property **vertical-align**.
- Most browsers may slightly shift text lines below a **<sub>** tag.

<sup> (Superscript)

This element renders its content as superscripted text.

Syntax

```
<sup
     class="class name(s)"
     dir="ltr | rtl"
     id="unique alphanumeric string"
     lang="language code"
     style="style information"
     title="advisory text">

</sup>
```

Attributes Defined by Internet Explorer

```
     accesskey="key" (5.5)
     contenteditable="false | true | inherit" (5.5)
     hidefocus="true | false" (5.5)
     language="javascript | jscript | vbs | vbscript" (4)
     tabindex="number" (5.5)
     unselectable="on | off" (5.5)
```

Standard Event Attributes

```
onclick, ondblclick, onkeydown, onkeypress, onkeyup, onmousedown, onmousemove,
onmouseout, onmouseover, onmouseup
```

Events Defined by Internet Explorer

```
onactivate, onbeforeactivate, onbeforecopy, onbeforecut, onbeforedeactivate,
onbeforeeditfocus, onbeforepaste, onblur, oncontextmenu, oncontrolselect, oncopy,
oncut, ondeactivate, ondrag, ondragend, ondragenter, ondragleave, ondragover,
ondragstart, ondrop, onfocus, onfocusin, onfocusout, onhelp, onlosecapture,
onmouseenter, onmouseleave, onmousewheel, onmove, onmoveend, onmovestart, onpaste,
onpropertychange, onreadystatechange, onresize, onresizeend, onresizestart,
onselectstart, ontimeerror
```

Examples

```
Here is some <sup>superscripted</sup> text.
x<sup>2</sup> = 4 when x = 2
```

Compatibility

HTML 3.2, 4, 4.01	Internet Explorer 2, 3, 4, 5, 5.5, 6
XHTML 1.0	Netscape 2, 3, 4, 4.5–4.8, 6, 7
	Opera 4–7

Notes

- The HTML 3.2 specification supports no attribute for **<sup>**.
- The **<sup>** tag is removed from XHTML 1.1 since it can be created using the CSS property **vertical-align**.
- Most browsers may slightly shift text lines above a **<sup>** tag.

<table> (Table)

This element is used to define a table. Tables are used to organize data as well as to provide structure for laying out pages when not using CSS.

Standard Syntax

```
<table
     align="center | left | right" (transitional only)
     bgcolor="color name | #RRGGBB" (transitional only)
     border="pixels"
     cellpadding="pixels"
     cellspacing="pixels"
     class="class name(s)"
     dir="ltr | rtl"
     frame="above | below | border | box | hsides |
            lhs | rhs | void | vsides"
     id="unique alphanumeric identifier"
     lang="language code"
     rules="all | cols | groups | none | rows"
     style="style information"
     summary="summary information"
     title="advisory text"
     width="percentage | pixels">

  caption, col, colgroup, thead, tbody, tfoot, and tr elements only

</table>
```

Nonstandard Attributes Commonly Supported

```
     background="url of image" file
     bordercolor="color name | #RRGGBB"
     cols="number of columns"
     height="percentage | pixels"
     hspace="pixels" (Netscape variants only)
     vspace="pixels" (Netscape variants only)
```

Attributes Defined by Internet Explorer

```
     accesskey="key" (5.5)
     bordercolordark="color name | #RRGGBB" (4)
     bordercolorlight="color name | #RRGGBB" (4)
     datapagesize="number of records to display" (4)
     datasrc="data source id" (4)
     hidefocus="true | false" (5.5)
     language="javascript | jscript | vbs | vbscript" (4)
     tabindex="number" (5.5)
     unselectable="on | off" (5.5)
```

Standard Event Attributes

```
onclick, ondblclick, onkeydown, onkeypress, onkeyup, onmousedown, onmousemove,
onmouseout, onmouseover, onmouseup
```

Events Defined by Internet Explorer

```
onactivate, onbeforeactivate, onbeforecut, onbeforedeactivate, onbeforeeditfocus,
onbeforepaste, onblur, oncontextmenu, oncontrolselect, oncopy, oncut, ondeactivate,
ondrag, ondragend, ondragenter, ondragleave, ondragover, ondragstart, ondrop,
onfilterchange, onfocus, onfocusin, onfocusout, onhelp, onlosecapture, onmouseenter,
onmouseleave, onmousewheel, onmove, onmoveend, onmovestart, onpaste, onpropertychange,
onreadystatechange, onresize, onresizeend, onresizestart, onscroll, onselectstart,
ontimeerror
```

Element-Specific Attributes

align This attribute specifies the alignment of the table with respect to surrounding text. The HTML 4.01 specification defines **center**, **left**, and **right**. Some browsers also might support alignment values, such as **absmiddle**, that are common to block objects.

background This nonstandard attribute, which is supported by nearly every browser, specifies the URL of a background image for the table. The image is tiled if it is smaller than the table dimensions. Note that some early versions of Netscape display the background image in each table cell, rather than behind the complete table, as in Internet Explorer.

bgcolor This attribute specifies a background color for a table. Its value can be either a named color, such as **red**, or a color specified in the hexadecimal *#RRGGBB* format, such as **#FF0000**.

border This attribute specifies, in pixels, the width of a table's borders. A value of **0** makes a borderless table, which is useful for graphic layout.

bordercolor This attribute, supported by Internet Explorer and Netscape, is used to set the border color for a table. The attribute should be used only with a positive value for the **border** attribute. The value of the attribute can be either a named color, such as **green**, or a color specified in the hexadecimal *#RRGGBB* format, such as **#00FF00**. The color applications may be slightly different in the two browsers, since Netscape colors only the outer border of the table.

bordercolordark This Internet Explorer–specific attribute specifies the darker of two border colors used to create a three-dimensional effect for cell borders. It must be used with the **border** attribute set to a positive value. The attribute value can be either a named color, such as **blue**, or a color specified in the hexadecimal *#RRGGBB* format, such as **#00FF00**.

bordercolorlight This Internet Explorer–specific attribute specifies the lighter of two border colors used to create a three-dimensional effect for cell borders. It must be used with the **border** attribute set to a positive value. The attribute value can be either a named color, such as **red**, or a color specified in the hexadecimal *#RRGGBB* format, such as **#FF0000**.

cellpadding This attribute sets the width, in pixels, between the edge of a cell and its content.

cellspacing This attribute sets the width, in pixels, between individual cells.

cols This attribute specifies the number of columns in the table and is used to help quickly calculate the size of the table. This attribute was part of the preliminary specification of HTML 4.0, but was later dropped. A few browsers, notably Netscape and Internet Explorer, support it.

datapagesize The value of this Microsoft-specific attribute is the number of records that can be displayed in the table when data binding is used.

datasrc The value of this Microsoft-specific attribute is an identifier indicating the data source that data will be pulled from for data binding. See Chapter 7 for an example.

frame This attribute specifies which edges of a table are to display a border frame. A value of **above** indicates only the top edge; **below** indicates only the bottom edge; and **border** and **box** indicate all edges, which is the default when the **border** attribute is a positive integer. A value of **hsides** indicates only the top and bottom edges should be displayed, **lhs** indicates the left-hand edge should be displayed, **rhs** indicates the right-hand edge should be displayed, **vsides** indicates the left and right edges both should be displayed, and **void** indicates no border should be displayed.

height This attribute specifies the height of the table in pixels or percentage of the browser window. Be careful, because some browser versions may not support percentage values on height or may have variations in this calculation when they do support it.

hspace This Netscape-specific attribute indicates the horizontal space, in pixels, between the table and surrounding content, similar to the same attribute on **<img>**.

rules This attribute controls the display of dividing rules within a table. A value of **all** specifies dividing rules for rows and columns. A value of **cols** specifies dividing rules for columns only. A value of **groups** specifies horizontal dividing rules between groups of table cells defined by the **thead**, **tbody**, **tfoot**, or **colgroup** elements. A value of **rows** specifies dividing rules for rows only. A value of **none** indicates no dividing rules and is the default.

summary This attribute is used to provide a text summary of the table's purpose and structure. This element is used for accessibility, and its presence is important for non-visual user agents.

vspace This Netscape attribute indicates the vertical space in pixels between the table and surrounding content, similar to the same attribute on **<img>**.

width This attribute specifies the width of the table either in pixels or as a percentage of the enclosing window.

Examples

```
<table bgcolor="white" border="2">
   <tr>
      <td>Cell 1</td>
      <td>Cell 2</td>
      <td>Cell 3</td>
      <td>Cell 4</td>
   </tr>

   <tr>
      <td>Cell 5</td>
      <td>Cell 6</td>
   </tr>
</table>
<table rules="all" bgcolor="yellow">
<caption>Widgets by Area</caption>
<thead align="center" bgcolor="green" valign="middle">
   <tr>
   <td>This is a Header</td>
   </tr>
</thead>

<tfoot align="right" bgcolor="red" valign="bottom">
   <tr>
```

```
   <td colspan="2">This is part of the footer.</td>
   <td>This is also part of the footer.</td>
   </tr>
</tfoot>

<tbody>
   <tr>
      <td> </td>
      <th>Regular Widget</th>
      <th>Super Widget</th>
   </tr>

   <tr>
      <th>West Coast</th>
      <td>10</td>
      <td>12</td>
   </tr>

   <tr>
      <th>East Coast</th>
      <td>1</td>
      <td>20</td>
   </tr>
</tbody>
</table>
```

Compatibility

HTML 3.2, 4, 4.01	Internet Explorer 2, 3, 4, 5, 5.5, 6
XHTML 1.0, 1.1, Basic	Netscape 1.1, 2, 3, 4, 4.5–4.8, 6, 7
	Opera 4–7

Notes

- In addition to displaying tabular data, tables are used to support graphic layout and design.
- The HTML 4 specification reserved the attributes **datasrc**, **datafld**, **dataformatas**, and **datapagesize** for future versions. However, XHTML dropped these attributes. They are supported in Internet Explorer 4 and later.
- At the time of this writing, most browsers have problems with **char** and **charoff** attributes in all table-related tags.
- The HTML 3.2 specification defines only the **align**, **border**, **cellpadding**, **cellspacing**, and **width** attributes for the **table** element.
- The **cols** attribute might provide an undesirable result under some versions of Netscape, which assumes the size of each column in the table is exactly the same.

<tbody> (Table Body)

This element is used to group the rows within the body of a table so that common alignment and style defaults can easily be set for numerous cells.

Standard Syntax

```
<tbody  align="center | char | justify | left | right"
        char="character"
        charoff="offset"
        class="class name(s)"
```

```
        dir="ltr | rtl"
        id="unique alphanumeric identifier"
        lang="language code"
        style="style information"
        title="advisory text"
        valign="baseline | bottom | middle | top">

tr elements only

</tbody>
```

Attributes Defined by Internet Explorer

```
accesskey="key" (5.5)
bgcolor="color name | #RRGGBB" (4)
hidefocus="true | false" (5.5)
language="javascript | jscript | vbs | vbscript" (4)
tabindex="number" (5.5)
unselectable="on | off" (5.5)
```

Standard Event Attributes

onclick, ondblclick, onkeydown, onkeypress, onkeyup, onmousedown, onmousemove, onmouseout, onmouseover, onmouseup

Events Defined by Internet Explorer

onactivate, onbeforeactivate, onbeforecut, onbeforedeactivate, onbeforepaste, onblur, oncontextmenu, oncontrolselect, oncopy, oncut, ondeactivate, ondrag, ondragend, ondragenter, ondragleave, ondragover, ondragstart, ondrop, onfocus, onfocusin, onfocusout, onhelp, onlosecapture, onmouseenter, onmouseleave, onmousewheel, onmove, onmoveend, onmovestart, onpaste, onpropertychange, onreadystatechange, onresize, onresizeend, onresizestart, onselectstart, ontimeerror

Element-Specific Attributes

align This attribute is used to align the contents of the cells within a **<tbody>** tag. Common values are **center**, **justify**, **left**, and **right**. The specification also defines a value of **char**. When **align** is set to **char**, the attribute **char** must be present and set to the character to which cells should be aligned. A common use of this approach would be to set cells to align on a decimal point. Unfortunately, browsers do not support the **char** align value well.

bgcolor This attribute specifies a background color for the cells within a **<tbody>** tag. Its value can be either a named color, such as **red**, or a color specified in the hexadecimal *#RRGGBB* format, such as **#FF0000**.

char This attribute is used to define the character to which element contents are aligned when the **align** attribute is set to the **char** value.

charoff This attribute contains an offset as a positive or negative integer to align characters as related to the **char** value. A value of **2** would align characters in a cell two characters to the right of the character defined by the **char** attribute.

valign This attribute is used to set the vertical alignment for the table cells within a **<tbody>** tag. The HTML specification defines **baseline**, **bottom**, **middle**, and **top**. Internet Explorer also supports **center**, which should act like **middle**.

Example

```
<table rule="all" bgcolor="yellow">
<tbody align="center" bgcolor="red" style="bodystyle"
       valign="baseline">
   <tr>
      <td> </td>
      <th>Regular Widget</th>
      <th>Super Widget</th>
   </tr>
   <tr>
      <th>West Coast</th>
      <td>10</td>
      <td>12</td>
   </tr>
   <tr>
      <th>East Coast</th>
      <td>1</td>
      <td>20</td>
   </tr>
</tbody>
</table>
```

Compatibility

HTML 4, 4.01	Internet Explorer 4, 5, 5.5, 6
XHTML 1.0, 1.1	Netscape 6, 7
	Opera 5–7

Notes

- This element is found only in a **<table>** tag and contains one or more table rows, as indicated by **<tr>** tags.
- For XHTML compatibility, the closing **</tbody>** tag must be used with this element; however, it is optional under traditional HTML.

<td> (Table Data)

This element specifies a data cell in a table. The element should occur within a table row as defined by the **tr** element.

Standard Syntax

```
<td
     abbr="abbreviation"
     align="center | justify | left | right"
     axis="group name"
     bgcolor="color name | #RRGGBB" (transitional only)
     char="character"
     charoff="offset"
     class="class name"
     colspan="number of columns to span"
     dir="ltr | rtl"
     headers="space-separated list of associated header
              cells' id values"
     height="pixels or percentage" (transitional only)
     id="unique alphanumeric identifier"
     lang="language code"
```

```
     nowrap="nowrap" (transitional only)
     rowspan="number or rows to span"
     scope="col | colgroup | row | rowgroup"
     style="style information"
     title="advisory text"
     valign="baseline | bottom | middle | top"
     width="pixels or percentage">  (transitional only)

</td>
```

Nonstandard Attributes Commonly Supported

```
background="url of image file"
bordercolor="color name | #RRGGBB"
```

Attributes Defined by Internet Explorer

```
accesskey="key" (5.5)
background="url of image file" (4)
bordercolor="color name | #RRGGBB" (4)
bordercolordark="color name | #RRGGBB" (4)
bordercolorlight="color name | #RRGGBB" (4)
hidefocus="true | false" (5.5)
language="javascript | jscript | vbs | vbscript" (4)
tabindex="number" (5.5)
unselectable="on | off" (5.5)
```

Standard Event Attributes

```
onclick, ondblclick, onkeydown, onkeypress, onkeyup, onmousedown, onmousemove,
onmouseout, onmouseover, onmouseup
```

Events Defined by Internet Explorer

```
onactivate, onbeforeactivate, onbeforecopy, onbeforecut, onbeforedeactivate,
onbeforeeditfocus, onbeforepaste, onblur, oncontextmenu, oncontrolselect, oncopy,
oncut, ondeactivate, ondrag, ondragend, ondragenter, ondragleave, ondragover,
ondragstart, ondrop, onfilterchange, onfocus, onfocusin, onfocusout, onhelp,
onlosecapture, onmouseenter, onmouseleave, onmousewheel, onmove, onmoveend,
onmovestart, onpaste, onpropertychange, onreadystatechange, onresizeend,
onresizestart, onselectstart, ontimeerror
```

Element-Specific Attributes

abbr The value of this attribute is an abbreviated name for a header cell. This might be useful when attempting to display large tables on small screens.

align This attribute is used to align the contents of the cells. Supported values are **center**, **justify**, **left**, and **right**.

axis This attribute is used to provide a name for a group of related headers.

background This nonstandard attribute, which is supported by major browsers, specifies the URL of a background image for the table cell. The image is tiled if it is smaller than the cell's dimensions.

bgcolor This attribute specifies a background color for a table cell. Its value can be either a named color, such as **red**, or a color specified in the hexadecimal *#RRGGBB* format, such as **#FF0000**. Note that some older versions of Netscape Navigator may not render a cell with a colored background unless a nonbreaking space, at least, is inserted in the cell.

bordercolor This attribute, supported by Internet Explorer and Netscape, is used to set the border color for a table cell. The attribute should be used only with a positive value for the **border** attribute. The value of the attribute can be either a named color, such as **green**, or a color specified in the hexadecimal *#RRGGBB* format, such as **#00FF00**.

bordercolordark This Internet Explorer–specific attribute specifies the darker of two border colors used to create a three-dimensional effect for a cell's borders. It must be used with the **border** attribute set to a positive value. The attribute value can be either a named color, such as **blue**, or a color specified in the hexadecimal *#RRGGBB* format, such as **#00FF00**.

bordercolorlight This Internet Explorer–specific attribute specifies the lighter of two border colors used to create a three-dimensional effect for a cell's borders. It must be used with the **border** attribute set to a positive value. The attribute value can be either a named color, such as **red**, or a color specified in the hexadecimal *#RRGGBB* format, such as **#FF0000**.

char This attribute is used to define the character to which element contents are aligned when the **align** attribute is set to the **char** value.

charoff This attribute contains an offset, specified as a positive or negative integer, to align characters as related to the **char** value. A value of **2**, for example, would align characters in a cell two characters to the right of the character defined by the **char** attribute.

colspan This attribute takes a numeric value that indicates how many columns wide a cell should be. This is useful for creating tables with cells of different widths.

headers This attribute takes a space-separated list of **id** values that correspond to the header cells related to this cell.

height This attribute indicates the height of the cell in pixels or percentage. Some browsers may have rendering problems with percentage values.

nowrap This attribute keeps the content within a table cell from automatically wrapping. The **nowrap** attribute takes no value under HTML but should be set to the value **nowrap** under XHTML.

rowspan This attribute takes a numeric value that indicates how many rows high a table cell should span. This attribute is useful in defining tables with cells of different heights.

scope This attribute specifies the table cells that the current cell provides header information for. A value of **col** indicates that the cell is a header for the rest of the column below it. A value of **colgroup** indicates that the cell is a header for its current column group. A value of **row** indicates that the cell contains header information for the rest of the row it is in. A value of **rowgroup** indicates that the cell is a header for its row group. This attribute might be used in place of the **header** attribute and is useful for rendering assistance by nonvisual browsers. This attribute was added very late to the HTML 4 specification, and support for this attribute is still minimal.

valign This attribute is used to set the vertical alignment for the table cell. The specification defines **baseline**, **bottom**, **middle**, and **top**. Internet Explorer also supports **center**, which should be the same as **middle**.

width This attribute specifies the width of a cell in pixels or percentage value.

Examples

```
<table>
<tr>
```

```
  <td align="left" valign="top" width="100">
  Put me in the top left corner.
  </td>
  <td align="right" bgcolor="red" valign="bottom" width="100">
  Put me in the bottom right corner.
  </td>
</tr>
</table>

<table border="1" width="80%">
   <tr>
      <td colspan="3">
      A pretty wide cell
      </td>
   <tr>
      <td>Item 2</td>
      <td>Item 3</td>
      <td>Item 4</td>
   </tr>
</table>
```

Compatibility

HTML 3.2, 4, 4.01	Internet Explorer 2, 3, 4, 5, 5.5, 6
XHTML 1.0, 1.1, Basic	Netscape 1.1, 2, 3, 4, 4.5–4.8, 6, 7
	Opera 4–7

Notes

- Under the XHTML 1.0 specification, the closing **</td>** tag ceases to be optional.
- The HTML 3.2 specification defines only **align**, **colspan**, **height**, **nowrap**, **rowspan**, **valign**, and **width** attributes.
- This element should always be within the **tr** element.

<textarea> (Multiline Text Input)

This element specifies a multiline text input field contained within a form.

Standard Syntax

```
<textarea
     accesskey="character"
     class="class name"
     cols="number"
     dir="ltr | rtl"
     disabled="disabled"
     id="unique alphanumeric identifier"
     lang="language code"
     name="unique alphanumeric identifier"
     readonly="readonly"
     rows="number"
     style="style information"
     tabindex="number"
     title="advisory text">

</textarea>
```

Attributes Defined by Internet Explorer

```
contenteditable="false | true | inherit" (5.5)
datafld="column name" (4)
datasrc="data source ID" (4)
hidefocus="true | false" (5.5)
language="javascript | jscript | vbs | vbscript" (4)
wrap="off | physical | virtual" (4)
```

Attributes Defined by Netscape 4

```
wrap="hard | off | soft"
```

Standard Event Attributes

onblur, onchange, onclick, ondblclick, onfocus, onkeydown, onkeypress, onkeyup, onmousedown, onmousemove, onmouseout, onmouseover, onmouseup, onselect

Events Defined by Internet Explorer

onactivate, onafterupdate, onbeforeactivate, onbeforecopy, onbeforecut, onbeforedeactivate, onbeforeeditfocus, onbeforepaste, oncontextmenu, oncontrolselect, oncopy, oncut, ondeactivate, ondrag, ondragend, ondragenter, ondragleave, ondragover, ondragstart, ondrop, onerrorupdate, onfilterchange, onfocus, onfocusin, onfocusout, onhelp, onlosecapture, onmouseenter, onmouseleave, onmousewheel, onmove, onmoveend, onmovestart, onpaste, onpropertychange, onreadystatechange, onresize, onresizeend, onresizestart, onselectstart, ontimeerror

Element-Specific Attributes

accesskey This attribute specifies a keyboard navigation accelerator for the element. Pressing ALT or a similar key in association with the specified character selects the form control correlated with that key sequence. Page designers are forewarned to avoid key sequences already bound to browsers.

cols This attribute sets the width in characters of the text area. The typical default value for the size of a **<textarea>** tag when this attribute is not set is **20** characters.

datafld This attribute is used to indicate the column name in the data source that is bound to the content enclosed by the **<textarea>** tag.

datasrc The value of this attribute is an identifier indicating the data source to pull data from.

disabled This attribute is used to turn off a form control. Elements will not be submitted, nor can they receive any focus from the keyboard or mouse. Disabled form controls will not be part of the tabbing order. The browser also can gray out the form that is disabled in order to indicate to the user that the form control is inactive. This attribute requires no value.

name This attribute allows a form control to be assigned a name so that it can be referenced by a scripting language. **Name** is supported by older browsers, such as Netscape 2–generation browsers, but the W3C encourages the use of the **id** attribute. For compatibility purposes, both attributes might have to be used.

readonly This attribute prevents the form control's value from being changed. Form controls with this attribute set might receive focus from the user but might not be modified. Because they receive focus, a **readonly** form control will be part of the form's tabbing order. Finally, the control's value will be sent on form submission. Under XHTML, the value of the **readonly** attribute should be set to **readonly**.

rows This attribute sets the number of rows in the text area. The value of the attribute should be a positive integer.

tabindex This attribute takes a numeric value indicating the position of the form control in the tabbing index for the form. Tabbing proceeds from the lowest positive **tabindex** value to the highest. Negative values for **tabindex** will leave the form control out of the tabbing order. When tabbing is not explicitly set, the browser can tab through items in the order they are encountered. Form controls that are disabled due to the presence of the **disabled** attribute will not be part of the tabbing index, although read-only controls will be.

wrap In some versions of Netscape and Microsoft browsers, this attribute controls word-wrap behavior. A value of **off** for the attribute forces the **<textarea>** not to wrap text, so the viewer must manually enter line breaks. A value of **hard** causes word wrap and includes line breaks in text submitted to the server. A value of **soft** causes word wrap but removes line breaks from text submitted to the server. Internet Explorer supports a value of **physical**, which is equivalent to Netscape's **hard** value, and a value of **virtual**, which is equivalent to Netscape's **soft** value. If the **wrap** attribute is not included, text will still wrap under Internet Explorer, but older versions of Netscape, notably Netscape 4, will scroll horizontally in the text box. Given this problem, even though it is nonstandard, it may be a good idea to include the **wrap** attribute.

Examples

```
<textarea name="CommentBox" id="CommentBox" cols="40" rows="8">
Default text in field
</textarea>

<textarea name="comment" id="comment" rows="10" cols="40" wrap="virtual"
          align="center">
</textarea>
```

Compatibility

HTML 2, 3.2, 4, 4.01	Internet Explorer 2, 3, 4, 5, 5.5, 6
XHTML 1.0, 1.1	Netscape 1, 2, 3, 4, 4.5–4.8, 6, 7
	Opera 4–7

Notes

- Any text between the **<textarea>** and **</textarea>** tags is rendered as the default entry for the form control. Content within a **textarea** is not interpreted, so white space is preserved and tags themselves are ignored.
- The HTML 2.0 and 3.2 specifications define only the **cols**, **name**, and **rows** attributes for this element.
- The **textarea** element lacks a maxlength attribute, which causes a potential security risk. Potential intruders to a site may copy and paste large amounts of text or script code into a **textarea** element in an attempt to break a Web application. All submissions from a **textarea** should be checked carefully to avoid security risks.
- The HTML 4.01 specification reserves the **datafld** and **datasrc** attributes for future use with the **textarea** element.

<tfoot> (Table Footer)

This element is used to group the rows within the footer of a table so that common alignment and style defaults can easily be set for numerous cells. This element might be particularly useful when setting a common footer for tables that are dynamically generated.

Standard Syntax

```
<tfoot
     align="center | char | justify | left | right"
     char="character"
     charoff="offset"
     class="class name(s)"
     dir="ltr | rtl"
     id="unique alphanumeric identifier"
     lang="language code"
     style="style information"
     title="advisory text"
     valign="baseline | bottom | middle | top">

    tr elements only

</tfoot>
```

Attributes Defined by Internet Explorer

```
     accesskey="key" (5.5)
     hidefocus="true | false" (5.5)
     language="javascript | jscript | vbs | vbscript" (4)
     tabindex="number" (5.5)
     unselectable="off | on" (5.5)
     valign="center" (4)
```

Standard Event Attributes

onclick, ondblclick, onkeydown, onkeypress, onkeyup, onmousedown, onmousemove, onmouseout, onmouseover, onmouseup

Events Defined by Internet Explorer

onactivate, onbeforeactivate, onbeforecut, onbeforedeactivate, onbeforepaste, onblur, oncontextmenu, oncontrolselect, oncopy, oncut, ondeactivate, ondrag, ondragend, ondragenter, ondragleave, ondragover, ondragstart, ondrop, onfocus, onfocusin, onfocusout, onhelp, onlosecapture, onmouseenter, onmouseleave, onmousewheel, onmove, onmoveend, onmovestart, onpaste, onpropertychange, onreadystatechange, onresize, onresizeend, onresizestart, onselectstart, ontimeerror

Element-Specific Attributes

align This attribute is used to align the contents of the cells within a **<tfoot>** tag. Common values are **center**, **justify**, **left**, and **right**. The HTML and XHTML specifications also define a value of **char**. When **align** is set to **char**, the attribute **char** must be present and set to the character to which cells should be aligned. A common use of this approach would be to set cells to align on a decimal point.

char This attribute is used to define the character to which element contents are aligned when the **align** attribute is set to the **char** value.

charoff This attribute contains an offset, as a positive or negative integer, for aligning characters as related to the **char** value. A value of **2**, for example, would align characters in a cell two characters to the right of the character defined by the **char** attribute.

valign This attribute is used to set the vertical alignment for the table cells within a **<tfoot>** tag. The specification defines **baseline**, **bottom**, **middle**, and **top**. Internet Explorer also supports **center**, which should be the same as **middle**.

Example

```
<table border="1" bgcolor="yellow" width="80%">
<tfoot align="center" bgcolor="red" class="footer"
       valign="bottom">
 <tr>
   <td>This is part of the footer.</td>
   <td>This is also part of the footer.</td>
 </tr>
</tfoot>
<tbody class="tablebody">
   <tr>
      <td>The contents of the table!</td>
   </tr>
</tbody>
</table>
```

Compatibility

HTML 4, 4.01	Internet Explorer 4, 5, 5.5, 6
XHTML 1.0, 1.1	Netscape 6, 7
	Opera 5–7

Notes

- This element is contained only by the **table** element and contains table rows as delimited by **tr** elements.
- While it would seem that this element should come after a **<tbody>** tag, it actually should come before it within a **<table>** tag.
- Under the XHTML 1.0 specification, the closing **</tfoot>** tag ceases to be optional.

<th> (Table Header)

This element specifies a header cell in a table. The element should occur within a table row as defined by a **tr** element. The main difference between this element and **td** is that browsers might render table headers slightly differently, usually bolding and centering contents. However, the element is logical in nature and should be used to structure tables.

Standard Syntax

```
<th
     abbr="abbreviation"
     align="center | justify | left | right"
     axis="group name"
     bgcolor="color name | #RRGGBB" (transitional only)
     char="character"
     charoff="offset"
     class="class name"
```

```
    colspan="number"
    dir="ltr | rtl"
    headers="space-separated list of associated header
            cells' id values"
    height="pixels" (transitional only)
    id="unique alphanumeric identifier"
    lang="language code"
    nowrap="nowrap" (transitional only)
    rowspan="number"
    scope="col | colgroup | row | rowgroup"
    style="style information"
    title="advisory text"
    valign="baseline | bottom | middle | top"
    width="pixels">  (transitional only)

</th>
```

Nonstandard Attributes Commonly Supported

```
    background="url of image file"
    bordercolor="color name | #RRGGBB"
```

Attributes Defined by Internet Explorer

```
    accesskey="key" (5.5)
    bordercolordark="color name | #RRGGBB" (4)
    bordercolorlight="color name | #RRGGBB" (4)
    hidefocus="true | false" (5.5)
    language="javascript | jscript | vbs | vbscript" (4)
    tabindex="number" (5.5)
    valign="center" (4)
```

Standard Event Attributes

```
onclick, ondblclick, onkeydown, onkeypress, onkeyup, onmousedown, onmousemove,
onmouseout, onmouseover, onmouseup
```

Events Defined by Internet Explorer

```
onactivate, onbeforeactivate, onbeforecopy, onbeforecut, onbeforedeactivate,
onbeforeeditfocus, onbeforepaste, onblur, oncontextmenu, oncontrolselect, oncopy,
oncut, ondeactivate, ondrag, ondragend, ondragenter, ondragleave, ondragover,
ondragstart, ondrop, onfilterchange, onfocus, onfocusin, onfocusout, onhelp,
onlosecapture, onmouseenter, onmouseleave, onmousewheel, onmove, onmoveend,
onmovestart, onpaste, onpropertychange, onreadystatechange, onresizeend,
onresizestart, onselectstart, ontimeerror
```

Element-Specific Attributes

abbr The value of this attribute is an abbreviated name for a header cell. This might be useful when attempting to display large tables on small screens.

align This attribute is used to align the contents of the cells within a **<tbody>** tag. Common values are **center**, **justify**, **left**, and **right**.

axis This attribute is used to provide a name for a group of related headers.

background This nonstandard attribute, which is supported by most browsers, specifies the URL of a background image for the table cell. The image is tiled if it is smaller than the cell's dimensions.

bgcolor This attribute specifies a background color for a table cell. Its value can be either a named color, such as **red**, or a color specified in the hexadecimal *#RRGGBB* format, such as **#FF0000**.

bordercolor This attribute, supported by Internet Explorer and Netscape, is used to set the border color for a table cell. The attribute should be used only with a positive value for the **border** attribute. The value of the attribute can be either a named color, such as **green**, or a color specified in the hexadecimal *#RRGGBB* format, such as **#00FF00**.

bordercolordark This Internet Explorer–specific attribute specifies the darker of two border colors used to create a three-dimensional effect for a cell's borders. It must be used with the **border** attribute set to a positive value. The attribute value can be either a named color, such as **blue**, or a color specified in the hexadecimal *#RRGGBB* format, such as **#00FF00**.

bordercolorlight This Internet Explorer–specific attribute specifies the lighter of two border colors used to create a three-dimensional effect for a cell's borders. It must be used with the **border** attribute set to a positive value. The attribute value can be either a named color, such as **red**, or a color specified in the hexadecimal *#RRGGBB* format, such as **#FF0000**.

char This attribute is used to define the character to which element contents are aligned when the **align** attribute is set to the **char** value.

charoff This attribute contains an offset, specified as a positive or negative integer, for aligning characters as related to the **char** value. A value of **2**, for example, would align characters in a cell two characters to the right of the character defined by the **char** attribute.

colspan This attribute takes a numeric value that indicates how many columns wide a cell should be. This is useful for creating tables with cells of different widths.

headers This attribute takes a space-separated list of **id** values that correspond to the header cells related to this cell.

height This attribute indicates the height of the cell in pixels or percentage. Some browsers may have rendering problems with percentage values.

nowrap This attribute keeps the content within a table cell from automatically wrapping. The **nowrap** attribute takes no value under HTML but should be set to the value **nowrap** under XHTML.

rowspan This attribute takes a numeric value that indicates how many rows high a table cell should span. This attribute is useful in defining tables with cells of different heights.

scope This attribute specifies the table cells for which the current cell provides header information. A value of **col** indicates that the cell is a header for the rest of the column below it. A value of **colgroup** indicates that the cell is a header for its current column group. A value of **row** indicates that the cell contains header information for the rest of the row it is in. A value of **rowgroup** indicates that the cell is a header for its row group. This attribute can be used in place of the **header** attribute and is useful for rendering assistance by nonvisual browsers. This attribute was added very late to the HTML 4.0 specification, and support for this attribute is still minimal in browsers.

valign This attribute is used to set the vertical alignment for the table cell. The specification defines **baseline**, **bottom**, **middle**, and **top**. Internet Explorer also supports **center**, which should be the same as **middle**.

width This attribute specifies the width of a cell in pixels or percentage value.

Examples

```
<table border="1">
   <tr>
      <th>Names</th>
      <th>Apples</th>
      <th>Oranges</th>
   </tr>
   <tr>
      <td>Bobby</td>
      <td>10</td>
      <td>5</td>
   </tr>
   <tr>
      <td>Ruby Sue</td>
      <td>20</td>
      <td>3</td>
   </tr>
</table>
```

Compatibility

HTML 3.2, 4, 4.01	Internet Explorer 2, 3, 4, 5, 5.5, 6
XHTML 1.0, 1.1, Basic	Netscape 1.1, 2, 3, 4, 4.5–4.8, 6, 7
	Opera 4–7

Notes

- The HTML 3.2 specification defines only **align**, **colspan**, **height**, **nowrap**, **rowspan**, **valign**, and **width** attributes.
- This element should always be within the **tr** element.
- Under the XHTML 1.0 specification, the closing **</th>** tag ceases to be optional.

<thead> (Table Header)

This element is used to group the rows within the header of a table so that common alignment and style defaults can easily be set for numerous cells. This element might be particularly useful when setting a common head for tables that are dynamically generated.

Standard Syntax

```
<thead
     align="center | char | justify | left | right"
     char="character"
     charoff="offset"
     class="class name(s)"
     dir="ltr | rtl"
     id="unique alphanumeric identifier"
     lang="language code"
     style="style information"
     title="advisory text"
     valign="baseline | bottom | middle | top">

   tr elements only

</thead>
```

Attributes Defined by Internet Explorer

```
accesskey="key" (5.5)
hidefocus="true | false" (5.5)
language="javascript | jscript | vbs | vbscript" (4)
tabindex="number" (5.5)
unselectable="off | on" (5.5)
valign="center" (4)
```

Standard Event Attributes

onclick, ondblclick, onkeydown, onkeypress, onkeyup, onmousedown, onmousemove, onmouseout, onmouseover, onmouseup

Events Defined by Internet Explorer

onactivate, onbeforeactivate, onbeforecut, onbeforedeactivate, onbeforepaste, onblur, oncontextmenu, oncontrolselect, oncopy, oncut, ondeactivate, ondrag, ondragend, ondragenter, ondragleave, ondragover, ondragstart, ondrop, onfocus, onfocusin, onfocusout, onhelp, onlosecapture, onmouseenter, onmouseleave, onmousewheel, onmove, onmoveend, onmovestart, onpaste, onpropertychange, onreadystatechange, onresize, onresizeend, onresizestart, onselectstart, ontimeerror

Element-Specific Attributes

align This attribute is used to align the contents of the cells within a **<thead>** tag. Common values are **center**, **justify**, **left**, and **right**. The specification also defines a value of **char**. When **align** is set to **char**, the attribute **char** must be present and set to the character to which cells should be aligned. A common use of this approach would be to set cells to align on a decimal point.

char This attribute is used to define the character to which element contents are aligned when the **align** attribute is set to the **char** value.

charoff This attribute contains an offset, specified as a positive or negative integer, for aligning characters as related to the **char** value. A value of **2**, for example, would align characters in a cell two characters to the right of the character defined by the **char** attribute.

valign This attribute is used to set the vertical alignment for the table cells with a **<thead>** tag. The specification defines **baseline**, **bottom**, **middle**, and **top**. Internet Explorer also supports **center**, which should be the same as **middle**.

Example

```
<table border="1" bgcolor="yellow" width="80%">
<thead align="center" bgcolor="red" class="footer"
       valign="bottom">
  <tr>
   <td>This is the Important Table Headline</td>
</thead>

<tbody class="tablebody">
   <tr>
    <td>The contents of the table!</td>
   </tr>
</tbody>
</table>
```

Compatibility

HTML 4, 4.01	Internet Explorer 4, 5, 5.5, 6
XHTML 1.0, 1.1	Netscape 6, 7
	Opera 5–7

Notes

- This element is contained only by a **<table>** tag and contains table rows as delimited by **<tr>** tags.
- Under the XHTML 1.0 specification, the closing **</thead>** tag ceases to be optional.

<title> (Document Title)

This element encloses the title of an HTML document. It must occur within a document's **head** element and must be present in all valid documents. Meaningful titles are very important because they are used for bookmarking a page and might be used by search engines attempting to index the document.

Standard Syntax

```
<title
     dir="ltr | rtl"
     id="unique alphanumeric identifier"
     lang="language code">

</title>
```

Events Defined by Internet Explorer

```
onlayoutcomplete, onreadystatechange
```

Example

```
<head><title>Big Company: Products: Super Widget</title></head>
```

Compatibility

HTML 2, 3.2, 4, 4.01	Internet Explorer 2, 3, 4, 5, 5.5, 6
XHTML 1.0, 1.1, Basic	Netscape 1, 2, 3, 4, 4.5–4.8, 6, 7
	Opera 4–7

Notes

- The **title** should be the first element found in the **head**.
- Meaningful names should provide information about the document. A poor title would be something like "My Home Page," whereas a better title would be "Joe Smith Home."
- Browsers can be extremely sensitive to the **<title>** tag. If the **title** element is malformed or not closed, the page might not even render in the browser.
- The HTML 2.0 and 3.2 specifications define no attributes for the **title** element.

<tr> (Table Row)

This element specifies a row in a table. The individual cells of the row are defined by the **th** and **td** elements.

Syntax

```
<tr
     align="center | justify | left | right"
     bgcolor="color name | #RRGGBB" (transitional only)
     char="character"
     charoff="offset"
     class="class name(s)"
     dir="ltr | rtl"
     id="unique alphanumeric identifier"
     lang="language code"
     style="style information"
     title="advisory text"
     valign="baseline | bottom | middle | top">

    td or th elements only

</tr>
```

Attributes Defined by Internet Explorer

```
     accesskey="key" (5.5)
     bordercolor="color name | #RRGGBB" (4)
     bordercolordark="color name | #RRGGBB" (4)
     bordercolorlight="color name | #RRGGBB" (4)
     hidefocus="true | false" (5.5)
     language="javascript | javascript | vbs | vbscript" (4)
     tabindex="number" (5.5)
     valign="center" (4)
```

Standard Event Attributes

```
onclick, ondblclick, onkeydown, onkeypress, onkeyup, onmousedown, onmousemove,
onmouseout, onmouseover, onmouseup
```

Events Defined by Internet Explorer

```
onactivate, onbeforeactivate, onbeforecopy, onbeforecut, onbeforedeactivate,
onbeforepaste, onblur, oncontextmenu, oncontrolselect, oncopy, oncut, ondeactivate,
ondrag, ondragend, ondragenter, ondragleave, ondragover, ondragstart, ondrop,
onfilterchange, onfocus, onfocusin, onfocusout, onhelp, onlosecapture, onmouseenter,
onmouseleave, onmousewheel, onmove, onmoveend, onmovestart, onpaste, onpropertychange,
onreadystatechange, onresize, onresizeend, onresizestart, onselectstart, ontimeerror
```

Element-Specific Attributes

align This attribute is used to align the contents of the cells within the element. Common values are **center**, **justify**, **left**, and **right**.

bgcolor This attribute specifies a background color for all the cells in a row. Its value can be either a named color, such as **red**, or a color specified in the hexadecimal *#RRGGBB* format, such as **#FF0000**.

bordercolor This attribute, supported by Internet Explorer and Netscape, is used to set the border color for table cells in the row. The attribute should be used only with a positive value for the **border** attribute. The value of the attribute can be either a named color, such as **green**, or a color specified in the hexadecimal *#RRGGBB* format, such as **#00FF00**.

bordercolordark This Internet Explorer–specific attribute specifies the darker of two border colors used to create a three-dimensional effect for the cell's borders. It must be used with the

border attribute set to a positive value. The attribute value can be either a named color, such as **blue**, or a color specified in the hexadecimal *#RRGGBB* format, such as **#00FF00**.

bordercolorlight This Internet Explorer–specific attribute specifies the lighter of two border colors used to create a three-dimensional effect for a cell's borders. It must be used with the **border** attribute set to a positive value. The attribute value can be either a named color, such as **red**, or a color specified in the hexadecimal *#RRGGBB* format, such as **#FF0000**.

char This attribute is used to define the character to which element contents are aligned when the **align** attribute is set to the **char** value.

charoff This attribute contains an offset, specified as a positive or negative integer, for aligning characters as related to the **char** value. A value of **2**, for example, would align characters in a cell two characters to the right of the character defined by the **char** attribute.

valign This attribute is used to set the vertical alignment for the table cells with a **<tr>** tag. The specification defines **baseline**, **bottom**, **middle**, and **top**. Internet Explorer also allows **center**, which should be the same as **middle**.

Example

```
<table width="300" border="1">
   <tr bgcolor="red" align="center" valign="middle">
      <td>3</td>
      <td>5.6</td>
      <td>7.9</td>
   </tr>
</table>
```

Compatibility

HTML 3.2, 4, 4.01 XHTML 1.0, 1.1, Basic	Internet Explorer 2, 3, 4, 5, 5.5, 6 Netscape 1.1, 2, 3, 4, 4.5–4.8, 6, 7 Opera 4–7

Notes

- This tag is contained only in the **<table>**, **<thead>**, **<tbody>**, and **<tfoot>** tags. It contains the **<th>** and **<td>** tags.
- The HTML 3.2 specification defines only the **align** and **valign** attributes for this element.
- Under the XHTML 1.0 specification, the closing **</tr>** tag ceases to be optional.

<tt> (Teletype Text)

This element is used to indicate that text should be rendered in a monospaced font similar to teletype text.

Standard Syntax

```
<tt
     class="class name(s)"
     dir="ltr | rtl"
     id="unique alphanumeric identifier"
     lang="language code"
     style="style information"
     title="advisory text">

</tt>
```

Attributes Defined by Internet Explorer

```
accesskey="key" (5.5)
contenteditable="false | true | inherit"
disabled="false | true" (5.5)
hidefocus="true | false" (5.5)
language="javascript | jscript | vbs | vbscript" (4)
tabindex="number" (5.5)
unselectable="on | off" (5.5)
```

Standard Event Attributes

onclick, ondblclick, onkeydown, onkeypress, onkeyup, onmousedown, onmousemove, onmouseout, onmouseover, onmouseup

Events Defined by Internet Explorer

onactivate, onbeforeactivate, onbeforecopy, onbeforecut, onbeforedeactivate, onbeforeeditfocus, onbeforepaste, onblur, oncontextmenu, oncontrolselect, oncopy, oncut, ondeactivate, ondrag, ondragend, ondragenter, ondragleave, ondragover, ondragstart, ondrop, onfocus, onfocusin, onfocusout, onhelp, onlosecapture, onmouseenter, onmouseleave, onmousewheel, onmove, onmoveend, onmovestart, onpaste, onpropertychange, onreadystatechange, onresize, onresizeend, onresizestart, onselectstart, ontimeerror

Examples

```
Here is some <tt>monospaced text</tt>.
Source code in this tag: <tt>main() { printf("hello world"); }</tt>
```

Compatibility

HTML 2, 3.2, 4, and 4.01 XHTML 1.0	Internet Explorer 2, 3, 4, 5, and 5.5 Netscape 1, 2, 3, 4, 4.5–4.8, 6, 7 Opera 4–7

Notes

- This element has been deprecated by the W3C under XHTML 1.1. The look of the tag can be replicated with the CSS properties **font** or **font-family**.

<u> (Underline)

This element indicates that the enclosed text should be displayed underlined.

Standard Syntax (Transitional Only)

```
<u
     class="class name(s)"
     dir="ltr | rtl"
     id="unique alphanumeric string"
     lang="language code"
     style="style information"
     title="advisory text">

</u>
```

Attributes Defined by Internet Explorer

```
accesskey="key" (5.5)
contenteditable="false | true | inherit" (5.5)
hidefocus="true | false" (5.5)
```

```
    language="javascript | jscript | vbs | vbscript" (4)
    tabindex="number" (5.5)
    unselectable="on | off" (5.5)
```

Standard Event Attributes

```
onclick, ondblclick, onkeydown, onkeypress, onkeyup, onmousedown, onmousemove,
onmouseout, onmouseover, onmouseup
```

Events Defined by Internet Explorer

```
onactivate, onbeforeactivate, onbeforecopy, onbeforecut, onbeforedeactivate,
onbeforeeditfocus, onbeforepaste, onblur, oncontextmenu, oncontrolselect, oncopy, oncut,
ondeactivate, ondrag, ondragend, ondragenter, ondragleave, ondragover, ondragstart,
ondrop, onfocus, onfocusin, onfocusout, onhelp, onlosecapture, onmouseenter,
onmouseleave, onmousewheel, onmove, onmoveend, onmovestart, onpaste, onpropertychange,
onreadystatechange, onresize, onresizeend, onresizestart, onselectstart, ontimeerror
```

Examples

```
Here is some <u>underlined text</u>.

Be careful with <u>underlined</u> text; it looks like
<a href="http://www.yahoo.com/">links</a>.
```

Compatibility

HTML 3.2, 4, 4.01 (transitional)	Internet Explorer 2, 3, 4, 5, 5.5, 6
XHTML 1.0 (transitional)	Netscape 3, 4, 4.5–4.8, 6, 7
	Opera 4–7

Notes

- This element has been deprecated by the W3C. Under the strict HTML and XHTML specifications, the **<u>** tag is not defined. The look provided by this element is supported by the CSS property **text-decoration**.
- Underlining text can be problematic because it looks similar to a link, especially in a black-and-white environment.

<ul> (Unordered List)

This element is used to indicate an unordered list, namely a collection of items that do not have a numerical ordering. The individual items in the list are defined by the **li** element, which is the only allowed element within a <**ul**> tag.

Standard Syntax

```
<ul
     class="class name(s)"
     compact="compact" (transitional only)
     dir="ltr | rtl"
     id="unique alphanumeric identifier"
     lang="language code"
     style="style information"
     title="advisory text"
     type="circle | disc | square"> (transitional only)

          List items specified by <li> tags

</ul>
```

Attributes Defined by Internet Explorer

```
accesskey="key" (5.5)
contenteditable="false | true | inherit" (5.5)
hidefocus="true | false" (5.5)
language="javascript | jscript | vbs | vbscript" (4)
tabindex="number" (5.5)
unselectable="on | off" (5.5)
```

Standard Event Attributes

onclick, ondblclick, onkeydown, onkeypress, onkeyup, onmousedown, onmousemove, onmouseout, onmouseover, onmouseup

Events Defined by Internet Explorer

onactivate, onbeforeactivate, onbeforecopy, onbeforecut, onbeforedeactivate, onbeforeeditfocus, onbeforepaste, onblur, oncontextmenu, oncontrolselect, oncopy, oncut, ondeactivate, ondrag, ondragend, ondragenter, ondragleave, ondragover, ondragstart, ondrop, onfocus, onfocusin, onfocusout, onhelp, onlosecapture, onmouseenter, onmouseleave, onmousewheel, onmove, onmoveend, onmovestart, onpaste, onpropertychange, onreadystatechange, onresize, onresizeend, onresizestart, onselectstart, ontimeerror

Element-Specific Attributes

compact This attribute indicates that the list should be rendered in a compact style. Few browsers actually change the rendering of the list, regardless of the presence of this attribute. The **compact** attribute requires no value.

type The **type** attribute is used to set the bullet style for the list. The values defined under HTML 3.2 and the transitional version of HTML and XHTML are **circle, disc**, and **square**. A user agent might decide to use a different bullet depending on the nesting level of the list, unless the **type** attribute is used. The **type** attribute is dropped under the strict versions of HTML 4 and XHTML because style sheets can provide richer bullet control.

Examples

```
<ul compact="compact" title="Sushi Short List" type="circle">
   <li>Maguro</li>
   <li>Ebi</li>
   <li>Hamachi</li>
</ul>

<!-- Common but bad example -->
<ul>Indentation using lists should not be used, though it is common.</ul>

<!-- Correct list nesting -->

<ul compact title="Sushi Short List" type="circle">
   <li>Item 1
   <ul>
       <li>Item A</li>
       <li>Item B</li>
</ul></li>
   <li>Item 2</li>
</ul>
```

Compatibility

HTML 2, 3.2, 4, 4.01	Internet Explorer 2, 3, 4, 5, 5.5, 6
XHTML 1.0, 1.1, Basic	Netscape 1, 2, 3, 4, 4.5–4.8, 6, 7
	Opera 4–7

Notes

- HTML 2.0 supports only the **compact** attribute.
- The HTML 3.2 specification supports **compact** and **type**.
- Under the strict HTML and XHTML specifications, the **ul** element does not support the **compact** attribute or the **type** attribute. Both of these attributes can be safely replaced with style rules.
- Due to XHTML's deprecation of attribute minimization, the **compact** attribute must have a quoted attribute when used in the transitional variant:

  ```
  <ul compact="compact"></ul>
  ```
- Many Web page designers and page development tools use the **<ul>** tag to indent text. The only element that should occur within a **ul** element is **li**, so such markup does not conform to standards. However, this common practice is likely to continue.
- Since the content model of **ul** says list items should be the only item within **<ul>** tags. Nested lists should occur within **<li>** tags rather than outside them as they are commonly found.
- Style sheets provide much better support for bullet control. See Appendix B or Chapter 10 for more information.

<var> (Variable)

This element is used to indicate a variable (an identifier that occurs in a programming language or a mathematical expression). The element is logical, although enclosed text is generally rendered in italics.

Standard Syntax

```
<var
     class="class name(s)"
     dir="ltr | rtl"
     id="unique alphanumeric value"
     lang="language code"
     style="style information"
     title="advisory text">

</var>
```

Attributes Defined by Internet Explorer

```
     accesskey="key" (5.5)
     contenteditable="false | true | inherit" (5.5)
     hidefocus="true | false" (5.5)
     language="javascript | jscript | vbs | vbscript" (4)
     tabindex="number" (5.5)
     unselectable="on | off" (5.5)
```

Standard Event Attributes

```
onclick, ondblclick, onkeydown, onkeypress, onkeyup, onmousedown, onmousemove,
onmouseout, onmouseover, onmouseup
```

Events Defined by Internet Explorer

```
onactivate, onbeforeactivate, onbeforecopy, onbeforecut, onbeforedeactivate,
onbeforeeditfocus, onbeforepaste, onblur, oncontextmenu, oncontrolselect, oncopy, oncut,
ondeactivate, ondrag, ondragend, ondragenter, ondragleave, ondragover, ondragstart,
ondrop, onfocus, onfocusin, onfocusout, onhelp, onlosecapture, onmouseenter,
onmouseleave, onmousewheel, onmove, onmoveend, onmovestart, onpaste, onpropertychange,
onreadystatechange, onresize, onresizeend, onresizestart, onselectstart, ontimeerror
```

Examples

```
Assign the value 5 to the variable <var>x</var>.
The variable <var>total</var> holds the total order value.
```

Compatibility

HTML 2, 3.2, 4, 4.01 XHTML 1.0, 1.1, Basic	Internet Explorer 2, 3, 4, 5, 5.5, 6 Netscape 1, 2, 3, 4, 4.5–4.8, 6, 7 Opera 4–7

Notes

- As a logical element, **var** is a perfect candidate for style sheet binding.
- The HTML 2.0 and 3.2 specifications support no attributes for this element.

<wbr> (Word Break)

This nonstandard element is used to indicate a place where a line break can occur if necessary. This element is used in conjunction with the **nobr** element, which is used to keep text from wrapping. When used this way, **wbr** can be thought of as a soft line break in comparison to a **
** tag. This element is common to many Netscape and Microsoft implementations, though it is not part of any HTML standard.

Proprietary Syntax

```
<wbr
     id="unique alphanumeric value">
```

Example

```
<nobr>A line break can occur here<wbr>but not elsewhere, even if the line is really
long.</nobr>
```

Compatibility

No standards support	Internet Explorer 2, 3, 4, 5, 5.5, 6 Netscape 1.1, 2, 3, 4, 4.5–4.8

Notes

- Older versions of Internet Explorer documentation defined **class**, **language**, **style**, and **title** for this tag. However, they have little meaning, given this tag's purpose, and have since been eliminated from the documentation, though they may effectively be recognized in some manner by the browser parser.
- Though this is an empty element and should be written as **<wbr />** under XHTML, it does not need to be. It is not standard and will not validate anyway.
- Standards-based browsers, such as Mozilla and Opera, do not support this tag but oddly seem to support **<nobr>**.

xml (XML Data Island)

This proprietary element introduced by Microsoft can be used to embed islands of XML (Extensible Markup Language) data into HTML documents; this will work only under Internet Explorer 5.0

or later. An **<xml>** tag can be used to reference outside data sources using the **src** attribute, or surround XML data in the HTML document itself.

Internet Explorer Syntax

```
<xml
    id="unique alphanumeric value"
    src="url of xml data file">

       ...embedded xml code...
</xml>
```

Events Defined by Internet Explorer

`ondataavailable, ondatasetchanged, ondatasetcomplete, onreadystatechange, onrowenter, onrowexit, onrowsdelete, onrowsinserted`

Element-Specific Attributes

src This attribute references an external XML data file.

Examples

```
<!-- This code embeds xml data directly into a document.
     All code between the xml tags is not HTML, but a
     hypothetical example of xml. -->

<xml id="tasty">
   <combomeal>
      <burger>
       <name>Tasty Burger</name>
         <bun bread="white">
            <meat />
            <cheese />
            <meat />
         </bun>
      </burger>
      <fries size="large" />
      <drink size="large" flavor="Cola" />
   </combomeal>
</xml>

<!-- This code fragment uses the src attribute to reference an
     external file containing xml data. -->

<xml src="combomeal.xml"></xml>
```

Compatibility

No standards support	Internet Explorer 5, 5.5, 6

Notes

- Support for the **<xml>** tag is limited to Internet Explorer 5 or better. Mozilla's approach is more focused on embedding HTML within XML documents.
- For a more detailed discussion of the element and demonstrations of its use, refer to "Embedding XML into HTML Documents" in Chapter 18.

<xmp> (Example)

This deprecated but still widely supported element indicates that the enclosed text is an example. Example text generally is rendered in a monospaced font, and the spaces, tabs, and returns are preserved, as with the **pre** element.

Syntax (Defined by HTML 2; Deprecated Under HTML 4)

```
<xmp>
</xmp>
```

Attributes Defined by Internet Explorer

```
accesskey="key" (5.5)
class="class name(s)" (4)
contenteditable="false | true | inherit" (5.5)
hidefocus="true | false" (5.5)
id="unique alphanumeric value" (4)
lang="language code" (4)
language="javascript | jscript | vbs | vbscript" (4)
style="style information" (4)
tabindex="number" (5.5)
title="advisory text" (4)
unselectable="on | off" (5.5)
```

Events Defined by Internet Explorer

```
onactivate, onbeforeactivate, onbeforecopy, onbeforecut, onbeforedeactivate,
onbeforeeditfocus, onbeforepaste, onblur, onclick, oncontextmenu, oncontrolselect,
oncopy, oncut, ondeactivate, ondblclick, ondrag, ondragend, ondragenter, ondragleave,
ondragover, ondragstart, ondrop, onfocus, onfocusin, onfocusout, onhelp, onkeydown,
onkeypress, onkeyup, onlosecapture, onmousedown, onmouseenter, onmouseleave,
onmousemove, onmouseout, onmouseover, onmouseup, onmousewheel, onmove, onmoveend,
onmovestart, onpaste, onpropertychange, onreadystatechange, onresize, onresizeend,
onresizestart, onselectstart, ontimeerror
```

Example

```
<xmp>This is a large block of text used as an example. Note that returns

  as well as    S P A C E S are preserved.</xmp>
```

Compatibility

HTML 2	Internet Explorer 2, 3, 4, 5, 5.5, 6 Netscape 1, 2, 3, 4, 4.5–4.8, 6, 7 Opera 4–7

Note

- This element was first deprecated under HTML 3.2, yet all major browsers continue to support it, and it is well documented and even extended for Internet Explorer. The **<pre>** tag or style sheets should be used instead of this tag.

APPENDIX B

CSS1 and CSS2 Reference

Cascading style sheets, covered in Chapters 10 and 11, offer a powerful new tool for Web page layout. When used properly, style sheets separate style from document structure, as was originally intended for HTML. Most style properties defined by the Cascading Style Sheets 1 (CSS1) specification are supported by major browsers. However, many of the properties in the CSS2 specification are not. A full listing of CSS1 is presented in this appendix. The visual properties of CSS2 are presented in their entirety; however, the aural properties are only briefly summarized given their lack of use. The appendix concludes with an overview of some of the proprietary CSS properties supported by Internet Explorer, some of which appear slated for inclusion in CSS3.

Style Inclusion Methods

This section defines the basic methods to associate CSS-based style information with HTML or XHTML documents.

Embedded Styles

Document-wide styles can be embedded in a document's **head** element using the **<style>** tag. Note that styles should be commented out to avoid interpretation by nonstyle-aware browsers. However, be aware that comment masking is frowned upon in XHTML and linked styles should be used or a CDATA section employed.

Example

```
<style type="text/css">
<!--
p  {font-size: 14pt; font-face: Times; color: blue;
    background-color: yellow;}
em {font-size: 16pt; color: green;}
-->
</style>
```

Inline Styles

You can apply styles directly to elements in a document using the core attribute **style**. As the closest style inclusion method to a tag, inline styles will take precedence over document wide or linked styles.

Example

```
<h1 style="font-size: 48pt; font-family: Arial;
         color: green;">CSS1 Test</h1>
```

Linked Styles

Styles can be contained in an external style sheet linked to a document or a set of documents (see Chapter 10), as shown in the following example. Linked information should be placed inside the **<head>** tag.

Example

```
<link rel="stylesheet" type="text/css" href="newstyle.css" />
```

The **rel** attribute is generally set to the value **stylesheet** but may also have a value of **alternate stylesheet** with an associated *title* value to provide different looks for the same page.

Examples

```
<link rel="stylesheet" href="standard.css" title="standard" />
<link rel="alternate stylesheet" href="bigred.css" title="Red Sheet" />
```

Chapter 11 has examples and more information on using alternative style sheets.

The **media** attribute may also be used to define the media to which a style sheet is applied. The keyword values **screen** or **print** are commonly used. The default value of **all** is applied when media is not specified.

Examples

```
<link rel="stylesheet" href="screenstyle.css" media="screen"
     type="text/css" />
<link rel="stylesheet" href="printstyle.css" media="print"
     type="text/css" />
```

CSS2 does define a rich set of media values as shown in Table B-1, but practice shows few are supported.

Imported Styles

Styles can be imported from an external file and expanded in place, similar to a macro. Importing can be used to include multiple style sheets. An imported style is defined within a **<style>** tag using **@import** followed optionally by a **type** attribute and a URL for the style sheet.

Media Type	Definition
all	For use with all devices
aural	For use with speech synthesizers
Braille	For use with tactile Braille devices
embossed	For use with Braille printers
handheld	For use with handheld devices
print	For use with printed material and documents viewed onscreen in print preview mode
projection	For use with projected media (direct computer-to-projector presentations), or printing transparencies for projection
screen	For use with color computer screens
tty	For use with low-resolution teletypes, terminals, or other devices with limited display capabilities
tv	For use with television-type devices

TABLE B-1 Media Types Defined Under CSS2

Example

```
<style type="text/css">
@import url(newstyle.css)
</style>
```

The **@import** directive allows style sheets to be grouped and joined together. While this was the design of the feature, unfortunately most CSS developers use it to perform a weak form of browser selection because many older CSS implementations do not support the directive. The basic idea of the trick is to put sophisticated style rules in an **@import** style sheet and leave basic styles in the style block. This trick should be avoided, particularly given that some browsers, notably versions of Internet Explorer, will cause a disturbing flash effect when loading imported styles.

CSS Measurements

CSS supports a number of measurements including absolute units such as inches, centimeters, points, and so on, as well as relative measures such as percentages and em units. Table B-2 summarizes these units of measure.

CSS Color Values

Style sheets support a variety of color measurement values, as shown in Table B-3. Appendix E provides a greater discussion of possible color values and names.

Measurement	Description	Example
%	Defines a measurement as a percentage relative to another value, typically an enclosing element.	p {font-size: 14pt; line-height: 150%;}
cm	Defines a measurement in centimeters.	div {margin-bottom: 1cm;}
em	A relative measurement for the height of a font in em spaces. Because an **em** unit is equivalent to the size of a given font, if you assign a font to 12pt, each "**em**" unit would be 12pt; thus, 2em would be 24pt.	p {letter-spacing: 5em;}
ex	This value defines a measurement relative to a font's x-height. The x-height is determined by the height of the font's lowercase letter *x*.	p {font-size: 14pt; line-height: 2ex;}
in	Defines a measurement in inches.	p {word-spacing: .25in;}
mm	Defines a measurement in millimeters.	p {word-spacing: 12mm;}
pc	Defines a measurement in picas. A pica is equivalent to 12 points; thus, there are 6 picas per inch.	p {font-size: 10pc;}
pt	Defines a measurement in points. A point is defined as $1/72^{nd}$ of an inch.	body {font-size: 14pt;}
px	Defines a measurement in screen pixels.	p {padding: 15px;}

TABLE B-2 CSS1 and CSS2 Length Measurement Units

Color Format	Description	Example
Specification-defined named colors	CSS color values can be defined using 16 color names: **aqua**, **black**, **blue**, **fuchsia**, **gray**, **green**, **lime**, **maroon**, **navy**, **olive**, **purple**, **red**, **silver**, **teal**, **white**, and **yellow.**	body {font-family: Arial; font-size: 12pt; color: red;}
Browser-defined named colors	Browsers define a variety of their own colors like **mintcream**. Appendix E provides a complete list of these extended colors, which should be avoided because of potential browser compatibility problems.	#gap {color: khaki;}
Six-digit hexadecimal	CSS's six-digit hexadecimal format is the same as HTML/XHTML. The format specifies color as #RRGGBB where RR is the amount of red, GG the amount of green, and BB the amount of blue all specified in a hexadecimal value ranging from 00 to FF.	div {font-family: Courier; font-size: 10pt; color: #00CCFF;}
Three-digit hexadecimal	The three-digit hexadecimal format is unique to CSS and specifies color in the format of #RGB where R,G, and B are hexadecimal ranging from 0 to F. Given the lesser number of digits, it is obviously less expressive than the six-digit format.	span {font-family: Helvetica; font-size: 14pt; color: #0CF;}
RGB	CSS colors can also be defined using the keyword **rgb**, followed by three numbers between 0 and 255, contained in parentheses and separated by commas, with no spaces between them. RGB color values can also be defined using percentages. The format is the same, except that the numbers are replaced by percentage values between **0%** and **100%**.	#p1 {color: rgb(204,0,51);} p {color: rgb(0%,10%,50%);}

TABLE B-3 CSS1 and CSS2 Color Measurement Units

TIP *For maximum compatibility with older CSS implementations, developers are encouraged to use known name values or the six-digit hexadecimal format when specifying color.*

Selectors

CSS1 and 2 support a rich set of selectors for specifying which particular element(s) that a CSS rule applies to. CSS1 selectors are presented in Table B-4.

CSS2 introduces a number of new selectors as summarized in Table B-5. Many of these selectors use document context to determine how styles should be applied to elements, potentially reducing reliance on HTML/XHTML selectors such as **class** and **id**. For more information, see Chapter 11.

Selector	Description	Example
element	Selects all elements of the name specified in the rule.	h1 {color: red;} /* makes all h1 tags red */
#id	Selects any tag with an **id** attribute set.	#test {color: green;} /* makes a tag with id='test' green */
.class	Selects any tag with the specified class value.	.note {color: yellow;} /* makes all tags with class='note' yellow */
element.class	Selects the specified elements with a particular class value.	h1.note {text-decoration: underline;} /* underlines all H1 tags with class='note' */
Grouping	Applies the same rules to a group of tags.	h1,h2,h3 {background-color: orange;} /* sets the background color of all h1,h2, and h3 elements to orange */
Contextual	Selects descendent tags.	p strong {color: purple;} /* sets all strong tags that are descendents of p tags purple */
:first-line	Selects the first line of an element.	p:first-line {color: red;} /* makes the first lines of a paragraph red */
:first-letter	Selects the first letter of an element.	p:first-letter {font-size: larger;} /* makes the first letter of a paragraph larger */
a:link	Specifies the unvisited link.	a:link {font-weight: bold;} /* makes unvisited links bold */
a:active	Specifies the link as it is being pressed.	a:active {color: red;} /* makes links red as they are pressed */
a:visited	Specifies the link after being pressed.	a:visited {text-decoration: line-through;} /* puts a line through visited links */

TABLE B-4 CSS1 and CSS2 Color Measurement Units

Selector	Description	Examples
*	The wildcard selector is used to apply a match to any element. It can be used for a global rule or, more commonly, in contextual or child selection rules.	* {background-color: red;} div * span {background-color: yellow;}
>	This selector defines a rule that matches only elements that are directly enclosed within another element, such as a **<p>** tag with a document body.	body > p {background-color: yellow;}
+	The adjacent sibling selector defines a rule that applies a style to the first incidence of an element immediately after the first element. In other words, the two tags are adjacent siblings in their parse tree.	h1 + p {color: red;}
[ ]	The attribute selector has many uses. Unfortunately, many browsers do not support it. The basic inclusion of an attribute name in brackets matches when the attribute is used on the selected element. A specific attribute value can be matched with = and pieces of an attribute can also be matched. The symbol ~= can be used to match space-separated attribute values while |= is used to match dash-separated attribute values. It is also possible to match multiple attribute values at once.	a[href] {background-color: yellow;} a[href="http://www.htmlref.com"] {font-weight: bold;} p[title~="Test match"] { font-style: italic; } p[lang|="en"] { color: red; } /* English text in red */ p[title="Test Selector"][lang|="en"] {border-style: dashed; border-width: 1px; }
@media	Defines style rules for multiple media types in a single style sheet. See "Media-Dependent Style Sheets" in Chapter 11.	@media screen {body {font-family: sans-serif; font-size: 18 pt;} }
@page	Used to define rules for page sizing and orientation rules for printing.	@page {size: 8.5in 11in;}
:left	Sets page layout rules for a left-hand page when printing.	@page :left {margin-left: 4cm; margin-right: 3cm;}
:right	Sets page layout rules for a right-hand page when printing.	@page :right {margin-left: 3cm; margin-right: 4cm;}
:first	Sets page layout rules for the first page in a document when printing.	/* Top margin on first page 10cm */ @page :first {margin-top: 10cm;}
:first-child	Applies a style to the first child element of an element.	p:first-child {color: red;}
:focus	Changes the display of an element when the element receives focus (generally, **<input="text">**).	input:focus{background-color: yellow;}
:hover	Changes the display of an element when a cursor passes over the element. Commonly supported for links, but defined for nearly every element.	a:hover {text-decoration: underline;} p:hover {background-color: yellow;}
:lang	Applies style to an element according to what language the element is in.	*:lang(fr) {color: blue;} *:lang(en) {color: red;}
:before	Defines content to be placed before an element. See the **content** property for more information on use.	div:before {content: url(sectionstart.gif);}
:after	Defines content to be placed after an element. See the **content** property for more information on use.	div:after {content: url(sectionend.gif);}

TABLE B-5 CSS2 Selector Summary

TIP *Developers should proceed with caution when using CSS2 selectors; many of the more complex ones are buggy or not supported even in modern browsers. However, they should not be avoided because when supported they can be used to create very powerful rules.*

Miscellaneous CSS Constructs

This section discusses some miscellaneous constructs associated with style sheets.

/* comments */

Comments can be placed within style sheets. HTML comment syntax (**<!-- comment -->**) does not apply. However, HTML comments are often used to mask style blocks. Style sheets use the comment syntax used in C programming (**/*comment*/**).

Example

```
<style type="text/css">
p {font-face: Courier; font-size: 14pt; font-weight: bold;
   background-color: yellow;}
/*This style sheet was created at Demo Company, Inc.
  All rights reserved.*/
</style>
```

! Important

This property specifies that a style takes precedence over any different, conflicting styles. A style specified as important by an author takes precedence over a rule set by an end user. This construct should be used sparingly.

Example

```
div {font-size: 14pt; line-height: 150%; font-family: Arial ! important;}
```

CSS1 and CSS2 Properties

This section presents the CSS1 and 2 properties in alphabetical order. Readers should note that the properties tend to come in groups and that most groups have shorthand notation. For example, the **background** property is shorthand for **background-color**, **background-image**, **background-position**, and **background-attachment**. The primary property for a set may contain extra details that should be noted.

background

This property sets any or all background properties in a shorthand form. Property order should not matter but the typical syntax is

```
background:  background-color  background-image  background-repeat
             background-attachment  background-position;
```

Any properties not specified use their default values. As with all shorthand forms, document authors should experiment with individual property values before condensing to a short form.

APPENDIX B

Examples

```
body {background: white url(picture.gif) repeat-y center;}
.red {background: #ff0000;}
#div1 {background: white url(logo.gif) no-repeat fixed 10px 10px;}
```

Browser and CSS Support Notes

CSS1	IE 4, 5, 5.5, 6	Nav 4, 4.5–4.8 (buggy), 6, 7	Opera 4, 5, 6, 7

background-attachment

This property sets the background image to scroll or not to scroll with its associated element's content. The default value is **scroll**, which sets the background to scroll with the associated content, typically text. The alternate value, **fixed**, is intended to make the background static with associated content such as text scrolls on top. This property is often used to create a watermark effect similar to the proprietary attribute, **bgproperties**, of the **<body>** tag introduced by Microsoft.

Examples

```
body {background-image: url(tile.gif); background-attachment: scroll;}
#logo {background-image: url(logo.gif); background-attachment: fixed;}
```

Browser and CSS Support Notes

CSS1	IE 4, 5, 5.5 ,6	Nav 6, 7	Opera 4, 5, 6, 7

background-color

This property sets an element's background color. It is often used in conjunction with the **color** property, which sets text color. If both are not set it is possible to have rendering problems and the W3C CSS validator will warn of this issue. Used with block elements, this property colors content and padding but not margins. The default value, **transparent**, allows any underlying content to show through. See Appendix E for browser support of color values.

Examples

```
p    {background-color: #00CCFF;}
body {background-color: orange;}
.red {background-color: rgb(255, 0, 0;}
```

Browser and CSS Support Notes

CSS1	IE 4, 5, 5.5, 6	Nav 4, 4.5–4.7 (buggy; may not fit entire region), 6, 7	Opera 4, 5, 6, 7

background-image

This property associates a background image with an element. Underlying content may show through transparent regions in the source image. The background image requires a URL (complete or relative) to link it to the source image specified with the **url( )** syntax. The default value is **none** and sets the background so that it doesn't display an image.

Examples

```
body    {background-image: url(yellowpattern.gif);}
p       {background-image: none;}
.robot {background-image: url(http://www.democompany.com/images/robot.gif);}
```

Browser and CSS Support Notes

CSS1	IE 4, 5, 5.5, 6	Nav 4, 4.5–4.7 (buggy; may not fit entire region), 6, 7	Opera 4, 5, 6, 7

background-position

This property determines how a background image is positioned within the canvas space used by its associated element. The position of the background image's upper-left corner can be specified as an absolute distance in pixels from the surrounding element's origin. It can also be specified as a percentage along the horizontal and vertical dimensions. Finally, the position can be specified as named values that describe the horizontal and vertical dimensions. The named values for the horizontal axis are **center**, **left**, and **right**; those for the vertical axis are **top**, **center**, and **bottom**. The default value for an unspecified dimension is assumed to be **center**.

Examples

```
body  {background-image: url(yellowpattern.gif);
       background-position: 50px 100px;}
#div1 {background-image: url(bricks.gif); background-position: 10% 45%;}
body  {background-image: url(logo.gif); background-position: top center;}
```

Browser and CSS Support Notes

CSS1	IE 4, 5, 5.5, 6	Nav 6, 7	Opera 4, 5, 6, 7

background-repeat

This value determines how background images tile when they are smaller than the canvas space used by their associated elements. It is used in conjunction with the **background-image** property. Possible values are **repeat** (repeats in both direction), **repeat-x** (repeats only horizontally), **repeat-y** (repeats vertically), and **no-repeat**. The default value is **repeat**.

Examples

```
body  {background-image: url(yellowpattern.gif) background-repeat: repeat;}
#div1 {background-image: url(tile.gif); background-repeat: repeat-x;}
p     {background-image: url(tile2.gif); background-repeat: repeat-y;}
.mark {background-image: url(logo.png); background-repeat: no-repeat;}
```

Browser and CSS Support Notes

CSS1	IE 4, 5, 5.5, 6	Nav 4, 4.5–4.8 (buggy may not fit entire region), 6, 7	Opera 4, 5, 6, 7

border

This property defines the width, style, and color for all four sides of an element's border in a shorthand form. There are five specific properties for setting the width of borders: **border-top-width**, **border-bottom-width**, **border-right-width**, **border-left-width**, and **border-width**. The first four set the width of specific borders; **border-width** is used to set all four. The **border** property by itself can set all of them. Values for border widths can be set in numeric measurements or with the named values **thin**, **medium**, or **thick**. Border colors and styles can be set with the properties **border-color** and **border-style**, respectively, as well as with the shorthand. The properties **border-top**, **border-bottom**, **border-right**, and **border-left** can be used to set width, style, and color values for different sides of a border. Given all these properties, the **border** property sets the width, style, and color of all sides of an element's border, typically in that order. The syntax is shown here:

border: *border-width border-style border-color;*

Given the complexity of the rule, like many shorthand properties, individual properties should probably be set and then condensed to shorthand form.

Examples

```
div     {border: 2px double red;}
.dashed {border: .5em dashed #f00;}
```

Browser and CSS Support Notes

CSS1,	IE 4, 5 (buggy), 5.5, 6	Nav 4, 4.5–4.8 (buggy), 6, 7	Opera 5, 6, 7

border-bottom

This property defines the width, style, and color for the bottom border of an element in a shorthand form. The syntax for the rules should be in order, as follows:

border-bottom: *border-width border-style border-color;*

Given that CSS1 did not support **border-bottom-color** and **border-bottom-style,** this property is useful for setting the characteristics of the bottom of boxes for older browsers.

Example

```
#redbottom  {border-top: thin solid red;}
```

Browser and CSS Support Notes

CSS1	IE 4, 5, 5.5, 6	Nav 6, 7	Opera 4, 5, 6, 7

border-bottom-color

This property defines the color of an element's bottom border. See Appendix E for information on browser support of color values.

Example

```
p {border-style: solid; border-width: thin; border-bottom-color: orange;}
```

Browser and CSS Support Notes

CSS2	IE 4, 5, 5.5, 6	Nav 6, 7	Opera 7

border-bottom-style

This property defines the style for the bottom border of an element. Allowed values are **none**, **dotted**, **dashed**, **solid**, **double**, **groove**, **ridge**, **inset**, and **outset**. See **border-style** property for specific information on each style.

Example

```
#box {border-width: 10px; border-style: solid; border-bottom-style: double;}
```

Browser and CSS Support Notes

CSS2	IE 4, 5, 5.5, 6	Nav 6, 7	Opera 7

border-bottom-width

This property sets the width of an element's bottom border. Values can be keywords (**thin**, **medium**, or **thick**) and numerical lengths such as pixels (**px**), inches (**in**), and so on.

Examples

```
.low {border-bottom-width: thick;}
p    {border-bottom-width: 15px;}
```

Browser and CSS Support Notes

CSS1	IE 4, 5 (buggy), 5.5, 6	Nav 4, 4.5–4.8 (buggy), 6, 7	Opera 5, 6, 7

border-collapse

This CSS2 property defines if table cell borders are connected or separate. Allowed values are **separate** and **collapse**. With a value of **collapse**, the borders appear to collapse on each other so that there's no more spacing between the borders. A rendering here in Internet Explorer 6 should illustrate the idea of the property.

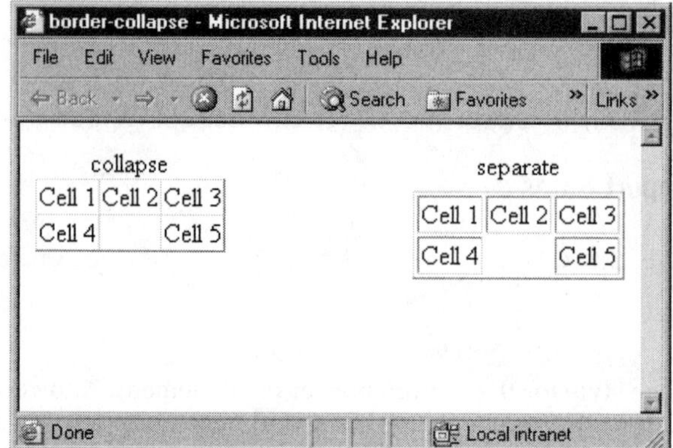

Example

```
<table border="1" style="border-collapse: collapse;">
<tr>
 <td>Cell 1</td><td>Cell 2</td><td>Cell 3</td>
</tr>
 <tr>
   <td>Cell 4</td><td></td><td>Cell 5</td>
</tr>
</table>
```

Browser and CSS Support Notes

CSS2	IE 5, 5.5, 6 (buggy)	Nav 6, 7	Opera 5, 6, 7

TIP *There are significant rendering differences in browsers even when the border-collapse property is supported.*

border-color

This property defines the color of an element's border. All borders are set at once but individual color values can be set with the shorthand **border-top**, **border-right**, **border-bottom**, and **border-left**. See Appendix E for information on browser support of color values.

Examples

```
p   {border-style: solid; border-width: thin; border-color: blue;}
#d1 {border-style: double; border-color: #0000EE;}
```

Browser and CSS Support Notes

CSS1	IE 4, 5 (buggy), 5.5, 6	Nav 4, 4.5–4.8 (buggy), 6, 7	Opera 4, 5, 6, 7

border-left

This property defines the width, style, and color for the left border of an element in a shorthand form. The syntax for the rules should be in order, as follows:

```
border-left: border-width border-style border-color;
```

Given that CSS1 did not support **border-left-color** and **border-left-style**, this property is useful for setting the characteristics of the left of boxes for older browsers.

Example

```
#leftout  {border-left: thin dashed red;}
```

Browser and CSS Support Notes

CSS1	IE 4, 5, 5.5, 6	Nav 6, 7	Opera 4, 5, 6, 7

border-left-color

This property defines the color of an element's left border. See Appendix E for information on browser support of color values.

Example

```
p {border-style: solid; border-width: thin; border-left-color: red;}
```

Browser and CSS Support Notes

CSS2	IE 4, 5, 5.5, 6	Nav 6, 7	Opera 7

border-left-style

This property defines the style for the left border of an element. Allowed values are **none**, **dotted**, **dashed**, **solid**, **double**, **groove**, **ridge**, **inset**, and **outset**. See **border-style** property for specific information on each style.

Example

```
#box {border-width: 5px; border-style: solid; border-left-style: dotted;}
```

Browser and CSS Support Notes

CSS2	IE 4, 5, 5.5, 6	Nav 6, 7	Opera 7

border-left-width

This property sets the width of an element's left border. Values can be keywords (**thin**, **medium**, or **thick**) and numerical lengths such as pixels (**px**), inches (**in**), and so on.

Examples

```
.thin {border-style: dashed; border-left-width: thin;}
p {border-style: solid; border-left-width: 5px;}
```

Browser and CSS Support Notes

CSS1	IE 4, 5 (buggy), 5.5, 6	Nav 4, 4.5–4.8 (buggy), 6, 7	Opera 5, 6, 7

border-right

This property defines the width, style, and color for the bottom border of an element in a shorthand form. The syntax for the rules should be in order, as follows:

`border-right``:` *`width style color`*`;`

Given that CSS1 did not support **border-right-color** and **border-right-style**, this property is useful for setting the characteristics of the right of boxes for older browsers.

Example

```
#greenzone  {border-right: thick dashed green;}
```

Browser and CSS Support Notes

CSS1	IE 4, 5, 5.5, 6	Nav 6, 7	Opera 4, 5, 6, 7

border-right-color

This property defines the color of an element's right border. See Appendix E for information on browser support of color values.

Example

```
p {border-style: solid; border-width: thin; border-right-color: green;}
```

Browser and CSS Support Notes

CSS2	IE 4, 5, 5.5, 6	Nav 6, 7	Opera 7

border-right-style

This property defines the style for the right border of an element. Allowed values are **none**, **dotted**, **dashed**, **solid**, **double**, **groove**, **ridge**, **inset**, and **outset**. See **border-style** property for specific information on each style.

Example

```
#box {border-width: 5px; border-style: solid; border-right-style: ridge;}
```

Browser and CSS Support Notes

CSS2	IE 4, 5, 5.5, 6	Nav 6, 7	Opera 7

border-right-width

This property sets the width of an element's right border. Values can be keywords (**thin**, **medium**, or **thick**) and numerical lengths such as pixels (**px**), inches (**in**), and so on.

Examples

```
div         {border-right-width: medium;}
.superfat   {border-right-width: 40px;}
```

Browser and CSS Support Notes

CSS1	IE 4, 5 (buggy), 5.5, 6	Nav 4,4.5–4.8 (buggy), 6, 7	Opera 5, 6, 7

border-spacing

This CSS2 property is similar to the **cellspacing** attribute on the **table** element in HTML/XHTML and defines the space between cells in a table. Its value can be an arbitrary length, but not negative. If one length is specified, it gives both the horizontal and vertical spacing. If two are specified, the first gives the horizontal spacing and the second the vertical spacing between cells.

Examples

```
table       {border-spacing: 10px;}
#table2     {border-spacing: 10px 5px;}
```

Browser and CSS Support Notes

CSS2	No IE support	Nav 6, 7	Opera 5, 6, 7

border-style

The **border-style** property defines the style of up to four different sides of a border, using the values **none**, **dotted**, **dashed**, **solid**, **double**, **groove**, **ridge**, **inset**, and **outset**. A value of **none** overrides any borders currently set. **Dashed** and **dotted** values are distinctly different but many browsers will set them the same. **Solid** is the default value. **Double** sets a double line border. **Groove** sets an edge line style border while a **ridge** value sets the border to resemble a raised ridge by reversing the shading of the grooved rendering. An **inset** value sets the border to display a lighter shade of the border color on its right and bottom sides while an **outset** value sets the border to display a lighter shade of the border color on its top and left sides. Examples of these styles are shown here:

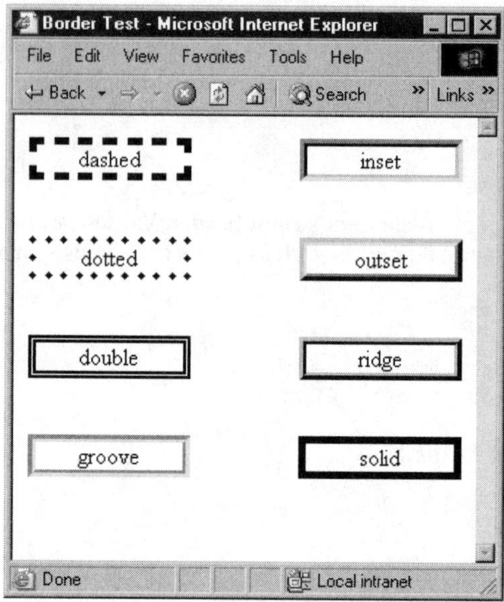

The shorthand style allows individual borders to be set. A single value copies to all border sides. With two values, the first sets the border style of top and bottom, and the second sets the right and left values. With three values, the first sets the top style, the second sets the right and left, and the third sets the bottom style. With four values, each is set individually in the order top, right, bottom, and left. In general, missing values are inferred from the value defined for the opposite side.

Examples

```
p          {border-style: solid;}
.twosides  {border-style: dashed solid;}
.allsides  {border-style: solid dashed groove inset;}
```

Browser and CSS Support Notes

CSS1	IE 4, 5 (no dotted/dashed), 5.5, 6	Nav 4, 4.5–4.8 (buggy), 6, 7	Opera 5, 6, 7

NOTE *Netscape 4 supports only one value for* **border-style**. *Use of multiple values will create erratic display under that browser.*

border-top

This property defines the width, style, and color for the top border of an element in a shorthand form. The syntax for the rules should be in order, as follows:

border-top: *border-width border-style border-color;*

Given that CSS1 did not support **border-top-color** and **border-top-style**, this property is useful for setting the characteristics of the top of boxes for older browsers.

Example

```
#boxtop  {border-top: thin solid blue;}
```

Browser and CSS Support Notes

CSS1	IE 4, 5, 5.5, 6	Nav 6, 7	Opera 4, 5, 6, 7

border-top-color

This property defines the color of an element's top border. See Appendix E for information on browser support of color values.

Example

```
p {border-style: solid; border-width: thin; border-top-color: red;}
```

Browser and CSS Support Notes

CSS2	IE 4, 5, 5.5, 6	Nav 6, 7	Opera 7

border-top-style

This property defines the style for the top border of an element. Allowed values are **none**, **dotted**, **dashed**, **solid**, **double**, **groove**, **ridge**, **inset**, and **outset**. See **border-style** property for specific information on each style.

Example

```
#box {border-width: 1px; border-style: solid; border-top-style: dashed;}
```

Browser and CSS Support Notes

CSS2	IE 4, 5, 5.5, 6	Nav 6, 7	Opera 7

border-top-width

This property sets the width of an element's top border. Values can be keywords (**thin**, **medium**, or **thick**) and numerical lengths such as pixels (**px**), inches (**in**), and so on.

Examples

```
p         {border-top-width: thin;}
#thicktop {border-top-width: 25px;}
```

Browser and CSS Support Notes

CSS1	IE 4, 5 (buggy), 5.5, 6	Nav 4, 4.5–4.8 (buggy), 6, 7	Opera 5, 6, 7

border-width

This property sets the width of an element's complete border. Values can be keywords (**thin**, **medium**, or **thick**) and numerical lengths. The **border-width** property can also be used to specify all four borders individually in the standard top, right, bottom, left style. A single value copies to all border sides. With two values, the first sets the border width of top and bottom, and the second sets the right and left values. With three values, the first sets the top width, the second sets the right and left, and the third sets the bottom width. With four values, each is set individually in the order top, right, bottom, and left.

Examples

```
div {border-width: medium;}    /* all sides set medium */
#d1 {border-width: 10px 5px;} /* 10px top-bottom, 5px right and left */
#fun {border-width: 10px 1px 4px 50px;} /* sides set individually */
```

Browser and CSS Support Notes

CSS1	IE 4, 5 (buggy), 5.5, 6	Nav 4, 4.5–4.8 (buggy), 6, 7	Opera 5, 6, 7

bottom

This property defines the *y* (vertical) coordinate for a positioned element, relative to the bottom of the enclosing element or browser window. Values can be specified as lengths (inches, pixels, and so on), as a percentage of the containing object's dimensions, or as **auto**, which lets this property function as determined by the browser or as defined by the parent element.

Examples

```
#div1 {position: absolute; left: 100px; bottom: 150px;}
#div2 {position: absolute; left: 50%; bottom: 30%;}
#div3 {position: absolute; left: auto; bottom: auto;}
```

Browser and CSS Support Notes

CSS2	IE 5, 5.5, 6	Nav 6, 7	Opera 5, 6, 7

caption-side

This property defines the position of a **caption** element within a **table**. It may take **left**, **right**, **top** or **bottom** as a value. A value of **top** will typically default in a browser.

Examples

```
caption {caption-side: bottom;}
.right  {caption-side: right;}
```

Browser and CSS Support Notes

CSS2	No IE support	Nav 6, 7	Opera 6, 7

clear

This property specifies the placement of an element in relation to floating objects. Possible values are **left**, **right**, **both**, and **none**. The property acts much like the **clear** attribute for the **
** tag and continues to return until the left, right, or both columns are clear. The default value is **none**.

Examples

```
br.clearright {clear: right;}
#clearboth    {clear: all;}
```

Browser and CSS Support Notes

CSS1	IE 4, 5 (buggy), 5.5, 6	Nav 4, 4.5–4.8 (buggy), 6, 7	Opera 5, 6, 7

clip

This property sets the coordinates of the clipping rectangle that houses the content of elements. The allowed clipping shape is a rectangle defined **rect (***top right bottom left***)** where the values specify offsets from the respective sides of the containing box. Eventually, other shapes may be possible.

Example

```
#div1 {position: absolute; left: 20px; top: 20px;
       width:100px; height:100; clip: rect(10px 90px 90px 10px);}
```

Browser and CSS Support Notes

CSS2	IE 4, 5 (buggy), 5.5, 6	Nav 6, 7	Opera 5, 6, 7

color

This property sets the color of text. Values can be specified as color names, hex values in three or six-digit format, or red-green-blue (RGB) values (numbers or percentages). For more information on color values, see Appendix E.

Examples

```
.sunflower {color: yellow;}
#sunburn   {color: #FF0000;}
p          {color: #FF0;}
#sunburn2  {color: rgb(255,0,0);}
body       {color: rgb(100%,100%,100%);}
```

Browser and CSS Support Notes

CSS1	IE 3, 4, 5, 5.5, 6	Nav 4, 4.5–4.7 6, 7	Opera 4, 5, 6, 7

content

This property generates content in a document and is used with the **:before** and **:after** pseudo-elements. Values for the property include ***string***, ***url***, ***counter***, **open-quote**, **close-quote**, **no-open-quote**, **no-close-quote**, and **attr(*X*)**. The ***string*** value simply inserts the defined string either before or after the selected element, depending on the rule in use. The ***url*** value is used to insert an external resource, typically an image. ***Counter*** values can be specified and used to automatically add a sequential indicator. The values **open-quote** and **close-quote** insert quotation symbols specified by the **quotes** property or, if undefined, default to the user-agent's default quote style. The **no-open-quote** and **no-close-quote** values do not insert quotation symbols but do increment or decrement the nesting level for quotes. The **attr(*X*)** returns a string value for the attribute *X* for the element the rule is associated with. If the related element does not have an attribute named *X*, an empty string is used.

Examples

```
div.section:before {content: "Section: ";}
div:before         {content: url(sectionstart.gif);}
div:after          {content: url(sectionend.gif);}
blockquote:before  {content: open-quote;}
blockquote:after   {content: close-quote;}
p:before           {content: counter(par-num, upper-roman); ". " }
p:before           {content: attr(title); }
```

Browser and CSS Support Notes

CSS2	IE not yet supported	Nav 6, 7 (no counter support)	Opera 7

counter-increment

This property accepts one or more names of counter names, each one optionally followed by an integer. The integer indicates by how much the counter is incremented or decremented for every occurrence of the element. The default increment is 1. Zero and negative integers are allowed. By default, counters are formatted as decimal numbers, but the styles supported by the **list-style-type** property are also available for counters and are specified with the syntax **counter(*name*, *list-style-type*)**.

Examples

```
div.section:before {content: "Section: " counter(section) ". ";
                    counter-increment: section;}  /* Add 1 to section */
h1.chapter:before  {content: counter(chno, upper-latin) ". ";
                    counter-increment: chno; }
.topten:before     {content: counter(countdown) ". ";
                    counter-increment: countdown -1; }
```

Browser and CSS Support Notes

CSS2	IE not yet supported	No Mozilla or Nav support yet	Opera 7

counter-reset

This property contains a list of one or more counter names, each one optionally followed by an integer. The integer gives the value that the counter is set to on each occurrence of the element. The default value is 0.

Examples

```
div.section:before {content: "Section: " counter(section) ". ";
                    counter-increment: section;}  /* Add 1 to section */
div.chapter:before {counter-reset: section;}      /* Set section to 0 */
```

Browser and CSS Support Notes

CSS2	IE not yet supported	Nav and Mozilla not yet supported	Opera 7

cursor

This property determines how the cursor displays when passed over the affected element. The **auto** value leaves the display to be determined by the user agent, so the cursor will display according to either the browser default settings or the user settings. The **crosshair** value renders the cursor as a simple cross, whereas **default** displays the system's default cursor (usually an arrow). Various other values listed in the CSS2 specification can indicate that something is a link (**pointer**), that text can be selected (**text**), that something can be resized in various directions (**e-resize, ne-resize, nw-resize, n-resize, se-resize, sw-resize, s-resize, w-resize**), or that the user must wait while a program is busy (**wait**). Table B-6 details the cursors supported in CSS2.

The value **url** can be used to reference a cursor source; multiple cursor sources can be listed. As with fonts, the user agent should attempt to render the first cursor listed, try the second one if necessary, and ultimately default to the generic cursor value listed last.

Examples

```
.help {cursor: help;}
p.clickable {cursor: hand;} /* non-standard */
a:longload  {cursor: wait;}
p {cursor:url("mything.cur"), url("second.cur"), text; }
```

Browser and CSS Support Notes

CSS2	IE 5, 5.5, 6	Nav 6, 7	Opera 7

TIP *Internet Explorer 6 custom cursor support includes animated cursors. While custom cursors may not be supported in all browsers, a variety of JavaScript tricks are often employed to imitate this CSS2 property.*

CSS Cursor Property Values	Description	Typical Rendering
auto	The browser determines the cursor to display based on the current context.	N/A
crosshair	A simple crosshair generally resembles a plus symbol.	
default	The browser's default cursor is generally an arrow.	
hand	A hand pointer (nonstandard but commonly supported).	
move	This indicates something is to be moved; usually rendered as four arrows together.	
e-resize	This indicates resizing as a double arrow pointing east-west (left-right).	
ne-resize	This indicates resizing as a double arrow pointing northeast-southwest.	
nw-resize	This indicates resizing as a double arrow pointing northwest-southeast.	
n-resize	This indicates resizing as a double arrow pointing north-south.	
pointer	Typically renders similar to the browser's default pointing cursor, which is generally a hand.	
se-resize	This indicates resizing as a double arrow pointing southeast-northwest.	
sw-resize	This indicates resizing as a double arrow pointing southwest-northeast.	
s-resize	This indicates resizing as a double arrow pointing north-south.	
w-resize	This indicates resizing as a double arrow pointing west-east.	

TABLE B-6 CSS2 Cursor Properties

CSS Cursor Property Values	Description	Typical Rendering
text	This indicates text that may be selected or entered; generally rendered as an I-bar.	I
wait	This indicates that the page is busy; generally rendered as an hourglass.	
help	This indicates that Help is available; the cursor is generally rendered as an arrow and a question mark.	?

TABLE B-6 CSS2 Cursor Properties *(continued)*

direction

The **direction** property is used to control the text direction much like the attribute **dir** for various HTML/XHTML tags. The allowed values are **rtl** (right to left) and **ltr** (left to right). While the direction property can easily affect block elements, for it to affect inline-level elements, the **unicode-bidi** property value must be **embed** or **override**.

Example

```
<div><span style="unicode-bidi: embed; direction: rtl;
background-color: yellow;">here doing I am  What!
</span> This is just a test</div>
```

Browser and CSS Support Notes

CSS2	IE 5, 5.5, 6	Nav 6, 7	No Opera support

display

This property specifies an element's display type and can override an element's defined display type. For example, block-level elements can be redefined as inline elements so that extra lines will not be placed between them. The allowed values for display under CSS1 are **inline**, **block**, **list-item**, and **none**. The value of **none** completely removes an element from the document tree and unlike the **hidden** value of the **visibility** property, **none** does not preserve an element's canvas space.

CSS2 adds **run-in**, **compact**, **marker**, **table**, **inline-table**, **table-row-group**, **table-header-group**, **table-footer-group**, **table-row**, **table-column-group**, **table-column**, **table-cell**, and **table-caption**.

Examples

```
p        {display: inline;}
b        {display: block;}
.removed {display: none;}
```

Browser and CSS Support Notes

CSS1	IE 4, 5, 5.5, 6	Nav 4, 4.5–4.8 (buggy), 6, 7	Opera 5, 6, 7

TIP *While the display property itself is generally implemented, most of the CSS2 display properties are not widely supported.*

empty-cells

This CSS2 property is used to control whether or not borders show on empty table cells. It takes two values: **show** or **hide**. The example here shows the subtle difference.

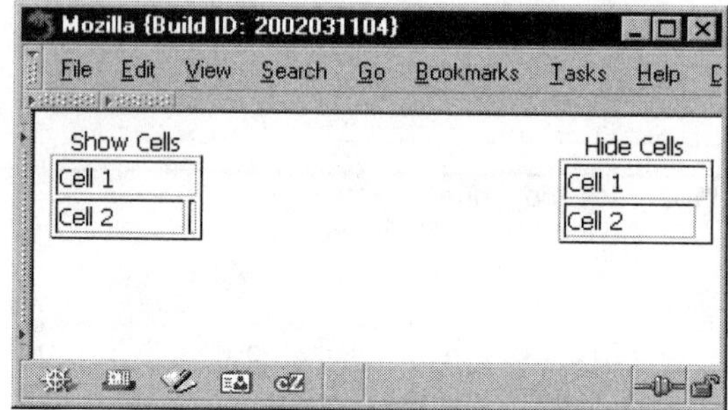

In most browsers that do not support this property, empty table cell borders are generally hidden.

Examples

```
<table border="1" style="empty-cells:show; width: 80px;">
<caption>Show Cells</caption>
<tr>
    <td colspan="2">Cell 1</td>
 </tr>
 <tr>
    <td>Cell 2</td>
    <td></td>
 </tr>
</table>
```

Browser and CSS Support Notes

CSS2	IE does not support except IE Mac	Nav 6, 7	Opera 5, 6, 7

float

This property influences the horizontal alignment of an element, making it “float” toward the left or right margin of its containing element. Possible values are **left**, **right**, and **none**. Floated regions act much like **<img>** tags that have been aligned left or right with respect to text.

Examples

```
#myimage {float: left;}
#pullquote {border-style: double; border-width: 5px;
            background-color: yellow; float: right;}
```

Browser and CSS Support Notes

CSS1	IE 4, 5 (buggy), 5.5, 6	Nav 4, 4.5–4.8 (buggy), 6, 7	Opera 6, 7

font

This property provides a shorthand way to specify all font properties with one style rule. The shorthand syntax is shown here:

```
font: font-style font-variant font-weight font-size/line-height font-family;
```

It is not necessary to include all properties and the lists of variant fonts should be separated by commas with those font names consisting of more than one word placed in quotes. You shouldn't use shorthand rules until the individual property values are correctly set.

Example

```
p {font: normal small-caps bold 12pt/18pt "Times New Roman", Courier, serif;}
.super {font: italic 18pt sans-serif;}
```

Browser and CSS Support Notes

CSS1	IE 3 (incomplete) 4, 5, 5.5, 6	Nav 4 (incomplete on Mac), 4.5–4.8, 6, 7	Opera 6, 7

font-family

This property sets the font face for text. It is equivalent to the **face** attribute of a **<font>** tag. Fonts may be named specifically or a generic font family name may be used. When multiple font names are specified and separated by commas, they are read in descending order looking for the first match. Generally, a generic font name will be listed at the end of a font list. There are five generic font names currently available: **serif**, **sans-serif**, **cursive**, **fantasy**, and **monospace**. Their renderings under modern browsers are shown here, but beware that they may not render the same in all browsers.

Examples

```
.modern  {font-family: "Arial, Helvetica, sans-serif";}
p        {font-family: "Times New Roman";}
body     {font-family: "Times New Roman, Courier";}
#special {font-family: fantasy;}
```

Browser Support Notes

CSS1	IE 4, 5, 5.5, 6	Nav 4, 4.5–4.8, 6, 7	Opera 4, 5, 6, 7

font-size

This property sets the font size of text. Options include exact sizes set with points (**pt**), pixels (**px**), picas (**pc**), inches (**in**), millimeters (**mm**), and centimeters (**cm**). Standard relative sizing units in em (**em**) and x-height (**ex**) may also be used, as well as the relative size keywords **larger** and **smaller** and percentage value (for example, 90%). Percentage values set the font size to a percentage of the primary font size of a section or document. For example, if the **font-size** for the **body** element was set to 12pt, and font size for a <p> tag inside the **body** was set to 200%, the text within the **<p>** tag would be 24pt. The property also supports size keywords (**xx-small**, **x-small**, **small**, **medium**, **large**, **x-large**, **xx-large**). The size keywords are roughly equivalent to the 1–7 size values for a **<font>** tag and the use of **larger** or **smaller** will increase or decrease the text size one relative size.

Examples

```
body      {font-size: 18pt;}
#heading1 {font-size: 36px;}
p         {font-size: 2em;}
h6        {font-size: xx-small;}
.special  {font-size: 75%;}
```

Browser Support Notes

CSS1	IE 4, 5, 5.5, 6	Nav 4, 4.5–4.8, 6, 7	Opera 4, 5, 6, 7

TIP *Keyword sizes such as* ***xx-large*** *may vary noticeably in browser implementations. Point (**pt**) size value may also vary across systems that measure screen resolution differently.*

font-size-adjust

This property is used for scaled fonts to make sure that text takes up the same amount of room regardless of the availability of a particular font or not. According to specification, when used properly the property helps ensure the x-height of the first font in a font selection list is maintained for subsequent fonts in the list. This property takes a number, which specifies the scaling factor to be used to adjust fonts. The default value of **none** does not preserve the font's x-height.

Browser Support Notes

CSS2	No IE support	No Nav or Mozilla support	No Opera support

font-size-stretch

This property is used to stretch or condense a font and takes values of **ultra-condensed**, **extra-condensed**, **condensed**, **semi-condensed**, **normal**, **semi-expanded**, **expanded**, **extra-expanded**, and **ultra-expanded**. The property also can take a relative value of **wider** or **narrower** to modify the appearance of text relative to a parent font. The default value is **normal** and is used to override inherited **font-size-stretch** values. At the time of this edition's writing, this property was yet to be supported by any major browser.

Examples

```
.narrow         {font-stretch: narrower;}
#arialstretch   {font-family: Arial; font-stretch: ultra-expanded;}
```

Browser Support Notes

CSS2	No IE support	No Nav or Mozilla support	No Opera support

font-style

This property sets the style of a font to **normal**, **oblique**, or **italic**. Sometimes font style can be controlled using a specific font (for example, Times New Roman Italic).

Examples

```
.backToNormal {font-style: normal;}
#special      {font-style: oblique;}
p.emphasis    {font-style: italic;}
```

Browser Support Notes

CSS1	IE 4, 5, 5.5, 6	Nav 4, 4.5–4.8, 6, 7	Opera 4, 5, 6, 7

font-variant

This property sets a variation of the specified or default font family. Values currently supported are **normal** and **small-caps**. The **small-caps** value sets text in smaller size all capitals. This style is often used in legal documents and license agreements. The **normal** value would be used to override any inherited font-variant value.

Examples

```
.legalese  {font-variant: small-caps;}
.nolegal   {font-variant: normal;}
```

Browser Support Notes

CSS1	IE 4, 5, 5.5, 6	Nav 4, 4.5–4.8, 6, 7	Opera 4, 5, 6, 7

font-weight

This property sets the weight, or relative boldness, of a font. Values can be set with named values (**normal** or **bold**) or with numbered values (**100–900**). Numeric weight values run from lightest (**100**) to boldest (**900**) in increments of 100. In practice, under most browsers the values **100–500** display as normal text; **600–900** display as bold. Browser screen support for other values is inconsistent at best, though print output may show variations. Relative values of **lighter** or **bolder** will increase or decrease the **font-weight** value relative to its surrounding weight. However, onscreen this generally means simply toggling the boldness on or off. There is some consideration for mapping various weight fonts into associated font families. For example, text in Helvetica at **font-weight: 900** would be mapped into Helvetica Black. However, while described in the specification, the support for weight to font family mapping appears nonexistent in browsers at this edition's writing.

Examples

```
em           {font-weight: bold;}
#light       {font-weight: 300;}
.superbold   {font-weight: 900;}
strong       {font-weight: normal; color: red;}
/* note override of default tag presentation */
```

Browser Support Notes

CSS1	IE 4, 5, 5.5, 6	Nav 4, 4.5–4.8, 6, 7	Opera 4, 5, 6, 7

height

This property sets the height of an element's content region (excluding padding, border, and margin). It is generally used on positioned block elements. Absolute measurements as well as percentage values are allowed. Percentage values are based on the height of the containing element. The default value **auto** automatically calculates the height of an element, based on the height of the containing element and the size of the content. Negative values are not allowed.

Examples

```
p {height: 200px; padding: 10px; border: solid 5px;}
#div1 {height: 50%; width: 50%;}
```

Browser Support Notes

CSS1	IE 4, 5, 5.5, 6	Nav 4, 4.5–4.8, 6, 7	Opera 4, 5, 6, 7

left

This property defines the *x* (horizontal) coordinate for a positioned element, relative to the left side of the containing element or browser window. Given that the containing element itself may be positioned, the value of left does not always relate to the distance from the browser window. Values can be specified as lengths (inches, pixels, and so on), as a percentage of the containing object's dimensions, or as **auto**.

Examples

```
#div1 {position: absolute; left: 120px; top: 50px;}
#div2 {position: absolute; left: 30%; top: 50%;}
#div3 {position: absolute; left: auto; top: auto;}
```

Browser Support Notes

CSS2	IE 4, 5, 5.5, 6	Nav 4, 4.5–4.8, 6, 7	Opera 5, 6, 7

letter-spacing

This property sets the amount of spacing between letters. Values can be set in various units (negative values are permitted) or to the default value **normal**. Because you can't cross tags, you may not have full control over inter-character spacing; in other words, the **letter-spacing** property should not be confused with the ability to fully kern text.

Example

```
.tight {font-family: Arial; font-size: 14pt; letter-spacing: 2pt;}
p      {letter-spacing: 1em;}
p.norm {letter-spacing: normal;}
```

Browser and CSS Support Notes

CSS1	IE 4, 5, 5.5, 6	Nav 6, 7	Opera 4, 5, 6, 7

line-height

This property sets the height (leading) between lines of text in a block-level element such as a paragraph. Values can be specified as a number of lines, a number of units (pixels, points, inches, centimeters, and so on), or a percentage of the font size. This property is often used in conjunction with the **font-size** property. Alternatively, the **line-height** can be set through the shorthand **font** property.

Examples

```
.double {line-height: 2;}
p       {font-size: 14px; line-height: 16px;}
p.norm  {line-height: normal;}
body    {line-height: 4ex;}
div     {line-height: 125%;}
```

Browser and CSS Support Notes

CSS1	IE 3, 4, 5, 5.5, 6	Nav 4, 4.5–4.7 (some problems with number of lines value), 6, 7	Opera 4, 5, 6, 7

list-style

This shorthand property sets **list-style-type, list-style-position** and **list-style-image**. In practice, the properties can appear in any order, but they ought to be written in the presented order.

Examples

```
ul       {list-style: inside url("bullet.gif");}
#square  {list-style: outside square;}
ol       {list-style: lower-roman inside;}
```

Browser and CSS Support Notes

CSS1	IE 4, 5, 5.5, 6	Nav 6, 7	Opera 4, 5, 6, 7

list-style-image

This property assigns a graphic image to a list label, using the URL of the image. The value for **list-style-image** other than a URL is **none**.

Example

```
ul {list-style-image: url(ball.gif);}
```

Browser and CSS Support Notes

CSS1	IE 4, 5, 5.5, 6	Nav 6, 7	Opera 4, 5, 6, 7

list-style-position

This property specifies whether the labels for an element's list items are positioned **inside** or **outside** the "box" defined by the list. The difference is illustrated clearly here.

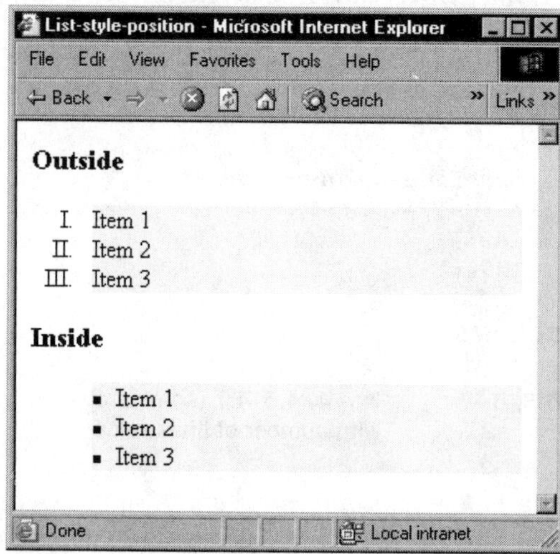

Example

```
ol {list-style-type: upper-roman; list-style-position: outside;
    background: yellow;}
ul {list-style-type: square; list-style-position: inside;
    background: yellow;}
```

Browser and CSS Support Notes

CSS1	IE 4, 5, 5.5, 6	Nav 6, 7	Opera 4, 5, 6, 7

list-style-type

This property defines labels for ordered and unordered lists or elements that have their **display** property set to **list-item**. The value **none** prevents a list label from displaying. CSS1 defines **disc**, **circle**, and **square**, which are typically used on unordered lists (**<ul>**). The values **decimal**, **lower-roman**, **upper-roman**, **lower-alpha**, and **upper-alpha** are typically used on ordered lists **(<ol>).** These property types correspond to the HTML/XHTML type attributes for lists. CSS2 adds more type values primarily for ordered lists in foreign languages. The CSS2 values include **decimal-leading-zero**, **lower-greek**, **lower-latin**, **upper-latin**, **hebrew**, **armenian**, **georgian**, **cjk-ideographic**, **hiragana**, **katakana**, **hiragana-iroha**, and **katakana-iroha**.

Examples

```
ol       {list-style-type: upper-roman;}
ol.none  {list-style-type: none;}
.ichi-ni {list-style-type: hiragana;}
```

Browser and CSS Support Notes

CSS1	IE 4, 5, 5.5, 6	Nav 4, 4.5–4.8, 6, 7	Opera 4, 5, 6, 7

TIP *Many of the CSS2 values for **list-style-type** are not supported in browsers.*

margin

The **margin** property sets a consistent margin on all four sides of the affected element. Margin values can be set to a specific length (**15pt**, **2em**, and so on) or to a percentage value of the block element's width. Margins can be set to negative values but content may be clipped. The value **auto** attempts to calculate the margin automatically. However, this value is buggy in many CSS implementations, particularly older browser versions, and might be avoided for compatibility reasons.

As a shorthand form, it is possible to set the four margins (**margin-top, margin-bottom, margin-right**, and **margin-left**) independently with this property. A single value will be copied to all four margins. With two values, the first value will specify top and bottom margins and the second value will specify the top right and left margins. If three values are specified, the first defines the top margin, the second defines the left and right margins, and the third defines the bottom margin. Note that the unspecified margin is inferred from the value defined for its opposite side. Lastly, all four values can also be set in order of top, right, bottom, and left.

Examples

```
p {margin: 15pt;} /* all sides  15pt */
#div1 {margin: 20px 10px;} /* 20px top-bottom, 10px left-right */
#div2 {margin: 10px 10px 5px 10px;}
/* 10px top, 10px right 5px bottom, 10px left */
```

Browser and CSS Support Notes

CSS1	IE 4 (buggy), 5, 5.5, 6	Nav 4,4.5–4.8 (buggy), 6, 7	Opera 4, 5, 6, 7

margin-bottom

This property sets an element's bottom margin and can be any normal measurement value as well as a negative value.

Example

```
p {margin-bottom: 10pt;}
```

Browser and CSS Support Notes

CSS1	IE 4 (buggy), 5, 5.5, 6	Nav 4, 4.5–4.8 (buggy), 6, 7	Opera 4, 5, 6, 7

margin-left

This property sets an element's left margin and can be any normal measurement value as well as a negative value.

Examples

```
p    {margin-right: 15pt;}
.off {margin-left: -10px;}
```

Browser and CSS Support Notes

CSS1	IE 4 (buggy), 5, 5.5, 6	Nav 4, 4.5–4.8 (buggy), 6, 7	Opera 4, 5, 6, 7

margin-right

This property sets an element's right margin and can be any normal measurement value as well as a negative value.

Example

```
p {margin-right: 15pt;}
```

Browser and CSS Support Notes

CSS1	IE 4 (buggy), 5, 5.5, 6	Nav 4, 4.5–4.8 (buggy), 6, 7	Opera 4, 5, 6, 7

margin-top

This property sets an element's top margin and can be any normal measurement value as well as a negative value.

Example

```
p {margin-top: 15pt;}
```

Browser and CSS Support Notes

CSS1	IE 4 (buggy), 5, 5.5, 6	Nav 4, 4.5–4.8 (buggy), 6, 7	Opera 4, 5, 6, 7

marker-offset

This property specifies the distance between the nearest border edges of a marker box and its associated surrounding box. The value may be specified in any length unit either relative or absolute. Lengths may be negative. So far, this property is not supported by any major browser.

Example

```
li:before { display: marker; marker-offset: 3em;
            content: counter(mycounter, lower-roman) ".";
            counter-increment: mycounter;}
```

Browser and CSS Support Notes

CSS2	No IE support	No Nav or Mozilla support	No Opera support

marks

Defines if during printing cross marks (**cross**) or crop marks (**crop**) are rendered just outside a page box edge. In order to see these indications, your printed page size may have to be adjusted smaller.

Example

```
body {marks: crop;}
```

Browser and CSS Support Notes

CSS2	No IE support	No Netscape or Mozilla support	No Opera support

max-height

Defines the maximum height a region may expand to if it is relatively sized. Measurements are generally in fixed values although relative units such as percentages may be used.

Example

```
#div1 {height: 50%; max-height: 500px; overflow: hidden;}
```

Browser and CSS Support Notes

CSS2	No IE support	Nav 6, 7	Opera 7

max-width

Defines the maximum width a region may expand to if it is relatively sized. Useful to constrain large regions of text from having overly long lines, which can result in readability problems. Measurements are generally in fixed values although relative units such as percentages may be used.

Example

```
#div1 {width: 50%; max-width: 800px;}
```

Browser and CSS Support Notes

CSS2	No IE support	Nav 6, 7	Opera 7

min-height

Defines the minimum height a region may reduce to if it is relatively sized and the browser window is adjusted. Measurements are generally in fixed values although relative units such as percentages may be used.

Example

```
#div1 {min-height: 100px; height: 50%;}
```

Browser and CSS Support Notes

CSS2	No IE support	Nav 6, 7	Opera 7

min-width

Defines the minimum width a region may reduce to if it is relatively sized and the browser window is adjusted. Measurements are generally in fixed values although relative units such as percentages may be used.

Example

```
#div1 {width: 50%; max-width: 800px; min-width: 400px;}
```

Browser and CSS Support Notes

CSS2	No IE support	Nav 6, 7	Opera 7

orphans

Defines the minimum number of lines of a paragraph that must be left at the bottom of a page. This property is really only meaningful in a paged environment such as print output. The default value is **2** if unspecified.

Examples

```
#hateorphans  {orphans: 5;}
.orphaned     {orphans: 1;}
```

Browser and CSS Support Notes

CSS2	No IE support	Nav 6, 7	Opera 7

outline

This property is a shorthand form that sets all outline properties at once. Outlines resemble borders but take up no additional space, and can be set to a shape different from that of the image, form field, or other element to which they are applied. Outlines are drawn over an item, rather than around it, thus causing no reflow. The shorthand syntax is as follows:

```
outline: outline-color outline-style outline-width;
```

While outlines are similar to borders, their individual sides cannot be set. All outline properties, both specific and shorthand, apply to the whole outline.

Examples

```
p:hover  {outline: dashed;}
.test    {outline: green solid 10px;}
```

Browser and CSS Support Notes

CSS2	No IE support	Nav 6, 7 use a proprietary style	Opera 7

TIP *Mozilla also supports an outline style with a proprietary syntax:* ***-moz-outline****.*

outline-color

This property accepts all CSS color values as discussed earlier in the appendix as well as in Appendix E. The keyword **invert** is also supported and should perform a color inversion on the pixels on the screen.

Examples

```
p:hover  {outline-style: dashed; outline-color: green;}
.test    {outline-width: 10px; outline-style: solid; outline-color: #f00;}
```

Browser and CSS Support Notes

CSS2	No IE support	Nav 6, 7 use a proprietary style	Opera 7

outline-style

This property defines a style for an element's outline, which is generally the same as its **border-style**. While outlines resemble borders, they are not supposed to take up canvas space, and theoretically could appear as a different shape than borders, potentially wrapping around the edges of content. Since outlines are drawn over an item, rather than around it, there is no reflow. The allowed values for this property are the same as **border-style** and include **none**, **dotted**, **dashed**, **solid**, **double**, **groove**, **ridge**, **inset**, and **outset**. See **border-style** property for specific information on each style.

Examples

```
p:hover  {outline-style: dashed;}
.test    {outline-width: 10px; outline-style: solid; outline-color: black;}
```

Browser and CSS Support Notes

CSS2	No IE support	Nav 6, 7 use a proprietary style	Opera 7

outline-width

This property defines a width for an element's outline, which is generally the same as its **border-width**. While outlines resemble borders, they are not supposed to take up canvas space, and theoretically could appear as a different shape than borders. Furthermore, outlines are drawn over an item, rather than around it, thus causing no reflow. Like **border-width**, this property's values can be keywords (**thin**, **medium**, or **thick**) and numerical lengths such as pixels (**px**), inches (**in**), and so on.

Examples

```
p     {outline-style: dashed; outline-width: thick;}
.test {outline-width: 10px; outline-style: solid; outline-color: black;}
```

Browser and CSS Support Notes

CSS2	No IE support	Nav 6, 7 use a proprietary style	Opera 7

overflow

This property determines an element's behavior when its content doesn't fit into the space defined by the element's other properties. Possible values are **visible**, **hidden**, **scroll**, **auto** or **inherit**. By default, content will be visible, but a value of **hidden** will clip content that extends past the defined region size. A value of **scroll** adds scroll bars appropriately so content can be viewed.

Examples

```
#div1 {position: absolute; left: 20px; top: 20px;
      width: 100px; height: 100px; overflow: scroll;}
#div2 {height: 100px; width: 100px; overflow: hidden;}
```

Browser and CSS Support Notes

CSS2	IE 4, 5, 5.5 (buggy), 6	Nav 4, 4.5–4.8 (buggy), 6, 7	Opera 4, 5, 6, 7

TIP *Printing content in a region with* ***overflow*** *set to* ***scroll*** *can be troublesome.*

padding

The padding properties set the space between an element's border and its content. The **padding** property sets the padding for all four sides; the other four properties set the padding for specific sides. Values can be specified as specific values (pixels, points, and so on) or as a percentage of the element's overall width. The shorthand **property** is similar to **margin**. A single value creates equal padding on all sides. Up to four values can be used, in the following clockwise order: **top**, **right**, **bottom**, and **left**. Any missing value defaults to the value defined for the side opposite to it. However, unlike the **margin** property, the **padding** property cannot take negative values.

Examples

```
#div1 {border-style: solid; padding: 10px 20px 10px;}
#div2 {border-style: dashed; padding: 50px;}
#div3 {padding: 10px 20px;}
```

Browser and CSS Support Notes

CSS1	IE 4, 5, 5.5 (buggy), 6	Nav 4, 4.5–4.8 (buggy), 6, 7	Opera 4, 5, 6, 7

padding-bottom

This property sets the distance between an element's bottom border and the bottom of its contained content.

Example

```
#div1 {padding-bottom: 5px;}
```

Browser and CSS Support Notes

CSS1	IE 4, 5 (buggy), 5.5, 6	Nav 4, 4.5–4.8 (buggy), 6, 7	Opera 4, 5, 6, 7

padding-left

This property sets the distance between an element's left border and the left edge of its content.

Example

```
#div1 {padding-left: 3em;}
```

Browser and CSS Support Notes

CSS1	IE 4, 5 (buggy), 5.5, 6	Nav 4, 4.5–4.8 (buggy), 6, 7	Opera 4, 5, 6, 7

padding-right

This property sets the distance between an element's right border and the rightmost edge of its content.

Example

```
#div1 {padding-right: .5in;}
```

Browser and CSS Support Notes

CSS1	IE 4, 5 (buggy), 5.5, 6	Nav 4, 4.5–4.8 (buggy), 6, 7	Opera 4, 5, 6, 7

padding-top

This property sets the distance between an element's top border and the top of its content.

Example

```
#div1 {padding-top: 25px;}
```

Browser and CSS Support Notes

CSS1	IE 4, 5 (buggy), 5.5, 6	Nav 4, 4.5–4.8 (buggy), 6, 7	Opera 4, 5, 6, 7

page

Defines the type of page where an element should be displayed. The page is defined and named with an **@page** selector.

Example

```
/* sets tables to be on landscape pages */
@page land {size: landscape;}
table {page: land;}
```

Browser and CSS Support Notes

CSS2	IE 5.5, 6	No Nav or Mozilla support	No Opera support

page-break-after

This property is used to control page breaks when printing a document. The property is set relative to the end of an element. A value of **always** forces a page break after the element. A value of **avoid** attempts to avoid a page break after the element. A value of **left** forces one or two page breaks after the element so that the next page is considered a left page. A value of **right** forces one or two page breaks after the element so the next page is considered a right page. The default value of **auto** neither forces nor forbids a page break.

Examples

```
#breakitdown {page-break-after: always;}
.getitright  {page-break-after: right;}
```

Browser and CSS Support Notes

CSS2	IE 4, 5, 5.5, 6	Nav 6, 7	Opera 7

page-break-before

This property is used to control page breaks when printing a document. This property is set relative to the start of an element. A value of **always** forces a page break before the element. A value of **avoid** attempts to avoid a page break before the element. A value of **left** forces one or two page breaks before the element so that the next page is considered a left page. A value of **right** forces one or two page breaks before the element so the next page is considered a right page. The default value of **auto** neither forces nor forbids a page break.

Examples

```
#breakitdown {page-break-before: always;}
.lefty       {page-break-before: left;}
```

Browser and CSS Support Notes

CSS2	IE 4, 5, 5.5, 6	Nav 6, 7	Opera 7

page-break-inside

This property is used to force or prohibit a printing page break within an element. A value of **always** forces a page break within the element. A value of **avoid** attempts to avoid a page break within the element. A value of **left** forces one or two page breaks within the element so that the next page is considered a left page. A value of **right** forces one or two page breaks within the element so the next page is considered a right page. The default value of **auto** neither forces nor forbids a page break.

Examples

```
#breakitdown {page-break-inside: always;}
.nobreaks    {page-break-inside: avoid;}
```

Browser and CSS Support Notes

CSS2	No IE support	Nav 6, 7	Opera 7

position

This property defines how an element is positioned relative to other elements, using the values **static**, **absolute**, **fixed**, and **relative**. When positioned **absolute**, the **left**, **right**, **top**, and **bottom** properties define the element's precise location, using the affected element's upper-left corner (0,0) as reference. Because elements can contain other elements, 0,0 is not necessarily the upper-left corner of the browser window. When a **relative** position is used, offsets will be related to the object's natural position in the document flow. An element with absolute position will be set at the defined coordinates regardless to its position within the document, but will scroll with a window. An object with a **fixed** position will stay in position onscreen as things scroll. The default value static places elements according to the natural order in which they occur in a document.

Examples

```
span    {position: relative; left: 190px; top: 30px;}
#div1   {position: absolute; left: 120px; top: 50px;}
#navbar {position:fixed; left: 0px; top: 0px;}
```

Browser and CSS Support Notes

CSS2	IE 4, 5, 5.5, 6	Nav 4, 4.5–4.8, 6, 7	Opera 4, 5, 6, 7

NOTE *The **fixed** position value is not supported in Internet Explorer versions although it is supported in later versions of standards-compliant browsers such as Mozilla and Opera.*

quotes

This property defines the style of quotation marks to be used with embedded quotations. A value of **none** produces no quotation marks. Two strings can also be given for the left and rightmost quotation symbols.

Examples

```
<style type="text/css">
 q { quotes: '"[' ']"'  }
</style>

<p>Hey <q>You can <q>quote</q> me</q> on this</p>
```

Browser and CSS Support Notes

CSS2	No IE support	Nav 6, 7	Opera 7 claims support but testing indicates it is inconsistent and occasionally broken.

right

This property defines the *x* (horizontal) coordinate for a positioned element, relative to the right side of either the containing element or browser window if directly within the **<body>**. Values can be specified as lengths (inches, pixels, and so on), as a percentage of the containing object's dimensions, or as **auto**. Most browsers assume pixels as the measure if not defined explicitly.

Examples

```
#div1 {position: absolute; right: 120px; top: 50px;}
#div2 {position: absolute; right: 30%; top: 50%;}
#div3 {position: absolute; right: auto; top: auto;}
```

Browser and CSS Support Notes

CSS2	IE 4, 5, 5.5, 6	Nav 6, 7	Opera 4, 5, 6, 7

size

This property specifies the size and orientation of a page box for printing. The **size** may either be "absolute" (fixed size) or "relative" (scalable, i.e., fitting available sheet sizes). Relative values include **landscape** and **portrait**. The default value is **auto**.

Examples

```
@page {size: landscape;}
@page {size: 6in 10in;} /* funny width and height */
```

Browser and CSS Support Notes

CSS2	No IE support but similar proprietary facilities available.	Nav 6, 7	Opera 7

table-layout

This property controls the algorithm used to lay out the table cells, rows, and columns. A value of **fixed** uses the fixed table layout algorithm, which relays not the content of the cells but simply the width of the tables, columns, borders, and defined cell spacing. This should result in faster page rendering. The default value of **auto** uses the standard automatic table layout algorithm, which may require multiple passes or take perceptible time to calculate, particularly when the table is complex or heavily nested.

Example

```
table {table-layout: fixed;}
```

Browser and CSS Support Notes

CSS2	IE 5, 5.5, 6	Nav 6, 7	Opera 7

text-align

This property sets the horizontal alignment of elements. Values are **left**, **right**, **center**, and **justify**. The default value is **left**. This property is similar to the **align** attribute available with HTML/XHTML block-level tags such as **<p>**. Justification may produce poor results: showing white space "rivers" in large text bodies because of screen resizing.

Examples

```
.goleft {text-align: left;}
p       {text-align: justify;}
h1.cent {text-align: center;}
```

Browser and CSS Support Notes

CSS1	IE 3, 4 (no justification), 5, 5.5, 6	Nav 4, 4.5–4.7 (quirks), 6, 7	Opera 4, 5, 6, 7

text-decoration

This property defines specific text effects. Possible values are **blink**, **line-through**, **overline**, **underline**, and **none**. The **blink** value is actually part of the CSS2 specification but is not supported in IE up to version 6. The **text-decoration** property is often used with the **a** element and its associated pseudoclasses (**a:active**, **a:hover**, **a:link**, and **a:visited**) to turn off link underlining or set different looks for hover or visited states.

Example

```
a            {text-decoration: none;}
a:visited    {text-decoration: line-through;}
a:hover      {text-decoration: underline;}
.onsale      {text-decoration: blink;}
.underlined {text-decoration: underline;}
.struck      {text-decoration: line-through;}
```

Browser and CSS Support Notes

CSS1	IE 4, 5, 5.5, 6 (no support for **blink**)	Nav 4, 4.5–4.8 (incomplete), 6, 7	Opera 6, 7

text-indent

This property indents the text in the first line of a block-level element. Values can be defined as length values (**.5cm**, **15px**, **12pt**, and so on) or as a percentage of the width of the block element. The default value is **0**, which indicates no indentation.

Examples

```
p           {text-indent: 5pt;}
#section1  {text-indent: 15%;}
```

Browser and CSS Support Notes

CSS1	IE 3, 4, 5, 5.5, 6	Nav 4, 4.5–4.7, 6, 7	Opera 4, 5, 6, 7

text-shadow

This as yet unimplemented CSS2 property sets a shadow effect for text. The shadow is defined by a comma-separated list of shadow effects to be applied to the text of the element. The shadow effects are applied in the order specified and may overlay each other, but they will never overlay the text itself. Each shadow effect must specify a shadow offset and may optionally specify a blur radius and a shadow color.

A shadow offset is specified with two length values usually in absolute measurement that indicate the distance from the text. The first length value specifies the horizontal distance to the right of the text. A negative horizontal length value places the shadow to the left of the text. The second length value specifies the vertical distance below the text. A negative vertical length value places the shadow above the text.

An optional blur radius may be specified after the shadow offset. The blur radius is a length value that indicates the boundaries of the blur effect.

A color value may optionally be specified before or after the length values of the shadow effect. The color value will be used as the basis for the shadow effect. If no color is specified, the value of an inherited color property is used.

Examples

```
h3 {text-shadow: 0.2em 0.2em; }
/* shadow to right and below */

span {text-shadow: 3px 3px 5px red; }
/* red blurry shadow right and below */

.solar{background: white; color: white; text-shadow: black 0px 0px 5px;}
/* sets an outline effect on the text */
```

Browser and CSS Support Notes

CSS2	No IE support	No Netscape or Mozilla support	No Opera support

text-transform

This property transforms the case of the affected text. Possible values are **capitalize**, **uppercase**, **lowercase**, and **none**. Note that a value of **capitalize** will affect every word in the selected text rather than first word only. The value of **none** is used to override any inherited **text-transform** values.

Examples

```
h1           {text-transform: capitalize;}
h1.nocap     {text-transform: none;}
.allsmall    {text-transform: lowercase;}
#bigletters {text-transform: uppercase; font-size: larger;}
```

Browser and CSS Support Notes

CSS1	IE 4, 5, 5.5, 6	Nav 4 (incomplete for Mac), 4.5–4.8, 6, 7	Opera 6, 7

top

This property defines the *y* (vertical) coordinate for a positioned element, relative to the top of the enclosing object or browser window. Values can be specified as lengths (inches, pixels, and so on), as a percentage of the containing object's dimensions, or as **auto**, which lets this property function as determined by the browser or as defined by the parent element. Browsers often assume pixels as a default measurement if none is specified.

Examples

```
#div1 {position: absolute; left: 100px; top: 150px;}
#div2 {position: absolute; left: 50%; top: 30%;}
#div3 {position: absolute; left: auto; top: auto;}
```

Browser and CSS Support Notes

CSS1	IE 4, 5, 5.5, 6	Nav 4, 4.5–4.8, 6, 7	Opera 6, 7

unicode-bidi

This property allows the text direction to be overridden to support multiple languages in the same document. The value **normal** uses the standard direction and rendering. A value of **embed** allows a new level of embedding to change direction while **bidi-override** allows the direction property to override any predefined direction.

Example

```
<div><span style="unicode-bidi: embed; direction: rtl;
      background-color: yellow;">?here doing I am  What</span>
 This is just a test.</div>
```

Browser and CSS Support Notes

CSS2	IE 5, 5.5, 6	Nav 6, 7	No Opera support

vertical-align

This property sets the vertical positioning of text and images with respect to the baseline setting. Possible values are **baseline**, **sub**, **super**, **top**, **text-top**, **middle**, **bottom**, and **text-bottom**. A value of **top** aligns the top of text or images with the top of the tallest element, relative to the baseline. A value of **text-top** aligns the top of text or images with the top of the font in the containing element while **text-bottom** aligns things with the bottom of the font. A value of **middle** aligns the middle of text or images to the middle of the x-height of the containing element. A value of **bottom** aligns the bottom of text or images with the bottom of the lowest element, relative to the baseline. The **sub** and **super** values provide subscript and superscript style. Percentages can also be given as values. The default value is **baseline**.

Examples

```
p      {vertical-align: top;}
.dive  {vertical-align: sub;}
.climb {vertical-align: super;}
```

Browser and CSS Support Notes

CSS1	IE 4, 5 (buggy), 5.5, 6	Nav 4, 4.5–4.8 (buggy), 6, 7	Opera 4, 5, 6, 7

visibility

This property determines whether or not an element is visible. Possible values are **hidden**, **visible**, and **inherit**. Be aware that a hidden element still occupies its full canvas space, but because this property is often used in conjunction with **z-index**, this may not matter. The default value **inherit** specifies that an element inherits its visibility state from the element that contains it. CSS2 defines a **collapse** value for this property that is often used with table cells. This property is commonly accessed via JavaScript to show and hide page objects in a manner often dubbed DHTML (Dynamic HTML).

Examples

```
p             {visibility: inherit;}
 peek-a-boo  {visibility: hidden;}
```

Browser and CSS Support Notes

CSS2	IE 4, 5, 5.5, 6	Nav 4, 4.5–4.8, 6, 7	Opera 4, 5, 6, 7

white-space

This property controls how spaces, tabs, and newline characters are handled in an element. Possible values are **normal**, **pre**, and **nowrap**. The normal value collapses multiple white space characters into single spaces and automatically wraps lines, as in normal HTML/XHTML. The **pre** value makes the element act much like a **<pre>** tag and preserves all white space. The value of **nowrap** prevents lines from wrapping if they exceed the element's content width.

Examples

```
p             {white-space: pre;}
pre           {white-space: normal;}
.sourcecode {white-space: nowrap;}
```

Browser and CSS Support Notes

CSS1	IE 5.5, 6	Nav 4, 4.5–4.8 (partial), 6, 7	Opera 4, 5, 6, 7

widows

Defines the minimum number of lines in a paragraph to be left at the top of a page. This property is really only meaningful in a paged environment such as print output. The default value is **2** if unspecified.

Examples

```
#hatewidows   {widows: 5;}
.widowmaker   {widows: 1;}
```

Browser and CSS Support Notes

CSS2	No IE support	Nav 6, 7	Opera 7

width

This property sets the width of an element's content region (excluding padding, border, and margin). Standard length units can be used and pixels (**px**) is often the assumed measurement in browsers. Percentage values, based on the width of the containing element, can also be used. The default value of **auto** automatically calculates the width of an element, based on the width of the containing element and the size of the content.

Examples

```
p     {width: 400px; padding: 10px; border: solid 5px;}
#div1 {width: 80%; padding: 10px; border: solid 5px;}
```

Browser and CSS Support Notes

CSS1	IE 4, 5, 5.5, 6	Nav 4, 4.5–4.8, 6, 7	Opera 4, 5, 6, 7

word-spacing

This property sets the spacing between words. Values can be set in inches (**in**), centimeters (**cm**), millimeters (**mm**), points (**pt**), picas (**pc**), em spaces (**em**), or pixels (**px**). Negative values are possible with this property, and may be used either for interesting effects or to create unreadable text. A default value of **normal** sets word spacing to the standard browser setting.

Examples

```
p         {font-family: Arial; font-size: 16pt; word-spacing: 3pt;}
p.normal  {font-family: Helvetica; font-size: 12pt; word-spacing: normal;}
```

Browser and CSS Support Notes

CSS1	IE 6	Nav 4, 4.5–4.8, 6, 7	Opera 4, 5, 6, 7

z-index

This property defines a layering context with relative or absolute positioning for elements containing other elements. By default, overlapping elements stack in the order in which they are defined in an HTML/XHTML document. This property can override default layering by assigning numeric layering values to an element, with higher numbers layering above lower numbers. The **auto** value tries to determine the z-placement of an element automatically by its order in the document.

Example

```
#div1 {position: absolute; top: 20px; left: 20px; height: 50px; width: 50px;
      background-color: blue; z-index: 2;}
```

Browser and CSS Support Notes

CSS2	IE 4, 5, 5.5, 6	Nav 4, 4.5–4.8, 6, 7	Opera 4, 5, 6, 7

CSS2 Aural Style Properties

CSS2 specifies a number of properties for use with speech-based browsers, which are listed here. No major browsers currently support these properties; however, in the future they may be useful for defining how speech-enabled browsers will "read" a document, right down to rate of speech, pauses before and after words, and when reading should be cued. Table B-7 lists the CSS2 aural style properties: more details on these properties are presented in Chapter 11.

TIP *While aural properties may seem to have little use, some CSS authors like to use aural style sheet rules to confuse certain browser versions to overload properties. This technique is not suggested and scripting logic should be used instead.*

Microsoft Extensions to CSS

Microsoft has introduced a number of proprietary extensions to CSS, many of which have also been proposed as additions to the CSS specification. The following section provides a quick overview of these, and notes the earliest version of Internet Explorer to support each one. For a more comprehensive overview of these properties, and of Microsoft's CSS support in general, see http://www.msdn.microsoft.com/workshop/author/css/reference/attributes.asp.

background-position-x

This Microsoft-proposed CSS property defines the x-coordinate of the **background-position** property. Introduced in Internet Explorer 4.

TABLE B-7 CSS2 Aural Style Properties

azimuth	**cue**
cue-after	**cue-before**
elevation	**pause**
pause-after	**pause-before**
pitch	**pitch-range**
play-during	**richness**
speak	**speak-header**
speak-numeral	**speak-punctuation**
speech-rate	**stress**
voice-family	**volume**

Example

```
<body style="background-image: url(picture.gif);
      background-repeat: no-repeat;
      background-position-x: 25%;">
```

background-position-y

This Microsoft-proposed CSS property defines the y-coordinate of the **background-position** property. Introduced in Internet Explorer 4.

Example

```
<body style="background-image: url(picture.gif);
            background-repeat: no-repeat;
            background-position-y: 200px;">
```

behavior

This Microsoft-proposed CSS property is used to define the URL for a script providing DHTML behavior. Introduced in Internet Explorer 5.0.

Example

```
<h1 style="behavior: url(colorchange.js);">What a dynamic header!</h1>
```

filter

This Microsoft-proposed CSS property is used to apply filter effects to associated HTML elements. Introduced in Internet Explorer 4.

Example

```
<h2 style="filter: Blur(Add = 1, Direction = 90, Strength = 20);
    width: 100%;">This header is all blurry.</h2>
```

ime-mode

This Microsoft-proposed CSS property is used to set the state of an Input Method Editor (IME); for use with Chinese, Japanese, and Korean character sets. Introduced in Internet Explorer 5.0.

Example

```
<textarea style="ime-mode:active;"></textarea>
```

layout-grid

This Microsoft-proposed CSS property defines a grid to be used in laying out Japanese or Chinese characters in a Web document. This is a shorthand property for the layout grid properties discussed next. Introduced in Internet Explorer 5.0.

Example

```
<p style="layout-grid: char line 12px 12px .5in;">
   A short text sample.</p>
```

layout-grid-char

This Microsoft-proposed CSS property defines the size of the character grid used for laying out Japanese or Chinese characters in a Web document. Introduced in Internet Explorer 5.0.

Example

```
<p style="layout-grid-char: 50px;">
  A short text sample.</p>
```

layout-grid-line

This Microsoft-proposed CSS property defines the gridline value used for laying out Japanese or Chinese characters in a Web document. Introduced in Internet Explorer 5.0.

Example

```
<p style="layout-grid-line: 100px">
A short text sample<br />
   with line breaks so<br />
   the meaning of this<br />
   property will be obvious.</p>
```

layout-grid-mode

This Microsoft-proposed CSS property defines if the text layout grid uses one or two dimensions. Introduced in Internet Explorer 5.0.

Example

```
<p style="layout-grid-mode: none; layout-grid-line: 100px;">
   A short text sample<br />
   with layout-grid-mode<br />
   set to a value of none<br />
   to turn off the grid.</p>
```

layout-grid-type

This Microsoft-proposed CSS property defines the type of grid to be used for laying out Japanese or Chinese characters in a Web document. Introduced in Internet Explorer 5.0.

Example

```
<p style="layout-grid-type: strict; layout-grid-line: 55px;">
   A short text sample.</p>
```

line-break

This Microsoft-proposed CSS property defines line-breaking rules for Japanese text. Introduced in Internet Explorer 5.0.

Example

```
p {line-break: normal;}
```

overflow-x

This Microsoft-proposed CSS property defines how content should behave when it exceeds the width of its enclosing element. Introduced in Internet Explorer 4.

Example

```
<p style="overflow-x: scroll; width: 100px;">
ABCDEFGHIJKLMNOPQRSTUVWXYZ
</p>
```

overflow-y

This Microsoft-proposed CSS property defines how content should behave when it exceeds the height of its enclosing element. Introduced in Internet Explorer 4.

Example

```
<p style="overflow-y: scroll; height: 25px; width: 50px;
          background-color: lightblue;">
ABC<br />
DEF<br />
GHI<br />
JKL<br />
MNO<br />
PQR<br />
STU<br />
VWXYZ
</p>
```

ruby-align

This Microsoft-proposed CSS property defines the alignment of ruby text as defined by the **<rt>** element, in relation to base text defined by the **<ruby>** tag (see entries for **<ruby>** and **<rt>** in Appendix A). Introduced in Internet Explorer 5.0.

Example

```
<ruby style="ruby-align: right;">
This is the base text defined by the ruby element.

<rt>This is the ruby text defined by the rt element.</rt>
</ruby>
```

ruby-overhang

This Microsoft-proposed CSS property defines the overhang of ruby text as defined by the **<rt>** tag, in relation to base text defined by the **<ruby>** tag (see entries for **<ruby>** and **<rt>** in Appendix A). Introduced in Internet Explorer 5.0.

Example

```
<ruby style="ruby-overhang: auto;">
This is the base text defined by the ruby element

<rt>This is the ruby text defined by the rt element
and it's a lot longer than the base text in this example.
A lot longer.</rt>
</ruby>

This is text outside of the ruby element.
```

ruby-position

This Microsoft-proposed CSS property defines the position of ruby text as defined by the **<rt>** tag, in relation to base text defined by the **<ruby>** tag (see entries for **<ruby>** and **<rt>** in Appendix A). Introduced in Internet Explorer 5.0.

Example

```
<ruby style="ruby-position: inline;">
This is the base text defined by the ruby element.

<rt>This is the ruby text defined by the rt element but it won't
look that way in IE 5.5 because it has been defined as inline in
relation to the base text.
</rt>
</ruby>
```

scrollbar-3d-light-color

This Microsoft extension to CSS defines a color for the top and left edges of the scroll box in a scrollbar; this and the related scrollbar properties can be applied to the browser window scrollbar when used with the **body** element, or to other elements when used in conjunction with clipping properties. Introduced in Internet Explorer 5.5.

Example

```
body {scrollbar-3d-light-color: lightblue;}
```

scrollbar-arrow-color

This Microsoft extension to CSS defines a color for the arrows in a scrollbar. Introduced in Internet Explorer 5.5.

APPENDIX B

Example

```
body {scrollbar-arrow-color: red;}
```

scrollbar-base-color

This Microsoft extension to CSS defines the base color for a scrollbar. Introduced in Internet Explorer 5.5.

Example

```
body {scrollbar-base-color: green;}
```

scrollbar-dark-shadow-color

This Microsoft extension to CSS defines a shadow color for the right and bottom edges of a scrollbar. Introduced in Internet Explorer 5.5.

Example

```
body {scrollbar-dark-shadow-color: #0000FF;}
```

scrollbar-face-color

This Microsoft extension to CSS defines a color for the face of a scrollbar. Introduced in Internet Explorer 5.5.

Example

```
body {scrollbar-face-color: #CC00FF;}
```

scrollbar-highlight-color

This Microsoft extension to CSS defines a color for the top and left edges of a scrollbar. Introduced in Internet Explorer 5.5.

Example

```
body {scrollbar-highlight-color: #CCFFFF;}
```

scrollbar-shadow-color

This Microsoft extension to CSS defines a color for the right and bottom edges of a scrollbar. Introduced in Internet Explorer 5.5.

Example

```
body {scrollbar-shadow-color: purple;}
```

TIP *Scrollbar color changes may not show in Internet Explorer if the browser is in strict compatibility mode as set by the doctype statement.*

text-autospace

This Microsoft-proposed CSS property defines spacing values for text; used when combining different types of characters, such as regular text, ideographic text, and numeric characters. Introduced in Internet Explorer 5.0.

text-justify

This Microsoft-proposed CSS property provides greater control over how justified text should be aligned and spaced. Introduced in Internet Explorer 5.0.

Example

```
<p style="text-align: justify; text-justify: distribute-all-lines;
         width: 250px;">
This paragraph is not only justified, but the text-justify property
is set to a value that makes the last line justify as well.
</p>
```

text-kashida-space

This Microsoft-proposed CSS property defines the ratio between kashida expansion and white space expansion in justified text (kashida is a typographic effect used with Arabic writing systems). Introduced in Internet Explorer 5.5.

text-underline-position

This Microsoft-proposed CSS property defines the position of underlining set with the text-decoration property. Introduced in Internet Explorer 5.0.

Example

```
<p style="text-decoration: underline;
          text-underline-position: above;">
This example uses the text-underline-position property to
place the underlining on top of the text. Why not just set
text-decoration to overline instead?</p>
```

word-break

This Microsoft-proposed CSS property can be used to allow line breaks within words, primarily for use with Asian languages. Introduced in Internet Explorer 5.0.

Example

```
<div style="word-break: break-all; width:50px;">
Words can break in this code example. Like this one:
Sesquipedalianism</div>
```

word-wrap

This Microsoft extension to CSS can be set to allow line breaks within words when content exceeds the limits of its containing element. Introduced in Internet Explorer 5.5.

Example

```
<p style="word-wrap: break-word; width: 30px;">
Words can break in this code example. Here is another long one:
Transcendentalism</p>
```

writing-mode

This Microsoft-proposed CSS property can be used to set text flow appropriate for European alphabets or East Asian alphabets. Values are **lr-tb** (left-to-right, top-to-bottom) and **tb-rl** (top-to-bottom, right-to-left). Introduced in Internet Explorer 5.5.

Example

```
<p style="writing-mode: tb-rl;">
This example will really turn your head if you
view it in Internet Explorer 5.5.</p>
```

zoom

This Microsoft extension to CSS can be used to define a magnification scale for an element. Can be used with scripting to create rollover effects. Introduced in Internet Explorer 5.5 and appears to be slated for CSS3 inclusion.

Example

```
<p onmouseover="this.style.zoom='150%';"
   onmouseout="this.style.zoom='normal';">
    Careful, this text might jump out at you!</p>
```

APPENDIX C

Special Characters

This appendix lists the special characters available in both standard HTML versions and XHTML. Note that browser support of elements in Appendix C is based on testing in the following browser versions: Netscape 1.22, Netscape 2.02, Netscape 3.01, Netscape Communicator 4.0, Netscape Communicator 4.5, Netscape Communicator 4.73, Netscape 6.0, Netscape 7.01, Internet Explorer 3.02, Internet Explorer 4.0, Internet Explorer 5.0, Internet Explorer 5.5, Internet Explorer 6.0, Opera 4.02, Opera 5.0, Opera 6.2, Opera 7.0, and MSN TV's browser simulator. In the tables in this appendix, the following abbreviations are used for the different Netscape, Internet Explorer, and Opera versions:

N1 = Netscape 1.22	IE3 = Internet Explorer 3.02
N2 = Netscape 2.02	IE4 = Internet Explorer 4.0
N3 = Netscape 3.01	IE5 = Internet Explorer 5.0
N4 = Netscape 4.0	IE5.5 = Internet Explorer 5.5
N4.5 = Netscape 4.5	IE6 = Internet Explorer 6.0
N4.7 = Netscape 4.73	O4 = Opera 4.02
N6 = Netscape 6.0	O5 = Opera 5.0
N7 = Netscape 7.01	O6 = Opera 6.2
	O7 = Opera 7.0

"Standard" HTML Character Entities

As discussed throughout the book, Web browsers do not render certain characters if they appear in an HTML document. Some keyboard characters such as < and > have special meanings to HTML because they are part of HTML tags. Other characters such as certain foreign language accent characters and special symbols can be difficult to insert as well. HTML uses a set of character entity codes in order to display these special characters. These codes consist of numbered entities and some, but not all, of these numbered entities have corresponding named entities. For example, the numbered entity **Ë** produces the character **Ë**. The named entity **Ë** produces the same character. Note that the named entity suggests the intended rendering of the character (a capital E with an umlaut), which provides a handy mnemonic device for dedicated

HTML coders. While **Ë** is widely supported, not all character entities work in all browsers. Theoretically, a browser vendor could even create arbitrary interpretations of these codes. For instance, some versions of MSN TV have their own unique renderings for the entities numbered 128 and 129. Opera 7 also seems to render some characters at **€**, ****, ****, and ****. Under the traditional HTML specifications, many of these such as 128 and 129 are not assigned a character. The codes numbered 32 through 255 (with some gaps) were assigned standard keyboard characters. Some of these codes duplicate characters that Web browsers can already interpret. For example, the entity **5** represents the numeral five, while **A** represents "A." Character entities become more practical when it is necessary to employ characters used in foreign languages, such as Œ or Å, or special characters such as ¶. The following chart lists these "standard" entities and their intended renderings, and identifies which browsers support each.

Named Entity	Browser Support	Numbered Entity	Browser Support	Intended Rendering	Description
			N: 1, 2, 3, 4, 4.5, 4.7, 6, 7 IE: 3, 4, 5, 5.5, 6 O: 4.02, 5, 6.2, 7 MSN TV		Space
		!	N: 1, 2, 3, 4, 4.5, 4.7, 6 IE: 3, 4, 5, 5.5, O: 4.02, 5 MSN TV	!	Exclamation point
"	N: 1, 2, 3, 4, 4.5, 4.7, 6, 7 IE: 3, 4, 5, 5.5, 6 O: 4.02, 7 MSN TV	"	N: 1, 2, 3, 4, 4.5, 4.7, 6, 7 IE: 3, 4, 5, 5.5, 6 O: 4.02, 5, 6.2, 7 MSN TV	"	Double quotes
		#	N: 1, 2, 3, 4, 4.5, 4.7, 6, 7 IE: 3, 4, 5, 5.5, 6 O: 4.02, 5, 6.2, 7 MSN TV	#	Number symbol
		$	N: 1, 2, 3, 4, 4.5, 4.7, 6, 7 IE: 3, 4, 5, 5.5, 6 O: 4.02, 5, 6.2, 7 MSN TV	$	Dollar symbol
		%	N: 1, 2, 3, 4, 4.5, 4.7, 6, 7 IE: 3, 4, 5, 5.5, 6 O: 4.02, 5, 6.2, 7 MSN TV	%	Percent symbol
&	N: 1, 2, 3, 4, 4.5, 4.7, 6, 7 IE: 3, 4, 5, 5.5, 6 O: 4.02, 5, 6.2, 7 MSN TV	&	N: 1, 2, 3, 4, 4.5, 4.7, 6, 7 IE: 3, 4, 5, 5.5, 6 O: 4.02, 5, 6.2, 7 MSN TV	&	Ampersand
		'	N: 1, 2, 3, 4, 4.5, 4.7, 6, 7 IE: 3, 4, 5, 5.5, 6 O: 4.02, 5, 6.2, 7 MSN TV	'	Single quote
		(	N: 1, 2, 3, 4, 4.5, 4.7, 6, 7 IE: 3, 4, 5, 5.5, 6 O: 4.02, 5, 6.2, 7 MSN TV	(	Opening parenthesis
		)	N: 1, 2, 3, 4, 4.5, 4.7, 6 IE: 3, 4, 5, 5.5 O: 4.02, 5 MSN TV	)	Closing parenthesis

Named Entity	Browser Support	Numbered Entity	Browser Support	Intended Rendering	Description
		*	N: 1, 2, 3, 4, 4.5, 4.7, 6 IE: 3, 4, 5, 5.5 O: 4.02, 5 MSN TV	*	Asterisk
		+	N: 1, 2, 3, 4, 4.5, 4.7, 6, 7 IE: 3, 4, 5, 5.5, 6 O: 4.02, 5, 6.2, 7 MSN TV	+	Plus sign
		,	N: 1, 2, 3, 4, 4.5, 4.7, 6, 7 IE: 3, 4, 5, 5.5, 6 O: 4.02, 5, 6.2, 7 MSN TV	,	Comma
		-	N: 1, 2, 3, 4, 4.5, 4.7, 6, 7 IE: 3, 4, 5, 5.5, 6 O: 4.02, 5, 6.2, 7 MSN TV	-	Minus sign (hyphen)
		.	N: 1, 2, 3, 4, 4.5, 4.7, 6, 7 IE: 3, 4, 5, 5.5, 6 O: 4.02, 5, 6.2, 7 MSN TV	.	Period
		/	N: 1, 2, 3, 4, 4.5, 4.7, 6, 7 IE: 3, 4, 5, 5.5, 6 O: 4.02, 5, 6.2, 7 MSN TV	/	Slash/virgule/ bar
		0	N: 1, 2, 3, 4, 4.5, 4.7, 6, 7 IE: 3, 4, 5, 5.5, 6 O: 4.02, 5, 6.2, 7 MSN TV	0	Zero
		1	N: 1, 2, 3, 4, 4.5, 4.7, 6, 7 IE: 3, 4, 5, 5.5, 6 O: 4.02, 5, 6.2, 7 MSN TV	1	One
		2	N: 1, 2, 3, 4, 4.5, 4.7, 6, 7 IE: 3, 4, 5, 5.5, 6 O: 4.02, 5, 6.2, 7 MSN TV	2	Two
		3	N: 1, 2, 3, 4, 4.5, 4.7, 6, 7 IE: 3, 4, 5, 5.5, 6 O: 4.02, 5, 6.2, 7 MSN TV	3	Three
		4	N: 1, 2, 3, 4, 4.5, 4.7, 6, 7 IE: 3, 4, 5, 5.5, 6 O: 4.02, 5, 6.2, 7 MSN TV	4	Four
		5	N: 1, 2, 3, 4, 4.5, 4.7, 6, 7 IE: 3, 4, 5, 5.5, 6 O: 4.02, 5, 6.2, 7 MSN TV	5	Five
		6	N: 1, 2, 3, 4, 4.5, 4.7, 6, 7 IE: 3, 4, 5, 5.5, 6 O: 4.02, 5, 6.2, 7 MSN TV	6	Six

Named Entity	Browser Support	Numbered Entity	Browser Support	Intended Rendering	Description
		7	N: 1, 2, 3, 4, 4.5, 4.7, 6, 7 IE: 3, 4, 5, 5.5, 6 O: 4.02, 5, 6.2, 7 MSN TV	7	Seven
		8	N: 1, 2, 3, 4, 4.5, 4.7, 6, 7 IE: 3, 4, 5, 5.5, 6 O: 4.02, 5, 6.2, 7 MSN TV	8	Eight
		9	N: 1, 2, 3, 4, 4.5, 4.7, 6, 7 IE: 3, 4, 5, 5.5, 6 O: 4.02, 5, 6.2, 7 MSN TV	9	Nine
		:	N: 1, 2, 3, 4, 4.5, 4.7, 6, 7 IE: 3, 4, 5, 5.5, 6 O: 4.02, 5, 6.2, 7 MSN TV	:	Colon
		;	N: 1, 2, 3, 4, 4.5, 4.7, 6, 7 IE: 3, 4, 5, 5.5, 6 O: 4.02, 5, 6.2, 7 MSN TV	;	Semicolon
<	N: 1, 2, 3, 4, 4.5, 4.7, 6 IE: 3, 4, 5, 5.5, O: 4.02, 5 MSN TV	<	N: 1, 2, 3, 4, 4.5, 4.7, 6, 7 IE: 3, 4, 5, 5.5, 6 O: 4.02, 5, 6.2, 7 MSN TV	<	Less than symbol
		=	N: 1, 2, 3, 4, 4.5, 4.7, 6, 7 IE: 3, 4, 5, 5.5, 6 O: 4.02, 5, 6.2, 7 MSN TV	=	Equal sign
>	N: 1, 2, 3, 4, 4.5, 4.7, 6, 7 IE: 3, 4, 5, 5.5, 6 O: 4.02, 5, 6.2, 7 MSN TV	>	N: 1, 2, 3, 4, 4.5, 4.7, 6, 7 IE: 3, 4, 5, 5.5, 6 O: 4.02, 5, 6.2, 7 MSN TV	>	Greater than symbol
		?	N: 1, 2, 3, 4, 4.5, 4.7, 6, 7 IE: 3, 4, 5, 5.5, 6 O: 4.02, 5, 6.2, 7 MSN TV	?	Question mark
		@	N: 1, 2, 3, 4, 4.5, 4.7, 6, 7 IE: 3, 4, 5, 5.5, 6 O: 4.02, 5, 6.2, 7 MSN TV	@	"At" symbol
		A	N: 1, 2, 3, 4, 4.5, 4.7, 6, 7 IE: 3, 4, 5, 5.5, 6 O: 4.02, 5, 6.2, 7 MSN TV	A	
		B	N: 1, 2, 3, 4, 4.5, 4.7, 6, 7 IE: 3, 4, 5, 5.5, 6 O: 4.02, 5, 6.2, 7 MSN TV	B	
		C	N: 1, 2, 3, 4, 4.5, 4.7, 6, 7 IE: 3, 4, 5, 5.5, 6 O: 4.02, 5, 6.2, 7 MSN TV	C	

Named Entity	Browser Support	Numbered Entity	Browser Support	Intended Rendering	Description
		D	N: 1, 2, 3, 4, 4.5, 4.7, 6, 7 IE: 3, 4, 5, 5.5, 6 O: 4.02, 5, 6.2, 7 MSN TV	D	
		E	N: 1, 2, 3, 4, 4.5, 4.7, 6, 7 IE: 3, 4, 5, 5.5, 6 O: 4.02, 5, 6.2, 7 MSN TV	E	
		F	N: 1, 2, 3, 4, 4.5, 4.7, 6, 7 IE: 3, 4, 5, 5.5, 6 O: 4.02, 5, 6.2, 7 MSN TV	F	
		G	N: 1, 2, 3, 4, 4.5, 4.7, 6, 7 IE: 3, 4, 5, 5.5, 6 O: 4.02, 5, 6.2, 7 MSN TV	G	
		H	N: 1, 2, 3, 4, 4.5, 4.7, 6, 7 IE: 3, 4, 5, 5.5, 6 O: 4.02, 5, 6.2, 7 MSN TV	H	
		I	N: 1, 2, 3, 4, 4.5, 4.7, 6, 7 IE: 3, 4, 5, 5.5, 6 O: 4.02, 5, 6.2, 7 MSN TV	I	
		J	N: 1, 2, 3, 4, 4.5, 4.7, 6, 7 IE: 3, 4, 5, 5.5, 6 O: 4.02, 5, 6.2, 7 MSN TV	J	
		K	N: 1, 2, 3, 4, 4.5, 4.7, 6, 7 IE: 3, 4, 5, 5.5, 6 O: 4.02, 5, 6.2, 7 MSN TV	K	
		L	N: 1, 2, 3, 4, 4.5, 4.7, 6, 7 IE: 3, 4, 5, 5.5, 6 O: 4.02, 5, 6.2, 7 MSN TV	L	
		M	N: 1, 2, 3, 4, 4.5, 4.7, 6, 7 IE: 3, 4, 5, 5.5, 6 O: 4.02, 5, 6.2, 7 MSN TV	M	
		N	N: 1, 2, 3, 4, 4.5, 4.7, 6, 7 IE: 3, 4, 5, 5.5, 6 O: 4.02, 5, 6.2, 7 MSN TV	N	
		O	N: 1, 2, 3, 4, 4.5, 4.7, 6, 7 IE: 3, 4, 5, 5.5, 6 O: 4.02, 5, 6.2, 7 MSN TV	O	
		P	N: 1, 2, 3, 4, 4.5, 4.7, 6, 7 IE: 3, 4, 5, 5.5, 6 O: 4.02, 5, 6.2, 7 MSN TV	P	

Named Entity	Browser Support	Numbered Entity	Browser Support	Intended Rendering	Description
		Q	N: 1, 2, 3, 4, 4.5, 4.7, 6, 7 IE: 3, 4, 5, 5.5, 6 O: 4.02, 5, 6.2, 7 MSN TV	Q	
		R	N: 1, 2, 3, 4, 4.5, 4.7, 6, 7 IE: 3, 4, 5, 5.5, 6 O: 4.02, 5, 6.2, 7 MSN TV	R	
		S	N: 1, 2, 3, 4, 4.5, 4.7, 6, 7 IE: 3, 4, 5, 5.5, 6 O: 4.02, 5, 6.2, 7 MSN TV	S	
		T	N: 1, 2, 3, 4, 4.5, 4.7, 6, 7 IE: 3, 4, 5, 5.5, 6 O: 4.02, 5, 6.2, 7 MSN TV	T	
		U	N: 1, 2, 3, 4, 4.5, 4.7, 6, 7 IE: 3, 4, 5, 5.5, 6 O: 4.02, 5, 6.2, 7 MSN TV	U	
		V	N: 1, 2, 3, 4, 4.5, 4.7, 6, 7 IE: 3, 4, 5, 5.5, 6 O: 4.02, 5, 6.2, 7 MSN TV	V	
		W	N: 1, 2, 3, 4, 4.5, 4.7, 6, 7 IE: 3, 4, 5, 5.5, 6 O: 4.02, 5, 6.2, 7 MSN TV	W	
		X	N: 1, 2, 3, 4, 4.5, 4.7, 6, 7 IE: 3, 4, 5, 5.5, 6 O: 4.02, 5, 6.2, 7 MSN TV	X	
		Y	N: 1, 2, 3, 4, 4.5, 4.7, 6, 7 IE: 3, 4, 5, 5.5, 6 O: 4.02, 5, 6.2, 7 MSN TV	Y	
		Z	N: 1, 2, 3, 4, 4.5, 4.7, 6, 7 IE: 3, 4, 5, 5.5, 6 O: 4.02, 5, 6.2, 7 MSN TV	Z	
		[	N: 1, 2, 3, 4, 4.5, 4.7, 6, 7 IE: 3, 4, 5, 5.5, 6 O: 4.02, 5, 6.2, 7 MSN TV	[	Opening bracket
		\	N: 1, 2, 3, 4, 4.5, 4.7, 6, 7 IE: 3, 4, 5, 5.5, 6 O: 4.02, 5, 6.2, 7 MSN TV	\	Backslash
		]	N: 1, 2, 3, 4, 4.5, 4.7, 6, 7 IE: 3, 4, 5, 5.5, 6 O: 4.02, 5, 6.2, 7 MSN TV	]	Closing bracket

Named Entity	Browser Support	Numbered Entity	Browser Support	Intended Rendering	Description
		^	N: 1, 2, 3, 4, 4.5, 4.7, 6, 7 IE: 3, 4, 5, 5.5, 6 O: 4.02, 5, 6.2, 7 MSN TV	^	Caret
		_	N: 1, 2, 3, 4, 4.5, 4.7, 6 IE: 3, 4, 5, 5.5 O: 4.02, 5 MSN TV	_	Underscore
		`	N: 1, 2, 3, 4, 4.5, 4.7, 6, 7 IE: 3, 4, 5, 5.5, 6 O: 4.02, 5, 6.2, 7 MSN TV	`	Grave accent, no letter
		a	N: 1, 2, 3, 4, 4.5, 4.7, 6, 7 IE: 3, 4, 5, 5.5, 6 O: 4.02, 5, 6.2, 7 MSN TV	a	
		b	N: 1, 2, 3, 4, 4.5, 4.7, 6 IE: 3, 4, 5, 5.5 O: 4.02, 5 MSN TV	b	
		c	N: 1, 2, 3, 4, 4.5, 4.7, 6, 7 IE: 3, 4, 5, 5.5, 6 O: 4.02, 5, 6.2, 7 MSN TV	c	
		d	N: 1, 2, 3, 4, 4.5, 4.7, 6, 7 IE: 3, 4, 5, 5.5, 6 O: 4.02, 5, 6.2, 7 MSN TV	d	
		e	N: 1, 2, 3, 4, 4.5, 4.7, 6, 7 IE: 3, 4, 5, 5.5, 6 O: 4.02, 5, 6.2, 7 MSN TV	e	
		f	N: 1, 2, 3, 4, 4.5, 4.7, 6, 7 IE: 3, 4, 5, 5.5, 6 O: 4.02, 5, 6.2, 7 MSN TV	f	
		g	N: 1, 2, 3, 4, 4.5, 4.7, 6, 7 IE: 3, 4, 5, 5.5, 6 O: 4.02, 5, 6.2, 7 MSN TV	g	
		h	N: 1, 2, 3, 4, 4.5, 4.7, 6, 7 IE: 3, 4, 5, 5.5, 6 O: 4.02, 5, 6.2, 7 MSN TV	h	
		i	N: 1, 2, 3, 4, 4.5, 4.7, 6, 7 IE: 3, 4, 5, 5.5, 6 O: 4.02, 5, 6.2, 7 MSN TV	i	
		j	N: 1, 2, 3, 4, 4.5, 4.7, 6, 7 IE: 3, 4, 5, 5.5, 6 O: 4.02, 5, 6.2, 7 MSN TV	j	

Named Entity	Browser Support	Numbered Entity	Browser Support	Intended Rendering	Description
		k	N: 1, 2, 3, 4, 4.5, 4.7, 6, 7 IE: 3, 4, 5, 5.5, 6 O: 4.02, 5, 6.2, 7 MSN TV	k	
		l	N: 1, 2, 3, 4, 4.5, 4.7, 6, 7 IE: 3, 4, 5, 5.5, 6 O: 4.02, 5, 6.2, 7 MSN TV	l	
		m	N: 1, 2, 3, 4, 4.5, 4.7, 6, 7 IE: 3, 4, 5, 5.5, 6 O: 4.02, 5, 6.2, 7 MSN TV	m	
		n	N: 1, 2, 3, 4, 4.5, 4.7, 6, 7 IE: 3, 4, 5, 5.5, 6 O: 4.02, 5, 6.2, 7 MSN TV	n	
		o	N: 1, 2, 3, 4, 4.5, 4.7, 6, 7 IE: 3, 4, 5, 5.5, 6 O: 4.02, 5, 6.2, 7 MSN TV	o	
		p	N: 1, 2, 3, 4, 4.5, 4.7, 6, 7 IE: 3, 4, 5, 5.5, 6 O: 4.02, 5, 6.2, 7 MSN TV	p	
		q	N: 1, 2, 3, 4, 4.5, 4.7, 6, 7 IE: 3, 4, 5, 5.5, 6 O: 4.02, 5, 6.2, 7 MSN TV	q	
		r	N: 1, 2, 3, 4, 4.5, 4.7, 6, 7 IE: 3, 4, 5, 5.5, 6 O: 4.02, 5, 6.2, 7 MSN TV	r	
		s	N: 1, 2, 3, 4, 4.5, 4.7, 6, 7 IE: 3, 4, 5, 5.5, 6 O: 4.02, 5, 6.2, 7 MSN TV	s	
		t	N: 1, 2, 3, 4, 4.5, 4.7, 6, 7 IE: 3, 4, 5, 5.5, 6 O: 4.02, 5, 6.2, 7 MSN TV	t	
		u	N: 1, 2, 3, 4, 4.5, 4.7, 6, 7 IE: 3, 4, 5, 5.5, 6 O: 4.02, 5, 6.2, 7 MSN TV	u	
		v	N: 1, 2, 3, 4, 4.5, 4.7, 6, 7 IE: 3, 4, 5, 5.5, 6 O: 4.02, 5, 6.2, 7 MSN TV	v	
		w	N: 1, 2, 3, 4, 4.5, 4.7, 6, 7 IE: 3, 4, 5, 5.5, 6 O: 4.02, 5, 6.2, 7 MSN TV	w	

Named Entity	Browser Support	Numbered Entity	Browser Support	Intended Rendering	Description
		x	N: 1, 2, 3, 4, 4.5, 4.7, 6, 7 IE: 3, 4, 5, 5.5, 6 O: 4.02, 5, 6.2, 7 MSN TV	x	
		y	N: 1, 2, 3, 4, 4.5, 4.7, 6, 7 IE: 3, 4, 5, 5.5, 6 O: 4.02, 5, 6.2, 7 MSN TV	y	
		z	N: 1, 2, 3, 4, 4.5, 4.7, 6, 7 IE: 3, 4, 5, 5.5, 6 O: 4.02, 5, 6.2, 7 MSN TV	z	
		{	N: 1, 2, 3, 4, 4.5, 4.7, 6, 7 IE: 3, 4, 5, 5.5, 6 O: 4.02, 5, 6.2, 7 MSN TV	{	Opening brace
				N: 1, 2, 3, 4, 4.5, 4.7, 6, 7 IE: 3, 4, 5, 5.5, 6 O: 4.02, 5, 6.2, 7 MSN TV			Vertical bar
		}	N: 1, 2, 3, 4, 4.5, 4.7, 6, 7 IE: 3, 4, 5, 5.5, 6 O: 4.02, 5, 6.2, 7 MSN TV	}	Closing brace
		~	N: 1, 2, 3, 4, 4.5, 4.7, 6, 7 IE: 3, 4, 5, 5.5, 6 O: 4.02, 5, 6.2, 7 MSN TV	~	Equivalency symbol (tilde)
			n/a		No character (Note: In the standard, the values from 127 to 159 are not assigned. Authors are advised not to use them. Many of them only work under Windows or produce different characters on other operating systems or with different default font sets.)
		€	MSN TV (nonstandard)* O: 6.2, 7*	See note*	No character defined

APPENDIX C

Named Entity	Browser Support	Numbered Entity	Browser Support	Intended Rendering	Description
™	IE: 3, 4, 5, 5.5, 6 N: 7 O: 6.2, 7 MSN TV		MSN TV (nonstandard) **	™	Trademark symbol (Nonstandard numeric value; use **™** or **™** instead.)
		‚	N: 2, 3, 4, 4.5, 7 IE: 3, 4, 5, 5.5, 6 O: 4.02, 5, 6.2, 7 MSN TV	‚	Low-9 quote (nonstandard)
		ƒ	N: 3, 4, 4.5, 4.7, 6, 7 IE: 3, 4, 5, 5.5, 6 O: 4.02, 5, 6.2, 7 MSN TV	ƒ	Small "f" with hook (nonstandard)
		„	N: 2, 3, 4, 4.5, 4.7, 6, 7 IE: 3, 4, 5, 5.5, 6 O: 4.02, 5, 6.2, 7 MSN TV	„	Low-9 double quotes (nonstandard)
		…	N: 2, 3, 4, 4.5, 4.7, 6, 7 IE: 3, 4, 5, 5.5, 6 O: 4.02, 5, 6.2, 7 MSN TV	…	Ellipsis (nonstandard)
		†	N: 2, 3, 4, 4.5, 4.7, 6, 7 IE: 3, 4, 5, 5.5, 6 O: 4.02, 5, 6.2, 7 MSN TV	†	Dagger (nonstandard)
		‡	N: 2, 3, 4, 4.5, 4.7, 6, 7 IE: 3, 4, 5, 5.5, 6 O: 4.02, 5, 6.2, 7 MSN TV	‡	Double dagger (nonstandard)
		ˆ	N: 3, 4, 4.5, 4.7, 6, 7 IE: 3, 4, 5, 5.5, 6 O: 4.02, 5, 6.2, 7 MSN TV	^	Circumflex accent, no letter (nonstandard)
		‰	N: 2, 3, 4, 4.5, 4.7, 6, 7 IE: 3, 4, 5, 5.5, 6 O: 4.02, 5, 6.2, 7 MSN TV	‰	Per thousand (nonstandard)
		Š	N: 3, 4, 4.5, 4.7, 6, 7 IE: 3, 4, 5, 5.5, 6 O: 4.02, 5, 6.2, 7 MSN TV	Š	Uppercase S with caron (nonstandard)
		‹	N: 2, 3, 4, 4.5, 4.7, 6, 7 IE: 3, 4, 5, 5.5, 6 O: 4.02, 5, 6.2, 7 MSN TV	<	Opening single-angle quote (nonstandard)
		Œ	N: 3, 4, 4.5, 4.7, 6, 7 IE: 3, 4, 5, 5.5, 6 O: 4.02, 5, 6.2, 7 MSN TV	Œ	Uppercase "OE" ligature (nonstandard)

Named Entity	Browser Support	Numbered Entity	Browser Support	Intended Rendering	Description
			None	Ÿ	Uppercase "Y" with umlaut (nonstandard)
		Ž	N: 7 IE: 6 O: 5, 6, 7	Ž	Uppercase "Z" with caron
			n/a		No character
			n/a		No character
		‘	N: 1, 2, 3, 4, 4.5, 4.7, 6, 7 IE: 3, 4, 5, 5.5, 6 O: 4.02, 5, 6.2, 7 MSN TV	‘	Opening "smart" single quote (nonstandard)
		’	N: 1, 2, 3, 4, 4.5, 4.7, 6, 7 IE: 3, 4, 5, 5.5, 6 O: 4.02, 5, 6.2, 7 MSN TV	’	Closing "smart" single quote (nonstandard)
		“	N: 2, 3, 4, 4.5, 4.7, 6, 7 IE: 3, 4, 5, 5.5, 6 O: 4.02, 5, 6.2, 7 MSN TV	“	Opening "smart" double quote (nonstandard)
		”	N: 2, 3, 4, 4.5, 4.7, 6, 7 IE: 3, 4, 5, 5.5, 6 O: 4.02, 5, 6.2, 7 MSN TV	”	Closing "smart" double quote (nonstandard)
		•	N: 2, 3, 4, 4.5, 4.7, 6, 7 IE: 3, 4, 5, 5.5, 6 O: 4.02, 5, 6.2, 7 MSN TV	•	Bullet (nonstandard)
		–	N: 2, 3, 4, 4.5, 4.7, 6, 7 IE: 3, 4, 5, 5.5, 6 O: 4.02, 5, 6.2, 7 MSN TV	–	En dash (nonstandard)
		—	N: 2, 3, 4, 4.5, 4.7, 6, 7 IE: 3, 4, 5, 5.5, 6 O: 4.02, 5, 6.2, 7 MSN TV	—	Em dash (nonstandard)
		˜	N: 3, 4, 4.5, 4.7, 6, 7 IE: 3, 4, 5, 5.5, 6 O: 4.02, 5, 6.2, 7 MSN TV	˜	Tilde (nonstandard)
™	IE: 3, 4, 5, 5.5, 6 N: 2, 3, 4, 4.5, 4.7, 6 7 O: 4.02, 5, 6.2, 7 MSN TV	™***	N: 2, 3, 4, 4.5, 4.7, 6, 7 IE: 3, 4, 5, 5.5, 6 O: 4.02, 5, 6.2, 7 MSN TV	™	Trademark symbol
		š	N: 3, 4, 4.5, 4.7, 6, 7 IE: 3, 4, 5, 5.5, 6 O: 4.02, 5, 6.2, 7 MSN TV	š	Lowercase S with caron (nonstandard)

APPENDIX C

Named Entity	Browser Support	Numbered Entity	Browser Support	Intended Rendering	Description
		›	N: 2, 3, 4, 4.5, 4.7, 6, 7 IE: 3, 4, 5, 5.5, 6 O: 4.02, 5, 6.2, 7 MSN TV	>	Closing single-angle quote (nonstandard)
		œ	N: 3, 4, 4.5, 4.7, 6, 7 IE: 3, 4, 5, 5.5, 6 O: 4.02, 5, 6.2, 7 MSN TV	œ	Lowercase "oe" ligature (nonstandard)
			n/a		No character
		ž	n/a		No character
		Ÿ	N: 4, 4.5, 4.7, 6, 7 IE:3, 5, 5.5, 6 O: 6.2, 7 MSN TV	Ÿ	Uppercase "Y" with umlaut (nonstandard)
	N: 1, 3, 4, 4.5, 4.7, 6, 7 IE: 3, 4, 5, 5.5, 6 O: 4, 5, 6, 7 MSN TV		N: 1, 2, 3, 4, 4.5, 4.7, 6 IE: 3, 4, 5, 5.5, 6 O: 5, 6, 7 MSN TV		Nonbreaking space
¡	N: 3, 4, 4.5, 4.7, 6, 7 IE: 3, 4, 5, 5.5, 6 O: 4.02, 5, 6.2, 7 MSN TV	¡	N: 1, 3, 4, 4.5, 4.7, 6, 7 IE: 3, 4, 5, 5.5, 6 O: 4.02, 5, 6.2, 7 MSN TV	¡	Inverted exclamation point
¢	N: 3, 4, 4.5, 4.7, 6, 7 IE: 3, 4, 5, 5.5, 6 O: 4.02, 5, 6.2, 7 MSN TV	¢	N: 1, 3, 4, 4.5, 4.7, 6, 7 IE: 3, 4, 5, 5.5, 6 O: 4.02, 5, 6.2, 7 MSN TV	¢	Cent symbol
£	N: 3, 4, 4.5, 4.7, 6, 7 IE: 3, 4, 5, 5.5, 6 O: 4.02, 5, 6.2, 7 MSN TV	£	N: 1, 3, 4, 4.5, 4.7, 6, 7 IE: 3, 4, 5, 5.5, 6 O: 4.02, 5, 6.2, 7 MSN TV	£	Pound sterling symbol
¤	N: 3, 4, 4.5, 4.7, 6, 7 IE: 3, 4, 5, 5.5, 6 O: 4.02, 5, 6.2, 7 MSN TV	¤	N: 1, 2, 3, 4, 4.5, 4.7, 6, 7 IE: 3, 4, 5, 5.5, 6 O: 4.02, 5, 6.2, 7 MSN TV	¤	Currency symbol
¥	N: 3, 4, 4.5, 4.7, 6, 7 IE: 3, 4, 5, 5.5, 6 O: 4.02, 5, 6.2, 7 MSN TV	¥	N: 1, 3, 4, 4.5, 4.7, 6, 7 IE: 3, 4, 5, 5.5, 6 O: 4.02, 5, 6.2, 7 MSN TV	¥	Japanese Yen
¦	N: 3, 4, 4.5, 4.7, 6, 7 IE: 3, 4, 5, 5.5, 6 O: 4.02, 5, 6.2, 7 MSN TV	¦	N: 2, 3, 4, 4.5, 4.7, 6, 7 IE: 3, 4, 5, 5.5, 6 O: 4.02, 5, 6.2, 7 MSN TV	¦	Broken vertical bar
§	N: 3, 4, 4.5, 4.7, 6, 7 IE: 3, 4, 5, 5.5, 6 O: 4.02, 5, 6.2, 7 MSN TV	§	N: 1, 2, 3, 4, 4.5, 4.7, 6, 7 IE: 3, 4, 5, 5.5, 6 O: 4.02, 5, 6.2, 7 MSN TV	§	Section symbol
¨	N: 3, 4, 4.5, 4.7, 6, 7 IE: 3, 4, 5, 5.5, 6 O: 4.02, 5, 6.2, 7 MSN TV	¨	N: 1, 3, 4, 4.5, 4.7, 6, 7 IE: 3, 4, 5, 5.5, 6 O: 4.02, 5, 6.2, 7 MSN TV	¨	Umlaut, no letter

Named Entity	Browser Support	Numbered Entity	Browser Support	Intended Rendering	Description
©	N: 1, 2, 3, 4, 4.5, 4.7, 6, 7 IE: 3, 4, 5, 5.5, 6 O: 4.02, 5, 6.2, 7 MSN TV	©	N: 1, 2, 3, 4, 4.5, 4.7, 6, 7 IE: 3, 4, 5, 5.5, 6 O: 4.02, 5, 6.2, 7 MSN TV	©	Copyright symbol
ª	N: 3, 4, 4.5, 4.7, 6, 7 IE: 3, 4, 5, 5.5, 6 O: 4.02, 5, 6.2, 7 MSN TV	ª	N: 1, 3, 4, 4.5, 4.7, 6, 7 IE: 3, 4, 5, 5.5, 6 O: 4.02, 5, 6.2, 7 MSN TV	ª	Feminine ordinal indicator
«	N3, 4, 4.5, 4.7, 6, 7 IE: 3, 4, 5, 5.5, 6 O: 4.02, 5, 6.2, 7 MSN TV	«	N: 1, 2, 3, 4, 4.5, 4.7, 6, 7 IE: 3, 4, 5, 5.5, 6 O: 4.02, 5, 6.2, 7 MSN TV	«	Opening double-angle quote
¬	N: 3, 4, 4.5, 4.7, 6, 7 IE: 3, 4, 5, 5.5, 6 O: 4.02, 5, 6.2, 7 MSN TV	¬	N: 1, 2, 3, 4, 4.5, 4.7, 6, 7 IE: 3, 4, 5, 5.5, 6 O: 4.02, 5, 6.2, 7 MSN TV	¬	Logical "not" symbol
	N: 3, 4, 4.5, 4.7, 6 IE: 3, 4, 5, 5.5, O: 4.02, 5 MSN TV		N: 1, 2, 3, 4, 4.5, 4.7, 6 IE: 3, 4, 5 MSN TV	- [no display in IE 5.5, 6, N7, O7]	Soft hyphen
®	N: 1, 2, 3, 4, 4.5, 4.7, 6, 7 IE: 3, 4, 5, 5.5, 6 O: 4.02, 5, 6.2, 7 MSN TV	®	N: 1, 2, 3, 4, 4.5, 4.7, 6, 7 IE: 3, 4, 5, 5.5, 6 O: 4.02, 5, 6.2, 7 MSN TV	®	Registered trademark symbol
¯	N: 3, 4, 4.5, 4.7, 6, 7 IE: 3, 4, 5, 5.5, 6 O: 4.02, 5, 6.2, 7 MSN TV	¯	N: 1, 3, 4, 4.5, 4.7, 6, 7 IE: 3, 4, 5, 5.5, 6 O: 4.02, 5, 6.2, 7 MSN TV	¯	Macron
°	N: 3, 4, 4.5, 4.7, 6, 7 IE: 3, 4, 5, 5.5, 6 O: 4.02, 5, 6.2, 7 MSN TV	°	N: 1, 2, 3, 4, 4.5, 4.7, 6, 7 IE: 3, 4, 5, 5.5, 6 O: 4.02, 5, 6.2, 7 MSN TV	°	Degree symbol
±	N: 3, 4, 4.5, 4.7, 6, 7 IE: 3, 4, 5, 5.5, 6 O: 4.02, 5, 6.2, 7 MSN TV	±	N: 1, 2, 3, 4, 4.5, 4.7, 6, 7 IE: 3, 4, 5, 5.5, 6 O: 4.02, 5, 6.2, 7 MSN TV	±	Plus/minus symbol
²	N: 3, 4, 4.5, 4.7, 6, 7 IE: 3, 4, 5, 5.5, 6 O: 4.02, 5, 6.2, 7 MSN TV	²	N: 1, 3, 4, 4.5, 4.7, 6, 7 IE: 3, 4, 5, 5.5, 6 O: 4.02, 5, 6.2, 7 MSN TV	^{2}	Superscript 2
³	N: 3, 4, 4.5, 4.7, 6, 7 IE: 3, 4, 5, 5.5, 6 O: 4.02, 5, 6.2, 7 MSN TV	³	N: 1, 3, 4, 4.5, 4.7, 6, 7 IE: 3, 4, 5, 5.5, 6 O: 4.02, 5, 6.2, 7 MSN TV	^{3}	Superscript 3
´	N: 3, 4, 4.5, 4.7, 6, 7 IE: 3, 4, 5, 5.5, 6 O: 4.02, 5, 6.2, 7 MSN TV	´	N: 1, 3, 4, 4.5, 4.7, 6, 7 IE: 3, 4, 5, 5.5, 6 O: 4.02, 5, 6.2, 7 MSN TV	´	Acute accent, no letter
µ	N: 3, 4, 4.5, 4.7, 6, 7 IE: 3, 4, 5, 5.5, 6 O: 4.02, 5, 6.2, 7 MSN TV	µ	N: 1, 2, 3, 4, 4.5, 4.7, 6, 7 IE: 3, 4, 5, 5.5, 6 O: 4.02, 5, 6.2, 7 MSN TV	µ	Micron

Named Entity	Browser Support	Numbered Entity	Browser Support	Intended Rendering	Description
¶	N: 3, 4, 4.5, 4.7, 6, 7 IE: 3, 4, 5, 5.5, 6 O: 4.02, 5, 6.2, 7 MSN TV	¶	N: 1, 2, 3, 4, 4.5, 4.7, 6, 7 IE: 3, 4, 5, 5.5, 6 O: 4.02, 5, 6.2, 7 MSN TV	¶	Paragraph symbol
·	N: 3, 4, 4.5, 4.7, 6, 7 IE: 3, 4, 5, 5.5, 6 O: 4.02, 5, 6.2, 7 MSN TV	·	N: 1, 3, 4, 4.5, 4.7, 6, 7 IE: 3, 4, 5, 5.5, 6 O: 4.02, 5, 6.2, 7 MSN TV	·	Middle dot
¸	N: 3, 4, 4.5, 4.7, 6, 7 IE: 3, 4, 5, 5.5, 6 O: 4.02, 5, 6.2, 7 MSN TV	¸	N: 1, 3, 4, 4.5, 4.7, 6, 7 IE: 3, 4, 5, 5.5, 6 O: 4.02, 5, 6.2, 7 MSN TV	¸	Cedilla
¹	N: 3, 4, 4.5, 4.7, 6, 7 IE: 3, 4, 5, 5.5, 6 O: 4.02, 5, 6.2, 7 MSN TV	¹	N: 1, 3, 4, 4.5, 4.7, 6, 7 IE: 3, 4, 5, 5.5, 6 O: 4.02, 5, 6.2, 7 MSN TV	¹	Superscript 1
º	N: 3, 4, 4.5, 4.7, 6, 7 IE: 3, 4, 5, 5.5, 6 O: 4.02, 5, 6.2, 7 MSN TV	º	N: 1, 3, 4, 4.5, 4.7, 6, 7 IE: 3, 4, 5, 5.5, 6 O: 4.02, 5, 6.2, 7 MSN TV	º	Masculine ordinal indicator
»	N: 3, 4, 4.5, 4.7, 6, 7 IE: 3, 4, 5, 5.5, 6 O: 4.02, 5, 6.2, 7 MSN TV	»	N: 1, 2, 3, 4, 4.5, 4.7, 6, 7 IE: 3, 4, 5, 5.5, 6 O: 4.02, 5, 6.2, 7 MSN TV	»	Closing double-angle quotes
¼	N: 3, 4, 4.5, 4.7, 6, 7 IE: 3, 4, 5, 5.5, 6 O: 4.02, 5, 6.2, 7 MSN TV	¼	N: 1, 3, 4, 4.5, 4.7, 6, 7 IE: 3, 4, 5, 5.5, 6 O: 4.02, 5, 6.2, 7 MSN TV	¼	One-quarter fraction
½	N: 3, 4, 4.5, 4.7, 6, 7 IE: 3, 4, 5, 5.5, 6 O: 4.02, 5, 6.2, 7 MSN TV	½	N: 1, 3, 4, 4.5, 4.7, 6, 7 IE: 3, 4, 5, 5.5, 6 O: 4.02, 5, 6.2, 7 MSN TV	½	One-half fraction
¾	N: 3, 4, 4.5, 4.7, 6, 7 IE: 3, 4, 5, 5.5, 6 O: 4.02, 5, 6.2, 7 MSN TV	¾	N: 1, 3, 4, 4.5, 4.7, 6, 7 IE: 3, 4, 5, 5.5, 6 O: 4.02, 5, 6.2, 7 MSN TV	¾	Three-fourths fraction
¿	N: 3, 4, 4.5, 4.7, 6, 7 IE: 3, 4, 5, 5.5, 6 O: 4.02, 5, 6.2, 7 MSN TV	¿	N: 1, 3, 4, 4.5, 4.7, 6, 7 IE: 3, 4, 5, 5.5, 6 O: 4.02, 5, 6.2, 7 MSN TV	¿	Inverted question mark
À	N: 1, 3, 4, 4.5, 4.7, 6, 7 IE: 3, 4, 5, 5.5, 6 O: 4.02, 5, 6.2, 7 MSN TV	À	N: 1, 3, 4, 4.5, 4.7, 6, 7 IE: 3, 4, 5, 5.5, 6 O: 4.02, 5, 6.2, 7 MSN TV	À	Uppercase "A" with grave accent
Á	N: 1, 3, 4, 4.5, 4.7, 6, 7 IE: 3, 4, 5, 5.5, 6 O: 4.02, 5, 6.2, 7 MSN TV	Á	N: 1, 3, 4, 4.5, 4.7, 6, 7 IE: 3, 4, 5, 5.5, 6 O: 4.02, 5, 6.2, 7 MSN TV	Á	Uppercase "A" with acute accent
Â	N: 1, 3, 4, 4.5, 4.7, 6, 7 IE: 3, 4, 5, 5.5, 6 O: 4.02, 5, 6.2, 7 MSN TV	Â	N: 1, 3, 4, 4.5, 4.7, 6, 7 IE: 3, 4, 5, 5.5, 6 O: 4.02, 5, 6.2, 7 MSN TV	Â	Uppercase "A" with circumflex

Named Entity	Browser Support	Numbered Entity	Browser Support	Intended Rendering	Description
Ã	N: 1, 3, 4, 4.5, 4.7, 6, 7 IE: 3, 4, 5, 5.5, 6 O: 4.02, 5, 6.2, 7 MSN TV	Ã	N: 1, 3, 4, 4.5, 4.7, 6, 7 IE: 3, 4, 5, 5.5, 6 O: 4.02, 5, 6.2, 7 MSN TV	Ã	Uppercase "A" with tilde
Ä	N: 1, 3, 4, 4.5, 4.7, 6, 7 IE: 3, 4, 5, 5.5, 6 O: 4.02, 5, 6.2, 7 MSN TV	Ä	N: 1, 3, 4, 4.5, 4.7, 6, 7 IE: 3, 4, 5, 5.5, 6 O: 4.02, 5, 6.2, 7 MSN TV	Ä	Uppercase "A" with umlaut
Å	N: 1, 3, 4, 4.5, 4.7, 6, 7 IE: 3, 4, 5, 5.5, 6 O: 4.02, 5, 6.2, 7 MSN TV	Å	N: 1, 3, 4, 4.5, 4.7, 6, 7 IE: 3, 4, 5, 5.5, 6 O: 4.02, 5, 6.2, 7 MSN TV	Å	Uppercase "A" with ring
Æ	N: 1, 3, 4, 4.5, 4.7, 6, 7 IE: 3, 4, 5, 5.5, 6 O: 4.02, 5, 6.2, 7 MSN TV	Æ	N: 1, 3, 4, 4.5, 4.7, 6, 7 IE: 3, 4, 5, 5.5, 6 O: 4.02, 5, 6.2, 7 MSN TV	Æ	Uppercase "AE" ligature
Ç	N: 1, 3, 4, 4.5, 4.7, 6, 7 IE: 3, 4, 5, 5.5, 6 O: 4.02, 5, 6.2, 7 MSN TV	Ç	N: 1, 3, 4, 4.5, 4.7, 6, 7 IE: 3, 4, 5, 5.5, 6 O: 4.02, 5, 6.2, 7 MSN TV	Ç	Uppercase "C" with cedilla
È	N: 1, 3, 4, 4.5, 4.7, 6, 7 IE: 3, 4, 5, 5.5, 6 O: 4.02, 5, 6.2, 7 MSN TV	È	N: 1, 3, 4, 4.5, 4.7, 6, 7 IE: 3, 4, 5, 5.5, 6 O: 4.02, 5, 6.2, 7 MSN TV	È	Uppercase "E" with grave accent
É	N: 1, 3, 4, 4.5, 4.7, 6, 7 IE: 3, 4, 5, 5.5, 6 O: 4.02, 5, 6.2, 7 MSN TV	É	N: 1, 3, 4, 4.5, 4.7, 6, 7 IE: 3, 4, 5, 5.5, 6 O: 4.02, 5, 6.2, 7 MSN TV	É	Uppercase "E" with acute accent
Ê	N: 1, 3, 4, 4.5, 4.7, 6, 7 IE: 3, 4, 5, 5.5, 6 O: 4.02, 5, 6.2, 7 MSN TV	Ê	N: 1, 3, 4, 4.5, 4.7, 6, 7 IE: 3, 4, 5, 5.5, 6 O: 4.02, 5, 6.2, 7 MSN TV	Ê	Uppercase "E" with circumflex
Ë	N: 1, 3, 4, 4.5, 4.7, 6, 7 IE: 3, 4, 5, 5.5, 6 O: 4.02, 5, 6.2, 7 MSN TV	Ë	N: 1, 3, 4, 4.5, 4.7, 6, 7 IE: 3, 4, 5, 5.5, 6 O: 4.02, 5, 6.2, 7 MSN TV	Ë	Uppercase "E" with umlaut
Ì	N: 1, 3, 4, 4.5, 4.7, 6, 7 IE: 3, 4, 5, 5.5, 6 O: 4.02, 5, 6.2, 7 MSN TV	Ì	N: 1, 3, 4, 4.5, 4.7, 6, 7 IE: 3, 4, 5, 5.5, 6 O: 4.02, 5, 6.2, 7 MSN TV	Ì	Uppercase "I" with grave accent
Í	N: 1, 3, 4, 4.5, 4.7, 6, 7 IE: 3, 4, 5, 5.5, 6 O: 4.02, 5, 6.2, 7 MSN TV	Í	N: 1, 3, 4, 4.5, 4.7, 6, 7 IE: 3, 4, 5, 5.5, 6 O: 4.02, 5, 6.2, 7 MSN TV	Í	Uppercase "I" with acute accent
Î	N: 1, 3, 4, 4.5, 4.7, 6, 7 IE: 3, 4, 5, 5.5, 6 O: 4.02, 5, 6.2, 7 MSN TV	Î	N: 1, 3, 4, 4.5, 4.7, 6, 7 IE: 3, 4, 5, 5.5, 6 O: 4.02, 5, 6.2, 7 MSN TV	Î	Uppercase "I" with circumflex
Ï	N: 1, 3, 4, 4.5, 4.7, 6, 7 IE: 3, 4, 5, 5.5, 6 O: 4.02, 5, 6.2, 7 MSN TV	Ï	N: 1, 3, 4, 4.5, 4.7, 6, 7 IE: 3, 4, 5, 5.5, 6 O: 4.02, 5, 6.2, 7 MSN TV	Ï	Uppercase "I" with umlaut

Named Entity	Browser Support	Numbered Entity	Browser Support	Intended Rendering	Description
Ð	N: 1, 3, 4, 4.5, 4.7, 6, 7 IE: 3, 4, 5, 5.5, 6 O: 4.02, 5, 6.2, 7 MSN TV	Ð	N: 1, 3, 4, 4.5, 4.7, 6, 7 IE: 3, 4, 5, 5.5, 6 O: 4.02, 5, 6.2, 7 MSN TV	Đ	Capital "ETH"
Ñ	N: 1, 3, 4, 4.5, 4.7, 6, 7 IE: 3, 4, 5, 5.5, 6 O: 4.02, 5, 6.2, 7 MSN TV	Ñ	N: 1, 3, 4, 4.5, 4.7, 6, 7 IE: 3, 4, 5, 5.5, 6 O: 4.02, 5, 6.2, 7 MSN TV	Ñ	Uppercase "N" with tilde
Ò	N: 1, 3, 4, 4.5, 4.7, 6, 7 IE: 3, 4, 5, 5.5, 6 O: 4.02, 5, 6.2, 7 MSN TV	Ò	N: 1, 3, 4, 4.5, 4.7, 6, 7 IE: 3, 4, 5, 5.5, 6 O: 4.02, 5, 6.2, 7 MSN TV	Ò	Uppercase "O" with grave accent
Ó	N: 1, 3, 4, 4.5, 4.7, 6, 7 IE: 3, 4, 5, 5.5, 6 O: 4.02, 5, 6.2, 7 MSN TV	Ó	N: 1, 3, 4, 4.5, 4.7, 6, 7 IE: 3, 4, 5, 5.5, 6 O: 4.02, 5, 6.2, 7 MSN TV	Ó	Uppercase "O" with acute accent
Ô	N: 1, 3, 4, 4.5, 4.7, 6, 7 IE: 3, 4, 5, 5.5, 6 O: 4.02, 5, 6.2, 7 MSN TV	Ô	N: 1, 3, 4, 4.5, 4.7, 6, 7 IE: 3, 4, 5, 5.5, 6 O: 4.02, 5, 6.2, 7 MSN TV	Ô	Uppercase "O" with circumflex
Õ	N: 1, 3, 4, 4.5, 4.7, 6, 7 IE: 3, 4, 5, 5.5, 6 O: 4.02, 5, 6.2, 7 MSN TV	Õ	N: 1, 3, 4, 4.5, 4.7, 6, 7 IE: 3, 4, 5, 5.5, 6 O: 4.02, 5, 6.2, 7 MSN TV	Õ	Uppercase "O" with tilde
Ö	N: 1, 3, 4, 4.5, 4.7, 6, 7 IE: 3, 4, 5, 5.5, 6 O: 4.02, 5, 6.2, 7 MSN TV	Ö	N: 1, 3, 4, 4.5, 4.7, 6, 7 IE: 3, 4, 5, 5.5, 6 O: 4.02, 5, 6.2, 7 MSN TV	Ö	Uppercase "O" with umlaut
×	N: 3, 4, 4.5, 4.7, 6, 7 IE: 3, 4, 5, 5.5, 6 O: 4.02, 5, 6.2, 7 MSN TV	×	N: 1, 3, 4, 4.5, 4.7, 6, 7 IE: 3, 4, 5, 5.5, 6 O: 4.02, 5, 6.2, 7 MSN TV	×	Multiplication symbol
Ø	N: 1, 3, 4, 4.5, 4.7, 6, 7 IE: 3, 4, 5, 5.5, 6 O: 4.02, 5, 6.2, 7 MSN TV	Ø	N: 1, 3, 4, 4.5, 4.7, 6, 7 IE: 3, 4, 5, 5.5, 6 O: 4.02, 5, 6.2, 7 MSN TV	Ø	Uppercase "O" with slash
Ù	N: 1, 3, 4, 4.5, 4.7, 6, 7 IE: 3, 4, 5, 5.5, 6 O: 4.02, 5, 6.2, 7 MSN TV	Ù	N: 1, 3, 4, 4.5, 4.7, 6, 7 IE: 3, 4, 5, 5.5, 6 O: 4.02, 5, 6.2, 7 MSN TV	Ù	Uppercase "U" with grave accent
Ú	N: 1, 3, 4, 4.5, 4.7, 6, 7 IE: 3, 4, 5, 5.5, 6 O: 4.02, 5, 6.2, 7 MSN TV	Ú	N: 1, 3, 4, 4.5, 4.7, 6, 7 IE: 3, 4, 5, 5.5, 6 O: 4.02, 5, 6.2, 7 MSN TV	Ú	Uppercase "U" with acute accent
Û	N: 1, 3, 4, 4.5, 4.7, 6, 7 IE: 3, 4, 5, 5.5, 6 O: 4.02, 5, 6.2, 7 MSN TV	Û	N: 1, 3, 4, 4.5, 4.7, 6, 7 IE: 3, 4, 5, 5.5, 6 O: 4.02, 5, 6.2, 7 MSN TV	Û	Uppercase "U" with circumflex accent
Ü	N: 1, 3, 4, 4.5, 4.7, 6, 7 IE: 3, 4, 5, 5.5, 6 O: 4.02, 5, 6.2, 7 MSN TV	Ü	N: 1, 3, 4, 4.5, 4.7, 6, 7 IE: 3, 4, 5, 5.5, 6 O: 4.02, 5, 6.2, 7 MSN TV	Ü	Uppercase "U" with umlaut

Named Entity	Browser Support	Numbered Entity	Browser Support	Intended Rendering	Description
Ý	N: 1, 3, 4, 4.5, 4.7, 6, 7 IE: 3, 4, 5, 5.5, 6 O: 4.02, 5, 6.2, 7 MSN TV	Ý	N: 1, 3, 4, 4.5, 4.7, 6, 7 IE: 3, 4, 5, 5.5, 6 O: 4.02, 5, 6.2, 7 MSN TV	Ý	Uppercase "Y" with acute accent
Þ	N: 1, 3, 4, 4.5, 4.7, 6, 7 IE: 3, 4, 5, 5.5, 6 O: 4.02, 5, 6.2, 7 MSN TV	Þ	N: 1, 3, 4, 4.5, 4.7, 6, 7 IE: 3, 4, 5, 5.5, 6 O: 4.02, 5, 6.2, 7 MSN TV	Þ	Capital "thorn"
ß	N: 1, 3, 4, 4.5, 4.7, 6, 7 IE: 3, 4, 5, 5.5, 6 O: 4.02, 5, 6.2, 7 MSN TV	ß	N: 1, 3, 4, 4.5, 4.7, 6, 7 IE: 3, 4, 5, 5.5, 6 O: 4.02, 5, 6.2, 7 MSN TV	ß	"SZ" ligature
à	N: 1, 3, 4, 4.5, 4.7, 6, 7 IE: 3, 4, 5, 5.5, 6 O: 4.02, 5, 6.2, 7 MSN TV	à	N: 1, 3, 4, 4.5, 4.7, 6, 7 IE: 3, 4, 5, 5.5, 6 O: 4.02, 5, 6.2, 7 MSN TV	à	Lowercase "a" with grave accent
á	N: 1, 3, 4, 4.5, 4.7, 6, 7 IE: 3, 4, 5, 5.5, 6 O: 4.02, 5, 6.2, 7 MSN TV	á	N: 1, 3, 4, 4.5, 4.7, 6, 7 IE: 3, 4, 5, 5.5, 6 O: 4.02, 5, 6.2, 7 MSN TV	á	Lowercase "a" with acute accent
â	N: 1, 3, 4, 4.5, 4.7, 6, 7 IE: 3, 4, 5, 5.5, 6 O: 4.02, 5, 6.2, 7 MSN TV	â	N: 1, 3, 4, 4.5, 4.7, 6, 7 IE: 3, 4, 5, 5.5, 6 O: 4.02, 5, 6.2, 7 MSN TV	â	Lowercase "a" with circumflex
ã	N: 1, 3, 4, 4.5, 4.7, 6, 7 IE: 3, 4, 5, 5.5, 6 O: 4.02, 5, 6.2, 7 MSN TV	ã	N: 1, 3, 4, 4.5, 4.7, 6, 7 IE: 3, 4, 5, 5.5, 6 O: 4.02, 5, 6.2, 7 MSN TV	ã	Lowercase "a" with tilde
ä	N: 1, 3, 4, 4.5, 4.7, 6, 7 IE: 3, 4, 5, 5.5, 6 O: 4.02, 5, 6.2, 7 MSN TV	ä	N: 1, 3, 4, 4.5, 4.7, 6, 7 IE: 3, 4, 5, 5.5, 6 O: 4.02, 5, 6.2, 7 MSN TV	ä	Lowercase "a" with umlaut
å	N: 1, 3, 4, 4.5, 4.7, 6, 7 IE: 3, 4, 5, 5.5, 6 O: 4.02, 5, 6.2, 7 MSN TV	å	N: 1, 3, 4, 4.5, 4.7, 6, 7 IE: 3, 4, 5, 5.5, 6 O: 4.02, 5, 6.2, 7 MSN TV	å	Lowercase "a" with ring
æ	N: 1, 3, 4, 4.5, 4.7, 6, 7 IE: 3, 4, 5, 5.5, 6 O: 4.02, 5, 6.2, 7 MSN TV	æ	N: 1, 3, 4, 4.5, 4.7, 6, 7 IE: 3, 4, 5, 5.5, 6 O: 4.02, 5, 6.2, 7 MSN TV	æ	Lowercase "ae" ligature
ç	N: 1, 3, 4, 4.5, 4.7, 6, 7 IE: 3, 4, 5, 5.5, 6 O: 4.02, 5, 6.2, 7 MSN TV	ç	N: 1, 3, 4, 4.5, 4.7, 6, 7 IE: 3, 4, 5, 5.5, 6 O: 4.02, 5, 6.2, 7 MSN TV	ç	Lowercase "c" with cedilla
è	N: 1, 3, 4, 4.5, 4.7, 6, 7 IE: 3, 4, 5, 5.5, 6 O: 4.02, 5, 6.2, 7 MSN TV	è	N: 1, 3, 4, 4.5, 4.7, 6, 7 IE: 3, 4, 5, 5.5, 6 O: 4.02, 5, 6.2, 7 MSN TV	è	Lowercase "e" with grave accent
é	N: 1, 3, 4, 4.5, 4.7, 6, 7 IE: 3, 4, 5, 5.5, 6 O: 4.02, 5, 6.2, 7 MSN TV	é	N: 1, 3, 4, 4.5, 4.7, 6, 7 IE: 3, 4, 5, 5.5, 6 O: 4.02, 5, 6.2, 7 MSN TV	é	Lowercase "e" with acute accent

Named Entity	Browser Support	Numbered Entity	Browser Support	Intended Rendering	Description
ê	N: 1, 3, 4, 4.5, 4.7, 6, 7 IE: 3, 4, 5, 5.5, 6 O: 4.02, 5, 6.2, 7 MSN TV	ê	N: 1, 3, 4, 4.5, 4.7, 6, 7 IE: 3, 4, 5, 5.5, 6 O: 4.02, 5, 6.2, 7 MSN TV	ê	Lowercase “e” with circumflex
ë	N: 1, 3, 4, 4.5, 4.7, 6, 7 IE: 3, 4, 5, 5.5, 6 O: 4.02, 5, 6.2, 7 MSN TV	ë	N: 1, 3, 4, 4.5, 4.7, 6, 7 IE: 3, 4, 5, 5.5, 6 O: 4.02, 5, 6.2, 7 MSN TV	ë	Lowercase “e” with umlaut
ì	N: 1, 3, 4, 4.5, 4.7, 6, 7 IE: 3, 4, 5, 5.5, 6 O: 4.02, 5, 6.2, 7 MSN TV	ì	N: 1, 3, 4, 4.5, 4.7, 6, 7 IE: 3, 4, 5, 5.5, 6 O: 4.02, 5, 6.2, 7 MSN TV	ì	Lowercase “i” with grave accent
í	N: 1, 3, 4, 4.5, 4.7, 6, 7 IE: 3, 4, 5, 5.5, 6 O: 4.02, 5, 6.2, 7 MSN TV	í	N: 1, 3, 4, 4.5, 4.7, 6, 7 IE: 3, 4, 5, 5.5, 6 O: 4.02, 5, 6.2, 7 MSN TV	í	Lowercase “i” with acute accent
î	N: 1, 3, 4, 4.5, 4.7, 6, 7 IE: 3, 4, 5, 5.5, 6 O: 4.02, 5, 6.2, 7 MSN TV	î	N: 1, 3, 4, 4.5, 4.7, 6, 7 IE: 3, 4, 5, 5.5, 6 O: 4.02, 5, 6.2, 7 MSN TV	î	Lowercase “i” with circumflex
ï	N: 1, 3, 4, 4.5, 4.7, 6, 7 IE: 3, 4, 5, 5.5, 6 O: 4.02, 5, 6.2, 7 MSN TV	ï	N: 1, 3, 4, 4.5, 4.7, 6, 7 IE: 3, 4, 5, 5.5, 6 O: 4.02, 5, 6.2, 7 MSN TV	ï	Lowercase “i” with umlaut
ð	N: 1, 3, 4, 4.5, 4.7, 6, 7 IE: 3, 4, 5, 5.5, 6 O: 4.02, 5, 6.2, 7 MSN TV	ð	N: 1, 3, 4, 4.5, 4.7, 6, 7 IE: 3, 4, 5, 5.5, 6 O: 4.02, 5, 6.2, 7 MSN TV	ð	Lowercase “eth”
ñ	N: 1, 3, 4, 4.5, 4.7, 6, 7 IE: 3, 4, 5, 5.5, 6 O: 4.02, 5, 6.2, 7 MSN TV	ñ	N: 1, 3, 4, 4.5, 4.7, 6, 7 IE: 3, 4, 5, 5.5, 6 O: 4.02, 5, 6.2, 7 MSN TV	ñ	Lowercase “n” with tilde
ò	N: 1, 3, 4, 4.5, 4.7, 6, 7 IE: 3, 4, 5, 5.5, 6 O: 4.02, 5, 6.2, 7 MSN TV	ò	N: 1, 3, 4, 4.5, 4.7, 6, 7 IE: 3, 4, 5, 5.5, 6 O: 4.02, 5, 6.2, 7 MSN TV	ò	Lowercase “o” with grave accent
ó	N: 1, 3, 4, 4.5, 4.7, 6, 7 IE: 3, 4, 5, 5.5, 6 O: 4.02, 5, 6.2, 7 MSN TV	ó	N: 1, 3, 4, 4.5, 4.7, 6, 7 IE: 3, 4, 5, 5.5, 6 O: 4.02, 5, 6.2, 7 MSN TV	ó	Lowercase “o” with acute accent
ô	N: 1, 3, 4, 4.5, 4.7, 6, 7 IE: 3, 4, 5, 5.5, 6 O: 4.02, 5, 6.2, 7 MSN TV	ô	N: 1, 3, 4, 4.5, 4.7, 6, 7 IE: 3, 4, 5, 5.5, 6 O: 4.02, 5, 6.2, 7 MSN TV	ô	Lowercase “o” with circumflex accent
õ	N: 1, 3, 4, 4.5, 4.7, 6, 7 IE: 3, 4, 5, 5.5, 6 O: 4.02, 5, 6.2, 7 MSN TV	õ	N: 1, 3, 4, 4.5, 4.7, 6, 7 IE: 3, 4, 5, 5.5, 6 O: 4.02, 5, 6.2, 7 MSN TV	õ	Lowercase “o” with tilde
ö	N: 1, 3, 4, 4.5, 4.7, 6, 7 IE: 3, 4, 5, 5.5, 6 O: 4.02, 5, 6.2, 7 MSN TV	ö	N: 1, 3, 4, 4.5, 4.7, 6, 7 IE: 3, 4, 5, 5.5, 6 O: 4.02, 5, 6.2, 7 MSN TV	ö	Lowercase “o” with umlaut

Named Entity	Browser Support	Numbered Entity	Browser Support	Intended Rendering	Description
÷	N: 3, 4, 4.5, 4.7, 6, 7 IE: 3, 4, 5, 5.5, 6 O: 4.02, 5, 6.2, 7 MSN TV	÷	N: 1, 3, 4, 4.5, 4.7, 6, 7 IE: 3, 4, 5, 5.5, 6 O: 4.02, 5, 6.2, 7 MSN TV	÷	Division symbol
ø	N: 1, 3, 4, 4.5, 4.7, 6, 7 IE: 3, 4, 5, 5.5, 6 O: 4.02, 5, 6.2, 7 MSN TV	ø	N: 1, 3, 4, 4.5, 4.7, 6, 7 IE: 3, 4, 5, 5.5, 6 O: 4.02, 5, 6.2, 7 MSN TV	ø	Lowercase "o" with slash
ù	N: 1, 3, 4, 4.5, 4.7, 6, 7 IE: 3, 4, 5, 5.5, 6 O: 4.02, 5, 6.2, 7 MSN TV	ù	N: 1, 3, 4, 4.5, 4.7, 6, 7 IE: 3, 4, 5, 5.5, 6 O: 4.02, 5, 6.2, 7 MSN TV	ù	Lowercase "u" with grave accent
ú	N: 1, 3, 4, 4.5, 4.7, 6, 7 IE: 3, 4, 5, 5.5, 6 O: 4.02, 5, 6.2, 7 MSN TV	ú	N: 1, 3, 4, 4.5, 4.7, 6, 7 IE: 3, 4, 5, 5.5, 6 O: 4.02, 5, 6.2, 7 MSN TV	ú	Lowercase "u" with acute accent
û	N: 1, 3, 4, 4.5, 4.7, 6, 7 IE: 3, 4, 5, 5.5, 6 O: 4.02, 5, 6.2, 7 MSN TV	û	N: 1, 3, 4, 4.5, 4.7, 6, 7 IE: 3, 4, 5, 5.5, 6 O: 4.02, 5, 6.2, 7 MSN TV	û	Lowercase "u" with circumflex
ü	N: 1, 3, 4, 4.5, 4.7, 6, 7 IE: 3, 4, 5, 5.5, 6 O: 4.02, 5, 6.2, 7 MSN TV	ü	N: 1, 3, 4, 4.5, 4.7, 6, 7 IE: 3, 4, 5, 5.5, 6 O: 4.02, 5, 6.2, 7 MSN TV	ü	Lowercase "u" with umlaut
ý	N: 1, 3, 4, 4.5, 4.7, 6, 7 IE: 3, 4, 5, 5.5, 6 O: 4.02, 5, 6.2, 7 MSN TV	ý	N: 1, 3, 4, 4.5, 4.7, 6, 7 IE: 3, 4, 5, 5.5, 6 O: 4.02, 5, 6.2, 7 MSN TV	ý	Lowercase "y" with acute accent
þ	N: 1, 3, 4, 4.5, 4.7, 6, 7 IE: 3, 4, 5, 5.5, 6 O: 4.02, 5, 6.2, 7 MSN TV	þ	N: 1, 3, 4, 4.5, 4.7, 6, 7 IE: 3, 4, 5, 5.5, 6 O: 4.02, 5, 6.2, 7 MSN TV	þ	Lowercase "thorn"
ÿ	N: 1, 3, 4, 4.5, 4.7, 6, 7 IE: 3, 4, 5, 5.5, 6 O: 4.02, 5, 6.2, 7 MSN TV	ÿ	N: 1, 3, 4, 4.5, 4.7, 6, 7 IE: 3, 4, 5, 5.5, 6 O: 4.02, 5, 6.2, 7 MSN TV	ÿ	Lowercase "y" with umlaut

** MSN TV renders € as a right-pointing arrowhead, while O: 7 defines it as a Euro symbol.*

*** MSN TV renders  as a left-pointing arrowhead.*

**** Support for ™ (™) is inconsistent across platforms, although this has improved much in more recent browsers. Designers concerned with backward compatibility might want to consider using a workaround such as **^{<small>**TM**</small>}**.*

APPENDIX C

HTML 4.0 Character Entities

The HTML 4.0 specification introduced a wide array of new character entities that expand the presentation possibilities of HTML, particularly in the presentation of foreign languages. These include additional Latin characters, the Greek alphabet, special spacing characters, arrows, technical symbols, and various shapes. Some of these entities have yet to be supported by browser vendors. Netscape versions 4.0 through 4.8 support only a few of the extended Latin characters, and some entities that duplicate characters already are available in the "standard" list (32 through 255). Internet Explorer versions 4.0 and higher support many of these entities, including the Greek alphabet and mathematical symbols, but do have notable holes. Netscape 6.*x*/7.*x*, Opera 7, and Mozilla browsers support pretty much all the entities.

Latin Extended-A

Named Entity	Browser Support	Numbered Entity	Browser Support	Intended Rendering	Description
&Oelig;	IE: 4, 5, 5.5, 6 N: 6, 7 O: 6.2, 7	Œ	IE: 4, 5, 5.5, 6 N: 4, 4.5, 4.7, 6, 7 O: 6.2, 7	Œ	Uppercase ligature "OE"
œ	IE: 4, 5, 5.5, 6 N: 6, 7 O: 6.2, 7	œ	IE: 4, 5, 5.5, 6 N: 4, 4.5, 4.7, 6, 7 O: 6.2, 7	œ	Lowercase ligature "oe"
Š	IE: 4, 5, 5.5, 6 N: 6, 7 O: 6.2, 7	Š	IE: 4, 5, 5.5, 6 N: 4, 4.5, 4.7, 6, 7 O: 6.2, 7	Š	Uppercase "S" with caron
š	IE: 4, 5, 5.5, 6 N: 6, 7 O: 6.2, 7	š	IE: 4, 5, 5.5, 6 N: 4, 4.5, 4.7, 6, 7 O: 6.2, 7	š	Lowercase "s" with caron
Ÿ	IE: 4, 5, 5.5, 6 N: 6, 7 O: 6.2, 7	Ÿ	IE: 4, 5, 5.5, 6 N: 4, 4.5, 4.7, 6, 7 O: 6.2, 7	Ÿ	Uppercase "Y" with umlaut

NOTE *Internet Explorer 5 for Macintosh displays Š, Š, š, and š with the caron shifted one space to the left of the "s" or "S" character it should be over.*

Latin Extended-B

Named Entity	Browser Support	Numbered Entity	Browser Support	Intended Rendering	Description
ƒ	IE: 4, 5, 5.5, 6 N: 6, 7 O: 6.2, 7	ƒ	IE: 4, 5, 5.5, 6 N:4, 4.5, 4.7, 6, 7 O: 6.2, 7	*f*	Latin small "f" with hook

Spacing Modifier Letters

Named Entity	Browser Support	Numbered Entity	Browser Support	Intended Rendering	Description
ˆ	IE: 4, 5, 5.5, 6 N: 6, 7 O: 4.02, 5, 6.2, 7	ˆ	IE: 4, 5, 5.5, 6 N: 4, 4.5, 4.7, 6, 7 O: 4.02, 5, 6.2, 7	ˆ	Circumflex accent
˜	IE: 4, 5, 5.5, 6 N: 6, 7 O: 4.02, 5, 6.2, 7	˜	IE: 4, 5, 5.5, 6 N: 4, 4.5, 4.7, 6, 7 O: 4.02, 5, 6.2, 7	˜	Small tilde

General Punctuation

Named Entity	Browser Support	Numbered Entity	Browser Support	Intended Rendering	Description
	N: 6, 7		N: 6, 7		En space
	N: 6, 7		N: 6, 7		Em space
	N: 6, 7		N: 6, 7		Thin space
‌	IE: 4, 5, 5.5, 6	‌	IE: 4, 5, 5.5, 6	ǀ	Zero width nonjoiner
‍	IE: 4, 5, 5.5, 6	‍	IE: 4, 5, 5.5, 6	ᛉ	Zero width joiner
‎	None	‎	None	Non-visible	Left-to-right mark
‏	None	‏	None	Non-visible	Right-to-left mark
–	IE: 4, 5, 5.5, 6 N: 6, 7 O: 6.2, 7	–	IE: 4, 5, 5.5, 6 N: 4, 4.5, 4.7, 6, 7 O: 6.2, 7	–	En dash
—	IE: 4, 5, 5.5, 6 N: 6, 7 O: 6.2, 7	—	IE: 4, 5, 5.5, 6 N: 4, 4.5, 4.6, 6, 7 O: 6.2, 7	—	Em dash
‘	IE: 4, 5, 5.5, 6 N: 6, 7 O: 6.2, 7	‘	IE: 4, 5, 5.5, 6 N: 4, 4.5, 4.6, 6, 7 O: 6.2, 7	‘	Open single quotation mark
’	IE: 4, 5, 5.5, 6 N: 6, 7 O: 6.2, 7	’	IE: 4, 5, 5.5, 6 N: 4, 4.5, 4.6, 6, 7 O: 6.2, 7	’	Close single quotation mark
‚	IE: 4, 5, 5.5, 6 N: 6, 7 O: 6.2, 7	‚	IE: 4, 5, 5.5, 6 N: 4, 4.5, 4.6, 6, 7 O: 6.2, 7	‚	Single low-9 quotation mark
“	IE: 4, 5, 5.5, 6 N: 6, 7 O: 6.2, 7	“	IE: 4, 5, 5.5, 6 N: 4, 4.5, 4.6, 6, 7 O: 6.2, 7	“	Open double quotation mark
”	IE: 4, 5, 5.5, 6 N: 6, 7 O: 6.2, 7	”	IE: 4, 5, 5.5, 6 N: 4, 4.5, 4.6, 6, 7 O: 6.2, 7	”	Close double quotation mark
„	IE: 4, 5, 5.5, 6 N: 6, 7 O: 6.2, 7	„	IE: 4, 5, 5.5, 6 N: 4, 4.5, 4.6, 6, 7 O: 6.2, 7	„	Double low-9 quotation mark
†	IE: 4, 5, 5.5, 6 N: 6, 7 O: 6.2, 7	†	IE: 4, 5, 5.5, 6 N: 4, 4.5, 4.6, 6, 7 O: 6.2, 7	†	Dagger
‡	IE: 4, 5, 5.5, 6 N: 6, 7 O: 6.2, 7	‡	IE: 4, 5, 5.5, 6 N: 4, 4.5, 4.6, 6, 7 O: 6.2, 7	‡	Double dagger
•	IE: 4, 5, 5.5, 6 N: 6, 7 O: 6.2, 7	•	IE: 4, 5, 5.5, 6 N: 4, 4.5, 4.6, 6, 7 O: 6.2, 7	•	Bullet

APPENDIX C

Named Entity	Browser Support	Numbered Entity	Browser Support	Intended Rendering	Description
…	IE: 4, 5, 5.5, 6 N: 6, 7 O: 6.2, 7	…	IE: 4, 5, 5.5, 6 N: 4, 4.5, 4.6, 6, 7 O: 6.2, 7	…	Horizontal ellipsis
‰	IE: 4, 5, 5.5 N: 6	‰	IE: 4, 5, 5.5, 6 N: 4, 4.5, 4.6, 6, 7 O: 6.2, 7	‰	Per thousand sign
′	IE: 4, 5, 5.5, 6 N: 6, 7 O: 6.2, 7	′	IE: 4, 5, 5.5, 6 N: 6, 7 O: 6.2, 7	′	Prime, minutes, or feet
″	IE: 4, 5, 5.5, 6 N: 6, 7 O: 6.2, 7	″	IE: 4, 5, 5.5, 6 N: 6, 7 O: 6.2, 7	″	Double prime, seconds, or inches
‹	IE: 4, 5, 5.5, 6 N: 6, 7 O: 4, 5.0, 6.2, 7	‹	IE: 4, 5, 5.5, 6 N: 4, 4.5, 4.7, 6, 7 O: 4, 5.0, 6.2, 7	<	Single left-pointing angle quotation mark
›	IE: 4, 5, 5.5, 6 N: 6, 7 O: 4, 5.0, 6.2, 7	›	IE: 4, 5, 5.5, 6 N: 4, 4.5, 4.7, 6, 7 O: 4, 5.0, 6.2, 7	>	Single right-pointing angle quotation mark
‾	IE: 4, 5, 5.5, 6 N: 6, 7	‾	IE: 4, 5, 5.5, 6 N: 6, 7	‾	Overline
⁄	IE: 4, 5, 5.5, 6 N: 6, 7 O: 4, 5.0, 6.2, 7	⁄	IE: 4, 5, 5.5, 6 N: 6, 7 O: 4, 5.0, 6.2, 7	/	Fraction slash

Greek

Named Entity	Browser Support	Numbered Entity	Browser Support	Intended Rendering	Description
Α	IE: 4, 5, 5.5, 6 N: 6, 7 O: 6.2, 7	Α	IE: 4, 5, 5.5, 6 N: 6, 7 O: 6.2, 7	Α	Greek capital letter alpha
Β	IE: 4, 5, 5.5, 6 N: 6, 7 O: 6.2, 7	Β	IE: 4, 5, 5.5, 6 N: 6, 7 O: 6.2, 7	Β	Greek capital letter beta
Γ	IE: 4, 5, 5.5, 6 N: 6, 7 O: 6.2, 7	Γ	IE: 4, 5, 5.5, 6 N: 6, 7 O: 6.2, 7	Γ	Greek capital letter gamma
Δ	IE: 4, 5, 5.5, 6 N: 6, 7 O: 6.2, 7	Δ	IE: 4, 5, 5.5, 6 N: 6, 7 O: 6.2, 7	Δ	Greek capital letter delta
Ε	IE: 4, 5, 5.5, 6 N: 6, 7 O: 6.2, 7	Ε	IE: 4, 5, 5.5, 6 N: 6, 7 O: 6.2, 7	Ε	Greek capital letter epsilon
Ζ	IE: 4, 5, 5.5, 6 N: 6, 7 O: 6.2, 7	Ζ	IE: 4, 5, 5.5, 6 N: 6, 7 O: 6.2, 7	Ζ	Greek capital letter zeta

Named Entity	Browser Support	Numbered Entity	Browser Support	Intended Rendering	Description
Η	IE: 4, 5, 5.5, 6 N: 6, 7 O: 6.2, 7	Η	IE: 4, 5, 5.5, 6 N: 6, 7 O: 6.2, 7	Η	Greek capital letter eta
Θ	IE: 4, 5, 5.5, 6 N: 6, 7 O: 6.2, 7	Θ	IE: 4, 5, 5.5, 6 N: 6, 7 O: 6.2, 7	Θ	Greek capital letter theta
Ι	IE: 4, 5, 5.5, 6 N: 6, 7 O: 6.2, 7	Ι	IE: 4, 5, 5.5, 6 N: 6, 7 O: 6.2, 7	Ι	Greek capital letter iota
Κ	IE: 4, 5, 5.5, 6 N: 6, 7 O: 6.2, 7	Κ	IE: 4, 5, 5.5, 6 N: 6, 7 O: 6.2, 7	Κ	Greek capital letter kappa
Λ	IE: 4, 5, 5.5, 6 N: 6, 7 O: 6.2, 7	Λ	IE: 4, 5, 5.5, 6 N: 6, 7 O: 6.2, 7	Λ	Greek capital letter lambda
Μ	IE: 4, 5, 5.5, 6 N: 6, 7 O: 6.2, 7	Μ	IE: 4, 5, 5.5, 6 N: 6, 7 O: 6.2, 7	Μ	Greek capital letter mu
Ν	IE: 4, 5, 5.5, 6 N: 6, 7 O: 6.2, 7	Ν	IE: 4, 5, 5.5, 6 N: 6, 7 O: 6.2, 7	Ν	Greek capital letter nu
Ξ	IE: 4, 5, 5.5, 6 N: 6, 7 O: 6.2, 7	Ξ	IE: 4, 5, 5.5, 6 N: 6, 7 O: 6.2, 7	Ξ	Greek capital letter xi
Ο	IE: 4, 5, 5.5, 6 N: 6, 7 O: 6.2, 7	Ο	IE: 4, 5, 5.5, 6 N: 6, 7 O: 6.2, 7	Ο	Greek capital letter omicron
Π	IE: 4, 5, 5.5, 6 N: 6, 7 O: 6.2, 7	Π	IE: 4, 5, 5.5, 6 N: 6, 7 O: 6.2, 7	Π	Greek capital letter pi
Ρ	IE: 4, 5, 5.5, 6 N: 6, 7 O: 6.2, 7	Ρ	IE: 4, 5, 5.5, 6 N: 6, 7 O: 6.2, 7	Ρ	Greek capital letter rho
Σ	IE: 4, 5, 5.5, 6 N: 6, 7 O: 6.2, 7	Σ	IE: 4, 5, 5.5, 6 N: 6, 7 O: 6.2, 7	Σ	Greek capital letter sigma
Τ	IE: 4, 5, 5.5, 6 N: 6, 7 O: 6.2, 7	Τ	IE: 4, 5, 5.5, 6 N: 6, 7 O: 6.2, 7	Τ	Greek capital letter tau
Υ	IE: 4, 5, 5.5, 6 N: 6, 7 O: 6.2, 7	Υ	IE: 4, 5, 5.5, 6 N: 6, 7 O: 6.2, 7	Υ	Greek capital letter upsilon
Φ	IE: 4, 5, 5.5, 6 N: 6, 7 O: 6.2, 7	Φ	IE: 4, 5, 5.5, 6 N: 6, 7 O: 6.2, 7	Φ	Greek capital letter phi
Χ	IE: 4, 5, 5.5, 6 N: 6, 7 O: 6.2, 7	Χ	IE: 4, 5, 5.5, 6 N: 6, 7 O: 6.2, 7	Χ	Greek capital letter chi

Named Entity	Browser Support	Numbered Entity	Browser Support	Intended Rendering	Description
Ψ	IE: 4, 5, 5.5, 6 N: 6, 7 O: 6.2, 7	Ψ	IE: 4, 5, 5.5, 6 N: 6, 7 O: 6.2, 7	Ψ	Greek capital letter psi
Ω	IE: 4, 5, 5.5, 6 N: 6, 7 O: 6.2, 7	Ω	IE: 4, 5, 5.5, 6 N: 6, 7 O: 6.2, 7	Ω	Greek capital letter omega
α	IE: 4, 5, 5.5, 6 N: 6, 7 O: 6.2, 7	α	IE: 4, 5, 5.5, 6 N: 6, 7 O: 6.2, 7	α	Greek small letter alpha
β	IE: 4, 5, 5.5, 6 N: 6, 7 O: 6.2, 7	β	IE: 4, 5, 5.5, 6 N: 6, 7 O: 6.2, 7	β	Greek small letter beta
γ	IE: 4, 5, 5.5, 6 N: 6, 7 O: 6.2, 7	γ	IE: 4, 5, 5.5, 6 N: 6, 7 O: 6.2, 7	γ	Greek small letter gamma
δ	IE: 4, 5, 5.5, 6 N: 6, 7 O: 6.2, 7	δ	IE: 4, 5, 5.5, 6 N: 6, 7 O: 6.2, 7	δ	Greek small letter delta
ε	IE: 4, 5, 5.5, 6 N: 6, 7 O: 6.2, 7	ε	IE: 4, 5, 5.5, 6 N: 6, 7 O: 6.2, 7	ε	Greek small letter epsilon
ζ	IE: 4, 5, 5.5, 6 N: 6, 7 O: 6.2, 7	ζ	IE: 4, 5, 5.5, 6 N: 6, 7 O: 6.2, 7	ζ	Greek small letter zeta
η	IE: 4, 5, 5.5, 6 N: 6, 7 O: 6.2, 7	η	IE: 4, 5, 5.5, 6 N: 6, 7 O: 6.2, 7	η	Greek small letter eta
θ	IE: 4, 5, 5.5, 6 N: 6, 7 O: 6.2, 7	θ	IE: 4, 5, 5.5, 6 N: 6, 7 O: 6.2, 7	θ	Greek small letter theta
ι	IE: 4, 5, 5.5, 6 N: 6, 7 O: 6.2, 7	ι	IE: 4, 5, 5.5, 6 N: 6, 7 O: 6.2, 7	ι	Greek small letter iota
κ	IE: 4, 5, 5.5, 6 N: 6, 7 O: 6.2, 7	κ	IE: 4, 5, 5.5, 6 N: 6, 7 O: 6.2, 7	κ	Greek small letter kappa
λ	IE: 4, 5, 5.5, 6 N: 6, 7 O: 6.2, 7	λ	IE: 4, 5, 5.5, 6 N: 6, 7 O: 6.2, 7	λ	Greek small letter lambda
μ	IE: 4, 5, 5.5, 6 N: 6, 7 O: 6.2, 7	μ	IE: 4, 5, 5.5, 6 N: 6, 7 O: 6.2, 7	μ	Greek small letter mu
ν	IE: 4, 5, 5.5, 6 N: 6, 7 O: 6.2, 7	ν	IE: 4, 5, 5.5 N: 6	ν	Greek small letter nu
ξ	IE: 4, 5, 5.5, 6 N: 6, 7 O: 6.2, 7	ξ	IE: 4, 5, 5.5 N: 6	ξ	Greek small letter xi
ο	IE: 4, 5, 5.5, 6 N: 6, 7 O: 6.2, 7	ο	IE: 4, 5, 5.5, 6 N: 6, 7 O: 6.2, 7	ο	Greek small letter omicron

Named Entity	Browser Support	Numbered Entity	Browser Support	Intended Rendering	Description
π	IE: 4, 5, 5.5, 6 N: 6, 7 O: 6.2, 7	π	IE: 4, 5, 5.5, 6 N: 6, 7 O: 6.2, 7	π	Greek small letter pi
ρ	IE: 4, 5, 5.5, 6 N: 6, 7 O: 6.2, 7	ρ	IE: 4, 5, 5.5, 6 N: 6, 7 O: 6.2, 7	ρ	Greek small letter rho
ς	IE: 4, 5, 5.5, 6 N: 6, 7 O: 6.2, 7	ς	IE: 4, 5, 5.5, 6 N: 6, 7 O: 6.2, 7	ς	Greek small letter final sigma
σ	IE: 4, 5, 5.5, 6 N: 6, 7 O: 6.2, 7	σ	IE: 4, 5, 5.5, 6 N: 6, 7 O: 6.2, 7	σ	Greek small letter sigma
τ	IE: 4, 5, 5.5, 6 N: 6, 7 O: 6.2, 7	τ	IE: 4, 5, 5.5, 6 N: 6, 7 O: 6.2, 7	τ	Greek small letter tau
υ	IE: 4, 5, 5.5, 6 N: 6, 7 O: 6.2, 7	υ	IE: 4, 5, 5.5, 6 N: 6, 7 O: 6.2, 7	υ	Greek small letter upsilon
φ	IE: 4, 5, 5.5, 6 N: 6, 7 O: 6.2, 7	φ	IE: 4, 5, 5.5, 6 N: 6, 7 O: 6.2, 7	φ	Greek small letter phi
χ	IE: 4, 5, 5.5, 6 N: 6, 7 O: 6.2, 7	χ	IE: 4, 5, 5.5, 6 N: 6, 7 O: 6.2, 7	χ	Greek small letter chi
ψ	IE: 4, 5, 5.5, 6 N: 6, 7 O: 6.2, 7	ψ	IE: 4, 5, 5.5, 6 N: 6, 7 O: 6.2, 7	ψ	Greek small letter psi
ω	IE: 4, 5, 5.5, 6 N: 6, 7 O: 6.2, 7	ω	IE: 4, 5, 5.5, 6 N: 6, 7 O: 6.2, 7	ω	Greek small letter omega
ϑ	IE: 5 (Mac only) N: 6, 7	ϑ	IE: 5 (Mac only) N: 6	X	Greek small letter theta symbol
ϒ	IE: 5 (Mac only) N: 6, 7	ϒ	IE: 5 (Mac only) N: 6, 7	ϒ	Greek upsilon with hook symbol
&piv	IE: 5 (Mac only) N: 6, 7	ϖ	IE: 5 (Mac only) N: 6, 7	ϖ	Greek pi symbol

Letter-like Symbols

Named Entity	Browser Support	Numbered Entity	Browser Support	Intended Rendering	Description
℘	N: 6, 7 O: 6.2, 7	℘	N: 6, 7 O: 6.2, 7	℘	Script capital P, power set
ℑ	N: 6, 7 O: 6.2, 7	ℑ	N: 6, 7 O: 6.2, 7	ℑ	Blackletter capital I, or imaginary part symbol

Named Entity	Browser Support	Numbered Entity	Browser Support	Intended Rendering	Description
ℜ	N: 6, 7 O: 6.2, 7	ℜ	N: 6, 7 O: 6.2, 7	ℜ	Blackletter capital R, or real part symbol
™	IE: 3, 4, 5, 5.5, 6 N: 6, 7 O: 4, 5.0, 6.2, 7 MSN TV	™	IE: 4, 5, 5.5, N: 4, 4.5, 6 4.7, 6, 7 O: 4, 5.0, 6.2, 7	™	Trademark symbol
ℵ	N: 6, 7 O: 6.2, 7	ℵ	N: 6, 7 O: 6.2, 7	ℵ	Alef symbol, or first transfinite cardinal

Arrows

Named Entity	Browser Support	Numbered Entity	Browser Support	Intended Rendering	Description
←	IE: 4, 5, 5.5, 6 N: 6, 7 O: 6.2, 7	←	IE: 4, 5, 5.5, 6 N: 6, 7 O: 6.2, 7	←	Left arrow
↑	IE: 4, 5, 5.5, 6 N: 6, 7 O: 6.2, 7	↑	IE: 4, 5, 5.5, 6 N: 6, 7 O: 6.2, 7	↑	Up arrow
→	IE: 4, 5, 5.5, 6 N: 6, 7 O: 6.2, 7	→	IE: 4, 5, 5.5, 6 N: 6, 7 O: 6.2, 7	→	Right arrow
↓	IE: 4, 5, 5.5, 6 N: 6, 7 O: 6.2, 7	↓	IE: 4, 5, 5.5, 6 N: 6, 7 O: 6.2, 7	↓	Down arrow
↔	IE: 4, 5, 5.5, 6 N: 6, 7 O: 6.2, 7	↔	IE: 4, 5, 5.5, 6 N: 6, 7 O: 6.2, 7	↔	Left-right arrow
↵	N: 6, 7 O: 6.2, 7	↵	N: 6, 7 O: 6.2, 7	↵	Down arrow with corner leftward
⇐	N: 6, 7 O: 6.2, 7	⇐	N: 6, 7 O: 6.2, 7	⇐	Left double arrow
⇑	N: 6, 7 O: 6.2, 7	⇑	N: 6, 7 O: 6.2, 7	⇑	Up double arrow
⇒	IE: 5.5, 6 N: 6, 7 O: 6.2,	⇒	IE: 5.5, 6 N: 6, 7 O: 6.2, 7	⇒	Right double arrow
⇓	N: 6, 7 O: 6.2, 7	⇓	N: 6, 7 O: 6.2, 7	⇓	Down double arrow
⇔	IE: 5.5, 6 N: 6, 7 O: 7	⇔	IE: 5.5, 6 N: 6, 7 O: 7	⇔	Left-right double arrow

Mathematical Operators

Named Entity	Browser Support	Numbered Entity	Browser Support	Intended Rendering	Description
∀	IE: 6 N: 6, 7 O: 6.2, 7	∀	IE: 6 N: 6, 7 O: 6.2, 7	∀	For all
∂	IE: 4, 5, 5.5, 6 N: 6, 7 O: 6.2, 7	∂	IE: 4, 5, 5.5, 6 N: 6, 7 O: 6.2, 7	∂	Partial differential
∃	IE: 6 N: 6, 7 O: 6.2, 7	∃	IE: 6 N: 6, 7 O: 6.2, 7	∃	There exists
∅	N: 6, 7 O: 6.2, 7	∅	N: 6, 7 O: 6.2, 7	∅	Empty set, null set, diameter
∇	IE: 6 N: 6, 7 O: 6.2, 7	∇	IE: 6 N: 6, 7 O: 6.2, 7	∇	Nabla, or backward difference
∈	IE: 6 N: 6, 7 O: 6.2, 7	∈	IE: 6 N: 6, 7 O: 6.2, 7	∈	Element of
∉	N: 6, 7	∉	N: 6, 7	∉	Not an element of
∋	IE: 6 N: 6, 7 O: 6.2, 7	∋	IE: 6 N: 6, 7 O: 6.2, 7	∋	Contains as member
∏	IE: 4, 5, 5.5, 6 N: 6, 7 O: 6.2, 7	∏	IE: 4, 5, 5.5, 6 N: 6, 7 O: 6.2, 7	∏	N-ary product, or product sign
∑	IE: 4, 5, 5.5, 6 N: 6, 7 O: 6.2, 7	∑	IE: 4, 5, 5.5, 6 N: 6, 7 O: 6.2, 7	∑	N-ary summation
−	IE: 4, 5, 5.5, 6 N: 6, 7 O: 4, 5.0, 6.2, 7	−	IE: 4, 5, 5.5, 6 N: 6, 7 O: 4, 5.0, 6.2, 7	−	Minus sign
∗	N: 6, 7	∗	N: 6, 7	∗	Asterisk operator
√	IE: 4, 5, 5.5, 6 N: 6, 7 O: 6.2, 7	√	IE: 4, 5, 5.5, 6 N: 6, 7 O: 6.2, 7	√	Square root, radical sign
∝	IE: 6 N: 6, 7 O: 6.2, 7	∝	IE: 6 N: 6, 7 O: 6.2, 7	∝	Proportional to
∞	IE: 4, 5, 5.5, 6 N: 6, 7 O: 6.2, 7	∞	IE: 4, 5, 5.5, 6 N: 6, 7 O: 6.2, 7	∞	Infinity
∠	IE: 6 N: 6, 7 O: 6.2, 7	∠	IE: 6 N: 6, 7 O: 6.2, 7	∠	Angle

Named Entity	Browser Support	Numbered Entity	Browser Support	Intended Rendering	Description
∧	IE: 6 N: 6, 7 O: 6.2, 7	⊥	IE: 6 N: 6, 7 O: 6.2, 7	⊥	Logical and
∨	N: 6, 7	⊦	N: 6, 7	⊦	Logical or
∩	IE: 4, 5, 5.5, 6 N: 6, 7 O: 6.2, 7	∩	IE: 4, 5, 5.5, 6 N: 6, 7 O: 6.2, 7	∩	Intersection, cap
∪	N: 6, 7 O: 6.2, 7	∪	N: 6, 7 O: 6.2, 7	∪	Union, cup
∫	IE: 4, 5, 5.5, 6 N: 6, 7 O: 6.2, 7	∫	IE: 4, 5, 5.5, 6 N: 6, 7 O: 6.2, 7	∫	Integral
∴	IE: 6 N: 6, 7 O: 6.2, 7	∴	IE: 6 N: 6, 7 O: 6.2, 7	∴	Therefore
∼	IE: 6 N: 6, 7 O: 6.2, 7	∼	IE: 6 N: 6, 7 O: 6.2, 7	~	Tilde operator
≅	N: 6, 7	≅	N: 6, 7	≅	Approximately equal to
≈	IE: 4, 5, 5.5, 6 N: 6, 7 O: 6.2, 7	≈	IE: 4, 5, 5.5, 6 N: 6, 7 O: 6.2, 7	≈	Almost equal to, asymptotic to
≠	IE: 4, 5, 5.5, 6 N: 6, 7 O: 6.2, 7	≠	IE: 4, 5, 5.5, 6 N: 6, 7 O: 6.2, 7	≠	Not equal to
≡	IE: 4, 5, 5.5, 6 N: 6, 7 O: 6.2, 7	≡	IE: 4, 5, 5.5, 6 N: 6, 7 O: 6.2, 7	≡	Identical to
≤	IE: 4, 5, 5.5, 6 N: 6, 7 O: 6.2, 7	≤	IE: 4, 5, 5.5, 6 N: 6, 7 O: 6.2, 7	≤	Less than or equal to
≥	IE: 4, 5, 5.5, 6 N: 6, 7 O: 6.2, 7	≥	IE: 4, 5, 5.5, 6 N: 6, 7 O: 6.2, 7	≥	Greater than or equal to
⊂	IE: 6 N: 6, 7 O: 6.2, 7	⊂	IE: 6 N: 6, 7 O: 6.2, 7	⊂	Subset of
⊃	IE: 6 N: 6, 7 O: 6.2, 7	⊃	IE: 6 N: 6, 7 O: 6.2, 7	⊃	Superset of
⊄	N: 6, 7	⊄	N: 6, 7	⊄	Not a subset of
⊆	IE: 6 N: 6, 7 O: 6.2, 7	⊆	IE: 6 N: 6, 7 O: 6.2, 7	⊆	Subset of or equal to
⊇	IE: 6 N: 6, 7 O: 6.2, 7	⊇	IE: 6 N: 6, 7 O: 6.2, 7	⊇	Superset of or equal to
⊕	N: 6, 7	⊕	N: 6, 7	⊕	Circled plus, direct sum

Named Entity	Browser Support	Numbered Entity	Browser Support	Intended Rendering	Description
⊗	N: 6, 7	⊗	N: 6, 7	⊗	Circled times, vector product
⊥	IE: 6 N: 6, 7 O: 6.2, 7	⊥	IE: 6 N: 6, 7 O: 6.2, 7	⊥	Perpendicular
⋅	N: 6, 7	⋅	N: 6, 7	·	Dot operator

Technical Symbols

Named Entity	Browser Support	Numbered Entity	Browser Support	Intended Rendering	Description
⌈	N: 6, 7	⌈	N: 6, 7	⌈	Left ceiling
⌉	N: 6, 7	⌉	N: 6, 7	⌉	Right ceiling
⌊	N: 6, 7	⌊	N: 6, 7	⌊	Left floor
⌋	N: 6, 7	⌋	N: 6, 7	⌋	Right floor
⟨	N: 7	〈	N: 7	<	Left-pointing angle bracket
⟩	N: 7	〉	N: 7	>	Right-pointing angle bracket

Geometric Shapes

Named Entity	Browser Support	Numbered Entity	Browser Support	Intended Rendering	Description
◊	IE: 4, 5, 5.5, 6 N: 6, 7 O: 6.2, 7	◊	IE: 4, 5, 5.5, 6 N: 6, 7 O: 6.2, 7	◊	Lozenge

Miscellaneous Symbols

Named Entity	Browser Support	Numbered Entity	Browser Support	Intended Rendering	Description
♠	IE: 4, 5, 5.5, 6 N: 6, 7 O: 6.2, 7	♠	IE: 4, 5, 5.5, 6 N: 6, 7 O: 6.2, 7	♠	Spade suit
♣	IE: 4, 5, 5.5, 6 N: 6, 7 O: 6.2, 7	♣	IE: 4, 5, 5.5, 6 N: 6, 7 O: 6.2, 7	♣	Club suit
♥	IE: 4, 5, 5.5, 6 N: 6, 7 O: 6.2, 7	♥	IE: 4, 5, 5.5, 6 N: 6, 7 O: 6.2, 7	♥	Heart suit
♦	IE: 4, 5, 5.5, 6 N: 6, 7 O: 6.2, 7	♦	IE: 4, 5, 5.5, 6 N: 6, 7 O: 6.2, 7	♦	Diamond suit

D

APPENDIX

Fonts

This appendix contains a quick reference for the commonly available fonts and a brief discussion of downloadable fonts.

Specifying Fonts

Under HTML 4.01 and transitional XHTML 1.0, you can use the **<font>** tag to set a font in a page by setting the **face** attribute:

```
<font face="Britannic Bold">This is important</font>
```

The Web browser reads this HTML fragment and renders the text in the font named in the **face** attribute—but only for users who have the font installed on their systems. Multiple fonts can be listed using the **face** attribute:

```
<font face="Arial, Helvetica, Sans-serif">
This should be in a different font</font>
```

Here, the browser reads the comma-delimited list of fonts until it finds a font it supports. Given the fragment shown here, the browser would first try Arial, then Helvetica, and finally a sans-serif font before giving up and using the current browser font.

CSS supports the same approach to setting fonts using **font-family** and **font** properties. For example, to set the font to Arial for all text in paragraph tags, you would use a rule like the following:

```
p {font-family: Arial;}
```

Of course, the same restriction of fonts available on the local system applies, so a comma-delimited list of fonts should be specified like so:

```
p {font-family: Verdana, Arial, Helvetica, Sans-serif;}
```

Regardless of the approach, you can apply a little guesswork to use fonts properly if you consider that most Macintosh, Windows, and UNIX users have a standard set of fonts. If equivalent fonts are specified, it may be possible to provide similar page renderings across platforms.

Fonts for Microsoft Platforms and Browsers

The following fonts are available for Microsoft browsers and systems; they are displayed in Figure D-1.

Font	Systems
Andale Mono	IE4.5 and IE5
Arial	Windows XP, Windows 2000, Windows ME, Windows 98, Windows 95, Windows 3.1*x*, Windows NT 3.*x*, Windows NT 4.*x*, IE4.5, 5, and 6
Arial Bold	Windows XP, Windows 2000, Windows ME, Windows 98, Windows 95, Windows 3.1*x*, Windows NT 3.*x*, Windows NT 4.*x*
Arial Italic	Windows XP, Windows 2000, Windows ME, Windows 98, Windows 95, Windows 3.1*x*, Windows NT 3.*x*, Windows NT 4.*x*
Arial Bold Italic	Windows XP, Windows 2000, Windows ME, Windows 98, Windows 95, Windows 3.1*x*, Windows NT 3.*x*, Windows NT 4.*x*
Arial Black	Windows XP, Windows 2000, Windows ME, Windows 98, IE3, IE4, IE5, and IE6
Comic Sans MS	Windows XP, Windows 2000, Windows ME, IE3, IE4, IE5, and IE6
Comic Sans MS Bold	Windows XP, Windows 2000, Windows ME, IE3, IE4, 5, and IE6
Courier New	Windows XP, Windows 2000, Windows ME, Windows 98, Windows 95, Windows 3.1*x*, Windows NT 3.*x*, Windows NT 4.*x*
Courier New Bold	Windows XP, Windows 2000, Windows ME, Windows 98, Windows 95, Windows 3.1*x*, Windows NT 3.*x*, Windows NT 4.*x*
Courier New Italic	Windows XP, Windows 2000, Windows ME, Windows 98, Windows 95, Windows 3.1*x*, Windows NT 3.*x*, Windows NT 4.*x*
Courier New Bold Italic	Windows XP, Windows 2000, Windows ME, Windows 98, Windows 95, Windows 3.1*x*, Windows NT 3.*x*, Windows NT 4.*x*
Georgia	Windows XP, Windows 2000, IE4, IE5, and IE6 (add-on)
Georgia Bold	Windows XP, Windows 2000, IE4, IE5, and IE6 (add-on)
Georgia Italic	Windows XP, Windows 2000, IE4, IE5, and IE6 (add-on)
Georgia Bold Italic	Windows XP, Windows 2000, IE4, IE5 & IE6 (add-on)
Impact	Windows XP, Windows 2000, Windows ME, Windows 98, Internet Explorer 3, 4, 5, and 6
Lucida Console	Windows XP, Windows 2000, Windows ME, Windows 98, Windows NT 3.*x* (except NT 3.0), Windows NT 4.*x*
Lucida Sans Unicode	Windows XP, Windows 2000, Windows 98, Windows NT 3.*x* (except NT 3.0), Windows NT 4.*x*

Font	Systems
Marlett	Windows XP, Windows 2000, Windows ME, Windows 98, Windows 95, Windows NT 4.*x*
Minion Web (Adobe)	Microsoft lists this as one of its "core fonts," but it seems to be available (for sale) only from Adobe (http://www.adobe.com).
Monotype.com	Old version of Andale Mono, still available for Windows 3.1 and 3.11 (add-on)
Symbol	Windows XP, Windows 2000, Windows ME, Windows 98, Windows 95, Windows 3.1*x*, Windows NT 3.*x*, Windows NT 4.*x*
Times New Roman	Windows XP, Windows 2000, Windows ME, Windows 98, Windows 95, Windows 3.1*x*, Windows NT 3.*x*, Windows NT 4.*x*
Times New Roman Bold	Windows XP, Windows 2000, Windows ME, Windows 98, Windows 95, Windows 3.1*x*, Windows NT 3.*x*, Windows NT 4.*x*
Times New Roman Italic	Windows XP, Windows 2000, Windows ME, Windows 98, Windows 95, Windows 3.1*x*, Windows NT 3.*x*, Windows NT 4.*x*
Times New Roman Bold Italic	Windows XP, Windows 2000, Windows ME, Windows 98, Windows 95, Windows 3.1*x*, Windows NT 3.*x*, Windows NT 4.*x*
Tahoma	Windows XP, Windows 2000, Windows ME, Windows 98
Trebuchet MS	Windows XP, Windows 2000, IE4, IE5, and IE6 (add-on)
Trebuchet MS Bold	Windows XP, Windows 2000, Windows 2000, IE4, IE5, and IE6 (add-on)
Trebuchet MS Italic	Windows XP, Windows 2000, IE4, IE5, and IE6 (add-on)
Trebuchet MS Bold Italic	Windows XP, Windows 2000, IE4, IE5, and IE6 (add-on)
Verdana	Windows XP, Windows 2000, Windows ME, Windows 98, IE3, IE4, IE5, and IE6
Verdana Bold	Windows XP, Windows 2000, Windows ME, Windows 98, IE3, IE4, IE5, and IE6
Verdana Italic	Windows XP, Windows 2000, Windows ME, Windows 98, IIE3, 4, 5, and 6
Verdana Bold Italic	Windows XP, Windows 2000, Windows ME, Windows 98, Internet Explorer 3, IE4, IE5, and IE6
Webdings	Windows XP, Windows 2000, Windows ME, Windows 98, IE4, IE5, and IE6
Wingdings	Windows XP, Windows 2000, Windows ME, Windows 98, Windows 95, Windows 3.1*x*, Windows NT 3.*x*, Windows NT 4.*x*

NOTE *For more reference on Microsoft related fonts, please see http://www.microsoft.com/typography/fonts.*

FIGURE D-1 Font families available for Microsoft browsers and systems

Andale Mono
Arial
Arial Bold
Arial Italic
Arial Bold Italic
Arial Black
Comic Sans MS
Comic Sans MS Bold
Courier New
Courier New Bold
Courier New Bold Italic
Courier New Italic
Georgia
Georgia Bold
Georgia Italic
Georgia Bold Italic
Impact
Lucida Console
Lucida Sans Unicode
M✓✕ (Marlett)
Minion Web
Σψμβολ (Symbol)
Times New Roman
Times New Roman Bold
Times New Roman Bold Italic
Times New Roman Italic
Tahoma
Trebuchet MS
Trebuchet MS Bold
Trebuchet MS Italic
Trebuchet MS Bold Italic
Verdana
Verdana Bold
Verdana Bold Italic
Verdana Italic
? (Webdings)
(Wingdings)

Fonts for Apple Macintosh System 7

The following fonts are available for Macintosh System 7; they are displayed in Figure D-2.

Chicago	Courier Regular	Geneva
Helvetica	Monaco	New York
Palatino	Symbol	Times

FIGURE D-2 Font families available with Macintosh System 7

Chicago
Courier Regular
Geneva
Helvetica
Monaco
New York
Palatino
Σψμβολ (Symbol)
Times

Additional Fonts for Apple Macintosh System 8 and Higher

In addition to the fonts shown for System 7, Macintosh System 8 offers the following fonts; they are displayed in Figure D-3.

Apple Chancery	Hoefler Text	Hoefler Text Ornaments
Skia		

Additional Fonts for Apple Macintosh System 8.5 and Higher

In addition to the fonts shown for System 8, Macintosh System 8.5 offers the following fonts; they are displayed in Figure D-4.

Capitals	Charcoal	Gadget
Sand	Techno	Textile

Additional Fonts for Apple Macintosh OS X

In addition to the fonts shown for System 8.5, Macintosh OS X offers the following fonts; they are displayed in Figure D-5.

American Typewriter	Andale Mono	Arial
Arial Black	Brush Script	Baskerville
Big Caslon	Comic Sans MS	Copperplate
Courier New	Didot	Georgia
Gill Sans	Futura	Herculanum
Impact	Lucida Grande	Marker Felt
Optima	Osaka	Papyrus
Times New Roman	Trebuchet MS	Verdana
Webdings	Zapf Dingbats	Zapfino

FIGURE D-3 Additional font families available with Macintosh System 8

Apple Chancery
Hoefler Text 
(Hoefler Text Ornaments)
Skia

FIGURE D-4 Additional font families available with Macintosh System 8.5

CAPITALS
Charcoal
Gadget
Sand
Techno
Textile

Fonts for UNIX Systems

The following fonts are available for most UNIX systems; they are displayed in Figure D-6.

Charter	Clean	Courier
Fixed	Helvetica	Lucida
Lucidabright	Lucida Typewriter	New Century Schoolbook
Symbol	Terminal	Times
Utopia		

Most users may have many other fonts in addition to the ones shown in the tables. Users of Microsoft's Office will probably also have access to fonts such as Algerian, Book Antiqua, Bookman Old Style, Britannic Bold, Desdemona, Garamond, Century Gothic, Haettenschweiller, and many others. The various browsers are also trying to make new fonts available. Microsoft's Webdings font provides many common icons for use on Web pages viewed in Internet Explore 4.0

FIGURE D-5 Additional fonts for Apple Macintosh OS X

American Typewriter
Andale Mono
Arial
Arial Black
Brush Script
Baskerville
Big Caslon
Comic Sans MS
COPPERPLATE
Courier New
Didot
Georiga
Gill Sans
Futura
HERCULANUM
Impact
Lucida Grande
Marker Felt
Optima
Osaka
Papyrus
Times New Roman
Trebuchet MS
Verdana

FIGURE D-6 Font families available on common UNIX systems

Charter
Clean
Courier
Fixed
Helvetica
Lucida
Lucidabright
New Century Schoolbook
Σψμβολ (Symbol)
Terminal
Times
Utopia

or higher. Some of these icons may be useful for navigation, like arrows, while others look like audio or video symbols that could provide an indication of link content.

Downloadable Fonts

The best solution for fonts on the Web is to come up with a cross-platform font that could be downloaded to the browser on the fly. Both of the major browser vendors have developed their own versions of downloadable fonts. Microsoft's solution can be found at www.microsoft.com/typography. Netscape's solution, called Dynamic Fonts, is based on TrueDoc, but this technology was discontinued with version 6.0 of the Netscape browser and should be avoided. A cross-platform solution to the font issue using Flash or another binary format is possible but rather involved. Some have tried to address this issue by performing font substitutions on the server side (www.glyphgate.com), but so far such an approach is not commonplace. The next section briefly discusses the only viable downloadable font technology in use at the time of this edition's writing: Microsoft Embedded fonts.

Microsoft's Dynamic Fonts

Microsoft Internet Explorer for Windows provides a fairly robust way to embed fonts in a Web page. To include a font, you must first build the page using the **font** element or style sheet rules that set fonts. When creating your page, don't worry about whether or not the end user has the font installed; it will be downloaded. Next, use Microsoft's Web Embedding Fonts Tool or a similar facility to analyze the font usage on the page. The program should create an .eot file that contains the embedded fonts. Then, add the font usage information to the page in the form of cascading style sheets (CSS) style rules, as shown here:

```
<!DOCTYPE HTML PUBLIC "-//W3C//DTD HTML 4.01 Transitional//EN"
"http://www.w3.org/TR/html4/loose.dtd">
<html>
<head>
<title>Microsoft Font Test</title>
<style type="text/css">
<!--

  @font-face {
    font-family: Ransom;
```

```
    font-style:  normal;
    font-weight: normal;
    src: url(fonts/ransom.eot);
  }

  .special {font-family: Ransom; color: green; font-size: 28pt;}
-->
</style>
</head>
<body>
<font face="Ransom" size="6">Example Ransom Note Font</font><br>
<span class="special">This is also in Ransom</span>
</body>
</html>
```

Notice how it is possible to use both typical style sheet rules like a **class** binding as well as the normal **<font>** tag. A possible rendering of font embedding is shown in Figure D-7.

You must first create a font file and reference it from the file that uses the font. It may be useful to define a font's directory within your Web site to store font files, similar to storing image files for site use.

The use of the **@font-face** acts as a pseudo-element that allows you to bring any number of fonts into a page. For more information on embedded fonts under Internet Explorer as well as links to font file creation tools like Web Embedding Font Tool (WEFT), see the Microsoft Typography site (http://www.microsoft.com/typography/web/embedding/weft3/).

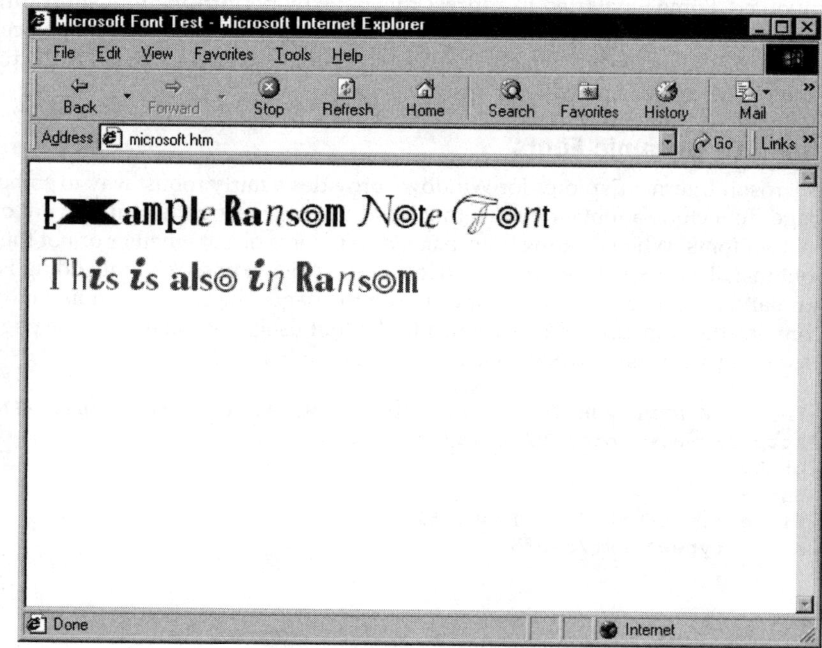

FIGURE D-7 Embedded fonts increase design choices

E

APPENDIX

Color Reference

This appendix provides basic information about the use of colors on the Web, from how to calculate browser-safe colors, adjust unsafe colors, and form hybrid colors, to the use of color names and their numerical equivalents as used in HTML and CSS, and browser support of color names.

Browser-Safe Colors

While 8-bit GIF images support 256 colors, cross-platform issues leave a palette of only 216 colors that are completely safe to use on the Web. This group of Web-safe colors is often called the *browser-safe palette*. Since it is difficult to present this information visually in a black and white book, the palette can be viewed online at http://www.htmlref.com/reference/AppE. Use of other colors beyond this safe set can lead to poor-looking images when viewed under limited color conditions such as 8-bit (256 color) VGA. Selecting a set of colors from the safe color palette and mixing them together in a process called *dithering* will approximate colors outside the safe range. In short, dithering attempts to imitate colors by placing similar colors near them, but generally creates irregularities that render the image unappealing.

The selection of the 216 safe colors is fairly obvious if you consider the additive nature of RGB color. Consider a color to be made up of varying amounts of red, green, or blue that could be set by adjusting an imaginary color dial from the extremes of no color to maximum color saturation. The safe colors use six possible intensity settings for each value of red, green, or blue. The settings are 0%, 20%, 40%, 60%, 80%, and 100%. A value of 0%, 0%, 0% on the imaginary color dial would be equivalent to black. A value of 100%, 100%, 100% would indicate pure white, while a value of 100%, 0%, 0% is pure red, and so on. The safe colors are those that have an RGB value set only at one of the safe intensity settings. The hex conversions for saturation are shown in Table E-1.

TABLE E-1 Color Intensity Conversion Table

Color Intensity	Hex Value	Decimal Value
100%	FF	255
80%	CC	204
60%	99	153
40%	66	102
20%	33	51
0%	00	0

Setting a safe color is simply a matter of selecting a combination of safe hex values. In this case, #9966FF is a safe hex color; #9370DB is not. Most Web design tools like Macromedia Dreamweaver contain safe color pickers as do imaging tools like Macromedia Fireworks or Adobe PhotoShop. Designers looking for color palettes, including improved color pickers and swatches, should visit http://www.visibone.com/colorlab/.

Setting an unsafe color to its nearest safe color is fairly easy—just round each particular red, green, or blue value up or down to the nearest safe value. A complete conversion of hex to decimal values is shown in Table E-2. Safe values are indicated in bold.

00=00	01=01	02=02	03=03	04=04	05=05
06=06	07=07	08=08	09=09	10=0A	11=0B
12=0C	13=0D	14=0E	15=0F	16=10	17=11
18=12	19=13	20=14	21=15	22=16	23=17
24=18	25=19	26=1A	27=1B	28=1C	29=1D
30=1E	31=1F	32=20	33=21	34=22	35=23
36=24	37=25	38=26	39=27	40=28	41=29
42=2A	43=2B	44=2C	45=2D	46=2E	47=2F
48=30	49=31	50=32	**51=33**	52=34	53=35
54=36	55=37	56=38	57=39	58=3A	59=3B
60=3C	61=3D	62=3E	63=3F	64=40	65=41
66=42	67=43	68=44	69=45	70=46	71=47
72=48	73=49	74=4A	75=4B	76=4C	77=4D
78=4E	79=4F	80=50	81=51	82=52	83=53
84=54	85=55	86=56	87=57	88=58	89=59
90=5A	91=5B	92=5C	93=5D	94=5E	95=5F
96=60	97=61	98=62	99=63	100=64	101=65
102=66	103=67	104=68	105=69	106=6A	107=6B
108=6C	109=6D	110=6E	111=6F	112=70	113=71
114=72	115=73	116=74	117=75	118=76	119=77
120=78	121=79	122=7A	123=7B	124=7C	125=7D
126=7E	127=7F	128=80	129=81	130=82	131=83
132=84	133=85	134=86	135=87	136=88	137=89
138=8A	139=8B	140=8C	141=8D	142=8E	143=8F
144=90	145=91	146=92	147=93	148=94	149=95

TABLE E-2 RGB to Hexadecimal Color Conversion Chart

150=96	151=97	152=98	**153=99**	154=9A	155=9B
156=9C	157=9D	158=9E	159=9F	160=A0	161=A1
162=A2	163=A3	164=A4	165=A5	166=A6	167=A7
168=A8	169=A9	170=AA	171=AB	172=AC	173=AD
174=AE	175=AF	176=B0	177=B1	178=B2	179=B3
180=B4	181=B5	182=B6	183=B7	184=B8	185=B9
186=BA	187=BB	188=BC	189=BD	190=BE	191=BF
192=C0	193=C1	194=C2	195=C3	196=C4	197=C5
198=C6	199=C7	200=C8	201=C9	202=CA	203=CB
204=CC	205=CD	206=CE	207=CF	208=D0	209=D1
210=D2	211=D3	212=D4	213=D5	214=D6	215=D7
216=D8	217=D9	218=DA	219=DB	220=DC	221=DD
222=DE	223=DF	224=E0	225=E1	226=E2	227=E3
228=E4	229=E5	230=E6	231=E7	232=E8	233=E9
234=EA	235=EB	236=EC	237=ED	238=EE	239=EF
240=F0	241=F1	242=F2	243=F3	244=F4	245=F5
246=F6	247=F7	248=F8	249=F9	250=FA	251=FB
252=FC	253=FD	254=FE	**255=FF**		

TABLE E-2 RGB to Hexadecimal Color Conversion Chart *(continued)*

Although mathematically translating to the closest browser-safe color seems appropriate, it might not look correct to many people. Consider creating a hybrid color by combining multiple safe colors together. This is done simply by creating a checkerboard effect with a GIF image, in which two or more non-dithering colors are placed side by side to give the appearance of a third color. A variety of PhotoShop plug-ins such as Colorsafe (www.boxtopsoft.com) exist for mixing colors.

Color Names and Numerical Equivalents

Table E-3 lists all the color names commonly supported by the major browsers (Netscape 3.0 and better through Netscape 7, Internet Explorer 3.0 and better, Opera 6 and better). The HTML specification defines 16 named colors: aqua, black, blue, fuchsia, gray, green, lime, maroon, navy, olive, purple, red, silver, teal, white, and yellow. (Out of these colors, only seven are considered safe in the reproduction sense discussed previously.) Many other color names have been introduced by the browser vendors—particularly Netscape—and are fairly commonly used. Color names are easier to remember than numerical codes, but might cause trouble when viewed under old or uncommon browsers. It is advisable to stick with the hexadecimal approach to colors, as it is generally safer. The corresponding hexadecimal code is shown next to each color name shown in Table E-3, and generally is interchangeable with the corresponding name. Thus, the code **<body bgcolor="lightsteelblue">** would produce the same result as **<body bgcolor= "#b0c4de">** under any browser that supported these color names. Identical colors might be reproducible with different names. For example, "magenta" and "fuchsia" are both equivalent to #FF00FF. Regardless of named color support, keep in mind that not all numeric values are completely browser safe either. Although these names and numbers probably won't be an issue for users with high-resolution monitors and higher degrees of color support, don't forget that these users are not the only people on the Web. Browser-safe colors in Table E-3 appear in bold; RGB equivalents are also included.

NOTE *While earlier versions of the Opera browser had highly inconsistent support of color names, more recent releases (Opera 6 and Opera 7) are greatly improved. Color names now display the same as their numerical equivalents in the newer Opera browsers, with the single exception of **navyblue**. This color name displays the same as **navy** in the Opera browsers. The color name **navyblue** is also problematic in Netscape's browser versions 6 and 7, which display it as black.*

Hexadecimal Code	Name	RGB Equivalent	Notes
#F0F8FF	aliceblue	240,248,255	The name "aliceblue" is not supported by versions of Netscape prior to version 4.0.
#FAEBD7	antiquewhite	250,235,215	
#00FFFF	aqua	0,255,255	
#7FFFD4	aquamarine	127,255,212	
#F0FFFF	azure	240,255,255	
#F5F5DC	beige	245,245,220	
#FFE4C4	bisque	255,228,196	
#000000	black	0,0,0	
#FFEBCD	blanchedalmond	255,235,205	
#0000FF	blue	0, 0,255	
#8A2BE2	blueviolet	138, 43,226	
#A52A2A	brown	165, 42, 42	
#DEB887	burlywood	222,184,135	
#5F9EA0	cadetblue	95,158,160	
#7FFF00	chartreuse	127,255, 0	
#D2691E	chocolate	210,105, 30	
#FF7F50	coral	255,127, 80	
#6495ED	cornflowerblue	100,149,237	
#FFF8DC	cornsilk	255,248,220	

TABLE E-3 Color Names and Their Numerical Equivalents

Hexadecimal Code	Name	RGB Equivalent	Notes
#DC143C	crimson	220,20,60	
#00FFFF	cyan	0,255,255	
#00008B	darkblue	0,0,139	
#008B8B	darkcyan	0,139,139	
#B8860B	darkgoldenrod	184,134, 11	
#A9A9A9	darkgray	169,169,169	
#006400	darkgreen	0,100, 0	
#BDB76B	darkkhaki	189,183,107	
#8B008B	darkmagenta	139, 0,139	
#556B2F	darkolivegreen	85,107, 47	
#FF8C00	darkorange	255,140, 0	
#9932CC	darkorchid	153, 50,204	
#8B0000	darkred	139, 0, 0	
#E9967A	darksalmon	233,150,122	
#8FBC8F	darkseagreen	143,188,143	
#483D8B	darkslateblue	72, 61,139	
#2F4F4F	darkslategray	47, 79, 79	
#00CED1	darkturquoise	0,206,209	
#9400D3	darkviolet	148, 0,211	
#FF1493	deeppink	255, 20,147	
#00BFFF	deepskyblue	0,191,255	
#696969	dimgray	105,105,105	
#1E90FF	dodgerblue	30,144,255	
#B22222	firebrick	178, 34, 34	
#FFFAF0	floralwhite	255,250,240	
#228B22	forestgreen	34,139, 34	
#FF00FF	fuchsia	255,0,255	
#DCDCDC	gainsboro	220,220,220	
#F8F8FF	ghostwhite	248,248,255	
#FFD700	gold	255,215, 0	
#DAA520	goldenrod	218,165, 32	
#808080	gray	127,127,127	

TABLE E-3 Color Names and Their Numerical Equivalents *(continued)*

APPENDIX E

Hexadecimal Code	Name	RGB Equivalent	Notes
#008000	green	0,128,0	
#ADFF2F	greenyellow	173,255, 47	
#F0FFF0	honeydew	240,255,240	
#FF69B4	hotpink	255,105,180	
#CD5C5C	indianred	205, 92, 92	
#4B0082	indigo	75,0,130	
#FFFFF0	ivory	255,255,240	
#F0E68C	khaki	240,230,140	
#E6E6FA	lavender	230,230,250	
#FFF0F5	lavenderblush	255,240,245	
#7CFC00	lawngreen	124,252, 0	
#FFFACD	lemonchiffon	255,250,205	
#ADD8E6	lightblue	173,216,230	
#F08080	lightcoral	240,128,128	
#E0FFFF	lightcyan	224,255,255	
#FAFAD2	lightgoldenrodyellow	250,250,210	
#90EE90	lightgreen	144,238,144	
#D3D3D3	lightgrey	211,211,211	
#FFB6C1	lightpink	255,182,193	
#FFA07A	lightsalmon	255,160,122	
#20B2AA	lightseagreen	32,178,170	
#87CEFA	lightskyblue	135,206,250	
#778899	lightslategray	119,136,153	
#B0C4DE	lightsteelblue	176,196,222	
#FFFFE0	lightyellow	255,255,224	
#00FF00	lime	0,255,0	
#32CD32	limegreen	50,205, 50	
#FAF0E6	linen	250,240,230	
#FF00FF	magenta	255, 0,255	
#800000	maroon	128,0,0	
#66CDAA	mediumaquamarine	102,205,170	
#0000CD	mediumblue	0,0,205	

TABLE E-3 Color Names and Their Numerical Equivalents *(continued)*

Hexadecimal Code	Name	RGB Equivalent	Notes
#BA55D3	mediumorchid	186, 85,211	
#9370DB	mediumpurple	147,112,219	
#3CB371	mediumseagreen	60,179,113	
#7B68EE	mediumslateblue	123,104,238	
#00FA9A	mediumspringgreen	0,250,154	
#48D1CC	mediumturquoise	72,209,204	
#C71585	mediumvioletred	199, 21,133	
#191970	midnightblue	25, 25,112	
#F5FFFA	mintcream	245,255,250	
#FFE4E1	mistyrose	255,228,225	
#FFE4B5	moccasin	255,228,181	
#FFDEAD	navajowhite	255,222,173	
#000080	navy	0, 0,128	
#9FAFDF	navyblue	159,175,223	
#FDF5E6	oldlace	253,245,230	
#808000	olive	128,128,0	
#6B8E23	olivedrab	107,142, 35	
#FFA500	orange	255,165, 0	
#FF4500	orangered	255, 69, 0	
#DA70D6	orchid	218,112,214	
#EEE8AA	palegoldenrod	238,232,170	
#98FB98	palegreen	152,251,152	
#AFEEEE	paleturquoise	175,238,238	
#DB7093	palevioletred	219,112,147	
#FFEFD5	papayawhip	255,239,213	
#FFDAB9	peachpuff	255,218,185	
#CD853F	peru	205,133, 63	
#FFC0CB	pink	255,192,203	
#DDA0DD	plum	221,160,221	
#B0E0E6	powderblue	176,224,230	
#800080	purple	128,0,128	
#FF0000	red	255, 0, 0	

TABLE E-3 Color Names and Their Numerical Equivalents *(continued)*

APPENDIX E

Hexadecimal Code	Name	RGB Equivalent	Notes
#BC8F8F	rosybrown	188,143,143	
#4169E1	royalblue	65,105,225	
#8B4513	saddlebrown	139,69,19	
#FA8072	salmon	250,128,114	
#F4A460	sandybrown	244,164, 96	
#2E8B57	seagreen	46,139, 87	
#FFF5EE	seashell	255,245,238	
#A0522D	sienna	160, 82, 45	
#C0C0C0	silver	192,192,192	
#87CEEB	skyblue	135,206,235	
#6A5ACD	slateblue	106, 90,205	
#708090	slategray	112,128,144	
#FFFAFA	snow	255,250,250	
#00FF7F	springgreen	0,255,127	
#4682B4	steelblue	70,130,180	
#D2B48C	tan	210,180,140	
#008080	teal	0,128,128	
#D8BFD8	thistle	216,191,216	
#FF6347	tomato	255, 99, 71	
#40E0D0	turquoise	64,224,208	
#EE82EE	violet	238,130,238	
#F5DEB3	wheat	245,222,179	
#FFFFFF	white	255,255,255	
#F5F5F5	whitesmoke	245,245,245	
#FFFF00	yellow	255,255, 0	
#9ACD32	yellowgreen	139,205,50	

TABLE E-3 Color Names and Their Numerical Equivalents *(continued)*

Many online color references claim that further color variations can be introduced by adding the numbers 1 through 4 to color names. If this were correct, cadetblue1, cadetblue2, cadetblue3, and cadetblue4 would display as different shades of the same color, with 1 being the lightest and 4 the darkest. Opera still partially supports this concept, but given the complete lack of support by the major browsers, there seems little sense in using this approach.

Some online color references also claim that gray supports up to 100 color variations (gray10, gray50, gray90, and so forth). Testing reveals that this does not work under Netscape or Internet Explorer. Opera supports this concept by displaying lighter grays for higher numerical values.

CSS Color Values

Cascading style sheets (CSS) support the color names and values listed above and also offer a number of other formats not available in HTML.

Three-Digit Hexadecimal Color Values

Under CSS, color values can be defined using three-digit hexadecimal color values, a concise version of the six-digit values just noted. This approach is supported by Internet Explorer 3 and higher and Netscape Navigator 4 and higher.

```
span {font-family: Helvetica; font-size: 14pt; color: #0CF;}
```

RGB Color Values

Under CSS, color values can be defined using RGB values. Colors are defined by the letters *rgb,* followed by three numbers between 0 and 255 that are contained in parentheses, separated by commas, and with no spaces between them. This approach is supported by Internet Explorer 4 and higher and Netscape Navigator 4 and higher.

```
p {color: rgb(204,0,51);}
```

RGB Color Values Using Percentages

Under CSS, RGB color values can also be defined using percentages. The format is the same, except that the numbers are replaced by percentage values between 0% and 100%. This approach is supported by Internet Explorer 4 and higher and Netscape Navigator 4 and higher.

```
p {color: rgb(75%,10%,50%);}
```

F

APPENDIX

Reading a Document Type Definition

This appendix presents the Document Type Definitions (DTDs) for XHTML 1.0. Traditional HTML "dialects" are defined using SGML (Standard Generalized Markup Language), a complex language with many nuances. Modern XHTML dialects are developed in XML (eXtensible Markup Language), which is a subset of SGML and slightly easier to work with. This appendix presents the small amount of SGML or XML knowledge needed to read the various DTDs directly.

Element Type Declarations

Two common types of declarations should be familiar to Web developers: element type declarations and attribute list declarations. Beyond these, the less familiar declarations for general and parameter entities are not very complicated.

An *element type declaration* defines three characteristics:

- The element type's name, also known as its *generic identifier*
- Whether start and end tags are required, forbidden (end tags on empty elements), or may be omitted
- The element type's *content model,* or what content it can enclose

All element type declarations begin with the keyword **ELEMENT** and have the following form:

```
<!ELEMENT name content_model >
```

The declaration for the XHTML **br** element gives a simple example:

```
<!ELEMENT br EMPTY>
```

This case says we have a **br** element that contains no content at all—it is empty, as shown by the keyword **EMPTY**.

In the case of traditional HTML, which is defined using SGML, we see a different syntax that defines

```
<!ELEMENT name minimization content_model >
```

In the traditional HTML 4.0 DTD we see

```
<!ELEMENT BR - O EMPTY>
```

Here, tag minimization is declared by two parameters that indicate the start and end tags. These parameters may take one of two values. A hyphen indicates the tag is required. An uppercase "O" indicates it may be omitted. The combination of "O" for the end tag and the content model **EMPTY** means the end tag is forbidden. Thus, under traditional HTML the **
** tag requires a start tag but not an end tag. Because the **
** tag does not contain content, its content model is defined by the keyword **EMPTY** just as it did in the XHTML specification.

Most HTML and XHTML elements enclose content. If a content model is declared, it is enclosed within parentheses and known as a *model group*. The HTML 4.0 declaration for a selection list option gives an example:

```
<!ELEMENT OPTION - O (#PCDATA)*>
```

The XHTML equivalent is almost identical save the casing of the element itself and the lack of the minimization information.

```
<!ELEMENT option (#PCDATA)>
```

Note in both cases the content model group contains the keyword **#PCDATA**. This stands for *parsed character data*—character content that contains no element markup but that may contain entity symbols for special characters. Keywords such as #PCDATA and CDATA are discussed in the section "SGML and XML Keywords."

Occurrence Indicators

In the previous example, also note the asterisk appended to the model group. This is an *occurrence indicator*—a special symbol that qualifies the element type or model group to which it is appended, indicating how many times it may occur. There are three occurrence indicators:

- ? Means optional and at most one occurrence (zero or one occurrence)
- * Means optional and any number of occurrences (zero or more occurrences)
- + Means at least one occurrence required (one or more occurrences)

Content models can also define an element type as containing element content, illustrated by the SGML declaration for a definition list (**<DL>**) under HTML 4:

```
<!ELEMENT DL - - (DT | DD)+>
```

The XML declaration for **dl** under XHTML is again only slightly different as it omits the minimization information and cases the elements differently.

```
<!ELEMENT dl (dt | dd)+>
```

Logical Connectors

Note in the previous example that the model group contains **dt** and **dd**, the names of element types that a **<dl>** tag may enclose. Note also the vertical bar separating **dt** and **dd**. This is a *logical connector*—a special symbol indicating how the content units it connects relate to each other. There are three logical connectors:

- | Means "or" (one and only one of the connected content units must occur)

- **&** Means "and" (all of the connected content units must occur)
- **,** Means "sequence" (the connected content units must occur in the specified order)

Thus, the content model in the previous declaration says that the **<dl>** tag must contain either a **<dt>** or **<dl>** tag and can contain any additional number of **<dt>** or **<dd>** tags.

- **( )** Used to group content units together

Model groups can be nested inside other model groups. Very flexible content models can be declared by combining this with the capability to qualify content units with occurrence indicators and logical operators. The XHTML declaration for the **<table>** tag illustrates this point:

```
<!ELEMENT table (caption?, (col*|colgroup*), thead?, tfoot?, (tbody+|tr+))>
```

The content model for the table element type reads as follows:

- Table content begins with zero or one <**caption**> tags.
- This must be followed by a content group.
- The content group must contain zero or more **<col>** tags or zero or more **<colgroup>** tags.
- This must be followed by zero or one **<thead>** tags.
- This must be followed by zero or one **<tfoot>** tags.
- This must be followed by one or more **<tbody>** or **<tr>** tags.

SGML Content Exclusion and Inclusion

Occasionally, the need arises to declare that an element type cannot contain certain other element types. This is known as a *content exclusion*. The excluded tags follow the model group, enclosed by parentheses and preceded by the minus sign under an SGML doctype:

```
(model group) -(excluded tags)
```

A *related special need* is the capability to declare that an element type can occur anywhere inside a content model. This is known as a *content inclusion*. The included tags follow the model group, and are enclosed by parentheses and preceded by the plus sign:

```
(model group) +(included tags)
```

As an example, the HTML 4.0 declaration for the **<BODY>** tag illustrates both excluded and included elements:

```
<!ELEMENT BODY O O (%block;) -(BODY) +(INS|DEL)>
```

Why are insertions and deletions used in this declaration? The content inclusion says that the **<INS>** and **<DEL>** tags can occur anywhere in the content enclosed by **<BODY>** and **</BODY> tags.** While the content exclusion says that a **BODY** element cannot contain another **BODY** element, in this case it's necessary because of the curious "**%block**" declaration used in the model group. The leading % character identifies this as a *parameter entity*, essentially a macro symbol that refers to a longer character string declared elsewhere in the DTD. Parameter entities, which commonly occur in DTDs, are discussed shortly (see the section "Parameter Entities"). The "**%block**" entity reference is a shorthand way of referring to all block element types that happen to include **<BODY>**. It is easier to exclude **<BODY>** from the list of block elements than to define a special purpose declaration. Interestingly, XML eliminates the use of content inclusion and exclusion from the XHTML DTD, and thus it is both more verbose and in some ways simpler to read.

Attribute Declarations

Once an element's syntax has been defined, we have to address its attributes. All attribute declarations begin with the keyword **ATTLIST** followed by the element name, attribute name, attribute type, and default data information, as you can see in the following:

```
<!ATTLIST element-name attribute-name attribute-type default-data>
```

The HTML 4.0 **<BDO>** tag type illustrates a small attribute declaration:

```
<!ATTLIST   BDO
      lang  NAME        #IMPLIED
      dir   (ltr|rtl)   #REQUIRED
>
```

The XML syntax that defines the **<bdo>** tag under XHTML is similar but you should notice that more attributes are not available for this tag

```
<!ATTLIST bdo
  %coreattrs;
  %events;
  lang        %LanguageCode; #IMPLIED
  xml:lang    %LanguageCode; #IMPLIED
  dir         (ltr|rtl)      #REQUIRED
>
```

SGML and XML Keywords

The previous SGML example declares the **lang** attribute as having values of type **NAME**, an alphabetic string. **NAME** is one of several SGML/XML keywords occurring in HTML and XHTML's declarations of an attribute's type:

- **CDATA** Unparsed character data
- **ID** A document-wide unique identifier
- **IDREF** A reference to a document-wide identifier
- **NAME** An alphabetic character string plus a hyphen and a period
- **NMTOKEN** An alphanumeric character string plus a hyphen and a period
- **NUMBER** A character string containing decimal numbers

Notice in early DTD fragment for **<bdo>** that the **dir** attribute does not declare its type using a keyword. Instead, the type is specified using an enumerated list containing two possible values, **ltr** and **rtl**. In that example for either SGML or XML, the attribute's default behavior is specified with a keyword. A default value may be specified using a quoted string.

- **#REQUIRED** A value must be supplied for the attribute.
- **#IMPLIED** The attribute is optional.
- **#FIXED** The attribute has a fixed value that is declared in quotes using an additional parameter. Because the attribute/value pair is assumed to be constant, it does not need to be used in the document instance.

Parameter Entities

An *entity* is essentially a macro that allows a short name to be associated with replacement text. Parameter entities define replacement text used in DTD declarations. Syntactically, a parameter entity is distinguished by using the percent (%) symbol. Its general form is shown here:

```
<!ENTITY % name "replacement text">
```

It is used in DTDs as follows:

```
%name;
```

Parameter entities are a convenient way to define commonly occurring pieces of a DTD so that changes only need to be made in one place. We see in XHTML a parameter entity to define the core attributes common to most elements.

```
<!ENTITY % coreattrs
 "id          ID             #IMPLIED
  class       CDATA          #IMPLIED
  style       %StyleSheet;   #IMPLIED
  title       %Text;         #IMPLIED"
>
```

Notice that entity **%coreattrs** further references entities (%StyleSheet; and %Text;) to define values for the style and title attributes. Once defined, the core attributes could be added to an attribute list declaration for an element, as follows:

```
<!ATTLIST some-element  %coreattrs;>
```

Oftentimes, you will see entities that in turn contain further entities. For example, under HTML 4.0 the **coreattrs** parameter entity is used with the **%i18n** and **events** parameter entities to define the expansion text for an aggregate entity called **attrs**.

```
<!ENTITY % attrs "%coreattrs %i18n %events">
```

Comments

DTDs in both SGML and XML contain the type of comments familiar to Web page authors:

```
<!-- this is a comment -->
```

Comments can also be embedded inside SGML declarations for explanatory purposes. Embedded comments are delimited by two dashes, and a single declaration may contain many embedded comments.

```
<!ATTLIST PARAM
  name       CDATA      #REQUIRED -- property name --
  value      CDATA      #IMPLIED  -- property value --
  valuetype (DATA|REF|OBJECT) DATA -- How to interpret value --
  type       CDATA      #IMPLIED  -- Internet media type --
  >
```

However, XML does not use this comment style, so you will not see it in the XHTML specification.

APPENDIX F

The DTDs

The rest of this appendix presents the Document Type Definitions for XHTML 1.0, starting with the transitional DTD, which is recommended for use in most Web documents. This is followed by the strict definition, which removes the presentational elements from markup in favor of CSS. The latest versions of these DTDs can be retrieved from the W3C:

- **XHTML 1 Transitional** http://www.w3.org/TR/xhtml1/DTD/xhtml1-transitional.dtd
- **XHTML 1 Strict** http://www.w3.org/TR/xhtml1/DTD/xhtml1-strict.dtd
- **XHTML 1 Frameset** http://www.w3.org/TR/xhtml1/DTD/xhtml1-frameset.dtd

Other DTDs can also be found online, including:

- **HTML 2** http://www.w3.org/MarkUp/html-spec/html.dtd
- **HTML 3** http://www.w3.org/TR/REC-html32#dtd
- **HTML 4 Transitional** http://www.w3.org/TR/html4/loose.dtd
- **HTML 4 Strict** http://www.w3.org/TR/html4/strict.dtd
- **HTML 4 Frameset** http://www.w3.org/TR/html4/frameset.dtd
- **XHTML 1.1** http://www.w3.org/TR/xhtml11/

XHTML 1.0 Transitional DTD

```
<!--
   Extensible HTML version 1.0 Transitional DTD

   This is the same as HTML 4 Transitional except for
   changes due to the differences between XML and SGML.

   Namespace = http://www.w3.org/1999/xhtml

   For further information, see: http://www.w3.org/TR/xhtml1

   Copyright (c) 1998-2002 W3C (MIT, INRIA, Keio),
   All Rights Reserved.

   This DTD module is identified by the PUBLIC and SYSTEM identifiers:

   PUBLIC "-//W3C//DTD XHTML 1.0 Transitional//EN"
   SYSTEM "http://www.w3.org/TR/xhtml1/DTD/xhtml1-transitional.dtd"

   $Revision: 1.2 $
   $Date: 2002/08/01 18:37:55 $

-->

<!--================ Character mnemonic entities =========================-->

<!ENTITY % HTMLlat1 PUBLIC
   "-//W3C//ENTITIES Latin 1 for XHTML//EN"
   "xhtml-lat1.ent">
%HTMLlat1;
```

```
<!ENTITY % HTMLsymbol PUBLIC
   "-//W3C//ENTITIES Symbols for XHTML//EN"
   "xhtml-symbol.ent">
%HTMLsymbol;

<!ENTITY % HTMLspecial PUBLIC
   "-//W3C//ENTITIES Special for XHTML//EN"
   "xhtml-special.ent">
%HTMLspecial;

<!--================== Imported Names ====================================-->

<!ENTITY % ContentType "CDATA">
    <!-- media type, as per [RFC2045] -->

<!ENTITY % ContentTypes "CDATA">
    <!-- comma-separated list of media types, as per [RFC2045] -->

<!ENTITY % Charset "CDATA">
    <!-- a character encoding, as per [RFC2045] -->

<!ENTITY % Charsets "CDATA">
    <!-- a space separated list of character encodings, as per [RFC2045] -->

<!ENTITY % LanguageCode "NMTOKEN">
    <!-- a language code, as per [RFC3066] -->

<!ENTITY % Character "CDATA">
    <!-- a single character, as per section 2.2 of [XML] -->

<!ENTITY % Number "CDATA">
    <!-- one or more digits -->

<!ENTITY % LinkTypes "CDATA">
    <!-- space-separated list of link types -->

<!ENTITY % MediaDesc "CDATA">
    <!-- single or comma-separated list of media descriptors -->

<!ENTITY % URI "CDATA">
    <!-- a Uniform Resource Identifier, see [RFC2396] -->

<!ENTITY % UriList "CDATA">
    <!-- a space separated list of Uniform Resource Identifiers -->

<!ENTITY % Datetime "CDATA">
    <!-- date and time information. ISO date format -->

<!ENTITY % Script "CDATA">
    <!-- script expression -->

<!ENTITY % StyleSheet "CDATA">
    <!-- style sheet data -->

<!ENTITY % Text "CDATA">
    <!-- used for titles etc. -->

<!ENTITY % FrameTarget "NMTOKEN">
    <!-- render in this frame -->
```

```
<!ENTITY % Length "CDATA">
    <!-- nn for pixels or nn% for percentage length -->

<!ENTITY % MultiLength "CDATA">
    <!-- pixel, percentage, or relative -->

<!ENTITY % Pixels "CDATA">
    <!-- integer representing length in pixels -->

<!-- these are used for image maps -->

<!ENTITY % Shape "(rect|circle|poly|default)">

<!ENTITY % Coords "CDATA">
    <!-- comma separated list of lengths -->


<!-- used for object, applet, img, input and iframe -->
<!ENTITY % ImgAlign "(top|middle|bottom|left|right)">

<!-- a color using sRGB: #RRGGBB as Hex values -->
<!ENTITY % Color "CDATA">

<!-- There are also 16 widely known color names with their sRGB values:

    Black  = #000000    Green  = #008000
    Silver = #C0C0C0    Lime   = #00FF00
    Gray   = #808080    Olive  = #808000
    White  = #FFFFFF    Yellow = #FFFF00
    Maroon = #800000    Navy   = #000080
    Red    = #FF0000    Blue   = #0000FF
    Purple = #800080    Teal   = #008080
    Fuchsia= #FF00FF    Aqua   = #00FFFF
-->

<!--=================== Generic Attributes ===============================-->

<!-- core attributes common to most elements
  id       document-wide unique id
  class    space separated list of classes
  style    associated style info
  title    advisory title/amplification
-->
<!ENTITY % coreattrs
 "id          ID             #IMPLIED
  class       CDATA          #IMPLIED
  style       %StyleSheet;   #IMPLIED
  title       %Text;         #IMPLIED"
  >

<!-- internationalization attributes
  lang        language code (backwards compatible)
  xml:lang    language code (as per XML 1.0 spec)
  dir         direction for weak/neutral text
-->
<!ENTITY % i18n
 "lang        %LanguageCode; #IMPLIED
  xml:lang    %LanguageCode; #IMPLIED
  dir         (ltr|rtl)      #IMPLIED"
  >
```

```
<!-- attributes for common UI events
  onclick     a pointer button was clicked
  ondblclick  a pointer button was double clicked
  onmousedown a pointer button was pressed down
  onmouseup   a pointer button was released
  onmousemove a pointer was moved onto the element
  onmouseout  a pointer was moved away from the element
  onkeypress  a key was pressed and released
  onkeydown   a key was pressed down
  onkeyup     a key was released
-->

<!ENTITY % events
 "onclick     %Script;       #IMPLIED
  ondblclick  %Script;       #IMPLIED
  onmousedown %Script;       #IMPLIED
  onmouseup   %Script;       #IMPLIED
  onmouseover %Script;       #IMPLIED
  onmousemove %Script;       #IMPLIED
  onmouseout  %Script;       #IMPLIED
  onkeypress  %Script;       #IMPLIED
  onkeydown   %Script;       #IMPLIED
  onkeyup     %Script;       #IMPLIED"
  >

<!-- attributes for elements that can get the focus
  accesskey   accessibility key character
  tabindex    position in tabbing order
  onfocus     the element got the focus
  onblur      the element lost the focus
-->

<!ENTITY % focus
 "accesskey   %Character;    #IMPLIED
  tabindex    %Number;       #IMPLIED
  onfocus     %Script;       #IMPLIED
  onblur      %Script;       #IMPLIED"
  >

<!ENTITY % attrs "%coreattrs; %i18n; %events;">

<!-- text alignment for p, div, h1-h6. The default is
     align="left" for ltr headings, "right" for rtl -->

<!ENTITY % TextAlign "align (left|center|right|justify) #IMPLIED">

<!--=================== Text Elements ====================================-->

<!ENTITY % special.extra
   "object | applet | img | map | iframe">

<!ENTITY % special.basic
   "br | span | bdo">

<!ENTITY % special
   "%special.basic; | %special.extra;">

<!ENTITY % fontstyle.extra "big | small | font | basefont">

<!ENTITY % fontstyle.basic "tt | i | b | u
```

```
                    | s | strike ">

<!ENTITY % fontstyle "%fontstyle.basic; | %fontstyle.extra;">

<!ENTITY % phrase.extra "sub | sup">
<!ENTITY % phrase.basic "em | strong | dfn | code | q |
                   samp | kbd | var | cite | abbr | acronym">

<!ENTITY % phrase "%phrase.basic; | %phrase.extra;">

<!ENTITY % inline.forms "input | select | textarea | label | button">

<!-- these can occur at block or inline level -->
<!ENTITY % misc.inline "ins | del | script">

<!-- these can only occur at block level -->
<!ENTITY % misc "noscript | %misc.inline;">

<!ENTITY % inline "a | %special; | %fontstyle; | %phrase; | %inline.forms;">

<!-- %Inline; covers inline or "text-level" elements -->
<!ENTITY % Inline "(#PCDATA | %inline; | %misc.inline;)*">

<!--================== Block level elements ==============================-->

<!ENTITY % heading "h1|h2|h3|h4|h5|h6">
<!ENTITY % lists "ul | ol | dl | menu | dir">
<!ENTITY % blocktext "pre | hr | blockquote | address | center | noframes">

<!ENTITY % block
    "p | %heading; | div | %lists; | %blocktext; | isindex |fieldset | table">

<!-- %Flow; mixes block and inline and is used for list items etc. -->
<!ENTITY % Flow "(#PCDATA | %block; | form | %inline; | %misc;)*">

<!--================== Content models for exclusions =====================-->

<!-- a elements use %Inline; excluding a -->

<!ENTITY % a.content
   "(#PCDATA | %special; | %fontstyle; | %phrase; | %inline.forms; |
 %misc.inline;)*">

<!-- pre uses %Inline excluding img, object, applet, big, small,
     font, or basefont -->

<!ENTITY % pre.content
   "(#PCDATA | a | %special.basic; | %fontstyle.basic; | %phrase.basic; |
   %inline.forms; | %misc.inline;)*">

<!-- form uses %Flow; excluding form -->

<!ENTITY % form.content "(#PCDATA | %block; | %inline; | %misc;)*">

<!-- button uses %Flow; but excludes a, form, form controls, iframe -->

<!ENTITY % button.content
   "(#PCDATA | p | %heading; | div | %lists; | %blocktext; |
      table | br | span | bdo | object | applet | img | map |
      %fontstyle; | %phrase; | %misc;)*">
```

```
<!--================ Document Structure ===================================-->

<!-- the namespace URI designates the document profile -->

<!ELEMENT html (head, body)>
<!ATTLIST html
  %i18n;
  id          ID             #IMPLIED
  xmlns       %URI;          #FIXED 'http://www.w3.org/1999/xhtml'
  >

<!--================ Document Head =======================================-->

<!ENTITY % head.misc "(script|style|meta|link|object|isindex)*">

<!-- content model is %head.misc; combined with a single
     title and an optional base element in any order -->

<!ELEMENT head (%head.misc;,
     ((title, %head.misc;, (base, %head.misc;)?) |
      (base, %head.misc;, (title, %head.misc;))))>

<!ATTLIST head
  %i18n;
  id          ID             #IMPLIED
  profile     %URI;          #IMPLIED
  >

<!-- The title element is not considered part of the flow of text.
     It should be displayed, for example as the page header or
     window title. Exactly one title is required per document. -->

<!ELEMENT title (#PCDATA)>
<!ATTLIST title
  %i18n;
  id          ID             #IMPLIED
  >

<!-- document base URI -->

<!ELEMENT base EMPTY>
<!ATTLIST base
  id          ID             #IMPLIED
  href        %URI;          #IMPLIED
  target      %FrameTarget;  #IMPLIED
  >

<!-- generic metainformation -->
<!ELEMENT meta EMPTY>
<!ATTLIST meta
  %i18n;
  id          ID             #IMPLIED
  http-equiv  CDATA          #IMPLIED
  name        CDATA          #IMPLIED
  content     CDATA          #REQUIRED
  scheme      CDATA          #IMPLIED
  >

<!--
  Relationship values can be used in principle:
```

APPENDIX F

```
   a) for document specific toolbars/menus when used with the link element
      in document head e.g. start, contents, previous, next, index, end, help
   b) to link to a separate style sheet (rel="stylesheet")
   c) to make a link to a script (rel="script")
   d) by stylesheets to control how collections of html nodes are rendered into
      printed documents
   e) to make a link to a printable version of this document
      e.g. a PostScript or PDF version (rel="alternate" media="print")
-->

<!ELEMENT link EMPTY>
<!ATTLIST link
  %attrs;
  charset     %Charset;      #IMPLIED
  href        %URI;          #IMPLIED
  hreflang    %LanguageCode; #IMPLIED
  type        %ContentType;  #IMPLIED
  rel         %LinkTypes;    #IMPLIED
  rev         %LinkTypes;    #IMPLIED
  media       %MediaDesc;    #IMPLIED
  target      %FrameTarget;  #IMPLIED
  >

<!-- style info, which may include CDATA sections -->
<!ELEMENT style (#PCDATA)>
<!ATTLIST style
  %i18n;
  id          ID             #IMPLIED
  type        %ContentType;  #REQUIRED
  media       %MediaDesc;    #IMPLIED
  title       %Text;         #IMPLIED
  xml:space   (preserve)     #FIXED 'preserve'
  >

<!-- script statements, which may include CDATA sections -->
<!ELEMENT script (#PCDATA)>
<!ATTLIST script
  id          ID             #IMPLIED
  charset     %Charset;      #IMPLIED
  type        %ContentType;  #REQUIRED
  language    CDATA          #IMPLIED
  src         %URI;          #IMPLIED
  defer       (defer)        #IMPLIED
  xml:space   (preserve)     #FIXED 'preserve'
  >

<!-- alternate content container for non script-based rendering -->

<!ELEMENT noscript %Flow;>
<!ATTLIST noscript
  %attrs;
  >

<!--====================== Frames ========================================-->

<!-- inline subwindow -->

<!ELEMENT iframe %Flow;>
<!ATTLIST iframe
  %coreattrs;
  longdesc    %URI;          #IMPLIED
```

```
  name        NMTOKEN        #IMPLIED
  src         %URI;          #IMPLIED
  frameborder (1|0)          "1"
  marginwidth %Pixels;       #IMPLIED
  marginheight %Pixels;      #IMPLIED
  scrolling   (yes|no|auto)  "auto"
  align       %ImgAlign;     #IMPLIED
  height      %Length;       #IMPLIED
  width       %Length;       #IMPLIED
  >

<!-- alternate content container for non frame-based rendering -->

<!ELEMENT noframes %Flow;>
<!ATTLIST noframes
  %attrs;
  >

<!--=================== Document Body ====================================-->

<!ELEMENT body %Flow;>
<!ATTLIST body
  %attrs;
  onload      %Script;       #IMPLIED
  onunload    %Script;       #IMPLIED
  background  %URI;          #IMPLIED
  bgcolor     %Color;        #IMPLIED
  text        %Color;        #IMPLIED
  link        %Color;        #IMPLIED
  vlink       %Color;        #IMPLIED
  alink       %Color;        #IMPLIED
  >

<!ELEMENT div %Flow;>  <!-- generic language/style container -->
<!ATTLIST div
  %attrs;
  %TextAlign;
  >

<!--=================== Paragraphs =======================================-->

<!ELEMENT p %Inline;>
<!ATTLIST p
  %attrs;
  %TextAlign;
  >

<!--=================== Headings =========================================-->

<!--
  There are six levels of headings from h1 (the most important) to
h6 (the least important).
-->

<!ELEMENT h1  %Inline;>
<!ATTLIST h1
  %attrs;
  %TextAlign;
  >

<!ELEMENT h2 %Inline;>
```

```
<!ATTLIST h2
  %attrs;
  %TextAlign;
  >

<!ELEMENT h3 %Inline;>
<!ATTLIST h3
  %attrs;
  %TextAlign;
  >

<!ELEMENT h4 %Inline;>
<!ATTLIST h4
  %attrs;
  %TextAlign;
  >

<!ELEMENT h5 %Inline;>
<!ATTLIST h5
  %attrs;
  %TextAlign;
  >

<!ELEMENT h6 %Inline;>
<!ATTLIST h6
  %attrs;
  %TextAlign;
  >

<!--=================== Lists =============================================-->

<!-- Unordered list bullet styles -->

<!ENTITY % ULStyle "(disc|square|circle)">

<!-- Unordered list -->

<!ELEMENT ul (li)+>
<!ATTLIST ul
  %attrs;
  type        %ULStyle;     #IMPLIED
  compact     (compact)     #IMPLIED
  >

<!-- Ordered list numbering style

    1   arabic numbers      1, 2, 3, ...
    a   lower alpha         a, b, c, ...
    A   upper alpha         A, B, C, ...
    i   lower roman         i, ii, iii, ...
    I   upper roman         I, II, III, ...

    The style is applied to the sequence number which by default
    is reset to 1 for the first list item in an ordered list.
-->
<!ENTITY % OLStyle "CDATA">

<!-- Ordered (numbered) list -->

<!ELEMENT ol (li)+>
<!ATTLIST ol
```

```
  %attrs;
  type        %OLStyle;      #IMPLIED
  compact     (compact)      #IMPLIED
  start       %Number;       #IMPLIED
  >

<!-- single column list (DEPRECATED) -->
<!ELEMENT menu (li)+>
<!ATTLIST menu
  %attrs;
  compact     (compact)     #IMPLIED
  >

<!-- multiple column list (DEPRECATED) -->
<!ELEMENT dir (li)+>
<!ATTLIST dir
  %attrs;
  compact     (compact)     #IMPLIED
  >

<!-- LIStyle is constrained to: "(%ULStyle;|%OLStyle;)" -->
<!ENTITY % LIStyle "CDATA">

<!-- list item -->

<!ELEMENT li %Flow;>
<!ATTLIST li
  %attrs;
  type        %LIStyle;      #IMPLIED
  value       %Number;       #IMPLIED
  >

<!-- definition lists - dt for term, dd for its definition -->

<!ELEMENT dl (dt|dd)+>
<!ATTLIST dl
  %attrs;
  compact     (compact)      #IMPLIED
  >

<!ELEMENT dt %Inline;>
<!ATTLIST dt
  %attrs;
  >

<!ELEMENT dd %Flow;>
<!ATTLIST dd
  %attrs;
  >

<!--=================== Address =======================================-->

<!-- information on author -->

<!ELEMENT address (#PCDATA | %inline; | %misc.inline; | p)*>
<!ATTLIST address
  %attrs;
  >

<!--=================== Horizontal Rule ===================================-->
```

```
<!ELEMENT hr EMPTY>
<!ATTLIST hr
  %attrs;
  align       (left|center|right) #IMPLIED
  noshade     (noshade)      #IMPLIED
  size        %Pixels;       #IMPLIED
  width       %Length;       #IMPLIED
  >

<!--==================== Preformatted Text ================================-->

<!-- content is %Inline; excluding
        "img|object|applet|big|small|sub|sup|font|basefont" -->

<!ELEMENT pre %pre.content;>
<!ATTLIST pre
  %attrs;
  width       %Number;      #IMPLIED
  xml:space   (preserve)    #FIXED 'preserve'
  >

<!--==================== Block-like Quotes ================================-->

<!ELEMENT blockquote %Flow;>
<!ATTLIST blockquote
  %attrs;
  cite        %URI;          #IMPLIED
  >

<!--==================== Text alignment ===================================-->

<!-- center content -->
<!ELEMENT center %Flow;>
<!ATTLIST center
  %attrs;
  >

<!--==================== Inserted/Deleted Text ============================-->

<!--
  ins/del are allowed in block and inline content, but its inappropriate to
  include block content within an ins element occurring in inline content.
-->
<!ELEMENT ins %Flow;>
<!ATTLIST ins
  %attrs;
  cite        %URI;          #IMPLIED
  datetime    %Datetime;     #IMPLIED
  >

<!ELEMENT del %Flow;>
<!ATTLIST del
  %attrs;
  cite        %URI;          #IMPLIED
  datetime    %Datetime;     #IMPLIED
  >

<!--================== The Anchor Element =================================-->

<!-- content is %Inline; except that anchors shouldn't be nested -->
```

```
<!ELEMENT a %a.content;>
<!ATTLIST a
  %attrs;
  %focus;
  charset     %Charset;      #IMPLIED
  type        %ContentType;  #IMPLIED
  name        NMTOKEN        #IMPLIED
  href        %URI;          #IMPLIED
  hreflang    %LanguageCode; #IMPLIED
  rel         %LinkTypes;    #IMPLIED
  rev         %LinkTypes;    #IMPLIED
  shape       %Shape;        "rect"
  coords      %Coords;       #IMPLIED
  target      %FrameTarget;  #IMPLIED
  >

<!--====================== Inline Elements ===================================-->

<!ELEMENT span %Inline;> <!-- generic language/style container -->
<!ATTLIST span
  %attrs;
  >

<!ELEMENT bdo %Inline;>  <!-- I18N BiDi over-ride -->
<!ATTLIST bdo
  %coreattrs;
  %events;
  lang        %LanguageCode; #IMPLIED
  xml:lang    %LanguageCode; #IMPLIED
  dir         (ltr|rtl)      #REQUIRED
  >

<!ELEMENT br EMPTY>   <!-- forced line break -->
<!ATTLIST br
  %coreattrs;
  clear       (left|all|right|none) "none"
  >

<!ELEMENT em %Inline;>   <!-- emphasis -->
<!ATTLIST em %attrs;>

<!ELEMENT strong %Inline;>   <!-- strong emphasis -->
<!ATTLIST strong %attrs;>

<!ELEMENT dfn %Inline;>   <!-- definitional -->
<!ATTLIST dfn %attrs;>

<!ELEMENT code %Inline;>   <!-- program code -->
<!ATTLIST code %attrs;>

<!ELEMENT samp %Inline;>   <!-- sample -->
<!ATTLIST samp %attrs;>

<!ELEMENT kbd %Inline;>  <!-- something user would type -->
<!ATTLIST kbd %attrs;>

<!ELEMENT var %Inline;>   <!-- variable -->
<!ATTLIST var %attrs;>

<!ELEMENT cite %Inline;>   <!-- citation -->
```

```
<!ATTLIST cite %attrs;>

<!ELEMENT abbr %Inline;>   <!-- abbreviation -->
<!ATTLIST abbr %attrs;>

<!ELEMENT acronym %Inline;>   <!-- acronym -->
<!ATTLIST acronym %attrs;>

<!ELEMENT q %Inline;>   <!-- inlined quote -->
<!ATTLIST q
  %attrs;
  cite        %URI;         #IMPLIED
  >

<!ELEMENT sub %Inline;> <!-- subscript -->
<!ATTLIST sub %attrs;>

<!ELEMENT sup %Inline;> <!-- superscript -->
<!ATTLIST sup %attrs;>

<!ELEMENT tt %Inline;>   <!-- fixed pitch font -->
<!ATTLIST tt %attrs;>

<!ELEMENT i %Inline;>   <!-- italic font -->
<!ATTLIST i %attrs;>

<!ELEMENT b %Inline;>   <!-- bold font -->
<!ATTLIST b %attrs;>

<!ELEMENT big %Inline;>   <!-- bigger font -->
<!ATTLIST big %attrs;>

<!ELEMENT small %Inline;>   <!-- smaller font -->
<!ATTLIST small %attrs;>

<!ELEMENT u %Inline;>   <!-- underline -->
<!ATTLIST u %attrs;>

<!ELEMENT s %Inline;>   <!-- strike-through -->
<!ATTLIST s %attrs;>

<!ELEMENT strike %Inline;>   <!-- strike-through -->
<!ATTLIST strike %attrs;>

<!ELEMENT basefont EMPTY>  <!-- base font size -->
<!ATTLIST basefont
  id          ID            #IMPLIED
  size        CDATA         #REQUIRED
  color       %Color;       #IMPLIED
  face        CDATA         #IMPLIED
  >

<!ELEMENT font %Inline;> <!-- local change to font -->
<!ATTLIST font
  %coreattrs;
  %i18n;
  size        CDATA         #IMPLIED
  color       %Color;       #IMPLIED
  face        CDATA         #IMPLIED
  >
```

```
<!--==================== Object ======================================-->
<!--
  object is used to embed objects as part of HTML pages. param elements should
  precede other content. Parameters can also be expressed as attribute/value
  pairs on the object element itself when brevity is desired.
-->

<!ELEMENT object (#PCDATA | param | %block; | form | %inline; | %misc;)*>
<!ATTLIST object
  %attrs;
  declare     (declare)      #IMPLIED
  classid     %URI;          #IMPLIED
  codebase    %URI;          #IMPLIED
  data        %URI;          #IMPLIED
  type        %ContentType;  #IMPLIED
  codetype    %ContentType;  #IMPLIED
  archive     %UriList;      #IMPLIED
  standby     %Text;         #IMPLIED
  height      %Length;       #IMPLIED
  width       %Length;       #IMPLIED
  usemap      %URI;          #IMPLIED
  name        NMTOKEN        #IMPLIED
  tabindex    %Number;       #IMPLIED
  align       %ImgAlign;     #IMPLIED
  border      %Pixels;       #IMPLIED
  hspace      %Pixels;       #IMPLIED
  vspace      %Pixels;       #IMPLIED
  >

<!--
  param is used to supply a named property value. In XML it would seem natural to
  follow RDF and support an abbreviated syntax where the param elements are
  replaced by attribute value pairs on the object start tag.
-->
<!ELEMENT param EMPTY>
<!ATTLIST param
  id          ID             #IMPLIED
  name        CDATA          #REQUIRED
  value       CDATA          #IMPLIED
  valuetype   (data|ref|object) "data"
  type        %ContentType;  #IMPLIED
  >

<!--=================== Java applet ==================================-->
<!--
  One of code or object attributes must be present. Place param elements before
other content.
-->
<!ELEMENT applet (#PCDATA | param | %block; | form | %inline; | %misc;)*>
<!ATTLIST applet
  %coreattrs;
  codebase    %URI;          #IMPLIED
  archive     CDATA          #IMPLIED
  code        CDATA          #IMPLIED
  object      CDATA          #IMPLIED
  alt         %Text;         #IMPLIED
  name        NMTOKEN        #IMPLIED
  width       %Length;       #REQUIRED
  height      %Length;       #REQUIRED
  align       %ImgAlign;     #IMPLIED
```

```
  hspace      %Pixels;       #IMPLIED
  vspace      %Pixels;       #IMPLIED
  >

<!--=================== Images ===========================================-->

<!--
   To avoid accessibility problems for people who aren't able to see the image,
   you should provide a text description using the alt and longdesc attributes.
   In addition, avoid the use of server-side image maps.
-->

<!ELEMENT img EMPTY>
<!ATTLIST img
  %attrs;
  src         %URI;          #REQUIRED
  alt         %Text;         #REQUIRED
  name        NMTOKEN        #IMPLIED
  longdesc    %URI;          #IMPLIED
  height      %Length;       #IMPLIED
  width       %Length;       #IMPLIED
  usemap      %URI;          #IMPLIED
  ismap       (ismap)        #IMPLIED
  align       %ImgAlign;     #IMPLIED
  border      %Length;       #IMPLIED
  hspace      %Pixels;       #IMPLIED
  vspace      %Pixels;       #IMPLIED
  >

<!-- usemap points to a map element which may be in this document or an external
     document, although the latter is not widely supported -->

<!--=================== Client-side image maps ============================-->

<!-- These can be placed in the same document or grouped in a separate document
     although this isn't yet widely supported -->

<!ELEMENT map ((%block; | form | %misc;)+ | area+)>
<!ATTLIST map
  %i18n;
  %events;
  id          ID             #REQUIRED
  class       CDATA          #IMPLIED
  style       %StyleSheet;   #IMPLIED
  title       %Text;         #IMPLIED
  name        CDATA          #IMPLIED
  >

<!ELEMENT area EMPTY>
<!ATTLIST area
  %attrs;
  %focus;
  shape       %Shape;        "rect"
  coords      %Coords;       #IMPLIED
  href        %URI;          #IMPLIED
  nohref      (nohref)       #IMPLIED
  alt         %Text;         #REQUIRED
  target      %FrameTarget;  #IMPLIED
  >
```

```
<!--================== Forms ==================================================-->

<!ELEMENT form %form.content;>   <!-- forms shouldn't be nested -->

<!ATTLIST form
  %attrs;
  action      %URI;          #REQUIRED
  method      (get|post)     "get"
  name        NMTOKEN        #IMPLIED
  enctype     %ContentType;  "application/x-www-form-urlencoded"
  onsubmit    %Script;       #IMPLIED
  onreset     %Script;       #IMPLIED
  accept      %ContentTypes; #IMPLIED
  accept-charset %Charsets;  #IMPLIED
  target      %FrameTarget;  #IMPLIED
  >

<!--
  Each label must not contain more than ONE field
  Label elements shouldn't be nested.
-->
<!ELEMENT label %Inline;>
<!ATTLIST label
  %attrs;
  for         IDREF          #IMPLIED
  accesskey   %Character;    #IMPLIED
  onfocus     %Script;       #IMPLIED
  onblur      %Script;       #IMPLIED
  >

<!ENTITY % InputType
  "(text | password | checkbox | radio | submit | reset | file |
    hidden | image | button)"
   >

<!-- the name attribute is required for all but submit & reset -->

<!ELEMENT input EMPTY>     <!-- form control -->
<!ATTLIST input
  %attrs;
  %focus;
  type        %InputType;    "text"
  name        CDATA          #IMPLIED
  value       CDATA          #IMPLIED
  checked     (checked)      #IMPLIED
  disabled    (disabled)     #IMPLIED
  readonly    (readonly)     #IMPLIED
  size        CDATA          #IMPLIED
  maxlength   %Number;       #IMPLIED
  src         %URI;          #IMPLIED
  alt         CDATA          #IMPLIED
  usemap      %URI;          #IMPLIED
  onselect    %Script;       #IMPLIED
  onchange    %Script;       #IMPLIED
  accept      %ContentTypes; #IMPLIED
  align       %ImgAlign;     #IMPLIED
  >

<!ELEMENT select (optgroup|option)+>  <!-- option selector -->
<!ATTLIST select
```

```
  %attrs;
  name        CDATA          #IMPLIED
  size        %Number;       #IMPLIED
  multiple    (multiple)     #IMPLIED
  disabled    (disabled)     #IMPLIED
  tabindex    %Number;       #IMPLIED
  onfocus     %Script;       #IMPLIED
  onblur      %Script;       #IMPLIED
  onchange    %Script;       #IMPLIED
  >

<!ELEMENT optgroup (option)+>   <!-- option group -->
<!ATTLIST optgroup
  %attrs;
  disabled    (disabled)     #IMPLIED
  label       %Text;         #REQUIRED
  >

<!ELEMENT option (#PCDATA)>     <!-- selectable choice -->
<!ATTLIST option
  %attrs;
  selected    (selected)     #IMPLIED
  disabled    (disabled)     #IMPLIED
  label       %Text;         #IMPLIED
  value       CDATA          #IMPLIED
  >

<!ELEMENT textarea (#PCDATA)>     <!-- multi-line text field -->
<!ATTLIST textarea
  %attrs;
  %focus;
  name        CDATA          #IMPLIED
  rows        %Number;       #REQUIRED
  cols        %Number;       #REQUIRED
  disabled    (disabled)     #IMPLIED
  readonly    (readonly)     #IMPLIED
  onselect    %Script;       #IMPLIED
  onchange    %Script;       #IMPLIED
  >

<!--
  The fieldset element is used to group form fields. Only one legend element
  should occur in the content and if present should only be preceded by
  whitespace.
-->
<!ELEMENT fieldset (#PCDATA | legend | %block; | form | %inline; | %misc;)*>
<!ATTLIST fieldset
  %attrs;
  >

<!ENTITY % LAlign "(top|bottom|left|right)">

<!ELEMENT legend %Inline;>     <!-- fieldset label -->
<!ATTLIST legend
  %attrs;
  accesskey   %Character;    #IMPLIED
  align       %LAlign;       #IMPLIED
  >

<!--
 Content is %Flow; excluding a, form, form controls, iframe
```

```
-->

<!ELEMENT button %button.content;>  <!-- push button -->
<!ATTLIST button
  %attrs;
  %focus;
  name        CDATA          #IMPLIED
  value       CDATA          #IMPLIED
  type        (button|submit|reset) "submit"
  disabled    (disabled)     #IMPLIED
  >

<!-- single-line text input control (DEPRECATED) -->
<!ELEMENT isindex EMPTY>
<!ATTLIST isindex
  %coreattrs;
  %i18n;
  prompt      %Text;         #IMPLIED
  >

<!--======================= Tables =======================================-->

<!-- Derived from IETF HTML table standard, see [RFC1942] -->

<!--
 The border attribute sets the thickness of the frame around the table. The
 default units are screen pixels.

 The frame attribute specifies which parts of the frame around the table should be
 rendered. The values are not the same as CALS to avoid a name clash with the
 valign attribute.
-->
<!ENTITY % TFrame "(void|above|below|hsides|lhs|rhs|vsides|box|border)">

<!--
 The rules attribute defines which rules to draw between cells:

 If rules is absent then assume:
     "none" if border is absent or border="0" otherwise "all"
-->

<!ENTITY % TRules "(none | groups | rows | cols | all)">

<!-- horizontal placement of table relative to document -->
<!ENTITY % TAlign "(left|center|right)">

<!-- horizontal alignment attributes for cell contents

  char        alignment char, e.g. char=':'
  charoff     offset for alignment char
-->
<!ENTITY % cellhalign
  "align      (left|center|right|justify|char) #IMPLIED
   char       %Character;     #IMPLIED
   charoff    %Length;        #IMPLIED"
  >

<!-- vertical alignment attributes for cell contents -->
<!ENTITY % cellvalign
  "valign     (top|middle|bottom|baseline) #IMPLIED"
  >
```

APPENDIX F

```
<!ELEMENT table
     (caption?, (col*|colgroup*), thead?, tfoot?, (tbody+|tr+))>
<!ELEMENT caption  %Inline;>
<!ELEMENT thead    (tr)+>
<!ELEMENT tfoot    (tr)+>
<!ELEMENT tbody    (tr)+>
<!ELEMENT colgroup (col)*>
<!ELEMENT col      EMPTY>
<!ELEMENT tr       (th|td)+>
<!ELEMENT th       %Flow;>
<!ELEMENT td       %Flow;>

<!ATTLIST table
  %attrs;
  summary     %Text;         #IMPLIED
  width       %Length;       #IMPLIED
  border      %Pixels;       #IMPLIED
  frame       %TFrame;       #IMPLIED
  rules       %TRules;       #IMPLIED
  cellspacing %Length;       #IMPLIED
  cellpadding %Length;       #IMPLIED
  align       %TAlign;       #IMPLIED
  bgcolor     %Color;        #IMPLIED
  >

<!ENTITY % CAlign "(top|bottom|left|right)">

<!ATTLIST caption
  %attrs;
  align       %CAlign;       #IMPLIED
  >

<!--
colgroup groups a set of col elements. It allows you to group several semantically
related columns together.
-->
<!ATTLIST colgroup
  %attrs;
  span        %Number;       "1"
  width       %MultiLength;  #IMPLIED
  %cellhalign;
  %cellvalign;
  >

<!--
 col elements define the alignment properties for cells in one or more columns.

 The width attribute specifies the width of the columns, e.g.
     width=64        width in screen pixels
     width=0.5*      relative width of 0.5

 The span attribute causes the attributes of one col element to apply to more than
one column.
-->
<!ATTLIST col
  %attrs;
  span        %Number;       "1"
  width       %MultiLength;  #IMPLIED
  %cellhalign;
```

```
  %cellvalign;
  >

<!--
    Use thead to duplicate headers when breaking table across page boundaries, or
    for static headers when  tbody sections are rendered in scrolling panel.

    Use tfoot to duplicate footers when breaking table across page boundaries, or
    for static footers when tbody sections are rendered in scrolling panel.

    Use multiple tbody sections when rules are needed between groups of table
    rows.
-->

<!ATTLIST thead
  %attrs;
  %cellhalign;
  %cellvalign;
  >

<!ATTLIST tfoot
  %attrs;
  %cellhalign;
  %cellvalign;
  >

<!ATTLIST tbody
  %attrs;
  %cellhalign;
  %cellvalign;
  >

<!ATTLIST tr
  %attrs;
  %cellhalign;
  %cellvalign;
  bgcolor     %Color;         #IMPLIED
  >

<!-- Scope is simpler than headers attribute for common tables -->
<!ENTITY % Scope "(row|col|rowgroup|colgroup)">

<!-- th is for headers, td for data and for cells acting as both -->

<!ATTLIST th
  %attrs;
  abbr        %Text;          #IMPLIED
  axis        CDATA           #IMPLIED
  headers     IDREFS          #IMPLIED
  scope       %Scope;         #IMPLIED
  rowspan     %Number;        "1"
  colspan     %Number;        "1"
  %cellhalign;
  %cellvalign;
  nowrap      (nowrap)        #IMPLIED
  bgcolor     %Color;         #IMPLIED
  width       %Length;        #IMPLIED
  height      %Length;        #IMPLIED
  >
```

```
<!ATTLIST td
  %attrs;
  abbr        %Text;         #IMPLIED
  axis        CDATA          #IMPLIED
  headers     IDREFS         #IMPLIED
  scope       %Scope;        #IMPLIED
  rowspan     %Number;       "1"
  colspan     %Number;       "1"
  %cellhalign;
  %cellvalign;
  nowrap      (nowrap)       #IMPLIED
  bgcolor     %Color;        #IMPLIED
  width       %Length;       #IMPLIED
  height      %Length;       #IMPLIED
  >
```

XHTML 1.0 Strict DTD

```
<!--
   Extensible HTML version 1.0 Strict DTD

   This is the same as HTML 4 Strict except for changes due to the differences
   between XML and SGML.

   Namespace = http://www.w3.org/1999/xhtml

   For further information, see: http://www.w3.org/TR/xhtml1

   Copyright (c) 1998-2002 W3C (MIT, INRIA, Keio),
   All Rights Reserved.

   This DTD module is identified by the PUBLIC and SYSTEM identifiers:

   PUBLIC "-//W3C//DTD XHTML 1.0 Strict//EN"
   SYSTEM "http://www.w3.org/TR/xhtml1/DTD/xhtml1-strict.dtd"

   $Revision: 1.1 $
   $Date: 2002/08/01 13:56:03 $

-->

<!--================ Character mnemonic entities =========================-->

<!ENTITY % HTMLlat1 PUBLIC
   "-//W3C//ENTITIES Latin 1 for XHTML//EN"
   "xhtml-lat1.ent">
%HTMLlat1;

<!ENTITY % HTMLsymbol PUBLIC
   "-//W3C//ENTITIES Symbols for XHTML//EN"
   "xhtml-symbol.ent">
%HTMLsymbol;

<!ENTITY % HTMLspecial PUBLIC
   "-//W3C//ENTITIES Special for XHTML//EN"
   "xhtml-special.ent">
%HTMLspecial;
```

```
<!--================== Imported Names ====================================-->
<!ENTITY % ContentType "CDATA">
    <!-- media type, as per [RFC2045] -->

<!ENTITY % ContentTypes "CDATA">
    <!-- comma-separated list of media types, as per [RFC2045] -->

<!ENTITY % Charset "CDATA">
    <!-- a character encoding, as per [RFC2045] -->

<!ENTITY % Charsets "CDATA">
    <!-- a space separated list of character encodings, as per [RFC2045] -->

<!ENTITY % LanguageCode "NMTOKEN">
    <!-- a language code, as per [RFC3066] -->

<!ENTITY % Character "CDATA">
    <!-- a single character, as per section 2.2 of [XML] -->

<!ENTITY % Number "CDATA">
    <!-- one or more digits -->

<!ENTITY % LinkTypes "CDATA">
    <!-- space-separated list of link types -->

<!ENTITY % MediaDesc "CDATA">
    <!-- single or comma-separated list of media descriptors -->

<!ENTITY % URI "CDATA">
    <!-- a Uniform Resource Identifier, see [RFC2396] -->

<!ENTITY % UriList "CDATA">
    <!-- a space separated list of Uniform Resource Identifiers -->

<!ENTITY % Datetime "CDATA">
    <!-- date and time information. ISO date format -->

<!ENTITY % Script "CDATA">
    <!-- script expression -->

<!ENTITY % StyleSheet "CDATA">
    <!-- style sheet data -->

<!ENTITY % Text "CDATA">
    <!-- used for titles etc. -->

<!ENTITY % Length "CDATA">
    <!-- nn for pixels or nn% for percentage length -->

<!ENTITY % MultiLength "CDATA">
    <!-- pixel, percentage, or relative -->

<!ENTITY % Pixels "CDATA">
    <!-- integer representing length in pixels -->

<!-- these are used for image maps -->

<!ENTITY % Shape "(rect|circle|poly|default)">

<!ENTITY % Coords "CDATA">
```

```
    <!-- comma separated list of lengths -->

<!--=================== Generic Attributes ===============================-->

<!-- core attributes common to most elements
  id       document-wide unique id
  class    space separated list of classes
  style    associated style info
  title    advisory title/amplification
-->

<!ENTITY % coreattrs
 "id          ID              #IMPLIED
  class       CDATA           #IMPLIED
  style       %StyleSheet;    #IMPLIED
  title       %Text;          #IMPLIED"
  >

<!-- internationalization attributes
  lang        language code (backwards compatible)
  xml:lang    language code (as per XML 1.0 spec)
  dir         direction for weak/neutral text
-->

<!ENTITY % i18n
 "lang        %LanguageCode; #IMPLIED
  xml:lang    %LanguageCode; #IMPLIED
  dir         (ltr|rtl)      #IMPLIED"
  >

<!-- attributes for common UI events
  onclick     a pointer button was clicked
  ondblclick  a pointer button was double clicked
  onmousedown a pointer button was pressed down
  onmouseup   a pointer button was released
  onmousemove a pointer was moved onto the element
  onmouseout  a pointer was moved away from the element
  onkeypress  a key was pressed and released
  onkeydown   a key was pressed down
  onkeyup     a key was released
-->

<!ENTITY % events
 "onclick     %Script;       #IMPLIED
  ondblclick  %Script;       #IMPLIED
  onmousedown %Script;       #IMPLIED
  onmouseup   %Script;       #IMPLIED
  onmouseover %Script;       #IMPLIED
  onmousemove %Script;       #IMPLIED
  onmouseout  %Script;       #IMPLIED
  onkeypress  %Script;       #IMPLIED
  onkeydown   %Script;       #IMPLIED
  onkeyup     %Script;       #IMPLIED"
  >

<!-- attributes for elements that can get the focus
  accesskey   accessibility key character
  tabindex    position in tabbing order
  onfocus     the element got the focus
  onblur      the element lost the focus
```

```
-->

<!ENTITY % focus
 "accesskey  %Character;    #IMPLIED
  tabindex   %Number;       #IMPLIED
  onfocus    %Script;       #IMPLIED
  onblur     %Script;       #IMPLIED"
  >

<!ENTITY % attrs "%coreattrs; %i18n; %events;">

<!--=================== Text Elements ======================================-->

<!ENTITY % special.pre
   "br | span | bdo | map">

<!ENTITY % special
   "%special.pre; | object | img ">

<!ENTITY % fontstyle "tt | i | b | big | small ">

<!ENTITY % phrase "em | strong | dfn | code | q |
                   samp | kbd | var | cite | abbr | acronym | sub | sup ">

<!ENTITY % inline.forms "input | select | textarea | label | button">

<!-- these can occur at block or inline level -->
<!ENTITY % misc.inline "ins | del | script">

<!-- these can only occur at block level -->
<!ENTITY % misc "noscript | %misc.inline;">

<!ENTITY % inline "a | %special; | %fontstyle; | %phrase; | %inline.forms;">

<!-- %Inline; covers inline or "text-level" elements -->
<!ENTITY % Inline "(#PCDATA | %inline; | %misc.inline;)*">

<!--================== Block level elements ================================-->

<!ENTITY % heading "h1|h2|h3|h4|h5|h6">
<!ENTITY % lists "ul | ol | dl">
<!ENTITY % blocktext "pre | hr | blockquote | address">

<!ENTITY % block
     "p | %heading; | div | %lists; | %blocktext; | fieldset | table">

<!ENTITY % Block "(%block; | form | %misc;)*">

<!-- %Flow; mixes block and inline and is used for list items etc. -->
<!ENTITY % Flow "(#PCDATA | %block; | form | %inline; | %misc;)*">

<!--================== Content models for exclusions ======================-->

<!-- a elements use %Inline; excluding a -->

<!ENTITY % a.content
   "(#PCDATA | %special; | %fontstyle; | %phrase; | %inline.forms; | %misc.inline;)*">

<!-- pre uses %Inline excluding big, small, sup or sup -->
```

```
<!ENTITY % pre.content
   "(#PCDATA | a | %fontstyle; | %phrase; | %special.pre; | %misc.inline;
      | %inline.forms;)*">

<!-- form uses %Block; excluding form -->

<!ENTITY % form.content "(%block; | %misc;)*">


<!-- button uses %Flow; but excludes a, form and form controls -->

<!ENTITY % button.content
   "(#PCDATA | p | %heading; | div | %lists; | %blocktext; |
    table | %special; | %fontstyle; | %phrase; | %misc;)*">

<!--================ Document Structure ==================================-->

<!-- the namespace URI designates the document profile -->

<!ELEMENT html (head, body)>
<!ATTLIST html
  %i18n;
  id          ID             #IMPLIED
  xmlns       %URI;          #FIXED 'http://www.w3.org/1999/xhtml'
  >

<!--================ Document Head =======================================-->

<!ENTITY % head.misc "(script|style|meta|link|object)*">

<!-- content model is %head.misc; combined with a single title and an
     optional base element in any order -->

<!ELEMENT head (%head.misc;,
     ((title, %head.misc;, (base, %head.misc;)?) |
      (base, %head.misc;, (title, %head.misc;))))>

<!ATTLIST head
  %i18n;
  id          ID             #IMPLIED
  profile     %URI;          #IMPLIED
  >

<!-- The title element is not considered part of the flow of text. It should be
     displayed, for example as the page header or window title. Exactly one title
     is required per document.-->

<!ELEMENT title (#PCDATA)>
<!ATTLIST title
  %i18n;
  id          ID             #IMPLIED
  >

<!-- document base URI -->

<!ELEMENT base EMPTY>
<!ATTLIST base
  href        %URI;          #REQUIRED
  id          ID             #IMPLIED
  >
```

```
<!-- generic metainformation -->
<!ELEMENT meta EMPTY>
<!ATTLIST meta
  %i18n;
  id          ID             #IMPLIED
  http-equiv  CDATA          #IMPLIED
  name        CDATA          #IMPLIED
  content     CDATA          #REQUIRED
  scheme      CDATA          #IMPLIED
  >

<!--
  Relationship values can be used in principle:

   a) for document specific toolbars/menus when used with the link element in
      document head e.g. start, contents, previous, next, index, end, help
   b) to link to a separate style sheet (rel="stylesheet")
   c) to make a link to a script (rel="script")
   d) by stylesheets to control how collections of html nodes are rendered into
      printed documents
   e) to make a link to a printable version of this document
      e.g. a PostScript or PDF version (rel="alternate" media="print")
-->

<!ELEMENT link EMPTY>
<!ATTLIST link
  %attrs;
  charset     %Charset;      #IMPLIED
  href        %URI;          #IMPLIED
  hreflang    %LanguageCode; #IMPLIED
  type        %ContentType;  #IMPLIED
  rel         %LinkTypes;    #IMPLIED
  rev         %LinkTypes;    #IMPLIED
  media       %MediaDesc;    #IMPLIED
  >

<!-- style info, which may include CDATA sections -->
<!ELEMENT style (#PCDATA)>
<!ATTLIST style
  %i18n;
  id          ID             #IMPLIED
  type        %ContentType;  #REQUIRED
  media       %MediaDesc;    #IMPLIED
  title       %Text;         #IMPLIED
  xml:space   (preserve)     #FIXED 'preserve'
  >

<!-- script statements, which may include CDATA sections -->
<!ELEMENT script (#PCDATA)>
<!ATTLIST script
  id          ID             #IMPLIED
  charset     %Charset;      #IMPLIED
  type        %ContentType;  #REQUIRED
  src         %URI;          #IMPLIED
  defer       (defer)        #IMPLIED
  xml:space   (preserve)     #FIXED 'preserve'
  >

<!-- alternate content container for non script-based rendering -->

<!ELEMENT noscript %Block;>
```

```
<!ATTLIST noscript
  %attrs;
  >

<!--=================== Document Body ====================================-->

<!ELEMENT body %Block;>
<!ATTLIST body
  %attrs;
  onload          %Script;   #IMPLIED
  onunload        %Script;   #IMPLIED
  >

<!ELEMENT div %Flow;>  <!-- generic language/style container -->
<!ATTLIST div
  %attrs;
  >

<!--=================== Paragraphs =======================================-->

<!ELEMENT p %Inline;>
<!ATTLIST p
  %attrs;
  >

<!--=================== Headings =========================================-->

<!--
  There are six levels of headings from h1 (the most important)
  to h6 (the least important).
-->

<!ELEMENT h1  %Inline;>
<!ATTLIST h1
   %attrs;
   >

<!ELEMENT h2 %Inline;>
<!ATTLIST h2
   %attrs;
   >

<!ELEMENT h3 %Inline;>
<!ATTLIST h3
   %attrs;
   >

<!ELEMENT h4 %Inline;>
<!ATTLIST h4
   %attrs;
   >

<!ELEMENT h5 %Inline;>
<!ATTLIST h5
   %attrs;
   >

<!ELEMENT h6 %Inline;>
<!ATTLIST h6
   %attrs;
   >
```

```
<!--=================== Lists ===============================================-->

<!-- Unordered list -->

<!ELEMENT ul (li)+>
<!ATTLIST ul
  %attrs;
  >

<!-- Ordered (numbered) list -->

<!ELEMENT ol (li)+>
<!ATTLIST ol
  %attrs;
  >

<!-- list item -->

<!ELEMENT li %Flow;>
<!ATTLIST li
  %attrs;
  >

<!-- definition lists - dt for term, dd for its definition -->

<!ELEMENT dl (dt|dd)+>
<!ATTLIST dl
  %attrs;
  >

<!ELEMENT dt %Inline;>
<!ATTLIST dt
  %attrs;
  >

<!ELEMENT dd %Flow;>
<!ATTLIST dd
  %attrs;
  >

<!--=================== Address =============================================-->

<!-- information on author -->

<!ELEMENT address %Inline;>
<!ATTLIST address
  %attrs;
  >

<!--=================== Horizontal Rule =====================================-->

<!ELEMENT hr EMPTY>
<!ATTLIST hr
  %attrs;
  >

<!--=================== Preformatted Text ===================================-->

<!-- content is %Inline; excluding "img|object|big|small|sub|sup" -->

<!ELEMENT pre %pre.content;>
```

```
<!ATTLIST pre
  %attrs;
  xml:space (preserve) #FIXED 'preserve'
  >

<!--=================== Block-like Quotes ================================-->

<!ELEMENT blockquote %Block;>
<!ATTLIST blockquote
  %attrs;
  cite        %URI;          #IMPLIED
  >

<!--=================== Inserted/Deleted Text ============================-->

<!--
  ins/del are allowed in block and inline content, but it's inappropriate to
  include block content within an ins element occurring in inline content.
-->

<!ELEMENT ins %Flow;>
<!ATTLIST ins
  %attrs;
  cite        %URI;          #IMPLIED
  datetime    %Datetime;     #IMPLIED
  >

<!ELEMENT del %Flow;>
<!ATTLIST del
  %attrs;
  cite        %URI;          #IMPLIED
  datetime    %Datetime;     #IMPLIED
  >

<!--================== The Anchor Element ================================-->

<!-- content is %Inline; except that anchors shouldn't be nested -->

<!ELEMENT a %a.content;>
<!ATTLIST a
  %attrs;
  %focus;
  charset     %Charset;      #IMPLIED
  type        %ContentType;  #IMPLIED
  name        NMTOKEN        #IMPLIED
  href        %URI;          #IMPLIED
  hreflang    %LanguageCode; #IMPLIED
  rel         %LinkTypes;    #IMPLIED
  rev         %LinkTypes;    #IMPLIED
  shape       %Shape;        "rect"
  coords      %Coords;       #IMPLIED
  >

<!--===================== Inline Elements ================================-->

<!ELEMENT span %Inline;> <!-- generic language/style container -->
<!ATTLIST span
  %attrs;
  >
```

```
<!ELEMENT bdo %Inline;>  <!-- I18N BiDi over-ride -->
<!ATTLIST bdo
  %coreattrs;
  %events;
  lang        %LanguageCode; #IMPLIED
  xml:lang    %LanguageCode; #IMPLIED
  dir         (ltr|rtl)      #REQUIRED
  >

<!ELEMENT br EMPTY>   <!-- forced line break -->
<!ATTLIST br
  %coreattrs;
  >

<!ELEMENT em %Inline;>   <!-- emphasis -->
<!ATTLIST em %attrs;>

<!ELEMENT strong %Inline;>   <!-- strong emphasis -->
<!ATTLIST strong %attrs;>

<!ELEMENT dfn %Inline;>   <!-- definitional -->
<!ATTLIST dfn %attrs;>

<!ELEMENT code %Inline;>   <!-- program code -->
<!ATTLIST code %attrs;>

<!ELEMENT samp %Inline;>   <!-- sample -->
<!ATTLIST samp %attrs;>

<!ELEMENT kbd %Inline;>  <!-- something user would type -->
<!ATTLIST kbd %attrs;>

<!ELEMENT var %Inline;>   <!-- variable -->
<!ATTLIST var %attrs;>

<!ELEMENT cite %Inline;>   <!-- citation -->
<!ATTLIST cite %attrs;>

<!ELEMENT abbr %Inline;>   <!-- abbreviation -->
<!ATTLIST abbr %attrs;>

<!ELEMENT acronym %Inline;>   <!-- acronym -->
<!ATTLIST acronym %attrs;>

<!ELEMENT q %Inline;>   <!-- inlined quote -->
<!ATTLIST q
  %attrs;
  cite        %URI;          #IMPLIED
  >

<!ELEMENT sub %Inline;> <!-- subscript -->
<!ATTLIST sub %attrs;>

<!ELEMENT sup %Inline;> <!-- superscript -->
<!ATTLIST sup %attrs;>

<!ELEMENT tt %Inline;>   <!-- fixed pitch font -->
<!ATTLIST tt %attrs;>

<!ELEMENT i %Inline;>   <!-- italic font -->
```

```
<!ATTLIST i %attrs;>

<!ELEMENT b %Inline;>   <!-- bold font -->
<!ATTLIST b %attrs;>

<!ELEMENT big %Inline;>   <!-- bigger font -->
<!ATTLIST big %attrs;>

<!ELEMENT small %Inline;>   <!-- smaller font -->
<!ATTLIST small %attrs;>

<!--===================== Object ======================================-->
<!--
  object is used to embed objects as part of HTML pages.
  param elements should precede other content. Parameters can also be
  expressed as attribute/value pairs on the object element itself when
  brevity is desired.
-->

<!ELEMENT object (#PCDATA | param | %block; | form | %inline; | %misc;)*>
<!ATTLIST object
  %attrs;
  declare     (declare)       #IMPLIED
  classid     %URI;           #IMPLIED
  codebase    %URI;           #IMPLIED
  data        %URI;           #IMPLIED
  type        %ContentType;   #IMPLIED
  codetype    %ContentType;   #IMPLIED
  archive     %UriList;       #IMPLIED
  standby     %Text;          #IMPLIED
  height      %Length;        #IMPLIED
  width       %Length;        #IMPLIED
  usemap      %URI;           #IMPLIED
  name        NMTOKEN         #IMPLIED
  tabindex    %Number;        #IMPLIED
  >

<!--
  param is used to supply a named property value.  In XML it would seem
  natural to follow RDF and support an abbreviated syntax where the param
  elements are replaced by attribute value pairs on the object start tag.
-->

<!ELEMENT param EMPTY>
<!ATTLIST param
  id          ID              #IMPLIED
  name        CDATA           #IMPLIED
  value       CDATA           #IMPLIED
  valuetype   (data|ref|object) "data"
  type        %ContentType;   #IMPLIED
  >

<!--=================== Images ==========================================-->

<!--
   To avoid accessibility problems for people who aren't able to see the image,
   you should provide a text description using the alt and longdesc attributes.
   In addition, avoid the use of server-side image maps. Note that in this DTD
   there is no name attribute. That is only available in the transitional and
   frameset DTD.
```

```
-->

<!ELEMENT img EMPTY>
<!ATTLIST img
  %attrs;
  src         %URI;          #REQUIRED
  alt         %Text;         #REQUIRED
  longdesc    %URI;          #IMPLIED
  height      %Length;       #IMPLIED
  width       %Length;       #IMPLIED
  usemap      %URI;          #IMPLIED
  ismap       (ismap)        #IMPLIED
  >

<!-- usemap points to a map element which may be in this document
     or an external document, although the latter is not widely supported -->

<!--================== Client-side image maps ============================-->

<!-- These can be placed in the same document or grouped in a separate document
     although this isn't yet widely supported -->

<!ELEMENT map ((%block; | form | %misc;)+ | area+)>
<!ATTLIST map
  %i18n;
  %events;
  id          ID             #REQUIRED
  class       CDATA          #IMPLIED
  style       %StyleSheet;   #IMPLIED
  title       %Text;         #IMPLIED
  name        NMTOKEN        #IMPLIED
  >

<!ELEMENT area EMPTY>
<!ATTLIST area
  %attrs;
  %focus;
  shape       %Shape;        "rect"
  coords      %Coords;       #IMPLIED
  href        %URI;          #IMPLIED
  nohref      (nohref)       #IMPLIED
  alt         %Text;         #REQUIRED
  >

<!--================ Forms ===============================================-->
<!ELEMENT form %form.content;>   <!-- forms shouldn't be nested -->

<!ATTLIST form
  %attrs;
  action      %URI;          #REQUIRED
  method      (get|post)     "get"
  enctype     %ContentType;  "application/x-www-form-urlencoded"
  onsubmit    %Script;       #IMPLIED
  onreset     %Script;       #IMPLIED
  accept      %ContentTypes; #IMPLIED
  accept-charset %Charsets;  #IMPLIED
  >

<!--
  Each label must not contain more than ONE field
```

```
  Label elements shouldn't be nested.
-->

<!ELEMENT label %Inline;>
<!ATTLIST label
  %attrs;
  for         IDREF          #IMPLIED
  accesskey   %Character;    #IMPLIED
  onfocus     %Script;       #IMPLIED
  onblur      %Script;       #IMPLIED
  >

<!ENTITY % InputType
  "(text | password | checkbox |
    radio | submit | reset |
    file | hidden | image | button)"
   >

<!-- the name attribute is required for all but submit & reset -->

<!ELEMENT input EMPTY>     <!-- form control -->
<!ATTLIST input
  %attrs;
  %focus;
  type        %InputType;    "text"
  name        CDATA          #IMPLIED
  value       CDATA          #IMPLIED
  checked     (checked)      #IMPLIED
  disabled    (disabled)     #IMPLIED
  readonly    (readonly)     #IMPLIED
  size        CDATA          #IMPLIED
  maxlength   %Number;       #IMPLIED
  src         %URI;          #IMPLIED
  alt         CDATA          #IMPLIED
  usemap      %URI;          #IMPLIED
  onselect    %Script;       #IMPLIED
  onchange    %Script;       #IMPLIED
  accept      %ContentTypes; #IMPLIED
  >

<!ELEMENT select (optgroup|option)+>  <!-- option selector -->
<!ATTLIST select
  %attrs;
  name        CDATA          #IMPLIED
  size        %Number;       #IMPLIED
  multiple    (multiple)     #IMPLIED
  disabled    (disabled)     #IMPLIED
  tabindex    %Number;       #IMPLIED
  onfocus     %Script;       #IMPLIED
  onblur      %Script;       #IMPLIED
  onchange    %Script;       #IMPLIED
  >

<!ELEMENT optgroup (option)+>   <!-- option group -->
<!ATTLIST optgroup
  %attrs;
  disabled    (disabled)     #IMPLIED
  label       %Text;         #REQUIRED
  >
```

```
<!ELEMENT option (#PCDATA)>     <!-- selectable choice -->
<!ATTLIST option
  %attrs;
  selected    (selected)     #IMPLIED
  disabled    (disabled)     #IMPLIED
  label       %Text;         #IMPLIED
  value       CDATA          #IMPLIED
  >

<!ELEMENT textarea (#PCDATA)>     <!-- multi-line text field -->
<!ATTLIST textarea
  %attrs;
  %focus;
  name        CDATA          #IMPLIED
  rows        %Number;       #REQUIRED
  cols        %Number;       #REQUIRED
  disabled    (disabled)     #IMPLIED
  readonly    (readonly)     #IMPLIED
  onselect    %Script;       #IMPLIED
  onchange    %Script;       #IMPLIED
  >

<!--
  The fieldset element is used to group form fields. Only one legend element
  should occur in the content and if present should only be preceded by
  whitespace.
-->
<!ELEMENT fieldset (#PCDATA | legend | %block; | form | %inline; | %misc;)*>
<!ATTLIST fieldset
  %attrs;
  >

<!ELEMENT legend %Inline;>     <!-- fieldset label -->
<!ATTLIST legend
  %attrs;
  accesskey   %Character;    #IMPLIED
  >

<!--
 Content is %Flow; excluding a, form and form controls
-->
<!ELEMENT button %button.content;>  <!-- push button -->
<!ATTLIST button
  %attrs;
  %focus;
  name        CDATA          #IMPLIED
  value       CDATA          #IMPLIED
  type        (button|submit|reset) "submit"
  disabled    (disabled)     #IMPLIED
  >

<!--======================= Tables =======================================-->

<!-- Derived from IETF HTML table standard, see [RFC1942] -->

<!--
 The border attribute sets the thickness of the frame around the
 table. The default units are screen pixels.
 The frame attribute specifies which parts of the frame around the table
 should be rendered. The values are not the same as CALS to avoid a name
```

```
 clash with the valign attribute.
-->
<!ENTITY % TFrame "(void|above|below|hsides|lhs|rhs|vsides|box|border)">

<!--
 The rules attribute defines which rules to draw between cells:

 If rules is absent then assume:
     "none" if border is absent or border="0" otherwise "all"
-->

<!ENTITY % TRules "(none | groups | rows | cols | all)">

<!-- horizontal alignment attributes for cell contents

  char       alignment char, e.g. char=':'
  charoff    offset for alignment char
-->
<!ENTITY % cellhalign
  "align      (left|center|right|justify|char) #IMPLIED
   char       %Character;    #IMPLIED
   charoff    %Length;       #IMPLIED"
  >

<!-- vertical alignment attributes for cell contents -->
<!ENTITY % cellvalign
  "valign     (top|middle|bottom|baseline) #IMPLIED"
  >

<!ELEMENT table
     (caption?, (col*|colgroup*), thead?, tfoot?, (tbody+|tr+))>
<!ELEMENT caption  %Inline;>
<!ELEMENT thead    (tr)+>
<!ELEMENT tfoot    (tr)+>
<!ELEMENT tbody    (tr)+>
<!ELEMENT colgroup (col)*>
<!ELEMENT col      EMPTY>
<!ELEMENT tr       (th|td)+>
<!ELEMENT th       %Flow;>
<!ELEMENT td       %Flow;>

<!ATTLIST table
  %attrs;
  summary     %Text;         #IMPLIED
  width       %Length;       #IMPLIED
  border      %Pixels;       #IMPLIED
  frame       %TFrame;       #IMPLIED
  rules       %TRules;       #IMPLIED
  cellspacing %Length;       #IMPLIED
  cellpadding %Length;       #IMPLIED
  >

<!ATTLIST caption
  %attrs;
  >

<!--
colgroup groups a set of col elements. It allows you to group several semantically
related columns together.
-->
```

```
<!ATTLIST colgroup
  %attrs;
  span         %Number;        "1"
  width        %MultiLength;  #IMPLIED
  %cellhalign;
  %cellvalign;
  >

<!--
 col elements define the alignment properties for cells in one or more columns.

 The width attribute specifies the width of the columns, e.g.
     width=64        width in screen pixels
     width=0.5*      relative width of 0.5

 The span attribute causes the attributes of one col element to apply to
 more than one column.
-->
<!ATTLIST col
  %attrs;
  span         %Number;        "1"
  width        %MultiLength;  #IMPLIED
  %cellhalign;
  %cellvalign;
  >

<!--
    Use thead to duplicate headers when breaking table across page boundaries, or
    for static headers when tbody sections are rendered in scrolling panel.

    Use tfoot to duplicate footers when breaking table across page boundaries, or
    for static footers when tbody sections are rendered in scrolling panel.

    Use multiple tbody sections when rules are needed between groups of table
    rows.
-->
<!ATTLIST thead
  %attrs;
  %cellhalign;
  %cellvalign;
  >

<!ATTLIST tfoot
  %attrs;
  %cellhalign;
  %cellvalign;
  >

<!ATTLIST tbody
  %attrs;
  %cellhalign;
  %cellvalign;
  >

<!ATTLIST tr
  %attrs;
  %cellhalign;
  %cellvalign;
  >
```

```
<!-- Scope is simpler than headers attribute for common tables -->
<!ENTITY % Scope "(row|col|rowgroup|colgroup)">

<!-- th is for headers, td for data and for cells acting as both -->

<!ATTLIST th
  %attrs;
  abbr        %Text;        #IMPLIED
  axis        CDATA         #IMPLIED
  headers     IDREFS        #IMPLIED
  scope       %Scope;       #IMPLIED
  rowspan     %Number;      "1"
  colspan     %Number;      "1"
  %cellhalign;
  %cellvalign;
  >

<!ATTLIST td
  %attrs;
  abbr        %Text;        #IMPLIED
  axis        CDATA         #IMPLIED
  headers     IDREFS        #IMPLIED
  scope       %Scope;       #IMPLIED
  rowspan     %Number;      "1"
  colspan     %Number;      "1"
  %cellhalign;
  %cellvalign;
  >
```

XHTML 1.0 Frameset DTD

```
<!--
   Extensible HTML version 1.0 Frameset DTD

   This is the same as HTML 4 Frameset except for changes due to the differences
   between XML and SGML.

   Namespace = http://www.w3.org/1999/xhtml

   For further information, see: http://www.w3.org/TR/xhtml1

   Copyright (c) 1998-2002 W3C (MIT, INRIA, Keio),
   All Rights Reserved.

   This DTD module is identified by the PUBLIC and SYSTEM identifiers:

   PUBLIC "-//W3C//DTD XHTML 1.0 Frameset//EN"
   SYSTEM "http://www.w3.org/TR/xhtml1/DTD/xhtml1-frameset.dtd"

   $Revision: 1.2 $
   $Date: 2002/08/01 18:37:55 $

-->

<!--================ Character mnemonic entities =========================-->

<!ENTITY % HTMLlat1 PUBLIC
   "-//W3C//ENTITIES Latin 1 for XHTML//EN"
   "xhtml-lat1.ent">
```

```
%HTMLlat1;

<!ENTITY % HTMLsymbol PUBLIC
   "-//W3C//ENTITIES Symbols for XHTML//EN"
   "xhtml-symbol.ent">
%HTMLsymbol;

<!ENTITY % HTMLspecial PUBLIC
   "-//W3C//ENTITIES Special for XHTML//EN"
   "xhtml-special.ent">
%HTMLspecial;

<!--================== Imported Names ====================================-->

<!ENTITY % ContentType "CDATA">
    <!-- media type, as per [RFC2045] -->

<!ENTITY % ContentTypes "CDATA">
    <!-- comma-separated list of media types, as per [RFC2045] -->

<!ENTITY % Charset "CDATA">
    <!-- a character encoding, as per [RFC2045] -->

<!ENTITY % Charsets "CDATA">
    <!-- a space separated list of character encodings, as per [RFC2045] -->

<!ENTITY % LanguageCode "NMTOKEN">
    <!-- a language code, as per [RFC3066] -->

<!ENTITY % Character "CDATA">
    <!-- a single character, as per section 2.2 of [XML] -->

<!ENTITY % Number "CDATA">
    <!-- one or more digits -->

<!ENTITY % LinkTypes "CDATA">
    <!-- space-separated list of link types -->

<!ENTITY % MediaDesc "CDATA">
    <!-- single or comma-separated list of media descriptors -->

<!ENTITY % URI "CDATA">
    <!-- a Uniform Resource Identifier, see [RFC2396] -->

<!ENTITY % UriList "CDATA">
    <!-- a space separated list of Uniform Resource Identifiers -->

<!ENTITY % Datetime "CDATA">
    <!-- date and time information. ISO date format -->

<!ENTITY % Script "CDATA">
    <!-- script expression -->

<!ENTITY % StyleSheet "CDATA">
    <!-- style sheet data -->

<!ENTITY % Text "CDATA">
    <!-- used for titles etc. -->

<!ENTITY % FrameTarget "NMTOKEN">
```

```
    <!-- render in this frame -->

<!ENTITY % Length "CDATA">
    <!-- nn for pixels or nn% for percentage length -->

<!ENTITY % MultiLength "CDATA">
    <!-- pixel, percentage, or relative -->

<!ENTITY % MultiLengths "CDATA">
    <!-- comma-separated list of MultiLength -->

<!ENTITY % Pixels "CDATA">
    <!-- integer representing length in pixels -->

<!-- these are used for image maps -->

<!ENTITY % Shape "(rect|circle|poly|default)">

<!ENTITY % Coords "CDATA">
    <!-- comma separated list of lengths -->

<!-- used for object, applet, img, input and iframe -->
<!ENTITY % ImgAlign "(top|middle|bottom|left|right)">

<!-- a color using sRGB: #RRGGBB as Hex values -->
<!ENTITY % Color "CDATA">

<!-- There are also 16 widely known color names with their sRGB values:

    Black  = #000000    Green  = #008000
    Silver = #C0C0C0    Lime   = #00FF00
    Gray   = #808080    Olive  = #808000
    White  = #FFFFFF    Yellow = #FFFF00
    Maroon = #800000    Navy   = #000080
    Red    = #FF0000    Blue   = #0000FF
    Purple = #800080    Teal   = #008080
    Fuchsia= #FF00FF    Aqua   = #00FFFF
-->

<!--=================== Generic Attributes ===============================-->

<!-- core attributes common to most elements
  id       document-wide unique id
  class    space separated list of classes
  style    associated style info
  title    advisory title/amplification
-->

<!ENTITY % coreattrs
 "id          ID             #IMPLIED
  class       CDATA          #IMPLIED
  style       %StyleSheet;   #IMPLIED
  title       %Text;         #IMPLIED"
  >

<!-- internationalization attributes
  lang        language code (backwards compatible)
  xml:lang    language code (as per XML 1.0 spec)
  dir         direction for weak/neutral text
-->
```

```
<!ENTITY % i18n
 "lang        %LanguageCode; #IMPLIED
  xml:lang    %LanguageCode; #IMPLIED
  dir         (ltr|rtl)      #IMPLIED"
  >

<!-- attributes for common UI events
  onclick     a pointer button was clicked
  ondblclick  a pointer button was double clicked
  onmousedown a pointer button was pressed down
  onmouseup   a pointer button was released
  onmousemove a pointer was moved onto the element
  onmouseout  a pointer was moved away from the element
  onkeypress  a key was pressed and released
  onkeydown   a key was pressed down
  onkeyup     a key was released
-->

<!ENTITY % events
 "onclick     %Script;       #IMPLIED
  ondblclick  %Script;       #IMPLIED
  onmousedown %Script;       #IMPLIED
  onmouseup   %Script;       #IMPLIED
  onmouseover %Script;       #IMPLIED
  onmousemove %Script;       #IMPLIED
  onmouseout  %Script;       #IMPLIED
  onkeypress  %Script;       #IMPLIED
  onkeydown   %Script;       #IMPLIED
  onkeyup     %Script;       #IMPLIED"
  >

<!-- attributes for elements that can get the focus
  accesskey   accessibility key character
  tabindex    position in tabbing order
  onfocus     the element got the focus
  onblur      the element lost the focus
-->
<!ENTITY % focus
 "accesskey   %Character;    #IMPLIED
  tabindex    %Number;       #IMPLIED
  onfocus     %Script;       #IMPLIED
  onblur      %Script;       #IMPLIED"
  >

<!ENTITY % attrs "%coreattrs; %i18n; %events;">

<!-- text alignment for p, div, h1-h6. The default is align="left" for ltr
     headings, "right" for rtl -->

<!ENTITY % TextAlign "align (left|center|right|justify) #IMPLIED">

<!--=================== Text Elements ====================================-->

<!ENTITY % special.extra
   "object | applet | img | map | iframe">

<!ENTITY % special.basic
   "br | span | bdo">

<!ENTITY % special
```

APPENDIX F

```
   "%special.basic; | %special.extra;">

<!ENTITY % fontstyle.extra "big | small | font | basefont">

<!ENTITY % fontstyle.basic "tt | i | b | u
                  | s | strike ">

<!ENTITY % fontstyle "%fontstyle.basic; | %fontstyle.extra;">

<!ENTITY % phrase.extra "sub | sup">
<!ENTITY % phrase.basic "em | strong | dfn | code | q |
                 samp | kbd | var | cite | abbr | acronym">

<!ENTITY % phrase "%phrase.basic; | %phrase.extra;">

<!ENTITY % inline.forms "input | select | textarea | label | button">

<!-- these can occur at block or inline level -->
<!ENTITY % misc.inline "ins | del | script">

<!-- these can only occur at block level -->
<!ENTITY % misc "noscript | %misc.inline;">


<!ENTITY % inline "a | %special; | %fontstyle; | %phrase; | %inline.forms;">

<!-- %Inline; covers inline or "text-level" elements -->
<!ENTITY % Inline "(#PCDATA | %inline; | %misc.inline;)*">

<!--================== Block level elements ===============================-->

<!ENTITY % heading "h1|h2|h3|h4|h5|h6">
<!ENTITY % lists "ul | ol | dl | menu | dir">
<!ENTITY % blocktext "pre | hr | blockquote | address | center">

<!ENTITY % block
    "p | %heading; | div | %lists; | %blocktext; | isindex | fieldset | table">

<!-- %Flow; mixes block and inline and is used for list items etc. -->
<!ENTITY % Flow "(#PCDATA | %block; | form | %inline; | %misc;)*">

<!--================== Content models for exclusions =====================-->

<!-- a elements use %Inline; excluding a -->

<!ENTITY % a.content
   "(#PCDATA | %special; | %fontstyle; | %phrase; | %inline.forms; |
     misc.inline;)*">

<!-- pre uses %Inline excluding img, object, applet, big, small,
     sub, sup, font, or basefont -->

<!ENTITY % pre.content
   "(#PCDATA | a | %special.basic; | %fontstyle.basic; | %phrase.basic; |
     %inline.forms; | %misc.inline;)*">


<!-- form uses %Flow; excluding form -->

<!ENTITY % form.content "(#PCDATA | %block; | %inline; | %misc;)*">
```

```
<!-- button uses %Flow; but excludes a, form, form controls, iframe -->

<!ENTITY % button.content
   "(#PCDATA | p | %heading; | div | %lists; | %blocktext; |
     table | br | span | bdo | object | applet | img | map |
     %fontstyle; | %phrase; | %misc;)*">

<!--================ Document Structure ==================================-->

<!-- the namespace URI designates the document profile -->

<!ELEMENT html (head, frameset)>
<!ATTLIST html
  %i18n;
  id          ID             #IMPLIED
  xmlns       %URI;          #FIXED 'http://www.w3.org/1999/xhtml'
  >

<!--================ Document Head =======================================-->

<!ENTITY % head.misc "(script|style|meta|link|object|isindex)*">

<!-- content model is %head.misc; combined with a single
     title and an optional base element in any order -->

<!ELEMENT head (%head.misc;,
     ((title, %head.misc;, (base, %head.misc;)?) |
      (base, %head.misc;, (title, %head.misc;))))>

<!ATTLIST head
  %i18n;
  id          ID             #IMPLIED
  profile     %URI;          #IMPLIED
  >

<!-- The title element is not considered part of the flow of text. It should be
     displayed, for example as the page header or window title. Exactly one title
     is required per document.
    -->
<!ELEMENT title (#PCDATA)>
<!ATTLIST title
  %i18n;
  id          ID             #IMPLIED
  >

<!-- document base URI -->

<!ELEMENT base EMPTY>
<!ATTLIST base
  id          ID             #IMPLIED
  href        %URI;          #IMPLIED
  target      %FrameTarget;  #IMPLIED
  >

<!-- generic metainformation -->
<!ELEMENT meta EMPTY>
<!ATTLIST meta
  %i18n;
  id          ID             #IMPLIED
  http-equiv  CDATA          #IMPLIED
  name        CDATA          #IMPLIED
```

APPENDIX F

```
  content     CDATA          #REQUIRED
  scheme      CDATA          #IMPLIED
  >

<!--
  Relationship values can be used in principle:

   a) for document specific toolbars/menus when used with the link element in
      document head e.g. start, contents, previous, next, index, end, help
   b) to link to a separate style sheet (rel="stylesheet")
   c) to make a link to a script (rel="script")
   d) by stylesheets to control how collections of html nodes are rendered into
      printed documents
   e) to make a link to a printable version of this document
      e.g. a PostScript or PDF version (rel="alternate" media="print")
-->

<!ELEMENT link EMPTY>
<!ATTLIST link
  %attrs;
  charset     %Charset;      #IMPLIED
  href        %URI;          #IMPLIED
  hreflang    %LanguageCode; #IMPLIED
  type        %ContentType;  #IMPLIED
  rel         %LinkTypes;    #IMPLIED
  rev         %LinkTypes;    #IMPLIED
  media       %MediaDesc;    #IMPLIED
  target      %FrameTarget;  #IMPLIED
  >

<!-- style info, which may include CDATA sections -->
<!ELEMENT style (#PCDATA)>
<!ATTLIST style
  %i18n;
  id          ID             #IMPLIED
  type        %ContentType;  #REQUIRED
  media       %MediaDesc;    #IMPLIED
  title       %Text;         #IMPLIED
  xml:space   (preserve)     #FIXED 'preserve'
  >

<!-- script statements, which may include CDATA sections -->
<!ELEMENT script (#PCDATA)>
<!ATTLIST script
  id          ID             #IMPLIED
  charset     %Charset;      #IMPLIED
  type        %ContentType;  #REQUIRED
  language    CDATA          #IMPLIED
  src         %URI;          #IMPLIED
  defer       (defer)        #IMPLIED
  xml:space   (preserve)     #FIXED 'preserve'
  >

<!-- alternate content container for non script-based rendering -->

<!ELEMENT noscript %Flow;>
<!ATTLIST noscript
  %attrs;
  >
```

```
<!--======================= Frames =========================================-->

<!-- only one noframes element permitted per document -->

<!ELEMENT frameset (frameset|frame|noframes)*>
<!ATTLIST frameset
  %coreattrs;
  rows         %MultiLengths; #IMPLIED
  cols         %MultiLengths; #IMPLIED
  onload       %Script;       #IMPLIED
  onunload     %Script;       #IMPLIED
  >

<!-- reserved frame names start with "_" otherwise starts with letter -->

<!-- tiled window within frameset -->

<!ELEMENT frame EMPTY>
<!ATTLIST frame
  %coreattrs;
  longdesc     %URI;           #IMPLIED
  name         NMTOKEN         #IMPLIED
  src          %URI;           #IMPLIED
  frameborder (1|0)            "1"
  marginwidth %Pixels;         #IMPLIED
  marginheight %Pixels;        #IMPLIED
  noresize     (noresize)      #IMPLIED
  scrolling    (yes|no|auto)   "auto"
  >

<!-- inline subwindow -->

<!ELEMENT iframe %Flow;>
<!ATTLIST iframe
  %coreattrs;
  longdesc     %URI;           #IMPLIED
  name         NMTOKEN         #IMPLIED
  src          %URI;           #IMPLIED
  frameborder (1|0)            "1"
  marginwidth %Pixels;         #IMPLIED
  marginheight %Pixels;        #IMPLIED
  scrolling    (yes|no|auto)   "auto"
  align        %ImgAlign;      #IMPLIED
  height       %Length;        #IMPLIED
  width        %Length;        #IMPLIED
  >

<!-- alternate content container for non frame-based rendering -->

<!ELEMENT noframes (body)>
<!ATTLIST noframes
  %attrs;
  >

<!--=================== Document Body ====================================-->

<!ELEMENT body %Flow;>
<!ATTLIST body
  %attrs;
  onload       %Script;        #IMPLIED
```

APPENDIX F

```
  onunload    %Script;        #IMPLIED
  background  %URI;           #IMPLIED
  bgcolor     %Color;         #IMPLIED
  text        %Color;         #IMPLIED
  link        %Color;         #IMPLIED
  vlink       %Color;         #IMPLIED
  alink       %Color;         #IMPLIED
  >

<!ELEMENT div %Flow;>  <!-- generic language/style container -->
<!ATTLIST div
  %attrs;
  %TextAlign;
  >

<!--=================== Paragraphs =========================================-->

<!ELEMENT p %Inline;>
<!ATTLIST p
  %attrs;
  %TextAlign;
  >

<!--=================== Headings ===========================================-->

<!--
  There are six levels of headings from h1 (the most important)
  to h6 (the least important).
-->

<!ELEMENT h1  %Inline;>
<!ATTLIST h1
  %attrs;
  %TextAlign;
  >

<!ELEMENT h2 %Inline;>
<!ATTLIST h2
  %attrs;
  %TextAlign;
  >

<!ELEMENT h3 %Inline;>
<!ATTLIST h3
  %attrs;
  %TextAlign;
  >

<!ELEMENT h4 %Inline;>
<!ATTLIST h4
  %attrs;
  %TextAlign;
  >

<!ELEMENT h5 %Inline;>
<!ATTLIST h5
  %attrs;
  %TextAlign;
  >

<!ELEMENT h6 %Inline;>
```

```
<!ATTLIST h6
  %attrs;
  %TextAlign;
  >

<!--==================== Lists ============================================-->

<!-- Unordered list bullet styles -->

<!ENTITY % ULStyle "(disc|square|circle)">

<!-- Unordered list -->

<!ELEMENT ul (li)+>
<!ATTLIST ul
  %attrs;
  type        %ULStyle;     #IMPLIED
  compact     (compact)     #IMPLIED
  >

<!-- Ordered list numbering style

    1   arabic numbers      1, 2, 3, ...
    a   lower alpha         a, b, c, ...
    A   upper alpha         A, B, C, ...
    i   lower roman         i, ii, iii, ...
    I   upper roman         I, II, III, ...

    The style is applied to the sequence number which by default is reset to 1
    for the first list item in an ordered list.
-->
<!ENTITY % OLStyle "CDATA">

<!-- Ordered (numbered) list -->

<!ELEMENT ol (li)+>
<!ATTLIST ol
  %attrs;
  type        %OLStyle;      #IMPLIED
  compact     (compact)      #IMPLIED
  start       %Number;       #IMPLIED
  >

<!-- single column list (DEPRECATED) -->
<!ELEMENT menu (li)+>
<!ATTLIST menu
  %attrs;
  compact     (compact)     #IMPLIED
  >

<!-- multiple column list (DEPRECATED) -->
<!ELEMENT dir (li)+>
<!ATTLIST dir
  %attrs;
  compact     (compact)     #IMPLIED
  >

<!-- LIStyle is constrained to: "(%ULStyle;|%OLStyle;)" -->
<!ENTITY % LIStyle "CDATA">
```

```
<!-- list item -->

<!ELEMENT li %Flow;>
<!ATTLIST li
  %attrs;
  type        %LIStyle;      #IMPLIED
  value       %Number;       #IMPLIED
  >

<!-- definition lists - dt for term, dd for its definition -->

<!ELEMENT dl (dt|dd)+>
<!ATTLIST dl
  %attrs;
  compact     (compact)      #IMPLIED
  >

<!ELEMENT dt %Inline;>
<!ATTLIST dt
  %attrs;
  >

<!ELEMENT dd %Flow;>
<!ATTLIST dd
  %attrs;
  >

<!--=================== Address ===========================================-->

<!-- information on author -->

<!ELEMENT address (#PCDATA | %inline; | %misc.inline; | p)*>
<!ATTLIST address
  %attrs;
  >

<!--=================== Horizontal Rule ===================================-->

<!ELEMENT hr EMPTY>
<!ATTLIST hr
  %attrs;
  align       (left|center|right) #IMPLIED
  noshade     (noshade)      #IMPLIED
  size        %Pixels;       #IMPLIED
  width       %Length;       #IMPLIED
  >

<!--=================== Preformatted Text =================================-->

<!-- content is %Inline; excluding
        "img|object|applet|big|small|sub|sup|font|basefont" -->

<!ELEMENT pre %pre.content;>
<!ATTLIST pre
  %attrs;
  width       %Number;       #IMPLIED
  xml:space   (preserve)     #FIXED 'preserve'
  >

<!--=================== Block-like Quotes =================================-->
```

```
<!ELEMENT blockquote %Flow;>
<!ATTLIST blockquote
  %attrs;
  cite        %URI;          #IMPLIED
  >

<!--=================== Text alignment ===================================-->

<!-- center content -->
<!ELEMENT center %Flow;>
<!ATTLIST center
  %attrs;
  >

<!--=================== Inserted/Deleted Text ============================-->


<!--
  ins/del are allowed in block and inline content, but it's inappropriate to
  include block content within an ins element occurring in inline content.
-->
<!ELEMENT ins %Flow;>
<!ATTLIST ins
  %attrs;
  cite        %URI;          #IMPLIED
  datetime    %Datetime;     #IMPLIED
  >

<!ELEMENT del %Flow;>
<!ATTLIST del
  %attrs;
  cite        %URI;          #IMPLIED
  datetime    %Datetime;     #IMPLIED
  >

<!--================== The Anchor Element ================================-->

<!-- content is %Inline; except that anchors shouldn't be nested -->

<!ELEMENT a %a.content;>
<!ATTLIST a
  %attrs;
  %focus;
  charset     %Charset;      #IMPLIED
  type        %ContentType;  #IMPLIED
  name        NMTOKEN        #IMPLIED
  href        %URI;          #IMPLIED
  hreflang    %LanguageCode; #IMPLIED
  rel         %LinkTypes;    #IMPLIED
  rev         %LinkTypes;    #IMPLIED
  shape       %Shape;        "rect"
  coords      %Coords;       #IMPLIED
  target      %FrameTarget;  #IMPLIED
  >

<!--===================== Inline Elements ================================-->

<!ELEMENT span %Inline;> <!-- generic language/style container -->
<!ATTLIST span
  %attrs;
```

```
  >

<!ELEMENT bdo %Inline;>  <!-- I18N BiDi over-ride -->
<!ATTLIST bdo
  %coreattrs;
  %events;
  lang        %LanguageCode; #IMPLIED
  xml:lang    %LanguageCode; #IMPLIED
  dir         (ltr|rtl)      #REQUIRED
  >

<!ELEMENT br EMPTY>   <!-- forced line break -->
<!ATTLIST br
  %coreattrs;
  clear       (left|all|right|none) "none"
  >

<!ELEMENT em %Inline;>   <!-- emphasis -->
<!ATTLIST em %attrs;>

<!ELEMENT strong %Inline;>   <!-- strong emphasis -->
<!ATTLIST strong %attrs;>

<!ELEMENT dfn %Inline;>   <!-- definitional -->
<!ATTLIST dfn %attrs;>

<!ELEMENT code %Inline;>   <!-- program code -->

<!ATTLIST code %attrs;>

<!ELEMENT samp %Inline;>   <!-- sample -->
<!ATTLIST samp %attrs;>

<!ELEMENT kbd %Inline;>  <!-- something user would type -->
<!ATTLIST kbd %attrs;>

<!ELEMENT var %Inline;>   <!-- variable -->
<!ATTLIST var %attrs;>

<!ELEMENT cite %Inline;>   <!-- citation -->
<!ATTLIST cite %attrs;>

<!ELEMENT abbr %Inline;>   <!-- abbreviation -->
<!ATTLIST abbr %attrs;>

<!ELEMENT acronym %Inline;>   <!-- acronym -->
<!ATTLIST acronym %attrs;>

<!ELEMENT q %Inline;>   <!-- inlined quote -->
<!ATTLIST q
  %attrs;
  cite        %URI;          #IMPLIED
  >

<!ELEMENT sub %Inline;> <!-- subscript -->
<!ATTLIST sub %attrs;>

<!ELEMENT sup %Inline;> <!-- superscript -->
<!ATTLIST sup %attrs;>
```

```
<!ELEMENT tt %Inline;>   <!-- fixed pitch font -->
<!ATTLIST tt %attrs;>

<!ELEMENT i %Inline;>   <!-- italic font -->
<!ATTLIST i %attrs;>

<!ELEMENT b %Inline;>   <!-- bold font -->
<!ATTLIST b %attrs;>

<!ELEMENT big %Inline;>   <!-- bigger font -->
<!ATTLIST big %attrs;>

<!ELEMENT small %Inline;>   <!-- smaller font -->
<!ATTLIST small %attrs;>

<!ELEMENT u %Inline;>   <!-- underline -->
<!ATTLIST u %attrs;>

<!ELEMENT s %Inline;>   <!-- strike-through -->
<!ATTLIST s %attrs;>

<!ELEMENT strike %Inline;>   <!-- strike-through -->
<!ATTLIST strike %attrs;>

<!ELEMENT basefont EMPTY>  <!-- base font size -->
<!ATTLIST basefont
  id          ID              #IMPLIED
  size        CDATA           #REQUIRED
 color       %Color;         #IMPLIED
  face        CDATA           #IMPLIED
  >

<!ELEMENT font %Inline;> <!-- local change to font -->
<!ATTLIST font
  %coreattrs;
  %i18n;
  size        CDATA           #IMPLIED
  color       %Color;         #IMPLIED
  face        CDATA           #IMPLIED
  >

<!--==================== Object ========================================-->
<!--
  object is used to embed objects as part of HTML pages.
  param elements should precede other content. Parameters can also be expressed as
  attribute/value pairs on the object element itself when brevity is desired.
-->

<!ELEMENT object (#PCDATA | param | %block; | form |%inline; | %misc;)*>
<!ATTLIST object
  %attrs;
  declare     (declare)       #IMPLIED
  classid     %URI;           #IMPLIED
  codebase    %URI;           #IMPLIED
  data        %URI;           #IMPLIED
  type        %ContentType;   #IMPLIED
  codetype    %ContentType;   #IMPLIED
  archive     %UriList;       #IMPLIED
  standby     %Text;          #IMPLIED
  height      %Length;        #IMPLIED
```

```
  width       %Length;        #IMPLIED
  usemap      %URI;           #IMPLIED
  name        NMTOKEN         #IMPLIED
  tabindex    %Number;        #IMPLIED
  align       %ImgAlign;      #IMPLIED
  border      %Pixels;        #IMPLIED
  hspace      %Pixels;        #IMPLIED
  vspace      %Pixels;        #IMPLIED
  >

<!--
  param is used to supply a named property value. In XML it would seem natural to
  follow RDF and support an abbreviated syntax where the param elements are
  replaced by attribute value pairs on the object start tag.
-->
<!ELEMENT param EMPTY>
<!ATTLIST param
  id          ID              #IMPLIED
  name        CDATA           #REQUIRED
  value       CDATA           #IMPLIED
  valuetype   (data|ref|object) "data"
  type        %ContentType;   #IMPLIED
  >

<!--=================== Java applet ==================================-->
<!--
  One of code or object attributes must be present.
  Place param elements before other content.
-->
<!ELEMENT applet (#PCDATA | param | %block; | form | %inline; | %misc;)*>
<!ATTLIST applet
  %coreattrs;
  codebase    %URI;           #IMPLIED
  archive     CDATA           #IMPLIED
  code        CDATA           #IMPLIED
  object      CDATA           #IMPLIED
  alt         %Text;          #IMPLIED
  name        NMTOKEN         #IMPLIED
  width       %Length;        #REQUIRED
  height      %Length;        #REQUIRED
  align       %ImgAlign;      #IMPLIED
  hspace      %Pixels;        #IMPLIED
  vspace      %Pixels;        #IMPLIED
  >

<!--=================== Images ===========================================-->

<!--
   To avoid accessibility problems for people who aren't able to see the image,
   you should provide a text description using the alt and longdesc attributes.
   In addition, avoid the use of server-side image maps.
-->

<!ELEMENT img EMPTY>
<!ATTLIST img
  %attrs;
  src         %URI;           #REQUIRED
  alt         %Text;          #REQUIRED
  name        NMTOKEN         #IMPLIED
  longdesc    %URI;           #IMPLIED
```

```
  height      %Length;        #IMPLIED
  width       %Length;        #IMPLIED
  usemap      %URI;           #IMPLIED
  ismap       (ismap)         #IMPLIED
  align       %ImgAlign;      #IMPLIED
  border      %Pixels;        #IMPLIED
  hspace      %Pixels;        #IMPLIED
  vspace      %Pixels;        #IMPLIED
  >

<!-- usemap points to a map element which may be in this document
     or an external document, although the latter is not widely supported -->

<!--=================== Client-side image maps ============================-->

<!-- These can be placed in the same document or grouped in a separate document
     although this isn't yet widely supported -->

<!ELEMENT map ((%block; | form | %misc;)+ | area+)>
<!ATTLIST map
  %i18n;
  %events;
  id          ID              #REQUIRED
  class       CDATA           #IMPLIED
  style       %StyleSheet;    #IMPLIED
  title       %Text;          #IMPLIED
  name        NMTOKEN         #IMPLIED
  >

<!ELEMENT area EMPTY>
<!ATTLIST area
  %attrs;
  %focus;
  shape       %Shape;         "rect"
  coords      %Coords;        #IMPLIED
  href        %URI;           #IMPLIED
  nohref      (nohref)        #IMPLIED
  alt         %Text;          #REQUIRED
  target      %FrameTarget;   #IMPLIED
  >

<!--================ Forms ===============================================-->

<!ELEMENT form %form.content;>   <!-- forms shouldn't be nested -->

<!ATTLIST form
  %attrs;
  action      %URI;           #REQUIRED
  method      (get|post)      "get"
  name        NMTOKEN         #IMPLIED
  enctype     %ContentType;   "application/x-www-form-urlencoded"
  onsubmit    %Script;        #IMPLIED
  onreset     %Script;        #IMPLIED
  accept      %ContentTypes;  #IMPLIED
  accept-charset %Charsets;   #IMPLIED
  target      %FrameTarget;   #IMPLIED
  >

<!--
  Each label must not contain more than ONE field
```

```
  Label elements shouldn't be nested.
-->
<!ELEMENT label %Inline;>
<!ATTLIST label
  %attrs;
  for         IDREF          #IMPLIED
  accesskey   %Character;    #IMPLIED
  onfocus     %Script;       #IMPLIED
  onblur      %Script;       #IMPLIED
  >

<!ENTITY % InputType
  "(text | password | checkbox | radio | submit | reset |
    file | hidden | image | button)"
   >

<!-- the name attribute is required for all but submit & reset -->

<!ELEMENT input EMPTY>     <!-- form control -->
<!ATTLIST input
  %attrs;
  %focus;
  type        %InputType;    "text"
  name        CDATA          #IMPLIED
  value       CDATA          #IMPLIED
  checked     (checked)      #IMPLIED
  disabled    (disabled)     #IMPLIED
  readonly    (readonly)     #IMPLIED
  size        CDATA          #IMPLIED
  maxlength   %Number;       #IMPLIED
  src         %URI;          #IMPLIED
  alt         CDATA          #IMPLIED
  usemap      %URI;          #IMPLIED
  onselect    %Script;       #IMPLIED
  onchange    %Script;       #IMPLIED
  accept      %ContentTypes; #IMPLIED
  align       %ImgAlign;     #IMPLIED
  >

<!ELEMENT select (optgroup|option)+>  <!-- option selector -->
<!ATTLIST select
  %attrs;
  name        CDATA          #IMPLIED
  size        %Number;       #IMPLIED
  multiple    (multiple)     #IMPLIED
  disabled    (disabled)     #IMPLIED
  tabindex    %Number;       #IMPLIED
  onfocus     %Script;       #IMPLIED
  onblur      %Script;       #IMPLIED
  onchange    %Script;       #IMPLIED
  >

<!ELEMENT optgroup (option)+>   <!-- option group -->
<!ATTLIST optgroup
  %attrs;
  disabled    (disabled)     #IMPLIED
  label       %Text;         #REQUIRED
  >

<!ELEMENT option (#PCDATA)>     <!-- selectable choice -->
```

```
<!ATTLIST option
  %attrs;
  selected    (selected)     #IMPLIED
  disabled    (disabled)     #IMPLIED
  label       %Text;         #IMPLIED
  value       CDATA          #IMPLIED
  >

<!ELEMENT textarea (#PCDATA)>     <!-- multi-line text field -->
<!ATTLIST textarea
  %attrs;
  %focus;
  name        CDATA          #IMPLIED
  rows        %Number;       #REQUIRED
  cols        %Number;       #REQUIRED
  disabled    (disabled)     #IMPLIED
  readonly    (readonly)     #IMPLIED
  onselect    %Script;       #IMPLIED
  onchange    %Script;       #IMPLIED
  >

<!--
  The fieldset element is used to group form fields. Only one legend element
  should occur in the content and if present should only be preceded by
  whitespace.
-->
<!ELEMENT fieldset (#PCDATA | legend | %block; | form | %inline; | %misc;)*>
<!ATTLIST fieldset
  %attrs;
  >

<!ENTITY % LAlign "(top|bottom|left|right)">

<!ELEMENT legend %Inline;>     <!-- fieldset label -->
<!ATTLIST legend
  %attrs;
  accesskey   %Character;    #IMPLIED
  align       %LAlign;       #IMPLIED
  >

<!--
 Content is %Flow; excluding a, form, form controls, iframe
-->
<!ELEMENT button %button.content;>  <!-- push button -->
<!ATTLIST button
  %attrs;
  %focus;
  name        CDATA          #IMPLIED
  value       CDATA          #IMPLIED
  type        (button|submit|reset) "submit"
  disabled    (disabled)     #IMPLIED
  >

<!-- single-line text input control (DEPRECATED) -->
<!ELEMENT isindex EMPTY>
<!ATTLIST isindex
  %coreattrs;
  %i18n;
  prompt      %Text;         #IMPLIED
  >
```

```
<!--======================= Tables =======================================-->

<!-- Derived from IETF HTML table standard, see [RFC1942] -->

<!--
 The border attribute sets the thickness of the frame around the table. The
 default units are screen pixels.

 The frame attribute specifies which parts of the frame around the table should be
 rendered. The values are not the same as CALS to avoid a name clash with the
 valign attribute.
-->
<!ENTITY % TFrame "(void|above|below|hsides|lhs|rhs|vsides|box|border)">

<!--
 The rules attribute defines which rules to draw between cells:

 If rules is absent then assume:
     "none" if border is absent or border="0" otherwise "all"
-->

<!ENTITY % TRules "(none | groups | rows | cols | all)">

<!-- horizontal placement of table relative to document -->
<!ENTITY % TAlign "(left|center|right)">

<!-- horizontal alignment attributes for cell contents

  char        alignment char, e.g. char=":"
  charoff     offset for alignment char
-->
<!ENTITY % cellhalign
  "align      (left|center|right|justify|char) #IMPLIED
   char       %Character;    #IMPLIED
   charoff    %Length;       #IMPLIED"
  >

<!-- vertical alignment attributes for cell contents -->
<!ENTITY % cellvalign
  "valign     (top|middle|bottom|baseline) #IMPLIED"
  >

<!ELEMENT table
     (caption?, (col*|colgroup*), thead?, tfoot?, (tbody+|tr+))>
<!ELEMENT caption  %Inline;>
<!ELEMENT thead    (tr)+>
<!ELEMENT tfoot    (tr)+>
<!ELEMENT tbody    (tr)+>
<!ELEMENT colgroup (col)*>
<!ELEMENT col      EMPTY>
<!ELEMENT tr       (th|td)+>
<!ELEMENT th       %Flow;>
<!ELEMENT td       %Flow;>

<!ATTLIST table
  %attrs;
  summary     %Text;         #IMPLIED
  width       %Length;       #IMPLIED
  border      %Pixels;       #IMPLIED
  frame       %TFrame;       #IMPLIED
```

```
  rules       %TRules;        #IMPLIED
  cellspacing %Length;        #IMPLIED
  cellpadding %Length;        #IMPLIED
  align       %TAlign;        #IMPLIED
  bgcolor     %Color;         #IMPLIED
  >

<!ENTITY % CAlign "(top|bottom|left|right)">

<!ATTLIST caption
  %attrs;
  align       %CAlign;        #IMPLIED
  >

<!--
colgroup groups a set of col elements. It allows you to group several semantically
related columns together.
-->
<!ATTLIST colgroup
  %attrs;
  span        %Number;        "1"
  width       %MultiLength;   #IMPLIED
  %cellhalign;
  %cellvalign;
  >

<!--
 col elements define the alignment properties for cells in one or more columns.

 The width attribute specifies the width of the columns, e.g.
     width=64        width in screen pixels
     width=0.5*      relative width of 0.5

 The span attribute causes the attributes of one col element to apply to more than
 one column.
-->
<!ATTLIST col
  %attrs;
  span        %Number;        "1"
  width       %MultiLength;   #IMPLIED
  %cellhalign;
  %cellvalign;
  >

<!--
    Use thead to duplicate headers when breaking table across page boundaries, or
    for static headers when tbody sections are rendered in scrolling panel.

    Use tfoot to duplicate footers when breaking table across page boundaries, or
    for static footers when tbody sections are rendered in scrolling panel.

    Use multiple tbody sections when rules are needed between groups of table
    rows.
-->
<!ATTLIST thead
  %attrs;
  %cellhalign;
  %cellvalign;
  >
```

```
<!ATTLIST tfoot
  %attrs;
  %cellhalign;
  %cellvalign;
  >

<!ATTLIST tbody
  %attrs;
  %cellhalign;
  %cellvalign;
  >

<!ATTLIST tr
  %attrs;
  %cellhalign;
  %cellvalign;
  bgcolor     %Color;         #IMPLIED
  >

<!-- Scope is simpler than headers attribute for common tables -->
<!ENTITY % Scope "(row|col|rowgroup|colgroup)">

<!-- th is for headers, td for data and for cells acting as both -->

<!ATTLIST th
  %attrs;
  abbr        %Text;          #IMPLIED
  axis        CDATA           #IMPLIED
  headers     IDREFS          #IMPLIED
  scope       %Scope;         #IMPLIED
  rowspan     %Number;        "1"
  colspan     %Number;        "1"
  %cellhalign;
  %cellvalign;
  nowrap      (nowrap)        #IMPLIED
  bgcolor     %Color;         #IMPLIED
  width       %Pixels;        #IMPLIED
  height      %Pixels;        #IMPLIED
  >

<!ATTLIST td
  %attrs;
  abbr        %Text;          #IMPLIED
  axis        CDATA           #IMPLIED
  headers     IDREFS          #IMPLIED
  scope       %Scope;         #IMPLIED
  rowspan     %Number;        "1"
  colspan     %Number;        "1"
  %cellhalign;
  %cellvalign;
  nowrap      (nowrap)        #IMPLIED
  bgcolor     %Color;         #IMPLIED
  width       %Pixels;        #IMPLIED
  height      %Pixels;        #IMPLIED
  >
```

Index

See Appendix A for a listing of HTML and XHTML elements. See Appendix B for a listing of properties in CSS1 and CSS2. Asterisks (*) after entries represent variable information.

Symbols and Numbers

B

D

G

H

I

J

N

O

Q

R

S

U

V

W

Y

Z

INTERNATIONAL CONTACT INFORMATION

AUSTRALIA
McGraw-Hill Book Company Australia Pty. Ltd.
TEL +61-2-9900-1800
FAX +61-2-9878-8881
http://www.mcgraw-hill.com.au
books-it_sydney@mcgraw-hill.com

CANADA
McGraw-Hill Ryerson Ltd.
TEL +905-430-5000
FAX +905-430-5020
http://www.mcgraw-hill.ca

GREECE, MIDDLE EAST, & AFRICA
(Excluding South Africa)
McGraw-Hill Hellas
TEL +30-210-6560-990
TEL +30-210-6560-993
TEL +30-210-6560-994
FAX +30-210-6545-525

MEXICO (Also serving Latin America)
McGraw-Hill Interamericana Editores S.A. de C.V.
TEL +525-117-1583
FAX +525-117-1589
http://www.mcgraw-hill.com.mx
fernando_castellanos@mcgraw-hill.com

SINGAPORE (Serving Asia)
McGraw-Hill Book Company
TEL +65-6863-1580
FAX +65-6862-3354
http://www.mcgraw-hill.com.sg
mghasia@mcgraw-hill.com

SOUTH AFRICA
McGraw-Hill South Africa
TEL +27-11-622-7512
FAX +27-11-622-9045
robyn_swanepoel@mcgraw-hill.com

SPAIN
McGraw-Hill/Interamericana de España, S.A.U.
TEL +34-91-180-3000
FAX +34-91-372-8513
http://www.mcgraw-hill.es
professional@mcgraw-hill.es

UNITED KINGDOM, NORTHERN,
EASTERN, & CENTRAL EUROPE
McGraw-Hill Education Europe
TEL +44-1-628-502500
FAX +44-1-628-770224
http://www.mcgraw-hill.co.uk
computing_europe@mcgraw-hill.com

ALL OTHER INQUIRIES Contact:
McGraw-Hill/Osborne
TEL +1-510-420-7700
FAX +1-510-420-7703
http://www.osborne.com
omg_international@mcgraw-hill.com